# LEGAL PROTECTION FOR THE INDIVIDUAL EMPLOYEE

## Fourth Edition

■ ■ ■

By

## Kenneth G. Dau–Schmidt

*Willard and Margaret Carr*
*Professor of Labor and Employment Law*
*Indiana University—Bloomington, Maurer School of Law*

## Robert N. Covington

*Professor of Law Emeritus*
*Vanderbilt University Law School*

## Matthew W. Finkin

*Albert J. Harno and Edward W. Cleary*
*Chair in Law*
*University of Illinois College of Law*

for

**THE LABOR LAW GROUP**

**AMERICAN CASEBOOK SERIES®**

**WEST®**

A Thomson Reuters business

Mat #41005494

*American Casebook Series* is a trademark registered in the U.S. Patent and Trademark Office.

To: Nick, Nathan and Ellie who have provided a constant source of love, amusement and adventure over the years, and have somehow managed to grow into wonderful adults! Also to Betsy, my muse and partner, and the mother of my three kids:

> "She walks in beauty, like the night
>> Of cloudless climes and starry skies;
> And all that's best of dark and bright
>> Meet in her aspect and her eyes:
> Thus mellow'd to that tender light
>> Which heaven to gaudy day denies."

Lord Byron

K.D.S.

To The Late Clyde Summers, *Psalm 112:5,* and to Paula, *Proverbs 31:29.*

R.N.C.

To The late Peter O. Steiner, whose life conjoined the profession of economics of analytical rigor with a deep-seated respect for human dignity.

M.W.F.

# FOREWORD

## The Labor Law Group

The Labor Law Group had its origins in the desire of scholars to produce quality casebooks for instruction in labor and employment law. Over the course of its existence, the hallmarks of the group have been collaborative efforts among scholars, informed by skilled practitioners, under a cooperative non-profit trust in which royalties from past work finance future meetings and projects.

At the 1946 meeting of the Association of American Law Schools, Professor W. Willard Wirtz delivered a compelling paper criticizing the labor law course books then available. His remarks so impressed those present that the "Labor Law Roundtable" of the Association organized a general conference on the teaching of labor law to be held in Ann Arbor in 1947. The late Professor Robert E. Mathews served as coordinator for the Ann Arbor meeting and several conferees agreed to exchange proposals for sections of a new course book that would facilitate training exemplary practitioners of labor law. Beginning in 1948, a preliminary mimeographed version was used in seventeen schools; each user supplied comments and suggestions for change. In 1953, a hard-cover version was published under the title *Labor Relations and the Law*. The thirty-one "cooperating editors" were so convinced of the value of multi-campus collaboration that they gave up any individual claims to royalties. Instead, those royalties were paid to a trust fund to be used to develop and "provide the best possible materials" for training students in labor law and labor relations. The Declaration of Trust memorializing this agreement was executed November 4, 1953, and remains the Group's charter.

The founding committee's hope that the initial collaboration would bear fruit has been fulfilled. Under Professor Mathews' continuing chairmanship, the Group's members produced *Readings on Labor Law* in 1955 and *The Employment Relation and the Law* in 1957, edited by Robert Mathews and Benjamin Aaron. A second edition of *Labor Relations and the Law* appeared in 1960, with Benjamin Aaron and Donald H. Wollett as co-chairmen, and a third edition was published in 1965, with Jerre Williams at the helm.

In June of 1969, the Group, now chaired by William P. Murphy, sponsored a conference to reexamine the labor law curriculum. The meeting, held at the University of Colorado, was attended by practitioners and by full-time teachers including nonmembers as well as members of the Group. In meetings that followed the conference, the Group decided to reshape its work substantially. It restructured itself into ten task forces, each assigned a unit of no more than two hundred pages on a discrete topic such as employment discrimination or union-member relations. An individual teacher could then choose two or three of these units as the material around which to build a particular course. This multi-unit approach dominated the Group's work throughout much of the 1970s under Professor Murphy and his successor as chairman, Herbert L. Sherman, Jr.

As the 1970's progressed and teachers refined their views about what topics to include and how to address them, some units were dropped from the series while others increased in scope and length. Under Professor Sherman's chairmanship, the Group planned a new series of six enlarged books to cover the full range of topics taught by labor and employment law teachers. Professor James E. Jones, Jr., was elected chairman in 1978 and shepherded to completion the promised set of six full-size, independent casebooks. The Group continued to reevaluate its work and eventually decided that it was time to convene another conference of law teachers.

In 1984, the Group, now chaired by Robert Covington, sponsored another general conference to discuss developments in the substance and teaching of labor and employment law, this time at Park City, Utah. Those discussions and a subsequent working session led to the conclusion that the Group should devote principal attention to three new conventional length course books, one devoted to employment discrimination, one to union-management relations, and one to the individual employment relationship. In addition, work was planned on more abbreviated course books to serve as successors to the Group's earlier works covering public employment bargaining and labor arbitration.

In 1989, with Alvin Goldman as Chair, the Group met in Breckenridge, Colorado, to assess its most recent effort and develop plans for the future. In addition to outlining new course book projects, the Group discussed ways to assist teachers of labor and employment law in their efforts to expand conceptual horizons and perspectives. In pursuit of the latter goals it co-sponsored, in 1992, a conference held at the University of Toronto Faculty of Law at which legal and nonlegal specialists examined alternative models of corporate governance and their impact on workers.

When Robert J. Rabin became Chair in 1996, the Group and a number of invited guests met in Tucson, Arizona, to celebrate the imminent fiftieth anniversary of the Group. The topics of discussion included the impact of the global economy and of changing forms of representation on the teaching of labor and employment law, and the impact of new technologies of electronic publishing on the preparation of teaching materials. The Group honored three of its members who had been present at the creation of the Group, Willard Wirtz, Ben Aaron, and Clyde Summers. The Group next met in Scottsdale, Arizona in December, 1999, to discuss the production of materials that would more effectively bring emerging issues of labor and employment law into the classroom. Among the issues discussed were integration of international and comparative materials into the labor and employment curriculum and the pedagogical uses of the World Wide Web.

Laura J. Cooper became Chair of the Group in July, 2001. In June, 2003, the Group met in Alton, Ontario, Canada. The focus there was on labor law on the edge, looking at doctrinal synergies between workplace law and other legal and social-science disciplines, and workers on the edge, exploring the legal issues of highly-compensated technology workers, vulnerable immigrant employees, and unionized manufacturing employees threatened by foreign competition. The Group also heard a report from its study of the status of the teaching of labor and employment law in the nation's law schools and discussed the implications of the study for the Group's future projects. Members of the Group began work on this case book on international labor law at this meeting. During Professor Cooper's term the Group also finished its popular reader *Labor Law Stories* which examines the stories behind many of the most important American labor law cases.

In July 2005, Kenneth G. Dau–Schmidt became the Chair of the Labor Law Group. Shortly after his election, the Group held a meeting in Chicago with national recognized practitioners to discuss how best to teach students about the practice of labor law in the new global economy of the information age. The outline that resulted from this meeting served as the basis for *Labor Law in the Contemporary Workplace*. Since the Chicago meeting, the Group has met again three times to discuss and work on new editions of its books and new projects: June 2006 in Saratoga Springs, New York, June 2007 in St. Charles, Illinois, and June 2010 in Arrowhead, California. Other Group projects that grew out of or benefited from these meetings include *International Labor Law: Cases and Materials on Workers' Rights in the Global Economy* and *A Concise Hornbook on Employment Law*. The Group has also hosted: a November 2007 symposium on the problems of low-wage workers, the proceedings of which were published in the Minnesota Law Review; a February 2009 symposium on the American Law Institute's Proposed Restatement of Employment Law, the proceedings of which were published in the Employee Rights and Employment Policy Journal; and a November 2010 symposium on labor and employment law policies under the Obama administration, the proceedings of which will be published in the Indiana Law Journal.

At any one time, roughly twenty-five to thirty persons are actively engaged in the Group's work; this has proven a practical size, given problems of communication and logistics. Coordination and editorial review of the projects are the responsibility of the executive committee, whose members are the successor trustees of the Group. Governance is by consensus; votes are taken only to elect trustees and to determine whom to invite to join the Group. Since 1953, more than eighty persons have worked on Group projects; in keeping the original agreement, none has ever received anything more than reimbursement of expenses.

The Labor Law Group currently has eight books in print. In addition to this volume, Thomson/West has published: *Principles of Employment Law* by Rafael Gely, Ann C. Hodges, Peggie R. Smith, and Susan J. Stabile; *Labor Law in the Contemporary Workplace,* by Kenneth G. Dau–Schmidt, Martin H. Malin, Roberto L. Corrada, Christopher David Ruiz Cameron and Catherine L. Fisk; *International Labor Law: Cases and Materials on Workers' Rights in the Global Economy,* by James Atleson, Lance Compa, Kerry Rittich, Calvin William Sharpe, Marley S. Weiss; *Employment Discrimination Law: Cases and*

*Materials on Equality in the Workplace* (Eighth Edition), by Dianne Avery, Maria L. Ontiveros, Roberto L. Corrada, Michael L. Selmi and Melissa Hart; *ADR in the Workplace* (Second Edition), by Laura J. Cooper, Dennis R. Nolan and Richard A. Bales; and *Public Sector Employment* (Second Edition), by Martin H. Malin, Ann C. Hodges and Joseph E. Slater. Foundation Press has published the Group's eighth book, *Labor Law Stories*, edited by Laura J. Cooper and Catherine L. Fisk.

THE EXECUTIVE COMMITTEE
OF THE LABOR LAW GROUP

# PREFACE

This book is designed for an introductory course in employment law and employee benefits law. Care has been taken to integrate theory and policy discussions into a rigorous case based course on the legal principles every practitioner in employment law should master. The material can be taught selectively in one three credit course, or can be divided into a pair of two credit courses: Employment Law (chapters 1–6); and Employee Benefit Law (chapters 7–11). We have found that students in the area appreciate buying one book for two courses and the material flows more naturally between the two courses because it has been integrated by one set of authors. We hope that you and your students enjoy the materials we have put together and benefit from their reading and class discussion. We have committed considerable effort to those ends.

# ACKNOWLEDGMENTS

Of course no work of this length and breadth can be efficiently accomplished by just three individuals. Although this edition is a substantial reworking of the prior text, the authors would like to thank the Labor Law Group members who worked on prior editions of this book: Clyde W. Summers and Alvin L. Goldman. Professors Dau–Schmidt and Covington would also like to thank their research assistants who worked so hard collecting material and proof-reading pages of the text, including: Katie Feary, Jessica Bauml, Kristine Kohlmeier, Ryan MacDonald and Rebekah Shulman. Professor Finkin, who avails himself neither of student help nor resort to a computer, owes a special debt of gratitude to his faithful amanuensis Stacey Ballmes. The authors would also like to thank the members of the Labor Law Group who gave comments on chapters of the book, including: Rick Bales, Melissa Hart, Ann Hodges, Michael Selmi and Peggie Smith. Finally, the authors would like to thank our students at the University of Illinois, Indiana University—Bloomington, Vanderbilt University and the Peking University School of Transnational Law, for working out of drafts of this edition and giving us comments and ideas for improving the text. Our efforts on this project could not have been successful without the help and contributions of all of these people.

# THE LABOR LAW GROUP

## Executive Committee

**Kenneth G. Dau–Schmidt**
*Chair*
*Indiana University–Bloomington*

**Richard Bales**
*Northern Kentucky University*

**Lance Compa**
*Cornell University*

**Laura Cooper**
*University of Minnesota*

**Marion G. Crain**
*Washington University—St. Louis*

**Catherine L. Fisk**
*University of California, Irvine*

**Martin H. Malin**
*Illinois Institute of Technology, Chicago–Kent College of Law*

**Dennis Nolan**
*University of South Carolina*

---

**Peggie Smith**
*Washington University—St. Louis*

# THE LABOR LAW GROUP

## Currently Participating Members

Steven D. Anderman
*University of Essex*

James Atleson
*State University of New York, Buffalo*

Dianne Avery
*State University of New York, Buffalo*

Richard A. Bales
*Northern Kentucky University*

Stephen Befort
*University of Minnesota*

Robert Belton
*Vanderbilt University*

Dr. Roger Blanpain
*Institut voor Arbeidsrecht*

Christopher David Ruiz Cameron
*Southwestern Law School, Los Angeles*

Lance Compa
*Cornell University*

Laura Cooper
*University of Minnesota*

Robert Corrada
*University of Denver*

Robert N. Covington
*Vanderbilt University*

Marion G. Crain
*Washington University—St. Louis*

Kenneth G. Dau–Schmidt
*Indiana University—Bloomington*

Cynthia Estlund
*New York University*

Matthew Finkin
*University of Illinois*

**xvii**

Catherine L. Fisk
*University of California—Irvine*

Joel W. Friedman
*Tulane University*

Ruben J. Garcia
*California Western School of Law*

Rafael Gely
*University of Missouri*

Melissa Hart
*Colorado University*

Ann Hodges
*University of Richmond*

Alan Hyde
*Rutgers University*

Brian A. Langille
*University of Toronto*

Pauline T. Kim
*Washington University B St. Louis*

Tom Kohler
*Boston College*

Orly Lobel
*University of San Diego*

Deborah Malamud
*New York University*

Martin H. Malin
*Illinois Institute of Technology, Chicago–Kent College of Law*

Mordehai Mironi
*University of Haifa*

Robert B. Moberly
*University of Arkansas*

Dennis R. Nolan
*University of South Carolina*

Maria L. Ontiveros
*University of San Francisco*

Kerry Rittich
*University of Toronto*

Michael Selmi
*George Washington University*

Calvin W. Sharpe
*Case Western Reserve University*

# SUMMARY OF CONTENTS

———

# TABLE OF CONTENTS

# TABLE OF CASES

The principal cases are in bold type. Cases cited or discussed in the text are in roman type. References are to pages. Cases cited in principal cases and within other quoted materials are not included.

# LEGAL PROTECTION FOR THE INDIVIDUAL EMPLOYEE

## Fourth Edition

# CHAPTER I

## THE EMPLOYMENT RELATIONSHIP

■ ■ ■

## A.  INTRODUCTION

The employment relationship has historically been a blend of status and contract, a relationship governed by a mixture of legally imposed rules expressing customs or public policies, and voluntarily bargained rules expressing mutual assent. Prior to the nineteenth century the relationship was predominantly one of status described as "master and servant," with the legally imposed rules implementing a dominant-servient relation. Entry into the relationship was by contract, and terms as to wages and duration of employment might be bargained, though often within legally imposed limits, but other terms were prescribed by law. It was not contemplated that the parties would design their own relationship. In the words of Holdsworth,

> until political economists of the earlier half of the nineteenth century converted the legislature to the belief that freedom of contract was the cure for all social ills, no one ever imagined that wages and prices could be settled merely at the will and pleasure of the parties to each particular bargain, or that the contract between employer and work-men could be regarded as precisely similar to any other contract.

4 SIR WILLIAM S. HOLDSWORTH, HISTORY OF ENGLISH LAW 394 (1924).

As contract supplanted status in regulating the employment relation-ship, there developed an awareness, more often in the legislatures than in the courts, that the employment contract was not like other contracts. This difference was dramatically expressed by the labor historians Commons and Andrews:

> When a bushel of wheat is bought and sold * * * the rights and duties created thereby can be fulfilled by delivering something external and inhuman. But when a laborer agrees to work he must deliver himself into the control of another * * *. The latter is a bargain which involves not only wages, but also hours of labor, speed and fatigue, safety and health, accident and disease, even life itself.

JOHN R. COMMONS & JOHN B. ANDREWS, PRINCIPLES OF LABOR LEGISLATION 1–2 (1st ed. 1916).

1

The employment contract is distinguished, not only because it subjects one person to the control of another and deals with human values of sustenance, security and survival, but also because it frequently leads to bargains which are socially unacceptable. As Commons and Andrews explained the Supreme Court's decision in *Holden v. Hardy*, 169 U.S. 366, 18 S.Ct. 383, 42 L.Ed. 780 (1898), upholding legislation limiting the work of women and children in the mines:

> the court recognized what has been dimly seen or implied from the beginning of labor legislation, that inequality of bargaining power is a justification under which the state may come to the aid of the weaker party * * * Inequality of bargaining power has long been a ground for legislative and judicial protection of the weaker party.

COMMONS & ANDREWS, *supra*, at 529.

This perspective of the employment relation articulates two of the major premises which pervade the material in the following chapters: the employment contract is not an "ordinary" contract, one usually being thought of as a singular and discrete transaction in a commercial market; and, it is an appropriate function for the law to aid the weaker party. These premises, however, supply only the beginning of analysis, for they raise persistent questions of degree: To what extent should the employment contract be treated as a special kind of contract? To what extent should the law come to the aid of the weaker party? To what extent should the employment relationship subordinate the employee to the interests and control of the employer?

Nor is the law constrained solely to achieving fairness between the parties, for it is equally concerned, sometimes more concerned, with the consequences to others, or to society generally. Society has an important interest that workers and their families have a minimum standard of income and security, and that their health and safety be protected. These are values which society need not allow employees to bargain away.

Toward these ends the law has established systems of insurance against unemployment, illness, old age, and other incidents which erode earnings or create hardships. These include social insurance which cannot be sufficiently provided by individual employment contracts, regardless of bargaining power. These insurance programs raise their special problems. What risks are to be covered, how do we ascertain the nature and amount of loss sustained, and what measure of protection is to be provided? How shall the cost of the insurance be distributed between the employer, the employees, and society.

In all of these areas, the substantive problems are matched, and sometimes overshadowed, by administrative problems. How effective are the remedies in protecting the employee's rights; to what extent are those rights more symbolic than real? How do we design legal procedures to resolve a multitude of small claims, or administrative processes to distribute insurance or benefits to 100 million employees?

These are questions that pervade this book. They run directly from the textile mills of the late eighteenth century—the prototypical factory—to the contemporary computerized work station. Accordingly, engagement with them usefully proceeds under the light of the last two hundred years' experience.

## B. THE ASCENDANCE—AND AMBIGUITIES—OF "FREE WAGE LABOR": FROM THE FEDERAL PERIOD TO THE GILDED AGE

For most of recorded history, crops were grown and marketed, goods were made and sold, and services were rendered by persons under a variety of legal regimes in which unfree labor—various forms of slavery, serfdom, peonage, and bound labor—often predominated. In the pre-Revolutionary period in the United States goods were made and services rendered by self-employed artisans, bound apprentices, indentured servants, slaves (who in some locales were able to rent themselves out to work in return for a fee to their masters), journeymen, and day laborers, each subject to different economic and social circumstances and different legal regimes. *See generally* Christopher Tomlins, *Early British America, 1585–1830: Freedom Bound, in* MASTERS, SERVANTS, AND MAGISTRATES IN BRITAIN AND THE EMPIRE, 1562–1995 ch. 2 (Douglas Hay & Paul Craven eds., 2004) (especially of the early colonial period); WORK AND LABOR IN EARLY AMERICA (Stephen Innes ed., 1988).

White indentured service, however, which had been a major feature of the seventeenth and eighteenth centuries, ceased to be of significance in America by the early nineteenth century. This development has been attributed in part to the lower cost of trans-Atlantic passage, making it easier for even the relatively poor to migrate as free labor (and so creating, in effect, an international labor market). But it has also been explained in domestic economic terms as well: the labor market had become much more unstable, wage rates had fallen below the cost of bound labor (whose support was the employer's responsibility), and the supply of labor was such that master craftsmen were better advised to rely upon free, that is wage, workers. *See generally* SHARON SALINGER, "TO SERVE WELL AND FAITHFULLY": LABOR AND INDENTURED SERVANTS IN PENNSYLVANIA, 1686–1800, at 150–56 (1987).

The process of "manufacture" theretofore and at the time was predominantly artisanal. The master's role, supervising his wife and children, apprentices and journeymen was inseparable from his role as head of the household and father; even journeymen could reside in the master's house and often were paid in kind—in clothing, firewood, room and board. *See generally* ALAN DAWLEY, CLASS AND COMMUNITY: THE INDUSTRIAL REVOLUTION IN LYNN 17–19 (1976).

The law of "master and servant," in which the servant was considered as a dependant, akin to a child, was applied in Great Britain to the emerging class of workers in manufactures. As Otto Kahn–Freund pointed out, that translation was oblivious to the critical differences between servants and children. Otto Kahn–Freund, *Blackstone's Neglected Child: The Contract of Employment*, 93 L.Q.R. 508 (1997). The status of the free wage earner in the United States was defined similarly in law; this even as a better word than "servant" had to be found in common usage—"hand," "operative," "mechanic" (especially of more sophisticated artisanal and technical work), and, in a borrowing from the French, *emplôyé*—a termed descriptive in France of those of higher status.

The worldview of the mechanical class in the antebellum period was often at odds with the assumptions of mastery and service upon which the common law rested.

> In the years following the American Revolution, artisan workers espoused a republicanism that emphasized their role in upholding the values of virtue, equality, citizenship, and especially, independence ... Artisans' confidence in their position in the new republic included an expectation that industrious apprentices and journeymen could achieve the goal of a "competence" or independence as master mechanics.

L. DIANE BARNES, ARTISAN WORKERS IN THE UPPER SOUTH: PETERSBURG, VIRGINIA, 1820–1865, at 178–79 (2008) (extensive references omitted). Journeymen hatters, coopers, printers, and other skilled trades insisted on controlling their pace of work and, abetted by their nascent trade unions, sometimes even the price of it; drinking on the job was a jealously guarded prerogative in an age when Americans consumed prodigious amounts of alcohol. DAVID BENSMAN, THE PRACTICE OF SOLIDARITY: AMERICAN HAT FINISHERS IN THE NINETEENTH CENTURY 53 (1985). Artisan workers manifested their independence by collective protest, in refusals to obey orders they deemed unreasonable, by striking the shop (called "turnouts" at the time), or simply by quitting. They rarely summoned the common law to their aid.

However, the hatters, coopers, printers, and kindred journeymen may be seen as exceptional, for the degree of independence they could realize was closely linked to the demand for their skills and so, even then, to fluctuating economic conditions. The semi-skilled, unskilled, and day laborers eked out a precarious existence in which resort to law figures primarily in disputes over eligibility for poor relief. *See* SETH ROCKMAN, SCRAPING BY: WAGE LABOR, SLAVERY, AND SURVIVAL IN EARLY BALTIMORE (2009).

Industrialization, which began in earnest after the Civil War and continued through the first half of the twentieth century, changed forever the employment relationship, posing a challenge to both the social conception of free labor and the legal conception of employment. Each of these conceptions needs be addressed.

On the social conception of free labor, the sheer growth in the scale of employment—of waged labor—abetted by the growth of scale in employing enterprises accompanied by the accelerating substitution of semi-skilled and, in some cases, relatively unskilled workers for the skilled independent artisans of the federal period. As historian Daniel Rodgers has explained:

> Well after 1850 the economy still presented a patchwork array of contrasts. In Philadelphia, handloom weavers worked in their own homes virtually in the shadow of the mechanized textile mills. In New York City, tiny tenement cigar shops competed with factory establishments of several hundred employees. * * * As late as 1889, David A. Wells, one of the nation's leading economists, could depreciate the importance of the factory system altogether and insist that no more than one-tenth of the gainfully employed were properly described as factory hands. Yet for all the variety and confusion, the drift of change was evident. As the century progressed, the mills grew larger, labor discipline more exacting, and the work processes more minutely subdivided and dependent on machinery.
>
> At times and in places, moreover, the transition to the factory economy took place with wrenching, unsettling speed. The shoe industry was for most nineteenth-century Americans the preeminent example of the rate at which the new could obliterate the old. As late as the 1840s the typical New England shoe shop was a 10′ × 10′ cottage housing a handful of skilled workers who made shoes by time-honored hand methods according to their personal, often eccentric, notions of size and fit. Some subdivision of tasks set in during that decade under the pressures of the merchants who controlled the trade, but the real revolution in shoemaking came in the 1860s with a rash of inventions, beginning with a sewing machine capable of stitching soles to uppers. Aggressive subdivision of labor, mechanization, and factory building quickly followed. By the 1870s, the shoemaking cottages were empty, and the men who had once been shoemakers now found themselves factory machine operators: beaters, binders, bottomers, buffers, burnishers, channellers, crimpers, cutters, dressers, edge setters, and so on through some thirty or forty subdivided occupations. * * *.
>
> Size, discipline, and displacement of skill characterized the factories. The physical growth of the workplace was evident at every hand. The Baldwin locomotive works had been a giant among factories in the mid–1850s with 600 employees. Twenty years later there were 3,000 factory hands at Baldwin, and by 1900 there were more than 8,000. The McCormick reaper plant in Chicago followed the same course, growing from about 150 employees in 1850 to 4,000 in 1900. But the manufacturing colossi of the early twentieth century dwarfed even these. By 1916 the McCormick plant had grown to 15,000 workers; and in that year the payroll at the Ford Motor Company works at Highland Park reached 33,000. Workshops of the size that had characterized the antebellum economy, employing a handful or a score of workers, persisted amid these immense establishments. But they employed a smaller and smaller fraction of the workers. By 1919,

in the Northern states between the Mississippi River and the Atlantic
Ocean, three-fourths of all wage earners in manufacturing worked in
factories of more than 100 employees, and 30 percent in the giants of
more than 1,000.

DANIEL T. RODGERS, THE WORK ETHIC IN INDUSTRIAL AMERICA 1850–1920, at
22–25 (1978). These changes in size of manufacturing establishments and
the skill of the workers had an impact on how employees were viewed and
managed.

In plants of this size, the informality of the small workshop was an
inevitable casualty. From the beginning the great textile mills had
laid down extensive regulatory codes and enforced them with heavy
fines and the threat of discharge. Other industries adopted such
measures more slowly. The Winchester Repeating Arms plant in New
Haven, for example, did not begin to insist that employees arrive on
time until the 1890s, and in the piecework trades workers clung for a
long time to their traditional right to set their own hours of labor. By
the 1890s, however, gates were common around factories, supplemented by the exacting eye of the first factory time clocks. Inside the
plants the baronial foremen, who had commonly hired, fired, and
cajoled the necessary labor out of their workers on their own whim
and responsibility, slowly disappeared. In their place the larger factories evolved tighter, more systematic, and more centralized schemes
of management. By 1920 personnel departments, rational and precise
cost accounting, central planning offices, and production and efficiency engineers had become fixtures of the new factory bureaucracies.
Defenders of the new management techniques argued that they were
fairer than the old. Certainly by the end of the century there was
little to be envied in the lot of the workers left behind in the
sweatshops and tenement rooms. But neither qualification lessened
the growing distance between a factory hand and his employer or the
subordination of the rhythms of work to the increasingly exacting
demands of efficiency.

*Id.**

The legal conception of free labor during this time derived from the
defense of this institution mounted during the Civil War against the
charge that industrialized workers were mere "wage slaves" no better and
possibly worse off than the chattel slaves of the south. The worry was that
industrialization separated people from the moral value of their work and
created a pauperized and subordinated working class.

Americans were wedded to the self-sustaining family farm as the
norm of social and economic organization and the locus of public
virtue. * * * Industrial production radically altered the accustomed
link between work and value—between the quantity of work invested
and the economic value realized and between the quality of work done

and the value of self-esteem. In this new "factory system," initiative, autonomy, and skill began to be replaced by passive attention, external discipline, and a predetermined, uniform product.

THE PHILOSOPHY OF MANUFACTURERS: EARLY DEBATES OVER INDUSTRIALIZATION IN THE UNITED STATES, at xxii–xxiii (Michael Brewster Folsom & Steven D. Lubar eds., 1982). At a minimum, the "pastoral moralists" of the antebellum world who "cherished liberal 'principles of individuality, of individual interests, of individual aims' " had to concede that America was becoming a "society," not a "community." STEVEN DAVENPORT, FRIENDS OF THE UNRIGHTEOUS MAMMON: NORTHERN CHRISTIANS & MARKET CAPITALISM, 1815–1860, at 194 (2008). One simply had to muddle through the moral ambiguities of free labor; but the very meaning of "free labor" was not free of ambiguity.

The defenders of free labor—"more likely to hire labor than to perform it," ROCKMAN, *supra*, at 241—proceeded from what Rockman calls a set of "social functions" but which neo-classical economists would no doubt call a model,

> that buyers and sellers of labor met in a metaphorical marketplace; that they did so as legal equals; that impartial forces of supply and demand set the rate of wages; and that the market distributed its rewards fairly to those who earned them through diligence and industry.

*Id.* It was enough that there be, as John Fabian Witt put it, a "consensual relationships among autonomous private actors." JOHN FABIAN WITT, THE ACCIDENTAL REPUBLIC: CRIPPLED WORKINGMEN, DESTITUTE WIDOWS, AND THE REMAKING OF AMERICAN LAW 39 (2004). Their conception of freedom or liberty was a negative conception, to be autonomous market actors free from government interference. But, as Witt also points out, liberal advocates of free labor posited a different conception of liberty, a positive one based on *individual independence*.

> Though similar in some respects to the liberal ideal of autonomy, independence stood for a different principle. Those who valued autonomy supported the maintenance of procedures for unconstrained freedom of choice, without regard to the substance of the choices that individuals made. Free markets in labor thus formed a critically important part of the liberal conception of free labor, for labor markets institutionalized the consensual formation of social relations. The labor movement, however, emphasized not procedures for the realization of autonomous choice, but substantive outcomes that established citizens' independence. In particular, the labor movement drew on the long tradition in modern political thought, harkening back to the American revolutionary period and beyond, that was concerned with the importance of an economically independent citizenry.

*Id.* (endnote omitted).

The conceptual and ideological conflict flowed over into the common law whose path, charted in the last quarter of the nineteenth century, continues to guide—or obstruct—us today.

## PAYNE v. THE WESTERN & ATLANTIC RAILROAD CO.

Supreme Court of Tennessee, 1884
81 Tenn. 507

[Payne owned a store near the railroad's depot in Chattanooga. He had developed a profitable business largely catering to employees of the Western and Atlantic. J.C. Anderson, the railroad's general agent in Chattanooga, issued an order that any employee trading with Mr. Payne be discharged. Payne sued in tort, but the defendant's demurrer was sustained.]

INGERSOLL, SP. J.

The novelty, interest and importance of the questions demand a careful examination of the cases and the principles involved. The case turns upon the common law. The first question is: Is it unlawful for one person, or a number of persons in conspiracy, to threaten to discharge employes if they trade with a certain merchant? Would it be unlawful to discharge them for such reason? If not, it surely would not be unlawful to "threaten" it.

If the employes are engaged for fixed terms, it may be assumed that a discharge by the employer for such a reason would be unwarranted, and would give the employe an action for breach of contract. But no one else, except a privy, could complain of the breach of contract, and the ground of the employe's action would be the refusal of the employer to pay him for the period promised in the contract of service. If the service is terminable at the option of either party, it is plain no action would lie even to the employe; for either party may terminate the service, for any cause, good or bad, or without cause, and the other cannot complain in law. Much less could a stranger complain. No action could accrue either to employe or stranger for breach of contract; for no contract is broken. If the act is unlawful it must be on other grounds than breach of contract, as, that it unjustly deprives plaintiff of customers and trade to which his fair dealing entitles him, and thus destroys his business.

For any one to do this without cause is censurable and unjust. But is it legally wrong? Is it unlawful? May I not refuse to trade with any one? May I not forbid my family to trade with any one? May I not dismiss my domestic servant for dealing, or even visiting, where I forbid? And if my domestic, why not my farm-hand, or my mechanic, or teamster? And, if one of them, then why not all four? And, if all four, why not a hundred or a thousand of them? * * * Nor can it be better determined by effect than by number. To keep away one customer might not perceptibly affect the merchant's trade; deprived of a hundred of them he might fail in business. On the contrary, my own dealings may be so important that, if I cease to trade with him, he must close his doors. Shall my act in keeping away a hundred of my employes be unlawful, because it breaks up the merchant's business, and yet it be lawful for me to accomplish the same result by withholding my own custom?

Obviously the law can adopt and maintain no such standards for judging human conduct; and men must be left, without interference to buy and sell where they please, and to discharge or retain employes at will for good cause or for no cause, or even for bad cause without thereby being guilty of an unlawful act *per se*. It is a right which an employe may exercise in the same way, to the same extent, for the same cause or want of cause as the employer. He may refuse to work for a man or company, that trades with any obnoxious person, or does other things which he dislikes. He may persuade his fellows, and the employer may lose all his hands and be compelled to close his doors; or he may yield to the demand and withdraw his custom or cease his dealings, and the obnoxious person he thus injured or wrecked in business. Can it be pretented [sic] that for this either of the injured parties has a right of action against the employes? Great loss may result, indeed has often resulted from such conduct; but loss alone gives no right of action. Great corporations, strong associations, and wealthy individuals may thus do great mischief and wrong; may make and break merchants at will; may crush out competition, and foster monopolies, and thus greatly injure individuals and the public; but power is inherent in size and strength and wealth* * *. The great and rich and powerful are guaranteed the same liberty and privilege as the poor and weak. All may buy and sell when they choose; they may refuse to employ or dismiss whom they choose, without being thereby guilty of a legal wrong, though it may seriously injure and even ruin others.

Railroad corporations have in this matter the same right enjoyed by manufacturers, merchants, lawyers and farmers. All may dismiss their employes at will, be they many or few, for good cause, for no cause or even for cause morally wrong, without being thereby guilty of legal wrong. *A fortiori* they may "threaten" to discharge them without thereby doing an illegal act, *per se*. The sufficient and conclusive answer to the many plausible arguments to the contrary, portraying the evil to workmen and to others from the exercise of such authority by the great and strong, is: They have the right to discharge their employes. The law cannot compel them to employ workmen, nor to keep them employed. If they break contracts with workmen they are answerable only to them; if in the act of discharging them, they break no contract, then no one can sue for loss suffered thereby. Trade is free; so is employment. The law leaves employer and employe to make their own contracts; and these, when made, it will enforce; beyond this it does not go. * * *. This secures to all civil and industrial liberty. A contrary rule would lead to a judicial tyranny as arbitrary, irresponsible and intolerable as that exercised by Scroggs and Jeffreys.[*] * * *

---

* Sir William Scroggs served as the Lord Chief Justice of England from 1678 to 1681. He lived a debauched life and had coarse and violent manners; and these qualities were conspicuous in his

FREEMAN, J., delivered the following dissenting opinion. TURNEY, J., concurring:

It is true this case is one of first impression in our State, and we have no precedent precisely covering the facts to guide us. It might even be conceded, that the precise principle involved had never been adjudicated by our courts, and still a remedy might well be found growing out of the analogies of our law, taking other principles that are settled as the basis on which the rule should be formulated, and its correctness reasoned out and indicated.

We might even go further and say if the exigencies of our advancing civilization demanded it, a new principle might be formulated to meet that demand, and this principle embodied in the well established forms of remedy found in our system of remedial jurisprudence. It is as much a part of the common law, that it has growth and expansive power to meet the wants of an advancing and necessarily complex system of civilization, as that precedent shall have its due influence in settling what that law is at any period of that growth. * * *

It is argued that a man ought to have the right to say where his employes shall trade. I do not recognize any such right. A father may well control his family in this, but an employer ought to have no such right conceded to him. In the case in hand and like cases under the rule we have maintained, the party may always show by way of defense that he has had reasons for what he has done; that the trader was unworthy of patronage; that he debauched the employe, or sold, for instance, unsound food, or any other cause, that affected his employes' usefulness to him, or justified the withdrawal of custom from him. This is not in any way to interfere with the legal right to discharge an employe for good cause, or without any reason assigned if the contract justifies it, but only that he shall not do this solely for the purpose of injury to another, or hold the threat over the employe *in terrorem* to fetter the freedom of the employe, and for the purpose of injuring an obnoxious party.

Such conduct is not justifiable in morals, and ought not to be in law, and when the injury is done as averred in this case the party should respond in damages. The principle will not interfere with any proper use of the legal rights of the employer, an improper and injurious use is all it forbids.

In view of the immense development and large aggregations of capital in this favored country—a capital to be developed and aggregated within the life of the present generation more than a hundred fold—giving the command of immense numbers of employes, by such means as we have

---

demeanor on the bench. Scroggs presided over a number of famous cases in which he dished out cruel words and harsh sentences to the defendants. George Jeffreys, 1st Baron Jeffreys of Wem, served in the position of Lord Chancellor during the reign of King James II and presided over the trials of supporters of the Duke of Monmouth's rebellion. His harsh treatment of the defendants (almost 200 hanged and more than 800 transported to the colonies as indentured laborers) earned him the nickname "the hanging judge". EDWARD FOSS, THE JUDGES OF ENGLAND (9 VOLS, LONDON, 1848–1864).—Eds.

before us in this case, it is the demand of a sound public policy, for the future more especially, as well as now, that the use of this power should be restrained within legitimate boundaries. * * * It will be to their interest to have free competition in the purchase of supplies for their wants, and its beneficial influences in keeping prices at the normal standard. The merchant and groceryman, and other traders should be untrammelled to furnish these, and the employes untrammelled in the exercise of his right to purchase where his interest will best be subserved. If, however, these masters of aggregated capital can use their power over their employes as in this case, all other traders except such as they choose to permit will be driven away or crushed out, and their capital probably alone have a monopoly to furnish his employes at his own rates freed from competition. The result is that capital may crush legitimate trade, and thus cripple the general property of the country and the employe be subject to its grinding exactions at will.

The principle of the majority opinion will justify employers, at any rate allow them to require employes to trade where they may demand, to vote as they may require, or do anything not strictly criminal that employer may dictate, or feel the wrath of employer by dismissal from service. Employment is the means of sustaining life to himself and family to the employe, and so he is morally though not legally compelled to submit. Capital may thus not only find its own legitimate employment, but may control the employment of others to an extent that in time may sap the foundations of our free institutions. Perfect freedom in all legitimate uses is due to capital, and should be zealously enforced but public policy and all the best interests of society demands it shall be restrained within legitimate boundaries, and any channel by which it may escape or overleap these boundaries, should be carefully but judiciously guarded. For its legitimate uses I have perfect respect, against its illegitimate use I feel bound, for the best interests both of capital and labor, to protest. * * *

## NOTES AND QUESTIONS

1. The English rule of master and servant presumed all contracts of service to be for a fixed period—as agreed to by the parties or, if not, as set by the custom or usage of the trade; and such was translated into the early law of the United States. This presumption was thought to protect both parties from opportunistic behavior by the other. For example, in agriculture the presumed period was one year or a cycle of the seasons so that the master had to maintain the servant in the winter when there was little work to do and the servant could not abandon the master in the fall when the harvest was due. During the fixed period of employment, servants could only be let go only upon "reasonable notice" or "for cause." The servant was obligated to obey all lawful and reasonable orders the master might give; failing to do so would be cause to discharge. Where, for example, an employer, for reasons of safety, forbad employees to smoke on the premises, the rule was held to be reasonable as a matter of law; and so an employee's willful disobedience gave cause

to dismiss. *Honigstein v. Hollingsworth*, 39 Misc. 314, 79 N.Y.S. 867 (N.Y. App. Term 1902); *Forsyth v. McKinney*, 8 N.Y.S. 561 (N.Y. Gen. Term 1890).

In *Payne* the court applied what became known as "the American rule" or "at-will" rule in evaluating the employees' contractual rights. Under this rule, there is no presumption of a definite term of employment, and any contract for an indefinite term is presumed to be "at-will" in that the employer can discharge the employee at any time for any reason, good or bad, or even for no reason. However, if the employment contract *does* specify a definite term, for example "employment for one year," then it is presumed that the employee can only be discharge "for good cause" during that term. H.G. Wood, A Treatise on the Law of Master & Servant: Covering the Relation, Duties and Liabilities of Employers and Employees § 134, at 272 (1872). The "at-will" rule, and several modern exceptions, will be discussed at length in Chapter IV.

2. The Tennessee Supreme Court opined that *if* the employees of the railroad were under contracts of fixed terms of service, termination during the term of the contract for a refusal to obey the Superintendant's order would not be "warranted, and would give the employee an action for breach of contract." Why should the presence of a contract for a fixed term make such a difference? As the law of master and servant obligated the servant to obey all lawful and reasonable orders of an employer, it was always a question for a court—a question for public disposition—whether the order was lawful and reasonable, was one the employee *ought* to have obeyed. In *International & G. N. Ry. Co. v. Greenwood*, 2 Tex.Civ.App. 76, 21 S.W. 559 (1893), for example, the railroad had ordered about 1,000 of its workers in Houston not to eat or drink at the plaintiff's hotel, resulting in the hotel owner's suit against the railroad. In this case, identical to *Payne*, the plaintiff prevailed. The appellate court said that as the employees had the right to eat and drink where they chose and such an order was not within the company's power to issue, at least to persons already employed. *Id.* at 561. (Why should *that* distinction be drawn?) No mention was made of whether any of these 1,000 employees were serving on contracts of fixed term.

3. In 1880, of a total labor force of over seventeen million workers, over 1.1 million were employed in domestic service, *i.e.*, about 6.5% of the total workforce. Given the absence of modern labor saving household devices, domestic help was a necessity for the maintenance of middle class domesticity, presumably including the home economics of the judiciary. Could a maid be told where to shop on her employer's account? Where to shop on her own account or, for that matter, what places she might frequent or her spare time? That would be so because, as a domestic, she was, like a child, an extension of the household. Is that rationale applicable to Superintendent Anderson's order to road's locomotive engineers, firemen, and brakemen?

4. Note how robustly the majority embraces *laissez-faire* even to the point of being oblivious to the irony of the observation that, "The great and rich and powerful are guaranteed the same liberty and privilege as the poor and weak. All may buy and sell where they choose; they may refuse to employ or dismiss whom they choose." Twenty-five years later, the ascerbic social critic Anatole France was to employ virtually the same words for that very

purpose: "The law in its majestic equality forbids both the rich and the poor from sleeping under the bridges and begging in the streets...." ANATOLE FRANCE, LE LYS ROUGE (1910). Howsoever straight-faced, the court proclaims the complete ascendance of the "market autonomy" conception of free labor over the "individual independence" embraced by the dissent. The historian Walter Licht has observed, echoed later by Jonathan Witt, that such a robust notion of *laissez-faire* "would have appeared foreign to Americans" of the early Republic. WALTER LICHT, INDUSTRIALIZING AMERICA: THE NINETEENTH CENTURY 191 (1995). Nor, as we have seen, was it consistent with the antecedent law of master and servant. The law had been transformed.

Philip Selznik explains the transformation thusly: the ascendance of market autonomy retained an appearance of continuity even as it worked at making a major change.

> The contractual theory ostensibly gave full discretion to the parties in defining the nature and scope of authority. In fact, however, the law imported into the employment contract a set of implied terms reserving full authority of direction and control to the employer. Once the contract was defined as an *employment* contract, the master-servant model was brought into play. The natural and inevitable authority of the master could then be invoked, for that authority had already been established as the defining characteristic of the master-servant relation. In this way, the continuing master-servant imagery lent a legal foundation to managerial prerogative.

> But the old master-servant model was only *partially* incorporated into the new law of employment. The traditional association of "master" and "authority" was welcomed, but in its modern dress authority was impersonalized, stripped of the sense of personal duty, commitment, and responsibility that once accompanied it, at least in theory. Although many employers felt such obligations, the new legal doctrine showed little interest in managerial benevolence. It presumed that each party would take care of his own interests and provide for them in a freely bargained agreement. The limited moral commitment of the employer justified any arrangement he could impose. The terms of the agreement, not the law of the employment contract, would have to be relied on for substantive justice in the plant.

> The prerogative contract gave the employer an open-ended sovereign power. But * * * a contract impliedly giving broad powers of decision to one party, and establishing the subordination of another, was hardly an ordinary contract. It was at best a Hobbesian social compact giving full discretion to the sovereign employer. This violated the spirit of nineteenth-century contractualism, which looked to voluntary agreements, based on bargaining over specific terms, as the substitute for prescriptive regulation by government.

PHILIP SELZNICK, LAW, SOCIETY, AND INDUSTRIAL JUSTICE 136 (1969) (italics in original).

5. In *Hutton v. Watters*, 132 Tenn. 527, 179 S.W. 134 (1915), the Supreme Court of Tennessee overruled *Payne* to the extent it had denied that a tort would be available under those facts. The court held that a boarding-

house owner could sue the president of a school who had told his employees that they would be fired if they boarded with her, this out of a "feeling of ill will" toward her on the president's part. However, the court also quoted Justice Freeman's dissent in *Payne*, set out above, as an accurate statement of the law. Justice Freeman's opinion, after rejecting the analogy of an employee to a domestic, went on to observe: "This is not in any way to interfere with the legal right to discharge an employee for good cause, or without any reason assigned *if the contract justifies it....*" (Italics added). What does "justify" mean? That the terms of the contract allow an employee to discharge "without assigning any reason"? *I.e.*, without having to state and so prove the existence of cause to dismiss? To discharge arbitrarily? Would the contract not have to set that out as an express term? Or would that be a default rule—one to be implied in the absence of an express term?

## C.　THE POLITICAL RESPONSE

Of course the courts were not the only institution grappling with the question of the appropriate bounds of property and contract in American law. During this time, Congress was called upon to determine once and for all "the great question of the time," whether a person and his or her labor could be the property of another, either against that person's will or after consent through contract. Even after that fundamental decision had been made, Congress and state legislatures had to deal with a growing number of petitions to intercede into the employment relationship to specify terms of employment or require the provision of some right or benefit. Perhaps not surprisingly, in responding to their constituencies' demands, the legislatures tended to have a more expansive view of the appropriate role of the government intervention into contractual relations than the early courts.

## 1.　ABOLITION OF INVOLUNTARY SERVITUDE

The Thirteenth Amendment provides:

"Neither slavery nor involuntary servitude except as a punishment for a crime whereof the party shall have been duly convicted, shall exist within the United States."

Congress implemented this Amendment by a statute in 1867 which declared that, "The holding of any person to service on labor under the system known as peonage is abolished and forever prohibited" and that any laws which enforce "the voluntary or involuntary service or labor of any person as peons in liquidation of any debt or obligation, or otherwise, are declared null and void." 42 U.S.C. § 1994.

### NOTES AND QUESTIONS

1.　The following is a form contract used by an employer of farm labor in South Carolina in 1903:

"I agree at all times to be subject to the orders and commands of said
_____ or his agents, perform all work required of me _____ or his
agents shall have the right to use such force as he or his agents may deem
necessary to compel me to remain on his farm and to perform good and
satisfactory services. He shall have the right to lock me up for safekeeping, work me under the rules and regulations of his farm, and if I should
leave his farm or run away he shall have the right to offer and pay a
reward of not exceeding $25 for my capture and return, together with the
expenses of same, which amount so advanced, together with any other
indebtedness, I may owe _____ at the expiration of above time, I agree
to work out under all rules and regulations of this contract at same wages
as above, commencing _____ and ending _____.

"The said _____ shall have the right to transfer his interest in this
contract to any other party, and I agree to continue work for said
assignee same as the original party of the first part."

Reprinted in RICHARD T. ELY, STUDIES IN THE EVOLUTION OF INDUSTRIAL SOCIETY 407
(1903).

According to Professor Ely, the employees working under these contracts
professed themselves "satisfied and contented with the arrangements." Is the
contract lawful under the Thirteenth Amendment? If it is, should specific
enforcement be granted? Does such private enforcement constitute "involuntary servitude" when the employment contract has been entered into voluntarily? Compare *Robertson v. Baldwin*, 165 U.S. 275, 17 S.Ct. 326, 41 L.Ed.
715 (1897) (allowing the compulsory return of seamen who "jump ship" to
complete the voyage they agreed to work) (Harlan, J., dissenting) with *Bailey
v. Alabama*, 219 U.S. 219, 31 S.Ct. 145, 55 L.Ed. 191 (1911) (holding violative
of the 13th Amendment a law making a quitting of work conclusive evidence
of an intent not to perform a contract of employment which then subjects the
employee to prosecution for criminal fraud) (Holmes, J., dissenting).

2. The unenforceability of any private agreement poses a bit of a puzzle
for liberal economists: why not enforce contracts that both sides agree to and
which they presumably benefit from? With respect to agreements to enter into
servitude or slavery economists have acknowledged the following arguments
supporting prohibition:

(a) to prevent us from making contracts we will later regret ("self-
paternalism");

(b) to prevent relationships that are offensive to most people and so, even
though they might benefit the parties involved, impose "external" psychic
costs on other members of society;

(c) that it is so rare that such a contract would be advantageous for the
servant that it minimizes adjudicatory costs to adopt an irrebuttable
presumption that such contracts are procured by duress or fraud. MORTON
J. HOROWITZ, THE TRANSFORMATION OF AMERICAN LAW, 1790–1860, at 187–88
(1977).

Suffice it to say, arguments based on the immorality of such agreements or on
judgments that it is not in a person's best interests to enter into such
agreements ("true paternalism") carry little weight in the economic lexicon.

There is another argument, grounded in political economy, to the negative externalities of even freely entered contracts of slavery: that there is a social and, especially, a political detrimental consequence, not just a psychic insult, to a society in which any number of its citizens become non-persons incapable of voluntary political association or engagement. From the perspective of the market autonomy model of free labor, however, why contracts to create a master-slave relationship should not be enforced "remains a very hard question." RICHARD EPSTEIN, FORBIDDEN GROUNDS: THE CASE AGAINST EMPLOYMENT DISCRIMINATION LAWS 20 n.6 (1992). Why is this a *very* hard question? *See* STEPHEN MAGLIN, THE DISMAL SCIENCE: HOW THINKING LIKE AN ECONOMIST UNDERMINES COMMUNITY (2008).

## 2. LABOR PROTECTIVE LEGISLATION

The regulation of labor was a feature of colonial government. In the face of labor scarcity the colonies often enacted limits on the wages a worker could exact. RICHARD B. MORRIS, GOVERNMENT AND LABOR IN EARLY AMERICA ch. 1 (1946). In the post-Revolutionary period, there were collective protests—pamphlets and "broadsides," legislative remonstrances, demonstrations, marches, protests, and strikes—over wages, hours, and working conditions. *See, e.g.,* PAUL A. GILJE & HOWARD B. ROCK, KEEPERS OF THE REVOLUTION: NEW YORKERS AT WORK IN THE EARLY REPUBLIC (1992); DAVID ZONDERSMAN, ASPIRATIONS & ANXIETIES: NEW ENGLAND WORKERS AND THE MECHANIZED FACTORY SYSTEM, 1815–1850 (1992). These grew apace in tandem with industrialization resulting in calls for protective legislation assuring payment in U.S. currency, limiting work hours—first for children and women, then in more hazardous occupations such as mining and baking (where long hours in dank tenement conditions and continuous exposure to flour dust could lead to or exacerbate lung disease), and eventually for all workers in the "ten hour day" and the later "eight hour day" movements—dealing with occupational health and safety and the consequences of industrial accidents and opening on to more protective schemes, often influenced or legitimated by experience in Europe. *See generally* DAVID MONTGOMERY, THE FALL OF THE HOUSE OF LABOR: THE WORKPLACE, THE STATE, AND AMERICAN LABOR ACTIVISM, 1865–1925 (1987); DAVID T. RODGERS, ATLANTIC CROSSINGS: SOCIAL POLITICS IN A PROGRESSIVE AGE (1998). Labor unrest and collective bargaining became the subject of a separate body of federal law following enactment of the National Labor Relations Act in 1935, the subject we call "labor law" today. But a patchwork floor of labor protective rights was set, plank by plank, first at the state and later at the federal level.

These kinds of laws proved vexing to the state and federal courts at the turn of the century, for they were enacted when the prevailing economic philosophy was *laissez-faire,* and its judicial off-spring was "freedom of contract." *See generally* RICHARD HOFSTADTER, SOCIAL DARWINISM IN AMERICAN THOUGHT 1860–1915 (1945); William E. Forbath, *The Ambiguities of Free Labor: Labor and Law in the Guilded Age,* 1985 WIS. L. REV. 767 (1985).

The high water mark of economic substantive due process was thought to have been reached in *Lochner v. New York*, 198 U.S. 45, 25 S.Ct. 539, 49 L.Ed. 937 (1905), striking down a law providing maximum hours of work for bakers. It has been argued, however, that *Lochner* did not "usher in a reign of terror for social legislation." David P. Currie, *The Constitution in the Supreme Court: The Protection of Economic Interests, 1889–1910*, 52 U. CHI. L. REV. 324, 381 (1985). Apart from *Adair v. United States*, 208 U.S. 161, 28 S.Ct. 277, 52 L.Ed. 436 (1908), which struck down a law forbidding the railroads to discriminate against union members in employment, the Court actually continued to uphold most challenged legislation. *See, e.g., Knoxville Iron Co. v. Harbison*, 183 U.S. 13, 22 S.Ct. 1, 46 L.Ed. 55 (1901) (sustaining a Tennessee law requiring that vouchers given in payment for work be redeemable in money). But some state courts struck down labor protective legislation on freedom of contract grounds. For example, in *Jordan v. State*, 51 Tex.Crim. 531, 103 S.W. 633 (App. 1907), the court struck down a Texas law forbidding the payment of wages in goods or merchandise in an opinion drenched in the market autonomy conception of free labor:

> In this country the employee today may be the employer next year, and protective legislation belittle their intelligence, and reflect upon their standing as free citizens. It is our boast that no class distinctions exist in this country. An interference by the Legislature with the freedom of the citizen in making contracts, denying to a part of the people, possessing sound minds and memory, the right to bargain concerning the equivalent they may desire to receive as compensation for their labor, is to create or carve out a class from a body of the people, and place that class within the pale of protective laws which invidiously distinguish them from other free citizens; thus dividing by arbitrary fiat equally free and intelligent people into distinctive classes or grades, the one marked by law as the object of legislative solicitude, and the other not.

Others, however, saw a similarity between coercion accomplished through fraud and coercion accomplished through dominant bargaining power. Learned Hand, for example, opined:

> For the state to intervene to make more just and equal the relative strategic advantages of the two parties to the contract, of whom one is under the pressure of absolute want, while the other is not, is as proper a legislative function as that it should neutralize the relative advantages arising from fraudulent cunning or from superior physical force. At one time the law did not try to equalize the advantages of fraud, but we have generally come to concede that the exercise of such mental superiority as fraud indicates, has no social value, but the opposite. It may well be that the uncontrolled exercise of the advantages derived from possessing the means of living of other men will also become recognized as giving no social benefit corresponding to the evils which result. If so, there is no ground for leaving it uncontrolled in the hands of individuals.

Learned Hand, *Due Process of Law and the Eight–Hour Day*, 21 HARV. L. REV. 495, 506 (1908).

The issue came to a head during the throes of the Great Depression. On "Black Thursday" October 24, 1929 a speculative bubble in the stock market burst, driving the stock market down and triggering the many bank failures. As the nation's wealth and money supply contracted, aggregate demand for goods and services declined, resulting in massive layoffs. For over a decade, the nation's unemployment rate exceeded 10% and reached heights estimated at 25–30%. In this economic environment, employees' had little or no ability to address their needs and concerns through individual contractual rights. Many employees could not find work and even those who retained their jobs had little bargaining power. Desperate employers reneged on promised wages and benefits and unilaterally imposed new contract terms. The facility with which employers were able to jettison long term commitments and benefits to employees under the existing regime of freedom of contract contributed to a growing political consensus on the need for government regulation and guarantees of benefits. Moreover, the disintegration of employees' livelihood further contributed to the decrease in aggregate demand and the severity of the economic downturn.

In 1932, Franklin Delano Roosevelt (FDR) and the Democrats were swept to office on a tidal wave of discontent with President Hoover and the policies of the Republican Party. In his presidential campaign, FDR had promised a "New Deal" for the American people that would provide work, security and a voice in the running of the economy. On the basis of his mandate for government action, FDR and his "New Dealer" Democrats enacted a series of protective statutes designed to rationalize the market, specify minimum terms and conditions of employment and provide the "social security" of government sponsored life and pension benefits and unemployment insurance. Social Security Act, ch. 531, 49 Stat. 620, codified as 42 U.S.C. ch.7. Their purpose in enacting these statutes was to present capitalism with "a human face" that constrained the terms within which individuals could operate under freedom of contract. Their purpose was also to get money back in the hands of working men and women in hopes that this would help the economy spiral up, rather than down.

In the early Constitutional tests of New Deal legislation, the Supreme Court clung doggedly to the conception of the limited role of government contained in the *Lochner* doctrine. In *A.L.A. Schechter Poultry Corp. v. United States*, 295 U.S. 495, 55 S.Ct. 837, 79 L.Ed. 1570 (1935), the Supreme Court struck down "codes of fair competition" under the National Industrial Recovery Act as constituting an unconstitutional delegation of legislative authority and exceeding Congressional authority under the commerce clause. Because of their resistance to his legislative agenda, FDR proposed expanding the membership of the Court by adding a new Justice for every sitting member over the age of 70½, up to a maximum of six. Whether because of the threat of FDR's "court-packing plan" or the economic exigencies of the time, the Court came to accept a more active role for government in the running of the economy and interceding on workers' behalf in the employment relationship.

The Court's new view on freedom of contract was announced in *West Coast Hotel v. Parrish*, 300 U.S. 379, 57 S.Ct. 578, 81 L.Ed. 703 (1937), where the Court sustained a Washington state minimum wage law covering women and minors. The Court opined in pertinent part:

> In each case the violation alleged by those attacking minimum wage regulation for women is deprivation of freedom of contract. What is this freedom? The Constitution does not speak of freedom of contract. It speaks of liberty and prohibits the deprivation of liberty without due process of law. In prohibiting that deprivation the Constitution does not recognize an absolute and uncontrollable liberty. Liberty in each of its phases has its history and connotation. But the liberty safeguarded is liberty in a social organization which requires the protection of law against the evils which menace the health, safety, morals and welfare of the people. Liberty under the Constitution is thus necessarily subject to the restraints of due process, and regulation which is reasonable in relation to its subject and is adopted in the interests of the community is due process. * * *

> This power under the Constitution to restrict freedom of contract has had many illustrations. That it may be exercised in the public interest with respect to contracts between employer and employee is undeniable. Thus statutes have been sustained limiting employment in underground mines and smelters to eight hours a day * * * in requiring redemption in cash of store orders or other evidences of indebtedness issued in the payment of wages * * * in forbidding the payment of seamen's wages in advance * * * in making it unlawful to contract to pay miners employed at quantity rates upon the basis of screened coal instead of the weight of the coal as originally produced in the mine * * * in prohibiting contracts limiting liability for injuries to employees * * * in limiting hours of work of employees in manufacturing establishments * * * and in maintaining workmen's compensation laws * * * In dealing with the relation of employer and employed, the legislature has necessarily a wide field of discretion in order that there may be suitable protection of health and safety, and that peace and good order may be promoted through regulations designed to insure wholesome conditions of work and freedom from oppression. * * *

> The point that has been strongly stressed that adult employees should be deemed competent to make their own contracts was decisively met nearly forty years ago in *Holden v. Hardy*, [169 U.S. 366, 397, 18 S.Ct. 383, 390, 42 L.Ed. 780], * * * where we pointed out the inequality in the footing of the parties. * * *

>> "The legislature has also recognized the fact, which the experience of legislators in many States has corroborated, that the

proprietors of these establishments and their operatives do not stand upon an equality, and that their interests are, to a certain extent, conflicting. The former naturally desire to obtain as much labor as possible from their employees, while the latter are often induced by the fear of discharge to conform to regulations which their judgment, fairly exercised, would pronounce to be detrimental to their health or strength. In other words, the proprietors lay down the rules and the laborers are practically constrained to obey them. In such cases self-interest is often an unsafe guide, and the legislature may properly interpose its authority."

And we added that the fact "that both parties are of full age and competent to contract does not necessarily deprive the State of the power to interfere where the parties do not stand upon an equality, or where the public health demands that one party to the contract shall be protected against himself." "The State still retains an interest in his welfare, however reckless he may be. The whole is no greater than the sum of all the parts, and when the individual health, safety and welfare are sacrificed or neglected, the State must suffer."

Although the Supreme Court in *Parrish* did not explicitly overrule *Lochner*, it clearly gave state legislatures more deference in determining the terms and conditions of employment. The actual end of the doctrine of economic substantive due process was announced several years later in *Williamson v. Lee Optical of Oklahoma*, 348 U.S. 483, 75 S.Ct. 461, 99 L.Ed. 563 (1955) where a unanimous Supreme Court declared: "The day is gone when this Court uses the Due Process Clause of the Fourteenth Amendment to strike down state laws, regulatory of business and industrial conditions, because they may be unwise, improvident, or out of harmony with a particular school of thought."

## 3. THE ECONOMICS OF EMPLOYMENT REGULATION

The legal debate over the virtues of freedom of contract and the potential benefits of protective employment regulation has an analogy in economic analysis that is useful and instructive. In economics this debate takes place under the rubric of the neoclassical economic analysis of employment regulation and the qualifications or amendments that might need to be made to this analysis due to the complexities of the nature of workers and the employment relationship or "market failures."*

### (a.) The Neoclassical Analysis

The neoclassical analysis of employment regulation begins with a set of assumptions known, appropriately, as "the neoclassical model." In

---

* The exposition of the relevant economic arguments in this section relies heavily on Bruce Kaufman's work in Bruce E. Kaufman, *The Economics of Regulating the Labor Market, in* LABOR AND EMPLOYMENT LAW AND ECONOMICS 24–51 (Kenneth G. Dau–Schmidt, Seth D. Harris & Orley Lobel eds., 2009).

brief, these assumptions include: (1) *zero transaction costs*, or that there are no time, travel or information costs to any transaction; (2) *perfect information*, in that all information on prices, availability and production are free and equally available to all parties; (3) individuals have *stable preferences* that are rational and complete in that they give the individual a preferred choice in all situations; (4) *rational maximization*, in that individuals act to rationally maximize their utility according to their preferences and firms act to rationally maximize profits according to their production technology; and (5) *competitive markets* in that market forces, rather than individuals or firms, determine prices and wages and there is free entry and exit into all markets. In fact these assumptions are never literally true, and, as will be discussed later, when characteristics of the examined phenomenon violate these assumptions in important ways, economists are obliged to move to an analysis that relaxes the offending assumption to yield a more accurate and useful model. However, economists have focused on the neoclassical set of assumptions, at least as a first cut in examining problems, because they yield a mathematically tractable model that is useful in examining a wide variety of phenomena.

Based on these assumptions, the neoclassical analysis of employment regulation can be presented in a series of simple supply and demand curves. In presenting the analysis it is useful to distinguish between two basic kinds of employment regulation: "labor market regulations" and "employment mandates." Labor market regulations are those that constrain or supplant the competitive market in determining wages and thereby directly change the negotiated terms of the labor contract. Examples include: a minimum wage law, a law to foster collective bargaining as means of raising workers' wages, a law prohibiting child labor, or a law prohibiting differences in pay based on race. Employment mandates require that employers provide a particular term or condition of employment, either directly or through a government program funded by an employment tax or employer contribution. These mandates may shift either or both the demand and supply curves for labor and thus indirectly affect the terms of the labor contact. Examples include: workers' compensation, unemployment compensation, paid maternity leave, advance warning of plant closure, and equal opportunity in job assignments and promotions. Although in practice the concepts of labor market regulations and employment mandates overlap, in theory they are distinct and must be presented separately.

The neoclassical analysis of a labor market regulation, such as a minimum wage law, is presented in Figure 1.1, panels (a) and (b). Panel (a) represents a competitive labor market with supply curve $S_C$ and demand curve $D_C$ that becomes "covered" by the minimum wage law, while Panel (b) represents a closely connected competitive labor market, for the same type of labor, with supply curve $S_U$ and demand curve $D_U$ that that remains "uncovered" by the law. Before the minimum wage law is instituted, the markets come to equilibrium at the point at which supply equals demand yielding the same equilibrium wage ($W_1$) in both markets.

At wages above $W_1$, labor supply exceeds demand and wages are driven down, while at wages below $W_1$, labor demand exceeds demand and wages are driven down. This equilibrium is "efficient" in that employers purchase labor up to the point where its marginal productivity equals its marginal cost ($W_1$) and efficiently combine this labor with capital in production. Efficient consumption of the good produced also ensues as consumers purchase the good up until the point where their marginal utility from the good equals its price. Once the minimum wage law is passes, it introduces a price floor of $W_2$ into the covered labor market, raising the wage from $W_1$ to $W_2$, above the market level.

Figure 1.1. Neoclassical Model: Economic Effects of a Labor Market Regulation

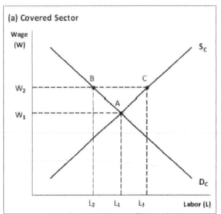
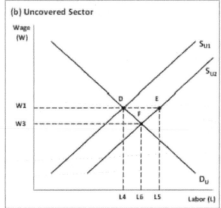

When the minimum wage is instituted, a number of adverse things are predicted to happen. First, the higher wage leads to involuntary unemployment ($L_3$–$L_1$) as employers cut back their level of demand from $L_1$ to $L_2$ and the higher wage draws more people into the covered labor market increasing the quantity of labor supplied from $L_1$ to $L_3$. Second, some of the $L_3$–$L_1$ unemployed workers become discouraged by lack of jobs in the covered sector and shift to the uncovered sector, shifting out the labor supply curve from $S_{U1}$ to $S_{U2}$. This shift in the supply curve depresses wages in the uncovered market, driving them down from $W_1$ to $W_3$. Third, the institution of the minimum wage causes inefficient methods of production among the covered employers in that they now have incentive to purchase more capital to save on the employees' higher wages. Finally, the minimum wage causes inefficient consumption in that the employers are forced to raise the price of their good to consumers and as a result the consumers will cut their consumption below the efficient level. Thus the neoclassical model predicts that labor market regulation results in higher wages for some, but lower wages and increased prices for others, causing inefficient production and consumption and a net transfer of wealth from some members of society to others.

The neoclassical analysis of an employment mandate, such as unemployment compensation, is similar, but sufficiently different to warrant a distinct graphical analysis. Figure 1.2 depicts a competitive labor market before and after the imposition of an employment mandate. Before the employment mandate is imposed, the amount of labor demanded by the employers at each possible wage is given by $D_1$, while the amount of labor supplied by the employees at each possible wage level is given by $S_1$. The market equilibrium occurs at $W_1/L_1$ where supply equals demand. Now assume the government requires all employers to provide workers with a good, such as unemployment insurance, funded by a tax on the employers. Such a mandate has two effects. First, because the mandate increases the cost of labor to the employers at any given wage, it shifts the demand curve down by the amount of the tax, from $D_1$ to $D_2$. Second, because the mandate increases the benefit of working to the employees at any given wage, it shifts the supply curve down by the amount of the value of the mandate to the workers, from $S_1$ to $S_2$. The result is that, after the imposition of the unemployment compensation system, the labor market reaches a new equilibrium $W_2/L_2$ where demand equals supply according to the new demand and supply curves. The actual impact of the mandate on wages and employment depends on: how expensive the mandate is to employers, how much it is valued by the employees, and the slopes of the demand and supply curves. As depicted in Figure 1.2, the effect of the legal mandate on this market is a new equilibrium with a lower wage ($W_2$) and lower employment level ($L_2$).

Figure 1.2. Neoclassical Model: Economic Effects
of an Employment Mandate

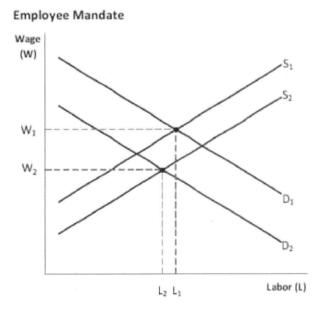

**Employee Mandate**

Within the context of the neoclassical model, an employment mandate is always inefficient, or at best provides no increase in efficiency. This is because, in the context of the neoclassical model, the government would only have to mandate a program, such as unemployment compensation, if the cost of the program to employers exceeded the value of the program to the employees. If the cost of the program to employers was less than the value of the program to employees, it would be part of the efficient contract for employment and the employers would voluntarily provide it in a competitive labor market. In the case in which the cost of the program to employers is the same as the value of the program to employees, the employers and employees are indifferent as to whether the program exists and it provides no increase or loss in social welfare.* However, in the case in which the program must be mandated because the cost to employers is greater than the value of the program to the employees, the mandate results in a deadweight loss in efficiency because the it forces employers to provide a term of employment that is wasteful because it is worth less to the employees than it costs the employers. The employees would be better off if the employers just paid the cost of the program to the employees in wages. This situation is the one depicted in Figure 1.2 where the demand curve shifts down by more than the supply curve and the level of employment drops from $L_1$ to $L_2$.

The results of the neoclassical model are consistent with many of the legal arguments that have been posed in favor of freedom of contract in *Lochner* and other cases. Under the neoclassical model, private agreements enhance wealth to the benefit of both parties, otherwise they would not agree to them. The efficient role for the state is merely to protect private property rights and enforce voluntary agreements as a means of channeling resources to their most valuable use. Any regulation beyond these basic functions is inefficient and only serves to decrease total wealth at best benefiting some people at the expense of others. Some law and economics scholars who champion the neoclassical analysis have gone further to add a normative dimension to their analysis arguing that private voluntary exchange also promotes such virtues as individual autonomy, initiative and responsibility. RICHARD EPSTEIN & JEFFREY PAUL, Labor Law and the Employment Market (1985); MILTON FRIEDMAN & ROSE FRIEDMAN, Free to Choose (1980). They see freedom of contract as an important principle in support of decentralized decision-making that supports freedom of choice in basic life decisions such as where to live, how to earn a living, how to spend your time and how to spend your wealth. MICHAEL TREBILCOCK, The Limits of Freedom of Contract (1993). Thus they advocate for the negative conception of liberty associated with freedom of contract, the right to be free from government intervention.

---

* There is also a qualification to the analysis to be made if either the demand or supply curves are perfectly vertical or horizontal.

## (b.) Economic Analyses Beyond the Neoclassical Model

Economists have also recognized that the neoclassical model is too simple to capture all of the features of the employment relationship. When an examined problem involves, in some important way, features of the employment relationship that are not captured by the neoclassical model, then the model does not adequately describe the problem and its prescription against regulation may be wanting. It is in the complexities of the employment relationship and the imperfections of the market that the economic case for regulation is made.

Some economists have raised fundamental objections to the neoclassical analysis. Several have pointed out that human labor is not a commodity. JOHN R. COMMONS, INSTITUTIONAL ECONOMICS: ITS PLACE IN POLITICAL ECONOMY (1934); BRUCE E. KAUFMAN, THE GLOBAL EVOLUTION OF INDUSTRIAL RELATIONS: EVENTS, IDEAS AND THE IIRA (2004); JOHN W. BUDD, EMPLOYMENT WITH A HUMAN FACE: BALANCING EFFICIENCY, EQUITY AND VOICE 43 (2004). The labor of a human being requires the investment of a portion of that person's life and, even though employment necessarily requires some subordination to the will of another, human beings have rights independent of any value of their labor as property or wealth. Thus, for example, we do not allow slavery, or even allow people to sell themselves into slavery, regardless of any possible impact such an arrangement would have on efficiency.* As a result, it is imperative that we take account of values other than efficiency in the regulation of the labor market. John W. Budd has summarized the relevant concerns as efficiency, equity and voice. *Id.* at 13. In other words, in addition to trying to promote the efficient use of resources, when regulating the employment relationship we have to remember that workers are people and try to promote equity between employees and employers and give workers a voice in the relationship. These concerns are lost in the simple neoclassical model.

Other economists have pointed to market imperfections that require amendment of the neoclassical analysis. Indeed some have argued that labor markets are *always* and *everywhere* imperfect. Bruce E. Kaufman, *The Non-existence of the Labor Demand/Supply Diagram and Other Theorems of Institutional Economics*, 29 J. LAB. RES. 285 (2008). This is evident in the fact that, contrary to the prediction of the neoclassical model, labor markets never clear in that the unemployment rate is never zero. Bruce Kaufman persuasively argues that the employment relationship would not even exist under the neoclassical assumptions. As the Nobel laureate Ronald Coase has asserted, in the absence of transaction costs there would be no firms. Accordingly, there would be no reason to employ another person and the entirety of General Motors Corporation would costlessly

---

* Historical data suggests that slave labor on the large plantations of the antebellum South was more productive than free labor on farms in the north, largely due to the gang system and economies of scale. Patrick Belser, *The Economics of Slavery, Forced Labor and Human Trafficking, in* LABOR AND EMPLOYMENT LAW AND ECONOMICS 424 (Kenneth G. Dau–Schmidt, Seth D. Harris & Orley Lobel eds., 2009). Never-the-less, we fought a just war to decide to end this horrible institution. Query how much normative weight should be given to the idea that slavery might be "efficient" when the slaves themselves have no say in the market?

assemble each day and transact business as tens of thousands of independent artisans and contractors. As a result, it is somewhat paradoxical to analyze the employment relationship and labor markets within the context of the pure neoclassical model. Bruce E. Kaufman, *The Economics of Regulating the Labor Market, in* LABOR AND EMPLOYMENT LAW AND ECONOMICS 3, 28–29 (Kenneth G. Dau–Schmidt, Seth D. Harris & Orley Lobel eds., 2009). These imperfections or "market failures" present opportunities for useful regulation of the labor market.

One commonly cited failure of the labor market is that employers generally have much more bargaining power than their employees. JOHN R. COMMONS & JOHN B. ANDREWS, PRINCIPLES OF LABOR LEGISLATION (1916); Karl Klare, *Countervailing Workers' Power as a Regulatory Strategy, in* LEGAL REGULATION OF THE EMPLOYMENT RELATIONSHIP 63–82 (Hugh Collins, M. Davies & Rodger Rideout eds., 2000). Bargaining power is defined as the ability to influence negotiations to gain a larger share of the benefits of the bargain. A party's bargaining power is determined by his or her alternatives and the party's ability to resist agreement relative to the other party to the agreement. There are a variety of reasons why employers enjoy more bargaining power than employees. Employers generally have a choice among many employees who might do a job, where as employees are generally lucky to have any choice among jobs. Large employers are generally not significantly inconvenienced by the loss of an employee, while an employee loses his or her livelihood for some time with the loss of a job. Labor is perishable in that a day of unemployment is a day of labor (and wages) that is forever lost to the employee. Employers also generally enjoy advantages in resources, information and legal rules. As a result they can hold out better in bargaining and enjoy advantages in negotiation and enforcement of the agreement. Sometimes employers are so dominant in a labor market that they enjoy monopsonistic power to set wages. A monopsonist, broadly defined,* is a buyer who enjoys market power because it is the only buyer, or one of only a few buyers, in a market. William M. Boal & Michael R. Ransom, *Monopsony in the Labor Market*, 35 J. ECON. LIT. 86 (1997); ALAN MANNING, MONOPSONY IN MOTION: IMPERFECT COMPETITION IN LABOUR MARKETS (2003). As a result the employer recognizes its ability to set wages and maximizes profits by cutting wages and cutting employment.

The case of a monopsonistic employer is presented graphically in Figure 1.3. In the case of a monopsonistic employer, the market supply curve is the labor supply curve the employer faces and it is upward sloping, reflecting the fact that the employer is not a price-taker, but instead can instead drive wages down, at the expense of eliciting less labor. The employer's marginal cost of labor curve (MCL) lies above the supply curve, reflecting the fact that, as the employer buys more labor, it has to not only pay the new labor an increased wage, but also pay all of its

---

\* I define Monopsony here broadly to include oligopsony, monopsonistic competition, and other market situations in which the labor supply curve of a single firm is upward sloping.

prior workers an increased wage.** As a result, the marginal addition to total cost of each additional unit of labor is greater than the labor's wage and the marginal cost of labor curve lies above the supply curve. Also, in the case of the monopsonistic employer, the employer's demand for labor is the market demand, although as we will see it does not follow the dictates of the firm's production technology in the same way it would in a competitive market. The relevant production technology is represented by the firm's marginal revenue product curve (MRP), which would be the market labor demand curve in the competitive case. The firm maximizes profits by employing each unit of labor for which its addition to total revenue (marginal revenue product) exceeds its addition to total cost (marginal revenue cost). Accordingly the employer employs labor up until the point $L_1$ where the marginal cost of labor equals its marginal revenue product (point A) and paying all labor the necessary wage according to the labor supply curve, $W_1$ (point B). Comparing this solution with the equilibrium that would have resulted cost in the competitive case where demand equals supply (point C), we see that the monopsonistic employer increases profits by choking back both wages and employment below the competitive levels.** In such a case regulation can improve both workers' lot and efficiency. For example, if the government set a minimum wage of $W_2$, the employer could no longer realize greater profits by cutting wages and employment and would decide to employ $L_2$ employees at $W_2$, increasing both wages and employment to the efficient level that would exist in a competitive market.

Another commonly cited imperfection of the labor market is significant transaction costs. Benjamin Klein, *Transaction Costs Determinants of 'Unfair' Contractual Arrangements*, 70 AM. ECON. REV. PAPERS & PROC. 356 (1980); Kenneth R. Vogel, *Analysis of Labour Contracts and their Administration Using Transaction Costs Economics*, 5 L. & POL. Q. 129 (1983). Although some employment relationships are fairly simple, for example paying home workers a piece rate for sewn sleeves, most are longer and more complicated relationships involving employee development, difficulties in monitoring production and deferred rewards. Long complicated relationships are more costly to fully specify and formally enforce than short one-time exchanges, and as a result, almost all employment contracts are less than fully specified and subject to implicit terms. This creates potential for employer and employee opportunistic behavior in the absence of attentive legal doctrines or statutes. For example, prior to the passage of ERISA, some unscrupulous employers discharged valuable employees in their twenty-ninth year of service merely to prevent them

---

** It is assumed that the employer cannot discriminate among workers with respect to wages, but instead must pay all workers the same wage.

** Alternatively, a monopsonistic firm may pay a competitive wage but exploit workers by reducing other terms and conditions of employment, such as benefits or safety expenditures; another option is to exercise its power through oppressive or onerous work supervision and discipline. In such cases government regulation to increase benefits or decrease oppression would improve workers' lives, and efficiency.

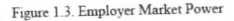

Figure 1.3. Employer Market Power

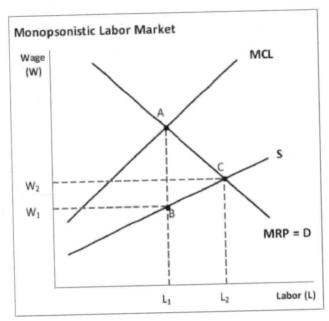

from earning the thirty year pension. Such pensions were promised to "good employees" as an inducement for hard work and investment in their job, but often not reduced to enforceable writings due to the costs of managing such a promise over time. As you will learn in Chapter 11, the vesting requirements of ERISA have solved this problem. Similarly, even if an employee has a well established contractual or common law right in the employment relationship, it may be too costly for the employee to enforce that right through a court of law. For example, in the early twentieth century, employees signed away meritorious tort suits against their employers for a pittance because had no resources to litigate with their employer and needed money and a job now. Workers' Compensation laws have eased this problem, providing workers with a low cost administrative means to receive compensation for their injuries, protect their jobs in filing a claim and give employers incentive to adequately account for the costs of injuries in production and price.

Yet another cited failure of the labor market is imperfect information. Ann–Sophie Vandenberghe, *Employment Contracts, in* LABOR AND EMPLOYMENT LAW AND ECONOMICS 83–86 (Kenneth G. Dau–Schmidt, Seth D. Harris & Orley Lobel eds., 2009). On this count, it may be that both the employer and the employee suffer from the same lack of information, or it may be that one of the parties has an advantage in gaining information so that there is an "information asymmetry" in the negotiation of the employment relationship. For example, a small employer may prefer that his janitorial staff use a certain cleaner because it is both cheap and effective. Unbeknownst to both the employer and the employees, the cleaner is effective because it contains a powerful agent that also significantly increases the risk of cancer in people with long-term exposure. The use of the cleaner is in fact inefficient in that if the parties knew how dangerous it was, the employees would not be willing to work with it without a significant compensating wage that would price the use of the cleaner out of the employer's consideration. However, due to imperfect information the parties would use the cleaner, leaving some of the janitorial staff to contract cancer several years later, perhaps even several years after leaving this employment relationship. This market imperfection presents an opportunity for beneficial and efficient regulation of working conditions by an agency that evaluates health and safety risks and promulgates rules for safe work practices. In essence such regulation attempts to minimize distortions due to the costs of information by having a centralized agency collect such information on behalf of both employees and employers and distributing that information in the form of rules.

A final form of market failure that is commonly attributed to the labor market is that many terms of employment are "public goods." John Addison & Barry Hirsch, *The Economic Effects of Employment Regulation: What are the Limits?, in* GOVERNMENT REGULATION OF THE EMPLOYMENT RELATIONSHIP 125–78 (Bruce E. Kaufman ed., 1997). A public good is a good that is non-rivalrous, in that many people can enjoy the same good, and non-excludable, in that if one person enjoys the good they cannot exclude others from enjoying the good. Thus, for example, slowing the speed of the assembly line, break-time away from coordinated production, improved light and air quality of the plant, perhaps even the choice of a better insurer for the health insurance plan, all are public goods in the workplace in that if the change is made many workers will benefit from it and the employer cannot make the change just for one employee and not others. The problem with public goods is that no individual employee has adequate incentive to negotiate for the improvement in that good because the benefits of the improvement will be shared by others while the costs of concessions to gain the benefit will be born by the individual employee. All employees have incentive to hold back and "free ride," hoping that some other employee will negotiate the benefit and that they will then share in the benefit without having to concede anything more to the employer. As a result, economists predict that individual bargaining will result in less than the efficient amount of public goods being negotiated in the workplace. This imperfection raises the possibility of beneficial regulation to increase such public goods to their efficient level.

In addition to fundamental objections to the neoclassical model and market failures, some economists have argued that there are macroeconomic reasons why employment regulation might sometime be beneficial that are not represented in the simple neoclassical analysis. Bruce E. Kaufman, *The Economics of Regulating the Labor Market, in* LABOR AND EMPLOYMENT LAW AND ECONOMICS 36–46 (Kenneth G. Dau–Schmidt, Seth D. Harris & Orley Lobel eds., 2009). Some have pointed out that the simple neoclassical model provides just a snap shot of the labor market at one

instance in time. In fact the economy exists over time and can grow or shrink as the economy "cycles up" or "cycles down." They argue that, by promoting a stable employment relationship and better wages and working conditions over time, government regulation can encourage workers to invest in their human capital (education), which will allow employers to pay more for the workers' time and demand more of the workers' services and the economy can cycle up to a higher equilibrium.* This possibility is represented in Figure 1.4. As workers invest in their training and become more productive, their productivity rises and employers can pay more for their time and demand more of them. As a result in the graph, the employers' demand curve shifts out from $D_1$ to $D_3$, raising both the equilibrium wage and the amount of labor demanded. Similarly, an economy can "cycle down." As the American public has learned recently, when the economy goes into recession and people are laid off, their loss of earning power can serve to further aggravate the recession by causing a decline in aggregate demand for goods. In this case, the employers' demand curve for labor shifts in to a lower wage and lower employment equilibrium, for example from $D_3$ to $D_2$ in Figure 1.4. It is an important policy consideration behind the adoption of our unemployment compensation system that such a system would be "counter-cyclical" in that it would provide money to laid off workers during recessions not only to help maintain those workers, but also to help maintain aggregate demand so that the recession does not worsen.

The criticisms and amendments to the neoclassical model that have been made by some economists are consistent with the legal arguments for limiting the doctrine of freedom of contract and allowing regulation of the employment relationship. The prospect of employer dominance in bargaining power has led some economists to champion the positive conception of individual liberty which advocates protecting worker independence from coercion by state *or* corporate power. AMARTYA SEN, COMMODITIES AND CAPABILITIES (1999). Imperfections in the labor market present opportunities for useful regulation that benefits workers *and* increases efficiency. Moreover, regulation of the labor market might help us foster investment in human capital and the supply of labor that promotes economic growth and a better life for all. Of course in each case whether a particular regulation is inefficient and decreases wealth or efficient and increases wealth depends on whether the examined problem fits better into the neoclassical analysis or its amendments. Whether employment regulation is good or bad for society is both an empirical question of whether it appropriately addresses a market failure, and also a normative question of whether any costs or inefficiencies occasioned by the regulation are warranted by other benefits from the law in promoting equity or worker voice.

---

* It is useful to think of this argument as an analogy to the economic arguments that are often made regarding encouraging small businesses. Just as we want to promote profitable stable markets to encourage small business men to invest in their business, so too we want to encourage profitable stable labor markets and employment relationships to encourage people to invest in their training. As one wag said: "You can't make a nation rich by making its workers poor."

Figure 1.4 "Cycling Up" or "Cycling Down"

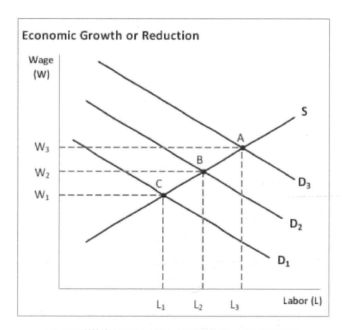

## 4. WHO IS AN "EMPLOYEE"?

In interpreting and applying any employment statute, one must confront the question of who is covered by the statute: who is a protected statutory "employee" and who is an excluded statutory non-employee. But what defines an "employee"? Sometimes the statute provides a definition or some guidance. The Fair Labor Standards Act (FLSA), our basic wage and hour law, defines a a covered "employee" as "any individual who is employed by an employer." 29 U.S.C. § 203(e). How the courts have dealt with this broad definition is explored in Chapter VII. By the same token, sometimes the statutory guidance can be restrictive: the National Labor Relations Act, our basic law dealing with unionization and collective bargaining, was amended in 1947 to exclude "any individual having the status of an independent contractor." Most often the word "employee" is used without further elaboration and left to fend for itself.

All these laws assume that there are persons producing goods or performing services for others who have need for protection in that relationship, that there are persons producing goods and performing services for others who do not need that protection, and that the law must find a way to distinguish the one from the other. This issue is instinct in every such labor protective regime.

## D'ANNUNZIO v. PRUDENTIAL INS. CO. OF AMERICA

Supreme Court of New Jersey, 2007
192 N.J. 110, 927 A.2d 113

JUSTICE LAVECCHIA delivered the opinion of the Court.

New Jersey's Conscientious Employee Protection Act (CEPA), *N.J.S.A.* 34:19–1 to –8, protects workers who blow the whistle on their employers' illegal, fraudulent, or otherwise improper activities that implicate the health, safety, and welfare of the public. The statute extends to "any individual who performs services for and under the control and direction of an employer for wages or other remuneration." *N.J.S.A.* 34:19–2(b) (defining "[e]mployee[s]" entitled to CEPA protection). The question here is who is included in that definition. We have recognized previously [in *Pukowsky v. Caruso*, 711 A.2d 398 (N.J. App. Div. 1998)] that that definition is not limited to a narrow band of traditional employees. In this appeal, we reaffirm the appropriateness of the *Pukowsky* test for assessing the status of an alleged "independent contractor" claiming protection as an "employee" under CEPA.

### I.

The appeal comes to us on a summary judgment record that focused solely on the "independent contractor" versus "employee" issue. Because the defendants claimed an entitlement to judgment based on that record, we view the facts in the light most favorable to the party opposing that motion and, therefore, accord to plaintiff all favorable inferences that support his claim to CEPA's protection.

In February 2000, defendant Prudential Property and Casualty Insurance Company (Prudential) hired plaintiff George D'Annunzio as a chiropractic medical director in its Personal Injury Protection (PIP) Department. Prudential's PIP Department reviews and pre-approves treatment plans submitted by the doctors who treat Prudential's insureds and other covered claimants injured in automobile accidents. It is the responsibility of the medical directors and nurse case managers to determine whether the proposed treatments are medically necessary, consistent with the PIP reforms authorized by the Automobile Insurance Cost Reduction Act (AICRA), *N.J.S.A.* 39:6A–1.1 to –35. Insurers engage licensed medical professionals to provide independent medical judgments as to the medical necessity of treatment plans submitted for approval. *See N.J.S.A.* 39:6A–3.1(a); *N.J.A.C.* 11:3–4.7(c)(4). Prudential opted to meet that requirement by having a cadre of licensed professionals in-house to perform the review function, but it designated those professionals as "independent contractors." Indeed, Prudential required every licensed medical director to maintain an active private professional practice and to agree that their hours billed to Prudential would not exceed fifty percent of their total professional practice.

Prudential sent D'Annunzio a one-year "Medical Director Consultant Agreement" that was described as "standard" for the position. For tax purposes, D'Annunzio executed the agreement in the name of his professional association (George D'Annunzio D.C.P.A.) rather than as a licensed individual, although the parties apparently agree that only a licensed individual could perform the tasks for which D'Annunzio was retained. Pursuant to the agreement, D'Annunzio was paid $125 per hour for twenty hours of work per week. D'Annunzio agreed to perform his services at a designated Prudential PIP claims office, Monday through Friday, from 8:00 a.m. until noon.

In respect of the relationship between the parties, the agreement stated that

> [t]he relationship between Prudential and the Medical Director is that of independent contractor. The Medical Director will maintain his own private practice and provide Medical Director services on a part time basis.... None of the provisions of this agreement are intended to create or be construed as creating any agency, partnership, joint venture or employer-employee relationship.

> As an independent contractor, [t]he Medical Director will have the sole responsibility for the payment of all self employment and applicable federal state and local taxes.

Both parties had the right to terminate the relationship without cause on sixty-days notice. Prudential also had the option of terminating the agreement immediately if D'Annunzio committed a material breach.

According to D'Annunzio, when he signed the agreement he expected to be permitted to perform his review function in an independent manner, as one might expect from a contractor of professional services. Instead, from his first day in Prudential's PIP Department, D'Annunzio found that Prudential sought to exert extensive control over him. D'Annunzio received a list of duties, workflow instructions, and a time sheet. The list of duties required that D'Annunzio (1) provide leadership and education to the staff; (2) review claims for medical appropriateness; (3) discuss treatment alternatives with doctors; (4) help to develop Prudential's care guidelines; (5) participate in peer reviews of colleagues; (6) participate in data analysis; and (7) provide in-house coverage through his physical presence or by being telephonically accessible during required hours. The workflow instructions included step-by-step directions for D'Annunzio to use in his review of PIP claims. In addition to requiring D'Annunzio to record his billable hours on Prudential's time sheet forms, other accouterments of the job appeared to D'Annunzio to be designed to make him essentially a cog in the machinery of Prudential's PIP Department.

As it turned out, D'Annunzio's tenure with Prudential was short-lived. During the summer of 2000 he informed supervisors of his objection to insurance violations that he perceived were being perpetrated by Prudential and its employees. D'Annunzio allegedly expressed concern about Prudential's failure to pay MRI bills, its hiring of non-medical vendors to perform independent medical evaluations, and the improper use of nurse case managers in the approval of medical care. In August and early September, D'Annunzio's supervisors Kathy Savvas, Linda Fraistat, Frank Hruska, and Anthony LoCastro informed him that his performance was not meeting expectations. D'Annunzio was advised to speed up his review of treatment files, to limit his reviews to claims involving chiropractic evaluations, and to reduce the number of treatment plans that he was denying. On September 11, 2000, Prudential gave D'Annunzio written notice that it was terminating its agreement with him based on the sixty-day notice provision.

D'Annunzio filed this action against Prudential, its parent company, as well as several officers and employees of Prudential. He alleged that he was fired because he had complained about Prudential's "lack of regulatory and contractual compliance" and that therefore his termination was in violation of CEPA. In addition, D'Annunzio asserted common law claims for breach of contract and wrongful discharge. * * *

[The trial court held that D'Annuzio was an independent contractor. The Appellate Division reversed.]

## II.

New Jersey's "conscientious employee" protection policy has as its genesis the decision of this Court in *Pierce v. Ortho Pharmaceutical Corp.,* 84 *N.J.* 58, 72, 417 *A.*2d 505 (1980), where we held that an at-will employee, wrongfully discharged in violation of "a clear mandate of public policy," has a common law cause of action against an employer. Following *Pierce,* the Legislature enacted CEPA, codified at *N.J.S.A.* 34:19–1 to –8. CEPA is remedial social legislation designed to promote two complementary public purposes: " 'to protect and [thereby] encourage employees to report illegal or unethical workplace activities and to discourage public and private sector employers from engaging in such conduct.' " *Yurick v. State,* 184 *N.J.* 70, 77, 875 *A.*2d 898 (2005) (quoting *Abbamont v. Piscataway Twp. Bd. of Educ.,* 138 *N.J.* 405, 431, 650 *A.*2d 958 (1994)). Specifically, in this dispute we are called on to address the scope of CEPA's protection of "employees" from retaliatory employment action.

Our goal in the interpretation of a statute is always to determine the Legislature's intent. *Wollen v. Borough of Fort Lee,* 27 *N.J.* 408, 418, 142 *A.*2d 881 (1958). To decipher that intent, we look first to the plain language of the statute, *Lane v. Holderman,* 23 *N.J.* 304, 313, 129 *A.*2d 8 (1957), and we ascribe to the statutory language its ordinary meaning, *DiProspero v. Penn,* 183 *N.J.* 477, 492, 874 *A.*2d 1039 (2005). "It is not the function of this Court to 'rewrite a plainly-written enactment of the Legislature [ ] or presume that the Legislature intended something other than that expressed by way of the plain language.' " *Ibid.* (quoting *O'Connell v. State,* 171 *N.J.* 484, 488, 795 *A.*2d 857 (2002)). When the plain language of a statute is susceptible to multiple interpretations, however, then recognized principles of statutory construction allow resort to extrinsic tools to determine the Legislature's likely intent. *See Aponte–Correa v. Allstate Ins. Co.,* 162 *N.J.* 318, 323, 744 *A.*2d 175 (2000).

CEPA prohibits an employer from taking adverse employment action against any "employee" who exposes an employer's criminal, fraudulent, or corrupt activities. *N.J.S.A.* 34:19–3. It authorizes an aggrieved employee to bring a civil suit against an employer who retaliates in violation of the statute. *N.J.S.A.* 34:19–5. Workers are thus protected from retaliation and employers are deterred from activities that are illegal or fraudulent, or otherwise contrary to a clear mandate of public policy concerning the safety, health, and welfare of the public. *See N.J.S.A.* 34:19–3; *Mehlman v. Mobil Oil Corp.*, 153 *N.J.* 163, 179, 707 *A.*2d 1000 (1998). When enacted, CEPA was "the most far reaching 'whistleblower statute' in the nation." *Mehlman, supra,* 153 *N.J.* at 179, 707 *A.*2d 1000. A single guiding principle has instructed our interpretation of CEPA in the decades since its enactment. As broad, remedial legislation, the statute must be construed liberally. . . .

CEPA defines an "employee" as

> any individual who performs services for and under the control and direction of an employer for wages or other remuneration.

The question is who is included in that definition. As the Appellate Division noted, the definition does not exclude, explicitly, persons who are designated as independent contractors performing services for an employer for remuneration. *D'Annunzio, supra,* 383 *N.J.Super.* at 279, 891 *A.*2d 673. It is beyond cavil that it includes more than the narrow band of traditional employees. In *Feldman, supra,* 187 *N.J.* at 241, 901 *A.*2d 322, when we considered the term's application in the context of a shareholder-director of a professional corporation, we specifically instructed courts to "look to the goals underlying CEPA and focus not on labels but on the reality of plaintiff's relationship with the party against whom the CEPA claim is advanced." *See also MacDougall v. Weichert,* 144 *N.J.* 380, 388, 677 *A.*2d 162 (1996) (emphasizing same for *Pierce* wrongful discharge claim).

Our courts have long recognized that, in certain settings, exclusive reliance on a traditional right-to-control test to identify who is an "employee" does not necessarily result in the identification of all those workers that social legislation seeks to reach. * * *

Taken out of context, labels can be illusory as opposed to illuminating. When CEPA or other social legislation must be applied in the setting of a professional person or an individual otherwise providing specialized services allegedly as an independent contractor, we must look beyond the label attached to the relationship. The considerations that must come into play are three: (1) employer control; (2) the worker's economic dependence on the work relationship; and (3) the degree to which there has been a functional integration of the employer's business with that of the person doing the work at issue. *See Lowe v. Zarghami,* 158 *N.J.* 606, 615–18, 731 *A.*2d 14 (1999). The test for determining those aspects of a non-traditional work relationship was set out in *Pukowsky* and we have already indicated our acceptance of that test as appropriate for CEPA purposes. In *Feldman,* *supra,* in which our dissenting colleague joined, we referenced *Pukowsky* as the standard for determining the independent-contractor status of an individual claiming entitlement to bring a CEPA action. 187 *N.J.* at 242, 901 *A.*2d 322.

In *Pukowsky,* the Appellate Division identified twelve factors to be considered when determining whether a plaintiff qualifies as an employee for purposes of the New Jersey Law Against Discrimination (LAD):

> (1) the employer's right to control the means and manner of the worker's performance; (2) the kind of occupation-supervised or unsupervised; (3) skill; (4) who furnishes the equipment and workplace; (5) the length of time in which the individual has worked; (6) the method of payment; (7) the manner of termination of the work relationship; (8) whether there is annual leave; (9) whether the work is an integral part of the business of the "employer;" (10) whether the worker accrues retirement benefits; (11) whether the "employer" pays social security taxes; and (12) the intention of the parties.

The *Pukowsky* test is a hybrid that reflects the common law right-to-control test, *see Restatement (Second) of Agency* § 220 (1957) (setting forth control test for assessing whether master-servant relationship is established under common law agency principles creating liability obligations), and an economic realities test, *Pukowsky, supra,* 312 *N.J.Super.* at 182–83, 711 *A.*2d 398. The *Pukowsky* test focuses heavily on work-relationship features that relate to the employer's right to control the non-traditional employee, and allows for recognition that the requisite "control" over a professional or skilled person claiming protection under social legislation may be different from the control that is exerted over a traditional employee. An employer cannot be expected to exert control over the provision of specialized services that are beyond the employer's ability. Yet, the work may be an essential aspect of the employer's regular business.

Therefore, the test further allows for examination of the extent to which there has been a functional integration of the employer's business with that of the person doing the work. Several questions elicit the type of facts that would demonstrate a functional integration: Has the worker become one of the "cogs" in the employer's enterprise? Is the work continuous and directly required for the employer's business to be carried out, as opposed to intermittent and peripheral? Is the professional routinely or regularly at the disposal of the employer to perform a portion of the employer's work, as opposed to being available to the public for professional services on his or her own terms? Do the "professional" services include a duty to perform routine or administrative activities? If so, an employer-employee relationship more likely has been established.

Finally, the test includes consideration of the worker's economic dependence on the employer's work, but does not insist on the same financial indicia one might expect to be present in the case of a traditional employee, such as the payment of wages, income tax deductions, or provision of benefits and leave time. Workers who perform their duties independently may nevertheless require CEPA's protection against retaliatory action when they speak against or refuse to participate in illegal or otherwise wrongful actions by their employer. Such individuals should benefit from CEPA's remedies. Moreover, CEPA's deterrent function would be undermined if such individuals were declared ineligible for its protection. The public at large benefits from a less restricted approach to who may sue under CEPA as an employee of a business enterprise. It is unlikely to us that the Legislature meant to sanction a restricted approach to CEPA's reach.

### III.

A reasonable application of CEPA's definition of "employee" should include adjustment for the modern reality of a business world in which professionals and other workers perform regular or recurrent tasks that further the business interests of the employer's enterprise, notwithstanding that they may receive remuneration through contracts instead of through the provision of wages and benefits. Therefore, in order that CEPA's scope fulfill its remedial promise, the test for an "employee" under CEPA's coverage must adjust to the specialized and non-traditional worker who is nonetheless integral to the business interests of the employer. We reaffirm that the *Pukowsky* test fulfills that purpose. The test is familiar and addresses most routine questions in respect of the status of an individual as either an independent contractor or employee. It also offers consistency because the test is known and has been subject to general application. * * *

We agree ... [that the test] appropriately examines the relationship to determine whether the professional's services have been incorporated into the work of the business (factor nine), and looks at the impact of that work relationship on the professional's ability to offer his or her services to the public (the overall economic realities of the relationship beyond method of payment and provision, or not, of benefits and leave). As to the former, one cannot help but note that D'Annunzio's treatment plan review function was an integral, indeed essential, aspect of Prudential's PIP Department's operations. Although Prudential may not have told him whether to approve or disapprove individual claims, the whole overlay of expectations placed on D'Annunzio made him a necessary part in its day-to-day operations. We glean that from the demand for his physical presence for half of the entire business workweek, spread over every business day, ensuring not only his professional discretionary judgment on individual cases, but also his ready availability to other professionals performing tasks for Prudential for consultation and educational purposes.

Moreover, D'Annunzio presented evidence that, although designated an independent contractor in his agreement with Prudential (a matter that we view as informative but not dispositive because the designation was stated by the parties to be for a purpose unrelated to CEPA's interests), his day-to-day activities were controlled in minute detail. The step-by-step instructions provided to him set forth every single particular as to how to review a claim, including direction on how much information to provide in his written reviews. Although that is not to say that a professional cannot be told to be succinct without converting him to the status of an employee under CEPA, D'Annunzio certainly can argue that he was essentially under the control of Prudential and that he was a veritable "cog" in the PIP Department's operations.

D'Annunzio's time spent at Prudential's operations was continuous, week to week, and daily, for a substantial period of time during business hours. That Prudential exacted a not-inconsequential amount of time from him, on its premises, caused D'Annunzio to be away from attending to his private practice. The impact on D'Annunzio cannot be said to be minor. Moreover, his duties included numerous administrative tasks, all to be performed in accordance with protocols devised by Prudential to meet their business plan for the review and approval of PIP treatment plans. In fact, all of the detailed requirements expected of D'Annunzio were in furtherance of Prudential's operation.

In sum, D'Annunzio pointed to many facts that support the creation of an employment relationship for CEPA purposes, notwithstanding that his agreement described him as an independent contractor. Therefore, and in view of the premature stage of these proceedings and the truncation of discovery, we agree with the Appellate Division panel that reversed the entry of summary judgment for Prudential and remanded the matter to the Law Division. In affirming the panel's judgment, we intend to express no opinion whatsoever on the merits of the substance of D'Annunzio's claimed CEPA violations. * * *

JUSTICE RIVERA-SOTO, dissenting. * * *

I.

As a matter of statutory interpretation, there is no need to engage in the *Pukowsky* analysis embraced by the majority. The requirement that a CEPA claimant be a defined "employee"—as opposed to an "independent contractor"—was imposed by the Legislature, not by judicial fiat. * * *

[T]he Legislature is no stranger to the differences between an employee and an independent contractor; it has repeatedly made a distinction between the two. Thus, in those instances when the Legislature has seen fit to do so, it has made the terms "employee" and "independent contractor" synonymous. *See, e.g., N.J.S.A.* 12A:3–405(a)(1) (providing that, in respect of employer's responsibility for forged endorsements on negotiable instruments, " '[e]mployee' includes an independent contractor and employee of an independent contractor retained by the employer"); *N.J.S.A.* 17B:27A–17 (defining, for health insurance benefit purposes, "[e]ligible employee" to "include[ ] . . . an independent contractor, if the . . . independent contractor is included as an employee under a health benefits plan of a small employer"); *N.J.S.A.* 34:15–3 (providing, for purposes of

Workers' Compensation Act, *N.J.S.A.* 34:15–1 to –69.3, that "[i]f an employer enters into a contract, written or verbal, with an independent contractor to do part of such employer's work . . . such contract . . . shall not bar the liability of the employer for injury caused to an employee of such [independent] contractor"); *N.J.S.A.* 46:2F–10(d)(4) (exempting, from Rule Against Perpetuities, transfers to "current or deferred benefit plan[s] for one or more employees, independent contractors, or their beneficiaries or spouses"); *N.J.S.A.* 54:32B–2(i)(1)(C) (defining, for purposes of Sales and Use Tax Act, *N.J.S.A.* 54:32B–1 to –43, "seller" as "[a] person who solicits business either by employees, independent contractors, agents or other representatives"). * * *

In contrast, the Legislature has acknowledged the difference between employees and independent contractors and, where it has discerned a need to do so, it has not hesitated to explicitly differentiate between them. * * *

Also, when it has deemed it appropriate, the Legislature has specifically defined the term "independent contractor" without regard to any concept of employment. *See N.J.S.A.* App. A:9–79, A9–80, A9–82, A9–83, A:9–84 (eff. Sept. 15, 2007) (comprehensively defining, for domestic security purposes, "[i]ndependent contractor" as "a person, firm, company or organization which enters into a contract to work within, supply or deliver materials to a designated facility [defined, by *N.J.S.A.* 13:1K–21, as a 'building, equipment, and contiguous area'] and whose employees have physical access to a designated facility").

In other instances and in a wide variety of contexts, the Legislature has used the term "independent contractor" without any particular definition, further acknowledging both its meaning separate and apart from, and its differences with, the term "employee." . . . [Reference to an extensive recitation of statutes throughout omitted.] The brute force of those disparate statutory provisions is clear: the Legislature can and repeatedly does set forth when it wishes its reach to cover independent contractors and when it does not.

In that context, CEPA is illustrative of how the Legislature acts when it does not wish to equate "independent contractors" with "employees." When the Legislature has chosen to eliminate any distinctions between "employees" and "independent contractors" it has displayed no reticence or difficulty in doing so. Yet, it cannot be disputed that CEPA protects employees and only employees. Against that backdrop, any extension of CEPA's reach is an unwarranted intrusion into the Legislature's realm.

In the end, the majority's interpretation of CEPA's definition of an "employee" stretches that definition to an unrecognizable—and ultimately meaningless—shape. Thus, as a matter of statutory construction, CEPA should be interpreted in a manner true to its legislative origins: as the Conscientious *Employee* Protection Act. Any further expansion of its reach properly belongs to the Legislature.

## II.

Even if one accepts the majority's interpretation of CEPA's reach, D'Annunzio is emblematic of how the majority's construct goes badly astray. In this case, D'Annunzio, for his own purposes, negotiated with Prudential to provide certain services in exchange for a contractually agreed on hourly rate; he created a professional corporation to enter into that contract with Prudential; and he in fact entered into a written contract with Prudential. Section II of that contract, titled "Legal Relationship between the Medical Director and Prudential," plainly states as follows:

> *The relationship between Prudential and [D'Annunzio] is that of independent contractor.* The Medical Director will maintain his own private practice and provide Medical Director services on a part time basis. Prudential makes no representations as to the volume of referrals and [D'Annunzio] acknowledges [that] this agreement is not exclusive. *None of the provisions of this agreement are intended to create or be construed as creating any* agency, partnership, joint venture or *employer-employee relationship.*

> As an independent contractor, [D'Annunzio] will have the sole responsibility for the payment of all self employment and applicable federal[,] state and local taxes.

> [Emphasis supplied.]

Despite that clear language, D'Annunzio now claims that, because he was provided stationery on which to write, because he was told the format in which reports were to be prepared, and because he was asked to do what he contracted in writing to do—that Prudential would provide him "adequate working space and necessary resources" and that he would "maintain office hours at the Prudential PIP claims office[,] Monmouth Executive Center, 3 Paragon Way Bldg. 3 [,] Freehold, NJ 07728 from 8 am until 12 pm (Monday through Friday)"—and even though his contract with Prudential required that he maintain a separate, viable private practice, somehow Prudential exercised sufficient "control and direction" over him to invoke CEPA's protections. That claim is legal gibberish.

The contract between D'Annunzio and Prudential could not have been clearer. D'Annunzio contracted to perform professional services on a part-time basis for Prudential. For his own economic purposes, D'Annunzio insisted on Prudential contracting for his services through his professional corporation. By his own design, then, D'Annunzio was an employee of his own professional corporation, while his professional corporation was an independent contractor to Prudential. That contract made clear that the relationship between the parties was one of an independent contractor (D'Annunzio, through his professional corporation) providing services to Prudential. Yet, when it suits his purpose in seeking to invoke CEPA's protections, D'Annunzio readily renounces all that he bargained for in exchange for a chance at a recovery under CEPA.

CEPA represents all of the salutary goals and aspirations the majority eloquently describes. It is, as the majority notes, "remedial social legislation designed to promote two complimentary public purposes: to protect and [thereby] encourage employees to report illegal or unethical workplace activities[,] and to discourage public and private sector employers from engaging in such conduct." . . . However, when we pervert its intendment solely to extend its reach to one who proudly wears the mantle of an independent contractor when it is convenient to him—only to shed it for the greener pastures of a hoped-for litigation recovery—we devalue CEPA's worth and cheapen its meaning. Prudential negotiated its contract with D'Annunzio in good faith, and Prudential abided by all of the contract's terms, including its termination on notice provisions. In those circumstances, D'Annunzio should be required to abide by the terms of the contract—the basis of the bargain—he knowingly, intelligently, and intentionally negotiated, not rewarded with a breath of renewed life to this rightly defunct claim. * * *

### NOTES AND QUESTIONS

1. The distinction between an employee and an independent contractor goes back to Roman law. One could render services under a *locatio conductio operarum* or a *locatio conductio operis*: the former a contract to work, the latter a contract to produce a work or a certain result, *e.g.*, to make a ring, build a house, arrange for a game to be given. But the contractual form of the transaction—*locatio conductio*—was the same. REINHARD ZIMMERMANN, THE LAW OF OBLIGATIONS: ROMAN FOUNDATIONS OF THE CIVILIAN TRADITION ch. 12 (1996).

2. In discussing the definition of an employee under New Jersey's CEPA, the court in *D'annunzio* refers to "the right-to-control test," "the economic realities test" and then adopts "a hybrid test" that shares attributes of the other two.

The right-to-control test is a creation of American common law and developed in tort law as a means of distinguishing between employees, for whose torts the employer is liable under the doctrine of *respondeat superior*, and independent contractors, who are solely responsible for their own torts. As stated in Chapter 7 of the Restatement (third) of Agency (2006):

Chapter 7. Torts—Liability Of Agent And Principal

Topic 2. Principal's Liability

§ 7.07   Employee Acting Within Scope Of Employment

(1) An employer is subject to vicarious liability for a tort committed by its employee acting within the scope of employment.

(2) An employee acts within the scope of employment when performing work assigned by the employer or engaging in a course of conduct subject to the employer's control. An employee's act is not within the scope of employment when it occurs within an independent course of conduct not intended by the employee to serve any purpose of the employer.

(3) For purposes of this section,

(a) an employee is an agent whose principal controls or has the right to control the manner and means of the agent's performance of work, and

(b) the fact that work is performed gratuitously does not relieve a principal of liability.

In determining whether a person is an employee under the right-to-control test, certain factors will be considered which, while not controlling, serve as general guidance to the Court. These factors include: whether the employer has the right to control the manner that work is to be done; whether the worker is integrated into the employer's business, or operates a distinct business; whether the worker is low skill; whether the employer provides tools and materials; whether the worker is employed in a continuous and long-term capacity; whether the worker is paid by the hour or week, rather than by the job; whether the worker's work is integrated into the employer's regular business; and whether the parties intended to create an employment relationship. *Lynch v. W.C.A.B.*, 123 Pa.Cmwlth. 299, 554 A.2d 159 (1989).

The economic realities test of who is an employee was developed by the courts in determining who was an employee covered by protective federal employment laws. The test examines whether, under the economic realities of the situation, the worker is economically dependent on the purported employer and thus it would fulfill the purposes of the protective legislation to cover the worker. The test also looks at a variety of factors similar to those considered under the right-to-control test, but with an eye toward determining whether the worker is dependent, rather than determining who has the right-to-control how the work is done. These factors include: whether the employer retains a certain degree of control over the work; whether the worker provides services that are a part of the employer's regular business; whether the worker has no investment in the work facilities and equipment; whether the worker does not have the opportunity to make a profit or incur a loss; whether the work does not require any special or unique skills or judgment; whether the worker has a permanent or extended relationship with the business. The economic realities test is broader than the right-to-control test and includes workers who are independent contractors under the right-to-control test, but who are economically dependent on the employer. See *United States Dept. of Labor v. Lauritzen*, 835 F.2d 1529 (7th Cir. 1987); Myra H. Barron, *Who's an Independent Contractor? Who's an Employee?*, 14 LAB. LAW 457 (1999).

The courts often borrow from either or both the right-to-control test and the economic realities test in interpreting federal and state law. The economic realities test is probably the default test for determining who is an employee under federal protective legislation when the statute gives little or no explicit direction. However, where a statute or its legislative history refers to the common law right-to-control test, it is applied. Federal statutes that use the right-to-control test include: the National Labor Relations Act; the Employment Retirement and Income Security Act; the Federal Unemployment Tax Act; the Immigration Reform and Control Act; the Federal Insurance Contributions Act; and the Federal Income tax Act. Federal statutes that use the economic realities test include: the Fair Labor Standards Act; Title VII of the Civil Rights Act; the Age Discrimination in Employment Act; the Americans with Disabilities Act; the Family and Medical Leave Act. Federal statutes that apply a hybrid test that combine features of both tests include: the Age Discrimination in Employment Act; and the Americans with Disabilities Act. Charles J. Muhl, *What is an employee? The Answer Depends on the Law*, 125 MONTHLY LAB. REV. 3 (2002).

As noted above, the right-to-control test was developed to determine whether the employer is liable for the torts of the worker under the doctrine of *respondeat superior*. The tests focus on whether the employer has the right to control the worker makes sense in this regard since if the employer can control how the work is done, she can control the standard of care the worker uses in undertaking the work. Accordingly, it makes sense to hold the employer liable for the torts of the employee to give the employer incentive to promote safe work practices. Does this same rationale make sense for any employment laws? If not, why use the tort right-to-control test to determine who is an employee covered by an employment statute?

3. The calculus of factors at play in the employee/independent contractor distinction is variable; thus one factor may weigh heavily in one case and then be discounted in another. This gives those who do the weighing rather broad and, at times almost unfettered discretion. Work through each of the separate indicia employment used by both the majority and the dissent in *D'Annunzio*: do they direct the decision definitively one way or the other?

4. Notably, the majority in *D'Annunzio* goes beyond a strict accounting under each of the factors—this factor goes that way, that factor goes this—to focus on the purpose of the legislation: to protect whistleblowing in the public interest. Is it not clear that, to the majority, the fundamental question is: will protecting D'Annunzio's action (if it is statutory whistleblowing) further the purpose of the law? To this the dissent replies: "when we pervert its [the statute's] intendment solely to extend its reach to one who proudly wears the mantle of an independent contractor ... we devalue [the Act's] worth and cheapen its meaning." Has the public purpose of protecting and so encouraging whistleblowing been "devalued" or "cheapened"? Has its intent in that regard been *perverted*? How?

5. A number of states, believing that employers have mischaracterized employees as independent contractors in order to avoid payment of unemployment compensation and workers' compensation taxes and withholding of income tax, have legislated to impose penalties for "misclassification," *e.g.*, COLO. REV. STAT. § 8–72–114 (2009). Some have gone on to distinguish a contractor from an employee either for the purpose of a specific industry where abuse is thought to be most likely, *e.g.*, Illinois Employee Classification Act, 820 ILCS 185/1 *et seq.* (Illinois' Employee Classification Act dealing with contractors in the construction industry), or at large as has Oregon. OR. REV. STAT. § 670.600 (2009). Under this Act an "independent contractor" is one who provides services for remuneration and who in doing so:

(a) Is free from direction and control over the means and manner of providing the services, subject only to the right of the person for whom the services are provided to specify the desired results; [and]

(b) ... is customarily engaged in an independently established business. ...

(Subsections (c) and (d) deal with mandated state licensure.) One is "customarily engaged" within the meaning of (b) of any three of five requirements—(a) through (e)—are met. *I.e.*:

(a) The person maintains a business location:

(A) That is separate from the business or work location of the person for whom the services are provided; for

(B) That is in a portion of the person's residence and that portion is used primarily for the business.

(b) The person bears the risk of loss related to the business or the provision of services as shown by factors such as:

(A) The person enters into fixed-price contracts;

(B) The person is required to correct defective work;

(C) The person warrants the services provided; or

(D) The person negotiates indemnification agreements or purchases liability insurance, performance bonds or errors and omissions insurance.

(c) The person provides contracted services for two or more different persons within a 12–month period, or the person routinely engages in business advertising, solicitation or other marketing efforts reasonably calculated to obtain new contracts to provide similar services.

(d) The person makes a significant investment in the business, through means such as:

(A) Purchasing tools or equipment necessary to provide the services;

(B) Paying for the premises or facilities where the services are provided; or

(C) Paying for licenses, certificates or specialized training required to provide the services.

(e) The person has the authority to hire other persons to provide or to assist in providing the services and has the authority to fire those persons.

The creation of a business entity such as a cooperation or limited liability company for the purpose of providing services does not establish independent contractorship per se. *Id.* at subsection (5). Under this definition would Mr. D'Annuzio have been an employee or an independent contractor?

6. Artist models for the Philadelphia Academy of Fine Arts sign a form contract with the Academy which sets a standard hourly rate of pay. They are

free to work as many hours as are available and may work elsewhere. The number of hours worked varies from model to model; last year one model worked only 1.5 hours while another worked 226. They are not subject to evaluation or discipline but may be discharged for tardiness, absenteeism, and the like. The contract form gives the Academy's instructors the right to determine the general pose assumed by the model but it states the "specific form of a pose, including wardrobe, will be left to [the models'] discretion, so long as the form meets the general requirement requested by the instructor for said pose." The models bring their own robe and shoes to wear on their breaks, and some sort of cloth "for their private areas" for sitting and reclining poses. If they wish, the models may bring additional equipment such as padding and poles to support poses. The Academy provides timers, heaters, lamps, and other equipment to the models. The form contract prohibits the models from speaking with the students while posing and sets the length of the poses and breaks. They do not receive employee benefits and are given IRS 1099 forms (for self-employment) rather than W–2 forms. They wish to form a union and bargain collectively for an increase in the hourly rate of pay. Do they have the statutory right to do so? Pennsylvania Academy of Fine Arts, 343 NLRB No. 93 (2004) (no). Are they entitled to unemployment compensation? *Glatfelter Barber Shop v. Unemployment Comp. Bd. of Review*, 957 A.2d 786 (Pa. Commw. Ct. 2008) (barbers working under similar contracts are employees).

7. As noted at the outset of these Notes and Questions, whenever a statute sets out to deal with workers as a class the question of coverage is inevitable. When in the late 14th century Henry B. contracted with Thomas F. for the latter to serve as Henry's chaplain for a fixed term and Thomas departed Henry's service during that term the Court of Common Pleas held him not to be a "laborer" within the meaning of the Statute of Laborers, 25 Edw. III (1351), that forbad a laborer from quitting service during the contract term. YEAR BOOK, 50 EDW. III, fol. 13, pl. 3 (1376). The employee/contractor (or own-account worker) distinction today permeates the law in all developed countries yet the courts in the United States tend to draw the distinction rather more woodenly than elsewhere, often failing to address the question of statutory purpose. *See generally* Guy Davidov, *The Three Axes of Employment Relationships: A Characterization of Workers in Need of Protection*, 52 TORONTO L.J. 357 (2002); Orsola Razzolini, *The Need to Go Beyond Contract: "Economic" and "Bureaucratic" Dependence in Personal Work Relations*, 31 COMP. LAB. L. & POL'Y J. 267 (2010). Some countries have developed intermediate categories where coverage depends upon the specific labor protective purpose at hand, *e.g.*, of "employee-like persons" in Germany, of "parasubordinated" persons in Italy, of "dependent contractors" in Canada, and, most recently in Spain. *See,* Various Authors, *Self–Employed Workers*, 31 COMP. LAB. L. & POL'Y J. 231–66 (2010) (discussing Spanish, German, and Canadian law). If foreign law may be looked to for "best ideas," might the courts as well as the legislatures here consider these as legitimating a more flexible, statutorily-focused analysis?

## D.  THE EMERGENCE OF THE MODERN EMPLOYMENT RELATIONSHIP

### EMPLOYMENT IN THE NEW AGE OF TRADE AND TECHNOLOGY: IMPLICATIONS FOR LABOR AND EMPLOYMENT LAW

Kenneth G. Dau–Schmidt
76 Ind. L.J. 1, 10–14 (2001)

### B.  The New Age of Trade and Technology and the Rise of Short–Term and Contingent Employment

[The United States emerged from WWII as the only intact industrial power in the world. Indeed due to government investment in production facilities during the war, the United States emerged from the war even stronger economically than when it entered. During the next three decades, while the rest of the world rebuilt, the United States economy operated largely free of international competition. As a result, American industry and labor enjoyed profits and wages unburdened by the pressure of international competition, and the American regulatory scheme, operated effectively without the need to coordinate with an international legal regime.

During this post-war period, America's captains of industry believed that the "best" management practices were to build a large vertically integrated firm, supported by a stable workforce. Firms "vertically integrated," performing all of the stages of producing their product in house, to ensure coordination of production and to achieve economies of scale. A classic example of such integration was Ford's River Rouge plant where it was bragged that the production process went "from iron ore to Mustangs under one roof!" Firms wanted a stable workforce to ensure their supply of this valuable resource in coordinating production. To maintain workforce stability, firms developed administrative rules for the retention, training, and promotion of workers within the organization. Economists refer to these systems of administrative rules as the "internal labor market," because, although these decisions are made in reference to external market forces, they define the terms of compensation and promotion within the firm in a way that is not directly determined by the "external" market.

The vertical integration of firms facilitated the retention of employees over the course of their careers because integrated firms had layers of positions within the firm for employee advancement. For example, at IBM from the 1950s to the 1980s, Thomas Watson, Jr., was famous for fostering a program of hiring employees largely on the basis of "character" and then training them for different positions within the firm as they progressed through their career. Thus, the employer became a major source of training and security throughout the course of the employee's life.]

During the last three decades of the twentieth century, the conditions that fostered lifetime employment and internal labor markets began to change. First, international competition became a much more important  factor for most American firms. The complete victory of the proponents of free trade, as represented in a variety of international treaties, has combined with a retooled Europe and Japan and with industrial development in previously third-world countries, to ensure that American companies across the entire breadth of our economy now feel the pressures of international competition. Indeed, the breadth of this change, in concert with a growth in American consumer demand for services, has caused the transformation of the American economy from one dominated by manufacturing to one dominated by its service sector. Together with the deregulation movement over the same period, the increase in international trade in the last quarter of the twentieth century has ensured that most American firms operate in a much more competitive environment than they previously did.

Second, new information technology has both facilitated the movement of capital from country to country and allowed new methods of  managing firms and organizing production that bring the market inside the firm. Increased communication and information processing capabilities allow companies to keep track of and manage plants and investments in other countries. The increased mobility of capital in the international economy has meant that employees must now compete with workers in other countries merely to retain the allegiance of their employer. The improvements in information gathering and processing capabilities have also allowed employers to trim mid-level management positions and devolve some management responsibilities to lower-level employees. As a result, the managerial ranks are much leaner than in times past and some of the past distinctions between managers and the managed have disappeared. Furthermore, the new information technology has allowed employers to collect and manage data on rivals and potential suppliers and use this information as a "benchmark" for the performance of their own divisions and operations. As a result, individual departments and divisions within firms have been placed in direct competition with their rivals in a way not previously experienced in the modern corporation. Finally, the new information technology allows employers to collect and manage information on the current capabilities and capacities of component suppliers to an extent not previously possible outside a single firm. Thus, it is no longer necessary for firms to be vertically integrated to ensure the adequate quality and quantity of their component parts, and methods of production increasingly rely on the subcontracting of important production work.

The economic environment in the new age of trade and technology is much less hospitable to internal labor markets and lifetime employment. The increased level of competition to which firms are subject has increased the risk of fixed investments such as employee training, and caused firms to put new emphasis on flexibility in methods of production.

As the level of competition has increased, firms have tended to focus on ever smaller areas of "core competency" in which they enjoy some competitive advantage. With the narrowing of corporate interests, fixed investments, such as specialized employee skills, run a greater risk of becoming useless to the firm.

Moreover, with greater competition, American firms are more subject to the dictates of the market place and want to remain flexible in order to respond to changes in demand. As a result, firms are less amenable to accepting the risk that employee skills will become obsolete and to locking themselves into long-term employment commitments.

In addition, the new information technology has allowed the reorganization of firms in leaner ways that are internally more subject to the machinations of the market and less integrated in their levels of production. The paring of midlevel managers from the operations of the firms and the availability of market-oriented management strategies such as benchmarking has made the administration necessary for internal labor markets relatively more expensive. Why maintain a large and costly human resources apparatus when the rest of your management tasks are being streamlined and reoriented to the market?

Finally, the disintegration of the firm allows for the subcontracting of work to various suppliers. Such subcontracting changes the firm's concerns back to payment for product and dismantles the larger corporate enterprises that served as vehicles for long-term careers. It is perhaps not surprising then that currently the "best" management practices identified by managers and academics are those that focus on flexibility and an immediate orientation to the market.

No single example demonstrates all of the many ways in which the employment relationship is changing in the new age of trade and technology, but perhaps the most talked about is the Volkswagen truck assembly plant in Resende, Brazil. Although most employers usually retain at least a core of "permanent" employees, supplementing them with temporary employees or subcontractors to handle particular components or seasonal variations in demand, the Volkswagen truck plant in Resende employs  almost no permanent employees. Instead, truck production is undertaken in four "modules" which are produced by four different subcontractors within the Volkswagen plant. Once employees from one subcontractor assemble the chassis, it makes its way down the main assembly line as employees from other subcontractors assemble and attach their components. Yellow lines on the floor of the plant delineate the area in which each subcontractor is supposed to operate. Volkswagen's relationship with the subcontractors runs on a quarterly basis and the subcontractors accordingly make no commitment of long-term employment to their employees. Employees of the subcontractors earn about a third of the wage of unionized Volkswagen workers in São Paulo, Brazil. Although this "virtual Volkswagen" plant is still somewhat unique, there are plans to emulate its system of subcontracted modular production in the industry. General

Motors is currently engaged in negotiations to undertake subcontracted modular production at four of its American plants, including the new Saturn plant, under its "project Yellowstone."

## III.  IMPLICATIONS OF THE NEW AGE OF TRADE AND TECHNOLOGY FOR LABOR AND EMPLOYMENT LAW

Not every worker will experience the changes in the employment relationship I have outlined above. Even employers who replace permanent employees with temporary employees and subcontractors or adopt new market-oriented methods of management, commonly retain a core of "permanent" employees, especially among their high-skilled or managerial workers. Moreover, many workers, especially unskilled low-wage workers, have never enjoyed the benefits of internal labor markets and lifetime employment. Indeed, because of the inadequacy of our data on temporary workers and subcontractors there has been a fair amount of controversy among academics about the number of employees who have been directly affected by these changes.

Nevertheless, as in economics, where it is the marginal worker who determines the wage and conditions of employment, so too in law is it the marginal worker, the one whose legal status might change or is changing, who determines the current legal issues to be addressed by the legislatures and the courts. There is no doubt that lifetime employment relationships have ceded ground to short-term employment relationships in the American economy and that the market has been interjected into the employment relationship in a way not experienced in the recent past. What do these changes mean for us in our efforts to address the current needs of employers and employees through labor and employment law?

The short answer is that, as the paradigm of lifetime employment under an internal labor market recedes, all of the problems of the employment relationship that this paradigm addressed will once again come to the forefront of the employment relationship and labor and employment law. As turnover rates increase with the rise of contingent employment, firms will place new emphasis on finding ways to evaluate the potential productivity of new hires. These efforts will undoubtedly raise issues in the conflict between employers' need for information and employees' right to privacy, including questions about defamation and the proper use of employee references. Similarly, as the employment relationship shortens and wages become more closely tied with the employee's current product, employers will strive to find new ways to monitor employees on the job. These efforts will also bring employers in conflict with employees' right to privacy. Moreover, as employees move from one employer to another over the course of their careers, employers will be less willing to finance employee training. Society will have to find new ways to ensure that employees can obtain the requisite skills. As workers' pay becomes more directly tied to current productivity, employers will be less likely to offer benefits that maintain employees during times of decreased productivity. Society will have to readdress existing public programs or find new ways to ensure that employees can maintain themselves and their families during times of slack demand, infirmity, and retirement. Finally, as employees become more transient they will become harder to organize and less likely to address public goods in the workplace. Society will have to find new ways to encourage workplace democracy and give expression to employees' collective voice. What does the above analysis tell us about how we should address these issues?

One central conclusion that can be drawn from the analysis is that remedies that attempt to adapt the parties and the employment relationship to the new information technology and global economy will be more successful than those that attempt to resist these changes. The underlying causes of the changes in the employment relationship that I have identified are not passing fads, but instead constitute fundamental changes in our economy. Employers are not going to forget how to use the new information technology and it seems extremely unlikely that efforts to restrict how that technology can be used would be popular or successful. Similarly, although in the future there may be the occasional small retreat from international free trade as the nation-state grapples with international business to maintain the rule of law, the march toward a global economy in manufactured goods and even many services seems relentless. Accordingly, it would be best to find solutions to the above problems that were consistent with or made use of the new information technology or global trade.

## NOTES AND QUESTIONS

1.  What are the implications for employment law of the move from long-term employment relationships governed by corporate administrative rules (the "internal labor market") in large firms to more short-term contingent relationships governed by the market in smaller sub-contracting firms? Who is the employer in the Resende Volkswagon plant, the small sub-contracting firms that depend on Volkswagon for their economic lives, or Volkswagon? Who controls the plant for the purposes of workplace safety, workers' compensation claims or OSHA complaints? Will employers who envision only a short-term relationship with employees want to provide extensive training for those employees? Will they want to provide benefits? How will they provide long-term benefits such as pensions? These are the questions you can look forward to working on in the course of your legal career.

2.  As economist Richard Freeman has pointed out, during the 1990s there was a near doubling of the relevant global labor force with a concomitant downward pressure on wages and benefits. Since 1990, the collapse of Communism, India's turn from autarky, and China's adoption of market capitalism have lead to an increase in the global economy's available labor force from 3.3 billion to 6 billion! Because all of these countries were relatively capital poor, their entry into the global economy has brought no corresponding increase in global capital, and as a result, the capital-to-labor ratio in the global economy has dropped approximately forty percent. This abrupt change

in the ratio of available labor and capital in the global economy has put tremendous downward pressure on the wages and benefits of workers in developed countries that are subject to global competition. The downward pressure on wages and benefits exists not only in manufacturing, but in any service in which work can be digitalized and sent to qualified people elsewhere in the world. RICHARD B. FREEMAN, AMERICA WORKS: CRITICAL THOUGHT ON THE EXCEPTIONAL U.S. LABOR MARKET 128–40 (2007).

3.   During the past two decades there has been a substantial increase in "market mediated jobs" or "contingent employment:" part-time employees, short-time hires (often on a project specific basis and legally characterized as "independent contractors"), temporary or "leased" workers, casual or "on call" employees, and contract workers. The most recent figures available show that fully 30.6% of all workers are in "nonstandard" work arrangements, the predominant form being part-time work. BUREAU OF LABOR STATISTICS, U.S. DEPT. OF LABOR, CONTINGENT WORK SUPPLEMENT (2005). Even for those in "standard" work arrangements the expectancy of long-term stability with a single employer has declined. From 1973 to 2006 the share of workers who had been in their jobs for 10 years fell by about 5%: from about 30% of the labor force age 35–44 to 25%, and from 46% of the labor force age 45–54 to 41%. "Long-term jobs (ones that last, say, at least 10 years) typically are the kinds of employment situations that provide workers with the best potential for sustained wage growth, good fringe benefits, and a feeling of employment security." LAWRENCE MISCHEL, JARED BERSTEIN & HEIDI SHIERHOLZ, THE STATE OF WORKING AMERICA 2008/2009, at 258 (2009).

Employers are interested in retaining contingent employees because it gives them flexibility in the size of their work force and saves money because contingent employees usually don't get benefits and sometimes are not paid as much as permanent employees. Some employees take these jobs because permanent, better paid, work is unavailable, but some take them because they want the flexibility of hours and commitment. *Id.* at 253. "In other words," as one observer put it, "part-time jobs are good or bad for the same reasons that full-time jobs are." Chris Tilly, *Two Faces of Part–Time Work: Good and Bad Part–Time Jobs*, in WORKING PART-TIME: RISKS AND OPPORTUNITIES 227–238 (Barbara Warme, Katherina Lundy & Larry A. Lundy eds., 1992).

Notable in the employment of low-wage low benefit contingent employees is the nation's largest employer, Walmart. Wal–Mart employs over one million workers in the U.S. It maintains a low-wage, low-benefit policy: only about 7% of Wal–Mart's hourly employees try to support a family on a single Wal–Mart income—"some academics have concluded that 'the company's ability to pay such low wages [about 25% below other 'big box' retailers] is possible only because state and federal tax, welfare, and health care programs subsidize the living standards of Wal–Mart employees far more than those of other U.S. workers." Nelson Lichtenstein, *Wal–Mart: A Template for Twenty–First Century Capitalism*, in WAL-MART: THE FACE OF TWENTY-FIRST CENTURY CAPITALISM 3, 30 (Nelson Lichtenstein ed., 2006). Most "associates" are kept to a maximum 32–hour work week and assigning overtime is considered as akin to a manager's having committed a corporate felony. The Company has a turnover rate of nearly 50% a year, which means an even higher rate at the entry level (where wages are even lower). The resulting chronic staffing shortage places enormous stress on managers to get the work done with an inadequate number of workers; this places stress in turn on Wal–Mart's workers akin to the "drive" system (or the sweatshop) of the nineteenth century. Ellen Rosen, *How to Squeeze More Out of a Penny, in* WAL-MART: THE FACE OF TWENTY-FIRST CENTURY CAPITALISM, 343 (Nelson Lichtenstein ed., 2006).

4. One factor not discussed in the excerpt from Dau–Schmidt's article above is the impact of the decline of unions in the American economy on the modern employment relationship. Since their peak in the mid–1950's when they represented 35% of private sector employees, American unions have declined steadily until they now represent slightly over 7% of private sector employees. Union representation in the public sector has increased from 11% to over 36% over the same period, but since the public sector accounts for only about 15% of the civilian work force, the impact of unions on our economy and the employment relationship has steadily decreased in recent times.

Union power during the post-war period played a large role in the formulation public policy, the conditions of employment and the corporate administrative rules that shaped the employment relationship at this time. As observed by Sanford Jacoby:

> The historical record indicates that the employment reforms introduced during World War I and after 1933 were attributable not so much to competitive market forces as to the growing power of the unions and the ascendance of the personnel department over other branches of management. These factors—along with the severity of the depression and changes in the composition of the labor force—led to changes in what Robert Solow has termed "social conventions or principles of appropriate behavior" and pushed firms to adopt policies that decasualized employment and curbed the excesses of the drive system.

> With the benefit of forty years' hindsight, we may observe that these policies often enhanced efficiency by reducing turnover and increasing morale, or by stimulating programs to upgrade the work force. But this effect was by no means obvious to the managers of firms in transition, who were skeptical that internal labor market arrangements would lower costs. Efficiency incentives were neither strong enough nor obvious enough to produce the modern internal labor market.

SANFORD M. JACOBY, EMPLOYING BUREAUCRACY: MANAGERS, UNIONS, AND THE TRANSFORMATION OF WORK IN AMERICAN INDUSTRY 1900–1945, at 275–80 (1985). The social compact that emerged in the 1950's from a pattern struck in unionized enterprises had a ripple effect throughout the economy: productivity gains would be shared with workers in terms of increased pay—which led to the growth of a blue collar middle class—and company defined benefits retirement plans (DB) would form a major element of support for workers in their post-employment years.

However, as union power began to seriously wane in the mid–1970s, the social compact established in the post-war period began to erode and wages and benefits began to decline. Table I sets out the gap between productivity and wages that has developed over time as unions decline.

Table I: Worker Productivity and Wages in the Private Sector, 1947–2009

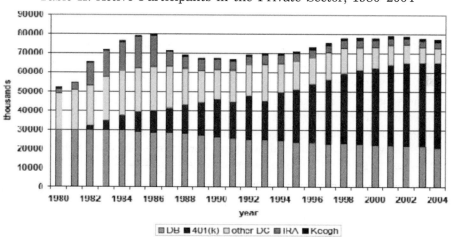

Table II sets out the prevalence of private pension systems. It shows a continuing and growing shift from defined benefits to money purchase plans (not all of which are employer-contributory) such as § 401(k) plans. This shifts the risk of loss of post-employment income from the employer to the employee.

Table II: Active Participants in the Private Sector, 1980–2004

**Source:** James Poterba, Steven Venti & David A. Wise, *The Changing Landscape of Pensions in the United States* (Nat'l Bureau of Econ. Research, Working Paper No. 13381, 2007).

These are market-mediated changes in employer policies; the law does not address them, not directly. Why then do U.S. employees not aggressively assume the role of market actors: by unionizing or engaging in collective protest—in strikes and mass demonstrations as American workers frequently did in the nineteenth century? Is it that American workers have lost the experience of and so the capacity for collective action? *Cf.* ROBERT PUTNAM, BOWLING ALONE: THE COLLAPSE AND REVIVAL OF AMERICAN COMMUNITY (2000). Or was Henry David Thoreau correct, that "most men lead lives of quiet desperation"?

5. What about the future? As the American economy continues to generate predominantly service jobs, the future labor force is likely to represent a mixture of persons in different labor markets, internal and market-mediated, full- and part-time (of secondary and primary wage earners) having greater or lesser inter-firm mobility and so greater or lesser bargaining power vis-a-vis incumbent or future employers. To those who adhere to the ideology of free wage labor as that of market interaction by autonomous participants there would seem to be little for the law to do; indeed for some, the law has already interfered in the market too much. To those who adhere to the ideology of free wage labor as that of autonomy in outcome in which the employee's independence is inadequately protected by the market, there is more for law to do. This raises the question of what we should expect the labor market to do for we can only judge the claim of "market failure" by the metric of our expectations. From the perspective of one market participant, the employee,

> Considerations other than material advantage enter into the relationship between employer and employee, for it is a relationship between people who look for loyalty, fairness, appreciation, and justice along with paychecks and productivity and who, if they believe they are denied them, can often respond with aggression, malice, and hatred.

RICHARD G. LIPSEY & PETER O. STEINER, ECONOMICS 354–55 (6th ed. 1981). Are these expectations limited to relational contracts only? Or do employees engaged in short-term "spot" labor market transactions for part-time as well as full-time work share them as well?

One solution to market failure of this kind, if we believe it to be such, is to collectivize the employment relationship and to require arms-length bargaining—"in good faith"—between the employer and employees' collective representative over wages and working conditions. Another solution is for positive law to set the floor of protection for all employees.

# CHAPTER II

## ENTERING THE EMPLOYMENT PORTAL: JOB SCREENING

■ ■ ■

## A. INTRODUCTION

Most labor markets are geographically localized; would-be applicants seek employment by job search engines, state and private employment agencies, want ads, and, commonly, via relatives and friends. Transportation time and commuting expenses, child care convenience, and other non-job-related factors may also limit the scope of an applicant's job search. Some labor markets are regional, national, or even international, especially for some highly sophisticated managerial and professional employments. Employers, too, use a variety of devices to seek applicants: some retail establishments, for example, place kiosks on the work floor in which a store visitor—usually a shopper—can log on to a company computer and fill out an online application. As we will see, employers can learn a good deal more about applicants than applicants can about employers. This is particularly true for employees who do not have friends or relatives in the shop or office who can clue the candidate in. There is, in other words, often an asymmetry of information in the labor market.

*[margin handwritten note: But not always]*

The selection process may be more or less rigorous depending on the job. At one factory in the Gilded Age a foreman tossed apples into the throng at the factory gate hoping to get work; a man who caught an apple got a job. SANFORD M. JACOBY, EMPLOYING BUREAUCRACY: MANAGERS, UNIONS, AND THE TRANSFORMATION OF WORK IN THE 20TH CENTURY 17 (1985). Today, there is usually at least an interview; but for low-wage positions even that can be rather perfunctory. *See, e.g.*, BARBARA EHRENREICH, NICKEL AND DIMED: ON (NOT) GETTING BY IN AMERICA (2001). Large employers tend to screen a greater number of applicants for each opening, seeking persons who will minimize the company's training and monitoring costs, than do smaller, less-well-financed companies. *See* John M. Barron, John Bishop & William C. Dunkelberg, *Employer Search: The Interviewing and Hiring of Employees*, 67 REV. ECON. & STAT. 43 (1985). Consequently, these larger and better-financed employers tend to deploy more sophisticated techniques of

*[margin handwritten note: Selection process]*

screening applicants; they also tend to offer higher wages and better benefits.

In a spot market for the sale of labor to perform an immediate task for a short term, the employer need be concerned only with the employee's immediate capacity to perform. In employment contemplating a longer term relationship, employers want to be assured that the persons selected will be competent, honest, dependable, able to work well in a group, able to be trained for and adapt to new job responsibilities and otherwise be cost effective. These employers may deploy a variety of screening devices once certain obvious threshold criteria have been met such as educational or training credentials, occupational licensure, citizenship or lawful resident status, possession of a driver's license, and the like. Among the most commonly used screening devices are: (1) questionnaires and interviews; (2) medical testing; (3) drug testing; and, increasingly, (4) background checking.

*[handwritten margin note: Potential screening devices]*

The use of these and kindred devices implicate the individual's interest in dignity and privacy in two senses: an interest in not being made an object of scrutiny or examination, *i.e.*, in not being treated as a mere utensil; and, an interest in informational self-determination. Of the latter, Elizabeth Neill observes:

> While each seeks for his own private or free life the status of an inherently private or free aspect of society, this can never be fully achieved because private or free lives, unlike innermost selves, constantly cross the boundaries of what is inherently public. So in seeking for ourselves a private or free life, we engage in ... the "dignity trade," or the "rights trade," wherein we stake claims, waive claims in exchange for other goods, and sometimes see claims overridden for the public good.

ELIZABETH NEILL, RITES OF PRIVACY AND THE PRIVACY TRADE: ON THE LIMITS OF PROTECTION FOR THE SELF 55 (2001).

Whether and to what extent dignity and privacy can be exchanged depends on the model of "free labor" we apply. Under the conception of the employee—or, here, the applicant—as an autonomous actor freely contracting in the labor market, these devices pose no issue of social or legal concern, for whatever "right" may be involved will have been bargained away freely in return for consideration for the job. *See, e.g.*, Bruce Kobayashi & Larry Ribstein, *Privacy and Firms*, 79 DENV. U. L. REV. 526 (2002). Under the conception of the free employee as one who retains a degree of independence from employer intrusion and control, some rights may not be traded away. A brief overview of employee screening will introduce the question of whether the law should strike a balance and how the balance might best be struck. Some of these questions recur in Chapter VI on Monitoring and Control.

# B.  BACKGROUND CHECKS

In a small nineteenth century community, an applicant's reputation—for drunkenness or temperance, diligence or sloth, intelligence or stupidity—would widely be known or readily be made known to a local employer. With industrialization, urbanization, immigration, and internal mobility came anonymity. How was a prospective employer to know whether an applicant was a promising hire? Antebellum employment bureaus cleared the references of domestic help (more on references a little later); in 1841, Louis Tappan founded the Mercantile Agency, which later became Dun & Bradstreet, to investigate the credit worthiness of prospective business partners or borrowers. Today, the explosion in information technology and its economies of scale has made background checking on prospective employees cheap and ubiquitous: with a social security number and a driver's license number, a prospective employer can learn about an applicant's entire life history, criminal history, driving history, credit card use, indebtedness, litigation (including workers' compensation claims), air travel, medical visits (though not diagnoses), and a good deal more.

## MONTGOMERY INVESTIGATIVE
## SERVICES, LTD. v. HORNE

Court of Special Appeals of Maryland, 2007
173 Md.App. 193, 918 A.2d 526

CHARLES E. MOYLAN, JR., JUDGE (RETIRED, SPECIALLY ASSIGNED).

The rule is that a defendant may not, without liability, publish defamatory information about a plaintiff. An exception to the rule is that sometimes a defendant enjoys a qualified privilege to publish defamatory information in order to serve some greater need. The exception to that exception is that the qualified privilege may be lost if it is abused. This case involves a couple of exceptions to the exception. * * *

### The Factual Background

In the Spring of 2002, Southern Services was in the business of providing termite and pest control to residential homeowners. The technicians for Southern Services would frequently have access to private homes at times when the homeowners were not present or at times when only a minor child was present. In order to protect its residential customers and to reduce the risk of harm, Southern Services requested criminal background checks on all of its technicians who would have access to residential homes. The criminal background checks were performed both during the initial hiring process and annually thereafter.

MIS was and is in the business of conducting various types of background checks for its clients. It conducts criminal, civil, traffic, and social security inquiries, as well as hospital record checks. MIS will conduct a simple computerized search through court databases for a fee of

$18 per inquiry, and will provide the client with a processed summary along with matching printouts. It will also conduct more thorough investigations, such as going to a courthouse to obtain copies of original documents from the court records. The client is charged a higher hourly rate for the more thorough investigations.

### The Initial Hiring of Horne

In early March of 2002, Horne applied for a job at the Silver Spring office of Southern Services. Horne was interviewed by James Lambert, the manager of the Silver Spring office. Lambert informed Horne that Southern Services would be performing a background check on him.

In the course of that interview, Horne informed Lambert about one brush that he had with the law. He had been arrested and charged with transporting a handgun and with impersonating a police officer. The charge of impersonating an officer resulted in a verdict of not guilty. In the Circuit Court for Montgomery County, Horne pleaded guilty to the charge of transporting a handgun, and the disposition of the case was probation before judgment, with one year of supervised probation. These charges had all been filed in the District Court on February 28, 1997. The cases were transferred to the Circuit Court and were disposed of by Judge Martha Kavanaugh on May 6, 1997. On March 12, 2002, Lambert hired Horne as a residential, pest-control technician.

*But hired*

### The Criminal Background Check

The routine background check on Horne was initiated on March 29, 2002, by Southern Services' district manager's office located in Manassas, Virginia. The district manager in Manassas was David Clayborn. The person initiating the request for a background check was Penny Clayborn, who also worked at the Manassas office. The request was for both a criminal records check and a civil records check, both for the State of Maryland.

The subject of the requested background check was listed as "Robert Horne," with no middle initial being given. Horne's address was given, however, as well as his social security number and his birthdate of "5–23–73."

### The Background Check Report

This case hinges entirely on the results of that background check as forwarded from MIS to Southern Services on April 2, 2002. When MIS received the request for the background check on March 29, 2002, the request was turned over to the appellant Tammy White, a background investigator for MIS.

The report of April 2, 2002, was faxed from Tammy White of MIS to Penny Clayborn of Southern Services. The report had been prepared by Tammy White. The singular subject of the investigation in that report was designated simply as "Robert Horne."

The bottom of the single page report summary showed an "Investigative Fee" of $54.00, reflecting "3 MD SEARCHES @ $18.00 EACH." The result of the first of these searches was unremarkable:

DISTRICT COURT OF MARYLAND, CRIMINAL
CASE NUMBER:                    4d00042046
CHARGE: 1: DEADLY WEAPON–CONCEAL        DISP: FORWARD TO CC
CHARGE: 2: HANDGUN ON PERSON             DISP: FORWARD TO CC
CHARGE: 3: PERSONATE POLICE OFFICER      DISP: FORWARD TO CC

Although no dates were given, those three charges were the charges filed against Horne in the District Court on February 28, 1997. They were all forwarded to the Circuit Court for ultimate disposition. These were the charges that Horne had described to James Lambert in his job interview.

The result of the second of the three searches was also unremarkable.

DISTRICT COURT OF MARYLAND, CIVIL
SEVERAL RECORDS MATCHING FIRST AND LAST NAME

Simply on the basis of the first and last names, the computerized records indicated sixteen different civil cases involving a "Robert Horne," with various middle initials, titles, and suffixes. If nothing else, the list was enough to alert the reader that "Robert Horne" was a common enough name to apply readily to more than one individual.

It was the third of the searches, that of the criminal records of the Montgomery County Circuit Court, that is critical to this appeal. Two Criminal Court Case Numbers were reported on and summarized, #35690 and #79341....

CASE NUMBER:    79341
CHARGE:1:       TRANSPORTING A HANDGUN BY VEHICLE
DISP:           GUILTY ONE YEAR SUPERVISED PROBATION[1]

CHARGE 2:       PERSONATING POLICE OFFICE
DISP:           NOT GUILTY

That Criminal Case Number clearly referred to the Robert Horne who was the subject of the requested background check. The record sheets that accompanied the report showed, as part of the antecedent District Court records, that the subject of the charges had, indeed, the date of birth of "5–23–73," precisely the date of birth of the subject of the requested background check.

What the April 2, 2002 report on the results of the background check on Robert Horne also included, however, was the following ostensible record from the "Montgomery County Circuit Court." The first of the criminal cases reported on was Criminal Case #35690. With no dates being shown, the report simply recorded:

---

**1.** Actually, even that part of the record was inaccurately summarized by MIS and reported to Southern Services. There was no verdict of guilty of transporting a handgun. The disposition was one of probation before judgment.

MONTGOMERY COUNTY CIRCUIT COURT:
CASE NUMBER:          35690
CHARGE: 1:            THEFT
DISP: GUILTY          6 MONTHS JAIL

CHARGE: 2:            CONSPIRACY
DISP: NOLLE PROSEQUI

No date of birth and no social security number connected the Robert Horne who was sentenced to serve six months for theft to the Robert Horne on whom Southern Services sought a background check and whom Southern Services had identified far more precisely. The Robert Horne who was convicted of theft was not the Robert Horne who is the appellee and cross-appellant in this case.

The report of April 2, 2002 from MIS nonetheless communicated to Southern Services the unmistakable message that the subject of Southern Services's inquiry had been convicted and incarcerated for theft. There was no alert about the possibility of a misidentification based on nothing more than a common name. To accuse someone falsely of theft, of course, is defamatory *per se*. It remains only to be seen whether that publication was somehow privileged.

### The Age Discrepancy

The Robert Horne who was convicted of theft had been sentenced for that crime by Judge John J. Mitchell on May 14, 1986, when the Robert Horne on whom the background check was sought was only twelve years old (still nine days shy of his thirteenth birthday even as of the date of sentencing). Tammy White was questioned about the age discrepancy between the Robert Horne of the theft conviction and the Robert Horne who was the subject of the background check. Her response was, at the very least, insensitive to the damage that a misleading report might cause.

Q. What's the date of the disposition for the theft charge in the Circuit Court for Montgomery County?

A. May 14th, 1986.

Q. All right. Now, *you were provided with the date of birth of Mr. Horne?*

A. *That's correct.*

Q. All right. *Did you compare the date of birth with the date of disposition?*

A. *No, I did not.*

Q. *Why not?*

A. I printed out—as I was requested, I printed out the information and faxed it back. *No one asked me to analyze it for them.*

Q.   When you faxed this cover sheet and the accompanying data sheets to Southern Pest Control on April 2nd, 2002, did you know that the individual mentioned in the theft disposition would have been 13 years old or so if he was the age that Mr. Horne was reported to on the transmittal sheet you got?

A.   No.

(Emphasis supplied).

Tammy White had been given very specific identifying data about the Robert Horne on whom she was requested to do a background check. A glance at the information on which she relied, and which she included in her report, would have revealed that the Robert Horne who had been sentenced for theft in 1986 could not have been the Robert Horne whom she had been asked to investigate.

Tammy White's testimony was also critical in pointing out the significance of the summary or cover sheet as opposed to the copies of the computer printouts that were her source material. The latter is a collection of raw data. The former is processed intelligence. Ms. White first referred to the cover sheet.

Q.   When you completed your search, you prepared a summary of the results of your investigation for your client, in this case, AA Southern Services, correct?

A.   *I prepared my cover sheet, yes.*

Q.   Which is a summary. It is your summary of the information, correct?

A.   Well, *it's a guideline to guide them through the information* that I sent them.

(Emphasis supplied).

She acknowledged that the computer printouts themselves may be difficult for a layman to interpret.

Q.   You prepared that because *you recognize these printouts may be difficult for the client to read?*

A.   *I use it as a tool to assist them in reading the printouts that I send to them, yes.*

Q.   And you recognize that *for people who are not trained in the reading of those printouts, that you need to provide them guidance?*

A.   *Yes.*

(Emphasis supplied).

Ms. White also acknowledged that her summary with respect to the civil records affirmatively alerted the recipient that "there may be more than one person reflected in those records." No such alert, however, was made in the case of the criminal records.

Q.  And you made a point of indicating with respect to the civil records that there may be more than one person reflected in those records, correct?

A.  Correct.

Q.  Now, *when it came to the District Court of Maryland, Criminal, everything was under one case number, correct?*

A.  *That's correct.*

Q.  And *when it came under the Montgomery County Circuit Court, everything was under that section, correct?*

A.  *That's correct.*

Q.  *You made no such representations to AA Southern Services that,* in the Montgomery County Circuit Court records, *there may be several individuals involved, did you?*

A.  *No, I did not.*

Q.  And *in that section, you reported two different sets of convictions, didn't you?*

A.  *Yes, I did.*

(Emphasis supplied).

### Consequences of the False Report

When the results of the background check were received by Penny Clayborn at the Manassas office, David Clayborn, the district manager, immediately forwarded to Robert McMichael, the president of Southern Services in Virginia Beach, Virginia, the report that the criminal background check on Horne had revealed a theft conviction resulting in six months of incarceration. McMichael decided to terminate Horne's employment and directed David Clayborn to direct James Lambert in Silver Spring to take action to that end. On April 12, 2002, Lambert fired Horne from his job, notwithstanding Horne's protests that he had never been convicted of or incarcerated for theft and he was not the "Robert Horne" who had been so convicted. It was established unequivocally that Horne would not have been fired from his employment with Southern Services if the report from MIS had not indicated that he had been convicted of and served a sentence of six months for theft.

We shall defer our factual summary of the circumstances surrounding Lambert's firing of Horne until we address directly Horne's cross-appeal against Southern Services.

### Qualified Privilege and the Proof of Malice

At the end of the plaintiff's case, the trial judge ruled that all three of the defendants still in the case—MIS, Tammy White, and Southern Services—were entitled to a qualified privilege and that Horne, therefore, had to prove actual malice in order to overcome that privilege. With respect to MIS and Tammy White, the judge ruled that Horne had produced a *prima facie* case that those two defendants had communicated the erroneous criminal background report to Southern Services with actual malice. The motion for judgment was, therefore, denied as to those two defendants, as it was again at the end of the entire case. The jury found actual malice and returned its verdict in favor of Horne on the claim of defamation. Both of the appellants' contentions focus on that element of malice.

With respect to Southern Services, on the other hand, the trial judge ruled that Horne had failed to produce legally sufficient evidence to generate an issue as to actual malice. The judge, therefore, granted the motion of Southern Services for a judgment in its favor. That is one of the two rulings that Horne challenges on his cross-appeal. The other challenge is to the judge's ruling that MIS and Tammy White enjoyed a qualified privilege in the first place. Horne does not argue that Southern Services was not entitled to a qualified privilege, only that Southern Services abused the privilege.

The entitlement of Southern Services to the qualified or conditional privilege is clear. Judge Karwacki wrote for this Court in *Happy 40, Inc. v. Miller,* 63 Md. App. 24, 31, 491 A.2d 1210 (1985):

> The conditional privilege accorded the defamatory remarks published to the fellow employees of the appellee was grounded upon the well settled privilege accorded to statements made within the context of the employer-employee relationship. * * *

### The Reciprocity of the Qualified Privilege

At this juncture, it is convenient to consider the second contention raised by Horne on his cross-appeal. He argues that the trial judge committed error in extending the qualified privilege enjoyed by Southern Services to MIS and Tammy White derivatively. We have no difficulty in affirming the trial judge's decision that MIS and Tammy White enjoyed a qualified privilege. * * *

Southern Services obviously had an important business-related interest in knowing the criminal record, if any, of its employees or prospective employees. Montgomery Investigative Services, as its name asserted, was in the business of investigating such criminal records. Southern Services hired MIS to conduct such an investigation and to report back its findings. The business-related need to obtain such information was reciprocal to the business-related job to report such information. The two are obviously flip sides of the same coin, and the privilege that the communication itself enjoys necessarily covers the communicator and the communicatee alike.

Accordingly, MIS and Tammy White enjoyed, just as Southern Services did, a qualified privilege. In order for Horne to prevail in his defamation suit against any of the three, it would have been necessary for him to have shown sufficient actual malice to overcome the privilege.

### Actual Malice On the Part of MIS and Tammy White

The trial judge, at the end of the entire case, denied the motion for judgment by MIS and Tammy White based on their argument that there was insufficient evidence of actual malice to permit the case against them to go to the jury. The jury then found that there was actual malice on their parts and returned verdicts against them. The appellants' first contention is that there was, as a matter of law, insufficient evidence of actual malice to generate a genuine jury issue in that regard. Their second contention is that the judge erroneously instructed the jury on the subject of actual malice.

### Jury Instruction on Actual Malice

It will be convenient to dispose of that second contention first. On the privilege enjoyed by MIS and Tammy White and on the actual malice that must be found to defeat the privilege, the total instruction was as follows:

> The Court has determined, as a matter of law, that *the Defendants are entitled to a qualified privilege.* In other words, the law recognizes that the publication of statements in certain situations advances social policies of greater importance than the vindication of a plaintiff's reputational interest, and thus, *the law gives a certain amount of protection to those persons making the statements.* The Defendants' qualified privilege, unless overcome, protects them from any liability to the Plaintiff for claims of defamation.
>
> *Upon the request of an employer, a person or corporation that communicates an employee's criminal background to the employer is provided with a qualified privilege.* The qualified privilege may protect the person making the statement from liability even if the statement is false.
>
> The qualified privilege given to the Defendants may only be overcome if a Plaintiff can prove, by clear and convincing evidence, that the Defendant abused the privilege by making the statements with actual malice. **ACTUAL MALICE EXISTS WHEN THE PERSON MAKING THE FALSE STATEMENT KNEW EITHER THAT THE STATEMENT WAS FALSE, OR THAT IT WAS ALMOST CERTAINLY FALSE, OR HAD OBVIOUS REASONS TO DISTRUST THE ACCURACY OF THE STATEMENT.**

(Emphasis supplied). * * *

### The Reckless Disregard of Truth

With respect to the appellants' first and primary contention, we affirm the decision of the trial judge to deny their motion for judgment. We agree with the trial judge that there was legally sufficient evidence to permit the jury reasonably to find that MIS and Tammy White acted with a reckless disregard of truth. A reckless disregard of truth would constitute the actual malice necessary to defeat the qualified privilege otherwise enjoyed by them.

The "reckless disregard" standard for measuring malice was analyzed and adopted by the Court of Appeals in *Marchesi v. Franchino*, 283 Md. 131, 387 A.2d 1129 (1978). Judge Levine's opinion for the Court could not be more clear.

> The view we take here finds support in the recent action of *the American Law Institute*, which, subject to an exception not relevant in this case, *adopted in Restatement (Second) of Torts § 600 (1977)*, *"Knowledge of Falsity or Reckless Disregard as to Truth"* as the malice necessary to defeat conditional privileges in defamation cases.
>
> . . .
>
> We hold, therefore, that *"knowledge of falsity or reckless disregard for truth"* is the standard by which the malice required to defeat the conditional privilege defense is to be measured in cases of private defamation.

283 Md. at 139, 387 A.2d 1129 (emphasis supplied). See also *Woodruff v. Trepel*, 125 Md.App. 381, 402, 725 A.2d 612 (1999) ("Malice means a reckless disregard of truth . . .").

Although the evidence would not have compelled a finding that MIS and Tammy White acted with a reckless disregard of truth, it was enough to permit such a finding. A report to an employer on a criminal records check of an employee is patently a highly serious and sensitive matter with possibly dire consequences for both the employer and the employee. It is a matter calling for both accuracy and a good faith effort to interpret correctly the raw data.

Particularly when dealing with investigations as cursory as computerized checks of judicial databases, some interpretative skill is indispensable. The printouts themselves provide information in so truncated a form as to be cryptic. It could readily have been inferred that MIS was alert to the need for interpretation in that it did not simply pass on to its customers the printouts themselves. Instead, it summarized and interpreted the raw data in its conclusory report to the customers.

In assessing the reckless disregard of truth, the jury may well have considered Tammy White's qualification, or lack thereof, for the job she was called on to perform. She had worked as a secretary for MIS since 1992. In 2001 she was assigned to do background investigations and was placed in charge of the background checks made on computer systems. She testified that she had received in-house training for her position from another MIS employee. When questioned in more detail, however, she described that training as instruction in "how to dial into the system and how to go into each criminal, civil, traffic level." There was no indication of any training in how to interpret the data that the records checks then revealed.

> Q. All right. *Did you receive any training on the criminal justice system* and how it works?
>
> A. *No.*

Q. *Did you receive any training on the juvenile justice system and how it works?*

A. *No.*

Q. *Have you ever had any experience or training in the juvenile justice system and what level individuals can be charged with different crimes at different ages?*

A. *No, I have not.*

(Emphasis supplied).

A perfect illustration of how the unskilled processing of raw data can easily lead to erroneous conclusions was the error with respect to Horne's trial for transporting a handgun. The actual disposition of the case in the Circuit Court for Montgomery County was one of "Probation Before Judgment." There was no criminal conviction. Tammy White's report to Southern Services, however, stated that Horne had been found guilty of the crime of transporting a handgun by vehicle.

In terms of Tammy White's inability to interpret the raw data, there were permissible inferences 1) that she was led astray by the initial plea of guilty and 2) that she was not trained to appreciate the critical difference between a disposition of "Guilty" and a disposition of "Probation Before Judgment." These are matters that could have entered into the jury's "reckless disregard" calculation.

The more devastating error made by MIS and Tammy White, of course, was to report to Southern Services that Horne had been convicted of theft and incarcerated for six months. The initial inquiry made by Southern Services, significantly, did not ask about anybody who happened to be named "Robert Horne." It asked about one particular Robert Horne with a particular social security number. It asked about the Robert Horne who had been born on May 23, 1973.

That inquiry, with that identifier, was sitting in front of Tammy White when she interpreted and summarized the printout that showed a May 14, 1986 conviction and sentencing for theft. It should have been immediately apparent that the Robert Horne who was the subject of the inquiry was only 12 years old on May 14, 1986 and could not have been the person sentenced to jail for theft. When asked whether she had compared the date of disposition with her subject's date of birth, her answer that "No one asked me to analyze it for them" betrayed a blithe indifference to the sensitive nature of the material she was processing. Blithe indifference to whether the subject of her inquiry had truly been convicted of theft is tantamount to "reckless disregard" of whether the subject of her inquiry had truly been convicted of theft. She nonetheless reported to Southern Services that there had been such a conviction of the Robert Horne who was the subject of the inquiry.

We affirm the trial judge's decision to let the defamation case against MIS and Tammy White go to the jury. * * *

[The portion of the opinion dealing with the Southern Services liability for the manner with which it disclosed MIS' report is omitted.]

### NOTES AND QUESTIONS

1. *Defamation in Employment Cases:* As summarized in the Restatement (Second) of Torts (1977), a plaintiff must show four elements to establish a claim for defamation.

§ 558.   Elements [of a Cause of Action for Defamation] Stated

To create liability for defamation there must be:

> (a) a false and defamatory statement concerning another;
>
> (b) an unprivileged publication to a third party;
>
> (c) fault amounting at least to negligence on the part of the publisher; and
>
> (d) either actionability of the statement irrespective of special harm or the existence of special harm caused by the publication.

There are several special rules that apply to defamation suites in the context of the employment relationship. First, although it is not defamatory merely to communicate that someone was fired or demoted, untrue communications that ascribe to another conduct, characteristics, or a condition that would adversely affect his fitness for his lawful business, trade, or profession is subject to liability without proof of special harm. Accordingly, false statements about an employee or why he was fired that cast aspersions on his ability to do his job are defamation *per se*. RESTATEMENT (SECOND) OF TORTS § 573 (2009). Second, as discussed in the *Horne* case, the conditional privilege of a common interest is frequently found in employment cases: either between the employer and a background-check company (as in *Horne*), between the employer and a referring employer, or between the employer and her employees. The rationale is that, because they are engaged the common interest or enterprise of finding good employees and running a business, a background-check company enjoys a privilege in its reports to the employer, a referring employer is privileged in its references, and an employer is privileged in its communications to other employees as to why an employee got fired. However, the privilege is conditional and can be lost if it is abused by making intentional or recklessly false statements, or by publishing the information beyond those who share the common interest. ALVIN L. GOLDMAN, LABOR AND EMPLOYMENT LAW IN THE UNITED STATES 75–76 (1996). Finally, although as a general rule a plaintiff cannot sue based on defamatory statements of the defendant that the *plaintiff* publishes, in some jurisdictions courts have held that defendants can be held liable for "compelled self publication" of defamatory statements by the plaintiff when it is reasonably foreseeable that the plaintiff will have to later publish them, for example in a future job interview. *See, e.g., Downs v. Waremart, Inc.,* 137 Or.App. 119, 903 P.2d 888, 888, 893–94 (1995), *aff'd in part, rev'd in part,* 324 Or. 307, 926 P.2d 314 (1996).

Because of the qualified privilege, in the vast majority of jurisdictions the law of defamation does not impose a duty to investigate the facts before pronouncing them; liability does not turn on mere negligence. The standard of "reckless or wanton disregard for the truth" applies to the facts as they were before the speaker at the moment she spoke. Of what relevance to MIS' (or Tammy White's) liability is that Ms. White was not well qualified and poorly trained? Is the Maryland court imposing a higher duty of care *sub silentio*?

2.  The federal Fair Credit Reporting Act (FCRA) (never mentioned in the *Horne* case) requires consumer reporting agencies—including those making background reports for "employment purposes"—to "follow reasonable procedures to assure maximum possible accuracy," § 1681e(b), but the Federal Trade Commission's implementing regulations opine that "error free reports" are not required. 16 C.F.R. 600 (Appx. 2009). The consumer reporting agency and the user of the report—the prospective employer—may be liable for a failure to comply with the Act, but neither the agency, the user, nor the supplier of information is liable "except to false information furnished with malice [*i.e.*, with knowledge of falsity or reason to believe in the falsity of what was uttered at the time] or willful intent to injure" the person reported on. In other words, there is a statutory qualified privilege as to information supplied in the background report.

3.  If the prospective employer contracts with a third party entity to conduct such a check "for employment purposes" the transaction must conform to the federal Fair Credit Reporting Act, 15 U.S.C. §§ 1681–1681t, especially in three key respects:

(1) A person may not procure a consumer report for "employment purposes" without first making a "clear and conspicuous disclosure" to the applicant in writing and in "a document that consists solely of the disclosure"—in other words, a separate letter or notice—and before the report is procured that one will be procured, and must secure a written authorization from the applicant for the report to be procured.

(2) A consumer reporting agency may not supply a report unless the person who obtains it, *i.e.* the prospective employer, certifies that these conditions have been met. Any report then supplied must be accompanied by or include a statement of the applicant's rights under the Act.

(3) Before taking any adverse action on the basis in whole or in part of a consumer report, the person who secured it must supply a copy of the report to the applicant and give the applicant a written statement of his or her rights.

The subject of the report (the job applicant) may demand that the consumer reporting agency correct any information the applicant believes is inaccurate. The reporting agency is must either make the correction or, if it believes the information is accurate, allow the applicant to add a written comment to it.

None of the Act's requirements were adhered to by Southern Services or MIS, but federal law was not involved in this case.

4.  May a prospective employer withdraw an offer of employment, conditioned on the conduct of a background check, after it receives a report, which is given to the applicant, that lists a criminal record the applicant believed in good faith he needn't have disclosed and which he asks the reporting agency to expunge? *Cf. Obabueki v. IBM Corp.*, 145 F.Supp.2d 371 (S.D.N.Y. 2001).

5. Mr. Horne sued Southern Services for defamation, for its further disclosure of MIS' erroneous report; more on that issue later. But why didn't Mr. Horne sue Southern Services for wrongful discharge? Should he have a cause of action? See Chapter IV.

6. After conducting a background check on a person applying for the position of assistant counsel with an FDIC insured bank, the prospective employer learns that the applicant has incurred a large amount of debt. Her written explanation in reply to the credit report is that she lacked medical insurance and had a child whose medical condition caused her extraordinary indebtedness. May the prospective employer withdraw its offer? In almost all jurisdictions the answer would be yes—but not in Hawaii or Oregon. In the latter, under OR. REV. STAT. 659A. 885 (2010),

> it is an unlawful employment practice for an employer to obtain or use for employment purposes information contained in the credit history of an applicant for employment or an employee, or to refuse to hire, discharge, demote, suspend, retaliate or otherwise discriminate against an applicant or an employee with regard to promotion, compensation or the terms, conditions or privileges of employment based on information in the credit history of the applicant or employee....

subject to exceptions for certain employments and subject to the following exemption:

> The obtainment or use by an employer of information in the credit history of an applicant or employee because the information is substantially job-related and the employer's reasons for the use of such information are disclosed to the employee or prospective employee in writing.

May the applicant be rejected in Oregon?

7. Federal law prohibits the discharge of an employee for any one wage garnishment to pay a debt. 15 U.S.C. § 1674(a). It does not mention a refusal to hire, and no private right of action has been held to be implied by it. But virtually nearly every state deals with the issue of wage garnishment, especially to allow it for the provision of child support and so to require the employee to be kept on the job and earning an income. Federal law also forbids private employers from terminating employees or from "discriminate[ing] with respect to employment" for filing for bankruptcy. 11 U.S.C. § 525(b). But discrimination "with regard to employment" has been held inapplicable to a refusal to hire. *Pastore v. Medford Sav. Bank*, 186 B.R. 553 (D. Mass. 1995). Should the insulation of bankruptcy or wage garnishment as a ground of termination extend to a refusal to hire?

8. In a job interview the company interviewer asks the applicant, a recent MBA or J.D. recipient, if she maintains a social networking website. She replies that she does. The interviewer asks to be given access to it and the applicant agrees even though her site contains material she thought would be seen only by her closest friends. The employer views the site and the job offer is not extended (or is withdrawn) due to the company's displeasure with her posted political sentiments or her display of revealing pictures of her and her boyfriend attending a beauty pageant at a nudist colony. A report issued in October, 2008, by the Society for Human Resource Management (SHRM)

indicated a "17% increase in HR Professionals at least occasionally using social network sites such as Facebook or MySpace for . . . applicant screening." BNA DAILY LABOR REPORT No. 196 at A–6 (Oct. 10, 2008).

May the applicant lie to the interviewer and deny that she maintains a social network Web site? If the company later learns that she did maintain such a Web site may it fire her for lying?

## A Note on the Employee Reference Problem

A time honored method of screening applicants was to require references from prior employers. Such references can provide useful information to prospective employers and serve as a valuable reward for good employees and a punishment for bad employees. However, references can also be abused. A spiteful employer may give an undeserved bad reference as revenge. Employers can also use the threat of a bad reference or the refusal to any reference as a means of gaining bargaining leverage with the employee. Toward the end of the nineteenth century, the railroads exchanged information on employees who had quit or had been discharged for bad performance, excessive absence, workplace protest, or union activity. At least with respect to workplace protest and union activity, such "blacklisting" was viewed as abusive and was dealt with in a spate of anti-blacklisting laws. These have become mostly dead letters as discrimination on the ground of union or other statutorily protected activity has been made the subject of separate statutory prohibitions. With respect to false and defamatory references that might be given out of spite or revenge, employees who discover the defamation have recourse to suit under tort law, subject to the employer's qualified privilege. As previously discussed, under the common law the employer enjoys a qualified privilege in communicating job references to other employers, but can still be held liable if that privilege is abused by making intentional or reckless false and defamatory statements.

Over the past two decades, employers have become increasingly reluctant to give any reference about their former employees to prospective employers beyond dates of hire or pay level (and, often, not even that). Data comparing corporate practices with respect to employee references in 1998 and 2004 are set out below.

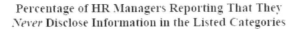

Percentage of HR Managers Reporting That They
*Never* Disclose Information in the Listed Categories

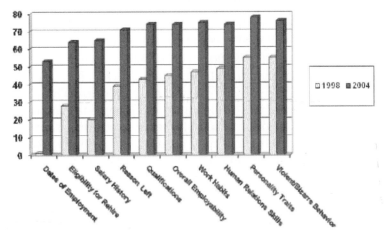

*Source:* Matthew W. Finkin & Kenneth G. Dau-Schmidt, *Solving the Employee Reference Problem: Lessons from the German Experience,* 57 AM. J. COMP. L. 387, 392 graph 1 (2009).

The reason for the decline in employee references is that employers fear suits for defamation, invasion of privacy, or interference in prospective economic advantage. It is not that the chance of liability on the basis of references is that large. Most employees never discover the content of their references and, as the *Horne* case illustrates, communications of this type are subject to a qualified privilege. Unless the former employer gives false information out of actual ill will or with reason to believe it to be false, the company would not be liable, but it might face the cost of having to move for the dismissal of the suit. The real problem is that, even though the chance of liability is small, the referring employer bears all the expected costs of such liability and enjoys none of the benefits of giving the reference, save the uncertain value of a promise to prospective and current employees that they will get references when they leave and an unenforceable hope that in the future other employers will give references on prospective employees. Thus, in deciding whether to give references, managers weigh unlikely but significant potential liability against no perceivable benefit and decide not to give references.

Many states have legislated on the matter to encourage employers to be more forthcoming with references. Most of these states have merely codified the common law qualified privilege to make it clear that employers enjoy a privilege in communicating references. Kansas, however, provides an absolute privilege—complete immunity from suit—to an employer who supplies the following upon the written request of a prospective employer:

(1) written employee evaluations which were conducted prior to the employee's separation from the employer and to which an employee shall be given a copy upon request; and

(2) whether the employee was voluntarily or involuntarily released from service and the reasons for the separation.

KAN. STAT. § 44–119a (2000). The problem with absolute immunity from liability is that then employers don't have adequate incentive not to intentionally or recklessly defame an employee. The Kansas statute attempts to mitigate this problem by requiring that the defamation be in a written report before the employee is fired, and that the employee be given a copy of the report upon request, but a job applicant would seem in a particularly bad position to rebut a defamation in his job reference, if he happened to know about it and requested and received a timely copy, in time to secure the job. Would you hire an employee who claimed he wasn't a thief when his past employer claimed he was? It is not clear whether this statute has led to any more employee references being given in Kansas.

## NOTES AND QUESTIONS

1. Assume that an employer believes an employee to have stolen or to have engaged in sexual assault and, in return for a resignation, agrees to give a "neutral" reference, one that would make no mention of these incidents. Assume further that that employee was hired, in part on the strength of the reference, and steals from the employer or sexually assaults a client. Can the new employer or the client sue the prior employer? *Compare Neptuno Treuhand-Und Verwaltungsgesellschaft Mbh v. Arbor*, 295 Ill.App.3d 567, 229 Ill.Dec. 823, 692 N.E.2d 812 (1998) *with Randi W. v. Moroc Joint Unified Sch. Dist.*, 14 Cal.4th 1066, 60 Cal.Rptr.2d 263, 929 P.2d 582 (1997).

2. The public interest in references is in promoting ready access to information that is accurate, complete, and fair, and at low transaction costs, both as a source of useful information for employers in making employment decisions and as a reward to good employees. Inasmuch as the accord of a qualified privilege has failed to encourage employers to be more forthcoming, does the Kansas law offer a better approach? Securities dealers are required to submit a Form U–5 to the relevant exchange whenever a broker leaves employment stating the reasons for the termination. These forms are a matter of public record. Should the brokerage enjoy absolute or qualified immunity in what it says for public consumption? *Compare Rosenberg v. Metlife, Inc.*, 8 N.Y.3d 359, 834 N.Y.S.2d 494, 866 N.E.2d 439 (2007) (finding absolute privilege) *with Galarneau v. Merrill Lynch, Pierce, Fenner & Smith Inc.*, 504 F.3d 189 (1st Cir. 2007) (no absolute privilege).

3. Would a mandatory disclosure law be a good alternative? Federal law requires prospective employers of commercial drivers to investigate an applicant's driving record and related matters. 49 C.F.R. §§ 391.21–.27 (2008). A private, industry-wide clearing house has been established to which reports on terminated drivers are submitted by their former employers and which are accessible to participating firms, *i.e.*, to prospective employers. *See Owner-Operator Indep. Drivers Ass'n v. USIS Commercial Servs., Inc.*, 537 F.3d 1184

(10th Cir. 2008). But in this system a driver has no ability to have truthful information that is unfair or misleading expunged. Would a pooled reference system that allowed for correction, not merely the addition of employee comment, be a better solution? How might it operate? *See* Finkin & Dau–Schmidt, *supra*.

4. After Southern Services' management received the report on Robert Horne from MIS it instructed James Lambert, manager of the Silver Springs office, to terminate Mr. Horne. Assume that Lambert summoned Horne to a private meeting—just the two of them—and told him that he was fired. Upon Horne's demand of a reason, Lambert said, "You're a thief, man. You've done six months in prison. We can't have you working here." Inasmuch as the words were spoken ("published" in terms of defamation law) only to Horne they would not be actionable in defamation against Lambert or Southern Services. But assume that Horne can prove: (1) that a prospective employer asked him for his employment history and the reasons given for any prior discharge; (2) that in compliance with this request he had stated that, based on an erroneous report, he had previously been discharged for misrepresenting his criminal record; and (3) that the prospective employer denied him employment. May he sue Southern Services at that point for a foreseeably compelled publication of its defamatory statement? The courts are divided on that issue. *Compare Rice v. Nova Biomedical Corp.*, 38 F.3d 909, 911 (7th Cir. 1994) (where Judge Posner terms the theory of compelled republication an "absurdity") *with McKinney v. County of Santa Clara*, 110 Cal.App.3d 787, 168 Cal.Rptr. 89, 94 (1980). If actionable, would the utterance be protected by qualified privilege?

# C.  INTERVIEWS

In conducting employee interviews, it is important for employers to keep in mind the requirements of Title VII of the Civil Rights Act, the American with Disabilities Act (ADA), and the Age Discrimination in Employment Act (ADEA). Taken together, these laws prohibit discrimination in employment on the basis of race, color, religion, sex, national origin, protected disability, or age. State anti-discrimination statutes often mirror these statutes, although they are sometimes written more broadly to prohibit discrimination on other bases, for example marital status and sexual orientation. Twenty-one states and the District of Columbia prohibit discrimination on the basis of marital status.* *See, e.g.*, WIS. STAT. § 111.31 (2002). Twenty states and the District of Columbia now have some prohibitions on discrimination on the basis of sexual orientation.** *See, e.g.*, MINN. STAT. §§ 363A.02–.03 (2004). Employers with fifteen em-

---

* Those states are: Alaska, California, Connecticut, Delaware, Florida, Hawaii, Illinois, Indiana, Maryland, Michigan, Minnesota, Montana, Nebraska, New Hampshire, New Jersey, New York, Oregon, North Dakota, Virginia, Washington, and Wisconsin. http://www.unmarriedamerica.org/ms-employment-laws.htm

** Those states are: California, Colorado, Connecticut, Hawaii, Illinois, Iowa, Maine, Maryland, Massachusetts, Minnesota, Nevada, New Hampshire, New Jersey, New Mexico, New York, Oregon, Rhode Island, Vermont, Washington, Wisconsin. http://www.lambdalegal.org/states-regions/

ployees are generally covered by Title VII and the ADA, while those with twenty employees are also subject to the ADEA. The firm must have the requisite number of employees for each working day in each of 20 or more calendar weeks in the current or preceding calendar year. 42 U.S.C. § 2000e(b) (2009); 29 U.S.C. § 621 (2009). Part-time employees are included as long as they worked on each working day of the week being counted. Absent such statutory limitations, however, employers are free to inquire into personal matters having no obvious connection to the job or the applicant's ability to perform it, *e.g.*, questions about property ownership, number of pets, and the like. *In* re *Delta Air Lines v. New York State Div. of Human Rights*, 91 N.Y.2d 65, 666 N.Y.S.2d 1004, 689 N.E.2d 898 (1997); Cort v. Bristol–Myers Co., 385 Mass. 300, 431 N.E.2d 908 (1982) (under a statutory guaranty of privacy from "unreasonable" intrusion).

In conducting interviews, two good general rules are to ask only questions that are pertinent to determining whether the person is suitable for the job and to ask the same basic questions of everyone. Beyond this, to avoid potential liability under federal or state anti-discrimination laws, employers should not ask questions designed to elicit information about an applicant's age, gender, religion, race, national origin, disability, marital status, or sexual orientation. Under Title VII, employers must avoid interview questions that might inadvertently establish disparate treatment of men and women. For example, employers should not ask only male applicants questions regarding whether they are available to travel or to work weekends or after hours. The same basic questions should be asked of all applicants regardless of gender. Under the ADA, employers may not inquire as to whether an applicant has a disability or ask the applicant about workers' compensation history until after an offer of employment is made.

Similarly, although an employer may need information regarding marital status to administer employee benefit programs, this information should be obtained only after the individual has been hired. Pursuant to both Title VII and the Pregnancy Discrimination Act (PDA), a female applicant should not be asked if she is pregnant or likely to become pregnant. Molly Hughes, *Lawyers As Employers: Hiring, Firing and Everything in Between (Part 1)*, 19 S.C. LAW. 30 (2008).

Beyond these anti-discrimination statutes there are other federal and state statutes that can limit what it is appropriate to ask during an employment interview. Most prominently, the National Labor Relations Act (NLRA) makes it an unfair labor practice to discriminate in employment on the basis of union support. Accordingly, employers should be advised not to ask job applicants about past union membership or support. Federal law also prohibits discrimination against veterans. Employers are also prohibited under the federal Bankruptcy Code from discriminating against job applicants because they are or have been debtors in bankruptcy, are bankrupt, or are associated with a bankruptcy. Some states also make it unlawful for employers to refuse to hire a person because he or she is subject to the garnishment of wages pursuant to a court order to make child support payments. Accordingly there are a lot of subjects on which to advise clients regarding job interviews.*

### NOTES AND QUESTIONS

1.  Should an employer be allowed to inquire into *any* matter that has no bearing on the job or the applicant's qualifications for it? Why? In several European countries, such as France and Germany, an employee cannot be dismissed for lying in response to a question that had no relevance to the job, as an invasion of the applicant's right of informational self-determination. Benjamin Belcher et. al., *Regulation of Information in the Labor Market: What Employers May Learn About Prospective Employees*, 21 COMP. LAB. L. & POL'Y J. 787 (2000). The National Labor Relations Board has held, with judicial approval, that an employee who is asked about union affiliation—a prohibited question—and lies about it to get the job cannot later be dismissed for lying. *Hartman Bros. Heating & Air Conditioning, Inc. v. NLRB*, 280 F.3d 1110 (7th Cir. 2002). Given the NLRB precedent, should the broader European approach be adopted in the United States?

2.  In public employment, questioning extensively into irrelevant personal matters has been enjoined, temporarily, as privacy-invasive. *Nelson v. NASA*, 530 F.3d 865 (9th Cir. 2008) (preliminary injunction authorized), *reh'g en banc den.*, 568 F.3d 1028 (9th Cir. 2009) *cert granted* (March 3, 2010). *Cf. Denius v. Dunlap*, 209 F.3d 944 (7th Cir. 2000). Should a private sector employer be given greater license? Why?

3.  May an employer ask about tobacco use if the job is to be performed in a state that does not protect consumers of tobacco from employment discrimination? *Cf. Rodrigues v. EG Sys., Inc.*, 639 F.Supp.2d 131 (D. Mass. 2009). Why? To the extent smokers incur greater medical costs, federal law allows employers to exclude smoking-related conditions from their group medical plans. *Christianson v. Poly–America, Inc. Med. Benefit Plan*, 412 F.3d 935 (8th Cir. 2005).

## D.  MEDICAL SCREENING

Employers may seek to hire employees who will minimize the costs associated with medical insurance, life insurance, absenteeism, and workers compensation. *See generally* MARK A. ROTHSTEIN, MEDICAL SCREENING AND THE EMPLOYEE HEALTH COST CRISIS (1989). At least three general questions are presented by the screening of employees for medical conditions: (1) Should any limit be imposed on the conditions employers are allowed to test for and use to disqualify an applicant? (2) What protection, if any, should be afforded concerning the disclosure of the screening results, in this case medical information? (3) What legal liability, if any, should flow from erroneous reports?

It is enough to observe here that, first, under the Americans With Disabilities Act (ADA) an employer may require an applicant to submit to

---

* A thorough list of "permissible questions" and "questions to be avoided" that was developed for the Equal Employment Opportunity Commission can be found at http://www.ncsu.edu/project/oeo-training/search/pre-employment_guidelines.pdf

a medical test only after an offer of employment has been made, as a prophylactic against discrimination on grounds of disability. *If* a medical test discloses a statutory disability, the employer must offer reasonable accommodation, but if the medical condition disclosed is not a disability, then the offer may be withdrawn with impunity. Second, both federal law and an extensive fabric of state laws govern the confidentiality of applicant and employee medical records. Third, the company-selected physician is not in a physician-patient relationship to the applicant insofar as any liability based upon that special relationship would be involved. *See also* ELAINE DRAPER, THE COMPANY DOCTOR: RISK, RESPONSIBILITY, AND CORPORATE PROFESSIONALISM (2003) (on the ethical situation of company-employed physicians). May a company-employed doctor refuse to turn an applicant's (or employee's) medical records over to company managers on the ground of patient confidentiality? *Cf. Horn v. New York Times*, 100 N.Y.2d 85, 760 N.Y.S.2d 378, 790 N.E.2d 753 (2003). The applicability of professional ethics as a limit on an employer's power to discharge will be treated in Chapter IV.

### NOTES AND QUESTIONS

1.    If an applicant is told that a "blood screen" will be required as a condition of employment, but is not told that that screen will include a test for HIV, and the applicant submits to the blood screen learning only later that that she had been tested for HIV, has the employer wrongly invaded the applicant's privacy? *Leonel v. American Airlines, Inc.*, 400 F.3d 702 (9th Cir. 2005).

2.    Under section 1211(c)(4)(A) of the ADA, a medical examination must be "job-related and consistent with business necessity." Is an airline permitted to test flight attendant applicants for HIV? *Cf. EEOC v. Prevo's Family Mkt.*, 135 F.3d 1089 (6th Cir. 1998); *Sanchez v. Lagoudakis*, 458 Mich. 704, 581 N.W.2d 257 (1998). If a personality inventory test is a medical test, is an employer permitted to use it?

3.    To anticipate Chapter IV, § 1211(c)(4)(A) is most often involved in employer demands for submission to "fitness for work" examinations required of employees returning to work after workplace injury or sick leave. A large body of law is beginning to accumulate on what is "job related" *and* consistent with "business necessity." *E.g.*, *Conroy v. New York Dep't of Correctional Servs.*, 333 F.3d 88 (2d Cir. 2003). So, too, under the Family and Medical Leave Act (FMLA), an employer may require the employee to supply medical certification for the condition giving rise to the leave request. The employer may approach the health care provider but only to "clarify" or "authenticate" the medical certification the employee has provided and then only through certain specified personnel explicitly *excluding* the employee's "direct supervisor." 29 C.F.R. § 825.306(a)(3) (2009). Why that exclusion?

# E.  GENETIC SCREENING

## IS GINA WORTH THE WAIT?

Mark A. Rothstein
36 J.L. MED. & ETHICS 174–178 (2008)

It has been pending in Congress for twelve years, despite the support of the last two presidential Administrations and the National Institutes of Health. It has been the subject of extensive affirmative lobbying by academic medical centers, pharmaceutical and biotech companies, genetic disease advocacy groups, and civil rights organizations. It has overcome vehement objections by employers and insurers. Its final passage, however, has been thwarted by a few Congressional leaders, who have prevented enactment despite overwhelming bipartisan support in both houses of Congress.

Based on this legislative history, one could not help but assume that the Genetic Information Nondiscrimination Act (GINA) is a revolutionary piece of legislation that, if finally enacted, would provide extensive, effective, and comprehensive protection against genetic discrimination in health insurance and employment. Unfortunately, such an assessment would be incorrect. Indeed, GINA may be a case of too much ado about too little. GINA is a fatally flawed bill, whose chances of achieving its noble goal of genetic nondiscrimination were doomed from the start by a health finance system in which individual health insurance is medically underwritten and by employment laws that fail to protect the privacy of employee health information. * * *

## *Need for GINA*

Proposals for state and federal legislation prohibiting genetic discrimination in health insurance and employment began by the mid–1990s, preceding any evidence of significant discriminatory conduct by health insurers or employers. The demands for federal legislation have intensified over the years, despite enactment of numerous state genetic nondiscrimination laws and the continued absence of any significant evidence of discrimination. Why?

There is considerable evidence that numerous individuals who are genetically at-risk for some serious disorders decline potentially efficacious genetic testing and medical intervention because they are concerned about the possibility of discrimination against themselves and family members. The supposed need for such defensive practices has motivated genetic disease advocacy and civil rights groups to support nondiscrimination legislation. In addition, genetics researchers, biotech companies, pharmaceutical companies, and genetic test developers realize that their efforts will be for nought unless individuals are willing to undergo genetic testing. Thus, researchers and commercial interests have been among the staunchest supporters of genetic nondiscrimination legislation. Federal legislation has been generally viewed as preferable to state legislation because it would be more consistent and comprehensive than the patch-work of state laws, even though GINA would not preempt more protective state laws.

There are four main concerns regarding the use of genetic informa-tion in employment and health insurance that have driven consumer efforts to obtain genetic nondiscrimination legislation.... First, individu-als are concerned about having their health privacy invaded by commer-cial entities searching their health records for the existence of genetic information. Second, individuals fear they will be required to undergo genetic testing as a condition of health insurance or employment and thereby to confront information about their health risks that they would prefer not to know. Third, individuals worry that a health insurer or employer will misunderstand the significance of the genetic information, resulting in their being erroneously disqualified from a job or insurance. Finally, individuals are concerned that even if the information is not misinterpreted, the results will be used to exclude them from access to something of great importance to them and to which they believe they have a degree of entitlement. * * *

### Employment Provisions

GINA would make it an unlawful employment practice for an employ-er, employment agency, labor organization, or training program to refuse to hire or to discharge any applicant or employee, or otherwise to discrimi-nate against any employee with respect to compensation, terms, condi-tions, or privileges of employment based on genetic information....

GINA also would make it unlawful for an employer, employment agency, labor organization, or training program to request, require, or purchase genetic information about an employee. One key exception is that it would be permissible for an employer to undertake genetic moni-toring of the biological effects of toxic substances in the workplace if: the employer provides written notice to the employee; the employee provides prior, knowing, voluntary, and written authorization, or the monitoring is required by law; the employee is informed of individual monitoring re-sults; the monitoring is in compliance with any applicable federal or state laws; and the employer receives only aggregate information that does not identify individual employees.

Despite the seemingly comprehensive prohibition on employer acquisi-tion of genetic information, it is likely that employers would continue to obtain genetic information on a routine basis. In accordance with section 102(d)(3) of the ADA, after a conditional offer of employment, employers are permitted to require, as a condition of employment, that individuals submit to a medical examination and sign an authorization for the release of their health records. There are no limits on the scope of the examina-tion or the records disclosed, although conditional offers may be with-drawn for medical reasons only if the examination or records indicate that the individual, with or without reasonable accommodation, is unable to perform the essential functions of the job.

Each year in the United States, conditional offerees sign an estimated 10.2 million authorizations for release of their health records. Because of the increasing interoperability of electronic health record networks, health record disclosures are becoming more comprehensive. Even if GINA resulted in employers requesting that custodians of health records (e.g., health care providers) release only nongenetic health information, there is no practical way to do so, and the entities are likely to continue the practice of routinely sending all of an individual's records. Thus, the number one concern of individuals today, that employers have access to their genetic test results, would remain their number one concern even if GINA were enacted. Effective protection of genetic information in the employment setting requires a ban on employer requests for comprehensive records at the post-offer stage; the research, development, and adoption of health information technology to facilitate the disclosure of only job-related health information; and the legal requirement to limit the scope of disclosures to job-related information.

### Genetic Exceptionalism

GINA, like numerous state genetic nondiscrimination laws, is based on an approach known as "genetic exceptionalism." This means that genetic information is treated separately and differently from other health information. To many observers and elected officials, the need for "genetic" nondiscrimination legislation has seemed self-evident to address what has been regarded as a "genetic" discrimination problem. For others, genetic exceptionalism represents poor public policy for the following reasons: (1) it is impossible to define "genetic" when scientists have identified that genes play a role in virtually every human health problem; (2) it is impossible to isolate genetic information in health records; (3) a general law is easier to apply than separate laws for various health conditions; (4) having a separate law for genetic information increases the stigma associated with genetic conditions; and (5) it is difficult to make a moral argument that it is impermissible to discriminate against people on the basis of genetic information but that it is permissible to do so if the condition is not genetic. * * *

### Conclusion

The main value of GINA is its symbolism. If enacted, federal law would declare a national policy against discrimination in health insurance and employment on the basis of genetic information. The symbolic value of many other forms of antidiscrimination laws has led to widespread changes in attitudes and actions by private parties. Enacting this legislation, however, is not without risks. First, the law's genetic exceptionalism approach could serve to increase the stigma of genetic conditions, genetic tests, and genetic information. Second, individuals might be convinced by public pronouncements of the value of GINA and rely upon it to their detriment, such as by undergoing predictive genetic testing and subsequently having their test results released to future employers. Third, perhaps the greatest risk posed by enacting GINA would be that lawmakers might become complacent and believe that the problem of genetic discrimination in health insurance and employment has been adequately addressed by the new federal law.

## NOTE AND QUESTION

*The Passage of GINA*: Despite Professor Rothstein's thoughtful critique of GINA, the Act was passed unanimously by the Senate, passed in the House by a vote of 414 to 1, and was signed into law by President Bush on May 21, 2008. Its effective date was set for 18 months later (after the next presidential election), November 21, 2009. Under 42 U.S.C. § 2000ff–1 (2008), the Act specifies that:

§ 2000ff–1. Employer practices

(a) Discrimination based on genetic information

It shall be an unlawful employment practice for an employer—

> (1) to fail or refuse to hire, or to discharge, any employee, or otherwise to discriminate against any employee with respect to the compensation, terms, conditions, or privileges of employment of the employee, because of genetic information with respect to the employee; or

> (2) to limit, segregate, or classify the employees of the employer in any way that would deprive or tend to deprive any employee of employment opportunities or otherwise adversely affect the status of the employee as an employee, because of genetic information with respect to the employee.

(b) Acquisition of genetic information

It shall be an unlawful employment practice for an employer to request, require, or purchase genetic information with respect to an employee or a family member of the employee except—

> (1) where an employer inadvertently requests or requires family medical history of the employee or family member of the employee;

> (2) where—

>> (A) health or genetic services are offered by the employer, including such services offered as part of a wellness program; * * *

> (3) where an employer requests or requires family medical history from the employee to comply with the certification provisions of section 2613 of Title 29 [The Family Medical Leave Act] or such requirements under State family and medical leave laws;

> (4) where an employer purchases documents that are commercially and publicly available (including newspapers, magazines, periodicals, and books, but not including medical databases or court records) that include family medical history;

(5) where the information involved is to be used for genetic monitoring of the biological effects of toxic substances in the workplace, but only if—

(A) the employer provides written notice of the genetic monitoring to the employee;

(B)(i) the employee provides prior, knowing, voluntary, and written authorization; or

(ii) the genetic monitoring is required by Federal or State law;

(C) the employee is informed of individual monitoring results;

(D) the monitoring is in compliance with [Federal and State monitoring requirements under OSHA and other laws] * * *

(E) the employer, excluding any licensed health care professional or board certified genetic counselor that is involved in the genetic monitoring program, receives the results of the monitoring only in aggregate terms that do not disclose the identity of specific employees; or

(6) where the employer conducts DNA analysis for law enforcement purposes as a forensic laboratory or for purposes of human remains identification, and requests or requires genetic information of such employer's employees, but only to the extent that such genetic information is used for analysis of DNA identification markers for quality control to detect sample contamination.

(c) Preservation of protections

In the case of information to which any of paragraphs (1) through (6) of subsection (b) applies, such information may not be used in violation of paragraph (1) or (2) of subsection (a) or treated or disclosed in a manner that violates section 2000ff–5 of this title.

As identified by Professor Rothstein, the Act has two broad prohibitions, but then adds numerous exceptions. Because of the recent effective date there has been little case law so far under the Act. GINA joins laws in 34 states and the District of Columbia in prohibiting or limiting genetic screening by employers and discrimination on the basis of genetic information.* *See, e.g.,* IOWA CODE § 729.6 (2007). Is the prohibition of genetic screening of job applicants and employees wise? *Compare* Colin S. Diver & Jane Maslow Cohen, *Genophobia: What is Wrong with Genetic Discrimination?*, 149 U. PA. L. REV. 1439 (2001) *with* Henry T. Greely, *Genotype Discrimination: The Complex Case for Some Legislative Protection*, 149 U. PA. L. REV. 1483 (2001). Will GINA be effective? Should we protect employees from discrimination on the basis of genetic information but not on the basis of other health-related information? A copy of the complete statute is included in the statutory supplement.

---

* Those states include: Arizona, Arkansas, California, Connecticut, Delaware, Hawaii, Idaho, Illinois, Iowa, Kansas, Louisiana, Maine, Maryland, Massachusetts, Michigan, Minnesota, Missouri, Nebraska, Nevada, New Hampshire, New Jersey, New Mexico, New York, North Carolina, Oklahoma, Oregon, Rhode Island, South Dakota, Texas, Utah, Vermont, Virginia, Washington, and Wisconsin. http://www.ncsl.org/IssuesResearch/Health/GeneticEmploymentLaws/tabid/14280/Default.aspx.

# F. DRUG SCREENING

Actually, employers rarely screen applicants for genetic traits (putting aside information on family medical histories), but screening for the consumption of one or more of a list of controlled substances is widespread. Prior to the mid–1980's, only a very small proportion of the workforce was subject to drug testing. However, with President Reagan's 1985 declaration of a "War on Drugs," the use of drug testing in the employment setting grew rapidly. In 1986, President Reagan issued Exec. Order No. 12,564, 51 Fed. Reg. 32,889 (Sept. 15, 1986), which required a "drug-free federal workplace" and directed each federal agency to "develop a plan for achieving the objective of a drug-free workplace" and to "establish a program to test for the use of illegal drugs by employees in sensitive positions." 5 U.S.C. §§ 7301(1), 7301(2)(a) (1986). After this Order, the use of drug testing became a common feature of federal employment and rapidly grew in the private sector. Although some firms were compelled to adopt drug testing programs under federal regulations requiring testing in industries such as railroads and trucking, many others voluntarily implemented drug testing programs. Pauline T. Kim, *Collective and Individual Approaches to Protecting Employee Privacy: The Experience With Workplace Drug Testing*, 66 La. L. Rev. 1009, 1011–12 (2006). An American Management Association's survey indicated that 55% of the companies surveyed screen applicants for drug use. More than forty-seven million employees work in workplaces that screen applicants for drug use.

Employers may decide to adopt an employee drug testing program to meet a number of concerns. One concern might be that employees who use drugs are a greater risk to public and workplace safety. This concern is paramount when employees operate dangerous machinery and is the basis for federal regulations requiring drug testing in the railway and trucking industries. A second objective might be to weed out less productive employees. Employers might be concerned that employees who use drugs will be less productive on the job, absent more often, or perhaps more likely to steal from the employer. Employers who provide health benefits might be concerned that employees who use drugs will be more likely to make claims against their insurance. Finally, employers might not want the company associated with illegal drug use. Especially for employees who represent the firm in sales or in public, an employer might want to take steps to insure that they don't use drugs. Scott S. Cairns & Carolyn V. Grady, *Drug Testing in the Workplace: A Reasoned Approach for Private Employers*, 12 Geo. Mason L. Rev. 491 (1990).

Employees also have important interests at stake in drug testing programs. Drug testing invokes important employee privacy interests. The collection of bodily fluids for testing involves a significant intrusion on privacy. Moreover, drug testing can yield a lot of private information beyond drug use including lawful prescription drug use, illness, and pregnancy. Employees also have an important interest in the accuracy of any test procedure so that they are not unfairly disciplined or have their character impugned, particularly if strict chain-of-custody rules are not followed to ensure the authenticity of the sample. Kim, *supra*, at 1013–14. Potential problems with the accuracy of employee drug tests is discussed below. But first, a brief introduction to the primary drug testing methods used in the employment setting.

## 1.  TESTING PROCEDURES

### URINALYSIS DRUG TESTING OF EMPLOYEES AT WILL: THE NEED FOR MANDATORY STANDARDS

Shane J. Osowski
11 N. Ill. U. L. Rev. 319, 321–327 (1991)

### A.  DRUG TESTING

Technology is rapidly advancing in the drug testing field, and drug testing may now be performed with samples of hair, breath, or saliva. However, these procedures all have deficiencies at their present state of refinement as compared to urinalysis and are not generally used in the employment setting. The discussion of this comment, therefore, is limited to urinalysis drug testing, the drug testing technique in mass use by employers.

Use of the term "drug" test in reference to urinalysis testing is really a misnomer. What is normally being tested for are metabolites, the inactive residue remaining after the body has processed the drug. This means that no urine detection system can measure "whether a drug is present in the blood, nor does it reveal the time or quantity of drug intake." The most any drug test can accomplish is to give a "positive" result when a metabolite is present in the test subject's urine.

This positive result may indicate any one of three separate inferences and does not justify the conclusion that the test subject is a drug user. First, the subject may have recently been exposed to a drug, which is possible through passive inhalation. Second, the subject may have previously used the drug, although that person is not necessarily presently impaired, and may have used the drug over 30 days previously. Finally, the test subject might have recently taken medication or other substances that produce the same metabolites as an illicit drug being tested for. This is very common considering that various over-the-counter medications, poppy seeds, or prescription medication can "cross react." * * *

This does not imply that fairly conclusive evidence of drug use cannot be obtained when drug test information is combined with further in-depth testing and a background medical check. Ideally, after an initial low-cost "screening" test indicates a positive result, a more expensive and highly accurate confirmation test is performed using a different scientific process to discern exactly which metabolite is present and in what quantity. This secondary procedure is required under mandatory guidelines for federal employer drug testing, although many private employers do not perform any confirmation testing. An interview with the test subject and a review of the subject's medical records by a competent physician would eliminate the possibility of an erroneous positive result caused by cross reactions or normal medication. While the federal guide-lines mandate this interview procedure for governmental testing, interviews are seldom given by non-governmental entities. * * *

### 1.   Common Urinalysis Tests

Of the numerous possible ways to test for drugs in body fluids, there are basically two testing methodologies that have come into common usage: the immunoassay and chromatography processes of urinalysis testing.... While other methods exist, most are either not suitable for large-scale use in an employment setting, or are so grossly inaccurate as to preclude acceptance even by nonregulated private employers....

### a.   Immunoassay

Immunoassay tests are the most widely used screening tests, as they are quick and inexpensive. The three most prevalent immunoassay tests are enzyme immunoassay, radioimmunoassay, and fluorescein polarization immunoassay. They are based on the principle that known "labels" and the unknown drug metabolites present in the urine will compete to bind to an antibody. First the "label" and antibody are combined, forming a chemical bond. When the urine is added, drug metabolites present in the urine will displace the "label" and bond in its place to the antibody. By measuring the unbound "label" with ordinary laboratory methods, the amount of drug metabolite originally present in the urine can be determined.

The simplest and least expensive test available is the enzyme immunoassay (EIA), making it the most commonly used test. The most prevalent EIA in the United States is the EMIT test produced by Syva Company which costs about $4.50 per use. EIA tests are extremely sensitive (they can detect very low levels of drug metabolite), however they tend to "cross-react" and are not specific as to the exact type of metabolite present. EIA tests are generally marketed as "screening" tests for use in culling out large numbers of test subjects, with those testing "positive" being confirmed using a more metabolite specific test such as gas chromatography/mass spectrometry (GC/MS). EIA has the added advantage of being easily automated to handle large quantities of samples. * * *

### b.   Chromatography

Chromatography methods are more accurate than immunoassay methods, but are also more complicated and expensive. In chromatography, the specimen is separated into various components, which are then identified and measured. Chromatography requires a stationary (fixed) phase which may be a solid or liquid, and a mobile (moving) phase which may be a liquid or gas. Substances from the urine sample are carried by the mobile phase across the stationary phase by capillary action, and the stationary phase interacts with these substances to separate them. After separation, a detection method distinguishes the components for identification and measurement.

Gas chromatography/mass spectrometry (GC/MS) is the "technique of choice" for identifying drug metabolites in urine. This combines the separating power of gas chromatography with the "high sensitivity and specificity of mass spectrometric detection." The first step of this process requires a gaseous mobile phase with ordinary chromatography. The detection phase next used to identify the separated drug metabolites utilizes a highly accurate mass spectrometry process. This mass spectrometry can detect a "fingerprint" pattern that is unique for each drug, and can be extremely accurate if there is a sufficiently high concentration of the drug to provide a good quality mass spectrum.

However, due to the complicated process and high cost [$80 to $100 per sample], this is generally used only to confirm positive tests from a less accurate method. This process also depends highly on the analyst's skill, but in a competent lab the results are almost conclusive. The federal guidelines, require this test to confirm any positive screening result when used in relation to the Federal government.

## NOTES AND QUESTIONS

1. *When to Test?*: Employers might seek to have employees take drug tests at various times. The most common time is probably pre-employment, but tests are also sometimes required after incidents raise a reasonable suspicion (for example, a truck driver is in an accident), or as part of a regular or random drug testing program. Federal regulations require random drug testing programs for certain railroad and trucking employees, and also require drug testing after accidents. Probably the greatest concerns about intrusion on the employee's rights occur in programs that require regular or random testing of current employees without reasonable suspicion. Alan Adler, *Civil Liberties and Ethical Concerns, in* NATIONAL INSTITUTE ON DRUG ABUSE, DEP'T OF HEALTH AND HUMAN SERVS., WORKPLACE DRUG ABUSE POLICIES 39 (1989). Why would this be?

2. *The Problem of Inaccurate Drug Tests*: A drug test can be inaccurate in two ways: either the test can fail to identify an actual drug user (a false negative) or it can falsely identify an employee who does not use illegal drugs as a drug use (a false positive). The rate at which a drug test accurately identifies actual drug users is called its "sensitivity." The rate at which it accurately identifies non-drug users is called its "specificity." A test result can be inaccurate for a number of reasons: contamination of the sample, lab error, or a positive result due to the presence of a "cross-reactant." A cross-reactant is a legal drug, chemical or food that is very similar chemically to the tested for illegal drug or its metabolite and thus causes the drug test to indicate that the illegal drug is or was in the worker's urine, when in fact it was not. Commonly known cross reactants are that ingesting poppy seeds can cause a person to test positive for heroin, while certain herbal teas can cause a person

to test positive for cocaine. Other troublesome cross-reactants and the drug they mimic are listed in the table below.

| Some Commonly Used Substances that Cross–React with Widely Tested for Illegal Drugs | |
| --- | --- |
| Drug | Cross–Reactant |
| Marijuana | Non-steroidal Anti Inflammatory Agents Ibuprofen (Advil, Motrin) |
| Amphetamines | Decongestants (Cold Medicines) Dietary Aids Asthma Medications Anti Inflammatory Agents |
| Barbiturates | Phenobarbital (Used to Treat Epilepsy) Anti Inflammatory Agents |
| LSD | Some Antihistamines Some Prescription Mind Agents Morning Glory Seeds |
| Cocaine | Local Anesthetics (Lidocaine, Novocain) Some Antibiotics (Amoxicillin, Ampicillin) Herbal Teas (Made from Cocoa Leaves) |
| Phencyclidine (PCP) | Prescription Cough Medicines Valium |
| Opiates | Codeine Quinine Prescription Analgesics Prescription Antitussives Over-the-Counter Cough Medicines Poppy Seeds |
| Safer Schools Web-site, Drug Testing, http://www.keystosaferschools.com/drug_testing_specifics. htm#falsepositives | |

Manufacturers of the Enzyme Multiple Immunoassay Test (EMIT) tests initially claimed an accuracy rate of 99% under "optimal conditions." Independent studies, however, demonstrated that under more realistic conditions the EMIT test yielded false positives up to 37% of the time. Due to improvements in the testing procedures, more recent studies indicate that a qualified lab with properly trained technicians can achieve an accuracy rate of 96% or higher. Some surveys have declared that the GC/MS test is nearly infallible. The GC/MS test eliminates the problem of cross-reactivity by identifying drugs by breaking compounds into electrically charged ion fragments. Of course the test needs properly trained and equipped technicians to achieve this accuracy. Cairns & Grady, *supra*, at 506–07.

3. *Drug Testing in a Low Drug Use Population*: The aggregate predictive value of a test will vary according to the prevalence of drug users in the tested population: the lower the percentage of drug users, the less likely it is that the aggregate results are accurate. To see why, consider the application

of a drug test to two different populations: one with a high percent of actual drug users, say 1000 convicts of whom 500 are drug users; and another with a low percent of drug users, for example, 1000 U.S. customs agents of whom only 20 are drug users. Assuming that an EMIT test is used with 99% sensitivity (it accurately identifies 99% of the true drug users) and 90% specificity (it accurately identifies 90% of drug-free workers as being drug free). Applying this test to the convicts, one would correctly identify 495 of the drug users (5 would slip through) while falsely identifying 50 of the drug-free convicts as drug users. Among the convicts, almost 91% of the 545 people who test positive are actually drug users. Applying the test to the custom agents, one would correctly identify almost all of the 20 drug users (1 might slip through) while falsely identifying 98 of the drug-free agents as drug users. Among the customs agents, less than 17% of the 118 people who test positive are actually drug users. The problem is that, even though the drug test is pretty accurate, among the customs agents there are so few actual drug users that the false positives swamp the true positives. This example demonstrates one of the conflicts between employers and employees on drug testing that is exacerbated by the disparity in importance the employer places on one employee and the importance that employee places on his job (bargaining power). Even though the employer does not want to get rid of drug-free employees on the basis of a bad test, it may be worth it to the employer to get rid 98 drug-free employees in order to get rid of the 20 actual drug users. From the employees' perspective, the drug test is an imposition that victimizes the vast majority of people who are fired under the program. Thus, even though the vast majority of employees don't use drugs and may favor a drug-free workplace, they may oppose and resent the drug testing program. *See, e.g., NTEU v. Von Raab*, 489 U.S. 656, 109 S.Ct. 1384, 103 L.Ed.2d 685 (1989) discussed below (union representing customs agents sued to block employee drug testing program).

4. *Required and Recommended Testing Procedures*: Pursuant to the executive order establishing the Drug–Free Federal Workplace, Exec. Order No. 12,564, 51 Fed. Reg. 32,889 (Sept. 15, 1986), the National Institute on Drug Abuse (NIDA) has established a set of guidelines for federal workplace drug testing. These Guidelines prescribe procedures and qualifications that a laboratory must meet to be certified to do federal testing. The guidelines also cover the collection and custody of samples and require storage of the samples for a period of time to allow further testing if a dispute arises.

The NIDA procedures require that initial drug screening must be done with an approved immunoassay procedure, and that any positive results must be confirmed with a follow-up "confirmatory test" using gas chromatography/mass spectrometry. The Guidelines also require that each agency employ a "Medical Review Officer" to interview any subject who tests positive on the confirmatory test in an effort to determine whether the positive test is the result of a lawfully ingested food or medicine cross reactant. Note that the requirement of an initial and confirmatory test not only employs the more reliable testing procedure when the worker's test is in question, but the employees who test positive on the first test constitute a population with a higher percentage of drug users, improving the aggregate predictive value of the second test.

The NIDA guidelines only apply to testing required by federal law for federal employees and certain employees in the railway and trucking industries. In the private sector, twenty-six states* and Puerto Rico have legislated with respect to drug testing most often requiring that, if employers want to test, they must follow testing procedures similar to the NIDA guidelines. Absent a statute, however, employers are unconstrained in all these regards, and, for the most part, the courts have found no legal barrier or constraint on a private employer's ability to require submission to a drug screen—even an unreliable one—as a condition of entering into (or retaining) employment. Unfortunately, many private employers, especially small employers, do not bother to use a confirmatory test or interview as part of their testing procedure. The worst testing procedures involve the use of "field tests" administered without any interview or confirmatory test by people without any training. This failure is certain to produce false accusations of drug abuse with potentially devastating consequences for the employee's career. An expert responding to a recent Journal of American Medical Association survey wrote: "It is almost beyond my ability to comprehend the fact that organizations are actually basing employee life-career decisions upon a single EMIT or RIA result." Shane J. Osowski, *Urinalysis Drug Testing of Employees At Will: The Need for Mandatory Standards*, 11 N. Ill. U. L. Rev. 319, 345 (1991). As a result, some commentators have called for mandatory testing guidelines to ensure accurate testing. See *id.* at 346–47.

## 2.   THE COURTS ON DRUG TESTING

### COLLECTIVE AND INDIVIDUAL APPROACHES TO PROTECTING EMPLOYEE PRIVACY: THE EXPERIENCE WITH WORKPLACE DRUGTESTING

Pauline T. Kim
66 La. L. Rev. 1009, 1015–31 (2006)

### III.   Contesting Workplace Drug Testing

### A.   The Leading Cases

In the mid–1980's, as employers began implementation of drug testing programs, employees or their representatives instituted a number of court cases challenging these policies. Because much of the early testing was undertaken by public employers, or as the result of federal mandates, the early cases most often raised constitutional challenges, alleging that the testing violated workers' Fourth Amendment rights to be free from unreasonable searches. This early litigation produced mixed results regarding the constitutionality of workplace drug testing; however, courts generally agreed that the testing implicated important privacy interests.
* * *

---

* These states are: Alaska, Alabama, Arizona, Connecticut, Delaware, Florida, Hawaii, Idaho, Iowa, Louisiana, Maine, Maryland, Massachusetts, Minnesota, Missouri, Montana, Nebraska, North Carolina, Ohio, Oklahoma, Oregon, Rhode Island, South Carolina, Utah, Vermont, and Washington. A total of twenty-nine states regulate drug testing among at least some public employees. http://www.aclu.org/files/FilesPDFs/testing_chart.pdf

Then, in 1989, the Supreme Court decided two high profile cases— *Skinner v. Railway Labor Executives' Association*[, 489 U.S. 602, 109 S. Ct. 1402 (1989).] and *National Treasury Employees Union v. Von Raab*[, 489 U.S. 656, 109 S. Ct. 1384 (1989)]—that directly addressed the constitutionality of drug tests under the Fourth Amendment. Skinner involved a challenge to the constitutionality of regulations promulgated by the Federal Railroad Administration (FRA) requiring drug and alcohol testing of railroad employees involved in a major train accident. Von Raab addressed the United States Customs Service's policy of requiring all employees transferred or promoted to certain positions to undergo urinalysis drug tests. Covered positions included those directly involved in drug interdiction, those requiring the incumbent to carry firearms, and those that entailed handling of "classified" material.

The Supreme Court in Skinner unambiguously recognized that the drug tests implicated significant privacy interests. It held that both the physical intrusion entailed in obtaining a blood sample, and the visual or aural monitoring of the act of urination required under the regulations infringed "expectations of privacy that society has long recognized as reasonable." Because testing bodily fluids "can reveal a host of private medical facts about an employee, including whether he or she is epileptic, pregnant, or diabetic," the Court found that the ensuing chemical analysis constituted a further invasion of privacy, and concluded that these intrusions "must be deemed searches under the Fourth Amendment." The Court noted, however, that the Fourth Amendment proscribes only unreasonable searches and seizures. Emphasizing the safety-sensitive nature of the railroad workers' jobs and the pervasive regulation of the railroad industry to ensure safety, the Court held that the government's "compelling" interest in testing without individualized suspicion outweighed the workers' interests in privacy. The Court reached a similar conclusion in Von Raab, referring to a "veritable national crisis" caused by the smuggling of illegal drugs, and finding that the Government had a compelling interest in ensuring that "front-line interdiction personnel are physically fit, and have unimpeachable integrity and judgment." * * *

In his dissent in Skinner, Justice Thurgood Marshall decried the "mass governmental intrusions upon the integrity of the human body that the majority allows to become reality," arguing that the decision will ultimately "reduce the privacy all citizens may enjoy." Justice Antonin Scalia, dissenting in Von Raab, found urinalysis drug testing to be "a type of search particularly destructive of privacy and offensive to personal dignity." Given the absence of any evidence of drug use among Customs Service employees, he concluded that the Customs Service testing program was "a kind of immolation of privacy and human dignity in symbolic opposition to drug use."

*Dissents o la- drug test*

Despite the clear recognition of a privacy interest in Skinner and Von Raab, those decisions made it more difficult for workers to challenge drug testing policies under the Fourth Amendment by accepting as compelling justifications the employers' asserted interests in safety in Skinner and in the "integrity" of the Customs Service in Von Raab. Prior to those decisions, published federal courts of appeals' decisions addressing Fourth Amendment challenges to workplace drug testing were evenly split. By contrast, in the years following the Court's decisions in Skinner and Von Raab, the courts of appeals overwhelmingly upheld government drug policies in the face of Fourth Amendment challenges.

### B.  A More Systematic Look at the Cases

Despite the considerable attention they received, Skinner and Von Raab were not representative of the bulk of legal disputes over employer drug testing. [Skinner and Von Raab] sought class-wide, injunctive relief based on a Fourth Amendment challenge. Most drug testing disputes, however, involved individual workers impacted by their employer's mandatory testing policies. Moreover, the constitutional claims raised in Skinner and Von Raab were not generally available to workers in the private sector. Private employees who wanted to challenge drug testing policies had to rely on common law or statutory claims, and if they were unionized, the remedies available through the collective bargaining system. * * *

In the private sector, employees relied primarily on common law theories to challenge adverse employment actions. Some directly challenged the intrusion entailed by testing policies, relying on the common law tort of invasion of privacy, which imposes liability for an "unreasonable intrusion upon the seclusion of another" that is "highly offensive to a reasonable person." Intrusion on seclusion claims were often accompanied by other claims focusing on dignitary harms such as defamation, intentional infliction of emotional distress, and negligent infliction of emotional distress. Because virtually all of the cases involved discharges, the employees also relied on theories suggesting limitations on the employer's right to terminate the employment. Thus, individual plaintiffs often alleged that their employer's actions breached a contract providing job security or promising to respect their privacy, or that they had been discharged in violation of public policy.

Because of the common law presumption that employment for an indefinite period is on an "at-will" basis, the employee discharged as a result of a drug testing policy faced an uphill battle. Very few workers in the private sector have contracts specifying a term of employment or guaranteeing job security. Unlike union employees who are typically protected by the collective bargaining agreement against discharge without "just cause," the non-union employee had fewer bases on which to challenge their employer's actions.... In the absence of a contractual limitation on the employer's right to discharge without cause, however, those arguments were simply unavailable to the non-union private sector employee. As a result, suits by non-union employees tended to focus on the dignitary harms threatened by drug testing.... One common argument was that discharges based on a drug testing policy fell within an exception to the at-will rule because they violated the public policy protecting employees' rights to privacy and freedom from unreasonable searches. Similarly, claims of breach of the implied covenant of good faith and fair dealing were often premised on the argument that employer testing that violated employee privacy constituted a bad faith breach. Thus, even the contract and wrongful discharge claims of non-union employees were often framed in terms of privacy interests.

In a small handful of cases, individual employees achieved some notable victories. In *Luck v. Southern Pacific Transportation Co.*, [267 Cal. Rptr. 618 (1990)] a California state court of appeal upheld a jury verdict for the plaintiff, a computer programmer terminated for refusing to submit to suspicion-less drug testing. The jury had rejected the employer's argument that Luck's job was "safety-sensitive" and awarded her damages. Agreeing with this factual conclusion, the court of appeal upheld the verdict on the grounds that Southern Pacific's attempt to invade Luck's privacy was unjustified. In another case, a drilling rig employee discharged after testing positive for marijuana was awarded damages on the grounds that direct observation of the act of urination by a representative of the defendant violated the plaintiff's right to privacy and caused him emotional distress. [*Kelley v. Schlumberger Tech. Corp.*, 849 F.2d 41 (1st Cir. 1988).] Despite the success of these plaintiffs in obtaining damages for dignitary harms, their experience was quite atypical. In the overwhelming majority of individual challenges to employer drug testing, courts ruled in favor of the employer, typically relying on the right to terminate at-will or finding that the employee's privacy interests were outweighed by the employer's interest in testing.

[Looking at litigated court cases, however, omits another important form of potential collective resistance to employer-mandated drug testing. In many workplaces, the issue of drug testing was addressed primarily through the collective bargaining process rather than litigation. In Johnson–Bateman, decided in 1989, the NLRB ruled that drug and alcohol testing is a mandatory subject of bargaining, and that therefore implementation of such a program by an employer without first bargaining with the union is an unfair labor practice. [295 N.L.R.B. 180 (1989).] ... Thus, the collective bargaining process at least offered the potential for workers to raise objections on a collective basis to employer-imposed drug testing policies, and to address issues such as which workers would be subject to testing, how and when tests would be conducted, and what consequences would follow a positive result.]

## IV. Assessing Collective v. Individual Approaches to Protecting Employee Privacy

\* \* \* Although privacy has traditionally been characterized as a personal right, a number of considerations suggest that workplace privacy raises collective concerns. First, the legal protection of privacy typically depends upon existing norms, which reflect collective values and social practices. For example, in applying the Fourth Amendment prohibition against unreasonable searches, courts first ask whether a person had a "legitimate expectation of privacy" intruded upon by the government search. Cases addressing common law invasion of privacy claims often undertake a similar inquiry. Determining the legitimacy of an employee's expectation of privacy often turns not only on general social norms, but also on the actual practices of that workplace. Thus, an individual employee's claim may well rise or fall depending upon the level of privacy afforded other employees in the same workplace or industry.

In the employment context, employees' interest in privacy might also be thought of as a type of "local public good." Some forms of protection— for example, freedom from video surveillance—are classic "non-excludable goods" in that all employees will avoid the intrusiveness of such surveillance if the employer agrees to forgo it, regardless of whether the particular worker would bargain for such a benefit. In theory, drug testing differs in that particular workers could be included or excluded from a testing program, depending upon individual agreements reached with the employer. As a practical matter, however, the utility of drug testing policies (excepting perhaps those based solely on reasonable suspicion) depends upon their application to workers as a class. Given the costs of establishing and implementing such policies, employers are unlikely to bargain for different testing rules for individual employees. Moreover, from the employee's perspective, individual bargaining about privacy in general and drug testing in particular is difficult to imagine, given the enormous signaling problems raised for an individual worker acting alone in objecting to a drug testing policy. To the extent that employee privacy rights have characteristics of a "local public good," individual bargaining is likely to be inefficient.

If it is difficult for the individual to act alone, how does the presence of a union affect the ability of workers to resist unwarranted intrusions of privacy? As seen from the examination of court cases above, unions played an important role in the early workforce-wide challenges to drug testing policies. Unions initiated suit in Skinner and Von Raab, the two cases in which the Supreme Court first addressed the constitutionality of workplace drug testing, as well as the overwhelming majority of early workforce-wide challenges to drug testing policies. Many of these cases directly asserted the privacy rights of workers, thereby forcing courts to assess the justifications for policies invading those rights. Thus, unions appear to offer at least the possibility of mobilizing a collective response to threats to employee privacy. * * *

What about an individual rights model for protecting employee privacy? As discussed above, individual litigants, in the absence of a union, are less likely to bring suit seeking workforce-wide relief. In addition, individual litigants are unlikely to seek any sort of prospective relief.... The typical plaintiff has suffered some sort of job-related detriment such as discipline or termination as a result of a testing policy, and seeks compensation for her individual losses. Given the incentives confronting the individual worker, this observation is not surprising. An employee acting alone has little incentive to step forward to challenge a proposed policy, even if she perceives it as intrusive and degrading. If she were to do so, she bears all the risk, not only of the costs of litigation, but also of incurring her employer's displeasure, while any potential benefits of challenging an employer's policies would accrue to her co-workers as well. The incentives are reversed, however, once a worker has suffered a job loss as a result of a workplace drug test. At that point, she risks very little by advancing a legal claim that an employer's testing policy violates her privacy rights, and, if she succeeds, she could potentially recover significant damages. * * *.

Although the cost-benefit calculus of litigation may look more attractive to the individual worker after termination, raising the policy and dignitary concerns that motivate resistance to workplace drug testing is significantly more difficult in after-the-fact challenges. Despite the very real possibility that chemical testing of urine will produce false positives, the worker fired for failing a drug test suffers from an implicit presumption of guilt. And where procedural safeguards such as ensuring sample integrity and permitting split samples are not in place, it is impossible for the worker to establish that a false positive has occurred in her case. Regardless of the accuracy of the result in a particular case, the purpose of bringing suit is typically to challenge the underlying policy by arguing that the intrusiveness of the drug testing policy outweighs any legitimate interest the employer has in testing. Although the worker who tests positive has the greatest incentive to bring the challenge, the fact that she did test positive will tend to weight any assessment in favor of the employer's position—after all, the test has "caught" a drug user.

The worker fired for refusing to submit to drug testing also faces difficulties. Although not tainted by a positive test result, her resistance to taking the test naturally raises questions about her motivation. Under both the Fourth Amendment and the common law tort of invasion of privacy, the question whether an individual has a reasonable expectation of privacy is crucial. Making the case that a particular testing protocol invades reasonable expectations of privacy is more difficult if the employee acts alone, while the rest of her co-workers submit to the test. Of course, it is possible that none of the other employees has any objection to the testing, and that the worker has no legitimate expectation of privacy in that particular context. However, given the enormous signaling problems faced by individual workers who object to drug testing, acquiescence cannot necessarily be taken as evidence that the employees had no legitimate expectation of privacy in the absence of a collective mechanism for raising privacy concerns.

Despite these difficulties, an individual rights approach to protecting employee privacy has at least one distinct advantage over collective challenges, at least under the current legal regime for collective bargaining. The individual privacy claim, asserting tort theories or violation of constitutional rights, brings with it the possibility of significant damages.... [U]nder collective bargaining agreements arbitrators generally do not award damages to redress dignitary harms. Thus, a worker fired for failing or refusing to take a drug test can grieve the discharge and seek reinstatement. However, the worker subjected to demeaning testing conditions who subsequently tested negative cannot get any meaningful remedy for the dignitary harm suffered under the current grievance arbitration system. Judging from published court opinions, individual privacy claims rarely succeed; nevertheless, the threat of legal liability for invasion of employee privacy may more effectively discourage unreasonably intrusive testing practices than the risks posed by individual grievances under a collective bargaining regime that offers no remedy for dignitary harm.

## NOTES AND QUESTIONS

1. The United States Supreme Court held that where drug screening or testing is imposed on public employees or on private sector employees by law, that imposition constitutes a search within the meaning of the Fourth Amendment, but that such action need only meet a standard of reasonableness requiring neither probable cause nor a warrant. *Skinner v. Railway Labor Executives' Ass'n*, 489 U.S. 602, 109 S.Ct. 1402, 103 L.Ed.2d 639 (1989); *NTEU v. Von Raab*, 489 U.S. 656, 109 S.Ct. 1384, 103 L.Ed.2d 685 (1989). The Court connected the constitutional standard of reasonableness to the job relatedness of the test, emphasizing especially that job safety would be a primary concern. How that has played out has given rise to some divisions of opinion. The Sixth Circuit has held in *Knox County Education Ass'n v. Knox County Board of Education* that teachers as a class occupy "safety sensitive" positions and may be tested. 158 F.3d 361 (6th Cir. 1998). But *Knox County* was expressly rejected in *American Federation of Teachers–West Virginia v. Kanawha County Board of Education*, 592 F.Supp.2d 883 (S.D. W. Va. 2009) and by the Ninth Circuit in treating the position of a library page. *Lanier v. City of Woodburn*, 518 F.3d 1147 (9th Cir. 2008).

2. Professor Kim argues that, even though privacy is commonly thought of as a quintessential personal right, there are important community and public good aspects to this interest. Both the Constitutional standard and the common law standard depend on what constitutes a legitimate or reasonable expectation in privacy. Thus, an individual's privacy rights depend on what other people tolerate as intrusions on their privacy. Moreover, many aspects of privacy in the workplace, for example whether the workplace is video-recorded, are public goods and individual employees will not have sufficient incentive to negotiate efficient limitations on these intrusions. This is particularly true because individual employees will not bargain to limit drug testing or surveillance because it makes them look like they have something to hide even if they don't. Note that if the question of privacy is left purely up to individual bargaining, the failure of individual employees to bargain for rights in turn undermines privacy norms and what constitutes a reasonable expectation of privacy. As Kim points out, one solution to this problem is collective bargaining—the employees bind together to collectively negotiate to uphold their privacy interests. Absent representation by a union, employee privacy rights depend ultimately on either statutes or common law principles that limit the employer's ability to impose intrusions through individual employment contracts. What limitations should there be on intrusions into employ-

ees privacy? Should employers be able to make job decisions on the basis of lawful off duty activities that do not affect the employee's ability to do his job? What if the activity involves the exercise of a fundamental right and only affects the employee's ability to do his job a little? What privacy rights should an employee have in the workplace?

## BAUGHMAN v. WAL–MART STORES, INC.

Supreme Court of Appeals of West Virginia, 2003
215 W.Va. 45, 592 S.E.2d 824

In the instant case, we uphold a grant of summary judgment by a circuit court in a case alleging invasion of privacy.

### I

In the instant case, the appellant, Stephanie Baughman, filed suit on July 5, 2001, against the appellee Wal–Mart Stores, Inc., in the Circuit Court of Harrison County. The appellant's complaint stated that the appellant was required to give a urine sample prior to her employment by a Wal–Mart store. That is, the appellant was offered a job by Wal–Mart— but prior to the appellant's starting work, Wal–Mart required her (and allegedly all other prospective employees) to first give a urine sample that Wal–Mart would test for results that may indicate illegal drug use. The appellant gave the urine sample and thereafter began working at Wal–Mart; she later left her employment at Wal–Mart for reasons apparently unrelated to the instant case.

The appellant's complaint stated that Wal–Mart's pre-employment requirement of giving a urine sample for drug testing after being offered a job, but before starting to work, was *per se* an actionable invasion of the appellant's privacy; and that Wal–Mart had, by requiring the sample, caused the appellant "embarrassment, indignity, humiliation, annoyance, inconvenience and other general damages."

Wal–Mart filed an answer admitting that the appellant had been required to submit a urine sample for drug testing, but denying that there was any illegality in or harm from this requirement. Thereafter, some limited amount of discovery took place. The appellant then filed a motion for partial summary judgment on the issue of liability. Wal–Mart filed a cross-motion for summary judgment on the same issue. The circuit court granted summary judgment to Wal–Mart, holding that the appellant had not shown an actionable invasion of privacy in Wal–Mart's requiring her to submit a urine sample for drug testing before she began to work for Wal–Mart.[2]

---

**2.** The appellee did not receive any adverse action from Wal–Mart as a result of the urine sample that she gave, so neither the circuit court nor this Court was or is called upon to address any issues involving policies or practices that Wal–Mart may have or used with respect to the methods, scope, nature, results, or range of consequences, if any, associated with pre-employment urine sample testing; nor is there any developed record on these practices and policies. Nor are there any allegations that the law against disability discrimination is implicated in the instant case.

## II

We review a grant of summary judgment *de novo.*

The appellant's principal argument is based on our holding in *Twigg v. Hercules Corp.,* 185 W.Va. 155, 406 S.E.2d 52 (1990). In *Twigg,* this Court stated in Syllabus Points 1 and 2:

1. It is contrary to public policy in West Virginia for an employer to require *an employee* to submit to drug testing since such test portends an invasion of an individual's right to privacy.

2. Drug testing will not be found to be violative of public policy grounded in the potential intrusion of a person's right to privacy where it is conducted by an employer based upon reasonable good faith objective suspicion of *an employee's* drug usage or while *an employee's* job responsibility involves public safety or the safety of others. [emphasis added]. * * *

We concluded in *Twigg* that in the case of current employment, the employee's right of privacy is not outweighed by the employer's rights and interests unless specific heightened safety concerns or well-grounded individualized suspicion is present—analogous to the kind of probable cause necessary for a warrant—and clearly outweighs the employee's important right to privacy.

However, in the pre-employment context, it is apparent—although not necessarily dispositive in every case—that a person clearly has a lower expectation of privacy. Employers regularly perform pre-employment background checks, seek references, and require pre-employment medical examinations, etc., that are far more intrusive than what would be considered tolerable for existing employees without special circumstances. Giving a urine sample is a standard component of a medical examination.

In light of the important issues involved, we are not prepared in deciding this case to paint with an unnecessarily broad brush—and to say that under no set of particular circumstances could a person successfully assert an invasion of privacy-based claim arising from a particular pre-employment drug testing requirement. Moreover, we strongly affirm our holding in *Twigg* regarding the appropriate balance that must be struck between privacy rights and employer's interests for an employer's current employees. We also point out that our ruling today relates only to the case of a private employer; and nothing in this opinion is to be seen as indicative of the scope of the legal rights of or restraints upon a public employer, the conduct of which directly implicates, *inter alia,* the constitutional prohibitions against searches without probable cause.

---

According to Befort, Stephen, *Pre-Employment Screening and Investigation: Navigating Between a Rock and a Hard Place,* 14 Hofstra Labor Law Journal 365, 394–398 (1997), in most if not all states that permit and regulate some form of pre-employment drug testing by statute, the right to the results of the tests, to request confirmatory tests, and the opportunity to challenge the results is afforded. We believe these practices are desirable, and adherence to such practices should be a factor in evaluating the fairness of any testing policies and practices.

In this regard, we are firmly committed to the unique and essential role of courts in protecting the individual's private life and "space" from well-intentioned but ultimately oppressive, insulting, degrading, and demeaning intrusions—whether these intrusions come from the omnipresent forces of the state, or from the equally omnipresent and inescapable forces of the market.

The principle and right of personal autonomy and privacy is just as important as the more traditional civil rights of freedom of assembly, speech, and religion. It is central to our constitutional system of government. Its protection needs strong and sometimes controversial and fearless, bulwarks—especially in an age of ever-more sophisticated and intrusive technologies, and cries for heightened surveillance and monitoring of every aspect of life. It is a crucial role of courts in a constitutional system to see that these bulwarks of privacy, autonomy, and ultimately freedom remain strong—even in the face of short-sighted efforts to erode them, or to make an end-run around them.[3]

Having said this, we agree with the circuit court that the principles of *Twigg* do not extend to the pre-employment situation and thus do not preclude the granting of summary judgment to Wal–Mart in the instant case. We conclude that the appellant put forth no facts that would show that her right to privacy was violated in the instant case simply as a result of Wal–Mart's requiring her, prior to starting work, to give a urine sample for drug testing purposes.

In making our decision, we are particularly mindful of the specter of a court-created "slippery slope" in this evolving area of law. Courts must guard against the inadvertent self-fulfilling "shrinking" of "expectations of privacy"—as incremental intrusions into areas of personal life and inviolability, traditionally viewed as private and protected, may perforce be validated in the light of similar and tolerated past erosions of the private sphere. It is for this reason that we necessarily must have some degree of hesitancy with respect to our ruling in the instant case—as we are putting a "stamp of approval" on a type of intrusion that we have not

---

**3.** In this regard, the following quotation from *Loder v. City of Glendale,* 14 Cal.4th 846, 921–922, 927 P.2d 1200, 1249, 59 Cal.Rptr.2d 696, 745 (1997) (Kennard, J., concurring and dissenting) (a case that involved drug testing of public employees) raises important and fundamental issues that cannot be lost sight of in balancing the competing interests in any drug testing case:

This case conjures up visions of an Orwellian nightmare in which the government, through intrusive bodily testing, microscopically scrutinizes the most intimate aspects of the bodies and lives of all individuals seeking government positions, justifying such scrutiny on the ground that the intrusions will enhance efficiency, productivity, and cost-effectiveness. In the words of one commentator: "[B]y submitting millions of Americans to systematic biochemical surveillance of their blood or urine, our level of expectations of individual privacy will greatly diminish, and we will, thereby, surrender a considerable amount of autonomy, dignity and sovereignty. We [will] have allowed the government and employers to transcend an invisible shield which stood at the edge of our bodies.... John Stuart Mill's aphorism, 'Over himself, over his own body and mind, the individual is sovereign,' no longer sounds relevant." (*Proposal for a Substance Abuse Testing Act: The Report of the Task Force on the Drug–Free Workplace, Institute of Bill of Rights Law* (1991) 33 Wal–Mart. [*sic*] [Wm.] & Mary L.Rev. 5, 3334 [Comment of task force member Cornish, italics omitted].)

sanctioned before (nor have we before disapproved it). Time will tell if we can hold to our resolve not to go further down a slippery slope. * * *

## NOTES AND QUESTIONS

*Why okay here?*

1. West Virginia is one of a very few jurisdictions to limit drug testing of employees to safety-sensitive positions, akin to the U.S. Supreme Court's application of the Fourth Amendment. But in *Baughman* the court refuses to take the same approach to the screening of applicants. Why? Of what job-related relevance is the passage of a drug test to the job of, say, greeter at a Wal–Mart?

2. The court acknowledges that submission to the test is intrusive but it distinguishes applicants as having a lower expectation of privacy as justifying *this* intrusion. But the court warns at the close about the prospect of incremental erosion of privacy—of each next privacy invasive step as being justified because it is no more intrusion than a prior privacy invasive step that has been found unobjectionable. (On just that manner of reasoning, *see City of North Miami v. Kurtz*, 653 So.2d 1025 (Fla. 1995).) Hasn't the court done just that?

3. Over a decade and a half ago, a comprehensive review of the scientific literature was undertaken by the National Research Council and the Institute of Medicine (NRC/IOM). UNDER THE INFLUENCE? DRUGS AND THE AMERICAN WORK FORCE (Jacques Normand, Richard O. Lempert & Charles P. O'Brien eds., 1994). On the use of drug testing to screen applicants, the NRC/IOM Report observed:

> Enough studies of preemployment drug-testing programs have been published with sufficiently consistent results that we can conclude that preemployment drug-test results are, in at least some job settings, valid predictors of some job-related behaviors. Those who test positive for drugs before employment are, as a group, likely to have higher rates of absenteeism, turnover, and disciplinary actions than those who test negative.

*Id.* at 227. But it also cautioned:

> These figures do not necessarily mean, however, the preemployment drug testing is a cost-effective selection program. Finding that job applicants' drug-test results are predictive of critical job behaviors means that employers can select, on average, more productive workers if they attend to drug test information than if that information is not used to make hiring decisions. However, as with any other type of selection program, the predictive efficacy of drug test results depends on a few critical selection parameters. In particular, the prevalence of drug use among potential job applicants has to be sufficiently large to yield meaningful measures of association between test results and the outcome measure and to justify the cost of testing. . . .

*Id.* at 227–85 (references omitted). And it further cautioned:

> It is also possible for employers to overweight preemployment drug-test results. In the best studies done to date, employers chose applicants using

the cues they ordinarily apply without reference to evidence of drug use. The research shows that, among this group, those who tested positive performed worse by certain job-related criteria than those who showed no evidence of recent drug use. The studies do not show that positive testers performed worse than those who would have replaced them had they been rejected on the basis of drug-test information. In particular, there is a danger that, if drug-test results trump other signs that warn of job difficulties, negative drug testers will be preferred to positive testers who exceeded them on job-related criteria. A major gap in the extant research is its failure to examine the interaction of recent drug usage and other job-related applicant characteristics. Although the studies show preemployment drug testing to be predictively valid, they also indicate that many applicants who test positive could be hired without producing any job-related difficulties.

*But can't overplay these findings*

*Id.* at 228. As for "for cause" and random drug testing, the study found no empirically based evidence of a relationship to work force productivity.

The report also touched upon the use of tests that measure one's readiness for the job in lieu of a drug test. It concluded that:

Alcohol and other drug use by work force members cannot be reliably inferred from performance assessments, since performance decrements may have many antecedents. Conversely, performance decrements are often not obvious despite alcohol and other drug use. More direct measures of the likely quality of worker performance hold promise for determining workers' fitness to perform specific jobs at specific times, regardless of the potential cause of impairment.

*Id.* at 10.

4. Assume that an employer makes a job offer contingent on the applicant's passing a drug test. The test result is a false positive, and the employer withdraws the offer. May the employee sue the laboratory? The employer? On what theory? *Compare Stinson v. Physicians Immediate Care, Ltd.*, 269 Ill.App.3d 659, 207 Ill.Dec. 96, 646 N.E.2d 930 (1995) *with Carroll v. Federal Express Co.*, 113 F.3d 163 (9th Cir. 1997).

5. A state has enacted a Medical Use of Marijuana Act that exempts from the reach of the criminal law a physician's prescribed use of marijuana for certain specified conditions. Jane Roe regularly consumes marijuana under a physician's prescription to treat migraine headaches. She applied for the job of telemarketer with a company that requires passage of a drug test. She notified management of her doctor-prescribed marijuana. The company has made a job offer conditioned on Ms. Roe's passage of a drug screen pursuant to its "drug free workplace policy." Ms. Roe has tested positive for marijuana. May the company withdraw its conditional offer of hire? *Roe v. TeleTech Customer Care Mgmt.* (Colorado), L.L.C., 152 Wash.App. 388, 216 P.3d 1055 (2009).

# G.  PSYCHOLOGICAL SCREENING

Since pre-industrial times, people have sought means other than judging a person's self-presentation to determine the person's true character. Gideon, for example, determined the courage of his warriors by how they drank water from a stream. Judges, Ch. 7, v. 1–8. And in the seventeenth century, witches could be detected by "swimming." The suspect was bound, stripped naked, and cast into a river. In England, if the subject floated, it was proof of witchcraft; but in southwest Germany, floating was evidence of innocence. F. ALLAN HANSON, TESTING TESTING: SOCIAL CONSEQUENCES OF THE EXAMINED LIFE 37–38 (1993).

More recently, scientific (or quasi-scientific) means of judging a subject's "true nature" have been developed. Polygraphy—mechanical "lie detection"—is one. Its use as a screening device in most employments is now forbidden by federal law; polygraphy will be treated later in this book, when used as an investigative device. Other common screening devices are explored below.

## 1. PERSONALITY TESTING

Personality tests attempt to develop a picture of the test-taker's emotional make-up. Some personality tests, such as the Rorschach and Thematic Apperception Tests, are projective. They ask the subject to explain to a psychologist what an ink blot depicts or the story behind a picture—in the latter, for example, of a woman lying in bed, breast exposed, behind a fully clothed male standing with his back to her. *See generally* ANNE ANASTASI, PSYCHOLOGICAL TESTING 602–04 (6th ed. 1988). More commonly used for employment purposes are objective tests that can be taken by paper and pencil such as the Minnesota Multiphase Personality Inventory (MMPI) (later reconfigured particularly for employee screening as the MMPI2), and others like it, such as the California Psychological Inventory.

The MMPI consists of several hundred questions which the subject answers about herself, such as:

I have nightmares every few nights.

It would be better if almost all laws were thrown away.

My soul sometimes leaves my body.

A minister can cure disease by praying and putting his hand on your head.

I see things or animals or people around me that others do not see.

Sometimes I am strongly attracted by the personal articles of others such as shoes, gloves, etc., so that I want to handle or steal them though I have no use for them.

Sometimes I feel as if I must injure either myself or someone else.

There are persons who are trying to steal my thoughts and ideas.

Efforts have been made more recently to eliminate or reduce questions concerning bodily functions and religion.

The results are scaled against a group of "normal" subjects. Originally the scales were of a clinical nature—paranoia, depression, psychopathic deviate, and the like; but the MMPI has been rescaled for employment screening purposes to measure non-clinical behavior or attitudes, e.g. anger, anxiety, cynicism, obsession, low self-esteem. Some of the questions help provide an estimate of the test's validity, because subjects may respond defensively in employment screening situations. One study found 6.8% of female applicants and 8.6% of male applicants produced invalid results. STARKE R. HATHAWAY, J.C. MCKINLEY & JAMES BUTCHER, MINNESOTA MULTIPHASIC PERSONALITY INVENTORY-2: USER'S GUIDE 1–2 (1989).

The purpose of asking these questions is to correlate the personality profile from the pattern of response that emerges against the profile of a normative group. For example, it may appear that a male's affirmative answer to the question "I like tall women," is an indication of impulsiveness. J. Block, *Personality Measurement: Overview, in* 12 INTERNATIONAL ENCYCLOPEDIA OF THE SOCIAL SCIENCES 32 (David L. Sills ed., 1968). The investigator is not interested in the subject's sexual interests, but in his degree of impulsiveness which, in turn, might arguably be related to the subject's likely response to stress on the job. But it is also true that in order to draw that inference—which may or may not be especially powerful, or may or may not accurately predict that response—one's inner state must be revealed through the questioning process.

Professional advocates are cautious about the use of personality inventories in employment screening. The MMPI User's Guide advises: "Routine use of clinically oriented tests like the MMPI–2 is not recommended for all personnel screening programs." Its use is recommended only for jobs involving safety or high degrees of stress such as firefighters and air traffic controllers. But a 1987 survey of 142 reporting companies (of 300 surveyed) indicated that 20% used some form of personality or psychological test. PAUL BLOCKLYN, PREEMPLOYMENT TESTING, PERSONNEL 66 (February 1988).

### NOTES AND QUESTIONS

1. To the extent a personality test provides evidence of a medical disorder or impairment, it would be considered a medical test governed by the ADA. *See* EEOC ENFORCEMENT GUIDANCE ON PRE-EMPLOYMENT INQUIRIES UNDER THE AMERICANS WITH DISABILITIES ACT, BNA DAILY LABOR REPORT No. 96 at D–1, D–10 (May 20, 1994).

2. Some of the criticism is directed to the methodology employed. *See, e.g.,* Thomas W. Zimmerer & Taylor G. Stephen, *Personality Tests for Potential Employees: More Harm Than Good,* 67 PERSONNEL J. 60 (1988); C.E. Johnson, R. Wood & S.F. Blinkhorn, *Spriouser and Spuriouser: The Use of Ipsative Personality Tests,* 61 J. OCCUPATIONAL PSYCHOL. 153 (1988). Some is predicated on philosophical grounds. *See generally* HANSON, *supra,* at 305:

> The capacity of the self to adopt such a rich variety of roles in social life is grounded in "privileged access." This term refers to the idea that other

people have no direct knowledge of what is going on in someone's mind—one's thoughts, desires, daydreams, fantasies, jealousies, and hidden agendas. The notion that the self can exclude all others from this inner sanctum (except, in some religious persuasions, God) ensures the ultimate uncertainty or mystery that the self can parlay into selective, creative, and variable presentations in the social world. Obviously, if this mystery were dispelled and all one's inner states were transparent to others, one's ability to mold one's public image would be drastically curtailed.

The effect of testing is precisely to dispel that mystery. Testing thwarts privileged access, intruding unchaperoned into the private realm formerly controlled by the self as gatekeeper and monitor of information. . . .

Production and presentation of knowledge about the self comes under the control of test givers. The self is no longer able, in a test situation, to temper or embellish it. Whatever tempering and embellishing takes place now stems from the tests themselves, which . . . regularly redefine or even fabricate the qualities they are intended to measure.

And some of the criticism has been placed on legal grounds. *See* Donald H.J. Hermann III, *Privacy the Prospective Employee, and Employment Testing: The Need to Restrict Polygraph and Personality Testing*, 47 WASH.L.REV. 73 (1971). *See also* ANNIE MURPHY PAUL, THE CULT OF PERSONALITY: HOW PERSONALITY TESTS ARE LEADING US TO MISEDUCATE OUR CHILDREN, MISMANAGE OUR COMPANIES, AND MISUNDERSTAND OURSELVES (2004).

3.  May a police department require applicants to take the MMPI? *See* Matter of Vey, 135 N.J. 306, 639 A.2d 718 (1994). May a discount store require it of applicants for store security agent? They Assume that store security agents are required to observe and apprehend shoplifters; they do not carry fire arms but they do carry handcuffs and may use force. *See Soroka v. Dayton Hudson Corp.*, 1 Cal.Rptr.2d 77 (Cal. Ct. App.1991), 24 Cal.Rptr.2d 587, 862 P.2d 148 (1993) (petition for review dismissed per settlement). May the test be used for the selection of managerial and sales personnel? *See New Ways of Testing Skills and Potential of Managers*, 39 INT'L MGMT. 7 (March 1984); *Personality Tests Beginning to Stage A Comeback*, 38 INT'L MGMT. 43 (November 1983); William F. Fortunato, *Personality Testing As An Aid to Good Sales Mgmt*, 105 BROADCASTING 16 (October 24, 1983); *Personality Tests Help When Hiring*, 106 SAVINGS INSTITUTIONS 158 (October 1985); Kevin O'Brien, *Star Producers Shine On Personality Test*, 90 NAT'L UNDERWRITER 3 (Sept. 1986).

4.  Assume that a personality test used to search for cooperative "team players," to screen out potential dissidents or malcontents, may also screen out those more likely to form, join, or assist a labor organization. Would the use of the test violate the National Labor Relations Act? *Cf.* Great Lakes Chem. Corp., 298 NLRB 615 (1990), *enforcement granted*, 967 F.2d 624 (D.C.Cir.1992).

5.  If an applicant is denied hire because, according to the testing agency, the applicant has an "extreme propensity" for alcoholism; but the applicant can prove that he has never had a problem with alcohol, could he have a cause of action against the testing agency? On what theory? What if he had signed a

"consent" or "release" as a condition of taking the test? *See, e.g., Pinger v. Behavioral Sci. Ctr.*, 52 Ohio App.3d 17, 556 N.E.2d 209 (1988).

## 2. HONESTY TESTING

A number of paper-and-pencil tests purport to measure a test-taker's honesty or, in some cases, the propensity for deviant workplace behavior such as drug use. *See generally* R.M. O'BANNON, L.A. GOLDINGER & G.S. APPLEBY, HONESTY AND INTEGRITY TESTING (1989); DAVID T. LYKKEN, A TREMOR IN THE BLOOD (1981) (from which the following illustrations are taken). These tests use one or more of four categories of questions: One elicits admission of illegal or other deviant activity, such as

*4 Types*
*①*

> What total value in merchandise and property have you taken without permission from employers? (Circle nearest value.)
>
> $5,000   $2,500   $1,000   $750   $500   $250   $100   $50   $0

A second elicits opinions toward illegal or disapproved behavior such as, *②*

> How many employees take small things from their employers from time to time?
>
> 95%    80%    60%    40%    20%    5%

A third elicits descriptions of one's own personality or thoughts, such as *③*

My philosophy is best described as:

    a.   The meek shall inherit the earth.

    b.   It's a dog eat dog world.

    c. No one owes you anything.

*④*

The fourth elicits reactions to hypothetical situations, such as

> How many employees take small things from their employers from time to time?
>
> 95%    80%    60%    40%    20%    5%

The first category, of self-reporting, is based upon the assumption that one who has stolen from an employer in the past is likely to do so in the future, though it has been pointed out that the question assumes the test-taker is answering truthfully. The other types of questions supply data from which inferences of a propensity toward dishonesty may be drawn.

*Assumes truth-telling in answers*

The predictive validity of these tests is controversial. In 1990, the Office of Technology Assessment reviewed the literature and concluded that "[t]he research on integrity tests has not yet produced data that clearly supports or dismisses the assertion that these tests can predict dishonest behavior." OFFICE OF TECHNOLOGY ASSESSMENT, THE USES OF INTEGRITY TESTS FOR PRE-EMPLOYMENT SCREENING 8 (1990). It, in turn, was criticized by the American Psychological Association on the ground that the OTA had chosen to include "only a small number of studies they considered to meet the highest levels of scientific credibility in evaluating integrity tests" rather than other "accepted methodologies." The OTA's conclusion was also strongly criticized by the Association of Personnel Test Publishers. *See* John W. Jones, David Arnold & William G. Harris, *Introduction to the Model Guidelines for Preemployment Integrity Testing*, 4 J. BUS. & PSYCHOL. 525 (1990). The debate has abated subsequently though the two statements remain as characterizing the state of knowledge thus far. One of the imponderables in arriving at a disinterested assessment of paper and pencil integrity testing is that most of these tests are proprietary, their scoring keys are kept secret by the testing companies that sell them, and much of the literature on validation is published either by those within the testing industry or who are supported by it.

A comprehensive review of the available professional literature, especially concerning more "personality based measures" rather than "overt" integrity questions, concluded that "integrity tests may be useful for institutional prediction but less so for individual prediction." Paul R. Sackett, Laura R. Burris & Christine Callahan, *Integrity Testing for Personnel Selection: An Update*, 42 PERSONNEL POL'Y 491, 529 (1989). They explain the distinction:

> An employer with a single opening and two applicants, one with a test profile indicating a 10% likelihood of theft and the other with a test profile indicating a 20% likelihood of theft, may find that the reasonable doubt standard is not met for either but may conclude that test use to choose between applicants is rational. This is the essence of institutional prediction: in the long run the employer using the test will be better off than the employer choosing haphazardly, assuming test validity.

*Id.* The conclusion (which assumes the only alternative to test use is "haphazard choice") reasons that the aggregate benefit to the employer in selecting from a large pool of applicants over time outweighs the consequences to individuals who are "honest"—in the sense that they would not steal if hired—but are turned away as a result of the employer's reliance upon the test. As the authors explain,

> Note that the typical passing rate for integrity tests is 40–70%; in order to use an integrity test an organization must be in a position to turn away a large proportion of applicants. As integrity tests are typically used as a final hurdle after screening for other factors such as ability and relevant job experience, the ratio of applicants to openings must be quite high. We note that the entry level retail, restaurant, and service jobs, for which integrity tests are commonly used, are the very jobs for which a scarcity of candidates is frequently reported. The employer who wants to identify potentially counterproductive employees without turning away a large portion of the applicant pool will not find integrity tests a viable solution to the problem.

*Id.* at 52–53. Does this observation remain sound in today's economy?

"Reliability" in test usage does not mean that the test is accurate in terms of what it is seeking to measure, but only that, within an acceptable range for error, one who passes or fails the test is likely to pass or fail if one takes the test again. Two critics have observed that *if* these tests are "reliable"—which means that a person who has failed one integrity test is very likely to fail another—and *if* these tests produce a high rate of false positives, as they appear to do, then an entire class of those wrongfully classified as dishonest may be condemned to underemployment or unemployment. Stephen J. Guastello & Mark L. Rieke, *A Review of a Critique of Honesty Test Research*, 9 Behav. Sci. & Law 501 (1991). *Cf.* Scott L. Martin, *Honesty Testing: Estimating and Reducing the False Positive Rate*, 3 J. Bus. & Psychol. 255 (1989).

### Notes and Questions

1. Paper and pencil honesty tests are not covered by the federal law governing polygraphs. 29 C.F.R. § 801.2(d)(2) (1993). Should they be prohibited as a screening device? Rhode Island seems to include all "written tests" in its proscription of lie detectors. R.I. Gen. Laws § 28–6.1 (1993). Massachusetts forbids such tests to be used as the "primary basis" for an employment decision. Mass. Gen. Laws ch. 149 § 19(B)(1) (1999). *See* Matthew W. Finkin, *From Anonymity to Transparence: Screening the Workforce in the Information Age*, 2000 Colum. Bus. L. Rev. 403; David C. Yamada, *The Regulation of Pre-Employment Honesty Testing: Striking a Temporary (?) Balance Between Self-Regulation and Prohibition*, 39 Wayne L. Rev. 1549 (1993); George A. Hanson, *To Catch a Thief: The Legal and Policy Implications of Honesty Testing in the Workplace*, 9 Law & Ineq. 497 (1991).

# CHAPTER III

## ESTABLISHING TERMS AND CONDITIONS OF EMPLOYMENT

■ ■ ■

### A.  INTRODUCTION

The formation of the employment relationship can be remarkably informal and malleable under American law. William Corbett has noted the basic legal framework:

> There is little law in the United States requiring specific steps in the formation of employment contracts. The employment relationship begins as it ends with few legal requirements and little formality, putting aside the Statute of Frauds. Accordingly, for most jobs there is very little negotiation over terms, and often terms are not reduced to writing. Additionally, the terms of employment change over the life of an employment relationship. Given the lack of bargaining for employment terms at the commencement of the employment relationship and the changes that occur over time, the traditional bargained-for exchange model of contract law may be inadequate to describe many employment contracts. As many have suggested, relational contract theory may provide a more relevant description of employment contracts.

William Corbett, *Working Group on Chapter 2 of the Proposed Restatement of Employment Law: Employment Contracts: Termination (Critique of § 2.02)*, 13 EMP. RTS. & EMP. POL'Y J. 93, 113 (2009) (references omitted).

As a result, the employment relationship and its supporting agreement can take a variety of forms. It might be short-term and very simple, for example when a landscaper picks up a day laborer in the parking lot of a home improvement store with a promise of "$100 for the day." Economists refer to such labor markets as a "spot market" for labor because laborers and employers come to one "spot" to trade labor for wages at the going rate akin to a commodity exchange. The employment relationship might be long-term and very complex, for example when an employee works for the same employer for 40 years and accrues vacation time, sick leave, life and disability insurance, and medical insurance, in addition to earning a salary with periodic raises. Economists refer to such employment as long-term employment subject to the "internal labor market" of administrative rules designed by the employer for the operation of the firm. *See generally* DAVID MARSDEN, A THEORY OF EMPLOYMENT SYSTEMS (1999). The employment relationship might be based purely on a brief verbal offer specifying little more than the wage, for example in the case of the day laborer, or it might be based on a detailed written contract, signed by both parties and purporting to encompass the "full extent" of the agreement between the parties, for example when a university hires a basketball coach. It might be that the terms are unilaterally set by the employer, as in the day laborer's case, or determined through bilateral negotiations as is typically the case with university basketball coaches. All of these situations are treated under the same general principles of contract law.

Usually the employment relationship and the supporting agreement fall somewhere between the extremes described in the previous paragraph. Usually the parties envision a relationship of significant, but indefinite, duration, and provide some important terms, but less than full specificity. How should the courts interpret an employment agreement when there is no express term to cover the dispute? The terms of employment may change over time and be represented in conversations and documents produced by various agents of the employer including: the application for employment; a conversation or phone call announcing the offer; a letter confirming the offer; announcements or documents describing company policies; conversations to retain the employee after s/he receives another offer of employment; and a company handbook. Which representations should bind the employer and employee? What if a representative of the employer sets out a benefit of employment as an inducement to recruit or retain the employee, but expressly disclaims being bound? Usually the terms are unilaterally offered by the employer, subject only to the employee finding a different job, without any real negotiation between the employer and the employees. Should there be limits on the terms an employer can unilaterally impose? Should there be any limits imposed on what the parties can agree to even in bilateral negotiations?

In considering these larger questions, recall the philosophical and economic limitations on the concept of freedom of contract discussed in Chapter 1. As previously observed, employers often have more bargaining power than employees in their relationship—sometimes oppressively so. The exercise of monopsony power by employers is neither equitable nor efficient. Should the courts give the same deference to contractual terms imposed on employees that courts give to terms arrived at through bargained exchange? For example, should an employer be able to impose a noncompete covenant on an employee late in the employee's career and then discharge that employee in favor of less expensive new hires? Moreover, market imperfections such as transaction costs, imperfect information, and the public good nature of many terms of employment can undermine employees' ability to adequately address their concerns through individual bargaining. For example, as we saw in the last Chapter, the level of privacy in the workplace is a public good about which individual employees have inadequate incentive to hold out for terms that would benefit all employees. This problem is exacerbated by an asymmetric information problem in that even good employees who value privacy will not insist on it because they fear signaling to their employer that they are up to no good. Should courts enforce any restrictions on privacy an employer should care to impose regardless of its necessity to the job?

## B.  EMPLOYER POLICY MANUALS AND EMPLOYEE HANDBOOKS

As we saw in Chapter I, the common law rule in the nineteenth century was that an employer had the power to issue work rules which, if lawful and reasonable, had to be obeyed by those subject to them. At the time the employer's work rules, if not brutish, were short; as much information as the employee needed to know was ordinarily conveyed by the foreman. *See, e.g.,* ANTHONY WALLACE, ROCKDALE 179 (1978). As late as 1935, only 13% of industrial firms had adopted employee rulebooks. But the bureaucratization of work, discussed in Chapter I, enmeshes the worker in a "web of rules." By 1948, 30% of industrial firms had adopted employee handbooks. A 1979 survey of 6,000 companies revealed that employee handbooks were distributed by approximately 75% of the companies responding.

### WOOLLEY v. HOFFMANN–LA ROCHE, INC.

Supreme Court of New Jersey, 1985
99 N.J. 284, 491 A.2d 1257, modified 101 N.J. 10, 499 A.2d 515 (1985)

WILENTZ, C.J.

### I

The issue before us is whether certain terms in a company's employment manual may contractually bind the company. We hold that absent a clear and prominent disclaimer, an implied promise contained in an employment manual that an employee will be fired only for cause may be enforceable against an employer even when the employment is for an indefinite term and would otherwise be terminable at will.

### II

Plaintiff, Richard Woolley, was hired by defendant, Hoffmann–La Roche, Inc., in October 1969, as an Engineering Section Head in defendant's Central Engineering Department at Nutley. There was no written employment contract between plaintiff and defendant. Plaintiff began work in mid-November 1969. Some time in December, plaintiff received and read the personnel manual on which his claims are based.

In 1976, plaintiff was promoted, and in January 1977 he was promoted again, this latter time to Group Leader for the Civil Engineering, the

Piping Design, the Plant Layout, and the Standards and Systems Sections. In March 1978, plaintiff was directed to write a report to his supervisors about piping problems in one of defendant's buildings in Nutley. This report was written and submitted to plaintiff's immediate supervisor on April 5, 1978. On May 3, 1978, stating that the General Manager of defendant's Corporate Engineering Department had lost confidence in him, plaintiff's supervisors requested his resignation. Following this, by letter dated May 22, 1978, plaintiff was formally asked for his resignation, to be effective July 15, 1978.

Plaintiff refused to resign. Two weeks later defendant again requested plaintiff's resignation, and told him he would be fired if he did not resign. Plaintiff again declined, and he was fired in July.

Plaintiff filed a complaint alleging breach of contract, intentional infliction of emotional distress, and defamation, but subsequently consented to the dismissal of the latter two claims. The gist of plaintiff's breach of contract claim is that the express and implied promises in defendant's employment manual created a contract under which he could not be fired at will, but rather only for cause, and then only after the procedures outlined in the manual were followed.[1] Plaintiff contends that he was not dismissed for good cause, and that his firing was a breach of contract.

Defendant's motion for summary judgment was granted by the trial court, which held that the employment manual was not contractually binding on defendant, thus allowing defendant to terminate plaintiff's employment at will.[2] The Appellate Division affirmed. We granted certification. 91 N.J. 548, 453 A.2d 865 (1982).

### III

Hoffmann–La Roche contends that [under the precedent of the *Savarese* case] the formation of the type of contract claimed by plaintiff to

---

**1.** According to the provisions of the manual, defendant could, and over the years apparently did, unilaterally change these provisions. Defendant concedes, for the purpose of these proceedings, that plaintiff's version of the provisions of the manual as of the date he was fired is accurate. At oral argument plaintiff's counsel claimed that defendant followed a fairly consistent pattern of firing only for cause and offered to prove that fact on remand.

**2.** The termination provisions of the employment manual are set forth in the Appendix to this opinion. It may be of some help to point out some of the manual's general provisions here. It is entitled "Hoffmann–La Roche, Inc. Personnel Policy Manual" and at the bottom of the face page is the notation "issued to: [and then in handwriting] Richard Woolley 12/1/69." The portions of the manual submitted to us consist of eight pages. It describes the employees "covered" by the manual ("all employees of Hoffmann–La Roche"), the manual's purpose ("a practical operating tool in the equitable and efficient administration of our employee relations program"); five of the eight pages are devoted to "termination." In addition to setting forth the purpose and policy of the termination section, it defines "the types of termination" as "layoff," "discharge due to performance," "discharge, disciplinary," "retirement" and "resignation." As one might expect, layoff is a termination caused by lack of work, retirement a termination caused by age, resignation a termination on the initiative of the employee, and discharge due to performance and discharge, disciplinary, are both terminations for cause. There is no category set forth for discharge without cause. The termination section includes "Guidelines for discharge due to performance," consisting of a fairly detailed procedure to be used before an employee may be fired for cause. Preceding these definitions of the five categories of termination is a section on "Policy," the first sentence of which provides: "It is the policy of Hoffmann–La Roche to retain to the extent consistent with company requirements, the services of all employees who perform their duties efficiently and effectively."

exist—Hoffmann–La Roche calls it a permanent employment contract for life—is subject to special contractual requirements: the intent of the parties to create such an undertaking must be clear and definite; in addition to an explicit provision setting forth its duration, the agreement must specifically cover the essential terms of employment—the duties, responsibilities, and compensation of the employee, and the proof of these terms must be clear and convincing; the undertaking must be supported by consideration in addition to the employee's continued work. Woolley claims that the requirements for the formation of such a contract have been met here and that they do not extend as far as Hoffmann–La Roche claims. Further, Woolley argues that this is not a "permanent contract for life," but rather an employment contract of indefinite duration that may be terminated only for good cause and in accordance with the procedure set forth in the personnel policy manual. Both parties agree that the employment contract is one of indefinite duration; Hoffmann–La Roche contends that in New Jersey, when an employment contract is of indefinite duration, the inescapable legal conclusion is that it is an employment at will; Woolley claims that even such a contract—of indefinite duration—may contain provisions requiring that termination be only for cause. * * *

We are thus faced with the question of whether this is the kind of employment contract—a "long-range commitment"—that must be construed as one of indefinite duration and therefore at will unless the stringent requirements of Savarese are met, or whether ordinary contractual doctrine applies. In either case, the question is whether Hoffmann–La Roche retained the right to fire with or without cause or whether, as Woolley claims, his employment could be terminated only for cause. We believe another question, not explicitly treated below, is involved: should the legal effect of the dissemination of a personnel policy manual by a company with a substantial number of employees be determined solely and strictly by traditional contract doctrine? Is that analysis adequate for the realities of such a workplace?

### IV

* * * This Court has clearly announced its unwillingness to continue to adhere to rules regularly leading to the conclusion that an employer can fire an employee-at-will, with or without cause, for any reason whatsoever. Our holding in *Pierce v. Ortho Pharmaceutical Corp.*, 84 N.J. 58, 72, 417 A.2d 505 (1980), while necessarily limited to the specific issue of that case (whether employer can fire employee-at-will when discharge is contrary to a clear mandate of public policy), implied a significant questioning of that rule in general.

> Commentators have questioned the compatibility of the traditional at will doctrine with the realities of modern economics and employment practices. * * * The common law rule has been modified by the enactment of labor relations legislation. * * * The National Labor Relations Act and other labor legislation illustrate the governmental policy of preventing employers from using the right of discharge as a

means of oppression. * * * Consistent with this policy, many states have recognized the need to protect employees who are not parties to a collective bargaining agreement or other contract from abusive practices by the employer. * * *

This Court has long recognized the capacity of the common law to develop and adapt to current needs. * * * The interests of employees, employers, and the public lead to the conclusion that the common law of New Jersey should limit the right of an employer to fire an employee at will. * * *

In recognizing a cause of action to provide a remedy for employees who are wrongfully discharged, we must balance the interests of the employee, the employer, and the public. Employees have an interest in knowing they will not be discharged for exercising their legal rights. Employers have an interest in knowing that they can run their businesses as they see fit as long as their conduct is consistent with public policy. The public has an interest in employment stability and in discouraging frivolous lawsuits by dissatisfied employees. [*Id.* at 66–67, 71, 417 A.2d 505 (citations omitted).]

The spirit of this language foreshadows a different approach to these questions. No longer is there the unquestioned deference to the interests of the employer and the almost invariable dismissal of the contentions of the employee. Instead, as Justice Pollock so effectively demonstrated, this Court was no longer willing to decide these questions without examining the underlying interests involved, both the employer's and the employees', as well as the public interest, and the extent to which our deference to one or the other served or disserved the needs of society as presently understood.

In the last century, the common law developed in a laissez-faire climate that encouraged industrial growth and approved the right of an employer to control his own business, including the right to fire without cause an employee at will. * * * The twentieth century has witnessed significant changes in socioeconomic values that have led to reassessment of the common law rule. Businesses have evolved from small and medium size firms to gigantic corporations in which ownership is separate from management. Formerly there was a clear delineation between employers, who frequently were owners of their own businesses, and employees. The employer in the old sense has been replaced by a superior in the corporate hierarchy who is himself an employee. We are a nation of employees. Growth in the number of employees has been accompanied by increasing recognition of the need for stability in labor relations. [*Id.* at 66, 417 A.2d 505 (citations omitted)].

The thrust of the thought is unmistakable. There is an interest to be served in addition to "freedom" of contract, an interest shared by practically all. And while "stability in labor relations" is the only specifically identified public policy objective, the reference to the "laissez-faire climate" and "the right to fire without cause an employee at will" as part of the "last century" suggests that any application of the employee-at-will rule (not just its application in conflict with "a clear mandate of public policy"—the precise issue in *Pierce*) must be tested by its legitimacy today and not by its acceptance yesterday. *See also Nicoletta v. North Jersey Dist. Water Supply Comm'n,* 77 *N.J.* 145, 390 *A.*2d 90 (1978) (at-will employee in public sector entitled, as a matter of constitutional right, to hearing prior to discharge).

Given this approach signaled by *Pierce, supra,* 84 *N.J.* 58, 417 *A.*2d 505, the issue is not whether the rules applicable to individual lifetime or indefinite long-term employment contracts should be changed, but rather whether a correct understanding of the "underlying interests involved," *supra* at 1261, in the relationship between the employer and its workforce calls for compliance by the employer with certain rudimentary agreements voluntarily extended to the employees.

## V

\* \* \* We acknowledge that most of the out-of-state cases demonstrate an unwillingness to give contractual force to company policy manuals that purport to enhance job security. \* \* \* These cases, holding that policy manual provisions do not give rise to any contractual obligation, have to some extent confused policy manuals with individual long-term employment contracts and have applied to the manuals rules appropriate only to the individual employment contract. When there was such an individual contract before them (often consisting of oral assurances or a skeletal written agreement) not specifying a duration or term, courts understandably ruled them to be "at-will" contracts. They did so since they feared that by interpreting a contract of indefinite duration to be terminable only for cause, the courts would be saddling an employer with an employee for many years. In order to insure that the employer intended to accept the burdens of such an unusual "lifetime employment," the courts understandably insisted that the contract and the surrounding circumstances demonstrate unmistakably clear signs of the employer's intent to be bound, leading to the requirements of additional independent consideration and convincing specificity.

Referring to these requirements, the Michigan Supreme Court noted:

> To the extent that courts have seen this rule as one of substantive law rather than construction, they have misapplied language and principles found in earlier cases where the courts were merely attempting to discover and implement the intent of the parties. [*Toussaint v. Blue Cross & Blue Shield of Mich.,* 408 *Mich.* 579, 600, 292 *N.W.*2d 880, 885 (1980).]

*See also Pine River State Bank v. Mettille,* 333 *N.W.*2d 622, 628 (Minn. 1983) (employee wrongfully terminated under provisions of employee handbook that was contractually binding on the employer).

Whatever their worth in dealing with individual long-term employment contracts, these requirements, over and above those ordinarily found in contract law, have no relevancy when a policy manual is involved. In that case, there is no individual lifetime employment contract involved, but rather, if there is a contract, it is one for a group of employees— sometimes all of them—for an indefinite term, and here, fairly read, one that may not be terminated by the employer without good cause.

More recently there have been some voices that sound this different note on the subject. See *Wagner v. Sperry Univac, Div. of Sperry Rand Corp.,* 458 F.Supp. 505 (E.D.Pa.1978), *aff'd,* 624 F.2d 1092 (3d Cir.1980); * * * *see also Salimi v. Farmers Insurance Group,* 684 P.2d 264 (Colo. App.1984) (employee's allegation that his demotion was a breach of contract based on procedures in the employment manual survives a motion to dismiss); *Kaiser v. Dixon,* 127 Ill.App.3d 251, 82 Ill.Dec. 275, 468 *N.E.*2d 822 (1984) (public employee entitled to notice and hearing before discharge as provided for in staff policy manual adopted by the village).[5] While the dividing line between these two groups of out-of-state cases may be explained by the different analyses of whether the requirements imposed by the law of contracts have been met, the results can also be explained by a difference in attitude, some courts continuing to be concerned with the adverse impact on employers of long-term employment contracts, while others are concerned with the adverse impact on employees when apparent commitments expressed in policy manuals are not honored.

*Ct sees changing attitude*

What is before us in this case is not a special contract with a particular employee, but a general agreement covering all employees. There is no reason to treat such a document with hostility.

The trial court viewed the manual as an attempt by Hoffmann–La Roche to avoid a collective bargaining agreement.[6] Implicit is the thought that while the employer viewed a collective bargaining agreement as an intrusion on management prerogatives, it recognized, in addition to the advantages of an employment manual to both sides, that unless this kind of company manual were given to the workforce, collective bargaining, and the agreements that result from collective bargaining, would more likely take place.

A policy manual that provides for job security grants an important, fundamental protection for workers. *See* F. Tanenbaum, *A Philosophy of Labor* 9 (1951), *quoted in* L. Blades, "Employment At Will *vs.* Individual Freedom: on Limiting the Abusive Exercise of Employer Power," 67

---

**5.** A recent article asserts that at least eighteen states have specifically held or pointed out in opinions that they recognize, to various extents, implied-in-fact contracts arising from employee manuals, other personnel policies, and/or oral or written representations regarding job security. F. Lopatka, "The Emerging Law of Wrongful Discharge—A Quadrennial Assessment of the Labor Law Issue of the 80's," 40 Bus.Law. 1, 17 (1984).

**6.** The trial court, after noting that if Hoffmann–La Roche had been unionized, Woolley would not be litigating the question of whether the employer had to have good cause to fire him, said "[T]here is no question in my mind that Hoffmann–La Roche offered these good benefits to their employees to steer them away from this kind of specific collective bargaining contract. * * * "

Colum.L.Rev. 1404, 1404 (1967) [hereinafter cited as Blades]. If such a commitment is indeed made, obviously an employer should be required to honor it. When such a document, purporting to give job security, is distributed by the employer to a workforce, substantial injustice may result if that promise is broken. * * *

VI

Given the facts before us and the common law of contracts interpreted in the light of sound policy applicable to this modern setting, we conclude that the termination clauses of this company's Personnel Policy Manual, including the procedure required before termination occurs, could be found to be contractually enforceable. Furthermore, we conclude that when an employer of a substantial number of employees circulates a manual that, when fairly read, provides that certain benefits are an incident of the employment (including, especially, job security provisions), the judiciary, instead of "grudgingly" conceding the enforceability of those provisions, *Savarese, supra,* 9 *N.J.* at 601, 89 *A.*2d 237, should construe them in accordance with the reasonable expectations of the employees.

The employer's contention here is that the distribution of the manual was simply an expression of the company's "philosophy" and therefore free of any possible contractual consequences. The former employee claims it could reasonably be read as an explicit statement of company policies intended to be followed by the company in the same manner as if they were expressed in an agreement signed by both employer and employees. From the analysis that follows we conclude that a jury, properly instructed, could find, in strict contract terms, that the manual constituted an offer; put differently, it could find that this portion of the manual (concerning job security) set forth terms and conditions of employment.

In determining the manual's meaning and effect, we must consider the probable context in which it was disseminated and the environment surrounding its continued existence. The manual, though apparently not distributed to all employees ("in general, distribution will be provided to supervisory personnel * * * "), covers all of them. Its terms are of such importance to all employees that in the absence of contradicting evidence, it would seem clear that it was intended by Hoffmann–La Roche that all employees be advised of the benefits it confers.

We take judicial notice of the fact that Hoffmann–La Roche is a substantial company with many employees in New Jersey. The record permits the conclusion that the policy manual represents the most reliable statement of the terms of their employment. At oral argument counsel conceded that it is rare for any employee, except one on the medical staff, to have a special contract. Without minimizing the importance of its specific provisions, the context of the manual's preparation and distribution is, to us, the most persuasive proof that it would be almost inevitable for an employee to regard it as a binding commitment, legally enforceable, concerning the terms and conditions of his employment. Having been employed, like hundreds of his co-employees, without any individual employment contract, by an employer whose good reputation made it so attractive, the employee is given this one document that purports to set forth the terms and conditions of his employment, a document obviously carefully prepared by the company with all of the appearances of corporate legitimacy that one could imagine. If there were any doubt about it (and there would be none in the mind of most employees), the name of the manual dispels it, for it is nothing short of the official *policy* of the company, it is the Personnel *Policy* Manual. As every employee knows, when superiors tell you "it's company policy," they mean business.

The mere fact of the manual's distribution suggests its importance. Its changeability—the uncontroverted ability of management to change its terms—is argued as supporting its non-binding quality, but one might as easily conclude that, given its importance, the employer wanted to keep it up to date, especially to make certain, given this employer's good reputation in labor relations, that the benefits conferred were sufficiently competitive with those available from other employers, including benefits found in collective bargaining agreements. The record suggests that the changes actually made almost always favored the employees.

Given that background, then, unless the language contained in the manual were such that no one could reasonably have thought it was intended to create legally binding obligations, the termination provisions of the policy manual would have to be regarded as an obligation undertaken by the employer. It will not do now for the company to say it did not mean the things it said in its manual to be binding. Our courts will not allow an employer to offer attractive inducements and benefits to the workforce and then withdraw them when it chooses, no matter how sincere its belief that they are not enforceable.

Whatever else the manual may deal with * * * one of its major provisions deals with the single most important objective of the workforce: job security. The reasons for giving such provisions binding force are particularly persuasive. Wages, promotions, conditions of work, hours of work, all of those take second place to job security, for without that all other benefits are vulnerable.

> We are dependent upon others for our means of livelihood, and most of our people have become completely dependent upon wages. If they lose their jobs they lose every resource, except for the relief supplied by the various forms of social security. Such dependence of the mass of the people upon others for *all* of their income is something new in the world. *For our generation, the substance of life is in another man's hands.* [F. Tanenbaum, A Philosophy of Labor, 9 (1951), *quoted in Blades, supra,* at 1404.]

*See Pugh v. See's,* 116 Cal. App. 3d 311, 320–21, 171 Cal. Rptr. 917, 921 (1981); *see also Blades, supra* at 1410 & n. 30 (right of discharge has been limited in collective bargaining agreements).

Job security is the assurance that one's livelihood, one's family's future, will not be destroyed arbitrarily; it can be cut off only "for good cause," fairly determined. Hoffmann–La Roche's commitment here was to what working men and women regard as their most basic advance. It was a commitment that gave workers protection against arbitrary termination.

Many of these workers undoubtedly know little about contracts, and many probably would be unable to analyze the language and terms of the manual. Whatever Hoffmann–La Roche may have intended, that which was read by its employees was a promise not to fire them except for cause.

Under all of these circumstances, therefore, it would be most unrealistic to construe this manual and determine its enforceability as if it were the same as a lifetime contract with but one employee designed to induce him to play on the company's baseball team. *See Savarese, supra,* 9 N.J. at 597, 89 A.2d 237.[8]

## VII

Having concluded that a jury could find the Personnel Policy Manual to constitute an offer, we deal with what most cases deem the major obstacle to construction of the terms as constituting a binding agreement, namely, the requirement under contract law that consideration must be given in exchange for the employer's offer in order to convert that offer into a binding agreement. The cases on this subject deal with such issues as whether there was a promise in return for the employer's promise (the offer contained in the manual constituting, in effect, a promise), or whether there was some benefit or detriment bargained for and in fact conferred or suffered, sufficient to create a unilateral contract; whether the action or inaction, the benefit or the detriment, was done or not done in reliance on the employer's offer or promise; whether the alleged agreement was so lacking in "mutuality" as to be insufficient for contractual purposes—in other words, whether the fundamental requirements of a contract have been met.

We conclude that these job security provisions contained in a personnel policy manual widely distributed among a large workforce are supported by consideration and may therefore be enforced as a binding commitment of the employer.

In order for an offer in the form of a promise to become enforceable, it must be accepted. Acceptance will depend on what the promisor bargained

---

**8.** The contract arising from the manual is of indefinite duration. It is *not* the extraordinary "lifetime" contract explicitly claimed in *Savarese*. For example, a contract arising from a manual ordinarily may be terminated when the employee's performance is inadequate; when business circumstances require a general reduction in the employment force, the positions eliminated including that of plaintiff; when those same circumstances require the elimination of employees performing a certain function, for instance, for technological reasons, and plaintiff performed such functions; when business conditions require a general reduction in salary, a reduction that brings plaintiff's pay below that which he is willing to accept; or when any change, including the cessation of business, requires the elimination of plaintiff's position, an elimination made in good faith in pursuit of legitimate business objectives: all of these terminations, long before the expiration of "lifetime" employment, are ordinarily contemplated in a contract arising from a manual, although the list does not purport to be exhaustive. The essential difference is that the "lifetime" contract purports to protect the employment against any termination; the contract arising from the manual protects the employment only from arbitrary termination.

for: he may have bargained for a return promise that, if given, would result in a bilateral contract, both promises becoming enforceable. Or he may have bargained for some action or nonaction that, if given or withheld, would render his promise enforceable as a unilateral contract. In most of the cases involving an employer's personnel policy manual, the document is prepared without any negotiations and is voluntarily distributed to the workforce by the employer. It seeks no return promise from the employees. It is reasonable to interpret it as seeking continued work from the employees, who, in most cases, are free to quit since they are almost always employees at will, not simply in the sense that the employer can fire them without cause, but in the sense that they can quit without breaching any obligation. Thus analyzed, the manual is an offer that seeks the formation of a unilateral contract—the employees' bargained-for action needed to make the offer binding being their continued work when they have no obligation to continue.

The unilateral contract analysis is perfectly adequate for that employee who was aware of the manual and who continued to work intending that continuation to be the action in exchange for the employer's promise; it is even more helpful in support of that conclusion if, but for the employer's policy manual, the employee would have quit. *See generally* M. Petit, "Modern Unilateral Contracts," 63 B.U.L.Rev. 551 (1983) (judicial use of unilateral contract analysis in employment cases is widespread).[9]

Those solutions seem to be technically correct. Among the cases holding that the document in question satisfied technical contractual requirements are *Toussaint, supra,* 408 Mich. 579, 292 *N.W.*2d 880, and *Anthony, supra,* 51 N.J. Super. 139, 143 *A.*2d 762. In *Toussaint* one main issue was the contractual force of an oral assurance given to the employee when he was hired that he would not be discharged so long as he was "doing his job." In addition to that assurance, Toussaint was at the same time handed a manual, which provided that an employee would not be discharged without cause and without following certain procedures. The court noted in *dictum* that the oral assurance was not necessary to its

---

**9.**    Third-party-beneficiary doctrines might be used to confer the benefits on all workers; or the employer's offer could be construed as inviting acceptance in the form of continuance of work by merely one worker in order to benefit all.

Similarly, the doctrine of promissory estoppel could be relied on as a rationale for enforcement of an employer's promises in a policy manual or similar document under certain circumstances. Under the formulation set forth in the *Restatement (Second) of Contracts,* that doctrine renders binding a promise when the promisor should reasonably expect the promisee or a third party to act or forbear to act in reliance on the promise, if the promisee or third party does so and justice requires. *Id.* at § 590. However, we do not pass on the applicability of this theory here, as it was not raised by the parties and does not seem appropriate to the facts presented. See Note, 93 Harv.L.Rev. 1816, 1820 & nn. 21–22 (1980).

The doctrine of unconscionability of the Uniform Commercial Code, codified at N.J.S.A. 12A:2–302, is analogous to the employment-at-will rule. The unconscionability doctrine developed to protect the disadvantaged party in a one-sided bargain. *See generally* J. White and R. Summers, *Uniform Commercial Code* (2d ed. 1980) (courts refuse to enforce unconscionable contract clauses); S. Marrinan, "Employment At–Will: Pandora's Box May have an Attractive Cover," 7 Hamline L.Rev. 155, 193 (1984) (doctrine of unconscionability used to overcome unequal bargaining positions of contracting parties).

holding. * * * A footnote concluded that "[i]t was therefore unnecessary for Toussaint to prove reliance on the policies set forth in the manual."

Similarly, in *Anthony v. Jersey Cent. Power & Light Co., supra,* 51 N.J. Super. 139, 143 *A.*2d 762, practically every contractual objection that could be made here was disposed of by the Appellate Division in the context of a claim for pension rights by supervisory personnel based on a company manual (entitled "General Rules"). There, the defendant-employer argued that its severance-pay rule was a mere gratuitous promise, not supported by consideration. The court responded, analyzing the promise as an offer of a unilateral contract and the employees' continued services as sufficient acceptance and consideration therefor. *Id.* at 143, 143 *A.*2d 762. To the defendant's argument that there was no evidence of reliance upon its promise, the *Anthony* court responded that reliance was to be presumed under the circumstances. *Id.* at 145–46, 143 *A.*2d 762. We agree.[10]

## VIII

The lack of definiteness concerning the other terms of employment— its duration, wages, precise service to be rendered, hours of work, etc., does not prevent enforcement of a job security provision.[12] The lack of terms (if the complete manual is similarly lacking) can cause problems of interpretation about these other aspects of employment, but not to the point of making the job security term unenforceable. Realistically, the objection has force only when the agreement is regarded as a special one between the employer and an individual employee. There it might be difficult to determine whether there was good cause for termination if one could not determine what it was that the employee was expected to do.

---

**10.** If reliance is not presumed, a strict contractual analysis might protect the rights of some employees and not others. For example, where an employee is not even aware of the existence of the manual, his or her continued work would not ordinarily be thought of as the bargained-for detriment. *See* S. Williston, *Contracts* §§ 101, 102A (1957). *But see* A. Corbin, *Contracts* § 59 (1963) (suggesting that knowledge of an offer is not a prerequisite to acceptance). Similarly, if it is quite clear that those employees who knew of the offer knew that it sought their continued work, but nevertheless continued without the slightest intention of putting forth that action as consideration for the employer's promise, it might not be sufficient to form a contract. *See* S. Williston, *Contracts* § 67 (1957). *But see Pine River, supra,* 333 *N.W.*2d at 627, 630. In this case there is no proof that plaintiff, Woolley, relied on the policy manual in continuing his work. Furthermore, as the Appellate Division correctly noted, Woolley did "not bargain for" the employer's promise. The implication of the presumption of reliance is that the manual's job security provisions became binding the moment the manual was distributed. Anyone employed before or after became one of the beneficiaries of those provisions of the manual. And if *Toussaint* is followed, employees neither had to read it, know of its existence, or rely on it to benefit from its provisions any more than employees in a plant that is unionized have to read or rely on a collective-bargaining agreement in order to obtain its benefits.

**12.** We do not agree with the distinction made by the courts below between a severance pay provision and the job security terms involved here, the former asserted to be specific, the latter too indefinite. The Appellate Division, referring to *Anthony,* noting that it involved a severance pay provision, characterized that as "a specific term of a contract [whose] parameters are clearly set forth [where the] conditions and factors involved are definite and easily ascertained." By contrast it referred to the "objections to a lifetime employment contract that make it contrary to public policy, *i.e.,* lack of definiteness, unequal burden of performance, etc.," * * * As implied above, we find that enforcing the provision that prohibits termination except for good cause is not so difficult as to warrant its invalidation on grounds of indefiniteness.

That difficulty is one factor that suggests the employer did not intend a lifetime contract with one employee. Here the question of good cause is made considerably easier to deal with in view of the fact that the agreement applies to the entire workforce, and the workforce itself is rather large. Even-handedness and equality of treatment will make the issue in most cases far from complex; the fact that in some cases the "for cause" provision may be difficult to interpret and enforce should not deprive employees in other cases from taking advantage of it. If there is a problem arising from indefiniteness, in any event, it is one caused by the employer. It was the employer who chose to make the termination provisions explicit and clear. If indefiniteness as to other provisions is a problem, it is one of the employer's own making from which it should gain no advantage. *Cf. In re Miller*, 90 *N.J.* 210, 221, 447 A.2d 549 (1982) (ambiguity should be resolved against party drafting contract). * * *

## XI

Our opinion need not make employers reluctant to prepare and distribute company policy manuals. Such manuals can be very helpful tools in labor relations, helpful both to employer and employees, and we would regret it if the consequence of this decision were that the constructive aspects of these manuals were in any way diminished. We do not believe that they will, or at least we certainly do not believe that that constructive aspect *should* be diminished as a result of this opinion.

All that this opinion requires of an employer is that it be fair. It would be unfair to allow an employer to distribute a policy manual that makes the workforce believe that certain promises have been made and then to allow the employer to renege on those promises. What is sought here is basic honesty: if the employer, for whatever reason, does not want the manual to be capable of being construed by the court as a binding contract, there are simple ways to attain that goal. All that need be done is the inclusion in a very prominent position of an appropriate statement that there is no promise of any kind by the employer contained in the manual; that regardless of what the manual says or provides, the employer promises nothing and remains free to change wages and all other working conditions without having to consult anyone and without anyone's agreement; and that the employer continues to have the absolute power to fire anyone with or without good cause.

Reversed and remanded for trial.

### NOTES AND QUESTIONS

1.  The majority view is that company policies circulated to the workforce in employee handbooks, company policy manuals and the like, if sufficiently definite, are binding on the employer. However, the doctrinal grounding for that result varies by jurisdiction. Some adhere strictly to traditional contact theory requiring offer, acceptance, and consideration—in this case the doing of the act rather than the giving of a promise—each of which must be

proved as to the particular employee should he or she make a claim grounded in the employer's policy. This is the approach taken by the Supreme Court of Illinois in *Duldulao v. Saint Mary of Nazareth Hosp. Ctr.*, 115 Ill.2d 482, 106 Ill.Dec. 8, 12, 505 N.E.2d 314, 318 (1987):

> [W]e hold that an employee handbook or other policy statement creates enforceable contractual rights if the traditional requirements for contract formation are present. First, the language of the policy statement must contain a promise clear enough that an employee would reasonably believe that an offer has been made. Second, the statement must be disseminated to the employee in such a manner that the employee is aware of its contents and reasonably believes it to be an offer. Third, the employee must accept the offer by commencing or continuing to work after learning of the policy statement. When these conditions are present, then the employee's continued work constitutes consideration for the promises contained in the statement, and under traditional principles a valid contract is formed.

*See also Phipps v. IASD Health Servs. Corp.*, 558 N.W.2d 198, 203 (Iowa 1997).

Note that it is conceivable, under this strict application of unilateral contract doctrine, that one co-worker could bind the employer to its policy while another could not if, at trial, it is found that the first had studied the policy and the second hadn't read it at all.

Michigan has rejected unilateral contract in favor of a theory that looks to the benefit the employer gets by its giving an assurance of job security or of the observance of progressive discipline:

> [A]n employer who chooses to establish desirable personnel policies, such as a discharge-for-cause employment policy, is not seeking to induce each individual employee to show up for work day after day, but rather is seeking to promote an environment conducive to collective productivity. *The benefit to the employer* of promoting such an environment, rather than the traditional contract-forming mechanisms of mutual assent or individual detrimental reliance, gives rise to a situation "instinct with an obligation."

*Bankey v. Storer Broad., Co.*, 432 Mich. 438, 443 N.W.2d 112, 119 (1989) (emphasis added).

Several jurisdictions have applied promissory estoppel, often along with but as an alternative ground to unilateral contract. *E.g., Taylor v. National Life Ins. Co.*, 161 Vt. 457, 652 A.2d 466, 475 (1993). Professor Stephen Befort has observed:

> The promissory estoppel analysis offers two advantages in the handbook arena. First, promissory estoppel appropriately focuses on the legitimacy of employee expectations rather than on the somewhat fictionalized search for the contract law technicalities of acceptance and consideration. Second, promissory estoppel theory goes beyond the promise principle to consider explicitly the underlying equities or "injustice" of enforcement or nonenforcement. While the equity factor may well drive many of the handbook cases under either theory, promissory estoppel analysis does so

openly and directly instead of covertly through a manipulation of other factors.

Stephen Befort, *Employee Handbook and the Legal Effect of Disclaimers*, 13 INDUS. REL. L.J. 326, 344 (1992) (citations omitted). But, as he has noted, that theory also has a drawback:

> [T]raditional promissory estoppel theory requires a showing of individualized reliance, and some courts have refused to enforce handbook promises where the employee in question has failed to prove detrimental reliance on specific handbook terms. This requirement imposes difficult proof problems and could result in inconsistent levels of job security among employees covered by the same policy language. [The same being so of strict unilateral contract theory, as we have seen.—Eds.] This drawback could be minimized by adopting the approach of those courts that dispense with the requirement of individual reliance in favor of a rule requiring only a showing of objectively established group reliance.

Stephen Befort, *Working Group on Chapter 2 of the Proposed Restatement of Employment Law: Employment Contracts: Termination (Critique of Section 2.04 and 2.05)*, 13 EMP. RTS. & EMP. POL'Y J. 93, 122–23 (2009) (citations omitted). In connection with the latter, Professor Befort adverts to the Michigan Supreme Court's decision in *Bankey*; but note that whereas *Bankey* focused on the benefit to the employer, *Woolley* focused on the "reasonable expectations of the employees." As we will see, this may make a profound difference.

There is yet another view which the *Woolley* opinion can be read to embrace. As noted earlier, as employers came to employ and so to manage ever larger numbers of employees in the nineteenth century they began to post (or distribute) rules uniformly to govern the workplace: *e.g.*, rules requiring notice of quitting (on pain of loss of accrued wages), forbidding smoking or the possession of alcohol on the premises, or governing the safe completion of work tasks. The courts treated these as implied contracts—implied in fact or by law—the question being whether the party "affected," usually the employee, had had such notice of the rule as to give rise to an inference of assent. H.G. WOOD, A TREATISE ON THE LAW OF MASTER AND SERVANT § 94 (2d ed. 1886). In the context of work rules, the non-observance of which would justify a finding of contributory negligence on the employee's part, a treatise of the period put the general rule thusly: " '[W]here rules are prescribed or regulations adopted for the government of employees in and about the discharge of their duties, it is the duty of the employer to give notice of their existence, and so to promulgate them as to afford to the employee a reasonable opportunity of ascertaining their terms'." 3 C.B. LABATT, COMMENTARIES ON THE LAW OF MASTER AND SERVANT § 1133 at p. 2993 (2d ed. 1913) (citation omitted). As in *Woolley*, the general promulgation of a rule governing the workplace would be given contractual effect as an implied in fact contract if it had been distributed widely enough or had been made known generally to the workforce even if the particular employee disclaimed knowledge.

Note also that the *Woolley* court draws an analogy between the employee handbook and a collective bargaining agreement. The fit is close, for reasons explained by David E. Feller. *A General Theory of the Collective Bargaining Agreement*, 61 CAL. L. REV. 663, 723–24 (1973) (references omitted):

> [I]n every organization, except the simplest in which ownership and management are coterminous, there must be a set of rules and limits controlling the actions of subordinate members of management in dealing with the work force. And as industrialization advances and business organizations grow in complexity, these rules tend to become more detailed and explicit.
>
> It is for these reasons that those studying non-union enterprises frequently find formalized personnel policies setting forth rules covering much of the substance usually contained in a collective bargaining agreement. Thus, studies of personnel practices in nonunion firms have found that an overwhelming majority specify such things as the application of seniority in layoffs, recalls from layoffs, and even promotions. Typically, formal rules govern the discipline or discharge of employees and rates of pay are determined by elaborate systems of job description and evaluation. . . .
>
> Collective bargaining is not, then, the occasion for introducing rules into the employment relationship. It is, rather, a method by which the employees participate in what would otherwise be a system of unilateral management rulemaking and administration.

Note accordingly that the terms of a collective agreement protect an individual employee even if he or she is totally unaware of its protection. *NLRB v. City Disposal Sys., Inc.*, 465 U.S. 822, 104 S.Ct. 1505, 79 L.Ed.2d 839 (1984).

And there is yet another theory, adopted in the *Restatement (Third) of Employment Law*, of "administrative estoppel." This is a doctrine of federal administrative law that holds that an administrative agency is bound by the *procedural* rules it adopts—in the leading case, rules on how to deal with accusations that an employee is a risk to national security—but only for so long as the rules are in effect. *E.g.*, *Vitarelli v. Seaton*, 359 U.S. 535, 79 S.Ct. 968, 3 L.Ed.2d 1012 (1959). *See* BERNARD SCHWARTZ, ADMINISTRATIVE LAW § 49 (3d ed. 1991). The *Restatement*'s adoption of that theory has been criticized by Stephen Befort on two grounds:

> First, no jurisdiction has adopted administrative agency estoppel as the underlying rationale for enforcing employer policy statements. As such, the draft *Restatement* here again proposes to change rather than to restate or clarify existing law.
>
> Second, it is not clear the rules governing administrative agency procedure are comparable in nature to the rules governing the substance of the employment relationship. While a procedural rule in an agency intends to determine substantive rights going into the future, a promissory statement made in the context of an ongoing employment relationship itself directly establishes the substantive rules governing that relationship. In some employment contexts, such as in the realm of procedural due process rights afforded by the Constitution to public employees, an employer's unilaterally promulgated rules and even practices have been found to be binding and not subject to unilateral alteration.

(criticism)

Stephen Befort, *Working Group on Chapter 2 of the Proposed Restatement of Employment Law: Employment Contracts: Termination (Critique of § 2.05)*, 13 EMP. RTS. & EMP. POL'Y J. 93, 132 (2009).

In other words, to deal with employer policies in the private sector the *Restatement* adopts a public sector administrative law theory that no court has applied to private employment and then misapplies it: a public employer's adoption of a rule conferring a *substantive* right on employees, including a right not to be dismissed without just cause, cannot be abrogated unilaterally. *See, e.g., Saxe v. Board of Trs.*, 179 P.3d 67 (Colo. App. 2007). Why the *Restatement* has taken this odd turn will be taken up under the discussion of the modification of terms of employment, *infra*.

Finally, some courts have declined to bind employers by their adopted policies at all on the ground, variously, that the transaction lacks "mutuality," that there is no consideration, or that as the policy may be revocable by the employer at any time it is an illusory promise.

2. Should employees be bound by their policies governing wrongful dismissal? If so, by what theory? Unilateral contract? Promissory estoppel? Estoppel by the benefit to the employer? Implied in fact contract? Or administrative estoppel?

3. As the *Woolley* court notes, the trial court had viewed the issuance of the job security rules as an "attempt by Hoffmann–La Roche to avoid a collective bargaining agreement," *i.e.*, to persuade its employees that they had no need for a union to secure the protection of just cause to discharge—a public good—because the company will have given that protection. The role of these rules as a means of union avoidance has been more pronounced in other cases. The Washington Court of Appeals considered a handbook that provided for progressive discipline and assured employees that a union was unnecessary because the company's rules provided all the benefits of a union. Noting the decision of the state's Supreme Court in *Swanson v. Liquid Air Corp.*, 118 Wash.2d 512, 826 P.2d 664 (1992), the Court of Appeals opined that

> In *Swanson*, the defendant "almost certainly offered [the handbook] in consideration for the employees' promise not to unionize and the employees almost certainly accepted it in consideration for the foregoing of their legal right to unionize." *Id*. Here, the handbook also exhorted employees not to unionize. . . . The employees did not unionize.

*Rowe v. Vaagen Bros. Lumber, Inc.*, 100 Wash.App. 268, 996 P.2d 1103, 1108 (2000). From this the court observed that, "A handbook can be offered and accepted as consideration for employees foregoing their legal right to unionize." *Id*.

It is perfectly lawful for an employer to exhort its employees not to unionize. It is also perfectly lawful for an employer to improve wages, benefits, and working conditions in an effort to persuade its employees that they have no need for a union—so long as these improvements are not timed to blunt a current organizing campaign. But it is perfectly *un*lawful for an employer to offer improved terms of employment "in consideration for the employees' promise not to unionize." In labor parlance, such an agreement is called a "yellow dog" contract and it is rendered unenforceable against the employee by the Norris–LaGuardia Act of 1932, 29 U.S.C. §§ 102, 103. The offer itself is unlawful under the National Labor Relations Act of 1935. How do you explain that in the year 2000 such a quid pro quo could be taken by a court as lawful contractual consideration for the company handbook's terms?

4. Some courts take a restrictive view of how specific the rules governing discipline or discharge must be to render them contractually binding. Thus, a list of grounds for discipline that distinguishes between offenses subject to summary discharge and offenses subject to progressive discipline, but that says it is a "non-exclusive" list, has been held to lack adequate specificity. *E.g., Semple v. Federal Exp. Corp.*, 566 F.3d 788 (8th Cir. 2009). If the employee's conduct clearly falls within an item on the list calling for progressive discipline instead of discharge, shouldn't the employee be able to enforce that "promise" by the employer?

# A Note on Disclaimers
## ORTEGA v. WAKEFIELD THERMAL SOLUTIONS, INC.

Superior Court of Massachusetts, 2006
20 Mass L. Rptr. 337

THOMAS E. CONNELLY, JUSTICE.

This is a wrongful discharge action brought by the plaintiff, Jose Ortega ("Ortega"), against his employer, Wakefield Thermal Solutions, Inc. d/b/a Wakefield Engineering ("Wakefield"). This matter is now before the court on Wakefield's motion for summary judgment. For the reasons discussed below, that motion is *Denied.*

### Facts

The jury would be entitled to believe the following facts.

Ortega was an employee of Wakefield for 22 years, and worked himself up within the company to the level of supervisor. Ortega was being paid $16.50 per hour at the time he was fired. As requested by Wakefield, Ortega generally worked fifteen (15) to twenty (20) overtime hours a week. On May 8, 2001, Ortega was supplied with a copy of the Wakefield Engineering Employee Handbook ("the Handbook"), and he signed a written acknowledgment that he had received said Handbook.[1] Also included in the signed acknowledgment was the following statement:

> I further acknowledge that if I have difficulty reading or understanding any of the provisions of the manual, that I am to contact the Human Resources Department for assistance.

The Handbook contains many extensive and detailed policies and practices in effect at Wakefield. It also contained the statement that "[t]he policies

---

1. The acknowledgment signed by Ortega on May 8, 2001, states in part:

1. That Ortega received the manual.

2. That the Manual contains important information about the Company's general personnel policies and about his privileges and obligation as an employee.

3. That he was expected to read, understand and adhere to the employer's policies and to familiarize himself with the material in the Corporate Manual.

and procedures that are contained in this manual are not terms and conditions of your employment nor a contract, and the manual itself is not a contract or an offer to enter a contract." Further, the Handbook provides that no employee is hired for a specific term, upon any specific conditions or pursuant to any contract of employment, and that the Company has the corresponding right to terminate any employee at any time with or without notice or cause.

*[handwritten margin note: Disclaimers in handbook]*

Prior to the incident involved, Ortega never had any problems, employment or otherwise, with his employer. He was a hard worker who worked 55 to 60 hours per week for his employer, and basically did what was asked of him by his employer.

The incident that triggered his termination was a vacation by Ortega to the Dominican Republic to visit family. He submitted a vacation request for April 8, 2002 through April 22, 2002, and planned on returning to work on April 23, 2002. On Saturday, April 6, 2002 he flew to the Dominican Republic. Ortega had a plane ticket for a return flight on Monday, April 22, 2002, but was not allowed to board the plane. Evidently, Ortega arrived about thirty (30) minutes before the flight was scheduled to depart and American Airlines personnel informed him that they had already sold his seat, and that there were no further seats available on the flight. Ortega stated that he made inquiries of the American Airlines personnel, but was informed that there were no other flights that day and that the next available flight was Thursday, April 25, 2002. Ortega states that he telephoned his supervisor, Tony Escobar ("Escobar") and told him that he could not make it back to work because he missed his flight and that there were no seats to Boston available until Thursday. Escobar did not indicate that Ortega's absence would create any problem for the company and indicated that Wakefield would continue to use supervisors to fill in for him. On Thursday, April 25, 2002, Ortega flew out of the Dominican Republic and on Friday April 26, 2002 returned to work. He was three days late in returning to work.

*[handwritten margin note: 3 days late b/c he missed flight]*

After he had been working for approximately one hour, Escobar came over to Ortega and brought Ortega to the Human Resources Manager, Mary Michaud ("Michaud"). After getting the necessary permissions, Wakefield, by Michaud, fired Ortega on the spot. Michaud stated that she called a travel agent in New Hampshire and was informed that there were seats available on American Airlines flights prior to Thursday, April 25, 2005, from the Dominican Republic to Boston. It was stated that Ortega was not fired for being late to return to work, but was fired for being dishonest to his employer.[2]

*[handwritten margin note: Fired for being dishonest b/c they believe he lied about earlier flights]*

---

**2.** The Court notes that Ortega applied for unemployment benefits with the State of New Hampshire. Wakefield opposed and contested the unemployment claim contending that the plaintiff was discharged for misconduct in connection with his work. At the hearing before the New Hampshire Security Appeal Tribunal, Wakefield contended that "[Ortega] was discharged because he was a supervisor. He set a poor example for his subordinates by not returning from vacation timely and the employer was fearful that others would do the same." Notwithstanding its statement at the time Ortega was fired, nothing was represented to the Appeal Tribunal by Wakefield that Ortega was in any way dishonest. There was no conversation by Wakefield with

*Discussion*

In a motion for summary judgment, the moving party bears the burden of showing that there are no genuine issues of material fact and that the moving party is entitled to judgment as a matter of law. Mass.R.Civ.P. 56(c); *Pederson v. Time, Inc.*, 404 Mass. 14, 17, 532 N.E.2d 1211 (1989). The burden need not be met with affirmative evidence negating an essential element of the plaintiff's case, but it may be satisfied by demonstrating that proof of the element is unlikely to be forthcoming at trial. *Kourouvacilis v. General Motors Corp.*, 410 Mass. 706, 711–12, 575 N.E.2d 734 (1991). In ruling on the motion, the judge should consider the evidence "with an indulgence in the [opposing party's] favor." *Anthony's Pier Four, Inc. v. Crandall Dry Dock Engineers, Inc.*, 396 Mass. 818, 822, 489 N.E.2d 172 (1986). The judge should not weigh the credibility of any evidence. "A toehold ... is enough to survive a motion for summary judgment." *Marr Equipment Corp. v. I.T.O. Corp. of New England*, 14 Mass.App.Ct. 231, 235, 437 N.E.2d 1076 (1982).

In opposition to the motion for summary judgment, the plaintiff points to Handbook policy "S3" which concerns disciplinary action and indicates "generally" that "the employee will be given advance notice that there is a serious problem with his performance, which may necessitate termination of employment at a future date." The objective of this advance notice is to give the employee a reasonable opportunity to alter his conduct or performance so as to salvage his employment with the Company. Furthermore, there are "Progressive Discipline" procedures in which an employee is subject to a verbal warning, a written warning, a three-day suspension, and termination. See Handbook Sections 3.0 to 3.5 (Disciplinary Action Policy).

Here, Wakefield gave Ortega no warning. They simply fired him about one hour after he arrived at work on Friday, April 26, 2005. Wakefield did not give this employee of twenty-two (22) years any progressive discipline as described in the Handbook. He was allegedly fired, without a hearing, based on the representations of a travel agent in New Hampshire.

The Employee Handbook states in part that it is not to be considered a contract, expressed or implied, between Ortega and Wakefield. Wakefield conspicuously states throughout the manual that it is not a contract and Wakefield reserves the right to change or eliminate its policies and procedures as necessary and without having to consult with or obtain the agreement of the employee.

In Massachusetts, "employment at will is terminable by either the employee or the employer without notice, for almost any reason or for no

---

the claimant about the incident prior to his discharge. After a hearing, the Appeal Tribunal concluded that "after a review of all the records and all the testimony ... the claimant was discharged but not for misconduct connected with his work." In reaching this conclusion, the tribunal chairman found that there was no pattern of negligence or disregard for the employer's best interest. Further, given Ortega's length of employment and the employer's failure to advise Ortega that his absence was a problem, the single incident was not severe to such a degree as to be considered misconduct. Wakefield did not appeal this decision or findings.

reason." *Jackson v. Action for Boston Community Development, Inc.,* 403 Mass. 8, 9, 525 N.E.2d 411 (1988). Here, Ortega is alleging that the defendant employer issued the Wakefield Engineering Employee Handbook to each employee of the company and that promises concerning disciplinary procedures made in this manual are binding on the employer.

"The principle that promises made in a personnel manual may be binding on an employer is accepted in a clear majority of American jurisdictions ... The idea that an employer may ignore promises made in personnel manual is in increasing disfavor in this country." *O'Brien v. New England Telephone & Telegraph Co.,* 422 Mass. 686, 691, 664 N.E.2d 843 (1996). The key inquiry is whether in light of context of the manual's preparation and distribution, as well as its specific provisions, it would be objectively reasonable for employees to regard the manual as a legally enforceable commitment concerning the terms and conditions of employment. *O'Brien,* 422 Mass. at 694, 664 N.E.2d 843; *Weber v. Teamwork Inc.,* 434 Mass. 761, 779–80, 752 N.E.2d 700 (2001) ("Where an employee signs a personnel policy ... or where an employer call special attention to the policy a finding that the terms of the policy on the basis of an implied contract may be justified"); *Ferguson v. Host International, Inc.,* 53 Mass.App.Ct. 96, 102, 757 N.E.2d 267 (2001). Negotiations of the terms of the contract between the employer and the employee is not an essential precondition to enforcement of the manual. *O'Brien,* 422 Mass. at 692, 664 N.E.2d 843.Further, any disclaimer clauses stating that a manual creates no contractual rights or reserving a unilateral right to modify or cancel the manual, while relevant, are *not dispositive* of whether an employee could reasonably believe that the procedures contained therein bind management. *O'Brien,* 422 Mass. at 693, 664 N.E.2d 843; *Ferguson,* 53 Mass.App.Ct. at 102–03, 757 N.E.2d 267.

If read as the manual sets out, an employee is informed of his rights and benefits in the policy manual, including the policy of progressive discipline (as set out in explicit detail in the five-page policy entitled Disciplinary Action, Policy No. S3), and then tells the employee, in essence, that by the way, you have no rights under this policy manual or under policy "S3" unless we, that is the employer, agrees at the time of your problem, that you have any rights at all. Wakefield always has the right to ignore the policy, with or without cause and with or without notice, but the employee does *not. De facto,* the Employee Handbook does *not* give the employee any rights, unless the Company agrees in its benevolence to give them. The privileges and rights given to its employees in the Handbook are totally illusionary. A jury could find that the manual is deceptively written by the employer, informing the employee that he has rights, but only if the Company agrees to give them to an employee [at] the time that he needs these rights. The contract could be considered by the jury to have been fraudulently written for the *sole* interest, financial or otherwise, of the employer. The manual does not set out the circumstances and conditions when an employer may disregard the Disciplinary Action policy and its progressive discipline procedures, but allows it to do whatever it wants to do. Contrast: *Weber v. Community Teamwork, Inc.*, 434 Mass. 761, 779 n. 36, 752 N.E.2d 700 (2001), when the employer specifically stated in the employee handbook when and for what reasons an employee may be terminated without going through its "progressive disciplinary procedures."

Further, the jury could find that Ortega relied on the employee manual and its policies as a condition of his continuing employment at Wakefield. This issue is discussed in both *O'Brien*, 422 Mass. at 692, 664 N.E.2d 843, and *Weber*, 434 Mass. at 780, 752 N.E.2d 700 ("Where an employee signs a personnel policy or where an employer calls special attention to the policy, a finding that the terms of the policy form the basis of an implied contract may be justified."). Here, there is evidence that Ortega signed the Corporate Policy Manual Acknowledgment on May 8, 2001, and therefore agreed, at least implicitly, that the Manual set out the Company's general personnel policies and about Ortega's privileges and obligations as an employee. He specifically knew of the progressive discipline provision of Policy S3. The fact that Ortega received the manual and signed an acknowledgment of its receipt may constitute sufficient evidence that there was an implied contract. *O'Brien*, 422 Mass. at 693, 664 N.E.2d 843. The jury could find that Ortega relied on the Manual and in particular on Policy S3 regarding progressive discipline, which he read and discussed with his fellow employees. After his receipt of the manual, he continued to work under provisions that would be in the nature of the acceptance of an offer of a unilateral contract. *O'Brien*, 422 Mass. at 693, 664 N.E.2d 843.

The question of the extent to which an employer may effectively reserve his rights to change or withdraw a manual, or some part of it, or the extent to which management may successfully provide that the manual from its inception or by amendment creates no rights at all is discussed in cases throughout the country. *O'Brien*, 422 Mass. at 694, 664 N.E.2d 843.However, before considering this point, it should be noted as discussed above, that any disclaimer clauses stating that the employer creates no contracted rights or reserves a unilateral right to modify or cancel the manual is *not dispositive* of whether the employee could reasonably believe that the procedures contained therein bind management. *O'Brien*, 422 Mass. at 692–93, 664 N.E.2d 843.

There are many cases around the country that deal with this issue. There is also a key law review article on the subject by Stephen F. Befort, *Employee Handbooks and The Legal Effect of Disclaimers*, 13 IND. REL. L.J. 326 (1993). In 1993, no fewer than 45 reported decisions over this past decade have declined to give effect to handbook disclaimers. *Id.* at 21, 664 N.E.2d 843, ni.#282 and Appendix *infra* at 382. This article describes situations where the employer sets out the privileges and benefits due an employee and then allow the employer, unilaterally and at will, to disclaim all those benefits. It is one thing to permit an employer to reap the benefits of a handbook by making explicit representations of job protections or job security, but quite another thing to allow the employer to avoid complying with these representations of job security or other rights, merely by including a disclaimer. As observed in a number of recent opinions, the situation becomes the quintessence of having "one's cake and eating it too." The following cases from around the country have addressed the issue:

> *Jones v. Central Peninsula General Hospital,* 779 P.2d 783, 788 (Alaska, 1989) (The manual therefore creates the impression, contrary to the "disclaimer" that employees are to be provided with certain job protections. Employers should not be allowed to instill . . . reasonable expectations of job security; in employees, and then withdraw the basis of those expectations when the employee's performance is no longer desired).

> *Thompson v. King's Entertainment Co.,* 674 F.Supp. 1194, 1198 (E.D.Va.1987) (Employers should be bound by therein expressed policies to preclude therein offering with one hand and they take away with the other).

> *Eldridge v. Evangelical Lutheran Good Samaritan Society,* 417 N.W.2d 797, 801 (N.D.1987) ("There are evident issues of fact about ambiguity and relevance created by an employer's disclaimer in an employee handbook that purports to "taketh" what the remainder of the handbook appears to give").

> See also: Matthew W. Finkin, The Bureaucratization of Work: Employer Policies and Contract Law, 1986 Wis.L.Rev. 733, 751–52 (1986) (stating that judicial enforcement of a boiler plate disclaimer "comes [close] to deference to a fraud").

> Comment, Unilateral Modification of Employment Handbooks: Further Encroachments on the Employment-at-Will Doctrine, 139 U.Pa. L.Rev. 197, 208–09 n. 76 (1990) (citing cases from thirty-three states and District of Columbia.)

In *O'Brien,* 422 Mass. at 694, 664 N.E.2d 843, the Court, by Judge Wilkins, perhaps summed up best the reasons why in a case like this, a company policy manual may be considered as a binding commitment, legally enforceable concerning the terms and conditions of Ortega's employment.

Management distributes personnel manuals because it is thought to be in its best interests to do so. Such a practice encourages employee security, satisfaction, and loyalty and a sense that every employee will be treated fairly and equally. See *Toussaint v. Blue Cross & Blue Shield of Mich.,* 408, 579, 613, 408 Mich. 579, 292 N.W.2d 880 (1980). Management expects that employees will adhere to the obligations that the manual sets forth. Courts recently have been reluctant to permit management to reap the benefits of a personnel manual and at the same time avoid promises freely made in the manual that employees reasonably believed were part of their arrangement with the employer. Management voluntarily offers, and defines the terms of, any benefit set forth in its unbargained for personnel manual. The employees may have a reasonable expectancy that management will adhere to a manual's provisions. "Without minimizing the importance of its specific provisions, the context of the manual's preparation and distribution is, to us, the most persuasive proof that it would be almost inevitable for an employee to regard it as a binding commitment, legally enforceable, concerning the terms and conditions of his employment," *Woolley v. Hoffmann–La Roche, Inc.*, 99 N.J. 284, 299, 491 A.2d 1257, modified on other grounds, 101 N.J. 10, 499 A.2d 515 (1985). In the circumstances of this case, an affected employee's reliance on the manual would be reasonable, and O'Brien, as one of those employees, is entitled to whatever rights that the manual sets forth.

In conclusion, this court believes that there are genuine issues of material fact in dispute and therefore, the motion for summary judgment should be denied. At best for Wakefield, it might be for a "close case." In any respect, the case should be tried, and depending on the jury verdict the Court may reconsider these issues on Motion JNOV. * * *

## NOTES AND QUESTIONS

1.   The *Woolley* court opined that a "clear and prominent disclaimer" of contractual status would be given legal effect. Not surprisingly, there has developed a textured body of law on just how clear and just how prominent the disclaimer must be. *See, e.g., Bowen v. Income Producing Mgmt. of Oklahoma, Inc.*, 202 F.3d 1282 (10th Cir. 2000); *Worley v. Wyoming Bottling Co., Inc.*, 1 P.3d 615 (Wyo. 2000). But many courts follow the line taken in *Wakefield Thermal Solutions* and submit the issue to a jury. As Professor Stephen Befort has observed, the jurisdictions that follow the promissory estoppel approach to handbook provisions are divided: some find the disclaimer negates the circumstance of a promise as a matter of law, while others take the disclaimer as an evidentiary factor to be weighed by a jury. Stephen Befort, *Working Group on Chapter 2 of the Proposed Restatement of Employment Law: Employment Contracts: Termination (Critique of Section 2.04) "Contextual Construction—The Particular Importance of Disclaimers"*, 13 EMP. RTS. & EMP. POL'Y J. 93, 123–26 (2009). Which is more persuasive? This question is expanded upon immediately below.

2.   Judge Posner addressed the case law apropos the following provision in the employee handbook of United Parcel Service: "[T]his Policy Book is not a contract of employment and does not affect your rights as an employee of UPS." *Workman v. United Parcel Serv., Inc.*, 234 F.3d 998, 1000 (7th Cir. 2000). He opined, with customary circumspection:

> We are mindful of cases that hold ... that it is not enough for the handbook to disclaim creating an employment contract; it must state in addition that the employee can be terminated at the will of the employer. . . .

> The decisions that refuse to give effect to the short-form disclaimer strike us as paternalistic in the extreme. Employment at will is the norm in the United States. An employee therefore has no reason to presume that he has tenure, and a disclaimer that a handbook creates a contract is a clear

statement that if he is fired he can't sue for breach of contract. What more is needed? . . .

One might wonder what function an employee handbook serves if it does not create enforceable obligations. The answer is that it conveys useful information to the employee. And more—for to the extent that it does contain promises, even if not legally binding ones, it places the employer under a moral obligation, or more crassly gives him a reputational incentive, to honor those promises. Such promises may not be worth as much to the promisee as a promise that the law enforces, but they are worth more than nothing, and it is nothing that the employee can expect if employers must choose between nothing and giving up employment at will.

*Id.* at 1001. Is that so?

a) "[M]any commentators maintain that employment policy is ill-served by a legal rule that gives preclusive effect to boilerplate disclaimers without regard to the actual expectations created by employer policy statements." Steven Befort, *"The Particular Importance of Disclaimers"*, *supra* at 125 (citations omitted). Is it "paternalism," *vide* Posner, J., to refuse to defer automatically to a clear and conspicuous disclaimer? There are cases, albeit of some vintage, holding that employers may not avoid obligations by simultaneously stating they will pay a bonus or other benefit while disclaiming their contractual obligation to pay: E.g. *George A. Fuller Co. v. Brown*, 15 F.2d 672 (4th Cir.1926); *Ellis v. Emhart Mfg. Co.*, 150 Conn. 501, 191 A.2d 546 (1963); *Wellington v. Con P. Curran Printing Co.*, 216 Mo.App. 358, 268 S.W. 396 (1925); *Molburg v. Hunter Hosiery, Inc.*, 102 N.H. 422, 158 A.2d 288 (1960); *Psutka v. Michigan Alkali Co.*, 274 Mich. 318, 264 N.W. 385 (Mich.1936); *Mabley & Carew Co. v. Borden*, 129 Ohio St. 375, 195 N.E. 697 (1935); *Schofield v. Zion's Co-op. Mercantile Inst.*, 85 Utah 281, 39 P.2d 342 (1934). Why were the reputational effects of dishonoring these commitments considered insufficient by these courts?

b) Is employment at-will really the "norm" in the workplace? Professor Pauline Kim conducted a survey of Missouri employees to test their understanding of the at-will doctrine in their state. She found that only about 10% accurately understood the doctrine and that the vast majority (around 80%) mistakenly believed they could not be lawfully discharged: so the employer could hire a lower wage employee to do the same job, in retaliation for reporting theft by another employee, because the employer mistakenly believed they were a thief when they could prove they were not, or merely because the employer did not like them personally. Pauline T. Kim, *Bargaining with Imperfect Information: A Study of Worker Perceptions of Legal Protection in an At–Will World*, 83 CORNELL L. REV. 105, at 134 (1997). If employees commonly have such a different view of the at-will doctrine, can we really say there is a "meeting of the minds" in accepting it as the default contractual term? Are there other reasons for accepting at-will as the default that do not depend on the idea of efficient voluntary exchange?

c) Even if employment at-will is "the norm" does it follow that employees can draw no legitimate expectation of fair treatment from an employer rule that runs counter to it? In the cases just cited, if these benefits were unusual at the time, were contrary to the then prevailing norm, did all these courts act wrongly—"paternalistically"—in refusing to defer to the employer's reservation of power not to observe its policy?

d) Is there any evidence of adverse "reputational effect" resulting from an employer's refusal to behave with moral responsibility regarding a legally disclaimed rule?

# C. PROMISSORY ESTOPPEL

## GROUSE v. GROUP HEALTH PLAN

Supreme Court of Minnesota, 1981
306 N.W.2d 114

OTIS, JUSTICE.

Plaintiff John Grouse appeals from a judgment in favor of Group Health Plan, Inc., in this action for damages resulting from repudiation of an employment offer. The narrow issue raised is whether the trial court erred by concluding that Grouse's complaint fails to state a claim upon which relief can be granted. In our view, the doctrine of promissory estoppel entitles Grouse to recover and we, therefore, reverse and remand for a new trial on the issue of damages.

The facts relevant to this appeal are essentially undisputed. Grouse, a 1974 graduate of the University of Minnesota School of Pharmacy, was employed in 1975 as a retail pharmacist at Richter Drug in Minneapolis. He worked approximately 41 hours per week earning $7 per hour. Grouse desired employment in a hospital or clinical setting, however, because of the work environment and the increased compensation and benefits. In the summer of 1975 he was advised by the Health Sciences Placement office at the University that Group Health was seeking a pharmacist.

Grouse called Group Health and was told to come in and fill out an application. He did so in September and was, at that time, interviewed by Cyrus Elliott, Group Health's Chief Pharmacist. Approximately 2 weeks later Elliott contacted Grouse and asked him to come in for an interview with Donald Shoberg, Group Health's General Manager. Shoberg explained company policies and procedures as well as salary and benefits. Following this meeting Grouse again spoke with Elliott who told him to be patient, that it was necessary to interview recent graduates before making an offer.

On December 4, 1975, Elliott telephoned Grouse at Richter Drug and offered him a position as a pharmacist at Group Health's St. Louis Park Clinic. Grouse accepted but informed Elliott that 2 week's notice to Richter Drug would be necessary. That afternoon Grouse received an offer from a Veteran's Administration Hospital in Virginia which he declined because of Group Health's offer. Elliott called back to confirm that Grouse had resigned.

Sometime in the next few days Elliott mentioned to Shoberg that he had hired, or was thinking of hiring, Grouse. Shoberg told him that company hiring requirements included a favorable written reference, a background check, and approval of the general manager. Elliott contacted two faculty members at the School of Pharmacy who declined to give references. He also contacted an internship employer and several pharmacies where Grouse had done relief work. Their responses were that they had not had enough exposure to Grouse's work to form a judgment as to his capabilities. Elliott did not contact Richter because Grouse's application requested that he not be contacted. Because Elliott was unable to supply a favorable reference for Grouse, Shoberg hired another person to fill the position.

On December 15, 1975 Grouse called Group Health and reported that he was free to begin work. Elliott informed Grouse that someone else had been hired. Grouse complained to the director of Group Health who apologized but took no other action. Grouse experienced difficulty regaining full time employment and suffered wage loss as a result. He commenced this suit to recover damages; the trial judge found that he had not stated an actionable claim.

In our view the principle of contract law applicable here is promissory estoppel. Its effect is to imply a contract in law where none exists in fact. *Del Hayes & Sons, Inc. v. Mitchell,* 304 Minn. 275, 230 N.W.2d 588 (1975). On these facts no contract exists because due to the bilateral power of termination neither party is committed to performance and the promises are, therefore, illusory. The elements of promissory estoppel are stated in *Restatement of Contracts* § 90 (1932):

> A promise which the promisor should reasonably expect to induce action or forbearance * * * on the part of the promisee and which does induce such action or forbearance is binding if injustice can be avoided only by enforcement of the promise.

Group Health knew that to accept its offer Grouse would have to resign his employment at Richter Drug. Grouse promptly gave notice to Richter Drug and informed Group Health that he had done so when specifically asked by Elliott. Under these circumstances it would be unjust not to hold Group Health to its promise.

The parties focus their arguments on whether an employment contract which is terminable at will can give rise to an action for damages if anticipatorily repudiated. Compare *Skagerberg v. Blandin Paper Co.,* 197 Minn. 291, 266 N.W. 872 (1936); *Degen v. Investors Diversified Services, Inc.,* 260 Minn. 424, 110 N.W.2d 863 (1961); and *Bussard v. College of St. Thomas, Inc.,* 294 Minn. 215, 200 N.W.2d 155 (1972) with *Hackett v. Foodmaker, Inc.,* 69 Mich.App. 591, 245 N.W.2d 140 (1976). Group Health contends that recognition of a cause of action on these facts would result in the anomalous rule that an employee who is told not to report to work the day before he is scheduled to begin has a remedy while an employee who is discharged after the first day does not. We cannot agree since under appropriate circumstances we believe section 90 would apply even after employment has begun.

When a promise is enforced pursuant to section 90 "[t]he remedy granted for breach may be limited as justice requires." Relief may be limited to damages measured by the promisee's reliance.

The conclusion we reach does not imply that an employer will be liable whenever he discharges an employee whose term of employment is at will. What we do hold is that under the facts of this case the appellant had a right to assume he would be given a good faith opportunity to perform his duties to the satisfaction of respondent once he was on the job. He was not only denied that opportunity but resigned the position he already held in reliance on the firm offer which respondent tendered him. Since, as respondent points out, the prospective employment might have been terminated at any time, the measure of damages is not so much what he would have earned from respondent as what he lost in quitting the job he held and in declining at least one other offer of employment elsewhere.

Reversed and remanded for a new trial on the issue of damages.

## NOTES AND QUESTIONS

1. The facts in *Grouse* reflect a recurring situation and a number of courts have declined to apply promissory estoppel on the ground—argued by Group Health but rejected by the *Grouse* court—that as an at-will job was offered., as the employer could have hired and then immediately fired, no damages could be due. *May v. Harris Mgmt. Corp.*, 928 So.2d 140 (La. Ct. App. 2005). A Connecticut court took this position but coupled it to an expression of regret. Petitte v. DSL.net, Inc., 102 Conn.App. 363, 925 A.2d 457, 459 (2007): "This case provides a clear illustration of how the employment at will doctrine can lead to seemingly harsh results." Why "seemingly"?

2. Economists have explained the doctrine of promissory estoppel as an effort to minimize transaction costs. If a promisor induces a promisee to incur costs in reasonable reliance upon the promise given, then the promisor should be liable for those costs if she breaks the promise. Otherwise, the promisor will not adequately take account of the promisee's costs in deciding whether to break the promise, with the result being too many broken promises and a waste of reliance costs. Is this a good explanation of the application of the doctrine of promissory *estoppel* in the *Grouse* case? If this analysis is correct, why would Grouse lose his cause of action under promissory estoppel after he has a "good faith" opportunity to do the job? See, Stewart J. Schwab, *Life–Cycle Justice: Accommodating Just Cause and Employment At Will*, 92 MICH. L. REV. 8, 39–43 (1993).

3. In *Grouse*, how should damages be measured? Out of pocket expenses? See *Hernandez v. UPS Supply Chain Solutions, Inc.*, 496 F.Supp. 2d 778 (W.D. Tex. 2007). The current discounted value of lost wages the employee would have earned from his former employer up to the time of retirement? See *Toscano v. Greene Music*, 124 Cal.App.4th 685, 21 Cal.Rptr.3d 732 (2004). The Alabama Supreme Court held that the measure of damages

for an employer's failure to abide by a promise to investigate any complaint against the employee and hear his side of the allegation before discharging him is the wages due for the period of time such a full investigation would have taken. *Wyatt v. BellSouth, Inc.*, 757 So.2d 403 (Ala. 2000). Two judges dissented on the ground that a jury could have found that the employee would not have been discharged after a full investigation and fair hearing, in which case the measure would be total wages lost.

## D. CHANGING TERMS OF EMPLOYMENT

As David Marsden has explained, employment, as a continuing, open-ended relationship allows the employer to assign work tasks and regulate the intensity of work without the transaction costs of a "spot market" for hiring into each task at an agreed-upon level of effort or productivity. But the obvious advantage of not having constantly to negotiate the terms may be offset by opportunistic behavior. "[T]he employer might take advantage of the employee's difficulties in finding alternative employment to impose new or unpleasant tasks outside the area on which they have agreed." To which the employee, faced with the costs of job loss and job search, might be impelled to acquiesce. DAVID MARSDEN, A THEORY OF EMPLOYMENT SYSTEMS 12 (1999). Alternatively, employees could demand only the most satisfying tasks restricting the employer's flexibility and causing it to pay higher rates than necessary—depending on the tightness of the labor market and the employer's costs of recruitment and training should the employees quit.

> Such problems could easily undermine the advantages of the employment transaction. Faced with a restrictive attitude from employees, the employer would lose the supposed flexibility, and faced with demands for flexibility beyond the bounds of agreement, workers may prefer the additional bargaining power that they have when they can quit easily. More generally, the resulting conflict is likely to reduce the gains to either party from rolling everything up into a single transaction. Hence, unless a solution can be found to the problem of regulating the bounds of the employment transaction, it is much less likely to be preferred to the sales transaction.

*Id.* at 13.

Where there is a contract fixing the terms and conditions of employment, both parties are bound by it, though they are free to agree to renegotiate. Where employment is at-will, the employee is free to demand a change (or quit) and the employer is free to announce and implement a change summarily. The ability of either party to effectively demand changes is constrained by market forces. If employers demand more than the market will bear, employees will quit or strike and prospective employees will not apply. If employees demand more than the market will bear, they will be quickly and easily replaced by the employerShould there be any role for the law in this situation or should the law stay out?

The Court of Appeals for the District of Columbia glossed the law—and the court's earlier decision in *National Rifle Ass'n v. Ailes*, 428 A.2d 816 (D.C. 1981)—thusly,

> In *Ailes* a number of employees who had been discharged as part of a reduction-in-force sued to recover monetary compensation for unused leave they had accrued in excess of a 225–hour limit that NRA had imposed by a policy change made during their employment. On the employer's appeal from an adverse jury verdict, this court agreed with the plaintiffs that, "as a general rule, an employee who accrues but does not take ... paid leave is entitled to monetary compensation for that leave upon discharge ... absent an agreement to the contrary." *Ailes*, 428 A.2d at 820. We held, however, that "once an employee learns about a new [employer] policy limiting compensation for unused leave upon termination, but elects to stay on the job and accept compensation, that decision is sufficient to imply an agreement to continue working subject to the new limitation." *Id.* at 822. This "implicit[ ]" or imputed agreement to a change, we said, required proof that the employee's "knowledge of the change was complete enough" to support an inference that his "decision to remain on the job was premised on acceptance of the new policy," *id.*, and further required proof that he had been given "at lease a brief period of time" to "remain on the job without prejudice"—*i.e.*, without having "impl[iedly] acquiesce[d]" in the change—while considering whether to accept the change or leave the employment. *Id.* at 822, 823. Applying these standards to the facts at hand, we sustained the jury's finding as to certain of the employees that there was an inadequate basis "for imputing [to them] a belief that the [225–hour policy] limit applied to them," *id.* at 824, but as to others, whose awareness of the change and its application to them was undisputed, we held that they "must be said as a matter of law to have agreed to that limitation." *Id.* at 825.

> *Ailes* did not expressly confine itself to agreement by at-will employees, though we think that is its clear implication. So viewed, the principle *Ailes* established for this jurisdiction is in keeping with the rule adopted by most courts considering the issue that an employer may prospectively modify the terms of at-will employment and that the employee's continued service amounts to acceptance of the modification. ... [Extensive recitation of authority omitted.] These courts hold that the ability to terminate the employment relationship at will necessarily includes the ability to alter its terms, and that permitting such modification avoids the undesirable result of encouraging employers to fire employees who do not expressly agree to new terms.

*Kaufman v. Int'l Bhd of Teamsters*, 950 A.2d 44, 47–48 (D.C. App. 2008).

*NOTES AND QUESTIONS*

1.   The *Ailes* court held that the new policy would not bind a continuing employee until the employee had knowledge of the policy "complete enough" to imply consent as a matter of law. What would determine that? The extent to which the policy was explained and distributed? The passage of time? Whether the employee had consulted a lawyer?

2.   Assume an employee with a fixed-term employment contract accrues a right to stock options or to commissions on continuing sales. Assume that upon the contract's termination, the employer offers to renew the contract on condition that the employee forego the accrued commissions or give back the stock option: she can have the old benefit or the "new" job but not both. Would the employee have a legal basis to contest the employer's demand? Would the doctrine of economic duress apply? *Compare Vines v. General Outdoor Adv. Co.*, 171 F.2d 487 (2d Cir. 1948) (per L. Hand, C.J.), *with Laemmar v. J. Walter Thompson, Co.*, 435 F.2d 680 (7th Cir. 1970). *See* John Dawson, *Economic Duress—An Essay in Perspective*, 45 MICH. L. REV. 251 (1947). Alternatively, and despite the appearance of a series of "spot market" transactions, what if the parties had had a long-term relationship, of renewal after renewal after a period of years, and which the employee expected to continue. Would a limitation on exercising the employer's power in "good faith" be applicable? *Cf. Tymshare, Inc. v. Covell*, 727 F.2d 1145 (D.C. Cir. 1984) (per Scalia, C.J.).

# DOYLE v. HOLY CROSS HOSPITAL

Supreme Court of Illinois, 1999
186 Ill.2d 104, 237 Ill.Dec. 100, 708 N.E.2d 1140

MILLER, JUSTICE. * * *

The plaintiffs in this case were nurses employed by the defendant, Holy Cross Hospital, in Chicago. The plaintiffs worked for the defendant continuously until they were discharged, effective November 1, 1991. The defendant hired Mary Doyle in 1960, Leni Serra in 1968, and Susan Valderrama and Valerie Zorek in 1972. In 1971, the defendant issued to existing employees and new hires an employee handbook, which contained a number of policies and provisions regarding employment with the defendant. One of the policies pertained to discharge, and it is the subject of the present appeal. According to the plaintiffs' amended complaint, policy number 7–G, "Economic Separation," stated:

> "Holy Cross Hospital is committed to providing a working environment where employees feel secure in their job. We understand that job security is important to an employee and to that employee's family. There are instances, though, that for economic or other reasons it becomes apparent that the permanent elimination of departments, job classifications, and/or jobs must be made, and there is no reasonable expectation that employees affected could be placed in other positions in the hospital or be recalled for work in one year or

less. To ensure that the economic separation is handled in an objective, structured, and consistent way, the following policies will be followed in determining which employees will be affected.

1. Job Classification
2. Length of Continuous Hospital Service
3. Ability and Fitness to Perform the Required Work. * * *

Because of the special needs of our patients, the following factors will be used in an economic separation affecting R.N.'s:

1. Nursing Areas of Expertise
2. Length of Service Within Each Area of Expertise
3. Ability and Fitness to Perform the Required Work * * *

Employees affected by an economic separation will be placed on a priority rehire list and will be contacted by the Human Resources Department if a position becomes available for which the separated employees may be eligible through experience, training, education and/or other qualifications. Priority rehire consideration shall be for a period of one year." * * *

In 1983, after all four of the plaintiffs had begun working for the defendant, the defendant promulgated policy 5–I, which provided:

> "The Personnel Policies and other various Hospital employee and applicant communications are subject to change from time to time and are not intended to constitute nor do they constitute an implied or express contract or guarantee of employment for any period of time.
>
> The employment relationship between the Hospital and any employee may be terminated at any time by the Hospital or the employee with or without notice."

The hospital discharged the four plaintiffs effective November 1, 1991. * * *

This court first recognized the enforceable effect of employee handbook provisions in *Duldulao v. Saint Mary of Nazareth Hospital Center*, 115 Ill.2d 482, 106 Ill. Dec. 8, 505 N.E.2d 314 (1987). The plaintiff in that case argued that an employee handbook that had been distributed to all employees and that set forth specific procedures for the dismissal of employees gave rise to a contract between the employer and employees. The *Duldulao* court concluded that an employee handbook or policy statement may create contractual rights if the traditional requirements for contract formation are satisfied. The court explained:

> "First, the language of the policy statement must contain a promise clear enough that an employee would reasonably believe that an offer has been made. Second, the statement must be disseminated to the employee in such a manner that the employee is aware of its contents and reasonably believes it to be an offer. Third, the employee must

accept the offer by commencing or continuing to work after learning of the policy statement. When these conditions are present, then the employee's continued work constitutes consideration for the promises contained in the statement, and under traditional principles a valid contract is formed." *Duldulao*, 115 Ill.2d at 490, 106 Ill.Dec. 8, 505 N.E.2d 314.

Given the contractual rationale of *Duldulao*, we find it difficult to reconcile the defendant's position with the requirements for contract formation and modification. Applying "traditional principles" of contract law, as *Duldulao* did, we conclude in this case that the defendant's unilateral modification to the employee handbook lacked consideration and therefore is not binding on the plaintiffs. A modification of an existing contract, like a newly formed contract, requires consideration to be valid and enforceable. ... Consideration consists of some detriment to the offeror, some benefit to the offeree, or some bargained-for exchange between them. ... In the present case, we are unable to conclude that consideration exists that would justify our enforcement of the modification against existing employees. Because the defendant was seeking to reduce the rights enjoyed by the plaintiffs under the employee handbook, it was the defendant, and not the plaintiffs, who would properly be required to provide consideration for the modification. But in adding the disclaimer to the handbook, the defendant provided nothing of value to the plaintiffs and did not itself incur any disadvantage. In fact, the opposite occurred: the plaintiffs suffered a detriment—the loss of rights previously granted to them by the handbook—while the defendant gained a corresponding benefit. * * *

[The court noted the decisions of other jurisdictions supporting this conclusion.]

* * * The defendant and *amicus* also contend that considerations of public policy argue in favor of allowing employers a free hand in modifying provisions of employee handbooks with respect to existing employees. The defendant and *amicus* note that under the appellate court's result here, an employer could be bound for a lengthy period to the terms of an employee handbook issued long ago. In addition, they assert that adoption of the appellate court's result in this case would mean that different employees could be subject to different contract terms and provisions, depending on when a particular person was hired and what the employee handbook provided at that time. Although we are aware of these potential draw-backs, we note that this is a matter of contract and see no compelling reason here to relieve the defendant of the obligations it has voluntarily incurred. Employers who choose to set forth policies in employee handbooks and manuals as an inducement to attracting and retaining a skilled and loyal work force cannot disregard those obligations at a later time, simply because the employer later perceives them to be inconvenient or burdensome.

[Two judges dissented on other grounds.]

## NOTES AND COMMENTS

1. The *Doyle* approach, consistent with the Illinois Supreme Court's application of traditional contract principles in *Duldalao*, is nevertheless a minority view. Most courts have permitted employers unilaterally to abrogate commitments to discharge only for good cause or upon observance of progressive discipline, sometimes without even a requirement of reserving that power beforehand.

The California Supreme Court, for example, allowed unilateral abrogation of an employment security policy, enforceable during its term as a matter of unilateral contract, by distinguishing unilateral from bi-lateral contracts. *Asmus v. Pacific Bell*, 23 Cal.4th 1, 96 Cal.Rptr.2d 179, 999 P.2d 71, 78 (2000):

> The general rule governing the proper termination of unilateral contracts is that once the promisor determines after a reasonable time that it will terminate or modify the contract, and provides employees with reasonable notice of the change, additional consideration is not required. The mutuality of obligation principle requiring new consideration for contract termination applies to bilateral contracts only. In the unilateral contract context, there is no mutuality of obligation. For an effective modification, there is consideration in the form of continued employee services. (citations omitted).

Is this doctrinally sound? Mutuality of obligation does not mean equality of obligation. It means that both parties are bound by something, *i.e.*, the employer's rules. Is there no mutuality of obligation in a unilateral contract? If so, how could the employer's job security policy have been enforceable in the first instance?

2. The Michigan Supreme Court, following the *sui generis* theory of enforcing handbook commitment to job security on the ground of the benefit employers get from giving employees a handbook, allowed unilateral abrogation in reasoning from that perspective:

> An employer who chooses to establish desirable personnel policies, such as a discharge-for-cause employment policy, is not seeking to induce each individual employee to show up for work day after day, but rather is seeking to promote an environment conducive to collective productivity. The benefit to the employer of promoting such an environment, rather than the traditional contract-forming mechanisms of mutual assent or individual detrimental reliance, gives rise to a situation "instinct with an obligation." When, as in the question before us, the employer changes its discharge-for-cause policy to one of employment-at-will, the employer's benefit is correspondingly extinguished, as is the rationale for the court's enforcement of the discharge-for-cause policy.

*Bankey v. Storer Broad. Co.*, 432 Mich. 438, 443 N.W.2d 112, 119 (1989). The *Restatement (Third) of Employment Law* adopts this rationale, which it appends as commentary to its adoption of the "administrative estoppel" rationale discussed in Note 1 at 122–123, *supra*. The theory of "administrative estoppel" was adopted specifically to allow employers to abrogate their assurances. The ALI's rationale has been criticized:

> The nub of the [*Restatement*'s] rationale is contained in the assertion that we should not assume that employers wish forever to constrain their flexibility in the matter of discharge, for the [*Restatement*] is candid about why employers provide these assurances in the first place. "Employers make such statements in their self-interest because they believe the policies ... will advance productivity, employee welfare, or some other organizational objective." In other words, when employers, acting in their self interest, decide that fear of job loss might be a better motivator than job satisfaction, they should be free to disregard their prior commitments. This logic elides the fact that the loyalty the employer's policy sought to instill rested upon creating reasonable employee expectations about how they will be treated in the future. The labor of a human being is a non-durable good. The individual's dwindling supply is expended, other opportunities ignored or foregone, at least partly because of the expectation of fair treatment the employer has engendered. If expectations of deferred income could estop the employer from abrogating retroactively its commitment to severance pay [which the *Restatement* acknowledges], it would seem much the same should apply in the matter of job security; or, less strongly, that the [*Restatement*] rather badly needs to explain why it would not, by reason other than that abrogability better serves an employer's interest.

Matthew Finkin, *Shoring Up the Citadel (At–Will Employment)*, 24 HOFSTRA LAB. & EMP. L.J. 1, 12 (2006). Much this view was expressed by the dissenting Justices *in Asmus v. Pacific Bell*, 23 Cal.4th 1, 96 Cal.Rptr.2d 179, 999 P.2d 71, 81 (2000).

3. Under *Doyle,* an employer would have to offer some consideration—an extra vacation day, a sum of money—in return for the employee's relinquishment of the right not be dismissed except for just cause. Some might accept; but some might not. As a result, an employer could treat some of its continuing complement of workers as at-will employees, but not all. Is that an intolerable or unworkable situation for employers? Note that employers may not abrogate vested benefits but can offer reduced benefits—or none at all—to new hires. This results in some workers having greater benefits than their coworkers in the same workplace doing the same work. So, too, have "two-tier" wage policies been adopted or negotiated with unions. If these distinctions between incumbent workers are tenable, why should a distinction between those who have bargained away their job security and those who have not be untenable?

# E. MANDATORY ARBITRATION

In 1925 Congress enacted the Federal Arbitration Act (FAA) at the behest of the Secretary of Commerce, Herbert Hoover, and the New York bar to expedite the disposition of commercial and maritime disputes. Section 2 of that statute provides that:

> A written provision in any maritime transaction or a contract evidencing a transaction involving commerce to settle by arbitration a contro-

versy thereafter arising out of such contract or transaction ... shall be valid, irrevocable, and enforceable, save upon such grounds as exist at law or in equity for the revocation of any contract.

9 U.S.C. § 2 (1988).

The applicability of an agreement to arbitrate future disputes to a claimed violation of law arising out of the transaction was tested in *Wilko v. Swan*, 346 U.S. 427, 74 S.Ct. 182, 98 L.Ed. 168 (1953). A customer's margin agreement with a broker for the purchase of corporate shares contained an arbitration clause that incorporated reference to a federal securities law protecting purchasers. The purchaser sued the broker for breach of the law and the broker sought to compel arbitration. The Securities Act voided any stipulation waiving compliance with any provision of the Act, but the broker argued that because the contract expressly incorporated the Securities Act, all the arbitration provision did was to substitute one forum for another and so waived no provision of law. A unanimous Supreme Court disagreed: the provision waived the buyer's right to sue in court, and the buyer's choice of forum *is* an advantage secured by the Securities Act. *Id.* at 435. The Court was influenced by other deficiencies it perceived in the arbitral process that rendered it unsuitable for the resolution of legal disputes: that arbitrators may not be lawyers; that a complete record need not be made nor a reasoned opinion given; that judicial review is limited both legally and practically.

In 1989, *Wilko* was overruled. *Rodriguez de Quijas v. Shearson/American Express, Inc.*, 490 U.S. 477, 109 S.Ct. 1917, 104 L.Ed.2d 526 (1989). In a series of cases the U.S. Supreme Court worked a complete reversal of the judicial posture regarding the submission of statutory claims to private arbitration—for securities transactions, banking, consumer credit and protection, and more. In 1991, in *Gilmer v. Interstate/Johnson Lane Corp.*, 500 U.S. 20, 111 S.Ct. 1647, 114 L.Ed.2d 26 (1991), the rules of a stock exchange mandating arbitration of all employment disputes of employees of the exchange's member employers were allowed to preclude judicial jurisdiction for an age discrimination claim. The Court's about-face was complete: "[B]y agreeing to arbitrate a statutory claim, a party does not forgo the substantive rights afforded by the statute; it only submits to their resolution in an arbitral, rather than a judicial forum." *Id.* at 26.

However, for those employers eager to avail themselves of this option, the Arbitration Act had a potentially vexing exemption. In contrast to the exchange rules involved in the *Gilmer* case, the Act expressly did *not* apply to "contracts of employment of seamen, railroad employees, or any other class of workers engaged in foreign or interstate commerce." 9 U.S.C. § 1.

All but one court of appeals held that that exemption applied only to those employees over whom Congress had jurisdiction when the law was enacted; that is, given the very narrow scope of Congress' power under the interstate commerce clause at the time, the exemption extracted from the Act only those workers who actually carried a good or a passenger across a state line. The Ninth Circuit disagreed, reasoning that it made no sense to *include* under the FAA that "class of workers engaged in foreign or interstate state" whom Congress could not have included in 1925 or for whom jurisdiction was most doubtful. The Ninth Circuit read the exemption in the context of the circumstances giving rise to it as excluding all employees from the reach of an Act.

In *Circuit City Stores, Inc. v. Adams*, 532 U.S. 105, 121 S.Ct. 1302, 149 L.Ed.2d 234 (2001), the Court, by a 5-to-4 majority, rejected the Ninth Circuit's reading. The Court purported to take the text at its plain meaning and rejected the historical context relied upon by the Ninth Circuit. The Court speculated (there is no other word for it) nevertheless on why Congress may have drawn the distinction as it did. The Court emphasized its strong commitment to arbitral deference, and it adverted to the need for certainty and uniformity:

> The considerable complexity and uncertainty that the construction of § 1 urged by respondent would introduce into the enforceability of arbitration agreements in employment contracts would call into doubt the efficacy of alternative dispute resolution procedures adopted by many of the Nation's employers, in the process undermining the FAA's proarbitration purposes and "breeding litigation from a statute that seeks to avoid it." The Court has been quite specific in holding that arbitration agreements can be enforced under the FAA without contravening the policies of congressional enactments giving employees specific protection against discrimination prohibited by federal law; as we noted in *Gilmer*, " '[b]y agreeing to arbitrate a statutory claim, a party does not forgo the substantive rights afforded by the statute; it only submits to their resolution in an arbitral, rather than a judicial, forum.' "

*Id.* at 123 (citations omitted). The Court's assumption, that federalizing what has come to be called "employment arbitration" (in contrast to arbitral systems created by collective bargaining agreements commonly referred to as "labor arbitration") would conduce toward uniformity, failed to account for the latter clause of § 2 that rendered arbitration provisions enforceable "*save* upon such grounds as exist at law or in equity for the revocation of any contract." *Id.* at 111–12 (Emphasis added.) This last clause tells us that the FAA preempts state laws that previously made arbitration agreements unenforceable, but not state law on the formation or revocation of contracts generally. As a result, private agreements to arbitrate employment disputes are enforceable unless there is some basis in a state's general contract law for finding that no arbitration agreement was formed or for finding that the agreement is revocable. Because each state has its own combination of contract law doctrines that apply to arbitration agreements (notice, consent, mutuality, consideration, unconscionability, etc.), the Court's belief that federalization would create uniformity was incorrect.

## DAVIS v. O'MELVENY & MYERS

United States Court of Appeals for the Ninth Circuit, 2007
485 F.3d 1066

Samuel P. King, Senior District Judge.

Plaintiff Jacqueline Davis (Davis) appeals the district court's order dismissing her action and compelling arbitration under 9 U.S.C. § 4 based upon an arbitration agreement with her former employer, Defendant O'Melveny & Myers (O'Melveny). On appeal, Davis challenges the enforceability of the arbitration agreement, contending that it is unconscionable under California law. The merits of the underlying claims in her complaint are not at issue here. Because the arbitration agreement is unconscionable under California law, we reverse and remand.

### BACKGROUND

On August 1, 2002, O'Melveny adopted and distributed to its employees a new Dispute Resolution Program (DRP) that culminated in final and binding arbitration of most employment-related claims by and against its employees. O'Melveny distributed the DRP via interoffice mail and posted it on an office intranet site. A cover memorandum stated: "Please read the attached and direct any questions you may have to a member of the Human Resources Department, the Legal Personnel Department, the Associate Advisory Committee or the Office of the Chair." Davis, who had worked as a paralegal at a Los Angeles, California, office of O'Melveny since June 1, 1999, received the DRP but apparently did nothing official to question the policy. * * *

On February 27, 2004, Davis filed this lawsuit under the Federal Fair Labor Standards Act (FLSA) and various other state and federal labor statutes, alleging failure to pay overtime for work during lunch time and rest periods and for other work exceeding eight hours a day and 40 hours a week, as well as denial of rest and meal periods. In addition to claims under the FLSA, her nine-count complaint included claims for violations of California Labor Code §§ 558, 2698 and 2699, and for declaratory relief seeking a declaration that the DRP is unconscionable and that O'Melveny's enforcement of its provisions and other allegedly illegal behavior constituted unfair business practices under California's Unfair Business Practices Act. The complaint sought damages and injunctive relief on an individual basis and for "all others similarly harmed."

The DRP covers most employment-related claims, as follows:

> Except as otherwise provided in this Program, effective November 1, 2002, you and the Firm hereby consent to the resolution by private arbitration of all claims or controversies, past, present or future . . . in any way arising out of, relating to, or associated with your employment with the Firm or the termination of your employment . . . that the Firm may have against you or that you may have against the

Firm. ... The Claims covered by this Program include, but are not limited to, claims for wages or other compensation due; ... and claims for violation of any federal, state or other governmental constitution, law, statute, ordinance, regulation or public policy. ...

Except as otherwise provided in the Program, neither you nor the Firm will initiate or pursue any lawsuit or administrative action (other than filing an administrative charge of discrimination with the Equal Employment Opportunity Commission, the California Department of Fair Employment and Housing, the New York Human Rights Commission or any similar fair employment practices agency) in any way related to or arising from any Claim covered by this Program.

In addition to administrative charges of discrimination as set forth above, the DRP also excluded certain other types of claims from mandatory arbitration as follows:

This Program does not apply to or cover claims for workers' compensation benefits; claims for unemployment compensation benefits; claims by the Firm for injunctive relief and/or other equitable relief for violations of the attorney-client privilege or work product doctrine or the disclosure of other confidential information; or claims based upon an employee pension or benefit plan, the terms of which contain an arbitration or other nonjudicial dispute resolution procedure, in which case the provisions of that plan shall apply.

It is undisputed that Davis's FLSA and related claims regarding overtime "arise out of," or "relate to," her employment for purposes of the scope of the DRP. The question here is whether the DRP is enforceable, in whole or in part.

Two other specific provisions of the DRP are also at issue in this appeal: (1) a "notice provision" requiring notice and a demand for mediation within one year from when the basis of the claim is known or should have been known; and (2) a confidentiality clause.

The notice provision provides as follows:

An employee must give written notice of any Claim to the Firm along with a demand for mediation. This notice must be given within one (1) calendar year from the time the condition or situation providing the basis for the Claim is known to the employee or with reasonable effort on the employee's part should have been known to him or her. The same rule applies to any Claim the Firm has against an employee.... ***Failure to give timely notice of a Claim along with a demand for mediation will waive the Claim and it will be lost forever.*** (Bold and underscore in original.)

The confidentiality clause provides as follows:

Except as may be necessary to enter judgment upon the award or to the extent required by applicable law, all claims, defenses and proceedings (including, without limiting the generality of the foregoing, the existence of a controversy and the fact that there is a mediation or an arbitration proceeding) shall be treated in a confidential manner by the mediator, the Arbitrator, the parties and their counsel, each of their agents, and employees and all others acting on behalf of or in concert with them. Without limiting the generality of the foregoing, no one shall divulge to any third party or person not directly involved in the mediation or arbitration the content of the pleadings, papers, orders, hearings, trials, or awards in the arbitration, except as may be necessary to enter judgment upon the Arbitrator's award as required by applicable law.

After Davis filed suit, O'Melveny moved to dismiss the action and to compel arbitration. The district court upheld the DRP and granted O'Melveny's motion. Davis filed a timely appeal. * * *

## DISCUSSION

Under California law, a contractual clause is unenforceable if it is both procedurally and substantively unconscionable. *See Armendariz v. Found. Health Psychcare Servs., Inc.,* 24 Cal.4th 83, 99 Cal.Rptr.2d 745, 6 P.3d 669, 690 (2000); *Nagrampa,* 469 F.3d at 1280. Courts apply a sliding scale: "the more substantively oppressive the contract term, the less evidence of procedural unconscionability is required to come to the conclusion that the term is unenforceable, and vice versa." *Armendariz,* 99 Cal.Rptr.2d 745, 6 P.3d at 690. Still, "both [must] be present in order for a court to exercise its discretion to refuse to enforce a contract or clause under the doctrine of unconscionability." *Id.* (quoting *Stirlen v. Supercuts, Inc.,* 51 Cal.App.4th 1519, 60 Cal.Rptr.2d 138, 145 (1997)). We address each prong in turn.

### 1. *Procedural Unconscionability*

In assessing procedural unconscionability, the court "focuses on whether the contract was one of adhesion. Was it 'imposed on employees as a condition of employment'? Was there 'an opportunity to negotiate'? ... '[The test] focuses on factors of oppression and surprise.' " *Soltani v. W. & S. Life Ins. Co.,* 258 F.3d 1038, 1042 (9th Cir.2001) (citations omitted).

The DRP was written by a sophisticated employer—a national and international law firm, no less—but there are no factors of adhesion such as surprise or concealment. The DRP was not hidden.[3] The terms were not concealed in an employee handbook. The binding nature of it was in bold and uppercase text. Terms were not buried in fine print. O'Melveny not only gave ample notice of the program and its terms, but also made efforts to have employment lawyers and human-resource personnel available to answer questions. There is no evidence (although the case did not progress very far) of undue pressure put on employees.

---

**3.** Whether the employees understood the terms and whether specific provisions "shock the conscience"—and in that sense would "surprise" an employee—are different questions, analyzed under the substantive prong.

Nevertheless, in a very real sense the DRP was "take it or leave it." The DRP's terms took effect three months after they were announced regardless of whether an employee liked them or not. An employee's option was to leave and work somewhere else. True, for current employees like Davis, three months might have been sufficient time to consider whether the DRP was reason to leave O'Melveny. In that sense, there could have been a meaningful opportunity to "opt out"—although to opt out of the entire employment relationship, not to retain the relationship but preserve a judicial forum.

In . . . [*Circuit City Stores, Inc. v. Adams*, 279 F.3d 889 (9th Cir. 2002) (on remand from the Supreme Court)], the Ninth Circuit, applying *Armendariz* (the controlling California Supreme Court case), found an arbitration agreement procedurally unconscionable because it was a "take it or leave it" proposition. 279 F.3d at 893. *Adams* reasoned that "[t]he agreement is a prerequisite to employment, and job applicants are not permitted to modify the agreement's terms—they must take the contract or leave it." *Id.* The Ninth Circuit found an agreement in *Ferguson v. Countrywide Credit Industries, Inc.*, 298 F.3d 778, 783 (9th Cir.2002), procedurally unconscionable for the same reason. California courts continue to apply the rationale from *Armendariz* to find such arbitration contracts procedurally unconscionable. *See, e.g., Martinez v. Master Prot. Corp.*, 118 Cal.App.4th 107, 12 Cal.Rptr.3d 663, 669 (2004) ("An arbitration agreement that is an essential part of a 'take it or leave it' employment condition, without more, is procedurally unconscionable.") (citations omitted).

Conversely, if an employee has a meaningful opportunity to opt out of the arbitration provision when signing the agreement and still preserve his or her job, then it is not procedurally unconscionable. *See, e.g., Circuit City Stores, Inc. v. Najd*, 294 F.3d 1104, 1108 (9th Cir.2002) (upholding agreement); *Circuit City Stores, Inc. v. Ahmed*, 283 F.3d 1198, 1200 (9th Cir.2002) (same). *Compare Mantor I*, 335 F.3d at 1106–07 (finding procedural unconscionability even if employee had been given an "opt out" form, because of undue pressure not to sign the "opt out" form, rendering the opportunity not meaningful).

O'Melveny concedes that its employees were not given an option to "opt out" and preserve a judicial forum. (It does note that employees were invited to ask questions about the DRP, but there is nothing to indicate that the terms were negotiable for employees such as Davis.) But, O'Melveny argues—and the district court agreed—that the three months of notice nevertheless satisfies the concern of oppression behind this factor. It relies on a "marketplace alternatives" theory used in cases outside the employment context. *See Dean Witter Reynolds, Inc. v. Superior Court*, 211 Cal.App.3d 758, 259 Cal.Rptr. 789 (1989).

[However,] *Dean Witter* addressed mandatory arbitration in a financial services contract. The court reasoned that if the consumer did not like the mandatory arbitration provision in an investment account contract, the consumer could get an account at another company. *Id.* at 798. The district court here accepted O'Melveny's argument extending *Dean Witter* by analogy to the employment context. The rationale is that if Davis did not want to work at O'Melveny (which was free to change most of the terms of her employment with reasonable notice) she had a "meaningful choice"—as in *Dean Witter*—to "do business elsewhere" by working somewhere else.

It is impossible, however, to square such reasoning with explicit language from *Ingle v. Circuit City Stores, Inc.*, 328 F.3d 1165, 1172 (9th Cir.2003) (*Ingle I*) and *Ferguson*, 298 F.3d at 784, specifically rejecting the argument that a "take it or leave it" arbitration provision was procedurally saved by providing employees time to consider the change. In *Ingle I*, the Ninth Circuit struck a Circuit City arbitration agreement as both procedurally and substantively unconscionable. 328 F.3d at 1172–73. As with O'Melveny's DRP, the employee Ingle did not have an opportunity to opt out by preserving a judicial forum. *Id.* at 1172. Circuit City argued that the agreement was enforceable because Ingle had time to consider the arbitration terms, but chose to accept the employment anyway. The *Ingle I* court rejected Circuit City's argument.

O'Melveny attempts to distinguish *Ingle I* in this regard because Davis had three *months*—not three days—to consider the arbitration agreement. The distinction, however, is not helpful because even if the opportunity to walk away was "meaningful," the DRP was still a "take it or leave it" proposition. More importantly, *Ingle I* reasoned that "[t]he amount of time [the employee] had to consider the contract is *irrelevant*." *Id.* (emphasis added). *Ingle I* addressed the availability of alternative employment by "follow[ing] the reasoning in *Szetela v. Discover Bank*, 97 Cal.App.4th 1094, 118 Cal.Rptr.2d 862 (2002), in which the California Court of Appeal held that *the availability of other options does not bear on whether a contract is procedurally unconscionable.*" *Ingle I*, 328 F.3d at 1172 (citing *Szetela*, 118 Cal.Rptr.2d at 867) (emphasis added); *see also Ferguson*, 298 F.3d at 784 ("[W]hether the plaintiff had an opportunity to decline the defendant's contract and instead enter into a contract with another party that does not include the offending terms *is not the relevant test for procedural unconscionability.*") (emphasis added) (citing *Szetela*, 118 Cal.Rptr.2d at 867). . . .

In *Nagrampa*, the Ninth Circuit reiterated these principles of California law and specifically rejected the argument that the availability of other employment can defeat a claim of procedural unconscionability when an employee is faced with a "take it or leave it" condition of employment. *Nagrampa*, 469 F.3d at 1283 ("The California Court of Appeal has rejected the notion that the availability in the marketplace of substitute employment, goods, or services *alone* can defeat a claim of procedural unconscionability.") (emphasis in original) (citations omitted). *Nagrampa* also distinguished *Dean Witter* by reasoning that the investor in that case was a sophisticated investor-attorney with specialized knowledge of financial institutions and financial service contracts. *Id.* In contrast, where—as is the case with Davis as a paralegal in an international law firm—the employee is facing an employer with "overwhelming bargaining power" that "drafted the contract, and presented it to [Davis] on a take-it-or-leave-it basis," the clause is procedurally unconscionable. *Id.* at 1284. . . .

In short, the DRP is procedurally unconscionable.

### 2. *Substantive Unconscionability*

Even if the DRP is procedurally unconscionable, we must also address whether the agreement is (or specific provisions of it are) substantively unconscionable before rendering it (or any of its terms) unenforceable. *Armendariz,* 99 Cal.Rptr.2d 745, 6 P.3d at 690; *Nagrampa,* 469 F.3d at 1280–81(reiterating that procedural unconscionability is to be analyzed in proportion to evidence of substantive unconscionability).

"Substantive unconscionability relates to the effect of the contract or provision. A 'lack of mutuality' is relevant in analyzing this prong. The term focuses on the terms of the agreement and whether those terms are so one-sided as to *shock the conscience.*" *Soltani,* 258 F.3d at 1043 (internal quotation marks and citations omitted) (emphasis in original). "A determination of substantive unconscionability . . . involves whether the terms of the contract are unduly harsh or oppressive." *Adams,* 279 F.3d at 893 (citation omitted). We proceed to examine individually the four provisions of the DRP that Davis challenges as substantively unconscionable or otherwise void. We then consider whether the provisions we conclude are void may be severed from the rest of the DRP or whether, instead, the DRP is unenforceable in its entirety.

### a. The "Notice Provision."

Davis challenges the DRP's notice provision. It allows one year within which to give notice from when any claim is "known to the employee or with reasonable effort . . . should have been known to him or her." Davis contends that this notice provision is a substantively-unconscionable shortened statute of limitations and that it deprives her of potential application of a "continuing violation" theory.

The challenged provision covers more than merely "notice"; it also requires a demand for mediation within a year ("***Failure to give timely notice of a Claim along with a demand for mediation will waive the Claim and it will be lost forever***") (bold and underscore in original). Under the DRP, then, mediation is a mandatory prerequisite to arbitration. The one-year notice provision thus functions as a statute of limitations. Because mediation precedes the arbitration, the "notice provision" requires the whole claim to be filed within a year. One cannot, for example, give written "notice" within a year, but otherwise file a claim later under a longer statute of limitations.[4] In short, if the claim is not filed within a year of when it should have been discovered, it is lost.

---

4. For example, there is a three-year limitation period for a willful FLSA violation, and two years otherwise. 29 U.S.C. § 255(a).

We have previously held that forcing employees to comply with a strict one-year limitation period for employment-related statutory claims is oppressive in a mandatory arbitration context. O'Melveny's "notice" provision is similar to the limitations provision in *Ingle I* .... We struck down that provision as substantively unconscionable. *Id.; see also Mantor I,* 335 F.3d at 1107 (adopting *Ingle I*'s statute-of-limitations holding). .... The fact that O'Melveny is also bound to litigate employment-related statutory claims within the one-year period is of no consequence, as these are types of claims likely only to be brought by employees. ...

In holding substantively unconscionable provisions shortening the time to bring employment-related statutory claims, we have been particularly concerned about barring a "continuing violations" theory by employees. Such a theory can be used, for example, when an employer has a "systematic policy of discrimination" consisting of related acts that began prior to period within the statute of limitations. *See, e.g., Richards v. CH2M Hill, Inc.,* 26 Cal.4th 798, 111 Cal.Rptr.2d 87, 29 P.3d 175, 183 (2001) (discussing various continuing violation theories). On this point, *Ingle I* reasoned:

> [A] 'strict one year statute of limitations on arbitrating claims ... would deprive [employees] of the benefit of the continuing violation doctrine available in FEHA suits.' ... While [the employer] insulates itself from potential damages, an employee foregoes the possibility of relief under the continuing violations doctrine. Therefore, because the benefit of this provision flows only to [the employer], we conclude that the statute of limitations provision is substantively unconscionable.

328 F.3d at 1175 (quoting *Adams,* 279 F.3d at 894–95) (citation omitted). Likewise, the provision imposed by O'Melveny functions to bar a "continuing violations" theory because it specifically bars any claims not brought within a year of when they were first known (or should have been known). \* \* \*

Under *Ingle I, Adams,* and *Mantor I* ... the DRP's one-year universal limitation period is substantively unconscionable when it forces an employee to arbitrate employment-related statutory claims.

### b.  *Confidentiality Provision.*

Next, Davis challenges the confidentiality provision. She argues that it is overly broad and therefore substantively unconscionable under *Ting v. AT&T,* 319 F.3d 1126 (9th Cir.2003).

In *Ting,* the Ninth Circuit found a confidentiality clause in an arbitration agreement substantively unconscionable. ...

Here, the DRP's confidentiality clause as written unconscionably favors O'Melveny. The clause precludes even mention to anyone "not directly involved in the mediation or arbitration" of "the content of the pleadings, papers, orders, hearings, trials, or awards in the arbitration" or even "the existence of a controversy and the fact that there is a mediation or an arbitration proceeding." Such restrictions would prevent an employee from contacting other employees to assist in litigating (or arbitrating) an employee's case. An inability to mention even the existence of a claim to current or former O'Melveny employees would handicap if not stifle an employee's ability to investigate and engage in discovery. The restrictions would also place O'Melveny "in a far superior legal posture" by preventing plaintiffs from accessing precedent while allowing O'Melveny to learn how to negotiate and litigate its contracts in the future. *Id.* Strict confidentiality of all "pleadings, papers, orders, hearings, trials, or awards in the arbitration" could also prevent others from building cases. *See id.* ("the unavailability of arbitral decisions may prevent potential plaintiffs from obtaining the information needed to build a case of intentional misconduct or unlawful discrimination"). It might even chill enforcement of Cal. Labor Code § 232.5, which forbids employers from keeping employees from disclosing certain "working conditions" and from retaliating against employees who do so.[5]

O'Melveny responds by arguing that the DRP allows parties to divulge information to those "directly involved" and would therefore allow fact investigation. . . . . It also relies upon a "savings clause" at the beginning of the provision ("Except as may be necessary to enter judgment upon the award or to the extent required by applicable law") as indicating that if there's something wrong with any of the confidentiality clause's terms, then the improper provision would be subordinated "to the extent required by applicable law"—i.e., ignored.

But such concessions depend upon overly generous readings of the confidentiality clause. We must deal with the terms as written. . . .

This does not mean that confidentiality provisions in an arbitration agreement are per se unconscionable under California law. . . . The parties to any particular arbitration, especially in an employment dispute, can always agree to limit availability of sensitive employee information (e.g., social security numbers or other personal identifier information) or other issue-specific matters, if necessary. Confidentiality by itself is not substantively unconscionable; the DRP's confidentiality clause, however, is written too broadly. * * *

[In this portion of the opinion the court explained the reasons why it found the exemption for attorney-client disputes, a non-mutual exception allowing O'Melveny & Myers a judicial remedy, to be "one-sided and thus substantively unconscionable."]

---

**5.** The section provides in part:

**§ 232.5. Working conditions; prohibition of sanctions against employee disclosure**

No employer may do any of the following:

(a) Require, as a condition of employment, that an employee refrain from disclosing information about the employer's working conditions.

(b) Require an employee to sign a waiver or other document that purports to deny the employee the right to disclose information about the employer's working conditions.

(c) Discharge, formally discipline, or otherwise discriminate against an employee who discloses information about the employer's working conditions.

### 3. *Availability of Statutory Rights*

Davis challenges as void against public policy the DRP's prohibition against most administrative actions. .... Arbitration is favored as a matter of policy regardless of whether it is in lieu of a judicial or administrative forum. . . .

Nevertheless, an arbitration agreement may not function so as to require employees to waive potential recovery for substantive statutory rights in an arbitral forum, especially for statutory rights established "for a public reason"—such as those under The Age Discrimination in Employment Act (ADEA) and the California Fair Employment and Housing Act (FEHA). *Gilmer,* 500 U.S. at 28, 111 S.Ct. 1647; *Armendariz,* 99 Cal. Rptr.2d 745, 6 P.3d at 680–81. That is, although such rights are arbitrable, an arbitration forum must allow for the pursuit of the legal rights and remedies provided by such statutes. *Armendariz,* 99 Cal.Rptr.2d 745, 6 P.3d at 681 (citing *Cole,* 105 F.3d at 1481–82). In this context, employment rights under the FLSA and California's Labor Code are "public rights" analogous to rights under the ADEA and FEHA. *See, e.g., Albertson's, Inc. v. United Food & Commercial Workers Union,* 157 F.3d 758, 761 (9th Cir.1998). * * *

[T]he DRP's all-inclusive bar to administrative actions (even given the listed exceptions for EEOC and California Department of Fair Housing ("DFEH") complaints) is contrary to U.S. Supreme Court and California Supreme Court precedent. O'Melveny recognizes that an exemption for EEOC and similar state-level administrative claims is necessary. *See Gilmer,* 500 U.S. at 28, 111 S.Ct. 1647 ("An individual ADEA claimant subject to an arbitration agreement will still be free to file a charge with the EEOC, even though the claimant is not able to institute a private judicial action."); *Armendariz,* 99 Cal.Rptr.2d 745, 6 P.3d at 679 n. 6 ("Nothing in this opinion, however, should be interpreted as implying that an arbitration agreement can restrict an employee's resort to the Department of Fair Employment and Housing, the administrative agency charged with prosecuting complaints made under the FEHA. . . .") (citing *Gilmer,* 500 U.S. at 28, 111 S.Ct. 1647). Presumably, the DRP specifically excludes such administrative complaints because of these cases. O'Melveny also acknowledges that the clause does not bar the EEOC or a similar state agency from seeking relief (in court) that is not individual-specific, such as a class action. The clause also could not bar an EEOC-instituted judicial action that might also seek victim-specific relief. *See EEOC v. Waffle House, Inc.,* 534 U.S. 279, 295–96, 122 S.Ct. 754, 151 L.Ed.2d 755 (2002). Therefore, under *Gilmer* and *Armendariz,* a clause that barred or required arbitration of administrative claims to the EEOC would be void as against public policy.

The exception (i.e., preclusion from arbitration) for administrative complaints to the EEOC and California DFEH was premised on the agencies' public purpose for the relief and their independent authority to vindicate public rights. *Gilmer,* 500 U.S. at 27, 111 S.Ct. 1647; *Waffle*

*House,* 534 U.S. at 291–92, 294–96, 122 S.Ct. 754. Indeed, the EEOC's enforcement scheme relies upon individual complaints. "Consequently, courts have observed that an individual may not contract away her right to file a charge with the EEOC [.]" *EEOC v. Frank's Nursery & Crafts, Inc.,* 177 F.3d 448, 456 (6th Cir.1999) (citations omitted); *cf. Waffle House,* 534 U.S. at 296 n. 11, 122 S.Ct. 754 ("We have generally been reluctant to approve rules that may jeopardize the EEOC's ability to investigate and select cases from a broad sample of claims.").

So it is with the Department of Labor and FLSA complaints—such complaints may not be waived with an arbitration clause because the statutory scheme is premised on an employee's willingness to come forward, in support of the public good. *See Mitchell v. Robert De Mario Jewelry, Inc.,* 361 U.S. 288, 292, 80 S.Ct. 332, 4 L.Ed.2d 323 (1960) ("Congress did not seek to secure compliance with prescribed standards [under the FLSA] through continuing detailed federal supervision or inspection of payrolls. Rather it chose to rely on information and complaints received from employees seeking to vindicate rights claimed to have been denied. Plainly, effective enforcement could thus only be expected if employees felt free to approach officials with their grievances."); *Lambert v. Ackerley,* 180 F.3d 997, 1003–04 (9th Cir.1999) (en banc) (explaining the importance of the FLSA's scheme of individual complaints by employees); *Painting & Drywall Work Pres. Fund, Inc. v. Dep't of Hous. & Urban Dev.,* 936 F.2d 1300, 1301 (D.C.Cir.1991) ("Both the Department of Labor and the Department of Housing and Urban Development ... enforce compliance with these [wage] laws. In doing so, they often rely on complaints from workers and unions.").

Even if the DRP does not preclude the Department of Labor or California Labor Commissioner from instituting independent actions, the DRP precludes any individual complaint or notification by an employee to such agencies. By not allowing employees to file or to initiate such administrative charges, the DRP is contrary to the same public policies relied upon in *Gilmer* and *Armendariz.* It follows that the same exception should apply. Therefore, the DRP's prohibition of administrative claims is void.

#### 4. *Severability*

That the arbitration agreement contains these flawed provisions does not necessarily mean that the entire DRP is substantively unconscionable. Rather, it might be possible to sever the one-year limitations provision (even though the DRP itself does not have a severability clause). ... The question is whether the offending clause or clauses are merely "collateral" to the main purpose of the arbitration agreement, or whether the DRP is "permeated" by unconscionability. *Armendariz,* 99 Cal.Rptr.2d 745, 6 P.3d at 696. * * * Despite a "liberal federal policy favoring arbitration agreements," *Moses H. Cone Memorial Hospital,* 460 U.S. at 24, 103 S.Ct. 927, a court cannot rewrite the arbitration agreement for the parties.

Given the scope of procedural and substantive unconscionability, the DRP is unenforceable. * * *

## CONCLUSION

The arbitration agreement is unconscionable under California law. We reverse and remand for proceedings not inconsistent with this opinion.

*Whole DRP is /onl-* [handwritten margin note]

### NOTES AND QUESTIONS

1. *Some aspects of a uniform law of employee arbitration.* The FAA requires a "written provision" in a contract. By its terms, it does not require that the employee sign the contract; but to be bound as a matter of contract there must be acceptance and consideration. If an employee is given an employer's "Rules of Arbitration," widely circulated and explained to the workforce, is directed to sign, refuses to do but continues to work, is the employee bound by it as a matter of contract? The Texas Supreme Court held he was. Dillard Dept. Stores, Inc., 198 S.W.3d 778 (Tex. 2006). Would the employer's declination to exercise its power to discharge an at-will employee who refused to opt in to the employer's arbitration scheme evidence an agreement to exempt the employee? Would that be a question of fact for a jury?

2. Does an employer's reservation of power to modify or revoke its arbitration system render the contract illusory? Several jurisdictions, including Texas, hold that it does. *J.M. Davidson, Inc. v. Webster*, 128 S.W.3d 223, 230 n.2 (Tex. 2003) (reviewing the caselaw). Why? And if so, would that not be so of all other policies contained in a handbook in which the employer has reserved a power to amend or abrogate?

3. If an employee reviews an Employee Handbook that sets out the company's arbitration plan early on in a lengthy document but which is not otherwise conspicuously identified, the terms of which company policies are generally explained, and he signs in acknowledgement at the Handbook's close, has the employee assented? *Compare Douglass v. Pflueger Hawaii, Inc.*, 110 Hawai'i 520, 135 P.3d 129 (2006) *with Morales v. Sun Constructors, Inc.*, 541 F.3d 218 (3rd Cir. 2008). What if the Handbook is in English, which the employee cannot read? *Morales, id.*

4. The California approach requires both procedural and substantive unconscionability. May the provision be procedurally conscionable whilst being substantively *un*conscionable? *Adler v. Fred Lind Manor*, 153 Wash.2d 331, 103 P.3d 773 (2004).

5. In California, a contract providing for arbitration of statutory claims is procedurally unconscionable if the employee cannot opt out, if it is "take it or leave it." In Tennessee, the employee must be " 'unable to find suitable employment'," *Seawright v. American Gen. Fin. Servs.*, 507 F.3d 967, 976 (6th Cir. 2007)—the very test rejected in California. Which is the better view?

6. Under the National Labor Relations Act (NLRA), an employee has a statutory right to talk to coworkers and customers about his or her work-related problems in an effort to enlist support—to engage in concerted activity

for mutual aid or protection. On its face, the confidentiality agreement would seem to violate the Act. Why was the NLRA never mentioned?

7. *More from the Supreme Court.* What if an employer's arbitration policy expressly reserves the question of unconscionability for the arbitrator to decide? The issue was decided, by vote of 5–4, in *Rent–A–Center, West v. Jackson*, 130 S.Ct. 2772, 78 USLW 4643 (2010). The employee had filed an employment discrimination suit against his employer and opposed arbitration on the ground that the arbitration provision was unconscionable but the question of unconscionability was delegated by the contract to the arbitrator. The Court had established that a challenge to the validity of the contract as a whole should be decided by the arbitrator but that a challenge to the agreement to arbitrate was reserved by the Federal Arbitration Act for judicial disposition. The *Rent–A–Center* majority, in an opinion written by Justice Scalia, held that a challenge to the enforceability of the arbitration agreement *as a whole* could be delegated to the arbitrator. Only a challenge directed to the delegation clause alone—giving jurisdiction to the arbitrator to decide unconscionability—could not be delegated: that question would have to be decided judicially if properly raised. (This distinction, which did not appear in the case law, was not argued to by any party or amicus in the case.) As Justice Stevens wrote for the dissenters:

> A claim that an *entire* arbitration agreement is invalid will not go to the court unless the party challenges the *particular sentences* that delegate such claims to the arbitrator, on some contract ground that is particular and unique to those sentences.

*Id.*, Stevens, J., dissenting (emphasis in original). In other words, a challenge that arbitration was unconscionable because of inadequate provision for discovery, excessive costs, lack of neutrality, or the like could be delegated to the arbitrator. What would an employee have to plead and prove about the delegation, and only the delegation, not implicating the larger features of the arbitration system, that would require a judicial determination of unconscionability?

8. May an arbitration provision require the employee to forego bringing or participating in a class arbitration? That issue will be taken up by the Supreme Court in *AT&T Mobility LLC v. Concepcion*, 130 S.Ct. 3322 (cert. granted May 24, 2010). *See also* Question 6, *supra*.

9. Section 7 of the National Labor Relations Act protects employee engagement in "concerted activity for mutual aid or protection." Such activity can involve collective resort to legal for a from the protection or advancement of the workers' interests as workers. Individual employment contracts may not be conditional on the waiver of § 7 rights. Would the waiver of class arbitration participation contained in an employer's arbitration policy violate the Labor Act? *See* NLRB General Counsel Memorandum 10–09 (June 16, 2010).

10. *The Rise of Employer–Sponsored Grievance and Arbitration Procedures:* Prior to the Supreme Court's decisions in *Gilmer* and *Circuit City*, most employers assumed that individual agreements to arbitrate employment disputes were unenforceable. As a result, such agreements were rare, covering less than 2% of the nonunion workforce. Peter Feuille & Denise R. Chachere,

*Looking Fair or Being Fair: Remedial Voice Procedure in Nonunion Work-places*, 21 J. MGMT. 27 (1995). Since the Court's decisions in *Gilmer* and *Circuit City*, employers have taken much greater interest in such agreements. Although no comprehensive survey exists, reliable estimates suggest that the percent of nonunion workplaces that employ grievance procedures that result in arbitration grew to about 10% in 1995, 16% in 1998, and currently is approximately 19%. Kenneth G. Dau–Schmidt and Timothy A. Haley, *Governance of the Workplace: the Contemporary Regime of Individual Contract*, 28 COMP. LAB. L. & POL'Y J. 313, 327–28 (2007). Moreover, it has been estimated that over 50% of the nonunion workforce currently has access to some form of dispute resolution procedure including mediation, ombudsmen, and/or arbitration. David Lewin, *Grievance Procedures in Nonunion Workplaces: Empirical Analysis of Usage, Dynamics, and Outcomes*, 66 CHI.-KENT L. REV. 823 (1990); HOYT N. WHEELER, BRIAN S. KLAAS & DOUGLAS M. MAHONY, WORKPLACE JUSTICE WITHOUT UNIONS 16–17 (2004). In comparison, 99% of collective bargaining agreements contain arbitration agreements. BNA, BASIC PATTERNS IN UNION CONTRACTS 7 (1995).

There are several reasons for employers' interest in sponsoring grievance procedures. The primary reason is concern about the costs of employment litigation. Katherine Stone has identified the increased number and costliness of discrimination suits in the 1990s as the driving factor, while Wheeler, Klass, and Mahoney would also cite employer concern over potential liability for wrongful discharge and breach of contract suits. Katherine Van Wetzel Stone, *Employment Arbitration Under the Federal Arbitration Act*, in EMPLOYMENT DISPUTE RESOLUTION AND WORKERS RIGHTS 27, 37 (ADRIENNE E. EATON & JEFFERY H. KEEFE EDS., 1999); HOYT N. WHEELER, BRIAN S. KLAAS & DOUGLAS M. MAHONY, WORKPLACE JUSTICE WITHOUT UNIONS 16–19 (2004). A secondary reason is the desire of employers to avoid employee organization by aping union communication and grievance procedures. In a national survey of 36 nonunion employers with grievance and arbitration procedures, Bickner, Ver Ploeg, and Feigenbaum found that 75% had adopted the procedures due to concerns over litigation costs, while 10% cited union avoidance as a motivating factor. Mei L. Bickner, Christine Ver Ploeg & Charles Feigenbaum, *Developments in Employment Arbitration*, 52 DISP. RES. J. 8, 78–83 (1997). In a survey of 3002 firms, Colvin found that both institutional factors, such as litigation costs, and human resource strategies, such as union avoidance, commonly contribute to employer decisions to adopt grievance and arbitration procedures. Alexander J.S. Colvin, *Institutional Pressures, Human Resource Strategies, and the Rise of Nonunion Dispute Resolution Procedures*, 56 INDUS. & LAB. REL. REV. 375 (2003).

11.  *Concerns About Employer–Sponsored Grievance and Arbitration Procedures:* The growth of employer sponsored individual grievance procedures resulting in binding arbitration has been a matter of some controversy in the legal literature. Critics have set forth a number of important criticisms particularly as it relates to arbitration of issues of individual rights under statutory law. First, arbitration often limits or eliminates important procedural protections. Arbitrators may not be expert in the area of law in question and generally do not follow the federal rules of evidence or procedure. The employer's grievance procedure may try to set a shorter time limit for filing or

may provide cursory or no discovery rights. Second, arbitration procedures may not afford employees all of the remedies they would have had at law. Arbitrators cannot grant injunctions and may not be able to hear class actions or grant attorneys' fees or costs. Third, arbitration may limit or interfere with our ability to develop a precedential body of law. Arbitrators are not required to issue a written opinion or give reasons for their decisions. For this reason, the EEOC, Department of Labor, and the NLRB have all, at various times, taken positions against pre-dispute agreements to arbitrate individual legal controversies. Fourth, employees are often asked to share in the costs of employing an arbitrator, and it is feared that this will unjustly discourage employee grievances. In union arbitration the union pays the employee's share while in administrative and court proceedings, the taxpayer foots the bill.

More generally, it is argued that, because of the asymmetry of the employment relationship, employers have unfair advantages in individual arbitrations that they don't enjoy in union arbitrations. As Malin has pointed out, individual agreements to arbitrate don't come from bargained for exchange, but instead are unilaterally imposed by the employer. Martin H. Malin, *Privatizing Justice—But By How Much? Questions that* Gilmer *Did Not Answer*, 16 OHIO ST. J. DISP. RES. 589 (2001). It is feared that the employer will use its unilateral power to impose arbitration procedures that are unfair or to select a biased arbitrator, and that fear has borne fruit in more than a few cases. See, e.g., *Hooters of America, Inc. v. Phillips*, 173 F.3d 933 (4th Cir. 1999) in which the Fourth Circuit found that the employer sponsored arbitration plan was a "sham system" "utterly lacking in the rudiments of even-handedness." Id. at 940. The unilateral nature of the agreement also raises serious questions about the effectiveness of the employee's waiver of the right to a jury trial. Even absent express bias, it is worried that arbitrators may cater to employer interests in order to secure future business. Arbitrators know that their being selected for future work will more likely depend on the employer's satisfaction in the case than on the satisfaction of an employee they will likely never see again. Bingham has also argued that the employer has the advantage of experience and the incentive of precedent as a "repeat player" in individual arbitration. Lisa B. Bingham, *Employment Arbitration: The Repeat Player Effect*, 1 EMP. RTS. & EMP. POL'Y J. 187 (1997), though more recent studies find the effect more tenuous or indiscernible. Under union arbitration, both sides to the dispute are repeat players with experience and interest in precedent.

Supporters of individual agreements to arbitrate counter with arguments of their own. Proponents contend that individual arbitration enjoys many of the same advantages as union arbitration. It is faster, less divisive and cheaper than litigation. RICHARD A. BALES, COMPULSORY ARBITRATION: THE GRAND EXPERIMENT IN EMPLOYMENT 9 (1997). The ease of arbitration makes grievance adjustment more accessible to employees. As a result, workers will be able to address more of their grievances than if they were left merely to litigate their disputes. Samuel Estreicher, *Predispute Agreements to Arbitrate Statutory Employment Claims*, 72 N.Y.U. L. REV. 1344 (1997). Supporters contend that individual employment arbitration can be fair if it complies with certain minimal procedural safeguards. Indeed, in *Cole v. Burns International Securi-*

*ty Services*, 105 F.3d 1465 (D.C. Cir. 1997) the Court of Appeals for the D.C. Circuit, in an opinion by Judge Harry Edwards, interpreted *Gilmer* to require five safeguards for any pre-dispute employment arbitration clause to be enforceable: a neutral arbitrator, opportunity for discovery, a written award, the availability of all remedies available at law, and no arbitrators' fee for the employee. Other courts and professional organizations have followed suit. Some also contest whether employers really enjoy advantages in individual arbitration. They point out that employers generally do better in litigation than in nonunion arbitration. Michael Z. Green, *Debunking the Myth of Employer Advantage from Using Mandatory Arbitration in Discrimination Claims*, 31 RUTGERS L.J. 399 (2000). For example, employers frequently prevail in litigation via summary judgment; summary judgment is rare in arbitration. Finally, supporters of nonunion arbitration pose a public policy argument stating that employment arbitration eases the caseload of our over-worked courts.

12. *Empirical Tests of the Efficacy and Fairness of Employer–Sponsored Grievance and Arbitration Procedures Relative to Litigation:* To empirically assess the efficacy and fairness of individual grievance arbitration relative to litigation is more difficult than one might initially suppose. With a few exceptions, empirical analyses have found that individual employees win individual grievances in greater proportion (52–62%) than they lose them (48–38%) and in about the same proportion as they win under state court adjudication and in greater proportion than they win in federal court. Unfortunately it is hard to infer much about the equity of an adjudicative process just by looking at won/loss rates. An employee's decision to take a claim to arbitration or trial, or even to file a grievance or suit, undoubtedly depends on the employee's assessment of the fairness of that procedure and his or her chances of winning. Similarly, an employer's decision to take a case to arbitration or trial depends on the employer's assessment of its chance of winning. Many arbitration agreements are part of a more comprehensive dispute resolution process that makes it easy for an employer to identify (and settle) the cases it likely would lose in arbitration; the prevalence of summary judgment in federal courts similarly skews the win/loss rates in that form. If the employee knows a process is unfair, he or she will grieve and arbitrate or file and try only the disputes where the employee's case is so strong that he or she has a reasonable chance of prevailing even under the biased procedure. Moreover, where only one party, here the employer, is a "repeat-player," with an interest in precedent because they will likely litigate similar cases in the future, one would expect that party to litigate worse cases on the off chance they will win, and thus have a worse won/loss ratio. Kenneth G. Dau–Schmidt and Timothy A. Haley, *Governance of the Workplace: the Contemporary Regime of Individual Contract*, 28 COMP. LAB. L. & POL'Y J. 313, 332–35 (2007).

Short of sampling all possible disputes as a comprehensive method of comparing the different methods of adjudication, there are a few ways scholars have attempted to deal with the problem of different filing and settlement rates between employees and employers. One method is to directly assess parties' perceptions of whether an adjudicative process is fair. In perhaps the best study to date using this methodology, Wheeler, Klaas, and Mahoney found that arbitrators perceive that individual arbitration serves employer interests better than employee interests with respect to all of the examined types of cases. HOYT N. WHEELER, BRIAN S. KLAAS & DOUGLAS M. MAHONY, WORKPLACE JUSTICE WITHOUT UNIONS 57 (2004). Another method to address the problem is to try to control for other variables and examine just the decisionmaking processes of arbitrators and judges by posing hypothetical cases to them and comparing the results. Bingham and Mesch conducted a study using this method and examining decisions from 743 subjects including traditional labor arbitrators, arbitrators for individual employment arbitration agreements, and law students. Bingham and Mesch found that "employment arbitrators" for individual agreements to arbitrate were less likely to grant reinstatement than either traditional labor arbitrators or law students, although when the analysis controlled for variables such as the profession of the arbitrator, no significant difference was observed. Lisa B. Bingham & Debra J. Mesch, *Decision Making in Employment and Labor Arbitration*, 39 INDUS. REL. 671 (2000).

The different methods of adjudication of workplace disputes have different costs and rewards. As previously discussed, the different costs to the employee of access to individual arbitration and litigation raises concerns about the equity of the process. Arbitrators charge about $2,000 a day for their services, while judges' salaries are paid by the taxpayers. Filing fees can also be higher for arbitrators, at about $500 plus $150 per day of hearing for the AAA. Court filing fees are generally between $100 to $200. However, arbitration appears to enjoy an advantage over litigation with respect to attorney's fees. In 1995, Howard estimated that the average cost of defending an arbitration was $20,000, while the average cost of defending an employment claim in court was $96,000. William M. Howard, *Arbitrating Claims of Employment Discrimination*, 50 DIS. RESOL. J. 40 (1995). Claimants' costs for representation are probably proportional, but less, and of course claimants' enjoy the advantage of contingent fees. Arbitration also seems to enjoy an advantage in the time necessary for determination of a case, taking on average half the time of litigation's average 12–18 months. WHEELER, KLAAS & MAHONY, *supra*, at 60. However, litigation seems to enjoy a distinct advantage with respect to the amounts that aggrieved employees recover upon final adjudication. The median nonunion arbitration award during the 1990s has been estimated at between $34,733 and $52,737, Samuel Estreicher, *Predispute Agreements to Arbitrate Statutory Employment Claims*, 72 N.Y.U. L. REV. 1344 (1997), while the median award for successful employment discrimination suits during the same time has been estimated at between $611,756 and $2,134,751. WHEELER, KLAAS & MAHONY, *supra*, at 57. A study of wrongful discharge cases in California for the years 1978–1987 found that employees won a median award of $124,150. David J. Jung & Richard Harkness, *The Facts of Wrongful Discharge*, 4 LAB. LAW. 257 (1988).

13.   The advent of mandatory arbitration has resulted in a substantial body of legal literature, reviewed by Richard Bales, *Normative Consideration of Employment Arbitration at* Gilmer's Quiñceanera, 81 TULANE L. REV. 331 (2006). The most prominent proponent of privatization of public law disputes is Samuel Estreicher, who represented Circuit City before the U.S. Supreme Court. Samuel Estreicher, *Saturns for Rickshaws: The Stakes in the Debate*

*over Predispute Employment Arbitration Agreements*, 16 OHIO ST. J. DISP. RESOL. 559 (2001). The most trenchant critic is Clyde Summers, *Mandatory Arbitration: Privatizing Public Rights, Compelling the Unwilling to Arbitrate*, 6 U. PA. J. LAB. & EMP. L. 5 (2004). Some effort at empirical research has been undertaken to find out whether the results of these systems differ from what the courts produce. The state of the empirical work has been summarized by Alexander Colvin, *Empirical Research on Employment Arbitration: Clarity Amidst Sound and Fury?*, 11 EMP. RTS. & EMP. POL'Y J. 405 (2007); and been made subject of stringent criticism by David Schwartz, *Mandatory Arbitration and Fairness*, 84 NOTRE DAME L. REV. 1247 (2009).

14. An "Arbitration Fairness Act" has been introduced in the U.S. Senate. It would render unenforceable boilerplate provisions to arbitrate future employment disputes. Would you endorse or oppose that legislation?

## F.  EMPLOYEES PARTICIPATION IN DE-TERMINING TERMS AND CONDI-TIONS OF EMPLOYMENT

This Chapter opened with a discussion of the labor market as the mediator of employer policies on wages and working conditions: the market aggregates employee preferences that, as expressed in the aggregate, induces employers to respond depending on the degree of monopsonistic power they enjoy. But as Martin Bronfenbrenner's observation of a half century ago noted, employer power is exercised "within limits which are sometimes wide." The responsiveness of employee policies to market conditions can be illustrated in the prevalence of drug testing conducted on incumbent employees: based on American Management Association data, random drug testing of incumbent workers fell from being deployed by about 70 percent of employers surveyed in 1996 to 47 percent in 2000. One explanation is that, faced with an extraordinarily tight labor market, faced, that is, with high recruitment costs for replacement, 23 percent of employers were much less eager in the late 1990s to find out what metabolites were in their employees' systems than they had been some years earlier. However influential market forces may be in the long run, in the short run they afford scant protection for the individual. In this case, an employee conscientiously opposed to being required to submit to suspicion-less drug testing, say, an employee of years of altogether satisfactory service faced with a newly instituted policy, would have to hope that the forces of demand and supply—on the former, to the robustness of the economy, on the latter, to conscription, the plague, and contraceptive decisions made in millions of bedrooms a generation before—will moderate the employer's insistence on submission. Consequently, the question that presses to the fore is whether, in lieu of acquiescence, willing or grudging, or quitting the job, a mechanism that will give employees a voice in framing the policies that govern them, their "public goods," is available.

# E.I. DU PONT DE NEMOURS & CO.

National Labor Relations Board, 1993
311 NLRB 893

[Section 8(a)(2) of the National Labor Relations Act forbids employers from dominating or interfering in the formation or administration of a statutory "labor organization" or to contribute financial or other support to it. Section 2(5) of the Act defines a "labor organization" as

> any organization of any kind, or any agency or employee representation committee or plan, in which employees participate and which exists for the purpose, in whole or in part, of dealing with employers concerning grievances, labor disputes, wages, rates of pay, hours of employment, or conditions of work.

An issue considered by the National Labor Relations Board in this case was whether six safety committees and one fitness committee were employer-dominated labor organizations. The Board held they were and ordered the employer to stop dealing with them or any successor to them. The Board's reasoning follows.] * * *

### 1.   Labor organization status under Section 2(5) of the Act

The threshold question for a determination of whether an employer has violated Section 8(a)(2) is whether the entity involved is a labor organization. Under the statutory definition set forth in Section 2(5), the entity is a labor organization if (1) employees participate, (2) the organization exists, at least in part, for the purpose of "dealing with" employers, and (3) these dealings concern "conditions of work," grievances, labor disputes, wages, rates of pay, or hours of employment. There is no question that each committee at issue herein is an organization in which employees participate. In addition, the committees discuss subjects such as safety, incentive awards for safety, or benefits such as employee picnic areas and jogging tracks. These subjects fall within the categories of subjects listed in Section 2(5). The committees, therefore, meet the first and third requirements for labor organization status. We turn now to the second requirement.

### The Limits of "dealing with"

The principal issue is whether the committees exist for the purpose, at least in part, of "dealing with" the employer on statutory subjects. The Supreme Court held in *NLRB v. Cabot Carbon Co.*[9] that the term "dealing with" in Section 2(5) is broader than the term "collective bargaining." The term "bargaining" connotes a process by which two parties must seek to compromise their differences and arrive at an agreement. By contrast, the concept of "dealing" does not require that the two sides seek to compromise their differences. It involves only a bilateral mechanism

---

**9.**   360 U.S. 203 (1959).

between two parties. That "bilateral mechanism" ordinarily entails a pattern or practice in which a group of employees, over time, makes proposals to management, management responds to these proposals by acceptance or rejection by word or deed, and compromise is not required. If the evidence establishes such a pattern or practice, or that the group exists for a purpose of following such a pattern or practice, the element of dealing is present. However, if there are only isolated instances in which the group makes ad hoc proposals to management followed by a management response of acceptance or rejection by word or deed, the element of dealing is missing.

Just as there is a distinction between "bargaining" and "dealing," there is a distinction between "dealing" and no "dealing" (and a fortiori no "bargaining"). For example, a "brainstorming" group is not ordinarily engaged in dealing. The purpose of such a group is simply to develop a whole host of ideas. Management may glean some ideas from this process, and indeed may adopt some of them. If the group makes no proposals, the "brainstorming" session is not dealing and is therefore not a labor organization.

Similarly, if the committee exists for the purpose of sharing information with the employer, the committee would not ordinarily be a labor organization. That is, if the committee makes no proposals to the employer, and the employer simply gathers the information and does what it wishes with such information, the element of dealing is missing, and the committee would not be a labor organization.

Likewise, under a "suggestion box" procedure where employees make specific proposals to management, there is no dealing because the proposals are made individually and not as a group.

The committees at issue here do not fall within any of these safe havens. They involve group action and not individual communication. They made proposals and management responded by word or deed. The committees made proposals to management representatives in different ways.

Some of the committees submitted proposals, concerning safety and fitness or recreational matters, to representatives of management outside the committees. Management representatives responded to these proposals. For example, the Antiknocks Committee proposed to various supervisors and managers that safety problems be corrected, and the managers responded to these proposals. The Fitness Committee proposed to higher management that tennis courts and a pavilion be constructed, and management rejected this proposal on the ground that it was too costly at the time. This activity between committees and management is virtually identical to that found to be "dealing" in *Cabot Carbon*.

All the committees discussed proposals with management representatives inside the committees. Each committee has management representatives who are full participating members. These representatives interact with employee committee-members under the rules of consensus decisionmaking as defined in the Respondent's Personal Effectiveness Process handbook. The handbook states: "consensus is reached when all members of the group, including its leader, are willing to accept a decision." Under this style of operation, the management members of the committees discuss proposals with ... employee members and have the power to reject any proposal. Clearly, if management members *outside* the committee had that power, there would be "dealing" between the employee committee and management. In our view, the fact that the management persons are on the committee is only a difference of form; it is not a difference of substance. As a practical matter, if management representatives can reject employee proposals, it makes no real difference whether they do so from inside or outside the committee. In circumstances where management members of the committee discuss proposals with employee members and have the power to reject any proposal, we find that there is "dealing" within the meaning of Section 2(5).

The mere presence, however, of management members on a committee would not necessarily result in a finding that the committee deals with the employer within the meaning of Section 2(5). For example, there would be no "dealing with" management if the committee were governed by majority decision-making, management representatives were in the minority, and the committee had the power to decide matters for itself, rather than simply make proposals to management. Similarly, there would be no "dealing" if management representatives participated on the committee as observers or facilitators without the right to vote on committee proposals. * * *

### 2.    Domination of the administration and/or formation of the committees

The structural operations of the committees warrant the finding that the Respondent dominated the administration of the committees. As discussed above, the Respondent ultimately retains veto power over any action the committee may wish to take. This power exists by virtue of the management members' participation in consensus decision-making. The committee can do nothing in the face of management members' opposition. In addition, the record shows that in each committee, a management member serves as either the leader or the "resource" (monitor or advisor) and therefore has a key role in establishing the agenda for each meeting and in conducting the meeting.[15]

The Respondent also controls such matters as how many employees may serve on each committee. In addition, the Respondent determines which employee volunteers will be selected in the event that the number of volunteers exceeds the number of seats designated for employees on the committees. [E]mployees had no independent voice in determining any

---

**15.** The committees operated under the Personal Effectiveness Process (PEP). The Respondent's PEP handbook indicates that each committee has a leader, a resource, and a scribe (note taker) who confer before each meeting and determine the agenda. The leader and the resource chair the meeting and keep it "on track." After the meeting, the leader, resource, and scribe evaluate the meeting and discuss how to improve the next meeting.

aspect of the composition, structure, or operation of the committees. In fact, as the record demonstrates, the Respondent can change or abolish any of the committees at will. In our view, all of these factors, taken together, establish that the Respondent dominated the administration of the committees. * * *

[In Crown Cork & Seal Co., 334 NLRB No. 92 (2001), the National Labor Relations Board held the company's "Socio–Tech System" of management, delegating to worker-management teams and committees the responsibility for production, training, product quality, attendance, safety, maintenance and discipline (short of suspension and discharge), did not implicate section 8(a)(2). These bodies were not labor organizations: They had decisional or effective recommendatory authority in the areas of their purview; they did not "deal with" management—they *were* management. The Board noted, however, that the General Counsel had not contended that the course of "dealing" occurred within the committees.]

## NOTES AND QUESTIONS

1.  Professor Michael LeRoy has criticized the role of § 8(a)(2) in the modern workplace. Suppose, he writes,

> [a]n employer wants to accommodate working parents by allowing more flexible scheduling. However, the employer does not know which employees want a more flexible schedule or how to make a series of flexible schedules to fit the organization's daily work requirements. A committee of employees and managers is formed [by management] and charged to discuss the matter with coworkers and develop a new scheduling plan. The committee eventually produces a plan that the employer considers and implements with some modifications.

Michael H. LeRoy, *Employee Participation in the New Millennium: Redefining a Labor Organization Under Section 8(a)(2) of the NLRA*, 72 S. CAL. L. REV. 1651, 1657 (1999). Would this violate federal law? He concludes that it would and from this he calls for legal change. Should the law be more accommodating in this scenario? One way to analyze that question is to explore not what § 8(a)(2) prohibits but that it allows: could the employer survey the employees about their preferences? Could the employer give work groups the power to set their schedules, subject only to the work being done? Could the employer have asked the workers to form a committee of their own choosing under rules of their own devising with which it could deal at arms-length as an independent body? Clyde Summers, *Effective Remedies for Employment Rights: Preliminary Guidelines and Proposals*, 141 U. PA. L. REV. 457 (1992). If so, why don't employers do this?

2.  Survey data indicate that in 2005 (the latest year available) a majority of American workers wished to be represented by unions whereas union density in the private sector is currently well below 8%. RICHARD B. FREEMAN & JOEL ROGERS, WHAT WORKERS WANT (updated ed. 2006). If employee voice is good for workplace efficiency—as a more effective way of dealing with the public goods aspect of employer policies than market mediation—why don't U.S.

employers respond to this demand by signaling their willingness to deal with representatives of their employees' own choosing?

3.   In 1990, Professor Paul Weiler recommended that the United States adopt a statutory requirement of worker-elected bodies with which employers had to share information and consult over employment related policies modeled on the German system of works councils. PAUL WEILER, GOVERNING THE WORKPLACE 283–95 (1990). That proposal has been echoed more recently. STEPHEN BEFORT & JOHN BUDD, INVISIBLE HANDS, INVISIBLE OBJECTIVES: BRINGING WORKPLACE LAW AND PUBLIC POLICY INTO FOCUS 181–88 (2009). Is that model translatable into the United States? Professor Estlund argues that as the proposal has no political support it is a " 'pleasant pipe dream'." CYNTHIA ESTLUND, REGOVERNING THE WORKPLACE 172 (2010).

# Chapter IV

# Termination of Employment: A Century After the Apotheosis of *Laissez-Faire*

■ ■ ■

It is well to reflect on the trajectory of the law of employment termination, of the extent to which the employer's behavior is subject to judicial oversight today. In the common law of master and servant the employer's policies or orders occasioning the discharge had to be lawful and reasonable. As the common law of status, of master and servant, was eclipsed by *laissez-faire*, by the market autonomy theory of "free" labor in the period of industrialization following the Civil War, the assumption of fixed duration gave way to the at-will rule, and that rule took on an ideological content that transcended the mere lack of specific duration, that is, that the law should stay out altogether. This was the ground of dispute between the majority and dissent in the *Payne* case. The rule, as it came commonly to be stated even well after the turn of the 20th century, was that an at-will employee could be discharged for no reason, for any reason, even for a morally opprobrious reason. Today the courts more commonly recast the rule as allowing the employers to dismiss for no reason or for any *lawful* reason, *i.e.*, without having to prove cause but often omitting the allowance of morally—and so potentially legally—opprobrious action. *E.g.*, *Theisen v. Covenant Med. Ctr., Inc.*, 636 N.W.2d 74, 79 (Iowa 2001): "The doctrine of employment-at-will, well established in Iowa law, permits an employer ... who is not under contract to terminate employment at any time for any lawful reason." Consequently, what follows is a snapshot of a body of law much in flux, as evidenced in the case set out below.

## A.  THE TENACITY—OR TENUOUSNESS— OF THE AT–WILL RULE

### WISEHART v. MEGANCK

Colorado Court of Appeals, 2002
66 P.3d 124

Opinion by Judge Casebolt.

In this civil case arising from termination of an employment relationship, plaintiff, Larry N. Wisehart, appeals the summary judgment in favor of defendants, Vectra Bank Colorado, NA and Michael Meganck, dismissing his claims for fraudulent misrepresentation and concealment. We affirm.

Plaintiff worked for the bank as a loan officer in an at-will relationship. Bank policy required him to obtain the approval of other bank officers when processing certain loans. While the bank's loan policy required written approval of the officers to be obtained before any closing, in practice the approvals were sometimes obtained afterwards.

On the day before the scheduled closing of a particular loan, plaintiff met with a senior loan officer to obtain his approval. That officer told plaintiff that he needed more detailed information regarding the loan and requested plaintiff to provide it. When plaintiff returned with the requested information later that afternoon, the officer had departed and could not be located.

Following the meeting with plaintiff, and without receiving the requested information, the officer informed another bank employee that he was not going to approve the loan. Nevertheless, in fact, neither the officer nor the bank had any objection to the loan.

Plaintiff's superiors knew the loan closing date well in advance and specifically were aware on the date of the closing that plaintiff intended to proceed with it. Despite opportunities to do so, no one informed plaintiff that the bank officer did not intend to give his approval.

While plaintiff was attending the closing the next day in another city, the bank issued his final paycheck in anticipation of termination. When plaintiff returned to the bank, Meganck, one of his supervisors, informed him that he was being terminated for failing to obtain the required written approvals before closing.

Plaintiff then initiated this action asserting claims for fraudulent misrepresentation and concealment against the bank and Meganck, essentially alleging that defendants had fraudulently set him up to be terminated. Plaintiff further alleged that the bank's stated reason for termination masked a plan to replace employees like himself who had been long-term employees of another financial institution that had merged with the bank.

Contending that Colorado does not recognize a claim of fraud in the employment at will context, defendants filed a motion for summary judgment. The trial court held, *inter alia*, that plaintiff's claims, even though couched in terms of fraud, essentially asserted a claim for wrongful termination, and the fact that his termination was achieved through fraud did not change the true nature of the claims. The court concluded that, even though defendants may have created a reason to terminate plaintiff's employment, that action did not give rise to a claim because defendants were free to terminate him without any reason whatsoever. Hence, the court dismissed plaintiff's claims, and this appeal followed.

*Still at will*

## I.

\* \* \*

### A.

In Colorado, an agreement of employment that is for an indefinite term is presumed to be at will. Either the employer or the employee may terminate at-will employment at any time with or without cause, and such termination generally does not give rise to a claim for relief. *Martin Marietta Corp. v. Lorenz,* 823 P.2d 100 (Colo.1992); *Continental Air Lines, Inc. v. Keenan,* 731 P.2d 708 (Colo.1987).

The at-will nature of the employment relationship reflects a matter of public policy. *Crawford Rehabilitation Services v. Weissman,* 938 P.2d 540 (Colo.1997). The at-will employment doctrine promotes flexibility and discretion for employees to seek the best position to suit their talents and for employers to seek the best employees to suit their needs. By removing encumbrances to quitting a job or firing an employee, the at-will doctrine promotes a free market in employment analogous to the free market in goods and services generally. *See Mackenzie v. Miller Brewing Co.,* 241 Wis.2d 700, 623 N.W.2d 739 (2001).

*Bot →* At the same time, strict application of the at-will doctrine may invite abuse and lead to injustice. Accordingly, legislation and the common law have restricted application of the at-will doctrine to balance the interests of employers and employees. *See Martin Marietta Corp. v. Lorenz, supra.* For example, certain federal and state statutes have created private claims for relief for wrongful discharge based on discrimination with respect to race, color, gender, national origin, ancestry, religious affiliation, disability, and age. State statutes also permit such claims in cases of termination resulting from an employee engaging in lawful activity off premises during nonworking hours, responding to a jury summons, and certain activities of "whistleblowing." *See Crawford Rehabilitation Services v. Weissman, supra.*

Colorado also recognizes a claim for relief for wrongful discharge in violation of public policy. This judicially crafted exception restricts an employer's right to terminate when the termination contravenes accepted and substantial public policies as embodied by legislative declarations, professional codes of ethics, or other sources. *Rocky Mountain Hospital & Medical Service v. Mariani,* 916 P.2d 519 (Colo.1996)(approving wrongful discharge claim based on accountant's refusal to violate code of profession-al conduct); *see also Martin Marietta Corp. v. Lorenz, supra* (proscribing termination for refusing to engage in illegal conduct); *Johnson v. Jefferson County Board of Health,* 662 P.2d 463 (Colo.1983)(government employer may not terminate at-will employee for exercising right of free speech); *Jones v. Stevinson's Golden Ford,* 36 P.3d 129 (Colo.App.2001)(approving wrongful discharge claim based on employee's refusal to violate Consumer Protection Act and Motor Vehicle Repair Act); *Lathrop v. Entenmann's, Inc.,* 770 P.2d 1367 (Colo.App.1989)(employer's retaliatory termination against employee for exercising right to apply for and receive workers' compensation benefits provided grounds for wrongful discharge claim).

These exceptions address societal concerns, while honoring the gener-al rule that employment affects private interests, and therefore parties generally are free to bargain for conditions of employment. *See Crawford Rehabilitation Services v. Weissman, supra* (claims that relate to a private contract or promise between an employer and an employee do not raise public policy concerns, other than the general interest society has in the integrity of the employment relationship).

Operating from the premise that parties are free to require cause for termination, Colorado also recognizes that an employer's failure to follow termination procedures contained in an employment manual can serve as the basis for a breach of contract or promissory tortuous claim. *Continen-tal Air Lines, Inc. v. Keenan, supra; see also Schoff v. Combined Insurance Co.,* 604 N.W.2d 43 (Iowa 1999); *Mackenzie v. Miller Brewing Co., supra.*

In addition, Colorado recognizes the viability of certain other tort claims that arise around the employment relationship. *See Jet Courier Service, Inc. v. Mulei,* 771 P.2d 486 (Colo.1989)(employee owes duty of loyalty to employer that prohibits soliciting employer's customers before terminating employment); *Berger v. Security Pacific Information Systems, Inc.,* 795 P.2d 1380 (Colo.App.1990)(employee induced to enter into at-will employment by employer's concealment may pursue fraud claim); *Cronk v. Intermountain Rural Electric Ass'n,* 765 P.2d 619 (Colo.App. 1988)(tortuous interference claim allowed against supervisor who induced employer to exercise its at-will termination power by presenting corrupt reason).

To summarize, employers operating under at-will employment princi-ples are generally free to discharge employees for any reason, even if that reason is wrong or incorrect, as long as the reason asserted does not trigger a recognized exception to the at-will termination doctrine noted above. Employees in such a relationship likewise may leave employment for any reason and at any time. Moreover, the presumption of at-will employment places the burden on the plaintiff to plead and prove circum-stances that would authorize application of one of the recognized excep-tions to the doctrine. *See Schur v. Storage Technology Corp.,* 878 P.2d 51 (Colo.App.1994).

Here, plaintiff's claims arise out of the termination of his at-will employment relationship under which his employer was free to terminate him any time, with or without any reason. Plaintiff's claims do not fall within any of the recognized exceptions to the doctrine of at-will employment, nor do they allege allowable theories or tort claims surrounding the employment relationship. * * *

*No basis*

Accordingly, unless there is another basis to allow a fraud claim under these circumstances, plaintiff's claims fail.

### B.

Plaintiff asserts that he is entitled to pursue claims that his termination resulted from fraudulent misrepresentation and concealment. He contends that an employer may not assert its right to terminate at will as a defense to a fraud claim. Plaintiff essentially asks us to recognize an exception to the at-will doctrine where the employer commits fraud to justify termination of an at-will employee. We decline to do so.

This is a question of first impression in Colorado. Most other courts that have considered such claims have concluded that the at-will doctrine precludes a claim for relief when fraud is the means used to effect termination. *See Salter v. Alfa Insurance Co.,* 561 So.2d 1050 (Ala.1990); *Hunter v. Up–Right, Inc.,* 6 Cal.4th 1174, 26 Cal.Rptr.2d 8, 864 P.2d 88 (1993); *Tatge v. Chambers & Owen, Inc.,* 219 Wis.2d 99, 579 N.W.2d 217 (1998); *see also Mackenzie v. Miller Brewing Co., supra* (*Tatge* holding equally applicable to intentional and negligent misrepresentation claims). *But cf. Mueller v. Union Pacific R.R.,* 220 Neb. 742, 371 N.W.2d 732 (1985).

*Salter v. Alfa Insurance Co., supra,* involved claims factually and legally similar to plaintiff's claims. In *Salter,* an insurance company instructed its agent not to investigate a particular claim. The agent complied with that instruction, but was subsequently terminated because she had failed to follow company policy requiring agents to cooperate with claims investigation. The court, noting that it did not sanction the insurance company's conduct, nevertheless recognized that the at-will doctrine permits termination for any reason, which necessarily includes grounds that are malicious or otherwise improper. The court therefore concluded that the agent's fraud claim failed as a matter of law. In its holding, the court recognized that the law will not punish a party for doing by misdirection that which it has a right to do forthrightly. *Salter v. Alfa Insurance Co., supra; see also Hunter v. Up–Right, Inc., supra.*

Here, while we likewise do not condone the bank's conduct, we find no basis to depart from the general rule that either party to an at-will employment contract may terminate the relationship for *any* reason, even if wrong, without giving rise to liability. *See Martin Marietta Corp. v. Lorenz, supra; Continental Air Lines, Inc. v. Keenan, supra.* Unless the plaintiff pleads and proves a recognized exception to the at-will employment doctrine, *see Schur v. Storage Technology Corp., supra,* the doctrine restrains courts from inquiring into the basis for termination and advances the value of a free market in employment for which the parties bargained.

We therefore decline to recognize an exception to the at-will employment doctrine for claims in which a fraud is employed to justify the termination of an at-will employment relationship. Plaintiffs' claims against the bank and Meganck therefore fail as a matter of law. *See Mackenzie v. Miller Brewing Co., supra* (at-will employment doctrine precludes recognition of fraud claims against both employer and supervisor). * * *

## II.

Plaintiff nevertheless contends that the bank, in its role as an employer, entered into a confidential relationship with him that gave rise to a duty to communicate honestly and openly regarding termination. We disagree.

*No reqd honesty*

The existence of a special relationship between contracting parties may trigger a tort duty of care in addition to duties arising from the contract. *See Town of Alma v. Azco Construction, Inc.,* 10 P.3d 1256 (Colo.2000)(recognizing special relationship giving rise to tort duty of care between attorney and client, physician and patient, and insurer and insured).

However, a special relationship that would give rise to a tort duty of honesty and disclosure is not recognized in the usual employment relationship. *See Decker v. Browning–Ferris Industries,* 931 P.2d 436 (Colo. 1997)(rejecting analogy of employer-employee relationship to that of insurer-insured); *see also Foley v. Interactive Data Corp.,* 47 Cal.3d 654, 254 Cal.Rptr. 211, 765 P.2d 373 (1988). *But cf. Jet Courier Service, Inc. v. Mulei, supra.*

*No Tort duty*

Here, the record does not suggest any departure from the usual employment relationship or any basis for a confidential relationship during plaintiff's tenure with the bank. Accordingly, we conclude the bank did not owe plaintiff a tort duty of honesty and disclosure relating to his at-will termination.

## III.

Plaintiff contends that, because the bank ostensibly terminated him for violating bank policy, and the bank has consistently maintained that his termination was for cause, we should review whether that cause was just. Essentially, he asks us to conclude that, although the bank had the right to terminate him with or without cause and for any reason, the fact that it claimed to have terminated him with cause and for a specific reason transformed the employment relationship from at will to one in which he could only be terminated for good cause. We reject this contention.

Any claim for relief arising because the bank terminated plaintiff's employment without cause or a valid reason requires as a predicate an agreement between the parties that cause or a valid reason is necessary for termination. Such a claim would also necessarily sound in contract. *See Continental Air Lines, Inc. v. Keenan, supra* (employment policy termination procedures imply existence of agreement to vary at-will relationship). To permit plaintiff to inquire into the cause for his termination in the guise of a tort claim would undo the parties' essential contractual bargain that there need be no such cause. *See Town of Alma v. Azco Construction, Inc., supra* (tort action is not permitted to enforce contractual obligations); *Mackenzie v. Miller Brewing Co., supra* (rejecting fraud claim in context of at-will employment on basis that it would envelop contract law with tort law).

At-will employment confers upon employer and employee the right to terminate with cause or without cause. The fact that the party that terminates the relationship claims that it had a good reason for doing so does not alter the nature of the relationship, nor does it give rise to a claim for relief.

## IV.

Plaintiff contends that *Berger v. Security Pacific Information Systems, supra,* compels a different result. We disagree.

In *Berger,* a division of this court recognized a claim for fraudulent inducement against a former employer that had misrepresented its financial condition and business prospects to lure the plaintiff to accept an employment offer. The employer later terminated the plaintiff's employment. As the *Berger* division noted when the defendant asserted the right to terminate at will, a fraudulent inducement claim does not implicate the at-will employment doctrine. In such an instance, the fraud is not related to the at-will termination right. Rather, the fraud arises prior to employment, before the at-will relationship is formed. *See Bernoudy v. Dura–Bond Concrete Restoration,* 828 F.2d 1316 (8th Cir.1987).

Other courts permit claims of fraudulent inducement in the at-will employment context while forbidding claims of fraud used to effect an at-will termination. *See Kidder v. AmSouth Bank,* 639 So.2d 1361 (Ala.1994); *Lazar v. Superior Court,* 12 Cal.4th 631, 49 Cal.Rptr.2d 377, 909 P.2d 981 (1996); *see also Mackenzie v. Miller Brewing Co., supra* (dicta approving fraudulent inducement claim).

Accordingly, we reject this contention.

## V.

To the extent plaintiff contends that his claims do not relate to his termination, but merely seek to hold his employer liable for acts of fraud that are generally actionable, we disagree.

Plaintiff describes defendants' fraudulent statements and acts as having been taken to set him up for termination. Plaintiff further asserts that he would not have acted as he did in reliance on defendants' fraud if he had known it would lead to his termination. *See Hunter v. Up–Right, Inc., supra* (plaintiff claiming fraud as means to effect termination fails to allege detrimental reliance as a matter of law). Likewise, all plaintiff's claimed damages arise directly from termination. *See Salter v. Alfa Insurance Co., supra* (plaintiff suffers no injury as a matter of law from misrepresentation resulting in termination).

Here, plaintiff's claims definitely relate to the termination of his employment. The employer used deception to justify a termination that it was entitled to carry out without explanation or reason. Limiting our decision to these circumstances, we conclude that plaintiff may not challenge his at-will termination by asserting a fraud claim.

*Could have fired him w/o fraud*

In light of our disposition, we need not address plaintiff's remaining contentions.

The judgment is affirmed.

JUDGE WEBB dissenting.

With respect, I dissent from the holding that plaintiff's nondisclosure claim depends on a "fraud exception" to the at-will employment rule. This is not a case of an employer that passively waited until it had cause to terminate an at-will employee, whether needed or not, but instead the bank allegedly resorted to fraud by nondisclosure. I find adequate support in Colorado tort law for applying basic fraud principles to plaintiff's employment relationship, despite his at-will status.

In *Berger v. Security Pacific Information Systems, Inc.*, 795 P.2d 1380 (Colo.App.1990), a division of this court upheld the fraud claim of an employee who relied on the employer's concealment of a fact that cast doubt on the longevity of their at-will relationship, without purporting to create an exception to the at-will employment rule. Both the claim in *Berger* and plaintiff's claim here share the fact that the employees suffered injury from the fraud when the employers terminated them for tainted reasons, rather than merely exercising their right to terminate without reason.

I disagree with the majority's limitation of *Berger* to fraud "not employed to effect termination." The fraud claim there arose because the employer terminated the employee for the reason that it had allegedly concealed. *Berger v. Security Pacific Information Systems, Inc., supra*, 795 P.2d at 1385 ("[The employee] did not know, when she accepted the job with SPIS, that there was a substantial risk that SPIS would discontinue [her project] in the near future.").

In my view, Colorado's recognition of a claim for tortuous interference with an at-will employment contract, *see e.g., Cronk v. Intermountain Rural Electric Ass'n*, 765 P.2d 619 (Colo.App.1988), also supports plaintiff's claim here. Tortious interference involves third party misconduct. Nevertheless, I discern no reason to recognize a claim against the supervisor in *Cronk*, who induced the employer to exercise its at-will termination power by presenting a corrupt reason concerning subordinates whom he had targeted, but here reject plaintiff's claim against the bank, which allegedly targeted plaintiff by contriving a reason for terminating him. * * *

*Policy*

Moreover, I am persuaded by the specific public policy of protecting employees against fraud by employers. *See* § 8–2–104, C.R.S.2001 (remedy for employees fraudulently induced to come to Colorado for work). Hence, I would allow plaintiff an opportunity to prove that, as in any fraud case, he was put in a worse position for having relied on the bank's alleged fraudulent concealment. *See generally* 37 C.J.S. *Fraud* § 41 (1943).

*Facts*

The background facts are undisputed: the bank acquired plaintiff's prior employer in 1998, retained him as its at-will employee, and acknowledged that he was an exemplary employee until it terminated him in 1999 for having violated credit policy. The termination memorandum read, in relevant part:

*show-used as cause*

> The loan has not been approved internally according to Vectra Bank Colorado credit policy, yet you have willfully disregarded this fundamental rule and completed the transaction. You leave me no alternative but to terminate your employment at Vectra Bank *for cause* effective this date. . . . (emphasis supplied)

*Facts symp to π*

The unrefuted complaint allegations and differing reasonable inferences from undisputed facts show a viable fraudulent nondisclosure claim because: (1) the bank wanted to replace officers of the predecessor with its own people; (2) the bank took no action against plaintiff for approximately one year following the acquisition; (3) as a matter of past practice, the three signatures required by the credit policy were sometimes obtained after a loan closed; (4) the afternoon before the scheduled loan closing, the senior officer told another employee that he did not intend to sign the approval form on the loan at issue, but neither communicated this information to plaintiff nor directed anyone else to do so; (5) the senior officer's statement to plaintiff at about the same time that he wanted more information on the loan created a false impression that he had not yet decided against signing the loan approval form; (6) the senior officer intended plaintiff to close the loan the following morning in ignorance of the officer's decision not to sign; (7) given the past practice, plaintiff closed the loan in reasonable reliance on this false impression; (8) ultimately, the bank did not object to the loan; and (9) but for plaintiff's having thereby violated credit policy, the bank would not have terminated his employment at that time.

The only element of plaintiff's fraud claim disputed by the majority is detrimental reliance. However, the bank's alleged plan to replace at-will employees inherited from the predecessor with its own people could have been implemented at any time since the acquisition. Yet the bank acted only after—and then immediately after—according to plaintiff it had fraudulently orchestrated cause.

The inference that but for this contrived cause the bank would not have acted against plaintiff when it did, even though it did not need cause at all, finds support in factors beyond the bank's alleged machinations.

First, termination without cause would have left the bank at risk of litigation because of the many and somewhat unpredictable exceptions to the at-will employment rule.

> Defense attorneys should not cause or allow their clients to believe in the vitality of the employment at-will doctrine. *The doctrine is so riddled with exceptions that it will rarely be the case that the termination of a particular employee does not fall within one of the exceptions.* In short, if an employer terminates an employee, *prudence dictates that the employer have a good reason for the termination, which should be documented.*

*Practitioner's Guide to Colorado Employment Law* 2–2 (Supp.2001) (emphasis supplied).

Second, absent clear cause for termination the bank could have been exposed to a claim by plaintiff under state and federal statutes protecting even at-will employees against age discrimination, because of the implication of age bias arising from plaintiff's status as a long-term and otherwise exemplary employee who was within the protected age group.

The narrow ground on which I would sustain plaintiff's claim—that the bank obtained through fraudulent nondisclosure a basis for termination without which it would not have terminated his employment when it did—does not contravene "the value of a free market in employment," as the majority fears. Fraud has long been recognized as an exception to caveat emptor. *See, e.g., Mastin v. Bartholomew,* 41 Colo. 328, 92 P. 682 (1907).

Even if employment at will is treated as a defense under basic tort principles, a jury question exists whether the bank's alleged contrivance of a reason for termination through fraudulent nondisclosure precludes a defense based on the at-will employment rule. *Cf. First Interstate Bank v. Piper Aircraft Corp.,* 744 P.2d 1197 (Colo.1987)(fraudulent concealment of a wrongful act tolls the limitations period). *See generally* F. HARPER ET AL., THE LAW OF TORTS 495 (2d ed. 1986) ("Misrepresentation may also avoid a defense.").

That the bank could have terminated plaintiff's at-will employment the very next day or any time thereafter, for some other reason or even for no reason, raises a dilemma equally inherent in many Colorado cases that recognize public policy wrongful termination claims by at-will employees. This factor may limit plaintiff's damages, but should not extinguish his claim. *See Berger v. Security Pacific Info. Sys., Inc., supra,* 795 P.2d at 1385 (rejecting the argument that fraud damages should be limited because the employee had "no guarantee of continued employment," because the jury "could reasonably infer from the evidence that [the

employee's] employment would have continued for a reasonable time").
* * *

The majority correctly concludes that most courts hold the at-will doctrine precludes a claim when "fraud is the means used to effect the termination." However, the other cases on which the majority relies do not discuss the three factors whose convergence I see as precluding summary judgment here: (1) an ulterior motive for terminating the at-will employee; (2) followed by a significant delay until the employer fraudulently fabricated a reason for termination; and (3) termination soon thereafter on the basis of that tainted reason. *See Salter v. Alfa Insurance Co.,* 561 So.2d 1050 (Ala.1990); *Mackenzie v. Miller Brewing Co.,* 241 Wis.2d 700, 623 N.W.2d 739 (2001); *Tatge v. Chambers & Owen, Inc.,* 219 Wis.2d 99, 579 N.W.2d 217 (1998).

Finally, I do not share the majority's concern that accepting plaintiff's fraud theory here would unduly conflate contract claims and tort claims. *See Town of Alma v. Azco Construction, Inc.,* 10 P.3d 1256 (Colo. 2000)(limiting negligence claims where the parties have a contractual relationship, but citing with approval *Brody v. Bock,* 897 P.2d 769, 776 (Colo.1995), which held, "The fact that such alleged representations constitute the substance of Bock's breach of contract claim does not require dismissal of his [fraud] claim.").

Accordingly, I would reverse the summary judgment order and allow the jury to consider plaintiff's fraud claim based on why the bank terminated him when it did, rather than foreclosing that inquiry because of what the bank legally could have done much earlier, but did not do.

### NOTES AND QUESTIONS

1. Inasmuch as Wisehart's job was held at-will, why would the bank have set him up for discharge? According to Wisehart, it did so because as the bank wanted to rid itself of the acquired bank's older workforce, including Wisehart, it could anticipate an age discrimination claim. Misconduct would give the bank plausible grounds to dispute an age discrimination claim. But Judge Webb gives another reason: that, given the pace of erosion in the at-will rule, the bank might insulate itself against an unanticipated need to prove cause to dismiss by manufacturing it. That may impute more legal depth than management's thinking warranted, but it captures the contemporary Swiss-cheese-like character of the exceptions to what was, a century ago, an absolute rule.

2. The Colorado Court of Appeals had previously held that the failure to inform a job applicant of the prospective employer's financial situation worked a fraud—sometimes called a "silent fraud"—to induce the applicant to enter employment. Consequently, the *Wiseheart* court was pressed to explain why an outright lie to justify termination would not be similarly actionable. The situations might be distinguished on the ground that Wiseheart had lost an at-will job. But fraud in the inducement of an at-will relationship is actionable in most jurisdictions, though some jurisdictions do require proof of specific

damages. *E.g.*, *Chires v. Cumulus Broad., LLC*, 543 F.Supp.2d 712 (E.D. Mich. 2008) (allowing "psychic injury" and lost job opportunities as elements of damage). As the California Court of Appeal put it, "an 'at-will' employer does not have carte blanche to lie to an employee about any matter whatsoever to trick him or her into accepting employment." *Agosta v. Astor*, 120 Cal.App.4th 596, 15 Cal.Rptr.3d 565, 572 (2004). Instead, the *Wisehart* majority sees no detrimental reliance on the falsehood when being terminated in contrast to reliance on a lie—or on silence when there is a duty to speak—when entering into employment. Is that persuasive? At least in terms of the tort of fraud. But in doing so, the court relies on the Supreme Court of Wisconsin's decision in *Mackenzie v. Miller Brewing Co.*, 241 Wis.2d 700, 623 N.W.2d 739 (2001). In that case the Wisconsin court rejected the test of fraud to induce an at-will employee to *remain* in employment. Isn't *Mackenzie* more like the inducement *into* employment? The dissent in *Mackenzie* thought so. Moreover, the *Mackenzie* majority went on to opine that to hold the employer liable would "conceivably stifle the free movement of employees"—a theme the *Wisehart* court echoes, and which will be returned to presently.

3. Contrary to its protestation did not the *Wisehart* majority conflate the issues of contract and tort? Of what relevance to the *tort* issue—of a departure from a societally-imposed, *non*-consensual obligation—is it that the employee was not protected by a *contractual* obligation allowing termination only for just cause?

4. Judge Webb points out that a supervisor who induces the company to discharge an employee out of malice or ill will, who, for example, fabricates evidence to cause the employee's termination, would be personally liable for the tort of interference in economic advantage. This is the law in many jurisdictions. *See, e.g.*, *Welch v. Ciampa*, 542 F.3d 927, 944 (1st Cir. 2008). Thus the manager who dishonestly causes the company to discharge the employee would be liable, but the company that discharges the employee dishonestly would not be liable. Does this make any sense?

5. If a duplicitous discharge of an at-will employee is not actionable in fraud, for the want of detrimental reliance by the employee, would the discharge be better analyzed as possible breach of the covenant of good faith and fair dealing? The case will be reconsidered under that head, *infra*.

———————

The *Wisehart* court recapitulates the variety of ways an employer's ability to discharge an employee is subject to legal scrutiny: under contract; by the application of torts grounded in public policy; and by a broad array of anti-retaliation, non-discrimination, and whistleblower statutes. These are canvassed below. After these are surveyed, the question of whether a general law of wrongful dismissal might supply a better, more coherent, and more efficient alternative to the system, or non-system, of our current law will be addressed.

# B. CONTRACT

## 1. CONTRACTS FOR A STATED TERM

### KRIZAN v. STORZ BROADCASTING CO.

Court of Appeals of Louisiana, 1962
145 So.2d 636

LANDRY, JUDGE.

\* \* \*

It is uncontroverted that on March 10, 1960, plaintiff arrived at his place of employment fifty-five minutes late without having called in to notify his employer of his tardiness and for such oversight he was summarily discharged.

Appellant contends plaintiff was discharged for tardiness and failure to follow instructions which constituted a breach of the employment contract by plaintiff and was, therefore, good and sufficient cause for defendant's termination of the employment agreement.

In considering the factual circumstances of the present case as hereinafter revealed, it must be borne in mind that, unlike employment for an indefinite period (wherein the employee is dischargeable at will without reason or cause), the instant case involves employment under a written contract for a fixed period. It is well settled in our jurisprudence that employment of the latter character carries with it the right of the employee to receive all wages or salary due under the contract excepting only those instances in which he is discharged for cause prior to the contract's termination. \* \* \*

Succinctly stated, defendant's contention is twofold, namely, (1) tardiness is sufficient cause in itself for discharge of an employee; and (2) plaintiff in the case at bar violated express instructions which required that he notify defendant by telephone of his expected tardy arrival on the day in question.

[W]hether tardiness constitutes ground for termination of employment is dependent upon the facts and circumstances of each individual case. Manifestly, in resolving such a question the attending facts and circumstances of each individual case must be taken into consideration such as (but not limited to) the type of occupation, profession, calling, business or undertaking involved, the custom regarding tardiness in the particular field of endeavor and the policies of the employer regarding late arrival as such policies are made known to his employees. We shall proceed to view the facts of the instant case in the light of the pronouncements hereinabove set forth.

The evidence herein reflects that Radio Station WTIX (operated by defendant corporation) was under the supervision of a General Manager, Fred Berthelson, who was also referred to as Station Manager. The announcers, (seven or eight in number, including plaintiff), were under the direct supervision and control of a Program Director which position was held by one Marshall H. Pearce at the time of plaintiff's discharge.

Plaintiff, an announcer or "disc jockey" was engaged to perform services on a 40 hour week basis. It appears that a disc jockey's daily duties and time schedule is divided into two categories, namely, "air time" and "production time". It further appears that "air time" refers to that portion of the announcer's schedule during which he is on the air "broadcasting live" by playing records, performing commercials in person and interspicing a live program with such patter, conversation and dialogue as is peculiar to his individual style of announcing. On the other hand, "production time" is shown to be that portion of the announcer's time utilized in the preparation of "taped" commercial announcements variously referred to in the profession as promotional and gimmick spots.

According to the testimony of the Station Manager, Berthelson, "air time" was performed by the several announcers on shifts allocated in accordance with a prearranged weekly schedule with which each announcer was familiar. Production work, according to Berthelson was also done by each announcer at specifically designated times which were usually fixed by the Program Director, Pearce, but sometimes established by Berthelson himself. It is readily conceded that none of the station's announcers were required to punch a time clock.

Of the several witnesses who testified herein concerning the policy of defendant-employer regarding late arrival for work all agree that the announcers employed by appellant were frequently tardy for work particularly so in reporting for production time. It further appears that at the time of trial in the court below some of these employees continued to report late for production time. * * *

The Station Manager, Berthelson, testified that in all probability he had warned all disc jockeys not to be late for work. However, Richard Celentano, a fellow employee of plaintiff (still employed by defendant at the time of trial) testified that announcers were told to use their own judgment about reporting to work on schedule. Celentano also testified that he understood that if he was going to be late for an hour or for a considerable length of time he was supposed to call in and report that he would be late. Herbert Lathrop, (professional name, Herb Holiday), a former employee of defendant presently employed by a rival station, testified that the only thing announcers were required to be punctual about were "air shows" and that such employees were frequently late for production time. * * *

The record establishes that with respect to production time there were instances when an announcer reporting on schedule would have no immediate services to perform. At other times, however, the press of business was such that in the event of a late arrival for production time the program manager would enlist the aid of a substitute in the event the scheduled employee did not arrive timely. From the foregoing it will readily appear that appellant's policy respecting punctuality was one of complete informality and laxness.

There is some evidence in the record, however, that the station manager and program director desired to improve the situation disclosed and that in this regard the program director, Pearce, had himself been criticized by his superior, the station manager, for arriving tardily. The record further reflects that both the station manager and program director, though desirous of improving the situation noted, were somewhat reluctant to initiate positive steps to effectuate a policy of promptness and make same known to the employees involved.

In essence Berthelson testified he instructed Pearce to advise plaintiff that plaintiff would be discharged if plaintiff did not call and report his inability to report on time. Pearce testified that upon orders from Berthelson he requested plaintiff to call him if plaintiff would be late thereafter. He stated positively that he did not inform plaintiff that plaintiff's failure to report would subject plaintiff to dismissal. Plaintiff conceded that Pearce spoke to him about calling if plaintiff were to be late. He further stated that nothing in Pearce's tone or language implied that failure to call would be considered cause for dismissal.

We believe the record in the instant case fails to establish with any degree of certainty that defendant's employees were properly notified that future tardiness would not be countenanced and that the former policy of laxity in this regard was being abandoned in favor of one which would henceforth require punctuality of arrival under penalty of dismissal. In this connection we note that not only did all of the announcers (saving Pearce) testify that they were not so instructed but also that had the Station Manager Berthelson wished to adopt such a policy he had ample opportunity to do so by virtue of his contacts with the several employees. In this connection it appears that Berthelson personally delivered weekly work schedules to each announcer. If he intended to establish a new policy with respect to prompt attendance it would be reasonable to expect him to mention the change to the employees at the time he personally handed each his weekly work schedule. * * *

We do not herein question or cast any doubt on the right of an employer to demand and require punctuality and promptness on the part of his employees with respect to their reporting for work. We do hold, however, that to expect punctuality after permitting and acquiescing in a policy of informality and laxity, the employer must make it clear to the employee that a change in policy has been placed in effect and that henceforth promptness will be demanded and required. The evidence convinces us, as it apparently did the learned trial court, that appellant has failed to establish that proper and adequate notice of a change in the former policy was communicated to plaintiff herein.

Appellant also contends that appellee breached the contract in question by failing to follow instructions. This contention is predicated upon a contract provision which in substance requires that the employee will promptly and faithfully comply with all reasonable requirements, directions and requests made by appellant. On this score Berthelson testified that approximately two weeks prior to plaintiff's release plaintiff arrived for work approximately one hour late which occurrence upset the Station Manager Berthelson and caused Berthelson to suggest to Pearce that the latter henceforth require all employees to report to work on time. When plaintiff arrived for work on this occasion, Pearce instructed plaintiff to henceforth call and report any tardiness. Pearce, however, did not warn plaintiff that if he were again late he would be dismissed.

Appellee readily conceded he was fifty-five minutes late in arriving for work on March 10, 1960, and failed to call and report his tardiness. He explained, however, that he remained awake until 4:00 A.M. of the morning of March 10, 1960, performing unscheduled work for his employer and as a consequence thereof overslept. He did not call the station because he was aware that his employer was cognizant of his remaining up during the early morning hours in the gratuitous performance of the business of the station. We will consider, in some detail, the circumstances surrounding the occurrence in question with the view of determining whether the single instance of failure to conform with instructions was a wilful disobedient act upon the part of plaintiff-employee, or whether under the circumstances shown, it was justified and therefore does not constitute ground for appellee's discharge.

On the date in question the station was in the process of conducting a promotional gimmick denominated a Walk-a-thon in the showroom of a furniture company. In this regard appellant's employee, Holiday, commenced a program on the morning of March 3, 1960, with the view of staying on the air continuously, as long as possible, in the hope of attaining the dubious distinction of setting a new record for sustained, uninterrupted broadcasting. The station manager, Berthelson, summoned the announcers to a meeting and instructed them to report to the furniture store in question from time to time during off hours to encourage their colleague Holiday in his endeavor and to prevent his falling asleep. Early in the morning of March 10, 1960, plaintiff was advised that Holiday's collapse was imminent. Plaintiff and his wife went immediately to the furniture store to assist in keeping Holiday awake but despite their efforts Holiday collapsed from exhaustion at 2:06 A.M. and could not be revived. Pending the arrival of a doctor who was summoned to Holiday's aid, a policeman attempted Holiday's revival. Plaintiff called the station manager and reported Holiday's collapse following which development plaintiff and a fellow employee continued the program until approximately 4:00 A.M., at which time plaintiff left to go home. Meanwhile, however, the station manager arrived at the scene and Holiday was taken to a hospital. Plaintiff and his wife arrived home at approximately 5:00 A.M. and plaintiff, being upset over Holiday's condition, was unable to sleep immediately. Eventually plaintiff fell asleep and did not awaken until approximately 2:00 P.M. that afternoon at which time he was scheduled to report for work. Upon awakening plaintiff immediately dressed and left for work arriving approximately fifty-five minutes late. For the aforesaid late arrival plaintiff, upon reporting for work, was discharged for being tardy and failing to call in and advise that he would not report on time. * * *

From the evidence of record herein, it is clear that plaintiff's one and only violation of the instruction to call and report his tardiness in reporting for production time did not amount to either disobedience or insubordination. There is no dispute that plaintiff's neglect in this regard was the first instance of its sort following the order or instruction. Neither can it be said that such action resulted from plaintiff's lack of concern over his employer's affairs since plaintiff's dedication to appellant's interest was amply demonstrated and established when plaintiff voluntarily assumed the duties of air time in the early morning during his off time when confronted with the emergency occasioned by Holiday's collapse. Under such circumstances it could hardly be contended with any degree of force or logic that his conduct was characterized by a wrongful or perverse mental attitude toward his employer. * * *

In view of the circumstances shown, we hold that the summary dismissal of appellee for the single act of non-compliance shown did not constitute disobedience, insubordination or defiance thereby rendering his discharge arbitrary and legally unjustifiable. * * *

Affirmed.

## NOTES AND QUESTIONS

*[handwritten margin note: If at will he'd be hosed.]*

1. It bears re-emphasis that had Kenneth Krizan not had a contract for a fixed term, that is, had he been an at-will employee, none of the court's fact-finding or analysis of whether the facts as found amounted to just cause would have been undertaken: he could have been arbitrarily discharged without legal recourse. Why would the radio station have agreed to a contract of a fixed term?

2. The courts routinely refer to "cause," "good cause," and "just cause," for discharge interchangeably in employment law cases. A variety of definitions of the concept can be found in judicial opinions and arbitrators' decisions concerned with various aspects of employment. Definitions of cause can be found in some statutes or regulations. *E.g.*, Montana Wrongful Discharge from Employment Act, MONT. CODE ANN. § 39–2–901 (1987) *et seq.*. "Good cause" may mean one thing for purposes of a collective bargaining agreement, *e.g.*, *Civil Serv. Comm'n of the City of Kelso v. City of Kelso*, 137 Wash.2d 166, 969 P.2d 474, 478 (1999), and something different for purposes of an individual employment contract, and can vary based on the nature of the employment. *Tricat Indus., Inc. v. Harper*, 131 Md.App. 89, 748 A.2d 48 (Ct. Spec. App. 2000), *cert. denied*, 359 Md. 334, 753 A.2d 1032 (2000).

Perhaps the most common formulation of the concept in the courts is that an employee's failure amounts to "good cause" for discharge if it constitutes a "material breach" of the employment contract such that it would warrant the employer ending the contract without liability for further compensation. In this formulation, "good cause" to terminate an employment contract is the same as legal cause to terminate any contract imposing continuing obligations on both parties. *See* RESTATEMENT (2D) AGENCY § 409(1); *Thomas v. Bourdette*, 45 Or.App. 195, 608 P.2d 178, 199 (1980) (applying the Restatement); *Spearman v. Delco Remy Div. of General Motors Corp.*, 717 F.Supp. 1351, 1358 (S.D. Ind. 1989). The Montana Wrongful Discharge from Employment Act (WDEA) defines "good cause" as "reasonable job-related grounds for dismissal based on a failure to satisfactorily perform job duties, disruption of the employer's operation, or other legitimate business reason." MONT. CODE ANN. § 39–2–903 (5) (1987). As set forth in the Model Employment Termination Act, "good cause" is defined as: "(i) a reasonable basis related to an individual employee for termination of the employee's employment in view of relevant factors and circumstances, which may include the employee's duties, responsibilities, conduct (on the job or otherwise), job performance, and employment record, or (ii) the exercise of business judgment in good faith by the employer...." MODEL EMPLOYMENT TERMINATION ACT § 1 (4) (1991).

Failures by employees that have found to be "good cause" for discharge include: failing substantially to perform the services that the employee was contracted to perform (*Davies v. Mansbach*, 338 S.W.2d 210 (Ky. Ct. App. 1960)); breaching his or her duty of loyalty to the employer (*In re Burris*, 263 N.C. 793, 140 S.E.2d 408 (1965)); and being insubordinate by willfully refusing to obey the employer's reasonable orders (*Parrish v. Worldwide Travel Service, Inc.*, 257 Va. 465, 512 S.E.2d 818 (1999)). Whether tardiness constitutes good cause for termination depends on the circumstances of the particular case, as the *Krizan* case evidences. However, an employer may not terminate an employee for refusing to obey an instruction in defense of his or her contract rights. *E.g.*, *Levine v. Zerfuss Offset Plate Serv. Co.*, 492 F.Supp. 946 (S.D.N.Y. 1980) (employer may not discharge employee for refusing to work a night shift when the contract provided for day work hours). Employee illness, incapacity, or death can constitute "good cause" if it renders the employee unable to substantially perform his or her duties. *Lee–Wright, Inc. v. Hall*, 840 S.W.2d 572 (Tex. Ct. App. 1992). The elimination of an employee's position as part of a reduction in force motivated by the economic interest of the business constitutes good cause for termination. *Gianaculas v. Trans World Airlines*, 761 F.2d 1391, 1395 (9th Cir. 1985); *Greenwood v. State Police Training Ctr.*, 127 N.J. 500, 606 A.2d 336 (1992).

3. If an employee under contract of stated duration is given a task virtually impossible to perform, would the employer's order constitute dismissal and thereby subject the employer to damages? *See Sanders v. May Broad. Co.*, 214 Neb. 755, 336 N.W.2d 92 (1983) (would work as a constructive discharge). And, *per contra*, if an executive is given no duties to perform but the employer continues full salary and benefits in the face of which the employee nevertheless quits, can the employee properly assert that he was discharged? *See Rudman v. Cowles Commc'ns, Inc.*, 30 N.Y.2d 1, 330 N.Y.S.2d 33, 280 N.E.2d 867 (1972) (yes).

4. The common law rule rejects an order of reinstatement as a remedy for employer breach of an employment contract. The reasons are the reluctance of the courts to compel an obnoxious personal relationship and the difficulties of policing an order of reinstatement. Are there circumstances

where such an order might nevertheless be the better remedy? *See American Ass'n of Univ. Professors v. Bloomfield Coll.*, 129 N.J.Super. 249, 322 A.2d 846 (1974), *aff'd* 136 N.J.Super. 442, 346 A.2d 615 (App. Div. 1975) (wrongfully dismissed faculty members ordered reinstated for college's breach of tenure contract). Reinstatement is an available remedy in union-management arbitration and under a variety of federal laws such as the Labor Management Relations Act, the Occupational Safety and Health Act, and Title VII of the 1964 Civil Rights Act. What factors should control whether such an order is appropriate?

*Botok here*

5. A survey of employers regarding the terms of their employment relationship with non-union employees found that 52% contract explicitly for an at-will relationship, while 15% contract expressly for just cause protection and 33% use no documents that specify the terms governing discharge. J. Hoult Verkerke, *An Empirical Perspective on Indefinite Term Employment Contracts: Resolving the Just Cause Debate*, 1995 WIS. L. REV. 837, 867 (1995). In the union setting, 92% of employees enjoy just cause protection under collective bargaining agreements. BUREAU OF NAT'L AFFAIRS, BASIC PATTERNS IN UNION CONTRACTS 7 (14th ed. 1995). When would an employer and employee agree to just cause protection through a contract for a definite term or express provision for just cause protection? Why is such protection so much more popular in collective bargaining agreements than individual agreements for employment? Economists have hypothesized that the parties will agree to such terms when the benefits of job security to employees in avoiding arbitrary or opportunistic discharge by the employer, outweigh the costs of job security to employers in the additional expense of suffering and getting rid of deficient employees. This might be true if the employees have strong preferences for job security, or because they are particularly vulnerable to employer opportunism in a career, perhaps due to high personal investments in training for the job. Some economists have argued that information imperfections result in too few provisions for job security in individual employment contracts. Good employees who want job security are afraid to ask for it in contract negotiations for fear the employer will take it as a sign that they are a slacker, and fail to hire them. Employers who may realize that job security is valuable even to good employees may be afraid to unilaterally offer such terms for fear of attracting a disproportionate number of slackers in their employee applicant pool. Walter Kamiat, *Labor and Lemons: Efficient Norms in the Internal Labor Market and the Possible Failures of Individual Contracting*, 144 U. PENN. L. REV. 1953, 1957–62 (1996). Bargaining through a union helps employees overcome this problem because the union asks for job security on behalf of all employees and there is no fear of being individually identified as a slacker. Unions also tend to represent the interests of the average employee who has a greater interest in job security than the most marketable and mobile employees who employers tend to cater to in individual bargaining. Finally, the cost of union enforcement of a just cause provision through arbitration is significantly lower than the cost of court enforcement of just cause provisions in individual employment contracts.

*Union Pos*

## Note on the Employee Who Quits

If an employee under a contract of stated duration quits without having his resignation accepted or, as it is sometimes said, abandons his employment, the employee may be liable for breach, the remedy for which is the employer's cost of replacing her. *See, e.g., Handicapped Children's Educ. Bd. of Sheboygan County v. Lukaszewski*, 112 Wis.2d 197, 332 N.W.2d 774 (1983). If an employee tenders a resignation, which is accepted, and, the very next day, changes her mind and seeks to withdraw it, must the employer accede? *Cf. Eggert v. Reed*, 130 Misc.2d 804, 497 N.Y.S.2d 810 (Sup. Ct. 1985) (employee cannot withdraw acceptance of termination benefits executed a day earlier).

## 2.  EMPLOYEE HANDBOOKS

## ORTEGA v. WAKEFIELD THERMAL SOLUTIONS, INC.

Massachusetts Superior Court, 2006
20 Mass. L. Rep. 337

[The case is reproduced at pages 124–130, *supra.*]

### NOTES AND QUESTIONS

1.  The company set out rules governing discipline and discharge requiring it to observe "progressive discipline," a graded series of penalties short of dismissal for those acts of misconduct that do not warrant summary dismissal and that would allow for corrective behavior or rehabilitation. This contractually binding system of rules meant that Mr. Ortega could not be dismissed except for good cause. Consequently, whether his conduct, even if wrongful— by no means obvious from the recitation of the facts on summary judgment— gave contractual cause to discharge would be for the jury to decide. As the Arizona Court of Appeals observed in a case involving the termination of the director of a choir:

> The contract provided that the appellee [the employee] could be discharged for neglect of duty or inappropriate behavior. There was evidence of discipline problems, some poor musical performances, poor business judgment, etc. However, as could be expected, there was a conflict in this evidence. Whether the Board [the employer] had cause is a question of fact, and the trial court implicitly found it did not. The appellant contends that as long as it acts in good faith it does not matter whether the appellee had neglected his duties or been guilty of inappropriate behavior. The appellant is wrong.

*Davis v. Tucson Arizona Boys Choir Soc.*, 137 Ariz. 228, 669 P.2d 1005, 1010 (Ct. App. 1983).

2.  Some jurisdictions, in the far West so far, have taken a different approach to the enforcement of just-cause provisions contained in an employer handbook or policy manual. The California Supreme Court saw the need to

allow a "sensible latitude for management decisionmaking," so to balance the employer's interest in "organizational efficiency" against the employee's interest in continuing employment. It struck the balance thusly:

> The proper inquiry for the jury ... is not, "Did the employee *in fact* commit the act leading to dismissal?" It is "Was the factual basis on which the employer concluded a dischargeable act had been committed reached honestly, after an appropriate investigation and for reasons that that are not arbitrary or pretextual?"

*Cotran v. Rollins Hudig Hall Int'l, Inc.*, 17 Cal.4th 93, 69 Cal.Rptr.2d 900, 948 P.2d 412 (1998).

If this approach were to have been adopted in Massachusetts, the question for the jury in *Wakefield Thermal Solutions* would have been: "Did the employer conduct an appropriate investigation and, if it did, was the decision that the employee was guilty of a summarily dischargeable offense—dishonesty—reached honestly?" Note that the answer to both questions might be "yes," resulting in judgment in favor of the company, even if Mr. Ortega proved that, in fact, he hadn't lied. Which is the better approach?

3. Is the employee's interest, which the California Supreme Court says is to be weighed in calculating the standard the jury is to apply, an interest in "continuing employment" or in not being dismissed wrongly? Does how one frames that interest affect whether or not to give greater deference to managerial judgment?

4. Other rationales have been offered in support of an employer-deferential standard. The *Cotran* court opined that to ignore management's determination of the facts, to have the jury find the facts de novo, would transform the workplace "into an adjudicative arena [where] effective decisionmaking will be thwarted?" Cotran, 948 P.2d at 421. Will it? In the case of the archetypical contract requiring just cause for discharge, the collective bargaining agreement, the burden of proof usually rests on the employer to prove (before a labor arbitrator) not that it had good reason to believe the employee had engaged in the specified misconduct but that the employee did in fact engage in that misconduct. Has the administration of thousands of collective agreements under this standard created an adjudicatory arena "where effective managerial decisionmaking is thwarted"? If not, why would it when applied to job security policies that attempt to further much the same end as collective agreements (and are often issued in order to avoid unionization)?

5. Another rationale, offered by the Supreme Court of Oregon, is that: "the meaning intended by the drafter, the employer, is controlling and there is no reason to infer that the employer intended to surrender its power to determine whether the facts constituting cause for termination exist." *Simpson v. Western Graphics Corp.*, 293 Or. 96, 643 P.2d 1276, 1279 (1982). Nowhere here—or in *Cotran*—is there mention of the maxim of contractual construction requiring that any contractual ambiguities be resolved *against* the drafting party. RESTATEMENT (SECOND) OF CONTRACTS § 206 (1981). The maxim is grounded in the assumption that because the drafter is in a position of greater power, enough to control the contract's terms, the interpreter should redress the balance in favor of the weaker party. Why is this time-honored maxim ignored by these courts? Should it play a role? Could the

employer policy incorporate the *Cotran* standard, *i.e.*, reserve to itself final authority to determine the facts? *Cf. Manes v. Dallas Baptist Coll.*, 638 S.W.2d 143 (Tex. App. 1982).

# C. TORT: DISCHARGE IN VIOLATION OF PUBLIC POLICY

## DANNY v. LAIDLAW TRANSIT SERVICES, INC.

Supreme Court of Washington (en banc), 2008
165 Wash.2d 200, 193 P.3d 128

OWENS, J.

The United States District Court for the Western District of Washington (District Court) certified the following question to this court:

> Has the State of Washington established a clear mandate of public policy prohibiting an employer from discharging an at-will employee because she experienced domestic violence and took leave from work to take actions to protect herself, her family, and to hold her abuser accountable?

Order at 1. We are unable to answer the question as written because parts of the original question would require us to make factual inquiries that the District Court itself must undertake. We choose to reformulate the question. The reformulated question is: Has the State of Washington established a clear mandate of public policy of protecting domestic violence survivors and their families and holding their abusers accountable? We answer the question in the affirmative. This policy is manifested in numerous legislative, judicial, constitutional, and executive expressions of public policy.

## FACTS

According to the statement of facts, defendant Laidlaw Transit Services, Inc. (Laidlaw) hired plaintiff Ramona Danny in February 1997. Laidlaw provides transit services in King County, Washington, working with big subcontractors on projects that provide public transit route bids to King County. In October 2002, Laidlaw promoted Danny to the position of scheduling manager.

While she was working at Laidlaw, Danny and her five children experienced ongoing domestic violence at the hands of her husband. She moved out of her house in February 2003 after suffering serious physical abuse but had to leave her children behind. In June 2003, she told Project Manager Jeff Kaeder about her domestic violence situation. In August 2003, Danny requested time off so she could move her children away from the abusive situation at their home. The project manager initially refused because Danny was working on a large project with an October deadline. The project was a route bid for Laidlaw's largest subcontractor; the route bid covered 3,000–4,500 of the call center rides each day, and it was

Danny's job to put the route bid together. On August 20, 2003, Danny's husband beat her 13–year–old son so badly that he had to be hospitalized. Danny immediately moved all five children out of the home. When she returned to work, Danny again requested time off to move her children to a shelter. The project manager approved paid time off between August 25 and September 8, 2003. The record reveals that during late August and early September 2003, Danny conferred with police regarding protection from her husband and assisted in the prosecution against him for the assault of her son. Danny Decl. at 1. During this time, Danny also used services from the King County Department of Community and Human Services to obtain transitional housing, domestic violence education, counseling and health services, and legal assistance. *Id.* at 2.

On October 9, 2003, about a month after returning to work, Laidlaw demoted Danny from manager and offered her the position of scheduler, which she accepted. Laidlaw terminated Danny's employment on December 3, 2003. Laidlaw's stated reason for termination was falsification of payroll records.

Danny filed her complaint against Laidlaw on May 10, 2005, alleging that Laidlaw terminated her employment in violation of public policy and Washington's Law Against Discrimination, chapter 49.60 RCW. On October 27, 2005, Laidlaw filed a motion for judgment on the pleadings seeking to dismiss Danny's public policy claim. The District Court stayed its decision on Laidlaw's motion and instead certified the above question to this court.

## ANALYSIS

*Wrongful Discharge in Violation of Public Policy.* Absent a contract to the contrary, Washington employees are generally terminable "at will." *Gardner v. Loomis Armored, Inc.,* 128 Wash.2d 931, 935, 913 P.2d 377 (1996). An at-will employee may quit or be fired for any reason. *Id.* The common law tort of wrongful discharge is a narrow exception to the terminable-at-will doctrine. *Id.* at 935–36, 913 P.2d 377. The tort of wrongful discharge applies when an employer terminates an employee for reasons that contravene a clearly mandated public policy. *Id.* As this court has previously stated, the tort of wrongful discharge " 'operates to vindicate the public interest in prohibiting employers from acting in a manner contrary to fundamental public policy.' " *Christensen v. Grant County Hosp. Dist. No. 1,* 152 Wash.2d 299, 313, 96 P.3d 957 (2004) (emphasis omitted) (quoting *Smith v. Bates Technical Coll.,* 139 Wash.2d 793, 801, 991 P.2d 1135 (2000)).

To sustain the tort of wrongful discharge in violation of public policy, Danny must establish (1) "the existence of a clear public policy (the *clarity* element);" (2) "that discouraging the conduct in which [she] engaged would jeopardize the public policy (the *jeopardy* element);" (3) "that the public-policy-linked conduct caused the dismissal (the *causation* element);" and (4) "[Laidlaw] must not be able to offer an overriding justification for the dismissal (the *absence of justification* element)."

*Gardner,* 128 Wash.2d at 941, 913 P.2d 377. Whether Washington has established a clear mandate of public policy is a question of law subject to de novo review. *Sedlacek v. Hillis,* 145 Wash.2d 379, 388, 36 P.3d 1014 (2001); *Parents Involved in Cmty. Schs. v. Seattle Sch. Dist. No. 1,* 149 Wash.2d 660, 670, 72 P.3d 151 (2003).

The reformulated certified question requires us to determine whether Danny has met the "clarity" element of wrongful discharge in violation of public policy. To determine whether a clear public policy exists, we must ask whether the policy is demonstrated in " 'a constitutional, statutory, or regulatory provision or scheme.' " *Thompson v. St. Regis Paper Co.,* 102 Wash.2d 219, 232, 685 P.2d 1081 (1984) (quoting *Parnar v. Americana Hotels, Inc.,* 65 Haw. 370, 380, 652 P.2d 625 (1982)). Although judicial decisions may establish public policy, " 'courts should proceed cautiously if called upon to declare public policy absent some prior legislative or judicial expression on the subject.' " *Id.* (emphasis omitted) (quoting *Parnar,* 65 Haw. at 380, 652 P.2d 625). To qualify as a public policy for purposes of the wrongful discharge tort, a policy must be "truly public" and sufficiently clear. *Sedlacek,* 145 Wash.2d at 389, 36 P.3d 1014; *see also Dicomes v. State,* 113 Wash.2d 612, 618, 782 P.2d 1002 (1989) (" '[P]ublic policy concerns what is right and just and what affects the citizens of the State collectively.' " (quoting *Palmateer v. Int'l Harvester Co.,* 85 Ill.2d 124, 130, 421 N.E.2d 876, 52 Ill.Dec. 13 (1981))).

*How to qualify*

This court has always been mindful that the wrongful discharge tort is narrow and should be "applied cautiously." *Sedlacek,* 145 Wash.2d at 390, 36 P.3d 1014. Washington courts have generally recognized the public policy exception when an employer terminates an employee as a result of his or her (1) refusal to commit an illegal act, (2) performance of a public duty or obligation, (3) exercise of a legal right or privilege, or (4) in retaliation for reporting employer misconduct. *Gardner,* 128 Wash.2d at 935–36, 913 P.2d 377.

Danny argues that she performed a public duty when she acted to protect herself and her children and that she exercised a legal right to obtain protection from her abuser. Danny points to several sources of this public policy from the legislative, executive, and judicial branches of government. We find a public policy of preventing domestic violence most clearly established in the State's legislative enactments. We also find the policy pronounced by executive and judicial sources. * * *

*Danny provide policy*

[The court catalogued legislative address to domestic violence which it summed up thusly:]

The legislature's consistent pronouncements over the last 30 years evince a clear public policy to prevent domestic violence—a policy the legislature has sought to further by taking clear, concrete actions to encourage domestic violence victims to end abuse, leave their abusers, protect their children, and cooperate with law enforcement and prosecution efforts to hold the abuser accountable. The legislature has created means for domestic violence victims to obtain civil and criminal protection from abuse, established shelters and funded social and legal services aimed at helping victims leave their abusers, established treatment programs for batterers, created an address confidentiality system to ensure the safety of victims, and guaranteed protection to victims exercising their duty to cooperate with law enforcement. The legislature's creation of means to prevent, escape, and end abuse is indicative of its overall policy of preventing domestic violence. This public policy is even more pronounced when a parent seeks, with the aid of law enforcement and child protective services, to protect his or her children from abuse.[1]

The legislature's articulated policy is "truly public" in nature. *Sedlacek*, 145 Wash.2d at 389, 36 P.3d 1014. The legislature has repeatedly and unequivocally declared that domestic violence is an immense problem that impacts entire communities. *E.g.*, LAWS OF 1992, ch. 111, § 1 (declaring that "[d]omestic violence is a problem of immense proportions affecting individuals as well as communities"); LAWS OF 2004, ch. 17, § 1(1) ("Domestic violence, sexual assault, and stalking are widespread societal problems that have devastating effects for individual victims, their children, and their communities."); RCW 10.99.010 (noting the "serious consequences of domestic violence to society and to the victims"); LAWS

---

**1.** Laidlaw argues that the extensive legislation establishing a public policy is irrelevant because the 2001 legislature failed to pass legislation that would have resulted in the protection Danny seeks. *See* S.B. 5329, 57th Leg., Reg. Sess. (Wash.2001). We disagree. Senate Bill 5329 would have required employers to grant as many as six weeks off to *all* crime victims. *Id.* at 3. We have no way of knowing whether the legislature would have rejected a narrower version of the statute covering only domestic violence victims who need to take limited leave from work to protect themselves or their children and hold their abusers accountable. The legislature's failure to pass a broad law covering all crime victims simply does not evince legislative intent to deny the narrower class of domestic violence victims protection from discharge in the limited situation presented in the certified question. *See Our Lady of Lourdes Hosp. v. Franklin County*, 120 Wash.2d 439, 453 n. 4, 842 P.2d 956 (1993) ("We refuse to speculate about the reasons for nonpassage of the bills. There are simply too many possibilities for us to reach the conclusion which DSHS has advanced."); *Red Lion Broad. Co. v. Fed. Commc'ns Comm'n*, 395 U.S. 367, 381 n. 11, 89 S.Ct. 1794, 23 L.Ed.2d 371 (1969) ("[U]nsuccessful attempts at legislation are not the best of guides to legislative intent.").

Laidlaw nevertheless argues that our prior case law requires us to hold the legislature's failure to pass Senate Bill 5329 dispositive. For support, Laidlaw relies on our holding in *Sedlacek*. In *Sedlacek*, we noted that the legislature failed to adopt language of a federal law on which *Sedlacek* relied for support of a public policy. 145 Wash.2d at 389–90, 36 P.3d 1014. We also noted, however, that the Washington Administrative Code and then-recent case law from this court had also rejected the public policy the *Sedlacek* plaintiffs asserted. *Id.* at 390, 36 P.3d 1014. Moreover, in *Roberts*, 140 Wash.2d 58, 993 P.2d 901, we allowed an employee to assert the common law tort of wrongful discharge even though the employee clearly lacked a statutory remedy. *Id.* at 69 n. 9, 993 P.2d 901 (noting the failure of bills that would have created a statutory remedy for Roberts by subjecting small employers to state antidiscrimination law).

The concurrence/dissent now refers to Substitute Senate Bill (SSB) 5900 from the most recent legislative session as an example of the legislature's "declin[ing] to enact" relevant legislation. Concurrence/dissent at 149. Far from declining to enact the legislation, the legislature unanimously passed an essentially identical bill the first time both houses voted on such a bill. The language of SSB 5900 was virtually the same as the recently passed Substitute House Bill (SHB) 2602, discussed below. *Compare* Substitute S.B. 5900, 60th Leg., Reg. Sess. (Wash.2008) *with* Laws of 2008, ch. 286. SSB 5900 passed the senate unanimously in February 2008, but the house did not vote on it before the parallel SHB 2602 passed both houses. *See* Bill Information, SB 5900–2007–08, http:// apps. leg. wa. gov/ billinfo/ summary. aspx? bill= 5900 (last visited September 29, 2008); Laws of 2008, ch. 286. Myriad reasons may explain why SSB 5900 did not come to a vote in either house in 2007, and its "nonpassage" says nothing about the legislature's intent with respect to the subject matter of the bill.

OF 1991, ch. 301, § 1 ("[T]he community has a vested interest in the methods used to stop and prevent future violence."); *see also* WASHINGTON STATE TASK FORCE ON GENDER AND JUSTICE IN THE COURTS, FINAL REPORT 18 (1989) (noting the idea that domestic violence is a " 'family matter' " is a gender biased belief).

Moreover, the legislature has specifically acknowledged that domestic violence negatively impacts victims *and* their employers. The legislature has declared "that domestic violence is the leading cause of injury among women" that often goes undiagnosed. RCW 43.70.610. The legislature has similarly recognized that domestic violence and its resulting trauma result in millions of dollars of costs in the form of "health care, *absence from work,* services to children, and more." LAWS OF 1992, ch. 111, § 1 (emphasis added); *accord* LAWS OF 1991, ch. 301, § 1 ("The collective costs to the community for domestic violence include the systematic destruction of individuals and their families, *lost lives, lost productivity, and increased health care."* (emphasis added)). We find ample evidence of a clear public policy in the legislature's pervasive findings and enactments over the past 30 years. * * *

[The court next catalogued address to domestic violence by the executive branch, *e.g.*, by executive order directing state workplaces to provide assistance to victims, and by the judiciary.]

Our court has also recognized a public policy of protecting human life from imminent harm. *Gardner,* 128 Wash.2d at 944, 913 P.2d 377. In *Gardner,* an employee left his armored truck against company policy to help a bank employee being chased by a man with a knife. This court held that "saving persons from life threatening situations" satisfied the clarity element. *Id.* at 945, 913 P.2d 377. Although the *Gardner* court recognized the policy in the context of *imminent* life threatening situations and the case alone does not establish the public policy that Danny seeks, its holding provides further evidence that this court has endorsed the protection of human life: "Society places the highest priority on the protection of human life." *Id.* at 944, 913 P.2d 377.

*The Significance of Evidence of Public Policy.* Laidlaw insists that any evidence of public policy is meaningless unless it directly addresses employers' responsibilities in preventing domestic violence. Resp't Br. at 16 ("[N]one of the statutes cited … mandate a clear public policy in the employment arena."). The dissent and the concurrence/dissent agree with Laidlaw that a court may not find a clear mandate of public policy absent a legislative expression of public policy specific to the employment arena. Both opinions cite *Thompson,* our seminal wrongful discharge case, for the proposition that in order to demonstrate a clear public policy and satisfy the "clarity" element, the plaintiff must show that the *employer* contravened the public policy. This interpretation conflates the elements of wrongful discharge.

The "clarity" element does not require us to evaluate the employer's conduct at all; the element simply identifies the public policy at stake.

Other elements of the tort serve to evaluate the employer's conduct in relation to that public policy. In *Gardner,* 12 years after *Thompson,* this court adopted the current four-part test for discharge in violation of public policy. *Gardner,* 128 Wash.2d at 941, 913 P.2d 377. The new test explicitly separated the requirement of a clear public policy (the "clarity" element) from the requirement that the employer's conduct threaten that policy (the "jeopardy" and "causation" elements). *Id.* at 941–42, 913 P.2d 377. The court specifically recognized that "[w]hereas prior decisions have lumped the clarity and jeopardy elements together, a more consistent analysis will be obtained by first asking if any public policy exists whatsoever, and then asking whether, on the facts of each particular case, the employee's discharge contravenes or jeopardizes that public policy." *Id.* at 941, 913 P.2d 377.

Because the "clarity" element does not concern itself with the employer's actions, the public policy need not specifically reference employment. In *Thompson* itself, the source of the public policy—the Foreign Corrupt Practices Act of 1977—did not specifically address employment but rather prohibited bribery of foreign officials. 102 Wash.2d at 234, 685 P.2d 1081. In *Ellis,* we found that a municipal fire code established a public policy against unauthorized disabling of a fire system without requiring the fire code to reference employment. 142 Wash.2d at 461, 13 P.3d 1065. In *Gardner,* this court examined a situation in which an employer terminated an employee who violated company policy in order to save a human life. 128 Wash.2d at 933, 913 P.2d 377. We recognized a clear public policy in support of preservation of human life without determining how such a duty might arise in the employment context. *Id.* at 944–45, 913 P.2d 377. In *Gardner,* we established that where a "fundamental public policy is clearly evidenced by countless statutes and judicial decisions," an employer may be liable for wrongful discharge if the employer fires an employee for taking actions necessary to protect that policy, regardless of whether the public policy itself addresses the employment context. *Id.*

The legislature's recent actions show that this state's clear and forceful public policy against domestic violence supports liability for employers who thwart their employees' efforts to protect themselves from domestic violence. The 2008 legislature unanimously passed Substitute House Bill 2602: "AN ACT Relating to increasing the safety and economic security of victims of domestic violence ..." SUBSTITUTE H.B. 2602, 60th Leg., Reg. Sess. (Wash. 2008). All 142 legislators who voted on the bill agreed that

> [i]t is in the public interest to reduce domestic violence, sexual assault, and stalking by enabling victims to maintain the financial independence necessary to leave abusive situations, achieve safety, and minimize physical and emotional injuries, and to reduce the devastating economic consequences of domestic violence, sexual assault, and stalking to employers and employees.

LAWS OF 2008, ch. 286, § 1(1). To that end, the new law provides for "reasonable leave" for domestic violence victims to seek legal remedies, law enforcement assistance, treatment for injuries, services from shelters and other agencies, or to relocate themselves or their families, among other things. LAWS OF 2008, ch. 286, § 3. Though the legislature had not yet considered such a bill at the time of Danny's discharge, the fundamental public policy underlying the bill had long been established at that time.

*Limitations of this Holding.* We are mindful of the employer's burden and the need to narrowly construe the public policy exception "in order to guard against frivolous lawsuits." *Gardner,* 128 Wash.2d at 936, 913 P.2d 377. In this case, we simply hold that Washington State has a clear public policy of protecting domestic violence survivors and their children and holding domestic violence perpetrators accountable.

Laidlaw argues that recognizing the clearly established public policy in this case will "require employers to serve as a functional equivalent of the Department of Social and Health Services." Resp't Br. at 11. Laidlaw also argues that "[a]n employee fearing discharge for what may be legitimate reasons need only claim to be a victim of domestic violence to be half way to a valid public policy claim when they are discharged." *Id.* at 39. Laidlaw's parade of horribles is unfounded. Our holding will in no way open the floodgates of litigation. The clarity element is merely one of the elements Danny and future plaintiffs must successfully establish in order to maintain a wrongful discharge claim. Plaintiffs like Danny must also satisfy the jeopardy, causation, and absence of justification elements of the wrongful discharge tort. *Korslund v. DynCorp Tri–Cities Servs., Inc.,* 156 Wash.2d 168, 178, 125 P.3d 119 (2005).

We reformulated the original certified question precisely because it implicated other elements of the tort beyond the "clarity" element. The original certified question asked whether the employer in this case was prohibited from discharging the employee for *taking time off work* to protect herself from domestic violence. Such a question requires a factual inquiry that is properly before the trial court under the "jeopardy" element.

To satisfy the "jeopardy" element, the employee "must prove that discouraging the conduct in which [she] engaged would jeopardize the public policy." *Gardner,* 128 Wash.2d at 941, 913 P.2d 377. This court was careful to note in *Gardner* that in order to satisfy the jeopardy element, the employee must show that her conduct *"directly relates* to the public policy, or was *necessary* for the effective enforcement of the public policy." *Id.* at 945, 913 P.2d 377. Accordingly, the employee must show that other means of promoting the policy are inadequate. *Id.*

The "jeopardy" element strictly limits the scope of claims under the tort of wrongful discharge. In this case, for example, in order for Danny to show that her conduct satisfies the "jeopardy" element, she will have to show that the time that she took off work was the *only available adequate means*[1] to prevent domestic violence against herself or her children or to hold her abuser accountable. This inquiry will turn on the nature of the danger, the particular actions that Danny took, and the details of her work schedule. For example, if she wished to get a protection order, but the court was only open during her scheduled work hours, time off may have been necessary. The amount of time off would turn on her distance from the court and other relevant factual circumstances. On the other hand, if she worked at night, her employer would likely not have been obligated to give her any time off work to seek a protection order. Time off would only be required if she could not obtain the order outside of work hours. Likewise, if she were called to testify against her abuser, time off would have been necessary if the hearing were during her work hours. If she needed to move her family to a shelter, the inquiry would turn on whether constraints such as the shelter's rules or her abuser's schedule made moving during work hours the *only adequate means* of protecting herself and her children.[2]

The concurrence/dissent would decide as a matter of law that time off work is never necessary to prevent domestic violence. We cannot decide the jeopardy element as a matter of law here because that which is "necessary" varies with the surrounding circumstances and cannot be determined without the factual record. Our case law makes it clear that a court must evaluate the facts of a case when deciding whether an employee's actions were "*necessary* for the effective enforcement of the public policy." *Id.* In *Ellis*, a case in which we reviewed a grant of summary judgment, we inquired (1) whether Ellis had a reasonable belief that his refusal to disable a fire alarm was necessary to prevent violation of the public policy and (2) whether his actions were in fact necessary given the city's claim that it would never have asked him to disable a fire alarm without fire department authorization. 142 Wash.2d at 461–64, 13 P.3d 1065. This court concluded that there were "at least two fact issues as to the [ "jeopardy"] prong of the *Gardner* test, both mandating reversal of the summary judgment." *Id.* at 464, 13 P.3d 1065. Similarly, in *Gardner,* the court stated that the "jeopardy" element required the court to ask "whether, on the facts of each particular case, the employee's discharge contravenes or jeopardizes [the] public policy." 128 Wash.2d at 941, 913 P.2d 377. The court examined the facts to determine whether the truck driver needed to leave his vehicle, including the screams and pleas for help of the woman as she was chased with a knife, *id.* at 934, 913 P.2d 377, the position of the truck, and the fact that no one else seemed ready to help, *id.* at 946, 913 P.2d 377.[3] We recognized again in *Korslund* that

---

**1.** Note that newly passed SHB 2602 provides a civil cause of action against employers who discharge employees for taking "reasonable" time off in response to domestic violence. LAWS OF 2008, ch. 286, § 12. The tort of wrongful discharge provides narrower protections for employees than does the new legislation.

**2.** Again, the factual circumstances would determine the amount of time off necessary. We stress, however, that time off would be necessary only to protect herself and her children from actual domestic violence. She would be entitled to time off to move her children directly from harm's way, but not to run errands or generally reorder her life.

**3.** The concurrence/dissent rejects "the proposition an employee's *need for leave* is an appropriate criterion for deciding the scope of" protected activity. Concurrence/ dissent at 148.

the "jeopardy" element "generally involves a question of fact." 156 Wash.2d at 182, 125 P.3d 119 (citing *Hubbard*, 146 Wash.2d at 715, 50 P.3d 602 (citing *Ellis*, 142 Wash.2d at 460–63, 13 P.3d 1065)). Only the trial court is equipped to make the requisite factual inquiries to decide the "jeopardy" element. We cannot decide it in this opinion because we simply lack the factual record to do so.

The concurrence/dissent's proposed holding would also require us to overrule *Gardner*. The concurrence/dissent would compel Danny to show that her employer discharged her simply because she acted to prevent domestic violence and not because she took time off work to take those actions. In *Gardner*, this court recognized that absenteeism is protected when it is part and parcel of the public-policy-protecting actions. There, the employer argued that it discharged the armored truck driver solely because he left the truck, not because he saved a woman's life. This court explicitly rejected that reasoning, saying, "Gardner's leaving the truck cannot be analyzed in isolation: his initial act of getting out of the truck is inextricably intertwined with his motive for leaving it and his subsequent actions." 128 Wash.2d at 947, 913 P.2d 377.[1]

In this case, like in *Gardner*, Danny was faced with a critical situation that was not related to her employment duties. Like in *Gardner*, she took action in response. Like in *Gardner*, those actions entailed leaving work for a period of time in an effort to further a clearly established public policy. If her actions were necessary to further the public policy, as the truck driver's actions were in *Gardner*, her conduct is protected. * * *

We keep in mind that the critical inquiry in the four-part wrongful discharge test is not whether the employer's actions *directly* contravene public policy, but whether the employer fired the employee because the *employee* took necessary action to comply with public policy. *See Gardner*, 128 Wash.2d at 941, 913 P.2d 377. The authors of all three opinions in this case agree that Washington State has a clearly defined public policy of protecting domestic violence survivors and their families and holding abusers accountable. The tort serves to safeguard that important public policy by allowing employees to do what they must to prevent domestic violence, without fear of losing their economic independence. But the concurrence/dissent's narrow reading of the jeopardy element tort would overly limit the tort's application. While it would protect employees from discharge based on their *status* as victims of domestic violence, it would leave exposed any employee who took an absolutely necessary morning off work to get a protection order, to give a statement to police, or to move her children out of imminent harm's way. Discouraging this conduct will directly endanger our community's efforts to end domestic violence. * * *

---

But the *Gardner* jeopardy analysis demonstrates that whether the employee's act of leaving work is factually "necessary" to protect the public policy is the very heart of the jeopardy inquiry.

**1.** Likewise, in the "jury duty" and "subpoena" cases cited by the concurrence/dissent, the employees were discharged because responding to these public duties required time off work, not because their employers disliked the actions of serving on a jury or testifying in court.

[Two Justices concurred in this opinion. Two Justices joined in a separate concurrence. Justice Madsen wrote separately and at length for himself and a fellow Justice. A portion is excerpted below.]

MADSEN, J. (concurring/dissenting).

The purpose of the tort claim for wrongful discharge in violation of public policy is to protect a clearly existing public policy mandate, not create one. * * *

The public policy tort exception to the at-will doctrine is not a vehicle by which this court may conscript employers to shoulder the burden of a societal problem. Rather, the purpose of the exception is to prevent an employer from using the power of discharge to shield itself from liability for wrongful conduct. *Smith v. Bates Technical Coll.*, 139 Wash.2d 793, 801, 991 P.2d 1135 (2000). *See generally* Lawrence E. Blades, *Employment at Will vs. Individual Freedom: On Limiting the Abusive Exercise of Employer Power*, 67 COLUM. L.REV. 1404 (1967). * * *

[Justice Madsen discussed the rule of tort law where a statute deals with the subject.]

In such instances, the legal component of the jeopardy analysis is whether the remedies provided by the legislature adequately protect the public policy. *See, e.g., Korslund*, 156 Wash.2d at 181, 125 P.3d 119 (concluding, as a matter of law, comprehensive statutory remedies against retaliation for reporting safety violations in nuclear industry adequately protects relevant public policy interests); *compare Smith*, 139 Wash.2d at 805, 991 P.2d 1135 (finding statutory remedies for wrongful discharge for filing a grievance inadequate where no recovery for emotional distress is available). However, when a statute does not directly address the employment relationship, a court must consider the clarity and jeopardy elements simultaneously, analyzing the nexus between the public policy and the workplace dispute to determine whether an important public policy would be jeopardized by permitting employee dismissals under the factual circumstances alleged. *See Gardner*, 128 Wash.2d at 946, 913 P.2d 377 (analyzing whether allowing employers to discharge employees for violating a work rule when necessary to save a life would contravene public policy favoring lifesaving activity).[1] ...

In this case, no applicable statute, constitutional provision, administrative regulation, or other source of public policy cited by the lead opinion directly addresses whether, and to what extent, public policy limits a private employer's power to discharge an employee who experiences

---

**1.** In *Gardner,* the majority inferred a "fundamental" public policy in favor of saving persons from life threatening situations from the emergency exception to the warrant requirement, recognition of self-defense as a defense to homicide, and the necessity defense to all other criminal charges. Specialists in the field point to *Gardner* as an anomaly in that the sources of law relied upon for the public policy impose no duty on either the employer or the employee to engage in, or refrain from, the conduct at issue. *See, e.g.,* Deborah A. Ballam, *Employment-at-Will: The Impending Death of a Doctrine*, 37 AM. BUS. L.J. 653, 671–72 (2000) (observing that the *Gardner* decision represents a "dramatic change in the existing precedent defining public policy for purposes of the wrongful discharge tort" and suggesting that it is "an anomaly based on unusual circumstances").

domestic violence. We have recognized a court may infer a public policy mandate from tangentially related constitutional and statutory provisions even in the absence of a direct expression of public policy. *Gardner,* 128 Wash.2d at 946, 913 P.2d 377. * * *

As apparent in *Gardner,* when the source of public policy does not itself address the employment relationship, a court must balance an employer's interest in operating its business as it sees fit, an employee's interest in job security, and society's interest in the protection of public policies to decide whether a clear mandate of public policy forbids an employer from discharging an employee for a particular reason. In striking this balance, a court must act with the greatest restraint to avoid intruding on the legislative prerogative of creating public policy or unfairly subjecting employers to liability for conduct they did not know was wrongful. *See Korslund,* 156 Wash.2d at 180, 125 P.3d 119 (narrow construction rule applies most forcefully to the identification of a clear mandate of public policy).

"Public policy" is an amorphous concept. Virtually every statute embodies a public policy. However, for purposes of defining the scope of an employer's liability for wrongful discharge, the public policy should be "clear" in the sense that it provides specific guidance to the employer....

We have recognized four general categories of cases that justify the imposition of tort liability: where an employer discharges an employee for (1) refusing to commit an illegal act,[1] (2) performing a public duty,[2] (3) exercising a legal right or privilege,[3] or (4) reporting an employer's illegal activity.[4] In such cases, the employee's interest in job security and society's interest in the fulfillment of public policies outweigh the employer's interest in controlling personnel decisions. We reasonably expect employers to recognize that discharging an employee for such socially undesirable reasons will expose them to liability for wrongful discharge.

In her complaint, Danny alleges her employer discharged her for "hold [ing] her abuser accountable" (complaint at 6), in violation of a clear public policy that favors "utilizing the state's legal system to obtain protection and to hold abusers accountable." *Id.* at 5. She further alleges her employer discharged her for "[taking] actions to protect herself [and]

---

**1.** *Hubbard,* 146 Wash.2d 699, 50 P.3d 602 (insisting on compliance with county zoning and building codes); *Ellis v. City of Seattle,* 142 Wash.2d 450, 13 P.3d 1065 (2000) (refusal to violate a fire code); *Thompson,* 102 Wash.2d 219, 685 P.2d 1081 (compliance with federal antibribery statute).

**2.** *Gardner,* 128 Wash.2d 931, 913 P.2d 377 (lifesaving activity); *Gaspar v. Peshastin Hi–Up Growers,* 131 Wash.App. 630, 128 P.3d 627 (2006) (cooperation with a police investigation of illegal activity by co-worker).

**3.** *Smith,* 139 Wash.2d 793, 991 P.2d 1135 (exercising right to file a grievance against an employer); *Roberts,* 140 Wash.2d 58, 993 P.2d 901 (opposition to sex discrimination); *Bravo,* 125 Wash.2d 745, 888 P.2d 147 (exercising statutory right to engage in concerted organizing activities); *Hume,* 124 Wash.2d 656, 880 P.2d 988 (asserting statutory right to overtime pay); *Wilmot,* 118 Wash.2d 46, 821 P.2d 18 (filing a worker's compensation claim).

**4.** *Korslund,* 156 Wash.2d 168, 125 P.3d 119 (reporting alleged violation of federal hazardous waste regulations); *Bennett,* 113 Wash.2d 912, 784 P.2d 1258 (opposition to age discrimination practices); *Dicomes v. State,* 113 Wash.2d 612, 782 P.2d 1002 (1989) (governmental misconduct).

her family," in violation of "a clear public policy encouraging domestic violence victims to seek alternative living arrangements and social services." *Id.* at 6.

As discussed in the lead opinion, Washington has clearly existing public policies to prevent crimes of domestic violence, protect the victims of domestic violence, and prosecute its perpetrators. These public policies are particularly jeopardized by the chilling effect the threat of dismissal could have on employees who experience domestic violence. Domestic violence is unlike most crimes in that its victims are often reluctant to report the crime or seek help to escape the perpetrator, due to fear, shame, or economic dependence. Employers may be expected to recognize they may not penalize employees for seeking legal recourse against the perpetrators of domestic violence or for accessing social services as doing so would thwart clearly existing public policies to prevent domestic violence, protect the victims of domestic violence, and effectively prosecute its perpetrators. In view of the importance of the public policies at issue, and the employer's minimal interest in discharging a person for engaging in such conduct, I agree that public policy clearly prohibits employers from discharging an employee for obtaining a protection order, filing a complaint against an abuser, cooperating with the investigation and prosecution of the alleged abuser, finding alternative living arrangements, or accessing support services for domestic violence victims.

But nothing in the sources of public policy cited by the lead opinion would have given an employer fair notice it may not discharge an employee for absenteeism resulting from domestic violence. Thus, I would hold that while an employer could not discharge an employee *because* he or she took such actions in response to domestic violence, before the legislature's enactment of Substitute House Bill 2602 no clear mandate of public policy prohibited an employer from discharging an employee who missed work or was unable to carry out his or her job functions as a result of domestic violence. * * *

In limited cases, an employee's performance of a public duty may require an employer to excuse an employee's absenteeism even in the absence of any express statutory or contractual requirement. In view of the importance of the jury system, and the need for diverse representation on juries, some courts have inferred a public policy mandate against discharging employees for missing work to perform jury service. *Nees v. Hocks*, 272 Or. 210, 536 P.2d 512 (1975); *Shaffer v. Frontrunner, Inc.*, 57 Ohio App.3d 18, 566 N.E.2d 193 (1990). An employer who refuses to allow an employee to miss work in order to serve on a jury places the employee in the "untenable position of choosing between his employment and [a statutorily] mandated duty." *Shaffer*, 566 N.E.2d at 196.

Similarly, courts have concluded public policy requires employers to excuse employees who miss work to respond to compulsory process, such as a subpoena. *Dunwoody v. Handskill Corp.*, 185 Or.App. 605, 60 P.3d 1135 (2003) (discharge for missing work to testify at murder trial violates public policy); Courts reason that allowing employers to discharge employees who miss work in order to fulfill jury duty or respond to legal summons would intolerably undermine the effective operation of our judicial system. *Nees,* 536 P.2d at 516. Accordingly, absent an overriding justification for the discharge, courts have determined employers may be held liable for wrongful discharge in such circumstances.

In contrast, as noted earlier, neither the parties nor my research has uncovered any case where a court has held an employer liable for wrongful discharge based on *absenteeism* where the employee is absent in order to report a crime, cooperate with law enforcement, or assist in the prosecution of a criminal offense. *Compare Gaspar v. Peshastin Hi–Up Growers,* 131 Wash.App. 630, 128 P.3d 627 (2006) (discharge in retaliation for cooperating with a police investigation violates public policy); *Little v. Windermere Relocation, Inc.,* 301 F.3d 958 (9th Cir.2001) (discharge in retaliation for reporting being raped during a business lunch with the employer's client); *Ludwick v. This Minute of Carolina, Inc.,* 287 S.C. 219, 337 S.E.2d 213 (1985) (discharge in retaliation for complying with a subpoena to testify at administrative hearing on alleged employer misconduct violates public policy); *Wiskotoni v. Mich. Nat'l Bank–W.,* 716 F.2d 378 (6th Cir.1983) (discharge in retaliation for testifying before a grand jury investigating co-worker's alleged wrongdoing violates public policy). * * *

Whether to provide victims of domestic violence with protected leave so they may obtain protection orders, participate in criminal prosecutions, and access social services is a policy decision for the legislature. In the most recent legislative session our legislature joined the ranks of those states that have enacted legislation providing the protection the petitioners here seek. S.B. Rep. on S.B. 5900, at 2, 60th Leg., Reg. Sess. (Wash.2007) (noting 34 other states provide similar protection).

The lead opinion downplays the significance of the legislature's action, stating, "though the legislature had not yet considered such a bill at the time of Danny's discharge, the fundamental public policy underlying the bill had long been established at that time." Lead opinion at 137–38. In fact, the legislature enacted Substitute House Bill 2602 after having considered the issue in three legislative sessions. *See* S.B. 5900, 59th Leg., Reg. Sess. (Wash.2007) (providing employment leave for domestic violence victims); S.B. 5329, 57th Leg., Reg. Sess. (Wash.2001) (providing employment leave for all crime victims, including domestic violence victims). Apparently impatient with the legislative process, the lead and concurring opinions would accomplish by judicial fiat what properly is a matter for the policy-making branch of government. As revealed by the statutes enacted by our legislature and other states, the issue of employment leave for domestic violence victims raises a number of practical considerations best left to legislative action.

The legislature is better equipped to balance the competing interests involved and create a specific statutory framework that provides adequate notice as to the amount of protective leave, which employers are subject to the leave, whether leave must be paid or unpaid, whether the leave is in addition to or cumulative of that available under the FMLA, whether notice is required, and the nature of the activities that are protected. These are policy decisions for the legislature, not this court.

Legislatures that have addressed the issue have formulated a wide variety of responses to these questions.[1] *See, e.g.,* California (Cal. LAB. CODE §§ 230, 230.1); Colorado (COLO.REV.STAT. § 24–34–402.7); Hawaii (HAW.REV.STAT. § 378–72); Illinois (820 Ill. COMP. STAT. 180/1–180/45); Maine (26 ME.REV.STAT. § 850); New York (N.Y. PENAL LAW § 215.14); North Carolina (N.C.GEN.STAT.95–270a).

The lead opinion finds no significance in the fact our legislature has twice considered and declined to enact legislation that would have provided the protection the petitioners seek. *See* Substitute S.B. 5900, at 2, 60th Leg., Reg. Sess. (Wash.2007). The lead opinion cites case law for the proposition we cannot infer legislative intent from the failure to enact legislation. However, legislative inaction is significant in the context of a public policy tort claim where the proposed legislation would have established a previously unrecognized public policy. * * *

## NOTES AND QUESTIONS

1. The rigidity of the *laissez-faire* element of the at-will rule, the assumption that the law must stay out when an employer discharges an employee even when the discharge is for a bad reason, began to erode when the courts confronted discharges for the refusal to do a criminal act, such as committing perjury, *Petermann v. International Bhd. of Teamsters, Warehousemen and Helpers of America*, 174 Cal.App.2d 184, 344 P.2d 25 (1959), or for complying with the law, such as service on a jury. *Nees v. Hocks*, 272 Or. 210, 536 P.2d 512 (1975). The law began to mushroom in the 1980s taking on a rich texture that varies significantly from jurisdiction to jurisdiction on what public policies justify the law's intervention and what sources can be looked to as expressing public policy. By 2007, the courts in 44 of the 51 jurisdictions had adopted a judicially recognized public policy exception.* The common notion nevertheless is that some discharges (or other seriously adverse action) so implicate the common weal, in contrast to being a purely personal wrong, as to require public intervention.

The Restatement (Third) of Employment Law has attempted to set out a consensus view of the current state of the law on discharge in violation of

---

**1.** Substitute House Bill 2602 enacted by our legislature provides relatively expansive protection for domestic violence victims. It contains no small employer exemption, entitles employees who experience domestic violence to take "reasonable leave" to seek legal, medical, and social services, with appropriate notice to employers, requires employers to restore employees to their original position, with no loss of benefits, prohibits employers from taking any adverse employment actions against employees who exercise their statutory privileges, and provides remedies for violations.

* The seven exceptions are Alabama, Florida, Georgia, Louisiana, Maine, New York and Rhode Island. Timothy A. Haley, *State Law Exceptions to the Employment at Will Doctrine, in* LEGAL RIGHTS IN THE WORKPLACE: STATUTORY SUPPLEMENT AND MATERIALS (Clyde W. Summers, Kenneth G. Dau–Schmidt & Alan Hyde 2007).

public policy. The Restatement identifies four sources of public policy: (1) constitutional texts; (2) statutes, ordinances, and decisional law; (3) administrative regulations and rules; and, (4) "principles of professional conduct"— codes of ethics—when these are "protective of the public interest" in contrast to being merely self-serving. Based on those sources, the Restatement abstracts five categories of discipline that violate public policy: (1) a refusal to do an act which the employee in good faith believes would violate a law or rule of ethics, (2) performing a public duty or obligation the employee believes in good faith to be imposed by law, (3) filing a charge or claiming a benefit under an "employment statute or law", (4) reporting (or inquiring about) "employer" conduct that the employee believes in good faith violates a law or principle of ethics, and (5) engaging in "any other activity directly furthering a substantial public policy."

The Labor Law Group's Working Group assigned to review this Chapter of the Restatement, though critical of much in the document's details, found its blackletter case clusters to reflect the consensus of those categories that have been well established. However, the Working Group also found it inadequate otherwise in recognizing the dynamic nature of this area of the law. Joseph Grodin et al., *Working Group on Chapter 4 of the Proposed Restatement of Employment Law: The Tort of Wrongful Discipline in Violation of Public Policy*, 13 EMP. RTS. & EMP. POL'Y J. 159, 160 (2009). For the detailed criticism the reader is directed to the Working Group's critique. Some of the larger issues are worth discussing here.

## 1. THE RESORT TO TORT

Why give an at-will employee who has no express contractual protection from discharge a cause of action for discharge in violation of public policy? There are several possible rationales. First, think of the implications of the employer's argument in which it wants to discharge an employee for refusing to violate the law. In essence, the employer is arguing it has a right, under the *law*, to discharge the employee for a reason that frustrates the *law*. It is a basic tenet of contract law that illegal contract terms are unenforceable and one cannot contract for an illegal purpose. This rationale argues for a cause of action in contract (not tort), with only ordinary contract (not punitive) damages. However, it is apparent in the public policy cases that there are public interests involved that will never be adequately represented in contract. The public's interest in people following the law, reporting violations of the law, and serving on juries constitutes a third-party interest that will never be adequately represented in contract negotiations between the employer and the employee. To uphold these public interests we give the employee a cause of action against the employer and because these public policies establish important community standards, this cause of action can lie in tort. The employer's actions in firing the employee assaults our social norms and values.

1. Sometimes the public policy giving rise to the tort claim is grounded in a statute (or other public regulatory measure) that does not provide for a private right of action. The question here is not whether a private right of action can be implied from the law but rather whether the law constitutes a statement of public policy upon which a tort may be founded. This whole area is "quite confused," in the words of the Labor Law Group's Working Group. The Restatement's black letter rule would have that question turn on whether the statutorily provided remedy is "adequate." The Working Group found this to beg the question and suggested more extended treatment. *Haley, supra* at 172–80.

2. An employee receives a summons for jury duty, notifies her employer that she will be absent because of the summons, and misses work. State law prohibits employers from discharging employees under this circumstance and subjects employers who violate the law to criminal contempt. The employer nonetheless violates the law and fires the employee. May the employee sue in tort for a discharge violative of public policy? *Cf. Di Blasi v. Traffax Traffic Network*, 256 A.D.2d 684, 681 N.Y.S.2d 147 (1998) (New York has not recognized the general concept of discharge wrongful due to public policy.)

## 2. THE SOURCES AND CLARITY OF PUBLIC POLICY

The singular focus of the Washington Supreme Court in *Laidlaw Transit Services* was on the element of the "clarity" of the public policy Ramona Danny invoked. As the opinions in that case evidence, most jurisdictions have required that the public policy be "clear," "definite," "well established," or the like, usually by reference to an authoritative non-judicial source. The consequence is sometimes scarcely edifying. The Illinois Supreme Court, for example, found "patient safety" even as expressed in the state's Medical Patient Rights Act, to lack sufficient specificity to allow the tort to apply to the discharge of an employee of a medical center who had informed the hospital's accrediting body of the hospital's failure meticulously to observe the agency's rules on patient charting. *Turner v. Memorial Med. Ctr.*, 233 Ill.2d 494, 331 Ill.Dec. 548, 911 N.E.2d 369 (2009). In contrast, confronted with an employee arguably discharged for complaining to management that its reports to the federal government of success in removing toxic substances were false, the Colorado Court of Appeals had no doubt that enough was stated to invoke public policy. *Kearl v. Portage Env't, Inc.*, 205 P.3d 496, 499 (Colo. App. 2008). The employee's legal complaint alleged that "he was terminated for his 'ongoing complaints' which were 'consistent with his professional duties as a scientist and academician' ..."

The Restatement aligns itself with those jurisdictions that allow judge-made law to be a source of public policy. That allowance, however, is circular as it gives no further guidance on what the courts may look to.

Are they restricted to the decisional law of the jurisdiction only? May the courts look to the decisional law of other jurisdictions, *i.e.*, of sister states that are, in our system, "foreign jurisdictions"? May they look to international law or even to courts abroad?

## NOTES AND QUESTIONS

1.   A well-respected journalist has accepted employment with a television production company for work on a news magazine. She is assigned to produce a segment entitled "To Catch a Predator." For this segment, the production company works with an organization called "Perverted Justice" which uses agents pretending to be minors to lure adult men into chat rooms. The parties make a date to meet and the men are led to believe they are arranging a sexual assignation with a minor. When the man arrives at the meeting place he is arrested while the confrontation scene is filmed. The reporter has objected to aspects of the manner in which this segment was arranged as violating the standards of ethics for journalism and, failing to persuade the company to change those aspects, has refused to participate. She has been discharged. Is the discharge actionable as violating public policy? *Compare Pierce v. Ortho Pharm. Corp.*, 84 N.J. 58, 417 A.2d 505 (1980) *with Bartel v. NBC Universal, Inc.*, 543 F.3d 901 (7th Cir. 2008).

## 3.   THE SCOPE OF PROTECTION

As the divisions within the Supreme Court of Washington in *Laidlaw Transiv Services* evidence the scope or reach of the invoked public policy is, by far, is the most contentious area. The Labor Law Group's Working Group concluded that the Restatement has captured the consensus on the case clusters most commonly held to be protected. But, even as it acknowledges the possibility of yet more common case clusters to emerge, the Restatement has defined the currently protected categories—by close cabining and omission—to preclude or, less strongly, to deter that from happening.

*Close cabining.* The Restatement would have the states sanction an employer who discharges an employee for claiming a benefit under an *"employment"* law. But there are cases involving a discharge for claiming a benefit that does not derive from an employment law. In *Bowman v. State Bank of Keysville*, 229 Va. 534, 331 S.E.2d 797 (1985), for example, the bank management ordered employees who were shareholders in the bank to vote their stock as management dictated, and discharged those who refused to do so. The Supreme Court of Virginia identified the issue as "whether this employer can, with absolute impunity, discharge employees in retaliation for the proper exercise of rights as stockholders, a reason which has nothing to do with the employee's job performance." *Id.* at 800. It held that the discharges violated public policy. The Restatement's formulation rejects the Virginia Supreme Court's approach without any explanation.

N<small>OTES AND</small> Q<small>UESTIONS</small>

1. The Restatement's formulation assumes that the public good is necessarily implicated when an employee invokes a right grounded in a law protecting employees as employees. That would seem to be the common sense of the matter, but some courts disagree even then. In *Crawford Rehabilitation Services, Inc. v. Weissman*, 938 P.2d 540 (Colo. 1997), an employee was dismissed for insisting on taking rest breaks employers were required to allow by law, of ten minutes for each four-hour work period. The court agreed that discharge for "exercising a job-related right" could violate public policy, but it stressed that to be actionable the employer's action must affect "society at large rather than a purely personal or proprietary interest." *Id.* at 552. According to the court, because discharge for insisting on her work breaks involved no "public health, safety, or welfare concern," it violated no "public policy related to an employee's basic rights." *Id.* at 553. Is that correct? Why were rest periods not a matter of "basic rights"? Why the legislature legislate on this matter at all? Does an employee, fired for demanding to be paid for overtime due under state law, have a cause of action for violation of public policy? See *Willard v. Golden Gallon–TN, LLC*, 154 S.W.3d 571 (Tenn. Ct. App. 2004) (yes). How does the public interest in requiring payment for overtime differ from the public interest in requiring rest breaks?

2. All the Justices in *Laidlaw Transit Service* agreed that discharge for being a victim of domestic violence would violate public policy. Is that correct? When a state's anti-discrimination law does not include marital status, would it be tortious to discharge an employee because she married? The R<small>ESTATE</small>-M<small>ENT</small> (T<small>HIRD</small>) <small>OF</small> E<small>MPLOYMENT</small> L<small>AW</small> restricts the tort to the exercise of an employment right. Under the R<small>ESTATEMENT</small> a discharge for being a victim of domestic violence—or, conceivably, of rape—would not be actionable. Which is the better approach?

3. Return to the Virginia case, *Bowman v. State Bank of Keysville*, 331 S.E.2d 797. The subject of the dispute between management and the employee shareholders does not appear in the court's account but it is fair to assume that the employees thought the measure, supported by management, was not to their economic interest. According to the Restatement, employees would be protected when they seek economic protections assured them by law *as employees*. Should it make a difference that they were retaliated against in employment for protecting the same economic interests by exercising a right not grounded in an employment law?

4. Must there be a close connection between the conduct for which the employee is discharged and public health or safety in order for public policy to be implicated? Does the injection of this element narrow the law within predictable limits? See *Bonidy v. Vail Valley Ctr. for Aesthetic Dentistry*, 186 P.3d 80 (Colo. App. 2008) (discharge of dental assistant for insisting on taking her legally mandated rest and lunch breaks *did* violate public policy because, here, the quality of her work might suffer—presumably due to hunger and fatigue—and so patient care might be adversely affected); *Silver v. CPC–Sherwood Manor, Inc.*, 84 P.3d 728 (Okla. 2004) (discharge of employee for leaving the job to seek medical assistance violates public policy where the

employee was a food service worker and requiring the worker to stay might threaten public health). * * *

5. A supervisor remonstrates his managers for stonewalling the worker compensation claims of two employees who worked under his supervision, to the point of telling his superiors, in frustration, that he'd advise the employees to seek legal counsel. He claims he was discharged for having done so. Would his discharge be actionable under the *Restatement*'s formulation? Should it be actionable? Cf. *Ballalatak v. All Iowa Agriculture Ass'n.*, 781 N.W.2d 272 (Iowa 2010).

6. Washington's "Little Norris–LaGuardia Act" states that it is the public policy of the state that employees be free to engage in "concerted activity for mutual aid or protection." Would it be tortious for an employer to discharge self-described managers of a non-profit organization assisting the disabled for demanding the discharge of the organization's executive director for mismanagement? *Briggs v. Nova Services*, 166 Wash.2d 794, 213 P.3d 910 (2009). Would their claim be preempted by the National Labor Relations Act? Cf. *Beasley v. Food Fair of No. Carolina, Inc.*, 416 U.S. 653, 94 S.Ct. 2023, 40 L.Ed.2d 443 (1974). The Washington Supreme Court does not mention the preemption issue. Why?

*More on close cabining*. The Restatement would extend public policy to a discharge for reporting an *employer's* unlawful conduct. Might the black-letter rule extend to include a report on a co-worker's unlawful activity when that activity affects the employer's business? *DeCarlo v. Bonus Stores, Inc.*, 989 So.2d 351 (Miss. 2008). In any event, the Restatement's rule cannot be extended to the report of unlawful behavior having no connection to the employer's business. Can an employee be discharged, as a matter of public policy, because she reported having been raped by her husband? *See Green v. Bryant*, 887 F.Supp. 798 (E.D. Pa. 1995). For filing a police report against him? *See Franklin v. Monadnock Co.*, 151 Cal.App.4th 252, 59 Cal.Rptr.3d 692 (Dist. 2007); *Rayburn v. Wady Indus. Inc.*, No. C07–1008., 2008 WL 1325914 (N.D. Iowa 2008). For reporting criminal activity as a "citizen crime fighter"? *Mackie v. Vaughan Chapter–Paralyzed Veterans of America, Inc.*, 354 Ill. App.3d 731, 289 Ill.Dec. 967, 820 N.E.2d 1042, 1045 (2004). The ALI's Reporters would exclude these from protection. Why? Do you agree?

7. If an employee is discharged for reporting to his manager that an outside sales firm the company had contracted with was engaging in fraudulent or deceptive sales practices would the discharge be actionable under the *Restatement*'s formulation? Should it be actionable? *Lamson v. Crater Lake Motors, Inc.*, 346 Or. 628, 216 P.3d 852 (2009).

*Omission*. The Labor Law Group's Working Group faults the ALI's Reporters for neglecting to mention lawful off-duty conduct as implicating public policy. *Haley, supra*, at 184. Recall that the *Wisehart* court adverted to the fact that "legislation and the common law have restricted application of the at-will doctrine to balance the interests of employers and employees," noting that state statutes permit claims in cases of termination "resulting from *an employee engaging in lawful activity off premises during nonworking hours*, responding to a jury summons, and certain activities of 'whistleblowing.' " (Italics added). Off-duty conduct will be treated in Chapter VI.

# D. THE IMPLIED COVENANT OF GOOD FAITH AND FAIR DEALING

## MITCHELL v. TECK COMINCO ALASKA, INC.

Supreme Court of Alaska, 2008
193 P.3d 751

WINFREE, JUSTICE.

## I. INTRODUCTION

Teck Cominco Alaska Incorporated is the operator of the Red Dog Mine ("Mine"), which is remotely located in the Kotzebue area on lands owned by NANA Regional Corporation, Inc. Teck Cominco fired Maurice Mitchell from his job as a warehouse supervisor at the Mine after concluding that Mitchell had sexually harassed a contractor's employee and lied during the ensuing investigation. Mitchell sued Teck Cominco, asserting a statutory claim for race-based discrimination and contract claims for breach of the covenant of good faith and fair dealing and wrongful discharge. * * *

## II. FACTS AND PROCEEDINGS

### A. Facts

Maurice Mitchell is an African–American who had worked for Teck Cominco at the Mine for fifteen years before he was fired in May 2005. In early 2005 Mitchell noticed L.B., an employee of a contractor at the Mine; he wanted to meet her and have a personal relationship with her. Mitchell's friend Carla W. knew L.B., and he asked Carla to approach L.B. to see if L.B. might be interested in getting to know him. Carla and Mitchell exchanged suggestive e-mails about L.B., and in one of them Mitchell mentioned summer work in the warehouse and the possibility that he might be able to help L.B. if she needed work.

Carla talked to L.B. in April 2005. According to Carla, she told L.B. that Mitchell was interested in meeting her and that Teck Cominco hired people for the summer. Carla later maintained that she did not link the possible employment and a relationship with Mitchell; she "made sure [L.B.] knew it was separate." L.B. interpreted the job possibility and relationship with Mitchell as linked, although she later acknowledged that Carla did not express a linkage. L.B. did not respond to Carla's inquiries on Mitchell's behalf and did not apply for a job with Teck Cominco.

Mitchell continued to be interested in L.B. and again e-mailed Carla about her. In May 2005 Carla wrote a note to L.B. about Mitchell: "He wanted to know if you were interested and I told him he would have to talk to you.... [I]f you decide to get involved or not with that situation, could you please let him know? Or if you want me to tell him something, let me know.... His name is Maurice Mitchell and he is the warehouse supervisor." Carla signed the note "Carlitta" and left it at L.B.'s dormitory. L.B. complained to her supervisor after seeing the note. L.B. and her supervisor then spoke with Jim Somers in Teck Cominco's human resources department. L.B. was asked to write a statement summarizing her complaint.

Somers and Jeff Sheardown, a Teck Cominco superintendent, then met briefly with Mitchell as he was about to fly home from the Mine at the end of his regular work rotation. The parties dispute what happened at the meeting; no one took notes or recorded the conversation. Mitchell asserts that no one told him he had been accused of offering a job in exchange for sex. The parties agree that Mitchell was shown a copy of the note Carla wrote to L.B. and that Mitchell asked who "Carlitta" was. Mitchell stated in an affidavit that during the meeting he denied having anything to do with writing the note; Somers testified at a deposition that Mitchell denied asking Carla to approach L.B. "on his behalf about possibilities of a summer job and of hooking up."

Teck Cominco continued its investigation after Mitchell left the Mine on rotation. Company e-mails between Mitchell and Carla were reviewed. Carla was interviewed about whether Mitchell had asked her to offer L.B. a job in exchange for sex. Carla prepared a short written statement at Somers's request, reflecting Carla's position that her discussion with L.B. about a summer warehouse position was separate from her discussion about Mitchell's personal interest in L.B. Teck Cominco did not contact Mitchell again during its investigation.

Robert Scott, then Teck Cominco's general manager at the Mine, decided to terminate Mitchell's employment based on the conclusion that Mitchell had offered L.B. a job in exchange for sex and had lied about it during the investigation. In its May 25, 2005, termination letter to Mitchell, Teck Cominco informed Mitchell that: (1) allegations that he tied a job offer to a personal relationship had "merit"; (2) he had been "considerably less than candid" when asked about the allegations; and (3) even if the allegations were not true, his "willingness to misrepresent facts to the detriment of [his] employer" would have been cause for discipline. Teck Cominco also stated that its reasons for firing Mitchell were "exacerbated" by his abuse of company e-mail and non-solicitation policies.

## B.  Proceedings

* * * Teck Cominco ... filed a motion for summary judgment on Mitchell's contract claim for breach of the covenant of good faith and fair dealing. Mitchell filed a cross-motion for summary judgment on that claim and on his contract claim for wrongful termination. Teck Cominco argued that it was entitled to judgment as a matter of law because (1) it had conducted an investigation, there were no minimal contractual or legal standards specifying how the investigation needed to be conducted, and Mitchell's termination was the result of the conclusions drawn from that investigation; and (2) the court had already ruled that Mitchell had not

been subjected to disparate treatment. Mitchell argued that he was entitled to judgment as a matter of law because (1) he in fact had not engaged in the conduct of which he was accused, making his termination per se unlawful; (2) Teck Cominco did not conduct a fair and impartial investigation of the allegations against him, in violation of its personnel policies; and (3) Teck Cominco treated Mitchell more severely than other employees who had violated its sexual harassment policy.

The court granted Teck Cominco's motion for summary judgment and denied Mitchell's cross-motion. The court determined that Mitchell's conduct violated Teck Cominco's sexual harassment policy because of the note Carla had written to L.B. after L.B. had ignored her first overture, stating: "If there had been ... no subsequent contact and [L.B.] made no response to the offer that had been communicated—all right—there would have been no case." The court found that because Mitchell was confronted with Carla's note, Mitchell "had clear indication of what the issues were ... prior to the termination." ... Apparently considering Mitchell's contract claim for wrongful termination dismissed along with the contract claim for breach of the covenant of good faith and fair dealing, the court later entered final judgment. * * *

### B. The Superior Court Should Not Have Granted Summary Judgment to Teck Cominco on Mitchell's Claim for Breach of the Covenant of Good Faith and Fair Dealing.

At-will employment contracts in Alaska include an implied covenant of good faith and fair dealing.[1] The covenant does not have a precise definition but generally requires employers to treat like employees alike and act in a manner that a reasonable person would regard as fair.[2] The covenant has both a subjective and an objective component: the subjective component "prohibits an employer from terminating an employee for the purpose of depriving the employee of the contract's benefits," and the objective component "prohibits the employer from dealing with the employee in a manner that a reasonable person would regard as unfair."[3] Mitchell's claim for breach of the covenant is under the objective component because he contends that Teck Cominco treated him unfairly in its investigation of the sexual harassment allegations and disciplined him more severely than it did other employees.

Teck Cominco based its summary judgment motion on its contentions that (1) it conducted an investigation that was legally sufficient to meet its obligation under its policies and procedures; (2) based on the facts available through its investigation, it reasonably could have concluded that Mitchell had offered a job to L.B. in exchange for sex, making his denial of wrongdoing irrelevant; and (3) the court's grant of summary judgment on

---

**1.** *See* Belluomini v. Fred Meyer of Alaska, Inc., 993 P.2d 1009, 1012 (Alaska 1999) (citing Ramsey v. City of Sand Point, 936 P.2d 126, 133 (Alaska 1997)).

**2.** *Id.* at 1012–13.

**3.** *Id.* at 1013 (citing *Luedtke v. Nabors Alaska Drilling, Inc.,* 834 P.2d 1220, 1223–24 (Alaska 1992)).

Mitchell's discrimination claim was a determination that it had not treated Mitchell disparately.

Teck Cominco agrees that under its policies and procedures, it was required to investigate the sexual harassment allegations against Mitchell before firing him. At oral argument before us Teck Cominco conceded that the implied covenant requires some minimal level of fairness to the employee during an employer's investigation. Mitchell testified that his interview lasted no more than five minutes and that he was never told that he was accused of offering a woman a job in exchange for sex or that he was being investigated for sexually harassing L.B. Somers testified that it would be "reasonable" to ask an employee being investigated to tell his side of the story and acknowledged that he had not given Mitchell this opportunity. If even this limited testimony is accepted and viewed in the light most favorable to Mitchell, it shows that Teck Cominco never advised him of the allegations against him and never gave him a fair opportunity to present his side of the story. This creates a triable issue of fact of whether, considering all of the circumstances, Teck Cominco conducted a fair and reasonable investigation.[4]

Mitchell also created a triable issue of fact about whether he was disparately treated. Mitchell presented evidence of several Teck Cominco employees who apparently violated the company's sexual harassment policy but were disciplined less severely than Mitchell. Teck Cominco did not assert that Mitchell's factual allegations were inaccurate, but rather argued that Mitchell's disparate treatment claim under the covenant of good faith and fair dealing was the same as under his already dismissed race discrimination claim. As noted above, the legal standards for the two claims are different—an employer can breach the covenant of good faith and fair dealing when it treats members of the *same* class disparately.[1] At a minimum, Mitchell's example of the white supervisor who sexually harassed a contractor's employee and whose discipline consisted of a letter of warning created a triable issue of fact about whether Teck Cominco treated Mitchell disparately. The fact that this incident happened after Mitchell's firing does not make it irrelevant.

We therefore vacate the superior court's entry of summary judgment for Teck Cominco on Mitchell's contract claims.

## C. Material Issues of Fact Precluded Summary Judgment on Mitchell's Cross–Motion.

Mitchell asked the superior court to grant him summary judgment on his contract claims that Teck Cominco violated the covenant of good faith

---

**4.** The reasonableness of any investigation is a fact-dependent question and may depend on the strength of the evidence of the underlying infraction. Here, Mitchell strenuously denies that he offered L.B. a job in return for sex and contends he was "fired for something he never did." An unreasonable or unfair investigation may lead to an unreasonable conclusion, although this is not always the case. But having concluded that there is a triable issue of fact about the fairness and reasonableness of Teck Cominco's investigation, the reasonableness of Teck Cominco's conclusion is also a triable issue of fact.

**1.** *See Charles*, 55 P.3d at 62.

and fair dealing and wrongfully terminated his employment. He offered evidence that Teck Cominco had not disciplined or terminated other employees for sexual harassment, and Teck Cominco did not dispute his evidence. Mitchell also argued that because he did not engage in quid pro quo sexual harassment as a matter of fact or law, Teck Cominco breached its employment contract with him as a matter of law. Finally, he argued that as a matter of law Teck Cominco breached the covenant of good faith and fair dealing because it did not give Mitchell an opportunity to tell his side of the story during the investigation. Mitchell asks us to reverse the court's denial of his summary judgment motion.

We conclude that the superior court properly denied Mitchell's summary judgment motion because disputed factual issues prevented entry of summary judgment on his claims. A party is not entitled to summary judgment simply because the non-moving party does not oppose summary judgment, so the fact that Teck Cominco did not dispute some of the evidence Mitchell presented about other employees who engaged in sexual harassment does not mean that he is automatically entitled to summary judgment on that issue.

Accepting and viewing the evidence in the light most favorable to Teck Cominco, as we must do when we evaluate Mitchell's motion: (1) Carla, at Mitchell's request, discussed both a summer job with Teck Cominco and a personal relationship with Mitchell, thus implicitly linking the two when she talked to L.B.; (2) Teck Cominco promptly and reasonably investigated L.B.'s complaint; (3) Teck Cominco reasonably concluded that Mitchell's conduct violated its sexual harassment policy; and (4) Teck Cominco reasonably terminated Mitchell because of his underlying conduct, his lack of candor during the investigation, and his abuse of company e-mail. This precludes the grant of Mitchell's cross-motion for summary judgment on his contract claims. * * *

### NOTES AND QUESTIONS

1. The background of the covenant of good faith and fair dealing was explored by the Labor Law Group's Working Group:

The implied obligation of good faith in carrying out the obligations of a contract has roots in Roman law, found expression in the medieval *jus commune*, and became a major feature in the civil law, notably in Germany—in the implied obligation of "fidelity and faith," *Treu und Glauben*, under 242 of the German Civil Code (BGB) of 1900—and elsewhere on the continent. In the United Kingdom, however, the common law was, generally speaking, hostile to the general implication of such an obligation. As late as 1963, for example, Lord Justice Pearson could opine with confidence that a "person who has a right under a contract ... is entitled to exercise it and can effectively exercise it for a good reason or bad reason or no reason at all." According to Robert Summers, such was essentially the state of the law in the United States at the same time.

Both Summers and Allan Farnsworth attribute the subsequent growth of law in the United States to two sources. First, to [sic] the Uniform Commercial Code (UCC) whose primary draftsman, Karl Llewellyn, drew upon the German conception of *Treu und Glauben*. And second, to [sic] section 205 of the *Restatement (Second) of Contracts*, which extended the obligation beyond transactions covered by the UCC to all contracts as a general principle of contract law. In other words, the covenant of good faith and fair dealing is a newcomer to American contract law; its content and meaning in application remain fully to be developed.

Matthew Finkin, *Working Group on Chapter 2 of the Proposed Restatement of Employment Law: Employment Contracts: Termination*, 13 EMP. RTS. & EMP. POL'Y J. 93, 135–36 (2009) (references omitted).

2. Not surprisingly, the development of an obligation of good faith in the employee relationship is thinly developed in the United States. In many jurisdictions, good faith is *per se* inapplicable to employment, not just to employment at-will. *See, e.g., Cenveo Corp. v. CelumSolutions Software GMBH & Co. KG et al.*, 504 F.Supp.2d 574, 577–78 (D. Minn. 2007). Some states apply the covenant to employment of fixed duration but exclude it from at-will employment. *See, e.g.. Gomez v. Trustees of Harvard Univ.*, 676 F.Supp. 13, 15 (D. D.C. 1987). In those instances, although a decision to terminate an at-will employee is not subject to scrutiny on grounds of good faith, a decision not to renew an employment contract of fixed duration would be. *See, e.g., Gaujacq v. Electricite de France Int'l N. Am., Inc.*, 601 F.3d 565, 580 (D.C. Cir. 2010). Some jurisdictions have applied the covenant to at-will employment but have limited it to a "bad faith" termination benefitting the employer financially at the employee's expense, such as a termination to deprive a salesman of commissioners that otherwise would become due. *See, e.g., Shen v. Biogen Idec Inc.*, 523 F.Supp.2d 48 (D. Mass. 2007). As of 2007, the courts in twenty-one states had accepted some form of the covenant of good faith and fair dealing in employment contracts.*

3. The leading jurisdictions to apply the covenant of good faith and fair dealing to at-will employment are Alaska, Delaware, and until succeeded by a general law of wrongful dismissal, Montana.

Alaska's law was summarized in *Teck Cominco Alaska, Inc.* (above). Delaware's is summarized in *Ulmer v. Home Depot, Inc.*, 471 F.Supp.2d 474, 477 (D. Del. 2007) (references omitted):

To establish a claim for breach of the covenant of good faith and fair dealing, the plaintiff must show that his claim falls into one of four exclusive categories: "(i) where the termination violated public policy; (ii) where the employer misrepresented an important fact and the employee relied 'thereon either to accept a new position or remain in a present one'; (iii) where the employer used its superior bargaining power to deprive an employee of clearly identifiable compensation related to the

---

* Alabama, Alaska, Arizona, Arkansas, California, Connecticut, Delaware, Idaho, Illinois, Indiana, Louisiana, Massachusetts, Nevada, New Hampshire, New Jersey, New York, Oklahoma, Pennsylvania, South Carolina, Vermont, Wyoming. Haley, *supra*.

employee's past service; and (iv) where the employer falsified or manipulated employment records to create fictitious grounds for termination."

In Montana, the covenant required an employer to have "a fair and honest reason for termination." *Flanigan v. Prudential Fed. Sav. & Loan Ass'n*, 221 Mont. 419, 720 P.2d 257 (1986). This common law obligation has now been codified.

Return to the *Wisehart* case. Would *Wisehart* have a cause of action in Alaska or Delaware today?

4.   Perhaps because the covenant is so poorly developed in the United States, it is not clear whether it sounds in tort or contract. Inasmuch as it is an imposed obligation, to observe community standards of decency—Restatement of Contracts (Second) § 205—tort damages, including punitive damages, would be arguable. But, as an obligation arising out of a contract it can be argued that only contractual damages would be available. If so, what would be added by a covenant of good faith?

Suits by insureds against insurance companies for bad-faith denials of claims are widely accepted as torts because the insurance contract creates a "special relationship." The problem the courts were seeking to solve was that when insurance companies were held liable for only contract damages for breach of the implied covenant of good faith and fair dealing, unscrupulous adjusters would deny claims they knew the company owed because there was some chance the claimant would give up and go away and if the claimant did sue, the worst that would happen is that the insurance company would have to pay what it owed the claimant anyway. By giving claimants a tort claim and punitive damages when adjusters made "bad faith" denials, the courts incentivized insurance companies to fulfill their contractual obligations. Although this doctrine developed in insurance contracts, commentators have argued for its expansion to contracts more generally where there are similar "special relationships" that exhibit four characteristics found in the insurance relationship: (1) one of the parties to the contract enjoys a superior bargaining position to the extent that it is able to dictate the terms of the contract; (2) the purpose of the weaker party in entering the contract is not primarily to profit but rather to secure an essential service or product, financial security, or peace of mind; (3) the relationship of the parties is such that the weaker party places its trust and confidence in the stronger entity; and (4) there is conduct on the part of the defendant indicating an intent to frustrate the weaker party's enjoyment of the contract rights. Charles M. Louderback & Thomas W. Jurika, *Standards for Limiting the Tort of Bad Faith Breach of Contract*, 16 U.S.F. L. REV. 187, 227 (1982).

In *Foley v. Interactive Data Corp.*, 47 Cal.3d 654, 254 Cal.Rptr. 211, 765 P.2d 373 (1988), the California Supreme Court rejected the idea that the employment relationship is a "special relationship" analogous to that between the insurer and insure, and thus rejected the allowance of punitive tort damages for a breach of the implied covenant of good faith and fair dealing. The court cautioned against an "uncritical incorporation of the insurance model into the employment context." *Id.* at 393. "We are not convinced," the court said, that a "special relationship" analogous to that between insurer and insured should be deemed to exist in the usual employment relationship which would warrant recognition of a tort action for breach of the implied covenant. Even if we were to assume that the special relationship model is an appropriate one to follow in determining whether to expand tort recovery, a breach in the employment context does not place the employee in the same economic dilemma that an insured faces when an insurer in bad faith refused to pay a claim or to accept a settlement offer within policy limits. When an insurer takes such actions, the insured cannot turn to the marketplace to find another insurance company willing to pay for the loss already incurred. The wrongfully terminated employee, on the other hand, can make reasonable efforts to seek alternative employment.

*Id.* at 395–96. Moreover, unlike the insurance situation—where the insurer and the insured's interests are financially at odds—the interests of employer and employee "are most frequently in alignment." *Id.* at 396. The court was also persuaded by three prudential or policy considerations as militating toward that result: (1) the need for economic predictability as important to commercial stability, (2) the concern that employers not be "unduly deprived of discretion to dismiss an employee by the fear" of tort liability, and (3) the need to formulate a rule to assure that only " 'deserving' " plaintiffs secure relief. *Id.* at 398–99.

Is the court in *Foley* right that the employer/employee relationship is not a "special" relationship like that of insurer/insured? If an employer fires a salesperson to prevent him from being paid a commission on a sale that has already been made, can the salesperson go to another employer to receive that commission, or is he like an insured who cannot go to a different insurance company to be compensated for an existing loss? Even though employers and employees have a common interest in the success of the firm, don't they have conflicting interests in how the proceeds of the firm are divided? *See* Kenneth G. Dau–Schmidt, *A Bargaining Analysis of American Labor Law and the Search for Bargaining Equity and Industrial Peace*, 91 MICH. L. REV. 419, 442–50 (1992). If an employer is liable for only ordinary contract damages for failure to pay commissions on sales an employee has already made, what incentive does an unscrupulous employer have not to withhold such commissions hoping the unfortunate employee will just go away? What about a case under a broader definition of the implied covenant of good faith and fair dealing? For example, if an employee is fired for doing what he is instructed to do, is he in a situation similar to that of the insurance claimant?

5. The Restatement (Third) of Employment Law acknowledges that a covenant of good faith and fair dealing applies to at-will employment, but only in such a fashion as to be "consistent" with the "at-will nature of the relationship." It limits the covenant to two—and only two—situations: a discharge to prevent the vesting or accrual of a right or benefit, and a retaliation against an employee for performing the employee's contractual obligations. Notably, unlike the Restatement's treatment of public policy, no category anticipating future development is added. Under the Restatement it is, in effect, "this and no more." But the Reporters do not explain why they

reject the law of Delaware or Alaska. Should there be more, or, less strongly, the possibility for more?

6.   The Labor Law Group's Working Group assessing this section of the Restatement noted that neither of the Restatement's two protected case clusters need not draw at all upon any idea of good faith or fair dealing, because each easily could be understood simply as a breach of contract To say "if you do x I will pay you y" is implicitly to say that, "and I will not fire you to deprive you of y"; to say "I authorize or order you to do x" is to say implicitly "and I will not fire you for doing x." *See, e.g., Hammond v. Heritage Commc'ns, Inc.,* 756 S.W.2d 152, 154 (Ky. Ct. App. 1988). Why does the Restatement adopt a duty of good faith but limit it to two situations where it's not needed?

7.   The Restatement requires that the duty of good faith be "consistent" with the at-will rule. If the rule today meant that an employer could discharge for a dishonest or malicious reason, then curtailing the power to do so would be inconsistent with the rule. But, as we have seen, that is no longer the at-will rule; and the Restatement agrees—it says only that the employer need not have to prove cause to dismiss an at-will employee. Is preclusion of a dishonest or malicious discharge, as a violation of good faith, "inconsistent" with the Restatement's formulation of the at-will relationship? If not, why wouldn't a malicious or duplicitous discharge violate the covenant of good faith under the Restatement? Wouldn't such discharges at least *possibly* be inconsistent with the commonly held standards of fairness and decency?

8.   Recall the *Wisehart* court adverted to the policy basis of its refusal to sanction a dishonesty grounded dismissal:

> The at-will employment doctrine promotes flexibility and discretion for employees to seek the best position to suit their talents and for employers to seek the best employees to suit their needs. *By removing encumbrances to quitting a job or firing an employee, the at-will doctrine promotes a free market in employment analogous to the free market in goods and services generally.*

66 P.3d at 126 (emphasis added). But the Uniform Commercial Code *does* impose a duty of good faith in commercial transactions governed by it, defined as "honesty in fact and the observance of reasonable commercial standards of fair dealing in the trade." In the free market for goods, a merchant could *not* engage in a "design to mislead." *Bunge Corp. v. H.A. Recker,* 519 F.2d 449, 452 (8th Cir. 1975) (sale of soybeans). And contracts in the market for services, in the opinion of the ALI Restatement (Second) of Contracts § 205, *are* subject to a duty of good faith and fair dealing. A bank must "exercise good faith with regard to notice when deciding to terminate" a loan. *Quality Auto. Co. v. Signet Bank/Maryland,* 775 F.Supp. 849, 852–53 (D. Md. 1991). Has the *Wisehart* court gotten it exactly backward? Why is the market for labor treated *differently* than the market for goods and the market for services provided by independent contractors?

# E.  STATUTORY REGULATION

## 1.  SPECIFIC ANTI–RETALIATION LAWS

There are over twenty federal laws that forbid employers from discharging or disciplining employees for exercising rights guaranteed under
them, Examples include filing for bankruptcy; serving on a federal jury;
complaining of motor vehicle, railroad, mine, or atomic energy safety; and
so on. Some of these anti-retaliation laws allow a private cause of action,
but many do not, allowing the employee only to seek to persuade an
administrative agency to pursue the complaint. Shortcomings of such an
administrative approach include delays in processing complaints; the
inability or disinclination of the administrative agency to pursue complaints due to budgetary, personnel, or other limitations; and the relative
ineffectiveness of the eventual remedy. The "whistleblower" protection of
the Sarbanes–Oxley Act has been notable for it defects. Richard E.
Moberly, *Unfulfilled Expectations: An Empirical Analysis of Why Sarbanes–Oxley Whistleblowers Rarely Win*, 49 WM. & MARY L. REV. 65 (2007).
In some instances, the federal scheme has been held to preempt state law,
including a state common law remedy for discharge for a reason violative
of public policy. *See, e.g., Chrisman v. Philips Industries, Inc.*, 242 Kan.
772, 751 P.2d 140 (1988) (reviewing authority on whether the Energy
Reorganization Act precludes a state tort action for discharge of a quality
control inspector for refusal to approve defective nuclear products, and
holding the action to have been preempted, relegating the inspector to a
complaint to the Department of Labor). *See also Day v. Staples, Inc.*, 555
Fed. 3d 42 (1st Cir. 2009) (no state law action can be grounded in the
public policy expressed by Sarbanes–Oxley).

A variety of specific anti-retaliation laws have been enacted at the
state level. Some deal with statutory programs of workplace health and
safety, workers' compensation, and the like. Many protect employees
against employer opposition to employees' exercise of civil liberties, such
as voting and the holding of political office. Some forbid employers to
coerce employees to deal with or refrain from patronizing particular
merchants, the very employer order issued in *Payne v. Western & Atl. Ry.
See, e.g.*, CAL. LAB. CODE § 450 (West 1971), FLA. STAT. § 448.03 (1999);
N.M. STAT. § 30–13–5 (1994). Sometimes the legislature may grind exceeding small, such as expressly insulating from discharge volunteer firefighters who leave their jobs to report to emergencies. *See, e.g.*, 43 PA. STAT.
ANN. § 1201 (West 1998) (providing a private right of action).

## 2.  "WHISTLE BLOWER" LAWS

### (a.) Anti-retaliation

The purpose of whistleblower laws is to enlist a company's employees—who are often the most knowledgeable about corporate malfeasance—in an effort to root it out. One way to do that is to give the

Reward

employee a reward. This approach is found in the federal False Claims Act, which allows a private person to sue a company that has defrauded the government, and rewards the whistleblower by allowing him or her to capture a portion of the proceeds. This "reward" approach is not widespread. The most common approach is to forbid retaliation against an employee who blows the whistle. Provisions doing this have been attached to a number of specific statutes, as we have seen, but in addition several states have enacted general protections for whistleblowers. What is protected and how it is protected varies widely. In some states, statutes are very narrowly drawn; in New York the law is virtually a trap for the unwary not only because the law is very narrowly drawn in what it protects but because the "institution" of an action under it is deemed to be a waiver—an election of remedy—foregoing any other source of relief. *See Reddington v. Staten Island Univ. Hosp.*, 11 N.Y.3d 80, 862 N.Y.S.2d 842, 893 N.E.2d 120 (2008). (Whether New York law can command that resort to a federal claim has been waived by instituting a state action has not yet been decided.) In other states, protections are more capacious. An example is New Jersey, where the Supreme Court has held that the common law of discharge against public policy exists alongside the state's whistleblower statute. *Tartaglia v. UBS PaineWebber Inc.*, 197 N.J. 81, 961 A.2d 1167 (2008). Some of the salient issues—and differences—are noted below.

*Who is protected:* As we saw in the *D'Annunzio* case in Chapter 1, New Jersey has given its whistleblower law broad reach. Others, by statute or judicial construction, have given a narrower reach. In one startling example, a report of violation of nursing standards by the nursing director of a nursing home to her supervisors was held to be within her job duties and so unprotected because Minnesota's Whistleblower law does not extend to reports made within the scope of an employee's job duties. *Skare v. Extendicare Health Serv., Inc.*, 515 F.3d 836 (8th Cir. 2008) (Quaere: wouldn't such an employee likely be the person most knowledgeable of her employer's malfeasance? Wouldn't her report likely be in the public interest?) The Maine Supreme Court held that an employee discharged for having engaged in statutorily protected conduct before she was hired—before she became an "employee"—is not protected. *Costain v. Sunbury Primary Care, P.A.*, 954 A.2d 1051 (Me. 2008). Why?

*What is protected*: There is considerable divergence in what these laws protect. Some are drafted narrowly or have been given narrowing constructions. New York protects disclosure to "a supervisor or to a public body" of a violation of law that "creates and presents a substantial and specific danger to the public health or safety." N.Y. LAB. LAW. § 740 (2006). Consequently, a report to the press would be unprotected even if it is of a violation of law that endangers public health. *Calabro v. Nassau Univ. Med. Cntr.*, 424 F.Supp.2d 465 (E.D.N.Y. 2006). Michigan protects reports of violations of federal or state law to public bodies unless the employee knows that the report is false. MICH. COMP. LAWS § 15.362 (1981).

But "public body" has been read to exclude complaint to a federal regulatory agency as the statutory definition lists only state agencies. *Lewandowski v. Nuclear Mgmt. Co.*, LLC, 272 Mich.App. 120, 724 N.W.2d 718 (2006). Illinois' protection of report to a public body has been read to exclude protection for making a report internal to the company; in that case, a report of toxic mold in a facility producing sterile respiratory therapy bottles. *Riedlinger v. Hudson Respiratory Care, Inc.*, 478 F.Supp.2d 1051 (N.D. Ill. 2007).

Others are drafted more broadly or have been given generous readings. Maine protects an employee's reporting "in good faith" that which the employee has "reasonable cause" to believe to be a violation of law "to his employer or a public body," but requires that the violation be "first brought * * * to the attention of a person having a supervisory authority with the employer, and has allowed the employer a reasonable opportunity to correct that violation." The latter is inapplicable, however, "where the employee has specific reason to believe that reports of violation to his employer will not result in promptly remedying the situation." ME. REV. STAT. ANN. TIT. 26, § 833 (2007). Thus, a security guard was protected in calling the Border Patrol about the authorization of Canadian employees of an affiliate of his employer to work in the United States. *Currie v. Indus. Sec., Inc.*, 915 A.2d 400 (Me. 2007). And whereas Pennsylvania protects only reporting to the employer or to governmental agencies, the protected report includes not only violations of law but also of "a code of conduct or ethics designed to protect the interest of the public or the employer." 43 PA. CONS. STAT. ANN. §§ 1422, 1423 (West 1988).

*What is the remedy:* In New Hampshire the Act is vindicated via complaint to the state's Commissioner of Labor who, after a hearing, may order reinstatement, fringe benefits, and injunctive relief. New York, Maine, and Connecticut allow the individual a cause of action, but provide only for reinstatement with back pay and attorney fees. Pennsylvania and Michigan provide for a civil action by the employee in which the court is authorized to order reinstatement, back pay, "actual damages," and attorney fees. New Jersey provides for a civil action in which the court is authorized to reinstate with back pay, award attorney fees, issue an injunction, and order either punitive damages or a civil fine to be paid into the General Fund.

### QUESTIONS

1.  Is a whistleblower statute necessary? If it is:

a.  Should the statute require an employee to exhaust an intramural complaint? If so, to whom? Should the statute require the employee complaint to be in writing?

b.  Should only complaints to a government agency be protected? To a private professional association? To a private "watchdog" organization? To the press?

c. What kinds of complaints should be protected? Of illegal activity? Unethical activity that violates no current statute or administrative regulation? Activity that the employee believes to be morally or socially undesirable? In the latter two cases, are the employee's own sincerely held beliefs enough to warrant protection or is some factual grounding required?

d. What should the remedy be?

### (b.) "Structural" Encouragement

Professor Richard Moberly has termed the legislative regime of the Sarbanes–Oxley Act the "structural" approach to protecting whistleblowers, as opposed the old "anti-retaliation" approach of most whistleblower laws. Richard E. Moberly, *Sarbanes–Oxley's Structural Model to Encourage Corporate Whistleblowers*, 2006 BYU. L. REV. 1107 (2006). The Sarbanes–Oxley Act provides that every audit committee of the Board of Directors of a publicly traded corporation "shall establish procedures for . . . the confidential, anonymous submission by employees of the issuer of concerns regarding questionable accounting or auditing matters." 15 U.S.C. § 78j–1(m)(4)(B) (2006). Thus the Act requires employers to enlist their employees in a joint effort to prevent malfeasance, rather than following the traditional anti-retaliation approach which pits the employee against the employer as an adversary. The Securities and Exchange Commission's implementing regulations for Sarbanes–Oxley do no more than to echo the statutory language. 17 C.F.R. § 240.10A–3(b)(ii) (2009). There has been no litigation on what this means or what the legal consequences are vis-à-vis erroneous reports of malfeasance.

### NOTES AND QUESTIONS

1. The whistleblower provision of Sarbanes–Oxley is silent on what type of "procedure" it mandates. The provision is commonly spoken of as a telephonic "hotline," but any form of communication is possible. Whatever it is the law requires anonymity for the speaker and confidentiality for the information covered by the Act.

a) Does the federal conferral of statutory anonymity preclude the compulsory disclosure of the name of the informant in a suit for defamation, malicious interference in prospective economic advantage, intentional infliction of emotional distress, or invasion of privacy?

b) Does the statutory conferral of confidentiality accord the informant or the company an absolute privilege as a defense in the event of such litigation? Does it preempt the states from applying these torts?

2. Because Sarbanes–Oxley applies to all U.S. publicly traded corporations, it applies also to their offices abroad. However, the data protection laws in Europe and elsewhere limit the transfer of personal information to countries that do not afford equivalent protection, which the U.S. does not. The French data protection authority, the CNIL, has allowed companies to institute whistleblowing systems, but they must be authorized by the CNIL and

meet certain of French data protection rules. The CNIL has strongly discouraged, but not forbidden, anonymity. CNIL, FAQs ON WHISTLEBLOWING SYSTEMS (2008). It opined:

> In most cases, anonymity is not a good solution, whether for the person issuing the report or for the organisation:
>
> — Being anonymous does not stop others from successfully guessing who raised the concern;
>
> — It is harder to investigate the concern if people can not ask follow-up questions;
>
> — It is easier to organise the protection of the whistleblower against retaliation if the report is made openly;
>
> — Anonymity can lead people to focus on the whistleblower, maybe suspecting that he or she is raising the concern maliciously;
>
> — The organisation may let a corporate culture of "anonymous letters" develop internally;
>
> — The social atmosphere within the organisation could deteriorate if the employees know that they can be anonymously reported at any time through the system.

Sarbanes–Oxley requires anonymity. Should it?

## 3. GENERAL LAW OF WRONGFUL DISMISSAL

It was argued more than three decades ago that the situation in the United States, a legal crazy-quilt which protects unionized employees against a wrongful discharge by collectively bargained grievance-arbitration systems, minority employees under anti-discrimination laws, and other employees only insofar as they can claim one of the statutory or common law exceptions to the at will rule, calls for statutory reform. *See, e.g.,* Clyde Summers, *Individual Protection Against Unjust Dismissal: Time for a Statute,* 62 VA. L. REV. 481 (1976). To some, the piling of exception upon exception to the "at-will" rule today, each exception taking on a legal life its own, makes the call for a coherent law of wrongful dismissal all that more pressing not only out of fairness to the individual but out of economic efficiency.

There have been some very modest efforts at general statutory reform on the subject of employee discharges. In 1987, Montana adopted the Wrongful Discharge from Employment Act (WDEA), MONT. CODE ANN. § 39–2–901—905 (1997). The Act provides that, after a probationary period, all covered employees are subject to dismissal only for good cause, and it gives the employee the right to challenge a termination in court or before an arbitrator. The WDEA encourages the parties to arbitrate disputes by providing that if a party rejects an offer to arbitrate, and then loses in court, that party is responsible for the other party's costs and attorney fees. Employees who are covered by a collective bargaining agreement or enjoy a fixed term contract are exempt from coverage of the Act. Students of the Montana law report that it has not lived up to its potential. Leonard Bierman, Karen Vinton & Stuart A. Youngblood, *Montana's Wrongful Discharge from Employment Act: The View from the Montana Bar*, 54 MONT. L. REV. 367, 379 (1993). One problem is that often lawyers are unwilling to pursue cases under the law because of the perceived lack of adequate compensation.

In 1991, The National Conference of Commissioners on Uniform State Law proposed a Model Employment Termination Act (META). This proposed act has three fundamental provisions: that employers have good cause for dismissal; the replacement of court trials with arbitration as the preferred method of litigating discharge suites; and strict limitations on employer liability for wrongful discharge suits. Employers are allowed to avoid the good-cause requirement by expressly contracting with the employee for severance pay instead. Employees covered by a collective bargaining agreement are exempt. To date, META has been introduced in only ten states and has been seriously considered in only one or two. No state has adopted it and it is not actively under consideration in any jurisdiction. James J. Brudney, *Mediation and Some Lessons from the Uniform State Law Experience*, 13 OHIO ST. J. ON DISP. RESOL. 795, 820 (1998); Jeremy B. Fox & Hugh D. Hindman, *The Model Employment Termination Act: Provisions and Discussion*, 6 EMP. RESP. & RTS. J. 33 (1993). The major elements of the META are compared with those of Montana's WDEA in Marc Jarsulic, *Protecting Workers from Wrongful Discharge: Montana's Experience With Tort and Statutory Regimes*. 3 EMP. RTS. & EMP. POL'Y J. 105 (1999).

The American territory of Puerto Rico has enacted the "Discharge Indemnity Law," which requires that an employer pay a discharged employee severance pay, unless the employer can show that the discharge is for "good cause." P.R. LAWS ANN. tit. 29, §§ 185a–185l (1985). The severance payment owed equal to one week's pay for each year of service plus: one month's pay if the employee has been employed less than 5 years, two months' pay if the employee has been employed 5–15 years, and 3 months' pay if the employee has been employed more than 15 years. The statute provides a detailed definition of good cause. The provisions of the law are mandatory, cannot be waived by contract, and provide the employee's exclusive remedy. The statute exempts employees who are not at-will because they are under a contact for a fixed term.

The U.S Virgin Islands have enacted the Wrongful Discharge Act (WDA). After a six-month probationary period, an employee can be discharged under the WDA only for one of nine specifically enumerated reasons.* In addition, an employer may terminate an employee as a result

---

\* Under the WDA, an employer may dismiss an employee:

a) who engages in a business which conflicts with his duties to his employer or renders him a rival of his employer

b) whose insolent or offensive conduct toward a customer of the employer injures the employer's business;

c) whose use of intoxicants or controlled substances interferes with the proper discharge of his duties;

of the cessation of business operations or as a result of a general cutback in the work force due to economic hardship, or as a result of the employee's participation in unprotected concerted activity. V.I. CODE ANN. TIT. 24 § 76 (1996). The employee's rights under the WDA can be modified by union contract. Some employees are specifically excluded from the WDA including: agricultural employees, firemen, domestic servants, executives, professionals, and some public employees. *Id.* § 62.

Even so, throughout much of the world—in the U.K., most of continental Europe, the federal sector in Canada, Japan, Brazil, and South Africa—so-called "typical" employees, those hired on indefinite employment, may not be dismissed without just a socially justifiable cause. They have access to public system of conciliation and adjudication of their claims, albeit under widely varying legal standards, burdens of proofs, and remedies. Many of these laws are summarized in INTERNATIONAL LABOR & EMPLOYMENT LAWS (Tim Darby & William Keller eds., 3d ed 2008–09).

*[handwritten margin note: Many countries require cause]*

The economic consequences of wrongful dismissal law have been the subject of intense theoretical debate and empirical investigation. Critics commonly model their argument on the view of such a law as a tax on employment: complex wrongful-dismissal laws make employers more cautious about hiring, reduce the job opportunities of higher risk applicants, and contribute to a higher rate of unemployment. Supporters of wrongful dismissal laws argue that such laws increase job attachment, reduce employee resistance to the introduction of new technologies and, closely related, encourage employers to invest in "human capital"—*i.e.*, because it *is* difficult to fire without having to justify it to a neutral adjudicator, employers have an interest in making sure the incumbent workforce is kept up to snuff in skills training and knowledge acquisition. *See* Christoph F. Buechtemann, *Introduction: Employment Security and Labor Markets*, *in* EMPLOYMENT SECURITY AND LABOR MARKET BEHAVIOR: INTERDISCIPLINARY APPROACHES & INTERNATIONAL EVIDENCE 3 (Christoph F. Buechtemann ed., 1993) (reviewing the theoretical debate).

At the empirical level, much turns on the design of the particular protective scheme: whether or not mass dismissals triggered by economic shocks are included or only dismissals for individual performance or behavior, what the standards of judgment are, how efficiently they are administered, and what the remedies are. *See, e.g.*, David Young, E.C. Directorate–General for Economic and Financial Affairs, *Employment*

---

d) who wilfully and intentionally disobeys reasonable and lawful rules, orders, and instructions of the employer; provided, however, the employer shall not bar an employee from patronizing the employer's business after the employee's working hours are completed;

e) who performs his work assignments in a negligent manner;

f) whose continuous absences from his place of employment affect the interests of his employer;

g) who is incompetent or inefficient, thereby impairing his usefulness to his employer;

h) who is dishonest; or

i) whose conduct is such that it leads to the refusal, reluctance or inability of other employees to work with him.

*Id.* § 76.

*Protection Legislation: Its Economic Impact and the Case for Reform*, Economic Papers No. 186 (July 2003); David H. Autor et al., *The Costs of Wrongful–Discharge Laws* (Nat'l Bureau of Econ. Research, Working Paper No. 9425, 2002). For a single-country study, see Dorothea Alewell, Eileen Schott, and Franziska Wiegand, *The Impact of Dismissal Protection on Employers' Cost of Terminating Employment Relations in Germany: An Overview of Empirical Research and Its White Spots*. 30 COMP. LAB. L. & POL'Y J. 667 (2009).

If one were to devise a system to deal with wrongfully discharged employees the desiderata would doubtless include the following:

1.   *Full Compensation*: The employee should be fully compensated for the wrong.

2.   *Expedition*: The wronged individual should be compensated as swiftly as possible—to maintain his or her standard of living, to secure psychological vindication, and, for the employer, to put the dispute to final rest, so also to dispel any lingering morale consequences to the remaining complement of employees. This may suggest the encouragement of a process of settlement.

3.   *Fairness*: Where the dispute is not settled, a neutral, unbiased adjudication is required. This could be a judge, a jury, an administrative hearing officer, or an arbitrator.

4.   *Accuracy*: Only those actually wronged should be afforded a remedy; those properly discharged should not. This may require an adversary proceeding with the participation of counsel before a neutral factfinder.

5.   *Low Transaction Costs*: The costs of the system, of attorney and other fees, should be as low as possible.

It should be immediately apparent that several of these desiderata are in conflict: the larger the compensation potentially involved, the greater the need for accuracy—certainly from the employer's perspective; the greater the need for accuracy, the greater the demand for due process—for pre-trial discovery, lengthier hearings, on the record and appellate review; the greater the demand for due process, the higher the transaction costs, especially attorney fees—and the greater the delay.

Tort litigation provides the fullest due process in terms of pre-trial discovery, use of expert witnesses, role of counsel, and the like. But the operation of the system as it has played out in individual employment litigation was summarized some years ago by Professor Clyde Summers, *Effective Remedies for Employment Rights: Preliminary Guidelines and Proposals*. 141 U. PA. L. REV. 457, 469 (1992) (references omitted):

The high costs of litigation in these cases raise a serious social question concerning transaction costs. In the median case, the wrongfully discharged employee ends up with a net payment of less than $74,500. For every wronged employee thus compensated, the employer pays legal fees of one and a half the estimated median fee, or about

$97,500, and the plaintiff's lawyer obtains $54,000, for a total of about $151,500 in fees. To this figure, one must add court and out of pocket costs to both sides of approximately $10,000. In short, more than $160,000 may be spent to transfer less than $74,500 of compensation to a wronged employee. This entire cost is ultimately borne by the employer while the wronged employee goes undercompensated. This is scarcely a legal remedy process but rather a redistribution device which enriches lawyers at the expense of both the employer and the employee.

In offering some guidance toward a better system—one entailing control of the claim by the employee, guaranteed protection against non-retaliation, the need for effective deterrence, and low transaction costs—Professor Summers argues that:

> Informal and simple procedures may provide less refined justice. Some *But* facts may not get discovered or fully explored; some legal arguments may not be as fully developed or understood; and the decisions may not be as carefully considered or articulated. Because the procedure is less formal and elaborate, there is less willingness to place large amounts at risk, so recoveries for emotional distress must be limited and punitive damages excluded. The employee's remedy, therefore, may be less. A balance, however, must be struck between more perfect outcomes and larger recoveries for a few on the one hand, and affordable costs with more limited damages to many on the other. Where the employment rights of individual workers with limited resources are involved, the balance tips heavily on the side of affordable costs and smaller recoveries. More perfect decision-making ought not to be bought by depriving most employees of any decision at all.

*Id.* at 534 (reference omitted).

Do any of the statutory schemes set forth in this section (Montana's WDEA, the META, Puerto Rico's Discharge Indemnity Law or the Virgin Island's WDA) satisfy either the desiderata set out above, Professor Summers' guidelines, or both? Can you propose a statutory solution that does?

# F. MANNER OF TERMINATION

## STRINGER v. WAL–MART STORES, INC.

Supreme Court of Kentucky, 2004
151 S.W.3d 781

### I. INTRODUCTION AND PROCEDURAL BACKGROUND

In June and July, 1995, Appellants, who were employees of a Monticello, Kentucky Wal–Mart, Inc. ("Wal–Mart") store, were terminated for "unauthorized removal of company property" and "violation of company policy"—specifically, for eating "claims candy," *i.e.,* candy from open or torn bags removed from the store's shelves that had been taken to the store's "claims area" to be processed by a claims clerk and then either discarded or returned. Appellants filed suit against Wal–Mart and their supervisor, Appellee Anthony Whitaker ("Whitaker") contending that, before, during, and after their termination, Wal–Mart committed the tortious acts of (1) intentional infliction of emotional distress (IIED)/outrage, by engaging in illegal surveillance of Appellants and conducting accusatory termination interviews; (2) defamation, through written and oral accusations to, and in the presence of, third parties to the effect that Appellants had been discharged for theft; and (3) an invasion of Appellant's privacy through violations of the provisions of KRS Chapter 526, which criminalizes conduct relating to eavesdropping.

A jury returned a verdict in Appellants' favor on each of their claims. In accordance with the jury's verdict, the Wayne Circuit Court entered judgment awarding each Appellant $2,000,000.00 in compensatory damages—$1,000,000.00 for "injury to reputation" and $1,000,000.00 for "embarrassment, humiliation, and mental anguish"—and $3,000,000.00 in punitive damages. Appellant Virginia Stringer ("Stringer") was awarded an additional $20,000.00 for her lost wages.

The Court of Appeals held that the trial court erred by failing to direct a verdict in Appellees' favor as to each of Appellants' claims and reversed the trial court's judgment in its entirety. We granted discretionary review and now affirm the Court of Appeals's holding with respect to the IIED/outrage claim and the invasion-of-privacy/eavesdropping claim, but reverse its holding as to Appellants' claim for defamation because the evidence at trial was sufficient to submit that claim to the jury. Because the jury's compensatory and punitive damages verdicts do not segregate the damages awarded for each claim, we vacate the previous damage awards and remand the case for the trial court to conduct a retrial solely to determine appropriate damages for Appellants' defamation claim.

[The court's treatment of the eavesdropping issue is omitted. The subject will be taken up in Chapter VI.]

## II. ANALYSIS

### A. STANDARD OF REVIEW

\* \* \*

### B. IIED / OUTRAGEOUS CONDUCT

Count I of Appellants' complaint stated a claim for IIED/outrage. Paragraphs 1–17 detailed Appellants' "conspiracy theory," *i.e.*, Appellants' claim that store policy actually permitted the consumption of claims candy and that the store's manager, Whitaker, installed the video equipment in order to fabricate a pretense for terminating Appellants when his actual motive was to prevent his own demotion by reducing payroll expenses and demonstrating a "get tough on inventory shrinkage" stance. The remainder of Count I alleged:

18.    That at the time of the discharge of the plaintiffs, they were told that they could not leave the store after having worked the entire night. The[y] were brought in one at a time and were abruptly told by Anthony Whitaker and Lee Scholenberger that they were being fired for "stealing" and that they had videotaped them. The plaintiff, Donnie H. Brummett, was told to make it easy on himself and admit to stealing stereos and electric razors. The plaintiff, Virginia Stringer, was questioned about missing items in the claims area such as fishing rods. The plaintiffs, during their discharge, were treated by the defendants and their representative as criminals (thieves). In fact, the plaintiff, Donnie H. Brummett, was told that if he did not sue them they would not press criminal charges. * * *

*Taped incident as pretext*

At trial, however, Appellants argued that Appellees' outrageous conduct consisted of more than the set-up, surveillance, and accusatory exit interviews. And, on appeal, Appellants advocate that the jury's verdict was supported by evidence demonstrating that Appellees: (1) escorted three of the four Appellants out of the store following their termination; (2) implied to other employees that Appellants were thieves (an assertion that is facially duplicative of Appellants' defamation claim); (3) attempted to deny Appellants their unemployment benefits; and (4) used the surveillance tape to train employees. * * *

*Extreme and outrageous conduct.* The cases thus far decided have found liability only where the defendant's conduct has been extreme and outrageous. It has not been enough that the defendant has acted with an intent which is tortious or even criminal, or that he has intended to inflict emotional distress, or even that his conduct has been characterized by "malice," or a degree of aggravation which would entitle the plaintiff to punitive damages for another tort. Liability has been found only where the conduct has been so outrageous in character, and so extreme in degree, as to go beyond all possible bounds of decency, and to be regarded as atrocious, and utterly intolerable in a civilized community. Generally, the case is one in which the recitation of the facts to an average member of the community would arouse his resentment against the actor, and lead him to exclaim, "Outrageous!"

The liability clearly does not extend to mere insults, indignities, threats, annoyances, petty oppression, or other trivialities. The rough edges of our society are still in need of a good deal of filing down, and in the meantime, plaintiffs will necessarily be expected and required to be hardened to a certain amount of rough language, and to occasional acts that are definitely inconsiderate and unkind. There is no reason for the law to intervene in every case where some one's feelings are hurt. There must still be freedom to express an unflattering opinion, and some safety valve must be left through which irascible tempers may blow off relatively harmless steam....[1]

---

**1.**  RESTATEMENT (SECOND) OF TORTS § 46(1) cmt. d (1965). *See also Kroger Company v. Willgruber,* Ky., 920 S.W.2d 61, 65 (1996) ("Citizens in our society are expected to withstand

With these goalposts in mind, Kentucky courts have found plaintiffs' proof of outrageous conduct sufficient to support an outrage/IIED claim in cases where the defendants: (1) harassed the plaintiff "by keeping her under surveillance at work and home, telling her over the CB radio that he would put her husband in jail and driving so as to force her vehicle into an opposing lane of traffic";[2] (2) intentionally failed to warn the plaintiff for a period of five months that defendant's building, in which plaintiff was engaged in the removal of pipes and ducts, contained asbestos;[3] (3) engaged in "a plan of attempted fraud, deceit, slander, and interference with contractual rights, all carefully orchestrated in an attempt to bring [plaintiff] to his knees";[4] (4) committed same-sex sexual harassment in the form of "frequent incidents of lewd name calling coupled with multiple unsolicited and unwanted requests for homosexual sex";[5] . . .

Outrageousness has been found lacking, however, in less-egregious cases where the defendant: (1) refused to pay medical expenses arising out of an injured worker's compensation claim;[6] . . . (5) wrongfully terminated the plaintiff;[7] . . . (8) wrongfully garnished plaintiff's wages pursuant to a forged agreement;[8] and (9) impregnated plaintiff's wife.[9] . . .

After examining the evidence in a light most favorable to Appellants, we agree with the Court of Appeals that the trial court erred when it denied Appellees' motion for a directed verdict. We have set a high threshold for IIED/outrage claims, i.e., that the conduct at issue must be "a deviation from all reasonable bounds of decency and is utterly intolerable in a civilized community," and, when measured against this standard, the jury's verdict in this case was flagrantly against the evidence. Appellants were at-will employees, and Wal–Mart could terminate their employ-

---

petty insults, unkind words and minor indignities. Such irritations are a part of normal, every day life and constitute no legal cause of action.") . . .

**2.** *Craft,* 671 S.W.2d at 248. *See also id.* at 250 ("The conduct alleged here is a deviation from all reasonable bounds of decency and is utterly intolerable in a civilized community. It qualifies as harassment intended to cause extreme emotional distress.").

**3.** *Bailey,* 873 S.W.2d at 196.

**4.** *Willgruber,* 920 S.W.2d at 64–67.

**5.** *Brewer,* 15 S.W.3d at 7. *Id.* at 6 ("As to whether Brewer's conduct was outrageous and intolerable to the point of being actionable . . . we have no trouble finding that it is.").

**6.** *Mitchell,* 712 S.W.2d at 341 ("The delay in the payment of medical bills demonstrated in this case cannot be the basis for an action for outrageous conduct pursuant to *Craft v. Rice.*"); *General Acc. Ins. Co. v. Blank,* Ky.App., 873 S.W.2d 580, 582 (1993) ("*Craft* is distinguishable from a situation involving a mere termination or delay of payments owned under a contract or a judgment which were being processed through judicial or administrative channels. Certainly, GA had just cause to question the necessity of back surgery, and its conduct simply did not rise to a level of extreme or outrageous conduct.").

**7.** *Bednarek,* 780 S.W.2d at 632 ("The conduct of Kroger or the Union as alleged in the complaint, and shown by the evidence in the record, does not reach that standard [of outrageousness.]").

**8.** *Kentucky Farm Bureau Mutual Ins. Co. v. Burton,* Ky.App., 922 S.W.2d 385 (1996) ("[W]e do not believe that [plaintiff] has shown that Farm Bureau's actions constituted outrageous conduct. . . . While the manner in which the proceedings were handled—from beginning to end— undoubtedly reflects ineptitude and indifference, we simply cannot agree that it rose to the level of intentional infliction of severe emotional distress according to the directives set forth under governing case law.").

**9.** *Arlinghaus v. Gallenstein,* Ky.App., 115 S.W.3d 351 (2003).

ment at any time "for good cause, for no cause, or for a cause that some might view as morally indefensible."[10] Accordingly, the "heart" of Appellant's IIED/outrage claim, *i.e.*, that Whitaker manufactured an excuse to fire them in order to save his own job, falls short of the extreme and outrageous conduct necessary to support such a claim. Although we recognized in *Willgruber* that an employer's conduct in connection with the termination of an employee can constitute outrageous conduct, Appellees' actions in this case do not approach those found actionable as IIED/outrage in *Willgruber*. We stress that "major outrage is essential to the tort; and the mere fact that the actor knows that the other will regard the conduct as insulting, or will have his feelings hurt, is not enough." The "indignities" associated with Appellees' escort of Appellants from the store premises and the other conduct identified at trial did not present a jury question as to IIED/outrage in this case. We thus affirm the Court of Appeals's holding that reversed the judgment for this claim in favor of Appellants.

## C. DEFAMATION

* * * At trial, Appellants introduced evidence concerning five separate allegedly defamatory oral or written statements made by Appellees: (1) oral statements made by Whitaker at a store-wide meeting he conducted in a public area of the store within a few weeks of Appellants' firing that were "more or less that some associates had been fired for stealing," that indicated that theft would not be tolerated at the store and "it didn't matter whether it was an associate or customers," and that "left the impression that there was more to it ... than just claims candy;" (2) an oral statement from James Carey, a Wal–Mart Assistant Manager, who, when asked whether Appellants had been terminated for eating candy from the claims area, responded " '[t]here was more to it than that' and that he couldn't talk about it" while in the employee lounge and in the presence of at least three employees; (3) a written document completed by Whitaker at the termination interview specifying that each employee had been terminated from employment because of "unauthorized removal of company property," that was forwarded to the store's personnel office and its contents were entered into the corporate computer system; (4) an oral statement made by Wal–Mart personnel at a district-wide meeting of Wal–Mart management to the effect that "[w]e had four people fired for stealing out of receiving [or for an integrity issue."—"the witness was equivocal regarding the exact phrasing]. I'm not going to tell you who it is or what store it is"; and (5) Whitaker's forwarding of the exit interview documents, which indicated the reason for termination as "unauthorized removal of company property," to Frankfort in connection with his decision to contest Appellants' unemployment claims. * * *

[The elements of the tort are]

   1.  defamatory language

---

**10.** *Firestone Textile Co. v. Meadows*, Ky., 666 S.W.2d 730, 731 (1983).

2.    about the plaintiff

3.    which is published and

4.    which causes injury to reputation.

The first three elements of the prima facie case are relatively easy to comprehend. "Defamatory language" is broadly construed as language that "tends so to harm the reputation of another as to lower him in the estimation of the community or to deter third persons from associating or dealing with him." And, "[i]t is for the jury to determine, on the basis of competent evidence, whether a defamatory meaning was attributed to it by those who received the communication. The terms should be construed in their most natural meaning and should be 'measured by the natural and probable effect on the mind of the average reader.'" Element two, "about the plaintiff" largely speaks for itself, but it is worth noting that the plaintiff need not be specifically identified in the defamatory matter itself so long as it was so reasonably understood by plaintiff's "friends and acquaintances ... familiar with the incident." The notion of "publication" is a term of art, and defamatory language is "published" when it is intentionally or negligently communicated to someone other than the party defamed. * * *

Generally, defamatory words written or spoken of another are divided into two classes in determining the extent to which they are actionable. Words may be actionable per se, or per quod. In the former class, damages are presumed and the person defamed may recover without allegation or proof of special damages. In the latter class, recovery may be sustained only upon an allegation and proof of special damages. * * *

We need not belabor this discussion ... however, because a "[f]alse accusation of theft is actionable per se—that is, libelous or slanderous per se." Accordingly, Appellants were not required to provide affirmative proof of injury to their reputations in order to recover for the defamatory statements at issue in this case:

We find that Appellants thus demonstrated a prima facie case for common law defamation per se.

To determine whether the evidence was sufficient to support the jury's verdict for Appellants, however, we must also address Appellees' defenses. First, it is beyond dispute that "[i]n this state, truth is a complete defense[,]" and thus a defendant able to prove the truth of the defamatory statement at issue cannot be held liable for defamation:

Accordingly, "if the evidence supports, without contradiction or room for reasonable difference of opinion, the defense that these [statements] were substantially true, it would necessarily follow that the jury should have been directed to find a verdict for the defendant, because the truth is always a complete defense."

Second, although the prima facie case for common law defamation presumes malice, and therefore does not require the plaintiff to make an affirmative showing of it, we have determined that strict liability of that sort is inappropriate in circumstances where the publisher, a third person, or the public has a cognizable interest in communicating the defamatory information. Accordingly, we have recognized a series of qualified or conditional privileges, including "where 'the communication is one in which the party has an interest and it is made to another having a corresponding interest, the communication is privileged if made in good faith and without actual malice.' " "The determination of the existence of privilege is a matter of law," and because of the common interests implicated in the employment context, Kentucky courts have recognized a qualified privilege for defamatory statements relating to the conduct of employees.

Qualified privileges exist where the circumstances "preclude any presumptions of malice, but still leave the party responsible for both falsehood and malice if affirmatively shown." When a qualified privilege is established, the presumption of malice disappears, and thus "false and defamatory statements will not give rise to a cause of action unless maliciously uttered." Stated otherwise, "[i]f a communication come[s] within the class denominated . . . qualifiedly privileged, no recovery can be had." However, the key word is "qualified," and the privilege can be lost if abused or exceeded:

The condition attached to all such qualified privileges is that they must be exercised *in a reasonable manner and for a proper purpose.* The immunity is forfeited if the defendant steps outside the scope of the privilege, or abuses the occasion. The qualified privilege does not extend . . . to the publication of irrelevant defamatory matter with no bearing upon the public or private interest which is entitled to protection.

Thus, a directed verdict in Appellees' favor would be appropriate despite Appellants' prima facie case of defamation per se if the jury could not have reasonably found both that the statements in question were false and that Appellees had waived any claim of privilege through abuse and/or malice. The Court of Appeals below found the "truth defense" to be Appellees' trump card:

The record clearly established that eating claims candy without paying was plainly against published company policy. The Associate Handbook specifically addresses such situation:

Dishonesty in any form will result in immediate termination. . . .

In a retail environment, taking anything, large or small, is dishonest. For example, eating candy from a broken bag without paying for it is dishonest.

Upon the foregoing, the act of eating claims candy without paying was considered a dishonest act and constituted grounds for dismissal. The simple fact is that [Appellants] "took" company property without paying; this constituted theft of company property. As a matter of law, we hold that Wal–Mart's alleged statements surrounding appellees' termination were not actionable as such statements were true. . . .

Although the parties' briefs address themselves primarily to this finding by the Court of Appeals, we conclude that it is unnecessary for us to wade into the issue of whether "company policy," as actually implemented in the Wal–Mart store in question, permitted or prohibited the consumption of claims candy because the defamatory statements in this case attributed larcenous actions beyond mere claims candy consumption to Appellants. In the second defamatory statement of which Appellants complain, the Assistant Manager stated that "there was more to" Appellants' termination than the theft of claims candy, which, in the context stated, could reasonably have been, and was, according to the testimony of Wal–Mart employee Joyce Floyd, who overheard the statement, interpreted as an assertion that Appellants had stolen items in addition to claims candy. This defamatory statement, for which Appellees were vicariously liable, appears to have no factual basis whatsoever, and thus Appellees cannot rely upon its truth in defense to Appellants' defamation claim. Although the context of the statement suggests the possibility of a qualified privilege, a jury could easily and reasonably have found that the privilege was exceeded in this case. It is clear that "when . . . there is any evidence of actual malice or malice in fact, the case should go to the jury." While actual malice "requires a showing of knowledge of falsity of the defamatory statement or reckless disregard of its truth or falsity," "[m]alice can be inferred from the fact of . . . falsity." Accordingly, regardless of the truth or falsity or privileged nature of any of the other defamatory statements, we cannot conclude that the jury's verdict as to defamation was flagrantly against the evidence, and we thus reverse the opinion of the Court of Appeals as to its disposition of the defamation claim and reinstate the trial court's liability judgment. * * *

GRAVES, JUSTICE, dissenting.

The majority presents a sound and thorough explanation of the law of defamation in Kentucky. However, the legal analysis presented in the majority opinion reminds me of Mark Twain's observation, "Truth is mighty and will prevail. There is nothing the matter with this, except that it ain't so." Truth is a complete defense to defamation claims; unfortunately, the sophistry of persuasive attorneys has convinced both the jury and this Court of an unreasonable interpretation of the alleged defamatory statement.

The statement that, " '[t]here was more to it than that' and that he couldn't talk about it" appears to be the jackpot in the majority's search for anything capable of a defamatory meaning. Unfortunately, there is nothing in that statement that a reasonable juror could find defamatory. The statement is clearly offensive to a disgruntled employee, and while I sympathize with Appellants' attitude toward their former employer, I fail to find any reasonable defamatory meaning to an objective observer that would establish Appellees' liability. Of all the facts alleged in Appellants' brief, I found the statement made by the Assistant Manager reflected a measure of decorum in that it conveyed nothing at all. "There's more to it than that" generally means, "I don't want to talk about it:" an interpretation that seems exceptionally reasonable when he continued to say exactly that. The statement would not imply any wrongdoing to a reasonable listener.

Here, Appellants' own admissions established the truth of Wal–Mart's statements regarding Appellants' terminations. Appellants' defamation claim is that Wal–Mart and Whitaker implied to others that Appellants were thieves. Yet, all four of these former employees admit that it was they—not their employer—who used the terminology "thief" to describe the reason for their discharge.

Even assuming that Mr. Whitaker "imputed" theft as the reason for Appellants' discharge, the statement is true. A thief is someone who takes something that does not belong to him. Or, as the Court of Appeals correctly reasoned: "The simple fact is that Appellees 'took' company property without paying; this constituted theft of such company property."

Even though the food Appellants admitted eating had no value to Wal–Mart and could not be paid for, Appellants' "destined for the dumpster" argument is wholly irrelevant to the fact that they violated the company's dishonesty policy. It is also disingenuous in that it ignores the fundamental distinction between taking merchandise from the claims area before the claims clerk is able to process it—which deprives Wal–Mart of receiving credit for damaged goods—and consuming merchandise in the employees' lounge with management approval after it has been processed and accounted for in order to maintain inventory control. For claims processing purposes, the candy had residual value to Wal–Mart and Appellants had no right to appropriate it.

Mr. Whitaker's policy is undisputed: employees cannot eat anything from claims before it is recorded and accounted for, and even then not without permission. Appellants admit this fact. At the employee meeting several days before Appellants were fired, Mr. Whitaker reiterated the policy in no uncertain terms: "And, if anyone has taken anything without paying for it, then you need to stop it immediately." * * *

It is true that Appellants consumed unprocessed claims merchandise belonging to Wal–Mart. It is also true that consuming claims merchandise is a violation of Wal–Mart's honesty policy. It is finally true, then, as marked on Appellants' termination forms, that they were discharged for violation of company policy and unauthorized removal of company property.

Based on the truth defense and the unreasonableness of a defamatory meaning to any of the alleged defamatory statements, I would affirm the Court of Appeals. The alleged defamation was not only substantially true, but also true in its essential parts.

COOPER, J., and WINTERSHEIMER, J., join in this dissent.

### NOTES AND QUESTIONS

1. Recall that in *Wakefield Thermal Solutions*, the employer was contractually required to investigate the employee's conduct before deciding on whether it merited discipline; the failure to conduct a sufficiently thorough investigation would be actionable in contract. In *Stringer* the employees had no such contractual protection; they complained only of an "accusatory termination interview." As a matter of common law, is an employer obligated to conduct an investigation before it dismisses an at-will employee? *Lambert v. Morehouse*, 68 Wash.App. 500, 843 P.2d 1116 (1993). If it is not but it does so anyway, and if it conducts the investigation negligently would the company be liable? *Theisen v. Covenant Med. Ctr., Inc.*, 636 N.W.2d 74 (Iowa 2001). If the answer is no to both, why?

2. According to the court, the nub of these employees' claims of emotional distress is that their employer fabricated a false (and very damaging) excuse to fire them (that was the same claim made in *Wisehart* to invoke the tort of fraud). Why isn't that outrageous?

3. If Wal–Mart's interrogation of these employees involved tactics that were sufficiently abusive to cause a judge to cry out "that's outrageous!" the Kentucky Supreme Court would allow liability in tort. Assume an employer's security department (often staffed by former police officers) uses the same techniques the police use in interrogating criminal suspects held in custody; indeed, assume that such are the "recognized standards" for the conduct of interrogation by industrial security personnel. Could such an interrogation give rise to liability in tort *as a matter of law*? *Compare Hall v. May Dep't Stores Co.*, 292 Or. 131, 637 P.2d 126 (1981) *with Kiphart v. Community Fed. Sav. & Loan Ass'n.*, 729 S.W.2d 510 (Mo. Ct. App. 1987).

4. The National Labor Relations Board had held that an employee in a non-unionized workplace who, faced within investigatory interview which the employee reasonably believes might result in discharge, asks for the presence of a coworker, has a right to have that coworker present. With a change of administration, and so in the Board's membership, the Board reversed itself. With another change of administration, the Board reverted to the prior rule. And with yet another change in administration it returned to the denial of such a right. IBM Corp., 341 N.L.R.B. No. 148 (2004) (reviewing the history). There is reason to expect an eventual return to the recognition of that right by the Obama Board. As either is, to the courts, a tenable reading of the Labor Act, it boils down to a question of policy. Which is the better policy?

5. The majority and dissent in *Stringer* differ on what the defamatory nature of the speech was. To the dissent, these employees were accused of "dishonesty" as Wal–Mart defined it, for which accusation was true. To the majority they were accused of "theft"—an allegation of broader conduct that does not draw its meaning from Wal–Mart's policy but from common parlance. That accusation, which the listeners would understand to cover actions that went beyond eating "claims candy," could not be defended on the basis of

their having eaten claims candy. Was there enough for the jury to conclude as it did?

6. That the accusation of theft was false is a necessary but not sufficient condition of liability. Even if false it could be privileged—as we are willing to tolerate some injurious falsehood where a greater social benefit is to be derived from the nature of the communication. A communication to those with a common interest is qualifiedly privileged, but the *Stringer* court held that the privilege was lost because it was communicated outside the circle of those with a "need to know." (In *Montgomery Investigative Services, Ltd. v. Horne*, discussed in Chapter II, the company was held liable for the hour-long harangue the employee's supervisor engaged in in front of the employee's co-workers accusing him of being a thief on the basis of a false background report as an abuse of his qualified privilege.) Note that the employees alleged that their supervisor, Anthony Whitaker, wanted to demonstrate that the store was getting "tough on inventory shrinkage," was serious about enforcing a policy that had not been strictly enforced if at all heretofore. Assume that toward that end—to show the entire workforce that management took its claims candy policy very seriously—Whitaker assembled the store's entire workforce at the close of business, had the accused appear before them, announced that they were being discharged for violation of Wal–Mart's honesty policy, and escorted them to the door. Would the communication be privileged as in furtherance of the common interest in manifesting to the workforce that the company took its honesty policy seriously? *See Wirig v. Kinney Shoe Corp.*, 461 N.W.2d 374 (Minn. 1990). *See generally* Matthew W. Finkin, *Discharge and Disgrace: A Comment on the "Urge to Treat People as Objects"*, 1 EMP. RTS. & EMP. POL'Y J. 1 (1997).

7. Note that three of the employees alleged that they were escorted from the premises after they'd been fired. Would it be actionable for an employer, after firing an employee (in private), to have the employee escorted by security personnel to the exit in full view of her coworkers? *Compare Phelan v. May Dep't Stores Co.*, 443 Mass. 52, 819 N.E.2d 550 (2004) *with Theisen v. Covenant Med. Ctr., Inc.*, 636 N.W.2d 74 (Iowa 2001).

8. Note that the employees were captured by a video surveillance camera. The subject of video surveillance will be treated in Chapter VI. Assume that they had not been videorecorded, but rather that the company had noticed that several bags of claimed goods had not been accounted for and that this group of employees were the only persons with authorized access to the area. The security department has requested that each of them submit to a polygraphy examination (in common parlance a "lie detector" test) on pain of discharge should the employee refuse. May the employer do that?

The federal Employee Polygraph Protection Act, 29 U.S.C. §§ 2001–2009, generally prohibits the use of polygraphy as a means of screening job applicants, but it permits polygraphy as an investigative tool vis-à-vis incumbent employees subject to specific restriction. *I.e.*, an employer may request an employee to submit to a polygraph test if—

**(1)** the test is administered in connection with an ongoing investigation involving economic loss or injury to the employer's business, such as theft, embezzlement, misappropriation, or an act of unlawful industrial espionage or sabotage;

**(2)** the employee had access to the property that is the subject of the investigation;

**(3)** the employer has a reasonable suspicion that the employee was involved in the incident or activity under investigation; and

**(4)** the employer executes a statement, provided to the examinee before the test, that—

> **(A)** sets forth with particularity the specific incident or activity being investigated and the basis for testing particular employees,
>
> **(B)** is signed by a person (other than a polygraph examiner) authorized to legally bind the employer,
>
> **(C)** is retained by the employer for at least 3 years, and
>
> **(D)** contains at a minimum—
>
> > **(i)** an identification of the specific economic loss or injury to the business of the employer,
> >
> > **(ii)** a statement indicating that the employee had access to the property that is the subject of the investigation, and
> >
> > **(iii)** a statement describing the basis of the employer's reasonable suspicion that the employee was involved in the incident or activity under investigation.

29 U.S.C. § 2006 (1988). Assume that all procedural requirements have been met. Would the company meet the "reasonable suspicion" test? *Compare Polkey v. Transtecs Corp.*, 404 F.3d 1264 (11th Cir. 2005) with *Taylor v. Epoc Clinic, Inc.*, 437 F.Supp.2d 1323 (M.D. Fla. 2006).

# Chapter V

## Obligations of Employees

■ ■ ■

### A. THE EMPLOYEE'S DUTY OF FAITHFULNESS AT COMMON LAW

#### NICHOL v. MARTYN

2 Esp. 732 (1799)

This was a special action on the case, against the defendant, for seducing the plaintiffs' customers.

The plaintiffs were wholesale ironmongers, who carried on a very extensive business; the defendant had been employed by them as their rider or traveller, to get orders in the course of their business; and the foundation of the action was, That the defendant, who at the time of bringing the action was in the same line of business with the plaintiffs, had, during the time that he was in their employment, endeavoured to seduce the several country shopkeepers who were in the habits of dealing with the plaintiffs, to leave off dealing with them, and to transfer their business to the defendant.

To prove the plaintiffs' case, they called some of those country shopkeepers. Their evidence proved that the defendant on his last coming to their shops as rider to the plaintiffs, and on their business, had told them that he was himself going into the same business with the plaintiffs after Christmas, and would then be obliged to them for an order on his own account.

It appeared, however, on the cross-examination of those witnesses, that he took the orders regularly for the plaintiffs on that journey, and that they were executed on the plaintiffs' account; and that no solicitation was used by the defendant for any order at that time, which might have been supplied by the plaintiffs.

It was also admitted, that in fact, the time of the defendant's engagement to serve the plaintiffs, expired at the beginning of the year; so that, in truth, in the month of March he would have been completely his own master.

235

LORD KENYON, CHIEF JUSTICE.—The conduct of the defendant in this case, may perhaps be accounted not handsome; but I cannot say that it is contrary to law. The relation in which he stood to the plaintiffs, as their servant, imposed on him a duty which is called of imperfect obligation, but not such as can enable the plaintiffs to maintain an action. A servant, while engaged in the service of his master, has no right to do any act which may injure his trade, or undermine his business; but every one has a right, if he can, to better his situation in the world; and if he does it by means not contrary to law, though the master may be eventually injured, it is *damnum abs. injuria*. There is nothing morally bad, or very improper in a servant, who has it in contemplation at a future period to set up for himself, to endeavour to conciliate the regard of his master's customers, and to recommend himself to them so as to procure some business from them as well as others. In the present case, the defendant did not solicit the present orders of the customers; on the contrary, he took for the plaintiffs all those he could obtain: his request of business for himself was prospective, and for a time when the relation of master and servant between him and the plaintiffs would be at an end.

It was suggested in the course of the cause, that the defendant had seduced some of the servants of the plaintiffs to quit their service, and to enter into his when he went into business.

Upon that point Lord Kenyon said, That seducing a servant, and enticing him to leave his master, while the master by the contract had a right to his services, was certainly actionable; but that to induce a servant to leave his master's service at the expiration of the time for which the servant had hired himself, although the servant had no intention at the time of quitting his master's service, was not the subject of an action.

The plaintiffs were nonsuited.

### NOTE

Little has changed in the two centuries since Lord Kenyon spoke: an employee must act in furtherance of her employer's interest, but she need not be unmindful of bettering her own situation in the world. Even when Lord Kenyon uttered these words, Adam Smith was extolling the benefit to society of enabling people to act in their self-interest. "It is not from the benevolence of the butcher, the brewer, or the baker that we expect our dinner, but from their regard to their own interest. .... [B]y directing that industry in such a manner as its produce may be of the greatest value, he intends only his own gain, and he is in this, as in many other cases, led by an invisible hand to promote an end which was no part of his intention. By pursuing his own interest he frequently promotes that of the society more effectually than when he really intends to promote it." ADAM SMITH, THE WEALTH OF NATIONS, 2.2.1, 4.2.9 (1776). Thus, the resolution of the tension between the implied obligation of faithfulness to one's employer and of faithfulness of one's own economic interest is infused with the question of how the public will fare in the balance the law strikes.

# QUALITY SYSTEMS, INC. v. WARMAN

United States District Court, District of Maryland, 2001
132 F.Supp.2d 349

LEGG, DISTRICT JUDGE.

[Samuel Warman worked for QSI, Inc., a supplier of computer talent to contractors, including the federal government. QSI competed with Windermere. Warman supervised six other managers known in the firm as "Friends of Dave." Warman quit QSI to work for Windmere. Within six weeks, these six managers and 31 technical employees left QSI for Windmere. QSI sued Warman for breach of the duty of loyalty. The court granted Warman's motion for summary judgment.] * * *

*Leaves for W, + many soon follow so*

In every employment contract, there is an implied duty that an employee must act solely for the benefit of his employer in all matters within the scope of his employment. *See Maryland Metals v. Metzner*, 282 Md. 31, 382 A.2d 564, 567 (1978). There is no set rule denoting when an employee has breached his fiduciary duty; rather, a court must examine the facts of each particular case. In analyzing the facts of the instant case, it is helpful to see what other courts have considered to be a breach of loyalty.

*Case by case*

An employee is free to search for another job prior to leaving his current position. *See id.* at 569. A group of employees may agree to leave together, such as when a partner at a law firm leaves with his associates. *See* Restatement (Second) of Agency § 393 cmt. e (1957). An employee may not, however, systematically induce other employees to leave their jobs if his purpose of enticement is to destroy an integral part of his employer's business. *See Morgan's Home Equipment Corp. v. Martucci*, 390 Pa. 618, 136 A.2d 838 (1957).

Briefly stated, an employee may discuss job offers with his circle of friends and the group may debate whether to leave together. Such discussions are a normal part of workplace intercourse. A breach of loyalty may occur, however, when an about-to-leave employee targets employees outside his normal circle and uses his position to induce them to defect.

*→ Can't target outside circle + induce.*

An employee may make arrangements to compete with his employer prior to leaving his job. *See Maryland Metals*, 382 A.2d at 569. The employee may also advise current customers that he is leaving. *See id.* at 569 n. 3. An employee is under no obligation to disclose the precise nature of his plans to his employer, unless he has acted inimically to the employer's interest. *See id.* at 569. Departing employees may purchase a rival business or equipment, secure land options, and obtain financing for a prospective new business. *See id.; C–E–I–R, Inc. v. Computer Dynamics Corp.*, 229 Md. 357, 183 A.2d 374, 379 (1962) (dictum). An employee may not, however, actively solicit business in competition with his employer. * * *

[The court held: (1) The "Friends of Dave" were privileged to leave *en masse*. Because individual defendants were part of the same circle, it would have been permissible for them to discuss joint employment oppor-tunities and hence they could have resolved to leave together without breaching a duty of loyalty. (2) One QSI client who had been contacted prior to Warman's departure, to solicit its business for Windmere, did not switch to Windmere and so no damages could be shown. (3) The second client was contacted only after Warman had left QSI.] * * *

## NOTES AND QUESTIONS

1. In a bit of an understatement, the Arizona Court of Appeals noted that the limits of proper conduct regarding securing the services of fellow employees to a competing venue "are not well marked." *Security Title Agency, Inc. v. Pope*, 219 Ariz. 480, 200 P.3d 977, 990 (App. 2008). Is it realistic to distinguish a mere "discussion" of one's future plans with co-workers from asking them to join in those plans? *Id.* at 990–92. Why? Why, in Maryland, may one not extend one's orbit of interest beyond those in the company one happens to know? As it is inherent in a competitive system that one competi-tor will lose out to another who offers a better product or more efficient service, how realistic is it to distinguish a mass exodus of disgruntled employees who seek to better themselves by forming a competing venture from a mass exodus designed to injure, even to destroy, the prior employer's profitability? *See Duane Jones Co. v. Burke*, 306 N.Y. 172, 117 N.E.2d 237 (N.Y. 1954). *See also* Comment, *Permissible Employee Disloyalty and the Duane Jones Case*, 22 U. CHI. L. REV. 278 (1954). If the employees are so valuable a business asset why were they not under contracts of fixed duration. Would such an arrangement protect the employer's interest? Where employ-ees left for a competitor "en masse," the Sixth Circuit sustained the grant of summary judgment for them and observed that the prior employer offered "no explanation why ordinary employees of a company may not meet with each other, openly or 'clandestinely,' to plan for the opening of a rival company for which they would rather work." *ATC Distrib. Group, Inc. v. Whatever It Takes Transmissions & Parts, Inc.*, 402 F.3d 700, 716 (6th Cir. 2005).

2. The court says that an employee is ordinarily under no obligation to inform the employer of his or her intent to engage in a competitive venture *unless* the employee has acted "inimically to the employer's interest." But isn't all preliminary competitive activity, including that which does not breach the employee's fiduciary duty, is in a sense "inimical" to the employer's interest. Or is it the failure to give notice that is the act inimical to the employer's interest? Where a physician, during the term of his contract, summarily left his employer's practice—so summarily as to strand patients—for a competing medical practice he and another former co-worker already had established, the Supreme Court of South Dakota held the physician had breached his implied obligation of faithfulness. *Reuben C. Setliff, III, M.D., P.C. v. Stewart*, 694 N.W.2d 859, 869–70 (S.D. 2005):

> Consistent with the highly fact intensive nature of the duty of loyalty inquiry, we do not announce a rule requiring employees in all instances to affirmatively notify an employer that they will be leaving. With regard to a preparation to establish a competing enterprise, "liability for breach of

fiduciary duty is not predicated upon ... failure to make full disclosure, but rather 'upon some particular circumstance which rendered the non-disclosure harmful to [the employer] or upon [the employee's] wrongful conduct apart from the omission.' " *Crawford & Co. v. M. Hayes & Assoc., L.L.C.*, No. 00–2574, 2001 WL 788652 at *2 (4th Cir.2001) (unpublished opinion) (quoting *Maryland Metals v. Metzner*, 282 Md. 31, 382 A.2d 564, 570 n.4 (Md. 1978)). This principle was illustrated in a case in which a court found that a dairy salesman, as part of his duty not to unfairly compete with his employer, was:

> obligated to give plaintiff sufficient notice of his intention to quit so that his employer could train a new man to continue the route and thus be in a position to compete openly and fairly for existing patrons. By lulling it into a belief that he had reconsidered his intention to quit, Wolf deprived plaintiff on an opportunity to compete with him on even terms.

*Sanitary Farm Dairies, Inc. v. Wolf*, 261 Minn. 166, 112 N.W.2d 42, 49 (1961). . . . . If the existence of a duty to notify depends on the question of whether circumstances indicate that the unannounced departure would harm the employer, then that question in turn partly depends on the role played by the employee within the business. "The scope of the duty of loyalty that an employee owes to an employer may vary with the nature of their relationship. Employees occupying a position of trust and confidence, for example, owe a higher duty than those performing low-level tasks." *Cameco, Inc. v. Gedicke*, 157 N.J. 504, 724 A.2d 783, 789 (N.J. 1999).

Under the facts presented at trial, the jury could have reasonably found a breach of this aspect of the duty of loyalty. Obviously Atkins was a crucial employee recruited by Setliff to join his practice. A witness testified that Atkins' abrupt departure with no notice resulted in general "chaos": the rescheduling of surgeries scheduled weeks in advance, the cancellation of appointments with existing and new patients, and the arrangement for follow-up care for patients on whom Atkins had operated up to the day before his departure. * * *

As Atkins breached his contract, which had two months to run, he would be liable for contractual damages measured, however, by the cost of securing a replacement. But he was sued, successfully, in tort for breach of a duty implied by law.

a) At what point should Atkins have given notice of his intent to leave?

b) Assume he was an at-will employee: would he still have had to give notice?

3. As summarized in Restatement (Third) of Agency § 8.01 (2006):

An agent has a fiduciary duty to act loyally for the principal's benefit in all matters connected with the agency relationship.

The Restatement of Agency elaborates in §§ 8.02–8.05 on how this duty applies to the agent: using his position with the principal to reap personal benefits from a third party; acting as, or on behalf of, a party with interest adverse to the principal; competing with the principal during the agency; and using the principal's property or confidential information for the agent's personal benefit. This duty sounds in tort and can give rise to tort damages including disgorgement, restitution, and punitive damages. The duty arises because: (1) the agent agrees to act subject to the principal's control and on her behalf, (2) the agent can take action with consequences for the principal's legal relations, and (3) the principal often must repose trust in the agent. At least in the Restatement's formulation, there is no corresponding duty placed on the employer. Should the employer have a corresponding duty? For example, in the *Stewart* case in note 2 above, what if the practice had summarily dismissed an at-will doctor in a specialty in which it routinely takes several months to find a new job and the practice of the industry is two months notice?

Recall from our prior discussion in Chapter 3, Section C, that several jurisdictions have applied the doctrine of the implied covenant of good faith and fair dealing to the employment relationship. This doctrine generally sounds in contract and gives rise only to ordinary contract damages. The most broadly accepted rationale for the doctrine is that every contract implicitly includes a covenant that one side cannot rob the other of the "benefit of the bargain," although some courts, such as the court in *Mitchell v. Teck Cominco Alaska, Inc.*, *supra*, also subscribe to a broader notion that the parties should be prohibited from treating each other "in a manner that a reasonable person would regard as unfair." Although the implied covenant of good faith and fair dealing applies to both employees and employers, the vast majority of suits under this doctrine are brought by employees.

Would it make sense to merge and rationalize these two doctrines? If the core purpose behind the implied covenant of good faith and fair dealing is to protect each party from being robbed of "the benefit of the bargain," isn't that the employer's complaint in a suit for breach of the employee's duty of faithfulness? If so, why do employers get tort damages for a breach of the duty of faithfulness while employees only get contract damages for a breach of the implied covenant of good faith and fair dealing? Why is the employee's duty of faithfulness commonly accepted in American jurisdictions, while the implied covenant of good faith and fair dealing is applied to employment contracts in only a minority of American jurisdictions? It's true, as the Restatement of Agency suggests, that principals have to trust agents with access to property and information in order for them to do their job, but don't employees, especially late in their work lives, trust employers with their future livelihoods? The common belief is that, in employment relationships, the employee is typically the more vulnerable of the two and the one with weaker bargaining power. Why then do employer interests get more protection under the law?

## A Note on Disparagement and Labor Speech

An employee who disparages her employer's product or service breaches the duty of faithfulness—as Lord Kenyon put it: to do no act that would undermine the employer's business. In the early nineteenth century, when the manager of Covent Garden said to a performer singing in the opera *Zampa*, "I wonder how you can perform in such rubbish," and was discharged for it, the court held it a fact question of whether his speech was so calculated to incite discontent as to be in breach of his obligation of faithfulness. *Lacy v. Osbaldiston*, 8 C&P 80, 173 ER 408 (1837).

Today, some speech that disparages the employer's product or service is sheltered from retaliation when it is spoken in the public interest—as covered by whistleblower law or by public policy. So, too, speech critical of an employer uttered during the course of a union organizing drive that is *intended* to incite discontent is sheltered by the right to unionize and to engage in "other concerted activity for mutual aid or protection" under § 7 of the National Labor Relations Act. An employee may accuse an employer of being a "Dictator," *El San Juan Hotel Corp.*, 289 NLRB 1453 (1988), or maintaining "slave labor" conditions, *Polynesian Cultural Ctr., Inc.*, 222 NLRB 1192 (1976). The purpose of this exception to the general rule forbidding disparagement is to foster robust debate on labor issues. *Cf. Linn v. United Plant Guard Workers, Local 114*, 383 U.S. 53, 86 S.Ct. 657, 15 L.Ed.2d 582 (1966).

## QUESTIONS

1. During a union organizing drive, the new management of the town's largest employer laid off 200 of its 2,000 workers, mostly from the engineering staff. The local newspaper created a website to discuss events at the company,. One posting criticized the union for the layoff. A union supporter replied on the website that, "This business is being tanked by a group of people who have no good ability to manage it." Would it violate the Labor Act, which makes it unlawful for an employer to "restrain" or "interfere" in § 7 rights, to discharge the speaker? *Compare Endicott Interconnect Techs., Inc. v. NLRB*, 453 F.3d 532 (D.C. Cir. 2006) (these statements were found detrimentally disloyal and so not protected under the NLRA) *with Fivecap, Inc. v. NLRB*, 294 F.3d 768 (6th Cir. 2002) (petition seeking removal of executives for their managerial failures was protected activity). If not, why? Matthew Finkin, *Disloyalty! Does* Jefferson Standard *Stalk* Still?, 28 BERKELEY J. EMP. & LAB. L. 541 (2007).

2. To persuade a school district not to let its contract for school bus service to a non-unionized company, employees of am incumbent, unionized contractor wrote letters to the school board urging that that contract not be let. Some of these letters criticized the safety record of the non-union bidder, but did not mention the issue of lower wages and benefits or the want of union representation. The school board let the contract nevertheless. Can the new company refuse to hire these drivers on the ground that their letters were "disloyal"? That because the safety of children is not a matter of wages or working conditions for school bus drivers under the Labor Act, "concerted activity for the mutual protection" of children's safety does not interfere or restrain these employees in exercising that right? Five Star Transp., Inc., 349 NLRB 42 (2007) (criticisms that non-union operation would result in lower wages protected, but criticisms that non-union operation would result in lower child safety not protected), *enf'd on other grounds* 522 F.3d 46 (1st Cir. 2008).

# B. TRADE SECRETS & CONFIDENTIAL BUSINESS INFORMATION

## DEL MONTE FRESH PRODUCE, N.A., INC. v. CHIQUITA BRANDS INT'L INC.

United States District Court, Northern District of Illinois, 2009
616 F.Supp.2d 805

William J. Hibbler, District Judge

## I. Factual Background

For such a complex case, the facts are quite simple. Kim Kinnavy worked in the Illinois office of Del Monte as district sales manager from 1999 until she resigned in 2007. As a sales manager, Kinnavy worked with customers who had banana supply contracts. Del Monte gave its sales managers—including Kinnavy—laptop computers and access to Del Monte's customer database. Two weeks before Kinnavy resigned, she used her laptop to e-mail herself files with the following titles: (a)Fuel surcharge: (b)Revised royal; (c)Contract renewals; (d) Pineapple update; (e)Phone list; (f) North American Customer Database 2005; (g) Fax List–Old Machine; (h) Fax List–III–6–06; and (i) CUSTMAST.xls, Kinnavy also e-mailed a copy of the "Fax List" and the "Phone List" to Mike Elsen, a broker working in Phoenix Arizona. Kinnavy denies she used the files for commercial purposes or that the files contained confidential information. After resigning, Kinnavy went to work for one of Del Monte's chief competitors: Chiquita Brands International.

Upon learning of Kinnavy's new employment, Del Monte sued Kinnavy in the Circuit Court of Cook County. Next, Del Monte removed the case to this Court on the basis of diversity jurisdiction and amended its pleadings to include Chiquita as a defendant. The essence of Del Monte's complaint is that Kinnavy violated federal law, and breached her employment agreements by working for a competitor and e-mailing confidential information to a third party. Del Monte also claims Chiquita tortiously interfered with Del Monte's business contracts and made intentional misrepresentations. Kinnavy and Chiquita move for summary judgment on all claims. * * *

[Only two of the many aspects of this case will be dealt with in this Chapter—the expropriation of trade secrets and confidential business information, and the covenant not to compete. Not also, however, that the employer claimed that Kinnavy violatied the federal Computer Fraud and Abuse Act by, without authority, accessing her employer's computer and transfering information from it. 18 U.S.C. § 1030. The Act provides for a private right of action to recover "damage" and "loss," but "damage" is defined as impairment of the data or program or information system and "loss" as the cost of conducting a damage assessment and restoration of the data. This claim was denied because no statutory "damage" or "loss" was incurred by the wrongful access and transmission,]

### F.  *Del Monte's Illinois Trade Secret Act Claim is Deficient*

Del Monte argues Kinnavy misappropriated certain confidential Del Monte data, and in doing so, she violated the Illinois Trade Secret Act. Specifically, Del Monte contends Kinnavy misappropriated: "prices, customer requirements, customer names, and contact information." ... In response, Kinnavy contends the type of information she allegedly misappropriated is not protected under the ITSA. The Court agrees. Under the Illinois Trade Secrets Act, a plaintiff may recover for damages incurred as a result of the misappropriation of a trade secret. 765 ILCS 1065/4 In order "to state a claim for trade secret misappropriation under the ITSA, a plaintiff must establish that it had: (1) a trade secret, (2) that the defendant misappropriated and (3) used for business purposes." ... At issue here is whether Del Monte satisfied the first element. The ITSA defines "trade secret" as:

> information, including but not limited to, technical or non-technical data, a formula, pattern, compilation, program, device, method, technique, drawing, process, financial data, or list of actual or potential customers or suppliers, that:
>
> (1) is sufficiently secret to derive economic value, actual or potential, from not being generally known to other persons who can obtain economic value from its disclosure or use; and
>
> (2) is the subject of efforts that are reasonable under the circumstances to maintain its secrecy or confidentiality.

765 ILCS 1065/2 Del Monte argues its price information qualifies as a trade secret. But, the "Illinois appellate courts which have addressed the issue have consistently held that price information which is disclosed by a business to any of its customers ... does not constitute trade secret information protected by the Act." *Applied Indus. Materials Corp. v. Brantjes,* 891 F.Supp. 432, 437–438 (N.D.Ill.1994); *Carbonic Fire Extinguishers, Inc. v. Heath,* 190 Ill.App.3d 948, 138 Ill.Dec. 508, 547 N.E.2d 675, 678 (1989) (holding that pricing information given to a customer that the customer is at liberty to divulge is not a trade secret.). For example, in *Trailer Leasing,* the court declined to find that pricing information was a trade secret:

> It is also unclear as to why general rate information constitutes a trade secret. By all accounts, this is a highly competitive business, and it is unlikely that rate information is ever secret, and if so, that it remains secret for very long. If competitor "A" gives a customer an advantageous rate, it will not be long before the customer shops that rate around and tries to get competitor "B" to go even lower; that is the nature of a competitive market.

*Trailer Leasing Co. v. Associates Commer. Corp.,* 1996 U.S. Dist. LEXIS 11366, at *3, 1996 WL 450801, *1 (N.D. Ill. Aug. 8 1996). There is no indication Del Monte's customers were prohibited from divulging the prices they paid for bananas. There is no indication Kinnavy misappropriated a pricing formula. As such, the Court finds that price information alone cannot constitute a trade secret.

Del Monte also asserts the identity of its customers is entitled to protection under the ITSA. This is incorrect. Rick Cooper—Vice President of Sales and Kinnavy's supervisor—gave the following testimony during his deposition:

Q:   Are you contending that Chiquita does not know who your customers are?

A:   No. No, I'm not

Q:   Do you know who Chiquita's customers are?

A:   Yes, we do.

Q:   Is there anything confidential about that?

A:   No.

. . . To be sure, Del Monte and Chiquita are fierce competitors. But, there seems to be little doubt about which customers are buying bananas from which company. Indeed, all one needs to do is go to the grocery store and look at the sticker on the bananas to see whether Del Monte or Chiquita is supplying the fruit. There is no protectable interest where a business' customers are known throughout the industry. For example, one of the clients Del Monte claims it lost because of Kinnavy—The Horton Fruit Company—prominently displays on its website that it is "a licensed Dole repacker." http://www.hortonfruit.com/fruits.htm (last accessed March 15, 2009). During Cooper's deposition, he admitted there would be nothing confidential or improper about someone walking into a grocery store and asking who supplied their bananas . . . The ITSA requires the protected information to be "sufficiently secret to derive economic value." 765 ILCS 1065/2. Here, the identity of customers buying fruit from Del Monte was not sufficiently secret to warrant protection under the ITSA. *See, e.g., A.J. Dralle, Inc. v. Air Technologies*, 255 Ill.App.3d 982, 194 Ill. Dec. 353, 627 N.E.2d 690, 697 (1994) (identity of customers is not a trade secret because, "Dralle's customers were known to others in the trade and could be easily ascertained by reference to telephone directories and trade journals.").

Customer contact information that takes little effort to compile is not protectable under the ITSA. Cooper acknowledged Del Monte and Chiquita are well aware of each other's customers. Thus, an individual would only need to look in the yellow pages to obtain the contact information of Del Monte customers. During his deposition Cooper was asked why the "phone list" Kinnavy e-mailed to Mike Elsen would be valuable to a competitor, he replied that it would "save somebody the time of looking Albertson's Denver location up in the phonebook." . . . A list of grocery stores' phone numbers is not "sufficiently secret" to confer trade secret status on Del Monte's contact list. *See, e.g., Carbonic Fire Extinguishers*, 190 Ill.App.3d 948 at 953, 138 Ill. Dec. 508, 547 N.E.2d 675 (customer contact list is not a trade secret where "names, addresses, and telephone numbers of the various customers were readily obtainable from the yellow pages of the telephone directory."); *Delta Med. Sys. v. Mid–America Med. Sys.,* 331 Ill.App.3d 777, 265 Ill. Dec. 397, 772 N.E.2d 768, 781 (medical supply company's customer contact list was not a trade secret where the names and contact information of the 72 "hospitals and medical clinics, could be derived by merely looking in the yellow pages."); *Hamer Holding Group v. Elmore,* 202 Ill.App.3d at 1001, 1011, 148 Ill. Dec. 310, 560 N.E.2d at 912, 919 (customer contact list not a trade secret because it could be easily duplicated by reviewing lists of non-profits from Secretary of State's office, distilling it by geographic region, and updating contacts and telephone numbers).

Finally, Del Monte contends information about its customers' needs and requirements is entitled to protection as a trade secret. The Seventh Circuit addressed a similar situation in *Curtis 1000, v. Suess,* where a stationery company sued an ex-employee who left to work for a competitor. 24 F.3d 941, 948 (7th Cir.1994). The Curtis 1000 company claimed the knowledge of its customers' requirements was entitled to trade secret protection. The court began by noting that an employee can gain valuable insight into the behavior of long-term customers: "Customers often conceal their real needs, preferences, and above all, reservation prices in order to induce better terms from sellers. Suess presumably had sniffed out those true needs, preferences, and reservation prices." *Id.* The operative question, however, is whether the employee is selling a service or whether the employee is selling goods where there is no qualitative differentiation across the marketplace, in other words, a mere commodity:

> Illinois cases distinguish between sellers of services, especially professional services such as accounting and consulting, and sellers of ordinary goods. In the former class, where the quality of the seller's service is difficult to determine by simple inspection, customers come to repose trust in a particular seller, and that trust is a valuable business asset, created by years of careful management, that the employee is not allowed to take away with him.
>
> In the latter class, involving the sale of goods, the element of trust is attenuated, particularly where as in this case the good is a simple and common one sold under competitive conditions. In these cases Illinois law does not permit the seller to claim a protectable interest in his relations with his customers ... For here current price and quality, rather than a past investment in meeting customers' needs, are the decisive factors in the continued success of the firm, and they of course are not appropriated by the departing employee.

*Curtis 1000 v. Suess,* 24 F.3d 941, 948 (7th Cir.1994).

Kinnavy handled banana supply contracts for Del Monte. Bananas are simple, non-unique goods. The Court concludes Kinnavy and Del Monte were selling a commodity, rather than providing a service. In other words, the "decisive factors" in customers choosing Del Monte are pricing and quality. These are things that cannot be appropriated by Kinnavy. For example, Sean Walsh—the director of produce for Spartan Grocery Stores, Inc.—testified Spartan switched its contract from Del Monte to Chiquita in large part because Chiquita's bananas were cheaper.... This would make sense given that Spartan was buying a commodity. Simply put, if Del Monte provides delicious bananas to its customers at prices below Chiquita its business will succeed. The record does not support Del Monte's claim that knowledge of its customers' requirements is a trade secret. The Court grants Kinnavy's motion for summary judgment as to Count VIII. * * *

[Del Monte then moved for reconsideration. It argued that Ms. Kinnavy's motion for summary judgment was directed to the *second* prong of the definition of a trade secret, *i.e.*, that Del Monte had failed to take reasonable efforts to maintain the secrecy of the information; but the court accepted a different argument, to the *first* prong of the definition, as matter not generally known, which argument was made only in. Kinnavy's reply brief. Del Monte argued that it had not been fully heard on that issue. The court agreed, reversed itself, and denied. Kinnavy's motion for summary judgment. The court turned to the company's IT Operations Management Guideline that prohibited employees from disclosing "internal information" to "unauthorized persons." It held that the Company policy constituted a "confidentiality agreement" binding on all the employees covered by it, including. Kinnavy.]

Del Monte relies heavily on Cooper's testimony in challenging Kinnavy's statement of the facts, arguing that it took many reasonable, protective steps to ensure the security of its information beyond entering into agreements with Kinnavy. In his affidavit, Cooper states that in order to access the database on Del Monte's computer system, Kinnavy needed a password and local network service. If she forgot her password, she had to call Del Monte's IT Department to give her access. According to Cooper, he disclosed certain sales and marketing data and information to Kinnavy "on a need to know basis." He states that Del Monte kept its files under password protection and sometimes locked and that it required each employee to have a computer login and a password that they had to change every thirty days and that they could not share with other employees. The company restricted access to confidential business-related files, Cooper says, as well as to the Arlington Heights office, and to certain floors of the Coral Gables headquarters. He states that Del Monte reminded its employees that its documents and information were confidential. After Kinnavy announced her resignation, Cooper says he asked her to return all Del Monte documents. He states the company sent Kinnavy a letter on May 24, 2007 which advised her "not to disclose confidential information (e.g., customer lists, pricing information, customer audit requirements) to any third party" and to return any such information in her possession immediately. In her response to Del Monte's statement of facts, Kinnavy admits many of these facts, including Cooper's statements about password-protection, restricted access to the local office, and the company's communications with her upon her resignation.

Del Monte cites two Illinois cases which rely on confidentiality agreements and limited access to hard copy and electronic files in finding that the second prong of the ITSA is met. In *Multiut Corp. v. Draiman,* 359 Ill.App.3d 527, 295 Ill.Dec. 818, 834 N.E.2d 43, 50 (Ill.App.Ct.2005), the court upheld a decision by a trial court that by "limiting access to both printed and computer-stored copies of the information and by requiring employees to sign confidentiality agreements," the plaintiff took sufficient steps to meet the trade secrets definition. In *Strata Marketing, Inc. v. Murphy,* 317 Ill.App.3d 1054, 251 Ill.Dec. 595, 740 N.E.2d 1166, 1177 (Ill.App.Ct.2000), the court denied the defendant's motion to dismiss because plaintiff's efforts included "keeping information under lock and key," "limiting computer access," and "requiring confidentiality agreements." Kinnavy, seemingly abandoning her original argument on reply in favor of the one discussed above, fails to provide any countervailing precedent in response to Del Monte's citations. In fact, in *Arcor,* the only case cited by Kinnavy, the court notes that if Arcor had taken additional measures beyond having employees sign confidentiality agreements, "such as limiting access to its customer information by computer password or keeping track of the hard copies of the information," it might have held that Arcor took sufficient steps to secure its information. 299 Ill.Dec. 526, 842 N.E.2d at 271. These cases indicate that the facts Del Monte points to in its response to Kinnavy's motion for summary judgment are material under the ITSA.

Kinnavy has failed to show that there is no genuine issue as to any material fact. * * *

## NOTES AND QUESTIONS

1. Note the balancing courts must do. On the one hand, an employee cannot be prohibited from selling her knowledge and skills—including the knowledge learned and skills perfected in her prior employment. There is a recognized societal interest in allowing individual freedom to practice a trade or profession and to increase the use of knowledge and skill in the economy. *See* Comment, *Industrial Secrets and the Skilled Employee,* 38 N.Y.U. L. Rev. 324 (1963). On the other hand, the employer's interest in its trade secrets— unique information that it may have expended considerable effort to acquire and that gives the employer a competitive advantage—is also worthy of protection.

2. Many states, like Illinois in the *Del Monte* case, have adopted the Uniform Trade Secrets act or some variation of it. The information capable of being a trade secret—a formula, a program, technical data, even a list of customers—must meet two requirements. First, it must be a secret from which economic value may be derived (some statutory formulations put it another way: it must be information that derives economic value from not being generally known or readily ascertainable).Second, it must be subject to reasonable efforts to be kept secret. The existence of a "confidentiality agreement" is one, but only one, factor bearing upon the latter. However, if, as the court held the first time, customer lists and banana prices were not

secret (or were readily ascertainable), why is it relevant that Del Monte password-protected those data subject? In *Southwest Stainless, LP v. Sappington*, 582 F.3d 1176 (10th Cir. 2009), the former employer, Metals, took the following measures to protect its pricing information: "Employees sign confidentiality agreements, passwords are used to restrict access to company information, employees are regularly reminded on the confidential nature of company information, and Metals has spent hundreds of thousands of dollars accumulating and maintaining its confidential information." However, large customers could access Metals's pricing—which allowed customer "feedback" to the company—and could share Metals's pricing information with others. Is Metals's pricing information a trade secret?

3. Is the court's disposition explained by the possibility that some of the data in the same files Ms. Kinnavy accessed and transmitted were trade secrets, some were not, and it would have all to be sorted out at trial? Even if not a trade secret subject to statutory protection, might the information be "confidential" subject to contractual non-disclosure?

4. Assume that an employee—who was not subject to a contractual non-competition agreement—downloads her employer's trade secrets and confidential business information shortly before leaving to join a competitor. The industry is composed of a very few competitors and the employee's knowledge and skills are limited to that industry. Her prior employer now sues her for misappropriation of its trade secrets and seeks an injunction not only against her using that information in her new job, but against her employment with the competitor in any position in which she "would have to use or disclose" that information. *I.e.*, in effect, any job with the competitor in which she could use her special knowledge and skills. Should the injunction issue? *See LeJeune v. Coin Acceptors, Inc.*, 381 Md. 288, 849 A.2d 451 (2004) (no). The American Law Institute's RESTATEMENT (THIRD) OF EMPLOYMENT LAW § 8.05 (2010), noting that some courts would enjoin the employee from working in a position where trade secrets or confidential information would be "inevitably" disclosed despite the absence of a covenant not to compete. Consistent with the Reporters' practice, no reason is given for taking that position. Which is the better approach?

5. In *Minnesota Mining & Manufacturing Co. v. Pribyl*, 259 F.3d 587 (7th Cir. 2001), three employees who had developed a critical material, kept by 3M as a trade secret, left 3M and set up a company to manufacture that material. (3M used the material in one of its products, but did not market it.) 3M sued for misappropriation of its trade secret. The trial court awarded damages equal to 3M's cost of developing the material(there were no lost profits to be disgorged because 3M had never sold the product), but the court declined to enjoin the former employees' use of the formula after the damages were paid. 3M has appealed, arguing that the trial court's approach amounts to a forced sale of the company's trade secret. Assume the former employees argue that because the company intended use the secret only in its own processes, the denial of an injunction would permit them to put the secret to better use, beneficial to a wider number and to the economy. How should the court rule?

6. Employee transmission and retention of proprietary information by computer plays a role in employer policies or practices monitoring employee computer use or conducting searches of company laptops. This will be discussed in Chapter VI.

## A Further Note on Confidential Information

As noted previously, the American Law Institute's projected *Restatement* of the common law of employment proceeds apace in the face of substantial academic criticism of its tendentiousness. No doubt detailed criticism of Chapter 8 on Employee Loyalty and Covenants Not to Compete will be forthcoming following the criticism discussed in Chapters III and IV, *supra*. Only a few of the more problematic aspects will be adverted to here.

Section 8.02 of the RESTATEMENT would have the law extend common law protection to "confidential information" as well as to trade secrets and such is indeed the law; but it defines that information as "commercially valuable" and it defines that value as being negative as well as positive in the sense that disclosure could injure the employer's business without advantaging a competitor. It gives an illustration:

> X opens a new supermarket and hires as deli workers two young people who were recently released from a juvenile correctional facility, having secured their time and having gained work experience in the prison's food-service facility while incarcerated. They are good employees but if their status as ex-juvenile offenders were publicized X knows that at least some of his customers would choose to shop elsewhere. The status of the workers as ex-offenders is information with negative commercial value and thus, if kept confidential, may be protected under this Section.

No authority is provided for this illustration nor is there any further discussion of this proposition. From what appears, so long as the employer has made adequate effort to keep this information secret, an employee who discloses this information can be liable, though the measure of damages is not discussed.

The common law rule is that an employee may not appropriate a trade secret or other confidential business information for her benefit or the benefit of a third party. Annot., 165 A.L.R. 1453 (1946). The *Restatement* eliminates the requirement of a benefit to the employee of a third party.

Moreover, the RESTATEMENT's rule makes no mention of the public interest in disclosure of confidential information that causes economic harm not the result of competition. The most obvious case is the whistleblowing employee. The common law is clear: "[T]here is no confidence as to the disclosure of iniquity." *Gartside v. Outram*, 26 L.J. Ch. 113, 114 (1856). "[A]ny misconduct of such a nature that it ought in the public interest to be disclosed," as Lord Denning put it, cannot be subject to confidentiality. *Initial Services Ltd. v. Putterill*, [1968] 1 Q.B. 396, 405. Yet the Reporters made no mention of this aspect of the rule they propose.

The permissibility of an employer shielding itself from the consequences of disclosure by confidentiality agreements when information in the former employee's possession affects the public interest is a debated question. *See* Terry Dworkin & Elletta Callahan, *Buying Silence*, 36 Am. Bus. L.J. 151 (1998). But the Reporter's rule would obviate the need for a contract.

If the supermarket maintains a confidential log of customer complaints against their former offender-employees engaged in delivery work with access restricted to key personnel, could the now retired custodian of the record be liable for testifying to the company's knowledge of the employee's proclivities in a suit for wrongful retention brought by a customer whom the employee assaulted? Would that disclosure be for "benefit" of a third party or would it be in the public interest?

Several states forbid discrimination in employment on the ground of having been incarcerated for a crime having no relation to the performance of the job. Assume an investigative reporter, pursuing an inquiry into how successful rehabilitative efforts have been, interviews the custodian of the record. Could the employee be discharged for disclosing the employer's hiring policies? Could she be sued for breach of the duty of loyalty, *i.e.*, for the loss of business resulting from the disclosure?

## C.  COVENANTS NOT TO COMPETE

### DEL MONTE FRESH PRODUCE, N.A., INC. v. CHIQUITA BRANDS INT'L, INC.

[Set out on page 242, *supra*]

D.  *The Non–Compete Agreement is Unenforceable*

. . . . The Non–Compete agreement states:

> For a period of 12 months from the date of Employee's separation from the employment with the Company, the Employee shall not be employed by ... or connected in any manner with, any business which represents, distributes, sells or brokers fresh vegetables, fresh fruit, and other fresh produce products: (a) to any person who or entity which is a customer of the Company on the date of termination of the Employee's employment ... or during the 12 month period prior thereto ... or (b) on behalf of or supplied by any person who or entity which is a supplier of the Company at the date of termination
> . . .
> This policy shall in all respects be subject to, and governed by, the laws of the state of Florida, without regard to its conflict of laws principles. * * *

*Non-Compete Larg,*

Before the Court can analyze whether this restrictive covenant is enforceable, the Court must determine whether to apply Florida or Illinois law. A federal court sitting in diversity must apply the conflict of laws rules of its forum state. *Utz v. Nationwide Mut. Ins. Co.,* 619 F.2d 7, 9 at n. 1 (7th Cir.1980). Illinois has adopted the Restatement (Second) of Conflict of Laws. *Gramercy Mills, Inc. v. Wolens,* 63 F.3d 569, 572 (7th Cir.1995). Section 187 of the Restatement governs situations like the present where the parties have included an explicit choice of law provision in their contract. Under that section, the parties' choice of law provision will control unless: (A) the chosen state has no substantial relationship to the parties or the transaction, and there is no reasonable basis for the parties choice, or (B) application of the law of the chosen state would be contrary to a fundamental policy of a state, which has a materially greater interest than the chosen state. Restatement (Second) § 187(a)(b) (1971).

Illinois law governs this dispute. To be sure, Del Monte has a reasonable basis for including Florida law in the contract: Del Monte—at least this particular entity—is incorporated in Florida. Nevertheless, (1) Del Monte chose to sue Kinnavy in the state court of Illinois; (2) Kinnavy is an Illinois resident; (3) Kinnavy worked in Del Monte's Illinois office; (4) Kinnavy signed the contract in Illinois and (4) the laws of Florida regarding restrictive covenants are contrary to the fundamental policy of the laws of Illinois. For example, in *Brown & Brown, Inc. v. Mudron,* the appellate court applied Illinois law to a restrictive covenant even though the employment contract contained a Florida choice of law provision:

> [I]t is clear that Illinois law will control the outcome of this dispute. Under Illinois law, in determining whether a restrictive covenant is reasonable, a court must consider the hardship the covenant imposes upon the individual employee. Florida law, however, specifically prohibits considering that factor. Fla. Stat. Ann. § 542.335(1)(g)(I) (West 2007)

> Thus, as a matter of fundamental public policy, Illinois has chosen to provide its workers greater protection from the negative effects of restrictive covenants. Florida law, which specifically prohibits considering the hardship a restrictive covenant imposes upon an individual employee, is contrary to Illinois's fundamental public policy.

*Brown & Brown, Inc. v. Mudron,* 379 Ill.App.3d 724, 727–28, 320 Ill.Dec. 293, 887 N.E.2d 437 (2008). The Court finds this reasoning persuasive and will apply the laws of its home-state.[10]

As a general rule, Illinois courts are reluctant to enforce restrictive covenants. *See, e.g., Francorp, Inc. v. Siebert,* 126 F.Supp.2d 543, 546 (N.D.Ill.2000) (invalidating an employee's non-compete agreement and

---

**10.** Fla. Stat. Ann. § 542.335(1)(g)(1) states: "In determining the enforceability of a restrictive covenant, a court: *Shall not consider any individualized economic or other hardship* that might be caused to the person against whom enforcement is sought." (emphasis added) By contrast, in Illinois: "A restrictive covenant's *reasonableness is measured by its hardship to the employee ...*" *Lawrence & Allen, Inc. v. Cambridge Human Resource Group, Inc.,* 292 Ill.App.3d 131, 138, 685 N.E.2d 434, 441, 226 Ill.Dec. 331 (1997) (emphasis added).

noting, "Illinois courts have long been hostile toward restrictive covenants as restraints on trade and contrary to sound public policy."); *Roberge v. Qualitek Int'l, Inc.,* 2002 U.S. Dist. LEXIS 1217, at \*12, 2002 WL 109360, \*4 (N.D.Ill. Jan. 28, 2002) (invalidating an employee's non-compete agreement and noting, "In Illinois, restrictive covenants are disfavored in the law and closely scrutinized because they are repugnant to the public policy encouraging an open and competitive marketplace."). Post-employment restrictive covenants "operate as partial restrictions on trade" and must be carefully scrutinized by the reviewing court. *Cambridge Eng'g, Inc. v. Mercury Partners 90 BI, Inc.,* 378 Ill.App.3d 437, 447, 316 Ill.Dec. 445, 879 N.E.2d 512 (2007). Nevertheless, a restrictive covenant may be enforceable if its terms are "reasonable and necessary to protect a legitimate business interest of the employer." *Id.* quoting *Lawrence & Allen, Inc. v. Cambridge Human Resource Group, Inc.,* 292 Ill.App.3d 131, 138, 685 N.E.2d 434, 226 Ill.Dec. 331 (1997). A "restrictive covenant's reasonableness is measured by its hardship to the employee, its effect upon the general public, and the reasonableness of the time, territory, and activity restrictions." *Cambridge Eng'g,* 378 Ill.App.3d at 447, 316 Ill.Dec. 445, 879 N.E.2d 512.

The Non–Compete agreement signed by Kinnavy is too broad and far-reaching to be enforceable. First, the Non–Compete contains no geographic restrictions. Thus, even if Kinnavy were to move to Lagos, Nigeria, she would still be bound by the restrictive covenant; this is unreasonable. In response, Del Monte argues extra restrictions are necessary because it is a multi-national firm that competes globally. This argument misses the mark. For example, in *Roberge v. Qualitek Int'l, Inc.,* the court analyzed a similar contention by an employer seeking to enforce a non-compete:

> Qualitek asserts that because it has customers globally and has competitors throughout the United States ... inserting an arbitrary boundary such as prohibiting Roberge from competing with Qualitek in the State of Illinois ... would not protect Qualitek's legitimate interests. While this is perhaps the most logical argument [Qualitek] could make ... *it is a position that has been rejected countless times by both state and federal courts in Illinois* [citing cases] Given this compelling authority we reject Qualitek's argument ...

2002 WL 109360, at \*6, 2002 U.S. Dist. LEXIS 1217, at \*16–17 (emphasis added); *see, also Hay Group, Inc. v. Bassick,* No. 02 C 8194, 2005 U.S. Dist. LEXIS 22095, at \*11, 2005 WL 2420415, \*3 (N.D.Ill. Sept. 29, 2005) (finding non-compete agreement lacking geographic boundaries unenforceable: "This non-compete effectively precludes Bassick from engaging in his occupation ... in any part of the world ... For this reason, the Bassick Noncompete is an unreasonable restraint on trade and is invalid."); *George S. May Int'l Co. v. International Profit Assocs.,* 256 Ill.App.3d 779, 195 Ill.Dec. 183, 628 N.E.2d 647, 655 (1993) (declining to enforce restrictive covenant which prevented employees from working in states in which they never worked for their employer.).

The Non–Compete agreement also contains blanket prohibitions on the *types* of employment Kinnavy can pursue. In Illinois, "an individual has a fundamental right to use his general knowledge and skills to purse the occupation for which he is best suited." *International Profit Assocs.,* 256 Ill.App.3d 779, 195 Ill.Dec. 183, 628 N.E.2d 647, at 653. But here, the Non–Compete prohibits Kinnavy from "being connected in *any manner* with" an entity that bought fruit, vegetables, or other produce from Del Monte. Under these terms, Kinnavy could not work as a cashier at a Piggly–Wiggly that bought produce from Del Monte. These restrictions are simply too broad to be enforceable. Judge Coar had this to say when faced with a similar restrictive covenant:

> As written, the covenant restricts Chase from working for any company, in any manner, in any business "leasing, renting selling, and using all sorts of transportation" or any similarly situation business dealing in related products. The universe of companies falling within the broad sweep of these loosely defined terms is simply too large to be considered reasonable.

*Trailer Leasing Co. v. Assocs Commercial Corp.,* 1996 U.S. Dist. LEXIS 9654., at *10, 1996 WL 392135, *3 (N.D.Ill. July 10, 1996). Similarly, in *Telxon Corp. v. Hoffman,* the court refused to enforce a non-compete agreement where the scope of the prohibited activities so broad that "the agreement would preclude Hoffman from working as a competitor's janitor." 720 F.Supp. 657, 665 (N.D.Ill.1989). Because agreements "which restrict the signor's ability to work for a competitor without regard to capacity have repeatedly been declared contrary to law" the Court finds Del Monte's Non–Compete agreement is unenforceable. *Id.* citing., *North American Paper Co. v. Unterberger,* 172 Ill.App.3d 410, 413, 122 Ill.Dec. 362, 364, 526 N.E.2d 621, 623 (1988) (finding restrictive covenant unenforceable because, "Unterberger is prohibited from associating with any competitor in any capacity whatsoever, even if Unterberger's job were merely menial and he had absolutely nothing to do with sales or purchasing,").

Finally, Del Monte asks the Court—in the event the Non–Compete is found to be invalid—to re-write the contract so it is in compliance with Illinois law. The Court declines Del Monte's invitation. The Non–Compete agreement is simply too broad and far-reaching to be salvageable. *See, e.g., Trailer Leasing Co.,* 1996 U.S. Dist. LEXIS 9654, at *12, 1996 WL 392135, *4 ("While this court has the option of blue-penciling the covenant, it declines to do so since substantial modification/deletions to the covenant would be required."); *Bassick,* 2005 U.S. Dist. LEXIS 22095, at *11, 2005 WL 2420415, at *3 ("Where as here, the restraint is patently 'unfair because of its over breadth,' courts will refuse to modify the agreement, even in the presence of a severability clause."). * * *

## NOTES AND QUESTIONS

1. As the difference between Illinois law and Florida law discussed by the *Del Monte* court suggests, states vary considerably in their receptivity to covenants not to compete. A covenant not to compete in employment, not connected to the sale of a business or partnership, is unenforceable in California per se, irrespective of any reasonableness in its terms. *Edwards v. Arthur Andersen LLP*, 44 Cal.4th 937, 81 Cal.Rptr.3d 282, 189 P.3d 285 (2008). In Texas, at-will employment alone will not support a covenant not to compete: the covenant must be ancillary to some other contract or be supported by separate consideration at the time it is entered into. *Tom James of Dallas, Inc. v. Cobb*, 109 S.W.3d 877 (Tex. App. 2003). In other jurisdictions, the covenant requires grounding in a legitimate business interest other than the desire to be free of competition: only then need the question of the reasonableness of the prohibition—to the jobs the employee is precluded from taking, to the locations where he may not work, and to duration—be reached. The need to protect trade secrets or confidential business information are recognized interests that will support a covenant not to compete. The *Del Monte* court does not attend to that question because it finds the covenant fails the test of reasonableness; but Illinois restricts the legitimate interest it is willing to recognize as supporting a valid covenant not to compete (apart from protecting confidential information) to "near permanent" customer relations. *Brown & Brown, Inc. v. Ali*, 592 F.Supp.2d 1009, 1044–45 (N.D. Ill. 2009) (sales of non-unique goods is rarely capable of showing such a relationship). New Hampshire extends the employer's protectable interests to

> an employee's special influence over the employer's customers, obtained during the course of employment; contacts developed during the employment; and the employer's development of goodwill and a positive image.
>
> . . .
>
> Moreover, when an employee holds a position involving client contact, it is natural that some of the goodwill emanating from the client is directed to the employee rather than to the employer, and the employer has a legitimate interest in preventing its employees from appropriating this goodwill to its detriment. . . .

*ACAS Acquisitions (Precitech) Inc. v. Hobert*, 155 N.H. 381, 923 A.2d 1076, 1085 (2007). Hawaii, following some other jurisdictions, allows specialized or "unique" training to be a protectable interest. *The 7's Enters., Inc. v. Del Rosario*, 111 Hawai'i 484, 143 P.3d 23 (2006). Some jurisdictions combine these. In Michigan, a physician's covenant not to compete can be grounded in the prevention of "unfair competition by presenting the loss of patients to departing physicians." *St. Clair Med., P.C. v. Borgiel*, 270 Mich.App. 260, 715 N.W.2d 914, 919 (2006).

> A physician who establishes patient contracts and relationships as the result of the goodwill of his employer's medical practice is in a position to unfairly appropriate that goodwill and thus unfairly compete with a former employer upon departure. See *Weber v. Tillman*, 259 Kan. 457, 467–69, 913 P.2d 84 (1996); . . . . This risk of unfair competition in this

context does not result from access to patient lists, but from the risk that patients will seek to follow a departing physician. Where the physician-patient relationship was facilitated by a physician's association with his employer or resulted from advertising dollars expended by that employer, a physician can unfairly take advantage of the employer's investments in advertising and goodwill when competing with the former employer to retain patients.

*Id.* at 920. The court held that the freedom of patient choice was not encumbered because the geographic restraint was limited to medical practice within only a seven-mile radius of the prior employment. The New Jersey Supreme Court rejected an outright prohibition of covenants not to compete among physicians along much this same line, but adding to the possible expropriation of the employer's good will the employer's interest in protecting its investment in skills development: the hospital "made a substantial investment in Dr. More [the employee] by giving him the opportunity to accumulate knowledge and hone his skills as a neurosurgeon. Indeed, Dr. More acknowledges that it 'takes years of education, practical experience and accumulated skills and knowledge, as well as an innate talent, for a doctor to reach [his] level of practice.'" *Community Hosp. Group, Inc. v. More*, 183 N.J. 36, 869 A.2d 884 (2005) (noting that the American Medical Association had endorsed the reasonable balancing approach).

2. Which, if any, of these interests claimed to provide legitimate support for a non-competition agreement do you find persuasive?

a) *Trade secrets and confidential information.* Because the law already provides a remedy for the misappropriation of trade secrets and other confidential business information, is additional contractual protection in terms of a non-competition agreement excessive? *See* Phillip Closius & Henry Schaffer, *Involuntary Nonservitude: The Current Judicial Enforcement of Employee Covenants Not to Compete—A Proposal for Reform*, 57 S. CAL. L. REV. 531 (1984).

b) *Customer contact.* This justification is grounded in the so-called "route driver" cases which a Missouri court explained thusly:

> [I]n the sales industry the goodwill of a customer frequently attaches to the employer's sales representative personally; the employer's product becomes associated in the customer's mind with that representative. The sales employee is thus frequently in a position to exert a special influence over the customer and entice that customer's business away from the employer. An employer may properly protect itself against such an eventuality for a reasonable period of time.

*West Group Broadcasting, Ltd. v. Bell*, 942 S.W.2d 934, 939 (Mo. App. 1997), (refusing to enforce a covenant for an on-the-air personality because the employee's new radio persona differed from that in her prior employment). But a California court scouted this theory as applied to an on-the-air reporter: "Actors, musicians, athletes, and others are frequently trained, tutored, and coached to satisfy the requirements of their sponsors and audiences, but their talents belong to them to contract away as they please...." *Metro Traffic Control, Inc. v. Shadow Traffic Network*, 22 Cal.App.4th 853, 27 Cal.Rptr.2d 573, 578–79 (1994).

A proposed but not yet adopted provision of the Restatement (Third) of Employment Law endorses a Texas decision—placing the illustration in Los Angeles, however—allowing a television station's investment in building an on-air personality's reputation to support a covenant not to compete. Section 8.07 Illustration 5. It does not note that that covenant would not be enforceable in California where the scenario is laid. Neither does it take note of the fact that several states that enforce covenants not to compete have carved out an exception for on-air personalities. *E.g.*, 820 ILCS 17/1–10 (2009 Supp.).

What would a route driver bring to the labor market, what would he or she have to offer a prospective employer, if not the knowledge and skills developed in prior employment? Why would these not include the value the customer attaches to the driver's person?

*Training costs.* In the New Jersey case, Dr. More acquired the skill that comes from the extended practice of neurosurgery. That is professional knowledge and skill we would expect any practitioner to acquire over time that he brings into the labor market. How does affording an *employee* the opportunity to perfect his surgical skill give the *employer* a protectable interest? The Hawaii court required the training to be "special" or "unique." In that case, the job was a "briefer," one who promotes and sells tourist items and tours. The "unique" training consisted of two months of memorizing scripts, observing "briefing" sessions, and responding to customers. Though the court does not say so, it may be that a period of training during which the employer gets no benefit represents a sunk cost that a covenant not to compete enables it to recoup. But that would be so of any training, not only of "special" training, would it not? Note also that the trainee in the case was paid $1,400 a month during her two-month training period and rose to $2,000 a month plus 1% commission on sales after her training was over. Wasn't the employee's utility to the employer during training reflected in the lower, training wage? If not, would a contractual requirement to repay training costs—$2,800 in her case—be a satisfactory and less drastic alternative to a covenant not to compete? *See* Gillian Lester, *Restrictive Covenants, Employee Training, and the Limits of Transaction–Cost Analysis*, 76 Ind. L.J. 49 (2001).

*Goodwill.* The Texas Supreme Court scoffed at this insofar as it applies to the "common calling" of an automobile trim repairman:

> When people leave a business to work for another or to open a firm of their own, many are capable of taking with them a sizeable number of the clients whom they had served at their previous place of employment. If they were not in possession of some type of personal magnetism or personal goodwill, they would be incapable of retaining those clients or customers. Shrewd employers and franchisers know this and seek to deprive the employee/franchisee of the fruits of his goodwill by requiring that he enter into an agreement containing a restrictive covenant. The covenant is generally unfair to the employee/franchisee, for when that person is placed in the position of being unable to compete with the former employer/franchiser, his personal goodwill is effectively neutralized.

*Hill v. Mobile Auto Trim, Inc.*,725 S.W.2d 168, 171–72 (Tex. 1987). As we saw, however, this is the very theory that undergirds enforcement of the covenant not to compete in the uncommon calling of medical doctors in Michigan. Apropos of that, what happens to the patients' interest in being served—or, at least, more conveniently served, depending upon the scope of the geographic restriction—by physicians of *their* choosing?

3. As we saw in the *Del Monte* case, even where supported by a legitimate business interest, the covenant must be reasonable, balancing not only the employer's and employees' interests, but also the public's interest. Does the public interest extend to maintaining a legal framework that encourages the broadest dissemination of knowledge and knowhow, to encourage employers and employees to develop new or better products and services? Professor Ronald Gilson has pointed out that employee mobility has spillover effects because they bring the knowledge and knowhow they have acquired at one employment to another:

> Suppose research and development in an industrial district takes place within a large number of firms, the results of which are then shared among firms through both voluntary and involuntary knowledge spillovers. Voluntary spillovers occur through such mechanisms as joint ventures and cooperative supply relationships in which a mutual exchange of technology between a customer and supplier takes place. The benefits of such knowledge spillovers then accrue to the suppliers' other customers. Involuntary spillovers occur through the movement of workers to new employers. Tacit information associated with an employer's technology is embedded in the human capital of its employees. When an employee changes jobs, that tacit information is available to the new employer. ... These knowledge spillovers supercharge the innovative capacity of the district with renewed agglomeration economies, facilitating the development of new technologies that create a new industrial life cycle.

Ronald Gilson, *The Legal Structure of High Technology Industrial Districts: Silicon Valley, Route 128, and Covenants Not to Compete*, 74 N.Y.U. L. REV. 575, 585–86 (1999) (references omitted). He attributes the success of Silicon Valley in California vis-à-vis Route 128 in Massachusetts, in part, to the fact that covenants not to compete are generally unenforceable in California, but generally enforceable (for a "reasonable period") in Massachusetts:

> Given the speed of innovation and the corresponding telescoping of product life cycles, knowledge more than a year or two old likely no longer has significant competitive value. The hiatus imposed by a covenant not to compete thus assures that a departing employee will bring to a new employer only her general and industry-specific human capital. The value of proprietary tacit knowledge embedded in the employee's human capital, or the value of inchoate inventions the employee has strategically chosen not to bring to conception during her employment, will have dissipated over the covenant's term. Nothing of value is left to spill over to a new employer or start-up venture.

> The availability of such a covenant has an obvious impact on the potential for an industrial district to develop a second-stage agglomeration economy like the one that has allowed Silicon Valley to reset its product cycle. The covenant puts a sharp brake on employee mobility, and thus on the

knowledge spillovers that give rise to the critical second-stage agglomeration economy. The widespread use and enforcement of covenants not to compete slow down high velocity employment to the point where the level of knowledge spillovers is too low to support a districtwide innovation cycle.

*Id.* at 603. Because Silicon Valley firms are unable to restrain employee mobility, they have developed a high-velocity employment environment where employees both leave to new ventures and are acquired from them, resulting in the acceleration of the transmission of knowledge and so of new ideas and new product development. Is this experience generalizable?

4. The RESTATEMENT (THIRD) OF EMPLOYMENT LAW proposes a uniform common law scheme favorable to the enforcement of covenants not to compete. Given the variety of approaches only hinted at in the preceding can there be said to be a uniform common law in the United States? If what is proposed is in the nature of law reform would not the economics of such covenants have to be addressed especially the effect on the development and dissemination of new products and services? If so, why does the RESTATEMENT make no reference to the extensive economic literature?

5. German law allows but strictly regulates covenants not to compete. They must be grounded in a legitimate business interest, *i.e.*, trade secrets and customer contact, and cannot be longer than two years. Because the employee loses the value of his special knowledge and skills for that period, the employer must pay the employee one-half of his prior compensation during the period of non-competition. German Commercial Code (HGB) § 74. Because this provision depends on the former employer's invoking its contract right, it allows the employer to calculate whether statutory compensation would cost more than enforcing the covenant would be worth. Does German law provide a model worth considering?

6. The *Del Monte* court refused to "blue-pencil" the covenant. To "blue-pencil" is to narrow the restriction to to legally acceptable limits and then to enforce it as narrowed. Illinois is not alone in refusing to "blue pencil" restrictive covenants. *See, e.g., Whimsical Expressions, Inc. v. Brown*, 275 Ga.App. 420, 620 S.E.2d 635 (2005). But other jurisdictions will. The argument against blue-penciling is that a court's willingness to re-draft encourages employers to draft overbroad protections knowing that, in the event of judicial challenge, the court will enforce a more reasonable restriction. Should a court blue-pencil or not?

7. May an at-will employee be discharged for refusing to sign an unenforceable covenant not to compete? Would such a discharge violate public policy? Oregon law declares void a noncompetition agreement not entered into upon initial employment (or, if entered into subsequently, one that is not tied to the employee's bona fide advancement). The Supreme Court of Oregon held the statute to confer an employment-related right, but not one expressing an important *public* interest; and so discharge for a refusal to sign was not tortious. *Dymock v. Norwest Safety Protective Equip. for Oregon Industry, Inc.*, 334 Or. 55, 45 P.3d 114, 116 (2002). A California Court of Appeal, noting that " 'public policy must involve a subject which affects the public at large rather than a purely personal or proprietary interest' " and which must " 'be

fundamental [or] substantial,' " held a discharge grounded in a refusal to sign an unenforceable restrictive covenant to be actionable as a termination in violation of public policy. *D'sa v. Playhut, Inc.*, 85 Cal.App.4th 927, 102 Cal.Rptr.2d 495, 499 (Ct. App. 2000). Which is the better view?

## D. EMPLOYEE CREATIVE WORK

The law of ownership of employee creative work and inventions has long been stable. In employments where employees are likely to generate ideas, the respective rights of the parties are commonly subjected to contractual treatment and often to state statutory regulation as well. For background, see Robert Gullette, *State Legislation Governing Ownership Rights in Inventions Under Employee Invention Agreements*, 62 J. PAT. OFF. SOC'Y 732 (1980) and Evelyn D. Pisegna–Cook, *Ownership Rights of Employee Inventions: The Role of Preinvention Assignment Agreements and State Statutes*, 2 U. BALT. INTELL. PROP. L.J. 163 (1994).

Ownership vests in the "author" of work that is subject to copyright protection. However, in a "work made for hire," the Copyright Act provides that the statutory "author" is the employer for whom the work was prepared. 17 U.S.C. § 201(b). Whether a work is one "made for hire" has been subject to a good deal of litigation and is commonly dealt with expressly by contract. *See, e.g., Archie Comic Publications, Inc. v. DeCarlo*, 258 F.Supp.2d 315 (S.D.N.Y. 2003).

Inventions are subject to patent protection, and, the human inventor generally has the right to the patent. Nevertheless, a body of common law has developed from *United States v. Dubilier Condenser Corp.*, 289 U.S. 178, 53 S.Ct. 554, 77 L.Ed. 1114 (1933). This common law regulates the rights of an employee vis-à-vis the employer depending upon the extent to which the employee uses the employer's facilities to develop the invention. In a nutshell:

(1) An employee who is employed to invent something specific may be required to assign the patent for it to the employer.

(2) An employee engaged in non-inventive work, or even inventive work of a general nature, who develops an invention on his own time and independent of the employer's facilities, retains full rights to the patent.

(3) An employee engaged in general inventive work; or even non-inventive work' who develops the invention using the employer's facilities, time, and resources; retains the legal right to the patent; but may be required to grant to the employer a non-exclusive royalty-free license to use the invention. This is called a "shop right."

Where inventive work is involved, individually negotiated contractual terms or company policies accorded contractual status will commonly treat the issue of the assignment of rights. An assignment agreement may be limited to inventions made or conceived during the period of employment, but the employer may also wish to reach post-termination inventions, on the theory that such inventions may be based upon the work done during employment. Such holdover or "trailer" provisions implicate a balancing between the employer's proprietary interests and the employee's interests in developing his ideas. However, an employer cannot enforce an agreement to assign all future inventions extending to any business with which the prior employer, its predecessor, or successor, may be concerned; such an obligation is unbounded as to duration and almost limitless as to substance.

Accordingly, courts consider several factors in striking the balance. First, a holdover clause must be limited to a reasonable period of time. Second, although a restriction limited to inventions based upon trade secrets or confidential information has been sustained, there is a difference of opinion on whether the latter is a necessary or merely a sufficient condition. The prevailing view is that the assignment need not be limited to using the prior employer's confidential information, but must be limited to "subject matter which an employee worked on or had knowledge of during his employment." *Dorr–Oliver, Inc. v. United States*, 432 F.2d 447, 452 (Ct. Cl. 1970).

## NOTES AND QUESTIONS

1. One student of the apportionment of rights set out above has been critical of it:

> The courts *have* sought to protect the right of individuals to make a living, to change jobs, and to be relieved from inequities, hardships, and harshness (although they have shown little disposition to look searchingly for such characteristics). Otherwise, however, public interest considerations have largely been ignored. There is virtually no suggestion, for instance, that inequality in bargaining power may exist and little concern over the dangers of monopoly—perhaps because the dangers seem too remote and indirect. Rarely do courts suggest strict construction of a contract on the time-honored ground that the employer drafted it. Most surprising, they show little concern over the possible adverse effects of employer-employee rules upon the stimulus to invent and the direction and scope of inventive activity. Lastly, they ignore the arguable proposition that an inventor may possess certain personal or inalienable rights in his invention that set it apart from other kinds of property.

John Stedman, *The Employed Inventor, the Public Interest, and Horse and Buggy Law in the Space Age*, 45 N.Y.U. L. Rev. 1, 16–17 (1970). Among his suggestions for reform are:

> We could retain our traditional law but apply it more strictly against the employer and with a hard look at its possible shortcomings. In applying the common law, for instance, we might inquire more closely whether a given result is fair or equitable, and rely more upon quantum meruit doctrines. In the area of contracts, we could look more searchingly for possible hardship and overreaching, and show more sensitivity to possible adverse effects in terms of restraining trade or discouraging inventive

activity—results that one associates with trailer clauses, restrictions upon changing jobs, and the like. Contracts might also be interpreted more strictly against the employer, be more freely subject to reformation where circumstances change and, where contrary to the public interest, be declared absolutely void instead of reformable. * * *

We might consider doctrines heretofore largely ignored in the field of invention which would recognize certain moral, possibly inalienable, rights in employees. These could include the right of an inventor to be identified as such—a right that already exists in the patent law although sometimes ignored, or it might include a right to share in the benefits of an invention to the extent that one had not already been compensated therefor. Management traditionally is rewarded, sometimes quite handsomely, in the form of bonuses, retirement benefits, and profit-sharing plans, for contributions beyond the call of duty. There is no clear reason why inventors should not be similarly rewarded—as, in fact, they are under the laws of some countries.

We might consider affording an employee an opportunity to get his invention into use, even though he owns no beneficial rights in it. Such a doctrine would accord with our general antitrust law approach which recognizes the right to hire inventors in order to acquire rights to inventions that can be put to use, but does not recognize the right to hire persons for the purpose of weakening one's competitors. It also accords with patent policy which looks askance at, even though it does not outrightly condemn, the suppression of patents. Such a right might be enforced in various ways. An employee might be given what amounts to a "shop right," or he might be given a right only in the event that the employer himself does not put the invention to use. "March-in" authority might be granted, under which the employee inventor could require, in such cases, that his employer grant licenses to others.

*Id.* at 23–24.

2. Are pre-invention agreements the best way to assure that improvements and new inventions find their way into the stream of commerce, *i.e.* produce societally optimal results? *Compare* Ann Bartow, *Inventors of the World, Unite! A Call for Collective Action by Employee–Inventors*, 37 SANTA CLARA L. REV. 673 (1997) and Steven Cherensky, Comment, *A Penny for Their Thoughts: Employee–Inventors, Preinvention Assignment Agreements, Property, and Personhood*, 81 CAL. L. REV. 597 (1993), *with* Robert Merges, *The Law and Economics of Employee Inventions*, 13 HARV. J.L. & TECH. 1 (1999).

3. Gil Grissom is a laboratory technician at Yo–Yo Dyne, Inc. His job is to test the tensile strength of the steel rope the company manufactures. Company policy in the Employee Handbook provides that the company retains ownership of all ideas conceived by any employee that "relates to" the company's business, whether perfected on the job or not, which is conceived during the employee's period of employment or within two years after the termination of employment. While conducting his routine testing work, Mr. Grissom conceived of a completely new method of fabricating steel rope. At home, on evenings and weekends, he "played around" with the idea using discarded parts taken from the company's dumpster. A year later, he quit Yo–

Yo Dyne to spend time developing his concept. Nine months later, he filed a patent application for it and approached Yo–Yo Dyne either to purchase the patent from him or to purchase a license to use it. Instead, Yo–Yo Dyne has sued to compel Grissom to assign the patent to it. Who should prevail? *Cf. Ingersoll–Rand Co. v. Ciavatta*, 110 N.J. 609, 542 A.2d 879 (1988).

4. Dr. John Marshall, a research scientist at a Yo–Yo Dyne subsidiary in the chemical business, had, pursuant to the company's intellectual property policy, requested his employer's permission to publish an article in a scientific journal based upon his research for the company, "The Potential of Immobilized Biocatalysts for Production of Industrial Chemicals." The company agreed and the article appeared. Marshall later learned that Yo–Yo Dyne planned to assign the copyright to a publication that enjoyed a very bad reputation in scientific circles. Could Marshall restrain his employer from assigning the copyright over his, the actual researcher/author's objection? *Cf. Marshall v. Miles Labs., Inc.*, 647 F.Supp. 1326 (N.D. Ind. 1986). If Dr. Marshall had submitted the article for publication without Yo–Yo Dyne's approval, could the company have withdrawn it from publication? *See Landrum v. J.F. Pritchard & Co.*, 139 Ga.App. 393, 228 S.E.2d 290 (1976). Could Yo–Yo Dyne have allowed the article to be published but have ordered Marshall's name deleted?

# CHAPTER VI

# MONITORING AND CONTROL

■ ■ ■

In Chapter I, we pointed out that perhaps nowhere in the conflict between the liberal concept of free labor as autonomy in the labor market and the conception of free labor as autonomy within the employment relationship quite as stark as in the area of worker privacy. To economic liberals, contract is the universal solvent; the law's essential function is to defer to terms of the bargain struck. *See* Bruce Kobayashi & Larry Ribstein, *Privacy and Firms*, 79 DENV. U. L. REV. 526 (2002). According to that view, state intervention—even to disallow an agreement authorizing video surveillance of employees in a toilet—would be "oppressive." *Id.* Critics of this robust neo-liberalism dispute that a contract of adhesion, especially one over "public goods" the individual is powerless to influence, is worthy of legal deference. *See* Matthew W. Finkin, *Employee Privacy and the "Theory of the Firm"*, 26 J. LAB. RES. 711 (2005).

The movement from the law of master and servant to freedom of contract was set out earlier in the excerpt from Philip Selznick. The shift has been explored as well by Spiros Simitis and it is well to review his account before proceeding further:

> If the market is to be accessible to everyone, all individuals must be able to rely upon their particular abilities and to exercise them freely. The inclusion of work universalizes access to the market and at the same time stresses the common denominator of all competitors. Behind the merchants, artisans, or workers there is always a *citoyen-propriétaire*. In each of these cases property is seen as the foundation of the individual actor's independence, the motive for his activities, and the incentive for economically rational behaviour. But in order to equate workers with merchants or artisans, labour had to be commodified.

Spiros Simitis, *The Case of the Employment Relationship: Elements of Comparison, in* PRIVATE LAW AND SOCIAL INEQUALITY IN THE INDUSTRIAL AGE: COMPARING LEGAL CULTURES IN BRITAIN, FRANCE, GERMANY, AND THE UNITED STATES 181, 187 (Willibald Steinmetz ed., 2000). But the consequence of the shift was often scarcely liberating:

The step from the proclamation to the application of the liberty of contract was in fact a step back into a social reality characterized by profound disparities between the various proprietors and not by their assumed equality. Therefore instead of improving the workers' chances to influence their employment conditions, contractual agreements simply sanctioned regulations as one-sided as the old masters' privileges had been.

*Id.* at 192.

Chapter III explored the legal status of rules employers promulgate to govern the workplace. These rules, policies, and practices, sometimes reflect a voracious appetite, employers seem to have to acquire information, to monitor and to control their workforces. If contract, meaning unilaterally promulgated employer policies, do not command the law's uncritical respect, the challenge for the law is to define the limits of the employer's "legitimate boundaries," in the words of the dissenters in *Payne v. Western Atlantic Railroad Co.*, discussed in Chapter I. What makes employee privacy a difficult question is that, as Elizabeth Neil observed, when we enter employment we cross the boundary of the purely private: "we stake claims, we waive claims in exchange for other good, and [we] sometimes see claims overridden for the public good." ELIZABETH NEILL, RITES OF PRIVACY AND THE PRIVACY TRADE: ON THE LIMITS OF PROTECTION FOR THE SELF 55 (2001). The law here is a complex web, state and federal, statutory and judge-made, sometimes writ large, sometimes of exquisite narrowness, characterized by large gaps and inconsistencies. *See generally* MATTHEW W. FINKIN, PRIVACY IN EMPLOYMENT LAW (3d ed. 2009). What follows touches on only the most salient or interesting issues.

## A.  VIDEO SURVEILLANCE

### HERNANDEZ v. HILLSIDES, INC.

Supreme Court of California, 2009
47 Cal.4th 272, 97 Cal.Rptr.3d 274, 211 P.3d 1063

BAXTER, J.

Defendants Hillsides, Inc., and Hillsides Children Center, Inc. (Hillsides) operated a private nonprofit residential facility for neglected and abused children, including the victims of sexual abuse. Plaintiffs Abigail Hernandez (Hernandez) and Maria–Jose Lopez (Lopez) were employed by Hillsides. They shared an enclosed office and performed clerical work during daytime business hours. Defendant John M. Hitchcock (Hitchcock), the director of the facility, learned that late at night, after plaintiffs had left the premises, an unknown person had repeatedly used a computer in plaintiffs' office to access the Internet and view pornographic Web sites. Such use conflicted with company policy and with Hillsides' aim of providing a safe haven for the children.

Concerned that the culprit might be a staff member who worked with the children, and without notifying plaintiffs, Hitchcock set up a hidden camera in their office. The camera could be made operable from a remote location, at any time of day or night, to permit either live viewing or videotaping of activities around the targeted workstation. It is undisputed that the camera was not operated for either of these purposes during business hours, and, as a consequence, that plaintiffs' activities in the office were not viewed or recorded by means of the surveillance system. Hitchcock did not expect or intend to catch plaintiffs on tape.

Nonetheless, after discovering the hidden camera in their office, plaintiffs filed this tort action alleging, among other things, that defendants intruded into a protected place, interest, or matter, and violated their right to privacy under both the common law and the state Constitution. The trial court granted defendants' motion for summary judgment and dismissed the case. The Court of Appeal reversed, finding triable issues that plaintiffs had suffered (1) an intrusion into a protected zone of privacy that (2) was so unjustified and offensive as to constitute a privacy violation. * * *

We agree with defendants that the trial court properly granted their motion for summary judgment. However, we reach this conclusion for reasons more varied and nuanced than those offered by defendants. * * *

## FACTS

* * * Plaintiffs Hernandez and Lopez performed clerical work during daytime business hours at Hillsides. When they were hired in 1996 and 1999, respectively, they signed disclosure statements and underwent background screening procedures required by law of persons working at licensed child care facilities. This process included fingerprint and criminal record checks, and an agreement to report any child abuse witnessed or suspected while working at Hillsides.

Beginning in 2001, plaintiffs shared an office in the administrative building at Hillsides. Each woman had her own desk and computer workstation. The office had three windows on exterior walls. Blinds on the windows could be opened and closed. The office also had a door that could be closed and locked. A "doggie" door near the bottom of the office door was missing its flap, creating a small, low opening into the office. Several people, besides plaintiffs, had keys to their office: five administrators, including Hitchcock, and all of the program directors. Hernandez estimated that there were five program directors. Hitchcock counted eight of them.

According to plaintiffs, they occasionally used their office to change or adjust their clothing. Hernandez replaced her work clothes with athletic wear before leaving Hillsides to exercise at the end of the day. Two or three times, Lopez raised her shirt to show Hernandez her postpregnancy figure. Both women stated in their declarations that the blinds were drawn and the door was closed when this activity occurred. Hernandez also recalled the door being locked when she changed clothes.

On or before August 22, 2002, Hillsides circulated an "E–Mail, Voicemail and Computer Systems Policy." This document stated that it was intended to prevent employees from using Hillsides' electronic communications systems in a manner that defamed, harassed, or harmed others, or that subjected the company to "significant legal exposure." Illegal and inappropriate activity was prohibited, such as accessing sexually offensive Web sites or displaying, downloading, or distributing sexually explicit material. The policy further contemplated the use of electronic "[p]ersonal passwords." However, it warned employees that they had "no reasonable expectation of privacy in any . . . use of Company computers, network and system." Along the same lines, the policy advised that all data created, transmitted, downloaded, or stored on the system was Hillsides' property, and that the company could "monitor and record employee activity on its computers, network . . . and e-mail systems," including "e-mail messages[,] . . . files stored or transmitted[,] and . . . web sites accessed."

Plaintiffs acknowledged the existence of the foregoing policy in their depositions. Indeed, both testified that, as employees of Hillsides, they were not allowed to access pornographic Web sites from their computers at work. They indicated that such conduct would conflict with Hillsides' mission to provide a safe environment for the abused and vulnerable children in its care. Hernandez described such conduct as "wrong," "illegal," and "unethical." Lopez agreed with this assessment.

In order to ensure compliance with Hillsides' computer policy and restrictions, Foster, the computer specialist, could retrieve and print a list of all Internet Web sites accessed from every computer on the premises. The network server that recorded and stored such information could pinpoint exactly when and where such Web access had occurred. In July 2002, Foster determined that numerous pornographic Web sites had been viewed in the late-night and early-morning hours from at least two different computers. One of them was located in the computer laboratory, or classroom. The other one sat on the desk Lopez used in the office she shared with Hernandez.

The evidence indicated that Lopez's computer could have been accessed after hours by someone other than her, because she did not always log off before going home at night. Hitchcock explained in his deposition that employees were expected to turn off their computers when leaving work at the end of the day, that a personal password was required to log onto the computer again after it had been turned off, and that this policy was communicated orally to employees when their computers were first assigned. He admitted that he did not remind plaintiffs of this procedure before taking the surveillance steps at issue here. Nonetheless, Lopez noted in her declaration that "[o]nce [her] computer at Hillsides was turned off, it required the input of a secret password in order to be accessed again."

Foster told defendant Hitchcock about the inappropriate Internet use, and showed him printouts listing the pornographic Web sites that had been accessed. Given the odd hours at which such activity had occurred, Hitchcock surmised that the perpetrator was a program director or other staff person who had unfettered access to Hillsides in the middle of the night . . .

In light of these circumstances, Hitchcock decided to use video equipment Hillsides already had in its possession to record the perpetrator in the act of using the computers at night. He told other administrators about the problem and his surveillance plan. Hitchcock explained in both his deposition and declaration that he sought to protect the children from any staff person who might expose them to pornography, emphasizing the harm they had endured before entering Hillsides.

With Foster's assistance, Hitchcock initially installed the video equipment in the computer laboratory from which some of the pornographic Web sites had been accessed. However, because so many people used the laboratory for legitimate reasons during and after business hours, Hitchcock decided instead to conduct surveillance in the office that plaintiffs shared. He did not inform plaintiffs of this decision. He reasoned that the more people who knew and "gossiped" about the plan, the greater the chance the culprit would hear about it and never be identified or stopped.

Hence, at some point during the first week of October 2002, Hitchcock and Foster installed video recording equipment in plaintiffs' office and in a storage room nearby. First, in plaintiffs' office, they positioned a camera on the top shelf of a bookcase, among some plants, where it apparently was obscured from view. They also tucked a motion detector into the lap of a stuffed animal or toy sitting on a lower shelf of the same bookcase. Second, these devices connected remotely to a television that Hitchcock and Foster moved into the storage room. A videocassette recorder was built into the unit. The television had a 19–inch monitor on which images could be viewed. * * *

Hitchcock rarely activated the camera and motion detector in plaintiffs' office, and never did so while they were there. His deposition testimony addressed these circumstances as follows: On three occasions, Hitchcock connected the wireless receptors to the television in the storage room after plaintiffs left work for the day, and then disconnected the receptors the next morning, before plaintiffs returned to work. On one such morning, he also removed the camera from the office, and returned it later, when plaintiffs were gone for the night. In short, the camera and motion detector were always disabled during the workday, such that "there was no picture showing" and "no recording going on" while plaintiffs were in their office. Hitchcock further stated that between installation of the equipment in early October 2002, and his decision to remove it three weeks later, no one was videotaped or caught using the computer in plaintiffs' office. He assumed that the culprit had learned about the camera and stopped engaging in unauthorized activity.

Meanwhile, about 4:30 p.m. on Friday, October 25, 2002, plaintiffs discovered the video equipment in their office. A red light on the motion detector flashed at the time. The cord attached to the camera was plugged into the wall and was hot to the touch.

Shocked by the discovery, plaintiffs immediately reported it to two supervisors, Sylvia Levitan and Toni Aikins. Levitan called Hitchcock, who was at home. A program director helped remove the camera from plaintiffs' office and lock it in Levitan's office for safekeeping.

A short time later, Hitchcock called Hernandez in her office. He apologized for installing the camera, and said the surveillance was not aimed at plaintiffs, but at an intruder who had used Lopez's computer to access inappropriate Web sites. Hernandez expressed concern that she was videotaped while changing her clothes or that "personal stuff" in her office was somehow disturbed. Hitchcock replied by assuring Hernandez that "the only time we activated that camera and the video recorder was after you left at night and [we] deactivated the two devices before you came to work in the morning. [¶] . . . [A]t no time did [we] ever capture [you] or [Lopez] on the tape." . . .

Plaintiffs did not return to work until Wednesday, October 30, 2002. That morning, they met for 30 minutes with both defendant Hitchcock and Aikins, their supervisor. Hitchcock essentially repeated the substance of his prior conversation with Hernandez. He apologized and explained the reason for installing the camera in plaintiffs' office, and assured them that they were not the target of the surveillance and had not been videotaped.

During this meeting, Lopez asked to see the surveillance videotape. Hitchcock agreed. The group went to Hitchcock's office and watched the tape on his television set. According to the depositions of both plaintiffs, there was not much to see. No one appeared on the tape except for Hitchcock, who was briefly seen setting up the camera and moving around inside plaintiffs' office. The only other recorded images were of Lopez's empty desk and computer, the surrounding work area, some closets, and the entrance to the office. No sound accompanied the playing of the tape. Hitchcock never indicated to plaintiffs that any audio recording was made, or that the camera could record sound. * * *

## DISCUSSION

### B. General Privacy Principles

* * * The . . . arguments have been framed throughout this action in terms of both the common law and the state Constitution. These two sources of privacy protection "are not unrelated" under California law. . . .

A privacy violation based on the common law tort of intrusion has two elements. First, the defendant must intentionally intrude into a place, conversation, or matter as to which the plaintiff has a reasonable expectation of privacy. Second, the intrusion must occur in a manner highly offensive to a reasonable person. . . . These limitations on the right to privacy are not insignificant.... Nonetheless, the cause of action recognizes a measure of personal control over the individual's autonomy, dignity, and serenity.... The gravamen is the mental anguish sustained when both conditions of liability exist....

As to the first element of the common law tort, the defendant must have "penetrated some zone of physical or sensory privacy ... or obtained unwanted access to data" by electronic or other covert means, in violation of the law or social norms.... In either instance, the expectation of privacy must be "objectively reasonable." ... In *Sanders v. American Broadcasting Companies* (1999) 20 Cal.4th 907, 85 Cal.Rptr.2d 909, 978 P.2d 67 (*Sanders*), a leading case on workplace privacy that we discuss further below, this court linked the reasonableness of privacy expectations to such factors as (1) the identity of the intruder, (2) the extent to which other persons had access to the subject place, and could see or hear the plaintiff, and (3) the means by which the intrusion occurred....

The second common law element essentially involves a "policy" determination as to whether the alleged intrusion is "highly offensive" under the particular circumstances.... Relevant factors include the degree and setting of the intrusion, and the intruder's motives and objectives.... Even in cases involving the use of photographic and electronic recording devices, which can raise difficult questions about covert surveillance, "California tort law provides no bright line on ['offensiveness']; each case must be taken on its facts." ...

The right to privacy in the California Constitution sets standards similar to the common law tort of intrusion....[1] Under this provision, which creates at least a limited right of action against both private and government entities ... the plaintiff must meet several requirements.

First, he must possess a legally protected privacy interest.... These interests include "conducting personal activities without observation, intrusion, or interference", as determined by "established social norms" derived from such sources as the "common law" and "statutory enactment." ... Second, the plaintiff's expectations of privacy must be reasonable. This element rests on an examination of "customs, practices, and physical settings surrounding particular activities" (*ibid.*), as well as the opportunity to be notified in advance and consent to the intrusion.... Third, the plaintiff must show that the intrusion is so serious in "nature, scope, and actual or potential impact as to constitute an egregious breach of the social norms." ...

*Hill* and its progeny further provide that no constitutional violation occurs, i.e., a "defense" exists, if the intrusion on privacy is justified by one or more competing interests.... For purposes of this balancing function—and except in the rare case in which a "fundamental" right of

---

**1.** Article I, section 1 of the California Constitution states: "All people are by nature free and independent and have inalienable rights. Among these are enjoying and defending life and liberty, acquiring, possessing, and protecting property, and pursuing and obtaining safety, happiness, and privacy."

personal autonomy is involved—the defendant need not present a " 'compelling' " countervailing interest; only "general balancing tests are employed." ... To the extent the plaintiff raises the issue in response to a claim or defense of competing interests, the defendant may show that less intrusive alternative means were not reasonably available. ... A relevant inquiry in this regard is whether the intrusion was limited, such that no confidential information was gathered or disclosed. ...

In light of the foregoing, we will assess the parties' claims and the undisputed evidence under the rubric of both the common law and constitutional tests for establishing a privacy violation. Borrowing certain shorthand language from *Hill, supra,* 7 Cal.4th 1, 26 Cal.Rptr.2d 834, 865 P.2d 633, which distilled the largely parallel elements of these two causes of action, we consider (1) the nature of any intrusion upon reasonable expectations of privacy, and (2) the offensiveness or seriousness of the intrusion, including any justification and other relevant interests. ...

## C. Intrusion upon Reasonable Privacy Expectations

For reasons we now explain, we cannot conclude as a matter of law that the Court of Appeal erred in finding a prima facie case on the threshold question whether defendants' video surveillance measures intruded upon plaintiffs' reasonable expectations of privacy. Plaintiffs plausibly maintain that defendants cannot prevail on this element of the cause of action simply because they "never intended to view or record" plaintiffs, or because defendants did not "capture [plaintiffs'] images at all." Other significant factors not considered by defendants point favorably in plaintiffs' direction on this issue.

Our analysis starts from the premise that, while privacy expectations may be significantly diminished in the workplace, they are not lacking altogether. In *Sanders, supra,* 20 Cal.4th 907, 85 Cal.Rptr.2d 909, 978 P.2d 67, a reporter working undercover for a national broadcasting company obtained employment alongside the plaintiff as a telepsychic, giving "readings" to customers over the phone. The reporter then secretly videotaped and recorded interactions with the plaintiff and other psychics using a small camera hidden in her hat and a microphone attached to her brassiere. The taping occurred in a large room containing 100 cubicles that were open on one side and on top, and from which coworkers could be seen and heard nearby. Visitors could not enter this area without permission from the front desk. Ultimately, the plaintiff sued the reporter and the broadcasting company for violating his privacy after one of his secretly taped conversations aired on television. A jury verdict in the plaintiff's favor was reversed on appeal. The appellate court concluded that the plaintiff could not reasonably expect that actions and statements witnessed by coworkers would remain private and not be disclosed to third parties. ...

Relying on the elements of the intrusion tort set forth in *Shulman, supra,* 18 Cal.4th 200, 74 Cal.Rptr.2d 843, 955 P.2d 469, we disagreed with the Court of Appeal in *Sanders,* and reversed the judgment. This court emphasized that privacy expectations can be reasonable even if they are not absolute."[P]rivacy, for purposes of the intrusion tort, is not a binary, all-or-nothing characteristic. There are degrees and nuances to societal recognition of our expectations of privacy: the fact that the privacy one expects in a given setting is not complete or absolute does not render the expectation unreasonable as a matter of law." . . .

In adopting this refined approach, *Sanders* highlighted various factors which, either singly or in combination, affect societal expectations of privacy. One factor was the identity of the intruder. . . . We noted that the plaintiff in that case, and other employees, were deliberately misled into believing that the defendant reporter was a colleague, and had no reason to suspect she worked undercover to secretly tape their interactions for use in a national television program. . . .

Also relevant in *Sanders, supra,* 20 Cal.4th 907, 85 Cal.Rptr.2d 909, 978 P.2d 67, was the nature of the intrusion . . . meaning, *both* the extent to which the subject interaction could be "seen and overheard" *and* the "means of intrusion." . . . These factors weighed heavily in the plaintiff's favor: "[T]he possibility of being overheard by coworkers does not, as a matter of law, render unreasonable an employee's expectation that his or her interactions within a nonpublic workplace will not be videotaped in secret by a journalist." We distinguished the situation in which "the workplace is regularly open to entry or observation by the public or press," or the subject interaction occurred between either the proprietor or employee of a business and a "customer" who walks in from the street.

The present case, of course, does not involve an imposter or "stranger to the workplace" who surreptitiously recorded and videotaped conversations that were later published without the speaker's consent. . . . Nor does it involve commercial interactions between the representatives of a business and its customers or other members of the public. Rather, defendants represent a private *employer* accused of installing electronic equipment that gave it the capacity to secretly watch and record employee activities behind closed doors in an office to which the general public had limited access. As we discuss later with respect to the "offensiveness" element of plaintiffs' claim, an employer may have sound reasons for monitoring the workplace, and an intrusion upon the employee's reasonable privacy expectations may not be egregious or actionable under the particular circumstances. However, on the threshold question whether such expectations were infringed, decisional law suggests that is the case here.

Consistent with *Sanders, supra,* 20 Cal.4th 907, 922, 85 Cal.Rptr.2d 909, 978 P.2d 67, which asks whether the employee could be "overheard or observed" by others when the tortious act allegedly occurred, courts have examined the physical layout of the area intruded upon, its relationship to the workplace as a whole, and the nature of the activities commonly performed in such places. At one end of the spectrum are settings in which work or business is conducted in an open and accessible space, within the sight and hearing not only of coworkers and supervisors, but also of customers, visitors, and the general public. (See *Wilkins v. National Broadcasting Co.* (1999) 71 Cal.App.4th 1066, 1072–1073, 1078, 84 Cal.Rptr.2d 329 [holding for purpose of common law intrusion tort that businessmen lacked privacy in lunch meeting secretly videotaped on crowded outdoor patio of public restaurant]; see also *Acosta v. Scott Labor LLC* (N.D.Ill.2005) 377 F.Supp.2d 647, 649, 652 [similar conclusion as to employer secretly videotaped by disgruntled employee in common, open, and exposed area of workplace]; *Melder v. Sears, Roebuck and Co.* (La.Ct. App.1999) 731 So.2d 991, 994, 1001 [similar conclusion as to department store employee captured on video cameras used to monitor customers as they shopped].)

At the other end of the spectrum are areas in the workplace subject to restricted access and limited view, and reserved exclusively for performing bodily functions or other inherently personal acts. (See *Trujillo v. City of Ontario* (C.D.Cal.2006) 428 F.Supp.2d 1094, 1099–1100, 1103, 1119–1122 (*Trujillo*) [recognizing that employees have common law and constitutional privacy interests while using locker room in basement of police station, and can reasonably expect that employer will not intrude by secretly videotaping them as they undress]; see also *Doe by Doe v. B.P.S. Guard Services, Inc.* (8th Cir.1991) 945 F.2d 1422, 1424, 1427 (*Doe*) [similar conclusion as to models who were secretly viewed and videotaped while changing clothes behind curtained area at fashion show]; *Liberti v. Walt Disney World Co.* (M.D.Fla.1995) 912 F.Supp. 1494, 1499, 1506 (*Liberti*) [similar conclusion as to dancers who were secretly viewed and videotaped while changing clothes and using restroom in dressing room at work].)

The present scenario falls between these extremes. (Cf. *Sacramento County Deputy Sheriffs' Assn. v. County of Sacramento* (1996) 51 Cal. App.4th 1468, 1482, 1487, 59 Cal.Rptr.2d 834 [rejecting common law intrusion claim of jail employee secretly videotaped while handling inmate property based on accessibility of his office to others and heightened security concerns inherent in custodial setting]; see also *Marrs v. Marriott Corp.* (D.Md.1992) 830 F.Supp. 274, 283 [similar conclusion as to security guard secretly videotaped while breaking into colleague's locked desk in open office used as common area by entire staff].)

Plaintiffs plausibly claim that Hillsides provided an enclosed office with a door that could be shut and locked, and window blinds that could be drawn, to allow the occupants to obtain some measure of refuge, to focus on their work, and to escape visual and aural interruptions from other sources, including their employer. Such a protective setting generates legitimate expectations that not all activities performed behind closed doors would be clerical and work related. As suggested by the evidence here, employees who share an office, and who have four walls that shield them from outside view (albeit, with a broken "doggie" flap on the door), may perform grooming or hygiene activities, or conduct personal conversations, during the workday. Privacy is not wholly lacking because the occupants of an office can see one another, or because colleagues, supervisors, visitors, and security and maintenance personnel have varying degrees of access. (See *Sanders, supra,* 20 Cal.4th 907, 917, 85 Cal.Rptr.2d 909, 978 P.2d 67 [" 'visibility to some people does not strip [away] the right to remain secluded from others' "]; *id.* at pp. 918–919, 85 Cal. Rptr.2d 909, 978 P.2d 67 [" 'business office need not be sealed to offer its occupant a reasonable degree of privacy' "].)

Regarding another relevant factor in *Sanders, supra,* 20 Cal.4th 907, 923, 85 Cal.Rptr.2d 909, 978 P.2d 67, the "means of intrusion," employees who retreat into a shared or solo office, and who perform work and personal activities in relative seclusion there, would not reasonably expect to be the subject of televised spying and secret filming by their employer. As noted, in assessing social norms in this regard, we may look at both the "common law" and "statutory enactment." . . .

Courts have acknowledged the intrusive effect for tort purposes of hidden cameras and video recorders in settings that otherwise seem private. It has been said that the "unblinking lens" can be more penetrating than the naked eye with respect to "duration, proximity, focus, and vantage point." (*Cowles v. State* (Alaska 2001) 23 P.3d 1168, 1182 (dis. opn. of Fabe, J.).) Such monitoring and recording denies the actor a key feature of privacy—the right to control the dissemination of his image and actions. (See *Shulman, supra,* 18 Cal.4th 200, 235, 74 Cal.Rptr.2d 843, 955 P.2d 469.) We have made clear that the " 'mere fact that a person can be seen by someone does not automatically mean that he or she can legally be forced to be subject to being seen by everyone.' " (*Sanders, supra,* 20 Cal.4th 907, 916, 85 Cal.Rptr.2d 909, 978 P.2d 67.)

Not surprisingly, we discern a similar legislative policy against covert monitoring and recording that intrudes—or threatens to intrude—upon visual privacy. Some statutes criminalize the use of camcorders, motion picture cameras, or photographic cameras to violate reasonable expectations of privacy in specified areas in which persons commonly undress or perform other intimate acts. Liability exists, under certain circumstances, where the lens allows the intruder to "look[ ]" into or "view[ ]" the protected area. (Pen.Code, § 647, subd. (j)(1).) Of course, the intruder also cannot "secretly videotape, film, photograph, or record" anyone in that private place where various conditions exist. (*Id.,* subd. (j)(3)(A); see *Trujillo, supra,* 428 F.Supp.2d 1094, 1119 [statute intended to protect visual privacy of persons in various states of undress].)

Other statutes authorize civil damages for certain invasions of privacy that involve either a physical trespass or other offensive conduct for the purpose of capturing a picture of someone engaged in personal or familial activities. The focus of such provisions is on the "intent to capture" a "visual image" (Civ.Code, § 1708.8, subd. (a)), or on the "attempt" to do so. (*Id.,* subd. (b).) Failure to capture or record the subject image is no defense to a statutory violation in this context. (*Id.,* subd. (j); see *Richardson–Tunnell v. Schools Ins. Program for Employees (SIPE)* (2007) 157

Cal.App.4th 1056, 1063, 69 Cal.Rptr.3d 176 [statute protects against aggressive, paparazzi-like, behavior of tabloid journalists].)

As emphasized by defendants, the evidence shows that Hitchcock never viewed or recorded plaintiffs inside their office by means of the equipment he installed both there and in the storage room. He also did not intend or attempt to do so, and took steps to avoid capturing them on camera and videotape. While such factors bear on the offensiveness of the challenged conduct, as discussed below, we reject the defense suggestion that they preclude us from finding the requisite intrusion in the first place. (See *Shulman, supra,* 18 Cal.4th 200, 232, 74 Cal.Rptr.2d 843, 955 P.2d 469 [requiring *either* a physical or sensory penetration into a private place or matter, *or* the gaining of unwanted access to private information].)

In particular, Hitchcock hid the video equipment in plaintiffs' office from view in an apparent attempt to prevent anyone from discovering, avoiding, or dismantling it. He used a camera and motion detector small enough to tuck inside and around decorative items perched on different bookshelves, both high and low. Plaintiffs presumably would have been caught in the camera's sights if they had returned to work after hours, or if Hitchcock had been mistaken about them having left the office when he activated the system. Additionally, except for the one day in which Hitchcock removed the camera from plaintiffs' office, the means to activate the monitoring and recording functions were available around the clock, for three weeks, to anyone who had access to the storage room. Assuming the storage room was locked, as many as eight to 11 employees had keys under plaintiffs' version of the facts (depending upon the total number of program directors at Hillsides).

In a related vein, plaintiffs cannot plausibly be found to have received warning that they would be subjected to the risk of such surveillance, or to have agreed to it in advance. We have said that notice of and consent to an impending intrusion can "inhibit reasonable expectations of privacy." ... Such factors also can " ' "limit [an] intrusion upon personal dignity" ' " by providing an opportunity for persons to regulate their conduct while being monitored. . . . Here, however, the evidence shows that no one at Hillsides told plaintiffs that someone had used Lopez's computer to access pornographic Web sites. Nor were they told that Hitchcock planned to install surveillance equipment inside their office to catch the perpetrator on television and videotape.

Moreover, nothing in Hillsides' written computer policy mentioned or even alluded to the latter scenario. As noted earlier, the version in effect at the relevant time made clear that any monitoring and recording of employee activity, and any resulting diminution in reasonable privacy expectations, were limited to "use of Company computers" in the form of "e-mail" messages, electronic "files," and "web site" data. Foster performed this administrative function when he used the network server to produce the list of pornographic Web sites accessed in both the computer laboratory and Lopez's office, and showed such computer-generated data to Hitchcock. There is no evidence that employees like plaintiffs had any indication that Hillsides would take the next drastic step and use cameras and recording devices to view and videotape employees sitting at their desks and computer workstations, or moving around their offices within camera range.

In sum, the undisputed evidence seems clearly to support the first of two basic elements we have identified as necessary to establish a violation of privacy as alleged in plaintiffs' complaint. Defendants secretly installed a hidden video camera that was both operable and operating (electricity-wise), and that could be made to monitor and record activities inside plaintiffs' office, at will, by anyone who plugged in the receptors, and who had access to the remote location in which both the receptors and recording equipment were located. The workplace policy, that by means within the computer system itself, plaintiffs would be monitored about the pattern and use of Web sites visited, to prevent abuse of Hillsides' computer system, is distinguishable from and does not necessarily create a social norm that in order to advance that same interest, a camera would be placed inside their office, and would be aimed toward a computer workstation to capture all human activity occurring there. Plaintiffs had no reasonable expectation that their employer would intrude so tangibly into their semi-private office.

### D. Offensiveness/Seriousness of the Privacy Intrusion

Plaintiffs must show more than an intrusion upon reasonable privacy expectations. Actionable invasions of privacy also must be "highly offensive" to a reasonable person ... and "sufficiently serious" and unwarranted as to constitute an "egregious breach of the social norms." ... Defendants claim that, in finding a triable issue in this regard, the Court of Appeal focused too narrowly on the mere presence of a functioning camera in plaintiffs' office during the workday, and on the inchoate risk that someone would sneak into the locked storage room and activate the monitoring and recording devices. Defendants imply that under a broader view of the relevant circumstances, no reasonable jury could find in plaintiffs' favor and impose liability on this evidentiary record. We agree.

For guidance, we note that this court has previously characterized the "offensiveness" element as an indispensible part of the privacy analysis. It reflects the reality that "[n]o community could function if every intrusion into the realm of private action" gave rise to a viable claim.... Hence, no cause of action will lie for accidental, misguided, or excusable acts of overstepping upon legitimate privacy rights.... In light of such pragmatic policy concerns ... a court determining whether this requirement has been met as a matter of law examines all of the surrounding circumstances, including the "degree and setting" of the intrusion and "the intruder's 'motives and objectives.'" ... Courts also may be asked to decide whether the plaintiff, in attempting to defeat a claim of competing interests, has shown that the defendant could have minimized the privacy intrusion through other reasonably available, less intrusive means. . . .

**1. Degree and Setting of Intrusion.** This set of factors logically encompasses the place, time, and scope of defendants' video surveillance efforts. In this case, they weigh heavily against a finding that the intrusion upon plaintiffs' privacy interests was highly offensive or sufficiently serious to warrant liability.

In context, defendants took a measured approach in choosing the location to videotape the person who was misusing the computer system. Evidently, plaintiffs' office was *not* the preferred spot. Hitchcock initially tried to capture the culprit in the computer laboratory. Based on the consistently high level of human traffic he described there, the laboratory apparently was far more accessible and less secluded than plaintiffs' office. The surveillance equipment was moved to the latter location only after Hitchcock determined it was too difficult to pinpoint who was using computers inappropriately in the open, more public laboratory setting.

Defendants' surveillance efforts also were largely confined to the area in which the unauthorized computer activity had occurred. Once the camera was placed in plaintiffs' office, it was aimed towards Lopez's desk and computer workstation. There is no evidence that Hitchcock intended or attempted to include Hernandez's desk in camera range. We can reasonably infer he avoided doing so, because no improper computer use had been detected there.

Likewise, access to the storage room and knowledge of the surveillance equipment inside were limited. A total of two people other than Hitchcock and Foster (Susanne Crummey and Stacey Brake) knew that the television/recorder was set up to monitor plaintiffs' office. Only one of them (Crummey) had a key to the lock on the storage room door. The spot was relatively remote and secure.

Timing considerations favor defendants as well. After being moved to plaintiffs' office and the storage room, the surveillance equipment was operational during a fairly limited window of time. Hitchcock decided to remove the equipment (and plaintiffs coincidentally discovered it) a mere 21 days later, during which time no one had accessed Lopez's computer for pornographic purposes. We can infer from the undisputed evidence that Hitchcock kept abreast of his own monitoring activities, and did not expose plaintiffs to the risk of covert visual monitoring or video recording any longer than was necessary to determine that his plan would not work, and that the culprit probably had been scared away.

Defendants' actual surveillance activities also were quite limited in scope. On the one hand, the camera and motion detector in plaintiffs' office were always plugged into the electrical circuit and capable of operating the entire time they were in place. On the other hand, Hitchcock took the critical step of connecting the wireless receptors and activating the system only three times. At most, he was responsible for monitoring and recording inside of plaintiffs' office an average of only once a week for three weeks. Such measures were hardly excessive or egregious. (Cf. *Wolfson v. Lewis* (E.D.Pa.1996) 924 F.Supp. 1413, 1420 [electronic surveillance that is persistent and pervasive may constitute a tortious intrusion on privacy even when conducted in a public or semi-public place].)

Moreover, on each of these three occasions, Hitchcock connected the wireless devices and allowed the system to remotely monitor and record events inside plaintiffs' office only after their shifts ended, and after they normally left Hillsides' property. He never activated the system during regular business hours when plaintiffs were scheduled to work. The evidence shows they were not secretly viewed or taped while engaged in personal or clerical activities.

On the latter point, we agree with defendants that their successful effort to avoid capturing plaintiffs on camera is inconsistent with an egregious breach of social norms. For example, in a case closely on point, one court has held that even where an employer placed a camera in an area reserved for the most personal functions at work, such that height-ened privacy expectations applied, the lack of any viewing or recording defeated the employee's invasion of privacy claim. (E.g., *Meche v. Wal-Mart, Stores, Inc.* (La.Ct.App.1997) 692 So.2d 544, 547 [camera concealed in ceiling of restroom to prevent theft].) This circumstance also distin-guishes plaintiffs' case from those we have discussed above, in which covert visual monitoring and video recording in an employment setting supported a viable intrusion claim. (E.g., *Doe, supra,* 945 F.2d 1422, 1424, 1427 [models' changing area]; *Trujillo, supra,* 428 F.Supp.2d 1094, 1100, 1119–1122 [police locker room]; *Liberti, supra,* 912 F.Supp. 1494, 1499 [dancers' dressing room].)

**2. Defendants' motives, justifications, and related issues.** This case does not involve surveillance measures conducted for socially repugnant or unprotected reasons. (See, e.g., *Shulman, supra,* 18 Cal.4th 200, 237, 74 Cal.Rptr.2d 843, 955 P.2d 469 [harassment, blackmail, or prurient curiosity].) Nor, contrary to what plaintiffs imply, does the record reveal the absence of any reasonable justification or beneficial motivation. The undisputed evidence is that defendants installed video surveillance equipment in plaintiffs' office, and activated it three times after they left work, in order to confirm a strong suspicion—triggered by publicized network tracking measures—that an unknown staff person was engaged in unauthorized and inappropriate computer use at night. Given the apparent risks under existing law of doing nothing to avert the problem, and the limited range of available solutions, defendants' conduct was not highly offensive for purposes of establishing a tortious intrusion into private matters. Our reasoning is as follows.

For legitimate business reasons, employers commonly link their net-work servers to the Internet, and provide employees with computers that have direct access to the network and the Internet. (*Delfino v. Agilent Technologies, Inc.* (2006) 145 Cal.App.4th 790, 805–806, 52 Cal.Rptr.3d

376 (*Delfino*) [noting trend over previous decade].) As this phenomenon has grown, employers have adopted formal policies regulating the scope of appropriate computer and Internet use. Such policies contemplate reasonable monitoring efforts by employers, and authorize employee discipline for noncompliance. (E.g., *Delfino, supra,* at p. 800, fn. 13, 52 Cal.Rptr.3d 376 [authorizing discharge for transmitting any threatening, sexually explicit, or harassing item on company computers]; *TBG Ins. Services Corp. v. Superior Court* (2002) 96 Cal.App.4th 443, 446, 117 Cal.Rptr.2d 155 (*TBG*) [similar policy as to derogatory, defamatory, or obscene material, coupled with notice that company would monitor employee computer use]; *id.* at p. 451, 117 Cal.Rptr.2d 155 [discussing American Management Association report stating that most large firms regulate and monitor employee Internet use]; cf. Chin et al., Cal. Practice Guide: Employment Litigation (The Rutter Group 2007) ¶ 5:782.5 et seq. [exploring limits on computer monitoring in workplace].)

Despite efforts to control the problem, the potential for abuse of computer systems and Internet access in the workplace is wide-ranging. (See, e.g., *Intel Corp. v. Hamidi* (2003) 30 Cal.4th 1342, 1347, 1 Cal. Rptr.3d 32, 71 P.3d 296 [holding that employee did not commit tort of trespass to chattels by sending mass emails on employer's electronic system, but otherwise declining to exempt Internet messages from general rules of tort liability]; *TBG, supra,* 96 Cal.App.4th 443, 446–447, 117 Cal.Rptr.2d 155 [employee terminated after repeatedly accessing pornographic Web sites on computer at work].) The consequences to employers may be serious. (E.g., *Delfino, supra,* 145 Cal.App.4th 790, 795–796, 800, 52 Cal.Rptr.3d 376 [third parties sued employer on various counts after receiving vile threats that employee sent over Internet from work computer]; *Monge v. Superior Court* (1986) 176 Cal.App.3d 503, 506–507, 509, 222 Cal.Rptr. 64 [employee stated claims for discrimination, harassment, and punitive damages against employer who failed to investigate her complaints about receiving sexually offensive message from supervisors on her work computer].)

Here, Hitchcock learned that the computer in plaintiffs' office was being used to access the Internet late at night, long after their shifts ended, by someone not authorized to use that equipment or office. Data recorded and stored inside the computer system itself convinced Hitchcock and the computer specialist, Foster, that the unauthorized user was viewing sexually explicit Web sites. Given the hour at which this unauthorized Internet activity occurred, Hitchcock strongly suspected that the responsible party was a program director or other staff person with keys and access to the administration building, which was otherwise locked at that hour.

Such use of Hillsides' computer equipment by an employee violated written workplace policies circulated both before and after the challenged surveillance activities occurred. As those policies warned, and case law confirms, the offending conduct posed a risk that the perpetrator might expose Hillsides to legal liability from various quarters. At the very least, parties on both sides confirmed that accessing pornography on company computers was inconsistent with Hillsides' goal to provide a wholesome environment for the abused children in its care, and to avoid any exposure that might aggravate their vulnerable state.

We also note that Hitchcock's repeated assurances that he installed the surveillance equipment solely to serve the foregoing purposes and not to invade plaintiffs' privacy are corroborated by his actions afterwards. When confronted by plaintiffs about the camera in their office, he explained its presence, and tried to assuage their concerns about being suspected of wrongdoing and secretly videotaped. To this end, he showed them the actual surveillance tape on demand and without delay. Against this backdrop, a reasonable jury could find it difficult to conclude that defendants' conduct was utterly unjustified and highly offensive.

Plaintiffs argue that even assuming defendants acted to prevent a rogue employee from accessing pornography on Hillsides' computers, and to minimize a genuine risk of liability and harm, no claim or defense of justification has been established as a matter of law. Plaintiffs insist triable issues exist as to whether defendants could have employed means less offensive than installing the camera in their office and connecting it to the monitor and recorder nearby. Examples include better enforcement of Hillsides' log-off/password-protection policy, installation of software filtering programs, closer nighttime monitoring of the camera outside the administration building, increased security patrols at night, and receipt of plaintiffs' informed consent to video surveillance.

Contrary to what plaintiffs imply, it appears defendants are not required to prove that there were no less intrusive means of accomplishing the legitimate objectives we have identified above in order to defeat the instant privacy claim. In the past, we have specifically declined to "impos[e] on a private organization, acting in a situation involving decreased expectations of privacy, the burden of justifying its conduct as the 'least offensive alternative' possible under the circumstances." (*Hill, supra,* 7 Cal.4th 1, 50, 26 Cal.Rptr.2d 834, 865 P.2d 633 [invoking language and history of state constitutional privacy provision and relevant case authority] ...

The argument lacks merit in any event. First, the alternatives that plaintiffs propose would not necessarily have achieved at least one of defendants' aims-determining whether a program director was accessing pornographic Web sites in plaintiffs' office. Rather, it is the same suspect group of program directors on whom plaintiffs would have had defendants more heavily rely to monitor exterior cameras and perform office patrols. Obtaining plaintiffs' consent also might have risked disclosing the surveillance plan to other employees, including the program directors. With respect to stricter regulation of employee computer use (software filters and log-off enforcement), such steps might have stopped the improper use of Lopez's computer. However, they would not have helped defendants identify the employee who performed such activity and who posed a risk of liability and harm in the workplace. (See *Hill, supra,* 7 Cal.4th 1, 50, 26 Cal.Rptr.2d 834, 865 P.2d 633 [rejecting proposed alternatives as "different in kind and character" than challenged acts].)

Second, for reasons suggested above, this is not a case in which "sensitive information [was] gathered and feasible safeguards [were] slipshod or nonexistent." ... Rather, privacy concerns are alleviated because the intrusion was "limited" and no information about plaintiffs was accessed, gathered, or disclosed. As we have seen, defendants did not suspect plaintiffs of using their computers improperly, and sought to ensure that they were not present when any monitoring or recording in their office occurred. The video equipment was rarely activated and then only at night, when plaintiffs were gone. There was no covert surveillance of them behind closed doors.

## CONCLUSION

We appreciate plaintiffs' dismay over the discovery of video equipment—small, blinking, and hot to the touch—that their employer had hidden among their personal effects in an office that was reasonably secluded from public access and view. Nothing we say here is meant to encourage such surveillance measures, particularly in the absence of adequate notice to persons within camera range that their actions may be viewed and taped.

Nevertheless, considering all the relevant circumstances, plaintiffs have not established, and cannot reasonably expect to establish, that the particular conduct of defendants that is challenged in this case was highly offensive and constituted an egregious violation of prevailing social norms. We reach this conclusion from the standpoint of a reasonable person based on defendants' vigorous efforts to avoid intruding on plaintiffs' visual privacy altogether. Activation of the surveillance system was narrowly tailored in place, time, and scope, and was prompted by legitimate business concerns. Plaintiffs were not at risk of being monitored or recorded during regular work hours and were never actually caught on camera or videotape. * * *

### NOTES AND QUESTIONS

1.  The American Management Association's 2007 Electronic Monitoring & Surveillance Survey indicates that almost 48% of the companies surveyed use video monitoring to counter theft, violence, or sabotage. This compares to 51% in 2005, but only 33% in 2001. Seven percent of employers videotape selected categories of employees in their job performance; in 2006, 6% videotaped all employees. In 2007, 78% of employers notified employees of antitheft video surveillance, and 89% of employers notified employees of job performance video monitoring. Video workplace monitoring has been used by employers to prove misconduct and has been relied upon to deny unemployment compensation benefits.

2.  In *Brazinski v. Amoco Petroleum Additives Co.,* 6 F.3d 1176 (7th Cir. 1993), the company had received information that a male supervisor and a

female worker, both assigned to the night shift, had been seen while on duty going into a locker room reserved for female employees. The company installed a video camera in the locker room, the lens, however, pointing toward the entry door, in an effort to document their dereliction from duty, which it did. Subsequently, several female workers and one female employed by a contractor sued for invasion of privacy, but only the latter was held to present a then-justiciable claim. However, the Court of Appeals for the Seventh Circuit sustained the dismissal of her claim. The court assumed *arguendo* that a person not herself the target, caught in an "unavoidably indiscriminate effort at surveillance" might have a cause of action, but the court held that for her privacy to have been invaded the employee must prove that she actually had been observed in a state of undress, whether on the monitor or on videotape, which allegation had not been made. The *Hillsides* court proceeds along a rather different analytical track, does it not? Which is more persuasive?

3. The *Hillsides* court asks whether the employee could be observed by others *when the tort occurred*; but other courts have had a different take on the question. *I.e.*, if the surreptitious video surveillance occurs in a work area that could have been observed by a co-worker or visitor, even though it was not and even though the employee was at pains to avoid being observed, the employee had no reasonable expectation of privacy. *See Nelson v. Salem State Coll.*, 446 Mass. 525, 845 N.E.2d 338 (2006) (under the fourth amendment). Which is more persuasive?

4. Questions 2 and 3 deal with the first prong of the analysis: whether a reasonable expectation of privacy was invaded. The second prong is whether the invasion was wrongful. The California Supreme Court adopts the Restatement of Torts' formulation—that to be wrongful the intrusion must be "highly offensive to a reasonable person." The drafter of the Restatement explained:

> It appears obvious that the interest protected by this branch of the tort is primarily a mental one. It has been useful chiefly to fill in the gaps left by trespass, nuisance, the intentional infliction of mental distress, and whatever remedies there may be for the invasion of constitutional rights.

William Prosser, *Privacy*, 48 CAL. L. REV. 383, 392 (1960). Return to *Springer v. Wal–Mart Stores, Inc.*, discussed in Chapter III. What "gap" in the tort of infliction of emotional distress does the tort of wrongful invasion of privacy fill? Would what *Hillsides* did be actionable under *Springer*?

5. Although the *Hillsides* court speaks in terms of "offensiveness", doesn't the court balance the nature of the intrusion against the business interest the employer was pursuing, its motives, and means? If so, has "offensiveness" been stripped of its "mental distress" content? Or does it mean that so long as business acts out of a legitimate motive and strives to minimize the impact on employee privacy, the employer's action is incapable of being "offensive" as measured by community standards? This case was decided on a motion for summary judgment Should a judge or a jury decide this question?

6.   Video surveillance of employee protected concerted activity under the National Labor Relations Act is subject to prohibition under the Act. *E.g.*, National Steel & Shipbuilding Co., 324 N.L.R.B. 499 (1997).

7.   A number of countries stringently regulate whether or not employers may videotape employees and, if permitted, under what circumstances and conditions. Remote surveillance is generally unlawful in Italy. In Germany, all aspect of video surveillance of employees must be agreed to with the employees' works council. (In a unionized enterprise in the United States, video surveillance is a mandatory subject of collective bargaining, but unlike Germany the agreement is not required for the employer to implement its demands.) The state of New South Wales (Australia) has enacted a comprehensive Workplace Surveillance Act (2005) that requires that any video monitoring of work areas be done openly and with notice to employees. Covert surveillance can be undertaken only with the approval of the "covert surveillance authority," a public officer akin to a magistrate, under conditions subject to public supervision. In other words, the employee interests to be protected in an unjustified covert video surveillance do not differ whether the surveillance is done by the police or by one's employer. Is prior official approval is a more effective (and less costly) means of regulation than tort litigation. Does New South Wales's approach commend itself for borrowing here?

## Note on Workplace Surveillance of the Spoken Word

Federal law prohibits intercepting of an "oral communication" not consented to by one of the parties. An "oral communication" is

> uttered by a person exhibiting an expectation that such communication is not subject to interception under circumstances justifying such expectation, but such term does not include any electronic communication...."

18 U.S.C. § 2510(2) (1998). Some cognate state laws require the consent of all parties to the conversation.

### QUESTIONS

1.   For the interception—commonly by a hidden tape recorder—to be actionable, must the person have a reasonable expectation of privacy in the place where the communication takes place, or only a reasonable expectation in non-interception? *E.g.*, may an employer secrete a microphone at a sales counter to monitor coworker and customer-worker conversations, that is, in a location where those conversations can easily be heard by those standing close by? *Compare Walker v. Darby*, 911 F.2d 1573 (11th Cir. 1990) *with State v. Duchow*, 310 Wis.2d 1, 749 N.W.2d 913 (2008).

2.   Because recorded conversations between workers and supervisors or managers may be the best evidence of unlawful activity, would an employee's discharge for surreptitiously recording her conversations be tortious, as violative of public policy? *Cf. NLRB v. Rockline Indus., Inc.*, 412 F.3d 962 (8th Cir.

2005); *Mena v. Key Food Stores Co–Op, Inc. et al.*, 195 Misc.2d 402, 758 N.Y.S.2d 246 (2003).

# B. ELECTRONIC MONITORING

The *Hillsides* court discussed the employer's policies on computer use; prohibiting the accessing of sexually explicit material and assigning passwords to employees. The policy

> warned employees that they had "no reasonable expectation of privacy in any . . . use of Company computers, network and system." Along the same lines, the policy advised that all data created, transmitted, downloaded, or stored on the system was Hillsides' property, and that the company could "monitor and record employee activity on its computers, network . . . and e-mail system," including "e-mail messages[,] . . . files stored or transmitted[,] and . . . web sites accessed."

*Hillside Privacy Policy*

211 P.3d at 280. Such policies are common, as we will see.

## 1. INTERCEPTION *OR* RETRIEVAL

The ability of an employer to monitor computer use is regulated by federal as well as cognate state statutory systems. Until 1968, the primary federal statute governing electronic interception was the Communications Act of 1934. In that year, Congress passed the Electronic Communications Privacy Act (ECPA) as part of the Omnibus Crime Control and Safe Streets Act, which has since been substantially amended. 18 U.S.C §§ 2510–21 (2006). Two portions of the now-amended ECPA—one termed the Wiretap Act, the other the Stored Communications Act—are of paramount importance, but they are also a skein of statutory opacity. The Wiretap Act prohibits the "interception" of any "electronic communication." This seemingly simple prohibition implicates the interplay of several complex definitional elements. An "electronic communication" is defined as "any transfer of signs, signals . . . data, or intelligence of any nature" by electronic means. Thus, the tracking in real time of the addressees of an employee's e-mail or his or her Internet connections would be an electronic communication. However, interception is defined as the "acquisition of the *contents*" of an electronic communication, and "contents" are defined to include "any information concerning the substance, purport or meaning of that communication." Consequently, although it is doubtful that tracking addressees alone would be a statutory "interception," devices or programs that screen the contents of communications for key words would seem much closer to securing "information concerning the substance" or "purport" of those communications. Even so, an interception of an employee's electronic communication by an employer is permitted if it meets one of two conditions: (1) when consented to, and (2) when made in the ordinary course of the employer's business.

A recurring issue concerns the distinction between "interception" of an electronic message, including one destined for storage, and "retrieval" of one already in storage. An employer may do the former under the Wiretap Act only with the consent of the employee or if in the ordinary course of its business. An employer is unfettered by the law in retrieving communications stored in its *own* system. In *Fraser v. Nationwide Mutual Insurance Co.*, 135 F.Supp.2d 623 (E.D. Pa. 2001), the company retrieved an e-mail message from its electronic file server and, finding an incriminating letter from one of the company's sales agents to a competitor, discharged him. He sued for violation of the ECPA, and the federal district court was called upon to decide whether the retrieval worked an "interception." The court held that it did not: an interception requires that the information be acquired contemporaneously with "the transmission *or transfer* of information from the sender to the recipient." Inasmuch as the Stored Communications Act permitted the company to access its own e-mail files, that Act was not violated; nor was the Wiretap Act for want of a statutory "interception."

## NOTES AND QUESTIONS

1.  Data for employer monitoring practice over time has been assembled by surveys concluded by the American Management Association:

### Employer Monitoring Practices, 2001–2007

|                                                    | 2001  | 2005 | 2007 |
| -------------------------------------------------- | ----- | ---- | ---- |
| Recording & review of telephone conversations      | 11.9% | 19%  | 16%  |
| Storage & review of voice mail messages            | 7.8%  | 15%  | 9%   |
| Storage & review of computer files                 | 36.1% | 50%  | 43%  |
| Storage & review of e-mail messages                | 46.5% | 55%  | N/A  |
| Monitoring Internet connections                    | 62.8% | 76%  | 66%  |
| Telephone use (time spent, numbers called)          | 43.3% | 51%  | 45%  |
| Computer use (time logged on, keystroke counts, etc.) | 18.9% | 36%  | 45%  |

2.  A majority of employers notify employees of their monitoring policies; but some do not. Federal law does not require notice, but notice, if sufficiently conspicuous, is evidence of consent, which is a defense to a claim of wrongful interception. Two states have legislated to require notice of electronic monitoring. *See* CONN. GEN. STAT. § 1–48 (1965); DEL. CODE tit. 19 § 705 (2002). In Connecticut, displaying a poster will satisfy the requirement. In Delaware, a "pop up" notice on the user's computer screen once a day will satisfy the requirement. Is notice alone equivalent to "consent"?

3.  Assume an employer has installed a "key logger" a "network analoger" on the employees' computers without any specific notice to employees

other than the *Hillsides* policy set out at the beginning of this Chapter. Key logging records every keystroke; it enables the detection of all addressees and the reading of the contents of all e-mail messages transmitted from the key logged computer. Does the key logging system constitute an "interception"? *Compare United States v. Ropp*, 347 F.Supp.2d 831 (C.D. Cal. 2004) *with Brahmana v. Lembo, No. C–09–00106 RMW*, 2009 WL 1424438 (N.D. Cal. 2009).

## 2.   SEARCH

### STENGART v. LOVING CARE AGENCY, INC.

Supreme Court of New Jersey, 2010
201 N.J. 300, 990 A.2d 650

CHIEF JUSTICE RABNER delivered of the opinion of the Court.

In the past twenty years, businesses and private citizens alike have embraced the use of computers, electronic communication devices, the Internet, and e-mail. As those and other forms of technology evolve, the line separating business from personal activities can easily blur.

In the modern workplace, for example, occasional, personal use of the Internet is commonplace. Yet that simple act can raise complex issues about an employer's monitoring of the workplace and an employee's reasonable expectation of privacy.

This case presents novel questions about the extent to which an employee can expect privacy and confidentiality in personal e-mails with her attorney, which she accessed on a computer belonging to her employer. Marina Stengart used her company-issued laptop to exchange e-mails with her lawyer through her personal, password-protected, web-based e-mail account. She later filed an employment discrimination lawsuit against her employer, Loving Care Agency, Inc. (Loving Care), and others.

In anticipation of discovery, Loving Care hired a computer forensic expert to recover all files stored on the laptop including the e-mails, which had been automatically saved on the hard drive. Loving Care's attorneys reviewed the e-mails and used information culled from them in the course of discovery. In response, Stengart's lawyer demanded that communications between him and Stengart, which he considered privileged, be identified and returned. Opposing counsel disclosed the documents but maintained that the company had the right to review them. Stengart then sought relief in court.

The trial court ruled that, in light of the company's written policy on electronic communications, Stengart waived the attorney-client privilege by sending e-mails on a company computer. The Appellate Division reversed and found that Loving Care's counsel had violated *RPC* 4.4(b) by reading and using the privileged documents.

We hold that, under the circumstances, Stengart could reasonably expect that e-mail communications with her lawyer through her personal account would remain private, and that sending and receiving them via a company laptop did not eliminate the attorney-client privilege that protected them. By reading e-mails that were at least arguably privileged and failing to notify Stengart promptly about them, Loving Care's counsel breached *RPC* 4.4(b). We therefore modify and affirm the judgment of the Appellate Division and remand to the trial court to determine what, if any, sanctions should be imposed on counsel for Loving Care.

I.

This appeal arises out of a lawsuit that plaintiff-respondent Marina Stengart filed against her former employer, defendant-appellant Loving Care, its owner, and certain board members and officers of the company. She alleges, among other things, constructive discharge because of a hostile work environment, retaliation, and harassment based on gender, religion, and national origin, in violation of the New Jersey Law Against Discrimination, *N.J.S.A.* 10:5–1 to –49. Loving Care denies the allegations and suggests they are an attempt to escape certain restrictive covenants that are the subject of a separate lawsuit.

Loving Care provides home-care nursing and health services. Stengart began working for Loving Care in 1994 and, over time, was promoted to Executive Director of Nursing. The company provided her with a laptop computer to conduct company business. From that laptop, Stengart could send e-mails using her company e-mail address; she could also access the Internet and visit websites through Loving Care's server. Unbeknownst to Stengart, certain browser software in place automatically made a copy of each web page she viewed, which was then saved on the computer's hard drive in a "cache" folder of temporary Internet files. Unless deleted and overwritten with new data, those temporary Internet files remained on the hard drive.

On several days in December 2007, Stengart used her laptop to access a personal, password-protected e-mail account on Yahoo's website, through which she communicated with her attorney about her situation at work. She never saved her Yahoo ID or password on the company laptop.

Not long after, Stengart left her employment with Loving Care and returned the laptop. On February 7, 2008, she filed the pending complaint.

In an effort to preserve electronic evidence for discovery, in or around April 2008, Loving Care hired experts to create a forensic image of the laptop's hard drive. Among the items retrieved were temporary Internet files containing the contents of seven or eight e-mails Stengart had exchanged with her lawyer via her Yahoo account. * * *

At least two attorneys from the law firm representing Loving Care ... reviewed the e-mail communications between Stengart and her attorney. The Firm did not advise opposing counsel about the e-mails until months later. In its October 21, 2008 reply to Stengart's first set of interrogatories, the Firm stated that it had obtained certain information from "e-mail correspondence" between Stengart and her lawyer from

Stengart's "office computer on December 12, 2007 at 2:25 p.m." In response, Stengart's attorney sent a letter demanding that the Firm identify and return all "attorney-client privileged communications" in its possession. The Firm identified and disclosed the e-mails but asserted that Stengart had no reasonable expectation of privacy in files on a company-owned computer in light of the company's policy on electronic communications.

Loving Care and its counsel relied on an Administrative and Office Staff Employee Handbook that they maintain contains the company's Electronic Communication policy (Policy). The record contains various versions of an electronic communications policy, and Stengart contends that none applied to her as a senior company official. Loving Care disagrees. We need not resolve that dispute and assume the Policy applies in addressing the issues on appeal.

The proffered Policy states, in relevant part:

> The company reserves and will exercise the right to review, audit, intercept, access, and disclose all matters on the company's media systems and services at any time, with or without notice. * * *

> E-mail and voice mail messages, internet use and communication and computer files are considered part of the company's business and client records. Such communications are not to be considered private or personal to any individual employee.

> The principal purpose of electronic mail (*e-mail*) is for company business communications. Occasional personal use is permitted; however, the system should not be used to solicit for outside business ventures, charitable organizations, or for any political or religious purpose, unless authorized by the Director of Human Resources.

The Policy also specifically prohibits "[c]ertain uses of the e-mail system" including sending inappropriate sexual, discriminatory, or harassing messages, chain letters, "[m]essages in violation of government laws," or messages relating to job searches, business activities unrelated to Loving Care, or political activities. The Policy concludes with the following warning: "Abuse of the electronic communications system may result in disciplinary action up to and including separation of employment."

Stengart's attorney applied for an order to show cause seeking return of the e-mails and other relief. The trial court converted the application to a motion, which it later denied in a written opinion. The trial court concluded that the Firm did not breach the attorney-client privilege because the company's Policy placed Stengart on sufficient notice that her e-mails would be considered company property. Stengart's request to disqualify the Firm was therefore denied.

The Appellate Division granted Stengart's motion for leave to appeal. The panel reversed the trial court order and directed the Firm to turn over all copies of the e-mails and delete any record of them. *Stengart v. Loving Care Agency, Inc.*, 408 *N.J.Super.* 54, 973 *A.2d* 390 (App.Div.2009).

Assuming that the Policy applied to Stengart, the panel found that "[a]n objective reader could reasonably conclude . . . that not all personal emails are necessarily company property." *Id.* at 64, 973 A.2d 390. In other words, an employee could "retain an expectation of privacy" in personal e-mails sent on a company computer given the language of the Policy. *Id.* at 65, 973 A.2d 390.

The panel balanced Loving Care's right to enforce reasonable rules for the workplace against the public policies underlying the attorney-client privilege. *Id.* at 66, 973 A.2d 390. The court rejected the notion that "ownership of the computer [is] the sole determinative fact" at issue and instead explained that there must be a nexus between company policies and the employer's legitimate business interests. *Id.* at 68–69, 973 A.2d 390. The panel concluded that society's important interest in shielding communications with an attorney from disclosure outweighed the company's interest in upholding the Policy. *Id.* at 74–75, 973 A.2d 390. As a result, the panel found that the e-mails were protected by the attorney-client privilege and should be returned. *Id.* at 75, 973 A.2d 390. * * *

## II.

Loving Care argues that its employees have no expectation of privacy in their use of company computers based on the company's Policy. In its briefs before this Court, the company also asserts that by accessing e-mails on a personal account through Loving Care's computer and server, Stengart either prevented any attorney-client privilege from attaching or waived the privilege by voluntarily subjecting her e-mails to company scrutiny. . . .

Stengart argues that she intended the e-mails with her lawyer to be confidential and that the Policy, even if it applied to her, failed to provide adequate warning that Loving Care would save on a hard drive, or monitor the contents of, e-mails sent from a personal account. Stengart also maintains that the communications with her lawyer were privileged. When the Firm encountered the arguably protected e-mails, Stengart contends it should have immediately returned them or sought judicial review as to whether the attorney-client privilege applied. * * *

## III.

Our analysis draws on two principal areas: the adequacy of the notice provided by the Policy and the important public policy concerns raised by the attorney-client privilege. Both inform the reasonableness of an employee's expectation of privacy in this matter. We address each area in turn.

## A.

We start by examining the meaning and scope of the Policy itself. The Policy specifically reserves to Loving Care the right to review and access "all matters on the company's media systems and services at any time."

In addition, e-mail messages are plainly "considered part of the company's business . . . records."

It is not clear from that language whether the use of personal, password-protected, web-based e-mail accounts via company equipment is covered. The Policy uses general language to refer to its "media systems and services" but does not define those terms. Elsewhere, the Policy prohibits certain uses of "the e-mail system," which appears to be a reference to company e-mail accounts. The Policy does not address personal accounts at all. In other words, employees do not have express notice that messages sent or received on a personal, web-based e-mail account are subject to monitoring if company equipment is used to access the account.

The Policy also does not warn employees that the contents of such e-mails are stored on a hard drive and can be forensically retrieved and read by Loving Care.

The Policy goes on to declare that e-mails "are not to be considered private or personal to any individual employee." In the very next point, the Policy acknowledges that "[o]ccasional personal use [of e-mail] is permitted." As written, the Policy creates ambiguity about whether personal e-mail use is company or private property.

The scope of the written Policy, therefore, is not entirely clear.

### B.

[The Court addressed the policies underlying the attorney-client privilege.]

The e-mail communications between Stengart and her lawyers contain a standard warning that their contents are personal and confidential and may constitute attorney-client communications. The subject matter of those messages appears to relate to Stengart's working conditions and anticipated lawsuit against Loving Care.

### IV.

Under the particular circumstances presented, how should a court evaluate whether Stengart had a reasonable expectation of privacy in the e-mails she exchanged with her attorney?

### A.

Preliminarily, we note that the reasonable-expectation-of-privacy standard used by the parties derives from the common law and the Search and Seizure Clauses of both the Fourth Amendment and Article I, paragraph 7 of the New Jersey Constitution. The latter sources do not apply in this case, which involves conduct by private parties only.[2]

The common law source is the tort of "intrusion on seclusion," which can be found in the *Restatement (Second) of Torts* § 652B (1977). That

---

**2.** In addition, a right to privacy can be found in Article I, paragraph 1 of the New Jersey Constitution. *Hennessey v. Coastal Eagle Point Oil Co.,* 129 *N.J.* 81, 95–96, 609 A.2d 11 (1992).

section provides that "[o]ne who intentionally intrudes, physically or otherwise, upon the solitude or seclusion of another or his private affairs or concerns, is subject to liability to the other for invasion of his privacy, if the intrusion would be highly offensive to a reasonable person." *Restatement, supra,* § 652B. A high threshold must be cleared to assert a cause of action based on that tort. *Hennessey, supra,* 129 *N.J.* at 116, 609 *A.*2d 11 (Pollock, J., concurring). A plaintiff must establish that the intrusion "would be highly offensive to the ordinary reasonable man, as the result of conduct to which the reasonable man would strongly object." *Restatement, supra,* § 652B cmt. d.

As is true in Fourth Amendment cases, the reasonableness of a claim for intrusion on seclusion has both a subjective and objective component. *See State v. Sloane,* 193 *N.J.* 423, 434, 939 *A.*2d 796 (2008) (analyzing Fourth Amendment); *In re Asia Global Crossing, Ltd.,* 322 *B.R.* 247, 257 (Bankr.S.D.N.Y.2005) (analyzing common law tort). Moreover, whether an employee has a reasonable expectation of privacy in her particular work setting "must be addressed on a case-by-case basis." *O'Connor v. Ortega,* 480 *U.S.* 709, 718, 107 *S.Ct.* 1492, 1498, 94 *L.Ed.*2d 714, 723 (1987) (plurality opinion) (reviewing public sector employment).

### B.

A number of courts have tested an employee's claim of privacy in files stored on company computers by evaluating the reasonableness of the employee's expectation. No reported decisions in New Jersey offer direct guidance for the facts of this case. In one matter, *State v. M.A.,* 402 *N.J.Super.* 353, 954 *A.*2d 503 (App.Div.2008), the Appellate Division found that the defendant had no reasonable expectation of privacy in personal information he stored on a workplace computer under a separate password. *Id.* at 369, 954 *A.*2d 503. The defendant had been advised that all computers were company property. *Id.* at 359, 954 *A.*2d 503. His former employer consented to a search by the State Police, who, in turn, retrieved information tied to the theft of company funds. *Id.* at 361–62, 954 *A.*2d 503. The court reviewed the search in the context of the Fourth Amendment and found no basis for the defendant's privacy claim in the contents of a company computer that he used to commit a crime. *Id.* at 365–69, 954 *A.*2d 503.

*Doe v. XYC Corp.,* 382 *N.J.Super.* 122, 887 *A.*2d 1156 (App.Div.2005), likewise did not involve attorney-client e-mails. In *XYC Corp.,* the Appellate Division found no legitimate expectation of privacy in an employee's use of a company computer to access websites containing adult and child pornography. *Id.* at 139, 887 *A.*2d 1156. In its analysis, the court referenced a policy authorizing the company to monitor employee website activity and e-mails, which were deemed company property. *Id.* at 131, 138–39, 887 *A.*2d 1156.

Certain decisions from outside New Jersey, which the parties also rely on, are more instructive. Among them, *National Economic Research Associates v. Evans,* 21 *Mass. L. Rptr.* No. 15, at 337, 2006 WL 2440008

(Mass.Super.Ct. Aug. 3, 2006), is most analogous to the facts here. In *Evans,* an employee used a company laptop to send and receive attorney-client communications by e-mail. In doing so, he used his personal, password-protected Yahoo account and not the company's e-mail address. *Ibid.* The e-mails were automatically stored in a temporary Internet file on the computer's hard drive and were later retrieved by a computer forensic expert. *Ibid.* The expert recovered various attorney-client e-mails; at the instruction of the company's lawyer, those e-mails were not reviewed pending guidance from the court. *Ibid.*

A company manual governed the laptop's use. The manual permitted personal use of e-mail, to "be kept to a minimum," but warned that computer resources were the "property of the Company" and that e-mails were "not confidential" and could be read "during routine checks." *Id.* at 338.

The court denied the company's application to allow disclosure of the e-mails that its expert possessed. *Id.* at 337. The court reasoned,

> Based on the warnings furnished in the Manual, Evans [(the employee)] could not reasonably expect to communicate in confidence with his private attorney if Evans e-mailed his attorney using his NERA [(company)] e-mail address through the NERA Intranet, because the Manual plainly warned Evans that e-mails on the network could be read by NERA network administrators. The Manual, however, did not expressly declare that it would monitor the *content* of Internet communications. . . . Most importantly, the Manual did not expressly declare, or even implicitly suggest, that NERA would monitor the content of e-mail communications made from an employee's personal e-mail account via the Internet whenever those communications were viewed on a NERA-issued computer. Nor did NERA warn its employees that the content of such Internet e-mail communications is stored on the hard disk of a NERA-issued computer and therefore capable of being read by NERA.

[*Id.* at 338–39.]

As a result, the court found the employee's expectation of privacy in e-mails with his attorney to be reasonable. *Id.* at 339.

In *Asia Global, supra,* the Bankruptcy Court for the Southern District of New York considered whether a bankruptcy trustee could force the production of e-mails sent by company employees to their personal attorneys on the *company's* e-mail system. 322 *B.R.* at 251–52. The court developed a four-part test to "measure the employee's expectation of privacy in his computer files and e-mail":

> (1) does the corporation maintain a policy banning personal or other objectionable use, (2) does the company monitor the use of the employee's computer or e-mail, (3) do third parties have a right of access to the computer or e-mails, and (4) did the corporation notify

the employee, or was the employee aware, of the use and monitoring policies?

[*Id.* at 257.]

Because the evidence was "equivocal" about the existence of a corporate policy banning personal use of e-mail and allowing monitoring, the court could not conclude that the employees' use of the company e-mail system eliminated any applicable attorney-client privilege. *Id.* at 259–61.

Both *Evans* and *Asia Global* referenced a formal ethics opinion by the American Bar Association that noted "lawyers have a reasonable expectation of privacy when communicating by e-mail maintained by an [online service provider]." *See id.* at 256 (citing ABA Comm. on Ethics and Prof'l Responsibility, Formal Op. 413 (1999)); *Evans, supra,* 21 *Mass. L. Rptr.* No. 15, at 339 (same).

Other courts have measured the factors outlined in *Asia Global* among other considerations. In reviewing those cases, we are mindful of the fact-specific nature of the inquiry involved and the multitude of different facts that can affect the outcome in a given case. No one factor alone is necessarily dispositive.

According to some courts, employees appear to have a lesser expectation of privacy when they communicate with an attorney using a company e-mail system as compared to a personal, web-based account like the one used here. *See, e.g., Smyth v. Pillsbury Co.,* 914 *F.Supp.* 97, 100–01 (E.D.Pa.1996) (finding no reasonable expectation of privacy in unprofessional e-mails sent to supervisor through internal corporate e-mail system); *Scott v. Beth Israel Med. Ctr., Inc.,* 17 *Misc.*3d 934, 847 *N.Y.S.*2d 436, 441–43 (N.Y.Sup.Ct.2007) (finding no expectation of confidentiality when company e-mail used to send attorney-client messages). *But see Convertino v. U.S. Dep't of Justice,* 674 *F.Supp.*2d 97, 110 (D.D.C.2009) (finding reasonable expectation of privacy in attorney-client e-mails sent via employer's e-mail system). As a result, courts might treat e-mails transmitted via an employer's e-mail account differently than they would web-based e-mails sent on the same company computer.

Courts have also found that the existence of a clear company policy banning personal e-mails can also diminish the reasonableness of an employee's claim to privacy in e-mail messages with his or her attorney. *Compare Scott, supra,* 847 *N.Y.S.*2d at 441 (finding e-mails sent to attorney not privileged and noting that company's e-mail policy prohibiting personal use was "critical to the outcome"), *with Asia Global, supra,* 322 *B.R.* at 259–61 (declining to find e-mails to attorney were not privileged in light of unclear evidence as to existence of company policy banning personal e-mail use). We recognize that a zero-tolerance policy can be unworkable and unwelcome in today's dynamic and mobile workforce and do not seek to encourage that approach in any way.

The location of the company's computer may also be a relevant consideration. In *Curto v. Medical World Communications, Inc.,* 99 *Fair*

*Empl. Prac. Cas.* (BNA) 298, 2006 WL 1318387 (E.D.N.Y. May 15, 2006), for example, an employee working from a home office sent e-mails to her attorney on a company laptop via her personal AOL account. *Id.* at 301. Those messages did not go through the company's servers but were nonetheless retrievable. *Ibid.* Notwithstanding a company policy banning personal use, the trial court found that the e-mails were privileged. *Id.* at 305.

We realize that different concerns are implicated in cases that address the reasonableness of a privacy claim under the Fourth Amendment. *See, e.g., O'Connor, supra,* 480 *U.S.* at 714–19, 107 *S.Ct.* at 1496–98, 94 *L.Ed.*2d at 721–24 (discussing whether public hospital's search of employee workplace violated employee's expectation of privacy under Fourth Amendment); *United States v. Simons,* 206 *F.*3d 392, 397–98 (4th Cir. 2000) (involving search warrants for work computer of CIA employee, which revealed more than fifty pornographic images of minors); *M.A., supra,* 402 *N.J.Super.* at 366–69, 954 *A.*2d 503 (involving Fourth Amendment analysis of State Police search of employee's computer, resulting in theft charges). This case, however, involves no governmental action. Stengart's relationship with her private employer does not raise the specter of any government official unreasonably invading her rights.

## V.

### A.

Applying the above considerations to the facts before us, we find that Stengart had a reasonable expectation of privacy in the e-mails she exchanged with her attorney on Loving Care's laptop.

Stengart plainly took steps to protect the privacy of those e-mails and shield them from her employer. She used a personal, password-protected e-mail account instead of her company e-mail address and did not save the account's password on her computer. In other words, she had a subjective expectation of privacy in messages to and from her lawyer discussing the subject of a future lawsuit.

In light of the language of the Policy and the attorney-client nature of the communications, her expectation of privacy was also objectively reasonable. As noted earlier, the Policy does not address the use of personal, web-based e-mail accounts accessed through company equipment. It does not address personal accounts at all. Nor does it warn employees that the contents of e-mails sent via personal accounts can be forensically retrieved and read by the company. Indeed, in acknowledging that occasional personal use of e-mail is permitted, the Policy created doubt about whether those e-mails are company or private property.

Moreover, the e-mails are not illegal or inappropriate material stored on Loving Care's equipment, which might harm the company in some way. *See Muick v. Glenayre Elecs.,* 280 *F.*3d 741, 742–43 (7th Cir.2002); *Smyth, supra,* 914 *F.Supp.* at 98, 101; *XYC Corp., supra,* 382 *N.J.Super.* at 136–40, 887 *A.*2d 1156. They are conversations between a lawyer and

*Hy of C atty-clien*

client about confidential legal matters, which are historically cloaked in privacy. Our system strives to keep private the very type of conversations that took place here in order to foster probing and honest exchanges.

In addition, the e-mails bear a standard hallmark of attorney-client messages. They warn the reader directly that the e-mails are personal, confidential, and may be attorney-client communications. While a pro forma warning at the end of an e-mail might not, on its own, protect a communication, *see Scott, supra,* 847 *N.Y.S.*2d at 444, other facts present here raise additional privacy concerns.

Under all of the circumstances, we find that Stengart could reasonably expect that e-mails she exchanged with her attorney on her personal, password-protected, web-based e-mail account, accessed on a company laptop, would remain private.

It follows that the attorney-client privilege protects those e-mails. *See Asia Global, supra,* 322 *B.R.* at 258–59 (noting "close correlation between the objectively reasonable expectation of privacy and the objective reasonableness of the intent that a communication between a lawyer and a client was given in confidence"). In reaching that conclusion, we necessarily reject Loving Care's claim that the attorney-client privilege either did not attach or was waived. In its reply brief and at oral argument, Loving Care argued that the manner in which the e-mails were sent prevented the privilege from attaching. Specifically, Loving Care contends that Stengart effectively brought a third person into the conversation from the start— watching over her shoulder—and thereby forfeited any claim to confidentiality in her communications. We disagree.

Stengart has the right to prevent disclosures by third persons who learn of her communications "in a manner not reasonably to be anticipated." *See N.J.R.E.* 504(1)(c)(ii). That is what occurred here. The Policy did not give Stengart, or a reasonable person in her position, cause to anticipate that Loving Care would be peering over her shoulder as she opened e-mails from her lawyer on her personal, password-protected Yahoo account. *See Evans, supra,* 21 *Mass. L. Rptr.* No. 15, at 339. The language of the Policy, the method of transmittal that Stengart selected, and the warning on the e-mails themselves all support that conclusion.

Loving Care also argued in earlier submissions that Stengart waived the attorney-client privilege. For similar reasons, we again disagree. * * *

### B.

Our conclusion that Stengart had an expectation of privacy in e-mails with her lawyer does not mean that employers cannot monitor or regulate the use of workplace computers. Companies can adopt lawful policies relating to computer use to protect the assets, reputation, and productivity of a business and to ensure compliance with legitimate corporate policies. And employers can enforce such policies. They may discipline employees and, when appropriate, terminate them, for violating proper workplace rules that are not inconsistent with a clear mandate of public policy. *See*

Hennessey, supra, *129 N.J.* at *99–100, 609 A.2d 11;* Woolley v. Hoffmann–LaRoche, Inc., *99 N.J. 284, 290–92, 491 A.2d 1257 (1985);* Pierce v. Ortho Pharm. Corp., *84 N.J. 58, 72–73, 417 A.2d 505 (1980). For example, an employee who spends long stretches of the workday getting personal, confidential legal advice from a private lawyer may be disciplined for violating a policy permitting only occasional personal use of the Internet. But employers have no need or basis to read the specific* contents *of personal, privileged, attorney-client communications in order to enforce corporate policy. Because of the important public policy concerns underlying the attorney-client privilege, even a more clearly written company manual—that is, a policy that banned all personal computer use and provided unambiguous notice that an employer could retrieve and read an employee's attorney-client communications, if accessed on a personal, password-protected e-mail account using the company's computer system—would not be enforceable.* * * *

## NOTES AND QUESTIONS

1. The reach of the Fourth Amendment into the monitoring of computer messages was presented in *City of Ontario v. Quon,* 130 S.Ct. 2619, 177 L.Ed.2d 216 (June 17, 2010). The city had issued members of its SWAT team electronic pagers. The city had a written e-mail policy that "[t]he use of City-owned computers and all associated equipment, software, programs, networks, Internet, e-mail and other systems operating on these computers is limited to City of Ontario related business. The use of these tools for personal benefit is a significant violation of City of Ontario Policy." The Policy also provided:

> C. Access to all sites on the Internet is recorded and will periodically reviewed by the City. The City of Ontario reserves the right to monitor and log all network activity including e-mail and Internet use, with or without notice. Users should have no expectation of privacy or confidentiality when using these resources.

> D. Access to the Internet and the e-mail system is **not** confidential; and information produced either in hard copy or in electronic form is considered City property. As such, these systems should not be sued for personal or confidential communications. Deletion of e-mail or other electronic information may not fully delete the information from the system.

The officers were told that this policy applied to the pagers as well. But the department administered the policy by charging each officer for the excess of characters used; it did not review the content of the messages. The officer administering pager told used the officers that review was not necessary so long as they paid for overage. That officer tired of collecting bills and informed the chief of police who requested that the messages be reviewed. They were secured from the service provider (which provision resulted in a separate suit against the service provider) and those messages transmitted whilst on duty were read. That review revealed extensive personal use especially in sexual badinage between an officer and his girlfriend. The officer sued the City for violation of his Fourth Amendment rights.

The plurality opinion of the Court in *O'Connor v. Ortega*, 480 U.S. 709, 107 S.Ct. 1492, 94 L.Ed.2d 714 (1987), held that whether a public employee had a "reasonable expectation of privacy" in the contents of the desk or files in his office had to be determined on a case-by-case assessment of the "operational realities" of the workplace. Thus an issue before the *Quon* Court was of the continuing vitality of that test: assuming the written policies applied, were they enough to dispel any expectation of privacy per se or would the manner in which these policies were applied—actually, not applied—give rise to a reasonable expectation of privacy despite the City's disclaimer to that effect and reservation of power to monitor? The Court refused to reach the question.

> Rapid changes in the dynamics of communication and information transmission are evident not just in the technology itself but in what society accepts as proper behavior. . . .

> Even if the Court were certain that the *O'Connor* plurality's approach were the right one, the Court would have difficulty predicting how employees' privacy expectations will be shaped by those changes or the degree to which society will be prepared to recognize those expectations as reasonable. . . . Cell phone and the text message communications are so pervasive that some persons may consider them to be essential means or necessary instruments for self-expression, even self-expectation of privacy. On the other hand, the ubiquity of those devices has made them generally affordable, so one could counter that employees who need cell phones or similar devices for personal matters can purchase and pay for their own. And employer policies concerning communications will of course shape the reasonable expectations of their employees, especially to the extent that such policies are clearly communicated.

> A broad holding concerning employees' privacy expectations vis-à-vis employer-provided technological equipment might have implications for future cases that cannot be predicted. It is preferable to dispose of this case on narrower grounds. For present purposes we assume several propositions *arguendo*: First, Quon had a reasonable expectation of privacy in the text messages sent on the pager provided to him by the City; second, petitioners' review of the transcript constituted a search within the meaning of the Fourth Amendment; and third, the principles applicable to a government employer's search of an employee's physical office apply with at least the same force when the employer intrudes on the employee's privacy in the electronic sphere.

It held the search reasonable under the Fourth Amendment assuming there to have been a reasonable expectation of privacy in them.

2. The *Stengart* court observes that, "different concerns are implicated in cases that address the reasonableness of a privacy claim under the Fourth Amendment." What are they? Insofar as an employee may or may not have a reasonable expectation of privacy in the content of electronic messages transmitted via an employer's system, in what way or ways does a private sector employee differ from a public sector one?

3. Assume that after Ms. Stengart returned her laptop Loving Care examined her hard drive for: (1) messages to competitors; (2) connections to porn sites; (3) other messages not related to the company's business; and, finding such, downloaded and read them. Will Loving Care have committed the tort of wrongful invasion of privacy in any of these?

# 3. ELECTRONIC MONITORING OF LOCATION

The American Management Association's 2007 Electronic Monitoring and Surveillance Survey indicated:

> Employers who use Assisted Global Positioning or Global Positioning Systems satellite technology are in the minority, with only 8% using GPS to track company vehicles; 3% using GPS to monitor cell phones; and fewer than 1% using GPS to monitor employee ID/Smartcards. The majority (52%) of companies employ Smartcard technology to control physical security access to buildings and data centers.

AMERICAN MANAGEMENT ASSOCIATION & EPOLICY INSTITUTE, 2007 ELECTRONIC MONITORING & SURVEILLANCE SURVEY (2008), *available at* http://press. amanet.org/press-releases/177/2007-electronic-monitoring-surveillance-survey/.

A telephone survey of its membership conducted by the United American Nurses union indicated that 40% were electronically tracked in the workplace—17% by Radio Frequency Tracking Devices (RFID) and 11.5% by global positioning systems among other devices. BNA Daily Labor Report, No. 226, A–6 (Nov. 27, 2009). (Hospital management has responded to nurses' protests by claiming that hard data produced by tracking devices protected nurses accused by patients of failing to respond to their calls.) Some critics have noted that the use of radio frequency identification chips (RFID) can allow management to monitor which employees associate with one another at breaks; for example, to identify those who associate with known union supporters.

## QUESTIONS

1. All cell phones sold in the United States today must be GPS traceable; but the GPS transmitter can be turned off. May an employer give company phones to its employees, require them to have it in their possession at all (even non-work) times, and to keep the GPS system on?

2. RFID chips can be subcutaneously implanted assuring they'll not be forgotten or mislaid. Four states forbid employers to "require" the subcutaneous implantation of RFID chips. May an employer request employees to have that minimally invasive procedure done? *See* Marisa Anne Pagnattaro, *Getting Under Your Skin—Literally: RFID in the Employment Context*, 2008 U. ILL. J.L. TECH. & POL'Y 237 (2008). What is the difference between request and require in practical terms? Should it make a difference that some other privacy protective law forbid "requests" that trench on the subject.

### A Note on Biometric Controls

As the Office of the Information and Privacy Commissioner of Alberta observed, there are several ways of verifying a person's identity for the purpose of control of entrance to (and exit from) a facility; these are so-called "factors of authentication." *Viz.*

    a) Something they know (*e.g.*, a password)

    b) Something they have (*e.g.*, an identity card)

    c) Something they are (*e.g.*, biometric information)

SOUTHWOOD CARE CENTRE, INFORMATION AND PRIVACY COMMISSION OF ALBERTA INVESTIGATION REPORT F2008–IR–1001, 26 (2008).

Facial identification, iris identification, and voice or handprint technology is in its infancy and is as yet rarely used. According to the 2007 American Management Association Electronic Monitoring and Surveillance Survey, only 2% of the companies surveyed used fingerprint scans; 0.4% used facial recognition and iris scans. But the United American Nurses' Survey, discussed earlier, indicated that almost 13% of the nurses responding were scanned by biometric systems. Managerial interest derives primarily from the fact that, in contrast to "swipe card" (or older time clock) technology, having a coworker swipe in (or punch in) for another is not possible. Thus far, although the Illinois Biometric Information Privacy Act, 740 ILL. COMP. STAT. 14/1 *et seq.* (2009) regulates the collection of data by biometric means, there is no statutory limit on or common law dealing with the deployment of this technology in the United States. There is in Canada, obviously, and in Europe. Under data protection laws in, for example, France and Italy, approval of the public data protection authority must be secured before biomonitoring technology may be deployed. Should the deployment of this technology be of legal concern? What are the issues? What would possible approaches be?

## C.  INFORMATIONAL SELF–DETERMINATION

### BODAH v. LAKEVILLE MOTOR EXPRESS, INC.

Supreme Court of Minnesota, 2003
663 N.W.2d 550

ANDERSON, RUSSELL A., JUSTICE.

[W]e consider an issue of first impression: whether allegations in the complaint that appellant Lakeville Motor Express, Inc.'s (LME) dissemination by facsimile of 204 employee names and social security numbers to 16 related or associated terminal managers in six states and "[t]hat upon information and belief the private information has not been redacted or erased and is still being shared or is accessible in general" constitute the requisite "publicity" under Minnesota law to support a claim for publication of private facts, an invasion of privacy tort. We adopt the definition of "publicity" from the Restatement (Second) of Torts § 652D cmt. a (1977).

Further, we hold that the complaint does not allege the requisite "publicity" to support a claim for publication of private facts. We reverse.

The facts recited in the pleadings may be summarized as follows. LME, a trucking company based in Minnesota, transports shipments throughout the upper Midwest, including Minnesota, Illinois, Iowa, North Dakota, South Dakota, and Wisconsin. In distributing freight, LME utilizes trucking terminals that are either owned by LME or its agents or are owned by independent trucking companies.

On January 4, 2001, LME Safety Director William Lowell Frame (Frame) sent a facsimile transmission to the terminal managers of 16 freight terminals. The cover sheet was addressed to "Terminal Managers," not to named individuals, and stated that the purpose of the fax was to allow LME to "keep computer records for terminal accidents-injuries etc." The cover sheet requested that the terminal managers "[p]lease review [the] list for your terminals[;] add or delete accordingly." Attached to the cover sheet was a five-page list of the names and social security numbers of 204 LME employees.

Shortly after LME disseminated the list, head Union Steward John Tonsager confronted Frame and LME President Peter Martin (Martin) about the dissemination of sensitive employee information and expressed his concern about identity theft. On May 1, 2001, Martin sent a letter to LME employees notifying them of the January 4 transmission. In the letter, Martin apologized for LME's mistake in sending the list to the other terminals and reported that the terminal managers were instructed to destroy or return the list immediately. Martin indicated that his instructions had been followed and that, as far as he knew, the terminal managers had not shared the information with anyone.

On or about September 6, 2001, respondents filed a class action lawsuit on behalf of themselves and all class members alleging that LME's dissemination of their social security numbers to the 16 terminal managers constituted an invasion of their right to privacy.

LME moved for dismissal of this action under Minn. R. Civ. P. 12.02(e) for failure to state a claim upon which relief may be granted. The district court determined that the dissemination did not constitute "publicity" under a claim for publication of private facts and granted LME's motion to dismiss. The court of appeals reversed and remanded, holding that "[a]n actionable situation requires a level of publication that unreasonably exposes the appellant to significant risk of loss under all the circumstances," and concluding that the appropriate consideration includes the nature of the private fact and the harm to which the plaintiff is exposed as a result of the dissemination as well as the breadth of disclosure. *Bodah v. Lakeville Motor Express, Inc.,* 649 N.W.2d 859, 866 (Minn.App.2002). * * *

In *Lake v. Wal–Mart Stores, Inc.,* this court adopted three separate causes of action which are generally referred to as the tort of invasion of privacy: intrusion of seclusion, appropriation of a name or likeness of another, and publication of private facts. 582 N.W.2d 231, 236 (Minn. 1998). The rationale behind recognizing the tort of invasion of privacy is that "[t]he right to privacy is an integral part of our humanity; one has a public persona, exposed and active, and a private persona, guarded and preserved. The heart of our liberty is choosing which parts of our lives shall become public and which parts we shall hold close." *Id.* at 235. According to *Lake,* to state a claim for publication of private facts, a plaintiff must demonstrate that one " 'gives publicity to a matter concerning the private life of another * * * if the matter publicized is of a kind that (a) would be highly offensive to a reasonable person, and (b) is not of legitimate concern to the public.' " *Id.* at 233 (quoting Restatement (Second) of Torts, § 652D). The *Lake* court did not define "publicity." . . .

Under the Restatement, " '[p]ublicity' * * * means that the matter is made public, by communicating it to the public at large, or to so many persons that the matter must be regarded as substantially certain to become one of public knowledge." Restatement (Second) of Torts § 652D cmt. a. The Restatement distinguishes "publicity" for purposes of invasion of privacy from "publication" for defamation:

> "Publicity," as it is used in this Section, differs from "publication," as that term is used in § 577 in connection with liability for defamation. "Publication," in that sense, is a word of art, which includes any communication by the defendant to a third person. * * * The difference is not one of the means of communication, which may be oral, written or by any other means. It is one of a communication that reaches, or is sure to reach, the public.

> Thus it is not an invasion of the right of privacy, within the rule stated in this Section, to communicate a fact concerning the plaintiff's private life to a single person or even to a small group of persons. On the other hand, any publication in a newspaper or a magazine, even of small circulation, or in a handbill distributed to a large number of persons, or any broadcast over the radio, or statement made in an address to a large audience, is sufficient to give publicity within the meaning of the term as it is used in this Section. The distinction, in other words, is one between private and public communication.

*Id.* For example, as the Restatement illustrates, the posting of a statement in a shop window, where it is read by passers-by, that a customer owes a debt, constitutes "publicity" under the Restatement. *Id.* at cmt. a, illus. 2. . . . By contrast, where defendants threatened to disseminate a "Dead–Beat Parent" poster to the public at large but in fact only delivered the poster to the plaintiff's employer and a few close relatives, distribution to this "handful of people" was insufficient to constitute "publicity." *Jones v. United States Child Support Recovery,* 961 F.Supp. 1518, 1520–21 (D.Utah 1997) . . .

LME maintains that the dissemination by fax of a list of 204 employee names and social security numbers to 16 associated or related terminal managers in six states and the allegation that the private information is being shared or is accessible in general does not constitute "publicity" to support an invasion of privacy claim. Specifically, because the complaint does not allege that the dissemination of the numbers was to the public at large or that the disclosure involved so many people that the numbers were substantially certain to become public knowledge, as required by the Restatement, it fails to allege the requisite "publicity." * * *

*Here.--*

Respondents contend that their complaint alleges sufficient "publicity" to defeat LME's Rule 12.02(e) motion. Respondents point to various facts: that LME disseminated the names and social security numbers to 16 trucking terminals across six states, that it is unknown whether the numbers were treated as confidential information after they were received because there was no warning to that effect on the fax cover sheet, that LME did not take action for as long as four months after the dissemination, and that the numbers may not have yet been redacted or destroyed. Furthermore, respondents embrace the court of appeals' unique approach to defining "publicity" which looks not only at the breadth of disclosure but also at "the nature of the private data and the damage [implicated by its disclosure]." *Bodah,* 649 N.W.2d at 866. * * *

*How Ct of App framed*

At the outset, we choose not to embrace the court of appeals' approach to defining "publicity." The court of appeals' hybrid approach uses the Restatement's breadth of disclosure analysis but adds as an additional factor "the nature of private data and the damage." *Bodah,* 649 N.W.2d at 866. Using both factors, the court of appeals fashioned a narrow publicity requirement under the facts of this case: "where the dissemination was not for profit or with malicious intent, [the publicity requirement] ought to be whether [the dissemination] unreasonably exposed appellants to a significant risk that their social security numbers would be misused." *Id.* at 867. We think this definition emasculates the distinction between public and private by suggesting that "publicity" can be established by "either widespread dissemination *or improper use." Id.* (emphasis added). Furthermore, by looking to the nature of the private data as part of the "publicity" element, the court blurs the distinction between the "publicity" element and the other elements of the tort of publication of private facts which require that the private data "not [be] of legitimate concern to the public" and that the publicity be "highly offensive." Restatement (Second) of Torts § 652D; *see also Bodah,* 649 N.W.2d at 866. Finally, a lack of reasonableness is neither an element of the invasion of privacy tort of publication of private facts nor part of the publicity analysis. As such, the court of appeals' determination that "[a]n actionable situation requires a level of publication that unreasonably exposes the appellant to significant risk of loss under all the circumstances" inappropriately emphasizes the reasonableness of the defendant's actions.[3] *Bodah,* 649 N.W.2d at 866.

---

**3.** Indeed, if an unauthorized transmission of private data actually resulted in pecuniary loss due to identity theft, a plaintiff may be able to bring a negligence action. *See Funchess ex rel. Haynes v. Cecil Newman Corp.,* 632 N.W.2d 666, 672 (Minn.2001) (listing the four elements of a negligence claim: "(1) the existence of a duty of care, (2) breach of that duty, (3) an injury, and (4)

We also reject the "special relationship" or "particular public" approach taken by some jurisdictions. These jurisdictions have concluded that certain situations—where there is a special relationship between the plaintiff and the public—warrant departure from the Restatement's stringent publicity requirement. *See, e.g.,* ... *Miller v. Motorola, Inc.,* 202 Ill.App.3d 976, 148 Ill.Dec. 303, 560 N.E.2d 900, 903 (1990) ("Where a special relationship exists between the plaintiff and the 'public' to whom the information has been disclosed, the disclosure may be just as devastating to the person even though the disclosure was made to a limited number of people. * * * Plaintiff's allegation that her medical condition was disclosed to her fellow employees sufficiently satisfies the requirement that publicity be given to the private fact."); *Beaumont v. Brown,* 401 Mich. 80, 257 N.W.2d 522, 531 (1977) (holding a disclosure made to a "particular public" with a special relationship to the plaintiff, such as co-workers, family, or neighbors, could be actionable), *overruled in part on other grounds by Bradley v. Saranac Cmt. Sch. Bd. of Educ.,* 455 Mich. 285, 565 N.W.2d 650, 658 (1997).

We decide, instead, to adopt the Restatement definition of "publicity." We conclude, therefore, that "publicity" means that "the matter is made public, by communicating it to the public at large, or to so many persons that the matter must be regarded as substantially certain to become one of public knowledge." Restatement (Second) of Torts § 652D cmt. a. In doing so, we have considered whether there are legitimate or compelling reasons of public policy that justify imposing liability for egregious but limited disclosures of private information. We conclude, nevertheless, that the Restatement's publicity requirement best addresses the invasion of privacy cause of action-absent dissemination to the public at large, the claimant's "private persona" has not been violated. *See Lake,* 582 N.W.2d at 235.

Furthermore, we think the Restatement definition appropriately limits the publication of private facts cause of action. Though much has been written on the subject, we reflect on the concerns of Samuel Warren and Justice Louis Brandeis—"the evil of the invasion of privacy by the newspapers" and "whether our law will recognize and protect the right to privacy in this and in other respects"—and Warren's and Brandeis' recognition of limitations to this right. Samuel D. Warren & Louis D. Brandeis, *The Right to Privacy,* 4 Harv. L.Rev. 193, 195, 196, 214–19 (1890). These concerns provided the foundation for all four invasion of privacy torts but resonate particularly with the tort of publication of private facts. William L. Prosser, *Privacy,* 48 Cal. L.Rev. 383, 383–89

---

the breach of the duty being the proximate cause of the injury"). Likewise, a plaintiff may have a cause of action for negligent infliction of emotional distress if, because private information was shared, the plaintiff suffered severe emotional distress with accompanying physical manifestations. *See Wall v. Fairview Hosp. & Healthcare Servs.,* 584 N.W.2d 395, 408 (Minn.1998) ("To establish a claim for negligent infliction of emotional distress, a plaintiff must show that she was within a zone of danger of physical impact, reasonably feared for her safety, and suffered severe emotional distress with accompanying physical manifestations."); *see, e.g., Navarre v. S. Washington County Sch.,* 633 N.W.2d 40 (Minn.App.2001), *aff'd in part, rev'd in part, and remanded,* 652 N.W.2d 9 (Minn.2002).

(1960) (tracing the evolution of the four invasion of privacy torts). As Warren and Brandeis noted more than 100 years ago:

> The design of the law must be to protect those persons with whose affairs the community has no legitimate concern, from being dragged into an undesirable and undesired publicity and to protect all persons, whatsoever; their position or station, from having matters which they may properly prefer to keep private, made public against their will.

Warren & Brandeis, *supra,* at 214–15. We understand the tort of publication of private facts to focus on a very narrow gap in tort law—to provide a remedy for the truthful but damaging dissemination of private facts, which is nonactionable under defamation rules. . . .

We turn now to the application of the Restatement's publicity requirement to the instant facts. We conclude that respondents' claim that LME disseminated 204 employees' social security numbers to 16 terminal managers in six states does not constitute publication to the public or to so large a number of persons that the matter must be regarded as substantially certain to become public. *See, e.g., C.L.D.,* 79 F.Supp.2d at 1084 (concluding that disclosure of private facts to only a few employees did not constitute publication); *Dancy v. Fina Oil & Chem. Co.,* 3 F.Supp.2d 737, 740 (E.D.Tex.1997) (finding insufficient publication where "the allegedly publicized facts, at worst, were made known to some workers in the refinery"); *Kuhn v. Account Control Tech., Inc.,* 865 F.Supp. 1443, 1448 (D.Nev.1994) (concluding that no "publicity" existed where dissemination of information regarding Kuhn's indebtedness was to a small group of co-workers); *Lewis v. Snap–On Tools Corp.,* 708 F.Supp. 1260, 1262 (M.D.Fla.1989) ("The mere conclusory allegation that the alleged disclosure was to 'large numbers of persons' does not meet the requirement that the publication be to the general public * * *."); *Wells v. Thomas,* 569 F.Supp. 426, 437 (E.D.Pa.1983) (determining that publication to community of employees at staff meetings "and discussions between defendants and other employees" does not constitute "publicity"); *Doe,* 690 N.E.2d at 692 (concluding that the disclosures to co-workers that plaintiff was HIV-positive did not satisfy the publicity element); *Eddy v. Brown,* 715 P.2d 74, 78 (Okla.1986) (holding that disclosure that plaintiff was undergoing psychiatric treatment to a limited number of co-workers was not "publicity"); *Vogel v. W.T. Grant Co.,* 458 Pa. 124, 327 A.2d 133, 137 (1974) (concluding there was no "publicity" where four persons— three relatives and one employer—were notified of plaintiff's indebtedness). * * *

*[handwritten margin note: Here, not publicity]*

## NOTES AND QUESTIONS

1. As the Minnesota Supreme Court noted, some jurisdictions have taken a less categorical approach to the breadth of publication where the information was especially sensitive. *E.g., Greenwood v. Taft, Stettinius & Hollister,* 105 Ohio App.3d 295, 663 N.E.2d 1030 (1995) (disclosure to others in the firm with no need to know that law firm associate had listed a male

partner on his benefits form was actionable for invading privacy). Which is the better view?

2.   The Minnesota Supreme Court did not reach the other element of the Restatement's view of what works a wrongful dissemination—that the facts disseminated must be embarrassing or offensive. Are social security numbers embarrassing or offensive?

3.   Several states have restricted employer distribution of social security numbers.

4.   The Data Protection Directive of the European Union requires the member states to enact laws safeguarding the confidentiality of personally sensitive information as well as limiting employers from gathering such information. The principles contained in the Directive has been widely adopted in countries as diverse as Canada, Morocco, Israel, and Hong Kong— in part because the Directive prohibits the transmission of personally sensitive information out of the EU to any country whose level of privacy protection is not "adequate" as measured by European standards. Should the U.S. follow that model which, in part, would substitute administrative regulation for tort litigation?

# D.   DRUG TESTING

Reconsider the discussion in Chapter II and recall the West Virginia Supreme Court's allowance of drug *screening* of applicants even as it limited the *testing* of incumbent employees to safety-sensitive or like jobs only. As that discussion noted, employers require incumbent employees to submit to drug testing for a variety of reasons: upon "reasonable suspicion" of drug use, upon return to work, after an accident causing injury or significant property loss, or on a random basis. If the drug test is a "medical examination" within the meaning of the Americans with Disabilities Act, it can be administered only if it is "job related and consistent with business necessity." 42 U.S.C. § 12112(c)(4)(A) (2009). However, under § 12114(d), "a test to determine the illegal use of drugs shall not be considered a medical examination."

A study of the effect of U.S. Department of Transportation rules on highway safety concluded that those drug testing policies had reduced highway facilities by 9 to 10 percent and that the benefits exceeded the cost on the order of 2 to perhaps 10 times the cost of the program. But the investigator also cautioned about generalizing these results: "In the typical job, where one worker's poor performance has few if any negative externalities, the benefits of testing may be small relative to its costs." Mireille Jacobson, *Drug Testing in the Trucking Industry: The Effect on Highway Safety*, 46 J.L. & Econ. 131 (2003). A study of post-accident drug testing (PADT) found that PADT can reduce workers' compensation claims, but that that may be the result of employees' either forgoing drug use or declining to report accidents, the latter explanation finding some support in the data. To the extent employees hide injuries as a result of PADT, the authors conclude that serious questions of public policy are raised. Alison D. Morantz & Alexandre Mas, *Does Post–Accident Drug Testing Reduce Injuries? Evidence from a Large Retail Chain*, 10 AM. L. & ECON. REV. 246 (2008).

In *Entrop v. Imperial Oil Ltd.*, [2000] 50 O.R. (3d) 18 (Ont. C.A.), the Ontario Court of Appeal confronted a challenge to the drug testing of employees in safety-sensitive positions:

> The drugs listed in the policy all have the capacity to impair job performance, and urinalysis is a reliable method of showing the presence of drugs or drug metabolites in a person's body. But drug testing suffers from one fundamental flaw. It cannot measure present impairment. A positive drug test shows only past drug use. It cannot show how much was used or when it was used. Thus, the Board found that a positive drug test provides no evidence of impairment or likely impairment on the job. It does not demonstrate that a person is incapable of performing the essential duties of the position. The Board also found on the evidence that no tests currently exist to accurately assess the effect of drug use on job performance and that drug testing programs have not been shown to be effective in reducing drug use, work accidents or work performance problems. On these findings, random drug testing for employees in safety-sensitive positions cannot be justified as reasonably necessary to accomplish Imperial Oil's legitimate goal of a safe workplace free of impairment. [2000] 50 O.R. (3d) 18 ¶ 99.

*Canada's View*

The court disallowed pre-employment screening for the same reason. *See also* Canadian Human Rights Commission, Executive Summary, *Canadian Human Rights Commission Policy on Alcohol and Drug Testing* (2002), *available at* http://www.chrc-ccdp.ca/pdf/poldrgalceng.pdf.

### QUESTIONS

1.   Return to the case of the user of medically prescribed marijuana who fails a random drug test and is fired. Inasmuch as under state law her use was not unlawful, was the test a medical examination under the ADA? If so, was it justified by job relatedness and business necessity?

2.   One of the policies claimed in support of the random testing of incumbent employees is a concern for safety and efficiency, *i.e.*, of subpar performance on the job. This was said of an accountant of six years' service, a recreational marijuana user, who tested positive in a random drug test and was fired. *See Seta v. Reading Rock, Inc.*, 100 Ohio App.3d 731, 654 N.E.2d 1061 (1995). As an accountant did she pose a threat to safety? Was there any evidence of subpar performance after six years on the job?

3.   Almost half the states regulate drug testing. Such regulation may cover the manner in which testing may be conducted and the disciplinary consequences for employees of positive test results. Drug use has been a major concern in professional sports. In football, it is regulated by collective agreement. The agreement provides for discipline of a player testing positive. It does not require a confirming test. However, Minnesota law forbids the

imposition of discipline without a confirming test. Must the Minnesota Vikings treat its players differently than a league member who is not based in a state with a cognate statute? *See Williams v. National Football League*, 582 F.3d 863 (8th Cir. 2009).

# E.   CONTROL OF EMPLOYEES

## 1.   PERSONAL RELATIONSHIPS

### RULON–MILLER v. INTERNATIONAL BUSINESS MACHINES CORP.

California Court of Appeal, 1984
162 Cal.App.3d 241, 208 Cal.Rptr. 524

RUSHING, ASSOCIATE JUSTICE.

International Business Machines (IBM) appeals from the judgment entered against it after a jury awarded $100,000 compensatory and $200,000 punitive damages to respondent (Virginia Rulon–Miller) on claims of wrongful discharge and intentional infliction of emotional distress. Rulon–Miller was a low-level marketing manager at IBM in its office products division in San Francisco. Her termination as a marketing manager at IBM came about as a result of an accusation made by her immediate supervisor, defendant Callahan, of a romantic relationship with the manager of a rival office products firm, QYX.

### Factual Background

IBM is an employer traditionally thought to provide great security to its employees as well as an environment of openness and dignity. The company is organized into divisions, and each division is, to an extent, independent of others. The company prides itself on providing career opportunities to its employees, and respondent represents a good example of this. She started in 1967 as a receptionist in the Philadelphia Data Center. She was told that "career opportunities are available to [employees] as long as they are performing satisfactorily and are willing to accept new challenges." While she worked at the data center in Philadelphia, she attended night school and earned a baccalaureate degree. She was promoted to equipment scheduler and not long after received her first merit award. The company moved her to Atlanta, Georgia where she spent 15 months as a data processor. She was transferred to the office products division and was assigned the position of "marketing support representative" in San Francisco where she trained users (i.e., customers) of newly-purchased IBM equipment. Respondent was promoted to "product planner" in 1973 where her duties included overseeing the performance of new office products in the marketplace. As a product planner, she moved to Austin, Texas and later to Lexington, Kentucky. Thereafter, at the urging of her managers that she go into sales in the office products division, she enrolled at the IBM sales school in Dallas. After graduation, she was assigned to San Francisco.

Her territory was the financial district. She was given a performance plan by her management which set forth the company's expectations of her. She was from time to time thereafter graded against that plan on a scale of one through five with a grade of one being the highest. After her first year on the job, she was given a rating of one and was felt by her manager to be a person who rated at the top of IBM's scale.

*Great perf*

A little over a year after she began in San Francisco, IBM reorganized its office products division into two separate functions, one called office systems and another called office products. Respondent was assigned to office systems; again she was given ratings of one and while there received a series of congratulatory letters from her superiors and was promoted to marketing representative. She was one of the most successful sales persons in the office and received a number of prizes and awards for her sales efforts.[1] IBM's system of rewarding salespersons has a formalistic aspect about it that allows for subtle distinctions to be made while putting great emphasis on performance; respondent exercised that reward system to its fullest. She was a very successful seller of typewriters and other office equipment.

She was then put into a program called "Accelerated Career Development Program" which was a way of rewarding certain persons who were seen by their superiors as having management potential. IBM's prediction of her future came true and in 1978 she was named a marketing manager in the office products branch.

IBM knew about respondent's relationship with Matt Blum well before her appointment as a manager. Respondent met Blum in 1976 when he was an account manager for IBM. That they were dating was widely known within the organization. In 1977 Blum left IBM to join QYX, an IBM competitor, and was transferred to Philadelphia. When Blum returned to San Francisco in the summer of 1978, IBM personnel were aware that he and respondent began dating again. This seemed to present no problems to respondent's superiors, as Callahan confirmed when she was promoted to manager. Respondent testified: "Somewhat in passing, Phil said: I heard the other day you were dating Matt Blum, and I said: Oh. And he said, I don't have any problem with that. You're my number one pick. I just want to assure you that you are my selection." The relationship with Blum was also known to Regional Manager Gary Nelson who agreed with Callahan. Neither Callahan nor Nelson raised any issue of conflict of interest because of the Blum relationship.

*Blum goes to rival but IBM knows*

Respondent flourished in her management position, and the company, apparently grateful for her efforts, gave her a $4,000 merit raise in 1979 and told her that she was doing a good job. A week later, her manager, Phillip Callahan, left a message that he wanted to see her.

*Costs to exceed*

---

**1.** In 1978 she fulfilled her annual sales quota in the fifth month of the year. She was given a "Golden Circle Award" in her third year of sales which is a recognition of superior sales by the company. She had been a member of the "100 Percent Club" for each of the years that she was in the San Francisco office.

When she walked into Callahan's office he confronted her with the question of whether she was *dating* Matt Blum. She wondered at the relevance of the inquiry and he said the dating constituted a "conflict of interest," and told her to stop dating Blum or lose her job and said she had a "couple of days to a week" to think about it.[2]

Fired for dating him

The next day Callahan called her in again, told her "he had made up her mind for her," and when she protested, dismissed her.[3] * * *

[The court held that IBM was bound by rules and regulations it had adopted for the benefit of employees].

In this case, there is a close question of whether those rules or regulations permit IBM to inquire into the purely personal life of the employee. If so, an attendant question is whether such a policy was

---

**2.** Because of the importance of this testimony, we set it out verbatim. Respondent testified: "I walked into Phil's office and he asked me to sit down and he said: Are you dating Matt Blum?

"And I said, What? I was kind of surprised he would ask me and I said: Well, what difference does it make if I'm dating Matt Blum? * * *

"And he said, well, something to the effect: I think we have a conflict of interest, or the appearance of a conflict of interest here.

"And I said: Well, gee, Phil, you've, you've pointed out to me that there are no problems in the office because I am dating Matt Blum, and I don't really understand why that would have any, you know, pertinency to my job. You said I am doing an okay job. I just got a raise.

"And he said: Well, I think we have a conflict of interest. * * *

"He said: No and he said: I'll tell you what. He said: I will give you a couple of days to a week. Think this whole thing over.

"I said: Think what over?

"And he said: You either stop dating Matt Blum or I'm going to take you out of your management job.

"And I was just kind of overwhelmed."

**3.** Respondent stated the next day she was again summoned to his office where Callahan sat ominously behind a desk cleared of any paperwork, an unusual scenario for any IBM manager.

She further testified: "I walked into Phil's office, and he asked me to shut the door, and he said he was removing me from management effectively immediately. And I said: What?

"And he repeated it. And I was taken aback, I was a little startled, and I think I said: Well, gee, I thought I had a couple of days to a week to think over the situation that we discussed yesterday.

"And he said: I'm making the decision for you.

"And I said: Phil, you've told me that I'm doing a good job. You told me that we are not losing anybody to QYX because I am dating Matt Blum, that we are not losing any equipment to QYX. I just don't understand what bearing dating has to do with my job.

"And he said: We have a conflict of interest. * * *

"I said: Well, what kind of a job would it be?

"And he said: Well, I don't have it, but it will be non-management. You won't be a manager again.

"Pardon me? * * *

"And I think I was getting very upset so I think I said something because of that respect for the individual tenet of IBM's that I really believed in I didn't think that he was following what I thought IBM, really did believe in. And he just said: You know, you are removed from management effective immediately.

"And I said: I think you are dismissing me.

"And he said: If you feel that way, give me your I.D. card and your key to the office. [¶] I want you to leave the premises immediately.

"And I was just about to burst into tears, and I didn't cry at work, so I basically fled his office.

"I felt he dismissed me."

applied consistently, particularly as between men and women. The distinction is important because the right of privacy, a constitutional right in California (*City and County of San Francisco v. Superior Court* (1981) 125 Cal.App.3d 879, 883, 178 Cal.Rptr. 435), could be implicated by the IBM inquiry. Much of the testimony below concerned what those policies were. The evidence was conflicting on the meaning of certain IBM policies. We observe ambiguity in the application but not in the intent. The "Watson Memo" (so called because it was signed by a former chairman of IBM) provided as follows:

*Right to privacy* [handwritten margin note]

*IBM policies* [handwritten margin note]

"TO ALL IBM MANAGERS:

"The line that separates an individual's on-the-job business life from his other life as a private citizen is at times well-defined and at other times indistinct. But the line does exist, and you and I, as managers in IBM, must be able to recognize that line.

"I have seen instances where managers took disciplinary measures against employees for actions or conduct that are not rightfully the company's concern. These managers usually justified their decisions by citing their personal code of ethics and morals or by quoting some fragment of company policy that seemed to support their position. Both arguments proved unjust on close examination. What we need, in every case, is balanced judgment which weighs the needs of the business and the rights of the individual.

"Our primary objective as IBM managers is to further the business of this company by leading our people properly and measuring quantity and quality of work and effectiveness on the job against clearly set standards of responsibility and compensation. This is performance— and performance is, in the final analysis, the one thing that the company can insist on from everyone.

"We have concern with an employee's off-the-job behavior only when it reduces his ability to perform regular job assignments, interferes with the job performance of other employees, or if his outside behavior affects the reputation of the company in a major way. When on-the-job performance is acceptable, I can think of few situations in which outside activities could result in disciplinary action or dismissal.

"When such situations do come to your attention, you should seek the advice and counsel of the next appropriate level of management and the personnel department in determining what action—if any—is called for. Action should be taken only when a legitimate interest of the company is injured or jeopardized. Furthermore the damage must be clear beyond reasonable doubt and not based on hasty decisions about what one person might think is good for the company.

"IBM's first basic belief is respect for the individual, and the essence of this belief is a strict regard for his right to personal privacy. This idea should never be compromised easily or quickly.

"/s/ Tom Watson, Jr."

It is clear that this company policy insures to the employee both the right of privacy and the right to hold a job even though "off-the-job behavior" might not be approved of by the employee's manager.

IBM had adopted policies governing employee conduct. Some of those policies were collected in a document known as the "Performance and Recognition" (PAR) Manual. IBM relies on the following portion of the PAR Manual:

> "A conflict of interest can arise when an employee is involved in activity for personal gain, which for any reason is in conflict with IBM's business interests. Generally speaking, 'moonlighting' is defined as working at some activity for personal gain outside of your IBM job. If you do perform outside work, you have a special responsibility to avoid any conflict with IBM's business interests.

> "Obviously, you cannot solicit or perform in competition with IBM product or service offerings. Outside work cannot be performed on IBM time, including 'personal' time off. You cannot use IBM equipment, materials, resources, or 'inside' information for outside work. Nor should you solicit business or clients or perform outside work on IBM premises.

> "Employees must be free of any significant investment or association of their own or of their immediate family's [sic], in competitors or suppliers, which might interfere or be thought to interfere with the independent exercise of their judgment in the best interests of IBM."

This policy of IBM is entitled "Gifts" and appears to be directed at "moonlighting" and soliciting outside business or clients on IBM premises. It prohibits "significant investment" in competitors or suppliers of IBM. It also prohibits "association" with such persons "which might interfere or be thought to interfere with the independent exercise of their judgment in the best interests of IBM."

Callahan based his action against respondent on a "conflict of interest." But the record shows that IBM did not interpret this policy to prohibit a romantic relationship. Callahan admitted that there was no company rule or policy requiring an employee to terminate friendships with fellow employees who leave and join competitors. Gary Nelson, Callahan's superior, also confirmed that IBM had no policy against employees socializing with competitors.

This issue was hotly contested with respondent claiming that the "conflict of interest" claim was a pretext for her unjust termination. Whether it was presented a fact question for the jury.

Do the policies reflected in this record give IBM a right to terminate an employee for a conflict of interest? The answer must be yes, but whether respondent's conduct constituted such was for the jury. We observe that while respondent was successful, her primary job did not give her access to sensitive information which could have been useful to competitors. She was, after all, a seller of typewriters and office equipment. Respondent's brief makes much of the concession by IBM that there was no evidence whatever that respondent had given any information or help to IBM's competitor QYX. It really is no concession at all; she did not have the information or help to give. Even so, the question is one of substantial evidence. The evidence is abundant that there was no conflict of interest by respondent.

*[handwritten margin note: She had no access to sensitive info]*

It does seem clear that an overall policy established by IBM chairman Watson was one of no company interest in the outside activities of an employee so long as the activities did not interfere with the work of the employee. Moreover, in the last analysis, it may be simply a question for the jury to decide whether, in the application of these policies, the right was conferred on IBM to inquire into the personal or romantic relationships its managers had with others. This is an important question because IBM, in attempting to reargue the facts to us, casts this argument in other terms, namely: that it had a right to inquire even if there was no evidence that such a relationship interfered with the discharge of the employee's duties *because* it had the effect of diminishing the morale of the employees answering to the manager. This is the "Caesar's wife" argument; it is merely a recast of the principal argument and asks the same question in different terms.[5] The same answer holds in both cases: there being no evidence to support the more direct argument, there is no evidence to support the indirect argument.

Moreover, the record shows that the evidence of rumor was not a basis for any decline in the morale of the employees reporting to respondent. Employees Mary Hrize and Wayne Fyvie, who reported to respondent's manager that she was seen at a tea dance at the Hyatt Regency with Matt Blum and also that she was not living at her residence in Marin, did not believe that those rumors in any way impaired her abilities as a manager. In the initial confrontation between respondent and her superior the assertion of the right to be free of inquiries concerning her personal life was based on substantive direct contract rights she had flowing to her from IBM policies. Further, there is no doubt that the jury could have so found and on this record we must assume that they did so find. * * *

### Intentional Infliction of Emotional Distress

The contract rights in an employment agreement or the covenant of good faith and fair dealing gives both employer and employee the right to breach and to respond in damages. Here, however, the question is whether

---

**5.** What we mean by that is that if you charge that an employee is passing confidential information to a competitor, the question remains whether the charge is true on the evidence available to the person deciding the issue, in this case, the respondent's managers at IBM. If you recast this argument in the form of the "Caesar's wife" argument attempted by IBM, it will be seen that exactly the same question arises, namely, "is it true?" Indeed, the import of the argument is that the rumor, or an unfounded allegation, could serve as a basis for the termination of the employee.

*Punitive dmgs?*

if IBM elected to exercise that right it should also be liable for punitive damages, because of its intentional infliction of emotional distress. The issue is whether the conduct of the marketing manager of IBM was "extreme and outrageous," a question involving the objective facts of what happened in the confrontation between the employee and employer as well as the special susceptibility of suffering of the employee.

The general rule is that this tort, in essence, requires the defendant's conduct to be so extreme and outrageous as to go beyond all possible bounds of decency, and to be regarded as atrocious and utterly intolerable in a civilized community. (*Alcorn v. Anbro Engineering, Inc.* (1970) 2 Cal.3d 493, 498–499, 86 Cal.Rptr. 88, 468 P.2d 216, particularly at fn. 5 quoting Rest.2d Torts § 46, comment d.)

The question is reduced to the inquiry of whether Callahan's statements and conduct could be found by the jury to fall within doctrinal requirements. " 'It is for the court to determine whether on the evidence severe emotional distress can be found; it is for the jury to determine whether, on the evidence, it has in fact existed.' " (*Fletcher v. Western National Life Ins. Co.* (1970) 10 Cal.App.3d 376, 397, 89 Cal.Rptr. 78.) "Where reasonable men may differ" the court must instruct the jury on the law and entrust the factual determination to it. (*Fuentes v. Perez* (1977) 66 Cal.App.3d 163, 172, 136 Cal.Rptr. 275.) The finding on this cause of action as reflected herein is sufficient to support the award of punitive damages. (*Fletcher, supra,* 10 Cal.App.3d at p. 404, 89 Cal.Rptr. 78.)

The jury was entitled to consider the evidence of extreme and outrageous conduct in light of the June 7 exchange followed by Callahan's conduct and pretextual statements, as well as in light of express corporate policy as manifested by the Watson memo. Indeed, the concern of the Watson memo is also a right protected by law. As we earlier noted "the right of privacy is unquestionably a 'fundamental interest of our society' " (*City and County of San Francisco v. Superior Court, supra,* 125 Cal. App.3d 879, 883, 178 Cal.Rptr. 435.) It is guaranteed to all people by article I, section 1, of the state Constitution. So the question is whether the invasion of plaintiff's privacy rights by her employer, in the setting of this case, constitutes extreme and outrageous conduct. The jury by special verdict so found.

*Deception Disregard for policy*

To determine if Callahan's conduct could reach the level of extreme, outrageous, and atrocious conduct, requires detailed examination. First, there was a decided element of deception in Callahan acting as if the relationship with Blum was something new. The evidence was clear he knew of the involvement of respondent and Blum well before her promotion. Second, he acted in flagrant disregard of IBM policies prohibiting him from inquiring into respondent's "off job behavior." By giving respondent "a few days" to think about the choice between job and lover, he implied that if she gave up Blum she could have her job. He then acted without giving her "a few days to think about it" or giving her the right to choose.

So far the conduct is certainly unfair but not atrocious. What brings Callahan's conduct to an actionable level is the way he brought these several elements together in the second meeting with respondent. He said, after calling her in, "I'm making the decision for you." The implications of his statement were richly ambiguous, meaning she could not act or think for herself, or that he was acting in her best interest, or that she persisted in a romantic involvement inconsistent with her job. When she protested, he fired her.

The combination of statements and conduct would under any reasoned view tend to humiliate and degrade respondent. To be denied a right granted to all other employees for conduct unrelated to her work was to degrade her as a person. His unilateral action in purporting to remove any free choice on her part contrary to his earlier assurances also would support a conclusion that his conduct was intended to emphasize that she was powerless to do anything to assert her rights as an IBM employee. And such powerlessness is one of the most debilitating kinds of human oppression. The sum of such evidence clearly supports the jury finding of extreme and outrageous conduct.

Accordingly we conclude that the emotional distress cause of action was amply proved and supports the award of punitive damages. (*Neal v. Farmers Ins. Exchange, supra,* 21 Cal.3d 910, 927–928, 148 Cal.Rptr. 389, 582 P.2d 980.)

The judgment is affirmed.

### NOTES AND QUESTIONS

1. On what legal theory did the court ground Ms. Rulon–Miller's claim of wrongful discharge? In contract, based upon IBM's policies—especially the "Watson Memo"? In tort, grounded in the public policy expressed it the California constitution's grant of privacy to all persons? In the covenant of good faith and fair dealing?

2. Compare *Rulon–Miller* with *Springer v. Wal–Mart*, discussed in Chapter IV, on the issue of emotional distress. Are these cases reconcilable? Or must one's mental hide be tougher in Kentucky than in California?

3. May an employer (outside of California) adopt (and apply without discrimination) a "no-fraternization" policy prohibiting any romantic involvement ("no dating") between *any* two employees of the company? *See Ellis v. United Parcel Service, Inc.,* 523 F.3d 823 (7th Cir. 2008). A 2001 American Management Survey indicated that 11% of the employers surveyed had such a policy. Why would a company adopt such a rule?

4. Colorado insulates employees from discharge for engaging in any lawful off-duty activity that has no impact in the workplace. COLO. REV. STAT. § 24–34–402.5 (2005). Presumably, a date would be such a lawful off-duty activity. What evidence of adverse workplace impact would an employer need

to show to enforce a prohibition in any particular case? Is this law an excessive intrusion into managerial prerogative? *Cf.* Erich Shiners, *Keeping the Boss Out of the Bedroom: California's Constitutional Right of Privacy as a Limitation on Private Employers' Regulation of Employees' Off–Duty Intimate Association*, 37 McGEORGE L. REV.449 (2006).

5.   Two co-workers share a house. The employer discharges one and directs the other to evict her roommate and to have no further contact with her. If she refuses and is discharged for that refusal, would she have an action for discharge in violation of public policy? *Cf. Privette v. University of N.C. at Chapel Hill*, 96 N.C.App. 124, 385 S.E.2d 185 (1989). If she agrees, would the former roommate have a valid cause of action? Under what theory? *See Creditwatch, Inc. v. Jackson*, 157 S.W.3d 814 (Tex. 2005).

## 2.   POLITICAL SPEECH AND ASSOCIATION

The Pennsylvania Constitution, as do several others, contains a free speech clause that, unlike the federal First Amendment, is drafted as a grant of power to persons and not as a limit only upon government:

> The free communication of thoughts and opinions is one of the invaluable rights of man, and every citizen may freely speak, write and print on any subject, being responsible for the abuse of that liberty.

John Novosel, a district claims manager of the Nationwide Insurance Company and a fifteen-year employee, was discharged for refusing to join in the company's effort to support a "No–Fault Reform Act" then before the state legislature. The court held the discharge violatived public policy found in the First Amendment and in the Pennsylvania Constitution.

*[handwritten margin note: Violative discharge]*

> The key question in considering the tort claim is therefore whether a discharge for disagreement with the employer's legislative agenda or a refusal to lobby the state legislature on the employer's behalf suffi-ciently implicate a recognized facet of public policy. The definition of a "clearly mandated public policy" as one that "strikes at the heart of a citizen's social right, duties and responsibilities," set forth in *Palma-teer v. International Harvester Co.*, 85 Ill.2d 124, 52 Ill.Dec. 13, 421 N.E.2d 876 (1981), appears to provide a workable standard for the tort action. While no Pennsylvania law directly addresses the public policy question at bar, the protection of an employee's freedom of political expression would appear to involve no less compelling a societal interest than the fulfillment of jury service or the filing of a worker's compensation claim.

*Novosel v. Nationwide Ins. Co.*, 721 F.2d 894, 899 (3d Cir.1983). The vitality of *Novosel* was reaffirmed in *Borse v. Piece Goods Shop, Inc.*, 963 F.2d 611 (3d Cir.1992), but it remains decidedly a minority view.

### NOTES AND QUESTIONS

1.   Many states forbid employment discrimination where the purpose is to influence how employees vote. Six states protect employee engagement in

"political activity" generally; and two—Louisiana and South Carolina—protect the holding of "political opinion." Michigan prohibits employers from keeping records of employee political association or activity. And at least two states provide protection generally for employee speech. *See* CONN. GEN. STAT. § 31–51q (1999); MASS. GEN. LAWS ch. 12, §§ 11H–11I (1988).

2. The Restatement of the Law (Third) Employment Law, § 4.02, would deny the protection of public policy to free speech, derived from a state constitution (presumably absent direct constitutional application to private employment as in California), either because the right asserted is not an "employment" right or because it is "waiveable." The Labor Law Group's Working Group criticized the latter for its impenetrability for the ALI's Reporters decline to supply any metric whatsoever by which the waiveable/non-waiveable distinction is to be drawn. Joseph Grodin et al., *Working Group on Chapter 4 of the Proposed Restatement of Employment Law: The Tort of Wrongful Discipline in Violation of Public Policy*, 13 EMP. RTS. & EMP. POL'Y J. 159, 188 (2009). If an employer cannot condition employment upon the employee's agreement not to report the employer's criminal wrongdoing—to "waive" the protection that would attach to doing so—why can it require the employee to relinquish the right publicly to demand a change in criminal law that would cause the employer to have compliance problems? Note that the employee would not be whistleblowing, because it is the failure of the law to cover the employer's action, not the employer's wrongdoing under extant law, that would be the focus of her public demand. Wouldn't the employee's expertise—her knowledge of how her employer had exploited a loophole in the law—be especially valued in informing the public?

The Restatement's refusal to extend public policy to retaliation for the exercise of a non-employment right was discussed in Chapter IV. According to the ALI, an employee may not be dismissed for demanding to be paid the minimum wage, but can be dismissed for demanding that the legislature increase the minimum wage. Does this make any sense?

3. Return to *Payne v. Western & Atlantic Railroad Co.*, in Chapter I. The dissent, challenging the majority's assumption of plenary employer control of lawful off-duty activity—shopping at Mr. Payne's store—reasoned that in consequence of according that power "Capital may thus not only find its own legitimate employment, but may control the employment of others to an extent that in time may sap the foundations of our free institutions." How does that observation fare a century and a quarter later? Should an employer be able to dismiss an employee (honored by the Governor of the state for his citizenship) of 22 years' service for his opposition to a political measure favorable to the Company? *See Edmondson v. Shearer Lumber Prods.*, 139 Idaho 172, 75 P.3d 733 (2003). For writing a letter critical of a company official's service on a local school board? See *Schultz v. Industrial. Coils, Inc.*, 125 Wis.2d 520, 373 N.W.2d 74 (Ct. App.1985). Could a waitress be dismissed for organizing a tax protest against the IRS? *See Young v. Anthony's Fish Grottos, Inc.*, 830 F.2d 993 (9th Cir.1987).

## 3.  WORKPLACE SPEECH AND ASSOCIATION

### NLRB v. COCA–COLA CO. FOODS DIV.

United States Court of Appeals, Seventh Circuit, 1982
670 F.2d 84

POSNER, CIRCUIT JUDGE.

We are presented with a question apparently of first impression regarding the power of the National Labor Relations Board to prohibit interference with concerted activities before they materialize.

Richard Geer, a mechanic at one of the respondent's plants, was promoted into a training program to become a roving mechanic, and then was released from the program, unjustly in his view, and returned to his previous job. Although the plant is not unionized, the company has a grievance procedure for its employees and Geer filed a grievance. His foreman decided that the grievance was without merit and the foreman's decision was sustained by the plant manager, Louderback. Geer then wrote a long letter to Louderback's superior, repeating his grievance and adding various accusations against Louderback personally. Louderback, angered by this, summoned Geer to his office. The evidence is conflicting on what was said there, but the administrative law judge believed Geer's version and we accept the ALJ's finding. According to Geer, Louderback abused him in various ways and then said: "If any talk gets around out there on that floor about this grievance and what it pertains and this meeting, I'm coming after you." The ALJ interpreted these remarks, and we accept his interpretation, as forbidding Geer to discuss his grievance with his fellow workers and as threatening retaliation if Geer did so; and such conduct, the ALJ concluded, violated section 8(a)(1) of the National Labor Relations Act, 29 U.S.C. § 158(a)(1), because it "clearly tend[ed] to interfere with and inhibit employees' free expression of their grievances." The NLRB affirmed the ALJ's decision, initially without an opinion; but later the Board added the following paragraph to its order:

> We agree with the Administrative Law Judge's conclusion that the Respondent violated Section 8(a)(1) of the Act by threatening to retaliate against employee Geer if he discussed his grievance with other employees. By such threat, the Respondent restrained and coerced Geer in his Section 7 right to discuss his grievance with other employees for the purpose of seeking their aid and support.

Section 8(a)(1) of the National Labor Relations Act makes it an unfair labor practice to interfere with, restrain, or coerce employees in the exercise of the rights guaranteed in section 7 of the Act, 29 U.S.C. § 157, and among these rights is the right of employees to engage in concerted activities for the purpose of mutual aid or protection. We accept the Board's finding that the respondent, through Louderback, interfered with Geer's discussing his grievance with his coworkers; the question is whether the respondent thereby interfered with concerted activity for the purpose of mutual aid or protection.

It is of no moment that the plant was not unionized and that Geer's complaint related to a personal grievance rather than to the general wage level or working conditions at the plant. If Geer had tried to enlist other workers in support of his grievance, he would have been engaged in a concerted activity protected by section 7. See, e.g., *Dreis & Krump Mfg. Co. v. NLRB,* 544 F.2d 320, 326 (7th Cir.1976). However, the ALJ made no finding that this is what Geer was trying to do or would have tried to do but for Louderback's threats. There was no evidence that Geer intended to discuss his grievance with other workers, let alone seek their aid and support. We thus do not know whether concerted activity protected by section 7 was aborted by Louderback's threats.

But we do not know this only because Louderback launched his preemptive strike. It would be absurd to conclude that if long before there were any stirrings of union activity at a plant the management threatened to shoot anyone who joined a union, section 8(a)(1) would not be violated because no one could prove that concerted activity protected by section 7 would ever have taken place in the absence of the threat. A right can be denied before its exercise is attempted or even contemplated.

*Pelton Casteel, Inc. v. NLRB,* 627 F.2d 23, 28–30 (7th Cir.1980), a recent decision of this circuit on which the respondent relies, is not in point. That case holds only that there is no section 7 "right to gripe"; that it is not protected concerted activity to complain to one's fellow workers. So if all Geer wanted to do was to gripe to his fellow workers, it would not have been a violation of the Act for the company to forbid him to do so. But it does not follow that by forbidding *all* communication with fellow employees, thereby prohibiting protected concerted activity along with unprotected griping, the company can insulate itself from liability.

Perhaps the distinction is a fine one, for the ALJ missed it. He thought Louderback's threats were bad because they inhibited the free expression of grievances. But *Pelton Casteel* holds that there is no section 7 right to such expression. That is presumably why the Board added the paragraph we have quoted. A fuller discussion might have been expected since the question presented by this case is, surprisingly, one of first impression. But the answer is free from doubt and the Board's order will therefore be

Enforced.

## NOTES AND QUESTIONS

1. If the individual's expression of her grievance to a coworker—a personal "gripe"—is not statutorily protected, how did Mr. Louderback's order violate the Act? On the other hand, why would a "personal gripe" not be protected? *See* Richard Michael Fischl, *Self, Others, and Section 7: Mutualism and Protected Protest Activities Under the National Labor Relations Act,*

89 COLUM. L. REV. 789 (1989); Robert A. Gorman & Matthew W. Finkin, *The Individual and the Requirement of "Concert" Under the National Labor Relations Act*, 130 U. PA. L. REV. 286 (1981).

2.  May employees appeal to non-employees—clients or customers—for aid in redress of their grievances? *See Handicabs v. NLRB*, 95 F.3d 681 (8th Cir. 1996).

3.  It is a common practice, and perfectly lawful under the Labor Act so long as employees are not threatened or promised benefits, for an employer to assemble its workforce—at large or in small groups—on paid time and require them to hear the employer's views, invariably negative, on unionization. (Sometimes such meetings address political, social, or even religious matters.) May a state legislate forbid an employer from retaliating or discriminating against employees who decline to attend such meetings? *See* N.J. REV. STAT. § 34119–10 (2009); OR. S.B. 519 (2009) (not yet codified). What legal grounding could legitimate this intervention on managerial control? *See generally* Symposium, *The Captive Audience*, 29 COMP. LAB. L. & POL'Y J. 67 (2008).

# 4. DRESS AND GROOMING

## JESPERSEN v. HARRAH'S OPERATING CO.

United States Court of Appeals for the Ninth Circuit, *en banc*, 2006
444 F.3d 1104

\* \* \*

Darlene Jespersen worked successfully as a bartender at Harrah's for twenty years and compiled what by all accounts was an exemplary record. During Jespersen's entire tenure with Harrah's, the company maintained a policy encouraging female beverage servers to wear makeup. The parties agree, however, that the policy was not enforced until 2000. In February 2000, Harrah's implemented a "Beverage Department Image Transformation" program at twenty Harrah's locations, including its casino in Reno. Part of the program consisted of new grooming and appearance standards, called the "Personal Best" program. The program contained certain appearance standards that applied equally to both sexes, including a standard uniform of black pants, white shirt, black vest, and black bow tie. Jespersen has never objected to any of these policies. The program also contained some sex-differentiated appearance requirements as to hair, nails, and makeup.

In April 2000, Harrah's amended that policy to require that women wear makeup. Jespersen's only objection here is to the makeup requirement. The amended policy provided in relevant part:

All Beverage Service Personnel, in addition to being friendly, polite, courteous and responsive to our customer's needs, must possess the ability to physically perform the essential factors of the job as set forth in the standard job descriptions. They must be well groomed, appealing to the eye, be firm and body toned, and be comfortable with maintaining this look while wearing the specified uniform. Additional factors to be considered include, but are not limited to, hair styles, overall body contour, and degree of comfort the employee projects while wearing the uniform. * * *

Beverage Bartenders and Barbacks will adhere to these additional guidelines:

- Overall Guidelines (applied equally to male/ female):
- Appearance: Must maintain Personal Best image portrayed at time of hire.
- Jewelry, if issued, must be worn. Otherwise, tasteful and simple jewelry is permitted; no large chokers, chains or bracelets.
- No faddish hairstyles or unnatural colors are permitted.
- Males:
- Hair must not extend below top of shirt collar. Ponytails are prohibited.
- Hands and fingernails must be clean and nails neatly trimmed at all times. No colored polish is permitted.
- Eye and facial makeup is not permitted.
- Shoes will be solid black leather or leather type with rubber (non skid) soles.
- Females:
- Hair must be teased, curled, or styled every day you work. Hair must be worn down at all times, no exceptions.
- Stockings are to be of nude or natural color consistent with employee's skin tone. No runs.
- Nail polish can be clear, white, pink or red color only. No exotic nail art or length.
- Shoes will be solid black leather or leather type with rubber (non skid) soles.
- *Make up (face powder, blush and mascara) must be worn and applied neatly in complimentary colors. Lip color must be worn at all times. (emphasis added).*

Jespersen did not wear makeup on or off the job, and in her deposition stated that wearing it would conflict with her self-image. It is not disputed that she found the makeup requirement offensive, and felt so uncomfortable wearing makeup that she found it interfered with her ability to perform as a bartender. Unwilling to wear the makeup, and not qualifying for any open positions at the casino with a similar compensation scale, Jespersen left her employment with Harrah's. * * *

In her deposition testimony, attached as a response to the motion for summary judgment, Jespersen described the personal indignity she felt as a result of attempting to comply with the makeup policy. Jespersen testified that when she wore the makeup she "felt very degraded and very demeaned." In addition, Jespersen testified that "it prohibited [her] from doing [her] job" because "[i]t affected [her] self-dignity ... [and] took away [her] credibility as an individual and as a person." Jespersen made no cross-motion for summary judgment, taking the position that the case should go to the jury. Her response to Harrah's motion for summary judgment relied solely on her own deposition testimony regarding her subjective reaction to the makeup policy, and on favorable customer feedback and employer evaluation forms regarding her work. * * *

[Ms. Jespersen argued that Harrah's policy constituted sex discrimination under Title VII of the Civil Rights Act either in its differential application as between men and women, as imposing a differentially higher burden on women, or as being based on unlawful sex stereotyping. She failed to persuade the court, three judges dissenting. Judge Kozinski, writing for the dissent, closed with an expression of "dismay" that the company would:

Didn't win

let go a valued, experienced employee who had gained accolades from her customers, over what, in the end, is a trivial matter. Quality employees are difficult to find in any industry and I would think an employer would long hesitate before forcing a loyal, long-time employee to quit over an honest and heartfelt difference of opinion about a matter of personal significance to her. Having won the legal battle, I hope that Harrahs' will now do the generous and decent thing by offering Jespersen her job back, and letting her give it her personal best—without the makeup.]

## NOTES AND QUESTIONS

1. Dress and grooming standards, especially "no beard" policies or limits on hair length for men, have been extensively litigated on sex discrimination grounds with a uniform lack of success. In *Fagan v. National Cash Register Co.*, 481 F.2d 1115 (D.C. Cir. 1973), for example, a male employee challenged the fact that he was forbidden to have long hair while female employees were not. The court found his real claim had nothing to do with sex discrimination:

Women's long hair ct doesn't care

We have then a situation where a male was indeed employed, and with full knowledge of the company's policy, insisted upon performing his work on his own terms and upon requiring the company to accommodate to his projection of his own image. He claimed the "right" to wear his hair "styled in my personal projection or image in the development of my personality."

*Id.* at 1122. The court would have none of it:

Perhaps no facet of business life is more important than a company's place in public estimation. That the image created by its employees dealing with the public when on company assignment affects its relations is so well known that we may take judicial notice of an employer's proper desire to achieve favorable acceptance. Good grooming regulations reflect a company's policy in our highly competitive business environment.

Reasonable requirements in furtherance of that policy are an aspect of managerial responsibility.

*Id.* at 1124–25.

2. Note the Swiss-cheese-like protection U.S. law affords an employee in Ms. Jespersen's position: She could not sue for an infringement of her common-law right to privacy, because the tort of invasion of privacy recognizes no right of an employee's presentation of herself to society; but if an authentic aspect of a sincerely held religious belief precluded her from wearing makeup, then as a matter of anti-discrimination in employment law her employer would have had to have made at least a minimal effort to accommodate her. *Cf. Cloutier v. Costco Wholesale Corp.*, 390 F.3d 126 (1st Cir. 2004). Because she had no such religious objection, however, we cannot learn whether any accommodation would have been possible. If her aversion to make-up was rooted in some medical or psychiatric condition that disabled her from performing a major life activity—or was perceived by her employer as being such—her employer would, again, have had to have made an effort to accommodate her under the Americans with Disabilities Act; but such was not the ground of her objection. If her employment had been in the District of Columbia, she might have been able to invoke that jurisdiction's prohibition on discrimination due to "personal appearance," but she was not employed there. If she were employed in one of the five states that protect "gender identification" from employer discrimination, she might have been able to invoke that protection; but she wasn't employed in one of them. Consequently, as female employees were required to wear make-up while men were forbidden to do so, she sued on the ground of sex discrimination—and lost.

3. Ms. Jespersen sought redress under sex discrimination law because it was at least arguable that the policy's distinction was unlawful on that ground; but, it really would have been of no consequence to her had male bartenders been subjected to the same proscription. Her real (not her legal) objection, as Judge Kozinski noted, lay not in the discriminatory aspect of her employer's order, but in the power it assumed to control the matter in which she chose to present herself, in an infringement of what she felt to be a private matter, felt so deeply as to lose her job over it. Other legal systems, *e.g.*, Germany and France, for example, acknowledge the right to present one's image as a legitimate claim which triggers a balancing test weighing the strength of the employer's justification—hygiene, safety, potential loss of business due to customer protest of offensive attire (*e.g.*, tongue posts), and even the need to project a professional image—against the employee's right of how to choose to present herself. In German law, contrary to the *Fagan* court, an employee *has* a right to the "free development of personality"—a literal translation of the German legal doctrine (*die freie Entfaltung der Persönlichkeit*).

If that were the issue in *Jesperesen*, how should the balance be struck? Given that employers already owe a duty of reasonable accommodation under a variety of federal and state laws for a variety of reasons and that American multi-national employers must accommodate employees abroad is the matter of hair length, beards, and self-presentation, why should the law not be similarly generalized here, for example, as a matter of good faith and fair dealing? *Per contra Miller v. Safeway, Inc.*, 170 P.3d 655 (Alaska 2007).

## 5. ECONOMIC LIBERTY

We return to the contemporary status of *Payne v. Western & Atlantic Railroad Co.*, of an employee's freedom from control by her employer in choosing what to buy and from whom to buy it. In the upwelling of antagonism toward the rise of corporate power in the late nineteenth century, especially in the South, that has come to be called the Populist Movement, laws limiting an employer's ability to require employers to purchase at company stores were passed in several states. Today, at the behest of the tobacco and alcohol lobbies, about half the states forbid employers from discriminating against employees because of the consumption of one of those products off duty (and having no consequence in the workplace) though a few forbid discrimination on the basis of the consumption of any "lawful product" and three insulate engagement in any lawful activity off the job—with New York separately protecting "recreational activities."

In sum, a century and a quarter after *Payne*, an at-will employee can be dismissed in most states for disobeying an employer's order on where he or she may not shop or what products to buy in what would seem to be a *reductio ad absurdum* of the market autonomy theory of free labor: that the employer's freedom from public accountability as a component of its economic liberty justifies it in constraining the economic liberties of its employees. That was the nub of the dispute between the *Payne* majority and the dissenters; and it continues apace. *Compare* Robert Howie & Laurence Shapero, *Lifestyle Discrimination Statutes: A Dangerous Erosion of At–Will Employment, a Passing Fad, or Both?*, 31 EMP. REL. L. J. 21 (2005) *with* Matthew W. Finkin, *Life Away from Work*, 66 LA. L.REV. 945 (2006).

### QUESTION

A law firm has just acquired a major soft drink company as a client. All employees of the firm have been instructed that they must purchase the client's products exclusively. At a small dinner given by an associate for a few of his colleagues and their significant others, one of the guests noted that her host was using a club soda of the client's competitor. She reported that fact to a senior partner and the associate was fired. Is the discharge actionable? Under what theory?

# CHAPTER VII

# REGULATING PAY AND HOURS OF WORK

■ ■ ■

## A.  INTRODUCTION

### 1.  IMPACT OF LAW ON LABOR COSTS

This chapter and Chapter XI deal with the two main components of employee compensation: pay (wages, salaries, commissions and the like) and benefits. These are the principal factors in "labor costs," a term that includes more than just compensation. For lawyers representing either employees or employers, it is important to see each of these cost factors in the context of others, in order to understand the perspective that employers likely to bring to negotiations, and to the settlement of controversies. This table, giving a quick and incomplete view of major components of labor costs and the principal laws that affect them, may help in understanding that perspective.

| Components | Relevant bodies of law |
|---|---|
| ***Wages*** <br> Regular periodic payments (E.g., hourly wages, weekly or monthly salaries) <br> Commission payments <br> Unit of production payments ("piece rates") <br> Bonuses | Contract doctrine <br> Federal and state wage/hour laws (E.g., Fair Labor Standards Act, state minimum wage laws and wage payment laws, "Living Wage" ordinances) <br> Garnishment restrictions |
| ***Benefits*** <br> Mandated benefit programs <br><br><br><br> Contract-based programs | Social Security laws, including Old Age and Disability Insurance, Medicare <br> Workers compensation laws <br> Unemployment Insurance <br> ERISA |
| ***Administrative costs*** <br> Wages for Human Resource personnel and fees paid to outside firms engaged in recruiting, monitoring, and discharging workers <br><br> Litigation costs in actions brought on behalf of workers <br><br><br><br> Collective bargaining costs for negotiating and administering agreements with unions | All the bodies of law listed above, plus costs of complying with duties imposed by tort law principles governing abusive discharge, defamation and the like; and complying with other regulatory statutes, such as the Occupational Safety and Health Act, various state, federal and local equal employment opportunity laws <br> National Labor Relations Act, Railway Labor Act |

## 2. EVOLUTION OF STATUTORY REGULATION OF PAY AND HOURS

Economically primitive societies can function without wages, work hours or even a clear distinction between work and other activities. However, when an economy relies upon the voluntary submission of some people to abide by the authority of others to direct their productive energies, it becomes necessary to distinguish between work and other activities, to establish means and levels of compensation, and to measure the duration or degree of work efforts.

Complex economic structures make it possible to mobilize the work of large numbers of people over long periods of time. This, in turn, makes it possible to increase both composite and individual productivity. However, complex economic systems also separate most people from the tools and resources for self-sufficiency. Survival, meeting the most basic needs, is available only through participation in that economic system. This poses two challenges. First, how can we ensure that those who depend on such a system have a real chance to participate; and, second, how should the system's production be divided among the participants.

Market economists assert that, all else being equal, if people are motivated to maximize their economic benefits, have perfect knowledge concerning their own and each other's economic activities, are trading in goods or services that are wholly interchangeable and are free to trade or not trade in the goods or services, then the price of the transactions and the level of activity will be established at the point at which there is an equilibrium between the demand and the supply for the particular item or service. Although such theoretical conditions rarely exist in the market for labor, experience demonstrates that the forces of supply and demand do have a significant impact upon the terms and conditions of employment. For example, a scarcity of labor in relation to the demand for workers usually enables the work force to improve wages, benefits and working conditions. An overabundance of workers in relation to the demand for labor usually is accompanied by reduced wages and benefits and less desirable working conditions. In addition, in the latter situation, many people seeking employment may be without work.

Economic changes that result in abrupt alteration of opportunities to participate in the labor market and that produce significant changes in the terms and conditions of employment often have stimulated governmental intervention into the market's adjustments of such matters. The earliest American experience with regulating wage rates probably was the attempt by the Massachusetts Bay Colony, in 1630, to impose a maximum limit upon the daily wage that workers could demand for their efforts. This legislation, adopted in the spirit of the British Statute of Labourers of 1349, was prompted by the fact that the scarcity of labor enabled colonial workers to extract higher wages than were being paid in the mother country. The availability of free cultivatable land provided a ready alternative for workers with the result that, in order to attract the necessary workforce, Massachusetts employers soon were paying more than the established rate.

The scarcity of labor in the New World colonies encouraged employers to seek alternatives to buying their labor through a market system in which the workers could alter their availability and demands. The legal system's toleration and enforcement of slave and indentured labor arrangements provided those alternatives. The latter form of servitude, however, gave rise to legal intervention in the form of what can be characterized as the first American minimum wage laws. As early as 1640, Maryland adopted a law requiring planters to give indentured workers 50 acres, at least five of which were tillable, upon the completion of their term of servitude. Other colonies imposed a variety of similar requirements, usually including the mandatory provision of specified items of clothing, tools and cash to the freed servant. In time, comparable requirements were adopted by many states for the benefit of apprentices who completed their terms of service. Of course, the motivation for such laws may not have been to ensure a minimum rate of compensation for the completed term of work; rather, their purpose may have been to keep such newly liberated workers from becoming impoverished wards of the community.

Although in recent decades minimum wage legislation generally has been combined with regulations limiting or discouraging working employees for an excessive number of daily or weekly hours, in early years legislatures dealt separately with the issues of wage laws and laws regulating the duration of work hours. And, in the development of American labor laws, demands for limits on the duration of work time were more common and more forcefully heard at an earlier era than were those for minimum wage standards. Thus, demands for limits on hours of work can be traced to the 1790s and early 1800s when various craft groups were advocating reduction of the work day from twelve to ten hours. By the mid–1830s, this goal had been achieved by the building trades in several large cities. In 1840, President Van Buren issued an Executive Order establishing a ten-hour day for government shipyard workers. In the next few decades several states adopted toothless laws urging employers to limit the work day to ten or even eight hours. However, until the mid–1930s, federal courts struck down statutes mandating limited work hours, reasoning that they violated a constitutionally protected "freedom of contract" unless the scope of regulation was restricted to very hazardous occupations or to women or children.

Australia and New Zealand adopted minimum wage legislation before the end of the 19th Century and the United Kingdom adopted such legislation in 1909. These examples often were cited by American proponents of minimum wage laws.

The initial American lobbying efforts for such legislation concentrated largely on minimum wage laws for women and children. By 1923, thirteen states had such laws and Congress had passed minimum wage legislation protecting women and children employed in the District of Columbia and Puerto Rico. At the same time, a growing list of other industrial nations were adopting broad minimum wage laws—France in 1915, Austria and Norway in 1918, Czechoslovakia in 1919 and Germany in 1923. However, a majority of the U.S. Supreme Court in *Adkins v. Children's Hospital*, 261 U.S. 525, 43 S.Ct. 394, 67 L.Ed. 785 (1923), ruled that the public interest served by such laws was insufficient to overcome constitutional protection of the worker's and employer's contractual autonomy. This constitutional barrier to state and federal minimum wage legislation persisted until overruled by the Court's decision in *West Coast Hotel Co. v. Parrish*, 300 U.S. 379, 57 S.Ct. 578, 81 L.Ed. 703 (1937). At that point, the nation was struggling to recover from the worst economic depression in the country's history. For example, it is estimated that by the summer of 1932, twenty-five percent of the labor force was unemployed. Minimum wage legislation, coupled with mandatory premium pay for overtime work, was viewed by many as a way to halt the decline of wage rates (e.g., from 1929 to 1933 the average wages of Pittsburgh steelworkers had dropped 38%), stimulate the economy through increased consumer spending, and provide wider distribution of work opportunities.

A different sort of wage statute—the "prevailing wage" law—was generally regarded as more likely to be constitutional, since grounded in the spending power. The general thrust of such laws was to require contractors performing work on government projects to pay the level of wages prevailing in the locality where the work was being done. Kansas enacted the first of these in 1891, and similar laws were eventually passed in more than 40 states (although some have been repealed, including the Kansas statute). A federal prevailing wage law applying to construction projects, the Davis–Bacon Act, was enacted in 1931, in part as a response to the early days of the Great Depression. A similar law applicable to the purchase of goods, the Walsh–Healey Act, came in 1936.

In 1937, several weeks after the Supreme Court upheld the constitutionality of the National Labor Relations Act, President Roosevelt sent a special message to Congress urging adoption of national minimum wage legislation. The initial proposal established a wage floor and would have given a five-member board authority to adopt regulations fixing higher minimum standards for different industries. Prominent union leaders such as John L. Lewis, of the United Mine Workers, and Sidney Hillman, of the Amalgamated Clothing Workers Union, differed with respect to the wisdom of allowing an agency to tailor standards to different industries. One expressed fear was that such regulating would supplant collective bargaining. Another, also expressed by unions, was that the minimum would become a ceiling as well as a floor. Many Southern representatives and senators resisted the concept of a national wage standard. They sought regional differentials that recognized the prevalence of lower wage rates and a lower cost of living in the South. (In 1937 median wages in the textile industry were about 20% lower in the South than in the Northeast. The differential was even greater when compared with the West.)

The legislative struggle continued for over a year, culminating in the adoption of the Fair Labor Standards Act (FLSA). As finally enacted, the statute prohibited various forms of child labor and established a progressively more rigorous system of minimum wages and mandatory premium payments for overtime work. The hourly minimum was set at 25 cents for the first year, 30 cents the next six years and 40 cents after that. However, the Administrator of the Act, who was appointed by the President with the advice and consent of the Senate, was given authority to increase the minimum rate, on an industry by industry basis, up to 40 cents per hour during the first seven years. Such modifications were to be based upon recommendations from industry committees consisting of an equal number of employer, employee and neutral representatives appointed by the Administrator. The Act also required an added premium equal to one half the employee's regular hourly rate to be paid for hours worked in excess of 44 hours a week during the first year of the Act, after 42 hours a week during the second year of the Act, and after 40 hours a week thereafter. The statute required employers to maintain records of hours worked and wages paid, and authorized the Secretary of Labor to develop a system for inspecting those records and investigating whether employers were complying with the law. The Act provided for civil suits by either the Secretary or affected workers as a means of enforcing the statute's requirements, and made some violations criminal offenses.

Adoption of minimum wage laws was motivated in part by a desire to establish a "safety net" of remuneration at a level that enables a worker to provide for the basic costs of existence in an industrial society. It also was motivated in part by the theories of economic planners who sought to stimulate economic growth by shifting more of the nation's wealth into the hands of those with the highest propensity to expend all of their income in consumption of goods and services. The overtime provisions were motivated predominantly by the desire to spread the available work among more workers. Accordingly, they penalize the employer by burdening the payroll with extra costs for meeting increased work demands with the existing work force rather than by expanding opportunities for the jobless. Premium pay requirements for overtime, however, serve a second purpose as well. From the vantage point of the worker who is required to work long hours, premium pay ensures that an added benefit is received to offset the sacrifice of the worker's ability to enjoy the normal amount of rest and leisure.

The statute has been amended several times since it was first placed on the books. The proportion of workers covered by the FLSA has gradually increased, and the minimum hourly wage required has moved in stages from the initial 25 cents to $7.25, as of July 2009. Part of that change, of course, is accounted for by inflation. The 25 cents a worker would earn in 1938 would be roughly equivalent in buying power to $3.72 in 2008.

## 3. EFFICACY OF WAGE AND HOUR REGULATION

Recall from Chapter I that economic analysis provides a logical basis for evaluating labor market regulations like the minimum wage. Under the traditional neoclassical analysis, assuming rational maximization, perfect competition, perfect information and zero transaction costs, the imposition of a minimum wage on a labor market results in some intended and unintended consequences. First, the minimum wage has the intended consequence of increasing the income of all the workers who had previously worked for less than the minimum wage and keep their job. On its own, this consequence might be justified as redistributive and increasing social welfare or allowing and encouraging human capital investment in and by low-wage workers. However, under this model the minimum wage will have other unintended and less desirable consequences. As shown in Figure 1.1 in Chapter I, setting a minimum wage above the market wage will cause employers to employ less low-wage workers, and when these workers are laid off they will go into any unregulated markets and depress wages there. Also, the minimum wage causes inefficiency in production and consumption as employers shift away from low-wage workers and consumers shift away from now more costly low-wage goods.

However, theories are only valuable in policy-making if they bear some relationship to what actually occurs in the real world. Despite the fairly straightforward prediction of the simple neoclassical model that a minimum wage law will lead to decreased employment among low-wage workers, the empirical evidence in support this proposition is remarkably weak. Most of the studies of the effect of minimum wage laws on employment focus on teenagers because for older workers any plausible variation in employment due to the minimum wage is swamped by other factors. It is also argued that any effect of the minimum wage will be larger for teenagers since they are considered more marginal as workers than adults. Early studies that examined variations in teenage employment over time with variations in the federal minimum wage found that an increase in the minimum wage of 10% would decrease teenage employment by 1 to 3%. Later studies that included data from the 1980's reduced the estimated impact on teenage employment from a 10% increase in the minimum wage to less than a 1% decrease in employment. Other studies have taken advantage of the fact that some states set minimum wages in excess of the federal minimum wage, and have studied variations in teenage employment among states with different minimum wages. In the 1990's, studies of this type found that a 10% increase in the minimum wage could result in anything from 8.7% decrease in teenage employment to a 3.7% *increase* in teenage unemployment, with most of the estimates between a decrease of 3% and an increase of 1%. Charles Brown, *Minimum Wages, Employment, and the Distribution of Income*, in HANDBOOK OF LABOR ECONOMICS, VOL. 3B (O. Ashenfelter and D. Card eds 1999) at 2115, 2116, 2134–39. Finally, other studies have examined changes in employment in low-wage industries, such as the retail trade and fast food restaurants, in response to changes in the minimum wage. The two most detailed surveys in this regard yielded estimates that low-wage employment slightly increased with modest increases in the minimum wage. Lawrence Katz and Alan Krueger, *The Effect of the Minimum Wage on the Fast Food Industry*, 46 IND. AND LAB. REL. REV. 6–21 (1992) and David Card and Alan Krueger, *Minimum Wages and Employment: a Case Study of the Fast Food Industry*, 84 AM. ECON. REV. 772–93 (1994). Although both of these studies have been subject to criticism, at the very least they make it hard to reject the hypothesis that modest changes in the minimum wage result in little or no decrease in employment.

Why has the simple economic model fared poorly in this case? Economists have offered various explanations. One explanation is that employer demand for low-wage workers does not vary much with the wage because labor costs are a small part of their cost of doing business, or because their technology of production requires a set number of workers. In Figure I this is the equivalent of arguing that the employers' labor demand curve is approximately vertical over the relevant range. Others have argued that the small observed employment effects from the minimum wage are due to lack of compliance by employers and the cutting of non-wage benefits to make up for improvements in the minimum wage. RONALD G. EHRENBERG AND ROBERT S. SMITH, MODERN LABOR ECONOMICS: THEORY AND PUBLIC POLICY (1982) at 77–78. Finally, some have argued that the ambiguous empirical results suggest that at least some low-wage employers enjoy monopsony power in the purchase of labor. DAVID CARD AND ALAN KRUEGER, MYTH AND MEASUREMENT: THE NEW ECONOMICS OF THE MINIMUM WAGE (1995). This would help explain increases in low-wage employment in response to increases in the minimum wage since the minimum wage reduces the monopsonistic employer's incentive to cut employment in order to drive down wages. GEORGE J. BORJAS, LABOR ECONOMICS (1996) at 177–78.

Of course, more fundamental criticisms of the neoclassical economic model are also possible. One challenge to the standard market theory is that its assumptions are far removed from the reality of how businesses operate and how business, financial, and personal decisions are made. It may be that the assumptions of the neoclassical model, that people are individual rational maximizers with perfect information, zero transaction costs and competitive markets, do not adequately capture significant phenomena in the labor market. It has been observed that: "The mere listing of these rigorous requirements for a perfect labor market makes it clear that actual labor markets depart from the model significantly. Much of the imperfection in the labor market derives from the fact that labor is not a commodity." JUANITA M. KREPS, PHILIP L. MARTIN, RICHARD PERLMAN, GERALD G. SOMERS, CONTEMPORARY LABOR ECONOMICS AND LABOR RELATIONS 43 (1980). As previously mentioned, wages are "sticky downward" and labor markets never "clear" in the sense of supply equaling demand under the simple neoclassical model, and periods of substantial "demand deficient" unemployment can persist for years, as the Great Recession is demonstrating at the time of the writing of this book, or even for more than a decade, as the Great Depression showed. "Since labor cannot be separated from human beings who perform it, adjustments in the supply of labor take longer to work out and may entail human suffering. Nevertheless, supply does adjust upward and downward in response to shifts in employer demand." ROY B. HELFGOTT, LABOR ECONOMICS, 2D ED. at 292–93 (1980).

Regardless of what one thinks of the adequacy or inadequacy of various economic models in analyzing changes in employment that might result from changes in the minimum wage, one could raise questions about the efficacy of the minimum wage law in raising the incomes of poor people. Even if modest increases in the minimum wage do not result in a large or any decrease in low-wage employment, does the minimum wage law significantly raise the incomes of poor people relative to wealthy people? As some minimum wage critics have pointed out, those who work for the minimum wage are not necessarily members of the poorest families. George Stigler, *The Economics of Minimum Wage Legislation*, 36 AM. ECON. REV. 358–65 (1946). Many families have multiple wage earners so that a minimum wage earner, and particularly a secondary earner such as a teenager, may be part of an affluent family. In contrast, many of the poorest families in America are poor precisely because they have no labor income and the minimum wage law does nothing to help them. What do empirical studies tell us about the usefulness of the minimum wage law in promoting a more egalitarian distribution of household income in our society?

Economists have approached this question in a variety of ways. Some have examined what percent of minimum wage workers are "poor" as compared with the rest of the working population.* One of the best studies in this regard found that 23% of adult minimum wage workers were "poor" as compared to 6% of the general population of adult workers. Edward Gramlich, *Impact of Minimum Wage Laws on Other Wages, Employment and Family Income*, 7 BROOKINGS PAPER ON ECONOMIC ACTIVITY 409 (1976). In contrast, the same study found that only 6.6% of minimum wage teenage workers were in poor families as compared with 8.2% of teenagers at all wages. Since minimum wage adults out number minimum wage teens by about two to one, the study's over-all estimate of minimum wage workers who were poor was 18%. Of course this percent may vary over time as the economy prospers or falters and people slip out of and into poverty. Richard Burkhauser & T. Aldrich Finegan, *The Minimum Wage and the Poor: the End of a Relationship*, 8 J. OF POL. ANAL & MANG'T 53 (1989). Others have examined what percent of poor people are minimum wage workers. The most recent study in this regard found that

---

* Of course, these results may vary depending on the definition of poverty that is used. The most common definition that has been used is to define someone as "poor" if their total family income is below the "poverty line," a constructed measure of the minimum family income necessary to maintain that family with a healthful diet and rudimentary clothing and shelter.

only 12.6% of poor families had minimum wage workers and that 25.7% of poor families had no worker at all. Richard Burkhauser, Kenneth Couch & Andrew Glenn, *Public Policies for the Working Poor: the Earned Income Credit Versus the Minimum Wage*, 15 RES. IN LAB. ECON. 65 (1996). Some economists have used these empirical estimates of the distributions of minimum wage and poor workers to run simulations of the impact of changes in the minimum wage on the distribution of income and found that increases in the minimum wage result in roughly equal increases in earnings across all deciles of the income distribution. Id. Of course, starting with an unequal distribution of income, if a policy causes equal increases in income across all deciles, the result of the policy will be a slightly more egalitarian distribution of income. Finally, empirical studies that have directly examined the relationship between the poverty rate and changes in the minimum wage have found a small and statistically insignificant decrease in the poverty rate associated with modest increases in the minimum wage. DAVID CARD & ALAN KRUEGER, MYTH AND MEASUREMENT: THE NEW ECONOMICS OF THE MINIMUM WAGE (Table 9.7) (1995). However, such studies may understate the effect of increases in the minimum wage on poverty since they are based on an absolute rather than a relative definition of poverty and the minimum wage may help people who are relatively poor even though they don't meet the study's definition of falling below the poverty line. Finally, some have argued that the minimum wage improves opportunities for low-wage workers by forcing less productive employers out of the market in favor of more productive employers "[T]he minimum wage helps marginal workers by forcing their inefficient employers either to rationalize [improve productivity by adopting sounder business policies] or to be driven out of business by more efficient competitors paying higher wages.... Increasing the minimum wage, by eliminating the chief prop of such low-productivity firms and industries, will force out of business those who cannot modernize." Marc Linder, *The Minimum Wage as Industrial Policy: A Forgotten Role*, 16 J. OF LEGIS. 151, 155–57 (1990). The more productive firms that are the survivors, can then expand their operations and their workforce, thereby creating higher wage jobs for those who had been employed at low wage firms.

Given what we know about the minimum wage, is it a useful policy? Are there better ways to fight poverty? What would be the result of raising or lowering the minimum wage, or doing away with it all together? Why is the minimum wage so politically controversial if it is in fact as empirically impotent as suggested by the studies above? Is it symbolically important or is it important to the people it affects? In weighing this last question, it might be worthwhile to read BARBARA EHRENREICH, NICKEL AND DIMED: ON (NOT) GETTING BY IN AMERICA (2001), an account of life as a minimum wage worker.

## B.  THE FAIR LABOR STANDARDS ACT

## 1.  COVERED EMPLOYMENT

As originally adopted, the FLSA applied only to work that was performed in the transportation of goods in interstate commerce or in the production of goods for shipment in interstate commerce. (The introductory language of sections 6 and 7 [29 U.S.C. §§ 206, 207] covered only those "engaged in commerce or in the production of goods for commerce.") Accordingly, it was possible for employers to segregate FLSA covered work activity along these lines, pay for that work in accordance with FLSA standards, and thereby pay less than the required FLSA amount for work not covered by the Act. This included paying the same worker in accordance with FLSA standards for the interstate portion of his work activity but a lower rate for the rest. The Act also authorized the Administrator to adopt regulations exempting learners and apprentices from the Act and to certify exemptions for handicapped workers.

A number of refinements were made to the FLSA with the adoption of the Portal-to-Portal Act in 1947. These changes were designed to resolve such questions as when work time begins and the extent to which an employer's good faith conduct excuses liability under the FLSA. Subsequent changes increased the minimum wage standard and substantially broadened the scope of FLSA coverage.

In its initial form, the FLSA reflected a very cautious reading of Congress' power to regulate wages based upon its authority to regulate interstate commerce. Over the next decade Commerce Clause doctrine was reshaped and by the 1960s Congress had little reason to doubt its authority to reach most wage rates. Resulting modifications in the FLSA— adding the concept of "enterprise" as a basis for coverage, discussed in the next case—eliminated the distinction between work performed in the production of goods for interstate commerce, or in the flow of such commerce, from other work. The Act now covers all employees of an enterprise that produces or handles goods produced for, moved in, or that have moved in, interstate commerce so long as the gross volume of annual business meets specified dollar levels or it is a business operating within one of a list of industries. Public employees were added to coverage in 1974. It is estimated that the FLSA originally covered 43% of all non-supervisory, non-agricultural privately employed persons. As a result of the later expansions, it presently covers 80–90% of all such privately employed persons and a significant portion of agricultural and state and local government employees.

The workers not covered by the statute are mostly those exempted from coverage by section 13 (29 U.S.C. § 213.) In its present form, the FLSA gives the Secretary of Labor rulemaking authority to exempt certain executive, administrative and professional employees from coverage. Because such personnel almost by definition are paid in excess of the minimum wage, these exemptions generally are of no importance with respect to the hourly rate. However, the exemption is significant in that it removes the requirement that such workers be paid time and a half for overtime.

Under current law, the Department of Labor has the authority to certify learners, full-time students, apprentices and handicapped employees to receive wages as low as 85% of the minimum rate in the case of learners, students and apprentices, and for the handicapped at a rate set by the employer below minimum but subject to disapproval by the Department of Labor. (The Act prohibits most employment of children under 12 and restricts the type and hours of employment of children 12 and over.)

## (a.) "Employer" Status (Including the Concept of "Enterprise")

The first question to be resolved in applying the FLSA is whether the particular employee is entitled to protection under the Act. The scope of coverage is largely defined by several provisions in section 3, 29 U.S.C.§ 203. Section 3(3) defines the word "employer," section 3(r) defines the word "enterprise," and section 3(s) defines the term "enterprise engaged in commerce or in the production of goods for commerce." Numerous exemptions from either the minimum wage or overtime pay provisions, or both, are scattered throughout the Act. For example, section 6(f) excludes certain household employees from the minimum wage provision and sections 7(i)–(p) partially exclude from the overtime pay provisions various categories of workers (e.g., certain commission salespersons, tobacco auction workers, state and local government workers) under specified conditions. Finally, section 13 exempts from minimum wage and overtime provisions a list of occupations including administrative, executive and professional employees; outside salespersons; employees of certain seasonal recreational or educational operations; catching and gathering marine life; small town newspaper, radio and television reporters; and certain casual employees. The same provision exempts from the mandated overtime premium pay requirement a variety of occupations including employees of certain motor vehicle, air and rail common carriers; seafarers; certain radio and television announcers, editors and engineers employed in small cities; sellers of motor vehicles and motor vehicle parts; agricultural workers; and taxicab drivers.

[The *Arnheim and Neely* case poses the problem of determining the extent to which particular forms of business affiliation alter the employing "enterprise" within the meaning of the FLSA.]

## BRENNAN v. ARNHEIM AND NEELY, INC.

Supreme Court of the United States, 1973
410 U.S. 512, 93 S.Ct. 1138, 35 L.Ed.2d 463

MR. JUSTICE STEWART delivered the opinion of the Court.

This case began when the Secretary of Labor sued the respondent real estate management company for alleged violations of the Fair Labor Standards Act of 1938, as amended, 52 Stat. 1060, 29 U.S.C. § 201 et seq. The Secretary sought an injunction against future violations of the minimum wage, overtime, and recordkeeping provisions of the Act, as well as back wages for the affected employees. An employee is entitled to the benefits of the minimum wage and maximum hours provisions of the Act, if he is, inter alia, "employed in an enterprise engaged in commerce or in the production of goods for commerce * * *." 29 U.S.C. §§ 206(a), 207(a).

 As stipulated in the District Court, the respondent company manages eight commercial office buildings and one apartment complex in the Pittsburgh area. With the exception of a minor ownership interest in one of the buildings, the respondent does not own these properties. Its services are provided according to management contracts entered into with the owners. Under these contracts, the respondent obtains tenants for the buildings, negotiates and signs leases, institutes whatever legal actions are necessary with respect to these leases, and generally manages and maintains the properties. The respondent collects rental payments on behalf of the owners, and deposits them in separate bank accounts for each building. These accounts, net of management expenses and the respondent's fees, belong to the owners of the properties. Payments are periodically made from the accounts to these owners.

The respondent's services with respect to the supervisory, maintenance, and janitorial staffs of the buildings are similarly extensive. The respondent conducts the hiring, firing, payroll operations, and job supervision of those employed in the buildings. It also fixes hours of work, and negotiates rates of pay and fringe benefits—subject to the approval of the owners. The respondent engages in collective bargaining on behalf of the owners where the building employees are unionized. D.C., 324 F. Supp. 987, 990–991. * * *

In order to resolve the intercircuit conflict, we granted the Secretary's petition for certiorari, 409 U.S. 840, 93 S. Ct. 56, 34 L. Ed.2d 79, which raises the question whether the management activities of the respondent at all of the buildings served should be aggregated as part of a single "enterprise" within the meaning of § 3(r) of the Act. Since no cross-petition for certiorari was filed by the respondent, the important issues of whether the respondent is in fact an "employer" of the building workers within the meaning of the Act, and whether gross rentals rather than gross commissions should serve as the measure of "gross sales," are not before us.

The concept of "enterprise" under the Fair Labor Standards Act came into being with the 1961 amendments, which substantially broadened the coverage of the Act. Rather than confining the protections of the Act to employees who were themselves "engaged in commerce or in the production of goods for commerce," 29 U.S.C. §§ 206(a), 207(a), the new amendments brought those "employed in an enterprise engaged in commerce" within the ambit of the minimum wage and maximum hours provisions. The Congress defined "enterprise engaged in commerce" to include a dollar volume limitation. The standard in the original amendments included "any such enterprise which has one or more retail or service establishments if the annual gross volume of sales of such enterprise is not less than $1,000,000 * * *," 75 Stat. 66, and has since been changed to include enterprises "whose annual gross volume of sales made or business done is not less than $500,000" for the period from February 1, 1967, to January 31, 1969, and those with annual gross sales of not less than $250,000 thereafter. 29 U.S.C. § 203(s)(1). The presence of this dollar-volume cutoff for coverage under the Act, in turn, places importance on the Act's definition of "enterprise."

*Dollar Value*

The term "enterprise" is defined by the statute as follows:

'Enterprise' means the related activities performed (either through unified operation or common control) by any person or persons for a common business purpose, and includes all such activities whether performed in one or more establishments or by one or more corporate or other organizational units * * *.

*Def in statute*

29 U.S.C. § 203(r) (emphasis added). Specific exemptions are noted, making clear that exclusive-dealership arrangements, collective-purchasing pools, franchises, and leases of business premises from large commercial landlords do not create "enterprises" within the meaning of the Act. Ibid.

The District Court correctly identified the three main elements of the statutory definition of "enterprise": related activities, unified operation or common control, and common business purpose. We believe the Court of Appeals erred in holding that the aggregate management activities of the respondent failed to meet these statutory criteria. Once the respondent is recognized to be the employer of all of the building employees, it follows quite simply that it is a single enterprise under the Act. The respondent is, after all, but one company. Its activities in all of the buildings are virtually identical, and are plainly "related" in the sense that Congress intended. As the Senate report accompanying the 1961 amendments indicated: "Within the meaning of this term, activities are 'related' when they are the same or similar * * *." S. Rep. No. 145, 87th Cong., 1st Sess., 41; U.S. Code Congressional & Admin. News, 1961, p. 1660. The respondent's activities, similarly, are performed "either through unified operation or common control." The respondent is a fully integrated management company directing operations at all nine buildings from its central office. For purposes of determining whether it is an "enterprise" under the Act, it is irrelevant that the relationship between the respondent and the owners is one of agency; that separate bank accounts are maintained for each building; and that the risk of loss and the chance of gain on capital investment belong to the owners, not the respondent. All that is required under the statutory definition is that the respondent's own activities be related and under common control or unified operation, as they plainly are.

In its analysis of this problem, the Court of Appeals placed great weight on the fact that the building owners have no relationship with one another, and have no common business purpose. This is true, but beside the point, for the owners are not defendants in this action and it is not *their* activities that are under examination. As Judge Winter wrote in the conflicting case from the Fourth Circuit, "It is *defendants'* activities at each building which must be held together by a common business purpose, not all the activities of all owners of apartment projects." *Shultz v. Falk,* 439 F.2d, at 346. In the present case, the respondent's activities at the several locations are tied together by the common business purpose of managing commercial properties for profit. The fact that the buildings are separate establishments is specifically made irrelevant by § 3(r).

The Court of Appeals also cited the portion of the Senate report explaining the exemptions to § 3(r), noted above, for exclusive-dealing contracts, franchises, leasing space in shopping centers, and the like:

> The bill also contains provisions which should insure that a small local independent business, not in itself large enough to come within the new coverage, will not become subject to the act by being considered a part of a large enterprise with which it has business dealings.

> The definition of 'enterprise' expressly makes it clear that a local retail or service establishment which is under independent ownership shall not be considered to be so operated and controlled as to be other than a separate enterprise because of a franchise, or group purchasing, or group advertising arrangement with other establishments or because the establishment leases premises from a person who also happens to lease premises to other retail or service establishments.

S. Rep. No. 145, 87th Cong., 1st Sess., 41.

The Court of Appeals went on to stress that the building owners should not be brought under the Act simply because they dealt with a large real estate management company. This is true, but also beside the point, since we deal here with that large management company as a party and, for purposes of this case, as an employer of the employees in question. We do not hold, nor could we in this case, that the individual building owners in their capacity as employers[5] are to be aggregated to

---

**5.** As both the District Court and the Court of Appeals noted, the statutory concept of "employer" is "any person acting directly or indirectly in the interest of an employer in relation to an employee * * *." 29 U.S.C. § 203(d). This definition was held to be broad enough that there might be "several simultaneous 'employers.'" 444 F.2d, at 611–612. See also 324 F. Supp. 987,

create some abstract "enterprise" for purposes of the Fair Labor Standards Act.[6]

It is argued that such a straight-forward application of the statutory criteria to the respondent's business ignores the significance of the dollar volume limitation included in the § 3(s) definition of "[e]nterprise engaged in commerce or in the production of goods for commerce." The Court of Appeals cited evidence in the legislative history of the 1961 amendments that indicates a purpose to exempt small businesses from the obligations of the Act. 444 F.2d, at 613; S. Rep. No. 145, 87th Cong., 1st Sess. 5. If the individual building owners are engaged in enterprises too small to come within the reach of the Fair Labor Standards Act, reasoned the Court of Appeals, it would be "anomalous" to treat them as a single enterprise subject to the Act "merely because they hire a rental agent who manages other buildings." 444 F.2d, at 614. Once again, however, the response to this argument is that it is the respondent management company not the individual building owners, that has been held in this case to be an "employer" of all the affected "employees." Furthermore, the proper measure of the respondent's size has been held to be the gross rentals produced by properties under its management. It is true that one purpose of the dollar-volume limitation in the statutory definition of "enterprise" is the exemption of small businesses, but this respondent is not such a business under these holdings of the Court of Appeals.[7] The argument to the contrary amounts to a collateral attack on the "employer" and "gross sales" determinations made below, and the respondent cannot make such an attack in the absence of a cross-petition for certiorari.[8]

We hold that the District Court was correct in aggregating all of the respondent's management activities as a single "enterprise." Accordingly, the judgment of the Court of Appeals is reversed and the case is remanded to the Court of Appeals for further proceedings consistent with this opinion.

It is so ordered. * * *

[JUSTICE WHITE dissented.]

---

992; *Wirtz v. Hebert*, 5 Cir., 368 F.2d 139; *Mid–Continent Pipe Line Co. v. Hargrave*, 10 Cir., 129 F.2d 655.

**6.** Contrary to the view taken by the dissent, we specifically do not hold that "the buildings and the management company collectively are an enterprise * * *." We deal solely with the management company and *its* "related activities performed * * * for a common business purpose."

**7.** It is stipulated that in all relevant years, the annual gross rental income collected by the respondent exceeded $1,000,000. 324 F. Supp., at 993.

**8.** We have granted certiorari in No. 72–844, *Falk v. Brennan*, sub nom. *Falk v. Brennan*, 410 U.S. 954, 93 S. Ct. 1419, 35 L.Ed.2d 686, to consider whether the proper measure of "gross sales" in this context is gross rentals collected or gross commissions, and whether maintenance employees are "employees" of the management company within the meaning of the Act.

## NOTES AND QUESTIONS

1.   In *Falk v. Brennan*, 414 U.S. 190, 94 S.Ct. 427, 38 L.Ed.2d 406 (1973), the Court held that the dollar volume of business done by a real estate management firm should be measured by the commissions earned rather than by the rents collected. Which figure do you think better reflects the management firm's impact upon interstate commerce? Upon wage rates affecting commerce?

Why does Congress draw jurisdictional lines for this law? At one time the answer may have been constitutional. But doesn't modern constitutional doctrine provide ways to avoid that? Are the lines drawn due to concern for the financial capacity of small businesses? Why should the employees of such businesses be less protected than others? Is it because Congress fears that bringing them within the federal standard would put the employer out of business and leave such workers jobless? Or, are the lines drawn as a matter of administrative convenience to ensure more effective use of limited enforcement resources? If the latter, would it be more reasonable to draw the lines based on the number of persons employed by an entity?

Often, Congress uses the number of employees in an enterprise as the threshold for applying employee rights legislation. Examples include Title VII of the 1964 Civil Rights Act, which protects against discrimination based on race, religion and national origin, and the Family and Medical Leave Act, which provides unpaid leave to attend to certain categories of personal needs. Is there a substantive difference in these approaches or are they rough proxies of each other?

2.   The "related activities" criterion often is difficult to delimit. In *Wirtz v. Savannah Bank & Trust*, 362 F.2d 857 (5th Cir.1966), a bank that owned a 15 story building occupied 4 floors for its banking operations and leased the remaining floors. The office rentals were held to be "related activities" because the rent helped the bank spread the high costs of occupying a downtown location, a location that enhanced the bank's stature in the community.

"Unified operation" and "common control" issues often involve situations in which the same group of individuals (sometimes family members) have ownership interests in several different corporate entities, and those entities have a single advertising program, employee selection process, or purchasing procedures. These cases frequently involve interlocking boards of directors as well. See, e.g., *Reich v. Bay, Inc.*, 23 F.3d 110 (5th Cir. 1994). Frequent interchange of employees or clients is also evidence of these factors. See *Chao v. A–One Medical Services, Inc.*, 346 F.3d 908 (9th Cir. 2003).

Suppose a group of affiliated companies owns an office building, a restaurant and a hotel that have a composite income that brings the enterprise within the FLSA. Assume, too, that none of the individual companies has adequate income to bring it within the Act. Under what conditions would the entire entity be treated as an enterprise covered by the FLSA? Even if the buildings were distant from each other, would the enterprise be covered if a single management firm handled all of the maintenance, repair, security and accounting for the three facilities? Do any of these variables make any difference to the welfare of the employees of the various facilities or their dependents? How should "enterprise" be defined in order to best carry out the purposes of the FLSA?

3. While the notion of what sorts of activity may have a sufficient connection to interstate commerce to trigger coverage has broadened over the years, there are still on occasion highly localized businesses that are held not to be "engaged in commerce." See, e,g., *Bien–Aime v. Nanak's Landscaping, Inc.*, 572 F. Supp. 2d 1312 (S.D. Fla. 2008).

4. Under section 3(d), 29 U.S.C. § 203(d), "employer" includes "any person acting directly or indirectly in the interest of an employer...." Under this language an individual who dominates the operation of a corporation may be held personally liable for violations of the FLSA. See the analysis in *Chao v. Hotel Oasis, Inc*, 493 F.3d 26 (1st Cir. 2007).

5. Many workers in the United States are hired through labor contractors, who recruit the workers and send them to perform duties for (and often under the supervision of) the labor contractors' clients. In such a situation, both the labor contractor and the contractor's client may be joint "employers" for FLSA purposes. Joint employment may also occur when the work of a contractor and subcontractor are performed in the same locale and with significant coordination. See, e.g., *Reyes v. Remington Hybrid Seed Co., Inc.* 495 F.3d 403 (7th Cir. 2007); *Schultz v. Capital International Security, Inc.*, 466 F.3d 298 (4th Cir. 2006) (security firm supplying guards and client Saudi prince both employers of guards); *Zheng v. Liberty Apparel Co.*, 355 F.3d 61 (2d Cir. 2003) (integrated production process involving careful supervision by contracting-out firm over work performed by sub-contractors); *Martinez–Mendoza v. Champion International Corp.*, 340 F.3d 1200 (11th Cir. 2003) (no joint employment when labor contractor rather than client provided great majority of supervision of workers). The *Zheng* case provides a melancholy reminder of how long it can take to obtain relief in cases involving FLSA violations in a multiple employer setting. The 26 worker-plaintiffs filed their action in August 1999, alleging repeated violations of the minimum wage, overtime and record-keeping requirements of the FLSA and also of New York state wage payment laws. Taking depositions about who knew of the violations, and just what business entities were involved in supervision of the work required considerable time. In 2002, the district court ruled against the plaintiffs on their claim that defendant Liberty Apparel, a company that farmed out garment work to a series of small firms, was an "employer" for FLSA purposes, and dismissed Liberty Apparel as a defendant. In 2003, in the opinion cited above, the Second Circuit reversed. Trial of the case got underway in late January 2009.

## (b.) "Employee" Status

## BAKER v. FLINT ENGINEERING & CONSTRUCTION COMPANY

U.S. Court of Appeals, Tenth Circuit, 1998
137 F.3d 1436

BRISCOE, CIRCUIT JUDGE.

Plaintiffs are a group of rig welders in the natural gas pipeline construction industry. They filed this action against Flint Engineering & Construction Company for overtime compensation under the Fair Labor Standards Act (FLSA), 29 U.S.C. § 201 et seq. Flint appeals the district court's entry of summary judgment in favor of plaintiffs, contending the court erred in concluding plaintiffs were employees of Flint rather than independent contractors. We exercise jurisdiction under 28 U.S.C. § 1291 and affirm.

I.

Flint is a corporation engaged in the construction, installation, and servicing of oil and gas pipelines and related facilities for the oil and gas industry in the "Four Corners" region of New Mexico. In particular, Flint is routinely hired as a general contractor by oil and gas companies to build natural gas pipelines and compressor stations which transport natural gas from the wellheads to the owner's main processing plants.

When Flint is the successful bidder on a project (or is otherwise hired to complete a project), it hires a variety of workers, including rig welders, to assist in completion of the project. Rig welders (a/k/a pipe welders) perform skilled welding on pipes, sheet metal, and other portions of gas industry facilities. They are routinely tested and certified by project owners to insure they can perform their jobs. They provide their own welding equipment, which is typically mounted on flat-bed pickup trucks. The equipped trucks are referred to as "welding rigs," and each welding rig costs between $35,000 and $40,000. Rig welders are also responsible for costs of stocking their welding rigs with supplies, as well as for necessary repairs to the rigs. Rig welders do not bid on jobs and do not have contractor's licenses that would enable them to do so.

Flint simply hires rig welders at a set hourly rate to work on particular projects. Flint does not negotiate the hourly rate, and sometimes pays on a "straight contract" basis at approximately $27 to $30 per hour, and sometimes on a "split check" basis at a rate of $10 per hour for labor and $17 per hour for rig rental.

Work on a project is typically conducted six days a week, twelve to fourteen hours per day. Rig welders are supervised by Flint foremen and are required to arrive, take breaks, and leave at times specified by the foremen. They are not allowed to complete their work when they want and, in most cases, it would be impossible for them to do so because they must coordinate their work with the other crafts and because other equipment and workers are necessary to move pipe for welding. Rig welders are not provided project blueprints. Instead, the foremen map out what pipes they want built and in what order. The foremen do not establish the welding specifications and standards, nor do they tell rig welders how to weld or how long a particular weld should take. Welding specifications and standards are established by the customer (i.e., the project owner) and the quality of welding is overseen by an inspector hired by the customer. Because of the nature of their work, rig welders (and other pipeline workers) would be unemployed after completion of a project if they did not seek work on new projects. Accordingly, it is common for rig welders to work for several different companies during the course of a year.

Prior to July 1, 1991, Flint considered rig welders as independent contractors and asked each rig welder to sign a document entitled "Agreement With Independent Contractor," which stated: "It is the intent of the parties involved to establish and maintain an 'independent relationship' rather than an employer-employee relationship. All Federal, State and Local laws, regulations, and guidelines should be adhered to accordingly. The Independent Contractor is responsible for maintaining adequate amounts of insurance."

The agreements did not indicate how long the "independent relationship" was to last, did not refer to specific projects or project specifications, and did not indicate how much the welder was to be paid. Although Flint began characterizing rig welders as employees on and after July 1, 1991, no other substantial changes took place in the way they were hired or treated.

Flint treats the majority of workers on each project as employees. For example, job foremen are treated and paid as employees, as are laborers, pipefitters, and welders' helpers (all of whom, like rig welders, are hired on a per project basis). Flint treats a few other workers (e.g., insulation workers, electrical workers) on each project as subcontractors or independent contractors. These subcontractors are paid on a lump-sum basis or a unit basis.

Plaintiffs filed this action on February 5, 1993, claiming violations of the FLSA. The parties filed cross-motions for summary judgment, all of which focused on whether plaintiffs were employees of Flint prior to July 1, 1991, for purposes of the FLSA. The district court conducted an evidentiary hearing and, on May 26, 1994, granted summary judgment in favor of plaintiffs on the independent contractor/employee issue, concluding plaintiffs were employees prior to July 1, 1991. * * *

## II.

The FLSA defines an employee as "any individual employed by an employer." 29 U.S.C. § 203(e)(1). In turn, "employer" is defined as including "any person acting directly or indirectly in the interest of an employer in relation to an employee." 29 U.S.C. § 203(d). The FLSA "defines the verb 'employ' expansively to mean 'suffer or permit to work.'" *Nationwide Mut. Ins. Co. v. Darden*, 503 U.S. 318, 326, 117 L. Ed.2d 581, 112 S. Ct. 1344 (1992) (quoting 29 U.S.C. § 203(g)). The Supreme Court has emphasized that the "striking breadth" of this latter definition "stretches the meaning of 'employee' to cover some parties who might not qualify as such under a strict application of traditional agency law principles." Id. Thus, in determining whether an individual is covered by the FLSA, "our inquiry is not limited by any contractual terminology or by traditional common law concepts of 'employee' or 'independent contractor.'" *Henderson v. Inter–Chem Coal Co., Inc.*, 41 F.3d 567, 570 (10th Cir.1994) (citing *Dole v. Snell*, 875 F.2d 802, 804 (10th Cir.1989)). Instead, the economic realities of the relationship govern, and "the focal point is 'whether the individual is economically dependent on the business to which he renders service ... or is, as a matter of economic fact, in business for himself.'" Id. The economic reality test includes inquiries into whether the alleged employer has the power to hire and fire employees, supervises and controls employee work schedules or conditions of employment, determines the rate and method of payment, and maintains employment records. *Watson v. Graves*, 909 F.2d 1549, 1553 (5th Cir. 1990).

In applying the economic reality test, courts generally look at (1) the degree of control exerted by the alleged employer over the worker; (2) the worker's opportunity for profit or loss; (3) the worker's investment in the business; (4) the permanence of the working relationship; (5) the degree of skill required to perform the work; and (6) the extent to which the work is an integral part of the alleged employer's business. *Henderson*, 41 F.3d at 570. In deciding whether an individual is an employee or an independent contractor under the FLSA, a district court acting as the trier of fact must first make findings of historical facts surrounding the individual's work. Second, drawing inferences from the findings of historical facts, the court must make factual findings with respect to the six factors set out above. Finally, employing the Findings with respect to the six factors, the court must decide, as a matter of law, whether the individual is an "employee" under the FLSA. Id. at 571. None of the factors alone is dispositive; instead, the court must employ a totality-of-the-circumstances approach. Id. at 570

In reviewing the district court's decision on appeal, we review the two types of factual findings (findings of historical fact, and findings with respect to the six factors) for clear error. The ultimate determination of whether an individual is an employee or an independent contractor for purposes of the FLSA is a question of law, which we review de novo. Id. at 571.

### Control

The district court found Flint's "degree of control over the rig welders, and the Plaintiffs' lack of independence over setting their work hours, work crews and other details of their welding work, is more consistent with employee rather than independent contractor status." R.I. 272. After carefully reviewing the record on appeal, we conclude this finding is not clearly erroneous.

 *Employee; not clearly erroneous.*

As in *Dole,* "the record does not support any inference that these [rig welders] act[] autonomously, or with any degree of independence which would set them apart from what one would consider normal employee status." 875 F.2d at 806. Instead, Flint's foremen tell the rig welders when to report to work, when to take breaks, on what portion of the project they will be working, and when their workday ends. The record indicates rig welders cannot perform their work on their own schedule; rather, pipeline work has assembly line qualities in that it requires orderly and sequential coordination of various crafts and workers to construct a pipeline. The record further indicates plaintiffs work on only one project at a time and do not offer services to third parties while a project is ongoing. Indeed, the hours plaintiffs are required to work on a project (ten to fourteen hours a day, six days a week), coupled with driving time between home and often remote work sites each day, make it practically impossible for them to offer services to other employers. In short, very little about plaintiffs' work situation makes it possible to view plaintiffs as persons conducting their own businesses. See id. at 808.

### Opportunity for profit or loss

In analyzing the second factor, the district court found plaintiffs are paid at a fixed hourly rate, plaintiffs have no opportunity to experience a loss on the job site, plaintiffs' ability to control costs of welding supplies does not necessarily enable them to make a profit, and plaintiffs' ability to maximize their wages by "hustling" new work is not synonymous with making a profit. Based on these findings, the court found "Plaintiffs had no opportunity to experience a profit or loss consistent with the characteristics of being independent businessmen." These findings are not clearly erroneous. ②

If plaintiffs could bid on jobs at a set amount and correspondingly set their own hours or schedule, they would have the opportunity for profit or loss. However, plaintiffs are hired on a per-hour basis rather than on a flat-rate-per-job basis. There is no incentive for plaintiffs to work faster or more efficiently in order to increase their opportunity for profit. Moreover, there is absolutely no risk of loss on plaintiffs' part. Plaintiffs exercise independent initiative only in locating new work assignments. While working on a particular assignment, there is little or no room for initiative (certainly none related to profit or loss). There is no indication plaintiffs share in the profits (or losses) of Flint's business. See *Dole,* 875 F.2d at 809. "In short, the [rig welders] have no control over the essential determinants of profits in a business, and no direct share in the success of the business." Id. at 810.

### Investment in business

The district court found plaintiffs have substantial investments in their welding rigs and that twenty-five to fifty percent of their compensation is based on their furnishing rigs. Although the court further found Flint's investment in the overall business far exceeds plaintiffs' investments, it nevertheless found "Plaintiffs' investment in this industry, and their compensation which is based on this investment, is more consistent with finding the rig welders independent contractors."

The investment "which must be considered as a factor is the amount of large capital expenditures, such as risk capital and capital investments, not negligible items, or labor itself." *Dole*, 875 F.2d at 810. This factor "is interrelated to the profit and loss consideration." *Lauritzen*, 835 F.2d 1529, 1537. "Courts have generally held that the fact that a worker supplies his or her own tools or equipment does not preclude a finding of employee status." *Dole*, 875 F.2d at 810. In making a finding on this factor, it is appropriate to compare the worker's individual investment to the employer's investment in the overall operation. See id. (comparing defendants' relative investment as cake decorators with employer's overall investment in bakery business); *Lauritzen*, 835 F.2d at 1537 (comparing migrant workers' capital investment with employer's overall investment in pickle-farming operation).

The district court is clearly correct in finding plaintiffs' investments in their welding rigs are significant (at least when compared to other workers), and in finding a significant portion of plaintiffs' pay is based on their furnishing rigs. However, plaintiffs' investments are disproportionately small when compared to Flint's investment in the overall business. Several witnesses testified that Flint routinely had hundreds of thousands of dollars of equipment at each work site. Compared to Flint's investment in the overall business, plaintiffs' investments are not so significant as to indicate they are independent contractors.

### Permanency of working relationship

The district court found plaintiffs rarely work for Flint more than two months at any one time, and rarely for more than three months during any twelve-month period. However, the court found plaintiffs remain on the job site until the necessary welding is done. Thus, the court found "Plaintiffs' lack of permanence is due to natural characteristics in the industry, and not the independent choice usually exhibited by one who intentionally chooses to be in business for oneself. Therefore, while rig welders are temporary workers, this finding is of little relevance in determining whether these Plaintiffs are employees or independent contractors."

Generally speaking, " 'independent contractors' often have fixed employment periods and transfer from place to place as particular work is offered to them, whereas 'employees' usually work for only one employer and such relationship is continuous and of indefinite duration." *Dole*, 875

F.2d at 811. However, "many seasonal businesses necessarily hire only seasonal employees, [and] that fact alone does not convert seasonal employees into seasonal independent contractors." *Lauritzen*, 835 F.2d at 1537.

We agree with the district court's findings on this factor. Although *Employee* plaintiffs exhibit characteristics generally typical of independent contractors as regards the short duration of their employment relationships and their frequent relocation to find employment, these characteristics of plaintiffs' employment are clearly due to the intrinsic nature of oil and gas pipeline construction work rather than any choice or decision on the part of plaintiffs. Notably, the record indicates the majority of workers employed by Flint (e.g., pipefitters, laborers, etc.) work on the same basis as plaintiffs and are nevertheless treated as employees. We conclude it is appropriate to characterize plaintiffs' relationship with Flint as "permanent and exclusive for the duration of" the particular job for which they are hired. Id. at 1537 (migrant workers' relationship with single farming operation was permanent and exclusive for duration of single harvest season).

### Degree of skill required to perform work

The district court found plaintiffs "are highly skilled individuals" and are, in fact, "the most skilled employees on a transmission systems project." However, the court further found plaintiffs do not "make any independent judgments on the job site," and thus do not exercise their skills "in any independent manner." Id. The court further found Flint does not attempt to hire the most skilled available rig welders nor does it negotiate pay depending on the level of skill possessed.

> Most independent contractors develop a business relationship with many contractors based on their expertise. If they do superior work they are often sought out in the future. Part of the reason is that the contractor comes to trust their skills and depends upon their judgment in completing their tasks. Here there is [sic] no such judgment decisions expected of the rig welders and, consequently, Defendant[] does not discriminate between rig welders [it] hires. In light of the fact that the Plaintiffs do not exercise any initiative or make any judgment decisions on the job site, the Court finds that Plaintiffs' skills are not indicative of independent contractor status.

Id. at 281–82.

The district court's findings on this factor are not clearly erroneous. Although "the lack of the requirement of specialized skills is indicative of employee status," *Dole*, 875 F.2d at 811, "the use of special skills is not itself indicative of independent contractor status, especially if the workers do not use those skills in any independent way." *Martin v. Selker Bros., Inc.*, 949 F.2d 1286, 1295 (3d Cir.1991). As noted by the district court, plaintiffs are highly skilled but they did not exercise those skills in any independent fashion in their employment with Flint. Although plaintiffs are not told by Flint how to complete a particular weld, they are told by Flint foremen when and where to weld. Accordingly, the fact that plaintiffs use special skills does not necessarily indicate they are independent contractors.

### Integral part of business

After noting this factor focuses on whether workers' services are a necessary component of the business, the district court found "rig welders are necessary in the construction of all transmission systems projects," and, although "they do not remain on the job site from start to finish, their work is a critical step on every transmission system project." These findings are not clearly erroneous. The evidence in the record on appeal clearly indicates rig welders' work is an important, and indeed integral, component of oil and gas pipeline construction work.

### Economic dependence of plaintiffs

Our final step is to review the findings on each of the above factors and determine whether plaintiffs, as a matter of economic fact, depend upon Flint's business for the opportunity to render service, or are in business for themselves. *Dole*, 875 F.2d at 804; *Brock v. Superior Care, Inc.*, 840 F.2d 1054, 1059 (2d Cir.1988). Although Flint urges us to focus on whether plaintiffs rely on Flint for their subsistence, we believe the question is whether plaintiffs are economically dependent upon Flint during the time period they work for Flint, however long or short that period may be. In other words, "the dependence at issue is dependence on that job for that income to be continued and not necessarily for complete sustenance." *Halferty v. Pulse Drug Co., Inc.*, 821 F.2d 261, 267 (5th Cir.1987).

In arguing plaintiffs are independent contractors, Flint relies heavily on *Carrell v. Sunland Const., Inc.*, 998 F.2d 330, 334 (5th Cir.1993), where the court held rig welders working for natural gas pipeline construction companies in Louisiana and other states were independent contractors for purposes of the FLSA. Although we agree the facts here are strikingly similar to those in *Carrell*, there are factual differences. For example, the court in *Carrell* emphasized the rig welders before it were highly skilled, but made no mention of whether those welders were free to exercise their judgment in completing their work. Here, the district court specifically found that although plaintiffs are highly skilled, they are not free to exercise those skills in any independent manner when they work for Flint. Plaintiffs are specifically told when and where to weld and have no authority to override those decisions. They are told when to report to work, when to take breaks, and when to end their workday.

Aside from differences in historical fact, we also disagree with the finding in *Carrell* that rig welders have an opportunity to maximize their profits by controlling the costs of their welding supplies and by consistently finding work with other companies. Instead, we agree with the district court that this is not the type of "profit" typically associated with an independent contractor. Generally speaking, an independent contractor has the ability to make a profit or sustain a loss due to the ability to bid on projects at a flat rate and to complete projects as it sees fit. Here, plaintiffs have neither the ability to bid on projects nor to complete their work in an independent fashion.

Ultimately, we agree with the district court and conclude plaintiffs are employees of Flint, rather than independent contractors, for purposes of the FLSA. In most respects, plaintiffs are no different from any other workers hired by Flint and treated as employees. Plaintiffs are hired to complete a job, are told their working hours, are told their hourly pay rate, and are told on what portion of the project they will be working during a given workday. Although plaintiffs are the most skilled workers on the job site, they are not asked to exercise their discretion in applying their skills; they are told what to do and when to do it. The only substantial difference between plaintiffs and the other workers on the job site is that plaintiffs are required to supply equipment to perform their jobs. This fact alone, however, does not alter the realities of their working situation. Nor does it allow them to make any type of substantial profit above wages they are paid. Ultimately, plaintiffs, like other workers hired by Flint, are dependent upon Flint for the opportunity to render services for however long a particular project lasts.

### NOTES AND QUESTIONS

1. What was the appropriate measure of damages for the welders? What do you think Flint assumed it would be paying welders when it bid on this work? Was the result fair to the employer? To competing bidders? Would these welders have been without this employment had Flint not won the bid?

2. Compare the facts in Sunland Construction (cited in *Flint*) with *Brennan v. A–1 Heating and Air Conditioning Service Company*, 73 CCH LC ¶ 33,043, 1973 WL 992 (D.Neb.1973), which similarly found an independent contractor relationship. In that case air conditioner installers operated out of an office provided by the company that sold the units, used its heavy duty tools and facilities for preparatory work, were paid weekly by the seller, and were paid for calls even if the customer was not at home and the work could not be done. On the other hand, the installers were not required to accept job assignments or the proposed amount of payment for a specific job. In addition, they provided their own hand tools, paid for helpers when needed, and controlled the manner in which they performed their work.

Professor Linder, borrowing from one of Justice Douglas' dissenting opinions, suggests that the test should be whether the person claiming FLSA protection is in the same boat as an employee. Accordingly, Linder would extend protection to "dependent contractors" as well as to employees. Would that approach help in deciding any of the above cases?

3. On a number of occasions courts have had to determine whether farmers employing "contract labor" to harvest crops are required to comply with the FLSA. For example, in *Donovan v. Brandel*, 736 F.2d 1114 (6th

Cir.1984), the issue was whether pickle harvesters were farm employees covered by the child labor and record keeping provisions of the FLSA, or were independent contractors. The farmer in this case contracted with the heads of several families, some migrant and some local, for family members to harvest the pickle crop. About half of the families returned each year. Each family was assigned a particular field and planting was scheduled so as to accommodate the family's availability. The harvesters worked 30–40 days and were paid weekly a 50% share of the price for which the harvested pickles were sold to processors. (This worked out to be $6–9 per hour.) Children helped by carrying containers and hauling drinking water. As they grew older, children helped by picking as well. Holding that the relationship in this case was one of independent contractor, the court made the following points: First, the issue of whether there is FLSA coverage is one of law; secondly, cases of this sort must be determined on a case-by-case basis in light of the whole business activity; third, economic dependence "may be the ultimate controlling factor in a given situation." The court also reasoned that the nature of the tenure of the parties' relationship was more "a product of a mutually satisfactory arrangement" than a permanent relationship. It also found that there were elements of skill and judgment required for maximum harvest production and that those elements worked to increase the harvesters' earnings. The court compared the harvesting method used on this farm with pickle harvesting by untrained pieceworkers or by mechanical methods and determined that the latter systems were less productive. Finally, the court was influenced by the fact that the services of the harvesting families were in demand in the region and the work did not involve either long hours or low wages.

*Secretary of Labor v. Lauritzen*, 835 F.2d 1529 (7th Cir.1987), cert. denied 488 U.S. 898, 109 S.Ct. 243, 102 L.Ed.2d 232 (1988), similarly involved the question of whether pickle harvesters are employees within the meaning of the Fair Labor Standards Act. Despite little factual distinction from *Brandel* (the evidence indicated that the farmer exercised somewhat more active control over harvesting), the court concluded that the harvesters were employees. It emphasized the lack of significant investment by the harvesters and the role of the harvesters as an integral part of the farm's productive operations. It concluded that because the harvesters are dependent on the farmer's investment and business activity for their continued livelihood, they are within the category of workers covered by the Act's protections.

*Beliz v. W.H. McLeod & Sons Packing Co.*, 765 F.2d 1317 (5th Cir.1985), involved a more typical agricultural harvesting situation. There, a South Carolina farm raising beets, tomatoes, squash and cucumbers engaged a farm labor contractor to recruit and transport migrant workers from Texas. The Farm Labor Contractor Registration Act regulates such activities and establishes minimum standards for recordkeeping, housing, transportation, and notification respecting the terms and conditions of proposed employment. The farm sent the contractor an advance payment to enable him to transport the workers he had recruited, provided housing and paid the contractor based on the number of buckets picked. The farm owner set the piece rate per bucket of crop harvested, assigned work locations on a daily basis, determined work schedules and checked to see that the crops were being picked without undue damage to plants and that the vegetables were properly sorted. The contractor was paid in cash and he in turn paid the workers. The families recruited by the contractor complained that their transportation and housing facilities were substandard and that their piecework pay, due to poor weather and crop conditions, fell below minimum wage requirements. The court concluded that, as a matter of law, the farm could be held liable as the workers' "employer" under the FLSA. It also found the farm liable for statutory damages resulting from recordkeeping violations under the Farm Labor Contractor Registration Act but concluded that damages based upon violations of other provisions of the latter statute may be assessed only against the contractor.

4. Judge Easterbrook separately concurred in the *Lauritzen* decision, cited in note 3, above. He observed that the fact-specific tests used by his colleagues in that decision, and by federal courts generally in enforcing the FLSA, pose a substantial evidentiary challenge in searching for all of the relevant facts and in large measure result in the courts weighing facts that have little or no relevance to the critical determination of whether the relationship is the sort Congress intended to be controlled by the FLSA. Thus, he argues:

> We should abandon these unfocused "factors" and start again. The language of the statute is the place to start. Section 3(g) ... defines "employ" as including "to suffer or permit to work". This is "the broadest definition '... ever included in any one act.'" ... No wonder the common law definition of "independent contractor" does not govern.... The definition, written in the passive, sweeps in almost any work done on the employer's premises, potentially any work done for the employer's benefit or with the employer's acquiescence. * * *

> [M]aybe, as Lauritzen says, the FLSA does more harm than good by foreclosing desirable packages of incentives (such as payment by reference to results rather than hours) or by reducing the opportunities for work, and hence the income, of those, such as migrant farm workers, who cannot readily enter white-collar professions and make more money while working fewer hours. The system in place on Lauritzen's farm may be the most efficient yet devised—best for owners, workers, and consumers alike—but whether it is efficient or not is none of our business. The judicial task is to implement what Congress did, not ask whether Congress did the right thing.

Having observed that much of what courts look to in deciding such cases is based on the common law concept of an independent contractor, Judge Easterbrook comments:

> All the details of the common law independent contractor doctrine having to do with the right to control the work are addressed to identifying the best monitor and precaution-taker. The reasons for blocking vicarious liability at a particular point have nothing to do with the functions of the FLSA.... The FLSA is designed to defeat rather than implement contractual arrangements. * * *

> The migrant workers are selling nothing but their labor. They have no physical capital and little human capital to vend. This does not belittle their skills. Willingness to work hard, dedication to a job, honesty, and good health, are valuable traits and all too scarce. Those who possess

these traits will find employment; those who do not cannot work (for long) even at the minimum wage in the private sector. But those to whom the FLSA applies must include workers who possess only dedication, honesty, and good health. So the baby-sitter is an "employee" even though working but a few hours a week, and the writer of novels is not an "employee" of the publisher even though renting only human capital. The migrant workers labor on the farmer's premises, doing repetitive tasks. Payment on a piecework rate (e.g., per pound of cucumbers) would not take these workers out of the Act, any more than payment of the sales staff at a department store on commission avoids the statute. The link of the migrants' compensation to the market price of pickles is not fundamentally different from piecework compensation. . . .

835 F.2d at 1543–45.

Would Judge Easterbrook reach a different result if he was deciding *Flint*? Are the welders selling nothing but their labor? Why do they invest so much money in their rigs?

5.   If Lauritzen's compensation system, paying the harvesting family a percentage of the price paid by the pickle processors, is "the most efficient yet devised," what is the effect of the court's decision on Lauritzen's interests, the interests of the harvesting families, the interests of the individual harvesters, the interests of other farm workers, the interests of consumers? Is that impact consistent with Congressional intent?

6.   Is the payment of time and a half for more than 40 hours a week detrimental to efficiency? To safety? To the economic well-being of our society? To the general social well-being of our society?

7.   Deciding whether someone is an independent contractor is just one of many FLSA issues that is very fact-specific. To what extent does the weighing of facts appear to be responsive to the pro-employee or pro-management predilections of the fact finder? What is the impact of allowing an administrative agency, a jury or a judge to be the primary fact-finder in such cases? The business community often complains about the burden of trying to comply with ever expanding government regulations. Would it be productive or counter-productive in terms of efficiency or in terms of equal treatment for employers, as well as for workers, to adopt more detailed administrative regulations? Is it feasible to reduce the need to engage in weighing competing factual considerations by adopting more detailed administrative regulations?

## McLAUGHLIN v. ENSLEY

United States Court of Appeals, Fourth Circuit, 1989
877 F.2d 1207

CHAPMAN, CIRCUIT JUDGE:

This case involves the meaning of "employee" as it applies to rights under the Fair Labor Standards Act, 29 U.S.C. § 201 et seq. (1982). More precisely, the issue is whether certain workers, who performed duties for an employer during a weeklong orientation period, were employees for purposes of the Fair Labor Standards Act's minimum wage and overtime provisions. Because we believe these workers should have been considered employees, we reverse.

*yes,*

I

The defendant in this action, Kirby Ensley, is the proprietor of a snack foods distribution business in Sylva, North Carolina. At the time of the events relative to this action, Ensley employed route men to drive his company trucks, to restock vending machines, and to sell "potato chips, candy, crackers, and peanuts" on a commission basis to retailers. The employees' income derived entirely from commission sales. They generally worked Monday through Friday, and sometimes on Saturday, for a total of about 50 to 60 hours per week.

*Route men*

Before hiring persons for route jobs, Ensley required them to participate in what was usually five days of exposure to the tasks they would be expected to perform. The parties agree that Ensley did not pay any form of compensation to the potential routemen during this week. During the week, which included about 50–60 hours of labor, the potential routeman traveled an ordinary route with an experienced routeman. They loaded and unloaded the delivery truck, restocked stores with Ensleys' product, were given instruction on how to drive the trucks, were introduced to retailers, were taught basic snack food vending machine maintenance, and occasionally helped in preparing orders of goods and with financial exchanges.

*orientation period is no pay*

At trial, conflicting evidence was introduced as to whether Ensley's business benefited from the new workers' activities. Ensley himself claimed that the trainees may have hindered normal operations. The testimony of two experienced drivers was that the extra hands naturally made their work load lighter. Similarly, there was disagreement as to the extent to which formal hiring was contingent on completion of the program. Ensley maintained that the training did not guarantee a future job. Yet there was evidence that no person, who had completed the training, was not subsequently hired.

After the government presented its case against Ensley to the jury, the defendant moved for a directed verdict, which, on the issue now before this court, was granted by the district court. Relying particularly on *Walling v. Portland Terminal Co.*, 330 U.S. 148, 67 S. Ct. 639, 91 L. Ed. 809 (1947), *Donovan v. American Airlines, Inc.*, 686 F.2d 267 (5th Cir. 1982), and *Isaacson v. Penn Community Services, Inc.*, 450 F.2d 1306 (4th Cir.1971), the court concluded that the determination of whether one is an employee for purposes of the Act is a legal question not reserved to the jury. After discussing generally the propositions that work under close scrutiny, work which does not displace other employees, and work which does not expedite a company's business are factors which help reveal whether a worker is an employee for purposes of the Act, the court determined that in light of plaintiff's evidence, the routemen in training were not employees. The court then proceeded to consider how the six-part test, developed by the Wage and Hour Division to aid in its own

*Notemfles*

determinations of when a so-called trainee is really an employee, should be applied in this case.[1]

The court believed that the instruction provided by Ensley was similar to that given in a vocational school for outside salesmen, that the training was for the benefit of the students, that the trainees did not displace regular workers, that Ensley derived no immediate advantage from the activities of the trainees, that the trainees were not necessarily entitled to a job, and that both parties understood that the new workers were not to receive wages.

## II

The starting point for an analysis of the question posed are the companion cases of *Portland Terminal, supra,* and *Walling v. Nashville, Chattanooga and St. Louis Ry.,* 330 U.S. 158, 67 S. Ct. 644, 91 L. Ed. 816 (1947). There, the Supreme Court addressed at some length the relationship between training that is not covered by the Act and employment that invokes its protection. The Court considered that "[w]ithout doubt the Act covers trainees, beginners, apprentices, or learners if they are employed to work for an employer for compensation." More accurately, however, the issue is whether such trainees are "employed," and the Act defines employ as "to suffer or permit to work." Despite the broadness of this definition, the Court believed that it "obviously" excluded those without a promise of compensation who worked for their own advantage on another's property, and did not "make a person whose work serves only his own interest an employee of another person who gives him aid and instruction." Similarly, the Act was not intended to penalize employers for instruction that will "greatly benefit" the trainees. Finally, it would be important to consider whether an employer received any work of "immediate advantage" from the employee. *Portland Terminal,* 330 U.S. at 151–53, 67 S. Ct. at 640–42.

*(4: "Broad but excluded")*

This court has not had many opportunities to consider Portland Terminal. Although it has applied the case from an early date, see *McComb v. Homeworkers' Handicraft Cooperative,* 176 F.2d 633, 639 (4th Cir.1949) (stating that *Portland Terminal* "merely held that learners or apprentices taking a training course under an agreement that compensation should not be paid them were not to be deemed employees within the meaning of the act."), and *Walling v. Norfolk Southern Ry. Co.,* 162 F.2d 95, 96 (4th Cir.1947) applying the holding of *Portland Terminal* to a factually identical case), it was not until *Wirtz v. Wardlaw,* 339 F.2d 785

---

**1.** The six criteria, all of which must be met before Wage and Hour determines there is no employment relationship, are: (1) the training, even though it includes actual operation of the facilities of the employer, is similar to that which would be given in a vocational school, (2) the training is for the benefit of the trainees, (3) the trainees do not displace regular employees, but work under close observation, (4) the employer that provides the training derives no immediate advantage from the activities of the trainees and on occasion his operations may actually be impeded, (5) the trainees are not necessarily entitled to a job at the completion of the training period, and, (6) the employer and the trainees understand that the trainees are not entitled to wages for the time spent in training. Wage and Hour Manual (BNA) 91:416 (1975).

(4th Cir.1964), and *Penn Community Services, supra,* that this court offered a broad discussion of the issue.

In *Wardlaw*, which involved the hiring by an insurance salesman of two women at less than minimum wages, the court held that the women were entitled to minimum wages and overtime compensation. Distinguishing the case from *Portland Terminal,* the court found it determinative that the employer's interests were served by the women's work and that he "benefited from their labors." *Wardlaw,* 339 F.2d at 788. In Penn Community Services, the court held that Portland Terminal had established that when "the employer received no 'immediate advantage' from the trainees' services," that is, when "the principal purpose of the seemingly employment relationship was to benefit the person in the employee status," the worker could not be brought under the Act. *Penn Community Services,* 450 F.2d at 1308. In sum, this court has concluded that the general test used to determine if an employee is entitled to the protections of the Act is whether the employee or the employer is the primary beneficiary of the trainees' labor.

### III

As a result, the proper legal inquiry in this case is whether Ensley or the new workers principally benefited from the weeklong orientation arrangement.[2] There are several facts that serve to illustrate the relative degrees of benefit. The most important of these relate directly to the nature of the training experience. The evidence established that the workers drove trucks, loaded and unloaded trucks, restocked retail store shelves and vending machines, learned basic food vending machine maintenance, and performed simple kinds of paperwork.

This recitation of the weeks' events establishes the very limited and narrow kinds of learning that took place, and requires a conclusion that the district court misapplied the controlling legal principle to the facts in evidence by granting the directed verdict. The prospective employees were simply helping to service a route, and the instruction they received did not rise to the level that one would receive in a general, vocational course in "outside salesmanship." The trainees were taught only simple specific job functions related to Ensley's own business.

By applying these factual circumstances to the legal question of which party received the principal benefit, it becomes plain that Ensley received more advantage than the workers. Ensley, without cost to himself, obtained employees able to perform at a higher level when they began to receive pay. Ensley also received a free opportunity to review job performance, and he received the benefit of aid to his regular employees while they performed their normal duties. These new workers were, in fact, helping Ensley to distribute his snack foods. On the other hand, it is clear that the workers received very little. As noted above, the skills learned

---

**2.** We do not rely on the formal six-part test issued by the Wage and Hour Division. Instead, because of the clear precedent of *Wardlaw* and *Penn Community Services,* we believe proper analysis derives from the principles stated in those cases.

were either so specific to the job or so general to be of practically no transferable usefulness. The brevity of the training period helps to underscore this fact. Finally, there was no credible evidence that a person who completed the training was not subsequently hired, suggesting that the new workers should be considered at-will employees from the beginning.

For the above reasons we conclude that those persons, who participated in the orientation program and are properly identified as such, are entitled to be considered as covered employees under the Fair Labor Standards Act and to receive minimum wages for one week of work. Accordingly, we reverse the judgment of the district court.

WILKINS, CIRCUIT JUDGE, dissenting:

The majority characterizes the "proper legal inquiry [as] whether Ensley or the new workers principally benefited from the weeklong orientation arrangement." However, the true legal issue is whether the trainees were "employees" within the definition of 29 U.S.C.A. §§ 203(e)(1), 203(g) (West 1978 & Supp.1989). The district court, in concluding that Ensley's trainees were not employees, applied the correct legal test and based its holding on factual findings that are not clearly erroneous. I would therefore affirm. * * *

## II.

Addressing the legal issue of whether trainees are employees during a training period, the Donovan court stated:

> The standard of review of the district court's decision is that of a legal, and not a factual, determination. Thus, although we are bound by the clearly erroneous standard in reviewing the individual findings of fact leading to the district court's conclusions, we review the determination that the [trainees] were not employees as we review any determination of law.

686 F.2d at 270 n. 4. See *Patel v. Wargo*, 803 F.2d 632, 634 (11th Cir.1986); *Beliz v. W.H. McLeod & Sons Packing Co.*, 765 F.2d 1317, 1327 (5th Cir.1985). In Donovan the court affirmed a district court resolution of the ultimate legal question that airline flight attendant trainees were not employees during their training period. 686 F.2d at 271. Before reaching the legal issue, the court reviewed, among other factors, the district court analysis of "the 'relative benefits flowing to trainee and company during the training period,'" id. at 271, and concluded that "the district court's finding that trainees gain the greater benefit from their experience is fully supported by the evidence." Id. at 272.

## III.

* * *

The majority's characterization of the training accomplished during the week ignores those attributes upon which the district court based its findings. While the trainees no doubt carried boxes and helped to load and unload trucks, the evidence presented supports the district court's findings that the trainees learned job-related skills, fundamental skills necessary to successfully perform the job of routeman in Ensley's company. In addition to vending machine maintenance and truck driving, the evidence shows that the trainees generally learned how to interact with store managers,[3] complete some of the paperwork necessary to process orders, read and understand a routebook, handle money and address credit and billing problems, and comply with Ensley's warehouse and delivery truck inventory control procedures. After the training period was over and employment began, a new routeman was taught other more technical job skills.

The majority emphasizes that the skills taught were specific to Ensley's operation or otherwise too general, either extreme producing "practically no transferable usefulness." This factor is of little significance. In Donovan, the district court found that American Airlines taught its trainees the skills necessary to perform jobs in its organization, and required applicants to complete the training regardless of prior experience in the airline industry. While some of the skills taught were no doubt transferable, American intended to teach its trainees "American's, and only American's," internal procedures, practices, grooming requirements, and " 'style.' " 686 F.2d at 269. The court held that while the training was "made more effective and less expensive by ... devoting it entirely to American's policies, [this did not] mean that trainees [were] working while receiving this instruction." Id. at 272. It makes no difference that Ensley chose not to teach more generally useful skills and that Ensley's program was "without cost to himself."

The majority alludes that Ensley "received the benefit of aid to his regular employees," but it fails to identify this alleged benefit. Since the snacks were sold from store shelves and vending machines, extra hands would not create any net increase in actual sales. There is no allegation that Ensley was able to reduce the number of trucks necessary to serve the area by requiring trainees to assist the drivers, so Ensley's delivery costs were in no way reduced. And since the drivers worked on a commission-based compensation plan and made deliveries to a set number of locations each day, any reduction in a driver's delivery time would not reduce Ensley's compensation costs to the routeman. In short, the district court did not clearly err in finding that Ensley received no immediate financial benefit from any assistance the trainees might have given to the supervising routemen during the training period.

Ensley did, of course, "benefit" from the training in that he was able to hire, at the end of the training period, a new routeman who was minimally qualified for the job. This "benefit," however, is present in every training-period case. For example, in Donovan the court held that "[a]lthough training benefits American by providing it with suitable

___
**3.** The trainees did not necessarily take over the route on which they trained, so while meeting the store managers may be considered mere orientation, learning how to interact with a manager was the relevant skill taught.

personnel, the trainees attend [the training] for their own benefit, to qualify for employment they could not otherwise obtain." 686 F.2d at 272. Thus the training of prospective employees does not, by itself, constitute an " 'immediate advantage' " to the employer. *Portland Terminal*, 330 U.S. at 153, 67 S. Ct. at 642.

## IV.

Finally, the majority's conclusion that Ensley's trainees are employees during the training period contravenes the policies underlying the trainee exclusion from the minimum wage law. The short term result of this contravention of policies produces a windfall to the small number of employees who have already completed Ensley's training program, and who had availed themselves of the training with no expectation of compensation. However, in the long term the majority's decision will tend to make it more difficult for young and/or unskilled persons seeking employment opportunities beyond that of an unskilled laborer to find employment.

Addressing the policies which support the statutory allowance of a sub-minimum wage for trainees, paid pursuant to special certifications issued under 29 U.S.C.A. § 214(1) (West 1965 & Supp.1989), the Supreme Court has said:

> Many persons . . . have so little experience in particular vocations that they are unable to get and hold jobs at standard wages. Consequently, to impose a minimum wage as to them might deprive them of all opportunity to secure work, thereby defeating one of the Act's purposes, which was to increase opportunities for gainful employment.

*Portland Terminal*, 330 U.S. at 151, 67 S. Ct. at 641.

*Some quit*

Ensley's trainees knew they would receive no compensation for the five days spent learning the rudiments of the job of routeman. Nonetheless they agreed to the arrangement, no doubt rationally concluding that the week of training was a suitable investment in their own future. Some had second thoughts after a few days of training, for the record shows that some trainees quit before the five days were completed. These individuals undoubtedly concluded that the investment was not worth it for them, most likely because the nature of the job for which they were training was not to their liking.

While Ensley might have chosen to pay his trainees in order to attract more skilled applicants, he opted for applicants who agreed to volunteer for a week of training with no compensation. The applicants volunteered for the training in order to obtain jobs they were seriously considering. As the Fifth Circuit has stated:

> We are aware that many companies hire persons as employees and then pay them while they attend company schools. These employers are governed . . . by the demands of the market place [sic] and by their own specialized needs. The FLSA does not require [all employers] to follow this course.

*Donovan*, 686 F.2d at 272.

I respectfully dissent.

### NOTES AND QUESTIONS

1. Courts differ respecting the importance of the six tests used by the Wage and Hour Division in distinguishing work from training. Rejecting the idea that each test must be satisfied, the Tenth Circuit describes the six criteria as important factors to be weighed in examining whether the totality of the circumstances justifies finding that the training is employment activity subject to FLSA wage standards. *Reich v. Parker Fire Protection Dist.*, 992 F.2d 1023 (10th Cir.1993).

2. Participants in formal apprenticeship programs may be required to attend a substantial number of hours of classroom instruction. So long as the apprenticeship program meets standards set by the Bureau of Apprenticeship and Training and that classroom instruction does not result in production of goods and services that can be sold by the employer, the time spent in the classroom is generally held not to be compensable. See *Loodeen v. Consumers Energy Co.*, 13 Wage & Hour Cases 2d 896 (W.D. Mich. 2008); *Merrill v. Exxon Corp.*, 387 F.Supp. 458 (S.D. Texas 1974). Training that is a prerequisite to being offered a job, and which does not involve productions of goods or services, is often also not compensable. See *Chao v. Tradesmen International, Inc.*, 310 F.3d 904 (6th Cir. 2002).

3. Enderby Corp. purchases three electric fork lift trucks and lays off 14 warehouse employees whose job was to move parts on hand carts. It tells the three most senior members of the laid off group that, if they successfully complete the employer's five-day fork lift truck training program, they can come back to work as fork lift operators. Does Enderby have to pay them for the five days' training? Can it pay them at the FLSA minimum rate rather than at their normal rate of pay during the training? What if instead of training them itself, Enderby sends them to a training program operated by the fork lift truck manufacturer?

4. "Volunteers" pose somewhat similar problems. The definition of "employee" in the FLSA expressly excludes people who volunteer services for state and interstate agencies if the work is unrelated to the work they are employed to perform. It also excludes "individuals who volunteer their services solely for humanitarian purposes to private non-profit food banks and who receive from the food banks groceries." 29 U.S.C. § 203(a)(4) and (5).

Assume that a local bank wants to promote its new debit card and sends letters offering free certificates for video rentals to those who sign up for the cards at the bank in the next two weeks. In order to handle the sign-ups, and answer customer questions about the debit cards, the bank contributes $1,000 to a local church on the condition that it supply church volunteers to staff the sign-up table. The church is obligated to provide two volunteers at the table at any given time for a total of 50 scheduled hours on each of the two weeks. Putting aside whether there may be payroll tax and income tax violations in this arrangement, are there any violations of the FLSA?

Other workers have been held simply not to fit into the "employee" category because of a clear understanding that the work they would perform would not be paid for. It is obvious that many people engage in substantial work—sometimes extended and demanding in nature—in volunteer projects. Habitat for Humanity volunteers, for example, frequently serve as carpenters, siding installers, insulation specialists, and so on. Those who purchase the houses do so with a combination of cash and "sweat equity" (work they perform in building not only their own house but houses for others). No one can doubt the value of such activity to society. Nonetheless, there is obviously an opportunity for abuse. The courts have recognized that there is a point at which those who organize such work and sell the end product may become "employers" and the alleged volunteers "employees." The best-known example of distinguishing between volunteer and employee doubtless is the case involving the Tony and Susan Alamo Foundation. The Foundation, a nonprofit religious organization, derived its income largely from 38 businesses that it operated in four states. These businesses included a motel, retail clothing outlets, pig farms, gasoline service stations, a record-keeping company, a candy manufacturing and distribution company, and an electrical and roofing construction operation. The founders of the Foundation supervised operations but most staffing was done by "associates" who were drug addicts, derelicts or criminals prior to becoming involved in the Foundation's program. The "associates" received food, lodging, clothing and other benefits but no wages. Current "associates" testified that they volunteered their efforts and expected no compensation for their labors. Rather, they considered such work their ministry. However, former "associates" testified that they were denied cafeteria privileges if they were absent from work for whatever reason and that they sometimes worked as much as 10–15 hours a day and 6 or 7 days a week. The district court estimated the actual value of benefits received by "associates" from the Foundation as "somewhat over $200 a month".

The Supreme Court unanimously upheld a decision finding the Foundation guilty of violating the minimum wage, overtime, and record-keeping requirements of the FLSA. The Court ruled that the Act does not exclude commercial activities of religious institutions and held that an employee's characterization of his activities as "voluntary" is not controlling. "The test of employment under the Act is one of 'economic reality.'" Therefore, reasoned the Court, the fact-finder could properly conclude that the in-kind benefits were received in exchange for services and constituted wages. *Tony and Susan Alamo Foundation v. Secretary of Labor*, 471 U.S. 290, 299–302, 105 S.Ct. 1953, 1961–62, 85 L.Ed.2d 278 (1985). The Court drew a distinction between the "associates'" volunteerism and voluntary services to the elderly, ill, indigent or disadvantaged without expectation of compensation. Moreover, the Court rejected the contention that application of the FLSA to the Alamo Foundation violated constitutional protections of religious freedom, noting that "there is nothing in the Act to prevent the associates from returning the monetary compensation [due under the FLSA] to the Foundation, provided they do so voluntarily." 471 U.S. at 303, 105 S. Ct. at 1963.

If the "volunteers" received or expected to receive nothing for their labors, would the result be the same? If an organization such as the Salvation Army asks its beneficiaries to do clean-up work in exchange for shelter, is that the sort of activity that requires minimum wage regulation? What about those seeking to purchase a home from Habitat for Humanity who are expected to perform work building homes for others as well as for themselves? If the answer is "no", what distinguishes that situation from Alamo?

Does the Alamo decision require religious orders to pay monks for their labors producing wine or cheese? If the volunteer returns 100% of the wage as a donation, will there still be payroll and income taxes to be paid?

For a proposed set of criteria to distinguish true volunteers from employees, see Note, *FLSA Restrictions on Volunteerism*, 78 CORNELL L. REV. 302, 332 (1993).

5.    Since a worker with the status of independent contractor or trainee or volunteer does not receive protection under the FLSA or most other labor and employment laws, the cost of that worker is probably less than the cost of an employee. Entrepreneurs thus have an incentive to avoid having the "employee" label applied to those performing work for them. Recognizing that business operators may therefore be tempted to characterize workers who are really employees as something else, a few jurisdictions have enacted "misclassification statutes," that penalize that sort of improper labeling. Enforcement of these laws has thus far been infrequent. See *Chicago Regional Council of Carpenters v. Joseph J. Sciamanna, Inc.*, 2008 WL 4696162 (N.D. Ill. 2008).

## (c.) Exclusions From Coverage

### (i.) *Executive, Administrative and Professional Employees*

Section 13(a)(1) [29 U.S.C. § 213(a)(1)] of the Fair Labor Standards Act excludes "bona fide executive, administrative, or professional employees," as well as outside salesmen, from the overtime premium pay requirement. The Act expressly includes as professional employees academic administrators and teachers in elementary and secondary schools as well as computer systems analysts, programmers, and software engineers. Section 13 additionally gives the Secretary of Labor authority to define who fits within these job classifications.

The regulations adopted by the Secretary to define and delimit who comes within the § 13(a)(1) overtime pay exemption, 29 C.F.R. Part 541, were revised substantially in 2004, as the following case discusses. The present regulations set a minimum salary level of $455 a week in order to be exempt. The "executive" employee exemption is a principal subject of the next opinion. An "administrative employee" is one who has a primary duty of office or nonmanual work related to management policies or general business operations, and who exercises discretion and independent judgment with respect to significant matters. A "professional employee" is one whose work is "primarily intellectual in character." A special provision exempts from overtime requirements the majority of employees who make $100,000 a year or more. At one time it was debated whether those in the computer programming field should be treated as executive, administrative or professional employees. Congress ended the debate by adopting

an amendment requiring the Secretary of Labor to adopt overtime exemption regulations to include persons involved in computer programming
work if paid on an hourly basis and at a rate of at least $27.63 an hour (at
the time, 6½ times the minimum wage).

## MORGAN v. FAMILY DOLLAR STORES, INC.

United States Court of Appeals, Eleventh Circuit, 2008
551 F.3d 1233

HULL, CIRCUIT JUDGE:

* * * An opt-in class of 1,424 store managers, in a collective action
certified by the district court, sued Family Dollar Stores, Inc. ("Family
Dollar") for unpaid overtime wages under the Fair Labor Standards Act
("FLSA"), 29 U.S.C. §§ 201–219. * * *

The jury found that the Plaintiff store managers were not exempt
executives and that Family Dollar had willfully denied them overtime pay.
* * * The court entered a final judgment of $35,576,059.48 against Family
Dollar consisting of $17,788,029.74 in overtime wages and an equal
amount in liquidated damages. * * *

### I.  PROCEDURAL HISTORY FROM 2001–2005

#### A.  Complaint

Family Dollar is a nationwide retailer that operates over 6,000 discount stores that sell a wide assortment of products, including groceries,
clothing, household items, automotive supplies, general merchandise, and
seasonal goods.[9] In January 2001, Janice Morgan and Barbara Richardson,
two store managers, filed a Complaint on behalf of themselves "and all
other similarly situated persons," alleging that Family Dollar willfully
violated the FLSA by refusing to pay its store managers overtime compensation. * * *

Family Dollar's Answer raised a number of affirmative defenses. It
asserted that its store managers were exempt executives and denied any
violations were willful. Family Dollar also argued that a collective action,
under § 216(b), was impermissible because (1) the store managers were
not similarly situated, (2) Plaintiffs' claims were not representative of
others in the group, and (3) Plaintiffs could not satisfy § 216(b)'s requirements for maintaining a collective action. * * *

[Some of the procedural aspects of the case are dealt with below in section
B.4 of this chapter.] * * *

### II.  SECOND JURY TRIAL IN 2006

* * * Given the jury's verdict and our standard of review, we outline
the trial evidence in the light most favorable to the Plaintiffs.

---

**9.** Family Dollar opens around 500 stores a year. Family Dollar had 2,900 stores in 1999,
4,545 stores in 2003, 5,700 stores in 2005, and has over 6,000 stores now. Here, we recite the
remaining facts in this case based on Family Dollar's organization during the time frame relevant
to this case, which is 1999 to 2005.

## A.  Corporate Structure

Family Dollar is a publicly held, nationwide retailer that operates over 6,000 discount stores in 40 states and the District of Columbia. It has annual sales of around $5 billion and annual net profits ranging from $200 to 263 million from 1999 to 2005. Its individual stores have average annual sales of $1 million, and average net profits of 5 to 7%, or $50,000 to $70,000. Family Dollar structures store operations into five divisions (each headed by a vice-president), 22 regions (each headed by a regional vice-president), and 380 districts (each overseen by a district manager). Each district contains multiple stores. Each district manager supervises the operations of 10 to 30 stores. Some districts are small with multiple stores in an urban area. Other districts are larger with small stores in small towns. The district manager's office is housed within one store in the district.

Family Dollar's corporate office issues instruction manuals with operating policies that apply uniformly to all stores nationwide. No matter the size of the store or the district, every detail of how the store is run is fixed and mandated through Family Dollar's comprehensive manuals.

## B.  Store Managers

Family Dollar has the same job description for all store managers and lists their "Essential Job Functions" as:

1.   Supervise all store personnel, including assigning tasks, ensuring compliance with merchandising and operational policies, and locking and unlocking store.

2.   Prepare, complete and transmit store reports as required.

3.   Count money/checks, prepare bank deposits and travel to bank.

4.   Count petty cash, get change from bank, unlock petty cash drawer and give change to cashiers as needed in registers.

5.   Post net sales in Beat Yesterday Book.

6.   Train Cashiers and Stock Clerks through verbal instructions and non-verbal demonstration.

7.   Count stock, calculate amount to order, use MSI machine to order and transmit, calculate additional goods needed for ad bulletins and endcap programs.

8.   Read, plan and stock schematics for proper merchandising.

9.   Practice cash control policies; including check approvals, refund and exchange approvals, layaway approvals (when applicable).

10.   Work as Cashier when needed and be able to perform all Cashier tasks, * * *

11.   Work as Stock Clerk when needed and be able to perform all Stock Clerk tasks * * *

The overwhelming evidence showed that Plaintiff store managers exercise little discretion and spend 80 to 90% of their time performing manual labor tasks, such as stocking shelves, running the cash registers, unloading trucks, and cleaning the parking lots, floors, and bathrooms. Even as to the assigned management tasks, such as paperwork, bank deposits, and petty cash, the store manual strictly prescribes them. And district managers closely scrutinize store managers to ensure compliance with the manual and corporate directives.

Family Dollar forbids outside janitorial help, and store managers lack authority to hire outside vendors. * * *

Store managers routinely perform janitorial duties. The manual even prescribes how janitorial tasks are to be performed * * *

Store managers lack discretion over the store's merchandise selection, prices, sales promotions, and layouts—all are set by the home office and district managers. For example, each store is provided a schematic layout and diagram of the store which shows (1) where each shelf must be, (2) what product goes on each shelf, (3) how all merchandise is to be displayed, (4) how all signs, merchandising, and display information is to be used, (5) how each "end cap" (the end of an aisle or gondola) should be displayed, and (6) what promotional product goes on the end cap. * * * The tiniest of details are governed by the manuals. * * * Further, each store has a preassigned "truck day" when the company truck delivers merchandise to the store. Because of the volume of unloading and stocking, the store manager always works "truck day." The store manager helps unload 800 to 1,500 cartons from the truck to the storeroom and stock the shelves. The evidence also showed that store managers are assigned a fixed payroll budget, with total labor hours to come from that budget each week, and are required to use only hourly employees. As detailed later, store managers have scant discretion to act independently of their district managers.

## C. *Family Dollar Executives*

Plaintiffs called two Family Dollar executives who testified about store managers' roles in the Family Dollar corporate hierarchy. Bruce Barkus started with Family Dollar in 1999, oversaw all stores, and reported to the President. He testified that Family Dollar classified store managers as executives, across the board, without ever determining how store managers spent their time: * * *

Barkus testified that in a study of how much time it took to unload trucks and get merchandise to the floor, that the "biggest chunk of the store manager's time was being spent on manual labor, unloading the trucks, getting it to the floor, and onto the shelves." Barkus also testified that district managers ensure that store managers do not exceed the fixed payroll budgets assigned by corporate management. A store manager that goes over budget, by even a penny, could be fired. Because store managers are under orders that overtime labor is not allowed, they are required to do any and all work, even if the payroll budget does not allocate enough hourly employees to get the job done. * * * Almost all of the store manager's job is standardized and controlled by superiors. Barkus confirmed that Family Dollar makes virtually no distinction between a store manager's job duties and an assistant store manager's job duties.

Plaintiffs also offered the testimony of Charles William Broome, a Senior Vice–President of Store Operations, who supervised 1,400 Family Dollar stores. Like Barkus, Broome confirmed that Family Dollar never studied whether store managers were exempt executives * * *

Family Dollar's corporate office generates a "staff scheduler" that uses the amount of money that the store may spend on labor and converts it into a document that delineates how many hours a week each employee should work and the total weekly labor hours for the store. According to the staff scheduler, each store manager is supposed to work 52 hours a week. Broome testified that, generally, store managers are expected to work between 48 to 52 hours, but that "as manager of the store, you're required to manage the store and do whatever it takes. I don't know that there is a specific number that's mandated." * * *

Although store managers can schedule what employees work what hours on the "weekly staff schedule" so long as the store does not exceed the payroll budget, certain corporate directives further constrain store managers' discretion, such as the prohibition on moving employee coverage from slower days (like weekdays that did not involve unloading truck shipments) to busier days. * * *

### D.  District Managers

Family Dollar's 380 district managers implement and enforce these policies and procedures. Their vigorous oversight ensures that store managers comply with the operations manual's precise dictates. The operations manual states that the district managers—not the store managers—head the "store team." * * *

Plaintiffs' witnesses explained how Family Dollar's corporate office sets a fixed payroll budget for each store and how that budget results in salaried store managers working long hours each week. * * *

For example, at a low volume, small store, the district manager sets the store's payroll budget at around $1,400 per week. The average store manager's salary of $600 per week comes out of this budget. The remaining $800 pays the hourly employees. The payroll budget is often only enough to pay one full-time hourly assistant manager and two or three hourly sales associates. Because the store is open seven days a week and store managers are not permitted to unilaterally schedule hourly staff for overtime, store managers routinely worked 60 to 70 hours a week to have enough floor coverage during the set store hours and to complete the required manual labor.

For higher volume, larger size stores, the corporate office sets a larger payroll budget, which usually covers more hourly employees (seven to ten). But larger stores have more merchandise to stock, more cartons to unload on truck day, a need for more cashiers, and more demand for cleaning. Because the payroll budget is fixed and strictly monitored, store managers at larger stores, just like those at smaller stores, routinely work 60 to 70 hours per week and spend 80 to 90% of their time on manual labor.

District managers closely supervise the hiring and firing process. They interview and hire store managers and interview and approve the hiring of assistant managers. Store managers initially interview assistant manager candidates and make recommendations to the district manager. The manual states that a "job offer is not to be made until ... Management has received authorization to hire." * * *

District managers set the rate of pay for all hourly employees (assistant managers and sales associates) and must approve all pay increases. District managers also evaluate hourly employee performance.

Only district managers have the power to close a store for bad weather. In the "Hurricane Warning Procedures" section, the manual instructs store managers that "[i]f the District manager cannot be located, contact the Regional Vice–President for recommendations regarding the course of action that should be taken."

### E. Salary Compared to Hourly Wages

Both parties submitted evidence documenting the average weekly salaries of all Plaintiffs and the average hourly wages of assistant managers. Plaintiffs' evidence showed that, from 1999 to 2005, Plaintiff store managers averaged $599.71 a week in salary. Despite the fact that the salary was intended to compensate a 52–hour workweek, store managers worked 60 to 70 hours a week. In other words, from 1999 to 2005, Plaintiff store managers averaged from $9.99 an hour (using Plaintiffs' average salary figures and a 60–hour workweek) to $8.57 an hour (using Plaintiffs' average salary figures and a 70–hour workweek). During the same years, assistant managers were paid hourly and averaged $7.60 an hour. Assuming a 70–hour workweek, store managers earned, on average, roughly the same (less than a dollar or more per hour) than assistant managers. Assuming a 60–hour week, store managers earned approximately $2 more per hour than assistant managers in 1999 to 2003 and approximately $3 more per hour in 2004 to 2005. * * *

### F. Judgment/Verdict

At the close of the evidence, the district court granted judgment as a matter of law to 163 of the 1,424 Plaintiff store managers, because, according to Family Dollar's charts, these 163 did not satisfy the third requirement in the executive exemption test, i.e., that they customarily and regularly directed the work of two or more other employees, as required by 29 C.F.R. § 541.1(f) (2003), 29 C.F.R. § 541.100(a) (2006). As to the remaining Plaintiffs, the jury determined Family Dollar failed to prove they were exempt executive employees.

The jury also found that Family Dollar acted willfully in denying overtime pay to all Plaintiffs. The jury awarded $1,575,932.12 in overtime pay to the 163 Plaintiffs and $17,516,071.27 in overtime pay to the remaining Plaintiffs. In calculating this over-time pay, the jury used Family Dollar's charts that documented (1) the number of hours that each of the Plaintiffs worked per week, and (2) the amount of back pay owed per Plaintiff for the applicable period.[10] * * *

## IV.  EXECUTIVE EXEMPTION DEFENSE

### A.  FLSA's Executive Exemption

* * * The exemption at issue here, the executive exemption, provides that the FLSA's requirements "shall not apply with respect to . . . any employee employed in a bona fide executive . . . capacity." 29 U.S.C. § 213(a)(1).

The Department of Labor's ("DOL") regulations interpret this defense. Because Plaintiffs' claims span from 1999 until 2005, two sets of DOL regulations apply. The regulations that were in effect prior to August 23, 2004 (the "old regulations") contain a short test that defines the phrase "employee employed in a bona fide executive capacity."[11] * * * This short test has three requirements: (1) an employee "is compensated on a salary basis at a rate of not less than $250 per week," (2) his "primary duty consists of the management of the enterprise in which the employee is employed or of a customarily recognized department or subdivision thereof," and (3) his work "includes the customary and regular direction of the work of two or more other employees." Id. (2003)[12] * * *

*Old test*

---

**10.**  This $1,575,932.12 to 163 Plaintiffs and $17,516,071.27 to the remaining Plaintiffs totaled $19,092,003.39. Although Plaintiffs requested a much larger amount of back pay based on a rate of pay using either a 40–hour or 48–hour workweek, the $19,092,003.39 sum represented Family Dollar's own calculation of overtime back pay based on Defendant's Trial Exhibit 1959, and reflected a rate of pay based on a salary intended to compensate for a 52–hour workweek. In other words, Family Dollar's chart divided the store managers' base salary by 52 hours (not 40 or 48 hours) to determine the hourly rate of pay for Family Dollar's overtime pay calculations. Thus, the jury's use of Family Dollar's calculations substantially reduced the verdict amount, and there is no cross-appeal on that issue.

After the verdict, the district court twice adjusted the back pay amount for certain Plaintiffs for various reasons (such as bankruptcy, judicial estoppel, and standing), and ultimately entered a March 31, 2006 judgment for back pay of $16,623,989.32, and increased the amount by $1,164,040.42 on April 6, 2007, for a total back pay judgment of $17,788,029.74.

**11.**  The old regulations had a long test and a short test. The long test applied to those who made not less than $155 a week. 29 C.F.R. § 541.1(a)–(f) (2003). The short test, on the other hand, applied to those making not less than $250 a week. 29 C.F.R. § 541.1(f) (2003). * * *.

The current regulations (effective August 23, 2004) abolished the distinction between the long and short tests. See Defining and Delimiting the Exemptions for Executive, Administrative, Professional, Outside Sales and Computer Employees, 69 Fed.Reg. 22,122, 22,122–25 (Apr. 23, 2004) (codified at 29 C.F.R. pt. 541) (explaining reasons for the August 23, 2004 change). The Plaintiffs whose claims involve conduct that occurred prior to August 23, 2004 all earned more than $250 a week. Therefore, only the short test under the old regulations and the August 23, 2004 regulations apply to this case.

**12.**  We cite the pre-August 23, 2004 regulations with a 2003 citation and the post-August 23, 2004 ones with a 2006 citation.

After August 23, 2004, the new regulations apply and add a fourth requirement. To establish an employee is a bona fide executive, an employer must show: (1) the employee is "[c]ompensated on a salary basis at a rate of not less than $455 per week"; (2) the employee's "primary duty is management of the enterprise in which the employee is employed or of a customarily recognized department or subdivision thereof"; (3) the employee "customarily and regularly directs the work of two or more other employees"; and (4) the employee "has the authority to hire or fire other employees or whose suggestions and recommendations as to the hiring, firing, advancement, promotion or any other change of status of other employees are given particular weight." 29 C.F.R. § 541.100(a) (2006).

The parties agree that the first element of the executive exemption test—the amount of salary—is met. But they hotly dispute the second element—whether the store managers' primary duty is management. Thus, we examine the second element.

### B. Primary Duty Is Management

Both regulations require that the employee's primary duty is management. The old regulations give these examples of managerial tasks:

> Interviewing, selecting, and training of employees; setting and adjusting their rates of pay and hours of work; directing their work; maintaining their production or sales records for use in supervision or control; appraising their productivity and efficiency for the purpose of recommending promotions or other changes in their status; handling their complaints and grievances and disciplining them when necessary; planning the work; determining the techniques to be used; apportioning the work among the workers; determining the type of materials, supplies, machinery or tools to be used or merchandise to be bought, stocked and sold; controlling the flow and distribution of materials or merchandise and supplies; providing for the safety of the men and the property.

29 C.F.R. § 541.102(b) (2003). The new regulations are similar and explain that generally, management includes, but is not limited to, the same conduct listed in the old regulations, but adds these examples of managerial tasks: "planning and controlling the budget; and monitoring or implementing legal compliance measures." 29 C.F.R. § 541.102 (2006).

The old and new regulations do not define primary duty. Both indicate the answer to the primary duty question "must be based on all the facts in a particular case." 29 C.F.R. § 541.700(a) (2006); 29 C.F.R. § 541.103 (2003). Both regulations identify factors to consider when determining whether an employee's primary duty is managerial. See 29 C.F.R. § 541.700(a) (2006); 29 C.F.R. § 541.103 (2003).

The old regulations list these five factors: (1) "[t]he amount of time spent in the performance of the managerial duties"; (2) "the relative importance of the managerial duties as compared with other types of duties"; (3) "the frequency with which the employee exercises discretionary powers"; (4) "his relative freedom from supervision"; and (5) "the relationship between [the employee's] salary and the wages paid other employees for the kind of nonexempt work performed by the supervisor." 29 C.F.R. § 541.103 (2003); see also *Rodriguez*, 518 F.3d at 1264 (listing factors in § 541.103 to be analyzed in determining whether an employee's primary duty is management). The old regulations explain: "In the ordinary case it may be taken as a good rule of thumb that primary duty means the major part, or over 50 percent, of the employee's time. Thus, an employee who spends over 50 percent of his time in management would have management as his primary duty." 29 C.F.R. § 541.103 (2003). The regulations then hedge a bit, and state that "[t]ime alone ... is not the sole test...." Id. (2003). Where the employee does not spend over 50% of his time on management, "he might nevertheless have management as his primary duty if the other pertinent factors support such a conclusion." Id. (2003).

*[margin note: old regs give 50% as guidance]*

The new regulations make a stronger effort to define primary duty, stating that "[t]he term 'primary duty' means the principal, main, major or most important duty that the employee performs." 29 C.F.R. § 541.700(a) (2006). The new regulations also add that this determination is to be made "with the major emphasis on the character of the employee's job as a whole." Id. (2006). The new regulations explicitly reference the same factors with one exception. The third factor—"the frequency with which the employee exercises discretionary powers"—has been deleted. Compare id. (2006), with 29 C.F.R. § 541.103 (2003).

*[margin note: Note the deletion]*

The new regulations, like the old, expand upon the time-spent-on-exempt-work factor. The new regulations state that this factor "can be a useful guide in determining whether exempt work is the primary duty of an employee" and that "employees who spend more than 50 percent of their time performing exempt work will generally satisfy the primary duty requirement." 29 C.F.R. § 541.700(b) (2006). As in the old ones, the new regulations specify that "[t]ime alone, however, is not the sole test" * * *.

The new regulations also clarify that "[c]oncurrent performance of exempt and nonexempt work does not disqualify an employee from the executive exemption if the requirements of § 541.100 are otherwise met." Id. § 541.106(a) (2006). In other words, an employee's performance of nonexempt work does not preclude the exemption if the employee's primary duty remains management. * * *

## C. *Family Dollar's Motion for Judgment as a Matter of Law*

Family Dollar bears the burden of proving its executive exemption affirmative defense. * * *

We have rejected a "categorical approach" to deciding whether an employee is an exempt executive. * * * Instead, we have noted the "necessarily fact-intensive nature of the primary duty inquiry," that "the answer is in the details," and that "[w]here an issue turns on the particular facts and circumstances of a case, it is not unusual for there to be evidence on both sides of the question, with the result hanging in the balance." Id. And "[t]he result reached must be left intact if there is evidence from which the decision maker, the jury in this instance, reasonably could have resolved the matter the way it did." * * *

As to the time-spent-on-exempt-work factor, the overwhelming evidence at trial showed Plaintiff store managers spent 80 to 90% of their time performing nonexempt, manual labor, such as stocking shelves, running the cash registers, unloading trucks, and cleaning the parking lots, floors, and bathrooms. Conversely, Plaintiff store managers spent only 10 to 20% of their time performing exempt work, a far cry from the DOL's 50% guideline for management tasks. See 29 C.F.R. § 541.700(b) (2006); 29 C.F.R. § 541.103 (2003). Family Dollar did not present evidence to the contrary. * * *

We recognize that the amount of time spent performing exempt tasks is not dispositive of the primary duty issue. But substantial evidence about the four other factors also supports the jury's verdict here.

As to the relative importance of store managers' managerial duties compared with their nonexempt duties, this factor weighs in favor of the jury's finding that store managers are not exempt executives. Admittedly, the store managers' job description includes managerial duties. But Family Dollar's job description of the store managers' "Essential Job Functions" provides that store managers must do the same work as stock clerks and cashiers. Store managers must work their store's preassigned merchandise delivery day, known as "truck day." Barkus acknowledged that store managers spent their delivery-day time doing manual labor. Rather than treat these manual tasks as an incidental part of a managerial job, Family Dollar describes them as essential. A large amount of manual labor by store managers was a key to Family Dollar's business model given each store's limited payroll budget and the large amount of manual labor that had to be performed. The jury was free to weigh the relative importance of the store managers' managerial and non-managerial duties, but ample evidence supported a finding that the non-managerial tasks not only consumed 90% of a store manager's time but were of equal or greater importance to a store's functioning and success.

The third factor in the old regulations—the frequency with which the employee exercises discretionary powers—also supports the jury's verdict. There was overwhelming evidence that store managers spent only 10 to 20% of their time on exempt (i.e., managerial) work. Plaintiffs presented evidence that store managers rarely exercised discretion because either the operations manuals or the district managers' directives controlled virtually every aspect of a store's day-to-day operations. * * *

As to the store managers' relative freedom from supervision, this factor likewise favors Plaintiffs. The evidence showed that * * * the combination of sweeping corporate micro-management, close district manager oversight, and fixed payroll budgets left store managers little choice in how to manage their stores and with the primary duty of performing manual, not managerial, tasks.

As to the last factor—the relationship between the store managers' salary and other wages for nonexempt work—the parties submitted evidence documenting the store managers' average salaries and the assistant managers' average hourly wages from 1999 to 2005. Using a 70–hour workweek, store managers earned, on average, roughly the same (less than a dollar or more per hour) as hourly assistant managers. Using a 60–hour workweek, store managers earned approximately two or three dollars more per hour than hourly assistant managers. * * * Given the relatively small difference between the store managers' and assistant managers' hourly rates, it was within the jury's province to conclude that this factor either did not weigh in Family Dollar's favor or at least did not outweigh the other factors in Plaintiffs' favor.

*[handwritten margin note: Jry okay where mgrs earned barely more than asst mgrs.]*

In sum, there was legally sufficient evidence for the jury, after considering all of the evidence and weighing the relevant factors, to have reasonably determined that Family Dollar failed to meet its burden of proving that Plaintiff store managers' primary duty was management.

### D.   Other Circuits' Cases

Despite these factors, Family Dollar insists its store managers were "in charge" of the store, and therefore, exempt as a matter of law. * * *

Even the retail-chain cases with standardized instructions did not involve fact patterns with the same level of corporate directives or district managers that constrained the powers of the employees-in-question in quite the same way. For example, in * * * Donovan v. Burger King Corp. ("Burger King II"), 675 F.2d 516, 517, 521–22 (2d Cir.1982), the assistant managers retained discretion over a number of operational decisions, and nothing suggested the Burger King restaurant manager, the position directly above the assistant manager, had oversight powers comparable to the ones exercised by Family Dollar district managers. The Second Circuit described restaurant managers as "available by phone" and "available for advice"—not as overarching remote micro-managers. * * *

### E.   163 Individual Plaintiffs Granted Judgment on Executive Exemption Defense

Family Dollar also appeals the district court's decision to grant judgment on the executive exemption defense as a matter of law to 163 of the 1,424 individual Plaintiffs. The court concluded that Family Dollar failed to prove these 163 Plaintiffs satisfied the third part of the executive exemption test, i.e., that they customarily and regularly directed the work of two or more other employees. * * *

Both regulations define "two or more other employees" as either two full-time workers or their equivalent. 29 C.F.R. § 541.104(a) (2006); 29 C.F.R. § 541.105(a) (2003). As to equivalency, an employee may supervise one full-time employee and two part-time employees. * * *

In applying the requirement that an employee "customarily and regularly directs the work of two or more other employees," the district court examined whether store managers supervised 80 subordinate hours of employee work per week at least 80% of the time. The district court did not require the store managers to be present when hourly employees worked those 80 hours-only that the store employ 80 hours of subordinate employee labor 80% of the time. Using Family Dollar's Exhibit 1742C, the district court granted judgment as a matter of law to 163 salaried Plaintiff store managers whose stores did not meet that requirement.

Family Dollar argues the court should have used Family Dollar's internal definition of full-time as a 30–hour workweek. Although the preamble to the new regulations states that the DOL declines to clarify the meaning of "full-time," it "stands by its current interpretation that an exempt supervisor generally must direct a total of 80 employee-hours of work each week." * * * Notably, the preamble does not suggest a work-week as short as 30 hours counts as "full-time" under the FLSA, much less 60 labor hours substituting for 80 hours. Further, Family Dollar's brief points to no evidence in the trial record suggesting that the industry standard in its line of retail business is a 30–hour workweek. While there may be instances where a deviation from the 40–hour workweek is appropriate, we cannot say that the district court, based on this record, erred in adopting 80 hours as constituting two full-time employees or their equivalent in this case. * * *

## VII.  JURY INSTRUCTIONS

Family Dollar's last claim involves the district court's jury instructions. * * *

Our practice is not to nitpick the instructions for minor defects. "[I]f the jury charge as a whole correctly instructs the jury, even if it is technically imperfect, no reversible error has been committed." * * * After review of the jury charge as a whole and counsels' entire closing arguments, we are convinced that the jury properly understood the issues and applicable law. Family Dollar has shown no reversible error in the charge.

## VIII.  CONCLUSION

For all of the above reasons, we affirm the district court's judgments.

## NOTE AND QUESTIONS

1.  The minimum weekly salary figure for the executive exemption is $455 a week under the 2004 revised regulation. A number of commentators have criticized this figure as much too low. See, e.g., MARC LINDER, TIME AND A HALF'S THE AMERICAN WAY: A HISTORY OF THE EXCLUSION OF WHITE–COLLAR WORKERS FROM OVERTIME REGULATION 1868–2004 (2004). The defense offered by the Department of Labor on this and other points appears at 69 Fed.Reg. §§ 22122 et seq.

2. The "salary" requirement has resulted in substantial litigation. Use of the amount of salary in defining the terms "executive, administrative or professional" was challenged early on, but upheld in a widely cited decision, *Walling v. Yeakley*, 140 F.2d 830 (10th Cir. 1944). In *Auer v. Robbins*, 519 U.S. 452, 117 S.Ct. 905, 137 L.Ed.2d 79 (1997), the Supreme Court dealt with whether police sergeants and lieutenants were salaried workers, when their pay could be docked for disciplinary reasons. The regulation in question spoke of "salary" as an amount "not subject to reduction because of variations in the quality or quantity of the work performed." The Court held that a mere theoretical possibility of docking did not prevent the employees in question from being exempt.

3. The decision in *Auer* is also important because it discusses application of the FLSA in the public sector. Extension of federally imposed minimum wage and overtime pay standards to state and local government employees has traveled a rocky road of constitutional challenge. In *Maryland v. Wirtz*, 392 U.S. 183, 88 S.Ct. 2017, 20 L.Ed.2d 1020 (1968), the Supreme Court upheld the extension of the Fair Labor Standards Act to public schools and hospitals. When Congress extended the Act to a broader range of state and local government workers, the Court, in *National League of Cities v. Usery*, 426 U.S. 833, 96 S.Ct. 2465, 49 L.Ed.2d 245 (1976), overruled its prior decision and held that constitutional respect for state sovereignty prevented Congress from regulating employment standards of those performing traditional governmental functions. However, when the Wage and Hour Administration attempted to enforce the Act in favor of government mass transportation workers in *Garcia v. San Antonio Metro. Trans. Auth.*, 469 U.S. 528, 105 S.Ct. 1005, 83 L.Ed.2d 1016 (1985), the Court reexamined the state sovereignty issue, overruled its *National League of Cities* decision, and held that the FLSA's standards apply to such workers.

Congress' expansion of the FLSA to state and local government workers does not treat all such workers in the same manner as private sector employees. Section 207(k) exempts duty tours of fire fighters and law enforcement personnel from overtime pay so long as 216 hours are not exceeded in a 28–day period. Section 207(o) allows public agencies to avoid premium pay for overtime by allowing them to grant, within specified parameters, compensatory time off.

Enforcement of the Act in favor of state (but not local government) workers received a setback in *Alden v. Maine*, 527 U.S. 706, 119 S.Ct. 2240, 144 L.Ed.2d 636 (1999), which held, 5–4, that the Constitution's structural respect for state sovereign immunity nullified the FLSA's grant to state employees of a right of action in state court to enforce a federal minimum wage claim. In *Seminole Tribe of Florida v. Florida*, 517 U.S. 44, 116 S.Ct. 1114, 134 L.Ed.2d 252 (1996); *Florida Prepaid Postsecondary Education Expense Board v. College Savings Bank*, 527 U.S. 627, 119 S.Ct. 2199, 144 L.Ed.2d 575 (1999), and *Kimel v. Florida Board of Regents*, 528 U.S. 62, 120 S.Ct. 631, 145 L.Ed.2d 522 (2000), the Court ruled that due to the 11th Amendment, the Commerce Clause of Article I, Section 8, does not give Congress authority to give access to federal courts for a private damages or injunctive suit against a state. Based on this most recent case law, absent a state's waiver of sovereign immunity, it must be assumed that FLSA standards can be enforced against a state only by an action brought by the U.S. Department of Labor—an agency with very limited resources to engage in such enforcement efforts. However, under the theory of *Ex parte Young*, 209 U.S. 123, 28 S.Ct. 441, 52 L.Ed. 714 (1908), it still may be possible to bring an individual injunctive action in federal court against a state government officer who exercises discretionary power in a manner that thwarts FLSA standards. *Board of Trustees of University of Alabama v. Garrett*, 531 U.S. 356, 121 S.Ct. 955, 148 L.Ed.2d 866 (2001).

4. The Department of Commerce characterizes about 25% of the American workforce as "managerial or professional." The revisions of the applicable regulations in 2004 made it easier for employees to be designated as "managerial," because the new regulations eliminated requirements that executive employees perform non-managerial duties no more than 40 per cent of the time. This may have accelerated an already observable trend. Professor Marc Linder has observed: "In the 1980s 'eating and drinking places' added almost 2 million new jobs, one-tenth of all new jobs in the United States and twice as many as any other industry, becoming the largest private sector employer. During this period the number of supervisory employees increased 61% as compared to a 41% increase in nonsupervisory workers. From 1964 to 1992, supervisory employees in eating and drinking places more than quadrupled...." Marc Linder, *Closing the Gap Between Rich and Poor*, 21 N.Y.U. REV. OF LAW & SOC. CHANGE 1, 22 (1993) (citations omitted). A sizable portion of such "managers" work more than 40 hours a week but earn not much more than the required $455 a week. Would the dual purposes of the Act be better served by restricting the managerial exemption to those who receive a more substantial premium above the minimum wage? This approach is used at § 213(a)(17), which exempts various categories of computer software specialists from the overtime provisions if they are paid at least $27.63 an hour. Another solution, which is used for some types of government employees, is to preserve the work spreading goal of the Act by requiring that those with true managerial responsibilities receive compensatory time off or extended vacations to offset excessive hours worked. See Peter D. DeChiara, *Rethinking the Management–Professional Exemption of the Fair Labor Standards Act*, 43 AMER. U.L. REV. 139 (1993).

5. How much "discretion" must one exercise in order to be exempt as an administrative employee? What of a "credit analyst" for a major bank who makes recommendations or decisions about whether a loan applicant is credit worthy, and in doing so applies criteria set out in a lengthy manual issued by the employer? See *Whalen v. J. P. Morgan Chase & Co.*, 569 F. Supp. 2d 327 (W.D.N.Y. 2008).

6. Section 13(a)(1) also provides an exemption for those who work "in the capacity of outside salesman." In an early opinion, one court discussed the reasons behind the exemption:

> The reasons for excluding an outside salesman are fairly apparent. Such salesm[a]n, to a great extent, works individually. There are no restrictions respecting the time he shall work and he can earn as much or as little, within the range of his ability, as his ambition dictates. In lieu of overtime, he ordinarily receives commissions as extra compensation. He

works away from his employer's place of business, is not subject to the personal supervision of his employer, and his employer has no way of knowing the number of hours he works per day. To apply hourly standards primarily devised for an employee on a fixed hourly wage is incompatible with the individual character of the work of an outside salesman.

*Jewel Tea Co. v. Williams*, 118 F.2d 202, 207–08 (10th Cir. 1941).

Recently, disputes have arisen about the status of representatives of drug companies who call on physicians to attempt to persuade those doctors to prescribe drugs produced by the representatives' employer. These representatives are not permitted by law to "sell" the drugs themselves, to a physician or a patient, but their compensation depends largely on how many prescriptions for particular drugs are written by doctors on particular representatives' lists. Most courts have held that these representatives are exempt under section 13(a)(1) and thus not entitled to overtime pay. See the discussion in *IMS Health Inc. v. Ayotte*, 550 F.3d 42 (1st Cir. 2008); *In re Novartis Wage & Hour Litigation*, 593 F.Supp.2d 637 (S.D.N.Y. 2009).

### *(ii.) Domestic Service Workers*

## LONG ISLAND CARE AT HOME, LTD. v. COKE

Supreme Court of the United States, 2007
551 U.S. 158, 127 S.Ct. 2339, 168 L.Ed.2d 54

JUSTICE BREYER delivered the opinion of the Court.

A provision of the Fair Labor Standards Act exempts from the statute's minimum wage and maximum hours rules

> any employee employed in domestic service employment to provide companionship services for individuals who (because of age or infirmity) are unable to care for themselves (as such terms are defined and delimited by regulations of the Secretary [of Labor]).

29 U.S.C. § 213(a)(15).

A Department of Labor regulation (labeled an "interpretation") says that this statutory exemption includes those "companionship" workers who "are employed by an employer or agency other than the family or household using their services." 29 CFR § 552.109(a) (2006). The question before us is whether, in light of the statute's text and history, and a different (apparently conflicting) regulation, the Department's regulation is valid and binding. See *Chevron U.S.A. Inc. v. Natural Resources Defense Council, Inc.*, 467 U.S. 837, 843–844 (1984). We conclude that it is.

### I

### A

In 1974, Congress amended the Fair Labor Standards Act of 1938 (FLSA or Act), 52 Stat. 1060, to include many "domestic service" employees not previously subject to its minimum wage and maximum hour requirements. * * * When doing so, Congress simultaneously created an exemption that excluded from FLSA coverage certain subsets of employees "employed in domestic service employment," including babysitters "employed on a casual basis" and the companionship workers described above. § 7(b)(3), 88 Stat. 62, (codified at 29 U.S.C. § 213(a)(15)).

The Department of Labor (Department or DOL) then promulgated a set of regulations that included two regulations at issue here. The first, set forth in a subpart of the proposed regulations entitled "General Regulations," defines the statutory term "domestic service employment" as

> services of a household nature performed by an employee in or about a private home ... of the person by whom he or she is employed ... such as cooks, waiters, butlers, valets, maids, housekeepers, governesses, nurses, janitors, laundresses, caretakers, handymen, gardeners, footmen, grooms, and chauffeurs of automobiles for family use [as well as] babysitters employed on other than a casual basis.

40 Fed. Reg. 7405 (1975) (emphasis added) (codified at 29 CFR § 552.3).

The second, set forth in a later subsection entitled "Interpretations," says that exempt companionship workers include those

> who are employed by an employer or agency other than the family or household using their services ... [whether or not] such an employee [is assigned] to more than one household or family in the same workweek....

40 Fed. Reg. 7407 (codified at 29 CFR § 552.109(a)).

This latter regulation (which we shall call the "third-party regulation") has proved controversial in recent years. On at least three separate occasions during the past 15 years, the Department considered changing the regulation and narrowing the exemption in order to bring within the scope of the FLSA's wage and hour coverage companionship workers paid by third parties (other than family members of persons receiving the services, who under the proposals were to remain exempt). * * * But the Department ultimately decided not to make any change. * * *

### B

In April 2002, Evelyn Coke (respondent), a domestic worker who provides "companionship services" to elderly and infirm men and women, brought this lawsuit against her former employer, Long Island Care at Home, Ltd., and its owner, Maryann Osborne (petitioners). * * * She alleged that the petitioners failed to pay her the minimum wages and overtime wages to which she was entitled under the FLSA and a New York statute, and she sought a judgment for those unpaid wages. * * * All parties assume for present purposes that the FLSA entitles Coke to the payments if, but only if, the statutory exemption for "companionship services" does not apply to companionship workers paid by third-party agencies such as Long Island Care. The District Court found the Department's third-party regulation valid and controlling, and it consequently dismissed Coke's lawsuit. * * *

On appeal, the Second Circuit found the Department's third-party regulation "unenforceable" and set aside the District Court's judgment. * * *

## II

We have previously pointed out that the " 'power of an administrative agency to administer a congressionally created ... program necessarily requires the formulation of policy and the making of rules to fill any gap left, implicitly or explicitly, by Congress.' " Chevron, 467 U.S., at 843, 104 S. Ct. 2778 * * *. When an agency fills such a "gap" reasonably, and in accordance with other applicable (e.g., procedural) requirements, the courts accept the result as legally binding. * * *

In this case, the FLSA explicitly leaves gaps, for example as to the scope and definition of statutory terms such as "domestic service employment" and "companionship services." 29 U.S.C. § 213(a)(15). It provides the Department of Labor with the power to fill these gaps through rules and regulations. Ibid.; 1974 Amendments, § 29(b), 88 Stat. 76 (authorizing the Secretary of Labor "to prescribe necessary rules, regulations, and orders with regard to the amendments made by this Act"). The subject matter of the regulation in question concerns a matter in respect to which the agency is expert, and it concerns an interstitial matter, i.e., a portion of a broader definition, the details of which, as we said, Congress entrusted the agency to work out.

The Department focused fully upon the matter in question. It gave notice, it proposed regulations, it received public comment, and it issued final regulations in light of that comment. 39 Fed. Reg. 35383 (1974); 40 Fed. Reg. 7404. See Mead, supra, at 230, 121 S. Ct. 2164. The resulting regulation says that employees who provide "companionship services" fall within the terms of the statutory exemption irrespective of who pays them. Since on its face the regulation seems to fill a statutory gap, one might ask what precisely is it about the regulation that might make it unreasonable or otherwise unlawful?

Respondent argues, and the Second Circuit concluded, that a thorough examination of the regulation's content, its method of promulgation, and its context reveals serious legal problems—problems that led the Second Circuit to conclude that the regulation was unenforceable. In particular, respondent claims that the regulation falls outside the scope of Congress' delegation; that it is inconsistent with another, legally governing regulation; that it is an "interpretive" regulation not warranting judicial deference; and that it was improperly promulgated. We shall examine each of these claims in turn.

## A

Respondent refers to the statute's language exempting from FLSA coverage those "employed in domestic service employment to provide companionship services for individuals who (because of age or infirmity) are unable to care for themselves." 29 U.S.C. § 213(a)(15). She claims that the words "domestic service employment" limit the provision's scope to those workers employed by persons who themselves receive the services (or are part of that person's household) and exclude those who are employed by "third parties." And she advances several arguments in favor of this position.

Respondent points to the overall purpose of the 1974 Amendments, namely to extend FLSA coverage, see, e.g., H.R. Rep. No. 93–232, pp. 2, 8 (1973); she notes that prior to the amendments the FLSA already covered companionship workers employed by certain third parties (e.g., private agencies that were large enough, in terms of annual sales, to qualify for the FLSA's "enterprise coverage" provisions, 29 U.S.C. §§ 206(a), 207(a)(1) (1970 ed.), see §§ 203(r), (s)(1) (defining "enterprise" and "enterprise engaged in commerce or the production of goods for commerce")); and she concludes that Congress must therefore have meant its "domestic service employment" language in the exemption to apply only to persons not employed by third parties such as Long Island Care. Respondent tries to bolster this argument by pointing to statements made by some Members of Congress during floor debates over the 1974 Amendments. See, e.g., 119 Cong. Rec. 24801 (1973) (statement of Sen. Burdick) ("I am not concerned about the professional domestic who does this as a daily living," but rather about "people who might have an aged father, an aged mother, an infirm father, an infirm mother, and a neighbor comes in and sits with them"). And she also points to a different statute, the Social Security statute, which defines "domestic service employment" as domestic work performed in "a private home of the employer." 26 U.S.C. § 3510(c)(1) (2000 ed.) (emphasis added; internal quotation marks omitted).

We do not find these arguments convincing. The statutory language refers broadly to "domestic service employment" and to "companionship services." It expressly instructs the agency to work out the details of those broad definitions. And whether to include workers paid by third parties within the scope of the definitions is one of those details.

Although the FLSA in 1974 already covered some of the third-party-paid workers, it did not at that point cover others. It did not cover, for example, companionship workers employed directly by the aged person's family; nor did it cover workers employed by many smaller private agencies. The result is that whether, or how, the definition should apply to workers paid by third parties raises a set of complex questions. Should the FLSA cover all companionship workers paid by third parties? Or should the FLSA cover some such companionship workers, perhaps those working for some (say, large but not small) private agencies, or those hired by a son or daughter to help an aged or infirm mother living in a distant city? Should it cover none? How should one weigh the need for a simple, uniform application of the exemption against the fact that some (but not all) third-party employees were previously covered? Satisfactory answers to such questions may well turn upon the kind of thorough knowledge of the subject matter and ability to consult at length with affected parties that an agency, such as the Department of Labor, possesses. And it is consequently reasonable to infer (and we do infer) that Congress intended its broad grant of definitional authority to the Department to include the authority to answer these kinds of questions. * * *

### B

Respondent says that the third-party regulation conflicts with the Department's "General Regulation" that defines the statutory term "domestic service employment." Title 29 CFR § 552.3 says that the term covers services "of a household nature performed by ... employee[s]" ranging from "maids" to "cooks" to "housekeepers" to "caretakers" and others, "in or about a private home ... of the person by whom he or she is employed" (emphasis added). See also § 552.101(a). A companionship worker employed by a third party to work at the home of an aged or infirm man or woman is not working at the "home ... of the person by whom he or she is employed" (i.e., she is not working at the home of the third-party employer). Hence, the two regulations are inconsistent, for the one limits the definition of "domestic service employee" for purposes of the 29 U.S.C. § 213(a)(15) exemption to workers employed by the household, but the other includes in the subclass of exempt companionship workers persons who are not employed by the household. Respondent adds that, given the conflict, the former "General Regulation" must govern (primarily because, in her view, only the former regulation is entitled to Chevron deference, an issue we address in Part II–C, infra).

Respondent is correct when she says that the literal language of the two regulations conflicts as to whether workers paid by third parties are included within the statutory exemption. The question remains, however, which regulation governs in light of this conflict. The Department, in its Advisory Memorandum, suggests that the third-party regulation governs, and we agree, for several reasons.

First, if we were to decide the contrary, i.e., that the text of the General Regulation, 29 CFR § 552.3, controls on the issue of third-party employment, our interpretation would create serious problems. Although § 552.3 states that it is supplying a definition of "domestic service employment" only "[a]s [that term is] used" in the statutory exemption, 29 U.S.C. § 213(a)(15), the rule appears in other ways to have been meant to supply a definition of "domestic service employment" for the FLSA as a whole (a prospect the Department endorses in its Advisory Memorandum). Why else would the Department have included the extensive list of qualifying professions, virtually none of which have anything to do with the subjects of § 213(a)(15), babysitting and companionship services? But if we were to apply § 552.3's literal definition of "domestic service employment" (including the "home ... of the [employer]" language) across the FLSA, that would place outside the scope of FLSA's wage and hour rules any butlers, chauffeurs, and so forth who are employed by any third party. That result seems clearly contrary to Congress' intent in enacting the 1974 Amendments, particularly if it would withdraw from FLSA coverage all domestic service employees previously covered by the "enterprise coverage" provisions of the Act.

If, on the other hand, § 552.3's definition of "domestic service employment" were limited to the statute's exemption provision, applying this definition literally (by removing all third-party employees from the exemption) would extend the Act's coverage not simply to third-party-employed companionship workers paid by large institutions, but also to those paid directly by a family member of an elderly or infirm person receiving such services whenever the family member lived in a different household than the invalid. Nothing in the statute suggests that Congress intended to make the exemption contingent on whether a family member chose to reside in the same household as the invalid, and it is a result that respondent herself seems to wish to avoid. See Brief for Respondent 34, n. 31.

Second, normally the specific governs the general. * * * The sole purpose of the third-party regulation, § 552.109(a), is to explain how the companionship services exemption applies to persons employed by third-party entities, whereas the primary (if not sole) purpose of the conflicting general definitional regulation, § 552.3, is to describe the kind of work that must be performed by someone to qualify as a "domestic service" employee. Given that context, § 552.109(a) is the more specific regulation with respect to the third-party-employment question.

Third, we concede that the Department may have interpreted these regulations differently at different times in their history. See, e.g., 58 Fed. Reg. 69311 (employees of a third-party employer qualify for the exemption only if they are also jointly employed "by the family or household using their services"); D. Sweeney, DOL Opinion Letter, Home Health Aides/Companionship Exemption, 6A LRR, Wages and Hours Manual 99:8205 (Jan. 6, 1999) (similar). But as long as interpretive changes create no unfair surprise—and the Department's recourse to notice-and-comment rulemaking in an attempt to codify its new interpretation, see 58 Fed. Reg. 69311, makes any such surprise unlikely here—the change in interpretation alone presents no separate ground for disregarding the Department's present interpretation. * * *

Fourth, we must also concede, as respondent points out, that the Department set forth its most recent interpretation of these regulations in an "Advisory Memorandum" issued only to internal Department personnel and which the Department appears to have written in response to this litigation. We have "no reason," however, "to suspect that [this] interpretation" is merely a " 'post hoc rationalizatio[n]' " of past agency action, or that it "does not reflect the agency's fair and considered judgment on the matter in question." * * *

For all these reasons, we conclude that the Department's interpretation of the two regulations falls well within the principle that an agency's interpretation of its own regulations is "controlling" unless "plainly erroneous or inconsistent with" the regulations being interpreted. * * *

## C

Respondent also argues that, even if the third-party regulation is within the scope of the statute's delegation, is perfectly reasonable, and otherwise complies with the law, courts still should not treat the regulation as legally binding. Her reason is a special one. She says that the regulation is an "interpretive" regulation, a kind of regulation that may be used, not to fill a statutory "gap," but simply to describe an agency's view of what a statute means. That kind of regulation may "persuade" a reviewing court, *Skidmore v. Swift & Co.*, 323 U.S. 134, 140, 65 S. Ct. 161, 89 L. Ed. 124 (1944), but will not necessarily "bind" a reviewing court. Cf. *[United States v]. Mead [Corp.]*, 533 U.S., at 232, 121 S. Ct. 2164 ("interpretive rules ... enjoy no Chevron status as a class" (emphasis added)).

Like respondent, the Court of Appeals concluded that the third-party regulation did not fill a statutory gap and hence was not legally binding. * * * It based its conclusion upon three considerations: First, when the Department promulgated a series of regulations to implement the § 213(a)(15) exemptions, 29 CFR pt. 552, it placed the third-party regulation in Subpart B, entitled "Interpretations," not in Subpart A, entitled "General Regulations." Second, the Department said that regulations 552.3, .4, .5, and .6, all in Subpart A, contained the "definitions" that the statute "require[s]." Third, the Department initially said in 1974 that Subpart A would "defin[e] and delimi[t] ... the ter[m] 'domestic service employee,' " while Subpart B would "se[t] forth ... a statement of general policy and interpretation concerning the application of the [FLSA] to domestic service employees." * * *

These reasons do not convince us that the Department intended its third-party regulation to carry no special legal weight. For one thing, other considerations strongly suggest the contrary, namely that the Department intended the third-party regulation as a binding application of its rulemaking authority. The regulation directly governs the conduct of members of the public, "affecting individual rights and obligations." * * * When promulgating the rule, the agency used full public notice-and-comment procedures, which under the Administrative Procedure Act an agency need not use when producing an "interpretive" rule. 5 U.S.C. § 553(b)(3)(A) (exempting "interpretative rules, general statements of policy, or rules of agency organization, procedure, or practice" from notice-and-comment procedures). Each time the Department has considered amending the rule, it has similarly used full notice-and-comment rulemaking procedures. * * * And for the past 30 years, according to the Department's Advisory Memorandum (and not disputed by respondent), the Department has treated the third-party regulation like the others, i.e., as a legally binding exercise of its rulemaking authority. * * *

For another thing, the Subpart B heading "Interpretations" (and the other indicia upon which the Court of Appeals relied) could well refer to the fact that Subpart B contains matters of detail, interpreting and applying the more general definitions of Subpart A. * * *

Finally, the ultimate question is whether Congress would have intended, and expected, courts to treat an agency's rule, regulation, application of a statute, or other agency action as within, or outside, its delegation to the agency of "gap-filling" authority. Where an agency rule sets forth important individual rights and duties, where the agency focuses fully and directly upon the issue, where the agency uses full notice-and-comment procedures to promulgate a rule, where the resulting rule falls within the statutory grant of authority, and where the rule itself is reasonable, then a court ordinarily assumes that Congress intended it to defer to the agency's determination. * * *

The three contrary considerations to which the Court of Appeals points are insufficient, in our view, to overcome the other factors we have mentioned, all of which suggest that courts should defer to the Department's rule. And that, in our view, is what the law requires.

D

Respondent's final claim is that the 1974 agency notice-and-comment procedure, leading to the promulgation of the third-party regulation, was legally "defective" because notice was inadequate and the Department's explanation also inadequate. We do not agree.

The Administrative Procedure Act requires an agency conducting notice-and-comment rulemaking to publish in its notice of proposed rulemaking "either the terms or substance of the proposed rule or a description of the subjects and issues involved." 5 U.S.C. § 553(b)(3). The Courts of Appeals have generally interpreted this to mean that the final rule the agency adopts must be "a 'logical outgrowth' of the rule proposed." * * *

Initially the Department proposed a rule of the kind that respondent seeks, namely a rule that would have placed outside the exemption (and hence left subject to FLSA wage and hour rules) individuals employed by third-party employers whom the Act had covered prior to 1974. 39 Fed. Reg. 35385 (companionship workers "not exempt" if employed by a third party that already was a "covered enterprise" under the FLSA). The clear implication of the proposed rule was that companionship workers employed by third-party enterprises that were not covered by the FLSA prior to the 1974 Amendments (e.g., most smaller private agencies) would be included within the § 213(a)(15) exemption.

Since the proposed rule was simply a proposal, its presence meant that the Department was considering the matter; after that consideration the Department might choose to adopt the proposal or to withdraw it. As it turned out, the Department did withdraw the proposal for special treatment of employees of "covered enterprises." The result was a determination that exempted all third-party-employed companionship workers from the Act. We do not understand why such a possibility was not reasonably foreseeable. * * *

Neither can we find any significant legal problem with the Department's explanation for the change. The agency said that it had "concluded that these exemptions can be available to such third party employers" because that interpretation is "more consistent" with statutory language that refers to " 'any employee' engaged 'in' the enumerated services" and with "prior practices concerning other similarly worded exemptions." 40 Fed. Reg. 7405. There is no indication that anyone objected to this explanation at the time. * * *

### III

For these reasons the Court of Appeals' judgment is reversed, and we remand the case for further proceedings consistent with this opinion.

It is so ordered.

### NOTES AND QUESTIONS

1. FLSA § 13(a)(15) [29 U.S.C. § 213(a)(15)], the provision involved in Coke, exempts baby-sitting that is on a "casual basis". What is the distinction between employment on a "casual basis" and employment on a "noncasual basis"? Does the term "casual basis" refer to frequency and duration or does it refer to the substantive nature of the activity? Is it employment on a casual basis to do such work every day for three weeks with no expectation of ever resuming the engagement? Is it employment on a casual basis to be engaged to do this two afternoons a week with an expectation of continuing to do so for several months? For several years? Are some types of jobs—e.g., part-time newspaper delivery, part-time baby-sitting—inherently casual in nature? Do considerations such as market efficiency, administrative effectiveness, or social needs justify treating "casual" employment as less protected than regular, long-term employment? Some such judgment seems to underlie the very broad language of § 13(d)[29 U.S.C. § 213(d)] that exempts any person "engaged in the delivery of newspapers to the consumer" and any "homeworker engaged in the making of wreaths from ... evergreens" not only from the requirements of the minimum wage and overtime provisions, but also from the prohibition on child labor. [For a history and critique of the exclusion of newspaper delivery work from American labor protective legislation, see Marc Linder, *From Street Urchins to Little Merchants: The Juridical Transvaluation of Child Newspaper Carriers*, 63 TEMPLE L. REV. 829 (1990).]

2. Section 13(b)(21) exempts from overtime protection any domestic service worker who resides in the household. Section 13(b)(24) excuses a nonprofit institution from paying overtime to resident "foster parents" of children living in the institution, if they receive a minimum cash payment of at least $10,000 a year.

### (iii.) Other Exemptions

Many exemptions that appeared in the original legislation have been eliminated or narrowed. Workers in many retail and service establishments were left totally outside the FLSA's protection, for example, by the 1938 Act's section 13(a)(2), but the statute now covers retail and service workers in establishments doing business of $500,000 or more a year. 29 U.S.C. § 203 (r), (s). The original exclusion of all agricultural workers from minimum wage requirements has been narrowed to those working on the smallest farms, although there is still a broad exemption from overtime requirements, not just for those on farms but for many workers in closely related work such as cotton ginning. 29 U.S.C. § 213(a)(6), (b)(5), (12), (13), (14), (15), (16), (28), (g), (h), (i), (j). Fishery workers are excluded from both wage and overtime requirements, as are members of crews of vessels sailing under flags. 29 U.S.C. § 213(5), (12). Several other exemptions apply to activities of very small businesses, particularly in rural areas, and to various types of seasonal work. See, e.g., 29 U.S.C. § 213(a)(3) (camps and seasonal recreational parks), (8) (small town newspapers), (10) (very small telephone utilities), (b)(9) (small town radio and TV stations, (20) (uniformed services with fewer than 5 employees). The FLSA includes a specific exemption for workplaces outside the United States and certain named U.S. territories.

Although the FLSA does not expressly exempt prison labor, in *Hale v. Arizona*, 993 F.2d 1387 (9th Cir.1993) (en banc), the court held that the Act does not protect prisoners sentenced to "hard-time" who perform work for a state-operated agency established to conduct industries using prison labor. The court reasoned that in such situations the relationship "is penological, not pecuniary." (993 F.2d at 1395) It noted, however, that the Act might apply when prisoners do work for outside employers.

Section 213(b)(1) of the Fair Labor Standards Act exempts from the overtime pay provisions "any employee with respect to whom the Secretary of Transportation has power to establish qualifications and maximum hours of service...." The Motor Carrier Act (49 U.S.C. § 3102) gives the Secretary authority to establish maximum hours for private carriers if necessary to promote safety. A private carrier includes an operator of a motor vehicle that transports property for sale, lease, rent or bailment, or to further a commercial enterprise. In *Friedrich v. U.S. Computer Services*, 974 F.2d 409 (3d Cir.1992), a divided court rejected an overtime claim filed by computer service employees who spent a considerable portion of their time traveling to customers in the employees' own vehicles or by airplane and rental cars. The employees installed, repaired and serviced computer software and carried with them about 35 pounds of tools, diagnostic materials, and replacement parts. The court ruled that the employees' travel placed them within the private carrier definition and that the failure of the Secretary of Transportation to establish maximum hour or other regulations respecting such motor vehicle operators was irrelevant. Since the Secretary had authority to regulate their hours, the employees came within the § 213(b)(1) exemption and they could not collect premium pay for hours worked in excess of 40 a week. A similar provision exempts many employees of railroads and airlines from the overtime requirements. 29 U.S.C. § 213(b)(3).

What is the impact of being excluded from some or all of the requirements of the FLSA? While workers and work opportunities are affected by failure to receive overtime premium pay, payment of wages below the minimum level has a more dramatic impact on employee welfare. A 1987 study estimated that close to 9% of all hourly workers earned below the federal minimum wage. Almost 60% earning below minimum were age 24 or younger; close to 40% of all who earned below minimum were under age 20, nearly 15% were 65 years of age or older. Sometimes earnings are below the minimum because employers violate federal law. Often, below minimum pay results from employment in a work category or for an employer that is exempt from FLSA coverage. Over half of all workers in the 1987 study whose hourly earnings were at or below the minimum lived in their parents' household. Women were twice as likely as men to be in the group earning at or below the minimum and part-time workers were six times as likely as full time workers to be in this category. Jobs paying such low wages were primarily sales or service positions. The demographics for those earning no more than thirty percent above the minimum wage are similar to those for persons employed at or below the minimum. See, Earl F. Mellor, *Workers at the Minimum Wage or Less*, 110 MONTHLY LAB. REV. 34 (Jul. 1987).

Does this remain the pattern? The Bureau of Labor Statistics figures for 2007 indicated that the proportion of workers being paid less than the minimum wage had decreased, according to the Bureau of the Census's Current Population Survey, to roughly one and one-half million workers. The age and other social characteristics patterns remained much the same. See Bureau of Labor Statistics, *Labor Force Statistics from the Current Population Survey: Characteristics of Minimum Wage Workers: 2007*, http://www.bls.gov/cps/minwage2007.htm. Because of difficulties with the statistical techniques involved, including undercounting of undocumented workers, it is likely that the estimates understate the number of persons at or below the minimum wage. See Steven E. Haugen and Earl F. Mellor, *Estimating the Number of Minimum Wage Workers*, MONTHLY LABOR REVIEW 70 (January 1990).

## 2.  COMPENSABLE ACTIVITY

### IBP, INC. v. ALVAREZ

Supreme Court of the United States, 2005
546 U.S. 21, 126 S.Ct. 514, 163 L.Ed.2d 288

JUSTICE STEVENS delivered the opinion of the Court.

These [two] consolidated cases raise questions concerning the coverage of the Fair Labor Standards Act of 1938 (FLSA), as amended by the Portal-to-Portal Act of 1947, with respect to activities of employees who must don protective clothing on the employer's premises before they engage in the productive labor for which they are primarily hired. The principal question, which is presented in both cases, is whether the time employees spend walking between the changing area and the production area is compensable under the FLSA. The second question ... is whether the time employees spend waiting to put on the protective gear is compensable under the statute.

I

As enacted in 1938, the FLSA, 29 U.S.C. § 201 et seq., required employers engaged in the production of goods for commerce to pay their employees a minimum wage of "not less than 25 cents an hour," § 6(a)(1), 52 Stat. 1062, and prohibited the employment of any person for workweeks in excess of 40 hours after the second year following the legislation "unless such employee receives compensation for his employment in excess of [40] hours ... at a rate not less than one and one-half times the regular rate at which he is employed," id., § 7(a)(3), at 1063. Neither "work" nor "workweek" is defined in the statute.

Our early cases defined those terms broadly. In *Tennessee Coal, Iron & R. Co. v. Muscoda Local No. 123*, 321 U.S. 590(1944), we held that time spent traveling from iron ore mine portals to underground working areas was compensable; relying on the remedial purposes of the statute and Webster's Dictionary, we described "work or employment" as "physical or mental exertion (whether burdensome or not) controlled or required by the employer and pursued necessarily and primarily for the benefit of the employer and his business." * * * The same year, in *Armour & Co. v. Wantock*, 323 U.S. 126 (1944), we clarified that "exertion" was not in fact necessary for an activity to constitute "work" under the FLSA. We pointed out that "an employer, if he chooses, may hire a man to do nothing, or to do nothing but wait for something to happen." * * * Two years later, in *Anderson v. Mt. Clemens Pottery Co.*, 328 U.S. 680 (1946), we defined "the statutory workweek" to "includ[e] all time during which an employee is necessarily required to be on the employer's premises, on duty or at a prescribed workplace." * * * Accordingly, we held that the time necessarily spent by employees walking from timeclocks near the factory entrance gate to their workstations must be treated as part of the workweek. * * *

The year after our decision in Anderson, Congress passed the Portal-to-Portal Act, amending certain provisions of the FLSA. Based on findings that judicial interpretations of the FLSA had superseded "long-established customs, practices, and contracts between employers and employees, thereby creating wholly unexpected liabilities, immense in amount and retroactive in operation," 61 Stat. 84, it responded with two statutory remedies, the first relating to "existing claims," id., at 85–86, and the second to "future claims," id., at 87–88. Both remedies distinguish between working time that is compensable pursuant to contract or custom and practice, on the one hand, and time that was found compensable under this Court's expansive reading of the FLSA, on the other. Like the original FLSA, however, the Portal-to-Portal Act omits any definition of the term "work."

With respect to existing claims, <u>the Portal-to-Portal Act provided that</u> <u>employers would not incur liability on account of their failure to pay</u> <u>minimum wages or overtime compensation for</u> any activity that was not <u>compensable by either an express contract</u> or an established custom or <u>practice.</u> With respect to "future claims," the Act preserved potential liability for working time not made compensable by contract or custom but narrowed the coverage of the FLSA by excepting two activities that had been treated as compensable under our cases: walking on the employer's premises to and from the actual place of performance of the principal activity of the employee, and activities that are "preliminary or postliminary" to that principal activity.

Specifically, Part III of the Portal-to-Portal Act, entitled "FUTURE CLAIMS," provides in relevant part:

*Future Claims 2*

SEC. 4. RELIEF FROM CERTAIN FUTURE CLAIMS UNDER THE FAIR LABOR STANDARDS ACT OF 1938 . . .—

(a) Except as provided in subsection (b) [which covers work compensable by contract or custom], no employer shall be subject to any liability or punishment under the Fair Labor Standards Act of 1938, as amended, . . . on account of the failure of such employer to pay an employee minimum wages, or to pay an employee overtime compensation, for or on account of any of the following activities of such employee engaged in on or after the date of the enactment of this Act—

(1) walking, riding, or traveling to and from the actual place of performance of the principal activity or activities which such employee is employed to perform, and

(2) activities which are preliminary to or postliminary to said principal activity or activities,

which occur either prior to the time on any particular workday at which such employee commences, or subsequent to the time on any particular workday at which he ceases, such principal activity or activities.

61 Stat. 86–87 (codified at 29 U.S.C. § 254(a)).

Other than its express exceptions for travel to and from the location of the employee's "principal activity," and for activities that are preliminary or postliminary to that principal activity, the Portal-to-Portal Act does not purport to change this Court's earlier descriptions of the terms "work" and "workweek," or to define the term "workday." A regulation promulgated by the Secretary of Labor shortly after its enactment concluded that the statute had no effect on the computation of hours that are worked "within" the workday. That regulation states: "[T]o the extent that activities engaged in by an employee occur after the employee commences to perform the first principal activity on a particular workday and before he ceases the performance of the last principal activity on a particular workday, the provisions of [§ 4] have no application." 29 CFR

*Actual change*

§ 790.6(a) (2005). Similarly, consistent with our prior decisions interpreting the FLSA, the Department of Labor has adopted the continuous workday rule, which means that the "workday" is generally defined as "the period between the commencement and completion on the same workday of an employee's principal activity or activities." § 790.6(b). These regulations have remained in effect since 1947, see 12 Fed. Reg. 7658 (1947), and no party disputes the validity of the continuous workday rule.

In 1955, eight years after the enactment of the Portal-to-Portal Act and the promulgation of these interpretive regulations, we were confronted with the question whether workers in a battery plant had a statutory right to compensation for the "time incident to changing clothes at the beginning of the shift and showering at the end, where they must make extensive use of dangerously caustic and toxic materials, and are compelled by circumstances, including vital considerations of health and hygiene, to change clothes and to shower in facilities which state law requires their employers to provide. . . ." *Steiner v. Mitchell*, 350 U.S. 247, 248 (1956). After distinguishing "changing clothes and showering under normal conditions" and stressing the important health and safety risks associated with the production of batteries, id., at 249, the Court endorsed the Court of Appeals' conclusion that these activities were compensable under the FLSA.

In reaching this result, we specifically agreed with the Court of Appeals that "the term 'principal activity or activities' in Section 4 [of the Portal-to-Portal Act] embraces all activities which are an 'integral and indispensable part of the principal activities,' and that the activities in question fall within this category." * * * Thus, under Steiner, activities, such as the donning and doffing of specialized protective gear, that are "performed either before or after the regular work shift, on or off the production line, are compensable under the portal-to-portal provisions of the Fair Labor Standards Act if those activities are an integral and indispensable part of the principal activities for which covered workmen are employed and are not specifically excluded by Section 4(a)(1)." * * *

The principal question presented by these consolidated cases—both of which involve required protective gear that the courts below found integral and indispensable to the employees' work—is whether postdonning and predoffing walking time is specifically excluded by § 4(a)(1). We conclude that it is not.

## II

Petitioner in No. 03–1238, IBP, Inc. (IBP), is a large producer of fresh beef, pork, and related products. At its plant in Pasco, Washington, it employs approximately 178 workers in 113 job classifications in the slaughter division and 800 line workers in 145 job classifications in the processing division. All production workers in both divisions must wear outer garments, hardhats, hairnets, earplugs, gloves, sleeves, aprons, leggings, and boots. Many of them, particularly those who use knives, must also wear a variety of protective equipment for their hands, arms, torsos, and legs; this gear includes chain link metal aprons, vests, plexi-glass armguards, and special gloves. IBP requires its employees to store their equipment and tools in company locker rooms, where most of them don their protective gear.

Production workers' pay is based on the time spent cutting and bagging meat. Pay begins with the first piece of meat and ends with the last piece of meat. Since 1998, however, IBP has also paid for four minutes of clothes-changing time. In 1999, respondents, IBP employees, filed this class action to recover compensation for preproduction and postproduction work, including the time spent donning and doffing protective gear and walking between the locker rooms and the production floor before and after their assigned shifts.

*about $ for walking + changing*

IBP does not challenge the holding below that, in light of Steiner, the donning and doffing of unique protective gear are "principal activities" under § 4 of the Portal-to-Portal Act. Moreover, IBP has not asked us to overrule Steiner. Considerations of stare decisis are particularly forceful in the area of statutory construction, especially when a unanimous interpretation of a statute has been accepted as settled law for several decades. Thus, the only question for us to decide is whether the Court of Appeals correctly rejected IBP's contention that the walking between the locker rooms and the production areas is excluded from FLSA coverage by § 4(a)(1) of the Portal-to-Portal Act.

IBP argues that the text of § 4(a)(1), the history and purpose of its enactment, and the Department of Labor's interpretive guidance compel the conclusion that the Portal-to-Portal Act excludes this walking time from the scope of the FLSA. We find each of these arguments unpersuasive.

*IBP's args*

### Text

IBP correctly points out that our decision in Steiner held only that the donning and doffing of protective gear in that case were activities "integral and indispensable" to the workers' principal activity of making batteries. 350 U.S., at 256. In IBP's view, a category of "integral and indispensable" activities that may be compensable because they are not merely preliminary or postliminary within the meaning of § 4(a)(2) is not necessarily coextensive with the actual "principal activities" which the employee "is employed to perform" within the meaning of § 4(a)(1). In other words, IBP argues that, even though the court below concluded that donning and doffing of unique protective gear are "integral and indispensable" to the employees' principal activity, this means only that the donning and doffing of such gear are themselves covered by the FLSA. According to IBP, the donning is not a "principal activity" that starts the workday, and the walking that occurs immediately after donning and immediately before doffing is not compensable. In effect, IBP asks us to create a third category of activities—those that are "integral and indispensable" to a "principal activity" and thus not excluded from coverage by § 4(a)(2), but that are not themselves "principal activities" as that term is defined by § 4(a)(1).

IBP's submission is foreclosed by Steiner. As noted above, in Steiner we made it clear that § 4 of the Portal-to-Portal Act does not remove activities which are " 'integral and indispensable' " to " 'principal activities' " from FLSA coverage precisely because such activities are themselves " 'principal activities.' " * * * While Steiner specifically addressed the proper interpretation of the term "principal activity or activities" in § 4(a)(2), there is no plausible argument that these terms mean something different in § 4(a)(2) than they do in § 4(a)(1). This is not only because of the normal rule of statutory interpretation that identical words used in different parts of the same statute are generally presumed to have the same meaning. * * *It is also because § 4(a)(2) refers to "said principal activity or activities." 61 Stat. 87 (emphasis added). The "said" is an explicit reference to the use of the identical term in § 4(a)(1).

Indeed, IBP has not offered any support for the unlikely proposition that Congress intended to create an intermediate category of activities that would be sufficiently "principal" to be compensable, but not sufficiently principal to commence the workday. Accepting the necessary import of our holding in Steiner, we conclude that the locker rooms where the special safety gear is donned and doffed are the relevant "place of performance" of the principal activity that the employee was employed to perform within the meaning of § 4(a)(1). Walking to that place before starting work is excluded from FLSA coverage, but the statutory text does not exclude walking from that place to another area within the plant immediately after the workday has commenced.

*Purpose*

IBP emphasizes that our decision in *Anderson v. Mt. Clemens Pottery Co.*, 328 U.S. 680, may well have been the proximate cause of the enactment of the Portal-to-Portal Act. In that case we held that the FLSA mandated compensation for the time that employees spent walking from timeclocks located near the plant entrance to their respective places of work prior to the start of their productive labor. Id., at 690–691. In IBP's view, Congress' forceful repudiation of that holding reflects a purpose to exclude what IBP regards as the quite similar walking time spent by respondents before and after their work slaughtering cattle and processing meat. Even if there is ambiguity in the statute, we should construe it to effectuate that important purpose.

This argument is also unpersuasive. There is a critical difference between the walking at issue in Anderson and the walking at issue in this case. In Anderson the walking preceded the employees' principal activity; it occurred before the workday began. The relevant walking in this case occurs after the workday begins and before it ends. Only if we were to endorse IBP's novel submission that an activity can be sufficiently "principal" to be compensable, but not sufficiently so to start the workday, would this case be comparable to Anderson.

Moreover, there is a significant difference between the open-ended and potentially expansive liability that might result from a rule that treated travel before the workday begins as compensable, and the rule at issue in this case. Indeed, for processing division knife users, the largest segment of the work force at IBP's plant, the walking time in dispute here consumes less time than the donning and doffing activities that precede or follow it. It is more comparable to time spent walking between two different positions on an assembly line than to the prework walking in Anderson.

*Regulations*

The regulations adopted by the Secretary of Labor in 1947 support respondents' view that when donning and doffing of protective gear are compensable activities, they may also define the outer limits of the workday. Under those regulations, the few minutes spent walking between the locker rooms and the production area are similar to the time spent walking between two different workplaces on the disassembly line. See 29 CFR § 790.7(c) (2005) (explaining that the Portal-to-Portal Act does not affect the compensability of time spent traveling from the place of performance of one principal activity to that of another). See also § 785.38 (explaining, in a later regulation interpreting the FLSA, that "[w]here an employee is required to report at a meeting place to receive instructions or to perform other work there, or to pick up and to carry tools, the travel from the designated place to the work place is part of the day's work, and must be counted as hours worked ...").

IBP argues, however, that two provisions in the regulations point to a different conclusion—the use of the phrase "whistle to whistle" in discussing the limits of the "workday," § 790.6, and a footnote stating that postchanging walking time is not "necessarily" excluded from the scope of § 4(a)(1), § 790.7(g), n. 49.

The "whistle to whistle" reference does reflect the view that in most situations the workday will be defined by the beginning and ending of the primary productive activity. But the relevant text describes the workday as "roughly the period 'from whistle to whistle.'" § 790.6(a) (emphasis added). Indeed, the next subsection of this same regulation states: "'Workday' as used in the Portal Act means, in general, the period between the commencement and completion on the same workday of an employee's principal activity or activities." § 790.6(b). IBP's emphasis on the "whistle to whistle" reference is unavailing.

The footnote on which IBP relies states:

Washing up after work, like the changing of clothes, may in certain situations be so directly related to the specific work the employee is employed to perform that it would be regarded as an integral part of the employee's 'principal activity.' This does not necessarily mean, however, that travel between the washroom or clothes-changing place and the actual place of performance of the specific work the employee is employed to perform, would be excluded from the type of travel to which section 4(a) refers.

§ 790.7(g), n. 49 (emphasis added; citations omitted).

This footnote does indicate that the Secretary assumed that there would be some cases in which walking between a locker room where the employee performs her first principal activity and the production line would be covered by the FLSA and some cases in which it would not be. That assumption is, of course, inconsistent with IBP's submission that such walking is always excluded by § 4(a), just as it is inconsistent with respondents' view that such walking is never excluded. Whatever the correct explanation for the Secretary's ambiguous (and apparently ambivalent) statement may be, it is not sufficient to overcome the clear statements in the text of the regulations that support our holding. And it surely is not sufficient to overcome the statute itself, whose meaning is definitively resolved by Steiner.

For the foregoing reasons, we hold that any activity that is "integral and indispensable" to a "principal activity" is itself a "principal activity" under § 4(a) of the Portal-to-Portal Act. Moreover, during a continuous workday, any walking time that occurs after the beginning of the employee's first principal activity and before the end of the employee's last principal activity is excluded from the scope of that provision, and as a result is covered by the FLSA.

### III

Respondent in No. 04–66, Barber Foods, Inc. (Barber), operates a poultry processing plant in Portland, Maine, that employs about 300 production workers. These employees operate six production lines and perform a variety of tasks that require different combinations of protective clothing. They are paid by the hour from the time they punch in to computerized timeclocks located at the entrances to the production floor.

Petitioners are Barber employees and former employees who brought this action to recover compensation for alleged unrecorded work covered by the FLSA. Specifically, they claimed that Barber's failure to compensate them for (a) donning and doffing required protective gear and (b) the attendant walking and waiting violated the statute. * * *

On appeal, petitioners argued, among other things, that the District Court had improperly excluded as noncompensable the time employees spend walking to the production floor after donning required safety gear and the time they spend walking from the production floor to the area where they doff such gear. The Court of Appeals rejected petitioners' argument, concluding that such walking time was a species of preliminary and postliminary activity excluded from FLSA coverage by §§ 4(a)(1) and (2) of the Portal-to-Portal Act. 360 F.3d, at 281. As we have explained in our discussion of IBP's submission, see Part II, *supra*, that categorical conclusion was incorrect.

Petitioners also argued in the Court of Appeals that the waiting time associated with the donning and doffing of clothes was compensable. The Court of Appeals disagreed, holding that the waiting time qualified as a "preliminary or postliminary activity" and thus was excluded from FLSA coverage by the Portal-to-Portal Act. 360 F.3d, at 282. Our analysis in Part II, *supra*, demonstrates that the Court of Appeals was incorrect with regard to the predoffing waiting time. Because doffing gear that is "integral and indispensable" to employees' work is a "principal activity" under the statute, the continuous workday rule mandates that time spent waiting to doff is not affected by the Portal-to-Portal Act and is instead covered by the FLSA.

The time spent waiting to don—time that elapses before the principal activity of donning integral and indispensable gear—presents the quite different question whether it should have the effect of advancing the time when the workday begins. Barber argues that such predonning waiting time is explicitly covered by § 4(a)(2) of the Portal-to-Portal Act, which, as noted above, excludes "activities which are preliminary to or postliminary to [a] principal activity or activities" from the scope of the FLSA. 29 U.S.C. § 254(a)(2).

By contrast, petitioners, supported by the United States as amicus curiae, maintain that the predonning waiting time is "integral and indispensable" to the "principal activity" of donning, and is therefore itself a principal activity. However, unlike the donning of certain types of protective gear, which is always essential if the worker is to do his job, the waiting may or may not be necessary in particular situations or for every employee. It is certainly not "integral and indispensable" in the same sense that the donning is. It does, however, always comfortably qualify as a "preliminary" activity.

We thus do not agree with petitioners that the predonning waiting time at issue in this case is a "principal activity" under § 4(a). As Barber points out, the fact that certain preshift activities are necessary for employees to engage in their principal activities does not mean that those preshift activities are "integral and indispensable" to a "principal activity" under Steiner. For example, walking from a timeclock near the factory gate to a workstation is certainly necessary for employees to begin their work, but it is indisputable that the Portal-to-Portal Act evinces Congress' intent to repudiate Anderson's holding that such walking time was compensable under the FLSA. We discern no limiting principle that would allow us to conclude that the waiting time in dispute here is a "principal activity" under § 4(a), without also leading to the logical (but untenable) conclusion that the walking time at issue in Anderson would be a "principal activity" under § 4(a) and would thus be unaffected by the Portal-to-Portal Act.

The Government also relies on a regulation promulgated by the Secretary of Labor as supporting petitioners' view. That regulation, 29 CFR § 790.7(h) (2005), states that when an employee "is required by his employer to report at a particular hour at his workbench or other place where he performs his principal activity, if the employee is there at that hour ready and willing to work but for some reason beyond his control there is no work for him to perform until some time has elapsed, waiting for work would be an integral part of the employee's principal activities." That regulation would be applicable if Barber required its workers to report to the changing area at a specific time only to find that no protective gear was available until after some time had elapsed, but there is no such evidence in the record in this case.

More pertinent, we believe, is the portion of § 790.7 that characterizes the time that employees must spend waiting to check in or waiting to receive their paychecks as generally a "preliminary" activity covered by the Portal-to-Portal Act. * * *

In short, we are not persuaded that such waiting—which in this case is two steps removed from the productive activity on the assembly line—is "integral and indispensable" to a "principal activity" that identifies the time when the continuous workday begins. Accordingly, we hold that § 4(a)(2) excludes from the scope of the FLSA the time employees spend waiting to don the first piece of gear that marks the beginning of the continuous workday.

## IV

For the reasons stated above, we affirm the judgment of the Court of Appeals for the Ninth Circuit in No. 03–1238. We affirm in part and reverse in part the judgment of the Court of Appeals for the First Circuit in No. 04–66, and we remand the case for further proceedings consistent with this opinion.

It is so ordered.

### NOTES AND QUESTIONS

1.  In *Barrentine v. Arkansas–Best Freight System, Inc.*, 750 F.2d 47 (8th Cir. 1984), the employer argued that the time a truck driver spent in carrying out a safety inspection required by federal regulation was not work time, since it was the regulatory agency, not the employer, that required time to be spent in this way. The Eighth Circuit rejected the argument since the employer as well as the general public benefited from the inspection. (Presumably the benefits were twofold: The employer would not be subject to penalties for failure to abide by the regulation, and its trucks would be less likely to malfunction.) What of time spent by a police officer donning a uniform or personal protective gear? See *Maciel v. City of Los Angeles*, 569 F. Supp. 2d 1038 (C.D. Cal. 2008).

2.  The Portal-to-Portal Act has been construed to distinguish between "waiting to be engaged" and "being engaged to wait". Thus, an employee who voluntarily arrives at his work station 15 minutes before starting time is waiting to be engaged and this time is not counted as FLSA work time. However, if an employee arrives at his work station at the time designated by

the employer but there is no work to do because the conveyor belt is stuck, he is engaged to wait and the time is counted as FLSA work time unless he is free to leave for a specified duration that is long enough to allow him to attend to his own affairs. (See 29 CFR §§ 785.15–.16.)

3. Under the Wage and Hour Division's enforcement policies, meal periods generally must be at least a half hour in length and must free the employee of all work duties to be excluded from compensable time. However, the mere fact that employees are prohibited from leaving the employer's premises does not require payment during a meal period. Similarly, the fact that an employee is on a business trip does not make meal time compensable under the FLSA. Rest periods are treated by the Division as noncompensable time if they are longer than 20 minutes and the worker is free to leave the work station. Shorter rest periods are deemed to be for the employer's mutual benefit even if the time is used for enjoying snacks or beverages. Thus, the worker is entitled to be paid. State laws sometimes compel breaks for employees, as a means of protecting employee safety and health (and sometimes the safety of those dealing with the employees). Breaks may also be a contract right, either under a collective bargaining agreement, or because an employee manual or some similar document creates an enforceable promise by the employer to provide these breaks. Failure to provide such breaks can lead to substantial liabilities. See, e.g., *Braun v. Wal–Mart, Inc.*, 2008 WL 2596918 (Minn. Dist. Ct. 2008).

4. An employee who works a shift for less than twenty-four hours is treated by the Wage and Hour Division as being entitled to compensation even though he is permitted to sleep during part of the scheduled time he is required to be present. However, the Division allows up to eight hours to be deducted for sleep time if the shift is at least 24 hours. The mere fact that a worker resides on the employer's premises does not determine whether the work schedule is more than or less than 24 hours a day. Rather, the work schedule is determined by the likelihood of the employee's rest being interrupted by a call to duty.

5. Generally, time spent by workers receiving training, instructions or education is compensable under the FLSA if it occurs during work hours or if attendance is required by the employer. However, training time in an apprenticeship program approved by the Department of Labor is exempt so long as it does not involve productive work or the performance of the employee's regular duties. See, e.g., *Ballou v. General Electric Co.*, 433 F.2d 109 (1st Cir.1970).

6. Time spent commuting to the work site is generally not compensable under the FLSA until the employee reaches the point of being required to perform a job duty. This rule is not altered by the fact that the employer provides the means of transportation. If the employer asks workers to report to a particular location from which they will be bused to work, is time on the bus or waiting for the bus to leave compensable? See *Gonzales v. Tanimura & Antle, Inc.*, 14 Wage & Hour Cases (BNA) 2d 364 (D.Ariz. 2008); *Preston v. Settle Down Enterprises, Inc.*, 90 F. Supp. 2d 1267 (N.D.Ga. 2000) (temporary employee provider). Travel to get to different sites where work is performed during the course of the work day is work time for which payment must be

made by the employer. Should being available to the employer on a cell phone while commuting to work transform that commute into work time? State laws may call for at least some commuting time to be compensated even though the FLSA does not. See, e.g., *Morillion v. Royal Packing Co.*, 22 Cal.4th 575, 94 Cal.Rptr.2d 3, 995 P.2d 139 (2000).

## PABST v. OKLAHOMA GAS & ELEC. CO.

United States Court of Appeals, Tenth Circuit, 2000
228 F.3d 1128

LUCERO, CIRCUIT JUDGE:

We again explore the question of when "on-call" time becomes sufficiently onerous to render it compensable under the Fair Labor Standards Act ("FLSA"). * * *

### I

Plaintiffs are Electronic Technicians in Oklahoma Gas & Electric's ("OG&E") Facility Operations Department. Plaintiffs Pabst and Gilley were Electronic Technician I's ("Tech 1s") and plaintiff Barton was an Electronic Technician II ("Tech 2"). The three plaintiffs, along with two other employees, monitored automated heat, fire, and security systems in several OG & E buildings. Prior to an August 1994 reduction in force, these duties required twelve on-site employees working three eight-hour shifts.

Plaintiffs were on call to monitor OG&E building alarms weekdays from 4:30 p.m. to 7:30 a.m. and twenty-four hours a day on weekends. During these hours, alarms went to computers at Pabst's and Gilley's homes, as well as to pagers for all plaintiffs. After October 1994, Barton began to receive alarms at home via lap-top computer. Plaintiffs were required to respond to the alarms initially within ten minutes, then, after October 1996, within fifteen minutes. Failure to respond within the time limit was grounds for discipline. Each plaintiff was assigned, and required always to carry, an alpha-numeric pager. These pagers were only 70% reliable. The short response time, coupled with unreliable pagers, forced plaintiffs to remain at or near their homes while on call.

The district court found that plaintiffs received an average of three to five alarms per night, not including pages for security issues. Although not all alarms required plaintiffs to report to the office—it appears many could be fixed by remote computer—the district court found it took an average of forty-five minutes to respond to each alarm. Neither party disputes those findings on appeal.

At trial, the parties did dispute whether a rotational on-call schedule was ever proposed or implemented. Acknowledging the dispute, the district court found that "[c]ontrary to OG&E's contention, an examination of the overtime hours actually billed by plaintiffs does not demonstrate that a rotational schedule was ever in effect; rather, the records reveal significant overlap among the technicians, which indicates to the court that no rotational schedule was ever implemented prior to June 1997." (I Appellant's App. at 57.) The district court also found a rotational schedule would not have been feasible because of the frequency of alarms and plaintiffs' differing areas of expertise.

According to plaintiffs, their supervisor instructed them to report only on-call time spent responding to an alarm. OG&E paid plaintiffs for at least one hour for each alarm to which they responded, and two hours if they had to return to OG&E facilities. Plaintiffs apparently reported some, but not all, of the alarms they answered, but did not claim as overtime the remainder of their time spent on call.

Considerable testimony was presented regarding the extent to which monitoring interfered with plaintiffs' personal activities. Most significantly, an average of three to five alarms per night, each requiring on average forty-five minutes of work, severely disrupted plaintiffs' sleep habits; indeed, they testified to rarely experiencing more than five hours of uninterrupted sleep per night. In addition, even during waking hours, plaintiffs were unable to pursue many personal activities while on call because of the need to come into their homes to check their computers every fifteen minutes.

The district court found plaintiffs' on-call time compensable under the FLSA and awarded them compensation for fifteen hours per weekday and twenty-four hours per Saturday and Sunday, less any hours already paid for responding to alarms. Because it found OG&E's violation was not willful, however, the district court limited recovery to the two-year limitations period. It also refused to award liquidated damages, finding that the FLSA violation was reasonable and in good faith. OG&E appeals the district court's rulings on liability, damages, and prejudgment interest, while plaintiffs cross-appeal the district court's ruling denying liquidated damages and its finding of no willful violation.

## II

"We review the district court's findings of fact under the clearly erroneous standard; conclusions of law we review de novo." *Armitage v. City of Emporia*, 982 F.2d 430, 431 (10th Cir.1992) (citations omitted).

With certain exceptions not relevant here, the FLSA requires an employer to pay a minimum wage for each hour it "employ[s]" an employee, as well as an overtime premium for hours in excess of forty per week. * * * "Employ" is defined as including "to suffer or permit to work." * * *. The pertinent question, and one with which courts have struggled, is whether on-call time is "work" for purposes of the statute. The FLSA does not explicitly address the issue of on-call time.[2] Courts,

---

**2.** Although regulations promulgated by the Department of Labor address that issue, they are unhelpful to our analysis because they fail to anticipate a scenario, like that in the present case, in which an on-call employee is able to perform his or her duties from a location away from the employer's premises. See 29 C.F.R. § 785.17 (stating that an "on call" employee is working if "required to remain on call on the employer's premises or so close thereto that he cannot use the time effectively for his own purposes"). More helpful are those regulations applicable to fire

however, have developed a jurisprudence of on-call time, based on the
Supreme Court cases of *Armour & Co. v. Wantock*, 323 U.S. 126, 65 S. Ct.
165, 89 L. Ed. 118 (1944), and Skidmore v. Swift & Co., 323 U.S. 134, 65
S. Ct. 161, 89 L. Ed. 124 (1944). Those cases determine the relevant
inquiry to be whether an employee is "engaged to wait" or "wait[ing] to
be engaged," *Skidmore*, 323 U.S. at 137, 65 S. Ct. 161, or, alternatively,
whether on-call time is spent predominantly for the benefit of the employer or the employee, see *Armour*, 323 U.S. at 133, 65 S. Ct. 165. Necessarily, the inquiry is highly individualized and fact-based, see *Skidmore*, 323
U.S. at 136–37, 65 S. Ct. 161; *Norton v. Worthen Van Serv., Inc.*, 839 F.2d
653, 654 (10th Cir.1988), and "requires consideration of the agreement
between the parties, the nature and extent of the restrictions, the relationship between the services rendered and the on-call time, and all
surrounding circumstances," *Boehm v. Kansas City Power & Light Co.*,
868 F.2d 1182, 1185 (10th Cir.1989) (citing *Skidmore*, 323 U.S. at 137, 65
S. Ct. 161). We also focus on the degree to which the burden on the
employee interferes with his or her personal pursuits. See *Armitage*, 982
F.2d at 432. Several facts are relevant in assessing that burden: number of
calls, required response time, and ability to engage in personal pursuits
while on call. See id.; *Renfro v. City of Emporia*, 948 F.2d 1529, 1537–38
(10th Cir.1991).

### A

OG&E argues that it did not know plaintiffs were working the entire
time they were on call and thus did not "suffer or permit" them to work.
29 U.S.C. § 203(g). Its theory goes as follows: Plaintiffs were responsible
for reporting their own overtime;[3] because they reported only time spent
responding to calls (and apparently not even all of that), rather than all of
their on-call time, OG&E lacked knowledge that they were working and
therefore did not suffer or permit them to work. This argument misinter-
prets the nature of the on-call time inquiry and borders on the disingenuous.

As a factual matter, OG&E's purported lack of actual knowledge is
dubious. Plaintiffs cite record testimony detailing a reprimand Pabst
received for attempting to report the entire time spent monitoring systems
as overtime. Although OG&E attempts to discount this testimony because
the incident occurred after the cessation of the particular on-call monitoring system at issue here, the testimony nevertheless lends support to
plaintiffs' assumption that it would have been futile—or even harmful—
for plaintiffs if they had attempted to report all of their on-call time as
overtime. More significantly, OG&E's policy informed plaintiffs they
would be compensated only for on-call time spent responding to an alarm.
The only logical inference was that they would not be compensated for

---

protection and law enforcement employees. See 29 C.F.R. § 553.221(d) (stating that time spent on
call is compensable if "the conditions placed on the employee's activities are so restrictive that
the employee cannot use the time effectively for personal pursuits").

**3.** Plaintiffs worked a forty-hour week in addition to their time on call. Thus, to the extent on-
call time was working time, it was compensable at the overtime rate. See 29 U.S.C. § 207.

time spent monitoring their computers and pagers, unless they took some specific action responding to an alarm. To claim, then, that OG&E did not know plaintiffs were working because they did not report every hour of their evenings and weekends as overtime is misleading. While OG&E arguably may have lacked knowledge of the legal proposition that the FLSA required compensating plaintiffs for their on-call time under the system at issue, OG&E certainly knew that plaintiffs were performing the duties they had been assigned.

OG&E relies heavily on *Davis v. Food Lion*, 792 F.2d 1274, 1276 (4th Cir.1986) for its knowledge theory. In *Davis*, 792 F.2d at 1275, the court found that "Food Lion has an established policy which prohibits employees from working unrecorded, so-called 'off-the-clock', hours." Davis argued that Food Lion's "Effective Scheduling" system required him to work such off-the-clock hours in order to perform his required duties and avoid reprimand. See id. at 1275–76. The Fourth Circuit held the FLSA "required Davis to prove Food Lion's actual or constructive knowledge of his overtime work," id. at 1276, and found no clear error in the district court's "factual finding that Food Lion has no actual or constructive knowledge of Davis's off-the-clock work," id. at 1277.

Davis is not applicable to the case before us. First, there is no evidence of anything like an explicit prohibition on plaintiffs' performing after-hours monitoring duties; on the contrary, such was the very essence of their responsibilities. Moreover, Davis was not, as plaintiffs correctly note, an on-call time case. In the on-call context, an employer who creates an on-call system obviously has constructive, if not actual, knowledge of employees' on-call duties. An employer must evaluate whether those duties are compensable under the FLSA, and if the employer concludes they are not, the employees do not bear the burden of submitting overtime requests for hours that fall outside the definition of what the employer classifies as compensable. Plaintiffs reported (apparently with some omissions) the hours to which they were entitled under OG&E's policy. That they did not report the entirety of their remaining on-call hours does not preclude the obvious conclusion that OG&E had knowledge of their on-call status.

OG&E's contention that the existence of a rotating on-call schedule prevented it from gaining actual or constructive knowledge of the full extent of plaintiffs' on-call hours implicates a disputed issue of fact. We review the district court's resolution of that dispute for clear error. See *Armitage*, 982 F.2d at 431. If plaintiffs were only on call one week out of three, there would certainly be a problem with each claiming on-call time for every week. However, as the district court noted, the alleged existence of a rotational schedule is contradicted by the significant overlap in the overtime hours reported by plaintiffs. Indeed, in its motion for reconsideration, OG&E conceded that even under its preferred "rotational schedule" analysis—under which one plaintiff was on call for a week running from 7:30 a.m Friday to 7:30 a.m. Friday, rather than calendar weeks—there were weeks when both Pabst and Barton recorded time. Given that concession the district court's resolution of the disputed factual question of the existence of a rotational schedule did not amount to clear error.

B

Whether a particular set of facts constitutes compensable "work" under the FLSA is a legal question we review de novo. * * * In *Renfro*, 948 F.2d at 1536–38, we granted FLSA compensation to firefighters for their on-call time. *Renfro*'s facts include the following:

> [T]he firefighter must be able to report to the stationhouse within twenty minutes of being paged or be subject to discipline; that the on-call periods are 24–hours in length; and primarily that the calls are frequent—a firefighter may receive as many as 13 calls during an on-call period, with a stated average frequency of 3–5 calls per on-call period.

Id. at 1535 (quoting *Renfro v. City of Emporia*, 729 F. Supp. 747, 751 (D.Kan.1990)).

OG&E emphasizes that all but one published Tenth Circuit case addressing on-call time have found it non-compensable. See, e.g., *Andrews v. Town of Skiatook*, 123 F.3d 1327, 1328–32 (10th Cir.1997); *Gilligan v. City of Emporia*, 986 F.2d 410, 413 (10th Cir.1993); *Armitage*, 982 F.2d at 432–33; *Boehm*, 868 F.2d at 1185; *Norton*, 839 F.2d at 654. But see *Renfro*, 948 F.2d at 1538. Counting published cases, however, is meaningless in resolving a fact-intensive question such as the compensability of on-call time. Rather, the proper question is which case is most analogous. Comparing *Renfro* with the cases cited by appellant reveals that a critical distinction in the highly fact-specific inquiry is the frequency of calls. See *Gilligan*, 986 F.2d at 412 ("[W]e noted in *Renfro* that the frequency of call backs was the factor which the *Renfro* district court cited as distinguishing that case from others which had previously held that on-call time was not compensable."); cf. *Armitage*, 982 F.2d at 432 (holding on-call time non-compensable, unlike in *Renfro*, because the plaintiffs were "called in on average less than two times per week"). As in *Renfro*, 948 F.2d at 1537, plaintiffs experienced three to five calls per on-call period. Additionally, although plaintiffs did not always actually report to OG&E's plant, they were required to take some action by computer within fifteen minutes, another burdensome element present in *Renfro*, id. In sum, this case is far more analogous to *Renfro* than to the more numerous precedents cited by OG&E.

Although OG&E complains bitterly against having to compensate plaintiffs for working twenty-four hours a day, seven days a week, the cost to an employer of an "always on call" arrangement does not mean that such a system is not cognizable under the FLSA, so long as the on-call time qualifies as work under the relevant FLSA precedents. While one circuit has held that always being on call, while extremely burdensome, does not in and of itself make the on-call time compensable for FLSA purposes, see *Bright v. Houston Northwest Med. Ctr. Survivor, Inc.*, 934

F.2d 671, 678–79 (5th Cir.1991) (en banc), another circuit found that requiring employees to monitor and respond all day, every day is a factor weighing in favor of compensability, see *Cross v. Arkansas Forestry Comm'n*, 938 F.2d 912, 916–17 (8th Cir.1991) (holding that on-call time is compensable under the FLSA because employees were required to continuously monitor transmissions and respond within thirty minutes, and because they were subject to on-call status twenty-four hours per day for every day of a work period). We agree with both Bright and Cross: Although always being on call is not dispositive, such an added burden is relevant in assessing the extent to which all-the-time on-call duty deprives employees of the ability to engage in personal activities.

The only significant difference between the burden on the plaintiffs in *Renfro* and the burden on Pabst, Gilley, and Barton is that plaintiffs here often did not have to report to the employer's workplace in order to respond to calls. This lighter burden, however, is offset by the fact that plaintiffs, unlike the firefighters in *Renfro*, were not on call for "six shifts of twenty-four hours each in a 19–day cycle," *Renfro*, 948 F.2d at 1531, but rather during all of their off-premises time. The frequency of calls here actually is greater than in *Renfro* because plaintiffs' calls during weekdays occurred during a fifteen hour, rather than a twenty-four hour, period. Additionally, in *Renfro*, we found on-call time compensable despite the fact that the firefighters "had participated in sports activities, socialized with friends and relatives, attended business meetings, gone shopping, gone out to eat, babysitted, and performed maintenance or other activities around their home." Id. at 1532 (citation and internal quotation omitted). *Renfro* controls the application of the FLSA to the facts before us, and leads us to hold that the district court was correct in finding plaintiffs' on-call time compensable.

### III

We next consider OG&E's claims that the award of overtime compensation should be reduced by subtracting out several time periods.

We reject, as a matter of law, OG&E's argument that time spent in personal pursuits should be subtracted. The relevant inquiry in on-call cases is not whether plaintiffs' duties prevented them from engaging in any and all personal activities during on-call time; rather it is "whether 'the time is spent predominantly for the employer's benefit or the employee's.'" *Boehm*, 868 F.2d at 1185 (quoting *Armour*, 323 U.S. at 133, 65 S. Ct. 165). This is a yes-no inquiry—whose benefit predominated? OG&E cites no authority for the proposition that a court must determine whose benefit predominated during each on-call hour. Cf. *Renfro*, 948 F.2d at 1532, 1538 (holding firefighters' on-call time compensable even though they engaged in some personal pursuits during that time). * * *

Finally, as discussed above, we find no clear error in the district court's factual finding that OG&E's alleged rotational schedule was never put into effect. We therefore decline to overturn the district court's award of overtime compensation.

IV

Prejudgment interest is ordinarily awarded in federal cases, although it is not available as a matter of right. See *Towerridge, Inc. v. T.A.O., Inc.,* 111 F.3d 758, 763 (10th Cir.1997). "[T]he standard of review on appeal is whether the trial court abused its discretion in awarding ... prejudgment interest." Id. (quoting *U.S. Indus., Inc. v. Touche Ross & Co.,* 854 F.2d 1223, 1255 n. 43 (10th Cir.1988)). OG&E first argues that the award was an abuse of discretion because it did not know of the alleged overtime, an equitable factor weighing against the award of interest. As discussed above, this ignorance argument is without merit because OG&E created the on-call policy and the terms under which plaintiffs could submit overtime.

OG&E advances a second argument-prejudgment interest should be awarded only from the time the complaint was filed, rather than for the entire period of recovery. The general rule, however, is that interest runs "from the time of the loss to the payment of judgment." *Zuchel v. City and County of Denver,* 997 F.2d 730, 746 (10th Cir.1993) (quoting *U.S. Indus., Inc.,* 854 F.2d at 1256). We thus discern no abuse of discretion in the district court's award of prejudgment interest.

V

Plaintiffs cross-appeal the district court's denial of liquidated damages. We review this issue for abuse of discretion: "[I]f the employer shows to the satisfaction of the court that the act or omission giving rise to such action was in good faith and that he had reasonable grounds for believing that his act or omission was not a violation of the [FLSA], the court may, in its sound discretion, award no liquidated damages...." *Department of Labor v. City of Sapulpa,* 30 F.3d 1285, 1289 (10th Cir. 1994) (quoting 29 U.S.C. § 260) (emphasis added). The district court found that OG&E's actions were reasonable and in good faith for several reasons: OG&E paid double time, rather than just time-and-a-half, for each hour of overtime plaintiffs reported; it permitted plaintiffs to report an hour every time they responded to an alarm, even if they actually spent as little as five minutes; and it was not fully aware of the extent of the burden on plaintiffs until some time in 1997, at which point it took corrective action.

Perhaps we might reach a different conclusion as fact-finders of the first instance, but we find it difficult to call the district court's conclusion an abuse of discretion. Admittedly, the record here is devoid of the sort of evidence—reliance on attorneys or other experts in personnel matters—that courts have found particularly persuasive in holding FLSA violations reasonable. * * * Nevertheless, because the law of on-call time under the FLSA is fact-sensitive, and because the facts relied upon by the district court lend at least some support to the conclusion that OG&E acted in good faith under a reasonable, albeit mistaken, belief that its particular on-call scheme was non-compensable under the statute, we find no abuse of discretion. * * *

Additionally, although we uphold the district court's finding that no rotational schedule was ever actually put into effect, the record could support a conclusion that OG&E supervisors at some times may have operated under a mistaken but good faith belief that such a schedule was in place. Detailed examination of plaintiffs' overtime records might have remedied this mistaken belief; however, given the lack of clarity in the record regarding when and how plaintiffs complained of their onerous on-call duties, we do not view the district court's finding of OG&E's reasonableness and good faith as an abuse of discretion.

## VI

Similarly, we reject plaintiffs' contention that the district court erred in holding OG&E's violation of the FLSA was not willful and consequently limiting the damages award to the statute's two year limitations period. See 29 U.S.C. § 255(a). "The standard for willful violations is whether the employer 'knew or showed reckless disregard for the matter of whether its conduct was prohibited by the [FLSA].' " *Reich v. Monfort, Inc.*, 144 F.3d 1329, 1334 (10th Cir.1998) (quoting *McLaughlin v. Richland Shoe Co.*, 486 U.S. 128, 133, 108 S. Ct. 1677, 100 L. Ed.2d 115 (1988)) (further citations omitted). "Whether an FLSA violation is willful is a mixed question of law and fact, but we believe the factual issues predominate and therefore consider the issue under a clearly erroneous standard of review." Id. (citing *Reich v. Newspapers of New England, Inc.*, 44 F.3d 1060, 1079 (1st Cir.1995)). We find no such error: The same facts that support the district court's conclusion that OG&E's failure to compensate plaintiffs for all of their on-call time was reasonable and in good faith support the district court's conclusion that OG&E's violation of the FLSA was not willful.

## VII

The judgment of the district court is AFFIRMED.

### NOTES AND QUESTIONS

1. Technological change has had considerable impact on the situation of "on call" workers. On the one hand, the spread of cellular phone coverage has made it much easier for an on-call employee to engage in a wide range of activities away from the workplace so long as within range of a transmission tower. But the availability of cellular phones and laptop computers has also encouraged employers, such as the defendant in this case, to reorganize work so that an on-call worker can do what once required a worker "on the spot" all the time. While it turned out that the reduction in force from twelve workers to four in this case was too great a change to succeed in practice, changes that resemble this are increasingly common and can often make operation of a facility more efficient, but also more demanding on workers.

2. Just how drastically must an on-call program limit a worker's personal activities for the on-call time to be work time? As the court's opinion

indicates, the interference must be very substantial indeed. The Tenth Circuit is not unusual in having only a few instances in which plaintiffs making such a claim have prevailed. Consider *Adair v. Charter County of Wayne*, 452 F.3d 482 (6th Cir. 2006). There, plaintiffs were required to live close enough to a major airport operated by the employer so that they would be able to reach the airport within 30 minutes, and to wear pagers at all times. Some were disciplined for failing to wear pagers or failing to respond to a page. Nonetheless, the court found they were not working while on call, since the pagers would operate statewide and most workers were paged only infrequently.

In *Owens v. Local No. 169, Association of Western Pulp and Paper Workers*, 971 F.2d 347 (9th Cir. 1992), the court surveyed the results in on-call cases to that date and found only three that had been resolved in favor of the workers. The court summarized the approach of the federal courts as one using a multi-factor analysis:

> Courts have considered a number of factors in determining whether an employee plaintiff had use of on-call time for personal purposes: (1) whether there was an on-premises living requirement; (2) whether there were excessive geographical restrictions on employee's movements; (3) whether the frequency of calls was unduly restrictive; (4) whether a fixed time limit for response was unduly restrictive; (5) whether the on-call employee could easily trade on-call responsibilities; (6) whether use of a pager could ease restrictions; and (7) whether the employee had actually engaged in personal activities during call-in time. Such a list is illustrative, not exhaustive. No one factor is dispositive. * * *

971 F.2d at 351.

3. *Davis v. Food Lion, Inc.* 792 F.2d 1274 (4th Cir. 1986) is one of several cases in which plaintiffs have sought to establish that an employer had put in place a system in which employees were prohibited from working overtime, but also assigned so many tasks to perform that the workers could not accomplish these tasks unless they worked beyond regular hours. The bulk of these cases have resulted in rulings for defendants, usually on the ground that the employer was unaware that its employees were engaged in overtime work. The employee plaintiffs would have filled out time sheets indicating compliance with the employer's policy, perhaps anticipating discipline or discharge if they did otherwise.

4. Idle time can occur during the course of scheduled work. Salaried workers are paid regardless of the lack of work load. Hourly workers in the U.S., on the other hand, typically are sent home early, without pay, or are given extended uncompensated meal periods ("off-the-clock") until sufficient work is available. In Denmark, Israel, Japan, and the United Kingdom, among other countries, workers are entitled to be paid for idle time if that "down time" is due to problems over which the employer should have control. In Japan, workers are additionally entitled to 60% of their average wages if business has been interrupted as a result of governmental intervention, efforts to introduce new production methods, poor planning in obtaining scarce materials, or because of problems caused by a parent company.

## 3. DETERMINING THE AMOUNT OF CASH PAYMENT REQUIRED

### (a.) "Regular Rate" and the Determination of Overtime Pay Liability

## DUFRENE v. BROWNING–FERRIS, INC.

United States Court of Appeals, Fifth Circuit, 2000
207 F.3d 264

RHESA HAWKINS BARKSDALE, CIRCUIT JUDGE:

\* \* \*

I.

Dufrene and the other plaintiffs (employees) are or were employed by BFI as drivers for recycling trucks or as drivers or hoppers for garbage trucks. (Hoppers ride on the truck, retrieve garbage, and empty it into the truck.)

BFI paid employees a day-rate: they were guaranteed a day's pay, regardless of the number of hours worked that day. After a 60–day probationary period, they received holiday pay, and certain sick days. After one year of service, they received one week paid vacation.

Employees state that BFI regularly required them to work in excess of 40 hours a week; and that they were almost never allowed to stop working after eight hours or less, even if that day's assigned route was completed, but, instead, were required to work additional routes.

In district court, the parties stipulated:

> The overtime compensation is calculated as follows: Employees are given their day rate and it is multiplied by the number of days worked to determine the amount of compensation due [for the week]. The total amount of compensation is then divided by the total number of hours worked to derive the hourly rate. The hourly rate is then divided by 2 and that amount is multiplied by the number of overtime hours. This calculation yields the total amount to be paid in overtime.

In March 1997, employees filed this action, claiming this method violated the FLSA. On cross motions for summary judgment, the district court held: employees were paid a day-rate; BFI's overtime method complied with 29 C.F.R. § 778.112; and, correspondingly, it did not violate the FLSA.

II.

A summary judgment is reviewed de novo. \* \* \* Such judgment is proper when the summary judgment record, viewed in the light most favorable to non-movant, establishes there is no material fact issue and movant is entitled to judgment as a matter of law. * * *.

Employees contend that the overtime method violates the FLSA; that 29 C.F.R. § 778.112 does not apply, because they did not clearly understand it would be used in calculating their overtime pay, and, alternatively, because they receive "other compensation", as referenced in that section; and finally, their collective bargaining agreement defines a day as eight hours, the day-rate compensates them only for working eight hours, and, correspondingly, they are entitled to additional compensation for hours worked in excess of that.

### A.

Employees maintain that the overtime method violates the FLSA requirement to pay time and a half for all hours worked in excess of 40 in a week. BFI responds that it pays such overtime in accordance with 29 C.F.R. § 778.112, one of the Department of Labor's interpretations of the FLSA's overtime payment requirements. An administrative agency's statutory interpretation is reviewed pursuant to *Chevron, U.S.A., Inc. v. Natural Resources Defense Council, Inc.*, 467 U.S. 837, 104 S. Ct. 2778, 81 L. Ed.2d 694 (1984) (if intent of Congress is clear, give it effect; if such intent ambiguous or silent, did Congress delegate to agency authority to interpret statute; and, if such delegation and if agency's interpretation permissible, court should defer to it).

### 1.

The interpretation at issue, 29 C.F.R. § 778.112, provides:

If the employee is paid a flat sum for a day's work or for doing a particular job, without regard to the number of hours worked in the day or at the job, and if he receives no other form of compensation for services, his regular rate is determined by totaling all sums received at such day rates or job rates in the workweek and dividing by the total hours actually worked. He is then entitled to extra half-time pay at this rate for all hours worked in excess of 40 in the workweek.

Addressed first is "whether Congress has directly spoken to the precise question at issue". *Chevron,* 467 U.S. at 842, 104 S. Ct. 2778. Section 7(a)(1) of the FLSA provides in pertinent part that

no employer shall employ any of his employees ... for a workweek longer than forty hours unless such employee receives compensation for his employment in excess of the hours above specified at a rate not less than one and one-half times the regular rate at which he is employed.

29 U.S.C. § 207(a)(1) (emphasis added).

At issue is what is that "regular rate" for employees paid by a day, not hourly, rate. Because the FLSA does not define "regular rate", Congress did not clearly express its intent on this precise question.

* * * By granting the Secretary of Labor the power to administer the FLSA, Congress implicitly granted him the power to interpret" 29 U.S.C. § 207(a)(1), the FLSA provision at issue. * * *.

The third inquiry is whether § 778.112 is a permissible interpretation of the FLSA; if it is, it is entitled to deference. *Chevron*, 467 U.S. at 844, 104 S. Ct. 2778. Employees make much of the undisputed fact that the greater the number of hours worked, the lower the regular rate, and, as a result, the lower the overtime compensation.

But, "that does not cause the system to run afoul of the FLSA if, as in this case, the regular rate remains constant within each workweek and the employee receives one and one-half his regular rate of compensation". *Condo*, 1 F.3d at 605. Cf. *Overnight Motor Transp. Co. v. Missel*, 316 U.S. 572, 580, 62 S. Ct. 1216, 86 L. Ed. 1682 (1942) (method for calculating overtime pay for weekly-wage employee did not violate FLSA simply because regular rate decreased as number of hours worked in a week increased, so long as employee received, as overtime compensation, 150% of his regular rate). Therefore, because each employee is receiving 100% of his regular rate for each hour worked, plus an additional one-half of that regular rate for each hour in excess of 40 in a week, § 778.112 is a permissible interpretation of the FLSA, entitled to deference.

*[handwritten margin note: permissible / deference]*

### 2.

For the reasons that follow, we conclude that § 778.112 applies to employees. The parties have stipulated that employees were paid a day-rate, paid regardless of the number of hours worked in a day. And, they are paid only for the number of days worked in a week.

Employees contend, however, that, before § 778.112 can be used to calculate their regular rate of pay, and, correspondingly, their overtime pay, they must clearly understand that the day-rate covers the hours the job may demand. They maintain that, because 29 C.F.R. § 778.114 requires a clear understanding prior to application, § 778.112 must as well.

The plain language of § 778.112 is directly contrary to this claim. It has no requirement that employees consent to its application. The triggering requirement is solely that employees are paid a day or job rate.

On the other hand, § 778.114(c) states: "The 'fluctuating workweek' method of overtime payment may not be used . . . unless the employee clearly understands that the salary covers whatever hours the job may demand in a particular workweek". (Emphasis added.) But, employees here are not paid a salary for a workweek. Instead, they are paid for the number of days they work in a week: a day-rate.

Accordingly, § 778.114 does not apply. For FLSA purposes, employee agreement to application of § 778.112 is not required.

### 3.

Next, employees assert that § 778.112 applies only if no other form of compensation is received; and that, because they received sick days, paid vacation, and other fringe benefits, the provision cannot be applied to them. * * *

Sick days and other fringe benefits are not "other compensation". See 29 C.F.R. § 778.200 (1999) (for calculating regular rate for overtime pay, payments for vacation, holiday, illness, retirement, health insurance, or similar benefits not compensation). There was no plain error.

### B.

Finally, employees seek assistance from their collective bargaining agreement (CBA).

### 1.

First, they note that the CBA defines a day as eight hours and the day-rate compensates them for such hours. They contend that, because a day is so defined, the day-rate compensates them only for up to eight hours worked, and, correspondingly, it cannot be used to compensate them for any hours worked in a day in excess of that. Consequently, they contend that BFI, in violation of the FLSA, has not paid them their regular rate for such excess hours.

This action, however, is for claimed violation of the FLSA overtime provisions, not of the CBA. Because the overtime payment method complies with § 778.112, this contention is without merit.

### 2.

Employees' contention that the CBA gives them an independent right to overtime pay after an eight-hour day is also without merit. The CBA states that this day-is-eight-hours-provision "shall not be construed as a basis for the calculation of overtime". Again, this dispute concerns, at best, a violation of the CBA, not the FLSA. (Needless to say, as employees concede, this action is not to enforce the CBA.)

### III.

For the foregoing reasons, the judgment is

AFFIRMED.

### NOTES AND QUESTIONS

1. As previously noted, a number of industries, occupations, and job classifications are expressly excluded from the overtime pay requirement. In addition, under some circumstances the Act allows an employer to contractually remove itself from this requirement if that contract satisfies established criteria. This is particularly important to workers and firms in lines of business in which the amount of work to be done changes radically from week to week, such as oil well drilling. Section 7(f) of the Act [29 U.S.C. § 207(f)] exempts hours worked in excess of 40 per week from time and a half for overtime "if the duties of such employee necessitate irregular hours of work,

and the contract" of employment provides for both a weekly guaranty of pay for up to 60 hours of work, and specifies both a pay rate and an overtime rate that meet the requirements of the FLSA. Such arrangements are known as "Belo plans". (The name is derived from the name of the employer involved in the first Supreme Court decision upholding such contracts.) Belo plan contracts can be in the form of provisions in a collectively bargained agreement or can be individual contracts.

Section 7(b)(1) of the FLSA similarly provides a method of exempting certain types of work arrangements from the rigid requirement of time and a half for hours worked in excess of 40 in any work week. Under § 7(b)(1), a union and an employer may enter into a written agreement with a guaranteed weekly wage that permits the worker to work more than forty hours a week at regular pay so long as the employee does not work more than 1040 hours during any period of 26 consecutive work weeks. In addition, § 7(b)(2) of the Act allows an employer and union to agree in writing to allow employees to work more than 40 hours a week without paying an overtime premium if the employee: a) is guaranteed between 1840 and 2080 hours of work over 52 consecutive weeks, b) receives overtime pay for hours worked in excess of the annual guaranty, and c) in no event is employed more than 2240 hours during the 52 week period. These so called 1040–2080 plans are available only through collective bargaining; unlike Belo plans, they cannot be individually negotiated. Their attractiveness to employers and workers is that they stabilize hours and earnings in seasonal industries.

2.   The *Dufrene* opinion illustrates the central importance of understanding the concept of the " 'regular rate' of pay for a given employee in a given workweek ...." As the opinion demonstrates, section 7(e) of the Act defines regular rate largely by listing various forms of remuneration that are excluded when determining the "regular rate." Among the exclusions are gifts for special occasions where the amount given does not bear a relationship to the number of hours worked. Some unworked paid time, including vacation pay, holiday pay, paid medical leave and call-in pay, is also excluded.

More difficult questions sometimes arise when expense reimbursement is involved. What of a fuel surcharge, for example, charged by a limousine company to a customer and then turned over to an employee driver who bought gas out of her own pocket. If the amount of the surcharge is not exactly the same as the increased cost of gasoline, should that surcharge be part of the regular rate or not? See *Powell v. Carey International, Inc.*, 514 F. Supp. 2d 1302 (S.D.Fla. 2007). Contributions to pension, medical insurance, life insurance and similar plans also are excluded in calculating the "regular rate" so long as a third party administers the program. In addition, § 7(e) excludes from "regular pay" other premium payments such as those paid for working weekends or daily overtime. Thus, if a worker receives 8 hours of holiday pay for Monday and then works eight hours a day Tuesday through Saturday, the Act does not require paying the overtime premium for that week.

3.   Commissions and incentive pay (extra pay for producing above a benchmark level) are included in determining the "regular rate" of pay but profit sharing is not. Why the difference in treatment?

4.  In *Minizza v. Stone Container Corp.*, 842 F.2d 1456 (3d Cir.), cert. denied 488 U.S. 909, 109 S.Ct. 261, 102 L.Ed.2d 249 (1988), the court held that a lump sum bonus is excluded from wages in calculating the "regular rate" of pay for the purpose of determining the proper FLSA overtime rate.

5.  The FLSA requires most employers to establish a regular work week, and the determination of whether more than 40 hours have been worked is based upon when that regular work week begins. As a result, if an employer wishes to give compensatory time off for work performed beyond the worker's normal hours, unless that time off is taken in the work week during which the extra hours were worked, it is likely to result in the statutory requirement of overtime pay (particularly in the private sector). For example, if Able's regular work week begins at 7:30 a.m. on Mondays and Able normally works eight hours a day Monday through Friday, Able's employer will be liable for overtime pay if in exchange for Able working an extra four hours on Friday, Able is told to report for work four hours late the next Monday. Indeed, under the FLSA, Able's employer will be liable for paying Able four hours of overtime premium pay even if Able is told to stay home all day the following Monday to compensate for the extra work the previous Friday.

Hospitals operate under a different scheme, one that uses two-week periods instead of one week, and provides for overtime rates after 80 hours during those two weeks. 29 U.S.C. § 207(j).

Fire and police services operate under another provision, under which overtime computation is done on a 28–day basis, and overtime pay is provided only for those whose tours of duty add up to more than 216 hours. 29 U.S.C. § 207(k).

Public sector employers have the privilege of using "compensatory time" plans on a broad scale. Under these plans, an employee receives time off from work at the rate of one and one-half hours for each overtime hour worked, rather than a cash payment. An employee may accumulate no more than 240 hours of "comp time" (480 hours for uniformed workers), and must be allowed to use that time off "within a reasonable time" after requesting to do so. See 29 U.S.C.§ 207(o).

That overtime computation under the FLSA must be done on a weekly basis does not mean that the employee must be paid weekly. Many states have wage payment laws that govern the frequency of pay periods. It is common for such statutes to permit an employer to pay hourly paid workers twice a month, salaried workers monthly. See, e.g., N.J.Stat.Ann. 34:11–4.2. Under some circumstances the Wage–Hour Administrator permits employers to use compensatory time off to avoid overtime cash liability where the workers are paid based on a biweekly, semi-monthly, or monthly pay period. This is permitted if the pay arrangement is constant and if the compensatory hours off from work are at least fifty percent greater than the number of overtime hours worked in the week during which the worker exceeds the weekly forty-hour threshold. See generally United States Department of Labor, Employment Standards Administration, Wage and Hour Division Field Operations Handbook 32j16, "Time Off and Prepayment Plans." Since the time off must be provided so soon after the overtime work occurs, such plans are (as the Handbook indicates) rare.

6. Requiring overtime pay can serve many purposes; promoting employee health, for example, by allowing time for rest and other activities. A principal reason for enacting this sort of hours limitation is that it "spreads the work"; by making the employer pay more for hours beyond 40 in a week, the law encourages the employer to hire a larger number of workers, so that none has to be paid at that higher rate. The exceptions discussed above obviously limit that work-spreading incentive.

Proposals to modify the FLSA would allow employers to avoid overtime pay if employees accept flextime and on average work no more than 40 hours a week. What would be the impact of such changes on spread-the-work goals or on safety and health concerns that are among reasons for requiring extra pay for overtime? Does such a change make more sense in a period of low unemployment but less sense when unemployment rates are high? Does such a change make more sense when dealing with white collar workers than when dealing with those who perform heavy labor or tedious physical tasks?

7. Why would an employer regularly work employees in excess of 40 hours a week, at premium pay, rather than hire part-time or additional full-time workers to meet the extra work hour needs? Are there aspects of the overtime premium requirement of the FLSA that frustrate sound employer and employee preferences? Are those preferences entitled to the same weight as are the public policy considerations that are served by the overtime pay requirement? Are there sound reasons for distinguishing between government and private sector workers in regulating the extent to which compensatory time off can substitute for paying an overtime premium?

## (b.) Allowable Payments in Kind

### CARO–GALVAN v. CURTIS RICHARDSON, INC.

United States Court of Appeals, Eleventh Circuit, 1993
993 F.2d 1500

KRAVITCH, CIRCUIT JUDGE:

\* \* \*

At issue in this case are certain provisions of the Migrant and Seasonal Agricultural Worker Protection Act, 29 U.S.C. §§ 1801–72 (1988) (AWPA), and the Fair Labor Standards Act, 29 U.S.C. §§ 201–19 (1988) (FLSA). The district court dismissed appellants' claims under those acts. We reverse and remand for further proceedings.

### I.

Appellants are indigent farmworkers. Appellee Curtis Richardson, Inc. (Richardson) owns and operates Fern Farms. [The farm principally grew and marketed ferns. Although it also grew and marketed some asparagus, for purposes of description and discussion the court referred to all crops as ferns.] Appellants worked for Richardson in Volusia County, Florida from 1983 to 1989, harvesting its fern crop and performing other field work.

Ferns are grown and harvested year-round. Most fern harvesting occurs from January through May, however, because weather conditions are more conducive to fern growth during those months and because the demand for ferns is greatest around the Valentine's Day, Easter, and Mother's Day holidays. This seasonal character of the fern industry was reflected in appellants' work. During the prime harvest season of January through May, appellants were able to cut enough ferns to earn more than minimum wage.* From June through December, appellants were unable to earn minimum wage cutting ferns. During this off-season period, Richardson offered appellants general field work at minimum wage, including weeding, pulling roots, cleaning, and performing other miscellaneous jobs. The off-season work was voluntary; Richardson allowed appellants to work elsewhere without risk of losing their jobs. Appellants rarely did so, however, because most employers in Volusia County similarly were affected by the cyclical demand for ferns and little alternative work was available.

While appellants were working for Richardson, they lived in trailers which Richardson owned. Richardson operated approximately twenty mobile homes at several sites around Volusia County. Appellants lived at one site where approximately eight trailers were located. All of the occupants at this trailer site were Richardson employees or their family members.[4] Living conditions in the Richardson trailers were substandard. The trailers were unsanitary, structurally unsound, riddled with holes in the ceilings and floors, infested by rodents and insects, and generally in a state of disrepair. Weeks often passed before Richardson made necessary repairs.

Richardson charged rent of $150.00 a month per unit regardless of the number of occupants. Rent and utility costs were deducted from appellants' paychecks. As a result of these deductions, appellants' take-home pay often fell below minimum wage. At times appellants' cash pay was zero. Richardson ordered appellants to vacate the trailers in May 1989 when it terminated their employment.

## II.

In April 1989, shortly before they were fired, appellants brought this action seeking damages and injunctive relief under AWPA and FLSA.[6] The

---

* Richardson paid appellants 17 or 18 cents for each bunch of ferns they cut, gathered, and loaded onto trailers. Appellants typically earned $900 to $1000 dollars per month during this period. (Editor)

**4.** Richardson rented units to nonemployees on at least two occasions for a rent of twice what it charged appellants. Those units were not at the location where appellants lived. * * *

**6.** In their second amended complaint, appellants alleged that Richardson violated AWPA by (1) failing to provide certain written disclosures at the time they began work; (2) failing conspicuously to post appellants' rights under AWPA; (3) providing incomplete wage statements; (4) failing to maintain certain records regarding their employment; (5) failing to provide adequate and safe housing; (6) failing to pay wages when due; and (7) discharging appellants in retaliation for exercising their rights under AWPA. See 29 U.S.C. §§ 1821–23, 1855. Appellants alleged that Richardson violated FLSA in that the deductions Richardson took from appellants' paychecks for rent and utilities unlawfully reduced their pay to below minimum wage. See 29 U.S.C. § 206. At

action was tried to the district court. After appellants rested their case, the court granted Richardson's motion for involuntary dismissal pursuant to Fed.R.Civ.P. 41(b). The court concluded that appellants were not "migrant agricultural workers" entitled to the protections of AWPA. The court also found that Richardson had not fired appellants in retaliation for bringing this lawsuit, but because they failed to perform work they had agreed to do. [This finding was not appealed.] Finally, the court held that the amounts Richardson deducted from appellants' paychecks for rent and utilities were reasonable, and thus lawful under FLSA. * * *

[The court found that the employees were covered by the AWPA because they were migrant agricultural workers engaged in seasonal work. Even though some fern gathering was performed year long, the workers could not rely on that employment during slack season. The court additionally found that because it was necessary to live in the employer's labor camp to get the seasonal work and to perform that work in order to rent the trailers, the Act's purposes required that these places of abode should not be treated as places of permanent residence. The court concluded that the district court erred when it dismissed the AWPA claims.]

## V.

The next issue is whether the district court erred in dismissing appellants' claims under FLSA. We believe it did.

FLSA requires employers to pay agricultural workers a minimum wage. 29 U.S.C. § 206(a)(5). Those payments must be made "free and clear," with one exception.... Under section 3(m) of FLSA, "wage" "includes the reasonable cost ... to the employer of furnishing [the] employee with board, lodging, or other facilities, if such board, lodging, or other facilities are customarily furnished by such employer to his employees." 29 U.S.C. § 203(m). Accordingly, the employer lawfully may deduct from an employee's pay the reasonable cost of employer provided housing, even if that deduction results in the employee's cash pay falling below the statutory minimum. Reasonable cost may not exceed the employer's actual cost. 29 C.F.R. § 531.3(a). The employer is responsible for maintaining and preserving records substantiating that cost. Id. § 516.27.

In *Donovan v. New Floridian Hotel, Inc.*, 676 F.2d 468 (11th Cir. 1982), we held that the plaintiff has the prima facie burden of showing "as a matter of just and reasonable inference that the wages paid to him did not satisfy the requirements of the FLSA." Id. at 475 n. 12; see *Anderson v. Mt. Clemens Pottery Co.*, 328 U.S. 680, 686–87, 66 S. Ct. 1187, 1192, 90 L. Ed. 1515 (1946), superseded by statute on other grounds as stated in *Carter v. Panama Canal Co.*, 463 F.2d 1289, 1293 (D.C.Cir.1972). Once the employee proves that the wages received were less than the statutory minimum, the burden shifts to the employer to prove with proper records the reasonable cost of the housing it furnished. *Donovan*, 676 F.2d at 475.

first, a Mr. Elmer Eden also was a plaintiff in this case. Eden sued Richardson as well as two other defendants, Betty Fowler and Joe Fowler, for alleged violations of AWPA. The district court dismissed Eden's claims before trial when Eden failed to appear.

"An employer's unsubstantiated estimate of his cost, where the employer has failed to comply with the recordkeeping provisions of the FLSA, and where there has been no determination of reasonable cost by the Wage and Hour Division does not satisfy the employer's burden of proving reasonable cost." Id. (citing *Marshall v. Debord*, 84 Lab.Cas. ¶ 33,721, at 48,476 (E.D.Okla.1978)).

In this case, appellants alleged that the deductions Richardson made from their paychecks for rent and utilities unlawfully brought their net pay below minimum wage. The district court dismissed appellants' claims because it found that appellants had not proved that the deductions were unreasonable. In so doing, the court erroneously placed the burden of proof on appellants. Appellants introduced evidence showing that the deductions resulted in their net pay falling below minimum wage on many occasions. At times appellants' take-home pay was nothing. Under *Donovan*, the burden thus shifted to Richardson to prove with records that the deductions were reasonable.

Richardson's only evidence of reasonableness was the bare, conclusory testimony of Curtis Richardson. *Donovan* explicitly rejects as insufficient such unsubstantiated estimates of cost. Richardson argues here that it was unable to introduce records in the district court because appellants never got beyond their case in chief. But this is precisely the point. The district court erred in granting Richardson's Rule 41(b) motion for involuntary dismissal. On remand, Richardson will have the opportunity to introduce records showing that its deductions were reasonable.

## VI.

The judgment of the district court is REVERSED. The case is REMANDED back to the district court for further proceedings consistent with this opinion.

## NOTES AND QUESTIONS

1. Employers sometimes compensate workers through "in-kind" payment of goods or services. In determining whether an employer has satisfied FLSA pay standards, credit is given for some in-kind forms of remuneration. The enforcement policy of the Wage and Hour Division permits employers to count as wages the reasonable cost to the employer of furnishing food, lodging, heat, hot water, cooking fuel, clothing and household effects if the following criteria are satisfied: 1) The in-kind service or goods must be furnished for the worker's primary benefit, 2) the in-kind goods or services must be voluntarily accepted by the worker, and 3) the furnishing of the goods or services must be customary to the type of business or occupation.

In applying the in-kind rules, employers have not been permitted to deduct the value of providing a salesman with an automobile where a vehicle is necessary to the conduct of the business. Thus, the wages before taking the deduction constitute the base for determining the amount of overtime premium due and the balance after such a deduction constitutes the base for determining whether the minimum wage has been paid. Similarly, employers have not been credited with the cost of meals provided to employees in order to facilitate the employee being available for calls to work that frequently occur during the meal period.

2. Migrant workers and foreign workers granted temporary work visas are often victims of exploitive practices involving deductions for employer-provided lodging, food, transportation and tools. Laws and regulations intended to protect these workers from exploitation often fail to deter such conduct due to inadequate enforcement resources and penalties. For example, in 1990 a Department of Labor study reported that the working conditions of 31% of migrant farm workers lack basic sanitation provisions (toilets or hand washing facilities) or drinking water. However, the Department's ability to respond to such conditions is encumbered not only by the size of its field staff but also by restrictions on enforcement against smaller farms. These restrictions are not in the basic legislation; rather they are imposed annually through Congress' appropriations bill for the Department.

Farm operators in many sections of the country hire foreign seasonal laborers who enter the country using the above-mentioned temporary work visas. The farmer (or group of farmers) initiates the application for such visas and in doing so must promise to pay the workers a minimum wage determined by the head of the U.S. Employment Service (a branch of the Department of Labor) to be the minimum that will ensure that the wages paid the foreign workers do not adversely affect the wages of similarly employed U.S. workers. In making that determination, the Employment Service may select a rate higher than that prevailing for similar work in the area if it is determined that "the use of aliens has depressed the wages of similarly employed U.S. workers." 20 C.F.R. § 655.200(c). See, generally, *Frederick County Fruit Growers Ass'n, Inc. v. Martin*, 968 F.2d 1265 (D.C.Cir.1992).

3. Deductions made by an employer for cash shortages or for breakage caused by the worker, or the like, are allowed under the FLSA so long as the net amount after deduction satisfies the minimum wage. However, state laws also place restraints on payroll deductions and often prohibit or regulate the extent to which and the manner in which deductions can be made for cash register shortages and the like. Such state protections are not pre-empted by the FLSA. An example appears later in this chapter, *Runyon v. Kubota Tractor Corp.*

4. If the Fern Farms operator proved that his cost of maintaining the unsanitary trailer was $150 per month, what argument could the employees' lawyer make to contend that that amount should not be included in calculating whether the workers were paid the FLSA minimum wage?

Had Fern Farms paid the full wage, rented the trailers and collected the $150 a month without taking it as a wage deduction, the FLSA would not have been implicated. The Migrant and Seasonal Agricultural Worker Protection Act, nevertheless, would still have applied because that statute requires employers to provide acceptable housing if it is necessary for workers to live in the work area.

## (c.) Tipped Employees

Few tipped workers were covered by the wage and hour law before 1961; until then most workers in all retail enterprises—including hotels and restaurants—were exempted by the now-repealed section 13(a)(2). In 1961, employees of relatively large retail enterprises were added to the statute's coverage; later amendments reduced the dollar volume required for coverage, so that now only the smallest restaurants and hotels fail to fall within the definition of "enterprise." Employers in those industries have regularly argued that their employees rely more on tips than on a pay packet. During hearings over proposed changes to the FLSA in the early 70s, for example, one representative of the American Hotel & Motel Association said: "Unless Congress is prepared to "outlaw" tips entirely, we believe that it should face squarely the fact that tipped employees receive income which far exceeds the purposes of any minimum wage and hour law." *Fair Labor Standards Amendments of 1971: Hearings on S. 1861 Before Subcommittee on Labor of the Committee on Labor and Public Welfare*, 92d CONGRESS 621 (1971) (statement of Arthur J. Packard).

Employee representatives paint a different picture of diners' tipping practices, describing them as at best erratic. One officer of the Hotel Workers made some diners sound a trifle lascivious:

> I oppose, in principle, the concept that a worker should be obliged to depend for his livelihood upon the benevolence and generosity of the public. * * * The amount of tips received for identical work will vary widely, depending on many factors—the area of the country, the season, the whim of the customers and—let's face it—often the physical attractiveness of the worker, which leads me to observe that under the Fair Labor Standards Act, the "wages of sin are not always death," but the cause of sub-minimal rates.

Resolving the issue is significant for the economy. The Bureau of Labor Statistics estimates there are roughly 3 million waiters, waitresses and bartenders in the United States, and if one adds in hotel bell service workers and other related groups, a total of about 5 million tipped workers seems likely. Whatever the true facts about guest generosity, the warring factions in Congress have created some truly complicated language about how much "tip credit" an employer may claim. The current version of the "tip credit" is part of the definition of "wages" in section 3(m):

> In determining the wage an employee is required to pay a tipped employee, the amount paid such employee by the employee's employer shall be an amount equal to—
>
> (1) the cash wage paid such employee which for the purposes of such determination shall be not less than the cash wage required to be paid such an employee on August 20, 1996; and
>
> (2) an additional amount on account of the tips received by such employee which amount is equal to the difference between the wage specified in paragraph (1) and the wage in effect under section 6(a)(1).

The additional amount on account of tips may not exceed the value of the tips actually received by an employee.

The preceding 2 sentences shall not apply with respect to any tipped employee unless such employee has been informed by the employer of the provisions of this subsection, and all tips received by such employee have been retained by the employee, except that this subsection shall not be construed to prohibit the pooling of tips among employees who customarily and regularly receive tips.

29 U.S.C. § 203(m).

To make matters more complicated, the term "tip" is not defined in the statute, although the term "tipped employee" is, in section 3(t):

"Tipped employee" means any employee engaged in an occupation in which he customarily and regularly receives more than $30 a month in tips.

29 U.S.C. § 203(t).

The basic concept of the tip credit is simple: An employer may pay a "tipped employee" as little as $2.13 an hour in cash compensation if the employee in fact has received "tips" during the workweek so that the total amount received in tips and in cash compensation for the week equal the product obtained by multiplying the number of hours worked times the minimum wage. (Overtime premiums may also be due, of course. The $2.13 figure is the result of the odd wording of paragraph (1). Under the pre–1996 law, the maximum amount an employer could claim as a tip credit was 50% of the minimum wage at the time the employee is paid. The 1996 amendments permit a larger tip credit, by freezing the required cash compensation at 50% of the minimum wage on the date of enactment of the 1996 amendments, i.e. $4.25 an hour.)

### Who Is a "Tipped Employee"?

Since a "tipped employee" is one who receives "tips" on a customary and regular basis, the obvious starting point for analysis is figuring out just what constitutes a "tip."

Ballentine's Law Dictionary defines it as "a gratuity given for personal services, as to a porter, table waiter, steward, etc." The Regulations issued by the Secretary are to the same effect, and make an important distinction:

A tip is a sum presented by a customer as a gift or gratuity in recognition of some service performed for him. It is to be distinguished from payment of a charge, if any, made for the service.

29 C.F.R. § 531.52

Thus we have a basic distinction: A "service charge" is not a "tip" for the purposes of the FLSA. From this flows an important principle: If the employer places a "service charge" on a customer's bill—as is typically done, for example, in the case of a banquet or large reception at a club or hotel—the money received as a service charge (a) belongs to the employer rather than to the employees, and (b) may be used to pay the employees' wages, to provide fringe benefits, or for other purposes.* If, on the other hand, the employer confiscates a "tip" that the waiter has received, then the employer is denied the benefit of the FLSA "tip credit."**

That an employer may use "service charge" money to pay basic wages or other costs under the FLSA does not, of course, mean that this is permitted under a state wage payment law or under an individual contract of employment or collective bargaining agreement. If such a contract requires that the employer pay over the entire sum collected as a service charge, either as part of or in addition to cash wages provided for by the agreement, that contract is fully lawful. The FLSA only permits a tip credit in the specified circumstances, it does not require an employer to take advantage of the credit opportunity. If the employer does not claim such a credit, and pays its employees the minimum wage, there is no violation of the FLSA, even if the employer confiscates tips in ways that would lead to its tip pooling arrangement (discussed in the next section) being invalid. Once again, employees might have a remedy under state law, but not under the federal statute.*

### What Is a Proper "Tip Pool" Under the FLSA?

It is common in some restaurants and hotels for employees to "pool" tips received by them. In this way, an employee is less subject to otherwise uncontrollable variations in income, variations associated with whether she waits on tables with "big spenders" or impecunious academics, or happens to be on bellhop duty when a large party of generous tippers check in. It also reduces the temptation for multiple servers to "compete" for tips from a single customer. If a tip pool is proper, the result is that the employer can take the "tip credit" against its wage obligation to each employee who participates in the pool. See 29 C.F.R. § 531.54. What the employer does is to wait until the "pool" distribution has been made, and then calculates the amount of tip credit for each employee.

---

* See *Marshall v. Newport Motel, Inc.*, 24 WH Cases 497 (S.D. Fla. 1979) (accepting the Secretary's regulations); Opinion Letter WH 305 (January 15, 1975), BNA Wage and Hour Manual 99:1187 (hereafter BNA WH Manual).

** See *Barcellona v. Tiffany English Pub*, 597 F.2d 464 (5th Cir. 1979); Opinion Letter WH 310 (February 19, 1975), BNA WH Manual 99:1191, disapproving a scheme under which an employer sought to confiscate all an employee's tips and then return them to the employee as "wages." The distinction between "tip" and "service charge" proved critical in two cases involving topless dancers, *Reich v. Priba Corp.*, 890 F.Supp. 586 (N.D. Texas 1995) and *Reich v. ABC/York–Estes Corp., d/b/a Heavenly Bodies*, 1997 WL 264379 (N.D.Ill. 1997). The dancers in each case were not paid any wage by the club at which they performed, but instead paid the club a "tip out fee" at the end of each shift worked. A major source of income for these dancers was performing "table dances," defined in one opinion as "a dance performed by one of the dancers exclusively for and in front of a particular seated customer." The clubs informed customers of a required minimum they must pay for this service, which the customer would hand over to the performer. Both courts found the amounts paid for table dances to be tips. The employer was therefore not entitled to treat any of the payments as wages. To the extent that the "tip out fee" constituted a confiscation of tips belonging to the dancers, those were to be returned to the dancers with interest.

* *Platek v. Duquesne Club*, 961 F.Supp. 831 (W.D. Penn. 1994). For an example of a statute requiring payment of certain service charge moneys to workers, see Tenn. Code Ann. § 50–2–107.

Two conditions are of primary importance in deciding whether a tip pool is proper or not: (1) who participates; (2) the knowledge of the participants. A third condition, the reasonableness of the amount of "contribution" exacted from each participant, has been mentioned at times, but has not always been recognized by the courts. See, e.g., *Kilgore v. Outback Steakhouse of Florida, Inc.*, 160 F.3d 294 (6th Cir. 1998).

The statute is clear on what categories of employees may participate: those who "customarily and regularly receive tips." In the restaurant context, this group includes food and drink servers, obviously, and bartenders. It is usually thought to include "captains," those individuals who direct the individual servers and sometimes assist in the service themselves, maitres d'hotels,* and wine stewards. The outer limit seems to be table bussers. The existing regulations indicate that it is legitimate to include these workers in tip pools. See 29 C.F.R. § 531.54. This is appropriate for two reasons. The average diner in an upscale restaurant probably thinks the tip she leaves is to show appreciation for all the service she has received, from the total serving staff,** bussers included. Historically, bussers have participated in such pools "customarily and regularly." The kitchen staff, however, are not among those who in the usual setting receive tips, and including them in the "pool" will deprive the employer of the "tip credit." See *Bonham v. Copper Cellar Corp.*, 476 F.Supp. 98 (E.D. Tenn. 1979).

That those who are expected to contribute to a "tip pool" must know of that arrangement and of how it affects their rights under the FLSA is also clear from the language of section 3(m). How is the employee to be informed? There is scant case law. In *Bonham v. Copper Cellar Corp.*, the court found that a notice inconspicuously posted in an employee work area was not enough. Id. Telling an employee when hired that the server's wage will be $2.13 an hour is not enough, even though that is clearly less than the minimum wage; the employer must go on to explain that the "real" minimum wage is a higher figure and that tips will be applied to make up the difference. *Reich v. Chez Robert, Inc.*, 821 F.Supp. 967, 977-978 (D.N.J. 1993), aff'd, 28 F.3d 401 (3d Cir. 1994). The burden of proof of notice is on the employer who wishes to take the tip credit, and the employer cannot rely simply on the argument that employees must understand about these arrangements or they would not accept jobs paying such low wages. *Martin v. Tango's Restaurant, Inc.*, 969 F.2d 1319 (1st Cir. 1992).

The Wage and Hour Administration has taken the position that if the participants in the pool are limited to those who regularly and customarily participate in such pools, and if the employer has informed the employee

---

* In some instances, maitres d'hotels may be sufficiently involved in management and direction of the enterprise to be "employers" within the meaning of the statute. If so, they are not to be included as beneficiaries of a tip pool. See *Fredette v. BVP Management Associates*, 905 F.Supp. 1034 (M.D. Fla. 1995).

** This is the attitude taken by the court in *Austin v. Colonial Williamsburg Hotel Properties, Inc.*, 3 Wage & Hour Cases 2d 579 (E.D. Va. 1996). The case involved claims by "wine runners."

of what is being done, it is not necessary that the employee in fact voluntarily agree to the tip pool arrangement. See Opinion Letter WH–380, March 26, 1976, BNA WH Manual 99:1232. A federal district court in Virginia approved this position in a case involving an ongoing squabble at Colonial Williamsburg between wine servers and the other members of a tip pool. *Austin v. Colonial Williamsburg Hotel Properties, Inc.*, 3 Wage & Hour Cases 2d 579 (E.D. Va. 1996).

Is there some limit to the amount an employee may be required to pay into the pool? The Wage and Hour Administration has taken the position that 15% of the amount of tips received is an outer limit, based on what it believes to be the custom and regular practice of the industry. See Opinion Letter WH–468, BNA WH Manual 99: 1286 (September 5, 1978). At least one court has differed with the Secretary, saying it could find "no statutory or regulatory authority" for this position. *Dole v. Continental Cuisine, Inc.*, 751 F.Supp. 799 (E.D. Ark. 1990).

## 4.  ENFORCEMENT ISSUES

### (a.)  FLSA Procedures

The Administrator of the Wage and Hour Division of the Department of Labor is appointed by the President with the advice and consent of the Senate. The Administrator is in charge of the investigation and discovery of wage and hour law violations. This includes authority to issue interpretive bulletins and manuals as well as procedural and interpretive rules and regulations. The Administrator also issues certificates providing partial exemptions from FLSA requirements for workers who are qualified apprentices, learners, handicapped, or full-time students. Additional regulations issued by the Secretary of Labor exercise delegated discretion to refine certain terms of the Act and determine the availability of specified exemptions. Included in the regulations adopted under the FLSA are employer payroll recordkeeping requirements and the requirement that government-prepared informational notices explaining employee rights under the FLSA be posted in places frequented by employees.

The Wage and Hour Division maintains offices throughout the country. Inspectors from these offices initiate periodic visits to places of employment where they check wage records in order to determine whether there has been compliance with the record keeping, minimum wage, and overtime payment requirements of the FLSA. Priority is given to inspection of repeat violators and of enterprises in industries or localities with a high incidence of violations. Investigators also respond to specific complaints by employees or others alleging violations of the Act.

Upon finding a violation, the investigator prepares an estimate of the amount of back wages that are due. The employer is given an opportunity to discover any errors in the calculations or in the information relied upon by the investigator. The amount of liability is confined by a two-year period of limitations (three years for willful violations) dating from the time the wages became due and payable to the employee. Because the investigation does not stay the running of the period of limitations until a suit is commenced, recovery for the deficiency is lost during the course of investigation and discussion to the extent that the deficiency dates back at least as long as the period of limitation. Therefore, delay in producing information and in resolving differences respecting the amount due works to reduce the employee's recovery. If an agreement is reached respecting the correct amount due, and if the employer is willing to make voluntary payments, a notice offering the agreed amount in full settlement of the employee's claim is sent to the worker by the Wage and Hour Division. Acceptance of such payments bars any further action by the employee. If an agreement is not reached, the Division, in its discretion, may request the Office of the Solicitor of Labor to initiate a federal district court suit for collection. Alternatively, and more often, the Wage and Hour Division simply sends the employee a notice setting forth the amount it believes is due together with an explanation of the employee's right to bring suit in federal or state court to collect the back wages. An employee can institute such a state or federal suit on his or her own initiative. If the Solicitor of Labor brings an enforcement suit, that action supersedes any suit brought by the employee claimant. The Solicitor may seek injunctive as well as monetary relief; an employee can only seek monetary relief. Through an administrative process, with appeals taken under the Administrative Procedure Act, a civil fine of up to $1,000 per violation can be imposed for willful or repeat violations of the minimum wage or overtime law. Additionally, in particularly aggravated cases of willful violation, criminal sanctions are available in an action initiated by the Department of Labor.

When suits are brought under the FLSA, statutorily defined liquidated damages, in an amount equal to the back wage claim, is added to the back wages. That is, the successful claimant receives double damages. In addition, the trial court is directed to award a reasonable attorney's fee and costs. Section 11 of the Portal-to-Portal Act (29 U.S.C. § 260), however, gives the trial court authority to reduce or eliminate the liquidated damages, but not the attorney's fee and costs, if it finds that the employer acted in good faith with reasonable grounds for believing it was complying with the FLSA. In addition, section 10 (29 U.S.C. § 259) of the Portal-to-Portal Act makes good faith reliance on administrative orders, regulations, rulings, approvals or interpretations, a complete defense to liability for minimum wage or overtime pay violations.

Suits may be brought by either the Secretary of Labor or an adversely affected employee to require reinstatement, back wages, statutorily defined damages (equal to the back wages), reasonable attorneys' fees and costs, for an employee who was discharged or discriminated against for instituting any proceeding or testifying under the FLSA. Employee suits for recovery of back wages due under the FLSA may be brought individually or by groups of similarly situated workers. Collective actions, however, are of the "opt-in" variety; an employee must specifically permit joining her claim in the action, a matter discussed in the following opinion. Unions are expressly prohibited from bringing collective FLSA actions in their representative capacity, since enactment of the Portal-to-Portal Act.

One problem in obtaining compliance with the statute is the limited enforcement activity possible with available resources. The number of Wage and Hour Division (WHD) investigators decreased from 945 at the end of 2000 to only 732 in 2007. The total number of "enforcement actions" went from 47,000 in 1997 to just under 30,000 a decade later. More than half the "enforcement actions" in the period from 2000 to 2007 were "conciliations," generally telephone conversations between an investigator and the employer in question. Most of these enforcement actions were the result of complaints by workers. A substantial majority of enforcement actions (75% in the period 2000–2007) resulted in a finding of liability. The most common violations involved failure to pay overtime. Most employers were willing to pay the amounts in question. In 2007, employers agreed to payments of roughly $230 million to remedy these violations. See Government Accountability Office, *Fair Labor Standards Act: Better Use of Available Resources and Consistent Reporting Could Improve Compliance*, GAO–08–926T, July 15, 2008. Case studies conducted by the GAO revealed that many investigations suffered from long delays in assigning a complaint to an investigator, and that investigators would often drop cases if they encountered significant employer opposition or difficulty in making contact with the employer or complainant. See Government Accountability Office, *Case Studies from Ongoing Work Show Examples in Which Wage and Hour Division Did Not Adequately Pursue Labor Violations*, GAO–08–973T (July 15, 2008).

The 2008 GAO studies reflect problems that have been subjects of comment and complaint for many years. One difficulty is that investigators routinely place primary reliance upon the employer's payroll records, but this is an unsatisfactory technique since records often are incomplete or false. Violation of the Act's record keeping requirements are subject to criminal prosecution, but such action is seldom pursued. Thus, it has been observed:

> At most, a court will issue an injunction ordering compliance with the record keeping requirement, but failure to comply with this order leads to only small monetary penalties. Employers learn that it pays not to keep records because the lack of records makes proof of violations and the imposition of back wage liability much more difficult. Thus, proof often must be obtained through employee testimony, but most employees have incomplete records and unreliable memories, and they may be reluctant to testify, or may have long since left the scene. Because the evidence is uncertain, cases often are settled for a portion of the wages due or are abandoned entirely. * * *

> [R]epeat violations are not deterred. The agency has had no pattern or policy of investigating violators to determine whether they have

changed their ways.... Even when an injunction has been obtained to prohibit future violations, the penalties for contempt are smaller than the costs of compliance, and the criminal penalties are rarely used.

Clyde W. Summers, *Effective Remedies for Employment Rights: Preliminary Guidelines and Proposals*, 141 U. PA. L. REV. 457, 493, 495–96 (1992).

Civil penalties of up to $1,000 for each repeated or willful violation of the minimum wage or overtime pay provisions of the Act were added to FLSA section 16(e) and became effective in 1990. However, the required administrative definitions were not adopted until late 1992. (See 29 C.F.R. § 578.3 for the administrative definitions of "repeated" and "willful.") Because an administrative procedure is required for assessing the fines, such action involves an enforcement undertaking separate from a suit to collect backpay. The 2008 GAO study criticized the WHD management practices for not making more consistent use of its statutory penalty authority for these violations. See GAO–08–962T at 17.

Studies indicate that noncompliance is more heavily concentrated in some areas of the country, in some industries and job categories, and in some segments of the workforce, and that a substantial portion of noncompliance goes undetected and unreported. Thus, a 1988 study by the GAO estimated that half of the 5,000 restaurants in Chicago with 25,000 employees were chronic labor law violators, that a fourth of the 100 apparel firms in New Orleans with 5,000 workers were multiple violators and that 3,000 apparel industry shops in New York and hundreds in Los Angeles similarly were sufficiently chronic violators to be classified as "sweatshops." These establishments employ a large number of aliens who are vulnerable to explicit and implied threats of being reported to federal authorities if they are in the country illegally and whose limited command of English reduces their work options even if legal residents.

Combating violations requires considerable persistence in some industries. Thus, Department of Labor targeted enforcement directed at the garment industry found only a third of Los Angeles garment manufacturing establishments in full compliance with the FLSA in 1999. However, this was an improvement over the 22% compliance rate found in 1994. Similarly, when in 1999 Department of Labor investigators reinspected vineyards found in violation of the FLSA and Migrant and Seasonal Agricultural Worker Protection Act, they found slightly more than half still in violation—a result that the Department's district office characterized as a positive development. 165 Labor Relations Reporter 28 (September 4, 2000).

The FLSA's child labor restrictions are enforced by suits brought by the Secretary of Labor to impose civil penalties of up to $10,000 per violation, by injunctive relief, and by criminal actions.

## (b.) Problems of Procedure and Proof

# MORGAN v. FAMILY DOLLAR STORES, INC.

United States Court of Appeals, Eleventh Circuit, 2008
551 F.3d 1233

HULL, CIRCUIT JUDGE:

[The principal facts of the case are set out earlier in this chapter in section B.1.] * * *

### I.  PROCEDURAL HISTORY FROM 2001–2005

* * *

#### B.  *April 2001 Motion to Facilitate Nationwide Notice*

In April 2001, Plaintiffs moved the district court to (1) certify the case as a collective action, (2) authorize notice "by first class mail to all similarly situated management employees employed by Family Dollar Stores, Inc. at any time during the three years prior to the filing of this action to inform them of the nature of the action and their right to opt-into this lawsuit," and (3) order Family Dollar to "produce a computer-readable data file containing the names, addresses, Social Security number and telephone numbers of such potential opt-ins so that notice may be implemented." In May 2001, the court denied the motion for immediate notice, but indicated the motion was "overruled without prejudice." * * *

[In the months that followed, the court supervised discovery, including the taking of depositions from Family Dollar executives and discovery of payroll and other records. In July 2002, the parties notified a sample of store managers of the action, 784 in all. One hundred forty-two indicated they would opt in, and were then sent lengthy questionnaires to fill out. The court also ruled on numerous motions.]

#### F.  *November 2002 Order and Fact Findings*

In November 2002, the district court, acting pursuant to § 216(b), granted Plaintiffs' motion to facilitate nationwide class notice to "all former and current Store Managers who work and/or worked for the Defendant over the last three years." The court found Family Dollar's store managers were similarly situated within the meaning of § 216(b) * * * Although the district court acknowledged that there existed "some differences between the named-Plaintiffs and the opt-ins in terms of pay scale and job duties," it concluded that "these differences do not preclude the facilitation of nationwide service." The court stressed that Plaintiffs must only be "similarly situated"—not "identically situated." The court considered Family Dollar's contention that its stores have "different locations, are of various sizes, and sell different volumes of merchandise." But the court found that those differences did not undermine the factual basis for concluding that Family Dollar's store managers were similarly situated. The court emphasized that it had the benefit of making its decision after twenty months of litigation, considering Plaintiffs' motion to facilitate nationwide notice on two previous occasions, and giving Family Dollar an opportunity to depose the named Plaintiffs. The court found that a sufficient number of similarly situated employees likely were interested in joining the suit and that the case could be managed and resolved in a single litigation. * * *

### H.   Discovery Disputes

Throughout the litigation, the district court resolved scores of discovery-related motions. * * *

[I]n June 2003, in a comprehensive order, the court (1) required Plaintiffs' counsel to produce the questionnaire responses used to support Plaintiffs' motion to facilitate nationwide notice; (2) ordered Family Dollar to produce the names, addresses, and telephone numbers of all former Family Dollar district managers since June 1999; (3) prohibited Plaintiffs' counsel from engaging in ex parte communication with former Family Dollar district managers; and (4) clarified that "this Court shall . . . treat each opt-in Plaintiff as a separate party for purposes of enforcement of the Scheduling Order." * * *

In January 2004, the district court issued a discovery management order resolving many issues. The court limited Family Dollar to "not more than" 250 depositions of the opt-in Plaintiffs, "including those who [had] already been deposed." The court did not restrict Family Dollar to written questions, but limited depositions to five per day (each three hours long). The order authorized Plaintiffs to select 250 opt-ins for Family Dollar to depose in-person. The court pushed the discovery deadline back to April 12, 2004, with dispositive motions due May 12, 2004. It denied both parties' motions for protective orders as moot. * * *

In addition to the 250 depositions of the opt-in Plaintiffs, the parties deposed Family Dollar's executives, district managers, various experts, and other witnesses. Family Dollar produced voluminous payroll records, store manuals, emails, and other communications. Plaintiffs produced the individual responses to the questionnaire. The record was fully developed before the next critical step in this case.

### I.   May 2004 Motion to Decertify the Collective Action

In May 2004, Family Dollar moved to decertify the collective action under § 216(b). Relying on affidavits and a wealth of information revealed during discovery, the parties briefed whether the case should proceed as 1,424 individual actions or as a § 216(b) collective action. Family Dollar argued (1) the opt-in Plaintiffs were not similarly situated under the FLSA, because their day-to-day job duties were too different; (2) the executive exemption defense is inherently individualized; and (3) discrepancies in the store managers' duties made a collective trial impossible and unfair. * * *

### J.  January 2005 Order and Fact Findings

In a January 2005 order, the district court denied Family Dollar's motion to decertify * * *.

In addition, the court found that the "evidence confirm[ed] that substantial similarities exist in the job duties of the named and opt-in Plaintiffs." The court found that 90% of the named and opt-in Plaintiffs (1) interview and train employees, (2) direct work of employees, and (3) maintain production and sales records.

The court also found that the named and opt-in Plaintiffs had similar restrictions on the scope of their responsibilities. Although classified as store managers, they lacked independent authority to hire, promote, discipline, or terminate assistant managers; award employees pay raises; or change weekly schedules of hourly employees. And 90% lacked the power to close the store in an emergency without the district manager's permission. The court concluded that none of the named and opt-in Plaintiffs were responsible for the "total operation of their stores," and that, in reality, district managers performed the relevant managerial duties. * * *

Viewing the evidence "as a whole," the court found that (1) the primary duties of Plaintiffs were not managerial; (2) the time spent performing non-managerial duties did not significantly differ from store to store, district to district, or region to region; and (3) the relative importance of the non-managerial duties (as compared to the limited number of managerial duties) did not vary significantly depending on the store or district. Further, "the basic pay rates of the named and opt-in Plaintiffs are also similar," * * *. The court determined that Family Dollar's defenses were not so individually tailored to each Plaintiff that a collective action would be unmanageable. Because substantial similarities existed in the Plaintiffs' job duties, and the same policies and procedures applied to each store, the court concluded that the case could be fairly tried as a collective action.

### K.  First Jury Trial

* * * In the first trial, the jury deadlocked. Therefore, the issues on appeal arise out of the second trial. * * *

The second jury trial lasted eight days. This time the jury reached a verdict, expressly finding the store managers were not exempt. The parties called 39 witnesses—store managers, district managers, corporate executives, payroll officials, and expert witnesses. In total, the testifying store managers worked at 50 different Family Dollar stores. The testifying district managers ran the operations of 134 different stores. Two testifying Family Dollar executives oversaw 1,400 stores, while a third testifying executive was in charge of all stores.

The parties presented hundreds of Family Dollar's records detailing its policies and procedures. * * * The parties also introduced a large volume of payroll records showing (1) the number of hours worked by each Plaintiff store manager each week, (2) each store manager's salary and rate of pay, and (3) the number of hours every employee worked each week. Both parties submitted multiple exhibits summarizing payroll data in easy-to-digest charts. * * *

### III.  DECERTIFICATION

#### A.  FLSA's Similarly Situated Requirement

* * * [T]o maintain a collective action under the FLSA, plaintiffs must demonstrate that they are similarly situated. See *Anderson v. Cagle's*, 488 F.3d 945, 952 (11th Cir.2007). * * *

Participants in a § 216(b) collective action must affirmatively opt into the suit. * * * That is, once a plaintiff files a complaint against an employer, any other similarly situated employees who want to join must affirmatively consent to be a party and file written consent with the court. * * * Therefore, the importance of certification, at the initial stage, is that it authorizes either the parties, or the court itself, to facilitate notice of the action to similarly situated employees. * * * After being given notice, putative class members have the opportunity to opt-in. The action proceeds throughout discovery as a representative action for those who opt-in.

The key to starting the motors of a collective action is a showing that there is a similarly situated group of employees. * * * The FLSA itself does not define how similar the employees must be before the case may proceed as a collective action. And we have not adopted a precise definition of the term.

Without defining "similarly," we provided some guidance in *Dybach v. State of Florida Department of Corrections*, 942 F.2d 1562, 1567 (11th Cir.1991). There, we emphasized that before facilitating notice, a "district court should satisfy itself that there are other employees . . . who desire to 'opt-in' and who are 'similarly situated' with respect to their job requirements and with regard to their pay provisions." Id. at 1567–68. Later, in *Grayson v. K Mart Corp.*, we instructed that under § 216(b), courts determine whether employees are similarly situated—not whether their positions are identical. 79 F.3d 1086, 1096 (11th Cir.1996). In other words, we explained what the term does not mean—not what it does. * * *

#### B.  Two–Stage Procedure for Determining Certification

While not requiring a rigid process for determining similarity, we have sanctioned a two-stage procedure for district courts to effectively manage FLSA collective actions in the pretrial phase. The first step of whether a collective action should be certified is the notice stage. * * * Here, a district court determines whether other similarly situated employees should be notified.

A plaintiff has the burden of showing a "reasonable basis" for his claim that there are other similarly situated employees. * * * We have described the standard for determining similarity, at this initial stage, as "not particularly stringent," * * * Nonetheless, there must be more than "only counsel's unsupported assertions that FLSA violations [are] wide-spread and that additional plaintiffs would come from other stores." * * *

The second stage is triggered by an employer's motion for decertification. * * * At this point, the district court has a much thicker record than it had at the notice stage, and can therefore make a more informed factual determination of similarity. Id. This second stage is less lenient, and the plaintiff bears a heavier burden. * * *

* * * Because the second stage usually occurs just before the end of discovery, or at its close, the district court likely has a more extensive and detailed factual record. * * *

### C. District Court's Denial of Decertification

Turning to this case and applying our circuit precedent, we conclude that Family Dollar has not shown that the district court abused its discretion in denying Family Dollar's motion for decertification. * * *

First, the district court not only properly followed the two-stage procedure for certifying a § 216(b) collective action but also demanded even more evidence than required before certifying the case at the first notice stage. * * * The district court denied stage one certification two times, without prejudice, and continued to reexamine its decision as the parties gathered and presented additional evidence. The district court conditionally certified the collective action only after the parties filed the depositions of the named Plaintiffs and multiple affidavits and after making detailed fact-findings that Plaintiffs' jobs were similar.

Subsequently, after three more years of discovery, the district court relied on a fully developed record when it denied Family Dollar's motion for decertification * * *.

Second, and more importantly, ample evidence supports the district court's fact-findings that the Plaintiff store managers were similarly situated under § 216(b). The district court, at the second stage, had a complete and comprehensive record and found that the opt-in store managers were factually similar in a number of respects including: (1) their universal classification as store managers with the same job duties; (2) the small fraction of time they spent on managerial duties; (3) the large amount of time they spent on non-managerial duties such as stocking shelves, running the cash registers, unloading trucks, and performing janitorial work; (4) the restrictions on their power to manage stores as compared to the district manager's sweeping managerial discretion; (5) the amount of close district manager supervision of store managers; (6) the lack of managerial discretion that Family Dollar corporate policies afforded to store managers; (7) their day-to-day responsibilities; (8) their receiving base salaries regardless of the hours worked and no overtime pay; (9) their sharing certain managerial duties with hourly employees; (10) their maintaining production and sales records; (11) their inability to authorize pay raises; (12) their power to train subordinates; (13) their restricted authority to close stores in the event of emergencies;

and (14) their inability to select outside vendors without district manager approval.

We recognize Family Dollar's assertion that the duties of store managers varied significantly depending on the store's size, sales volume, region, and district. But there was scant evidence to support this argument. Rather, the bulk of evidence demonstrated that the store managers were similarly situated and even Family Dollar perceived no such distinction. Indeed, it exempted all store managers from overtime pay requirements without regard to store size, sales volume, region, district, or hiring and firing authority.

As to the second factor, whether there were defenses individual to each Plaintiff, Family Dollar argues the executive exemption defense is always individualized and fact specific, thereby precluding this collective action. As discussed later, applying the executive exemption is "an inherently fact-based inquiry" that depends on the many details of the particular job duties and actual work performed by the employee seeking overtime pay. * * * But Family Dollar ignores the overwhelming evidence showing that the Plaintiffs, as a group, shared a number of factual details with respect to their job duties and day-to-day work. Just because the inquiry is fact-intensive does not preclude a collective action where plaintiffs share common job traits. Given the volume of evidence showing the store managers were similarly situated, and the fact that Family Dollar applied the executive exemption across-the-board to every store manager—no matter the size, region, or sales volume of the store—Family Dollar has not shown clear error in the district court's finding that its defenses were not so individually tailored to each Plaintiff as to make this collective action unwarranted or unmanageable.

As to the third factor, fairness and procedural considerations, we reject Family Dollar's contention that given the size of the class, the individualized application of the exemption defense, and the court's decision to allow representative testimony at trial, any collective action would be inherently unfair. There is nothing inherently unfair about collectively litigating an affirmative executive-exemption defense where the district court has made well-supported and detailed findings with respect to similarity. Indeed, the more similar the employees, the less likely that collectively litigating the executive-exemption issue can be fundamentally unfair. And to repeat, there was abundant evidence that Plaintiffs' actual jobs were the same, or, at a minimum, substantially similar.

In addition, Plaintiffs' evidence established that Family Dollar uniformly exempted all store managers from overtime pay requirements, and its exemption decision did not turn on any individualized factors. Not one. There is nothing unfair about litigating a single corporate decision in a single collective action, especially where there is robust evidence that store managers perform uniform, cookie-cutter tasks mandated by a one-size-fits-all corporate manual. Addressing whether Plaintiffs' claims could be tried fairly as a collective action also requires looking to the purposes of

§ 216(b) actions under the FLSA: (1) reducing the burden on plaintiffs through the pooling of resources, and (2) efficiently resolving common issues of law and fact that arise from the same illegal conduct. * * * We also bear in mind that the FLSA is a remedial statute that should be liberally construed. * * * Oddly, the thrust of Family Dollar's fairness argument butts up against the purpose of a collective action—to efficiently resolve a large number of plaintiffs' claims. Therefore, generally speaking, the size of an FLSA collective action does not, on its own, compel the conclusion that a decision to collectively litigate a case is inherently unfair. * * *

## V.   REPRESENTATIVE TESTIMONY

Family Dollar's challenge to the use of representative testimony proceeds as follows: Seven Plaintiffs testified. There are 1,424 Plaintiffs. Therefore, the verdict is based on only the representative testimony of less than 1% of the total number of Plaintiffs. Family Dollar argues that this was simply too small a sample size of testifying Plaintiffs, and therefore the jury verdict is unreliable and should be set aside.

Family Dollar's depiction of the trial is belied by the record. First, Plaintiffs did not use representative testimony to prove its prima facie case. Instead, Plaintiffs relied on Family Dollar's thorough payroll records for each of the 1,424 Plaintiffs to show (1) when each employee worked, (2) how many actual hours they worked, (3) how much they were paid, and (4) that they never received overtime pay. Rather than contesting Plaintiffs' prima facie case,[13] Family Dollar focused on its executive exemption defense at trial.

Second, Family Dollar's claim, stripped of its hyperbole, is reduced to an objection that not enough Plaintiffs testified to ensure a reliable verdict on whether the executive exemption defense applied. But the jury's verdict as to that defense was not based on the testimony of just seven Plaintiffs. Instead, the parties presented an abundance of trial evidence about the executive exemption issue, including (1) a vast array of corporate manuals; (2) testimony from 39 witnesses including Family Dollar executives, district managers who ran the operations of 134 stores, and store managers who worked at a total of 50 different stores; (3) detailed charts summarizing wages and hours; and (4) a wealth of exhibits including emails, internal Family Dollar correspondence, payroll budgets, and in-store schematics. If one factors in that Broome and Barkus oversaw thousands of stores, the witnesses go from representing hundreds of stores to thousands. In addition to the large quantity of testimonial evidence, the non-testimonial evidence was equally high in quality and largely comprised of Family Dollar's corporate records. The jury's verdict is well-supported not

---

**13.**   To establish its prima facie case, Plaintiffs demonstrated that: (1) Family Dollar employed them; (2) Family Dollar is an enterprise engaged in interstate commerce covered by the FLSA; (3) each Plaintiff actually worked in excess of a 40–hour workweek; and (4) Family Dollar did not pay any overtime wages to them. See 29 U.S.C. § 207(a).

simply by "representative testimony," but rather by a volume of good old-fashioned direct evidence.

Family Dollar's trial conduct is also revealing. It actually opposed the introduction of more witness testimony from Plaintiff store managers. After Family Dollar presented the deposition testimony of 12 opt-in store managers, Plaintiffs attempted to introduce into evidence the deposition testimony of 238 more opt-in store managers. But Family Dollar objected, and the district court sustained the objection. * * *

This leads us to a third flaw in Family Dollar's argument. Plaintiffs did not shoulder the burden of proof on the executive exemption defense. Family Dollar did. * * * Thus, Family Dollar cannot rely on an insufficient number of witnesses being called by the Plaintiffs to meet Family Dollar's burden of proof on its own affirmative defense.

We reject Family Dollar's argument that the executive exemption defense is so individualized that the testifying Plaintiffs did not fairly represent the non-testifying Plaintiffs. For the same reasons that the court did not err in determining that the Plaintiffs were similarly situated enough to maintain a collective action, it did not err in determining that the Plaintiffs were similarly situated enough to testify as representatives of one another.

In any event, the only issue we must squarely decide is whether there was legally sufficient evidence—representative, direct, circumstantial, in-person, by deposition, or otherwise—to produce a reliable and just verdict. There was.

## NOTES AND QUESTIONS

1. What considerations might lead one of the parties to request a jury trial in a case brought under section 16(b)?

2. The "opt-in" procedures of the FLSA are used not just in wage and hour disputes, but also in enforcement of the Equal Pay Act amendments to the Act; they are also used in cases under the Age Discrimination in Employment Act (ADEA).

3. As the opinion indicates, one area of controversy in "opt-in" cases is the extent to which it is appropriate for a "lead plaintiff" in an FLSA action to have the assistance of the court in gaining access to information about other potential claimants in order to contact them and invite them to join in the case. Is it proper, for instance, to order a defendant employer to produce names and addresses of other potential plaintiffs? The Supreme Court held "yes" in *Hoffmann–LaRoche v. Sperling*, 493 U.S. 165, 110 S.Ct. 482, 107 L.Ed.2d 480 (1989), an ADEA case. In that opinion, however, the Court also said it is important for a trial court not to compromise its appearance of neutrality between the parties in the way it manages the content and distribution of notices. Given that, should a court itself take an active role in notifying such potential plaintiffs? See, e.g., *De Asencio v. Tyson Foods, Inc.*, 342 F.3d 301 (3d Cir. 2003). The *Tyson Foods* litigation also illustrates problems that may crop up when plaintiffs seek relief under both the FLSA

and state laws. Joinder of state and federal claims is common, and when this is true, it may be possible for plaintiffs to obtain certification of both a collective FLSA action and a Rule 23 state law action simultaneously. See, e.g., *Iglesias–Mendoza v. LaBelle Farm*, 239 F.R.D. 363 (S.D.N.Y. 2007).

Since enactment of the Portal-to-Portal Act, unions have been expressly prohibited from bringing collective FLSA actions in their representative capacity.

4.   The success of plaintiffs in the *Morgan* case may have been one factor that has led to the filing of others. A number are now at the certification stage. See, e.g., AON Wage & Hour Employment Practices Litigation, 2010 WL 1433314 (N.D. Ill. 2010) (granting conditional certification); *Hernandez v. United Auto Credit Corp.*, 2010 WL 1337702 (N.D. Cal. 2010) (decertifying conditional class); *In re Dain Rauscher Overtime Litigation*, 2010 WL 1324938 (D.Minn. 2010) (granting conditional certification on specified counts but finding certain Rule 23 requirements not met).

5.   In deciding the "similarly situated" issues to determine whether a class action should be permitted, the court found itself addressing factual matters that overlapped with decisions the jury must ultimately make in deciding whether the executive exemption applied. What effect might this have on the conduct of the trial itself?

6.   Management of the litigation in a multi-plaintiff case involves not just notice, but also such matters as the number of witnesses to be deposed or called, and the amount of hours to be allotted to each party for examining those witnesses. This is true whether the action is brought by individual plaintiffs or by the Secretary of Labor.

An extreme case of limiting the time available for presentation of FLSA claims and defenses is *Secretary of Labor v. DeSisto*, 929 F.2d 789 (1st Cir. 1991). The district court limited the trial to a single day, even though the claims involved totaled roughly one million dollars. The Secretary was allowed to present two witnesses: a compliance officer from the Wage and Hour Division, and one employee of the defendant employer, a non-profit corporation that operated two boarding schools for troubled teenagers, one at West Stockbridge, Massachusetts, and one in Florida. The employees on whose behalf the Secretary was acting fell into several categories, principally dormitory parents and assistant dormitory parents. The employer was allowed to call only a single witness. The First-Circuit panel that reviewed the case on appeal criticized the severe limitations the trial court had placed on the parties:

> We have found no case, and the Secretary cited none at oral argument, holding that one employee can adequately represent 244 employees holding a variety of positions at different locations. ... Usually, an employee can only represent other employees only if all perform substantially similar work. ... In *Dole v. Snell*, 875 F.2d 802 (10th Cir.1989), for example, the DOL offered the testimony of one employee and the compliance officer to support an award to 32 employees. But in that case, unlike this one, all 32 employees held identical positions as cake decorators. Moreover, in *Dole v. Snell* the parties stipulated that the testifying employee was representative. Id. at 811. Where the employees fall into

several job categories, it seems to us that, at a minimum, the testimony of a representative employee from, or a person with first-hand knowledge of, each of the categories is essential to support a back pay award.... This testimony need not be given orally at trial, but it must be properly before the court as admitted evidence. * * *

[The witness] John Walsh worked at the farm program, which was not part of the main Stockbridge campus. Although he could certainly testify about his own hours and duties, and those of others employed at the farm program, and could, in the court's discretion, have been permitted to testify as to DP and ADP duties at the Massachusetts campus, he should not have been permitted to testify in a representative capacity for all other employees (including blue collar workers and those employed in Florida). * * * In this era of crowded dockets it is perhaps increasingly common for a trial court to attempt to speed things along by imposing limits on the attorneys. ... This court finds nothing at all to criticize in a district court's effort to eliminate needless time-wasting. * * *

In *Donovan v. Burger King Corp.*, 672 F.2d 221 (1st Cir.1982), the Secretary of Labor alleged FLSA violations at 44 Burger King restaurants. At issue was the exempt or non-exempt status of assistant managers. The district court evaluated the 44 restaurants and chose six that it considered representative. Testimony was then allowed from six witnesses, one assistant manager from each restaurant. On appeal, the defendant complained that the limitation was improper. We disagreed * * *.

While the *Burger King* case supports the proposition that the trial court has considerable leeway in molding the trial, it also demonstrates the importance of performing the Rule 403 balance and taking care to ensure that excluded evidence is merely cumulative. The case before us does not appear to have received the same degree of consideration. For that reason, we hold that the witness limitation constituted an abuse of discretion in that it prevented both parties from presenting sufficient evidence on which to base a reliable judgment. ... The appropriate remedy is a new trial.

7. The opinion in the *Morgan* case indicates that Family Dollar Stores did not keep records of the number of hours worked by its store managers, but did maintain payroll records indicating the amounts paid each plaintiff, as the FLSA requires. Not all employers do so, and this in turn can create additional proof problems. In the *DeSisto* case mentioned in the preceding note, that was the case, and the court indicated how this problem should be dealt with, on the basis of the Supreme Court's *Mt. Clemens Pottery* decision:

The burden of proof in FLSA cases was set forth by the Supreme Court over forty years ago in a case that has well withstood the passage of time. In *Anderson v. Mt. Clemens Pottery Co.*, 328 U.S. 680, 66 S.Ct. 1187, 90 L.Ed. 1515 (1946), the Court focused specifically on the problem manifested in this case: How can an employee demonstrate a violation of the Act when the duty and the ability to keep adequate records rests solely with the employer, the adverse party? Recognizing that "[t]he solution ... is not to penalize the employee by denying him any recovery on the ground that he is unable to prove the precise extent of uncompensated work," the Court imposed a significant burden on the employer. Id. at 687, 66 S. Ct. at 1192. The Court stated:

> In such a situation we hold that an employee has carried out his burden if he proves that he has in fact performed work for which he was improperly compensated and if he produces sufficient evidence to show the amount and extent of that work as a matter of just and reasonable inference. The burden then shifts to the employer to come forward with evidence of the precise amount of work performed or with evidence to negative the reasonableness of the inference to be drawn from the employee's evidence. If the employer fails to produce such evidence, the court may then award damages to the employee, even though the result may be only approximate.

Id. at 687–88, 66 S. Ct. at 1192. Plainly, then, although the initial burden is on the employee (or, as here, the Secretary of Labor on behalf of the employees), that burden is a minimal one. Where the employer has failed to keep adequate employment records, it pays for that failure at trial by bearing the lion's share of the burden of proof.

At times the proof available to the Secretary or an individual plaintiff will be the recollection of individual employees, whose depositions then form the basis on which the judge or jury will make a judgment about how many hours were worked (as in *Morgan*) and also about how much was paid.

## (c.) Time Limits and Liquidated Damages

### MORGAN v. FAMILY DOLLAR STORES, INC.

United States Court of Appeals, Eleventh Circuit, 2008
551 F.3d 1233

HULL, CIRCUIT JUDGE:

[The principal facts of the case are set out earlier in this chapter in section B.1.] * * *

### VI.  WILLFULNESS AND LIQUIDATED DAMAGES

* * *

#### A.  Willful Violation

The statute of limitations for a claim seeking unpaid overtime wages under the FLSA is generally two years. 29 U.S.C. § 255(a). But if the claim is one "arising out of a willful violation," the statute of limitations is extended to three years. Id.

"To establish that the violation of the [FLSA] was willful in order to extend the limitations period, the employee must prove by a preponderance of the evidence that his employer either knew that its conduct was prohibited by the statute or showed reckless disregard about whether it was." *Alvarez Perez*, 515 F.3d at 1162–63 (citing *McLaughlin*, 486 U.S. at 133, 108 S.Ct. at 1681). Federal regulations define "reckless disregard" as the " 'failure to make adequate inquiry into whether conduct is in compliance with the [FLSA].' " * * *

Family Dollar raises several challenges to the jury's willfulness finding. All fail. First, the evidence, detailed above, was legally sufficient to support the jury's finding that Family Dollar's FLSA violations were willful. For example, the Plaintiffs presented testimony from Family Dollar executives that it never studied whether the store managers were exempt executives. Executives also testified that Family Dollar's company-wide policy was that store managers were exempt from FLSA overtime requirements, but they had no idea who made that policy. Further, given the evidence at trial, the jury reasonably could have found that Family Dollar executives knew that store managers spent most of their time performing manual, not managerial, tasks, that corporate manuals micro-managed store managers' performance of those tasks, that the 380 district managers closely supervised their store managers, and that store managers had little discretion or freedom from supervision.

Second, we reject Family Dollar's suggestion that the complex and fact-intensive nature of the executive exemption inquiry means that, as a matter of law, the FLSA violations were not willful. Such a rationale would effectively preclude a willfulness finding in cases involving an executive exemption affirmative defense. While the jury could have well considered that factor in its willfulness determination, complexity alone does not preclude a willfulness finding. Third, we reject Family Dollar's argument that the court's decision to grant judgment as a matter of law for 163 Plaintiffs somehow biased the jury in its willfulness determination. This speculation has no support in the record. * * *

### B.   Good Faith and Liquidated Damages

When the jury finds an employer has violated the FLSA and assesses compensatory damages, the district court generally must add an award of liquidated damages in an equal amount. 29 U.S.C. § 216(b) * * * However, the district court has discretion to reduce or deny liquidated damages " 'if the employer shows to the satisfaction of the court that the act or omission giving rise to such action was in good faith and that he had reasonable grounds for believing that his act or omission was not a violation of the [FLSA].' " * * *

Here, the district court determined that Family Dollar failed to meet its burden of proving good faith on the liquidated damages issue because the jury already had found willfulness on the statute of limitations issue. Family Dollar argues that the district court erred because judges have the discretion to decide good faith regardless of the jury's willfulness finding.

While this was an open question in our circuit in 2006—the time of the second trial-our subsequent decision in Alvarez Perez forecloses Family Dollar's argument. In Alvarez Perez, we concluded that "in an FLSA case a jury's finding in deciding the limitations period question that the employer acted willfully precludes the court from finding that the employ-

er acted in good faith when it decides the liquidated damages question."
\* \* \* Accordingly, the district court did not err in awarding Plaintiffs
$17,788,029.32 in liquidated damages, representing an amount equal to
the back pay award.

NOTES AND QUESTIONS

1. The standard for determining "willfulness" was set by the Supreme
Court in *McLaughlin v. Richland Shoe Co.*, 486 U.S. 128, 108 S.Ct. 1677, 100
L.Ed.2d 115 (1988), as the *Morgan* court indicates. The competing standard,
for which three Justices argued, was one developed by the Fifth Circuit in
*Coleman v. Jiffy June Farms, Inc.*, 458 F.2d 1139 (5th Cir.), *cert. denied,* 409
U.S. 948, 93 S.Ct. 292, 34 L.Ed.2d 219 (1972). That opinion reasoned that an
action is willful whenever "there is substantial evidence in the record to
support a finding that the employer knew or suspected that his actions might
violate the FLSA. Stated most simply, we think the test should be: Did the
employer know the FLSA was in the picture?" 458 F.2d at 1142. How much
more precise or demanding is the "knowledge or reckless disregard" approach?

2. The Eleventh Circuit states that an action that is "willful" is necessarily an action not in "good faith." What about the converse? Is it possible to
be liable for liquidated damages even though the employer did not act
"willfully"? See *Rodriguez v. Farm Stores Grocery, Inc.* 518 F.3d 1259 (11th
Cir. 2008); *Martin v. Indiana Michigan Power Co.*, 381 F.3d 574 (6th Cir.
2004). The same issue arises under other statutes. See, e.g., *A.J. McNulty, Inc.
v. Secretary of Labor*, 283 F.3d 328 (D.C. Cir. 2002) (rejecting use of the
*Richland Shoe* standard for OSHA cases); *Hillstrom v. Best Western TLC
Hotel*, 354 F.3d 27 (1st Cir. 2003) (applying the *Richland Shoe* approach in an
FMLA case).

3. How important is it that an employer has been advised by the Wage
and Hour Division that its pay practices do not conform to the statute? What
if the employer has consulted an attorney who advises the employer that the
Wage and Hour Division analysis is wrong? See *Baystate Alternative Staffing,
Inc. v. Herman*, 163 F.3d 668 (1st Cir. 1998) (remanding a finding of
willfulness); but see *Smith v. Central Security Bureau, Inc.*, 231 F.Supp.2d
455 (W.D. Va. 2002).

## (d.) Compromised Claims

## LYNN'S FOOD STORES, INC. v. UNITED STATES

United States Court of Appeals, Eleventh Circuit, 1982
679 F.2d 1350

GOLDBERG, CIRCUIT JUDGE:

\* \* \*

After an official investigation, the Department of Labor concluded
that Lynn's Food Stores, Inc. ("Lynn's") had violated FLSA provisions

concerning, inter alia, minimum wage, overtime, and record-keeping. As a result, the Department of Labor determined that Lynn's was liable to its employees for back wages and liquidated damages. After the employer's unsuccessful attempts to negotiate a settlement with the Department of Labor, Lynn's approached its employees directly in an attempt to resolve the back wage claims. Specifically, Lynn's offered its employees $1000.00, to be divided among them on a pro rata basis, in exchange for each employee's agreement to waive "on behalf of himself (herself) and on behalf of the U.S. Department of Labor" any claim for compensation arising under the FLSA. Some fourteen Lynn's employees signed the agreements, thereby accepting pro rata shares of $1000.00 in exchange for back wages which, according to Department of Labor calculations, totaled more than $10,000.00. Lynn's then brought this action in district court seeking judicial approval of the settlement. * * *

There are only two ways in which back wage claims arising under the FLSA can be settled or compromised by employees. First, under section 216(c), the Secretary of Labor is authorized to supervise payment to employees of unpaid wages owed to them. An employee who accepts such a payment supervised by the Secretary thereby waives his right to bring suit for both the unpaid wages and for liquidated damages, provided the employer pays in full the back wages.

The only other route for compromise of FLSA claims is provided in the context of suits brought directly by employees against their employer  under section 216(b) to recover back wages for FLSA violations. When employees bring a private action for back wages under the FLSA, and present to the district court a proposed settlement, the district court may enter a stipulated judgment after scrutinizing the settlement for fairness. See *D.A. Schulte, Inc. v. Gangi*, 328 U.S. 108, 66 S. Ct. 925, 928 n. 8, 90 L. Ed. 1114; *Jarrard v. Southeastern Shipbuilding Corporation*, 163 F.2d 960, 961 (5th Cir.1947).[8]

It is clear that the agreements for which Lynn's seeks judicial approval fall into neither recognized category for settlement of FLSA claims. The agreements cannot be approved under section 216(c) because they were not negotiated or supervised by the Department of Labor; and because the agreements were not entered as a stipulated judgment in an

---

**8.** In *Schulte Co. v. Gangi, supra*, the Supreme Court invalidated a settlement agreement releasing the employer from liquidated damage claims even though there was a bona fide dispute about whether the employees were covered by the FLSA. Based on the reasoning in *O'Neil*, the Court concluded, "neither wages nor the damages for withholding them are capable of reduction by compromise of controversies over coverage." Id. at 929. However, the Court in dicta drew a distinction between a settlement agreement and a stipulated judgment entered in the adversarial context of an employees' suit for FLSA wages. Id. at 928 n.8.

Finally, in *Jarrard v. Southeastern Shipbuilding Corp., supra*, the Fifth Circuit held that the Supreme Court's decisions in O'Neil and Schulte regarding settlements did not prohibit approval of a "solemn and binding stipulated judgment entered upon disputed issues of both law and fact" in an FLSA suit brought by employees. Id. at 961. Thus, the lower court's decision to accord res judicata effect to a stipulated judgment entered by a state court, which awarded employees overtime compensation but not liquidated damages, was affirmed.

*This doesn't fit* action brought against Lynn's by its employees, the agreements cannot be approved under existing case law.

Lynn's takes the position that the circumstances in which its employees signed settlement agreements essentially duplicates the adversarial context of a lawsuit brought by employees to resolve a bona fide dispute over FLSA coverage. This is precisely the position rejected by the Supreme Court in both *Brooklyn Savings v. O'Neil, supra* and *Schulte, Inc. v. Gangi, supra;* and we take this opportunity to reject it once again.

Settlements may be permissible in the context of a suit brought by employees under the FLSA for back wages because initiation of the action by the employees provides some assurance of an adversarial context. The employees are likely to be represented by an attorney who can protect their rights under the statute. Thus, when the parties submit a settlement to the court for approval, the settlement is more likely to reflect a reasonable compromise of disputed issues than a mere waiver of statutory rights brought about by an employer's overreaching. If a settlement in an employee FLSA suit does reflect a reasonable compromise over issues, such as FLSA coverage or computation of back wages, that are actually in dispute; we allow the district court to approve the settlement in order to promote the policy of encouraging settlement of litigation. But to approve an "agreement" between an employer and employees outside of the adversarial context of a lawsuit brought by the employees would be in clear derogation of the letter and spirit of the FLSA. * * *

*Here no rep. v. os spirit.*

The facts of this case illustrate clearly why this is so. Lynn's employees had not brought suit against Lynn's for back wages. Indeed, the employees seemed unaware that the Department of Labor had determined that Lynn's owed them back wages under the FLSA, or that they had any rights at all under the statute. There is no evidence that any of the employees consulted an attorney before signing the agreements. Some of the employees who signed the agreement could not speak English.

*Yikes*

Lynn's offered for the record a transcription of the settlement "negotiations" between its representative and its employees. The transcript was offered as proof that the employees were not "pressured" to sign the agreements, that the settlements were strictly "voluntary." Ironically, the transcript provides a virtual catalog of the sort of practices which the FLSA was intended to prohibit. Lynn's representative repeatedly insinuated that the employees were not really entitled to any back wages, much less the amounts calculated by the Department of Labor. The employees were told that when back wages had been distributed as a result of past actions taken by the Department of Labor, "Honestly, most everyone returned the checks * * * " It was suggested that only malcontents would accept back wages owed them under the FLSA: the representative stated, "some [employees] * * * indicated informally to Mr. Lynn and to others within Lynn's Food Stores that they felt like they had been paid what they were due, and that they were happy and satisfied with the arrangements which had been made." Employees who attempted to suggest that they had been paid unfairly were told by the representative "we're not really here to debate the merits of it \* \* \*" and that the objections would be taken up at "another time". The representative summed up the proceedings with this comment, "[t]hose who feel like they've been paid fairly, we want to give them an opportunity to say so." In sum, the transcript is illustrative of the many harms which may occur when employers are allowed to "bargain" with their employees over minimum wages and overtime compensation, and convinces us of the necessity of a rule to prohibit such invidious practices.

### Conclusion

Other than a section 216(c) payment supervised by the Department of Labor, there is only one context in which compromises of FLSA back wage or liquidated damage claims may be allowed: a stipulated judgment entered by a court which has determined that a settlement proposed by an employer and employees, in a suit brought by the employees under the FLSA, is a fair and reasonable resolution of a bona fide dispute over FLSA provisions. Since the agreements presented by Lynn's to the district court meet none of the above criteria, the district court was correct in refusing to approve the agreements. Accordingly, the decision of the district court is affirmed.

*Affd*

AFFIRMED.

### NOTES AND QUESTIONS

1. The appellate court's dicta respecting the need for judicial approval of an FLSA settlement was favorably cited in *Walton v. United Consumers Club, Inc.*, 786 F.2d 303 (7th Cir.1986) (dicta). See also, *Boone v. City of Suffolk*, 79 F. Supp. 2d 603 (E.D.Va.1999).

2. Examine 29 U.S.C. §§ 216(b) and (c). What support, if any, does the statute provide for the proposition that an FLSA claim settlement is not binding until approved by the Department of Labor or a court? Assume that an employee who is represented by counsel brings an FLSA wage deficiency suit under § 216(b) and prior to going to court a settlement is reached between the parties' counsel. Under the Act, should it be sufficient to make a joint motion to dismiss? Does the dicta in *Lynn* and *Walton* add to, detract from, or have no impact upon the likelihood that such suits will be settled before trial?

## 5.  RETALIATION

### TRAVIS v. GARY COMMUNITY MENTAL HEALTH CENTER, INC.

United States Court of Appeals, Seventh Circuit, 1990
921 F.2d 108, cert. denied 502 U.S. 812, 112 S.Ct. 60, 116 L.Ed.2d 36 (1991)

EASTERBROOK, CIRCUIT JUDGE.

Elliott Cunningham filed suit contending that the Gary Community Mental Health Center, Inc., had not afforded him promised vacation, sick, and holiday pay, and had retaliated against him when he invoked his rights under the Fair Labor Standards Act. The FLSA forbids retaliation. 29 U.S.C. § 215(a)(3). Cunningham subpoenaed Denise Travis, his immediate supervisor, to be a witness at trial. Travis's testimony was helpful to Cunningham, who prevailed. Within the month, the Center fired both Cunningham and Travis. Travis was on leave expecting a child; the Center demanded that she immediately return her medical insurance card. At the trial in this case a witness explained that Travis was cast out because "she had cost us money". The jury concluded that Travis was the victim of retaliation. She received about $83,000 in damages plus $21,000 in attorney's fees. We must decide whether the remedy is authorized by law. (Defendants' challenge to the verdict was not argued in the opening brief and is waived.)

Instead of standing on § 215(a)(3), Travis put most of her reliance on 42 U.S.C. § 1985(2), which creates a remedy:

> If two or more persons ... conspire to deter, by force, intimidation, or threat, any party or witness in any court of the United States from attending such court, or from testifying to any matter pending therein, freely, fully, and truthfully, or to injure such party or witness in his person or property on account of his having so attended or testified....

Section 1985(2), unlike § 215(a)(3), requires proof of a conspiracy. Travis found the plurality of actors in the managers of the Center. She named as defendants three of the Center's senior executives: Charlie Brown, its Executive Director; Kenneth R. Phillips, its Director of Administration; and Wendell P. Robinson, its Director of Clinical Services. Brown, Phillips, and Robinson discussed discharging Travis, and Brown instructed Phillips to prepare the letter conveying the news.

This intra-corporate conspiracy approach runs smack into *Dombrowski v. Dowling*, 459 F.2d 190, 196 (7th Cir.1972) (Stevens, J.), which held that the conspiracy requirement in § 1985(3) "is not satisfied by proof that a discriminatory business decision reflects the collective judgment of two or more executives of the same firm." Travis asks us to distinguish or limit *Dombrowski*. Whittling away at a case is more attractive if its core principle is wrong than if it is right, for why strain to curtail the application of sound rules? Travis therefore reminds us that *Dombrowski* has not won universal approbation and invites us to rethink the subject. * * *

[The court concluded that intracorporate discussions are not conspiracies and, therefore, relief was not available under 42 U.S.C. § 1985(2).]

Travis's relief depends, then, on the FLSA. Most of the award ($45,500) represents punitive damages, and another $35,000 is compensation for emotional distress attributable to the discharge and revocation of health insurance while Travis was on leave to receive medical care for complications in her pregnancy. She suffered little loss in wages, because the firing caused such a ruckus within the Center that its managers reinstated her within two months. At oral argument, Travis's lawyer candidly remarked that he pursued the claim under § 1985(2) because, he believed, decisions of the Supreme Court limited the availability of compensatory and punitive damages under the FLSA. So they did, once upon a time, but the landscape changed in 1977.

As enacted in 1938, the FLSA established as remedies the statutory wages and overtime compensation plus "an additional equal amount as liquidated damages" plus attorneys' fees. 29 U.S.C. § 216(b). Compensatory and punitive damages were unavailable. Congress amended the remedial section by adding this language: "Any employer who violates the provisions of section 15(a)(3) of this Act [29 U.S.C. § 215(a)(3)] shall be liable for such legal or equitable relief as may be appropriate to effectuate the purposes of section 15(a)(3), including without limitation employment, reinstatement or promotion and the payment of wages lost and an additional equal amount as liquidated damages." Pub.L. 95–151, 91 Stat. 1252 (1977). This amendment authorizes "legal" relief, a term commonly understood to include compensatory and punitive damages.

Because the original text prescribed as a remedy double the shortfall of wages, and the amendment says that damages include this "without limitation", Congress has authorized other measures of relief. Which other forms? The answer has been left to the courts. We could not find any case interpreting this amendment. The legislative history is unhelpful. The language originated in the Senate; the committee report does not discuss it. The Conference Committee adopted the Senate's proposal, remarking that the bill authorizes suits "for appropriate legal or equitable relief" without describing what relief might be "appropriate". H.R.Conf.Rep. No. 95–497, 95th Cong., 1st Sess. 16 (1977).

Appropriate legal relief includes damages. Congress could limit these damages, but the 1977 amendment does away with the old limitations without establishing new ones. Compensation for emotional distress, and punitive damages, are appropriate for intentional torts such as retaliatory discharge. So although § 1985(2) does not support the jury's award, § 216(b) does. Fed.R.Civ.P. 54(c) requires courts to award the relief to which the prevailing party is entitled, even if that party did not request the relief or relied on the wrong statute. Misplaced reliance on § 1985(2) does not undercut the verdict; § 216(b) supplies all the authority the district court required.

AFFIRMED.

## NOTES AND QUESTIONS

1. In *Snapp v. Unlimited Concepts, Inc.*, 208 F.3d 928 (11th Cir.2000), the Eleventh Circuit rejected the approach of *Travis* on the ground that punitive damages are inconsistent with the statute's overall remedial design of using compensatory remedies. For a thoughtful discussion of the continuing disagreement, see *Lyles v. Flagship Resort Development Corp.*, 371 F. Supp. 2d 597 (D.N.J. 2005).

2. Section 15(a)(3) [29 U.S.C. § 215(a)(3)] has been held to prohibit a former employer from informing a prospective employer that the job applicant had filed an FLSA complaint. *Dunlop v. Carriage Carpet Co.*, 548 F.2d 139 (6th Cir.1977). Examine FLSA § 15(a)(3). Would the job applicant also have a claim against the prospective employer for hiring discrimination? Does the Act tolerate employers asking prospective job applicants if they ever filed an FLSA claim? If an employee was hired and it was later discovered that she lied in answering that question, would section 15(a)(3) allow the employer to dismiss her for submitting a false employment application? See the definition of employee in § 3(e) and § 3(g). In contrast, *Ball v. Memphis Bar–B–Q Co., Inc.*, 228 F.3d 360 (4th Cir.2000) held, 2–1, that § 15(a)(3) does not protect an employee who is dismissed five days after he tells the company president that, in an anticipated FLSA suit, he cannot testify in the manner suggested by the president. The court reasoned that the FLSA protection is inoperative until a suit is filed. There is an ongoing disagreement among lower federal courts over the extent to which the statute protects employees from retaliation for informal complaints. See the discussion in *Hicks v. Association of American Medical Colleges*, 503 F. Supp. 2d 48 (D.D.C. 2007).

3. As this book goes to press the Supreme Court is considering whether the FLSA retaliation provision protects an employee who made oral complaints about the location of the employer's time clocks (which would prevent employees from being paid for time spent in putting on and taking off protective gear). See *Kasten v. Saint–Gobain Performance Plastics Corp.*, 570 F.3d 834, *rehearing en banc denied,* 585 F.3d 310 (7th Cir. 2009), *cert. granted,* ___ U.S. ___, 130 S.Ct. 1890, 176 L.Ed.2d 361 (2010).

## 6. COMPARATIVE NOTE ON REGULATION OF REMUNERATION

Relative prosperity from country to country sometimes is examined by citing minimum and average earnings using the dollar equivalent for each nation. This can be misleading because there are substantial national differences in costs of living. An alternative approach to assessing the relative generosity of workforce remuneration is to compare the amount of work needed to attain the level of weekly earnings or a particular standard of living. For example, in material terms most American workers live reasonably well but, on average, Americans with full-time jobs work more hours per year than do workers in most industrial nations except Japan.

A study published by the Bureau of Labor Statistics compared the relative purchasing power of a dollar in 1996 with the equivalent exchange rate amount of local currency in 32 counties including all of the European Union nations. The study found that a dollar purchased a bit more in the U.S. than did the equivalent amount of local currency in Austria, Belgium, Denmark, Finland, France, Germany, Luxembourg, the Netherlands, and Sweden. Non–EU countries also in that list were Iceland, Japan, Norway and Switzerland. In other words, the cost of living was a bit higher in those countries than in the U.S. Of the countries studied, the dollar purchased less in the U.S. than in Australia, Canada, Czech Republic, Hungary, Mexico, New Zealand, Poland, Turkey, Greece, Ireland, Italy, Portugal, Spain, the United Kingdom, Israel, Russia, Slovak Republic, and Slovenia. Most of the difference in countries with lower prices came from the lower price for goods and services not involved in world trade (e.g., housing, basic foods, health care, recreation). Of course, for some of these items, quality comparisons are extremely difficult (e.g., a meal served at a Paris bistro versus the same priced meal served in a mid-Western U.S. town or an annual medical check-up in a third world country versus one in the U.S.). Similarly, climate often makes significantly different demands on the amount that must be expended for clothing and shelter to achieve a comparable degree of comfort.

Minimum standards of remuneration are justified as a means of insulating workers from the potential dehumanizing effect of market decisions that rely on depressed wage costs as a competitive tool. This is often described as providing workers with a "safety net" of protection from economic exploitation. The goal of the safety net can be perceived as having a biological function, an equitable function, or a political function. As a biological function, its purpose is to ensure survival of those who contribute work to the system; i.e., they will receive at least the minimum return necessary to sustain themselves and their families in food, shelter, and clothing. As an equitable function, the purpose of the safety net is to ensure that those who work have a stake in the growth and success of the economic system to which they contribute their work. Similarly, minimum standards of remuneration can carry out a political function of ensuring that those who get the least benefit from the wealth distribution system nevertheless are motivated to continue to support that system. When we examine the methods by which different countries mandate standards for minimum wages and premium pay, we find that they vary in the degree to which they are responsive to each of the above considerations.

If the function of a minimum wage is to provide a biological safety net, its basis should look to the cost of the shopping basket for goods and services that provide minimal sustenance. Thus, while a 1:2 ratio of minimum to average wage may be needed at one stage of economic development, as the economy prospers, a 1:2.2 or 1:3 or 1:5 ratio may be adequate to provide those needs. Some countries, including the U.S., have traditionally used a 1:2 ratio between the minimum and average wage rates as a guidepost for adjusting the minimum standard. How does one justify maintaining a fixed ratio of that sort if minimum sustenance justifies the safety net's function but the overall standard of living provided by the economy has experienced substantial improvement over the past half century? It was previously noted that for more than a decade, the U.S. minimum wage has drifted downward from that traditional ratio. Nevertheless, that same minimum wage provides less than a poverty level income if the earner is the sole household provider.

As an alternative goal, if a safety net minimum standard serves an equitable or political function, the needs of the economic and social system might dictate providing well in excess of bare sustenance for those earning the least, and, as the economy grows and changes, may call for a relative improvement for those at the bottom. Minimum wage standards can provide a means of strengthening an economic system and in some instances minimum standards have been designed to redistribute the total pool of earned income available to a workforce so as to create a more equal distribution of national wealth. For example, it has been stated that the goals of minimum wages in Japan include "raising the quality of the labor force and securing fair competition among undertakings and [promoting] the sound development of the national economy." KAZUO SUGENO, JAPANESE LABOR LAW at 192 (L. KANOWITZ, TRANS., 1992). A number of European countries adopted this approach in the post-recovery period after World War II. Thus, an intentional pattern of adjustments in France moved its minimum to over 60% of the average wage rate by the late 1970s. Similarly, by the late 1970s, national policies in The Netherlands had shifted its minimum to a level of about 75% of the average national wage.

Diverse methods are used for establishing minimum wage standards. Some years ago, French legislation adopted an initial standard with subsequent annual adjustments made by administrative decree. These are partly tied to changes in the cost of living. Japan has an advisory Council whose recommendations, based on its studies and analysis, are closely followed by the prefecture governments which establish separate minimum standards by industry. However, dominant patterns set by enterprise collective agreements are also used as a basis for prefecture decisions and on occasion for national minimum standards imposed by the Labor Ministry for a particular craft or industry. Until 1993, the United Kingdom used an administrative process to set minimum standards but adopted them only for those occupations or industries that traditionally had the lowest wages. Elimination of minimum standards was justified by the British government in 1993 on the thesis that such regulation distorts the labor market and reduces individual freedom.

A number of countries use collectively negotiated minimum wage standards as a benchmark for adopting broad-based legal standards. In Belgium, for example, government decree often imposes on all enterprises minimum standards that were established by collective bargaining negotiations between national federations of employers and national federations of unions. This technique is referred to as "extension" of the collective agreement. It is used for establishing wage standards as well as other minimum terms of employment on regional or industry levels in a large number of other countries including Germany, France and Finland. In Denmark, most wage rates are resolved under a system of collective bargaining. In the vast majority of situations, an industry-wide agreement establishes minimum wage rates which generally are between 50% and 65% of the average wage for those employed in the Danish industry. Specific wage rates above the average are collectively negotiated at the company level.

Minimum wage standards typically do not cover some categories of workers and industries. A common exemption is for enterprises with less than a threshold number of workers. Although in some countries agricultural workers are not covered, in other countries farm workers are prime beneficiaries of minimum wage laws. Domestic servants and professional workers also are commonly excluded from minimum wage standards. In Argentina, Belgium, Italy, and The Netherlands, among other countries, the minimum pay rate is reduced for young workers. Many countries have similar reductions for apprentices and handicapped workers. To what extent do such policy choices reflect differing perceptions respecting the nature of various types of employment relationships, the capacity of law to affect conduct, or the extent of social, economic and political needs for legal intervention into some but not other work situations?

Some nations use the same approach as the U.S. in requiring premium pay for hours worked in excess of 40 per week. This is done in Austria, which sets the premium at 50%, with the difference that the law also imposes a five-hour limit on the amount of weekly overtime that can be worked. Some countries mandate premium pay for daily overtime and higher premiums for weekend or holiday work. In Japan, responsive to legal requirements that each establishment adopt a maximum number of normal weekly work hours and work days, enterprises specify their normal daily and weekly work schedule. Employees must receive their base level pay for those hours regardless of whether work is available, and work beyond those hours must be compensated at a premium of 25% above the base rate. (The base rate does not include periodic bonuses, which in Japan often are in excess of 25% of the base pay.) In addition, the same premium must be paid for all work between 10 p.m. and 5:00 a.m. The premium is doubled if those late hours also involve work beyond the employee's normal work hours.

In 2000, in an effort to create new jobs, France reduced the standard work week to 35 hours for employers with over 20 employees. Smaller employers were required to adopt the 35 hour work week beginning in 2002. French law imposes premium pay for weekly hours worked in excess of 35. The law originally placed a stringent additional limitation on overtime: subject to waiver by administrative officials, a worker could not work more than 130 overtime hours a year. That figure was raised to 180 hours a year in 2002, and to 220 hours in 2005. In 2007, the law was again changed to permit employers to increase the use of overtime, by reducing the tax that an employer had been required to pay on overtime hours. The change was controversial and continues to provoke debate among French economists.

Mandatory minimum remuneration in industrial nations almost always includes health insurance financed in whole or part by the employer. Paid sick leave, often subsidized in whole or part by government tax credits or social security payments, is another common legal benefit provided in industrial countries as is a "family allowance" which provides extra pay in relation to the number of dependents the worker supports.

European Community Directive No. 92/85 requires member nations to provide a minimum of 14 weeks' paid leave covering prenatal confinement and postpartum recuperation. In addition, most nations legally mandate several paid holidays and paid annual vacation leave. European countries typically require a minimum of four weeks of paid vacation after a year's employment, and a fifth week is becoming common. In Argentina, by law employees are entitled to at least two weeks' annual paid vacation for the first five years of employment, three weeks a year for the next five years, four weeks annually for the next ten years, and five weeks annually after that.

European nations experienced significantly higher unemployment than the U.S. during much of the 1990s. Some argue this was due to reduced competitiveness resulting from much higher social insurance costs imposed on European employers. A related explanation is that European collective agreements and laws provide greater job security than in the U.S., with the result that European employers have less flexibility to adjust to economic and technological change. A very different explanation is that huge adjustment costs that largely have been shared by all European Union economies resulted from the absorption of East Germany, with its mass of workers who were not productively employed, into a united Germany. Still other explanations look to cultural and educational system differences that arguably enabled American workers, managers, and consumers more quickly to adjust to the electronic software and internet technologies. Whatever the reasons, Europeans have been seeking ways to reduce unemployment. One proposal is that income security costs be shifted from the employer to general wealth, income and consumption taxes so that a strong social welfare system can be maintained without interfering with market competitiveness. R. Blanpain, "The Changing World of Work," in COMPARATIVE LABOUR LAW AND INDUSTRIAL RELATIONS IN INDUSTRIALIZED MARKET ECONOMIES 23, 44–47 (R. BLANPAIN & C. ENGELS, eds., 6th ed., 1998). And, as previously noted, a more traditional approach, recently attempted in France, was the imposition of a shorter work week.

## 7.   CHILD LABOR REGULATION

In agrarian and pre-industrial societies, parents and other elders direct the performance of rudimentary work by children as a way of teaching them the skills and knowledge they will need as adult participants in the society's productive endeavors. When populations grow and social interactions become more complex, a need also develops to keep children occupied so that their energies are not absorbed in anti-social conduct. Thus, a provision for employing impoverished children that was included in the English Poor Law of 1601 has been described as adopted in part to banish idleness. Such benevolent concerns were soon overshadowed by the exploitation of employers who typically worked their charges long hours at arduous, menial tasks from which the children gained too little knowledge or skills to move into better paid trades when they reached adulthood. WALTER I. TRATTNER, CRUSADE FOR THE CHILDREN: A HISTORY OF THE NATIONAL CHILD LABOR COMMITTEE AND CHILD LABOR REFORM IN AMERICA 22 (1970).*

The importation of the factory system into America brought with it many of Britain's child labor practices. The proponents of using child labor proclaimed the benevolence of providing a means of sustenance to destitute children and the public benefit of a reduction of the burden of their public support. The "whipping room", a place for dealing with unruly child workers, could be found in many factories. Factory owners particularly sought those under age 12 and it was estimated in 1820 that children comprised 43% of the textile mill laborers in Massachusetts, 47% in Connecticut, and 55% in Rhode Island. *Id.* Although some state adopted laws prohibiting employment of children under 12 in textile factories and mines, generally they were not effectively enforced. It was estimated that over two million children under age 15 were gainfully employed in 1900.

*Unenforced laws*

> ... Many descended into the dark and dangerous coal mines each day, or worked above ground in the coal breakers, where [dust was so thick] that light could scarcely penetrate.... Others were forced to crouch for hours at a time and face the blinding glare and stifling heat of glass factory furnace rooms. Many children spent their days or nights in the dull, monotonous, noisy spinning rooms of cotton mills, where humid, lint-filled air made it difficult to breathe, and where they were kept awake by cold water thrown in their faces. Others, perhaps only five or six years old, shucked oysters and picked shrimp. Some worked in fruit and vegetable canneries sixteen hours a day, seven days a week, in sheds exposed to the weather.

WALTER I. TRATTNER, CRUSADE FOR THE CHILDREN: A HISTORY OF THE NATIONAL CHILD LABOR COMMITTEE AND CHILD LABOR REFORM IN AMERICA 41–42 (1970).

The National Child Labor Committee was organized early in the Twentieth Century to study child labor, educate the public and promote legislative reform. In 1912 it succeeded in its efforts to get Congress to establish the Children's Bureau, soon thereafter placed in the Department of Labor, which had research and educational responsibilities. The Bureau's efforts contributed to the adoption of the Child Labor Act of 1916 which prohibited the interstate transportation of goods produced or worked on by children under age 14 or by children under age sixteen who were employed more than eight hours a day or more than six days a week or earlier than 6 a.m. or later than 7 p.m. In *Hammer v. Dagenhart*, 247 U.S. 251, 38 S.Ct. 529, 62 L.Ed. 1101 (1918), the Supreme Court declared that law unconstitutional on the ground that Congress was improperly attempting to regulate local employment, a matter solely within the regulatory power of the states. That decision was expressly overruled when the Court upheld the FLSA in *United States v. Darby*, 312 U.S. 100, 61 S.Ct. 451, 85 L.Ed. 609 (1941).

*Lochner cases*

---

* See also, ELIZABETH L. OTEY, THE BEGINNINGS OF CHILD LABOR LEGISLATION IN CERTAIN STATES (1974).

The child labor provisions of the FLSA exempt from its coverage newspaper delivery, employment as an actor or performer, some specified agricultural related activities, and work for parents in businesses other than mining, manufacturing or hazardous occupations. All other child labor is prohibited for those under age 14. Between 14 and 16, a limited number of work hours is permitted within restrictions designed not to interfere with school attendance, and work must not be in manufacturing or mining nor involve occupations deemed hazardous by the Secretary of Labor for that age group. Children between 16 and 18 can be employed in any industry but must not be employed in occupations deemed hazardous by the Secretary of Labor for that age group. See FLSA §§ 203(*l* ), 212, 213(c), 214(b), 215(a)(4), and 216(e).

## MARTIN v. FUNTIME, INC.

United States Court of Appeals, Sixth Circuit, 1992
963 F.2d 110

CONTIE, SENIOR CIRCUIT JUDGE:

Appellant, Funtime, Inc., appeals a judgment for the plaintiff, the Secretary of Labor, finding violations of the wage and hour provisions of the Fair Labor Standards Act, 29 U.S.C. §§ 212, 215(a)(4), governing child labor.

### I.

Appellant, Funtime, Inc., is an Ohio corporation with its principal place of business in Aurora, Ohio. Funtime owns and operates three amusement parks—Geauga Lake Park located in Aurora, Ohio; Wyandot Lake Park located in Powell, Ohio; and Darien Lake Park located in Darien Center, New York.

Funtime employed numerous 14 and 15 year-old children in various occupations throughout the parks during the 1989 and 1990 operating seasons. These children were regularly required to work more hours than the Fair Labor Standards Act ("FLSA") permitted.

In the summer of 1985, Funtime's operations at Wyandot Lake Park came under investigation by the Wage and Hour Division of the United States Department of Labor. A compliance officer found that the park was employing children in violation of the FLSA. On August 13, 1985 the compliance officer discussed her findings with Mr. Ed McHale, the park's general manager, providing him with written results of the inquiry. As a result of this 1985 investigation, Funtime was assessed a civil money penalty. Joint Appendix at 814.

Five years later, in March 1990, another Wage and Hour compliance officer began investigating Funtime's operations at Geauga Lake Park. During this investigation, the officer reviewed the park's employment records for the 1988 and 1989 seasons. He was given a list of the names of the 14 and 15 year-olds employed at the park. The officer transcribed the park's employment figures, compiling a summary of all the hours worked and the ages of the employees. In order to verify the ages, the compliance officer compared the dates of birth contained on the park's records with dates he obtained from the childrens' school records.

In May 1990, the compliance officer notified Geauga Lake Park that as a result of his investigation he had discovered that 135 children had been employed in violation of the FLSA's child labor provisions during the 1988 and 1989 seasons. In response, the park attempted various corrective measures to prevent further violations.

In September 1990, the same compliance officer revisited Geauga Lake for a follow-up investigation to determine whether Funtime had come into compliance with the FLSA. The compliance officer conducted a similar review of the park's employment records. In that investigation, the officer found 22 additional violations. The results of the investigation were transmitted to the park's director of human resources, who challenged the validity of the officer's computations. Nevertheless, the park agreed to take further preventive measures, including the installation of an automatic time keeping system, and the reduction in the total number of minors employed.

In July 1990, another Wage and Hour compliance officer began investigating Funtime's Darien Lake amusement park. The officer reviewed the park's employment records, and prepared a transcription of the information found on the personnel records which indicated that child labor violations had occurred. The ages of all minor employees were verified by comparing the dates of birth that appeared on the park's records with the dates that appeared on certain proof of age certificates issued by New York schools.

The investigation of Darien Park continued in November 1990. The investigating officer reviewed the park's employment records for the 1988 and 1989 seasons. The ages of the children were verified and the records were transcribed by the officer into a summary which revealed that 230 minors were employed in violation of the FLSA.

In response, the park took various steps to avoid future child labor violations, recognizing however the "problems the park had encountered with minors using various efforts to avoid the restrictions placed on them." Appellant's Brief at 11. Funtime alleges that the Wage and Hour investigators "never mentioned the investigation at Geauga Lake to the Darien Lake representatives, and the Darien Lake representatives never indicated that they were aware of the Geauga Lake investigation." Id. at 10. Presumably, Funtime believes that being unaware of these other investigations relieved them of the duty of seeking more severe corrective measures.

In September 1990 a Wage and Hour compliance officer continued the investigation of Funtime's Wyandot Lake Park, reviewing their employment records for the 1989 and 1990 seasons. The officer made photo copies of the park's payroll and time records, which revealed that 82 minors were employed in violation of the FLSA. The ages of the minor employees were verified using school records.

In October 1990 Funtime was notified of the violations which occurred at Wyandot Lake. However, Wyandot Lake's director of personnel, Keith M. Swider, who was also notified of these violations, claimed to be unaware of the violations which were earlier uncovered by the 1985 investigation. Swider was not employed at the park at that time. Swider testified that in the middle of the summer of 1990 he was informed by Wyandot Lake's general manager that Funtime's Geauga Lake Park had been investigated that spring; however, the compliance officer never mentioned this investigation to him at the time that his park was being investigated. Apparently, Funtime now argues that this lack of knowledge precludes a finding that the 1989 and 1990 violations were willful or intentional.

In response to the above incidents, the Secretary of Labor filed a complaint against Funtime in the United States District Court. The Department of Labor sought injunctive relief against Funtime's Geauga Lake, Wyandot Lake and Darien Center parks. On March 27 and 28, 1991 the district court conducted a bench trial in this case. On April 24, 1991 the district court issued its Findings of Fact and Conclusions of Law, finding that during the 1990 season, each of the three parks owned by Funtime had employed minors in violation of the FLSA's child labor provisions, and that the violations had been substantial in number. Joint Appendix at 19. The court found that all of the violations had been properly investigated and verified. The district court also concluded that, because the violations continued long after the 1985 investigation of Wyandot Lake, Funtime's child labor violations were willful. Id. at 20. The court thus believed that this indicated that it was likely that the violations would continue to occur. It rejected Funtime's argument that its three parks were separate entities and thus that the officials at each park had no way of knowing that the other parks had been investigated. Id. at 23.[1] Accordingly, the district court held that the Secretary of Labor was "entitled to an injunction restraining [Funtime], its agents, and all other persons acting in concert with them" from violating the provisions of 29 U.S.C. §§ 212, 215(a)(4). Id.

Funtime filed a timely notice of appeal from the district court's judgment.

## II.

Funtime first argues that the district court abused its discretion in issuing an injunction against Funtime. For the following reasons, we believe that injunctive relief was proper in this case. Section 17 of the Fair Labor Standards Act, codified as amended at 29 U.S.C. § 217, authorizes a

---

1. Funtime does not have a centralized corporate personnel function; however, the general managers at each amusement park and the corporate officers meet periodically. Nevertheless, appellant claims that the various parks do not share personnel information. Appellant's Brief at 14.

court to enjoin violations of certain of the Act's provisions. Among those is section 12(c), codified as amended at 29 U.S.C. § 212(c), which prohibits the employment of "oppressive child labor," which is defined to mean "a condition of employment under which ... any employee under the age of sixteen years is employed by an employer ... in any occupation." 29 U.S.C. § 203(*l* )(1). Section 203(*l* ) also authorizes the Secretary of Labor to promulgate regulations defining what shall constitute oppressive child labor of children between the ages of 14 and 16 years. As such, regulations adopted pursuant to this authority restrict the hours during which a child may work. See Child Labor Regulation No. 3, 29 C.F.R. §§ 570.31–.49 (1991). The district court concluded that the appellant committed numerous violations of the above provisions, and thus the primary question on appeal is whether the district court properly ordered injunctive relief.

"The issuance of an injunction under the Fair Labor Standards Act is addressed to the reasonable discretion of the trial judge." *Wirtz v. Flame Coal Co.*, 321 F.2d 558, 560 (6th Cir.1963). The exercise of discretion is not unbridled, *Dunlop v. Davis*, 524 F.2d 1278, 1280 (5th Cir.1975), and "in exercising its discretion the court must give 'substantial weight to the fact that the Secretary seeks to vindicate a public, and not a private, right.'" *Brock v. Big Bear Market No. 3*, 825 F.2d 1381, 1383 (9th Cir.1987) (quoting *Marshall v. Chala Enterprises, Inc.*, 645 F.2d 799, 804 (9th Cir.1981)).

The purpose of issuing an injunction against future violations is to effectuate general compliance with the Congressional policy of abolishing substandard labor conditions by preventing recurring future violations. *Big Bear*, 825 F.2d at 1383; *Dunlop*, 524 F.2d at 1280. Prospective injunctions are essential because the cost of noncompliance is placed on the employer, id., which lessens the responsibility of the Wage and Hour Division in investigating instances of noncompliance. *Dunlop*, 524 F.2d at 1280. The imposition of an injunction is not punitive, nor does it impose a hardship on the employer "since it requires him to do 'what the Act requires anyway—to comply with the law.'" Id. at 1281; see, e.g., *Wirtz*, 321 F.2d at 561 (standard of public interest is not measured by the possible consequences which may befall the employer in complying with the law, but by the existence of substandard labor conditions).

In *Dunlop*, the Fifth Circuit held that "two factors [are] properly considered in determining whether a permanent injunction should be granted." *Dunlop*, 524 F.2d at 1281. These include: (1) the previous conduct of the employer; and (2) the dependability of his promises for future compliance. Id. Furthermore, the court must look at evidence of current compliance; however, "current compliance alone, particularly when achieved by direct scrutiny of government, is not a sufficient ground for denying injunctive relief." *Big Bear*, 825 F.2d at 1383 (citing *Dunlop*, 524 F.2d at 1281); *Marshall v. Lane Processing, Inc.*, 606 F.2d 518, 519 (8th Cir.1979), cert. denied, 447 U.S. 922, 100 S. Ct. 3013, 65 L. Ed.2d 1114 (1980).

Appellant argues that the injunction was improper because Funtime had taken "substantial steps to prevent child labor violations" and that it promised to "eliminate future violations through the imposition of additional, significant procedures" demonstrating "the likelihood of future compliance." Appellant's Brief at 18–20. However, as indicated above, an employer's efforts at current compliance, even if successful, are not sufficient grounds to deny injunctive relief. *Dunlop*, 524 F.2d at 1281. Rather, a court's primary concern is whether the violations are likely to reoccur in the future. *Big Bear*, 825 F.2d at 1383. "A dependable, bona fide intent to comply, or good faith coupled with extraordinary efforts to prevent recurrence," are factors which weigh against an injunction. Id. However, "an employer's pattern of repetitive violations or a finding of bad faith are factors weighing heavily in favor of granting a prospective injunction." Id. (citing *Dunlop*, 524 F.2d at 1281).

In the present case, we believe that the district court did not abuse its discretion in ordering an injunction. First, the facts demonstrate that appellant Funtime exercised less than good faith in attempting to comply with the FLSA. The investigation began in 1985, and Funtime was assessed a civil money penalty on September 25, 1985. Nevertheless, the violations continued into the 1989 and 1990 seasons. Furthermore, a July 1990 investigation of Geauga Lake Park disclosed a substantial number of violations. Funtime was notified of its lack of compliance. However, a follow-up investigation conducted in November 1990 revealed that Geauga Lake continued to employ minors in violation of the FLSA even though their operations had been subjected to the scrutiny of the Department of Labor. These failures to comply after initial investigations do not demonstrate "likelihood of future voluntary compliance" on Funtime's part. *Dunlop*, 524 F.2d at 1281. Funtime's attempt to avoid the shadow of bad faith by arguing that its parks were separate entities, and that the general manager of Wyandot Lake in 1990 was unaware of the violations which occurred in 1985, is unavailing. The penalty in 1985 was assessed against Funtime, and the present suit is against Funtime. Since Funtime had, or should have had, knowledge of this original violation, it is irrelevant that the manager of its Wyandot Lake Park had no such knowledge.

In addition, an employer's responsibility for child labor violations approaches strict liability, and an employer cannot avoid liability by arguing that its supervisory personnel were not aware of the violation, or by simply adopting a policy against employing children in violation of the Act. *Lenroot v. Interstate Bakeries Corp.*, 146 F.2d 325, 328 (8th Cir.1945). Therefore, we find that the employer was put on notice in 1985 that it was not complying with the FLSA, and thus it is of little value to argue, at this juncture, that the current violations came as a complete surprise.

Secondly, Funtime committed a substantial number of violations of the Act after the 1985 investigation. If the violations were merely isolated, then Funtime could more plausibly argue "good faith." However, in this case there were hundreds of additional violations occurring after the 1985 investigation. Under the present circumstances, the district court was justified in doubting whether Funtime would comply in the future, because it failed to comply after earlier being sanctioned. Therefore, Funtime's recent attempts to guarantee compliance came too late, and we find Funtime's promises of future compliance were not sufficient "to convince the district court that there is no reasonable probability of a recurrence of the violation," *Marshall v. Van Matre*, 634 F.2d 1115 (8th Cir.1980). ...

### III.

Funtime next argues that even if the district court applied the proper standard in determining whether an injunction was appropriate, the judgment should nevertheless be invalidated because the court's conclusion rested on inadmissible evidence. Funtime contends that the transcriptions and summaries of its personnel records, introduced by the Department of Labor, were hearsay and violated the Best Evidence Rule, Fed. R. Evid. 1002. * * *

[W]e believe that the admissibility of these documents hinges exclusively on Fed. R. Evid. 1006.

Fed. R. Evid. 1006 provides:

> The contents of voluminous writings ... which cannot conveniently be examined in court may be presented in the form of a ... summary. The originals, or duplicates, shall be made available for examination or copying, or both, by other parties at a reasonable time and place. The court may order that they be produced in court.

This rule provides an exception to the "Best Evidence Rule" which ordinarily requires the proponent, when attempting to prove the content of a document or writing, to produce the original. Fed. R. Evid. 1002. As an initial matter, there is little doubt that Rule 1006 applies to the present facts as it was not disputed that Funtime's original personnel records were voluminous.

"The admission of summaries under Rule 1006 is committed to the sound discretion of the trial court." *United States v. Campbell*, 845 F.2d 1374, 1381 (6th Cir.), cert. denied, 488 U.S. 908, 109 S. Ct. 259, 102 L. Ed.2d 248 (1988). Under Rule 1006, the summary must be "accurate, authentic and properly introduced before it may be admitted into evidence." *United States v. Scales*, 594 F.2d 558, 563 (6th Cir.), cert. denied, 441 U.S. 946, 99 S. Ct. 2168, 60 L. Ed.2d 1049 (1979). Funtime contends that the district court erred because the summaries themselves were hearsay, and thus not admissible. * * *

In this regard, it is certain the personnel records would be admissible under Fed. R. Evid. 803(6) as business records. The records in this case were compiled by Funtime or its employees; were kept in the course of a regularly conducted business activity, i.e. personnel management; and, it was the regular practice of Funtime to keep such records. Therefore, we find that these employment records would be admissible under the business records exception, thereby making summaries of their contents admissible by virtue of Rule 1006.

\* \* \* Therefore, all that remains to be established is that the summaries themselves were accurate. *Scales*, 594 F.2d at 562.

The district court held that it was "clear" that the summaries were reliable. Joint Appendix at 158–59. We agree. The records were summarized by Wage and Hour compliance officers who testified to their accuracy and authenticity. Joint Appendix at 44–45, 59–60, 103. Furthermore, if the summaries were inaccurate, Funtime, who was in possession of the originals, could have produced them to prove the inaccuracies. Funtime, however, points out specific discrepancies, such as the government's practice of including the employees' meal periods in calculating total hours worked, and improperly counting the hours of one employee who was over 18. Given the large total number of violations committed by Funtime, we believe that one or two computational errors would have a negligible effect on the reliability of the summaries as a whole. If the errors had been as significant as Funtime suggests, it could have produced the originals, thereby neutralizing any unfavorable consequences which would flow from their introduction into evidence. Therefore, we hold that the summaries were properly admitted under Rule 1006, and Funtime's challenges based on Rule 803(8)(C) are without merit.

### IV.

For the foregoing reasons, the district court's decision is hereby AFFIRMED.

### NOTES AND QUESTIONS

1. See FLSA §§ 16 and 17 (29 U.S.C. §§ 216 and 217) in the Appendix. The appellate and trial court opinions in Funtime refer to but a single occasion when a civil penalty was imposed, 1985, and the trial court reports that the fine collected on that occasion was reduced from the initial levy. What may have led the Department of Labor to seek an injunctive remedy in 1991?

2. The administrative civil penalty procedures include an optional appeal within the Department of Labor. Until those procedures are final, an employer is not entitled to seek judicial review of the agency's action. See *Acura of Bellevue v. Reich*, 90 F.3d 1403 (9th Cir. 1996).

3. Minors sometimes use false documents to persuade a prospective employer that they are old enough to qualify for employment. What steps can an employer take to be certain of the applicant's age? What standard of employer liability should be applied if the applicant is hired and it later is determined that the applicant lied? What penalty, if any, should be imposed on the applicant? Are the administrative problems of such a nature that local officials, not federal officials, are best equipped to handle them? Should the entire issue of regulating child labor be left to local law?

4. Contemporary economic activity relies on qualities of human capital that include knowledge, learning ability, adaptability, analytic capacity, and willingness and ability to coordinate activities. To what extent is that capital

developed in school, on playing fields, at the workplace? Whose interests are at stake if government limits the number of hours a child may work when school is in session or when it is not in session? Restrictions on hours sometimes are evaded when a child holds multiple jobs. Are there techniques for avoiding such evasions?

5.  Federal law places few restrictions on the type of work children can do when employed on a family-owned farm or when working, with parental permission, on farm operations that are too small to hire enough labor to come within FLSA minimum wage standards or when employed as seasonal hand-harvest laborers on a farm whose operations have been certified as meeting federal standards for safety, health, and harvesting urgency. Yet, it has been observed that agriculture is "the most dangerous industry, especially for children." STEVEN L. WILLBORN, STEWART J. SCHWAB & JOHN F. BURTON, JR., EMPLOYMENT LAW at 473 (1993). Does the agricultural exclusion demonstrate that the FLSA's child labor provisions intrude excessively upon the labor market, intrude insufficiently in the case of agricultural labor, or reflect a balance based on societal or political interests that are unique to farming?

# C.  WAGE PAYMENT, GARNISHMENT, AND ASSIGNMENT LAWS

## 1.  WAGE PAYMENT

At the beginning of the twentieth century, it was not uncommon, at least in certain industries, for employers to withhold two weeks or a month's pay on pain of forfeiture if the employee quit without providing that much notice, or to pay in goods or in scrip redeemable only at the company store. These practices were legislated against in a spate of state wage payment (or "truck") laws during the Progressive period. See generally, G. Paterson, *Wage-Payment Legislation in the United States* (BLS Bull. No. 229) (1918). See e.g., *Knoxville Iron Co. v. Harbison*, 183 U.S. 13, 22 S.Ct. 1, 46 L.Ed. 55 (1901), sustaining one such statute challenged as violative of freedom of contract.

These laws generally require payment in money, regulate the frequency of payment, require all wages earned at the time of termination to be paid within a set period of time (subject, in many jurisdictions, to statutory liquidated damages for unlawful delay), and limit what an employer may deduct or withhold. Many states provide that if the amount of wages due is in dispute, the employer must pay the amount the employer concedes to be due, acceptance of which by the employee shall not constitute a release of the balance of the claim. There is a division of authority, however, on whether the state wage payment law bears upon the employee's claim that he had been discharged to defeat the accrual of the wage or benefit under the law. Compare *Cook v. Alexander and Alexander of Conn., Inc.*, 40 Conn.Sup. 246, 488 A.2d 1295 (1985) (wage payment law states a public policy such that discharge to avoid the vesting of bonuses and thrift plan benefits states a cause of action) with *Sendi v.*

*NCR Comten, Inc.*, 619 F.Supp. 1577 (E.D.Pa.1985) (wage payment law has no application to wages for future services).

In *Livadas v. Bradshaw*, 512 U.S. 107, 114 S.Ct. 2068, 129 L.Ed.2d 93 (1994), the Court held that a state law requiring prompt payment of back wages to a dismissed worker is not preempted by the Labor Management Relations Act even though the employment is covered by a collectively-bargained agreement.

## RUNYON v. KUBOTA TRACTOR CORP.

Supreme Court of Iowa, 2002
653 N.W.2d 582

NEUMAN, JUSTICE.

This dispute is over a $3979 deduction taken from an employee's bonus check. The question is whether Iowa Code chapter 91A (1999), our wage payment collection law, governs the controversy and, if so, whether the deduction violated section 91A.5(2)(c), which prohibits deductions for "[l]osses due to . . . default of customer credit." * * *

### I.  Background Facts and Proceedings.

* * * In 1977 the plaintiff, Jake Runyon, was hired by the defendant, Kubota Tractor Corporation, as a regional sales manager. Kubota, a California corporation, manufactures high-quality compact tractors.

Runyon, who resided in Des Moines when he was hired, was assigned to a territory covering Iowa, Nebraska, and northern Missouri. He moved to Missouri in 1982 but has retained responsibility for the performance of nine dealerships in Iowa. He regularly visits the dealerships, keeps in contact by telephone, and attends trade shows here.

Runyon's compensation package with Kubota includes a fixed annual salary, a guaranteed commission based on sales, and a discretionary "Management by Objective" (MBO) bonus. Roughly seventy percent of Runyon's commissions are based on sales in Missouri, with the remaining thirty percent resulting from sales to Nebraska and Iowa dealers. As a Missouri resident, Runyon files and pays his income taxes there.

Kubota's financial relationship with its dealers is pertinent to the parties' dispute over Runyon's bonus for 1999. Essentially, Kubota extends credit to its dealers to finance the cost of all tractors and inventory on hand at the dealerships. The dealer "owns" the products but is not required to advance the cost to Kubota until a customer makes a purchase. Once the dealer receives payment, it must pay Kubota the dealer cost. When a tractor is sold but the dealer either cannot or will not pay Kubota, the product is considered "sold out of trust" (SOT). Kubota regards SOTs as a serious threat to asset management and thus considers them when calculating bonuses due under its MBO compensation plan.

In January 2000, Kubota issued Runyon a check for his 1999 MBO bonus of $19,895. The record reveals that Runyon would have been entitled to a bonus of $26,526 but for two deductions, only one of which is at issue here. * * * At issue is a $3979 deduction for four SOTs occurring at dealerships in Iowa and Missouri. The sum represents a fifteen percent reduction in the bonus to which Runyon would have otherwise been entitled.

Runyon sued Kubota for breach of contract and violation of the Iowa Wage Payment Collection Law, Iowa Code chapter 91A. Following discovery, he dismissed his breach of contract claim. * * *

## II.　Issues on Appeal.

A. *Constitutional claim.* At the outset Kubota claims the court committed an error of constitutional magnitude when it applied chapter 91A to "non-Iowa employers, such as Kubota, and non-Iowa employees, such as Plaintiff." Kubota fails to mention, however, how or where this constitutional claim was raised in the trial court. * * * We deem the issue waived and, accordingly, give it no further consideration * * *

B. *Applicability of Iowa's Wage Payment Collection Law.* The real question is whether Runyon is entitled to the protection and enforcement of Iowa Code chapter 91A. Kubota asserts that "[p]laintiff is not a statutory 'employee' and Kubota is not a statutory 'employer' under the Wage Payment Collection [Law]." Its argument rests on the straightforward assertion that "[s]urely the legislature did not intend for the Act to apply to employees when the employer is not located in Iowa, the employee does not reside in Iowa, and the employee is not paid in Iowa." Runyon counters that the governing statute, section 91A.2, renders irrelevant the criteria cited by Kubota. He frames the question this way: "Did the Iowa Legislature intend for employees who were hired in Iowa and required by their employers to work in Iowa on a regular, ongoing, and substantial basis to be unprotected by the Wage Payment Collection Law?"

Like the district court, we are convinced that Runyon has the better argument. We have observed that the purpose of chapter 91A is to "facilitate collection of wages by employees." *Condon Auto Sales*, 604 N.W.2d at 596. A bonus meets the statutory definition of "wages." *Dallenbach*, 459 N.W.2d at 488. The statute defines "employee" as "a natural person who is employed in this state for wages by an employer." Iowa Code § 91A.2(3). An "employer" under the statute means a person or entity "who in this state employs for wages a natural person." Id. § 91A.2(4).

Kubota contends that the phrase "in this state" in the foregoing definitions narrows the persons to whom the statute applies. We agree that the legislature evidently intended not to extend the statute's reach to persons not employed in the state of Iowa. See *Henriksen v. Younglove Constr.*, 540 N.W.2d 254, 260 (Iowa 1995) (intent must be discerned from legislative words). But it seems equally clear to us that the phrase "in this state" modifies the term "employed," not, as Kubota suggests, the words "employee" and "employer." In other words, the statute's focus is not on an individual employee's state of residence or an employer's home office but whether the employee is "employed in this state for wages by an employer." Iowa Code § 91A.2(3); see also id. § 91A.2(4) (employer is one who "in this state employs for wages a natural person").

The word "employ" is not defined in chapter 91A. * * * "Employ" is commonly defined as follows:

> To engage in one's service; to hire; to use as an agent or substitute in transacting business; to commission and intrust with the performance of certain acts or functions or with the management of one's affairs; ... the term is equivalent to hiring, which implies a request and a contract for a compensation. To make use of, to keep at work, to entrust with some duty.

*Employ*

Black's Law Dictionary 362 (abridged 6th ed.1991). * * *

As the common definition of "employ" reveals, neither the residence of the employee nor the location of the employer controls. Neither does chapter 91A condition its application on such criteria. The statutory term implies only the actual engagement of services in the transaction of business. Here, while Runyon did work out of his home in Missouri, the record reveals he transacted substantial business and routinely performed services on behalf of Kubota within Iowa's borders. Because Runyon's dispute with Kubota involved employment-related services rendered in Iowa for wages, the district court committed no error in applying the Iowa Wage Payment Collection Law.

C. *Sufficiency of the evidence.* Kubota next argues the evidence was insufficient to support Runyon's claim that the company violated chapter 91A by failing to pay his bonus when it was "due." See Iowa Code § 91A.3(1) ("employer shall pay all wages due its employees"). Kubota insists it timely paid Runyon the bonus to which he was "due" under the MBO compensation plan. Runyon counters that Kubota has missed the point of his claim. While conceding his bonus check was timely delivered, he claims it included an unlawful deduction. Therefore, he argues, he did not receive all he was "due" and is entitled to recover the difference in accordance with section 91A.8. Again, Runyon has the more persuasive argument.

Kubota rightly notes that in Dallenbach we suggested that a bonus cannot be "due"—as that term is used in section 91A.3(1)—until it can be accurately estimated in accordance with the parties' agreement. *Dallenbach*, 459 N.W.2d at 489. We have likewise held that a bonus is not "due" if an employee fails to meet the eligibility requirements for the pay out. *Phipps v. IASD Health Servs. Corp.*, 558 N.W.2d 198, 202 (Iowa 1997). Here, however, the issue is quite different. Runyon claims his bonus "due" included the $3979 deducted for SOTs. That brings us to the governing statute in the case and the parties' factual dispute over its application.

Iowa Code section 91A.5, captioned "Deductions from wages," states that the following "shall not be deducted from an employee's wages":

> Losses due to breakage, damage to property, default of customer credit, or nonpayment for goods or services rendered so long as such losses are not attributable to the employee's willful or intentional disregard of the employer's interests.

Iowa Code § 91A.5(2)(c) (emphasis added).

Kubota argued forcefully at trial, and urges on appeal, that the deduction taken from Runyon's bonus was not based on "losses" sustained by Kubota but on Runyon's failure to conduct required audits of his dealers' accounts, a failure that permitted the SOTs to occur. Runyon countered this testimony with proof that SOTs stem, in fact, from "default in customer credit" which, in this case, led to losses sustained by Kubota. The factual dispute centered on whether the sum deducted from Runyon's bonus, although not directly tied to a specific loss, was nevertheless intended by Kubota to penalize Runyon for SOTs occurring in Iowa dealerships during 1999.

Given this record, the district court determined that a jury question was engendered concerning Kubota's alleged violation of section 91A.5(2)(c). We find no error in this determination. The case is analogous to *Salter v. Freight Sales Co.*, 357 N.W.2d 38 (Iowa Ct.App.1984). In *Salter*, an employer reduced the commission paid the manager of its furniture store following a burglary that occurred at the store. After some months, the former commission rate was restored. *Salter*, 357 N.W.2d at 40. In the suit for unpaid wages that followed, the employer argued the reduced commission "was a valid modification of [the] contract which [the manager] chose to accept by continuing in defendant's employ." Id. at 41. A skeptical district court rejected the argument, a decision affirmed on appeal. Reasoning the trial court was right to "disregard the name given to the transaction and look at its substance," our court of appeals upheld the district court's finding that substantial evidence supported the employee's claim that his wages had been effectively reduced by the amount of the burglary loss in violation of section 91A.5(2)(c). Id. at 41–42.

Just as in *Salter*, the trial court here looked beyond mere semantics to determine that section 91A.5(2)(c) was implicated and left it to the jury to sort out the conflict in the evidence. * * *

D. *Liquidated damages.* Runyon asserts on cross-appeal that the district court erred when it refused to direct a verdict, or submit a jury instruction, on the question of his entitlement to liquidated damages. The governing statute is Iowa Code section 91A.8. It provides:

> When it has been shown that an employer has intentionally failed to pay an employee wages or reimburse expenses pursuant to section 91A.3, whether as the result of a wage dispute or otherwise, the employer shall be liable to the employee for any wages or expenses that are so intentionally failed to be paid or reimbursed, plus liqui-

dated damages, court costs and any attorney's fees incurred in recovering the unpaid wages and determined to have been usual and necessary. In other instances the employer shall be liable only for unpaid wages or expenses, court costs and usual and necessary attorney's fees incurred in recovering the unpaid wages or expenses.

Iowa Code § 91A.8.

Because Kubota's deduction from Runyon's bonus was plainly intentional, not mistaken, Runyon argues the court erred when it refused to award the liquidated damages authorized by section 91A.8. In support of the district court's ruling, Kubota contends the decision is controlled by the Dallenbach case. We agree.

In Dallenbach this court held that a wage dispute involving a bonus comes within the "other instances" category of section 91A.8, thus entitling the employee to recover the unpaid bonus and attorney fees but not liquidated damages. *Dallenbach*, 459 N.W.2d at 489. We reasoned that section 91A.8 limits the recovery of liquidated damages to unpaid wages as defined by section 91A.3, that is, "wages due ... in monthly, semimonthly, or biweekly installments on regular paydays." Id. A bonus, we concluded, does not commonly fit that definition. Id. As already noted, however, Dallenbach held a bonus does fit the section 91A.2 definition of "wages" so as to entitle the employee to recover not only the unpaid bonus but the costs and reasonable attorney fees expended to secure it. Id. at 488; Iowa Code § 91A.2(7) ("wages" means compensation owed by an employer for labor or service rendered by an employee).

The district court properly applied the statutes here consistent with our holding in Dallenbach. We are not inclined, as Runyon urges, to reverse Dallenbach because the parties' dispute over the bonus here alleged an unlawful deduction. Based on the language in the pertinent statutes, we still believe the legislature intended to reserve the liquidated damages provision of section 91A.8 for situations involving the intentional withholding of regular paychecks and commissions, rather than for disputes over the calculation of discretionary bonuses payable at year-end.

### III. Conclusion.

We affirm the judgment entered upon the jury's verdict in favor of Runyon and against Kubota for $3979 plus $30,004.64 in related attorney fees and litigation expense plus interest. We likewise affirm the district court's denial of Runyon's claim for liquidated damages.

[Concurring opinion omitted.]

### NOTES AND QUESTIONS

1. Incentive compensation schemes, such as the bonus plan involved in *Runyon*, regularly cause difficulties under wage payment laws. In *Rosen v. Smith Barney, Inc.*, 393 N.J.Super. 578, 925 A.2d 32 (2007), the plaintiffs had agreed to have some of their pay diverted in a "deferred stock compensation

plan." They left the employer to go to work for a major competitor. This triggered a forfeiture clause in the deferred compensation plan. Plaintiffs argued that this violated New Jersey's wage payment law. The court, however, decided that payment into the plan as directed by the plaintiffs was in fact lawful payment to them, that the forfeiture clause was authorized under applicable laws and regulations, and that the existence of the forfeiture clause was properly disclosed to the plaintiffs when they signed up to participate in the deferred compensation plan. In *Prachasaisoradej v. Ralphs Grocery Co.*, 42 Cal.4th 217, 64 Cal.Rptr.3d 407, 165 P.3d 133 (2007), a divided California Supreme Court decided that defendant's method for calculating profits for the purpose of an incentive compensation plan was lawful, even though it took into account merchandise shortages, workers compensation costs, and other items that would not be properly deducted directly from regular wages.

2.   A majority of states have held that wage payment laws protect undocumented workers, and some of these workers have been allowed to collect both the unpaid wages and statutory liquidated damages. See, e.g., *Coma Corp. v. Kansas Department of Labor*, 283 Kan. 625, 154 P.3d 1080 (2007).

3.   Consider the *Salter* decision discussed in *Runyon*. If a manager leaves cash in a less secure place than was usual, would the manager's employer have a cause of action against that manager for an ensuing burglary loss? If so, is a wage payment law appropriately used to cut off that employer's claim? What about a loss resulting from the manager's negligent operation of a company owned vehicle? What if the employee were not a manager, but a sales clerk?

## 2.   WAGE GARNISHMENT

### DONOVAN v. SOUTHERN CALIFORNIA GAS CO.

United States Court of Appeals, Ninth Circuit, 1983
715 F.2d 1405

PER CURIAM:

\* \* \*

The Secretary alleges that in discharging Dianne Allen because her wages had been garnished, the company violated section 304(a) of the Act. 15 U.S.C. § 1674(a). That section prohibits an employer from discharging an employee whose earnings "have been subjected to garnishment" on account of only one indebtedness. The Secretary contends that garnishment has not occurred until such time as earnings have actually been withheld, while the company contends that garnishment has occurred at the time the employer first receives a legally binding garnishment notice.

The parties stipulated to facts showing that while the company had received two garnishment notices from different creditors in connection with Ms. Allen's earnings, Ms. Allen had promptly secured a release from the second creditor, and therefore no wages had been withheld pursuant to the second order. On cross-motions for summary judgment on this issue of statutory construction, the district court ruled for the defendant. We reverse.

## FACTS:

Ms. Allen was employed by Southern California Gas as a collection control clerk from July 23, 1973 until December 8, 1977. On May 9, 1977 the company received a notice of garnishment and a writ of execution for a debt which she owed to National Business Factors, Inc. This debt had been incurred during her marriage. However, she was divorced by the time it became the subject of the garnishment. Upon receipt of the notice, the company informed Ms. Allen of its delivery and reviewed with her its written policy regarding garnishment. On May 18, 1977 and May 27, 1977, the company remitted amounts in partial satisfaction of the National Business Factors debt. The company counted these payments as Ms. Allen's first and second garnishments.

On May 31, 1977, the company received a second notice of garnishment and writ of execution against Ms. Allen pursuant to a judgment in favor of the Joseph Magnin Company, Inc. It considered this Ms. Allen's third garnishment. She immediately contacted Joseph Magnin and obtained an order of release, which was received by her employer on June 9, 1977. Between receipt of the writ and the release, no actual garnishment of Ms. Allen's wages occurred; however, under company policy, the Joseph Magnin debt counted as her third garnishment for two debts within a nine-month period. She was therefore required to take a two-day disciplinary lay-off. She was also reminded that should the company receive another garnishment within the nine-month period, she would be terminated.

On June 13, 1977, the company received a second order to release, dated June 7, 1977, from National Business Factors, which released the May 9, 1977 garnishment notice. For six months nothing further happened. However, on December 7, 1977, the company received another notice of garnishment and writ of execution arising from the original National Business Factors debt. On December 8, 1977, Ms. Allen was informed of its receipt and was also told that this was considered her fourth garnishment. She immediately contacted National Business Factors and made arrangements for a release, but at the end of that day she was informed that she was being terminated. She elected to resign rather than be discharged. A check for her final wages was prepared and those wages were garnished. On December 16, 1977, the company received an order of release from National Business Factors dated December 13, 1977. A check was then prepared and sent to Ms. Allen for the amount of the final garnishment.

The Secretary of Labor, who is charged with the enforcement of the Consumer Credit Protection Act, brought suit on behalf of Ms. Allen, seeking her reinstatement and back wages. The parties stipulated to the facts and filed cross-motions for summary judgment seeking judicial interpretation of the meaning of the underlined words of the Act: "No employer may discharge any employee by reason of the fact that his earnings have been subjected to garnishment for any one indebtedness." 15 U.S.C. § 1674(a).

After an interval of three years, the district court ruled for the defendant, reasoning that California's contemporaneous garnishment statute imposed a duty upon the employer to withhold a debtor's earnings from the time the writ was served and therefore brought the state within the purview of an Opinion Letter issued by the Wage and Hour Administrator in 1970. This appeal followed.

## DISCUSSION:

The district court granted summary judgment on a pure question of law, the construction of a statute. There are no disputed facts. The appellate standard of review is therefore de novo. *Radobenko v. Automated Equipment Corp.*, 520 F.2d 540, 543 (9th Cir.1975).

This statute has not previously been construed in the Ninth Circuit.

\* \* \* in a case of first impression, the courts look to the traditional signposts for statutory interpretation: first, the language of the statute itself; and second, its legislative history and the interpretation given by its administering agency, both as guides to the intent of Congress in enacting the legislation.

*Turner v. Prod*, 707 F.2d 1109, 1114 (9th Cir.1983).

### A.   The Language

The courts begin interpretation of a statute with the language itself. *Consumer Product Safety Commission v. GTE Sylvania*, 447 U.S. 102, 108, 100 S. Ct. 2051, 2056, 64 L. Ed.2d 766 (1980). In construing the same clause of this statute in a similar factual setting, the Seventh Circuit said:

> Garnishment is defined in § 302(c) of the Act, 15 U.S.C. § 1672(c), as "any legal or equitable procedure through which the earnings of any individual are required to be withheld for payment of any debt." \* \* \* [T]he use of the present tense, rather than the future tense, in the phrase "are required to be withheld" supports a construction that in order for the earnings to "have been subjected to garnishment" those earnings must first be actually withheld pursuant to a garnishment order.

*Brennan v. Kroger Co.*, 513 F.2d 961, 963 (7th Cir.1975) (emphasis added). We agree.

Moreover, the phrase "subjected to garnishment" in section 304(a) refers to "earnings." The district court held that the Magnin notice constituted a subjection to garnishment, despite the fact that nothing whatsoever happened to Ms. Allen's earnings as a consequence of it. The court's analysis thus does not comport with the express language of the statute.

## B.   Legislative History

In 1968 when the Consumer Credit Protection Act was passed, Congress was greatly concerned about the negative effects of garnishment upon individual workers, 15 U.S.C. § 1671(a); the termination of employment which often came in the train of garnishment, 15 U.S.C. § 1671(a)(2); the high correlation between garnishment and personal bankruptcy, Hearings on H.R. 11601 Before Subcomm. on Consumer Affairs of the House Comm. on Banking & Currency, 90th Cong., 1st Sess. pt. 1 at 540 (1967) [hereinafter Hearings]; and the unacceptably high level of damage to the country's economic well-being which it felt was created by the interaction between the two, 15 U.S.C. § 1671(a)(3); House Committee on Banking & Currency, Report on H.R. 11601, H.R. Rep. No. 1040, 90th Cong., 2d Sess. (1968), reprinted in 1968 U.S. Code Cong. & Admin. News 1962 at 1978 [hereinafter Committee Report]. Initially, it considered legislation which would have outlawed garnishment entirely. Id. However, it was persuaded that such an abolition would work hardship upon honest creditors, and so it enacted sections 303(a) and 304(a), which limited the amounts which could be taken by garnishment and restricted the employer's power to terminate as a consequence of garnishment. 15 U.S.C. §§ 1673(a), 1674(a); Committee Report at 1978.

It seems clear that the dominant purpose of Congress in enacting this legislation was to protect employees from the adverse effects of garnishment proceedings and discharges based upon them. Although the district court spoke in terms of Congress' balancing between the interests of the employer and the employee in garnishment proceedings (the expense and inconvenience for the employer against the livelihood of the employee), we see no evidence of this in the legislative history. The fact that Congress struck a balance between the interests of the debtor and creditor is not an invitation for the courts to extend that balance to the interests of the employer. The legislative history reveals the statute's dominant purpose as being the preservation of an employee's job. Brennan v. Kroger, 513 F.2d at 964. Such a purpose cannot be reconciled with a reading of the language which permits a termination upon the mere service of a second garnishment order. Id.

Ms. Allen falls squarely within the group whom Congress wished to protect. She had contracted heavy debts while married. She was working to liquidate them after her divorce. Three times in the nine months covered by the stipulated facts of this case she got releases from her creditors and appears to have been making payments on her debts; she did not resort to bankruptcy with its concomitant damage to the national economy. Her forced resignation would leave her without income to meet her obligations. To allow the construction of the statute which the company here urges undermines the purpose of Congress in enacting the statute. We will not do so.

## C.

* * * We therefore hold that "earnings have been subjected to garnishment" within the meaning of Section 304(a) only when they have

actually been withheld from the paycheck of the employee. We do not reach the question of which point in the paycheck preparation cycle constitutes that withholding since there is no contention in the record before us that Dianne Allen's check was in any state of preparation when she secured her release from Joseph Magnin. The district court is reversed and this case is remanded for further proceedings in accordance with this opinion.

### NOTES AND QUESTIONS

1. In *Brennan v. Kroger Co.*, 513 F.2d 961 (7th Cir.1975), it was held that an employer cannot discharge an employee upon being served with a garnishment notice by a second creditor while garnishment deductions were still being made upon the first garnished indebtedness. The court reasoned that under state law, deductions would not begin until the payment of the indebtedness for the first garnishment had been satisfied and that, therefore, the wages had not yet been "subjected" to the second garnishment. The court noted the possibility that the employee might obtain a release from the indebtedness underlying the second garnishment order prior to that order being executed for actual collection against the worker's wages.

Do the decisions in *Kroger* and in *Southern California Gas* serve only the interests of the employee and his or her dependents, or do they serve a social function as well? If the latter, why not totally ban dismissals due to having wages garnished?

2. Several federal courts of appeals have held that § 1674 of the Consumer Credit Protection Act creates a remedy only in the form of a suit by the Secretary of Labor and does not give rise to an implied private cause of action. *LeVick v. Skaggs Companies, Inc.*, 701 F.2d 777 (9th Cir.1983); *McCabe v. City of Eureka*, 664 F.2d 680 (8th Cir.1981) (2–1); *Smith v. Cotton Bros. Baking Co.*, 609 F.2d 738 (5th Cir.), cert. denied 449 U.S. 821, 101 S.Ct. 79, 66 L.Ed.2d 23 (1980). Would a private action be preempted if founded upon a state abusive discharge suit based on dismissal in violation of a specific law? Section 1677 of the Act says that it does not nullify state laws that protect employees from garnishment. Does that resolve the preemption issue?

3. In addition to prohibiting dismissal of an employee upon being subjected to wage garnishment for a single debt, the Consumer Credit Protection Act limits the portion of earnings that is subject to garnishment as follows:

15 U.S.C. § 1673 Restriction on garnishment.

(a) Maximum allowable garnishment. Except as provided in subsection (b) and in section 305 [15 USCS § 1675], the maximum part of the aggregate disposable earnings of an individual for any workweek which is subject to garnishment may not exceed

(1) 25 per centum of his disposable earnings for that week, or

(2) the amount by which his disposable earnings for that week exceed thirty times the Federal minimum hourly wage prescribed by section

6(a)(1) of the Fair Labor Standards Act of 1938 [29 USCS § 206(a)(1)] in effect at the time the earnings are payable,

whichever is less. In the case of earnings for any pay period other than a week, the Secretary of Labor shall by regulation prescribe a multiple of the Federal minimum hourly wage equivalent in effect to that set forth in paragraph (2).

(b) Exceptions.

(1) The restrictions of subsection (a) do not apply in the case of—

(A) any order for the support of any person issued by a court of competent jurisdiction or in accordance with an administrative procedure, which is established by State law, which affords substantial due process, and which is subject to judicial review.

(B) any order of any court of the United States having jurisdiction over cases under chapter 13 of title 11 of the United States Code [11 USCS §§ 1301 et seq.]

(C) any debt due for any State or Federal tax.

(2) The maximum part of the aggregate disposable earnings of an individual for any workweek which is subject to garnishment to enforce any order for the support of any person shall not exceed—

(A) where such individual is supporting his spouse or dependent child (other than a spouse or child with respect to whose support such order is used), 50 per centum of such individual's disposable earnings for that week; and

(B) where such individual is not supporting such a spouse or dependent child described in clause (A), 60 per centum of such individual's disposable earnings for that week;

except that, with respect to the disposable earnings of any individual for any workweek, the 50 per centum specified in clause (A) shall be deemed to be 55 per centum and the 60 per centum specified in clause (B) shall be deemed to be 65 per centum, if and to the extent that such earnings are subject to garnishment to enforce a support order with respect to a period which is prior to the twelve-week period which ends with the beginning of such workweek.

(c) * * *

4. What garnishment deduction limits are imposed by § 1673 if an employee is required both to make support payments and also pay a judgment creditor? Taking guidance from the Department of Labor's interpretative regulation, 29 C.F.R. § 870.11, an Illinois court has held that state law controls the order of priorities in executing wage garnishments and that under its state law a garnishment for support payments takes priority over a creditor garnishment regardless of which was executed first. Additionally, the court concluded that if 25% or more of the garnishee's earnings are withheld to pay support, no further withholding is available to satisfy a creditor's garnishment of wages. *Commonwealth Edison v. Denson*, 144 Ill.App.3d 383, 98 Ill.Dec. 859, 494 N.E.2d 1186 (3d Dist.1986).

The New Hampshire Supreme Court has ruled that the statutory limit is an absolute standard that cannot be equitably modified even if the wage earner has intentionally restricted his earnings. *Center for Gastrointestinal Medicine, Inc. v. Willitts*, 137 N.H. 67, 623 A.2d 752 (1993). The court observed, however, that the statute does not prevent execution against the support debtor's assets or possible contempt proceedings for "voluntary dissipation of talents". 623 A.2d at 754.

5.   An income tax refund is the property of the taxpayer, not "disposable earnings." Therefore, even though the taxes were withheld from earned income, § 1673 does not insulate a bankrupt's tax refund from a bankruptcy trustee's use of it, without restriction, as an asset available to pay the bankrupt's debts. *Kokoszka v. Belford*, 417 U.S. 642, 94 S.Ct. 2431, 41 L.Ed.2d 374 (1974). Based on this analysis, the Utah Supreme Court has held that creditors may garnish the full amount of a tax refund. *Funk v. Utah State Tax Comm'n*, 839 P.2d 818 (Utah 1992).

# 3.   ASSIGNMENT OF WAGES

Perhaps due to the instability of employment in the pre-World War II period, unsalaried workers had a difficult time securing bank loans. See generally EVANS CLARK, FINANCING THE CONSUMER 10 (1930) (prior to 1930, "the working man, with no security but his character, the expectation of future wages and, perhaps, some furniture, has not been able to borrow at any bank"). The practice developed for certain lending institutions to give small loans upon the employee's assignment of his future wages. See A. Fortas, *Wage Assignments in Chicago*, 42 YALE L.J. 526 (1933). Most states came to regulate wage assignment in order to protect the wage earner's spouse and dependents or to protect the employer from a loss of efficiency should the employee develop the sense that he is working not for his own benefit but for the benefit of the assignee.

## EXCERPTS FROM REPORT, FEDERAL TRADE COMMISSION

49 Fed. Reg. 7755–7758

A wage assignment is a contractual transfer by a debtor to a creditor of the right to receive wages directly from the debtor's employer. To activate the assignment, the creditor simply submits it to the debtor's employer, who then pays all or a percentage of debtor's wages to the creditor. The debtor releases the employer from any liability arising out of the employer's compliance with the wage assignment, and may waive any requirement that the creditor first establish or allege a default. Absent a statutory restriction, it is not necessary to obtain the employer's consent to enter into a wage assignment.

Wage assignment and wage garnishment are both methods by which a creditor can obtain the debtor's wages to apply to or satisfy a debt. Procedurally, however, the two remedies are very different. Garnishment requires that the creditor obtain a court judgment before wages can be garnished to collect the debt. The Supreme Court has held that prejudgment garnishment deprives the debtor of constitutional due process rights. Wage assignment, on the other hand, does not require a judgment. A creditor can file a wage assignment without any judicial review of the creditor's claim. The debtor does not have a hearing with an opportunity to assert any defenses. Unlike prejudgment garnishment, prejudgment wage assignment has usually survived constitutional challenge. There is no meaningful distinction between the effects of the two remedies, but when presented with challenges to wage assignments, courts generally have not found sufficient state action in the assignment to trigger the due process protections of the fourteenth amendment, thus courts have not reached the merits of challenges based on constitutional claims.

Some wage assignments are used as a method of making regular payments on a debt prior to delinquency rather than as a collection remedy. These wage assignments are essentially voluntary payroll deductions, and are used most frequently by credit unions and other creditors closely associated with the employer. This record does not indicate that payroll deduction wage assignments cause consumer injury; we have therefore exempted such assignments from the rule. Similarly, preauthorized electronic fund transfers to accounts from wages may be considered to be wage assignments, but they are used as methods of payment rather than as a collection remedy. Thus, they are exempted from the rule because this rulemaking record does not show that they cause consumer injury. * * *

Wage assignments are prohibited in the Uniform Consumer Credit Code States, several other states, and in the District of Columbia. A substantial majority of the remaining states have imposed restrictions on the use of wage assignments. Some of the more common restrictions are: a time limit for the assignment, a requirement that the employer or spouse consent to the assignment, and an absolute prohibition of assignment in certain kinds of transactions. In addition, some states require that the wage assignment be on a separate document, and some allow the debtor to contest a wage assignment by informing the employer that he or she has a defense.

Some states have enacted a limitation (generally 15 percent to 25 percent) on the amount of weekly or monthly wages that may be assigned. State provisions are inconsistent, however, and do not always offer adequate protection. Federal statutory limitations on wage garnishment do not apply to wage assignments. Thus, unless there is a state statutory limitation, creditors are restricted only by the terms of the wage assignment. * * *

[Additional problems noted in the FTC report included: a) Workers who made a wage assignment often were unaware of their right to assert defenses against the creditor's collection based on the creditor's fraud or breach of warranty. b) Because employers often resent the added adminis-

WAGE PAYMENT, GARNISHMENT

trative costs of paying a wage assignment, creditors can exploit the worker's fear of job loss if the creditor is forced to present the assignment to the employer for payment. c) Indebtedness in the form of a wage assignment can disrupt family finances and leave the worker without the ability to purchase necessities. Based on its findings respecting the impact of wage assignment practices, the FTC adopted the rule that follows.]

## RULE ADOPTED BY THE FTC

16 C.F.R. § 444.2(a)

In connection with the extension of credit to consumers in or affecting commerce, as commerce is defined in the Federal Trade Commission Act, it is an unfair act or practice within the meaning of Section 5 of that Act for a lender or retail installment seller directly or indirectly to take or receive from a consumer an obligation that:

\* \* \*

(3) Constitutes or contains an assignment of wages or other earnings unless:

(i) The assignment by its terms is revocable at the will of the debtor, or

(ii) The assignment is a payroll deduction plan or preauthorized payment plan, commencing at the time of the transaction, in which the consumer authorizes a series of wage deductions as a method of making each payment, or

(iii) The assignment applies only to wages or other earnings already earned at the time of the assignment. \* \* \*

### NOTES AND QUESTIONS

1. A wage garnishment can result from a worker's voluntary contractual undertakings or from such other causes as tort liability, tax liability, civil and criminal penalties, or the status indebtedness of maintenance and support for children and former spouses. In contrast, wage assignments are solely contractual undertakings, though the previously-quoted FTC findings suggest that such contracts are not always entered into knowingly or voluntarily.

What values are served by making the knowing, voluntary nature of wage assignments the critical factors in determining the constitutionality of enforcement procedures, or in establishing regulatory restrictions upon such enforcement?

2. In what ways does FTC regulation 16 C.F.R. § 444.2(a), quoted above, respond to the interests of the assignor's employer? To the interests of the assignor's dependents? To the interests of the assignee?

3. In *American Financial Services Ass'n v. FTC*, 767 F.2d 957 (D.C.Cir. 1985), cert. denied 475 U.S. 1011, 106 S. Ct. 1185, 89 L. Ed.2d 301 (1986), the court rejected several challenges to 16 C.F.R. § 444.2(a) among other FTC

consumer credit regulations. One challenge asserted that the agency's actions had improperly displaced all state regulation. Rejecting this contention, the court stated that Congress' delegation of regulatory authority to the FTC in this area was not intended to "occupy the field" and thereby wholly preempt local regulation. Accordingly, the court explained that state law survives the regulations to the extent that local law does not directly conflict with the federal agency's rules and does not give less protection than those rules to interests sought to be protected by the FTC.

4. For a "creditor's side" view of the practical and doctrinal problems posed by limitations on wage assignments, see John T. Hundley, *Assignments of Wages in Illinois: Pitfalls for Employer Businesses*, 14 DePaul Bus. L.J. 21 (2001).

## D.  COLLECTION OF PAY AND BENEFITS FROM INSOLVENT EMPLOYERS

Federal bankruptcy law controls the distribution of the assets of most financially failed enterprises. The Bankruptcy Code accepts the concept of secured indebtedness. Therefore, the liquidated proceeds of an asset that, by statute or a perfected security device is collateral for an indebtedness, is distributed first to satisfy that indebtedness. Any excess in the proceeds from the securing asset becomes part of the general assets of the bankrupt estate which are distributed in liquidation of the estate's general debts. Conversely, to the extent that a securing asset does not satisfy a secured debt, the debt balance becomes a general claim on the insolvent estate.

Two general categories of wages enjoy the status of secured claims in bankruptcy proceedings. Under federal maritime law, wages owed to seafarers have a statutory lien upon the vessel and the tariffs collected for the carriage of goods by the vessel. In addition, state statutes impose what is called a mechanic's lien on the work product of various types of workers. The wages of construction workers generally enjoy such a secured interest in the property improvements that result from their work. In some jurisdictions, other trades are also given a statutory lien on their work products.

Sovereign immunity bars execution of a mechanic's lien if the work product is government-owned property. As a substitute for such lost payment security, the Miller Act, 40 USC § 270a, requires employers performing construction, alteration or repair of federal buildings or other public works (e.g., a dam) to post a bond against which unpaid employees can execute claims for unpaid wages and benefits. Many states have similar statutes protecting wage claims of those who build or repair state-owned facilities.

To the extent that assets are available partially to satisfy the general claims on a bankrupt estate, the Bankruptcy Code creates a series of priorities that entitles some general creditors to collect all or part of their claim before an effort is made to satisfy the remaining claims of general creditors. (See 11 U.S.C. § 507.) Under this system, several priorities affect employee claims. First priority is given to claims for expenses of administering the bankrupt estate. This includes payment of wages and salaries for work performed after the estate comes under the jurisdiction of the bankruptcy trustee. Third priority is given to claims for wages, salaries and commissions, including vacation, severance and sick leave pay. However, the third priority is limited to claims for work performed within ninety days prior to the filing of the bankruptcy petition or the termination of the business, whichever occurred first. In addition, a cap of $4,650 per claim is imposed on this priority. Finally, claims for contributions to employee benefit plans are given fourth priority, subject to a maximum amount per protected employee and a limit on the period for which the contribution was due.

The protection provided by the Bankruptcy Code's priority preferences for earnings owed employees can be illusory. Typically, it takes months or years to resolve the bankruptcy proceeding; generally, payments are not made for third priority claims until the administrative process is nearing completion. More disastrous for employees is the possibility that there are insufficient unsecured assets to pay even part of the third priority claims.

*Citicorp Industrial Credit, Inc. v. Brock*, 483 U.S. 27, 107 S.Ct. 2694, 97 L.Ed.2d 23 (1987), involved an interesting end run around the dilemma created when secured creditors have claims on all of an insolvent employer's assets. In that case, a clothing manufacturer pledged substantially all of its assets to secure a loan for working capital. Business went poorly; the manufacturer defaulted on its obligations to the lender, the latter took possession of the securing collateral, and the manufacturer's employees were not paid for a period from January 27 to February 19. The Department of Labor intervened by seeking an injunction to prevent the lender from transporting finished goods (part of the seized collateral) in interstate commerce. The Supreme Court held that goods produced during the period for which the employees were not paid had been manufactured in violation of FLSA minimum wage requirements and, therefore, under § 15(a)(1) of the Act [29 U.S.C. § 215(a)] were banned from interstate commerce. The Court noted that the goods in the hands of the creditor could not be permitted to compete in interstate commerce with lawfully produced goods since they were tainted by the failure to provide FLSA minimum compensation. Even though the creditor had no direct responsibility to pay the workers, the Court observed that it could cure the violation, and vacate the lien, by paying the employees the statutorily-required wage. How to reconcile hot goods injunction procedures and procedures under the Bankruptcy Code remains difficult. See *Chao v. Hospital Staffing Services, Inc.*, 270 F.3d 374 (6th Cir. 2001).

# CHAPTER VIII

## PROTECTION OF PHYSICAL INTEGRITY— OCCUPATIONAL HEALTH AND SAFETY

■  ■  ■

### A.  INTRODUCTION

Legal protection of workers from the hazards of the workplace, whether by common law rules or statutory regulation, raises a fundamental question: How should the costs of those risks be allocated between the employer and the workers who are put at risk? Employers cannot provide entirely risk free workplaces; some accidents and injuries to health are unavoidable. But with proper precautions, safety devices, production methods and working conditions, many can be avoided. The question, at the first level, is how much cost of avoidance should employers be required to bear, and how much risk of injury should employers be allowed to impose on their workers.

Economists hypothesize that, in a perfectly competitive economy, the labor and product markets will efficiently allocate the costs of industrial accidents among employers, workers and consumers. In a perfect labor market, workers would realize the potential costs of the risks to which they are exposed and, having safer alternative jobs, demand higher wages to compensate them for these potential costs. The magnitude of the "compensating wages" that the workers can demand relative to the expected costs of accidents, will depend on the slopes of the workers' labor supply and demand curves.* Compensating wages not only give the employer incentive to provide safety equipment or insurance to mitigate workplace risks, but also provide a resource for workers to self-insure or purchase third party insurance against these risks. The costs of compensating wages, safety devices and employer provided insurance would be reflected in the price of the goods and split between the employer and the

---

* If the workers are essential to the operations of firm so that the firm's demand for them is insensitive to their wage, they will be able to demand compensating wages that fully compensate them for the expected costs of accidents. However, if the workers are less important to the firm, they will receive compensating wages that are less than the expected costs of accidents and will have to bear some of these costs themselves.

470

consumers of the good according to the slopes of the supply and demand curve for the good.**

Of course ideal circumstances are rarely attained. Workers may not be able to adequately evaluate all of the hazards they face in the workplace. This seems particularly true when considering complex long-term risks such as exposure to chemicals, radiation, dust or repetitive motion. It is hard for workers to ask for compensating wages for risks of which they are not fully aware. Indeed, it may be that workers systematically under-estimate workplace risks as a means of psychologically coping with the hazards to which they are exposed. Although this may be a sound strategy for dealing with some of the stress of working, it is probably not an optimal strategy for bargaining with your employer. Employers, who might have superior knowledge about the risks of a job, have little incentive to advertise those risks to workers in soliciting employees. In addition, some workers may not have good safe alternative jobs in negoti-ating with their employers. Without alternatives, the invisible hand of the marketplace does not work. Finally, it may be difficult or impossible for workers to translate all of the risks they suffer into the monetary equivalent of a compensating wage. The costs of accidents borne by workers include the human costs of pain and suffering, loss of ability to carry on a normal life of usefulness and enjoyment, and the shortening or loss of life itself. Ultimately, the level of health and safety protection we require of employers depends on the values we place on the fundamental right of workers to life and physical integrity. It is our unwillingness to place a dollar value on that right which underlies many disputed issues in legal regulation of the work environment.

Comprehensive legal regulation, even at lower levels of protection, raises major administrative problems. Modern industry has an unlimited number of production processes and job assignments with infinitely varied working conditions. It is estimated that more than 575,000 potentially toxic substances are now being used in industry, with thousands of new ones added every month. How is it possible to prescribe all the safety devices or measures required, or define health standards which will deal adequately with these hazards, and to adopt them by procedures which follow traditional due process? What kind of administrative structure, forms of procedure, and character of legal prescriptions and standards are required to accomplish this task?

Enforcement raises an additional range of problems. The Occupation-al Safety and Health Act covers some 110 million plus private sector workers employed in well over 6 million workplaces. What methods can be devised to discover more than a token number of violations? What sanctions are appropriate and at the same time effective in deterring

---

** If the good is a necessity with no reasonable substitutes, the consumers' demand for the good will be insensitive to price and consumers will bear most or all of the employer's costs associated with industrial accidents in producing the good. On the other hand, if the good is frivolous with many excellent substitutes so that the consumers' demand for the good is very sensitive to price, then the employer will bear most or all of his or her costs associated with industrial accidents in producing the good.

violators, particularly where the standards are necessarily general and the cost of compliance so substantial that employers are inclined to err on the side of savings rather than safety?

These problems of administration and enforcement, which are pervasive in all efforts to protect employees, are sharply focused in the regulation of occupational health and safety. They are major concerns and points for discussion in this chapter. The useful question is not whether the statute is now fulfilling its function, but what changes might make it more effective.

The common law duties of an employer for the safety and health of its employees have been somewhat redundantly summarized by Prosser in these broad terms:

1.   The duty to provide a safe place to work.

2.   The duty to provide safe appliance, tools and equipment for work.

3.   The duty to give warning of dangers which the employee might reasonably be expected to remain in ignorance.

4.   The duty to provide a sufficient number of suitable fellow servants.

5.   The duty to promulgate and enforce rules for the conduct of employees which would make the work safe.

PROSSER & KEETON, TORTS p. 569 (5th ed. 1984).

The potential protection provided by these duties was eviscerated by the "unholy trinity" of common law defenses—contributory negligence, assumption of risk and the fellow servant rule. The most devilish of these defenses was assumption of risk, which declared that a worker, by accepting employment, bargained away his right to hold the employer responsible for risks known to him or normally incident to his employment. Even though the employer had clearly violated its common law or statutory duties, the innocent worker could be barred because she "voluntarily" continued working and thereby consented to assume the risk. The fact that she continued under protest or threat of discharge did not, in the blind contract logic of the courts, make her consent any less "voluntary." As seen in the next chapter, this contract reasoning was extended by Chief Justice Shaw in the notorious case of *Farwell v. Boston & Worcester Rail Road*, 45 Mass. (4 Metc.) 49 (1842), to justify the fellow servant rule. The worker, by accepting employment, assumed the risk of the negligence of his fellow servants. It was a part of his bargained contract of employment. Due to the blessings of the unholy trinity, employers escaped liability in 85 to 90 percent of industrial accidents. When the injured worker did recover, it was after long delay, often under pressure to settle to obtain money to live, with lawyer's fees and expenses taking most of the recovery.

Eventually, the appalling number of deaths and serious injuries in the mines and factories and on the railroads, undermined the rationale that workers voluntarily agreed to these conditions. In some states, judges began to scale back employer defenses. For example, the fellow servant rule did not apply to the negligence of a "vice principal" such as a supervisor or sub-contractor. Where injured workers were able to get their case past the judge to the jury room, the verdicts were often substantial.

Legislative response to the dangers to life and limb which workers faced in industrial life took two directions. First, states, and to a lesser extent the federal government, passed safety laws requiring safeguards on dangerous machinery such as gears, presses, and cutting devices, protection against gas explosions and rock falls in mines, and safety equipment such as automatic couplers and warning devices on the railroads. By the turn of the century, more than half the states had some form of occupational safety and health laws, but these were narrowly focused on specific hazards and were poorly enforced.

The second, and by far most dominant response, was not to protect workers from danger but, as seen in the next chapter, to compensate the worker for injuries they suffered. The Federal Employees' Liability Act, applicable to employees on interstate railroads, preserved the common law tort duties, but eliminated the debilitating common law defenses of contributory negligence, assumption of risk and fellow servant rule. The measure of recovery for employer negligence in performing these duties was the tort measure, including recovery for pain and suffering. The response at the state level was the enactment of worker's compensation laws which made the employer liable regardless of fault, but limited the employee's recovery to medical costs and only a portion of lost wages, often less than half. Recovery from the employer under workers' compensation was made exclusive, barring potentially more substantial common law damages.

Although every state passed occupational health and safety laws by 1960, most existed more on paper than in the workplace. Some spent as little as two cents per year per worker in job safety enforcement. Half the states had fewer than twenty-five inspectors; a third had a dozen or fewer. Only a few, such as New York and California, had statutes and enforcement administrations which could be described as even half-hearted. In 1970, there were only 1600 inspectors enforcing all the various state laws. It was said that there were three times as many fish and game wardens as there were safety inspectors, so that trout and quail were better protected than working men and women. See, 116 Cong. Rec. 38, 393 (1970), reprinted in Leg. Hist. of Occupational Safety and Health Act of 1970, 92nd Cong. 1st sess. (1971) 1049. Senator Yarborough of Texas described existing job safety efforts "a sneeze in a hurricane."

Federal legislation was piecemeal and snail-paced, reaching only a few notorious evils in industry and on the railroads. In 1936, the Walsh–Healy Public Contracts Act included a provision that contracts for manufacturing or furnishing material to the federal government in an amount more than $10,000 must contain a stipulation that working conditions of the contractor must not be "unsanitary, or hazardous to health and safety." The statutory words were largely an empty promise, for only one out of twenty-five companies was inspected each year, resulting in only thirty-four complaints for 75,000 companies.

Mine safety legislation seemed always to come after the fact. When 119 Illinois miners were killed in December, 1951, Congress passed a Coal Mine Safety Act, but it took the death of seventy-eight miners in Farmington, West Virginia to stir Congress to pass the Coal Mine Health and Safety Act of 1969, arguably the most effective health and safety statute yet enacted.

Mine safety legislation in 1969 triggered a broader concern for occupational safety and health. The Construction Safety Act of 1969 established standards for construction on public works and the Federal Railway Safety Act in 1970 included provisions for employee safety.

This upsurge of concern led to the passage of the Occupational Safety and Health Act of 1970. Congressional hearings spotlighted the hazards that workers faced in modern industry. Secretary of Labor Schultz testified that in 1968 an estimated 14,500 workers were killed and 2.2 million were disabled each year in industrial accidents, resulting in a loss of 250 million man days of work and $8 billion loss in Gross National Product. This was 20% more than in 1958. The hazards to occupational health from dust, noise and toxic substances were even greater. The Public Health Service estimated there were 390,000 new occurrences of occupational disease each year. The Surgeon General, in a sample study of industrial plants, found that 65% of the workers were potentially exposed to harmful physical agents or toxic materials, and only 35% were adequately protected by controls or safety measures. In some states, 30% of textile workers in carding and spinning rooms suffered from "brown lung" caused by cotton dust. Although the dangers of asbestos had been known by manufacturers for more than half a century, 40% of the workers who had since entered insulation work were destined to die of asbestos or lung cancer. As many as 3.5 million workers had been exposed to the danger of breathing asbestos fibers. It was estimated that every twenty minutes a new and potentially toxic chemical was introduced into industry. Leg.Hist. *supra* 142–144.

The potential effectiveness of legislation was evidenced by the fact that states with good safety legislation had only one-sixth as many industrial accidents as states with poor legislation. Reliance, however, could not be placed on state legislation. Efforts by some states to protect against hazards were undermined by other states that sought to attract industry by permitting the hazards. Too often regulation by one state of toxic chemicals would not lead to corrective action, but to the employer moving to a more permissive state and subjecting a different group of workers to the toxic hazards. Similarly, reliance could not be placed on employers, for no matter how concerned an employer might be, its efforts would be penalized by its competitive disadvantage against less concerned employers. If the life and physical integrity of workers were to be protected, market forces required national legislation.

Impelled by these facts and considerations, Congress enacted the Occupational Safety and Health Act of 1970. Section 2 [29 U.S.C. § 651(b)] declared the purpose to be "to assure so far a possible every working man and woman in the Nation safe and healthful working conditions * * *." The prevailing temper of its enactment was expressed by Senator Yarborough:

> We know the costs would be put into consumer goods but that is the price we should pay for the 80 million workers in America. 116 Cong. Rec. 37,345 (1970), Leg.Hist., *supra* 444. * * * We are talking about people's lives, not the indifference of some cost accountants. We are talking about assuring the men and women who work in our plants and factories that they will go home after a day's work with their bodies intact. We are talking about assuring workers who work with deadly chemicals that when they have accumulated a few years seniority they will not have accumulated lung congestion and poisons in their bodies, or something that will strike them down before they reach retirement age. 116 Cong. Rec. 37,625 (1970), Leg.Hist. *supra* 510.

While OSHA is by far the broadest federal regulation of employee safety, there are other statutes and regulations aimed at particular occupational groups. Safety of vessels (including many oil drilling rigs in the Gulf of Mexico, such as the BP rig that blew in 2010 killing 11 workers) is largely entrusted to the Coast Guard. Much of the regulation of trucking safety is performed by the Federal Highway Administration, that of operating employees on railroads by the Federal Railroad Administration. Some aspects of mine worker safety are dealt with below. Section 4(b)(1) of the OSH Act, 29 U.S.C. § 653(b)(1), provides that those and other agencies retain their employee safety responsibilities, independent of OSHA. A number of interagency agreements seek to clarify which agency will deal with which types of problems.

# B. OVERVIEW OF THE OCCUPATIONAL SAFETY AND HEALTH ACT

## 1. SUBSTANTIVE DUTIES

Section 5(a) of the statute [29 U.S.C. § 654(a)] imposes on employers two kinds of duties. The so-called "general duty clause," applicable where no specific standard has been adopted or is applicable to the special situation, provides:

> Each employer—(1) shall furnish to each of his employees employment and a place of employment which are free from recognized hazards that are causing or are likely to cause death or serious physical harm to his employees.

This duty was built on the common law principle that individuals are obliged to refrain from actions which cause harm to others. In the words of the Senate Committee Report:

The committee believes that employers are equally bound by this general and common duty to bring no adverse effects to the life and health of their employees throughout the course of their employment. Employers have primary control of the work environment and should insure that it is safe and healthful. Section 5(a) * * * merely restates that each employer shall furnish this degree of care. S. Rep. No. 91–1282, 9 (1970) Leg.Hist. *supra* 9 at 149.

The second kind of duty is imposed by the "specific duty" or standards clause, which requires that:

"Each employer—(2) shall comply with occupational safety and health standards promulgated under this Act."

Section 2(8) [29 U.S.C. § 652(8)] defines an occupational safety and health standard as a required condition, practice, means, operation or process "reasonably necessary to provide safe or healthful employment and places of employment."

Section 6 [29 U.S.C. § 655] prescribes the procedure for the Secretary of Labor to establish national standards for safety and health. Because of the desire to establish national standards as soon as possible, the Secretary of Labor was authorized to adopt during the first two years of the statute any "established Federal standard" and any "national consensus standard" without resorting to the lengthy rule-making procedures required by Section 6 or by the Administrative Procedure Act. The "established federal standards" were those adopted under the Walsh–Healey Act, and six other federal acts. The "national consensus standards" were those adopted by private organizations such as the American National Standards Institute, National Fire Protection Institute and the American Society for Testing and Materials. Such standards were required to be adopted by procedures which afforded opportunity for consideration of diverse views and the persons affected had to reach substantial agreement. Most of those standards are still in force.

Section 6 provides that the Secretary may modify or revoke any of these standards, or establish new standards only through the procedures prescribed by Section 6 and the Administrative Procedure Act. Section 6(c) provides for establishing temporary emergency standards effective for six months pending these procedures where there is "grave danger" of exposure to toxic substances or new hazards. Any person adversely affected by any standard may challenge its validity directly by an immediate petition in a U.S. court of appeals, or may challenge its validity in proceedings brought by the Secretary to enforce it in a specific case.

In the first twenty years of the statute only thirty-five new health standards and forty safety standards were promulgated, with procedures taking up to fifteen years or more from the time a standard was proposed until it was upheld by a court of appeals. Emergency temporary standards are not always treated favorably by the courts, see *Asbestos Information Association/North America v. OSHA*, 727 F.2d 415 (5th Cir.1984), but the limitation to six months effectiveness severely restricts their usefulness in any case.

## 2.  ENFORCEMENT PROCEDURE

Responsibility for enforcement of the statute is vested nominally in the Secretary of Labor, but is administratively located in the Occupational Safety and Health Administration (OSHA), an agency in the Labor Department under an Assistant Secretary of Labor. Enforcement is through inspection of the work place by compliance officers. (See 29 U.S.C. §§ 658–59). Inspections may be triggered by complaints of employees, reports from any source of imminent dangers of serious injury, or reports of fatal or multiple injuries. In addition, programmed investigations are scheduled by OSHA with priorities as to the types of workplaces or establishments to be inspected.

Following the inspection, the Compliance Officer makes a report to the Area Director who then issues citations with abatement orders and proposed penalties. The penalties (See 29 U.S.C. § 666) may range up to $7,000 for non-serious or serious violations, and from $5,000 up to $70,000 for repeated and willful violations. Failure to obey an abatement order may result in a civil penalty of up to $7,000 a day. An employer who willfully violates the statute and thereby causes the death of an employee may be criminally prosecuted and, as a result of 18 U.S.C. §§ 2 and 3571, subject to a fine of up to $500,000 if a corporation, and $250,000 and six months imprisonment for a first offense by an individual. Up to one year of imprisonment may be imposed for further criminal offenses. Criminal violations are not prosecuted by OSHA, but by the Department of Justice.

If the employer does not contest the citation in fifteen working days, it becomes a final order and binding. If the employer files a timely notice of contest, the case goes to the Occupational Safety and Health Review Commission (OSHRC), an independent three member body. It is then assigned to an Administrative Law Judge for a hearing and decision. Any party aggrieved by that decision may petition for "discretionary review," which can be granted by any member of the Commission. If review is not granted, the ALJ's decision becomes a final order of the Commission. (See 29 U.S.C. § 659). Appeals from final orders of the Commission are to the federal courts of appeal. Review may include not only findings of fact, interpretation of the statute and applicable standard, and the assessment of penalty in the specific case, but also the validity of the standard applied. (See 29 U.S.C. § 660).

In the proceedings for enforcement, from the issuance of citation to petition for judicial review, the Assistant Secretary of Labor for OSHA acts as prosecutor of the alleged violations. Thus, before the ALJ and the Commission, the Secretary is an "aggrieved party" and may appeal from an unfavorable decision of the Commission that does not uphold the citations or the penalties.

## 3.   ROLE OF STATE LEGISLATION

Although the Occupational Safety and Health Act was passed because state legislation was inadequate, Congress did recognize that at least a few states provided substantial protection. Also, strong arguments were made for encouraging and permitting state regulation. Section 18 [29 U.S.C. § 667] generally preempts state legislation where any federal standard is in effect, but it provides that the Secretary can cede jurisdiction over any area where the state submits a plan with standards comparable to those of OSHA and enforcement meeting certain criteria. Federal grants are made to the states for operation of certified plans, but those grants are less than half the state's costs, leaving more than half of the costs to be borne by the states. Approximately one-half of the states now have certified plans covering part or all of the areas covered by the federal statute.

## 4.   NATIONAL INSTITUTE FOR OCCUPATIONAL SAFETY AND HEALTH

The OSH Act created the National Institute for Occupational Safety and Health (NIOSH) in the Department of Health and Human Services. Its function is to conduct research and make recommendations to the Secretary of Labor for adopting new standards and revising old standards. Its focus is on providing optimum protection of employees. In formulating a recommendation, NIOSH research includes analyzing all existing literature on the problem, collecting data and making field studies, or contracting for such research by outsiders.

The research may involve inspection of workplaces and questioning of employers and employees to obtain industry data. NIOSH, however, has no authority to issue citations or impose penalties, but can only collect information. On the basis of this research, which in case of health standards may take three to five years, NIOSH prepares tentative recommendations which are reviewed by NIOSH experts, consultants, professional societies and other government agencies. It then makes its recommendations to the Secretary of Labor, who then decides what action to take.

## 5.   COORDINATION WITH ACTIVITIES OF OTHER FEDERAL AGENCIES

Section 4(b)(1) of the OSH Act provides: that the Act does not apply to "working conditions with respect to which other Federal agencies and State agencies acting under section 274 of the Atomic Energy Act of 1954 ... exercise statutory authority to prescribe or enforce standards or regulations affecting occupational safety or health." In *Chao v. Mallard*

*Bay Drilling, Inc.,* 534 U.S. 235, 122 S.Ct. 738, 151 L.Ed.2d 659 (2002) the Supreme Court held that OSHA jurisdiction is not preempted unless the other Federal agency has in fact exercised its authority to regulate the working conditions in questions. It is not enough that the agency has the power to regulate those conditions, or that the agency has exercised its power in some minimal way that does not reach the working conditions that an OSHA citation addresses.

# C.  FEDERAL MINE SAFETY AND HEALTH ACT

Protection of safety and health in the mines under the Federal Mine Safety and Health Act (MSHA) as amended in 1977 and 2006, 30 U.S.C. § 801 et seq., follows the same general pattern as OSHA. The Secretary of Labor, acting through the Mine Safety and Health Administration (MSHA), is responsible for establishing standards and enforcing those standards. Enforcement is through inspection, by mine inspectors who issue citations, with contested citations heard by an administrative law judge subject to appeals to the Mine Safety and Health Review Commission (MSHRC).

There are, however, a number of significant differences. First, the MSH Act has no general duty clause, but the long history of mine regulation had established a comprehensive set of specific standards which were incorporated as interim standards in the 1977 Act. Second, inspections are both more frequent and often more effective than those carried out under OSHA. While the number of MSHA inspectors dropped sharply from 2000 to 2008, the ratio of inspectors to mines remains significantly higher than the ratio of OSHA inspectors to non-mine workplaces. As a result, mines are generally inspected multiple times a year, while the most hazardous workplaces elsewhere are often not inspected once in four years, and many workplaces are never inspected. Because mine inspection is specialized, the inspectors are generally better trained and are required to have five years experience in the mines. Third, the inspector has authority to order immediate closing of part or all of a mine where he finds imminent danger or repeated "unwarrantable failure" to comply with mandatory health or safety standards, even though these do not create an imminent danger. The mine must remain closed until a subsequent inspection discloses no similar violations. During the period the mine is closed the miners are entitled to pay for up to one week. Fourth, employers are required to provide health and safety training for all employees. New miners must be given at least forty hours of training if they work underground and twenty-four hours if they work on the surface. In addition, all miners must receive eight hours of refresher training each year. Employees must be paid their normal rate for all training time, and travel and meal costs if the training is not at their normal place of work. See Galloway, McAteer & Webb, *A Miner's Bill of Rights,* 80 W. VA. L. REV. 397 (1978); *Symposium: Thinking Outside the*

*Box: A Post–Sage Look at Coal Mine Safety*, 111 W.VA. L. REV. (2008). Despite these added protections for workers, mining, particularly underground mining, remains a notably hazardous occupation. The Bureau of Labor Statistics reported that in 2008, the incidence rate for non-fatal injuries was 3.9 cases for 100 full time workers, 4.4 per 100 for all coal mine workers, but 6.5 per 100 for bituminous coal underground mining. The contrast is even more striking when fatal injuries are considered. In private industry as a whole, the fatal injury incidence rate was 4.3 cases per 100,000 full time workers; in coal mining that rate was 24.8 per 100,000. A major disaster in the spring of 2010 took the lives of more than two dozen West Virginia coal miners, and has led to a variety of proposals for reorganizing the administration of coal mine safety.

# D.  ADOPTION OF STANDARDS

## AMERICAN IRON AND STEEL INSTITUTE v. OCCUPATIONAL SAFETY AND HEALTH ADMINISTRATION

United States Court of Appeals, Eleventh Circuit, 1999
182 F.3d 1261

ANDERSON, CHIEF JUDGE:

These consolidated cases seek judicial review of the Occupational Safety and Health Administration's ("OSHA") new standard for respiratory protection in the workplace. The separate challenges are brought by the American Iron and Steel Institute ("Industry") and the American College of Occupational and Environmental Medicine ("Doctors") and relate to different aspects of the new standard. For the reasons that follow, we conclude that OSHA correctly applied the law and that its factual determinations were supported by substantial evidence, and therefore the petitions for review are DENIED.

## I.  BACKGROUND

The Occupational Safety and Health Act of 1970 ("OSH Act"), 29 U.S.C. §§ 651–678, was enacted to ensure safe and healthy working conditions for employees. The OSH Act empowers OSHA to promulgate standards "dealing with toxic materials or harmful physical agents ... which most adequately assure, to the extent feasible, on the basis of the best available evidence, that no employee will suffer material impairment of health or functional capacity even if such employee has regular exposure to the hazard dealt with by such standard for the period of his working life." 29 U.S.C. § 655(b)(5). One such hazard is caused by harmful dusts, fumes, gases, and the like that contaminate the atmospheres in many workplaces. OSHA began to regulate employee exposure to such contaminants as early as 1971. In January 1998, OSHA issued a new regulatory standard representing a comprehensive revision of those portions of the old standard which addressed the manner and conditions of respirator use ("Standard"). See 63 Fed.Reg. 1152 (Jan. 8, 1998) (codified at 29 C.F.R. § 1910.134). It is the Standard that is at issue in this case.

## A. History of Respiratory Regulation

In 1971, while OSHA was still in its infancy, it promulgated an initial respiratory protection standard pursuant to § 6(a) of the OSH Act, 29 U.S.C. § 655(a). Section 6(a) authorized OSHA to adopt national consensus standards as occupational safety and health standards in a prompt manner, without the lengthy procedures normally incident to administrative rulemaking, during a period of two years from the OSH Act's effective date. Under that framework, OSHA adopted the American National Standards Institute ("ANSI") Standard Z88.2–1969, "Practices for Respiratory Protection." That standard reflected a preference for engineering controls over respirators;1 in effect, it allowed respirators only "[w]hen effective engineering controls are not feasible, or while they are being instituted." This restriction on the use of respirators, sometimes referred to as the Hierarchy-of-Controls Policy, thus became an ingrained part of OSHA's regulatory framework, and was codified at 29 C.F.R. § 1910.134(a)(1).

The authority that was conferred by § 6(a) to codify national consensus standards as federally mandated occupational safety and health standards expired in 1973, but the respiratory protection standard remained intact. After 1973, OSHA was bound to follow § 6(b) of the OSH Act, 29 U.S.C. § 655(b), in promulgating, modifying, or revoking standards. Section 6(b) requires the notice and comment procedures typical to administrative rulemaking. Various parts of the old respiratory protection standard were revised and updated over the years pursuant to § 6(b), but the changes were relatively minor.

The issuance of the Standard in 1998 was the culmination of several years of regulatory debate, hearings, and comment from industry, labor, and other interested persons. The Standard was limited to issues relating to the manner and conditions of use of respirators, and retained the Hierarchy-of-Controls Policy as reflected in § 1910.134(a)(1). OSHA first published an advance notice of proposed rulemaking on May 14, 1982. See 47 Fed.Reg. 20803. On September 17, 1985, OSHA announced the availability of a preliminary draft of a new respiratory protection standard. On November 4, 1994, OSHA published a proposed version of the new respiratory protection standard, and the hearing required by 29 U.S.C. § 655(b)(3) was held June 6, 1995. Following the hearing, OSHA obtained additional comments from interested parties. The final Standard was published on January 8, 1998 and became effective on April 8, 1998.

## B. Highlights of the Standard

The Standard retains the Hierarchy-of-Controls Policy, which as a general matter prefers engineering controls over respirators worn by individual employees. 29 C.F.R. § 1910.134(a)(1). However, the employer is required to provide respirators for its employees when respirators are necessary to protect their health. 29 C.F.R. § 1910.134(a)(2). The Standard requires certain employers to develop and implement a written respiratory protection program that includes several mandatory items. 29 C.F.R. § 1910.134(c). Employers are required to select particular types of respirators based on certain criteria, such as the nature of harmful contaminants and workplace and user factors. 29 C.F.R. § 1910.134(d). In this regard, atmospheres in workplaces are classified into two categories: "immediately dangerous to life and health" ("IDLH"), and non-IDLH. Only certain highly effective types of respirators may be used in IDLH atmospheres. 29 C.F.R. § 1910.134(d)(2). With respect to non-IDLH atmospheres, the Standard permits an employer to choose between atmosphere-supplying respirators (i.e., those with a self-equipped oxygen tank) and the less burdensome air-purifying respirators (i.e., those which merely filter the incoming air). 29 C.F.R. § 1910.134(d)(3)(iii). However, air-purifying respirators are usable only if certain specified steps are taken to ensure that the filtering device is working and maintained properly. 29 C.F.R. § 1910.134(d)(3)(iii)(B). The medical evaluation provisions of the Standard require the employer "to provide a medical evaluation to determine the employee's ability to use a respirator, before the employee is fit tested or required to use the respirator in the workplace." 29 C.F.R. § 1910.134(e)(1). The medical evaluation provisions spell out the procedures in this regard much more specifically than the prior standard. In addition, whereas licensed physicians were responsible for such medical evaluations under the prior standard, the Standard allows non-physician "licensed health care professionals" to perform such evaluations to the extent allowed under state law. 29 C.F.R. § 1910.134(e)(2). The new Standard also contains detailed provisions relating to initial and periodic fit-testing to ensure respirators fit an employee-user's face properly, 29 C.F.R. § 1910.134(f), proper day-to-day use of respirators, 29 C.F.R. § 1910.134(g), maintenance and care of respirators, 29 C.F.R. § 1910.134(h), the required quality of the breathing gases used in conjunction with an air-supplying respirator, 29 C.F.R. § 1910.134(i), proper identification and labeling of filters, cartridges, and canisters, 29 C.F.R. § 1910.134(j), provision of training and information to employees, 29 C.F.R. § 1910.134(k), periodic self-evaluations of an employer's written respiratory protection program to ensure that it continues to work properly, 29 C.F.R. § 1910.134(l), and appropriate record-keeping regarding medical evaluations and fit-testing, 29 C.F.R. § 1910.134(m).

### C. Provisions Under Attack and Alignment of the Parties

The instant petitions for review are brought by the Industry and the Doctors. The Industry challenges three particular aspects of the Standard. First, it challenges the retention of the Hierarchy-of-Controls Policy in § 1910.134(a)(1), and OSHA's failure even to consider revising or abrogating that policy in light of its revision of the rest of the regulation. Second, it challenges § 1910.134(d)(3)(iii)(B) and the conditions placed upon the use of air-purifying respirators, as opposed to air-supplying respirators. Third, it challenges the requirements in § 1910.134(f)(2) and § 1910.134(k)(5) regarding, respectively, annual fit-testing and annual retraining, contending that less frequent fit-testing and retraining would have sufficed.

The Doctors, on the other hand, challenge only one aspect of the Standard: the provision in § 1910.134(e) enabling non-physician licensed health care professionals (e.g., nurses, physician's assistants, etc.) to perform the medical evaluation services that were previously conducted only by physicians ("Non–Physician Involvement Provision"). They contend that the Non–Physician Involvement Provision is defective because OSHA failed to notify interested parties that it was considering the elimination of mandatory physician involvement, that it is void for vagueness, and that it is not amply supported by the factual evidence.

The United Steelworkers of America ("Steelworkers") have intervened in this litigation; the Steelworkers defend the Standard against the Industry's attack, but adopt the Doctors' argument regarding the Non–Physician Involvement Provision. The American Association of Occupational Health Nurses and the American Nurses Association (collectively, "Nurses") have intervened in defense of the Non–Physician Involvement Provision against the Doctors' attack.

## II. DISCUSSION

### A. Standard of Review

We must uphold OSHA's factual determinations underlying its regulations if they are supported by substantial evidence in the record considered as a whole. Substantial evidence is "such relevant evidence as a reasonable mind might accept as adequate to support a conclusion." *American Textile Mfrs. Inst., Inc. v. Donovan*, 452 U.S. 490, 522, 101 S.Ct. 2478, 2497, 69 L.Ed.2d 185 (1981) (internal quotation marks omitted). "All that need be shown is that OSHA's determination is supported by substantial evidence presented to or produced by it and does not rest on faulty assumptions or factual foundations." *Color Pigments Mfrs. Ass'n v. OSHA*, 16 F.3d 1157, 1160 (11th Cir.1994). OSHA's policy decisions are entitled to the same deference. *AFL–CIO*, 965 F.2d at 970. Of course, questions of law are reviewed de novo.

### B. The Industry's Challenge

#### 1. Retention of the Hierarchy-of-Controls Policy

The Industry's first challenge to the Standard is addressed to the retention of the Hierarchy-of-Controls Policy from the prior standard.[1] The Hierarchy-of-Controls Policy reflects a general preference for engineering controls, which eliminate or arrest pollution at the source, over respirators in reducing employee exposure to airborne contaminants.

---

**1.** The Hierarchy-of-Controls Policy provides that the prevention of atmospheric contamination must be "accomplished as far as feasible by accepted engineering control methods (for example, enclosure or confinement of the operation, general and local ventilation, and substitution of less toxic materials). When effective engineering controls are not feasible, or while they are being instituted, appropriate respirators shall be used pursuant to this section." 29 C.F.R. § 1910.134(a)(1).

Although it comprehensively revised those aspects of the prior standard relating to the manner and conditions of respirator use, OSHA altogether excluded the Hierarchy-of-Controls Policy from the rulemaking proceeding. Consequently, the Hierarchy-of-Controls Policy was not open to comment or scrutiny. In the issuing release for the Standard, OSHA explained its position in the following way:

> By leaving paragraphs (a)(1) and (a)(2) of the final rule unchanged from the corresponding paragraphs of the respiratory protection standard that has been in effect since 1971, OSHA.... continues the protection that employees have relied on,.... retains the language that employers are familiar with,.... [and] allows OSHA and the affected public to continue to rely on OSHA interpretations....

The unchanged language of paragraph (a)(1) was included in the language of the proposed rule only to enable interested parties to view the rule as it would ultimately appear in the Code of Federal Regulations in its entirety. Since OSHA neither proposed nor adopted modifications to proposed paragraph (a)(1), the Agency believes that it is not legally required to reconsider this issue at this time. OSHA has the authority to identify which regulatory requirements it is proposing to revise and which issues are to receive regulatory priority. Limiting this rulemaking to issues concerning respirator programs is appropriate because such programs are the exclusive focus of this rulemaking and to collect comments and data on additional issues would divert resources from the task at hand. 63 Fed.Reg. at 1180.

The Industry, for its part, contends that this position is unsupportable because it allows OSHA selectively to insulate favored aspects of a standard from public scrutiny and judicial review. The Industry also contends that since 1971, when the original Hierarchy-of-Controls Policy was adopted, the factual circumstances have changed dramatically and now respirators may be every bit as effective as engineering controls. The Industry also notes that the Hierarchy-of-Controls Policy was originally adopted as part of a § 6(a) standard, which means that it has never been subject to the notice and comment procedures and scrutiny attendant to most rulemakings.

Thus, the legal issue for our consideration is whether OSHA, when it was comprehensively revising those aspects of the Standard relating to the manner and conditions of respirator use, could exclude the Hierarchy-of-Controls Policy from the rulemaking proceeding. Logic dictates that an agency must have some discretion in setting an agenda for rulemaking and excluding some matters categorically. Otherwise rulemaking would be very difficult because an agency would be unable to concentrate its scarce resources on a particular problem. Our decision in *AFL–CIO v. OSHA*, 965 F.2d 962 (11th Cir.1992), is instructive on this issue. In AFL–CIO, this Court reviewed OSHA's Air Contaminants Standard, a comprehensive set of permissible exposure limits ("PELs") for 428 toxic substances. The notice of proposed rulemaking for the Air Contaminants Standard proposed to issue new or revised PELs for a number of substances, but "limited the scope of [the] rulemaking to those substances for which [a private standard-setting organization] recommended limits that were either new or more protective than the existing PELs." Id. at 969 (citing the notice of proposed rulemaking). After issuance of the Air Contaminants Standard, industry and labor unions attacked it from both sides in this Court.

The unions in AFL–CIO argued that by limiting the rulemaking to those substances that either (1) had no existing PEL, or (2) for which the standard-setting organization had recommended a limit more protective than the existing PEL, OSHA had violated the command of the OSH Act that it set standards " 'which most adequately assure[ ] ... that no employee will suffer material impairment of health or functional capacity.' " Id. at 984 (quoting 29 U.S.C. § 655(b)(5) (alterations in original)). The court rejected this argument:

> [W]e [do not] find a requirement that OSHA include all possible substances in one rulemaking. OSHA has never claimed that the Air Contaminants Standard constituted the entire universe of substances needing regulation, and it seems reasonable that some limit needed to be set as to what substances could be considered in this rulemaking. The list of [the standard-setting organization's] recommendations is a rational choice as the source for that limitation. [Those] recommendations are well known to industry and the safety and health community. Therefore, we find that the agency's choice to so limit this rulemaking is a valid exercise of OSHA's authority to set priorities for rulemaking.

The union brought a separate challenge to a decision by OSHA "to defer issuing standards for monitoring and medical surveillance of the new PELs until a later rulemaking." Id. at 985. Under § 6(b)(7) of the OSH Act, occupational safety and health standards are required to provide for "monitoring or measuring employee exposure," and to prescribe medical examinations and tests, where appropriate. 29 U.S.C. § 655(b)(7). The union claimed that OSHA violated this requirement by promulgating the Air Contaminants Standard without simultaneously promulgating monitoring and medical surveillance rules with respect to that standard. We also dismissed this argument, holding that this was "purely a matter of regulatory priority" with respect to which the agency had ample discretion. AFL–CIO, 965 F.2d at 985. Thus, OSHA was permitted to wait and address monitoring and medical surveillance at another point.

While AFL–CIO suggests that the agency's chosen scope of rulemaking is a matter subject to judicial review, it also stands for the proposition that such review is rather limited and deferential in nature. With respect to avoiding consideration of substances for which the private standard-setting organization had not recommended a more protective PEL, we held that it was reasonable for OSHA to confine its rulemaking in that manner. With respect to monitoring and medical surveillance, we allowed

OSHA to postpone consideration of those issues until a later date. AFL–CIO did not precisely define the standard of review of an agency's choice of scope for a particular rulemaking, and we need not do so today. It is clear, however, that the standard of review is at least as deferential as a reasonableness standard.

We hold that the decision to exclude the Hierarchy-of-Controls Policy from revision was reasonable. The Standard deals with appropriate measures for employers to take with respect to respirator use; for example, training, maintenance, quality of device, etc., are included within its ambit. These matters are not necessarily factually intertwined with the propriety of implementing engineering controls, if feasible, rather than resorting to respirators. The Industry has presented nothing to this Court to lead us to believe that the alleged technological improvement in respirators substantially alters the comparative benefits of engineering controls versus respirators. To the contrary, it appears that the major rationale for engineering controls is that they make respiratory protection automatic, while respirators are dependent on use and constant attention and are subject to human error. Of course, technological improvement in respirators is not likely to reduce substantially the risk of human error, and in any event no such suggestion has been made in this case. Under these circumstances, it was not unreasonable for OSHA to determine that allowing submission of evidence about the relative merits of engineering controls and respirators would have distracted attention from and clouded the essential issues before it, namely, how respirators should be used if they are used. Like the AFL–CIO court, we hold that "the agency's choice to so limit this rulemaking" by excluding the Hierarchy-of-Controls Policy from consideration "is a valid exercise of OSHA's authority to set priorities for rulemaking." *AFL–CIO*, 965 F.2d at 984. The Industry has failed to demonstrate that OSHA's decision was unreasonable.

We also conclude that the fact that the original Hierarchy-of-Controls Policy was promulgated pursuant to § 6(a)'s abbreviated procedures, rather than the usual § 6(b) notice-and-comment proceedings, bears no special significance in this analysis. Section 6(a), 29 U.S.C. § 655(a), authorized OSHA for a limited time (through 1973) to adopt existing national consensus standards as occupational safety and health standards without the rigors of notice-and-comment proceedings. The Hierarchy-of-Controls Policy, having been originally adopted pursuant to § 6(a), has thus never undergone public scrutiny, unlike most of the standards that are in effect today. The Industry makes much of the fact that the Hierarchy-of-Controls Policy has eluded comment and scrutiny for 28 years in this manner. Although this situation may be undesirable from a public policy standpoint, it is fully consistent with the language Congress used for § 6(a). The plain language of § 6(a) causes it to operate "[w]ithout regard to ... the other subsections of this section." 29 U.S.C. § 655(a). Further, although OSHA's authority to promulgate standards under § 6(a) expired in 1973, there is no statutory provision causing standards adopted under § 6(a) themselves to expire at any time. Rather, a § 6(a) "start-up" standard continues in effect until it is modified or revoked by a new rulemaking initiated under § 6(b). See *AFL–CIO*, 965 F.2d at 968–69 (referring to the possibility of updating a § 6(a) standard, the court pointed out that the statute provides two mechanisms to revise existing standards, i.e., a § 6(b) proceeding or, in the case of a need for an emergency temporary standard, a § 6(c) proceeding). Because the statute treats § 6(a) standards and § 6(b) standards as having equal force of law once they are promulgated, the fact that the Hierarchy-of-Controls Policy originated under § 6(a) rather than under § 6(b) does not affect our analysis of whether OSHA was bound to reconsider it here.

The Industry also implies that the Hierarchy-of-Controls Policy has outlived its validity under § 6(a) because it no longer represents a national consensus standard. This argument is without merit because the Industry has proffered no evidence that the Hierarchy-of-Controls Policy no longer represents the national consensus standard. To the contrary, the most recent national consensus standard, ANSI Standard Z88.2–1992, § 4.2, retains the Hierarchy-of-Controls Policy. Thus, the Industry has failed to demonstrate that OSHA's decision to limit the instant rulemaking to issues relating to the manner and conditions of respirator use was unreasonable.

For the foregoing reasons, we reject the Industry's challenge to the retention of the Hierarchy-of-Controls Policy. * * *

### 3. Annual Fit–Test and Retraining Requirements

We turn next to the Industry's challenge to the provisions in the Standard requiring annual fit-testing and retraining of respirator-using employees. See 29 C.F.R. § 1910.134(f)(2), (k)(5). With respect to the annual fit-testing requirement, a respirator cannot function properly unless it is properly fitted to the wearer's face. Accordingly, the Standard requires in paragraph (f) that an employee be fit tested with a respirator of the same make, model, style, and size as is proposed to be used, before he actually begins to use one in the course of employment. The Industry does not object to this initial-test requirement, but does object to a requirement in (f)(2) that wearers be tested at least annually following the initial test.

With respect to the annual retraining requirement, the Standard requires in paragraph (k) that "the employer ... provide effective training to employees who are required to use respirators." Training should address the necessity of respirators, fit, usage, maintenance, limitations and capabilities, emergency situations, malfunction, inspection, and storage. See 29 C.F.R. § 1910.134(k)(1)(i)–(vii). The Industry does not object to the initial training requirement, but does object to a requirement in (k)(5) that such training be re-administered to employees annually.

The Industry points out that some evidence indicates that annual fit-testing is unnecessary because only a tiny percentage of employees experience facial changes that necessitate changes in respirator fit, and those who do can easily be detected by physical appearance. OSHA noted that "[c]ommenters generally agreed that some additional fit testing beyond an initial test was necessary, but opinions varied widely on the appropriate intervals at which such tests should be performed." 63 Fed.Reg. at 1223. "[A] large number of rulemaking participants supported OSHA's proposal to require the testing of respirator fit on an annual basis." Id. at 1224. We conclude that the annual fit-testing requirement is supported by substantial evidence in the record considered as a whole.

We find that the annual retraining requirement is also supported by substantial evidence. "OSHA's compliance experience [had] demonstrated that inadequate respirator training is a common problem, and is often associated with respirator program deficiencies that could lead to employee exposures to workplace contaminants." 63 Fed.Reg. at 1261–62. OSHA stated that annual retraining is necessary so that "employees know about the respiratory protection program and . . . cooperate and actively participate in the program," "so that employees will be confident when using respirators," and to "eliminate complacency on the part of both the employer and employees." Id. at 1261. OSHA noted that commenters requesting less frequent or no retraining submitted no data indicating that less frequent training "would be sufficient for respirator users to retain information critical to the successful use of respirators on an individual basis." Id. Additionally, OSHA explained that annual retraining is the norm with respect to a number of other, substance-specific OSHA standards that involve respirators. Id.

While retraining at some other periodic interval might also be defensible, OSHA was entitled to require annual retraining as a precautionary measure to assure "that no employee will suffer material impairment of health or functional capacity even if such employee has regular exposure to the hazard." 29 U.S.C. § 655(b)(5). Moreover, OSHA could conclude based on the record that annual retraining is reasonably necessary to ensure that employee knowledge about respirators does not fall into obsolescence. Given that conscientiousness among employees is such a critical element in the formula for success of a respirator program, OSHA could reasonably find that the Industry's suggested alternative of screening employees to determine who needed retesting would not serve its goal of preventing misuse and "ensur[ing] a reasonable amount of recall and performance on the part of the respirator user." 63 Fed.Reg. at 1261. We see no basis for disturbing OSHA's factual conclusions and policy decisions in this regard.

1.  Medical Evaluations and the Non–Physician Involvement Provision

"Medical evaluation to determine whether an employee is able to use a given respirator . . . is necessary to prevent injuries, illnesses, and even, in rare cases, death from the physiological burden imposed by respirator use." 63 Fed.Reg. at 1207. To this end, 29 C.F.R. § 1910.134(e)(1) provides that "[t]he employer shall provide a medical evaluation to determine the employee's ability to use a respirator, before the employee is fit tested or required to use the respirator in the workplace."

The Standard does not distinguish between physicians and other licensed health care professionals. Rather, it allows all of the tasks associated with medical evaluations to be performed by any licensed health care professional to the same extent as they may be performed by a physician, to the extent permitted under state law.

### 2. Whether OSHA Gave Sufficient Notice

The Doctors' first challenge to the Non-Physician Involvement Provision is that OSHA failed to satisfy the statutory notice requirements of the OSH Act. See 29 U.S.C. § 655(b)(2) ("The Secretary shall publish a proposed rule promulgating, modifying, or revoking an occupational safety or health standard in the Federal Register and shall afford interested persons a period of thirty days after publication to submit written data or comments."). The thrust of this argument is that prior to issuance of the Standard, OSHA's proposed rule failed to give notice that OSHA was contemplating the total elimination of federally mandated physician involvement. Rather, the Doctors argue, OSHA had suggested merely that its revisions to the respiratory protection standard might allow non-physician health care professionals to function under the supervision of a physician, or to perform some but not all medical evaluation tasks. The Doctors argue that they were blindsided by an outcome that went further than any of the proposed alternatives.

The D.C. Circuit provided guidance on an analogous question in *National Mining Ass'n v. Mine Safety & Health Admin.*, 116 F.3d 520, 531 (D.C.Cir.1997). In *National Mining Association*, the regulation at issue abandoned the Mine Safety & Health Administration's ("MSHA") long-standing policy of requiring pre-shift examinations to determine methane and oxygen levels in a coal mine three hours before shifts begin, in favor of a new policy requiring examinations at fixed intervals. The abandonment of the old three-hour policy occurred suddenly in the final rule, whereas the proposed rule ("1994 Draft") had adhered to the three-hour policy and thus no comment had been submitted to MSHA on that matter. The petitioner protested that had it known MSHA was reconsidering the three-hour policy, it would have submitted comment pointing out that state law already required frequent examinations, making such a change unnecessary.

The D.C. Circuit, recognizing that "[a]gencies are not limited to adopting final rules identical to proposed rules" and that "[n]o further notice and comment is required if a regulation is a 'logical outgrowth' of the proposed rule," identified the controlling legal principle as "whether the purposes of notice and comment have been adequately served." *National Mining Association*, 116 F.3d at 531 (internal quotation marks omitted). Specifically, notice is inadequate if "the interested parties could not reasonably have anticipated the final rulemaking from the draft rule." Id. (internal quotation marks omitted).

In the instant notice of proposed rulemaking, OSHA opened its discussion of medical evaluation procedures by noting that "there appears to be considerable difference of opinion as to what circumstances should trigger a physical examination, what the physical examination should consist of, *who is to administer such an examination*, and what the specific criteria should be for passing or failing." 59 Fed.Reg. 58884, 58907 (Nov. 15, 1994) (emphasis added). Further and more specifically, OSHA said that "[c]ommenters questioned the preproposal draft requirement that the medical evaluation be performed by a licensed physician.... OSHA requests comments on this issue and on the extent of the role that should be given to [non-physician] health professionals." Id. at 58910. The extent of non-physicians' appropriate role was also thoroughly explored at the public hearings on the Standard, as is demonstrated by the transcripts of those hearings.

Under these circumstances, interested parties were adequately put on notice that the Standard might establish an expanded role for non-physician health care professionals and, concomitantly, a diminished mandatory role for physicians. The Doctors could reasonably have anticipated that the final Standard might eliminate a mandatory role for physicians.

We have reviewed the record and find OSHA's decision to be supported by substantial evidence.

For the foregoing reasons, the petitions for review are

DENIED

## NOTES AND QUESTIONS

1.  Most consensus standards were drafted by private organizations such as the American National Standards Institute (ANSI), which rely heavily on professional and trade associations and individual firms in the industry for funding and information. Would you expect such organizations to promulgate standards which fully reflect the policy of the Act?

2.  When the statute was passed, Congress assumed that national consensus standards would be used only as an interim measure so that the statute could be immediately effective without waiting on OSHA to develop standards. It is recognized that a large proportion of the voluntary standards are seriously out-of-date. Many represent the lowest common denominator of acceptance by interested private groups. Accordingly, supporters of the statute regarded it as essential that such standards be constantly improved and replaced as new knowledge and techniques are developed. S.Rep. No. 91–1282 (1970) 6, Leg.Hist. 146.

This assumption has failed, in major part because of the elongated rulemaking procedures prescribed by Congress. As a Government Accounting Office report noted in 2001, it is not only the language of the OSH Act itself that creates stringent procedural requirements; many other statutes add to the delay, including the Administrative Procedure Act, the Paperwork Reduction Act, the Regulatory Flexibility Act, and others. In addition, Executive Orders have made the process more difficult. See Government Accounting

Office, Federal Rulemaking: Procedural and Analytical Requirements at OSHA and Other Agencies (2001), GAO–01–852T In the present case, the procedure to develop the standard had taken sixteen years. Thus, the great bulk of specific standards are still consensus standards .. This is the case in spite of the present realization that the greatest hazards are presented by dust, chemical fumes, noise and toxic substances, and that new substances are being introduced in rapid suffocating succession.

Should the court take into account these considerations when confronted by a case such as this, where the wording of the consensus standard is susceptible to an interpretation that will provide greater protection?

3. In *Usery v. Kennecott Copper Corp.*, 577 F.2d 1113 (10th Cir. 1977), the ANSI consensus standard stated that "guard rails and toe boards should be installed" on platforms ten feet above the ground. As adopted by OSHA the word "should" was replaced by the word "shall"; in the court's judgment, this meant that it became mandatory rather than advisory. The court ruled that the regulation was invalid because it altered the ANSI standard and dismissed the citations.

Could Kennecott have been cited under the general duty clause and the "advisory" language be used to show that the lack of guard rails and toe boards was a recognized hazard? Indeed, where there is a consensus standard, is there any need for OSHA adoption of a specific standard? Does not a consensus standard prove a "recognized hazard?"

4. In establishing a noise exposure standard, OSHA set a permissible workplace limit of ninety decibels using an eight hour time-weighted average. In addition, it required that all employees exposed to eighty-five decibels or more be notified of the sound level to which they were exposed, and be tested annually to determine whether the employee had suffered hearing loss. If there were a hearing loss of ten decibels in either ear, the employee had to be provided hearing protectors, trained in their use, and required to use them. The employers objected that they were being made responsible for hearing loss, even though it was caused by age or aggravated by noise outside the workplace, listening to loud music, or other activities. This was dismissed by the court as having "simply no merit." Studies showed that ten to fifteen percent of those exposed to eighty-five decibels on an eight hour time weighted average suffered hearing loss, so abating workplace noise or protecting employees exposed to noise above that level was directed toward a primary risk factor.

Objections to requiring annual hearing tests were rejected because the tests protected employees suffering limited hearing loss before they suffered material impairment. Also, requiring employees to be notified of the noise level to which they were exposed enabled and encouraged employees to cooperate with measures to protect them from further loss. *Forging Industry Ass'n v. Secretary of Labor*, 773 F.2d 1436 (4th Cir.1985).

The preference for "engineering controls" over personal safety devices was also challenged in the case of the sound level standard, and a Ninth Circuit panel applied a cost-benefit standard that resulted in rejecting the Secretary's approach. See *Donovan v. Castle & Cooke Foods*, 692 F.2d 641 (9th Cir. 1982).

Where the employer is required to monitor the employees' condition by periodic medical examinations, it can be required to pay not only for the examination but for the employees' travel costs, and for the time spent in getting the examination, even though it is scheduled during non-working hours. This requirement was supported by evidence that when the employer paid for time and travel, there was 100% employee participation; when the employer did not pay there was only 58% participation. The statute gives OSHA, said the court, "a rather broad mandate to charge employers for whatever scheme of medical review it deems reasonably necessary." *Phelps Dodge Corp. v. OSHRC*, 725 F.2d 1237, 1239 (9th Cir.1984).

## AMERICAN TEXTILE MANUFACTURERS INSTITUTE INC. v. DONOVAN

United States Supreme Court, 1981
452 U.S. 490, 101 S.Ct. 2478, 69 L.Ed.2d 185

JUSTICE BRENNAN delivered the opinion of the Court.

In 1978, the Secretary, acting through the Occupational Safety and Health Administration (OSHA), promulgated a standard limiting occupational exposure to cotton dust, an airborne particle by product of the preparation and manufacture of cotton products, exposure to which induces a "constellation of respiratory effects" known as "byssinosis." 43 Fed.Reg. 27352, col. 3 (1978). This disease was one of the expressly recognized health hazards that led to passage of the Act.

Petitioners in these consolidated cases, representing the interests of the cotton industry, challenged the validity of the "Cotton Dust Standard" in the Court of Appeals for the District of Columbia Circuit pursuant to § 6(f) of the Act. They contend in this Court, as they did below, that the Act requires OSHA to demonstrate that its Standard reflects a reasonable relationship between the costs and benefits associated with the Standard. Respondents, the Secretary of Labor and two labor organizations, counter that Congress balanced the costs and benefits in the Act itself, and that the Act should therefore be construed not to require OSHA to do so. They interpret the Act as mandating that OSHA enact the most protective standard possible to eliminate a significant risk of material health impairment, subject to the constraints of economic and technological feasibility. The Court of Appeals held that the Act did not require OSHA to compare costs and benefits. We granted certiorari, 449 U.S. 817, 101 S.Ct. 68, 66 L.Ed.2d 19 (1980) to resolve the important question, which was presented but not decided in last Term's Industrial Union Dept. v. American Petroleum Institute, 448 U.S. 607, 100 S.Ct. 2844, 65 L.Ed.2d 1010 (1980), 4 and to decide other issues related to the Cotton Dust Standard.

I

Byssinosis, known in its more severe manifestations as "brown lung" disease, is a serious and potentially disabling respiratory disease primarily caused by the inhalation of cotton dust. * * * Byssinosis is a "continuum * * * disease," 43 Fed.Reg. 27354, col. 2 (1978), that has been categorized into four grades. In its least serious form, byssinosis produces both subjective symptoms, such as chest tightness, shortness of breath, coughing, and wheezing, and objective indications of loss of pulmonary functions. Id., at 27352, col. 2. In its most serious form, byssinosis is a chronic and irreversible obstructive pulmonary disease, clinically similar to chronic bronchitis or emphysema, and can be severely disabling. Ibid. At worst, as is true of other respiratory diseases including bronchitis, emphysema, and asthma, byssinosis can create an additional strain on cardiovascular functions and can contribute to death from heart failure. See Exhibit 6–73, App. 72 ("there is an association between mortality and the extent of dust exposure"). One authority has described the increasing seriousness of byssinosis as follows:

"In the first few years of exposure [to cotton dust], symptoms occur on Monday, or other days after absence from the work environment; later, symptoms occur on other days of the week; and eventually, symptoms are continuous, even in the absence of dust exposure." A. Bouhuys, Byssinosis in the United States, Exhibit 6–16, App. 15.9

Estimates indicate that at least 35,000 employed and retired cotton mill workers, or 1 in 12 such workers, suffer from the most disabling form of byssinosis. The Senate Report accompanying the Act cited estimates that 100,000 active and retired workers suffer from some grade of the disease. S.Rep. No. 91–1282, p. 3 (1970), Leg.Hist. 143. One study found that over 25% of a sample of active cotton-preparation and yarn-manufacturing workers suffer at least some form of the disease at a dust exposure level common prior to adoption of the current Standard. 43 Fed.Reg. 27355, col. 3 (1978); Exhibit 6–51, App. 44. Other studies confirm these general findings on the prevalence of byssinosis. * * *.

Not until the early 1960's was byssinosis recognized in the United States as a distinct occupational hazard associated with cotton mills. * * * In 1966, the American Conference of Governmental Industrial Hygienists (ACGIH), a private organization, recommended that exposure to total cotton dust be limited to a "threshold limit value" of 1,000 micrograms per cubic meter of air (1000 ug/m3) averaged over an 8–hour workday. * * * The United States Government first regulated exposure to cotton dust in 1968, when the Secretary of Labor, pursuant to the Walsh–Healey Act, 41 U.S.C. § 35(e), promulgated airborne contaminant threshold limit values, applicable to public contractors, that included the 1,000 ug/m3 limit for total cotton dust. * * * Following passage of the Act in 1970, the 1,000 ug/m3 standard was adopted as an "established Federal standard" under § 6(a) of the Act, * * * a provision designed to guarantee immediate protection of workers for the period between enactment of the statute and promulgation of permanent standards.

In 1974, ACGIH, adopting a new measurement unit of respirable rather than total dust, lowered its previous exposure limit recommendation to 200 ug/m3 measured by a vertical elutriator, a device that measures cotton dust particles 15 microns or less in diameter. * * * That same

year, the Director of the National Institute for Occupational Safety and
Health (NIOSH), pursuant to the Act, 29 U.S.C. §§ 669(a)(3), 671(d)(2),
submitted to the Secretary of Labor a recommendation for a cotton dust
standard with a permissible exposure limit (PEL) that "should be set at
the lowest level feasible, but in no case at an environmental concentration
as high as 0.2 mg lint-free cotton dust/cu m," or 200 ug/m3 of lint-free
respirable dust. * * * Several months later, OSHA published an Advance
Notice of Proposed Rulemaking, 39 Fed.Reg. 44769 (1974), requesting
comments from interested parties on the NIOSH recommendation and
other related matters. Soon thereafter, the Textile Worker's Union of
America, joined by the North Carolina Public Interest Research Group,
petitioned the Secretary, urging a more stringent PEL of 100 ug/m3.

On December 28, 1976, OSHA published a proposal to replace the
existing federal standard on cotton dust with a new permanent standard,
pursuant to § 6(b)(5) of the Act. * * * The proposed standard contained a
PEL of 200 ug/m3 of vertical elutriated lint-free respirable cotton dust for
all segments of the cotton industry. Ibid. It also suggested an implementation strategy for achieving the PEL that relied on respirators for the short
term and engineering controls for the long term. Id., at 56506, cols. 2 and
3. OSHA invited interested parties to submit written comments within a
90–day period.

Following the comment period, OSHA conducted three hearings in
Washington, D.C., Greenville, Miss., and Lubbock, Tex., that lasted over
14 days. Public participation was widespread, involving representatives
from industry and the work force, scientists, economists, industrial hygienists, and many others. By the time the informal rulemaking procedure
had terminated, OSHA had received 263 comments and 109 notices of
intent to appear at the hearings. * * * The voluminous record, composed
of a transcript of written and oral testimony, exhibits, and post-hearing
comments and briefs, totaled some 105,000 pages. * * * OSHA issued its
final Cotton Dust Standard—the one challenged in the instant case—on
June 23, 1978. Along with an accompanying statement of findings and
reasons, the Standard occupied 69 pages of the Federal Register. 43
Fed.Reg. 27350–27418 (1978); see 29 CFR § 1910.1043 (1980).

The Cotton Dust Standard promulgated by OSHA establishes mandatory PEL's over an 8–hour period of 200 ug/m3 for yarn manufacturing,
750 ug/m3 for slashing and weaving operations, and 500 ug/m3 for all
other processes in the cotton industry. 29 CFR § 1910.1043(c) (1980).
These levels represent a relaxation of the proposed PEL of 200 ug/m3 for
all segments of the cotton industry.

OSHA chose an implementation strategy for the Standard that de-
pended primarily on a mix of engineering controls, such as installation of
ventilation systems, and work practice controls, such as special floor-
sweeping procedures. Full compliance with the PEL's is required within
four years, except to the extent that employers can establish that the
engineering and work practice controls are infeasible. § 1910.1043(e)(1).

During this compliance period, and at certain other times, the Standard requires employers to provide respirators to employees. § 1910.1043(f). Other requirements include monitoring of cotton dust exposure, medical surveillance of all employees, annual medical examinations, employee education and training programs, and the posting of warning signs. A specific provision also under challenge in the instant case requires employers to transfer employees unable to wear respirators to another position, if available, having a dust level at or below the Standard's PEL's, with "no loss of earnings or other employment rights or benefits as a result of the transfer." § 1910.1043(f)(2)(v). * * *

In promulgating the Cotton Dust Standard, OSHA interpreted the Act to require adoption of the most stringent standard to protect against material health impairment, bounded only by technological and economic feasibility. * * * The agency expressly found the Standard to be both technologically and economically feasible based on the evidence in the record as a whole. Although recognizing that permitted levels of exposure to cotton dust would still cause some byssinosis, OSHA nevertheless rejected the union proposal for a 100 ug/m3 PEL because it was not within the "technological capabilities of the industry." Id., at 27359–27360. Similarly, OSHA set PEL's for some segments of the cotton industry at 500 ug/m3 in part because of limitations of technological feasibility. Id., at 27361, col. 3. Finally, the Secretary found that "engineering dust controls in weaving may not be feasible even with massive expenditures by the industry," id., at 27360, col. 2, and for that and other reasons adopted a less stringent PEL of 750 ug/m3 for weaving and slashing.

The Court of Appeals upheld the Standard in all major respects. * * * Rejecting the industry position that OSHA must demonstrate that the benefits of the Standard are proportionate to its costs, the court instead agreed with OSHA's interpretation that the Standard must protect employees against material health impairment subject only to the limits of technological and economic feasibility. Id., at 80–84, 617 F.2d, at 662–666. The court held that "Congress itself struck the balance between costs and benefits in the mandate to the agency" under § 6(b)(5) of the Act, and that OSHA is powerless to circumvent that judgment by adopting less than the most protective feasible standard. 199 U.S.App.D.C., at 81, 617 F.2d, at 663. Finally, the court held that the agency's determination of technological and economic feasibility was supported by substantial evidence in the record as a whole. Id., at 73–80, 617 F.2d, at 655–662.

We affirm in part, and vacate in part.

The principal question presented in these cases is whether the Occupational Safety and Health Act requires the Secretary, in promulgating a standard pursuant to § 6(b)(5) of the Act, to determine that the costs of the standard bear a reasonable relationship to its benefits. Relying on §§ 6(b)(5) and 3(8) of the Act, * * * petitioners urge not only that OSHA must show that a standard addresses a significant risk of material health impairment, see Industrial Union Dept. v. American Petroleum Institute,

448 U.S., at 639, 100 S.Ct., at 2863 (plurality opinion), but also that OSHA must demonstrate that the reduction in risk of material health impairment is significant in light of the costs of attaining that reduction. See Brief for Petitioners in No. 79–1429, pp. 38–41. Respondents on the other hand contend that the Act requires OSHA to promulgate standards that eliminate or reduce such risks "to the extent such protection is technologically and economically feasible." Brief for Federal Respondent 38; Brief for Union Respondents 26–27. To resolve this debate, we must turn to the language, structure, and legislative history of the Act.

## A

The starting point of our analysis is the language of the statute itself. * * * Section 6(b)(5) of the Act, 29 U.S.C. § 655(b)(5) (emphasis added), provides:

> "The Secretary, in promulgating standards dealing with toxic materials or harmful physical agents under this subsection, shall set the standard which most adequately assures, *to the extent feasible*, on the basis of the best available evidence, that no employee will suffer material impairment of health or functional capacity even if such employee has regular exposure to the hazard dealt with by such standard for the period of his working life."

Although their interpretations differ, all parties agree that the phrase "to the extent feasible" contains the critical language in § 6(b)(5) for purposes of these cases.

The plain meaning of the word "feasible" supports respondents' interpretation of the statute. According to Webster's Third New International Dictionary of the English Language 831 (1976), "feasible" means "capable of being done, executed, or effected." Accord, The Oxford English Dictionary 116 (1933) ("Capable of being done, accomplished or carried out"); Funk & Wagnalls New "Standard" Dictionary of the English Language 903 (1957) ("That may be done, performed or effected"). Thus, § 6(b)(5) directs the Secretary to issue the standard that "most adequately assures * * * that no employee will suffer material impairment of health," limited only by the extent to which this is "capable of being done." In effect then, as the Court of Appeals held, Congress itself defined the basic relationship between costs and benefits, by placing the "benefit" of worker health above all other considerations save those making attainment of this "benefit" unachievable. Any standard based on a balancing of costs and benefits by the Secretary that strikes a different balance than that struck by Congress would be inconsistent with the command set forth in § 6(b)(5). Thus, cost-benefit analysis by OSHA is not required by the statute because feasibility analysis is. See *Industrial Union Dept. v. American Petroleum Institute*, 448 U.S., at 718–719, 100 S.Ct. at 2902–2903 (MARSHALL, J., dissenting).

When Congress has intended that an agency engage in cost-benefit analysis, it has clearly indicated such intent on the face of the statute. One early example is the Flood Control Act of 1936, 33 U.S.C. § 701a:

"[T]he Federal Government should improve or participate in the improvement of navigable waters or their tributaries, including watersheds thereof, for flood-control purposes if *the benefits to whomsoever they may accrue are in excess of the estimated costs*, and if the lives and social security of people are otherwise adversely affected." (Emphasis added.)

A more recent example is the Outer Continental Shelf Lands Act Amendments of 1978, 43 U.S.C. § 1347(b) (1976 ed., Supp. III), providing that offshore drilling operations shall use

"the best available and safest technologies which the Secretary determines to be economically feasible, wherever failure of equipment would have significant effect on safety, health, or the environment, except where the Secretary determines that the incremental benefits are clearly insufficient to justify the incremental costs of using such technologies."

These and other statutes demonstrate that Congress uses specific language when intending that an agency engage in cost-benefit analysis. * * * Certainly in light of its ordinary meaning, the word "feasible" cannot be construed to articulate such congressional intent. We therefore reject the argument that Congress required cost-benefit analysis in § 6(b)(5).

B

Even though the plain language of § 6(b)(5) supports this construction, we must still decide whether § 3(8), the general definition of an occupational safety and health standard, either alone or in tandem with § 6(b)(5), incorporates a cost-benefit requirement for standards dealing with toxic materials or harmful physical agents. Section 3(8) of the Act, 29 U.S.C. § 652(8) (emphasis added), provides:

"The term 'occupational safety and health standard' means a standard which requires conditions, or the adoption or use of one or more practices, means, methods, operations, or processes, *reasonably necessary or appropriate* to provide safe or healthful employment and places of employment."

Taken alone, the phrase "reasonably necessary or appropriate" might be construed to contemplate some balancing of the costs and benefits of a standard. Petitioners urge that, so construed, § 3(8) engrafts a cost-benefit analysis requirement on the issuance of § 6(b)(5) standards, even if § 6(b)(5) itself does not authorize such analysis. We need not decide whether § 3(8), standing alone, would contemplate some form of cost-benefit analysis. For even if it does, Congress specifically chose in § 6(b)(5) to impose separate and additional requirements for issuance of a subcategory of occupational safety and health standards dealing with toxic materials and harmful physical agents: it required that those standards be issued to prevent material impairment of health to the extent feasible. Congress could reasonably have concluded that health standards should be subject to different criteria than safety standards because of the special problems presented in regulating them. See *Industrial Union Dept. v. American Petroleum Institute*, 448 U.S., at 649, n. 54, 100 S.Ct., at 2867, n. 54 (plurality opinion).

Agreement with petitioners' argument that § 3(8) imposes an additional and overriding requirement of cost-benefit analysis on the issuance of § 6(b)(5) standards would eviscerate the "to the extent feasible" requirement. Standards would inevitably be set at the level indicated by cost-benefit analysis, and not at the level specified by § 6(b)(5). For example, if cost-benefit analysis indicated a protective standard of 1,000 ug/m3 PEL, while feasibility analysis indicated a 500 ug/m3 PEL, the agency would be forced by the cost-benefit requirement to choose the less stringent point. We cannot believe that Congress intended the general terms of § 3(8) to countermand the specific feasibility requirement of § 6(b)(5). Adoption of petitioners' interpretation would effectively write § 6(b)(5) out of the Act. We decline to render Congress' decision to include a feasibility requirement nugatory, thereby offending the well-settled rule that all parts of a statute, if possible, are to be given effect. * * * Congress did not contemplate any further balancing by the agency for toxic material and harmful physical agents standards, and we should not " 'impute to Congress a purpose to paralyze with one hand what it sought to promote with the other.' " *Weinberger v. Hynson, Westcott & Dunning, Inc.*, [412 U.S. 609], at 631, quoting *Clark v. Uebersee Finanz–Korporation*, 332 U.S. 480 (1947)

## C

The legislative history of the Act, while concededly not crystal clear, provides general support for respondents' interpretation of the Act. The congressional Reports and debates certainly confirm that Congress meant "feasible" and nothing else in using that term. Congress was concerned that the Act might be thought to require achievement of absolute safety, an impossible standard, and therefore insisted that health and safety goals be capable of economic and technological accomplishment. Perhaps most telling is the absence of any indication whatsoever that Congress intended OSHA to conduct its own cost-benefit analysis before promulgating a toxic material or harmful physical agent standard. * * *

Not only does the legislative history confirm that Congress meant "feasible" rather than "cost-benefit" when it used the former term, but it also shows that Congress understood that the Act would create substantial costs for employers, yet intended to impose such costs when necessary to create a safe and healthful working environment. Congress viewed the costs of health and safety as a cost of doing business. Senator Yarborough, a cosponsor of the Williams bill, stated: "We know the costs would be put into consumer goods but that is the price we should pay for the 80 million workers in America." 116 Cong.Rec., at 37345, Leg.Hist. 444. * * * Senator Eagleton commented that "[t]he costs that will be incurred by employers in meeting the standards of health and safety to be established under this bill are, in my view, *reasonable and necessary costs of doing business.*" 116 Cong.Rec., at 41764, Leg.Hist. 1150–1151 (emphasis added).

Other Members of Congress voiced similar views. Nowhere is there any indication that Congress contemplated a different balancing by OSHA of the benefits of worker health and safety against the costs of achieving them. Indeed Congress thought that the financial costs of health and safety problems in the workplace were as large as or larger than the financial costs of eliminating these problems. In its statement of findings and declaration of purpose encompassed in the Act itself, Congress announced that "personal injuries and illnesses arising out of work situations impose a substantial burden upon, and are a hindrance to, interstate commerce in terms of lost production, wage loss, medical expenses, and disability compensation payments." 29 U.S.C. § 651(a).

> "[T]he economic impact of industrial deaths and disability is staggering. Over $1.5 billion is wasted in lost wages, and the annual loss to the Gross National Product is estimated to be over $8 billion. Vast resources that could be available for productive use are siphoned off to pay workmen's compensation benefits and medical expenses." S.Rep. No. 91–1282, p. 2 (1970). * * *

Senator Eagleton summarized: "Whether we, as individuals, are motivated by simple humanity or by simple economics, we can no longer permit profits to be dependent upon an unsafe or unhealthy worksite." 116 Cong.Rec. 41764 (1970), Leg.Hist. 1150–1151.

### III

Section 6(f) of the Act provides that "[t]he determinations of the Secretary shall be conclusive if supported by substantial evidence in the record considered as a whole." Petitioners contend that the Secretary's determination that the Cotton Dust Standard is "economically feasible" is not supported by substantial evidence in the record considered as a whole. In particular, they claim (1) that OSHA underestimated the financial costs necessary to meet the Standard's requirements; and (2) that OSHA incorrectly found that the Standard would not threaten the economic viability of the cotton industry.

* * * Since the Act places responsibility for determining substantial evidence questions in the courts of appeals, 29 U.S.C. § 655(f), we apply the familiar rule that "[t]his Court will intervene only in what ought to be the rare instance when the [substantial evidence] standard appears to have been misapprehended or grossly misapplied" by the court below. *Universal Camera Corp. v. NLRB, supra,* 340 U.S., at 491, 71 S.Ct., at 466; * * * Therefore, our inquiry is not to determine whether we, in the first instance, would find OSHA's findings supported by substantial evidence. Instead we turn to OSHA's findings and the record upon which they were based to decide whether the Court of Appeals "misapprehended or grossly misapplied" the substantial evidence test.

A

OSHA derived its cost estimate for industry compliance with the Cotton Dust Standard after reviewing two financial analyses, one prepared by the Research Triangle Institute (RTI), an OSHA-contracted group, the other by industry representatives (Hocutt–Thomas). The agency carefully explored the assumptions and methodologies underlying the conclusions of each of these studies. From this exercise the agency was able to build upon conclusions from each which it found reliable and explain its process for choosing its cost estimate. * * *

Petitioners criticize OSHA's adoption of the Hocutt–Thomas estimate, since that estimate was based on achievement of somewhat less stringent PEL's than those ultimately promulgated in the final Standard. Thus, even if the Hocutt–Thomas estimate was exaggerated, they assert that "only by the most remarkable coincidence would the amount of that overestimate be equal to the additional costs required to attain the far more stringent limits of the Standard OSHA actually adopted." Brief for Petitioners in No. 79–1429, p. 27; see Brief for Petitioner in No. 79–1583, pp. 14–15. The agency itself recognized the problem cited by petitioners, but found itself limited in the precision of its estimates by the industry's refusal to make more of its own data available. OSHA explained that, "in the absence of the [industry] survey data [of textile mills], OSHA cannot develop more accurate estimates of compliance costs." 43 Fed.Reg. 27373, col. 1 (1978). Since § 6(b)(5) of the Act requires that the Secretary promulgate toxic material and harmful physical agent standards "on the basis of the best available evidence," 29 U.S.C. § 655(b)(5), and since OSHA could not obtain the more detailed confidential industry data it thought essential to further precision, we conclude that the agency acted reasonably in adopting the Hocutt–Thomas estimate. While a cost estimate based on the standard actually promulgated surely would be preferable, we decline to hold as a matter of law that its absence under the circumstances required the Court of Appeals to find that OSHA's determination was unsupported by substantial evidence.

Therefore, whether or not in the first instance we would find the Secretary's conclusions supported by substantial evidence, we cannot say that the Court of Appeals in this case "misapprehended or grossly misapplied" the substantial evidence test when it found that "OSHA reasonably evaluated the cost estimates before it, considered criticisms of each, and selected suitable estimates of compliance costs." 199 U.S.App.D.C., at 79, 617 F.2d, at 661 (footnote omitted).

B

After estimating the cost of compliance with the Cotton Dust Standard, OSHA analyzed whether it was "economically feasible" for the cotton industry to bear this cost. OSHA concluded that it was, finding that "although some marginal employers may shut down rather than comply, the industry as a whole will not be threatened by the capital requirements of the regulation." 43 Fed.Reg. 27378, col. 2 (1978); see id., at 27379, col. 3

("compliance with the standard is well within the financial capability of the covered industries"). In reaching this conclusion on the Standard's economic impact, OSHA made specific findings with respect to employment, energy consumption, capital financing availability, and profitability. Id., at 27377–27378. To support its findings, the agency relied primarily on RTI's comprehensive investigation of the Standard's economic impact. * * *

RTI had estimated a total compliance cost of $2.7 billion for a 200 ug/m3 PEL, and used this estimate in assessing the economic impact of such a standard. As described in n. 44, *supra*, OSHA estimated total compliance costs of $656.5 million for the final Cotton Dust Standard, a standard less stringent than the across-the-board 200 ug/m3 PEL of the proposed standard. Therefore, the agency found that the economic impact of its Standard would be "much less severe" than that suggested by RTI for a 200 ug/m3 PEL estimate of $2.7 billion. 43 Fed.Reg. 27378, col. 2 (1978). Nevertheless, it is instructive to review RTI's conclusions with respect to the economic impact of a $2.7 billion cost estimate. RTI found:

> "Implementation of the proposed [200 ug/m3] standard will require adjustments within the cotton textile industry that will take time to work themselves out and that may be difficult for many firms. In time, however prices may be expected to rise and markets to adjust so that revenues will cover costs. Although the impact on any one firm cannot be specified in advance, nothing in the RTI study indicates that the cotton textile industry as a whole will be seriously threatened by the impact of the proposed standard for control of cotton dust exposure." Ex. 16, Co. of App.J.A. 1380; id., at 3620.

In reaching this conclusion, RTI analyzed the total and annual economic impact on each of the different sectors of the cotton industry. * * *

The Court of Appeals found that the agency "explained the economic impact it projected for the textile industry," and that OSHA has "substantial support in the record for its * * * findings of economic feasibility for the textile industry." 199 U.S.App.D.C., at 80, 617 F.2d, at 662. On the basis of the whole record, we cannot conclude that the Court of Appeals "misapprehended or grossly misapplied" the substantial evidence test.

## IV

The final Cotton Dust Standard places heavy reliance on the use of respirators to protect employees from exposure to cotton dust, particularly during the 4–year interim period necessary to install and implement feasible engineering controls. One part of the respirator provision requires the employer to give employees unable to wear a respirator the opportunity to transfer to another position, if available, where the dust level meets the Standard's PEL. 29 CFR § 1910.1043(f)(2)(v) (1980). When such a transfer occurs, the employer must guarantee that the employee suffers no loss of earnings or other employment rights or benefits. Petitioners do not object to the transfer provision, but challenge OSHA's authority under the

Act to require employers to guarantee employees' wage and employment benefits following the transfer. The Court of Appeals held that OSHA has such authority. 199 U.S.App.D.C., at 93, 617 F.2d, at 675. We hold that, whether or not OSHA has this underlying authority, the agency has failed to make the necessary determination or statement of reasons that its wage guarantee requirement is related to the achievement of a safe and healthful work environment.

Respondents urge several statutory bases for the authority exercised here. They cite § 2(b) of the Act, 29 U.S.C. § 651(b), which declares that the purpose of the Act is "to assure so far as possible every working man and woman in the Nation safe and healthful working conditions"; § 2(b)(5), which suggests achievement of the purpose "by developing innovative methods, techniques, and approaches for dealing with occupational safety and health problems"; § 6(b)(5), which requires the agency to "set the standard which most adequately assures * * * that no employee will suffer material impairment of health or functional capacity * * * "; and § 3(8), which provides that a standard must require "conditions, or the adoption or use of one or more practices, means, methods, operations, or processes, reasonably necessary or appropriate to provide safe or healthful employment." Brief for Federal Respondent 68. Whatever methods these provisions authorize OSHA to apply, it is clear that such methods must be justified on the basis of their relation to safety or health.

Section 6(f) of the Act, 29 U.S.C. § 655(f), requires that "determinations of the Secretary" must be supported by substantial evidence. Section 6(e), 29 U.S.C. § 655(e), requires the Secretary to include "a statement of the reasons for such action, which shall be published in the Federal Register." In his "Summary and Explanation of the Standard," the Secretary stated: "Each section includes an analysis of the record evidence and the policy considerations underlying the decisions adopted pertaining to specific provisions of the standard." 43 Fed.Reg. 27380, col. 2 (1978). But OSHA never explained the wage guarantee provision as an approach designed to contribute to increased health protection. Instead the agency stated that the "goal of this provision is to minimize any adverse economic impact on the employee by virtue of the inability to wear a respirator." Id., at 27387, col. 3. Perhaps in recognition of this fact, respondents in their briefs argue:

> "Experience under the Act has shown that employees are reluctant to disclose symptoms of disease and tend to minimize work-related health problems for fear of being discharged or transferred to a lower paying job. * * * It may reasonably be expected, therefore, that many employees incapable of using respirators would continue to breathe unhealthful air rather than request a transfer, thus destroying the utility of the respirator program." Brief for Federal Respondent 67.
> * * * *

Whether these arguments have merit, and they very well may, the post hoc rationalizations of the agency or the parties to this litigation cannot serve as a sufficient predicate for agency action. For Congress gave OSHA the responsibility to protect worker health and safety, and to explain its reasons for its actions. Because the Act in no way authorizes OSHA to repair general unfairness to employees that is unrelated to achievement of health and safety goals, we conclude that OSHA acted beyond statutory authority when it issued the wage guarantee regulation.

## V

When Congress passed the Occupational Safety and Health Act in 1970, it chose to place pre-eminent value on assuring employees a safe and healthful working environment, limited only by the feasibility of achieving such an environment. We must measure the validity of the Secretary's actions against the requirements of that Act. For "[t]he judicial function does not extend to substantive revision of regulatory policy. That function lies elsewhere—in Congressional and Executive oversight or amendatory legislation." *Industrial Union Dept. v. American Petroleum Institute, supra*, 448 U.S., at 663, 100 S.Ct., at 2875 (BURGER, C.J., concurring); \* \* \*

Accordingly, the judgment of the Court of Appeals is affirmed in all respects except to the extent of its approval of the Secretary's application of the wage guarantee provision of the Cotton Dust Standard at 29 CFR § 1910.1043(f)(2)(v) (1980). To that extent, the judgment of the Court of Appeals is vacated and the case remanded with directions to remand to the Secretary for further proceedings consistent with this opinion.

It is so ordered.

JUSTICE POWELL took no part in the decision of these cases.

JUSTICE STEWART, dissenting.

\* \* \*

Everybody agrees that under this statutory provision the Cotton Dust Standard must at least be economically feasible, and everybody would also agree, I suppose, that in order to determine whether or not something is economically feasible, one must have a fairly clear idea of how much it is going to cost. Because I believe that OSHA failed to justify its estimate of the cost of the Cotton Dust Standard on the basis of substantial evidence, I would reverse the judgment before us without reaching the question whether the Act requires that a standard, beyond being economically feasible, must meet the demands of a cost-benefit examination. \* \* \*

JUSTICE REHNQUIST, with whom THE CHIEF JUSTICE joins, dissenting.

A year ago I stated my belief that Congress in enacting § 6(b)(5) of the Occupational Safety and Health Act of 1970 unconstitutionally delegated to the Executive Branch the authority to make the "hard policy choices" properly the task of the legislature. *Industrial Union Dept. v. American Petroleum Institute*, 448 U.S. 607, 671, 100 S.Ct. 2844, 2878, 65 L.Ed.2d 1010 (1980) (concurring in judgment). Because I continue to believe that the Act exceeds Congress' power to delegate legislative au-

*Believes
OSHA
exceeds
Cong's power*

thority to nonelected officials, see *J.W. Hampton & Co. v. United States*, 276 U.S. 394, 48 S.Ct. 348, 72 L.Ed. 624 (1928), and *Panama Refining Co. v. Ryan*, 293 U.S. 388, 55 S.Ct. 241, 79 L.Ed. 446 (1935), I dissent. I will repeat only a little of what I said last Term. * * * *

As the Court correctly observes, the phrase "to the extent feasible" contains the critical language for the purpose of these cases. We are presented with a remarkable range of interpretations of that language. Petitioners contend that the statute requires the Secretary to demonstrate that the benefits of its "Cotton Dust Standard," in terms of reducing health risks, bear a reasonable relationship to its costs. Brief for Petitioners in No. 79–1429, pp. 38–41. Respondents, including the Secretary of Labor at least until his postargument motion, counter that Congress itself balanced costs and benefits when it enacted the statute, and that the statute prohibits the Secretary from engaging in a cost-benefit type balancing. Their view is that the Act merely requires the Secretary to promulgate standards that eliminate or reduce such risks "to the extent * * * technologically or economically feasible." Brief for Federal Respondent 38; Brief for Union Respondents 26–27. As I read the Court's opinion, it takes a different position. It concludes that, at least as to the "Cotton Dust Standard," the Act does not require the Secretary to engage in a cost-benefit analysis, which suggests of course that the Act permits the Secretary to undertake such an analysis if he so chooses. Ante, at 2491–2492.

Throughout its opinion, the Court refers to § 6(b)(5) as adopting a "feasibility standard" or a "feasibility requirement." Ante, at 2490–2497. But as I attempted to point out last Term in *Industrial Union Dept. v. American Petroleum Institute, supra*, 448 U.S., at 681–685, 100 S.Ct., at 2883–2885, the "feasibility standard" is no standard at all. Quite the contrary, I argued there that the insertion into § 6(b)(5) of the words "to the extent feasible" rendered what had been a clear, if somewhat unrealistic, statute into one so vague and precatory as to be an unconstitutional delegation of legislative authority to the Executive Branch. Prior to the inclusion of the "feasibility" language, § 6(b)(5) simply required the Secretary to "set the standard which most adequately assures, on the basis of the best available professional evidence, that no employee will suffer any impairment of health. * * * " Legislative History, Occupational Safety and Health Act of 1970, p. 943 (Comm. Print 1971) (hereinafter Leg.Hist.). Had that statute been enacted, it would undoubtedly support the result the Court reaches in these cases, and it would not have created an excessive delegation problem. The Secretary of Labor would quite clearly have been authorized to set exposure standards without regard to any kind of cost-benefit analysis.

But Congress did not enact that statute. The legislative history of the Act reveals that a number of Members of Congress, such as Senators Javits, Saxbe, and Dominick, had difficulty with the proposed statute and engaged Congress in a lengthy debate about the extent to which the

Secretary should be authorized to create a risk-free work environment. Congress had at least three choices. It could have required the Secretary to engage in a cost-benefit analysis prior to the setting of exposure levels, it could have prohibited cost-benefit analysis, or it could have permitted the use of such an analysis. Rather than make that choice and resolve that difficult policy issue, however, Congress passed. Congress simply said that the Secretary should set standards "to the extent feasible." Last year, Justice Powell reflected that "one might wish that Congress had spoken with greater clarity." American Petroleum Institute, 448 U.S., at 668, 100 S.Ct., at 2877 (POWELL, J., concurring in part and in judgment). I am convinced that the reason that Congress did not speak with greater "clarity" was because it could not. The words "to the extent feasible" were used to mask a fundamental policy disagreement in Congress. I have no doubt that if Congress had been required to choose whether to mandate, permit, or prohibit the Secretary from engaging in a cost-benefit analysis, there would have been no bill for the President to sign.

The Court seems to argue that Congress did make a policy choice when it enacted the "feasibility" language. Its view is that Congress required the Secretary to engage in something called "feasibility analysis." Ante, at 2490. But those words mean nothing at all. They are a "legislative mirage, appearing to some Members [of Congress] but not to others, and assuming any form desired by the beholder." American Petroleum Institute, supra, at 681, 100 S.Ct., at 2883. * * * *.

In believing that § 6(b)(5) amounts to an unconstitutional delegation of legislative authority to the Executive Branch, I do not mean to suggest that Congress, in enacting a statute, must resolve all ambiguities or must "fill in all of the blanks." Even the neophyte student of government realizes that legislation is the art of compromise, and that an important, controversial bill is seldom enacted by Congress in the form in which it is first introduced. It is not unusual for the various factions supporting or opposing a proposal to accept some departure from the language they would prefer and to adopt substitute language agreeable to all. But that sort of compromise is a far cry from this case, where Congress simply abdicated its responsibility for the making of a fundamental and most difficult policy choice—whether and to what extent "the statistical possibility of future deaths should * * * be disregarded in light of the economic costs of preventing those deaths." American Petroleum Institute, supra, at 672, 100 S.Ct. at 2879. That is a "quintessential legislative" choice and must be made by the elected representatives of the people, not by nonelected officials in the Executive Branch. As stated last Term:

> "In drafting § 6(b)(5), Congress was faced with a clear, if difficult, choice between balancing statistical lives and industrial resources or authorizing the Secretary to elevate human life above all concerns save massive dislocation in an affected industry. That Congress recognized the difficulty of this choice is clear. * * * That Congress chose, intentionally or unintentionally, to pass this difficult choice on to the

Secretary is evident from the spectral quality of the standard it selected." 448 U.S., at 685, 100 S.Ct., at 2885.

In sum, the Court is quite correct in asserting that the phrase "to the extent feasible" is the critical language for the purposes of these cases. But that language is critical, not because it establishes a general standard by which those charged with administering the statute may be guided, but because it has precisely the opposite effect: in failing to agree on whether the Secretary should be either mandated, permitted, or prohibited from undertaking a cost-benefit analysis, Congress simply left the crucial policy choices in the hands of the Secretary of Labor. As I stated at greater length last Term, I believe that in so doing Congress unconstitutionally delegated its legislative responsibility to the Executive Branch.

*Not Constitutional*

## NOTES AND QUESTIONS

1. Conceptually, under cost-benefit analysis the decision-maker simply weighs the costs of compliance against the benefits achieved. In deciding whether to undertake public works projects such as a dam or waterway for flood control, the responsible public agency would compare the expected construction costs with the economic benefits of reducing floods to determine whether the considered project would yield a net profit or loss, all expressed in dollar terms.

Applying cost-benefit analysis to safety regulations poses additional problems. The estimation of compliance costs poses problems similar to those encountered in estimating the construction costs of a dam, but the benefits of safety regulations are much more difficult to account and quantify than the expected property losses from floods. First there is the problem of estimating the number of injuries and lives saved by a safety regulation. Policy makers can use epidemiological studies based on animal subjects or humans to estimate the potential savings of life and limb from requiring a safety device or reducing workers' exposure to hazards such as cotton dust, but such exercises are expensive and very inexact. Second there is the problem of valuing in dollar terms the lives and limbs that one projects will be saved by the regulation. What dollar value should be placed on the use of a worker's arm or a worker's life to compare it with the costs of requiring employer compliance with the regulation?

Economists have proposed two methods of obtaining ball park figures for the value of human life and limb. The first is to estimate lost future earnings. Under this method, one would evaluate the value of a life or limb by estimating the future earnings that would be lost with the loss of the life or limb. Unfortunately this method systematically undervalues workers' lives and limbs since it takes no account of the non-pecuniary benefits of living and having limbs such as playing the piano, or playing with your kids. The method also suffers certain ethical deficiencies since, under it, high wage workers are worth more than low wage workers. At a minimum the method would seem to justify regulations permitting different levels of exposure to harmful chemicals for workers with different wages in the same workplace: for example doctors and nurses. In addition, based on estimated lost future earnings, on average, whites are worth more than blacks, men are worth more than women and young people are worth more than old people. If taken too seriously, this method of valuing human life might justify a regulation requiring that only old people work with toxic chemicals!

The second method of valuing human life and limb that economists have devised is based on the compensation workers demand to be exposed to health risks. Under this "willingness to pay" method of calculation, workers might be polled as to the amount they would have to be paid to risk life or limb, or the economist might examine actual wage data through statistical regression analysis to estimate the compensating wages workers receive for taking jobs with a greater risk of injury or death. Multiplying the wage premium workers say they need, or that they actually receive, to be subjected to a given risk, times the risk in question, gives you an estimate of the value of the life or limb at risk. This method of valuation is only valuable if workers adequately understand and evaluate the risks to which they are being subjected. As previously discussed in this book, it seems doubtful that workers fully understand all of the health risks to which they are subjected in the work place, and also doubtful that they ask for adequately compensating wages. If workers don't or can't command an adequate compensating wage for the risks to which they are subjected, then this method of estimation will yield valuations of life and limb that are too low. The empirical studies by economists using this method inspire little confidence since they yield estimates of the value of human life from as little as $50,000 to several million dollars. It makes a great deal of difference as to the amount and types of safety regulations you can justify using analysis, depending on whether you use $50,000 for estimating the value of lives saved, or $3 million.

The brief of the American Textile Manufacturer's Institute did not attempt to make a cost benefit calculation or argue that the costs of the standard outweighed the benefits. Its argument was simply that OSHA had not made a showing that reflected "an assessment of the costs and benefits of the standard (and available alternatives) sufficient to permit OSHA to determine that the risk reduction benefits of the standard bear a reasonable relation to its costs." (p. 36). The nearest the brief came to explaining what a "reasonable relation" might be was a footnote suggesting that a standard which reduced the number of deaths in a workplace from ten to 9 per year at a cost of $100,000 might satisfy the requirements, but if it cost one billion might not. (p. 38).

2. Section 6(b)(5) [29 U.S.C. § 655(b)(5)] applies to "toxic materials or harmful physical agents." This has been interpreted by OSHA as applicable only to "health" standards, which govern latent hazards such as carcinogens which develop slowly or after latency periods, as contrasted with "safety" standards, which address hazards that cause immediately visible physical harm and this has been upheld by the courts. *International Union, UAW v. OSHA,* 938 F.2d 1310 (D.C.Cir.1991).

"Safety" standards are governed by Section 3(8) [29 U.S.C. § 652(8)] which requires that the standard be "reasonably necessary or appropriate to provide safe or healthful employment." The courts have held that "reasonably necessary" imports "reasonableness." "The safety measures for which expenditures are made must be reasonable ones, which means first, that they produce an expected safety benefit commensurate to their cost; and second, that when compared with other possible safety measures, they represent an economical means of achieving the expected safety benefit." 938 F.2d at 1319 (quoting from *Consolidated Rail Corp. v. ICC*, 646 F.2d 642, 648 (D.C.Cir. 1981)). See also note 4 on p. 491.

The D.C. Court of Appeals acknowledged the criticism that valuation of lost years of life, suffering and other injury is impossible, but "that is so only in the sense that pin-point figures are necessarily arbitrary, so that the decisionmaker is effectively limited to considering some range of values." Id. at 1320. "Thus, cost-benefit analysis entails only a systematic weighing of pros and cons, or what Benjamin Franklin referred to as 'moral and prudential algebra'." Id. at 1321.

As expressed by other courts, with equally elusive language, the standard must on balance produce a benefit, the costs of which are not unreasonable. No formal cost-benefit analysis is required and the cost of compliance is not unreasonable if the standard in fact alleviates a grave danger. The statute requires only that "the expected costs of OSHA regulations be reasonably related to the expected benefits, leaving considerable discretion for the agency as long as it is exercised on substantial evidence and with an adequate statement of reasons." *National Grain and Feed Association v. OSHA*, 866 F.2d 717 (5th Cir.1988) (quoting *Texas Independent Ginners Ass'n v. Marshall*, 630 F.2d 398, 411 n. 44 (5th Cir.1980)).

Although the court refused to require cost-benefit analysis, can OSHA establish a standard without making findings as to costs and benefits? Is the practical issue here how OSHA shall make its inquiries and judgments, or how the courts shall review its standards?

3.  OSHA's authority to determine the issue of technological feasibility was described by the court in reviewing OSHA's arsenic expressive standard in *ASARCO, Inc. v. OSHA*, 746 F.2d 483 (9th Cir.1984).

In finding that a standard is "technologically feasible," the Secretary is not restricted to the state of the art in the regulated industry. *Boise Cascade*, 694 F.2d at 589. The Act is designed to be "technology-forcing." *United Steelworkers*, 647 F.2d at 1264. Hence, "[s]o long as [the Secretary] presents substantial evidence that companies acting vigorously and in good faith *can develop* the technology, OSHA can require industry to meet [standards] never attained anywhere." *Boise Cascade*, 694 F.2d at 589–90 (quoting *United Steelworkers*, 647 F.2d at 1264) (emphasis added). In fact, for our purposes here—reviewing OSHA's general rulemaking for the purpose of protecting worker health—all OSHA need demonstrate is that "modern technology has at least conceived some industrial strategies or devices which are likely to be capable of meeting the PEL and which the industries are generally capable of adopting." *United Steelworkers*, 647 F.2d at 1266. 746 F.2d at 495–96.

In *Public Health Research Group v. Department of Labor*, 557 F.3d 165 (3d Cir. 2009), a nonprofit advocacy group challenged a proposed OSHA standard governing hexavalent chromium exposure. The standard, issued pursuant to an earlier court order, would permit employee exposure at a level of five micrograms per cubic meter of air, despite evidence that exposure above a 1 microgram per cubic meter level could pose health risks. OSHA responded that reducing exposure levels below the proposed standard would not be technologically feasible. The court remanded the standard to OSHA to consider whether the monitoring and employee notice provision of the rule (which would require notice to employees only if monitoring showed that they were exposed above the permitted limit) might be changed. In March 2010, OSHA issued a revised version of the standard, requiring notice to employees of monitoring results, regardless of whether the exposure was above or below the permitted level.

4.  The term "economic feasibility" has been given more specific content by OSHA and other courts. In *American Iron and Steel Institute v. OSHA*, 939 F.2d 975 (D.C.Cir.1991), the standard governing worker exposure to airborne lead was upheld with the following explanation:

> OSHA approached the question of economic feasibility by estimating the probable costs of industry compliance and comparing those costs to the industry's financial profile in order to determine the likely effect of costs on the prices of the industry's product (if the costs were able to be passed through to customers) or on the viability of the industry (if the costs had to be absorbed). Economic feasibility was shown if the industry could either pass on the costs or absorb the costs without threatening the competitive structure of the industry.

> Compliance costs estimates for each industry were developed ... OSHA then compared annualized compliance costs to industry sales figures to determine the percentage the industry would have to raise prices in order to maintain existing profits. Where prices could not be passed on, OSHA compared annualized costs to annualized profits to determine the impact on the industry of absorbing those costs. Id. at 982.

5.  How persuasive is Justice Rehnquist's dissenting argument that the statute is an unconstitutional delegation to the Executive because, the words "to the extent feasible" were used to mask a fundamental policy disagreement in Congress? Does the general policy declared by Congress in Section 2 "to assure as far as possible every working man and woman in the Nation safe and healthful working conditions" fail to provide sufficient articulation of Congressional policy? Compare this language to that in the anti-trust laws, environmental legislation, the National Labor Relations Act, Graham–Rudman, or foreign trade legislation.

Consider the consequences of courts declaring statutes unconstitutional whenever they found broad or ambiguous statutory language was "used to mask fundamental policy disagreement in Congress." Would this not provide a charter for the courts to invalidate a wide range of social legislation? If Congress heeded the admonitions of Justice Rehnquist, what would be the effect on efforts to pass new social legislation? See Cass Sunstein, *Is OSHA Unconstitutional?*, 94 VA. L. REV. 1407 (2008).

6.  Establishing standards, particularly for exposure to toxic substances, commonly requires making determinations that are inescapably uncertain. First, is the extent of risks to health at various levels of exposure, and whether the standard is "reasonably necessary" to prevent a "significant

risk." Second, is whether the standard is technologically feasible, particularly where it is intended to be "technology forcing." The uncertainty rests in part on the indefiniteness of the substantive test, in part on the inadequacy or conflict in factual or scientific data, and in part on the necessity to predict future developments.

This uncertainty raises difficult questions for both the agency and the courts. How should OSHA and the Commission deal with the problems of uncertainties in performing their functions, and how should the courts review that performance? This involves questions both as to who should bear the burden of proof and what level of proof is required. These problems and proposed solutions are explored in depth in Howard A. Latin, *The Feasibility of Occupational Health Standards: An Essay on Legal Decisionmaking Under Uncertainty*, 78 Nw.U.L. REV. 583 (1983).

7. A problem not discussed in the principal case is who can challenge a standard. Section 656(f) provides that, "Any person who may be adversely affected" may file a petition in the United States court of appeals within 60 days. Challenges are commonly made by trade associations representing employers. However, challenges may be made by producers and sellers of products made less marketable by the standard. See *Asbestos Information Ass'n v. Reich*, 117 F.3d 891 (5th Cir.1997); *Color Pigments Manufactures Ass'n v. OSHA*, 16 F.3d 1157 (11th Cir. 1994); contra, *Calumet Industries v. Brock*, 807 F.2d 225 (D.C.Cir.1986). An employer may also challenge the validity of a standard by contesting a citation issued under the standard. *Boise Cascade Corp. v. Secretary of Labor*, 694 F.2d 584 (9th Cir.1982).

8. As the Court's opinion indicates, the Secretary enjoys considerable freedom in deciding which hazards to address through the adoption of a standard. Even after the standard setting process has been initiated, the courts have been reluctant to intrude into the process and set time goals. In a few instances, however, the process has been so glacial that a court has finally lost patience and ordered that the standard setting process be less dilatory. See, e.g., the opinions relating to regulating exposure to hexavalent chromium. *OCAW v. OSHA*, 145 F.3d 120 (3d Cir. 1998) (failure to publish standard in 1995, as agency had announced plans to do in 1993, not a sufficient basis to enter order requiring swifter progress); *Public Citizen Health Research Group v. Chao*, 314 F.3d 143 (3d Cir. 2002)) (ordering mediation between agency and petitioning group on issue of timetable for issuing standard); 2003 WL 22158985 (3d Cir. 2003) (adopting schedule based on recommendations of mediator calling for issuance of final standard in 2006); *Public Health Research Group v. Department of Labor*, 557 F.3d 165 (3d Cir. 2009) (remanding standard issued in October 2006 to agency to reconsider notice of hazard provision).

## UNITED STEELWORKERS OF AMERICA v. AUCHTER

United States Court of Appeals, Third Circuit, 1985
763 F.2d 728

GIBBONS, CIRCUIT JUDGE:

This case involves consolidated petitions for judicial review of the Hazard Communications Standard promulgated by the Secretary of Labor on the authority of the Occupational Safety and Health Act of 1970 (OSH Act), Pub.L. 91–596, 84 Stat. 1590, 29 U.S.C. § 651 *et seq.* (1982). Certain intervenors challenge our jurisdiction to consider the petitions pursuant to 29 U.S.C. § 655(f) (1982), contending that the action under review is a regulation rather than a standard. Petitioners and the Secretary urge that we have jurisdiction. Petitioners and intervenors challenge the standard on several substantive grounds, while the Secretary defends it. We conclude that the petitions for review are properly here, and thus address the substantive challenges.

I.

*Evolution of the Standard*

Section 6 of the OSH Act directs the Secretary of Labor to promulgate occupational safety and health standards to further the purpose of the Act "to assure so far as possible every working man and woman in the Nation safe and healthful working conditions * * *." 29 U.S.C. §§ 651(b) and 655(b)(1) (1982). Any standard promulgated by the Secretary shall prescribe the use of labels or other appropriate forms of warning as are necessary to insure that employees are apprised of all hazards to which they are exposed, relevant symptoms and appropriate emergency treatment, and proper conditions and precautions of safe use or exposure. 29 U.S.C. § 655(b)(7) (1982).

In 1974, the National Institute for Occupational Safety and Health (NIOSH), an agency created by section 22 of the OSH Act, 29 U.S.C. § 671 (1982), recommended that the Secretary promulgate a standard requiring employers to inform employees of potentially hazardous materials in the workplace. 47 Fed.Reg. 12095 (1982). Later that year the Secretary appointed an advisory committee to develop standards for implementation of the statutory provision requiring labels or other appropriate forms of warning. That advisory committee issued its report on June 6, 1975, recommending a classification of hazards, the use of warning devices such as labels and placards, disclosure of chemical data, and employee training programs. *Id.* at 12096.

The 1975 Committee report did not result in prompt action by the Secretary. In 1976 a House of Representatives subcommittee held oversight hearings during which several committee members expressed concern over the Secretary's failure to promulgate a comprehensive Hazard Communication Standard. *Control of Toxic Substances in the Workplace: Hearings Before the Subcomm. on Manpower and Housing of the House Comm. on Government Operations,* 94th Cong.2d Sess. 87, 89–90 (1976). Seventeen months later, the full House Committee on Government Operations issued a Report which criticized the agency for "miserly use of its delegated powers to deal with disease and death-dealing toxic substances." House Comm. on Government Operations, *Failure to Meet Commitments Made in the Occupational Safety and Health Act,* H.R.Rep. No. 710, 95th Cong., 1st Sess. 13 (1977). The Committee concluded that:

The Department of Labor should exercise its power under the Occupational Safety and Health Act to insure that employers and workers can and will know what kinds of toxic dangers are present in the Nation's workplaces. OSHA should require chemical formulators to identify any regulated substance in products they sell.

*Id.* at 15.

Eventually, on January 16, 1981, the agency published a notice of proposed rulemaking entitled "Hazards Identification." 46 Fed.Reg. 4412–53. The Standard proposed would be applicable to employers in Division D, Standard Industrial Classification Codes 20–39, which include only employers in the manufacturing sector. *Id.* at 4426. This classification of employers is made by type of activity for the purpose of promoting uniformity and comparability in the presentation of statistical data. Executive Office of the President, Office of Management and Budget, *Standard Industrial Classification Manual* 9 (1972). This initial proposal was withdrawn by the Secretary on February 12, 1981, for further consideration of regulatory alternatives. 46 Fed.Reg. 12214. The notice of proposed rulemaking which resulted in the rule challenged in the instant proceedings, entitled "Hazard Communication," was published on March 19, 1982. 47 Fed.Reg. 12091. Like the January 16, 1981 proposal, it was limited to employers in the manufacturing sector. The most significant difference from the rule proposed in 1981 was the inclusion in the March 19, 1982 proposal of a trade secret exception to the requirement that the chemical identities of all hazardous chemicals be disclosed. *Compare* 46 Fed.Reg. 4426 (1981) *with* 47 Fed.Reg. 12105 (1982).

The standard was published in its final form on November 25, 1983. 48 Fed.Reg. 53279. It requires that chemical manufacturers and importers "evaluate chemicals produced in their workplaces or imported by them to determine if they are hazardous." 29 C.F.R. § 1910.1200(d)(1) (1984). It refers to several compilations of toxic materials. These lists establish a floor of toxic substances which chemical manufacturers or importers must treat as hazardous. 29 C.F.R. § 1910.1200(d)(3) (1984). Chemicals not included in the designated compilations must be evaluated for hazardousness by reference to "available scientific evidence." 29 C.F.R. § 1910.1200(d)(2) (1984). A manufacturer or importer of chemicals found to be hazardous must "ensure that each container * * * leaving the workplace is labeled" with the chemical identity, with appropriate hazard warnings, and with the name and address of the source. 29 C.F.R. § 1910.1200(f)(1) (1984). Manufacturers or importers must also prepare a "material safety data sheet" (MSDS) containing the chemical common names of each hazardous ingredient, and information necessary for safe use of the product. 29 C.F.R. § 1910.1200(g) (1984). The MSDS must be provided to each employer in the manufacturing sector (Standard Industrial Classification Codes 20–39) purchasing a hazardous chemical. That employer must in turn make the MSDS available for employee inspection, 29 C.F.R. § 1910.1200(g)(8) (1984), and "shall provide employees with

information and training on hazardous chemicals in their work area
* * *." 29 C.F.R. § 1910.1200(h) (1984).

The rule allows an exception from the labeling and MSDS ingredient
disclosure requirements when a chemical manufacturer or importer claims
that the chemical identity is a trade secret. 29 C.F.R. § 1910.1200(i)
(1984). In such a case, the manufacturer or importer must provide a
MSDS disclosing the hazardous properties of the chemical and suggesting
appropriate precautions. In the case of a medical emergency, the manufacturer or importer must disclose the chemical identity to a treating physician or nurse, and may later require such a health professional to sign a
confidentiality agreement. 29 C.F.R. § 1910.1200(i)(2) (1984). Absent a
medical emergency, the manufacturer or importer may be required to
disclose the chemical identity to a health professional who makes a
written request detailing the occupational need for the information, and
who is willing to sign a confidentiality agreement containing a liquidated
damages clause. 29 C.F.R. § 1910.1200(i)(3) & (4) (1984). In no case is the
manufacturer required to disclose the precise formula, as opposed to the
identity of chemicals in the compound.

The rule provides expressly that:

> [t]his occupational safety and health standard is intended to address
> comprehensively the issue of evaluating and communicating chemical
> hazards to employees in the manufacturing sector, and to preempt
> any state law pertaining to this subject.

29 C.F.R. § 1910.1200(a)(2) (1984). Thus, at least insofar as they might
require hazard communication to employees in the manufacturing sector,
state hazard disclosure laws are claimed to be preempted by the rule.

## II.

### *Jurisdiction Under Section 6(f) of the OSH Act*

Congress has in section 6 of the OSH Act authorized the Secretary to
issue health and safety standards. 29 U.S.C. § 655 (1982). In section 8(c)
(3) of the Act, Congress also authorized the Secretary to issue regulation
requiring employers to keep records and inform employees of worker
exposure to potentially toxic materials or harmful physical agents. 29
U.S.C. § 657(c)(3) (1982). Classification of the Hazard Communication
Standard as a section 6 standard or a section 8 regulation will have two
interrelated consequences.

First, Congress has vested in the courts of appeals jurisdiction over
challenges to the validity of section 6 standards. 29 U.S.C. § 655(f) (1982).
Congress has made no such decision with respect to judicial review of
section 8 regulations. These are reviewable in the district courts pursuant
to the Administrative Procedure Act. 5 U.S.C. § 703 (1982). Thus if the
Hazard Communication Standard is a section 8 regulation the only course
open to us would be to transfer the petitions for review to an appropriate
district court. 28 U.S.C. § 1631 (1982). A court of appeals would reach the

merits of a dispute over a regulation, therefore, only on an appeal from a judgment of the district court.

Second, by whatever route the case arrived in a court of appeals, whether the challenged rule is a section 6 standard or a section 8 regulation affects its preemptive effect on state law. Section 18(a) of the OSH Act provides explicitly:

> Nothing in this chapter shall prevent any State agency or court from asserting jurisdiction under State law over any occupational safety or health issue with respect to which no standard is in effect under section 655 of this title.

29 U.S.C. § 667(a) (1982). If, however, a section 6 standard has been adopted, the role of the states is circumscribed by section 18(b) which provides:

> Any State which, at any time, desires to assume responsibility for development and enforcement therein of occupational safety and health standards relating to any occupational safety or health issue with respect to which a Federal standard has been promulgated under section 655 of this title shall submit a State plan for the development of such standards and their enforcement.

29 U.S.C. § 667(b) (1982). The Secretary must accept such a state plan if it "will be at least as effective in providing safe and healthful employment" as the OSHA standards. 29 U.S.C. § 667(c)(2) (1982).

The intervenor states all have hazard disclosure laws which, if not preempted, would be operative in the manufacturing sector. None contend, however, that they have submitted and have obtained approval of their plans pursuant to section 18. Given the explicit language of sections 18(b) and (c), the conclusion is inescapable that if the rule in issue is a section 6 standard it preempts state law until a state obtains section 18 approval of a state plan. It is not likely that the states challenging the rule will seek such approval, for section 18 contemplates that if they do so, they take on the fiscal burdens of enforcement now borne by the United States. 29 U.S.C. § 667(c)(5) (1982).

Since the disclosure requirements of laws adopted by the intervening states are in several respects stricter than those adopted by the Secretary, it is not surprising that those states would have us classify the challenged rule as a section 8 regulation rather than a section 6 standard. The preemptive effect of a section 8 regulation is not dealt with explicitly in the OSH Act, and any implied preemption would require a finding that it is impossible to comply with both federal and state law, or that "the state law stands as an obstacle to the accomplishment of the full purposes and objectives of Congress." *Silkwood v. Kerr–McGee Corporation,* 464 U.S. 238, 104 S.Ct. 615, 621, 78 L.Ed.2d 443 (1984). It is not likely that we could make either such finding. * * *

The states urge that the difference between section 6 standards and section 8 regulations must be determined by looking at the separate purposes behind the two provisions. Section 6 standards, they urge, serve two purposes: (1) to improve safety in the workplace by removing specific and already-identified hazards; and (2) to provide objective criteria capable of immediate application. Section 8 regulations, they urge, are designed, not for the elimination of specific and already-identified hazards, but for such purposes as the facilitation of investigation and enforcement. The states place principal reliance, in this regard, upon *Louisiana Chemical Association v. Bingham,* 657 F.2d 777, 782–83 (5th Cir.1981), in which the court classified the agency's Records Access rule as a section 8 regulation. The court in *Louisiana Chemical Association* held that before proceeding to the merits of a section 6(f) petition for review it must determine "whether the challenged rule reasonably purports to correct a particular 'significant risk' or instead is merely an enforcement or detection procedure designed to further the goals of the Act generally." *Id.* at 782. It concluded that the Records Access rule was a section 8 regulation.

The quoted distinction provides a convenient test for identifying standards, which this rule satisfies. While both the Records Access rule and the Hazards Communication rule have in common the object of communicating hazard information to employees, the former only provides for access to records maintained by an employer for other purposes, while the latter is aimed at eliminating the specific hazard that employees handling hazardous substances will be more likely to suffer impairment to their health if they are ignorant of the contents of those substances. The Secretary found that inadequate communication is itself a hazard, which the standard can eliminate or mitigate. 48 Fed.Reg. 53321 (1983). *See also* 48 Fed.Reg. 53282–83, 53323–24, 53327–29 (1983).

The State of New York urges that a communication rule can never be a standard, because it does not provide for diminution of risk through improved protection or reduced exposure. The Secretary found, however, that risk of harm can be greatly reduced by direct warning to employees, who are in the best position to assure that dangerous substances are handled in the safest possible manner. 47 Fed.Reg. 12112. Moreover New York's interpretation of section 6 is inconsistent with the inclusion therein of the direction to the Secretary to promulgate standards which "prescribe the use of labels or other appropriate forms of warning as are necessary to insure that employees are apprised of all hazards to which they are exposed * * *." 29 U.S.C. § 655(b)(7) (1982). Finally, while we exercise independent judgment as to the distinction between a section 6 standard and a section 8 regulation, the interpretation of those provisions of the OSH Act by the agency charged with its implementation should be afforded some degree of deference. The Secretary has classified the rule as a standard, and urges that the petition for review is properly here.

We conclude, therefore, that the Hazard Communication Standard is a section 6 standard reviewable in this court pursuant to section 6(f).

## III.

*Preemption of State Hazard Communication*
*Rules in the Manufacturing Sector*

Our analysis of the jurisdictional issue disposes of the states' objection to preemption of their hazard disclosure laws with respect to employees in the manufacturing sector. The Hazard Communication Standard, to the extent it is valid, as a section 6 standard, applies to the exclusion of state disclosure laws which have not been approved in accordance with section 18.

Massachusetts, Illinois, New Mexico, and West Virginia raise the question whether the federal Hazard Communication Standard operates to preclude state laws outside the manufacturing sector. The Secretary does not contend that the Standard has such an effect. 48 Fed.Reg. 53284; Respondent's Brief at 84–89. He urges, as well, that the issue of the standard's operation outside that sector is not ripe for review. To the extent that the states seek a declaration that their hazard disclosure laws may operate outside the manufacturing sector, we agree that it would be premature to make such a declaration in this case. The Secretary does not urge that they may not so operate, but other parties not before us might present reasons, such as unseverability as a matter of state law, which have not been litigated before this court. We hold only that, to the extent it is valid, the federal Hazard Communication Standard preempts state hazard disclosure laws with respect to disclosure to employees in the manufacturing sector.

### B. *Limitation of Coverage to the Manufacturing Sector*

None of the petitioners still before us contend that the manufacturing sector should not be covered by a hazard communication standard. The Secretary's decision to provide coverage only for employees in the manufacturing sector is based on a finding that this sector, which includes 32% of total employment, accounts for more than 50% of the reported cases of illness due to chemical exposure. 48 Fed.Reg. 53285 (1983). From this datum the Secretary determined that employees in the manufacturing sector have the greatest risk of experiencing health effects due to chemical exposure. *Id.* Agricultural employees have a higher chemical source incidence rate than manufacturing employees. The Secretary discounted this datum, however, because 80% of the reported chemical source cases among agricultural workers involved skin illnesses from handling plants, which would not be regulated by the proposed Hazard Communication Standard. *Id.* Moreover the Secretary concluded that the Environmental Protection Administration has, under the Federal Insecticide, Fungicide and Rodenticide Act, exercised jurisdiction over regulation of field use of pesticides. Excluding agricultural employees, there is substantial evidence in the record that the manufacturing sector has the highest incidence rate of chemical exposures which the Agency has authority to regulate.

Several petitioners, while conceding that the finding about incidence rate of illnesses in the manufacturing sector is supported by substantial evidence, contend that the Secretary's exclusion of other sectors, such as service, construction, and agriculture, is unsupported by reasons that are consistent with the purposes of the statute. They urge that while the incidence rate for employees in the manufacturing sector is high overall, some employees in specific non-manufacturing categories, such as hospital workers, are exposed to a greater number of toxic substances than are typical workers in the manufacturing sector. Moreover some workers in specific non-covered industries have higher reported rates of chemical source illness and injury than do workers in many covered industries. The Standard Industrial Classification breakdown, they contend, is not relevant to the statute, since that classification is made for a myriad of statistical purposes, mainly economic, having little to do with exposure to hazards. The result of the standard is that spray painters in the manufacturing sector, for example, must be provided with MSDS's and with information and training on hazardous chemicals in the products they use, while spray painters in the construction industry using the same products are not so protected.

In explaining the limited coverage, the Secretary reasoned:

> It should be emphasized that the Agency does not believe that employees in other industries are not exposed to hazardous chemicals, or that they should not be informed of those hazards. OSHA has merely exercised its discretion to establish rulemaking priorities, and chosen to first regulate those industries with the greatest demonstrated need.

45 Fed.Reg. 53286. Rejecting arguments of participants in the rulemaking proceeding that other workers, such as painters in the construction industry, are exposed to the same hazards as are workers in the manufacturing sector, the Secretary reasoned:

> As stated previously, OSHA acknowledges that exposures to hazardous chemicals are occurring in other industries as well. A limited coverage of them is included in the final standard since all containers leaving the workplace of chemical manufacturers, importers, or distributors will be labeled, regardless of their intended destination. This will alert downstream users to the presence of hazardous chemicals, and the availability of material safety data sheets. The Agency contends that the focus of this standard should remain on the manufacturing sector since that is where the greatest number of chemical source injuries and illnesses are occurring. This focus will also serve to ensure that hazard information is being generated for chemicals produced or imported into this country, and this increased availability will benefit all industry sectors.

*Id.* The Secretary's reasoning does not address the petitioners' contention that reliance on the Standard Industrial Classification is inappropriate because it ignores the high level of exposure in specific job settings outside the manufacturing sector.

The Secretary maintains that section 6(g) of the Act affords him unreviewable discretion to determine what industries shall be covered by a standard. That section provides in relevant part:

> In determining the priority for establishing standards under this section, the Secretary shall give due regard to the urgency of the need

for mandatory safety and health standards for particular industries, trades, crafts, occupations, businesses, workplaces or work environments.

29 U.S.C. § 655(g) (1982). We reject the Secretary's contention that his priority-setting authority under section 6(g) vitiates judicial review of his determination that only the manufacturing industry need be covered by the Hazard Communication Standard. Section 6(g) must be read in conjunction with section 0 which provides for judicial review of standards. Indeed the language "due regard to the urgency of the need for mandatory safety standards for particular industries" suggests to us a statutory standard by which to measure the exercise of the Secretary's priority-setting discretion. In *United Steelworkers of America v. Marshall,* 647 F.2d 1189, 1309–10 (D.C.Cir.1980), *cert. denied,* 453 U.S. 913, 101 S.Ct. 3148, 69 L.Ed.2d 997 (1981), the court reviewed under section 6(f) the Secretary's decision to exempt the construction industry from a standard limiting exposure to lead. Although the court did not explicitly address section 6(g), it implicitly rejected the contention that the Secretary's priority-setting authority is unreviewable. We do so explicitly.

* * * Section 6(g) clearly permits the Secretary to set priorities for the use of the agency's resources, and to promulgate standards sequentially. Once a standard has been promulgated, however, the Secretary may exclude a particular industry only if he informs the reviewing court, not merely that the sector selected for coverage presents greater hazards, but also why it is not feasible for the same standard to be applied in other sectors where workers are exposed to similar hazards. * * *

There is record evidence that workers in sectors other than manufacturing are exposed to the hazards associated with use of toxic materials or other harmful physical agents. The Secretary has given no statement of reasons why it would not be feasible to require that those workers be given the same MSDS's and training as must be given to workers in the manufacturing sector. * * * The Secretary has given reasons why the labeling, MSDS, and instruction requirements comply with section 6(c)(7) for employees in the manufacturing sector, but no explanation why the same information is not needed for workers in other sectors exposed to industrial hazards. Such a statement of reasons is required by section 6(f). *Synthetic Organic,* 503 F.2d at 1160.

We hold, therefore, that the petitions for review of those petitioners who object to the limitation of the Hazard Communication Standard must be granted. That standard may continue to operate in the manufacturing sector, but the Secretary's explanation for excluding other sectors does not withstand the scrutiny mandated by section 6(f). Thus the Secretary will be directed to reconsider the application of the standard to employees in other sectors and to order its application to other sectors unless he can state reasons why such application would not be feasible.

### D.  The Trade Secret Exemption

Several petitioners challenge the inclusion in the Hazard Communication Standard of a "trade secret" exception. 29 C.F.R. § 1910.1200(i) (1984). They contend that the agency has defined "trade secret" too broadly, and that the conditions under which workers may obtain information claimed to be a trade secret are unduly burdensome. * * *    *too broad?*

All information reported to or otherwise obtained by the Secretary or his representative in connection with any inspection or proceeding under this chapter which contains or which might reveal a trade secret referred to in section 1905 of Title 18 shall be considered confidential for the purpose of that section, except that such information may be disclosed to other officers or employees concerned with carrying out this chapter or when relevant in any proceeding under this chapter. In any such proceeding the Secretary, the Commission, or the court shall issue such orders as may be appropriate to protect the confidentiality of trade secrets.

Plainly the Secretary has provided greater protection for chemical manufacturers and importers than that afforded in those states utilizing the Restatement of Torts trade secret definition. Even the Restatement definition, moreover, goes beyond the protection afforded to trade secrets in other regulatory contexts. *See Public Citizen Health Research Group v. Food and Drug Administration*, 704 F.2d 1280, 1287 (D.C.Cir.1983) (Food and Drug Administration's adoption of Restatement of Torts trade secret definition inconsistent with Freedom of Information Act).

We agree that there is no legal justification for affording broader trade secret protection in the Hazard Communication Standard than state law affords. No petitioner urges that the Secretary's original proposal, which would have protected formula and process information but required disclosure of hazardous ingredients, is inadequate. That proposal was consistent with "[t]he general policy of OSHA * * * that the interests of employee safety and health are best served by full disclosure of chemical identity information." 48 Fed.Reg. 53312 (1983). The petition for review will therefore be granted and the proceedings remanded to the Secretary for reconsideration of the definition of trade secrets, which definition shall not include chemical identity information that is readily discoverable through reverse engineering.

### 2.  The Access Rule

In addition to objections to the definition of trade secrets, several petitioners challenge the provisions of the Hazard Communication Standard relating to access to the allegedly confidential information. The petitioners contend that once a manufacturer raises a claim of trade secret, the Standard places overly stringent procedural barriers to the discovery of information relevant to the assessment of health hazards. These objections go to: a) the requirement that the request be in writing with a statement of need; b) the limitation of access to "health professionals"; and c) the requirement that a confidentiality agreement with a liquidated damages clause be signed. 29 C.F.R. § 1910.1200(i).

### a) The Written Request Requirement

The Secretary justifies the requirement that a request for trade secret information be in writing with supporting documentation as a means of facilitating dispute resolution:

> Then if the matter is to be referred to OSHA to settle any dispute between the requesting party and the employer protecting a trade secret, the Agency will be able to base a decision upon a review of these written materials. Should the matter not be resolved to the satisfaction of all parties, it may result in a citation and referral to the Occupational Safety and Health Review Commission (OSHRC) for judicial review.

48 Fed.Reg. at 53315. The tendered justification is both reasonable and consistent with the purposes of the Act.

### b) The Restriction of Access to Health Professionals

The restriction limiting access to trade secrets to health professionals is more troublesome. Commentators on the proposed standard were generally in agreement that trade secret chemical identity information must be disclosed at least to a treating physician. *Id.* at 53316. The Secretary concluded that other health professionals, particularly those engaged in the prevention of disease or injury, had a legitimate need for chemical identity information. *Id.* at 53318. It declined, however, to authorize direct employee access to specific chemical identities of hazardous substances for which a trade secret is claimed. *Id.* The Secretary advances three rationales to justify restricting employee access to secret chemical identity information.

One reason is that "by and large professional training would be required" for any purpose that would amount to a "need to know" confidential information. *Id.* The United Steelworkers of America, AFL–CIO–CLC, a petitioner, points to a number of instances in the record, however, where non-health-professional workers used chemical identity information to improve workplace safety. They urge that employees and local union safety officers, although not health professionals, have often received training in health and safety, and thus know how to use the basic literature on chemical hazards, and know how to obtain technical assistance. Steelworkers' brief at 40.

A second reason advanced by the Secretary for allowing access only to health professionals, and not directly to employees, is that "providing access to trade secret chemical identities only to health professionals on a confidential basis will protect these employees adequately." 48 Fed.Reg. at 53318. The Steelworkers point to record evidence, however, that it is quite difficult for many workers to obtain the services of a health professional, at least prior to the need for treatment. Steelworkers' brief at 41–42.

There is no substantial evidence in the record that significant numbers of unorganized workers will be able to obtain the services of a health professional prior to the time that treatment becomes necessary. Even for organized workers, the record evidence suggests that few local unions retain health professionals.

The Secretary's final justification for limiting access to health professionals involves the risk of disclosure.

> This is not to say that "downstream" employees are more likely to disclose trade secrets or violate confidentiality agreements than health professionals, but it is an unmistakable fact that the more people who have access to confidential information, the more difficult it is to preserve its secrecy or to locate the source of a leak if one occurs.

48 Fed.Reg. at 53318. The Secretary correctly notes that the chance of a leak increases as the number of people having access to information increases. The issue posed by the petitioners, however, is not the number of persons obtaining access, but the type of persons. There is no record evidence supporting the Secretary's apparent conclusion that employees who are not health professionals will be more likely to breach a confidentiality agreement than would the same number of health professionals. We conclude that the restriction in the Hazard Communication Standard of access to trade secret information to health professionals is not supported by substantial evidence in the record, and is inconsistent with the mandate of section 6(b)(5) that OSHA promulgate the standard that "most adequately assures, to the extent feasible, on the basis of the best available evidence, that no employee will suffer material impairment of health * * *." 29 U.S.C. § 655(b)(5).

### c) The Confidentiality Agreement Requirement

The Standard requires that, except in a medical emergency, a manufacturer which receives a request for trade secret information may require that the requester sign a confidentiality agreement containing a liquidated damages clause. 29 C.F.R. § 1910.1200(i)(3)(v) (1984). The Standard minimizes the risk that employers will make excessive demands for liquidated damages clauses by providing that the agreement "[m]ay not include requirements for the posting of a penalty bond," but only "a reasonable pre-estimate of likely damages * * *." 29 C.F.R. § 1910.1200(i)(4)(ii) and (iii) (1984). Some petitioners contend that the requirement of a confidentiality agreement will deter health professionals from lending assistance. In Part IV(D)(2)(b) above we hold that the restriction on access to health professionals is invalid. But in any event, confidentiality agreements are a well-accepted traditional means of allowing access to trade secret information while effectively protecting the owners of that information from irreparable harm. Thus we reject petitioners' challenge to the Standard's requirement that requesters of trade secret information sign a confidentiality agreement.

V.

Conclusion

The petitions for review are properly filed in this court. The Hazard Communication Standard, to the extent that it is valid, preempts state hazard communication rules as they apply to employees in the manufacturing sector. The Standard may operate in that sector, but the Secretary will be directed to reconsider its application to employees in other sectors, and to order its application in those sectors unless he can state reasons why such application would not be feasible. The Secretary's [r]ejection of the RTECS list as overinclusive is supported by substantial evidence, consistent with the OSH Act's statutory purpose, and is therefore valid. The definition of trade secrets, which is broader than the protection afforded trade secrets by state law, is invalid, and the Secretary will be directed to reconsider a trade secret definition which will not include chemical identity information that is readily discoverable through reverse engineering. The trade secret access rule in the Standard is invalid insofar as it limits access to health professionals, but is otherwise valid, and the Secretary will be directed to adopt a rule permitting access by employees and their collective bargaining representatives.

JAMES McGIRR KELLY, DISTRICT JUDGE, concurring and dissenting: * * *

### NOTES AND QUESTIONS

1. Requiring manufacturers and importers of chemicals to determine whether the products they introduce into the workplace are potentially toxic relieves OSHA of the nearly insuperable task of monitoring new chemicals and determining if they are toxic. Manufacturers and importers have the scientific knowledge about the substances they supply and can more adequately and economically make that determination. In addition, the requirement expresses a broader principle that a supplier ought not put a product on the market without first determining whether it will endanger the health and safety of those who use it.

How effective will such a requirement be if violations of the standard are remedied by the customary civil penalties and orders of abatement? Compare the incentive provided by the statute with that to protect users provided by judicially developed rules of product liability. How will the labeling requirements affect tort suits against manufacturers and suppliers?

2. Following the *Auchter* decision, the Secretary did not act on the court's instruction to reconsider application of the standard to other sectors and to order it applicable unless he could state reasons why it would not be feasible. After two years of the Secretary's inaction, the petitioners moved to hold the Secretary in contempt. In *United Steelworkers of America v. Pendergrass*, 819 F.2d 1263 (3d Cir.1987), the court ordered the Secretary to publish a hazard communication standard applicable to all workers covered by the Act within sixty days or explain why this was not feasible. The Secretary, within the sixty days, issued a final rule extending coverage to all industries while

protesting that he should have been given more time to develop a feasibility study.

The amended standard was upheld against challenges by the construction industry. *Associated Builders & Contractors Inc. v. Brock*, 862 F.2d 63 (3d Cir. 1988). The OMB then disapproved the standard as violating the Paper Reduction Act because the standard required that at multi-employer work sites employers exchange material data safety sheets. The Supreme Court held that the OMB acted beyond its authority because agency action mandating disclosure to third parties was not within the Paper Reduction Act. *Dole v. United Steelworkers*, 494 U.S. 26, 110 S.Ct. 929, 108 L.Ed.2d 23 (1990). Congress later reversed *Dole* (prospectively) by amending the Paperwork Reduction Act in 1995.

3. Right to Know laws might be considered as serving several different purposes: (1) Inform employees of risks in their jobs so they can make an informed choice; (2) enable employees to inform their doctors of their exposure so as to aid diagnoses and treatments; (3) make employees, and their unions where there is collective bargaining, more aware of the risks and thereby lead to wage rates more commensurate with those risks; (4) trigger or encourage inquiry into the risks created by the toxic substances being used; and (5) disclose violations of specific standards or the general duty clause and enable employees or unions to file complaints.

How effective is the Hazard Communication Standard in promoting each of these purposes? To what extent is its effectiveness dependent on the presence of a union with the expertise and resources to examine the MSDSs, analyze its significance and take action on it? Would the union need to be the majority representative to perform this function?

4. Prior to adoption of the Hazardous Communications Standard, OSHA had published a list of 400 chemical substances, with their threshold limit values (TLVs), the level of airborne concentrations of the chemicals which can be tolerated by humans without negative consequences. No standard was adopted, however, requiring employers to observe these TLVs, primarily because of the time and resources needed to conduct rulemaking procedures.

Could OSHA have treated an employer's exceeding the published TLVs as a "recognized hazard," and cited the employers for violation of the general duty clause where employers knew or could have known that employees were being exposed?

5. The Hazard Communication Standard should be viewed in connection with the Toxic Substances Control Act of 1977, which prohibits the domestic manufacture or import into the United States of any new commercial chemical substance prior to review by the Environmental Protection Agency. Notice of intent to manufacture a new chemical or process an existing chemical for a "significant use" must be given to the EPA at least ninety days in advance, which then determines whether there is a "reasonable basis to conclude" that it "will present an unreasonable risk of injury to health or the environment."

Any person may petition the EPA to initiate proceedings for issuing or amending regulations, or for an order in a specific case. If the EPA denies the petition or fails to act within ninety days, the individual can obtain judicial review. Also, any person may sue any party (including the U.S. Government) who is alleged to be in violation of the Act or of certain regulations or orders, or may sue the Administrator of EPA to compel the performance of any act or duty under the statute which is not discretionary.

Compare the usefulness of the TSCA with the OSH Act in protecting employees from toxic substances in the workplace. Consider the role of the Hazard Communication Standard in enabling employees or their representatives to achieve enforcement of both the TSCA and the OSH Act. See, Nina G. Stillman & John R.Wheeler, *The Expansion of Occupational Safety and Health Law*, 62 NOTRE DAME L. REV. 969, 980–992 (1987).

6.   The complex issues involved in preemption are addressed again in *Gade v. National Solid Wastes Management Association*, 505 U.S. 88, 112 S.Ct. 2374, 120 L.Ed.2d 73 (1992), reproduced in part below at 615.

7.   In late 2009, OSHA proposed changes to the Hazard Communication standard that would use the United Nations Globally Recognized System of Classification and Labeling of Chemicals.

# E.  ADMINISTRATIVE INTERPRETATION OF STANDARDS

When a standard is ambiguous, the question arises whose interpretation shall control, the Secretary's or the Commission's? In *Martin v. OSHRC*, 499 U.S. 144, 111 S.Ct. 1171, 113 L.Ed.2d 117 (1991), the Commission vacated a citation on the grounds that the facts did not establish a violation of the regulation cited. The Court of Appeals affirmed, holding that where the relevant regulations were ambiguous, the court must defer to the Commission's reasonable interpretation, rather than the Secretary's reasonable interpretation.

The Supreme Court pointed out the unique "split enforcement" structure of the Act which gave the Secretary the rulemaking and enforcement powers and the Commission the adjudicative function of determining whether the facts support a finding of violation of those regulations. Congress did not endow the Commission with the normal adjudicative powers possessed by a traditional unitary agency which uses adjudication to engage in lawmaking.

"Congress intended to delegate to the Commission the type of non-policymaking adjudicatory powers typically exercised by a court in the agency review context. Under this conception the Commission is authorized to review the Secretary's interpretations only for consistency with the regulatory language and for reasonableness .... In addition, of course, Congress charged the Commission with making authoritative findings of fact and with applying the Secretary's standards to those facts.... The Commission need be viewed as possessing no more power than this to perform its statutory role as a neutral arbiter." 499 U.S. 154–55.

Although the Secretary's interpretation of an ambiguous standard is upheld as reasonable, it may be unenforceable in a particular case because it did not provide fair notice to the employer that its conduct was prohibited where it was not obviously hazardous. *Beaver Plant Operations, Inc. v. Herman*, 223 F.3d 25 (1st Cir. 2000).

# F. ENFORCEMENT OF EMPLOYER OBLIGATIONS

## 1. INSPECTION

Enforcement of the general duty clause and the specific standards begins with inspections of the workplace by OSHA compliance officers. The number of inspections per year has ranged from 90,000 in 1976 to 36,350 in 2000 and 38,591 in 2008. The compliance officer must present his or her credentials to the employer and obtain admission to the premises. The first step is to examine the accident and injury records which most employers of ten or more are required to maintain.

The second step is a tour of part or all of the workplace. In this "walkaround," the compliance officer is accompanied by a representative of the employer and "a representative authorized by his employees," if there is one. If there is no "authorized representative," the compliance officer is "to consult with a reasonable number of employees," and may do this without the employer representative present. At the end of the tour, the compliance officer informs the employer of any violations observed and discusses possibilities of abatement. The compliance officer does not issue citations; these are issued by the Area Director. An inspection may take a few hours to several days and divert a number of employees and management form their normal work.

*Walkaround*

Inspections are initiated in three ways: First, OSHA schedules "programmed inspections" (23,023 in 2008) on a random basis, with primary emphasis on larger employers in those industries which are most hazardous. Scheduled inspections begin with an examination of the company's safety records. This review may affect the scope of the remaining examination of the workplace.

Second, an inspection may be triggered by an accident resulting either in a fatality or in hospitalization of five or more employees. OSHA may learn of such accidents by news reports, employee complaints, or from reports employers are required to make to OSHA within forty-eight hours of such accidents.

Third, inspections may be triggered by written complaints, made usually by an employee or a union. No action is taken on telephoned complaints regardless of the seriousness of the claimed violation. If an informal written complaint is made, OSHA informs the employer and requests the employer to inform OSHA as to what steps have been taken to abate the hazard. If a formal complaint is filed, and the employer is in an industry with a high accident rate, an inspection will be conducted and it will be comprehensive. But if the complaint is in an industry with a low accident rate, the inspection will be limited to the hazard alleged in the complaint.

No advance notice is given of an inspection, and any person giving unauthorized advance notice is subject to criminal charges punishable by a fine of up to $1,000, and imprisonment to six months.

### (a.) Requirement of a Warrant

Not surprisingly, some employers have resisted such administrative incursions on business privacy by claiming protection of the Fourth Amendment, requiring the compliance officer to produce a search warrant. In *Marshall v. Barlow's Inc.*, 436 U.S. 307, 98 S.Ct. 1816, 56 L.Ed.2d 305 (1978), a divided Supreme Court held that an inspection was a search within the Fourth Amendment and that a warrant was required. However, probable cause in the criminal sense was not required. "A warrant showing that specific business has been chosen for OSHA search on a general administrative plan for the enforcement of the Act derived from neutral sources ... would protect the employer's Fourth Amendment rights."

The requirement of a warrant has posed no significant problems for programmed inspections. To obtain a warrant the Secretary need only show the general plan on which the schedule is based, that the employer was in the neutrally defined class, and that the employer was appropriately selected under that plan. *Brock v. Gretna Machine & Ironworks, Inc.*, 769 F.2d 1110 (5th Cir.1985); *Donovan v. Hackney, Inc.*, 769 F.2d 650 (10th Cir.1985). For example, construction work sites may be selected randomly by a computer taking into account dollar value of project, size in square feet, length of time of project, and type of project. See *National Engineering Company v. OSHRC*, 45 F.3d 476 (D.C.Cir.1995)

Inspections based on fatalities or catastrophic accidents, or on employee and union complaints have caused more problems. Reliance on a newspaper report that an employee had both hands amputated was held not enough, although the employer had been cited for violations four years before. The court declared, "newspaper reports are not of sufficient reliability to form the basis of Fourth Amendment probable cause determination." *Donovan v. Federal Clearing Die Casting Co.*, 655 F.2d 793, 794 (7th Cir.1981). Similarly, the courts have held that the mere filing of an employee complaint is not enough. There must be a showing of a general plan to inspect on the basis of complaints and that the complaint states facts justifying an inspection. *Burkart Randall Division of Textron, Inc. v. Marshall*, 625 F.2d 1313 (7th Cir.1980); *Reich v. Kelly–Springfield Tire Co.*, 13 F.3d 1160 (7th Cir.1994).

A "non-programmed" warrant will normally authorize the agency to inspect the cause of the accident or the specific complaint, not conduct a general inspection of the premises. The warrant may authorize review of the employer's required injury and accident record. If that indicates a full inspection is necessary, the Secretary may apply for a second warrant authorizing a wall to wall inspection. *Trinity Industries, Inc. v. OSHRC*, 16 F.3d 1455 (6th Cir.1994). In this case, the evidence obtained in a comprehensive inspection was not suppressed because the inspectors had an objectively good faith belief that their actions were authorized by the warrant. If an employer refuses to produce records, the agency may issue an administrative subpoena for them. The records sought by such a subpoena may go beyond the particulars of the original complaint, at least to a reasonable degree. See *Reich v. Montana Sulphur and Chemical Co.*, 32 F.3d 440 (9th Cir. 1994).

In *L. R. Willson & Sons, Inc. v. OSHRC*, 134 F.3d 1235 (4th Cir. 1998), an OSHA Compliance Officer received a call from a hotel patron that there were safety violations in the construction of a building across the street. He went to the roof of the hotel and took fifty minutes of video of men working eighty feet above the ground without any fall protection. The result was citing the contractor for serious violations. The contractor sought to exclude the video from evidence. The court held that here was no violation of the Fourth Amendment as there was no reasonable expectation of privacy because the work was plainly visible from the rooms in the hotel.

Employer refusal to honor a subpoena will lead to court proceedings to compel the employer to submit, in which the employer will likely seek to quash the subpoena on some ground. Such a "time buying" tactic may result in delay of a year or more in the actual inspection. See, e.g., *Martin v. International Matex Tank Terminals–Bayonne*, 928 F.2d 614 (3d Cir. 1991). In rare instances, OSHA has sought to avoid this delay by executing the warrant in the company of federal marshals despite the employer's refusal to submit. See *Trinity Marine Prods., Inc. v. Chao*, 512 F.3d 198 (5th Cir. 2007).

There is uncertainty whether the principles of *Barlow's* are generally applicable to the safety records that OSHA requires an employer to maintain, so that an inspector must get a warrant to examine them. See Carlos B. Castillo, *Discord Among Federal Courts of Appeal: The Constitutionally of Warrantless Searches of Employer's OSHA Records*, 45 U. OF MIAMI L. REV. 201 (1990). Challenges to the record-keeping requirements are generally made in the course of enforcement proceedings. See *Sturm, Ruger & Co., Inc. v. Chao*, 300 F.3d 867 (D.C. Cir. 2002).

### (b.) OSHA Efforts to Reduce Inspections

In 1982, OSHA instituted a program to encourage employer development of comprehensive safety programs. Those entities with a qualified program, known as a Voluntary Protection Program (VPP), are exempt from routine OSHA inspections, though they continue to be subject to inspections in response to specific complaints or catastrophic events. To be eligible for VPP status, an employer's injury incidents must not exceed the average industry rate. In addition, among other requirements, the program must include regular safety training; a procedure for surveying and evaluating existing hazards and the hazardous potential of new processes, materials, and equipment; monthly self-inspections; a vehicle for employee input respecting safety and health needs; a system for investigating and documenting any accidents; utilization of professional consultants; written safety rules and procedures; first aid trained personnel; and written annual performance evaluations. As of January 2010, there were nine corporate participants in the VPP program, the most recent being Morton Salt. There are also individual sites that qualify for the program.

In 1997, OSHA made another effort to reduce inspections. It identified 12,500 companies with high illness and injury rates, placed them on a "primary inspection list" for a comprehensive inspection, and began inspecting the 500 worst offenders. The Cooperative Compliance Program Directive provided that OSHA would remove workplaces from the list, and reduce the probability of inspection by 70 to 90 percent if the relevant employer cooperated in the Program. To participate the employer had to agree to identify and correct all hazards and implement a comprehensive health and safety program, provide a procedure which enabled employees to complain of unsafe practices, and address substantive problems of ergonomics and other safety and health problems. The effect was to require employers to go beyond the requirements of the law in preventing injuries and illness, including compliance with applicable "voluntary standards," "industry practices" and suppliers safety recommendations. More than 10,000 employers joined. The Chamber of Commerce, National Association of Manufacturers and other trade groups petitioned for review in the court of appeals on the grounds that the Directive was in substance a standard adopted without the required notice and hearing. The court held that although an employer was not subject to any penalty for failing to join the CCP, being subject to an inspection could be as onerous as paying a fine. Inspections might extend over several weeks, create disruption and impose lost time of employees escorting the inspector. The "agency was intentionally using the leverage it has by virtue of its power to inspect. The Directive is therefore the practical equivalent of a rule that requires an employer to comply or suffer the consequence." The court vacated the Directive without prejudice to OSHA repromulgating it after observing the required procedures. *Chamber of Commerce of the United States v. United States Department of Labor*, 174 F.3d 206 (D.C.Cir.1999) (on some points, the opinion has been questioned by *Sturm Ruger & Co., Inc. v. Chao*, 300 F.3d 867 (D.C. Cir. 2002)). For discussion of potential self-enforcement devices which have not been tried, see Neil Gunningham, *Toward Effective and Efficient Enforcement of the Occupational Safety and Health Regulation: Two Paths to Enlightenment*, 19 COMP.LAB.L. & POL.J. 547 (1998); Anne T. Nichting, *OSHA Reform: An Examination of Third Party Audits*, 75 CHI. KENT L. REV., 195 (1999).

## 2.  POST INSPECTION PROCEDURES

The compliance officer reports the findings made on the inspection to the Area Director, who, on the basis of that report, decides what, if any citations should issue, the proposed penalties to be imposed on the employer, and the steps to be taken by the employer to abate the violations. Citations are issued in the name of the Secretary. More than 80 percent of the inspections result in citations, with an average of more than two citations for each inspection.

The employer, on receipt of the citation, may either accept the citation and comply, or file a notice of contest with the Area Director. If no notice of contest is filed, the citation becomes a legally binding order, enforceable by a federal district court. The contest may be to the violation, to the penalty, or to the abatement order. When a notice of contest has been filed, the Secretary is required to immediately advise the Commission of the contest, and then the Secretary files a complaint. The complaint is heard by an Administrative Law Judge (ALJ), who after hearing decides whether there has been a violation, and if so, what penalty shall be assessed and what abatement measures are to be taken. Either the employer or the Secretary may file a Petition for Direct Review (PDR) with the Commission to challenge the ALJ's decision. Unless one of the three members of the Commission request review, the decision of the ALJ becomes the final order of the Commission. Appeal from that decision is to the federal courts of appeals. The result is that the case may come before the court of appeals without ever being heard by the Commission itself.

The percentage of contested cases has ranged from 21 percent in 1980 to a low of 2.8 percent in 1985. This drop in the 1980's probably reflected the Reagan administration's "non-confrontational" policy with the assessed penalties being reduced from $15 million in 1980 to less than $5 million in 1983. Settlements of many of the penalties were for less than 20 percent of those assessed. In 2008, the penalties assessed by OSHA totaled $92 million; an additional $70 million dollars in penalties were assessed under state plans.

Contested cases may be disposed of prior to hearing before the ALJ by the Secretary withdrawing the citation for lack of merit, the employer withdrawing its notice of contest, or by a settlement agreement between the Secretary and the employer. Ninety percent of the contested cases are thus settled prior to the ALJ hearing, and many of the ALJ decisions are not reviewed by the Commission. The net result is that only a fraction of the citations ever reach the Commission.

In *Cuyahoga Valley Ry. Co. v. United Transportation Union,* 474 U.S. 3, 106 S.Ct. 286, 88 L.Ed.2d 2 (1985), after a citation had been issued and the employer had contested, the Secretary filed a complaint with the Commission and the union intervened. At the hearing before the Administrative Law Judge, the Secretary moved to vacate the citation, and despite the union's objection, this motion was granted. The Commission directed review of the ALJ's order and remanded it for consideration of the union's objection. The Supreme Court held, "the Secretary has unreviewable discretion to withdraw a citation." 474 U.S. at 6, 106 S.Ct. at 287.

> [E]nforcement of the Act is the sole responsibility of the Secretary. * * * It is the Secretary, not the Commission, who sets the substantive standards for the workplace, and only the Secretary has the authority to determine if a citation should be issued to an employer for unsafe working conditions. * * * A necessary adjunct of that power is the authority to withdraw a citation and enter into settlement discussions with the employer * * *.

The Sixth Circuit's conclusion that the Commission can review the Secretary's decision to withdraw a citation would discourage the Secretary from seeking voluntary settlements with employers in violation of the Act, thus hampering enforcement of the Act. 474 U.S. 6–7, 106 S.Ct. at 287.

Special procedures potentially compelling the Secretary to act are provided in Section 13 of the Act in case of "imminent danger." This is defined as one "which could reasonably be expected to cause death or serious physical harm immediately or before the imminence of such danger can be eliminated through the enforcement procedures otherwise provided by the Act."

Imminent dangers might be noticed in any fashion—in a scheduled inspection, from news reports, or from employee or union complaints. OSHA policy is to give these cases first priority, conducting an inspection in twenty-four hours. Where the inspector finds an imminent danger, the Secretary may seek injunctive relief in the district court. The inspector is required to inform the affected employees of the imminent danger and that he is recommending that the Secretary act. If the Secretary "arbitrarily or capriciously fails to seek relief," any employee who may be injured may bring an action against the Secretary for a writ of mandamus to compel the Secretary to seek relief.

## 3. EMPLOYEE AND EMPLOYEE REPRESENTATIVE PARTICIPATION IN ENFORCEMENT

One characteristic of the Occupational Safety and Health Act is that, with one minor exception, it provides the workers whose lives and bodily security are to be protected no independent rights or ability to enforce the statute. OSHA does not give injured workers or their surviving families any cause of action against the employer for damages for violations which lead to injury or death. *Jeter v. St. Regis Paper Co.,* 507 F.2d 973 (5th Cir.1975). For employees other than those covered by the Federal Employers Liability Act and the Jones Act, recovery is normally only under the workers' compensation laws. Under most workers' compensation laws, the fact that the injury results from a violation of a safety or health standard does not result in a recovery any greater than the inadequate amounts allowed for a wholly unpreventable accident.

Employees do have limited participation in the enforcement process by filing a formal complaint which may lead to an inspection. If the Area Director decides not to make an inspection, the complaining employee is notified and may obtain an informal review. However, informal complaints often do not lead to an inspection: the Area Director will only write the employer a letter recommending corrective action.

When an inspection is conducted, "a representative authorized by his (the employer's) employees," if there is one, must be allowed to accompany the inspector on the walkaround, but the employee representative is not entitled to pay for the time spent in the walkaround. In practice, this right has substance only when there is a union to act as an authorized representative. In the absence of a union, which is by far the most common situation, only the employer representative participates in the walkaround; employees participate only to the extent that they are interviewed by the compliance officer or call conditions to his attention. The latter has limited value because employees may be unprepared or be afraid to come forward when an employer representative is present.

When the Area Director determines what, if any, action is to be taken as a result of the inspection, the affected employees must be informed. Copies of citations must be posted at or near where each cited violation occurred. Employees may not contest the Area Director's refusal to issue a citation before the Commission, but may obtain an informal review by OSHA. If a citation is issued, then complicated questions are presented as to the role of employees or their representatives in further proceedings before the Commission and in judicial review of Commission decisions. The technical and policy issues are marked out in the following case.

## OIL, CHEMICAL AND ATOMIC WORKERS v. O.S.H.R.C.

United States Court of Appeals, District of Columbia Circuit, 1982
671 F.2d 643

PER CURIAM:

Petitioner Oil, Chemical and Atomic Workers International Union and its Local 3–499 ("OCAW") seek review of a decision of the Occupational Safety and Health Review Commission ("OSHRC" or "Commission") dismissing a citation issued by the Secretary of Labor to the American Cyanamid Company. *Secretary of Labor v. American Cyanamid Company,* OSHRC Docket No. 79–5762 (April 27, 1981), reported at 9 BNA OSHC 1596. American Cyanamid has moved to intervene and has moved to dismiss OCAW's petition for review, arguing that OCAW is not a proper petitioner for review under the Occupational Safety and Health Act of 1970 ("Act"), and that OSHRC is not a proper respondent. 29 U.S.C. § 660(a).

American Cyanamid's motion raises several threshold issues that must be answered before we reach the merits of the petition. Those issues are:

*Review of a dismissed citation*

(1) Does the role of the Secretary as the exclusive prosecutor under the Act preclude the appeal of an OSHRC decision by OCAW, a labor union representing affected employees, when the union has participated as a party in the OSHRC proceeding?

(2) Does OCAW have the right to challenge a determination by the Secretary not to appeal a decision by the OSHRC dismissing a citation?

(3) May the OSHRC participate as an active party in the Court of Appeals on a petition for review of its decision?

(4) Is the company the proper party respondent in proceedings initiated by a petition filed by OCAW to review the OSHRC decision?

(5) Is the Secretary the proper party respondent in proceedings initiated by a petition filed by the company to review the OSHRC decisions?

We answer the first, second and third questions in the negative and the fourth and fifth questions in the affirmative. Accordingly, we sustain the OCAW's petition for review and we deny the company's motion to dismiss.

## I.  Background

The facts giving rise to this litigation are not in dispute. In 1977, American Cyanamid adopted a Fetus Protection Policy and implemented it at its Willow Island, West Virginia plant. This policy precluded female employees of presumed childbearing capacity from being assigned to, bidding into, or holding any production job at that plant which involved occupational exposure to toxic substances identified as harmful to the fetus. Any female production worker who failed to provide evidence of permanent infertility by April, 1978, would have to request a transfer to one of three departments where toxic substances were not used. Only seven job openings were available to the thirty women affected by this policy. To rebut the policy's presumption of the potential childbearing capacity of menstruating women, five female production workers underwent voluntary sterilizations. These women retained their production positions. All five stated that they would not have undergone the procedure but for the company's policy which threatened their livelihood. Late in 1978, two women presumed childbearing capacity who refused to be sterilized were transferred to the utility pool with subsequent loss of pay and benefits.

OCAW filed a complaint about the policy with the Occupational Safety and Health Administration ("OSHA"), pursuant to 29 U.S.C. § 657(f)(1), in December, 1978. Thereafter, OSHA inspectors conducted an inspection of the Willow Island plant. As a result of this inspection, OSHA issued a citation on October 9, 1979, alleging that Cyanamid had committed a willful violation of the general duty clause, 29 U.S.C. § 654(a)(1), by implementing a policy which required women employees to be sterilized in order to be eligible to work in certain areas of the plant. Cyanamid filed a timely notice of contest, and the Secretary issued a formal complaint. On November 16, 1979, OCAW elected party status pursuant to Commission Rule 20(a), 29 C.F.R. § 2200.20, in order to participate in hearings concerning this citation before the OSHRC. Cyanamid filed its answer to the Secretary's complaint and moved for summary judgment. The Administrative Law Judge granted the company's motion and dismissed the citation on two independent grounds: (1) that the citation was barred by the Act's six-month statute of limitations; and (2) that the action of the Equal Employment Opportunity Commission precluded the Secretary's jurisdiction over the alleged hazard.

*[handwritten: Citation dismissed]*

Both the union and the Secretary petitioned the full OSHRC for discretionary review of the judge's decision pursuant to section 12(j) of the Act, 29 U.S.C. § 661(i). After review was directed, the OSHRC affirmed the ruling on a third ground, finding that the citation did not allege the existence of a "hazard" within the meaning of the Act's general duty clause. Accordingly, the citation was vacated.

Pursuant to section 11 of the Act, 29 U.S.C. § 660(a), OCAW filed a timely petition for review. It named the OSHRC as a respondent. The Secretary elected not to file a petition.

## II.   The Right of OCAW to Appeal

As an initial matter, American Cyanamid challenges the jurisdiction of this court, arguing that OCAW's petition for review fails to present a case or controversy because the statute precludes the union from being heard on matters other than the reasonableness of the abatement period. Our jurisdictional basis for reviewing any OSHRC proceeding is 29 U.S.C. § 660, which provides for appellate review of commission decisions. It states:

> Any person adversely affected or aggrieved by an order of the Commission issued under subsection (c) of section 10 [29 U.S.C. § 659(c)] may obtain a review of such order in * * * the court of appeals for the District of Columbia Circuit * * *.

Cyanamid argues in its motion that the broad language of § 660(a) must be limited by Section 10(c) of the Act, 29 U.S.C. § 659(c). Section 10(c) is the cornerstone of the right of employees, or their authorized representatives, to participate in hearings before the OSHRC. It provides, in its entirety:

> If an employer notifies the Secretary that he intends to contest a citation issued under section 658(a) of this title or notification issued under subsection (a) or (b) of this section, or if, within fifteen working days of the issuance of a citation under section 658(a) of this title, any employee or representative of employees files a notice with the Secretary alleging that the period of time fixed in the citation for the abatement of the violation is unreasonable, the Secretary shall immediately advise the Commission of such notification, and the Commission shall afford an opportunity for a hearing (in accordance with

Section 554 of Title 5 but without regard to subsection (a)(3) of such section). The Commission shall thereafter issue an order, based on findings of fact, affirming, modifying, or vacating the Secretary's citation or proposed penalty, or directing other appropriate relief, and such order shall become final thirty days after its issuance. Upon a showing by an employer of a good faith effort to comply with the abatement requirements of a citation, and that abatement has not been completed because of factors beyond his reasonable control, the Secretary, after an opportunity for a hearing as provided in this subsection, shall issue an order affirming or modifying the abatement requirements in such citation. The rules of procedure prescribed by the Commission shall provide affected employees or representatives of affected employees an opportunity to participate as parties to hearings under this subsection.

29 U.S.C. § 659(c).

The company contends that section 10(c) limits employee participation in enforcement proceedings to contesting the reasonableness of the abatement period. It reasons that this limit on the initiation of and participation in commission adjudications should be carried over to the instigation of judicial review because Congress intended that the provisions be read together as part of a "detailed statutory scheme." *Whirlpool Corp. v. Marshall,* 445 U.S. 1, 10, 100 S.Ct. 883, 889, 63 L.Ed.2d 154 (1980). That scheme—says the company—may most consistently be interpreted to limit the rights of employees to initiate and participate in proceedings before the commission and to appeal commission decisions to issues challenging the reasonableness of the abatement period.

We reject the company's initial contention that employees have no right to be heard on matters other than the reasonableness of the abatement period. The starting point for our analysis is section 10(c) of the Act, 29 U.S.C. § 659(c). It is apparent that the first sentence of section 10(c) contemplates two types of hearings. The first is triggered by an employer who notifies the Secretary of an intention to contest a citation. In that hearing, employees are authorized to "participate as parties" by virtue of the last sentence of section 10(c). The second type of hearing is triggered by employees who notify the Secretary of their contention "that the period of time fixed in the abatement citation is unreasonable."

This second type of hearing—that initiated by *employees*—is tied to the agenda set by statute: contesting the reasonableness of the abatement period. *Marshall v. OSHRC and OCAW,* 635 F.2d 544, 552 (6th Cir.1980). Employees are prohibited from instituting a commission action on any matter other than the reasonableness of the abatement period. *UAW v. OSHRC,* 557 F.2d 607, 610 (7th Cir.1977). Nothing in the text of the statute, however, so confines employee/union participation as "parties" in the first type of hearing—that initiated by the *employer* to contest a citation.

Indeed, the section 10(c) limitation suggested by the company would, be an anomaly when viewed in the total context of the Act. Typically, as demonstrated by the instant case, an employee who believes a violation exists that threatens physical harm may request an inspection by giving the Secretary written notice. 29 U.S.C. § 657(f)(1). If, upon receipt of such notification, the Secretary determines there are reasonable grounds to believe a violation exists, he must conduct a special inspection as soon as possible. *Id.* A representative authorized by the employees shall be given the opportunity to accompany the Secretary or his representative during the physical inspection of the workplace. *Id.* § 657(e). If the Secretary believes that the employer has violated any portion of the Act, "he shall with reasonable promptness issue a citation to the employer." *Id.* § 658. The employer may then contest the citation if he disputes the Secretary's finding of a violation flowing from an investigation initiated by employees. At the hearing initiated by the employer, the employee may elect party status. *Id.* § 659(c). It is at this juncture that the company insists that the election of party status limits the employees to contesting the length of the abatement period. We find no support for this position in the statute. Moreover, we find the adoption of the company's premise inconsistent with the remainder of the statutory scheme. The company would have us hold that the employee's interest in and contribution to the enforcement process, protected by the statute throughout the enforcement process, abruptly ceases once the adjudicative process is initiated by the employer filing a notice of contest. By permitting employees to elect party status, and not qualifying this status with the same limits imposed on the employees' initiation of commission proceedings, it is apparent that Congress intended to continue the broad scope of employee participation in the enforcement of the Act through the adjudicative stages. * * *

In sum, the legislative history shows that Congress intended to allow employees to participate as parties in enforcement proceedings in two separate contexts—to initiate contests over the reasonableness of the abatement period and to participate as parties in an employer-initiated contest. We find that Congress did not intend to limit the interest assertable by the union in an employer-initiated proceeding to the length of the abatement period. The scheme of the Act enables employees to translate their concern for workplace safety into a demand for an inspection of the workplace, and, if a violation exists, into a citation. If the employer disputes the inspector's findings and files a notice of contest, the Act entitles employees to "participate as parties" in hearings before the OSHRC. The employees' request for party status confers jurisdiction on the commission to entertain the employees' objections on all matters relating to the citation in question.

We therefore hold that where a union or employee has elected party status in proceedings before the OSHRC, the union or employee has a right to appeal the decision of the OSHRC. As a party in an employer-initiated hearing before the OSHRC, the union will be "adversely affected or aggrieved" by an unfavorable OSHRC decision. Accordingly, the union can seek judicial review in a federal court of appeals under section 11(a) of the Act, 29 U.S.C. § 660(a). * * *

Our view does not impinge on the Secretary's unique role in administering the Act. As the Supreme Court has noted, the Act creates public rights that are to be vindicated by the Secretary through government management and enforcement of a complex administrative scheme. *Atlas Roofing Co. v. OSHRC,* 430 U.S. 442, 444–47, 97 S.Ct. 1261, 1264–65, 51 L.Ed.2d 464 (1977). We recognize that the Secretary has been vested with considerable discretion in the promulgation of standards. Thus, employees may not compel the Secretary to adopt a standard. *National Congress of Hispanic American Citizens v. Usery,* 554 F.2d 1196 (D.C.Cir.1977). Similarly, we are persuaded that enforcement of the Act is the sole responsibility of the Secretary. He is the exclusive prosecutor of OSHA violations. *Atlas Roofing Co.,* 430 U.S. at 445–47, 97 S.Ct. at 1264–65. Necessarily included within the prosecutorial power is the discretion to withdraw or settle a citation issued to an employer, and to compromise, mitigate or settle any penalty assessed under the Act, 29 U.S.C. § 655(e). Thus, employees may not contest the representation of a settlement agreement that abatement has occurred. *Marshall v. OCAW and OSHRC,* 647 F.2d 383, 388 (3d Cir.1981). They may not prosecute a citation before the commission after the Secretary has moved to withdraw it. *Marshall v. OSHRC and OCAW, supra,* 635 F.2d at 552. They may not argue that a particular method of abatement would be inefficacious. *Marshall v. Sun Petroleum Products Co.,* 622 F.2d 1176, 1184–86 (3d Cir.), *cert. denied,* 449 U.S. 1061, 101 S.Ct. 784, 66 L.Ed.2d 604 (1980). They may not challenge the substantive provision of an abatement plan. *UAW v. OSHRC, supra,* 557 F.2d at 610–11.

We endorse so broad a reading of prosecutorial discretion under the statute because we believe that such discretion comports with the Congressional intent that the Secretary be charged with the basic responsibilities for administering the Act. We agree with other courts that have considered the issue that the union has no right to challenge the refusal of the Secretary to proceed with a citation or to file a complaint. *See, e.g., Marshall v. OSHRC and OCAW, supra,* 635 F.2d at 550. The company, however, contends that these decisions prohibit employees from challenging the Secretary's prosecutorial decisions before the commission proceedings, except where the length of an abatement period is concerned. It reasons that the decision to seek review of a commission decision is a similar exercise of prosecutorial discretion and concludes that allowing employees to petition for judicial review of a commission decision impermissibly usurps the Secretary's prosecutorial discretion as enforcer of the Act.

We reject this position. We agree with the company that a decision of the Secretary not to appeal the OSHRC ruling is an exercise of prosecutorial discretion. Accordingly, we find that the union has no right to challenge the determination of the Secretary not to appeal. In this instance, however, the OCAW is not seeking review of the Secretary's decision; instead, it is seeking judicial review of an order of the OSHRC, an independent adjudicatory body.[8] Under the Act, we hold that a union has the right to appeal the ruling of the OSHRC, whether or not the Secretary simultaneously seeks review, as a person "adversely affected or aggrieved" within the meaning of section 11(a) of the Act.

The union's right to appeal OSHRC decisions where it has participated as a party in the commission proceedings is, however, subject to two conditions, derived from the general statutory scheme and purpose of the Act. First, the union must give the Secretary notice of its intention to appeal and must serve him with copies of all of the pleadings. This notice requirement is ordered so that the Secretary is made aware of the litigation and so that he may act to intervene if he deems it appropriate. Second, the case may become moot in those instances when the Secretary, participating in the appeal as an amicus curiae or as an intervenor, provides this court with a clear and unconditional statement that he will not prosecute the claim regardless of the disposition of the appeal by this court. The prosecutorial discretion with which the Secretary is vested empowers him not to renew his prosecution effort even if this court were to find that the citation dismissed by the OSHRC asserted a violation under the Act. *Marshall v. OSHRC and OCAW, supra,* 635 F.2d at 549–52. While we will not require the Secretary to furnish us with a statement of his intent, we may dismiss the appeal as moot in instances where the Secretary has voluntarily proffered such a statement after the union has filed a petition for review.[9]

### III.   The Proper Respondent in the Appeal

We must next decide if the OSHRC, the named respondent in this petition for review, has the authority to participate as a party in this court in a proceeding to review one of its decisions. American Cyanamid, in its motion to dismiss, contends that no case or controversy exists because the OSHRC cannot participate as a party. While we agree with the company that the Act limits the role of the OSHRC to that of an adjudicatory agency and precludes the OSHRC from independent representation in judicial proceedings before this court, we decline to dismiss these proceedings. We grant the motion to remove the OSHRC from these proceedings; concurrently, we grant the OCAW's motion to amend and reform the caption and to name the company as the proper party respondent in this petition for review.

---

**8.** The employee's right to appeal an adverse decision of an adjudicatory agency has never been interpreted as a review of the prosecutor's decision not to appeal. In many instances, appeals by private parties from the dismissal of an administrative action have gone forward without the filing of an appeal by the prosecutorial agency. *See, e.g., Newspaper Drivers v. Detroit Newspaper Publishers Assn.,* 382 U.S. 374, 86 S.Ct. 543, 15 L.Ed.2d 423 (1966). The power to seek judicial review of a decision of an adjudicatory agency has never been vested solely in the prosecutorial arm of that agency.

**9.** In instances where the Secretary has not furnished the court with a statement of his intent, we will review the decision of the commission. The fact that there is uncertainty as to whether the government will continue to prosecute the case upon remand does not mean that no justiciable controversy exists. *See Dunlop v. Bachowski,* 421 U.S. 560, 575, 95 S.Ct. 1851, 1861, 44 L.Ed.2d 377 (1975).

The circuits are sharply divided on the question of whether the commission is a proper party to an OSHA appeal. Three circuits have held that the commission is not a proper party. Two circuits have stated this position in dictum. The Second Circuit has noted that the commission is assigned the "relatively limited role of administrative adjudication." *General Electric Company v. OSHRC,* 583 F.2d 61, 63 n. 3 (2d Cir.1978). In *Brennan v. OSHRC,* 505 F.2d 869, 871 (10th Cir.1974), the Tenth Circuit found that the commission is "an adjudicatory body with no regulatory powers." * * *

In those instances where the commission rules in favor of the employer and dismisses the citation, two parties may appeal the commission's order. The Secretary may file a petition for review of the commission's action. 29 U.S.C. § 660(b). He may have an interest in seeking review of a decision of which he disapproves. In this instance, the employer would be the proper respondent. Like an appellee in the appeal of a district court decision, the employer has a concrete stake in having the commission's order affirmed.

In a case such as the instant one, where the union is appealing an adverse decision by the commission, the proper party respondent is the employer.[13] The deletion of the OSHRC does not trigger any jurisdictional problem potentially foreclosing the effective adjudication of the merits of the appeal. The rationale of Federal Rule of Appellate Procedure 15(a) which mandates that each petition for review of an agency order shall name the agency as respondent is inapplicable.

In most cases, a single private party is contesting the action of an agency, and the agency must appear and defend to assure the adversarial stance requisite to a case or controversy. In this case, however, sufficient adversity exists between the union and the company to insure proper litigation without the participation of the OSHRC. The company's interest is adverse to the interests of the petitioner union. It can be expected to litigate vigorously to sustain the ruling of the OSHRC. The union plainly has an interest in having the OSHRC decision reversed and the citation upheld, resulting in an invalidation of the company's Fetus Protection Policy and a fine assessed against the company. To require the OSHRC to appear as a party would parallel requiring a district court to appear and defend its decision upon direct appeal. Just as a district court may not defend its decision in the court of appeals, the OSHRC has no authority to defend its order before this court.

### NOTES AND QUESTIONS

1. Despite the ruling in the instant case, the Review Commission continues to be named as a party in many cases, usually as a joint party with either

---

**13.** We do not decide whether the employer is the only proper respondent in cases such as this one. We express no opinion as to whether the Secretary could participate as a respondent in petitions for review filed by the union. *Cf. Shahady v. Atlas Tile and Marble Co., et al.,* 673 F.2d 479 (D.C.Cir.1982).

the Secretary of Labor or the cited employer. See, e.g., *StarTran, Inc. v. Occupational Safety and Health Review Comm'n*, 290 Fed. Appx. 656 (5th Cir. 2008).

2.   The Secretary can settle a case with an employer at any time subject to the employees' or union's right to contest the period of abatement. After the employer has filed a protest so that the case is in the hands of the Commission, the Secretary can settle and the Commission has no authority to review the settlement, *Donovan v. OSHRC*, 713 F.2d 918 (2d Cir. 1983), and if employees or the union have intervened and become parties, the Secretary can settle without their consent, *United Steelworkers of America v. Herman*, 216 F.3d 1095 (D.C. Cir. 2000) (reviewing cases from many Circuits). They may, however, be able to object to the abatement period provided.

Nor does the individual employee have any right against OSHA for negligence in enforcing the statute. In *Irving v. United States*, 162 F.3d 154 (1st Cir.1998), an employee bent over to retrieve a glove and her hair was drawn by the high speed of an unguarded drive shaft. Compliance officers had twice made wall to wall inspections but did not report or call the employer's attention to this serious violation. The employee sued the government under the Federal Tort Claims Act (FTCA) for negligent failure to note and cite the unguarded drive shaft. A divided court held that the Act placed virtually no constraint on the Secretary's discretion to conduct inspections and that the regulations did not mandate a particular manner of inspection or materially restrict the compliance officer's flexibility conducting the inspection. The regulations "unambiguously grant OSHA compliance officers discretion over the scope, manner and details of conducting inspections" 162 F. 3d 164. The inspections were, therefore, "discretionary" under the FTCA, and the government could not be held liable for the compliance officer's negligence.

3.   In contrast to the limited role given by OSHA to employee representatives in regulating health and safety in the workplace, other countries rely heavily on employee participation. See Julie E. Korostoff et. al., Comment, *Rethinking the OSHA Approach to Workplace Safety: A Look at Worker Participation in the Enforcement of Safety Regulations in Sweden, France and Great Britain*, 13 COMP. LAB. L.J. 45 (1991). In Sweden, every workplace over fifty employees must have a safety committee of employer and employee representatives with a safety delegate chosen by the union. Employers must notify the safety delegates of any changes which might have a significant bearing on safety conditions. The safety delegates not only participate in inspections by a labor inspector, but make inspections on their own initiative and can call in a labor inspector. The employer must provide training for the safety delegates on work time. Some 30,000 safety delegates are given twenty to forty hours of training each year. The safety committee is consulted concerning new machinery, new production processes and new plant construction. Also, the safety committee oversees the company health service and approves the appointment of company doctors and safety engineers, who report to the safety committee.

Great Britain also provides for statutory safety committees appointed by the unions. Safety representatives are authorized to investigate potential hazards and employee complaints, inspect the workplace and employer safety records, and represent employees in dealing with government inspectors. Safety representatives are allowed time off with pay for performing their functions and for training classes. About 30,000 are given a ten day training course each year.

In Germany, safety matters are handled by the works councils, which are elected by the employees. The works council has broad responsibility for enforcing safety laws and regulations, preventing employment injuries, participating in inspections, and consulting on changes in jobs, work processes, machinery or plant construction which have an impact on the nature of the work and the demands on employees. Where changes impose a special burden on employees that are "in obvious contradiction to the established findings of ergonomics relating to the tailoring of jobs to meet human requirements," the works council may demand corrective measures and any dispute is resolved through arbitration. Works Constitution Act of Jan. 15, 1972, Sections 87(7), 88–91, BGB1.I, 13 at 30–31. The works council must approve of all appointments of plant physicians and safety specialists. Works council members are paid by the employer for all time spent in performing their duties and for all training.

In the United States, proposals have been introduced to amend OSHA to mandate the creation of safety committees so that in non-union plants employees would have some voice in safety matters and aid in enforcing the statute, but all such proposals have died aborning. Eighteen states mandate or authorize workplace safety committees in conjunction with their safety and health laws or their workers' compensation system. See Matthew Finkin, *Bridging The Representation Gap*, 3 U. OF PA. J. LAB. & EMPL. L. 39 (2001). Many employers establish safety committees on their own initiative. Establishing safety committees in nonunion settings, whether under state statute or employer initiative, however, poses risk of violating Section 8(a)(2) of the NLRA which prohibits employer domination of a labor organization. See *E. I. du Pont de Nemours & Co.*, 311 N.L.R.B. 893 (1993). But if the plan assures free election by the employees of their representatives and full freedom to propose, consider, and object or approve safety plans and problems, and full freedom to consult with employees, they could escape being labeled as "dominated" by the employer. The use of company time and company property would probably not constitute unlawful employer support and assistance. See *BASF Wyandotte Corp. v. O.C.A.W.*, 274 NLRB 978 (1985).

Several states mandate the creation of workplace safety committees that include employee representatives. The method of selection for these committee members varies from being appointed by the employer, to selected by lot from volunteers and elected by the employees. Their functions are generally described in terms that make them advisory to management, but they may inspect to discover health and safety hazards and make recommendations to management. They can perform one valuable function under the federal law, and that is providing an employee representative who is entitled to accompany an inspector on the "walk-around." Such safety committees have limited effectiveness in the absence of a union, but they provide a union an opportunity to organize. See David Weil, *Mandating Safety and Health Committees: Lessons from The States*, in PROCEEDINGS OF THE 47TH ANNUAL MEETING OF THE

IRRA 2723 (PAULA VOOS, ED.); Note, *Participation with Representation: Ensuring Workers' Rights in Cooperative Management*, 1994 ILL. L. REV. 729 (1994).

# G. ESTABLISHING VIOLATIONS OF THE GENERAL DUTY CLAUSE AND OF STANDARDS

## PRATT & WHITNEY AIRCRAFT v. SECRETARY OF LABOR

United States Court of Appeals, Second Circuit, 1981
649 F.2d 96

MESKILL, CIRCUIT JUDGE:

\* \* \*

## A.  The Regulatory Framework

This case presents the complex and often bewildering regulatory framework of OSHA. In this case, the Commission found that Pratt & Whitney had breached the "general duty" clause of the Act and had violated several of the regulations promulgated by the Secretary of Labor (the Secretary). See 29 C.F.R. §§ 1900–2000 (1980). The "general duty" provision, § 5(a)(1) of the Act, provides:

(a) Each employer—

> (1) shall furnish to each of his employees employment and a place of employment which are free from recognized hazards that are causing or are likely to cause death or serious physical harm to his employees.

29 U.S.C. § 654(a)(1) (1976). This section is intended as a catchall provision to cover dangerous conditions of employment not specifically covered by existing health and safety standards promulgated by the Secretary of Labor under the Act. *See* Morey, *The General Duty Clause of the Occupational Safety and Health Act of 1970,* 86 Harv.L. Rev. 988, 990 (1973). "To prove a violation of the general duty clause, 'the Secretary must prove (1) that the employer failed to render its workplace free of a hazard which was (2) recognized and (3) causing or likely to cause death or serious physical harm.' " *Usery v. Marquette Cement Manufacturing Co.,* 568 F.2d 902, 909 (2d Cir.1977) (quoting *National Realty & Construction Co. v. OSHRC,* 489 F.2d 1257, 1265 (D.C.Cir.1973)).

The violations in this case have been classified as both "serious" and "non-serious." Section 17(k) of the Act sets forth the requirements for a serious violation:

> For purposes of this section, a serious violation shall be deemed to exist in a place of employment if there is a substantial probability that death or serious physical harm could result from a condition which exists, or from one or more practices, means, methods, operations or

processes which have been adopted or are in use, in such place of employment unless the employer did not, and could not with the exercise of reasonable diligence, know of the presence of the violation.

29 U.S.C. § 666(j) (1976). Whether a violation of any of the health and safety standards promulgated by the Secretary may be deemed serious depends upon whether any accident that would result from the violation would present a substantial probability of death or serious physical injury. * * * It would appear, however, that any condition at a place of employment that violates the general duty clause would have to be deemed serious, since an element of a general duty violation is that the condition is "likely to cause death or serious physical harm." There seems to be little distinction between "substantial probability" as employed in § 17(k) and "likely" as employed in § 5(a)(1). With this background in mind, we turn to the facts of the case.

### B.   The OSHA Citations

In the spring of 1975, OSHA compliance officers inspected the Pratt & Whitney plant located in North Haven, Connecticut. More than 4,500 employees work at the facility, which has over one million square feet of manufacturing space. Citations were issued to Pratt & Whitney for two serious violations and several non-serious violations of the Act. Several of the citations for non-serious violations were set aside after a full hearing conducted before the administrative law judge, Abraham Gold. Judge Gold also vacated the citation issued to Pratt & Whitney for its serious violation of 29 C.F.R. § 1910.94(d)(7)(iii) (1980), a regulation which proscribes the use of a common exhaust system that poses a risk of fire, explosion, or hazardous chemical reaction. Judge Gold affirmed the citation issued to Pratt & Whitney for its serious violation of the general duty clause.

Both the Secretary and Pratt & Whitney appealed to the OSHRC for review of Judge Gold's decision. Moving at a glacial pace, the OSHRC rendered its decision three and one-half years after briefs were filed by the parties. The OSHRC reinstated the serious violation of 29 C.F.R. § 1910.94(d)(7)(iii) (1980) which had been vacated by Judge Gold, affirmed the citation for the serious violation of the general duty clause, and vacated several of the citations for non-serious violations.

Pratt & Whitney seeks review of the serious and non-serious violations affirmed by the OSHRC. The Secretary does not challenge the portions of the OSHRC's decision which vacated citations for several of the non-serious violations. For the purpose of clarity, we treat each of Pratt & Whitney's challenges to the citations separately.

### C.   The General Duty Clause Violation

During the course of the inspections at the North Haven facility, OSHA compliance officers discovered that Pratt & Whitney was storing large quantities of acids and cyanides in a common, indoor, bulk-chemical storage area. The parties agree that, if acid were to come in contact with the cyanides, a lethal gas, hydrogen cyanide (HCN), would be formed. The storage shed was about 40 feet long and 32 feet wide, and was partitioned lengthwise by a very hard asbestos-like substance. The partition was approximately seven feet high, and atop of it there was a chainlink fence which extended to the ceiling of the storage shed. On one side of the partition, the *wet-side,* acids were stored; on the other, the *dry-side,* potassium cyanide and sodium cyanide pellets were stored. The storage shed had only one drain, which was located on the dry-side about two feet from the partition. About 1/4 inch of space was left between the bottom of the partition and the floor so that liquids could pass to reach the drain.

The petitioner's expert, Mr. Doyle, testified that the likelihood of HCN gas being formed was "very remote," because such an occurrence would require "a series of disconnected events." A. 437–38. Notwithstanding that several acid spills had in fact occurred, Mr. Doyle testified that it would take approximately one and one-half hours for the most corrosive acid stored in the shed to eat through the steel drums containing the cyanide compounds. Petitioner's expert also claimed that the drain would have to be plugged and two containers of acid would have to spill for the acid to reach the cyanides. Furthermore, Mr. Doyle noted that the otherwise readily detectable fumes of such an acid spill would have to go undetected for the length of time necessary for the acid to corrode the cyanide drum.

The Secretary's expert, Mr. Padden, testified that he had visited 300 to 400 plants which stored acids and cyanides and that he had observed only two that had used a common drain. He added that those two plants "corrected the situation immediately" after being urged to do so. Mr. Padden stated that all of the other plants he had seen had used separate storage areas and separate drains for acids and cyanides.

The OSHRC determined that the cited conditions amounted to a serious violation of the general duty clause, concluding that the formation of HCN in Pratt & Whitney's chemical storeroom was "reasonably foreseeable," and that feasible methods of abatement—separately storing the chemicals with separate drains—were available. The OSHRC also concluded that in the event of an accident, a likely consequence would be death or serious injury. Thus the Commission determined that Pratt & Whitney's violation of the general duty clause was a serious one under § 17(k) of the Act, 29 U.S.C. § 666(j) (1976). In a dissenting opinion, Commissioner Barnako agreed that the reasonable foreseeability of a hazardous incident is an element of a violation under the general duty clause, but concluded that, under the facts presented, the occurrence of a hazardous incident at petitioner's storeroom was not reasonably foreseeable.

The only issue presented in connection with this citation is whether the conditions at Pratt & Whitney's indoor chemical storage facility amounted to a "recognized hazard" within the meaning of § 5(a)(1) of the Act, 29 U.S.C. § 654(a)(1) (1976). We are convinced that much of the confusion in this case was generated by a failure on the part of the

Secretary properly to define the "hazard" with which this citation is concerned. The Secretary has asserted from the outset that the recognized hazard it found at Pratt & Whitney's plant was "hydrogen cyanide formation." Of course, it cannot be denied that uncontrolled formation of HCN gas at a place of employment would constitute a recognized hazard within the meaning of § 5(a)(1). Indeed, petitioner concedes as much. However, there was not a scintilla of evidence that HCN had ever formed in petitioner's storeroom. Thus, the hazard evaluated at Pratt & Whitney's chemical storage area could not have been uncontrolled HCN gas formation, but rather must have been a condition that might result in the generation of that lethal gas. Because the Secretary defined the recognized hazard in terms of a potentiality, HCN formation, rather than the existing condition that might give rise to that potentiality, the manner in which the chemicals were stored, the parties found themselves debating over the relevance of the *probability* of a hazardous incident occurring at the petitioner's plant. Thus, Pratt & Whitney contends that the likelihood of HCN forming in its chemical storage area was too remote a possibility to support a violation of the general duty clause. The Secretary, on the other hand, asserts that since the hazard to be prevented—HCN formation—in and of itself constitutes a recognized hazard, all that had to be shown was that the condition under examination presented a *possibility* of its formation. The OSHRC apparently was uneasy about upholding a violation of the general duty clause where only a possibility of a hazardous incident occurring was demonstrated, since it imposed, without the urging of either party, a seemingly higher probability standard; as stated above, the Commission determined that the occurrence of a hazardous incident—*i.e.*, HCN formation—in Pratt & Whitney's storeroom was "reasonably foreseeable." Although we conclude that the condition cited constituted a violation of the general duty clause, we arrive at this determination by a different route than that taken by the OSHRC and the Secretary.

Section 5(a)(1) of the Act obligates employers to rid their workplaces not of possible or reasonably foreseeable hazards, but of recognized hazards. The intent of the legislature may be gleaned from the plain language of the statute. "Recognized" is defined in Webster's Third New International Dictionary (unabridged 1971) as follows: "to recall *knowledge* of: make out as or perceive to be something previously *known* * * * to perceive clearly: be fully aware of: REALIZE." (emphasis added). In short, the term "recognized hazard, the dangerous potential of a condition or activity must actually be known either to the particular employer or generally in the industry."

This definition is fully supported by the legislative history of the general duty clause. *See* Meeds, *A Legislative History of OSHA*, 9 Gonzaga L. Rev. 327, 346–47 (1974). The term "recognized hazard" is intended to cover dangerous conditions that can be detected by the human senses and are generally known as hazardous. *See* 116 Cong.Rec. 42206 (1970): A recognized hazard is a condition that is known to be hazardous, and is known not necessarily by each and every individual employer but is known taking into account the standard of knowledge in the industry. In other words, whether or not a hazard is "recognized" is a matter for objective determination; it does not depend on whether the particular employer is aware of it. 116 Cong.Rec. 38377 (1970) (quoted in *National Realty & Construction Co. v. OSHRC, supra,* 489 F.2d at 1265 n. 32). We find nothing in the legislative history of § 5(a)(1) to support an interpretation such as the Secretary's that any condition which presents a possibility of seriously injuring an employee constitutes a recognized hazard within the meaning of that section. * * *

As we stated in *Usery v. Marquette Cement Manufacturing Co., supra,* to be a recognized hazard, the dangerous potential of the condition or activity being scrutinized either must be known by the employer or known generally in the industry. Applying the appropriate standard avoids completely the task of speculation about probabilities of hazardous incidents occurring. Therefore, the burden was on the Secretary in this case to show that the manner in which Pratt & Whitney stored its chemicals was known by it to be hazardous or was generally recognized as such by the industry. Irrespective of the improper standard advanced by the Secretary, we are satisfied that the record contains substantial evidence to sustain a violation of the general duty clause under the *Marquette* standard. Mr. Padden's testimony that only two of the 300 to 400 plants he had visited had employed common drains, and that those two had corrected the situation immediately when advised, permitted the inference that the industry generally stored acids and cyanides separately with separate drains to guard against the formation of HCN gas in storage areas. Since the record reveals substantial evidence, 29 U.S.C. § 660(a), (b) (1976), that the industry generally recognized as hazardous the manner of storing chemicals utilized by Pratt & Whitney, the general duty clause violation must be affirmed. * * *

## D.   The Serious Violation Involving Common Ductwork

At its North Haven plant, Pratt & Whitney maintains an exhaust system that provides separate exhaust ducts over the various open tanks of cyanide, heated slushing oil, hydrogen peroxide, and glacial acetic acid used in its plating operations. The individual exhaust ducts have chimney-like "plenums" that are connected to a common duct for each of the plant's seven plating lines. Each of the seven common ducts feeds exhaust through a stack in the roof. Relying on 29 C.F.R. § 1910.94(d)(7)(iii) (1980), which prohibits the use of common exhaust systems where a combination of the vented substances "may constitute a fire, explosion, or chemical reaction hazard," the Secretary cited the company for a serious violation.

In connection with all seven plating lines, the Secretary contends that acid mists and cyanide mists could combine in the common duct to form HCN gas, a serious hazard to the employees. The Secretary asserts that the gas, if formed, conceivably could asphyxiate employees on the roof, or in the plant itself if a downdraft returned it inside the plating department.

Additionally, the Secretary claims that cyanide gas in the ducts would pose a serious fire or explosion hazard because of the low flash point of that vapor.

The Secretary also contends with respect to one of the plating lines that hydrogen peroxide and heating oil could combine in a common duct and create the potential for fire or explosion. Another possibility, according to the Secretary, is that the hydrogen peroxide could react with acetic acid in the common duct to form peracetic acid which also could create the risk of fire or explosion. For the latter to occur, the Secretary concedes that the ventilation system would have to malfunction, but notes that the system actually did break down during the OSHA inspection.

The Secretary argues that the plating industry recognizes that use of common exhaust systems for these chemicals is hazardous; that the practice in the industry is to vent these chemicals separately; that its own expert testified that the ventilation system constituted a hazard; and that Pratt & Whitney permitted cigarette smoking in the plating department, thus enhancing the danger of a fire or an explosion.

With respect to HCN formation, Pratt & Whitney points out that the OSHA compliance officer did not make any tests to detect the presence of HCN at any of the locations where it was alleged that the gas could form. Petitioner, however, tested for HCN concentration at each of the seven stacks on the roof, and not a trace of HCN was detected. The testing device, according to petitioner's employee, Mr. Dunstan, was sensitive to one-hundredth of the acceptable exposure limit of HCN. Tests were also performed to determine whether HCN was being formed in the common ducts as alleged. These tests also proved to be negative. Contrary to the contention of the Secretary, the company's expert witness, Mr. Doyle, testified before Judge Gold that he had seen plating lines in different companies that used common ducts and individual duct systems. Mr. Doyle testified that the results of the tests performed by the company's employee, Mr. Dunstan, were satisfactory. He concluded that the common duct system posed no hazard of HCN formation. In connection with the Secretary's allegation that heated oil mists or acetic acid could combine in the ducts with hydrogen peroxide vapors and create a hazard of fire or explosion, Mr. Dunstan concluded that such a reaction "will not likely occur." Jt.App. 478–80.

After a full administrative hearing, Judge Gold set aside the citation. Judge Gold stated: Complainant's evidence does not demonstrate the existence of hydrogen cyanide gas or peracetic acid in the common duct system. It does not establish that the hydrogen peroxide and slushing oil combine in the common duct. The Secretary has presented textbook theory, without obtaining readily available information which would show whether there existed at Respondent's facility those specific conditions required for the creation of a fire, explosion, or chemical reaction hazard. He has offered nothing more than conjecture. In addition, he suggests that a hazard might arise * * * by virtue of a ventilation breakdown, malfunction of the heating systems for the various solutions, spontaneous combustion caused by mechanical failure, a down-draft of effluent or "by some yet unimagined happening." We have no showing of any reasonable likelihood of such mishaps; the Secretary might just as well have suggested the possibilities of arson or insurrection. Jt.App. 50.

Despite the emphatic language employed by Judge Gold in his opinion setting aside this violation, the OSHRC reversed, stating:

> Section 1910.94(d)(7)(iii) is violated whenever the same exhaust system is used to remove two or more substances, when either one or a combination of the substances *may* constitute a fire, explosion or chemical reaction hazard in the duct system. The use of the word "may" makes it clear that a violation is established whenever a hazardous combination of the substances is possible. It is not necessary to prove that the chemical reaction is reasonably likely or that the prohibited hazards actually threaten employees at the time of the inspection. The standard is directed toward the control of possible or potential hazards. *Cf. Brennan v. OSHRC (Underhill Construction Corp.),* 513 F.2d 1032, 1039 (2d Cir.1975).

Jt.App. 81 (emphasis in original). The OSHRC determined that the evidence proffered by the Secretary demonstrated "the realistic possibility" both that HCN could be formed and that fire or explosion could result from a reaction in the duct of heated oil and either hydrogen peroxide or peracetic acid. The Commission concluded that "[d]espite the relatively low likelihood of an incident, a large number of employees could be immediately exposed if an incident occurred * * * [and] the consequences of employee exposure would be severe." Jt.App. 83.

Pratt & Whitney does not dispute that an occurrence of the hazardous reactions in its common duct system might be "possible." However, it is argued that a mere possibility that a chemical reaction might occur in its duct system is insufficient to support a violation of the safety regulation involved. Since there is no question that substantial evidence supports the OSHRC's determination under a "possibility" standard, our inquiry is limited to determining whether the OSHRC's interpretation of § 1910.94(d)(7)(iii) is valid. * * *

In a plurality decision, the Supreme Court stated in *Industrial Union Department, AFL–CIO v. American Petroleum Institute,* 448 U.S. 607, 100 S.Ct. 2844, 65 L.Ed.2d 1010 (1980) (*"Benzene"* case), that OSHA

> was not designed to require employers to provide absolutely risk-free workplaces whenever it is technologically feasible to do so, so long as the cost is not great enough to destroy an entire industry. Rather, both the language and structure of the Act, as well as its legislative history, indicate that it was intended to require the elimination, as far as feasible, of significant risks of harm.

448 U.S. at 641, 100 S.Ct. at 2864. The Court placed principal reliance upon § 3(8) of the Act, 29 U.S.C. § 652(8) (1976), in reaching this conclusion, stating:

By empowering the Secretary to promulgate standards that are "reasonably necessary or appropriate to provide safe or healthful employment and places of employment," the Act implies that, before promulgating any standard, the Secretary must make a finding that the workplaces in question are not safe. But "safe" is not the equivalent of "risk-free." There are many activities that we engage in every day—such as driving a car or even breathing city air—that entail some risk of accident or material health impairment; nevertheless, few people would consider these activities "unsafe." Similarly, a workplace can hardly be considered "unsafe" unless it threatens the workers with a significant risk of harm.

Therefore, before he can promulgate any permanent health or safety standard, the Secretary is required to make a threshold finding that a place of employment is unsafe—in the sense that significant risks are present and can be eliminated or lessened by a change in practice. 448 U.S. at 642, 100 S.Ct. at 2864. Thus, the *Benzene* case clearly teaches that the Act is intended only to guard against significant risks, not ephemeral possibilities. It follows that § 1910.94(d)(7)(iii) can properly be interpreted as proscribing an employer's use of a common exhaust system only where there exists a "significant risk" that a combination of the substances removed will cause a fire, explosion, or chemical reaction hazard. The risk must be something more than a mere possibility. The term "possible" can embrace anything that falls "within the bounds of what may * * * occur * * * within the framework of nature." Webster's Third New International Dictionary, *supra*. The occurrence of a freakish event constitutes a possibility, but we believe, especially in light of the Supreme Court's decision in the *Benzene* case, that safety standards may not be so broadly interpreted so as to embrace such slight risks of harm. We are convinced that the test employed by the OSHRC—that "a violation is established whenever a hazardous combination is possible"—would permit this safety standard to be applied to conditions posing insignificant risks that are beyond the scope of the Act. Thus, the decision of the OSHRC concerning this violation must be set aside. * * *

Based on the record before us, we cannot predict whether the OSHRC will conclude that the common ductwork at Pratt & Whitney's plant poses a *significant risk* of fire, explosion, or dangerous chemical reaction in violation of § 1910.94(d)(7)(iii). We feel compelled to point out, however, that implicit in the opinion of the ALJ is a determination that the Secretary failed to establish even the remotest possibility of such mishaps occurring. Judge Gold opined that "the Secretary might just as well have suggested the possibilities of arson or insurrection." Jt.App. 50. Clearly, Judge Gold would have held, under the appropriate test, that the Secretary failed to carry his burden of proof that the ductwork in petitioner's plating department posed a significant risk of a hazardous incident. In remanding this action we are constrained to remind the OSHRC that the burden of proof was upon the Secretary to demonstrate the violation by a preponderance of the evidence, *Olin Construction Co. v. OSHRC,* 525 F.2d

464, 466 (2d Cir.1975) (per curiam). That the scope of review available to the courts to scrutinize such agency determinations is strictly limited by the substantial evidence test in no way relieves the OSHRC of its obligation to determine whether the Secretary has established alleged violations of OSHA health or safety standards by a preponderance of the proof. Moreover, while the OSHRC is not bound to accept the factual findings of the ALJ, the latter's determinations are entitled to some weight and should not be disturbed without explanation. As Judge Lumbard stated in *NLRB v. Interboro Contractors, Inc.,* 388 F.2d 495, 499 (2d Cir.1967):

> [T]he Board's supporting evidence, in cases where it rejects the examiner's findings, must be stronger than would be required in cases where the findings are accepted, since in the former cases the supporting evidence must be deemed substantial when measured against the examiner's contrary findings as well as the opposing evidence.

Indeed, the Supreme Court in *Universal Camera Corp. v. NLRB,* 340 U.S. 474, 71 S.Ct. 456, 95 L.Ed. 456 (1951), indicated that the reviewing commission of an agency should show at least some deference to the factual findings of the ALJ:

> We do not require that the examiner's findings be given more weight than in reason and in the light of judicial experience they deserve. The "substantial evidence" standard is not modified in any way when the Board and its examiner disagree. We intend only to recognize that evidence supporting a conclusion may be less substantial when an impartial, experienced examiner who has observed the witnesses and lived with the case has drawn conclusions different from the Board's than when he has reached the same conclusion.

340 U.S. at 496, 71 S.Ct. at 468. In arriving at its determination that the ductwork of petitioner's plant posed a possibility that a hazardous event might occur, the OSHRC relied upon the "textbook theory" rejected by Judge Gold. Additionally, the OSHRC noted that the Secretary's expert, Mr. Padden, had not recalled seeing similar ductwork in the "100 or so" other plating departments he had visited. The latter testimony, however, conflicted with that of petitioner's expert, Mr. Doyle, who testified that of the plants he had visited, "some had individual ducts over the plating baths, * * * and others had common ducts." Furthermore, petitioner conducted scientific tests which revealed not a trace of the dangerous substances that the Secretary claimed might form. On remand, the OSHRC is obligated to weigh carefully all of the latter evidence in determining whether the Secretary has demonstrated by a preponderance of the evidence that the common ductwork at petitioner's plant violated § 1910.94(d)(7)(iii). Again, we express no view as to the proper outcome of this reconsideration; our concern is rather to assure that all the evidence is given appropriate weight and that the conclusion reached is adequately supported by a reasoned explanation.

The citation for this violation is set aside and remanded to the Commission for further proceedings consistent with this opinion.

### E.  The Non–Serious Violations

Petitioner seeks review of several non-serious violations for which it was cited. We find that only one of these merits discussion. At the heat treatment department in petitioner's North Haven plant, small metal parts are moved to and from a heating furnace on a contraption called a "spider." (See illustration in appendix). The spider consists of four circular trays arranged vertically on an axle. It weighs approximately 875 pounds and is about six feet tall. The spider hangs from the hook of an overhead crane, and is lifted about 4½ feet when being moved. Thus, while in motion, the top tray of the spider is about 10½ feet from the ground. A single employee stands about 2½ feet from the spider while it is moving. Each of the trays on the spider is bordered by a one inch lip to keep the small metal parts from falling.

The OSHA compliance officer cited petitioner for a violation of 29 C.F.R. § 1910.132(a) (1980), which requires necessary protective equipment for jobsite hazards, for failing to provide the operator of the spider with a hard hat. The OSHRC affirmed the violation, finding that "the employee was exposed to the hazard of parts falling on his head from the higher trays." Jt.App. 91–92.

Pratt & Whitney contends, as it did below, that the manner in which the spider was operated did not present a hazard to the employee operating it. The company claims that it was unreasonable for the OSHRC to conclude that metal parts could somehow be propelled off a tray of the spider over the one inch lip, travel over 2½ feet horizontally in the air, and strike an operator in the head. Petitioner notes that the tremendous weight of the spider makes it very difficult to jostle and points out that it travels at only 1½ miles per hour. Pratt & Whitney also claims that the Secretary offered absolutely no evidence to show under what circumstances the spider could be jostled other than the bare allegation that it could run into another employee.

Section 1910.132(a) provides in pertinent part:

> Protective equipment, including personal protective equipment for eyes, face, head, and extremities * * * shall be provided, used, and maintained * * * wherever it is necessary by reason of hazards or processes or environment.

29 C.F.R. § 1910.132(a) (1980). "To impart the requisite specificity to this provision, courts, construing it * * * have implied a general 'reasonableness' standard." *American Airlines, Inc. v. Secretary of Labor*, 578 F.2d 38, 41 (2d Cir.1978). The test adopted by this Circuit in the *American Airlines* case requires the OSHRC to determine whether a reasonable man familiar with the conditions of the industry would have instituted the protective measure which the Commission claims the alleged violator failed to implement. Our decision in *American Airlines* antedated the OSHRC's order in this case by almost two years; yet, the Commission nevertheless failed to make the required finding. We cannot, on the basis of the record before us, determine as a matter of law what result should be reached on

that issue. The order of the OSHRC affirming the violation of § 1910.132(a) is vacated and remanded for proceedings consistent with this opinion.

## Summary

The citation for the serious violation of the general duty clause is affirmed. The citations for violations of §§ 1910.94(d)(7)(iii) and 1910.132(a) are vacated and remanded for further proceedings consistent with this opinion. The remainder of the citations for the non-serious violations are affirmed. Each party shall bear its own costs.

## NOTES AND QUESTIONS

1. Could the use of a common drain for storage areas of acids and cyanides be a "recognized hazard" if it was customary in the industry and only a minority in the industry used separate drains?

2. In *Nelson Tree Services v. OSHRC*, 60 F.3d 1207 (6th Cir.1995), the employer was trimming and cutting trees obstructing utility lines. A tree, which was in the process of being cut, unexpectedly fell prematurely and killed an employee who was crossing in front of it. The employer argued that in utility line clearance, this was not a recognized hazard because, unlike in the logging industry, trees were typically topped before felling the trees. The court ignored arguments of industry practice saying, "simply put, it is dangerous for persons to walk in front of a notched tree." The court emphasized that the "potential hazard" could be easily avoided by preventing employees from entering the area where the tree would fall. The employer's actual knowledge of the hazard is sufficient to establish a recognized hazard.

3. Judge Learned Hand stated the tort standard of negligence in the algebraic formula of whether the burden of precaution (B) is less than the injury (L), multiplied by the probability (P) of the accident occurring. The standard of negligence has been identified by economists as the appropriate standard to induce a level of care in which potential tort feasor has incentive to undertake all the precautions for which the expected benefits of those precautions exceed the costs. How does the duty imposed by the general duty standard differ from this? Should it differ?

4. The common ductwork violation was not based on the general duty clause but on a specific standard. When the court interprets the words of the standard "may constitute a fire, explosion, or chemical reaction hazard" as requiring a "significant risk" does the standard impose any greater or different duty than would be imposed by the general duty clause? Can there be a "significant risk" without "recognized hazard"? On remand, the Commission reaffirmed its earlier findings, applying a "significant risk" approach. The court found the Commission's application of this approach unsatisfying and set aside the order affirming the citation. *Pratt & Whitney Aircraft Division v. Donovan*, 715 F.2d 57 (2d Cir. 1983).

5. The citation for failing to provide hard hats to an employee working near the "spider" was for violation of a special standard. Does this standard provide any specific guidance or notice to the employer? Why would the

Secretary promulgate such a standard, rather than relying on the general duty clause?

6. The Commission long held that an employer could not be cited for violation of the general duty clause when a specific standard was available. The rationale was that specific standards were intended to be the primary method of achieving the policies of the Act. This misstated formalistic rule has been reshaped by the courts.

In *Usery v. Marquette Cement Manufacturing Co.*, 568 F.2d 902 (2d Cir.1977), the employer was relining a kiln. The worn-out bricks were placed in a chute which led to an alley twenty-six feet below. The alley had no warning sign or barricade. An employee walking through the alley was struck by a load of bricks and instantly killed. The Secretary's complaint charged the employer with violating a specific standard of the construction industry concerning demolition of buildings. Because relining a kiln is not "construction" the Secretary moved at the hearing to amend the charge to allege a violation of the general duty clause. The Commission held that the complaint could not be amended. The court reversed and held that the employer could be held for a violation of the general duty clause, stating "it scarcely requires expertise in the industry to recognize that it is hazardous to dump bricks from an unenclosed chute into an unbarricaded alleyway." 568 F.2d at 910.

Similarly, in *International Union, UAW v. General Dynamics Land Systems Division*, 815 F.2d 1570 (D.C.Cir.1987) the court held that although the alleged violation of a specific standard was not proven, an employer could be found in violation of the general duty clause where the employer's own accident experience should have led it to recognize that the specific standard was not adequate to protect its employees from the hazard.

These were cases where a specific duty was alleged, but the specific duty was not applicable. *New York State Electric & Gas Corp. v. Secretary of Labor*, 88 F.3d 98 (2d Cir.1996), presented the obverse situation. The complaint alleged a violation of the general duty clause, but this was not applicable. The Commission *sua sponte* amended the charge to find a violation of a special duty, and this was upheld by the court. "The pivotal question," said the court, "is whether prejudice would result." Id. at 104.

7. The same conduct may violate the general duty clause and also one or more specific standards. Is there any reason why the employer should not be cited for either or both so long as only one fine is assessed?

8. In *R.L. Sanders Roofing Co. v. OSHRC*, 620 F.2d 97 (5th Cir.1980), a roofer fell from a flat roof on which he was working. The employer was cited for violation of the general duty clause for having employees working on the roof with no perimeter guard. A standard promulgated for the roofing industry required guard rails on sloped roofs where the slope of the roof was greater than four inches in twelve inches. The court held that the presence of the standard, which did not require guard rails on sloped roofs with slopes of four inches in twelve inches or less, impliedly exempted flat roofs from the requirement because the "accepted industry practice in roofing is not to use perimeter guard rails." It is "an obvious danger to which roofers are highly conscious." A safety standard, said the court, "must give an employer fair warning of the conduct it prohibits or requires." 620 F.2d at 100. Could the

employer in this situation reasonably believe that he was not required to install guard rails?

## CATERPILLAR INC. v. OCCUPATIONAL SAFETY AND HEALTH REVIEW COMMISSION

United States Court of Appeals, Seventh Circuit, 1997
122 F.3d 437

CUMMINGS JR., CIRCUIT JUDGE:

Petitioner Caterpillar Inc. ("Caterpillar") appeals a final decision of the Occupational Safety and Health Review Commission (the "Commission") issued September 4, 1996. This case arises out of an accident at Caterpillar's East Peoria, Illinois, facility involving the repair of a 6,000–ton forging press called the Erie 6000. The repair procedure required use of a gear pulling device that had four steel studs on it, each weighing 35 to 40 pounds and measuring 42 inches in length and 1 3/4 inches in diameter. The accident occurred when a steel stud broke off during the repair operation and was propelled 121 feet, where it hit an employee in the head, causing serious injury.

After the accident, the Secretary issued a citation alleging that Caterpillar willfully violated Section 5(a)(1), 29 U.S.C. § 654(a)(1)—the "general duty clause"—of the Occupational Safety and Health Act of 1970 (the "Act"), 29 U.S.C. § 651 *et seq.* The Administrative Law Judge (the "ALJ") assigned to the case affirmed the citation and assessed a penalty of $30,000. The Commission agreed with the ALJ that Caterpillar's violation of Section 5(a)(1) was willful, but concluded that a penalty of $49,000, the amount originally requested by the Secretary, was appropriate.

This Court has jurisdiction over the appeal pursuant to Section 11(a) of the Act, 29 U.S.C. § 660(a).

### Facts; Standard of Review

At issue in this case is a citation issued on or about January 13, 1993, by the Occupational Safety and Health Administration ("OSHA"). The citation alleged a violation of Section 5(a)(1) of the Act in that:

> On or about July 16, 1992, in building BB at the Erie 6,000 ton forging press, employees were exposed to the hazard of being struck by broken parts thrown through the air during maintenance procedures. The equipment, including the studs, as used in an attempt to pull the Erie 6,000 ton press's clutch hub off of its shaft, did not have a safety factor of four-to-one and the equipment was neither guarded nor retained.

In July 1992, a bearing failed on the hub of the Erie 6000, a 6,000–ton forging press that forges the track links of earthmoving equipment. As a result, the hub had to be removed from its crank shaft so that new bearings could be inserted, and Caterpillar scheduled this maintenance procedure for July 15, 1992, during a previously planned production shutdown. Prior to the operation, Ronald Williams, the day shift's lead repairman, met with his supervisor of three months, James Rhodes. As discussed below, prior to this time, Williams had held detailed discussions with his previous supervisor about his safety concerns regarding this type of operation and had made multiple suggestions regarding possible safety precautions. During his meeting with Rhodes, however, Williams suggested only that warning signs be posted and the area be cordoned off. Rhodes agreed and took care of the matter.

To remove the hub, Williams and two co-workers assembled a gear pulling device, which consisted in part of four steel studs screwed into the face of the hub, two on each side. Using two large hydraulic jacks, an outward pressure was placed against the hub. As had happened in the past with this type of assembled gear puller, when a high degree of pressure was placed on the steel bars spanning the area across the face of the crank shaft between the paired studs uneven pressure could cause the studs to bend or break.

The operation at issue in this case began during the night shift on July 15, 1992. That crew did not successfully remove the hub and quit after a stud snapped and a fragment flew 25 feet. Richard Hill, the night-shift supervisor, was in the vicinity and was aware of the broken stud and had observed studs break during maintenance operations on another forging press. Hill told Rhodes about the stud break, but Williams, the worker in charge of the pull, was not advised. The next day when Williams began preparing for the pull, he noticed that the area in front of the Erie 6000 was not "taped off" even though warning tape had been placed 40 to 60 feet away from the sides of the press, so he and Rhodes moved the warning tape to a distance of 90 to 100 feet away from the press on all sides. Williams warned Caterpillar employees Bonner and Dunn, who were performing unrelated work, that the operation was about to begin, and the men moved out of the way. However, when the crew began the pulling procedure, one of the studs broke, and the fragment, which weighed over nine pounds, flew 121 feet through the air. It struck Dunn in the back of the head, causing serious injury.

This was not the first experience Caterpillar had had with flying studs. In the Spring of 1989, Williams and a crew removed the hub on the Erie 6000 press in order to fix the brake wheel. During the process one of the studs broke and a fragment flew 60 feet through the air, stopping finally when it hit a heavy metal cabinet. The force of the impact indented the cabinet three inches. Both maintenance foreman Clay Parker (Williams's supervisor prior to Rhodes) and the shop superintendent, Darrel Seeyle, were aware of the incident. The stud came within 20–25 feet of hitting Seeyle.

During a July 1989 pull, the crew removed the hub from the other side of the Erie 6000 press, with Williams again acting as leadman. Eight to ten studs broke and flew during this procedure, one of the studs flying

35 to 40 feet and leaving a half-inch dent in the metal of a crane (co-incidentally, it was the accident victim in 1992, Dunn, who narrowly escaped injury from this stud).

As a result of these experiences, Williams had repeatedly requested, and repeatedly been denied, enhanced safety precautions. At various times, Williams suggested the use of: (i) a "furnace curtain," which was rejected by Parker as too expensive and time consuming; (ii) tapered studs, which were also rejected by Parker after one use as too expensive and time consuming; (iii) an "H-beam fixture," which was discussed with other employees, including a mechanical technician who was a member of management, but nothing came of the idea; and (iv) a "bridge" device of several pieces of plate welded together with bracing, which Parker rejected without comment.

This Court's review of the Commission's order is limited to a determination whether the factual basis of the Commission's decision is based upon substantial evidence and whether the legal basis for the decision is arbitrary or capricious and in accordance with law. Administrative Procedure Act, 5 U.S.C. § 706. Caterpillar's primary argument on appeal is that it took precautions commensurate with the foreseen hazards of the Erie 6000 operation by assigning the project to a skilled and experienced tradesman (Williams) with a positive safety record. It states the issue as being "whether an employer may rely on its assignment of a complicated and potentially hazardous skilled-trades level task to a skilled trades-trained employee, as a method of meeting the employer's obligations" under the general duty clause (Br. at 2). Caterpillar urges us to find that the Commission's decision was arbitrary and capricious and departed from prior Commission precedent and the applicable statutory scheme.

**The Commission's finding that Caterpillar's violation of the general duty clause was willful is fully supported by Commission precedent and is not arbitrary or capricious**

\* \* \* \* Commission precedent clearly establishes that a general duty clause violation requires the following elements: (i) the existence of a hazard likely to cause death or serious physical harm; (ii) the employer's recognition (*i.e.,* awareness) of the hazard; (iii) the availability of feasible means to abate the hazard; and (iv) the employer's failure to implement the feasible means of abatement. See *Secretary of Labor v. Kastalon, Inc.,* 1986 WL 53514, \*4 (O.S.H.R.C.). Of these factors, at issue in this appeal is, first, whether Caterpillar was aware of the hazard of studs shooting into the workplace during the type of maintenance procedure on the Erie 6000 that took place in July 1992, and, second, whether Caterpillar failed to implement a feasible means of abatement. An OSHA violation is willful if it is committed with intentional disregard of, or plain indifference to, the requirements of the statute. See *Valdak Corp. v. O.S.H.R.C.,* 73 F.3d 1466, 1468 (8th Cir.1996); *Ensign–Bickford Co. v. O.S.H.R.C.,* 717 F.2d 1419, 1422 (D.C.Cir.1983), *certiorari denied,* 466 U.S. 937, 104 S.Ct. 1909, 80 L.Ed.2d 458 (collecting cases). A willful violation "is differentiated from other types of violations by a heightened awareness—of the illegality of the conduct or conditions—and by a state of mind-conscious disregard or plain indifference." *Secretary of Labor v. Calang Corp.,* 1990 WL 140086, *2 (O.S.H.R.C.) (citations omitted).

The Commission's finding of willfulness was based on its conclusion that, in accordance with "well settled" principles of agency law, an employer is imputed with its supervisor's knowledge of a hazardous condition, even if the supervisor subsequently departs the employ of the employer, ... It found that Caterpillar was attempting to evade responsibility for its conduct by looking at the knowledge of Rhodes and its other new supervisory personnel in 1992, rather than looking back to the knowledge of the supervisors in place during the 1989 operations. In response, the Commission noted that it was Caterpillar's responsibility to disseminate to those entrusted with the health and safety of its employees the knowledge possessed by it regarding the "pervasive and continuing nature" of the flying stud problem. See *id.* at 3. In other words, it concluded that Caterpillar's "heightened awareness" of the problem remained with the corporation despite any turnover in personnel. See *id.* at 3–4.

After finding a "heightened awareness" of the problem, the Commission also concluded that Caterpillar showed a "plain indifference to employee safety" when it simply delegated authority to Williams, "whose prior safety concerns it had rebuffed," again citing *Tampa Shipyards. Id.* at 4. It noted that Caterpillar had both knowledge of the hazard and abundant resources to evaluate and abate it and found that Caterpillar's installation of the tape barrier and warning signs for the procedure at issue were not an "objectively reasonable means of abatement, especially where employees involved in the hub-pulling procedure were located within it." *Id.* at 4–5.

Caterpillar claims that it took all steps required by the general duty clause when it put Williams, a skilled craftsman, in charge of the operation and relied on him to make appropriate safety recommendations to his supervisor, Rhodes. We agree with the Commission's analysis, however. The mere fact that Parker and Seeyle, who both indisputably were aware of the hazard, ceased to be Williams's supervisors before the 1992 pull does not cancel Caterpillar's knowledge (*i.e.,* heightened awareness) of the risks of the operations and its responsibility for their impact on Williams and the safety of the operation. ... To hold otherwise would encourage corporate forgetfulness with possibly serious safety consequences. These supervisors consistently rejected Williams's recommendations for protecting workers from the flying studs. In light of these rejections, Caterpillar cannot now argue that it reasonably relied on Williams to ensure the safety of the hub pulling operation in 1992.

We also find that the Commission's conclusion that such reliance showed a plain indifference to employee safety—a prerequisite to a finding of willfulness—is supported by substantial evidence and Commission precedent and is neither arbitrary nor capricious. ... The ALJ's findings of fact, as adopted by the Commission, demonstrate this. Caterpillar became aware as early as 1989 that when studs broke from the hub, fragments were propelled erratically in different directions and for different distances. Despite this knowledge, and despite two incidents in which employees were nearly struck by flying fragments, Caterpillar rejected or ignored the recommendations of the very person it had put on the projects to eliminate the hazard. Williams had neither the power nor the authority independently to implement his rejected safety measures, nor could he commit Caterpillar resources to the measures. Caterpillar cannot now claim that it is not guilty of a willful violation because it put Williams in charge of the pull operation and relied on his expertise. The fact that Williams did not suggest additional safety measures during the July 1992 operation appears understandable given the rejection of his many suggestions over the preceding three years, and it does not excuse Caterpillar's failure to implement additional safety measures. After all, "[r]esponsibility under the Act for ensuring that employees do not put themselves into any unsafe position rests ultimately upon each employer, not the employees, and employers may not shift their responsibility onto their employees." *Secretary of Labor v. V.I.P. Structures, Inc.*, 1994 WL 362276, *3 (O.S.H.R.C.).

Caterpillar emphasizes that certain structural changes were made to the Erie 6000 press after 1989 to avoid the "galling" that had caused the studs to break off during the 1989 pulling operation and that, as noted above, the hub of the Erie 6000 was removed without incident during 1991. However, on the evening of July 15, 1992, the night *before* Dunn was struck by a flying stud fragment, galling occurred while the crew was removing the hub, causing a stud to snap and a fragment to fly through the air, just as had happened during the 1989 operation. Rhodes was aware of the stud break that evening. It should have been obvious then, if not before, that whatever modifications had been made to the press were not sufficient to eliminate the risk of flying studs.

Good faith efforts at compliance that are incomplete or not entirely effective can negate a willfulness finding provided that they were objectively reasonable under the circumstances. See *Tampa Shipyards*, 1992 WL 52938 at *10. However, we agree with the Commission that in this case Caterpillar's decision in July 1992 to install warning tape and signs was not an objectively reasonable safety plan. As the Commission noted, the tape certainly offered no protection to employees working within the danger zone and Caterpillar had no way of knowing on July 16, 1992, that a 100–foot zone would be adequate, given that a previous stud had been shot out to 60 feet, stopping only when it slammed into a steel cabinet, leaving a three-inch dent (the safety zone of 40–60 feet on the sides only of the Erie 6000 on July 15, 1992, was without question inadequate).

Despite Caterpillar's urging, this Court's decision in *McLaughlin v. Union Oil Co. of California*, 869 F.2d 1039 (7th Cir.1989), does not lead to a contrary result. In that case, this Court found that the employer's failure to inspect a pressure vessel for microscopic hydrogen stress corrosion cracking was merely negligent and not "willful." However, the Court emphasized as part of its reasoning that there had never been a serious accident to such a pressure vessel by reason of hydrogen stress corrosion cracking. See id. at 1047. We believe the facts of this case are simply distinguishable: Caterpillar's failure to take reasonable safety precautions after it was actually aware from other near-accidents that flying stud fragments posed a danger is far different conduct than Union Oil's failure to discover microscopic cracking before any accident had resulted or visibly been threatened.

Likewise, Caterpillar puts much emphasis on the Commission's decision in *Secretary of Labor v. Connecticut Light & Power Co.*, 1989 WL 223325 (O.S.H.R.C.), wherein it stated that, "An employer is justified in placing a great deal of reliance on the judgment of highly experienced and trained employees with good safety records." *Id.* at *6. However, Caterpillar's selective quote miscomprehends the thrust of the Commission's decision in that case. Unlike Caterpillar in this case, Connecticut Light & Power had not put an employee in charge of ensuring other employees' safety. The Commission found that Connecticut Light & Power had not violated the general duty clause because it had a very detailed safety protocol in place, which employees were expected to follow. It concluded that the Secretary had failed to meet her burden of proving the inadequacy of the safety program because she did not establish that the accident was the result of inadequate training or that more supervision by the foremen would have been both feasible and useful. It found instead that the employees involved in the accident were trained adequately to recognize the hazard posed by an energized lightning arrestor and that the company was justified in relying on those employees to discover the hazard and take proper precautions. *Id.* at *4–5.

Caterpillar's situation is completely different than that of Connecticut Light & Power. In this case, Caterpillar would like us to find that, because it "relied" on the expertise of Williams (while repeatedly rejecting or ignoring his recommendations), it did not violate the general duty clause. But, unlike Connecticut Light, it had no safety protocol in place and it had not trained Dunn, the accident victim, to recognize the hazard posed by flying studs. Unlike the injured Connecticut Light employee, who had been extensively briefed on safety issues, Dunn could not have been expected to take care of himself under the circumstances. Under Caterpillar's formulation, an employer would have almost no duty at all to its employees so long as it found one employee to take charge of a known, dangerous activity.

In light of the foregoing, the Commission's conclusion that Caterpillar willfully violated the Act's "general duty" clause is affirmed.

### The penalty was appropriate

Penalties under the Act must take into account the size of the employer's business, the gravity of the violation, the good faith of the employer and the employer's history of previous violations. See 29 U.S.C. § 661(j). The Commission increased the penalty imposed by the ALJ, finding that Caterpillar was not entitled to credit for good faith, which the ALJ had given, reasoning that Caterpillar's violation had been willful and that abatement had been prompted only by the accident at issue and not done independently before anyone was hurt. See Commission Decision at 6. After crediting Caterpillar only for its generally positive history with respect to previous violations, it determined that the proposed penalty of $49,000 was appropriate.

Caterpillar argues only that the Commission erred when it refused to give Caterpillar good faith credit, because Caterpillar co-operated in the accident investigation and immediately corrected identified hazards. It asserts that the Commission's theory is inconsistent with the policies of the Act and that the Commission's decision should be vacated, but it does so without citation to any legal authority that would lead us to agree.

This Court will not overturn the sanction imposed by the Commission unless it is unwarranted in law or without justification in fact. See *Butz v. Glover Livestock Commission Co., Inc.*, 411 U.S. 182, 185–186, 93 S.Ct. 1455, 1457, 36 L.Ed.2d 142; *Valdak*, 73 F.3d at 1470. The Commission's decision clearly reflects consideration of the statutory criteria and a careful review of the facts of the case. The penalty imposed by the Commission appropriately reflected the statutory criteria and was supported by the record.

The order of the Commission is AFFIRMED.

### NOTES AND QUESTIONS

1. The proof necessary to establish exposure to a hazard was summarized in *Mineral Industries & Heavy Construction Group v. OSHRC*, 639 F.2d 1289, 1294 (5th Cir.1981):

> The OSHRC need not prove that a given employee was actually endangered by the unsafe condition, but only that it was reasonably certain that employee was or would be exposed to that danger * * * The goal of the Act is to prevent the first accident, not to serve as a source of consolation for the first victim or his survivors. Hence, no proof of a specific instance where employees were exposed to the hazardous condition is necessary to support the finding of a violation.

In the words of the court in *Daniel International Corp. v. Donovan*, 705 F.2d 382, 388 (10th Cir.1983), "the Secretary need show only the existence of the hazardous condition and its accessibility to employees." Where an employer was cited for failing to require employees to wear hard hats, it was not necessary to show actual exposure to risk, but only "access to an area of danger." "Imminent risk of injury or death to employees should not be required before the Secretary can compel protective action." *Donovan v. Adams Steel Erection, Inc.*, 766 F.2d 804, 811 (3d Cir.1985).

2. Note that the opinion in *Caterpillar, Inc.* articulates a four-element burden of proof, rather than the three-element burden articulated in *Pratt &*

*Whitney.* Where no accident has occurred, the employer may appropriately insist that OSHA identify what additional preventative measures would be effective and feasible. But when an employee has been severely injured or killed, should the burden be on the employer to show that the accident was unavoidable? Where possible preventative measures are so self-evident as in this case, should the Commission be able to take judicial notice of them?

3. In *Titanium Metals Corp. of America v. Usery,* 579 F.2d 536 (9th Cir.1978), the employer was cited for a serious violation of the general duty clause following an explosion and fire which fatally burned an employee. The employer conceded that titanium dust was highly flammable, but pointed out that it was impossible to mass produce titanium without creating some dust. It argued that because the industry was in its infancy, no precise standards had developed as to what levels of accumulation of dust created a danger of explosion or serious fires. There was, therefore, no "recognized hazard * * * likely to cause death or serious injury." The court held that the lack of a precise standard was no defense. There was a recognized hazard of fire. This imposed on the employer the burden of minimizing accumulations to the extent feasible; "to err on the side of greater, not lesser caution." The Secretary had presented evidence that there were feasible measures for reducing the risk of explosion or major fire by daily sweepdowns and frequent washdowns of the area, elimination of sources of sparks, and cleaning up of spilled oil. The employer had violated its general duty by not taking known feasible measures to reduce the likelihood of a fire causing death or serious injury.

4. The definition of "willful" has been snarled in a semantic thicket. "Moral turpitude" or "malicious intent" is not required. Some courts say that the conduct must be voluntary with "an intentional disregard or plain indifference to the Act's requirement." See *McKie Ford, Inc. v. Secretary of Labor,* 191 F.3d 853, 856 (8th Cir.1999). The Third Circuit uses stronger words: "Willfulness connotes defiance or such reckless disregard of consequences as to be equivalent to a knowing, conscious and deliberate flaunting of the Act * * *. [I]t involves an element of obstinate refusal to comply." *Frank Irey Jr., Inc. v. OSHRC,* 519 F.2d 1200, 1207 (3d Cir.1974). This test was expressly repudiated in *Valdak v. OSHRC,* 73 F.3d 1466 (8th Cir.1996). A car wash had a spinning industrial spin dryer for towels. It had an interlocking device to prevent opening the lid while it was still spinning. The interlocking device was not working but the car wash continued to use it. A fifteen year old boy on his third day on the job stuck his arm in the machine while it was still spinning and his arm was severed above the elbow. The court said it was not necessary to show the employer "flaunted" or "obstinately refused." It was enough that the employer "knowingly permits a serious hazard to exist," 73 F.3d at 1469. The First Circuit, in an opinion by then Judge Breyer, added its clarification with the puzzling statement that the offender "need not be consciously aware that the conduct is forbidden at the time he performs it, but his state of mind must be such that, if he were informed of the rule, he would not care." *Brock v. Morello Brothers Construction, Inc.,* 809 F.2d 161, 164 (1st Cir.1987). The Seventh Circuit has indicated that a history of past violation may be relevant in deciding whether a given violation is willful.

*Lakeland Enterprises of Rhinelander, Inc. v. Chao,* 402 F.3d 739 (7th Cir. 2005).

## Note: OSHA Remedies

As already noted, the statute provides for three principal potential remedies: abatement orders, civil penalties, and criminal prosecutions.

Abatement orders can be analogized to "cease and desist" orders under other statutes, since their usual purpose is to require an employer to cease violating a standard or to discontinue a practice that violates the general duty clause. There is, however, a more "action oriented" tenor to OSHA abatement orders, since they affirmatively require the use of safety equipment, or the reduction of noise or dust, or some other affirmative step.

The Act, in Section 17, 29 U.S.C. § 666, sets out the civil penalties for various violations as follows:

Non-serious violations—Up to $7,000

Serious violation—Up to $7,000

Repeated violations—Up to $70,000

Willful violation—$5,000 to $70,000

Failure to correct a violation for which a citation has been issued—Up to $7,000 a day

Penalties are assessed when the citation is issued, but are frequently reduced in negotiations with the employer. If the employer contests the citation, then the ALJ assesses the penalties, subject to review by the Commission, "giving due consideration to the appropriateness of the penalty with respect to the size of the business of the employer being charged, the gravity of the violation, the good faith of the employer, and the history of previous violations."

A "serious" violation is defined by the statute as one where "there is a substantial probability that death or serious physical harm could result." There is no statutory definition of "repeated" or (as discussed in the preceding opinion and Note 4 following) "willful." Originally, for a violation to be repeated the employer had to have violated the standard on at least two previous occasions and "flaunted" the requirements of the statute. *Bethlehem Steel Corp. v. OSHRC,* 540 F.2d 157 (3d Cir.1976). After the 1990 amendments, the court defined "repeated" differently. There must now only be "a Commission final order against the same employer for a substantially similar violation.... A repeated violation requires no more than a second violation and does not require proof of 'flaunting.'" *Reich v. D. M. Sabia Co.,* 90 F.3d 854, 860 (3d Cir.1996).

During the first twenty years of the Act, the assessed penalties were modest, or even nominal. However, since the early 1990's, they have sometimes been more substantial. In 2000, ten companies were assessed fines of more than $400,000, with one of $2,500,000. In *Reich v. Sea Sprite*

*Boat Co. Inc.*, 50 F.3d 413 (7th Cir.1995), the employer ignored a series of citations, filed no protests and did not pay the fines. A settlement was negotiated but the employer ignored the settlement agreement and continued its violations. The OSHA inspector proposed a fine of $35,000 which was not contested nor paid. The Company president said that he decided not to pay because the firm had better use of its money. Finally OSHA obtained a court enforcement order, but the company behaved as if it did not exist. Seven years of defiance was too much for OSHA and it asked the court to hold the company in contempt. After two more years, the court assessed a fine of $2,000 a day from the time the contempt order was issued, $1,452,000, in addition to the $135,000, with any continued violation to be fined at $7,000 a day.

The rare high-dollar penalties are usually associated with violations that OSHA characterizes as "egregious," a term not found in the Act itself. In the case of such "egregious" violations, OSHA may issue separate citations for each employee exposed to a hazard. The courts have not always been receptive to this approach. In *Reich v. Arcadian Corp.* 110 F.3d 1192 (5th Cir. 1997), OSHA issued eighty-seven general duty citations, one for each employee exposed to a single hazard and proposed a $50,000 penalty for each of the eighty-seven violations, for a total $4,350,000. The court held that penalties were to be assessed on the number of hazards, not the number of workers exposed, a decision based largely on the way the particular standard involved in the case was worded. In *Chao v. OSHRC*, 401 F.3d 355 (5th Cir. 2005), on the other hand, the court held that the language of one standard involved would justify using a penalty-per-each-exposed-employee approach, but also found the Secretary's discretionary decision to use that approach "unreasonable" in the circumstances of the case. The preference of some courts for a "per instance" approach has underscored the importance of the record-keeping requirements imposed under the statute. Each failure to record a violation or injury on a required report can constitute an "instance" of a violation, and thus justify a higher total penalty. See, e.g., *Kaspar Wire Works, Inc. v. Secretary of Labor*, 268 F.3d 1123 (D.C. Cir. 2001). As one might expect, the frequency with which the agency has chosen to use the "egregious violation" approach has varied from one administration to another. The proposed penalties for such violations in the first quarter of 2010 seem likely to be the highest ever.

Despite these occasional high penalties, many critics have argued that the typical penalty imposed is far too low, and proposals have been made in Congress fairly often to increase them. As this book goes to press, the Congress is considering the Robert C. Byrd Miner Safety and Health Act (H.R. 5663) which would amend both the 1977 mine safety legislation and the OSH Act to increase civil penalties and make criminal prosecution more likely. The bill was reported out to the House floor on a strict party line vote in July 2010. Its future remains uncertain, given near-unanimous Republican opposition. See generally the criticisms offered by an AFL–CIO attorney in Lynn Rhinehart, *Workers at Risk: The Unfulfilled*

*Promise of the Occupational Safety and Health Act*, 111 W.VaL. Rev. 117 (2008). Attempts to measure the impact of penalties on the subsequent safety records of workplaces have led to mixed conclusions. See Wayne B. Gray and John Mendeloff, *The Declining Effects of OSHA Inspections on Manufacturing Injuries*, 58 INDUS. & LAB. REL. REV. 571 (2005).

Criminal prosecutions under section 17 (e)–(g) are rare, but criminal penalties are sometimes imposed for willful violation causing death to any employee. The punishment may be a fine up to $250,000 for an individual defendant and $500,000 for an organizational defendant. In *United States v. Pitt–Des Moines*, 168 F.3d 976 (7th Cir.1999), the employer failed to properly bolt girders in constructing a post office building in spite of repeated warnings that it was not complying with OSHA standards. As a result, the structure collapsed, killing two ironworkers. The employer was indicted for a criminal violation of the Act and found guilty. The court imposed a fine of $1,000,000, which was upheld on appeal.

In *S. A. Healy Company v. OSHRC*, 138 F.3d 686 (7th Cir.1998), three employees died of a methane explosion. After the Company had been convicted of three criminal violations and fined $750,000, the company was cited for sixty-eight violations of the Act. The employer, in defense, claimed that this constituted double jeopardy. On remand from the Supreme Court (522 U.S. 1025, 118 S.Ct. 623, 139 L.Ed.2d 604 (1997)), the court held that the penalty based on a citation is not a criminal penalty but a civil penalty. The employer can not be imprisoned, and money penalties have not been historically viewed as criminal punishment, and was therefore not double jeopardy.

Obstructing OSHA investigation activity and lying to OSHA compliance officers and other officials about such matters can also lead to significant criminal sentences. See *United States v. Atlantic States Cast Iron Pipe Co.*, 627 F.Supp.2d 180 (D.N.J. 2009).

# H. MULTI–EMPLOYER RESPONSIBILITY

## SOLIS v. SUMMIT CONTRACTORS, INC.

United States Court of Appeals, Eighth Circuit, 2009
558 F.3d 815

GRUENDER, CIRCUIT JUDGE.

The Occupational Safety and Health Review Commission ("OSHRC") held that the Secretary of Labor's ("Secretary") multi-employer worksite policy for "controlling" employers ("controlling employer citation policy") violated agency regulation 29 C.F.R. § 1910.12(a). The controlling employer citation policy provides that the Occupational Safety and Health Administration ("OSHA") may issue citations to general contractors at construction sites who have the ability to prevent or abate hazardous conditions created by subcontractors through the reasonable exercise of supervisory authority regardless of whether the general contractor created the hazard ("creating employer citation policy") or whether the general contractor's own employees were exposed to the hazard ("exposing employer citation policy"). The Secretary filed a petition for review. We grant the petition, vacate OSHRC's order and remand for further proceedings.

## I.  BACKGROUND

Because the development of the controlling employer citation policy provides the framework and context for this case, we start with a historical review of the policy before detailing the relevant factual background.

### A.  The Development of the Controlling Employer Citation Policy

Congress enacted the Occupational Safety and Health Act of 1970 ("OSH Act") to "establish[ ] a comprehensive regulatory scheme designed 'to assure so far as possible . . . safe and healthful working conditions' for 'every working man and woman in the Nation.'" *Martin v. OSHRC*, 499 U.S. 144, 147, 111 S.Ct. 1171, 113 L.Ed.2d 117 (1991) (quoting 29 U.S.C. § 651(b)). The OSH Act assigns distinct regulatory tasks to two different administrative actors: the Secretary and OSHRC. *Id.* The Secretary, through OSHA, creates and enforces workplace health and safety standards. * * * If the Secretary determines that an employer failed to comply with such a standard, the Secretary may issue a citation and assess a monetary penalty. * * * OSHRC carries out the adjudicatory functions of the OSH Act. 29 U.S.C. § 651(b)(3); *Martin*, 499 U.S. at 147, 111 S.Ct. 1171.

The OSH Act describes an employer's duties as follows:

(a)  Each Employer—

(1)  shall furnish to each of his employees employment and a place of employment which are free from recognized hazards that are causing or are likely to cause death or serious physical harm to his employees;

(2)  shall comply with occupational safety and health standards promulgated under this chapter.

*[handwritten margin note: Gen'l spec dutie]*

29 U.S.C. § 654. Subsection (a)(1) creates a general duty running only to an employer's own employees, while subsection (a)(2) creates a specific duty to comply with standards for the good of all employees on a multi-employer worksite. * * *.

Prior to the OSH Act, the Secretary had promulgated health and safety standards for construction sites for federally funded and federally assisted projects under the Construction Safety Act of 1969. 40 U.S.C. § 333, *incorporated into* 40 U.S.C. § 340 U.S.C. §§ 3704, 3705. As part of OSHA's inception, Congress authorized the Secretary to adopt numerous preexisting federal standards, including those of the Construction Safety Act, as OSHA standards without notice-and-comment rulemaking during a period of two years. * * *. In May 1971, the Secretary used his authority to adopt these established construction standards as OSHA standards when he promulgated 29 C.F.R. § 1910.12(a), the regulation at issue in this case, which provides:

> The standards prescribed in part 1926 of this chapter are adopted as occupational safety and health standards under section 6 of the Act and shall apply, according to the provisions thereof, to every employment and place of employment of every employee engaged in construction work. Each employer shall protect the employment and places of employment of each of his employees engaged in construction work by complying with the appropriate standards prescribed in this paragraph.

29 C.F.R. § 1910.12(a); *see* 29 C.F.R. §§ 1910.13–1910.16 (adopting other preexisting federal standards).

Nine days before the Secretary issued this regulation, OSHA published its first Field Operations Manual. This manual established the Secretary's multi-employer worksite policy, a policy that indicates which employers at a multi-employer construction site OSHA could cite for violations. According to this multi-employer worksite policy, OSHA may cite employers who exposed their own employees to hazardous conditions or who created a hazardous condition "endangering employees (whether his own or those of another employer)...." OSHA, Field Operations Manual ¶ 10, at VII–6–8 (May 20, 1971). Hence, the manual's initial multi-employer worksite policy adopted the creating employer and the exposing employer citation policies, but not the controlling employer citation policy.[2]

Initially, OSHRC narrowly construed the multi-employer worksite policy. In *City Wide Tuckpointing Serv. Co.*, OSHRC held that the Secretary could not issue a citation to a subcontractor who created a hazard but whose own employees were not exposed to or affected by the hazard. 3 OSAHRC 194, 195–96, 201 ¶ 6 (1973). In *Gilles & Cotting, Inc.*, a scaffold used by a subcontractor had collapsed and killed two of the subcontractor's employees. 4 OSAHRC 1080, 1080 (1973). None of the employees of the general contractor, Gilles & Cotting, Inc., used or was affected by the scaffold. Nevertheless, on January 29, 1972, the Secretary issued Gilles & Cotting a citation "because as general contractor it had control of the job site...." *Id.* at 1081. This was the first time the Secretary issued a citation based on the controlling employer theory. On review, OSHRC found that Congress intended that the obligations of 29 U.S.C. § 654(a) were "predicated upon the existence of an employment relationship" because § 654(a) imposes duties only on "each employer." *Id.* at 1081–82. Thus, OSHRC held that an employer is responsible for the safety and health of only those employees who work for the employer. Because Gilles & Cotting's own employees were not directly affected by the scaffold

---

**2.** Both the creating employer and the controlling employer citation policies allow OSHA to issue citations to the employer for violations that do not directly affect the employer's own employees.

violation, OSHRC vacated the citation. Other OSHRC cases reaffirmed the City Wide and Gilles decisions * * *

By 1975, two federal courts of appeals began to question these OSHRC decisions. For example, in *Brennan v. OSHRC*, the Second Circuit rejected OSHRC's interpretation of § 654(a) and stated that § 654(a)(2) was "in no way limited to situations where a violation of a standard is linked to exposure of his employees to the hazard." 513 F.2d at 1038. There, the court held that § 654(a)(2) permitted the Secretary to issue citations based on the controlling employer and creating employer citation policies, rejecting the prohibition imposed on these policies by City Wide and Gilles. *Id.* Likewise, in *Anning–Johnson Co. v. OSHRC*, the Seventh Circuit noted in dicta that: "[a]lthough it is not necessary for a decision in the present case, . . . we are not at all sure that a general contractor, who has no employees of his own exposed to a cited violation is necessarily excused from liability under the [OSH] Act." 516 F.2d 1081, 1091 n. 21 (7th Cir.1975).

In light of these decisions, OSHRC retreated from its position in *City Wide and Gilles*. See *Anning–Johnson Co.*, 4 BNA OSHC 1193, 1197, 1975–1976 CCH OSHD ¶ 20,690 (O.S.H.R.C. May 12, 1976) ("We find ourselves in general agreement with the principles enunciated in the cogent opinions of the Second and Seventh Circuit Courts of Appeals."). OSHRC announced its revised position that a contractor who has either created a hazard or controls a hazardous condition has a duty under § 654(a)(2) to comply with OSHA standards even if the contractor's own employees are not exposed to the hazard. *Id.* at 1197–99; *Grossman Steel & Aluminum Corp.*, 4 BNA OSHC 1185, 1188, 1975–1976 CCH OSHD ¶ 20,691 (O.S.H.R.C. May 12, 1976). * * * *

Throughout this period, the Secretary continued to address the multiemployer worksite policy. In 1974, after OSHRC's *City Wide* and *Gilles* decisions, OSHA altered its Field Operations Manual such that the multiemployer worksite policy included only the exposing employer citation policy. OSHA, Field Operations Manual X–14 (Jan. 22, 1974). In April 1976, after the decisions by the Second and Seventh Circuits, the Secretary sought to implement an OSHA regulation for its multi-employer worksite policy that would include the creating employer and the controlling employer citation policies. The Secretary requested public comment on such a proposed regulation. Citation Guidelines in Multi–Employer Worksites Request for Public Comment Notice, 41 Fed.Reg. 17,639, 17,-639–40 (Apr. 27, 1976). However, before the comment period ended on May 27, 1976, OSHRC had decided *Anning–Johnson* and *Grossman Steel*, which allowed the Secretary to issue citations based on the creating employer and controlling employer citation policies. After these decisions, the Secretary discontinued his efforts to promulgate through informal rulemaking an OSH Act regulation for the multi-employer worksite policy.

After 1976, the Secretary occasionally altered the multi-employer worksite policy. In 1981, the correcting employer citation policy was added. It allowed OSHA to issue citations to the employer responsible for correcting the hazard even if its own employees were not exposed to the hazard. OSHA, Field Operations Manual OSHA Instruction CPL 2.49 (Dec. 23, 1981). In 1994, the multi-employer worksite policy was amended to add the creating employer and the controlling employer citation policies. OSHA, Field Inspection Reference Manual OSHA § V.C.6 (Sept. 26, 1994). The current OSHA manual was published in 1999, and its multi-employer worksite policy contains the same four citation policies—exposing employer, correcting employer, creating employer and controlling employer—as the 1994 version. *See* OSHA, Field Inspection Reference Manual OSHA Instruction CPL 2.103 (Dec. 10, 1999).

Since *Anning–Johnson* and *Grossman Steel,* general contractors have challenged the Secretary's authority to cite them for violations when their own employees are not exposed to any hazards related to the violations. See, e.g.,* * * [Marshall v]. *Knutson* [*Constr. Co*], 566 F.2d 596 at 599 (8th Cir. 1977) * * * In *Knutson*, this circuit held that a general contractor, as the controlling employer, has a duty under § 654(a)(2) to protect not only its own employees from safety hazards but all the employees engaged at the worksite. 566 F.2d at 599.But see *Melerine v. Avondale Shipyards, Inc.*, 659 F.2d 706, 710–11 (5th Cir.1981) (holding that § 654(a)(2) does not extend employers' responsibility beyond their own employees). We, therefore, have found that the Secretary has statutory authority for the multi-employer worksite policy, including the controlling employer citation policy. See *Knutson*, 566 F.2d at 599.

Recently, the United States Court of Appeals for the District of Columbia Circuit has questioned whether the Secretary's controlling employer citation policy violates OSHA's regulatory framework. See *Anthony Crane Rental, Inc. v. Reich*, 70 F.3d 1298, 1306 (D.C.Cir.1995); see also *IBP*, 144 F.3d at 865–66. In *Anthony Crane*, the court stated in dicta that "it is not clear to us that the multi-employer [worksite] doctrine is consistent with the Secretary's own construction industry regulation, 29 C.F.R. § 1910.12(a).... [T]he language of § 1910.12 ... is in marked tension with the multi-employer [worksite] doctrine...." 70 F.3d at 1306. However, because it was unnecessary to the outcome of the case, the court indicated that "we leave to a later date the critical decision of whether to apply the multi-employer [worksite] doctrine where an employer has been cited under the construction industry regulations of 29 C.F.R. § 1910.12." Id. at 1307. To date, the only court to have addressed this issue has held that the Secretary's multi-employer worksite policy did not exceed the scope of § 1910.12(a). *Comm'r of Labor v. Weekley Homes, L.P.*, 169 N.C.App. 17, 609 S.E.2d 407, 414–15 (2005).

### B.  Factual Background

In this case, Summit Contractors, Inc. ("Summit") was the general contractor for the construction of a college dormitory in Little Rock, Arkansas. Because Summit had subcontracted the entire project, it had only four employees at the construction site: a project superintendent and three assistant superintendents. Summit subcontracted the exterior brick masonry work to All Phase Construction, Inc. ("All Phase"). On two or three separate occasions, Summit's project superintendent had observed All Phase employees operating without personal fall protection on scaffolds that lacked guardrails. The project superintendent had advised All Phase to correct these problems. However, when All Phase's employees moved the scaffold to another location, they would again work without fall protection and without guardrails.

In June 2003, an OSHA Compliance Safety and Health Officer observed All Phase employees working on scaffolds over ten feet above the ground without fall protection or guardrails in violation of 29 C.F.R. § 1926.451(g)(1)(vii). Although it is undisputed that none of Summit's employees were exposed to any hazard created by the scaffold violation, the OSHA officer issued Summit a citation for violation of 29 C.F.R. § 1926.451(g)(1)(vii) based on the controlling employer citation policy.

Summit contested the citation, and the matter was referred to an Administrative Law Judge ("ALJ"). Summit argued that § 1910.12(a) places a duty on employers to protect only its own employees, not those of any subcontractor. Therefore, according to Summit, § 1910.12(a) precludes the Secretary from citing controlling employers whose own employees were not exposed to the hazardous condition. The ALJ upheld the citation and rejected Summit's position because § 1910.12(a) "does not prohibit application of an employer's safety responsibility to employees of other employers."

OSHRC granted review and issued three separate opinions. Although one of these opinions agreed with the ALJ, the other two held that § 1910.12(a) requires each employer to protect only its own employees and thereby precludes the controlling employer citation policy. Therefore, OSHRC vacated the citation, and its decision became the final order. Because the alleged violation occurred in Arkansas, the Secretary filed a petition for review in our court pursuant to 29 U.S.C. § 660(b). The Secretary argues that the plain language of § 1910.12(a) does not preclude the controlling employer citation policy and that the courts should give deference to the Secretary's interpretation of the regulation. Hence, we are required to address the "critical decision" recognized by the D.C. Circuit. *See Anthony Crane*, 70 F.3d at 1306.

## II.  DISCUSSION

### A.  Standard of Review

We will uphold OSHRC's factual findings if they are "supported by substantial evidence on the record considered as a whole." 29 U.S.C. § 660(a); *Omaha Paper Stock Co. v. Sec'y of Labor*, 304 F.3d 779, 782 (8th Cir.2002). Pursuant to the Administrative Procedure Act, "[w]e will uphold [OSHRC's] legal conclusions unless they are 'arbitrary, capricious, an abuse of discretion, or otherwise not in accordance with law.'" *Id.* (citing 5 U.S.C. § 706(2)(A)).

"In situations in which the meaning of [regulatory] language is not free from doubt, the reviewing court should give effect to the agency's interpretation so long as it is reasonable, that is, so long as the interpretation sensibly conforms to the purpose and wording of the regulations." *Martin*, 499 U.S. at 150, 111 S.Ct. 1171 * * *. In those instances in which the Secretary's interpretation differs from OSHRC's, we afford substantial deference to the Secretary's reasonable interpretation. *Martin*, 499 U.S. at 158, 111 S.Ct. 1171. "[N]o deference is due if the interpretation is contrary to the regulation's plain meaning." *Advanta USA, Inc. v. Chao*, 350 F.3d 726, 728 (8th Cir.2003) (quoting *In re Old Fashioned Enters., Inc.*, 236 F.3d 422, 425 (8th Cir.2001)). However, "[d]eference is due when an agency has developed its interpretation contemporaneously with the regulation, when the agency has consistently applied the regulation over time, and when the agency's interpretation is the result of thorough and reasoned consideration." Id. (quoting *Sioux Valley Hosp. v. Bowen*, 792 F.2d 715, 719 (8th Cir.1986)).

### B.   Regulatory Interpretation

In examining the meaning of § 1910.12(a), our inquiry begins with the regulation's plain language. We look to see "whether the language at issue has a plain and unambiguous meaning with regard to the particular dispute in the case." *See Robinson v. Shell Oil Co.*, 519 U.S. 337, 340, 117 S.Ct. 843, 136 L.Ed.2d 808 (1997). "The Court will avoid an interpretation of a [regulation] that renders some words altogether redundant." *United States v. Alaska*, 521 U.S. 1, 59, 117 S.Ct. 1888, 138 L.Ed.2d 231 (1997) * * *. We also should "avoid a [regulatory] construction that would render another part of the same [regulation] superfluous." *United States v. Stanko*, 491 F.3d 408, 413 (8th Cir.2007) * * * Any interpretation of § 1910.12(a) generally should conform to the accepted rules of grammar. *See, e.g., Dep't of Hous. & Urban Dev. v. Rucker*, 535 U.S. 125, 131, 122 S.Ct. 1230, 152 L.Ed.2d 258 (2002) * * * Applying these construction rules, we must now determine whether § 1910.12(a) precludes the Secretary from adopting the controlling employer citation policy.

The first sentence of § 1910.12(a) indicates that OSHA adopted the federal construction standards and that these standards now apply to all construction sites covered under OSHA rather than only federally funded and federally assisted construction contracts. The second sentence states:

> Each employer shall protect the employment and places of employment of each of his employees engaged in construction work by complying with the appropriate standards prescribed in this paragraph.

29 C.F.R. § 1910.12(a). The subject of this sentence is "each employer," the verb is "shall protect," and the objects are "employment" and "places of employment." The rest of the sentence contains prepositional phrases; a preposition serves to "link[ ] an object (a noun or noun equivalent) to another word in the sentence to show the relationship between them." *Chicago Manual of Style*, 187 § 5.162 (15th ed.2003). In this case, the

preposition "of" serves to link the objects, "employment" and "places of employment," to "each of his employees." Hence, grammatically reconstructed, the language of the regulation requires: (1) that an employer shall protect the employment of each of his employees ("part (1)") and (2) that an employer shall protect the places of employment of each of his employees ("part (2)").

In this case, the prepositional phrase "of each of his employees" serves as an adjective that narrows the meaning of "employment" and "places of employment." See id. at 188 § 5.166 ("A prepositional phrase can be used as a noun, ... an adverb, ... or an adjective...."); id. at 165 § 5.66 (discussing limiting adjectives). Because the term "of each of his employees" limits the term "employment," part (1) provides that an employer shall protect only the employment of his employees. Stated differently, part (1) provides that an employer shall protect only his employees.[3] However, this is not the end of the analysis. In part (2), the term "of each of his employees" limits the term "places of employment" such that the employer shall protect the places of employment where the employer actually has employees. See Reich v. Simpson, Gumpertz & Heger, Inc., 3 F.3d 1, 4–5 (1st Cir.1993) (holding that the plain language of § 1910.12(a) establishes a duty of employers to protect only those construction sites where they have employees). Unlike part (1), part (2) of the regulation does not limit the employer's duty to protect only the employer's own employees. Therefore, the plain language of part (2) does not preclude an employer's duty to protect the place of employment, including others who work at the place of employment, so long as the employer also has employees at that place of employment. See Weekley Homes, 609 S.E.2d at 415.

Summit contends that the regulation requires the employer to protect only "his employees." Because the creating employer, correcting employer and controlling employer citation policies permit OSHA to issue citations to employers when their own employees are not exposed to the hazard, Summit's reading of § 1910.12(a) effectively precludes these policies and only permits the exposing employer citation policy. Although part (1) may support this interpretation, part (2) must provide something different to avoid being superfluous to part (1). Summit argues that part (2) requires the employer to protect only his employees at their places of employment. This interpretation creates two problems. First, Summit's interpretation is contrary to the grammatical construction of the sentence because it requires the term "each of his employees" to be the object of the sentence, rather than a prepositional phrase that modifies the actual objects of the sentence. Second, Summit's interpretation would make the term "places of employment" redundant of the term "employment" and, therefore, superfluous. * * *

---

**3.** We do not agree with the Secretary's argument that "his employees" does not mean "only his employees." The natural reading requires us to read "his employees" as "only his employees." Cf. Cooper Indus., Inc. v. Aviall Servs., Inc., 543 U.S. 157, 166, 125 S.Ct. 577, 160 L.Ed.2d 548 (2004) (holding that the "natural meaning" of "may seek contribution ... during or following any civil action" is that contribution may only be sought then).

Even if we were to find Summit's interpretation to be reasonable and that § 1910.12(a) was therefore ambiguous, we would defer to the Secretary's interpretation nonetheless. Summit contends that we should not give deference to the Secretary's interpretation of § 1910.12(a) because the Secretary did not adopt the controlling employer citation policy contemporaneously with the regulation and has not had a consistent multi-employer worksite policy since § 1910.12(a) was enacted. *See Advanta USA*, 350 F.3d at 728. However, Summit conflates the issues. We defer to the Secretary's interpretation of her regulation, § 1910.12(a), and not the Secretary's interpretation of her multi-employer worksite policy. The Secretary's application of the multi-employer worksite policy is only relevant to the extent that it sheds light on the Secretary's interpretation of § 1910.12(a).

First, the Secretary did not initially interpret § 1910.12(a) as limiting an employer's responsibility to its own employees. Contemporaneous with the enactment of the regulation in May 1971, OSHA issued its first Field Operations Manual that authorized the agency to cite employers who created a hazardous condition "endangering employees (whether his own or those of another employer)...." OSHA, Field Operations Manual ¶ 10, at VII–6–8 (May 20, 1971). By adopting the creating employer citation policy, OSHA held employers responsible for OSHA violations even when their own employees were not exposed to any hazards related to the violations. OSHA also started to issue citations based on the controlling employer theory only eight months after the promulgation of § 1910.12(a). See *Gilles*, 4 OSAHRC at 1085.

Nonetheless, Summit argues that the Secretary did not initially intend § 1910.12(a) to extend an employer's liability beyond the employer's own employees because § 1910.12(a) did not adopt 29 C.F.R. § 1926.16 when it adopted the construction standards of the Construction Safety Act. Section 1926.16 is a regulation of the Construction Safety Act published in Subpart B of 29 C.F.R. § 1926 that contains language specifically extending an employer's liability beyond its own employees. When the Secretary issued § 1910.12(a), the regulation adopted "the standards" published in Subpart C and later subparts of 29 C.F.R. § 1926, which do not include § 1926.16. See29 C.F.R. §§ 1910.11, 1910.12(c) (discussing which parts of § 1926 are adopted). However, without more, the Secretary's failure to adopt § 1926.16 does not prove that the Secretary interpreted § 1910.12(a) to preclude her from extending an employer's liability beyond its own employees, especially when the Secretary adopted the creating employer citation policy in the 1971 OSHA Field Operations Manual and started to issue citations based on the controlling employer theory shortly after the regulation was enacted.

Second, we disagree with Summit's contention that the Secretary has not consistently applied her interpretation of § 1910.12(a) over time. Although the Secretary altered the multi-employer worksite policy to include only the exposing employer citation policy in its 1974 OSHA Field Operations Manual, the Secretary appears to have done so in response to

OSHRC's *City Wide* and *Gilles* decisions, which held that the creating employer and controlling employer citation policies violated § 654(a)(2). Nonetheless, even after adopting this new multi-employer worksite policy, the Secretary continued to challenge the *City Wide* and *Gilles* decisions. See *Martin Iron Works*, 9 OSAHRC at 695; HRH, 8 OSAHRC at 841; *Hawkins*, 8 OSAHRC at 569. The Secretary had also requested public comment on a proposed regulation adopting the creating employer and the controlling employer citation policies. The Secretary appears to have done this in response to various federal court of appeals decisions indicating that § 654(a)(2) does not preclude the creating employer and the controlling employer citation policies. See *Brennan*, 513 F.2d at 1038; *Anning–Johnson*, 516 F.2d at 1091 n. 21. The Secretary abandoned the informal rulemaking process after OSHRC's adjudications in *Anning–Johnson* and *Grossman Steel*, which established the creating employer and the controlling employer citation policies and held that the policies did not violate § 654(a)(2).[4] Thus, the Secretary's actions during this time period may provide insight into the Secretary's, OSHRC's and several courts' interpretations of § 654(a)(2), but they do not provide insight into the Secretary's interpretation of § 1910.12(a). Therefore, because there is no evidence in the record that the Secretary has ever interpreted § 1910.12(a) to preclude her from holding an employer liable for OSHA violations that do not affect its own employees, we defer to the Secretary's reasonable interpretation that § 1910.12(a) does not preclude the controlling employer citation policy.

We find that the plain language of § 1910.12(a) does not preclude the Secretary's controlling employer citation policy. Even if the regulation were ambiguous, we would defer to the Secretary's reasonable interpretation. Therefore, OSHRC abused its discretion in determining that the controlling employer citation policy conflicted with § 1910.12(a), a legal conclusion that was not in accordance with the law.

## C.  Alternative Arguments

Summit argues that the controlling employer citation policy is premised on an expansive definition of employer and employee in violation of the Supreme Court's direction in *Nationwide Mutual Insurance v. Darden*, 503 U.S. 318, 322–25, 112 S.Ct. 1344, 117 L.Ed.2d 581 (1992). In Darden, the Supreme Court held that when Congress leaves the term "employee" insufficiently clear, courts are to construe the term according to the

---

**4.** The amici on behalf of Summit contend that the Secretary could not lawfully apply the multi-employer worksite policy without first adopting it through the informal rulemaking process of the Administrative Procedure Act. See 5 U.S.C. § 553. This argument may have some merit. *But see Universal Constr. Co.*, 182 F.3d at 728 n. 2 (rejecting this argument). The Supreme Court has stated that Congress did not intend for OSHRC to use its "adjudicatory power to play a policymaking role," *Martin*, 499 U.S. at 154, 111 S.Ct. 1171, as it appears OSHRC did in *Anning–Johnson* and *Grossman Steel*. Therefore, the Secretary may be required to submit its multi-employer worksite policy to the informal rulemaking process, unless the multi-employer worksite policy is an interpretive rule or a statement of policy. *See Air Transp. Assoc. v. Fed. Aviation Admin.*, 291 F.3d 49, 55 (D.C.Cir.2002); *Gen. Elec. Co. v. Envtl. Prot. Agency*, 290 F.3d 377, 382–85 (D.C.Cir.2002). However, we decline to consider this issue because it was raised to this court by the amici and not by the parties. * * * *

conventional master-servant relationship as understood by common-law agency doctrine. *Id.* at 322–23, 112 S.Ct. 1344. Based on statements by Commissioner Cleary in his dissenting opinions, Summit believes that the controlling employer citation policy is premised on a broad definition of employer and employee rather than the common-law definition. * * * *

Summit misconstrues *Anning–Johnson* and *Grossman Steel*. Nothing in those opinions remotely indicates that OSHRC relied on a broad definition of employer or employee. Rather, OSHRC premised the controlling employer citation policy upon § 654(a)(2), which, unlike § 654(a)(1), does not base an employer's liability on the existence of an employer-employee relationship. *Anning–Johnson*, 4 BNA OSHC at 1198–99; *Grossman Steel*, 4 BNA OSHC at 1188; see *Knutson*, 566 F.2d at 599. Therefore, the controlling employer citation policy is not premised on an expansive definition of employer or employee and does not conflict with the *Darden* decision. See *Sec'y of Labor v. Trinity Indus., Inc.*, 504 F.3d 397, 402 (3d Cir.2007) (holding that the multi-employer worksite policy did not violate *Darden*).

Summit also argues that the Secretary has no legal authority for the controlling employer citation policy. However, we held in *Knutson* that § 654(a)(2) provides statutory authority for the controlling employer citation policy. *Knutson*, 566 F.2d at 599. We are bound by this decision unless the en banc court or the Supreme Court reaches a different result. * * *

Nonetheless, Summit raises a novel argument asserting that § 654(a)(2) limits an employer's duty to provide a safe workplace for only his employees. Section 654(a)(2) uses the term "occupational safety and health standards," which is defined as "a standard which requires conditions ... reasonably necessary or appropriate to provide safe or healthful employment and places of employment." 29 U.S.C. § 652(8). Summit claims that employment must mean the common law master-servant relationship. * * *.

This argument contains the same defect as Summit's argument with respect to § 1910.12(a). Specifically, to make both terms meaningful, the use of the term "places of employment" must provide something different than the term "employment." We agree that the term "places of employment" limits the employer's duty to worksites where he has employees. However, it is not limited to only the "employment" of his employees because that interpretation would render the phrase "places of employment" redundant of "employment" and, therefore, superfluous. * * *

Alternatively, Summit contends that the controlling employer citation policy violates 29 U.S.C. § 653(b)(4) because it would increase the employer's liability at common law. The statute provides that "[n]othing in this chapter shall be construed to supersede or in any manner affect any workmen's compensation law or to enlarge or diminish or affect in any other manner the common law or statutory rights, duties, or liabilities of employers and employees under any law with respect to injuries, diseases, or death of employees arising out of, or in the course of, employment." 29 U.S.C. § 653(b)(4). The federal courts have held that this provision does not create a private cause of action and prevents federal preemption of state tort law and worker's compensation schemes. *Gade v. Nat'l Solid Wastes Mgmt. Ass'n*, 505 U.S. 88, 96, 112 S.Ct. 2374, 120 L.Ed.2d 73 (1992) (holding that § 653(b)(4) prevents federal preemption of state tort law and worker's compensation schemes); * * *; *Am. Fed'n of Gov't Employees, AFL–CIO v. Rumsfeld*, 321 F.3d 139, 143–44 (D.C.Cir.2003) (holding that § 653(b)(4) does not create a private cause of action); *Ries v. Nat'l R.R. Passenger Corp.*, 960 F.2d 1156, 1164–65 (3d Cir.1992) (holding that § 653(b)(4) prohibits private causes of action including the use of a violation of an OSHA regulation to establish negligence per se). Because the controlling employer citation policy neither creates a private cause of action nor preempts state law, the policy does not violate § 653(b)(4) by increasing an employer's liability at common law.

Finally, Summit and the amici argue that the controlling employer citation policy is an ill-conceived policy that is counterproductive to the goals of the OSH Act. It is uncertain what potential benefits are gained in citing both a subcontractor and a general contractor for a single OSHA violation when the general contractor had informed the subcontractor of the violation on prior occasions. Although a general contractor plays a role in setting safety standards at worksites, OSHA is an intricate and function-specific regulatory regime such that each employer on a worksite may be uniquely situated to know of the very specific regulatory requirements affecting its particular trade. Therefore, the controlling employer citation policy places an enormous responsibility on a general contractor to monitor all employees and all aspects of a worksite. However, these policy concerns should be addressed to Congress or to the Secretary and not to the courts. * * *

## III.  CONCLUSION

Because we conclude that OSHRC's holding was contrary to law, we grant the Secretary's petition, vacate OSHRC's order and remand for further proceedings consistent with this opinion.

BEAM, CIRCUIT JUDGE, dissenting.

I concur in the panel majority's (the court's) analysis that 29 U.S.C. § 654(a)(2) incorporates the requirements of 29 C.F.R. § 1910.12(a) within the governance imposed by the Occupational Safety and Health Act of 1970 (OSH Act). I also concur in the court's fundamental grammatic interpretation of § 1910.12(a). I disagree, however, with the court's conclusion that the regulation, as the court construes it, is sufficiently ambiguous to require this court to defer to the Secretary of Labor's decision to overrule the carefully reasoned decision of the Occupational Safety and Health Review Commission (Commission) vacating Summit's Occupational Safety and Health Administration (OSHA) "controlling employer" citation. Accordingly, I dissent. * * *

### NOTES AND QUESTIONS

1. Multi-employer situations vary, creating quite different questions of statutory interpretation. Reading Section 654 (a) literally (and carefully), consider the following:

(a) Carpenters of subcontractor A are working on the fifth floor of a building under construction. They threw waste lumber over the side to the ground below where bricklayers of subcontractor B are passing by. A bricklayer is hit by a plank and is killed. Can A be cited for violation of the general duty clause?

(b) A's carpenters stack lumber overhanging the outside perimeter of the building in violation of a specific standard prohibiting stacking of materials within six feet of the outside perimeter. This creates a risk to the bricklayers and the employees of other subcontractors below. Can B be cited for a violation of this specific standard? *See Brennan v. OSHRC*, 513 F.2d 1032 (2d Cir. 1975).

(c) C's electricians are working near an opening in the floor which the carpenters had left without a guard rail as required by a specific standard. When C is cited for a violation he argues that he had neither created nor controlled the hazard. Can the Commission's enforcement be upheld on the basis of the words of Section 654? *Dun–Par Engineered Form Co. v. Marshall*, 676 F.2d 1333 (10th Cir.1982). What if C protests to A and the general contractor but they do nothing and an electrician falls down the opening? Can these citations be upheld under the Chevron doctrine?

2. Why should a general contractor be responsible for a violation by a subcontractor who endangered only his own employees? Consider the following cases, the first decided by the same Circuit as the principal case:

> IBP, a meat processor, contracted out the cleaning of its machinery to DSC Sanitation Management. DSC employees engaged in gross violations of safety procedures. IBP Management inspectors told the DSC employees to stop, but the DSC employees ignored them, sometimes replying, "I don't work for you" and "You can't stop me." These violations were reported to DSC supervisors, but DSC took no steps to prevent the violations. Finally, a DSC employee was killed while trying to clean a machine without stopping it as required by lockout procedures. DSC was found guilty of three willful violators for "intentional disregard and plain indifference to the Act's requirement" and fined $210,000. *DSC Sanitation Management, Inc. v. OSHRC*, 82 F.3d 812 (8th Cir.1996).

At the same time IBP was cited under the "multi employer doctrine" for willfully failing to enforce its lockout procedure. The Commission found that IBP had control over the hazard because it had the right to cancel its contract with DSC. The court questioned OSHA's multiple employer doctrine, but held that in any case the contractual right of IBP to remove DSC from the job if DSC failed to follow required procedure was not enough control to hold IBP responsible. IBP had pointed out the safety violation to DSC supervisors and management which was the most it could be expected to do, "The Commission", said the court, "has defined 'control' in an irrational way." *IBP v. Herman*, 144 F.3d 861 (D.C. Cir. 1998).

In *R. P. Carbone Construction Co. v. OSHRC*, 166 F.3d 815 (6th Cir. 1998), the court upheld citations against the general contractor for violations of a subcontractor which endangered the subcontractor's own employees. The general contractor had not "inquired into the subcontractor's safety program and the violations were in plain view or should have been reasonably detected." Without even citing the IBP case, the court stated, "There is a presumption that a general contractor has sufficient control over its subcontractors to require them to comply with safety standards." Id. at 818.

3. Should a general contractor be held responsible for violations by a subcontractor which endanger only the subcontractor's own employees? Is not one penalty assessed against the primary violator enough? What would be the contractor's liability under tort law? Could IBP recover the amount of the assessed fine from DSC?

4. As the principal opinion indicates, one Circuit, the Fifth has rejected the Secretary's approach to the multi-employer issues. In *Universal Constr. Co. v. OSHRC*, 182 F.3d 726 (10th Cir. 1999), Judge Briscoe commented: "None of [the Fifth Circuit] cases persuasively explain the basis for the rejection of the doctrine."

5. In 2010, a divided OSHRC decided to abandon the position taken in its opinion in the principal case, and to return to its prior position accepting the Secretary's approach. *Summit Contractors, Inc.*, OSHRC Docket No. 05–0839v, August 19, 2010.

# I.  EMPLOYER DEFENSES

## P. GIOIOSO & SONS, INC. v. OCCUPATIONAL SAFETY AND HEALTH REVIEW COMMISSION

United States Court of Appeals for the First Circuit, 1997
115 F.3d 100

SELYA, CIRCUIT JUDGE:

The petitioner, P. Gioioso & Sons, Inc. (Gioioso), seeks review of a final order of the Occupational Safety and Health Review Commission (the Commission) determining that it violated the Occupational Safety and Health Act of 1970 (OSH Act), 19 U.S.C. §§ 651–678 (1994). The petition purports to raise six distinct objections to the Commission's order. The Secretary of Labor (the Secretary) maintains that we lack jurisdiction to hear three of these objections because Gioioso failed to raise them when it petitioned the Commission for review of the hearing examiner's adverse decision. The remaining objections, the Secretary tells us, are without force. The jurisdictional question is new to this court. We resolve it favorably to the Secretary and dispose of certain objections on that ground. We deny the remnants of the petition on the merits.

## II.  THE ORIGINS OF THE DISPUTE

Gioioso is in the construction industry, specializing in utilities. Some time ago, it contracted with the Massachusetts Water Resources Authority

(MWRA) to lay water lines in Winthrop, Massachusetts. During a lengthy period beginning in 1993, it laid several thousand feet of pipe under or near the access road to MWRA's Deer Island work site.

In the course of its endeavors, Gioioso dug an 18–foot–long trench at the intersection of Shirley and Taft Avenues. On October 6, 1994, Gioioso's foreman, Salvatore Santone, and a laborer, Fernando Camara, were standing in this trench. At that moment, several OSHA compliance officers happened to pass by the work site. The meandering traffic afforded the compliance officers a clear view of the trench and one of their number, Edward Wells, did not like what he saw: the trench's walls were unsloped and unsupported, the two workmen standing in the trench were visible only from the shoulders up, and a ten-foot section of cast metal pipe was suspended aloft from the bucket of a piece of heavy construction equipment located at one end of the trench. Wells sounded the alarm (figuratively speaking) and the driver stopped the car.

One of Wells' colleagues, Patrick Griffin, exited the vehicle and hurried toward the trench. Griffin noticed that the dangling pipe was connected to the bucket of a large excavating machine by only a single attachment point and watched as it rotated into a position parallel to the trench and directly over the workmen's heads. When Griffin reached the trench, he discovered that it measured no less than six feet deep and four feet wide and had been dug in gravelly soil. No trench box was in place to guard against a cave-in (although Santone claimed that he and Camara had been measuring the trench to ascertain if it could accommodate one). Moreover, because the trench lay adjacent to the only road providing access to Deer Island, vibrations from traffic increased the risk of a cave-in. A gas pipe, six inches in diameter, traversed the width of the trench. Wells corroborated many of Griffin's observations.

In due course, OSHA issued citations alleging three serious violations (one of which the Secretary later withdrew) and a repeat violation.[3] The two serious violations (which we shall label "A" and "B") were as follows:

A. Permitting employees to work beneath the suspended pipe in violation of *29 C.F.R. § 1926.651(e) (1996)* (which instructs that "[n]o employee shall be permitted underneath loads handled by lifting or digging equipment").

B. Permitting workers to use a ladder that did not extend at least three feet above the top of the trench in violation of *29 C.F.R. § 1926.1053(b)(1) (1996)* (which directs that "[w]hen portable ladders are used for access to an upper landing surface, the ladder side rails shall extend at least 3 feet (.9m) above the upper landing").

---

**3.** A serious violation occurs if there is a substantial probability that death or serious physical harm could result from a condition which exists, or from one or more practices, means, methods, operations, or processes which have been adopted or are in use ... unless the employer did not, and could not with the exercise of reasonable diligence, know of the presence of the violation. *29 U.S.C. § 666(k)*. While the OSH Act does not define the term "repeat violation," courts typically require proof that the respondent violated the same standard on an earlier occasion in a substantially similar fashion....

The repeat violation (which we shall label "C") was as follows:

C. Failing to provide an adequate protective system for workers in an unshored trench, in violation of *29 C.F.R. § 1926.652(a)(1) (1996)* (which provides that, except when excavations are made entirely in stable rock or are less than five feet in depth, "[e]ach employee in an excavation shall be protected from cave-ins by an adequate protective system").

The petitioner filed a timely notice of contest. At the outset of the hearing, it moved for disqualification on the ground that the ALJ, several years earlier (while employed as an attorney in the Department of Labor), had prosecuted one or more similar cases involving Gioioso. The ALJ refused to recuse himself. After considering the evidence, he found that the violations had in fact occurred, accepted OSHA's characterizations of them, and imposed penalties of $1,600 for each of the two serious violations and $8,000 for the repeat violation.

Gioioso filed with the Commission a petition for discretionary review (PDR) of the ALJ's decision. Its PDR called attention to only three issues (described *infra* Part IV). The PDR generated no interest and the ALJ's decision ripened into the Commission's final order.[4] Gioioso then sought a judicial anodyne.

## III.  THE JURISDICTIONAL ISSUE

We turn first to the jurisdictional quandary. In pressing its cause before this court, the petitioner raises not only the three issues which it enumerated in the PDR but also three additional issues, namely, whether the ALJ erred in (1) failing to recuse himself, (2) characterizing violation B as serious, and (3) assessing substantial penalties. The question, then, is whether Gioioso's failure to press these points in the PDR constitutes a forfeiture of the right to bring them before a reviewing court. We think that it does.

We begin with bedrock. In the administrative state, exhaustion of administrative remedies is "generally required." *Weinberger v. Salfi*, 422 U.S. 749, 765, 95 S.Ct. 2457, 2467, 45 L.Ed.2d 522 (1975). * * * *

The OSH Act warmly embraces the exhaustion doctrine. It provides in relevant part that persons such as Gioioso who are "adversely affected or aggrieved by an order of the Commission" may obtain judicial review in the "court of appeals for the circuit in which the violation is alleged to have occurred." *29 U.S.C. § 660(a)*. The right to judicial review, however, is carefully cabined. Congress specifically directed that "[n]o objection that has not been urged before the Commission shall be considered by the court, unless the failure or neglect to urge such objection shall be excused because of extraordinary circumstances." *Id.* The regulations complement the statute, explaining that an aggrieved party's failure to file a PDR

---

**4.** By its inaction, the Commission effectively adopted the ALJ's recommended findings and report. We sometimes will refer to these findings as if they had been made by the Commission in the first instance.

"may foreclose court review of the objections to the [ALJ's] decision." *29 C.F.R. § 2200.91(f).* * * *

We believe it follows from the bifurcation of duties contained in the statutory scheme, as well as from plain meaning, that the OSH Act precludes judicial review of those objections not urged in front of the Commission. To be specific, the OSH Act acknowledges the existence of two separate adjudicators—the Commission and the ALJs—and assigns very different responsibilities to each. The Commission members, whom the President appoints based on their training, expertise, and experience, see 29 U.S.C. § 661(a), carry out the broad adjudicatory functions required by the OSH Act. Conversely, the ALJs' functions are case-specific. This division of labor carries with it disparate responsibilities, leaving in the Commission's hands the task of ensuring the development of a cohesive body of decisional rules which comport with the objectives of the OSH Act.

Given this framework, we think that the wiser course is to construe the statute according to its letter. Only if an issue is actually called to the attention of the Commission, through the PDR or by a Commission member's spontaneous initiative, will the Commission have the informed opportunity that Congress intended—a meaningful chance to correct a mistake before an order becomes final. Thus, the model that Congress envisioned can function optimally only if the aggrieved party alerts the Commission to those issues which that party thinks are worthy of review. *Accord McGowan v. Marshall,* 604 F.2d 885, 890–91 (5th Cir.1979); *Keystone,* 539 F.2d at 963. * * *

Consistent with this conclusion, we next examine the PDR which Gioioso filed. We find absolutely no reference in it either to the alleged mischaracterization of the ladder violation or to the supposedly excessive nature of the penalty assessments. Because Gioioso failed to urge these objections before the Commission, we are without jurisdiction to entertain them.

The recusal issue presents a variation on the theme. Although the PDR did not list this objection as an issue for review, there was a glancing mention of it in a footnote. The petitioner claims to have preserved the issue in this fashion. But the exhaustion doctrine demands more than oblique references, and the statute's use of the verb "urge" in this contest is telling. *See* Webster's Collegiate Dictionary 1300 (10th ed.1993) (defining "urge" as meaning "to present, advocate, or demand earnestly or pressingly" or "to declare, advance, or press earnestly a statement, argument, charge or claim"); The American Heritage Dictionary of the English Language 1965 (3d ed.1992) (defining "urge" as "[t]o entreat earnestly and often repeatedly; exhort ... [t]o present a forceful argument, claim, or case"). In an OSHA case, an objection is not "urged" in the requisite sense (and will not be deemed preserved for judicial review) unless the PDR conveys the substance of the objection face up and squarely, in a manner reasonably calculated to alert the Commission to the crux of the perceived problem.

The petitioner's treatment of the recusal issue fails to meet this benchmark. As the PDR reads, the matter of recusal is little more than a passing comment, designed to provide information buttressing another argument rather than to carve out an independent ground for inquiry. Since the footnote failed to place the Commission on proper notice, it did not suffice to reserve the issue of recusal for judicial review. * * *

## IV.  THE MERITS

Our conclusion that we lack jurisdiction to hear three of the petitioner's six objections marks only the end of the beginning. We still must resolve the three preserved claims, namely, (1) whether substantial evidence supports the finding that the petitioner's employees worked below a suspended pipe (Violation A); (2) whether the Commission erred in finding that the petitioner's employees were exposed to trench-related hazards without an adequate protection system (Violation C); and (3) whether the record supports the rejection of the petitioner's unpreventable employee misconduct defense. * * * *

### b.  Violation A

The Commission found that Gioioso breached the excavation standard, 29 C.F.R. § 1926.651(e), which mandates that "[n]o employee shall be permitted underneath loads handled by lifting or digging equipment." The petitioner assigns error. We see none.

The citation underpinning Violation A states in relevant part that Gioioso's personnel "were exposed to serious injury while working in a trench in which a section of 12" water line was being lowered. In adjudicating this citation, the ALJ credited the testimony of two compliance officers who described seeing a ten-foot section of cast metal pipe suspended from the bucket of an excavating machine by a chain sling. As the pipe moved, it rotated around the single point of suspension and passed over the heads of the men who were working in the trench. While the observations of the two compliance officers were not entirely congruent, the ALJ determined that the modest discrepancies in their accounts were easily explained by the officers' differing vantage points. He also found that a photograph taken shortly thereafter corroborated their testimony. Keeping in mind the frailty of Gioioso's rebuttal—its foreman, Santone, stated only that he did not recall the pipe passing overhead—there is no principled basis on which a court could justify substituting its judgment for the factfinder's. *See General Dynamics*, 599 F.2d at 463.

### c.  Violation C

The Commission found that Gioioso failed to provide an adequate protective system within the trench, thereby violating 29 C.F.R. § 1926.652(a)(1). The petitioner again spies error. We do not. It is undisputed that the petitioner neglected to furnish a support system, shield system, or other adequate safeguarding within the trench as required by 29 C.F.R. § 1926.652(c). Additionally, the petitioner failed to comply with the provisions of 29 C.F.R. § 1926.652(b)(1)(i) (which delineates a protection option accomplished by the gradual sloping of the excavation's walls). But the regulations exempt some unsloped excavations that are less than five feet in depth, *see id.* § 1926.652(a)(1)(ii), and the petitioner seeks the shelter of this exemption. The petitioner hypothesizes that its workers never were exposed to the hazards inherent in an excavation exceeding five feet in depth because they were standing on a pipe that traversed the width of the trench. The ALJ rejected this defense: although he believed it was unlikely that the workmen were standing on the floor of the trench when the compliance officers arrived, he found that "no matter where they were standing, [they] were still inside a trench that was not protected in accordance with § 1926.652(a)(1)." We review this essentially legal judgment de novo. In reaching this conclusion, the ALJ relied heavily on *Ford Dev. Corp.,* 15 O.S.H. Cas. (BNA) 2003 (1992). There, the employer claimed that its employees were supposed to stand on a pipe while in a trench, and that in so doing they effectively would be exposed to a depth of only 3.5 feet (the distance from the upper surface of the pipe to the top of the trench). The Commission rejected this argument. It noted that the depth exception applies only if an excavation is "less than 5 feet (1.52m) in depth and examination of the ground by a competent person provides no indication of a potential cave-in." 29 C.F.R. § 1926.652(a)(1)(ii). The Commission then explained that "[t]he standard speaks of the depth of the trench, not of the position of employees in the trench." *Ford Dev. Corp.,* 15 O.S.H. Cas. at 2011. On this basis, the Commission held that the depth exception did not apply. *See id.* The reasoning in *Ford* embodies a sensible construction of the regulation—and one that comports with its wording and purpose. The safety standard is implicated by the depth of a particular trench, without regard to an individual worker's precise position in it. The notion that having workers stand on a laid pipe within a trench is a satisfactory method of protecting them from the risk of cave-ins is nonsense. While the regulations are performance-oriented, they only allow employers to choose from a limited universe of acceptable procedures, not to jury-rig convenient alternatives and impose them on an imperiled work force. *See Conie Constr., Inc. v. Reich,* 73 F.3d 382, 384 (D.C.Cir.1995). The record in this case aptly illustrates the wisdom of this conclusion. A compliance officer, Griffin, testified to the close proximity of traffic on the adjacent roads and warned that this could cause vibrations along the trench walls, thus heightening the risk of a cave-in. If a cave-in occurred in a trench of this depth, Griffin believed that workers within it would "probably ... be buried" regardless of where they were standing. We have said enough on this score. Because the excavation regulation applies to the trench in question whereas the depth exception does not, the Commission's resolution of Violation C must stand.

### d.   Unpreventable Employee Misconduct

The Commission rejected the petitioner's affirmative defense of unpreventable employee misconduct (the UEM defense). The petitioner challenges this determination as a matter of law and as a matter of fact. We reject both challenges.

The OSH Act requires that an employer do everything reasonably within its power to ensure that its personnel do not violate safety standards. But if an employer lives up to that billing and an employee nonetheless fails to use proper equipment or otherwise ignores firmly established safety measures, it seems unfair to hold the employer liable. To address this dilemma, both OSHRC and the courts have recognized the availability of the UEM defense.

The contours of the UEM defense are relatively well defined. To reach safe harbor, an employer must demonstrate that it (1) established a work rule to prevent the reckless behavior and/or unsafe condition from occurring, (2) adequately communicated the rule to its employees, (3) took steps to discover incidents of noncompliance, and (4) effectively enforced the rule whenever employees transgressed it. *See New York State Elec. & Gas Corp. v. Secretary of Labor,* 88 F.3d 98, 105 (2d Cir.1996). * * *

The mainstay of Gioioso's argument is that the ALJ unnecessarily required repetitive documentary proof referable to the UEM defense. But this is smoke and mirrors; the record reveals quite clearly that the ALJ applied the appropriate legal standard in a wholly unremarkable way and found that the employer failed to carry the devoir of persuasion on both the implementation and enforcement components of the defense. This deficit is fatal. Even if an employer establishes work rules and communicates them to its employees, the defense of unpreventable employee misconduct cannot be sustained unless the employer also proves that it insists upon compliance with the rules and regularly enforces them. *See Centex–Rooney Constr. Co.,* 16 O.S.H. CAS. (BNA) 2127, 2130 (1994).

Contrary to the petitioner's insinuations, the ALJ did not presume to establish a per se rule requiring documentation. Rather, he counted the absence of documentation against the proponent of the defense *in the circumstances of this case.* We cannot fault this approach. Given the nature of the issue, there is no reason why a factfinder must accept an employer's anecdotal evidence uncritically. And in this instance, we agree with the ALJ that the absence of any vestige of documentary proof was not only a relevant datum but a telling one.

The petitioner also questions whether the Commission's rejection of its UEM defense is supported by substantial evidence in the record. After giving due deference to the ALJ's credibility determinations, we conclude that the ruling passes muster.

While the record reflects that Gioioso made a meaningful effort to develop a satisfactory safety program, it is much less conclusive on the issues of implementation and enforcement. The petitioner's best case is that it distributes safety manuals to all new employees; that these manuals contain information regarding, *inter alia,* the lifting of loads, methods of trench protection, and the proper placement of ladders in trenches; and that it supplements these materials in various ways. The petitioner's safety chairman testified that the company sponsors weekly "toolbox talks" at its work sites, monthly safety meetings for supervisory personnel, and biennial safety seminars for all employees. But this evidence left some fairly conspicuous gaps as to the content of the training exercises, who conducted each session, and who attended them. Documentation— say, syllabi or attendance rosters—would have gone a long way toward filling these gaps, but the petitioner proffered none. Absent such documentation, it cannot persuasively argue that it effectively communicated the rules to its employees.

The ALJ found most compelling the lack of any substantial evidence in the record that the petitioner effectively enforced its safety program. It provided no evidence of unscheduled safety audits or mandatory safety checklists, and no documentation that it ever executed its four-tiered disciplinary policy. This lacuna in the proof undermines its attempt to mount a viable UEM defense. * * * * Even when a safety program is thorough and properly conceived, lax administration renders it ineffective (and, thus, vitiates reliance on the UEM defense). *See Brock,* 818 F.2d at 1274, 1278 (in which the ALJ rejected a UEM defense when the employer could not produce records evidencing employees' receipt of safety manuals, the occurrence of safety meetings, and the like).

*Brock* also illustrates another point which has pertinence here. The *Brock* court regarded the circumstances surrounding the actions of the employer's foreman as further evidence that the employer's program was lax. *See id.* at 1277. The case at hand is not dissimilar; Santone, the petitioner's foreman, in effect acknowledged that his actions directly contravened the company's safety policies. And while the petitioner argues that a foreman should not be regarded as a supervisor, the company's own safety manual identifies the foreman as the "safety foreman for his crew," instructs employees to "listen to your foreman" in respect to safety matters, and directs foremen (along with other company safety officers) to inspect work sites regularly and to enforce safety rules. Seen in the context of these instructions, the foreman's breach of safety rules supplies the basis for an inference that the employer's implementation of safety procedures and/or its enforcement policies left something to be desired. *See id.; see also H.B. Zachry,* 638 F.2d at 819. The same circumstance also buttresses the ALJ's finding that Gioioso's employees probably were unaware that a threat of disciplinary action existed for nonobservance of safety rules.

Finally, it bears mentioning that one of the violations (Violation C) is a repeat violation. Recent violations provide some evidence of ineffective safety enforcement. *See Jensen Constr. Co.,* 7 O.S.H. Cas. at 1479 & nn. 5– 6. The ALJ was entitled to draw such an inference here.

We need go no further. Taking into account the totality of the circumstances and the allocation of the burden of proof, we find the petitioner's claim that the Commission improperly rejected its UEM defense to be without merit.

## NOTES AND QUESTIONS

1.    In *D.A. Collins Construction Company v. Secretary of Labor*, 117 F.3d 691 (2d Cir.1997), carpenters working on a bridge were required to use safety belts with lanyards to attach to rods in the bridge at all times. In practice, carpenters often violated the Company's safety rules by not fastening their safety lines while walking on the platform going to and from lunch because they felt it was "too time consuming," and at times the supervisor also violated the rule. The court rejected the employer's defense of unforeseeable employee misconduct because the employer had not taken specific steps to insure that supervisors were fulfilling their duty to discover violations of the work rule. 117 F.3d at 695.

Section 654 (b) provides:

Each employee shall comply with occupational safety and health standards and all rules regulations and orders issued pursuant to this chapter which are applicable to his own actions and conduct.

In these cases, both the foreman and the other workmen were violating the employer's work rules and the safety standards; perforce they were violating Section 654 (b). Why should the employer be held responsible?

2.    Two electricians were assigned to connect a ground wire to a utility pole. They were given drawings and written instructions as to the height to install it, but they failed to follow the drawings and the written warning to keep below the live power line. One of the employees came in contact with the live line carrying 7200 volts and was killed. The Commission upheld citations for permitting employees to work in proximity to a live wire without grounding or guarding it effectively, and for failing to instruct employees to recognize the dangers of working near energized lines. In court, the employer argued that the Commission erred in failing to find unforeseeable misconduct by the employee, but the court disagreed, saying:

To establish employee misconduct as an affirmative defense, an employer must carry its burden of showing that due to the existence of a thorough and adequate safety program that is communicated and enforced as written, the conduct of the employees in violating that policy was idiosyncratic and unforeseeable.

There was no evidence that the employer had inspected the worksite or instructed its employees to recognize the hazard; it had no specific work rules preventing employees from working close to high voltage lines; and it failed to warn of dangers which the employer could have discovered with reasonable diligence. The employer, therefore, could not claim employee misconduct; it was not "idiosyncratic and unforeseeable." *CMC Electric, Inc. v. OSHA*, 221 F.3d 861 (6th Cir.2000).

A large portion of workplace accidents are the result of employee negligence or disregard of obvious dangers or safety violations. How much must an employer do to make such employee conduct "idiosyncratic and unforeseeable"? Can an employer rely on the usually good judgment of an employee or supervisor? See *Mass. Electric Construction Co. v. OSHA*, 215 F.3d 1312 (1st Cir.2000).

# NEW YORK STATE ELECTRIC & GAS CORP. v. SECRETARY OF LABOR

United States Court of Appeals, Second Circuit, 1996
88 F.3d 98

CARDAMONE, CIRCUIT JUDGE:

## A. Facts

On the morning of July 30, 1991 NYSEG employees Jim Webb, a first-class gas fitter, and Raymond Price, an equipment operator, drove in a company truck to the intersection of Front Street and Valley Street in Binghamton, New York. Their mission was to "tie in" a section of newly laid natural gas pipe. Upon arrival Webb put out cones and signs to protect the work site from vehicular traffic, while Price unloaded a backhoe to excavate the area surrounding the pipe. Because the existing break in the pavement was not wide enough for the tie-in, Price used a jackhammer from the truck to widen it.

While Price was so engaged, William Marzeski, an Occupational Safety and Health Administration (OSHA) compliance officer, happened to be driving through the intersection, and noticed that Price was operating the jackhammer without protective eyewear. He stopped and asked Price to identify his immediate supervisor, and was told that Webb was the crew leader. Marzeski then identified himself to Webb as an OSHA compliance officer and explained that Price was not wearing safety glasses. Webb agreed that Price should have been using protective goggles. Upon being further questioned, Price said he was not wearing steel-toe shoes either. At Webb's behest, Price then retrieved goggles and protective toe covers from the truck, put the equipment on, and resumed work.

## B. Citation and Complaint

As a result of the compliance officer's report, the respondent Secretary of Labor issued a citation alleging a violation of 29 C.F.R. § 1926.28, a regulation the Secretary had promulgated as head of OSHA. The regulation makes employers "responsible for requiring the wearing of appropriate personal protective equipment in all operations where there is an exposure to hazardous conditions or where this part indicates a need for using such equipment to reduce the hazards to the employees." To show that the Secretary's regulations indicated a need for relevant safety gear, the citation also referred to 29 C.F.R. § 1926.102(a)(1) (1995), which requires that employees be provided with eye and face protection equipment when there is a potential for eye or face injury. The allegations set forth in the citation stated that Price had been "exposed to eye and toe injuries while operating ... [a jackhammer] without using protective eye equipment and safety-toe footwear."

The Secretary subsequently filed a complaint with the Commission amending the citation and asserting a slightly different theory of liability. With respect to the lack of toe protection, the Secretary now asserted a violation of 29 C.F.R. § 1910.132(a) (1995), a standard requiring the use of "[p]rotective equipment, including personal protective equipment for eyes, face, head, and extremities ... wherever it is necessary by reason of hazards ... encountered in a manner capable of causing injury...." With respect to Price's failure to use eye protection, the complaint additionally alleged a violation of the "general duty clause" of the OSH Act, 29 U.S.C. § 654(a)(1).

## C. ALJ's Hearing and Decision

A hearing was held before an Administrative Law Judge (ALJ) pursuant to 29 U.S.C. § 659(c). The Secretary's case consisted primarily of Marzeski's testimony. He related his observations and conversation with Price and Webb at the work site on July 30, 1991. NYSEG called John Durfee, its manager of industrial relations for health and safety, Jack Jones, the supervisor for the Binghamton area in July of 1991, and John Hrywnak, the gas supervisor in charge of the Webb–Price crew when the citation was issued. Petitioner's witnesses described NYSEG's safety program, which included a rule requiring employees to wear eye and foot protection equipment when cutting pavement with a pneumatic tool.

Because Price and Webb were both newly hired employees of NYSEG—it had taken over their former employer's Binghamton business a few months earlier—they had been required to attend an orientation meeting covering safety practices and rules. As part of petitioner's safety program, safety meetings were held monthly to discuss selected topics. Supervisors were obligated to check work sites once or twice a day to ensure that safe work practices were being observed. When safety violations were discovered, they were corrected immediately, and NYSEG disciplined those responsible, imposing progressive discipline for further violations of its safety rules. In addition to the daily supervisor checks, Jones conducted quarterly safety audits of each work crew. Hrywnak testified it was company policy for crew members to report safety lapses to "the lead person on the crew"—in this case, Webb.

Following the hearing the ALJ sustained both violations alleged in the amended citation. With respect to the § 1910.132(a) violation (failure to wear protective footwear), the ALJ noted that the Secretary has the burden of showing, *inter alia,* that the employer knew or could have known of the violation of the standard requiring the wearing of protective equipment. The hearing officer also observed that such knowledge or constructive knowledge may be imputed to the employer through the employer's supervisory personnel. Here Webb was the "lead man" of the two-person crew at the site, and though he was not actually aware of the safety violation, he would have known had he exercised reasonable diligence. Thus, the ALJ concluded that Webb—and NYSEG, by imputation—had constructive knowledge of the safety violation.

The ALJ rejected the defense of "unpreventable employee misconduct" for two alternative reasons. He concluded that if Webb was indeed a supervisory employee, he did not do enough to discover Price's noncompliance; but, if Webb was not a supervisor, NYSEG's safety supervision was inadequate. Either way, NYSEG violated the relevant safety standards. The ALJ ruled on the "general duty clause" violation (failure to wear protective eyewear) in the same fashion.

### D.  The Commission's Decision

Reviewing the ALJ's decision, the Commission determined that the citation could not appropriately be based on the statutory "general duty clause." The Secretary may not rely on this general clause when it is "preempted" by a more specific standard, in this case 29 C.F.R. § 1926.28(a), which requires an employee to wear "appropriate personal protective equipment" where there is a need. The Commission therefore amended the complaint *sua sponte* to restore the original basis for the eye safety violation set forth in the citation—29 C.F.R. § 1926.28(a).

The Commission agreed with the ALJ's conclusion that Webb had constructive knowledge of Price's safety violations. It affirmed the hearing officer's findings that Webb was the "lead man" on the crew and reasonably should have known of the violation because he and Price were in close proximity to one another and the violations were readily observable. Although NYSEG challenged the ALJ's finding that Webb held a supervisory position for purposes of imputing knowledge to his employer, the Commission declined to reach that question. Instead it adopted the ALJ's reasoning concerning NYSEG's affirmative defense and found that if Webb was a supervisor, his constructive knowledge could be imputed to NYSEG; if not, then NYSEG failed to provide adequate safety supervision. Ruling in this fashion, the Commission determined that the Secretary carried his burden and proved that the petitioner had constructive knowledge of the safety violation regardless of whether Webb was or was not a supervisor.

With respect to the employer's defense of unpreventable employee misconduct, the Commission further held that NYSEG failed to demonstrate it enforced its safety rules effectively. The Commission declined to follow cases from the Third and Tenth Circuits placing the burden of proof for employee misconduct on the Secretary. Again, it stated that whether or not Webb was a supervisor was not relevant: in either case, the employer had failed to make sufficient efforts to detect violations of the safety rules. Were Webb not a supervisor, but simply Price's co-worker, then supervision was inadequate because it was limited to brief, twice-daily visits to work sites; if Webb was a supervisor, then NYSEG failed to show it did enough to prevent safety violations, including adequate training of its supervisors. The Commission observed that NYSEG's voluminous evidence regarding its safety programs dealt primarily with electrical utility operations rather than the natural gas operations in which Price and Webb were engaged. It declared that NYSEG had violated 29 C.F.R.

§ 1926.28(a) and § 1910.132(a) for the eye and foot safety violations respectively and affirmed the $1,500 assessed penalty for these violations. NYSEG appeals these determinations.

We set aside the Commission's determination, in part, affirm, in part, and remand the case to the Commission for further proceedings.

## DISCUSSION

We address several arguments advanced by petitioner. The first point we consider is a procedural one: NYSEG's insistence that the Commission acted beyond its authority when it amended, *sua sponte,* the portion of the complaint dealing with Price's failure to use eye protection. Next, we discuss the following questions: whether the Commission improperly required NYSEG to carry the burden of proving the adequacy of its safety program, instead of placing that burden on the Secretary; whether the Commission inappropriately concluded that NYSEG constructively knew of Price's safety violation; whether knowledge could be imputed to NYSEG through its employee Webb; and whether NYSEG should be absolved of liability because Price's conduct was unforeseeable. * * *

## I.  Amendment of the Complaint

We turn now to the issues raised, and consider NYSEG's procedural contention first. The question is whether the Commission should have dismissed, rather than amended, that part of the complaint alleging a violation of the Act's general duty clause stemming from Price's failure to use protective eyewear. The Commission adopted petitioner's contention that the general duty clause was an inappropriate basis for the citation because a specific standard—29 C.F.R. § 1926.28, the standard invoked in the original citation—applied to Price's conduct. But instead of dismissing, the Commission proceeded to amend the complaint itself, reading the complaint as though it had asserted a special duty clause violation. Petitioner believes such *sua sponte* amendment was error.

Proceedings before the Commission generally are governed by the Federal Rules of Civil Procedure. 29 U.S.C. § 661(g). Under the Federal Rules, pleadings are not ends in themselves, but are simply the means by which a case is presented to a tribunal. *See Mfg. Co.,* 568 F.2d 902, 906 (2d Cir.1977). In an administrative proceeding, w *Usery v. Marquette Cement* hich of course is the forum for the instant case, pleadings are liberally construed and easily amended. *Id.* And, because such matters are conducted informally, the form a pleading takes does not loom large, *see* 1 Kenneth C. Davis, Administrative Law Treatise § 8.04, at 523 (1st ed.1958) (administrative pleadings are unimportant). Further, under Fed. R.Civ.P. 15(b), "[w]hen issues not raised by the pleadings are tried by express or implied consent of the parties, they shall be treated in all respects as if they had been raised in the pleadings." In assessing whether the pleadings should conform to the proof, the pivotal question is whether prejudice would result. *See Marquette Cement,* 568 F.2d at 907.

Petitioner tells us that the applicability of the general duty clause was hotly disputed throughout the appeal before the Commission and that the Secretary never moved to amend the complaint at the hearing before the ALJ. However, a party cannot normally show that it suffered prejudice simply because of a change in its opponent's legal theory. Instead, a party's failure to plead an issue it later presented must have disadvantaged its opponent in presenting its case. *See D. Federico Co. v. New Bedford Redevelopment Auth.*, 723 F.2d 122, 126 (1st Cir.1983) ("The fact that [a Rule 15(b) amendment] involves a change in the nature of the cause of action, or the legal theory of the action, is immaterial so long as the opposing party has not been prejudiced in presenting its case."). Here, NYSEG does not dispute that the material fact issues to be tried would have been exactly the same regardless of whether or not the general duty clause was invoked. *Cf. Spancrete Northeast, Inc. v. OSHRC*, 905 F.2d 589, 593 (2d Cir.1990) (29 C.F.R. § 1926.28(a) is analogous to the general duty imposed by the Act). Hence, NYSEG was not prejudiced by the change in the theory of the safety infraction alleged against it. Nor is it helpful to the employer that the Secretary failed to move to amend because Rule 15(b) requires no motion or formal amendment of the pleadings. \* \* \* \*

Petitioner maintains, in addition, that allowing such *sua sponte* amendments would promote "sloppy drafting" by the Secretary, and that it would eliminate the need for safety standards by allowing the Secretary to plead a general duty violation in every case. These concerns are misplaced. First, although in the instant case the relevant standard is general in nature and raises the same issues as would the special duty clause, proving a general duty violation ordinarily will be more burdensome than proving a special duty violation. The former requires the Secretary to demonstrate that an employer exposed its employees to a "recognized" hazard likely to cause death or serious physical harm, and that the employer could have taken feasible steps to avoid the violation. *See Carlyle Compressor Co., Div. of Carrier Corp. v. OSHRC*, 683 F.2d 673, 676 (2d Cir.1982). The latter, in contrast, only requires proof that the employer's knowing failure to comply with a relevant safety standard exposed employees to an unsafe condition. Thus, contrary to NYSEG's concerns, the Secretary has an obvious incentive to plead a violation of the special duty clause.

Second, imprecise pleading is only tolerated where it does not prejudice the employer and has no effect on the outcome of the case. In the absence of prejudice, poorly pled theories in administrative proceedings are therefore without consequence. NYSEG fully litigated all the issues relevant to a special duty violation. We therefore reject its argument that the Commission improperly read the complaint as asserting *29 C.F.R. § 1926.28(a)* as a basis for liability.

II.   Employer's Knowledge and Adequacy of Safety Program

In carrying out the adjudicatory role assigned to it by the Act, the Commission has held that the Secretary's *prima facie* case to show a *[margin note: Element of spe duty (4 Carv)]*

violation of the special duty clause consists of four elements: (1) a relevant safety standard applies, (2) the employer failed to comply with it, (3) employees had access to the violative condition, and (4) the employer had knowledge or constructive knowledge of the condition. ... see *Carlisle Equip. Co. v. Secretary of Labor*, 24 F.3d 790, 792–93 (6th Cir.1994).

The fourth element, the knowledge requirement, may be satisfied by proof either that the employer actually knew, or "with the exercise of reasonable diligence, could have known of the presence of the violative condition." *Secretary of Labor v. Pride Oil Well Serv.*, 15 O.S.H. Cas. (BNA) 1809, 1814 (Review Comm'n 1992); see 29 U.S.C. § 666(k) ("Serious violation" cannot exist when "the employer did not, and could not with the exercise of reasonable diligence, know of the presence of the violation."); *Carlisle, 24 F.3d at 793.* Knowledge or constructive knowledge may be imputed to an employer through a supervisory agent. ... Further, constructive knowledge may be predicated on an employer's failure to establish an adequate program to promote compliance with safety standards. *Brock v. L.E. Myers Co.*, 818 F.2d 1270, 1277 (6th Cir.), cert. denied, 484 U.S. 989, 108 S.Ct. 479, 98 L.Ed.2d 509 (1987).

The Commission has also taken the position that when the Secretary has made out a *prima facie* case of a violation, the employer may still prevail by establishing the affirmative defense of unpreventable or unforeseeable employee misconduct. *E.g., Pride*, 15 O.S.H. Cas. at 1816. This defense requires an employer to demonstrate it (1) established a work rule to prevent the violative behavior, (2) adequately communicated the rule to its employees, (3) took steps to discover non-compliance, and (4) effectively enforced safety rules when violations were discovered. *E.g., Secretary of Labor v. Nooter Constr. Co.*, No. 91–237, 1994 WL 27750, at *6 (O.S.H.R.C. Jan. 31, 1994); *Dover*, 1993 O.S.H.D. at 41,480.

*[margin note: What we analyze]*

We discuss the merits of this issue by analyzing petitioner's several contentions: (a) the Commission erred in requiring NYSEG to shoulder the burden of proving the adequacy of its safety program, when that issue arose as part of the Secretary's *prima facie* case; (b) there was insufficient proof that NYSEG's safety program was inadequate and, therefore, the Secretary could not show NYSEG had knowledge of the violation; (c) the evidence was insufficient to permit Webb's knowledge to be ascribed to NYSEG on the basis of his purported supervisory status, because Webb was not a supervisor and, in any event, he had no actual or constructive knowledge; and (d) even if Webb had constructive knowledge of the violation, imputation was improper because the violation was unforeseeable.

## A. Burden of Proof

We first address whether the Commission erred in placing on NYSEG the burden of proof regarding the adequacy of its safety policy. The Secretary argues that the issue need not be reached because the Commission assumed the burden was on the Secretary. If we reach the question, however, the Secretary maintains that the burden should be borne by the employer. When determining that the employer's supervision was inadequate if Webb was simply Price's co-worker and not his supervisor, the Commission adopted the ALJ's ruling with respect to NYSEG's affirmative defense that it had an adequate safety program. In other words, the Commission relied on the ALJ's discussion of whether NYSEG proved its affirmative defense instead of asking whether the Secretary proved the knowledge component of his *prima facie* case. The ALJ's ruling on the affirmative defense placed the burden of proof squarely on the employer, and nothing in the Commission's opinion suggests it thought that placement wrong, even in the very different context of proving a *prima facie* case. We must therefore address the burden-of-proof question. * * *

NYSEG concedes that "unpreventable employee misconduct" is a defense that must be pleaded and proved by the employer. It argues, however, that the burden regarding the adequacy of the employer's safety policy must be borne by the Secretary when, as here, the issue arises as part of the Secretary's *prima facie* case. The proper allocation of the burden regarding whether a violation constituted unpreventable conduct—an issue closely related to, but not the same as, the burden-of-proof contention urged by NYSEG on this appeal—has split the Circuits. As one Justice of the Supreme Court observed, "There is a confusing patchwork of conflicting approaches to this issue," *L.E. Myers,* 484 U.S. at 989, 108 S.Ct. at 479 (1987) (White, J., dissenting from denial of certiorari). * * *

The majority of the Circuits have held that unpreventable employee misconduct is an affirmative defense that an employer must plead and prove. The First Circuit so held in a case involving the general duty clause, *General Dynamics Corp. v. OSHRC,* 599 F.2d 453, 459 (1st Cir.1979), as have the Fifth, Sixth, Eighth, and Eleventh Circuits in special duty cases, *H.B. Zachry Co. v. OSHRC,* 638 F.2d 812, 818 (5th Cir. Unit A Mar.1981); *L.E. Myers,* 818 F.2d at 1277; *Danco Constr. Co. v. OSHRC,* 586 F.2d 1243, 1246–47 (8th Cir.1978); *Daniel Int'l Corp. v. OSHRC,* 683 F.2d 361, 364 (11th Cir.1982).

Relying on the case law placing the burden of proving unpreventable conduct on the employer, the Secretary argues that NYSEG should also bear the burden with respect to whether it had *knowledge* of Price's conduct, at least where such knowledge is based on the inadequacy of its safety policy. As the Secretary acknowledges, and as noted above, when knowledge is based on shortcomings in the employer's safety policy, one issue raised in the *prima facie* case—the adequacy of the policy—is the same question that would arise if the employer were to raise the defense of unpreventable misconduct. The Secretary maintains that it would be illogical to require it to prove knowledge as part of its *prima facie* case when the adequacy of the safety policy is subsumed in an employer's affirmative defense.

But the fact that the employer might litigate a similar or even an identical issue as an affirmative defense does not logically remove an element from the complainant's case. The Commission has held—and the

Secretary appears to have conceded in the proceedings before the Commission—that a *prima facie* case of a special duty violation includes the element of knowledge. Without explicitly adopting a new rule, the Commission effectively ignored the usual rule it has followed that the Secretary must establish by a preponderance of the evidence that the employer knew or constructively knew of the violation. The Commission's opinion does not attempt to justify such a significant departure from its established precedent, nor did the Secretary give the Commission good reasons for modifying this element of its *prima facie* case.

When an administrative agency addresses a question in an inconsistent manner, departing from a position it has previously taken, it must make a clear statement of its new rule and articulate its reasons for making the change in order for an appellate court to conduct intelligible judicial review. *Atchison, Topeka & Santa Fe Ry. v. Wichita Bd. of Trade,* 412 U.S. 800, 808, 93 S.Ct. 2367, 2375, 37 L.Ed.2d 350 (1973). . . .

Perhaps the Commission could, without violating the Act, accept the Secretary's position as a permissible one, a proposition we do not now decide. What we do hold, however, is that without an explanation of the reasons for eliminating the Secretary's burden to prove knowledge of the safety violation as part of its *prima facie* case, the burden of showing an  employer's knowledge may not be shifted to an employer simply because the Secretary can assert no grounds for knowledge other than the inadequacy of the employer's safety policy. *Cf. Dunlop v. Rockwell Int'l,* 540 F.2d 1283, 1291 (6th Cir.1976) (a change in the Commission's position on whether knowledge is an element of a non-serious violation "must be clearly stated and accompanied by a statement of the reasoning behind the change").

Contrary to the Secretary's suggestion, the view of the majority of the Circuits—that unpreventable misconduct is an affirmative defense—does not compel a holding that the employer bears the burden on the adequacy of its safety policy in this case. The Secretary must first make out a *prima facie* case before the affirmative defense comes into play. *See L.E. Myers,* 818 F.2d at 1277. Knowledge may be proved in a variety of ways. The Commission might choose to adopt a rule akin to the shifting burdens of proof used in discrimination cases, *see, e.g., Texas Dep't of Community Affairs v. Burdine,* 450 U.S. 248, 252–56, 101 S.Ct. 1089, 1093–95, 67 L.Ed.2d 207 (1981), with the ultimate burden of showing employer knowledge remaining with the Secretary; or, the Commission might select some other rule. We think its experience and expertise in the occupational safety field place it in the best position to formulate a workable rule, one it must then apply in a consistent fashion.

Without deciding whether a given rule would be permissible under the OSH Act, we simply hold that—absent a clear and reasoned explanation for changing its prior rule—the burden of proof regarding the issue of knowledge may not be shifted to the employer even when knowledge charged to an employer is predicated on its alleged inadequate safety policy.

### B. Constructive Knowledge Arising From Inadequacy of NYSEG's Safety Program

Assuming, for purposes of its analysis, that Webb was not a supervisor, the Commission concluded that NYSEG had constructive knowledge of Price's conduct because it was not sufficiently diligent in providing supervision. NYSEG challenges this conclusion on two grounds, arguing first that there was no evidence in the Secretary's case-in-chief to show that it did not sufficiently monitor its employees, and second that there was not substantial evidence, taking the record as a whole, to support such a finding. * * *

We must nonetheless point out that in reaching the conclusion that NYSEG's safety program was inadequate if Webb was not a supervisor, the Commission improperly assumed—as explained above—that NYSEG bore the burden of proof with respect to showing employer knowledge. In addition, the Commission's reasoning was at odds with the OSH Act because it effectively subjected NYSEG to absolute liability for Price's conduct. Under the plain terms of the Act, worker safety is to be ensured only "so far as possible." OSH Act § 2(b), 29 U.S.C. § 651(b). The Commission's usual rule that an employer may be held liable if it has knowledge of a safety violation—whether such knowledge is imputed to it from a supervisor, stems from its failure to establish an adequate safety program, or arises from some other grounds—is consistent with the statute because it does not impermissibly insist upon safety measures beyond those that are reasonable. *See 29 U.S.C. § 666(k)* (no serious violation where employer could not have known, with the exercise of reasonable diligence, of the violation); *REA Express,* 495 F.2d at 826. But, as earlier stated, the Commission's opinion reveals it did not apply its usual rule in the present case.

Instead, it impaled NYSEG on the horns of a dilemma. If Webb was a supervisor, then his knowledge must be imputed and NYSEG therefore had knowledge. If, on the other hand, Webb was not a supervisor, then NYSEG's safety policy was inadequate because it conducted insufficient monitoring. In effect, the Commission found a single violation of the standard was enough to show that NYSEG's supervision was insufficient. By ruling that NYSEG's safety policy was inadequate if there was no supervisor constantly present to monitor Price's activities, the Commission imposed an unreasonable obligation on NYSEG. Depending upon the circumstances, close supervision may or may not be reasonably necessary to attain compliance with safety rules. *See Horne Plumbing,* 528 F.2d at 569. Insisting that each employee be under continual supervisor surveillance is a patently unworkable burden on employers. Thus, the Commission relied on a construction of the statute that is impermissible, *see Chevron,* 467 U.S. at 843, 104 S.Ct. at 2781–82, and its order must be set aside as arbitrary and capricious, *Bancker Constr.,* 31 F.3d at 34.

Although petitioner presented voluminous evidence of its safety practices, the Commission did not seriously analyze the reasonableness of this program. Rather, it applied a *per se* rule that a supervisor must be present at all times. Whether, given the evidence adduced at the hearing, the Commission would have been entitled to find that NYSEG's monitoring for purposes of ensuring its workers' safety was insufficient, is a matter we need not decide. On appeal, both parties advanced reasons for reaching opposite conclusions regarding the adequacy of NYSEG's safety program. But to accept the Secretary's position would be to "accept appellate counsel's *post hoc* rationalizations for agency action." *Metropolitan Life,* 380 U.S. at 444, 85 S.Ct. at 1064–65. We therefore must remand this issue to the Commission for its reconsideration.

C.   Imputation of Webb's Knowledge to His Employer

NYSEG avers it had no knowledge of Price's conduct by imputation from Webb because Webb was not a supervisory employee and, in any event, he had no knowledge or constructive knowledge of Price's conduct. Neither argument is persuasive.

Although the ALJ ruled that Webb's knowledge should be imputed to his employer because of his status as "crew leader," the Commission expressly declined to decide whether Webb was a supervisor for such purposes. Instead, the Commission held that the employer had knowledge of the safety violation regardless of whether Webb held a supervisory position. As already explained, when evaluating NYSEG's knowledge in the event Webb was not a supervisor, the Commission used an arbitrary rule inconsistent with the Act. Because a ruling that Webb was not a supervisor would not necessarily dispose of this case, and because Congress has given the Commission the primary role in making such factual findings, we decline to reach or decide the question. In remanding, we leave the issue of Webb's status for the Commission to decide.

The Commission did, however, determine as a fact that Webb—although he did not actually know of Price's infractions—had constructive knowledge if he was a supervisor because he was working nearby and the violations were easy to see. This finding, although its materiality is contingent upon Webb's supervisory status—a question yet to be resolved—is amply supported by substantial evidence. The testimony indicated that the two men were working at the same intersection on the same gas-line project. Although Webb says he did not actually notice that Price was not wearing the appropriate safety gear, the record strongly suggests that if he had looked at Price he could have known. The sound of a pneumatic jackhammer certainly put Webb on notice that Price was engaging in a potentially dangerous activity requiring the use of safety goggles and toe protectors. On remand NYSEG may not therefore avoid liability on the grounds that Webb, if he is found to be a supervisor, could not reasonably have known of the violation.

### D.  Unforeseeability of Price's Conduct

NYSEG maintains further that it should have prevailed regardless of whether Webb was a supervisor with constructive knowledge, because the evidence shows that its safety policy was adequate and the violation was unforeseeable. As earlier noted, when the Secretary attempts to prove constructive knowledge on the basis of the alleged inadequacy of the employer's safety policy, one element of the employer's "unforeseeable employee misconduct" defense is also necessarily relevant to the Secretary's *prima facie* case.

The Commission improperly analyzed this issue—insofar as it related to the Secretary's case—by departing from its own precedent and placing the burden of proof on the employer and by imposing absolute liability. A review of the Commission's opinion shows that the same *per se* liability analysis infected its ruling that the employer failed to establish the unforeseeable employee misconduct defense. On remand, if the Commission reaches the question of whether petitioner carried its burden of persuasion with respect to the defense, it must do so without applying a *per se* rule that a safety policy is inadequate unless employees are under constant supervision. Using the usual four-part test for this defense, *see, e.g., Dover,* 1993 O.S.H.D. at 41,480; *Pride,* 15 O.S.H. Cas. at 1816, would of course be permissible under the Act so long as the Commission only requires a reasonable policy and does not impose absolute liability. The Commission may not, however, infer that the employer's safety policy is inadequate simply because an employee worked at a field site where no supervisor was present.

### CONCLUSION

In sum, we hold that the Commission arbitrarily and capriciously concluded that NYSEG's safety policy was inadequate, first, by departing without explanation from its prior decisions placing the burden regarding knowledge on the Secretary and, second, by impermissibly construing the Act and applying a *per se* rule that a safety policy is inadequate if employees are not constantly monitored for safety violations. Accordingly, the Commission's order sustaining the validity of the citation against NYSEG must be set aside.

We decline to decide whether any of the following determinations are supported by substantial evidence: (1) that the employer's safety policy was or was not reasonably adequate, (2) that Webb was or was not a supervisor for purposes of imputing knowledge to his employer, or (3) that Price's misconduct was or was not unpreventable. However, the Commission's finding that Webb had constructive knowledge of Price's conduct, if indeed he was a supervisor, is affirmed.

For the reasons stated, the Commission's order is set aside, in part, affirmed, in part, and the case is remanded for further proceedings not inconsistent with this opinion.

## NOTES AND QUESTIONS

1. The court leaves somewhat in limbo the question whether knowledge of a supervisor is *per se* knowledge of the employer. In *Horne Plumbing and Heating Co. v. OSHRC*, 528 F.2d 564 (5th Cir.1976), the job foreman and another experienced foreman were killed when a trench collapsed because it had not been properly shored. Horne, the owner of the company, had instructed the employees to shore the trench but the two foremen, with a "cavalier attitude," ignored the order and the dangers, chiding other employees for their reluctance to work in the unshored trench. The court pointed out the employer's "outstanding safety program" and safety record, and that both of the men killed were highly experienced and had used shoring on other jobs. The court refused to impute the job foreman's conduct to the employer, holding: "(O)n the facts of this case, it was error to find Horne liable on an imputation theory for the unforeseeable, implausible, and therefore unpreventable acts of his employees. A contrary holding would not further the policies of the Act, and it would result in an imposition of a standard virtually indistinguishable from one of strict or absolute liability which Congress through Section 17(k) specifically eschewed." Id. at 571.

Why should not the employer be held liable for the safety violations of its foremen? An employer is liable for the torts of its employees, regardless of its instructions to the employee, and this is not considered strict or absolute liability. An employer is responsible under the National Labor Relations Act for the anti-union conduct of its supervisors even though they have been specifically instructed not to engage in such conduct. Is there any reason why the same principle should not apply under the OSH Act? Later cases have held that knowledge of a supervisor or the "competent person," that is the person responsible for enforcing OSHA standards can be attributed to the employer. *Lakeland Enterprises of Rhinelander, Inc. v. Chao*, 402 F.3d 739 (7th Cir. 2005); *Globe Contractors Inc. v. Herman*, 132 F.3d 367 (7th Cir. 1997). If an employer instructs a non-supervisor to conduct a "safety audit," the resulting report is likely to put the employer "on notice" of violations found, even if some management official seeks to suppress the report from higher-ups. See *A.E. Staley Mfg. Co. v. Secretary of Labor*, 295 F.3d 1341 (D.C. Cir. 2002).

2. The burden of proof issue has divided the federal courts. *In L. R. Willson & Sons, Inc. v. OSHRC*, 134 F.3d 1235 (4th Cir.1998), when an employee and a foreman admitted working seventy-five feet above the ground without the required fall protection, the Fourth Circuit held that the knowledge of a supervisor was not to be imputed to the employer and that the burden was on the Secretary to prove that the employee conduct was not unforeseeable or unpreventable as a part of his case in chief. The Supreme Court has refused to decide the issue, over the protest of two justices. See *Brock v. L.E. Myers Co.*, 818 F.2d 1270, (6th Cir.), *cert. denied*, 484 U.S. 989, 108 S.Ct. 479, 98 L.Ed.2d 509 (1987). See the discussion in *Three Sons, LLC v. Wyoming Occupational Safety & Health Comm'n*, 160 P.3d 58 (Wyo. 2007). The *Willson & Sons* decision is analyzed in Note, *L.R.Willson & Sons v.*

*OSHRC: The State of the Employee Misconduct Defense in OSHA Adjudications Involving Serious Violations*, 6 TEX. WESLEYAN L. REV. 187 (2000).

3. OSHA has acknowledged that there may be special circumstances where complying with a standard may be a greater hazard than noncompliance, but the burden is on the employer to establish this affirmative defense. The employer must prove (1) that compliance would result in a greater hazard than noncompliance, (2) that there are no alternative means of employee protection, and (3) that a variance was unavailable or appropriate. *E & R Erectors, Inc. v. Secretary of Labor*, 107 F.3d 157 (3d Cir.1997).

4. In *Union Tank Car Company, Inc. v. OSHA*, 192 F.3d 701 (7th Cir. 1999), the employer was cited for a serious violation of the standard that employees working in enclosed spaces (here tank cars) be equipped with a body harness so they can be pulled out without another employee entering. Instead of a body harness, the company used a wrist harness, claiming that it was safer because it allowed a worker to be extracted faster. The court held that, "good faith belief that one's policies are safer than those required by OSHA regulation is not a defense to a violation of those regulations" 192 F.3d 706.

## ATLANTIC & GULF STEVEDORES, INC. v. OCCUPATIONAL SAFETY & HEALTH REVIEW COMMISSION

United States Court of Appeals, Third Circuit, 1976
534 F.2d 541

GIBBONS, CIRCUIT JUDGE.

\* \* \*

The petitioners are stevedoring companies operating in the Port of Philadelphia. They employ longshoremen. The Secretary of Labor, pursuant to statutory authority, has adopted safety and health regulations for longshoring. Among those regulations is the so called "longshoring hardhat" standard:

> "Employees shall be protected by protective hats meeting the specifications contained in the American National Standard Safety Requirements for Industrial Head Protection, Z89.1 (1969)."

29 C.F.R. § 1918.105(a) (1975).

On April 10–11, 1973 an OSHA compliance officer inspected the Camden, New Jersey docks and discovered that nearly all of petitioners' longshoremen were working without hardhats. The Secretary cited petitioners for violation of § 5(a)(2) of OSHA, 29 U.S.C. § 654(a)(2), and proposed that civil penalties aggregating $455 be levied against the petitioners. Each citation also ordered immediate abatement of violations. Petitioners filed notices of contest, 29 U.S.C. § 659(a), which resulted in a hearing before the Commission's Administrative Law Judge. 29 U.S.C. § 659(c).

At the hearing the OSHA compliance officer testified that on the dates of his inspections, only a very small proportion of the longshoremen were wearing hardhats, that none of the petitioners had previously been cited for a violation of the hardhat standard, and that no injuries were involved. He also testified that between 1971, when the standard was adopted, and April 1973 there had been a moratorium in the Secretary's enforcement of it, because the longshoremen's unions opposed it and the rank-and-file preferred not to wear hardhats. In 1973 the Secretary changed his enforcement policy, apparently as a result of conversations between a representative of the Department of Labor and the president of the International Longshoremen's Association.

Witnesses for the petitioners testified that stevedores in the Port of Philadelphia had, beginning in 1971, undertaken strenuous but unsuccessful efforts to obtain compliance with the standard by their longshoring employees; had furnished the required hardhats; had encouraged use of the headgear at regular safety meetings; had posted hardhat signs on their working premises; had used payroll envelope stuffers advocating hardhat wearing; and had placed hardhat safety messages on the hiring tapes. All this was to little avail, and each employer witness testified to a firm belief that wildcat strikes or walkouts would attend attempts to enforce the standard by firing employees who refused to comply. There is undisputed testimony that in another port a strike over that issue did occur.[4] There is, however, no testimony that these petitioners ever denied work to a longshoreman for his refusal to wear a hardhat.

The petitioners urged that the Secretary's citations and proposed penalties should be vacated because in view of the longshoremen's intransigent opposition to and their union's lukewarm support for the standard, compliance *by them* with the hardhat standard was not achievable. The Administrative Law Judge found the three employers in violation of 29 C.F.R. § 1918.105(a), but vacated the Secretary's proposed penalties. A petition for discretionary review was filed with the Commission pursuant to § 12(j) of the Act, 29 U.S.C. § 661(i), and review was granted.

I

On April 11, 1975 the Commission handed down the decision and final order which we review. The Commission voted 2–1 to affirm the Administrative Law Judge's decision finding violations and vacating proposed penalties, but each Commissioner filed a separate opinion. Commissioner Cleary announced the decision of the Commission. He rejected as "largely speculative" the petitioners' contention that they had done all they could do without causing labor strife. In addition, citing *Brennan v. OSHRC (Gerosa, Inc.)*, 491 F.2d 1340 (2d Cir.1974), he concluded that, at least when non-compliance by employees was neither unpredictable nor

---

**4.** This strike occurred in the Port of New York in 1970, prior to the enactment of OSHA. The record also disclosed that stevedoring companies have successfully enforced the mandatory use regulation in the Port of Norfolk, but that longshoremen in the Port of San Francisco have resisted the use of hardhats.

idiosyncratic, final responsibility for compliance with the Act's requirements rested with the employers.

Commissioner Van Namee, concurring, did not agree that the evidence of potential labor unrest was speculative. Nor did he agree that employers could under the Act be held strictly liable in all instances of technical non-compliance. Yet he concluded that in this instance the employers would, because of the terms of their collective bargaining agreements, have a remedy under § 301 of the Labor Management Relations Act, 29 U.S.C. § 185, against a wildcat strike. Commissioner Van Namee surmised that the availability of such a remedy made the fear of a strike, or at least an effective one, "nothing more than an illusion."[6] He recognized, however, that the applicability of a particular safety and health standard should not turn on whether the parties to the collective bargaining agreement agreed upon a grievance-arbitration procedure that was broad enough to permit a *Boys Markets* injunction. Such an approach would admit of selective enforcement of OSHA safety standards. To meet this objection Commissioner Van Namee said that irrespective of the existence of a *Boys Markets* remedy, the Commission itself had the statutory authority to issue cease and desist orders running against employees. These orders could be enforced by injunction in the Courts of Appeals pursuant to §§ 11(a) and (b) of the Act, 29 U.S.C. §§ 660(a) and (b).

Chairman Moran dissented. Like Commissioner Van Namee, he rejected Commissioner Cleary's assessment of the evidence concerning the likelihood of walkouts over attempts to enforce the hardhat requirement. He concluded that the employers had taken all steps required of them under the Act. He also expressed doubt as to the availability of § 301 injunctive relief.

In summary, although the Commission order affirmed the citations, there is no opinion which can be said to represent a consensus. Two Commissioners, Moran and Van Namee, agree that the record contains substantial evidence tending to show that a work stoppage will occur if the petitioners take additional steps to enforce the hardhat requirement. Commissioner Van Namee concludes, however, that the availability of relief before the Commission against spontaneous employee obduracy renders this body of evidence irrelevant. Chairman Moran evidently does not share Commissioner Van Namee's expansive view of the Commission's

---

**6.** That a *Boys Markets, Inc. v. Retail Clerks, Local 770*, 398 U.S. 235, 90 S.Ct. 1583, 26 L.Ed.2d 199 (1970) remedy is available does not, of course, by itself conclusively answer petitioners' objection that employee recalcitrance makes compliance with the longshoring hardhat safety standard impossible. The stevedores could obtain a § 301 injunction only if they agreed to submit the hardhat dispute to arbitration. There can be no assurance, for example, that an arbitrator would decide that an employee who defied an express directive of his employer and ignored validly promulgated federal regulations could be discharged or otherwise disciplined for such conduct. We assume, however, that arbitration would most often sustain the employer prerogative in this regard. Where the collective bargaining agreement empowers the employer to seek § 301 relief, therefore, that remedy is likely to prove adequate. In those instances where it is demonstrably inadequate, the employers may nevertheless seek relief from liability by petitioning for a variance from the standard, 29 U.S.C. § 655(d), or for an extension of time in which to abate a cited violation 29 U.S.C. § 659(c). *See* Part IIIB, *infra*.

powers, although he did not in this case address the issue. Commissioner Cleary flatly rejects any interpretation of OSHA that would permit the Commission to issue cease and desist orders against employees. Nevertheless, he regards the threat of work stoppages posed in this instance as largely speculative. In any event, Commissioner Cleary suggests that where, as here, employee non-compliance is neither unpredictable nor idiosyncratic, the employer has an absolute statutory duty to enforce the terms of the Act.

## II

Section 11(a) of the Act, 29 U.S.C. § 660(a), directs the reviewing court to accept "[t]he findings of the Commission with respect to questions of fact, if supported by substantial evidence on the record considered as a whole * * *." *Brennan v. OSHRC (Interstate Glass Co.)*, 487 F.2d 438 (8th Cir.1973). Because there is no opinion in which a majority of the Commission joined, there is no Commission finding of fact with respect to the likelihood that enforcement of the hardhat standard would provoke a work stoppage. But two Commissioners appear to have credited the testimony of the petitioners' witnesses that such a work stoppage was likely if not inevitable. We believe that such a finding would be supported by substantial evidence on the record as a whole.[7] Indeed, Commissioner Cleary's rejection of the evidence as "largely speculative", if it represented a finding of the Commission, probably would have to be dismissed as unsupported by substantial record evidence. Thus we assume, for purposes of this petition for review, that the longshoremen in the Port of Philadelphia are intransigent on the hardhat issue and are likely to strike if more vigorous enforcement efforts are undertaken.

This assumption serves to focus the specific and relatively narrow issue presented by this petition, viz., whether when employee non-compliance with an occupational safety or health standard is both predictable and virtually uniform, the employer must nevertheless enforce compliance even at the risk of concerted employee work stoppages. Because any answer to this inquiry is an adjudicatory conclusion, the scope of our review is less narrowly jacketed than with factual determinations. The law of this circuit is that we may set aside such conclusions if we find them to be arbitrary, capricious, an abuse of discretion or otherwise not in accordance with law. *Brennan v. OSHRC (Hanovia Lamp Div.)*, 502 F.2d 946, 951 (3d Cir.1974); *Budd Co. v. OSHRC*, 513 F.2d 201, 204 (3d Cir.1975) (per curiam).

---

**7.** In addition to the evidence of the employers' futile attempts at friendly persuasion, and of the longshoremen's resistance in the Port of Philadelphia and elsewhere, *see* Part I *supra*, the evidence showed that while initial compliance in 1971 with the regulation was good (about 80%), the rate of compliance quickly deteriorated. Apparently many workers tried the hats, found them uncomfortable or cumbersome, and discontinued their use.

The evidence also showed that although the stevedores had never actually denied employment to a longshoreman who refused to wear a hardhat, a 1971 threat of such action triggered an angry demonstration of longshoring foremen. Statistics showing that head injuries comprised only a small fraction (perhaps 1%) of total longshoring injuries fueled employee sentiment that hardhats did not protect against a significant occupational hazard and hence were unnecessary.

## A

In urging us to vacate the citations, petitioners place principal reliance on our decision in the *Hanovia Lamp* case. There we followed the holding of the District of Columbia Circuit in *National Realty & Construction Co. v. OSHRC,* 160 U.S.App.D.C. 133, 489 F.2d 1257 (1973), rejecting a construction of the Act which would effectively make employers strictly liable for violations arising from employee misconduct. In *Hanovia Lamp* we held that an employer could be held answerable for a violation resulting from such misconduct only when "demonstrably feasible measures" existed for materially reducing its incidence. 502 F.2d at 952. In reply the Secretary correctly points out that both *National Realty Construction* and *Hanovia Lamp* involved citations for violation of the Act's general duty clause, while this case involves a citation for violation of a specific safety standard. It seems to be the Secretary's position that employers are to be held to a higher standard of care under specific regulations than under the general duty clause. We decline to bifurcate the statute in such a manner, and attach no significance to the proffered distinction. As the First Circuit observed in *Cape & Vineyard Division of New Bedford v. OSHRC,* 512 F.2d 1148 (1st Cir.1975), the employer's task of guarding against the aberrational action of specific employees who violate specific safety standards is essentially no less difficult than under the general duty clause. *Cf. Brennan v. Butler Lime & Cement Co.,* 520 F.2d 1011, 1017 (7th Cir.1975). Thus the *Hanovia Lamp* standard governing employer responsibility applies, in our view, to 29 C.F.R. § 1918.105(a) to the same extent as to the general duty clause.

But while *Hanovia Lamp, National Realty Construction* and *Cape & Vineyard Division* supply us with the standard of liability to be applied to the facts of this case, they offer precious little insight into the question whether the petitioner stevedoring companies have breached their statutory duty of care. Those cases involved the unpredictable and unforeseeable actions of individual employees. This case involves the predictable, nearly universal actions of all the longshoremen. There is a demonstrably feasible measure which can be taken to prevent such concerted disobedience: the employer can refuse employment to those who insist on violating the standard. The discussions of strict liability in the cases referred to have no application to the instant situation, except to the extent that they are authority for the proposition that we will not construe OSHA to impose completely unreasonable burdens on employers within the Act's coverage.

We find guidance on this difficult question in our recent decision in *AFL–CIO v. Brennan,* 530 F.2d 109 (3d Cir.1975). In that case we reviewed action of the Secretary adopting a "no hands in dies" standard for the mechanical power press industry. We recognized that the economic feasibility of an occupational safety and health standard was relevant to our assessment of its statutory validity. We pointed out that an economically impossible standard would in all likelihood prove unenforceable, and that the burden of policing a regulation uniformly ignored by a majority of industry members would prove to be overwhelming. Thus we held that in promulgating regulations the Secretary could take into account the economic impact of a proposed standard. *See* 530 F.2d at 122–123; *Industrial Union Department, AFL–CIO v. Hodgson,* 162 U.S.App.D.C. 331, 499 F.2d 467, 477–78 (1974).

## B

In the same case, however, we also recognized that OSHA must be viewed as technology-forcing legislation; that is, legislation looking to improvement in the techniques of industrial safety. *See* 530 F.2d at 120–122. The Secretary's rule-making task comprehends weighing the competing considerations of economic burden and improvement of safety. The approach we took in *AFL–CIO v. Brennan* suggests, although it does not compel, the conclusion that employee resistance to a safety standard having severe economic consequences is a relevant consideration in the instant case. That conclusion is not compelled because of the manifest differences between the Secretary's quasi-legislative rule-making, which we review under § 6(f) of the Act, 29 U.S.C. § 655(f), and Commission adjudication, which we review under § 11(a), 29 U.S.C. § 660(a).

[The court here discussed the legislative history and the legal and practical considerations as to the role of the Commission and the courts in reviewing the validity of a standard in a Section 6(f) proceeding directly challenging its validity immediately after the standard is promulgated and indirectly challenging its validity subsequently in an enforcement proceeding, reviewable under Section 11.]

In light of the foregoing discussion, it can be argued that because Congress in § 6(f) of the Act authorized direct review in the courts of appeals of standards promulgated by the Secretary, and limited the period of review to 60 days, we are without authority to entertain an attack upon the validity of any regulation in a § 11 enforcement proceeding. * * * § 11(a), while confining judicial review of fact findings in enforcement proceedings to the substantial evidence standard, is entirely silent as to legal issues. We do not find, from the availability of limited pre-enforcement judicial review permitted under § 6(f) and the silence with respect to legal issues in § 11(a), an intention to limit the scope of judicial review in the enforcement proceeding. Judicial review at that stage is, after all, the ordinarily preferred method. * * *

That being the case, it seems illogical to suggest that the Commission cannot in the first instance adjudicate both the fact of violation and the validity of the implicated standard. Certainly it would be an exercise in futility for the Commission to enforce a citation under a standard which it knew, perhaps from prior adjudications, would be held invalid by this court. * * *

## III

In this case the petitioners contend that the longshoring hardhat safety standard, insofar as it is applied to them, is invalid because attempts at enforcement would provoke a wildcat strike by their employees. The standard is, in their view, economically infeasible. They produced evidence tending to support this position in the proceeding before the Administrative Law Judge. We believe that petitioners have carried their burden of proof on the issue. The remaining question is the legal sufficiency of the defense. We turn, then, to the several grounds relied upon by the Commission in rejecting petitioners' challenge to the hardhat safety standard.

*We believe strike will occur, but*

A

If Commissioner Van Namee is correct that the Commission has the power to issue cease and desist orders against employees as well as employers, then the economic infeasibility argument against the standard disappears from this case. Unlike the no hands in dies standard which we reviewed in *AFL–CIO v. Brennan, supra,* the infeasibility claim in this case is bottomed not on the cost of forcing the technological change, but on the cost of a work stoppage caused by employee discontent with a simple, inexpensive and facially reasonable safety standard. If the Commission, and in turn this court, can issue coercive process against employees directly, the threat is eliminated and the defense overcome. It is far from clear, however, that the Commission enjoys the power for which Commissioner Van Namee argues.

Commissioner Van Namee finds the source of such coercive authority in a combination of § 2(b)(2) of the Act, 29 U.S.C. § 651(b)(2), § 5(b), 29 U.S.C. § 654(b), and § 10(c), 29 U.S.C. § 659(c). The latter provision authorizes the Commission to issue orders "affirming, modifying, or vacating the Secretary's citation * * * or directing other appropriate relief * * *." Section 2(b)(2), in the section of the Act setting forth congressional findings and a declaration of policy, provides:

> (b) The Congress declares it to be its purpose and policy * * * to assure so far as possible every working man and woman in the Nation safe and healthful working conditions and to preserve our human resources—* * *
>
> > (2) by providing that employers and employees have separate but dependent responsibilities and rights with respect to achieving safe and healthful working conditions * * *.

Section 5(b) provides that

> "[e]ach employee shall comply with occupational safety and health standards and all rules, regulations, and orders issued pursuant to this chapter which are applicable to his own actions and conduct."

According to Commissioner Van Namee the employees' separate responsibilities under § 5(b) would be "meaningless and a nullity" if the Commission and this court, in an enforcement proceeding, were powerless to sanction employee disregard of safety standards and commission orders. * * *

With considerable misgivings, we conclude that Congress did not intend to confer on the Secretary or the Commission the power to sanction employees. Sections 2(b)(2) and 5(b) cannot be read apart from the detailed scheme of enforcement set out in §§ 9, 10 and 17 of the Act. It seems clear that this enforcement scheme is directed only against employers. Sections 9(a) and 10(a) provide for the issuance of citations and notifications of proposed penalties only to employers. 29 U.S.C. §§ 658(a), 659(a). Section 10(a) refers only to an employer's opportunity to contest a citation and notification of proposed penalty. Only after an employer has filed a notice of contest does the Commission obtain general jurisdiction. Employees and their representatives may then elect to intervene under § 10(c). The only independent right granted employees by § 10(c) is to contest before the Commission the reasonableness of any time period fixed by the Secretary in a citation for the abatement of a violation. Section 17, 29 U.S.C. § 666, provides for the assessment of civil monetary penalties only against employers.[17] That the Act's use of the term "employer" is truly generic is made plain in § 3, the definitional section, where "employer" and "employee" are separately defined. *See* 29 U.S.C. § 652. We find no room for loose construction of the term of art.

We are likewise unable to find support in § 5(b) for the proposition that the Act's sanctions can be directed at employees. Although this provision's injunction to employees is essentially devoid of content if not enforceable, we reluctantly conclude that this result precisely coincides with the congressional intent. * * *

The Senate Report on the employee duty section, quoted in full, says:

The committee recognizes that accomplishment of the purposes of this bill cannot be totally achieved without the fullest cooperation of affected employees. In this connection, Section 5(b) expressly places upon each employee the obligation to comply with standards and other applicable requirements under the act.

It should be noted, too, that studies of employee motivation are among the research efforts which the committee expects to be undertaken under section 18, and it is hoped that such studies, as well as the programs for employee and employer training authorized by section 18(f), will provide the basis for achieving the fullest possible commitment of individual workers to the health and safety efforts of their employers. It has been made clear to the committee that the most successful plant safety programs are those which emphasize employee participation in their formulation and administration; every effort should therefore be made to maximize such participation throughout industry.

---

**17.** Compare in this regard the Federal Coal Mine Health and Safety Act of 1969, 30 U.S.C. §§ 801–960. Section 109(a)(1)–(2) provides for civil penalties against miners as well as employers. 30 U.S.C. § 819(a)(1)–(2). In contrast to OSHA, § 109(a)(4) preserves the right to jury trial in the civil penalty enforcement proceeding. 30 U.S.C. § 819(a)(4). *See Frank Irey, Jr., Inc. v. OSHRC,* 519 F.2d 1200 (3d Cir.1974) (en banc), *petition for cert. filed,* 44 U.S.L.W. 3363 (U.S. Nov. 21, 1975) (No. 75–748).

The committee does not intend the employee-duty provided in section 5(b) to diminish in anyway the employer's compliance responsibilities or his responsibility to assure compliance by his own employees. Final responsibility for compliance with the requirements of this act remains with the employer.

S.Rep. No. 91–1282, *supra,* at 10–11, U.S. Code Cong. & Admin. News 1970, p. 5187. We simply cannot accept the argument that a remedy for violations of § 5(b) can be implied from its terms. All the evidence points in the other direction.

Nor do we believe that the language in § 10(c) authorizing the Commission to issue orders "directing other appropriate relief" can be stretched to the point that it includes relief against employees. Rather, the generality of that language must be deemed limited by its context—relief in connection with the Secretary's citation. The Secretary appears not to have authority to issue a citation against an employee, and the Commission's powers cannot be any broader. "Other appropriate relief" refers to other appropriate relief against an employer.

This court's power under § 11(a) of the Act is framed in somewhat broader terms:

> Upon [the filing of a petition for review], the court shall have jurisdiction of the proceeding and of the question determined therein, and shall have power to grant such temporary relief or restraining order as it deems just and proper, and to make and enter upon the pleadings, testimony, and proceedings set forth in such record a decree affirming, modifying, or setting aside in whole or in part, the order of the Commission and enforcing the same to the extent that such order is affirmed or modified.

29 U.S.C. § 660(a).

Clearly we can, in deciding whether and to what extent we will enforce a Commission order affirming a Secretary's citation, take into account the fact that employee intransigence in spite of employer best efforts would make enforcement inequitable. In such a case we could deny or limit enforcement. But § 11(a) does not grant to this court any independent authority to sanction employees.

## B

We hold, then, that Commissioner Van Namee's reason for rejecting the petitioners' economic infeasibility defense cannot withstand analysis. We must face squarely the issue whether the Secretary can announce, and insist on employer compliance with, a standard which employees are likely to resist to the point of concerted work stoppages. To frame the issue in slightly different terms, can the Secretary insist that an employer in the collective bargaining process bargain to retain the right to discipline employees for violation of safety standards which are patently reasonable, and are economically feasible except for employee resistance?

We hold that the Secretary has such power. As Part IIIA of this opinion has indicated, the entire thrust of the Act is to place primary responsibility for safety in the work place upon the employer. That, certainly, is a decision within the legislative competence of Congress. In some cases, undoubtedly, such a policy will result in work stoppages. But as we observed in *AFL–CIO v. Brennan, supra,* the task of weighing the economic feasibility of a regulation is conferred upon the Secretary. He has concluded that stevedores must take all available legal steps to secure compliance by the longshoremen with the hardhat standard.

We can perceive several legal remedies which employers in petitioners' shoes might find availing. An employer can bargain in good faith with the representatives of its employees for the right to discharge or discipline any employee who disobeys an OSHA standard. Because occupational safety and health would seem to be subsumed within the subjects of mandatory collective bargaining—wages, hours and conditions of employment, *see* 29 U.S.C. § 158(d)—the employer can, consistent with its duty to bargain in good faith, insist to the point of impasse upon the right to discharge or discipline disobedient employees. *See NLRB v. American National Insurance Co.,* 343 U.S. 395, 72 S.Ct. 824, 96 L.Ed. 1027 (1952). Where the employer's prerogative in such matters is established, that right can be enforced under § 301. Should discipline or discharge nevertheless provoke a work stoppage, *Boys Markets* injunctive relief would be available if the parties have agreed upon a no-strike or grievance and arbitration provision. And even in those cases in which an injunction cannot be obtained, or where arbitration fails to vindicate the employer's action, the employer can still apply to the Secretary pursuant to § 6(d) of the Act, 29 U.S.C. § 655(d), for a variance from a promulgated standard, on a showing that alternative methods for protecting employees would be equally effective. *See Brennan v. OSHRC (Underhill Construction Corp.),* 513 F.2d 1032, 1036 (2d Cir.1975). Moreover, under § 10(c), 29 U.S.C. § 659(c), the Secretary has authority to extend the time within which a violation of a standard must be abated.

In this case petitioners have produced no evidence demonstrating that they have bargained for a unilateral privilege of discharge or discipline, that they have actually discharged or disciplined, or threatened to discharge or discipline, any employee who defied the hardhat standard, or that they have petitioned the Secretary for a variance or an extension of the time within which compliance is to be achieved. We conclude that as a matter of law petitioners have failed to establish the infeasibility of the challenged regulation.

The order of the Commission enforcing the Secretary's citations will be affirmed. The petition for review will be denied.

### NOTES AND QUESTIONS

1. The court suggests that the employer may bargain with the union for a contract provision expressly permitting discipline of employees who refuse

to wear hard hats or otherwise violate OSHA standards. Assume the union's response is to insist on some concession in return. Should the cost of the concession be viewed simply as the employer's cost of compliance, like many other more substantial costs of compliance?

2.   The union, however, may refuse to agree to such a provision because the members would not ratify the contract, and the impasse will result in a strike. Should the strike be viewed as one to compel the employer to agree to a contract countenancing violation of the OSH Act? If so, this would seem to be a violation by the union of its statutory duty to bargain in good faith and the striking employees would be subject to discharge. But the legal results might not produce the practical result of enabling the employers to resume operations and enforce the hard hat rule.

3.   The court suggests that if a collective agreement is in effect and the employees strike to protest the discharge of an employee for refusing to wear a hard hat, the employer may enjoin the strike. However, under *Boys Markets Inc. v. Retail Clerks Union, Local 770,* 398 U.S. 235, 90 S.Ct. 1583, 26 L.Ed.2d 199 (1970), such an injunction will issue only on the condition that the employer submit the discharge to arbitration. In the unlikely event that the arbitrator ruled that the discharge violated the collective agreement and the employee was ordered reinstated, should the district court refuse to enforce the award as contrary to public policy? See *United Paperworkers International Union v. Misco, Inc.,* 484 U.S. 29, 108 S.Ct. 364, 98 L.Ed.2d 286 (1987).

4.   The practical result of enforcing the OSHA hard hat standard might be to tell the employer, the union and the employees that the docks could not operate unless the employees wore hard hats. Is this an appropriate solution?

5.   It has been claimed that 80 to 90 percent of all occupational injuries are due to unsafe acts of employees rather than unsafe working conditions. The failure of the OSH Act to provide penalties against employees who violate safety and health standards has generated sharp criticism and some imaginative proposals, including one which would allow an employer to pass through to employees at fault all or a portion of the fine imposed on the employer. See Comment, *Employee Non–Compliance With The Occupational Safety and Health Act: Making The Worker Pay,* 31 AM.U.L. REV. 123 (1981). How effective would potential liability for fines be in influencing employee conduct? Will it be more or less effective than the employer's ability to discipline?

# J.  STATE EFFORTS TO PROMOTE SAFETY AND HEALTH

## 1.  SECTION 18 PLANS

### AFL–CIO INDUSTRIAL UNION DEPARTMENT v. MARSHALL

United States Court of Appeals, District of Columbia Circuit, 1978
570 F.2d 1030

LEVENTHAL, CIRCUIT JUDGE:

The Occupational Safety and Health Act of 1970 (OSHA) was intended to reduce the number and severity of work-related injuries and illnesses. At the time of the passage of OSHA, there was some concern that the Act not result in the wholesale federalization of occupational safety. Therefore, in § 18 of OSHA, 29 U.S.C. § 667 (1970), Congress provided that a state may reassume responsibility for occupational safety and health by submitting an acceptable plan to the Secretary of Labor. The issue presented by this case is the validity of the criteria used by the Secretary of Labor for approval of state plans.

## A. Background

There are two stages to the state plan approval process, initial approval and final approval, and the implementation of an approved plan is monitored at all times. Section 18(c) of OSHA sets out criteria for determining plan acceptability. "The Secretary shall approve the plan submitted by a State * * * if such plan in his judgment" satisfies the stated criteria. These initial approvals do not necessarily cede federal jurisdiction to the state nor affect the federal enforcement program's operation within the state. Instead, there is a concurrent jurisdiction period of at least three years during which the Secretary monitors the state program for compliance with § 18(c) and may enforce the federal program. See 29 U.S.C. § 667(e), (f) (1970).

This case requires us to focus on the standards for evaluating state plans set forth in § 18 of OSHA, and particularly the requirement of (c)(2), that the state standards be "at least as effective" as the federal standards, and of (c)(4) and (5), that there be adequate assurances that the state agency administering the plan will have sufficient "qualified personnel" and "adequate funds" to enforce the state standards.

The AFL–CIO challenged the regulations of the Secretary that interpreted "adequate funds" and "qualified personnel necessary for enforcement of [the state] standards." It claimed the regulations only parroted the language of the statute, established no rational criteria and guidelines for evaluating the sufficiency of a state's plan in terms of effective inspection and enforcement, and have resulted in state plans with wide disparities in manpower commitments and fund allotments.

The District Court upheld the Secretary of Labor's regulations on motions for summary judgment. It held that "the Secretary has promulgated rational, ascertainable standards for personnel and funding." The District Court interpreted those standards to require that the state effort be at least comparable to what the federal effort would have been in the absence of an approved state plan. The District Court also held that the Secretary of Labor had consistently and properly applied those standards. The AFL–CIO has appealed that decision to this court.

The AFL–CIO contends that the Secretary exceeded the scope of his authority by interpreting the requirements of § 18 to mandate only the provision of staff and funding levels "at least as effective as" the Federal enforcement program. It emphasizes that (4) and (5) do not contain the "at least as effective as" criterion explicitly used in (2) and (3) of § 18(c), and it argues that "adequate funds" and "qualified personnel necessary for the enforcement of such standards" mean force and funding levels sufficient to ensure that the normative standards are in fact enforced.

To demonstrate the invalidity of use of an "at least as effective as" standard for subsections (c)(4) and (5), the AFL–CIO notes that the federal benchmarks that have been employed by the Secretary are predicated on federal enforcement levels that are artificially low because the Secretary deliberately withheld commitment of adequate resources until he knew the full extent of likely state participation. It cites testimony given by Assistant Secretary of Labor George Guenther before the Senate Subcommittee on Appropriations on April 16, 1972.

> [W]e have consciously attempted to control the level of our staff resources until we get a better reading of State participation.
>
> We have had some pressure on us, as you are aware, to substantially increase our forces immediately. We have refrained from requesting those kinds of increases for the reason that we don't believe that it's responsible to beef up the Federal program to such a level, and then find the States coming onboard, and have to withdraw from that staff level.

The Secretary maintains that this attitude was prompted by a lack of funding and "by Congress' repeated expressions of concern regarding possible State dislocations produced by precipitous Federal movement in this delicate area."

The Secretary argues that subsections (4) and (5) must be read in light of subsection (2), which he characterizes as the "overriding criterion." Subsection (2) states that the Secretary shall approve the state plan if it, *inter alia,* "provides for the development and enforcement of safety and health standards relating to one or more safety or health issues, which standards (and the enforcement of which standards) are or will be at least as effective in providing safe and healthful employment and places of employment as the standards promulgated under section 6." The Secretary maintains that with the inclusion of the parenthetical phrase, Congress indicated that state plan approvals were to be governed by direct comparison of state funding and personnel with that of the federal program which would otherwise be operative. * * *

## C.  Court's View of OSHA § 18(c)

After consideration of the text, legislative history and purpose of OSHA, we reach a conclusion as to the meaning of the statute that is different from that of either party—but that comports, we think, both with an effective enforcement program and a dynamic federal-state partnership in occupational health and safety matters. We hold that in referring to personnel and funding levels in terms of adequacy or sufficiency, Congress clearly intended that the states assure effective enforcement programs. In granting initial approval to state plans, the Secretary can consider—as interim federal benchmarks—whether the state is willing to provide personnel and funding "at least as effective as" that provided by the federal government. But such interim federal benchmarks must be part of an articulated, coherent program calculated to achieve a fully effective program at some point in the foreseeable future. As we discuss in part D of this opinion, the interim federal benchmarks that have been used for initial approval of state plans are not part of such a program. To comply with the mandate of the statute, the regulations and program directives establishing the benchmarks must be supplemented.

We now set forth the several pertinent considerations that have led us to our interpretation of § 18(c).

### 1.  Statutory Language

We think, along with plaintiffs, that there is significance in the fact that the "at least as effective as" criterion was explicitly set forth in § 18(c)(2) as to standards in state plans, but was omitted when Congress moved from standards to enforcement in subsections (4) and (5). The omission of the "at least as effective as" language from (4) and (5), dealing with personnel and funds, is the more conspicuous in view of insertion of these words in subsection (3). The Secretary's argument that the use of the "at least as effective as" language in subsection (2) is an overriding criterion, with no need for explicit repetition in (4) and (5), is difficult to reconcile with the existence of such repetition in (3) of § 18(c).

In interpretation, we must serve the legislative purpose. The purpose of OSHA, as explicitly set forth in § 2(b)(10), is "to assure so far as possible every working man and woman in the Nation safe and healthful working conditions and to preserve our human resources * * * by providing an effective enforcement program." This clear statement of purpose in § 2 gives context for the use of such terms as "adequate" and "necessary" in § 18(c), the context of providing "an effective enforcement program." "It is our duty 'to give effect, if possible, to every clause and word of a statute' * * * rather than to emasculate an entire section."

### 2.  Legislative History

It is a well-known canon of construction that the language of a statute is the best indication of legislative intent. *Browder v. United States,* 312 U.S. 335, 338, 61 S.Ct. 599, 85 L.Ed. 862 (1941). Here we find that the legislative history also comports with our interpretation of the statutory language.

Subsections (2), (4) and (5) of 18(c) moved from introduction to passage virtually without change, and were not the subject of extensive discussion in Congressional committees or in floor debates. * * * *.

The language of both committee reports carefully distinguished between standards and the means to enforce them. As to the latter, once the standards were set there were to be assurances that the state would have the resources "necessary to do the job." The language straightforwardly expresses a Congressional intention that approved state programs assure sufficient resources to effectively enforce the standards set forth in those programs.

The foregoing recognizes a requirement for state plans. It does not, however, mandate a rigid approach toward state efforts that would make the perfect the enemy of the good. The legislative history develops another consideration of material importance—and that is time. Congress was aware that both the states and the federal government would need time to bring a program of this type on-line. Thus § 18(c)(4) states that a state plan must give "satisfactory assurances that such agency or agencies *have or will have* the legal authority and qualified personnel necessary for the enforcement of such standards." Time is needed to staff up enforcement efforts. Moreover, switching jurisdiction from the state to federal authority entails significant transition costs. Concern was expressed on the floor of the Senate lest precipitate federal preemption mean the loss of the services of the state occupational safety and health machinery to the detriment of the overall effort.

### 3. Overall Ascertainment of Legislative Purpose

If we were controlled by the text alone, it might be argued that the "at least as effective as" concept is completely irrelevant for subsections (c)(4) and (5), where those words are omitted. An overall ascertainment of legislative purpose, however, bids us take into account practical necessities, including the concern for precipitate preemption brought out in the legislative history. In the application of a new federal statute, there is a likely Congressional contemplation of maximizing use of existing state machinery. "Federalism" cannot be invoked categorically where it would defeat the national objective. A sensitivity to state participation has value, however, where the state administration can be integrated with federal application—either as a supplement, or as a stopgap measure, or as a delegation under federal control. We have been instructed that a federal statute should not be given a rigid interpretation that would "prevent States from undertaking supplementary efforts toward [the] very same end." *New York State Department of Social Services v. Dublino,* 413 U.S. 405, 419, 93 S.Ct. 2507, 2516, 37 L.Ed.2d 688 (1973).

Taking all these considerations into account, we hold that it is reasonable for the Secretary to employ federal "at least as effective" benchmarks under (4) and (5) of § 18(c), if those objectives are integrated with the objectives of "necessary" personnel and "adequate" funds. The resultant of these vectors of analysis is the approval of current federal levels of personnel and funds as benchmarks for state plans, provided they are part of a coherent program to realize a fully effective enforcement effort at some point in the foreseeable future. These benchmarks must be pragmatic in terms of time frame but not lax in goal, and sustain state efforts that are reasonably adapted to realize the Act's objectives within the same time frame as the federal effort. * * *

Given the obligation to provide "adequate" funds and "necessary" personnel, the Secretary's regulations would obviously be deficient if they contemplated that state plans that received approval on the basis of an interim benchmark could then stand still, without any obligation to keep pace with the improving federal effort. At oral argument, government counsel advised that the states were required to upgrade their programs. The court asked for supplemental memoranda on this matter. The government's memorandum states that state programs are required to keep pace with the federal effort throughout the initial and final approval stages. What is unclear is what was the Secretary's "reasoned course" in achieving OSHA's mandate—how did the lower initial benchmark levels relate to ultimate realization of the Act's goals. * * *

The Secretary submitted a "relatively final draft" of the "OSHA System for Enforcement Planning and Resource Allocations" which sets out the ideal number of inspectors for a total Federal–State program. These data are based on information concerning the relative hazardousness of various industries in different geographical areas and the number of safety inspections necessary as a result. We are informed that this system was developed for OSHA planning and budget reasons as well as state plan evaluation. "[I]ts Federal figures for nonplan States do not represent the actual Federal deployment in any State, but an even projection designed to provide a theoretical model of equitable Federal enforcement with available Federal funds." But the Secretary concludes "the ultimate test is still a direct comparison of Federal vis-a-vis State personnel to determine approved States' current 'as effective' status."

In the last analysis, the "OSHA System for Enforcement Planning and Resource Allocation" does nothing to justify the standards employed in granting initial plan approval. It remains the case that however poor the federal effort, a state plan is approved if it is marginally better. For the years 1972 to 1974 this was clearly the case. For 1975, again, the state effort is compared with the federal effort "as is". The federal effort is now described as a percentage of what is really needed, but all that is required of an approved state plan is that its percentage be at least as high as that of the federal effort. Although we think Congress conceded the Secretary some practical flexibility in administering OSHA, this rudderless scheme of plan approval cannot be reconciled with the mandate that state plans assure "necessary" personnel and "adequate" funds. The Secretary must have some plan to reach that objective and the states must subscribe to that timetable as a precondition to implementation of the state plan. * * *

### E. Relief

We declare that the Secretary has a duty to establish criteria that are part of an articulated plan to achieve a fully effective enforcement effort at some point in the foreseeable future. The "OSHA System for Enforcement Planning and Resource Allocation" has been drawn up with ideal benchmarks. Accordingly, with a planning horizon and an appreciation for administrative lags, the Secretary should be able to articulate a series of benchmarks clearly related to eventual achievement of the goals of the Act.

This is an action for equitable relief wherein considerations of the public interest weigh heavily. We decline to enjoin implementation of any of the state plans that have been approved to date by the Secretary. The problems we have identified do not necessarily mean that the Secretary erred in giving an initial approval based on present "as effective as" criteria. What those problems require is that in addition there be an articulated and coherent program moving from an initial "as effective as" approach toward the personnel and funding levels needed for satisfactorily effective enforcement. These criteria can be provided by supplements to the approval process. We contemplate that once the Secretary has articulated his program goals and objectives in terms of personnel and funding in accordance with this opinion, the necessary resources will be sought from Congress, and the underlying criteria will be applied in the state plan approval process.

The case will be remanded for entry of a decree not inconsistent with this opinion.

*So ordered.*

MacKINNON, CIRCUIT JUDGE, concurring:

Congress declared the scheme of the Act to be to "[encourage] the States to assume the fullest responsibility for the administration and enforcement of their occupational safety and health laws * * *." (84 Stat. 1591). The statutory alternative is federal administration. It is thus incongruous to suggest that a state OSHA plan must have "necessary" personnel and "adequate" enforcement funds which are substantially in excess of what the alternative federal administration would afford.

Such being the intent of the Act and Congress being its author, it is proper to gauge what Congress considered to be "necessary" and "adequate" for state administration by what amounts Congress has made available for the alternative federal administration.

The present lawsuit is overly ambitious and seeks extreme relief. Its objective is to wrap up the entire nation in one ball of wax and get a nationwide decree declaring how many inspections each state shall have and what sums each state shall appropriate for administration and enforcement. Raising issues in such a broad context prevents careful consideration of the basic problems. To my mind the largest approach should be on a state-by-state basis.

The scheme of the Act requires safety and health standards for particular hazards and these, which involve industrial activity and states of varying geographical size, differ greatly throughout the nation. The establishment of "disparate" numbers of inspectors in various states is thus a necessary fact of life. For a court to impose proper generalized personnel requirements for each state in the nation is a practical impossibility. A great deal of discretion must be left to federal and state administrators. Our task in this case is rendered more onerous by the fact that appellants are basically attacking the approval by the Secretary of some 25 state plans; but the record is devoid of the relevant facts with respect to the separate states. Under such circumstances, it is my view that the proper relief would be to remand the case for a more definite statement by appellants, order the necessary discovery, and thus develop some concrete facts upon which to determine whether the action of the Secretary has, or has not, been arbitrary and capricious. But the issues on that basis would be almost unmanageable. Thus, I join in Judge Leventhal's opinion which calls for action that is moulded in the vein in which the Secretary states he has been approaching the problems.

### NOTES AND QUESTIONS

1. States play a very significant role in protecting worker safety and health. At the beginning of 2010, twenty-one states (Alaska, Arizona, California, Hawaii, Indiana, Iowa, Kentucky, Maryland, Michigan, Minnesota, Nevada, New Mexico, North Carolina, Oregon, South Carolina, Tennessee, Utah, Vermont, Virginia, Washington and Wyoming) and Puerto Rico operate approved plans for both private and public sector workers. The Connecticut, Illinois, New Jersey, New York and Virgin Islands plans cover only public employees. In fiscal 2009, these plans conducted over 61,000 inspections.

2. State standards are in some cases path-breaking. For example, California adopted a repetitive motion injury standard in 1997, Washington adopted a comprehensive ergonomics standard in 2000, and Michigan uses the general duty clause to reach repetitive motion injuries. California and Minnesota have incorporated into their systems standards to avoid needlestick injuries which transmit HIV and Hepatitis B and C and other bloodborne pathogens. Washington pioneered special safety and health standards for late night retail industry in 1990. A number of states have implemented Cooperative Compliance Programs such as have been blocked by the federal courts at the national level. Might say something more about Cooperative Compliance Programs here?

3. The importance of budget decisions to effective enforcement of the Act is pervasive at both federal and state levels, but ceding jurisdiction to the states has special budget twists. Unions have charged that the Secretary has been too willing to approve state plans, not out of deference to the principle of federalism, but out of pressures on the Department's budget because of the federal deficit. The effort is to shift to the states as much budget burden as possible. On the other side, few states have developed full scale state plans because the federal grant is half the cost, or less. They prefer to have the federal government bear the whole cost rather than exercise their role as states in a federal system.

California is the one of the few major industrial states which has obtained approval of its comprehensive state plan, and it provided four times as many inspectors as the federal level. In 1988, Governor Dukemejian decided to help balance his budget by withdrawing the state plan and shifting the burden to the federal government. To fill gap created by this withdrawal, 318 out of the total 1200 federal inspectors were assigned to California. In November, 1988, the voters of California approved an initiative measure to restore full state enforcement of occupational health and safety standards and to require that the state budget include sufficient funds to enforce Cal—OSHA.

## 2.  PREEMPTION OF NON-APPROVED "PLANS"

### GADE v. NATIONAL SOLID WASTES MANAGEMENT ASSOCIATION

Supreme Court of the United States, 1992
505 U.S. 88, 112 S.Ct. 2374, 120 L.Ed.2d 73

JUSTICE O'CONNOR announced the judgment of the Court and delivered the opinion of the Court with respect to Parts I, III, and IV, and an opinion with respect to Part II in which THE CHIEF JUSTICE, JUSTICE WHITE, and JUSTICE SCALIA join.

In 1988, the Illinois General Assembly enacted the Hazardous Waste Crane and Hoisting Equipment Operators Licensing Act, Ill.Rev.Stat., ch. 111, §§ 7701–7717 (1989), and the Hazardous Waste Laborers Licensing Act, Ill.Rev.Stat., ch. 111, §§ 7801–7815 (1989) (together, licensing acts). The stated purpose of the licensing acts is both "to promote job safety" and "to protect life, limb and property." §§ 7702, 7802. In this case, we consider whether these "dual impact" statutes, which protect both workers and the general public, are pre-empted by the federal Occupational Safety and Health Act of 1970, 84 Stat. 1590, 29 U.S.C. § 651 *et seq.* (OSH Act), and the standards promulgated thereunder by the Occupational Safety and Health Administration (OSHA).

*Illinois acts sf preempted by OSHA?*

The OSH Act authorizes the Secretary of Labor to promulgate federal occupational safety and health standards. 29 U.S.C. § 655. In the Superfund Amendments and Reauthorization Act of 1986 (SARA), Congress directed the Secretary of Labor to "promulgate standards for the health and safety protection of employees engaged in hazardous waste operations" pursuant to her authority under the OSH Act. SARA, Pub.L. 99–499, Title I, § 126, 100 Stat. 1690–1692, codified at note following 29 U.S.C. § 655. In relevant part, SARA requires the Secretary to establish standards for the initial and routine training of workers who handle hazardous wastes.

In response to this congressional directive, OSHA, to which the Secretary has delegated certain of her statutory responsibilities, see *Martin v. Occupational Safety and Health Review Comm'n*, 499 U.S. 144, 147 n. 1, 111 S.Ct. 1171, 1174 n. 1, 113 L.Ed.2d 117 (1991), promulgated regulations on "Hazardous Waste Operations and Emergency Response," including detailed regulations on worker training requirements. 51 Fed. Reg. 45654, 45665–45666 (1986) (interim regulations); 54 Fed.Reg. 9294, 9320–9321 (1989) (final regulations), codified at § 1910.120 (1991). The OSHA regulations require, among other things, that workers engaged in an activity that may expose them to hazardous wastes receive a minimum of 40 hours of instruction off the site, and a minimum of three days actual field experience under the supervision of a trained supervisor. 29 CFR

§ 1910.120(e)(3)(i). Workers who are on the site only occasionally or who are working in areas that have been determined to be under the permissible exposure limits must complete at least 24 hours of off-site instruction and one day of actual field experience. §§ 1910.120(e)(3)(ii) and (iii). On-site managers and supervisors directly responsible for hazardous waste operations must receive the same initial training as general employees, plus at least eight additional hours of specialized training on various health and safety programs. § 1910.120(e)(4). Employees and supervisors are required to receive eight hours of refresher training annually. § 1910.120(e)(8). Those who have satisfied the training and field experience requirement receive a written certification; uncertified workers are prohibited from engaging in hazardous waste operations. § 1910.120(e)(6).

In 1988, while OSHA's interim hazardous waste regulations were in effect, the State of Illinois enacted the licensing acts at issue here. The laws are designated as acts "in relation to environmental protection," and their stated aim is to protect both employees and the general public by licensing hazardous waste equipment operators and laborers working at certain facilities. Both licensing acts require a license applicant to provide a certified record of at least 40 hours of training under an approved program conducted within Illinois, to pass a written examination, and to complete an annual refresher course of at least eight hours of instruction. Ill.Rev.Stat., ch. 111, §§ 7705(c) and (e), 7706(c) and (d), 7707(b), 7805(c) and (e), 7806(b). In addition, applicants for a hazardous waste crane operator's license must submit "a certified record showing operation of equipment used in hazardous waste handling for a minimum of 4,000 hours." § 7705(d). Employees who work without the proper license, and employers who knowingly permit an unlicensed employee to work, are subject to escalating fines for each offense. §§ 7715, 7716, 7814.

The respondent in this case, National Solid Wastes Management Association (Association), is a national trade association of businesses that remove, transport, dispose, and handle waste material, including hazardous waste. The Association's members are subject to the OSH Act and OSHA regulations, and are therefore required to train, qualify, and certify their hazardous waste remediation workers. 29 CFR § 1910.120 (1991). For hazardous waste operations conducted in Illinois, certain of the workers employed by the Association's members are also required to obtain licenses pursuant to the Illinois licensing acts. Thus, for example, some of the Association's members must ensure that their employees receive not only the 3 days of field experience required for certification under the OSHA regulations, but also the 500 days of experience (4,000 hours) required for licensing under the state statutes.

Shortly before the state licensing acts were due to go into effect, the Association brought a declaratory judgment action in United States District Court against Bernard Killian, the former Director of the Illinois Environmental Protection Agency (IEPA); petitioner Mary Gade is Killian's successor in office and has been substituted as a party pursuant to this Court's Rule 35.3. The Association sought to enjoin IEPA from enforcing the Illinois licensing acts, claiming that the acts were pre-empted by the OSH Act and OSHA regulations and that they violated the Commerce Clause of the United States Constitution. The District Court held that state laws that attempt to regulate workplace safety and health are not pre-empted by the OSH Act when the laws have a "legitimate and substantial purpose apart from promoting job safety." App. to Pet. for Cert. 54. Applying this standard, the District Court held that the Illinois licensing acts were not pre-empted because each protected public safety in addition to promoting job safety. *Id.,* at 56–57. * * *

On appeal, the United States Court of Appeals for the Seventh Circuit affirmed in part and reversed in part. *National Solid Wastes Management Assn. v. Killian,* 918 F.2d 671 (1990). The Court of Appeals held that the OSH Act pre-empts all state law that "constitutes, in a direct, clear and substantial way, regulation of worker health and safety," unless the Secretary has explicitly approved the state law. *Id.,* at 679. Because many of the regulations mandated by the Illinois licensing acts had not yet reached their final form, the Court of Appeals remanded the case to the District Court without considering which, if any, of the Illinois provisions would be pre-empted. *Id.,* at 684. The court made clear, however, its view that Illinois "cannot regulate worker health and safety under the guise of environmental regulation," and it rejected the District Court's conclusion that the State's 4,000–hour experience requirement could survive pre-emption simply because the rule might also enhance public health and safety. *Ibid.* Writing separately, Judge Easterbrook expressed doubt that the OSH Act pre-empts nonconflicting state laws. *Id.,* at 685–688. He concluded, however, that if the OSH Act does pre-empt state law, the majority had employed an appropriate test for determining whether the Illinois licensing acts were superseded. *Id.,* at 688.

We granted certiorari, 502 U.S. 1012, 112 S.Ct. 656, 116 L.Ed.2d 748 (1991), to resolve a conflict between the decision below and decisions in which other Courts of Appeals have found the OSH Act to have a much narrower pre-emptive effect on "dual impact" state regulations. See *Associated Industries of Massachusetts v. Snow,* 898 F.2d 274, 279 (C.A.1 1990); *Environmental Encapsulating Corp. v. New York City,* 855 F.2d 48, 57 (C.A.2 1988); *Manufacturers Assn. of Tri–County v. Knepper,* 801 F.2d 130, 138 (C.A.3 1986), cert. denied, 484 U.S. 815, 108 S.Ct. 66, 98 L.Ed.2d 30 (1987); *New Jersey State Chamber of Commerce v. Hughey,* 774 F.2d 587, 593 (C.A.3 1985). * * *

## II

In the OSH Act, Congress endeavored "to assure so far as possible every working man and woman in the Nation safe and healthful working conditions." 29 U.S.C. § 651(b). To that end, Congress authorized the Secretary of Labor to set mandatory occupational safety and health standards applicable to all businesses affecting interstate commerce, 29 U.S.C. § 651(b)(3), and thereby brought the Federal Government into a field that traditionally had been occupied by the States. Federal regulation of the workplace was not intended to be all encompassing, however. First, Congress expressly saved two areas from federal pre-emption. Section 4(b)(4) of the OSH Act states that the Act does not "supersede or in any manner affect any workmen's compensation law or ... enlarge or diminish or affect in any other manner the common law or statutory rights, duties, or liabilities of employers and employees under any law with respect to injuries, diseases, or death of employees arising out of, or in the course of, employment." 29 U.S.C. § 653(b)(4). Section 18(a) provides that the Act does not "prevent any State agency or court from asserting jurisdiction under State law over any occupational safety or health issue with respect to which no [federal] standard is in effect." 29 U.S.C. § 667(a).

Congress not only reserved certain areas to state regulation, but it also, in § 18(b) of the Act, gave the States the option of pre-empting federal regulation entirely. * * * *

About half the States have received the Secretary's approval for their own state plans as described in this provision. 29 CFR pts. 1952, 1956 (1991). Illinois is not among them.

In the decision below, the Court of Appeals held that § 18(b) "unquestionably" pre-empts any state law or regulation that establishes an occupational health and safety standard on an issue for which OSHA has already promulgated a standard, unless the State has obtained the Secretary's approval for its own plan. 918 F.2d, at 677. Every other federal and state court confronted with an OSH Act pre-emption challenge has reached the same conclusion, [FN1] and so do we.

Our ultimate task in any pre-emption case is to determine whether state regulation is consistent with the structure and purpose of the statute as a whole. Looking to "the provisions of the whole law, and to its object and policy," *Pilot Life Ins. Co. v. Dedeaux,* 481 U.S. 41, 51, 107 S.Ct. 1549, 1555, 95 L.Ed.2d 39 (1987) (internal quotation marks and citations omitted), we hold that nonapproved state regulation of occupational safety and health issues for which a federal standard is in effect is impliedly pre-empted as in conflict with the full purposes and objectives of the OSH Act, *Hines v. Davidowitz, supra.* The design of the statute persuades us that Congress intended to subject employers and employees to only one set of regulations, be it federal or state, and that the only way a State may regulate an OSHA-regulated occupational safety and health issue is pursuant to an approved state plan that displaces the federal standards.

The principal indication that Congress intended to pre-empt state law is § 18(b)'s statement that a State "shall" submit a plan if it wishes to "assume responsibility" for "development and enforcement ... of occupational safety and health standards relating to any occupational safety or health issue with respect to which a Federal standard has been promulgated." The unavoidable implication of this provision is that a State may not enforce its own occupational safety and health standards without obtaining the Secretary's approval, and petitioner concedes that § 18(b) would require an approved plan if Illinois wanted to "assume responsibility" for the regulation of occupational safety and health within the State. Petitioner contends, however, that an approved plan is necessary only if the State wishes completely to replace the federal regulations, not merely to supplement them. She argues that the correct interpretation of § 18(b) is that posited by Judge Easterbrook below: *i.e.*, a State may either "oust" the federal standard by submitting a state plan to the Secretary for approval or "add to" the federal standard without seeking the Secretary's approval. 918 F.2d, at 685 (Easterbrook, J., *dubitante*).

Petitioner's interpretation of § 18(b) might be plausible were we to interpret that provision in isolation, but it simply is not tenable in light of the OSH Act's surrounding provisions. "[W]e must not be guided by a single sentence or member of a sentence, but look to the provisions of the whole law." *Dedeaux, supra,* at 51, 107 S.Ct., at 1555 (internal quotation marks and citations omitted). The OSH Act as a whole evidences Congress' intent to avoid subjecting workers and employers to duplicative regulation; a State may develop an occupational safety and health program tailored to its own needs, but only if it is willing completely to displace the applicable federal regulations.

Cutting against petitioner's interpretation of § 18(b) is the language of § 18(a), which saves from pre-emption any state law regulating an occupational safety and health issue with respect to which no federal standard is in effect. 29 U.S.C. § 667(a). Although this is a saving clause, not a pre-emption clause, the natural implication of this provision is that state laws regulating the same issue as federal laws are not saved, even if they merely supplement the federal standard. Moreover, if petitioner's reading of § 18(b) were correct, and if a State were free to enact nonconflicting safety and health regulations, then § 18(a) would be superfluous: There is no possibility of conflict where there is no federal regulation. Because "[i]t is our duty 'to give effect, if possible, to every clause and word of a statute,'" *United States v. Menasche,* 348 U.S. 528, 538–539, 75 S.Ct. 513, 519–520, 99 L.Ed. 615 (1955) (quoting *Montclair v. Ramsdell,* 107 U.S. 147, 152, 2 S.Ct. 391, 395, 27 L.Ed. 431 (1883)), we conclude that § 18(a)'s preservation of state authority in the absence of a federal standard presupposes a background pre-emption of all state occupational safety and health standards whenever a federal standard governing the same issue is in effect.

Our understanding of the implications of § 18(b) is likewise bolstered by § 18(c) of the Act, 29 U.S.C. § 667(c), which sets forth the conditions that must be satisfied before the Secretary can approve a plan submitted by a State under subsection (b). State standards that affect interstate commerce will be approved only if they "are required by compelling local conditions" and "do not unduly burden interstate commerce." § 667(c)(2). If a State could supplement federal regulations without undergoing the § 18(b) approval process, then the protections that § 18(c) offers to interstate commerce would easily be undercut. It would make little sense to impose such a condition on state programs intended to supplant federal regulation and not those that merely supplement it: The burden on interstate commerce remains the same. * * *

Looking at the provisions of § 18 as a whole, we conclude that the OSH Act precludes any state regulation of an occupational safety or health issue with respect to which a federal standard has been established, unless a state plan has been submitted and approved pursuant to § 18(b). Our review of the Act persuades us that Congress sought to promote occupational safety and health while at the same time avoiding duplicative, and possibly counterproductive, regulation. It thus established a system of uniform federal occupational health and safety standards, but gave States the option of pre-empting federal regulations by developing their own occupational safety and health programs. In addition, Congress offered the States substantial federal grant moneys to assist them in developing their own programs. See OSH Act § 23, 29 U.S.C. §§ 672(a), (b), and (f) (for three years following enactment, the Secretary may award up to 90% of the costs to a State of developing a state occupational safety and health plan); 29 U.S.C. § 672(g) (States that develop approved plans may receive funding for up to 50% of the costs of operating their occupational health and safety programs). To allow a State selectively to "supplement" certain federal regulations with ostensibly nonconflicting standards would be inconsistent with this federal scheme of establishing uniform federal standards, on the one hand, and encouraging States to assume full responsibility for development and enforcement of their own OSH programs, on the other.

We cannot accept petitioner's argument that the OSH Act does not pre-empt nonconflicting state laws because those laws, like the Act, are designed to promote worker safety. In determining whether state law "stands as an obstacle" to the full implementation of a federal law, *Hines v. Davidowitz,* 312 U.S., at 67, 61 S.Ct., at 404, "it is not enough to say that the ultimate goal of both federal and state law" is the same, *International Paper Co. v. Ouellette,* 479 U.S. 481, 494, 107 S.Ct. 805, 813, 93 L.Ed.2d 883 (1987). "A state law also is pre-empted if it interferes with the methods by which the federal statute was designed to reach th[at] goal." * * *

### III

Petitioner next argues that, even if Congress intended to pre-empt all nonapproved state occupational safety and health regulations whenever a federal standard is in effect, the OSH Act's pre-emptive effect should not be extended to state laws that address public safety as well as occupational safety concerns. As we explained in Part II, we understand § 18(b) to mean that the OSH Act pre-empts all state "occupational safety and health standards relating to any occupational safety or health issue with respect to which a Federal standard has been promulgated." 29 U.S.C. § 667(b). We now consider whether a dual impact law can be an "occupational safety and health standard" subject to pre-emption under the Act.

The OSH Act defines an "occupational safety and health standard" as "a standard which requires conditions, or the adoption or use of one or more practices, means, methods, operations, or processes, reasonably necessary or appropriate to provide safe or healthful employment and places of employment." 29 U.S.C. § 652(8). Any state law requirement designed to promote health and safety in the workplace falls neatly within the Act's definition of an "occupational safety and health standard." Clearly, under this definition, a state law that expressly declares a legislative purpose of regulating occupational health and safety would, in the absence of an approved state plan, be pre-empted by an OSHA standard regulating the same subject matter. But petitioner asserts that if the state legislature articulates a purpose other than (or in addition to) workplace health and safety, then the OSH Act loses its pre-emptive force. We disagree.

Although "part of the pre-empted field is defined by reference to the purpose of the state law in question, ... another part of the field is defined by the state law's actual effect." *English v. General Electric Co.,* 496 U.S. 72, 84, 110 S.Ct. 2270, 2278, 110 L.Ed.2d 65 (1990) (citing *Pacific Gas & Elec. Co. v. State Energy Resources Conservation and Development Comm'n,* 461 U.S. 190, 212–213, 103 S.Ct. 1713, 1726–1727, 75 L.Ed.2d 752 (1983)). In assessing the impact of a state law on the federal scheme, we have refused to rely solely on the legislature's professed purpose and have looked as well to the effects of the law. As we explained over two decades ago:

> "We can no longer adhere to the aberrational doctrine ... that state law may frustrate the operation of federal law as long as the state legislature in passing its law had some purpose in mind other than one of frustration. Apart from the fact that it is at odds with the approach taken in nearly all our Supremacy Clause cases, such a doctrine would enable state legislatures to nullify nearly all unwanted federal legislation by simply publishing a legislative committee report articulating some state interest or policy—other than frustration of the federal objective—that would be tangentially furthered by the proposed state law.... [A]ny state legislation which frustrates the full effectiveness of federal law is rendered invalid by the Supremacy Clause."

*Perez v. Campbell,* 402 U.S., at 651–652, 91 S.Ct., at 1712–1713.

\* \* \*

Our precedents leave no doubt that a dual impact state regulation cannot avoid OSH Act pre-emption simply because the regulation serves several objectives rather than one. As the Court of Appeals observed, "[i]t would defeat the purpose of section 18 if a state could enact measures stricter than OSHA's and largely accomplished through regulation of worker health and safety simply by asserting a non-occupational purpose for the legislation." 918 F.2d, at 679. Whatever the purpose or purposes of the state law, pre-emption analysis cannot ignore the effect of the challenged state action on the pre-empted field. The key question is thus at what point the state regulation sufficiently interferes with federal regulation that it should be deemed pre-empted under the Act.

In *English v. General Electric Co., supra,* we held that a state tort claim brought by an employee of a nuclear-fuels production facility against her employer was not pre-empted by a federal whistle-blower provision because the state law did not have a "direct and substantial effect" on the federal scheme. *Id.,* 496 U.S., at 85, 110 S.Ct., at 2278. In the decision below, the Court of Appeals relied on *English* to hold that, in the absence of the approval of the Secretary, the OSH Act pre-empts all state law that "constitutes, in a direct, clear and substantial way, regulation of worker health and safety." 918 F.2d, at 679. We agree that this is the appropriate standard for determining OSH Act pre-emption. On the other hand, state laws of general applicability (such as laws regarding traffic safety or fire safety) that do not conflict with OSHA standards and that regulate the conduct of workers and nonworkers alike would generally not be pre-empted. Although some laws of general applicability may have a "direct and substantial" effect on worker safety, they cannot fairly be characterized as "occupational" standards, because they regulate workers simply as members of the general public. In this case, we agree with the court below that a law directed at workplace safety is not saved from pre-emption simply because the State can demonstrate some additional effect outside of the workplace.

In sum, a state law requirement that directly, substantially, and specifically regulates occupational safety and health is an occupational safety and health standard within the meaning of the Act. That such a law may also have a nonoccupational impact does not render it any less of an occupational standard for purposes of pre-emption analysis. If the State wishes to enact a dual impact law that regulates an occupational safety or health issue for which a federal standard is in effect, § 18 of the Act requires that the State submit a plan for the approval of the Secretary.

\* \* \*

We also reject petitioner's argument that the Illinois licensing acts do not regulate occupational safety and health at all, but are instead a "precondition" to employment. By that reasoning, the OSHA regulations themselves would not be considered occupational standards. SARA, however, makes clear that the training of employees engaged in hazardous waste operations is an occupational safety and health issue, and that certification requirements before an employee may engage in such work are occupational safety and health standards. See *supra,* at 2379–2380. Because neither of the OSH Act's saving provisions are implicated, and because Illinois does not have an approved state plan under § 18(b), the state licensing acts are pre-empted by the OSH Act to the extent they establish occupational safety and health standards for training those who work with hazardous wastes. Like the Court of Appeals, we do not specifically consider which of the licensing acts' provisions will stand or fall under the pre-emption analysis set forth above.

The judgment of the Court of Appeals is hereby

*Affirmed.*

JUSTICE KENNEDY, concurring in part and concurring in the judgment.

Though I concur in the Court's judgment and with the ultimate conclusion that the state law is pre-empted, I would find express pre-emption from the terms of the federal statute. I cannot agree that we should denominate this case as one of implied pre-emption. The contrary view of the plurality is based on an undue expansion of our implied pre-emption jurisprudence which, in my view, is neither wise nor necessary. * * *

A finding of express pre-emption in this case is not contrary to our longstanding rule that we will not infer pre-emption of the States' historic police powers absent a clear statement of intent by Congress. * * *

The statute is clear: When a State desires to assume responsibility for an occupational safety and health issue already addressed by the Federal Government, it must submit a state plan. The most reasonable inference from this language is that when a State does not submit and secure approval of a state plan, it may not enforce occupational safety and health standards in that area. Any doubt that this is what Congress intended disappears when subsection (b) is considered in conjunction with subsections (a), (c), and (f). *Ante,* at 2384–2385. I will not reiterate the plurality's persuasive discussion on this point. Unartful though the language of § 18(b) may be, the structure and language of § 18 leave little doubt that in the OSH statute Congress intended to pre-empt supplementary state regulation of an occupational safety and health issue with respect to which a federal standard exists. * * *

JUSTICE SOUTER, with whom JUSTICE BLACKMUN, JUSTICE STEVENS, and JUSTICE THOMAS join, dissenting.

* * *

Our cases recognize federal pre-emption of state law in three variants: express pre-emption, field pre-emption, and conflict pre-emption. Express pre-emption requires "explicit pre-emptive language." See *Pacific Gas & Elec. Co. v. State Energy Resources Conservation and Development Comm'n,* 461 U.S. 190, 203, 103 S.Ct. 1713, 1722, 75 L.Ed.2d 752 (1983), citing *Jones v. Rath Packing Co.,* 430 U.S. 519, 525, 97 S.Ct. 1305, 1309, 51 L.Ed.2d 604 (1977). Field pre-emption is wrought by a manifestation of congressional intent to occupy an entire field such that even without a federal rule on some particular matter within the field, state regulation on that matter is pre-empted, leaving it untouched by either state or federal law. 461 U.S., at 204, 103 S.Ct., at 1722. Finally, there is conflict pre-emption in either of two senses. The first is found when compliance with both state and federal law is impossible, *ibid.,* the second when a state law "stands as an obstacle to the accomplishment and execution of the full purposes and objectives of Congress," *Hines v. Davidowitz,* 312 U.S. 52, 67, 61 S.Ct. 399, 404, 85 L.Ed. 581 (1941).

The plurality today finds pre-emption of this last sort, discerning a conflict between any state legislation on a given issue as to which a federal standard is in effect, and a congressional purpose "to subject employers and employees to only one set of regulations." *Ante,* at 2383. Thus, under the plurality's reading, any regulation on an issue as to which a federal standard has been promulgated has been pre-empted. As one commentator has observed, this kind of purpose-conflict pre-emption, which occurs when state law is held to "undermin[e] a congressional decision in favor of national uniformity of standards," presents "a situation similar in practical effect to that of federal occupation of a field." L. Tribe, American Constitutional Law 486 (2d ed.1988). Still, whether the pre-emption at issue is described as occupation of each narrow field in which a federal standard has been promulgated, as pre-emption of those regulations that conflict with the federal objective of single regulation, or, as Justice KENNEDY describes it, as express pre-emption, see *ante,* at 2390 (opinion concurring in part and concurring in judgment), the key is congressional intent, and I find the language of the statute insufficient to demonstrate an intent to pre-empt state law in this way. * * *

The plurality errs doubly. First, its premise is incorrect. In the sense in which the plurality uses the term, there is the possibility of "conflict" even absent federal regulation since the mere enactment of a federal law like the Act may amount to an occupation of an entire field, preventing state regulation. Second, the necessary implication of § 18(a) is not that every federal regulation pre-empts all state law on the issue in question, but only that some federal regulations may pre-empt some state law. The plurality ignores the possibility that the provision simply rules out field pre-emption and is otherwise entirely compatible with the possibility that pre-emption will occur only when actual conflict between a federal regulation and a state rule renders compliance with both impossible. Indeed, if Congress had meant to say that any state rule should be pre-empted if it deals with an issue as to which there is a federal regulation in effect, the text of subsection (a) would have been a very inept way of trying to make the point. It was not, however, an inept way to make the different point that Congress intended no field pre-emption of the sphere of health and safety subject to regulation, but not necessarily regulated, under the Act. Unlike the case where field pre-emption occurs, the provision tells us, absence of a federal standard leaves a State free to do as it will on the issue. * * *

In sum, our rule is that the traditional police powers of the State survive unless Congress has made a purpose to pre-empt them clear. See *Rice,* 331 U.S., at 230, 67 S.Ct., at 1152. The Act does not, in so many words, pre-empt all state regulation of issues on which federal standards have been promulgated, and respondent's contention at oral argument that reading subsections (a), (b), and (h) could leave no other "logical" conclusion but one of pre-emption is wrong. Each provision can be read consistently with the others without any implication of pre-emptive intent. See *National Solid Wastes Management Assn. v. Killian,* 918 F.2d 671, 685–688 (C.A.7 1990) (Easterbrook, J., *dubitante*). They are in fact just as consistent with a purpose and objective to permit overlapping state and federal regulation as with one to guarantee that employers and employees would be subjected to only one regulatory regime. Restriction to one such regime by precluding supplemental state regulation might or might not be desirable. But in the absence of any clear expression of congressional intent to pre-empt, I can only conclude that, as long as compliance with federally promulgated standards does not render obedience to Illinois' regulations impossible, the enforcement of the state law is not prohibited by the Supremacy Clause. I respectfully dissent.

## NOTES AND QUESTIONS

1. Does the majority spell out how enforcement of the Illinois statute will "conflict with the full purpose and objective" of OSHA when it differs from the OSHA standard only in being more strict? A state can establish a safety or health standard on any subject for which OSHA does not have a standard. If Illinois had passed its statute before OSHA issued its standard with lower requirements, would the Illinois statute be preempted? Would that further the purposes and objectives of OSHA?

2. A state may get approval of a state plan for a single or limited number of subjects so Illinois could get approval for its hazardous waste handling license. After such approval, the employers must comply with the state standard. Is the practical result any different where the state standard is stricter than the OSHA standard?

3. In *Industrial Truck Association, Inc. v. Henry,* 125 F.3d 1305 (9th Cir.1997), California, pursuant to a referendum, adopted regulations requiring warnings of exposure of any employee in the workplace to listed chemicals that caused cancer, birth defects and other reproductive harm. Under court order, regulations were submitted to OSHA to be incorporated into the state plan and approved. As a result, California had two sets of regulations dealing with these warnings, with the OSHA approved plan applicable only to employers employing workers in the state and the original regulations applying to any person doing business in the state. A manufacturer and distributor of industrial trucks which emit fuel exhaust containing components on the hazard list sued to enjoin the California requirement that it put hazard labels on its trucks; a requirement not included in the OSHA approved plan. The court held that any regulations not submitted to OSHA as part of a state plan are preempted if they relate to the same "issue." The "issue" here was the Hazard Communications Standard which imposes comprehensive hazardous chemical warning requirements. OSHA has thereby occupied the field and the California regulation applicable to the manufacturers and distributors of truck was preempted.

4. Illinois passed a statute, the Structural Work Act, which required that all scaffolds, hoists and cranes used in construction be erected and operated in a "safe, suitable and proper manner." Violation was a criminal

offense and could be the basis for a tort action if anyone, employee or passerby was injured. Are the criminal and tort actions preempted by OSHA? See *Vukadinovich v. Terminal 5 Venture*, 834 F.Supp. 269 (N.D.Ill.1993).

5.   In *Puffer's Hardware, Inc. v. Donovan*, 742 F.2d 12 (1st Cir.1984), an employee was crushed by an elevator. The employer, when cited for violation of the general duty clause, contended that compliance with state safety laws was a complete defense because OSHA had no elevator standards. The court acknowledged that in the absence of federal regulations, state law applied. However, the court concluded that the absence of a specific standard did not preclude OSHA from enforcing the general duty clause. The purpose of the statute was to increase employee health and safety, and Congress did not intend that compliance with minimum state standards would exempt an employer from complying with the general duty clause of the federal statute.

# K.   ADDITIONAL MEANS TO PROTECT WORKERS: GOING BEYOND OSHA INSPECTION AND CITATION

## 1.   SELF-HELP—UNDER THE OSH ACT AND THE NATIONAL LABOR RELATIONS ACT

### WHIRLPOOL CORPORATION v. MARSHALL

Supreme Court of the United States, 1980
445 U.S. 1, 100 S.Ct. 883, 63 L.Ed.2d 154

MR. JUSTICE STEWART delivered the opinion of the Court.

The Occupational Safety and Health Act of 1970 (Act) prohibits an employer from discharging or discriminating against any employee who exercises "any right afforded by" the Act. The Secretary of Labor (Secretary) has promulgated a regulation providing that, among the rights that the Act so protects, is the right of an employee to choose not to perform his assigned task because of a reasonable apprehension of death or serious injury coupled with a reasonable belief that no less drastic alternative is available.[3] The question presented in the case before us is whether this regulation is consistent with the Act.

---

3.   The regulation, 29 CFR § 1977.12 (1979), provides in full:

"(a) In addition to protecting employees who file complaints, institute proceedings, or testify in proceedings under or related to the Act, section 11 also protects employees from discrimination occurring because of the exercise 'of any right afforded by this Act.' Certain rights are explicitly provided in the Act; for example, there is a right to participate as a party in enforcement proceedings (sec. 10). Certain other rights exist by necessary implication. For example, employees may request information from the Occupational Safety and Health Administration; such requests would constitute the exercise of a right afforded by the Act. Likewise, employees interviewed by agents of the Secretary in the course of inspections or investigations could not subsequently be discriminated against because of their cooperation.

"(b)(1) On the other hand, review of the Act and examination of the legislative history discloses that, as a general matter, there is no right afforded by the Act which would entitle employees to walk off the job because of potential unsafe conditions at the workplace. Hazardous conditions which may be violative of the Act will ordinarily be corrected by the employer, once brought to his attention. If corrections are not accomplished, or if there is dispute about the existence of a

I

The petitioner company maintains a manufacturing plant in Marion, Ohio, for the production of household appliances. Overhead conveyors transport appliance components throughout the plant. To protect employees from objects that occasionally fall from these conveyors, the petitioner has installed a horizontal wire-mesh guard screen approximately 20 feet above the plant floor. This mesh screen is welded to angle-iron frames suspended from the building's structural steel skeleton.

Maintenance employees of the petitioner spend several hours each week removing objects from the screen, replacing paper spread on the screen to catch grease drippings from the material on the conveyors, and performing occasional maintenance work on the conveyors themselves. To perform these duties, maintenance employees usually are able to stand on the iron frames, but sometimes find it necessary to step onto the steel mesh screen itself.

In 1973, the company began to install heavier wire in the screen because its safety had been drawn into question. Several employees had fallen partly through the old screen, and on one occasion an employee had fallen completely through to the plant floor below but had survived. A number of maintenance employees had reacted to these incidents by bringing the unsafe screen conditions to the attention of their foremen. The petitioner company's contemporaneous safety instructions admonished employees to step only on the angle-iron frames.

On June 28, 1974, a maintenance employee fell to his death through the guard screen in an area where the newer, stronger mesh had not yet been installed.[4] Following this incident, the petitioner effectuated some repairs and issued an order strictly forbidding maintenance employees

---

hazard, the employee will normally have opportunity to request inspection of the workplace pursuant to section 8(f) of the Act, or to seek the assistance of other public agencies which have responsibility in the field of safety and health. Under such circumstances, therefore, an employer would not ordinarily be in violation of section 11(c) by taking action to discipline an employee for refusing to perform normal job activities because of alleged safety or health hazards.

"(2) However, occasions might arise when an employee is confronted with a choice between not performing assigned tasks or subjecting himself to serious injury or death arising from a hazardous condition at the workplace. If the employee, with no reasonable alternative, refuses in good faith to expose himself to the dangerous condition, he would be protected against subsequent discrimination. The condition causing the employee's apprehension of death or injury must be of such a nature that a reasonable person, under the circumstances then confronting the employee, would conclude that there is a real danger of death or serious injury and that there is insufficient time due to the urgency of the situation, to eliminate the danger through resort to regular statutory enforcement channels. In addition, in such circumstances, the employee, where possible, must also have sought from his employer, and been unable to obtain, a correction of the dangerous condition."

**4.** As a result of this fatality, the Secretary conducted an investigation that led to the issuance of a citation charging the company with maintaining an unsafe walking and working surface in violation of 29 U.S.C. § 654(a)(1). The citation required immediate abatement of the hazard and proposed a $600 penalty. Nearly five years following the accident, the Occupational Safety and Health Review Commission affirmed the citation, but decided to permit the petitioner six months in which to correct the unsafe condition. Whirlpool Corp., 1979 CCH OSHD ¶ 23,552. A petition to review that decision is pending in the United States Court of Appeals for the District of Columbia Circuit.

from stepping on either the screens or the angle-iron supporting structure. An alternative but somewhat more cumbersome and less satisfactory method was developed for removing objects from the screen. This procedure required employees to stand on power-raised mobile platforms and use hooks to recover the material.

On July 7, 1974, two of the petitioner's maintenance employees, Virgil Deemer and Thomas Cornwell, met with the plant maintenance superintendent to voice their concern about the safety of the screen. The superintendent disagreed with their view, but permitted the two men to inspect the screen with their foreman and to point out dangerous areas needing repair. Unsatisfied with the petitioner's response to the results of this inspection, Deemer and Cornwell met on July 9 with the plant safety director. At that meeting, they requested the name, address, and telephone number of a representative of the local office of the Occupational Safety and Health Administration (OSHA). Although the safety director told the men that they "had better stop and think about what [they] were doing," he furnished the men with the information they requested. Later that same day, Deemer contacted an official of the regional OSHA office and discussed the guard screen.

The next day, Deemer and Cornwell reported for the night shift at 10:45 p.m. Their foreman, after himself walking on some of the angle-iron frames, directed the two men to perform their usual maintenance duties on a section of the old screen.[6] Claiming that the screen was unsafe, they refused to carry out this directive. The foreman then sent them to the personnel office, where they were ordered to punch out without working or being paid for the remaining six hours of the shift.[7] The two men subsequently received written reprimands, which were placed in their employment files.

A little over a month later, the Secretary filed suit in the United States District Court for the Northern District of Ohio, alleging that the petitioner's actions against Deemer and Cornwell constituted discrimination in violation of § 11(c)(1) of the Act. As relief, the complaint prayed, inter alia, that the petitioner be ordered to expunge from its personnel files all references to the reprimands issued to the two employees, and for a permanent injunction requiring the petitioner to compensate the two employees for the six hours of pay they had lost by reason of their disciplinary suspensions.

Following a bench trial, the District Court found that the regulation in question justified Deemer's and Cornwell's refusals to obey their foreman's order on July 10, 1974. The court found that the two employees had "refused to perform the cleaning operation because of a genuine fear of death or serious bodily harm," that the danger presented had been "real and not something which [had] existed only in the minds of the

---

**6.** This order appears to have been in direct violation of the outstanding company directive that maintenance work was to be accomplished without stepping on the screen apparatus.

**7.** Both employees apparently returned to work the following day without further incident.

employees," that the employees had acted in good faith, and that no reasonable alternative had realistically been open to them other than to refuse to work. The District Court nevertheless denied relief, holding that the Secretary's regulation was inconsistent with the Act and therefore invalid. *Usery v. Whirlpool Corp.*, 416 F.Supp. 30, 32–34.

The Court of Appeals for the Sixth Circuit reversed the District Court's judgment. 593 F.2d 715. Finding ample support in the record for the District Court's factual determination that the actions of Deemer and Cornwell had been justified under the Secretary's regulation, *id.*, at 719, n. 5, the appellate court disagreed with the District Court's conclusion that the regulation is invalid. *Id.*, at 721–736. It accordingly remanded the case to the District Court for further proceedings. *Id.*, at 736. We granted certiorari, 444 U.S. 823, 100 S.Ct. 43, 62 L.Ed.2d 29, because the decision of the Court of Appeals in this case conflicts with those of two other Courts of Appeals on the important question in issue. * * * *

## II

The Act itself creates an express mechanism for protecting workers from employment conditions believed to pose an emergent threat of death or serious injury. Upon receipt of an employee inspection request stating reasonable grounds to believe that an imminent danger is present in a workplace, OSHA must conduct an inspection. 29 U.S.C. § 657(f)(1). In the event this inspection reveals workplace conditions or practices that "could reasonably be expected to cause death or serious physical harm immediately or before the imminence of such danger can be eliminated through the enforcement procedures otherwise provided by" the Act, 29 U.S.C. § 662(a), the OSHA inspector must inform the affected employees and the employer of the danger and notify them that he is recommending to the Secretary that injunctive relief be sought. § 662(c). At this juncture, the Secretary can petition a federal court to restrain the conditions or practices giving rise to the imminent danger. By means of a temporary restraining order or preliminary injunction, the court may then require the employer to avoid, correct, or remove the danger or to prohibit employees from working in the area. § 662(a).

To ensure that this process functions effectively, the Act expressly accords to every employee several rights, the exercise of which may not subject him to discharge or discrimination. An employee is given the right to inform OSHA of an imminently dangerous workplace condition or practice and request that OSHA inspect that condition or practice. 29 U.S.C. § 657(f)(1). He is given a limited right to assist the OSHA inspector in inspecting the workplace, §§ 657(a)(2), (e), and (f)(2), and the right to aid a court in determining whether or not a risk of imminent danger in fact exists. See § 660(c)(1). Finally, an affected employee is given the right to bring an action to compel the Secretary to seek injunctive relief if he believes the Secretary has wrongfully declined to do so. § 662(d).

In the light of this detailed statutory scheme, the Secretary is obviously correct when he acknowledges in his regulation that, "as a general matter, there is no right afforded by the Act which would entitle employees to walk off the job because of potential unsafe conditions at the workplace.'' By providing for prompt notice to the employer of an inspector's intention to seek an injunction against an imminently dangerous condition, the legislation obviously contemplates that the employer will normally respond by voluntarily and speedily eliminating the danger. And in the few instances where this does not occur, the legislative provisions authorizing prompt judicial action are designed to give employees full protection in most situations from the risk of injury or death resulting from an imminently dangerous condition at the worksite.

As this case illustrates, however, circumstances may sometimes exist in which the employee justifiably believes that the express statutory arrangement does not sufficiently protect him from death or serious injury. Such circumstances will probably not often occur, but such a situation may arise when (1) the employee is ordered by his employer to work under conditions that the employee reasonably believes pose an imminent risk of death or serious bodily injury, and (2) the employee has reason to believe that there is not sufficient time or opportunity either to seek effective redress from his employer or to apprise OSHA of the danger.

Nothing in the Act suggests that those few employees who have to face this dilemma must rely exclusively on the remedies expressly set forth in the Act at the risk of their own safety. But nothing in the Act explicitly provides otherwise. Against this background of legislative silence, the Secretary has exercised his rulemaking power under 29 U.S.C. § 657(g)(2) and has determined that, when an employee in good faith finds himself in such a predicament, he may refuse to expose himself to the dangerous condition, without being subjected to ''subsequent discrimination'' by the employer.

The question before us is whether this interpretative regulation constitutes a permissible gloss on the Act by the Secretary, in light of the Act's language, structure, and legislative history. Our inquiry is informed by an awareness that the regulation is entitled to deference unless it can be said not to be a reasoned and supportable interpretation of the Act.
* * *

## A

The regulation clearly conforms to the fundamental objective of the Act—to prevent occupational deaths and serious injuries. The Act, in its preamble, declares that its purpose and policy is ''to assure so far as possible every working man and woman in the Nation safe and healthful working conditions and to *preserve* our human resources * * *.'' 29 U.S.C. § 651(b). (Emphasis added.)

To accomplish this basic purpose, the legislation's remedial orientation is prophylactic in nature. See *Atlas Roofing Co. v. Occupational Safety and Health Review Comm'n,* 430 U.S. 442, 444–445, 97 S.Ct. 1261, 1263–1264, 51 L.Ed.2d 464. The Act does not wait for an employee to die or become injured. It authorizes the promulgation of health and safety standards and the issuance of citations in the hope that these will act to prevent deaths or injuries from ever occurring. It would seem anomalous to construe an Act so directed and constructed as prohibiting an employee, with no other reasonable alternative, the freedom to withdraw from a workplace environment that he reasonably believes is highly dangerous.

Moreover, the Secretary's regulation can be viewed as an appropriate aid to the full effectuation of the Act's "general duty" clause. * * * As the legislative history of this provision reflects, it was intended itself to deter the occurrence of occupational deaths and serious injuries by placing on employers a mandatory obligation independent of the specific health and safety standards to be promulgated by the Secretary. Since OSHA inspectors cannot be present around the clock in every workplace, the Secretary's regulation ensures that employees will in all circumstances enjoy the rights afforded them by the "general duty" clause.

The regulation thus on its face appears to further the overriding purpose of the Act, and rationally to complement its remedial scheme. In the absence of some contrary indication in the legislative history, the Secretary's regulation must, therefore, be upheld, particularly when it is remembered that safety legislation is to be liberally construed to effectuate the congressional purpose. * * *

## B

In urging reversal of the judgment before us, the petitioner relies primarily on two aspects of the Act's legislative history.

## 1

Representative Daniels of New Jersey sponsored one of several House bills that led ultimately to the passage of the Act. As reported to the House by the Committee on Education and Labor, the Daniels bill contained a section that was soon dubbed the "strike with pay" provision. This section provided that employees could request an examination by the Department of Health, Education, and Welfare (HEW) of the toxicity of any materials in their workplace. If that examination revealed a workplace substance that had "potentially toxic or harmful effects in such concentration as used or found," the employer was given 60 days to correct the potentially dangerous condition. Following the expiration of that period, the employer could not require that an employee be exposed to toxic concentrations of the substance unless the employee was informed of the hazards and symptoms associated with the substance, the employee was instructed in the proper precautions for dealing with the substance, and the employee was furnished with personal protective equipment. If these conditions were not met, an employee could "absent himself from such risk of harm for the period necessary to avoid such danger without loss of regular compensation for such period."

This provision encountered stiff opposition in the House. Representative Steiger of Wisconsin introduced a substitute bill containing no "strike with pay" provision. In response, Representative Daniels offered a floor amendment that, among other things, deleted his bill's "strike with pay" provision. He suggested that employees instead be afforded the right to request an immediate OSHA inspection of the premises, a right which the Steiger bill did not provide. The House ultimately adopted the Steiger bill.

The bill that was reported to and, with a few amendments, passed by the Senate never contained a "strike with pay" provision. It did, however, give employees the means by which they could request immediate Labor Department inspections. These two characteristics of the bill were underscored on the floor of the Senate by Senator Williams, the bill's sponsor.

After passage of the Williams bill by the Senate, it and the Steiger bill were submitted to a Conference Committee. There, the House acceded to the Senate bill's inspection request provisions.

The petitioner reads into this legislative history a congressional intent incompatible with an administrative interpretation of the Act such as is embodied in the regulation at issue in this case. The petitioner argues that Congress' overriding concern in rejecting the "strike with pay" provision was to avoid giving employees a unilateral authority to walk off the job which they might abuse in order to intimidate or harass their employer. Congress deliberately chose instead, the petitioner maintains, to grant employees the power to request immediate administrative inspections of the workplace which could in appropriate cases lead to coercive judicial remedies. As the petitioner views the regulation, therefore, it gives to workers precisely what Congress determined to withhold from them.

We read the legislative history differently. Congress rejected a provision that did not concern itself at all with conditions posing real and immediate threats of death or severe injury. The remedy which the rejected provision furnished employees could have been invoked only after 60 days had passed following HEW's inspection and notification that improperly high levels of toxic substances were present in the workplace. Had that inspection revealed employment conditions posing a threat of imminent and grave harm, the Secretary of Labor would presumably have requested, long before expiration of the 60–day period, a court injunction pursuant to other provisions of the Daniels bill. Consequently, in rejecting the Daniels bill's "strike with pay" provision, Congress was not rejecting a legislative provision dealing with the highly perilous and fast-moving situations covered by the regulation now before us.

It is also important to emphasize that what primarily troubled Congress about the Daniels bill's "strike with pay" provision was its requirement that employees be paid their regular salary after having properly invoked their right to refuse to work under the section.[29] It is instructive

---

**29.** Congress' concern necessarily was with the provision's compensation requirement. The law then, as it does today, already afforded workers a right, under certain circumstances, to walk off their jobs when faced with hazardous conditions. Under Section 7 of the National Labor

that virtually every time the issue of an employee's right to absent himself from hazardous work was discussed in the legislative debates, it was in the context of the employee's right to continue to receive his usual compensation.

When it rejected the "strike with pay" concept, therefore, Congress very clearly meant to reject a law unconditionally imposing upon employers an obligation to continue to pay their employees their regular paychecks when they absented themselves from work for reasons of safety. But the regulation at issue here does not require employers to pay workers who refuse to perform their assigned tasks in the face of imminent danger. It simply provides that in such cases the employer may not "discriminate" against the employees involved. An employer "discriminates" against an employee only when he treats that employee less favorably than he treats others similarly situated.[31]

2

The second aspect of the Act's legislative history upon which the petitioner relies is the rejection by Congress of provisions contained in both the Daniels and the Williams bills that would have given Labor Department officials, in imminent-danger situations, the power temporarily to shut down all or part of an employer's plant. These provisions aroused considerable opposition in both Houses of Congress. The hostility engendered in the House of Representatives led Representative Daniels to delete his [v]ersion of the provision in proposing amendments to his original bill. The Steiger bill that ultimately passed the House gave the Labor Department no such authority. The Williams bill, as approved by the Senate, did contain an administrative shutdown provision, but the Conference Committee rejected this aspect of the Senate bill.

The petitioner infers from these events a congressional will hostile to the regulation in question here. The regulation, the petitioner argues, provides employees with the very authority to shut down an employer's plant that was expressly denied a more expert and objective United States Department of Labor.

Relations Act, 29 U.S.C. § 157, employees have a protected right to strike over safety issues. See *NLRB v. Washington Aluminum Co.*, 370 U.S. 9, 82 S.Ct. 1099, 8 L.Ed.2d 298. Similarly, Section 502 of the Labor Management Relations Act, 29 U.S.C. § 143, provides that "the quitting of labor by an employee or employees in good faith because of abnormally dangerous conditions for work at the place of employment of such employee or employees [shall not] be deemed a strike." The effect of this section is to create an exception to a no-strike obligation in a collective-bargaining agreement. *Gateway Coal Co. v. Mine Workers*, 414 U.S. 368, 385, 94 S.Ct. 629, 640, 38 L.Ed.2d 583. The existence of these statutory rights also make clear that the Secretary's regulation does not conflict with the general pattern of federal labor legislation in the area of occupational safety and health. See also 29 CFR § 1977.18 (1979).

**31.** Deemer and Cornwell were clearly subjected to "discrimination" when the petitioner placed reprimands in their respective employment files. Whether the two employees were also discriminated against when they were denied pay for the approximately six hours they did not work on July 10, 1974, is a question not now before us. The District Court dismissed the complaint without indicating what relief it thought would have been appropriate had it upheld the Secretary's regulation. The Court of Appeals expressed no view concerning the limits of the relief to which the Secretary might ultimately be entitled. On remand, the District Court will reach this issue.

As we read the pertinent legislative history, however, the petitioner misconceives the thrust of Congress' concern. Those in Congress who prevented passage of the administrative shutdown provisions in the Daniels and Williams bills were opposed to the unilateral authority those provisions gave to federal officials, without any judicial safeguards, drastically to impair the operation of an employer's business. Congressional opponents also feared that the provisions might jeopardize the Government's otherwise neutral role in labor-management relations.

Neither of these congressional concerns is implicated by the regulation before us. The regulation accords no authority to Government officials. It simply permits private employees of a private employer to avoid workplace conditions that they believe pose grave dangers to their own safety. The employees have no power under the regulation to order their employer to correct the hazardous condition or to clear the dangerous workplace of others. Moreover, any employee who acts in reliance on the regulation runs the risk of discharge or reprimand in the event a court subsequently finds that he acted unreasonably or in bad faith. The regulation, therefore, does not remotely resemble the legislation that Congress rejected.

### C

For these reasons we conclude that 29 CFR § 1977.12(b)(2) (1979) was promulgated by the Secretary in the valid exercise of his authority under the Act. Accordingly, the judgment of the Court of Appeals is affirmed.

### NOTES AND QUESTIONS

1. The Court remanded to the district court the question whether refusal to pay the employees for the rest of the day constituted discrimination. The district court awarded them back pay because they were not given a chance to perform safe work which was available. Sending them home was unnecessary. *Marshall v. Whirlpool Corp.*, 9 OSHC 1038, 1980 OSHD ¶ 24, 957 (N.D.Ohio 1980).

2. The OSHA regulation, somewhat ambiguously, requires that the condition be "of such a nature that a reasonable person * * * would conclude that there is a real danger of death or serious injury." Why should it not be enough that the employee "in good faith believe" there was such a danger? Should the employee bear the risk that at a later time the fact finder will have a different view of what a "reasonable person" would conclude? The Mine Safety and Health Act requires only that the employee have a good faith belief that conditions, such as excess dust, is a chronic long term threat to his health or safety due to violation of safety regulations. *Phillips v. Interior Bd. of Mine Operations Appeals*, 500 F.2d 772 (D.C.Cir.1974).

Should the danger be required to rise to the level of "death or serious injury"? Should the employer be allowed to discharge employees who refuse to expose themselves to hazards which are serious violations of the employer's statutory duties?

3. If the employee has justifiably refused to work because of the employer's safety violation, should the employer be liable for the resulting lost pay? Does denying the employee pay perpetuate the 19th century dogma that the worker has a free choice to either work under dangerous conditions created by the employer or go hungry?

The Mine Safety and Health Act provides that, in cases of imminent danger, the mine inspector can require that the operation or even the whole mine be closed down, and the employees be paid for the time lost up to one week. 30 USC § 821. Because mine inspectors can be called in by the union or the employees on short notice, this provides an important and potentially effective remedy.

In Sweden, the union safety delegate may order suspension of work if the job involves immediate or serious danger to the life or health of the employee and no immediate remedy can be obtained from the employer, and workers receive their pay during the suspension of work. The dispute is resolved by the labor inspector who is available on short notice.

4. In *NLRB v. Washington Aluminum Co.*, 370 U.S. 9, 82 S.Ct. 1099, 8 L.Ed.2d 298 (1962), cited in the Court's opinion, seven unorganized machinists were discharged when they walked out rather than work in an unheated and bitterly cold shop. The Court held that this was protected activity under Section 7 of the National Labor Relations Act and that they should be reinstated. Because the seven workers acted together it was "concerted" activity and was for mutual aid and protection; it was, therefore, within the scope of the Act's protection. A concerted refusal to work is protected whether there is in fact a hazardous condition. It is enough that the employees believe the conditions are objectionable and act on that belief. Where a single person acted alone protesting violation of safety regulations, the NLRB first held that this was "constructive concerted" activity because it was designed to benefit all employees and they were presumed to consent to the action in their common interest. *Alleluia Cushion Co. v. Henley*, 221 NLRB 999, 1975 WL 6526 (1975). The Reagan Board rejected the theory of "constructive concerted" activity and held that the discharge of a truck driver who, acting alone, refused to take out a truck did not violate the statute. The court of appeals, after giving the Board a second try at justifying its new position, held that this was a permissible interpretation of the statute. *Prill v. NLRB*, 835 F.2d 1481 (D.C.Cir.1987).

In a similar case in the Second Circuit, *Ewing v. NLRB*, 861 F.2d 353 (2d Cir.1988), the court upheld the Board after its third try at justifying its conclusion, saying:

> We now reluctantly conclude that the Board has offered a reasonable interpretation of the Act. 861 F.2d at 355. * * * By its own admission, the Board advocates an interpretation that condones "outrageous" employer conduct. The vast majority of American employees are not unionized. They do not work under the protections a collective bargaining agreement affords. Statutory employment rights provide the only protection they have against the arbitrary power of their employer. As it stands, the NLRB's interpretation of Section 7 would allow management to

discharge or discipline an individual worker for exercising statutory employment rights. Id. at 359.

For a discussion of the Board's handling of these cases, see Matthew Finkin, *Labor Law by Boz—A Theory of Meyers Industries, Inc., Sears Roebuck and Co., and Bird Engineering*, 71 Iowa L. Rev. 155 (1985).

5. Section 502 of the Labor Management Relations Act provides, in a backhanded fashion, a limited protection to strikes during the contract term because of health and safety conditions. The section states:

> nor shall the quitting of labor by an employee or employees in good faith because of abnormally dangerous conditions for work at the place of employment of such employee or employees be deemed a strike under this Act.

Despite the express terms of Section 502, the Supreme Court held that to justify a strike where there was an implied no-strike obligation in the collective agreement, it was not enough that the refusal to work was based on a good faith belief of danger, but there must also be "ascertainable objective evidence * * * that an abnormally dangerous condition for work exists." *Gateway Coal Co. v. U.M.W.A.*, 414 U.S. 368, 386–87, 94 S.Ct. 629, 641–42, 38 L.Ed.2d 583 (1974).

The courts have refused to find "abnormally dangerous conditions" unless there were substantial dangers of serious injury or death. See *NLRB v. Maryland Shipbuilding and Drydock Co.*, 683 F.2d 109 (4th Cir.1982); *Jones & Laughlin Steel Corp. v. UMWA*, 519 F.2d 1155 (3d Cir.1975). See also James Atleson, *Threats to Health and Safety: Employee Self–Help Under the NLRA*, 59 Minn.L. Rev. 647 (1975).

An employee has six months to file an unfair labor practice charge with the National Labor Relations Board if discriminated against because of a concerted refusal to work under abnormally dangerous working conditions. In contrast, section 660(c) gives an OSHA discriminatee only thirty days to file a complaint seeking protection and relief.

6. In *Paige v. Henry J. Kaiser Co.*, 826 F.2d 857 (9th Cir.1987), *cert. denied* 486 U.S. 1054, 108 S.Ct. 2819, 100 L.Ed.2d 921 (1988), two employees covered by a collective agreement refused to refuel gasoline generators because the engines had not cooled, the funnels leaked, the carrying containers spilled over, and refueling had to be done under a shower of sparks thrown off by a welder. They sued for wrongful discharge on the basis of California public policy as expressed in the Cal–OSHA law. Although the collective agreement provided that Kaiser would comply with the Cal–OSHA law, the court of appeals held that the existence of a remedy under the collective agreement did not preempt a tort remedy under state law. Congressional inclusion of provisions in the OSH Act for state regulation of employee health and safety demonstrated an intent to permit state regulation. The creating of a state cause of action and an additional remedy did not interfere with the collective bargaining process and enforcement of contract rights through the grievance procedure and arbitration.

The remedy through the collectively bargained grievance procedure may not always be wholly adequate because of the principle, sometimes mechanically applied, that when an order by supervision is improper, the employee must obey and then grieve. Refusal to obey is insubordination, even though the order is improper. This principle is generally qualified by the rule that the employee need not obey an order that creates a serious risk to health or safety, but a study of arbitration cases suggests that some arbitrators give dominant weight to management authority and discharges are upheld or reinstatement is without back pay. See J. Snow, *Health and Safety*, in LABOR AND EMPLOYMENT ARBITRATION § 39.06 (T. BORNSTEIN & A. GOSLINE, EDS.); James A.Gross and Patricia A.Greenfield, *Arbitral Value Judgments in Health and Safety Disputes: Management Rights Over Workers' Rights*, 34 BUFFALO L. REV. 645 (1985); James H. Swain, *Protecting Individual Employees: Is it Safe to Complain About Safety?*, 9 U. OF BRIDGEPORT L. REV. 59 (1988).

## ASARCO, INC. v. NATIONAL LABOR RELATIONS BOARD

United States Court of Appeals, Sixth Circuit, 1986
805 F.2d 194

JOHN W. PECK, SENIOR CIRCUIT JUDGE.

This case is before the court on the application of ASARCO, Inc., to set aside the decision and order of the National Labor Relations Board (the Board) which found that ASARCO violated §§ 8(a)(1) and (5) of the National Labor Relations Act, 29 U.S.C. § 158(a)(1), (5). The violations were based on ASARCO's refusal to give an industrial hygienist employed by the International Chemical Workers Union (the Union) access to its mine for the purpose of investigating a fatal accident, ASARCO's denial of the Union's request for photographs taken of the accident site, and ASARCO's failure to give the Union copies of its internal investigative accident report. For reasons stated herein, we grant enforcement of the Board's order in part, and set aside the order in part.

On July 31, 1984, Wade Fields, an ASARCO employee and member of the Union's Local 700, with which ASARCO has a collective bargaining agreement, apparently drove a tractor off a bench of ore materials and over an abrupt 30–foot drop-off inside ASARCO's Young Mine, an underground zinc mine. Co-workers found Fields after the accident to which there were no eye-witnesses. Fields died hours later on August 1, 1984.

ASARCO's safety director, Donald Ledbetter, immediately reported the accident to the Federal Mine Safety and Health Administration (MSHA). That same day an inspection team extensively investigated the accident site. The team included ASARCO representatives, the MSHA official, and Thales Miller, a member of Local 700 and its safety committee. After the on-site investigation, at which ASARCO took photographs, MSHA directed ASARCO to move the tractor to its shop area for inspection and gave ASARCO permission to clean up the accident site. The tractor was closely examined by the MSHA official, as well as by Ray Gann, the Local 700 president, and Dennis Gann, another member of the Local and its safety committee. Following this, MSHA, ASARCO, and

Union representatives interviewed employees who had worked on Fields' shift.

On August 2, 1984, the Union requested permission for the Union's industrial hygienist, Thurman Wenzl, to visit the accident site. ASARCO denied this request. ASARCO did agree to the Union's subsequent request that ASARCO representatives meet with Wenzl and other Union officials to discuss the accident.

At this meeting, which followed MSHA's "closeout" conference attended by the Union, ASARCO representatives again denied the Union's request for access. The Union also requested copies of the photographs taken of the accident site. ASARCO advised the Union that the photographs would be given to the MSHA. Upon learning at the meeting that ASARCO planned to prepare its own internal investigative report of the accident, the Union requested a copy of the report. ASARCO never fulfilled the Union's request. The Union did receive a copy of the MSHA accident investigation report. The record reflects that ASARCO otherwise cooperated with the Union in answering questions about the accident.

The Union filed unfair labor practice charges alleging that ASARCO violated §§ 8(a)(1) and (5) of the Act by refusing the Union's requests for access and information. After an evidentiary hearing, the administrative law judge (ALJ) found that ASARCO had violated the Act. By decision and order dated March 14, 1985, the ALJ ordered ASARCO to grant access to the Union hygienist and to turn over its photographs and internal investigative report. A three-member panel of the Board affirmed the ALJ's decision and adopted the ALJ's order as its own. ASARCO's petition for review followed. The Board filed a cross-petition for enforcement of its order. The Union has intervened. * * *

### The Union's Request for Access

The Board applied the balancing test set forth in *Holyoke Water Power Co.*, 273 NLRB 1369, *enforced sub nom. NLRB v. Holyoke Water Power Co.*, 778 F.2d 49 (1st Cir.1985), *cert. denied*, 477 U.S. 905, 106 S.Ct. 3274, 91 L.Ed.2d 565 (1986), in determining that ASARCO should have granted the Union's industrial hygienist access to the accident site. Under *Holyoke* the Board:

> balance[s] the employer's property rights against the employees' right to proper representation. Where it is found that responsible representation of employees can be achieved only by the union's having access to the employer's premises, the employer's property rights must yield to the extent necessary to achieve this end. However, the access ordered must be limited to reasonable periods so that the union can fulfill its representation duties without unwarranted interruption of the employer's operations. On the other hand, where it is found that a union can effectively represent employees through some alternate means other than by entering on the employer's premises, the em-

ployer's property rights will predominate, and the union may properly be denied access.

273 NLRB at 1370. The *Holyoke* standard is drawn from *NLRB v. Babcock & Wilcox Co.*, 351 U.S. 105, 112, 76 S.Ct. 679, 684, 100 L.Ed. 975 (1956), which balances the § 7 rights of self-organization that are implicated by access requests of non-employee union organizers against the employer's interest in preventing invasion of its private property rights. In *Holyoke* the Board also expressly overruled an earlier line of cases, including *Winona Industries, Inc.*, 257 NLRB 695 (1981), in which the Board treated requests for access as simple information requests. 273 NLRB at 1370. It is well settled that "[t]he duty to bargain collectively, imposed upon an employer by § 8(a)(5) of the National Labor Relations Act, includes a duty to provide relevant information needed by a labor union for the proper performance of its duties as the employees' bargaining representative." *Detroit Edison Co. v. NLRB*, 440 U.S. 301, 303, 99 S.Ct. 1123, 1125, 59 L.Ed.2d 333 (1979) (citations and footnote omitted). In evaluating an employer's obligation to fulfill the union's information requests, the Board and courts apply a "discovery type standard," under which the requested information need only be relevant and useful to the union in fulfilling its statutory obligations in order to be subject to disclosure. *NLRB v. Acme Industrial Co.*, 385 U.S. 432, 437, 87 S.Ct. 565, 568, 17 L.Ed.2d 495 (1967); *General Motors Corp. v. NLRB*, 700 F.2d 1083, 1088 (6th Cir. 1983).

ASARCO argues that the Union could satisfy its representation duties and accompanying need for information relevant to Field's accident and the safety issues raised thereby through means other than mine access— notably, the MSHA report and interviews with Union representatives who participated in the on-site investigation. In light of these alternate sources of relevant information, ASARCO contends that the Union did not meet the *Holyoke* test for access to employer property.

On the other hand, the intervenor Union asks this court to enforce the Board's order, but under the more liberal standard set forth in *Winona*, 257 NLRB at 697–98. The Union argues that *Holyoke* is flawed and should be overruled because it is premised upon *Babcock & Wilcox, supra*, which deals with § 7 rights of self-organization and the employer's duty under § 8(a)(1) to refrain from interfering with those rights and does not involve the employer's affirmative duty under § 8(a)(5) to bargain with the employer's representative. Because the outcome in this case is the same under either test, we decline to decide whether *Winona* or *Holyoke* is the proper test to be applied in situations involving the bargaining representative's request for access to employer property in order to gather information relevant to its representative responsibilities. As noted by the First Circuit in *Holyoke*, "[i]f the union's interest in obtaining information is substantial, and the employer's interest in keeping union representatives off its property is insignificant, both *Winona* and a balancing test point to the same result." 778 F.2d at 53. Employee safety, as a condition of employment, is a mandatory subject of collective bargaining. *Oil, Chemical & Atomic Workers Local Union,* 711 F.2d at 360. In addition, the collective bargaining agreement between ASARCO and the Union stated that the Union agreed "to cooperate and help management in the promotion of safety and the enforcement of safety rules and regulations;" the agreement also established a safety committee composed of union and management representatives whose function was "to make recommendations to management on accident prevention." The information regarding the fatal accident sought by the Union in this case was therefore clearly relevant and necessary to its duties as bargaining representative. ASARCO gave no reason for its flat refusal to permit the Union's industrial hygienist into the mine, nor did it attempt to strike a mutually acceptable compromise that would answer ASARCO's concerns later articulated before the ALJ regarding disruption of work and productivity. Finally, ASARCO's safety director Ledbetter conceded on cross-examination that without actually going through the mine one could not conduct a fair and complete investigation of the accident. On these facts, we agree with the Board's findings that absent access to the accident site the Union could not fulfill its obligation to represent the employees. We therefore enforce the portion of the Board's order which grants access to the Union's industrial hygienist to the mine and accident site for a reasonable period and at a reasonable time.

### The Request for Photographs

The Union's request for photographs must also be upheld. On appeal ASARCO does not contest the Board's finding that the photographs constituted information that was relevant and necessary to the Union's understanding of the accident and its duty to represent the employees with regard to safety conditions. ASARCO contends that it had no legal obligation to take the photographs in the first instance and therefore should be under no compulsion to give the "fruits of its investigation" to the Union now. This position is patently unsupportable, as perhaps is indicated by ASARCO's failure to cite any cases in support of its argument. Indeed, the case law is replete with instances in which employers have had the duty under § 8(a)(5) to give bargaining representatives data complied voluntarily and for the employers' own purposes. ASARCO's other argument is that the Union could have obtained the photographs from the MSHA, so that it had no legal duty to supply them. However, the availability of the requested information from another source does not alter the employer's duty to provide readily available relevant information to the bargaining representative. Accordingly, we enforce the portion of the Board's order which requires ASARCO to give the Union the requested photographs of the accident site.

### The Request for ASARCO's Internal Investigative Report

The appeal regarding the portion of the Board's order requiring disclosure of ASARCO's internal self-critical report presents a more difficult question. The Board was unable to cite, and we are unable to find, any prior case in which such a report was ordered to be disclosed. The Board argues that since the report would be subject to disclosure under federal discovery rules, ASARCO's report should also be disclosed pursuant to the "discovery-type standard" for disclosure in § 8(a)(5) cases. *See Acme,* 385 U.S. at 437, 87 S.Ct. at 568; *NLRB v. Rockwell–Standard Corp.,* 410 F.2d 953, 958 (6th Cir.1969). Although a liberal discovery-type standard is used in information request cases to determine relevance, this does not mean that anything that would be discoverable in litigation is automatically subject to disclosure in the collective bargaining context. Rather, relevance and any resulting duty to disclose must be evaluated in light of the rights and obligations created by the National Labor Relations Act.

The uncontradicted testimony of ASARCO's safety director Ledbetter established that ASARCO prepares extensive self-critical reports after serious accidents in order to improve safety and prevent future similar mishaps. The reports contain speculative material and opinions, criticisms of persons, events, and equipment, and recommendations for future practices. Ledbetter stated that if ASARCO were required to divulge these reports to the Union, much of their contents would have been omitted, adversely affecting, if not nullifying, the report's value. Ledbetter testified that ASARCO also prepares these reports in anticipation of litigation which frequently arises after serious accidents.

The ALJ, as affirmed by the Board, concluded that ASARCO's internal report was not prepared in anticipation of litigation and should be disclosed because no lawsuit was pending at the time of the Union's request and because, in the ALJ's view, the record failed to establish that the report would not have been prepared in the complete absence of the possibility of some liability for the accident. The ALJ gave no weight to ASARCO's other argument that disclosure of the self-critical analysis would seriously affect the candor of future critiques and have a chilling effect that would defeat the critique's primary purpose.

In this case the Board's position ignores the evidence that ASARCO's self-critical report is part of its effort to avoid future similar accidents. The practice of uninhibited self-critical analysis, which benefits both the union's and employer's substantial interest in increased worker safety and accident prevention, would undoubtedly be chilled by disclosure. As in *International Union of Electrical, Radio & Machine Workers, supra,* and *Anheuser–Busch, supra,* disclosure would seriously thwart the intended primary purpose of the document to the ultimate detriment of both parties' interests. The Board's position also ignores that the Union has available to it all relevant factual information regarding the accident by virtue of its extensive participation in the accident investigation with ASARCO officials and by virtue of the portions of the Board's order granting mine access and delivery of the photographs. Under these circumstances, access to ASARCO's internal report and self-critical thinking is not relevant or reasonably necessary to the Union's representative duties, and ASARCO's failure to disclose it was not a § 8(a)(5) violation.

Because we deny enforcement of this portion of the Board's order on this basis, we need not consider ASARCO's other argument that the report should be shielded because it was prepared in anticipation of litigation.

In accordance with the foregoing, the portions of the Board's order granting mine access to the Union's hygienist at a reasonable time and in a reasonable manner and giving the Union the photographs are upheld. Enforcement of the portion of the Board's order giving the Union ASARCO's internal report is denied.

*Holding*

## NOTES AND QUESTIONS

1. Why should the union insist that its own industrial hygienist have access to the mine when its members on the safety committee had full access? If it is explicitly acknowledged that employee members of safety committees need training to perform their functions effectively, should the employer be required to bear the burden of that training on the grounds that the employer is responsible for providing a safe and healthful place to work and members of the safety committee are aiding the employer in fulfilling that responsibility?

2. In *NLRB v. Holyoke Water Power Co.,* 778 F.2d 49 (1st Cir.1985), employees had complained of the noise level in the fan room. The Company had made studies, but the union questioned these studies and requested access for its own hygienist to make a study. The Board applied the *Babcock* test of balancing "the Union's interest in obtaining access against the Company's interest in preventing an invasion of its property," and held that the employer must grant access. The court questioned the application of this balancing test where the union represents the employees and the employer has a duty to bargain. Even if the balancing test is applied, said the court, the company's interest in denying access was insubstantial. "The potential for disruption is not great, since the union already represents the employees. The industrial hygienist's investigation will last a day or less. Since no employees are regularly stationed in the fan room, the hygienist will not disrupt employee work patterns." 778 F.2d at 53. Compare the disruption here with that in *Babcock,* where the Supreme Court held that union representatives could be barred from distributing handbills in the company parking lot because other channels of communication were available.

3. Where there is a safety committee, as in *ASARCO,* why should not the investigation be made by the safety committee, or the Company's full report be available to the safety committee? *ASARCO* stated that one of the purposes of the report was to prevent future mishaps. Does its refusal to make the report available indicate a lack of willingness to permit the union to participate fully in the safety program? Does this suggest a refusal to bargain in good faith concerning matters arising during the contract term?

The court says, "The practice of uninhibited self-critical analysis, which benefits both the union's and employer's substantial interest in increased worker safety and accident prevention, would be undoubtedly chilled by disclosure." What assumptions underlie this statement? Surely, it can not be that the union would object to improved safety measures which the report might suggest. Surely, it should not be that the report will disclose violations of the Act which the OSHA investigation did not discover. Surely, it must not be that the employer is not obligated to provide feasible safety measures. Is there an assumption that the level of safety to be provided is a management function in which the employees, through their representatives, have no right to share? Is there behind this an assumption that the employer could and would choose to leave its employees at risk rather than discuss with them what feasible measures might protect their health and safety?

4.   There is no dispute that health and safety matters are generally a subject over which management must bargain with the union. Consider the following:

(1) The union insists to impasse that the employer agree to notify and discuss with the union before introducing any new potentially hazardous substances or new hazardous processes into the plant.

(2) The union insists to impasse on a clause that makes any condition which would violate the OSH Act a violation of the collective agreement, and that this provision shall be subject to the grievance procedure and arbitration.

5.   In. *Oil, Chemical & Atomic Workers, Local Union No. 6–418 v. NLRB*, 711 F.2d 348 (D.C.Cir.1983), a case involving employee exposure to toxic substances, the D.C. Circuit upheld a Board order requiring the employer to provide medical records even though it might result in identification of some employees. Since the decision in that case, new legislation has been put in place that protects the confidentiality of medical records. In light of these provisions in the Americans with Disabilities Act, the Family and Medical Leave Act, and HIPPA, would the same result be reached today?

## 2.  DETERRING UNSAFE CONDITIONS THROUGH ACTIONS FOR DAMAGES

### TEAL v. E.I. DUPONT DE NEMOURS AND COMPANY

United States Court of Appeals, Sixth Circuit, 1984
728 F.2d 799

CELEBREZZE, SENIOR CIRCUIT JUDGE.

\* \* \*

The Daniel Construction Company (Daniel Construction) entered into a contract with DuPont to dismantle and remove hydraulic bailers from DuPont's plant. The bailers occupied three floor levels within the plant and were used to compress synthetic Dacron® fiber. Hydraulic "rams" provided the force necessary to compress the fiber. The rams were located below the ground floor in a "bailer pit", access to which was provided by a straight and permanently affixed ladder. On March 14, 1979, Richard Teal, an employee of Daniel Construction, fell approximately seventeen feet from the ladder to the floor of the bailer pit. Richard Teal brought this action against DuPont alleging that his fall and injuries were the direct and proximate result of DuPont's negligence. \* \* \*

During the course of the trial, appellants introduced evidence which indicated that DuPont's ladder failed to conform to federal regulations promulgated pursuant to the Occupational Safety and Health Act of 1970. 29 U.S.C. Sec. 651 *et seq.* Specifically, OSHA regulations require a clearance of not less than seven inches "from the centerline of the rungs, cleats or steps to the nearest permanent object in back of the ladder." 29 C.F.R. Sec. 1910.27(c)(4). The uncontroverted testimony of Robert B. Taylor, a director of the Division of Occupational Safety and Health for the Tennessee Department of Labor, indicated that the ladder failed to conform with the seven inch clearance requirement. Because DuPont had breached a regulatory obligation, appellants requested the trial court to instruct the jury on the issue of negligence *per se*. The trial court refused; instead, it informed the jury that the OSHA regulation "may be considered * * * as some evidence * * * of the (appropriate) standard of care." Appellants claim that the district court's refusal to charge on the issue of negligence *per se* is reversible error. * * *

Pursuant to Tennessee case law, a breach of a duty imposed by statute or regulation is negligence *per se* if the party injured is a member of the class of persons the statute or regulation was intended to protect. *E.g., Alex v. Armstrong,* 215 Tenn. 276, 385 S.W.2d 110 (1964); *Traylor v. Coburn,* 597 S.W.2d 319, 322 (Tenn.App.1980); *Berry v. Whitworth,* 576 S.W.2d 351, 353 (Tenn.App.1978). In this case, the parties agree that Richard Teal was, at the time of the accident, an employee of Daniel Construction, an independent contractor, and that Teal fell from a permanently affixed ladder in DuPont's plant. Further, the parties agree that the OSHA regulation established a duty owed by DuPont and that DuPont breached its duty to conform with the specifications of the regulation. Accordingly, the primary dispute is whether an employee of an independent contractor is a member of the class of persons that the OSHA regulation was intended to protect.

DuPont argues that the stated purposes for the Occupational Safety and Health Act of 1970 reveal that Congress did not intend to impose a duty upon employers to protect the safety of an independent contractor's employees who work in the employer's plant. In support of this proposition, DuPont relies upon the plain language of the Act which provides that "each employer shall furnish to each of *his* employees employment and a place of employment which are free from recognized hazards that are causing or are likely to cause death or serious physical harm to *his* employees." 29 U.S.C. Sec. 654(a)(1) (emphasis added). Although DuPont's legal position is not without support, *see Melerine v. Avondale Shipyards, Inc.,* 659 F.2d 706 (5th Cir.1981), we believe that an employer's duty to comply with OSHA regulations is broader than DuPont suggests. * * *

The difficulty which courts have experienced in attempting to define a particular employer's responsibilities under the Act is due primarily to the varying nature of the separate duty provisions. The general duty clause was intended by Congress to cover unanticipated hazards; Congress recognized that it could not anticipate all of the potential hazards that might affect adversely the safety of workers. Accordingly, it enacted the general duty clause to cover serious hazards that were not otherwise covered by specific regulations. *Southern Ohio Building Systems, Inc. v. OSHRC,* 649 F.2d 456, 458 (6th Cir.1981). Pursuant to Sec. 654(a)(1), every employer owes a duty of reasonable care to protect his employees from recognized hazards that are likely to cause death or serious bodily injury. The protection from *exposure* to serious hazards is the primary purpose of the general duty clause, *e.g., Anning–Johnson Co. v. United States O.S. & H.R. Com'n,* 516 F.2d 1081, 1086 (7th Cir.1975), and *every* employer owes this duty regardless of whether it controls the workplace, whether it is responsible for the hazard, or whether it has the best opportunity to abate the hazard. In contrast, Sec. 654(a)(2) is the specific duty provision. The class of employers who owe a duty to comply with the OSHA regulations is defined with reference to control of the workplace and opportunity to comply with the OSHA regulations. Accordingly, an employer's responsibilities under the Act depend upon which duty provision the employer is accused of breaching. Similarly, the class of persons for whom each of these duty provisions was enacted must be determined with reference to the particular duty in dispute.

In this case, DuPont is accused of breaching the specific duty imposed on employers by Sec. 654(a)(2). Accordingly, DuPont's reliance on the plain language of the general duty clause is misplaced. The very narrow question on appeal does not concern the scope of an employer's general duty to protect employees from exposure to recognized hazards, but rather, the scope of an employer's duty to comply with the specific OSHA regulations. If the special duty provision is logically construed as imposing an obligation on the part of employers to protect *all* of the employees who work at a particular job site, then the employees of an independent contractor who work on the premises of another employer must be considered members of the class that Sec. 654(a)(2) was intended to protect. In other words, one cannot define the scope of an employer's obligation under Sec. 654(a)(2) as including the protection of another's employees and, at the same time, claim that these "other" employees are unintended beneficiaries.

We believe that Congress enacted Sec. 654(a)(2) for the special benefit of *all* employees, including the employees of an independent contractor, who perform work at another employer's workplace. * * * Consistent with the broad remedial nature of the Act, we interpret the scope of intended beneficiaries of the special duty provision in a broad fashion. In our view, once an employer is deemed responsible for complying with OSHA regulations, it is obligated to protect every employee who works at its workplace. *See, e.g., Marshall v. Knutson Construction Co.,* 566 F.2d 596, 599 (8th Cir.1977) (duty of general contractor extends to protection of all employees). Thus, Richard Teal, an employee of an independent contractor, must be considered a member of the class of persons that the special duty provision was intended to protect.

As we have indicated, Tennessee case law establishes that the breach of a duty imposed by regulation is negligence *per se* if the plaintiff is a member of the class of persons which the regulation was intended to protect. DuPont concedes that it owed a duty to comply with the OSHA regulation in question and that it breached this duty. Because Richard Teal is a member of the class of persons that the OSHA regulation was intended to protect, the appellants were entitled to a jury instruction on their negligence *per se* claim. Accordingly, we hold that the district court erred by refusing to give the requested instruction on the issue of negligence *per se*.

*[handwritten margin note: Teal covered so neg. per se]*

## NOTES AND QUESTIONS

1. The great majority of actions for personal injury are governed by state tort law. The states have divided sharply on whether the *Teal* approach is proper. Some have embraced its reasoning fully. See, e.g., *Hargis v. Baize*, 168 S.W.3d 36 (Kentucky 2005). Others have rejected *Teal*'s reasoning. See, e.g., *Canape v. Petersen*, 897 P.2d 762 (Colo. 1995). One reason for the division is the different reading courts give to section 4(b)(4), 29 U.S.C. § 653(b)(4). That subsection provides: "Nothing in this Act shall be construed to supersede . . . any workmen's compensation law or to enlarge or affect . . . the common law or statutory rights, duties, or liabilities of employers and employees under any law with respect to injuries . . . arising out of, or in the course of, employment." The majority in *Canape* reasoned that this language precluded the use of OSHA standards to define the scope of duty owed by an employer. A vigorous dissent in that case argues that this language only precludes creating a new cause of action and that using an OSHA standard to define the scope of care that a reasonable person would take is perfectly consistent with general state law tort practice.

2. As the next chapter illustrates, a special federal tort law applies under the Federal Employers Liability Act to operating employees on railroads and to certain maritime workers. In *Pratico v. Portland Terminal Co.*, 783 F.2d 255 (1st Cir.1985), a railroad worker was injured while helping to lift a wheel-bearing on a railroad car with a jacking mechanism that did not comply with OSHA standards. The injured worker sued the railroad under the Federal Employers Liability Act, contending that violation of the OSHA standard constituted negligence *per se*. The railroad argued that Section 4(b)(4) of the Act barred application of negligence *per se*. The court rejected this argument, saying that use of OSHA regulations as a standard of care did not create any new rights, duties or liabilities, and should not be viewed as expanding the liability of employers under existing causes of action or negligence. "Rather it simply allows the presence of a statutory regulation to serve as irrefutable evidence that particular conduct is unreasonable." 783 F.2d at 265. "The legislative history of Section 4(b)(4) shows that the intent of the provision was merely to ensure that OSHA was not read to create a private right of action for injured workers which would allow them to bypass the otherwise exclusive remedy of worker's compensation." Id. at 266. Other federal circuits have disagreed. See the discussion in *Elliott v. S. D. Warren Co.* 134 F.3d 1 (1st Cir.1998).

3.  Even if a court is willing to give negligence *per se* effect to violation of an OSHA standard, it is necessary for the injured worker to establish first that the standard is truly applicable to the circumstances of her case. *Pelletier v. Main Street Textiles LP,* 470 F.3d 48 (1st Cir. 2006).

4.  A court that refuses to apply a negligence *per se* approach (so that violation of an OSHA standard is treated as a breach of the duty of reasonable care) may nonetheless permit proof of a breach of an OSHA standard to be admissible evidence on the issue of whether reasonable care was exercised. See, e.g., *Chilcutt v. Ford Motor Co.,* 662 F.Supp.2d 967 (S.D. Ohio 2009) (applying Ohio law).

5.  In *United Steelworkers of America v. Rawson,* 495 U.S. 362, 110 S.Ct. 1904, 109 L.Ed.2d 362 (1990), survivors of mine workers killed in an underground fire sued the union for negligence in the state court, alleging that the mine workers' deaths were caused by the negligence of the mine safety committee which was created by the collective agreement and composed of union and employer representatives. The court stated that the primary duty for safety was on the employer and not the union, but the union might assume a responsibility toward employees by accepting a duty of care through a collective agreement. However, defining that duty required interpretation of the collective agreement, which under Section 301 of the LMRA was governed by federal law and preempted application of state law. The union owed a contractual duty to the employees only if the promise made in the collective agreement was one specifically made to, or enforceable by individual employees. The union owed the employees a duty of fair representation, but this duty was not violated by mere negligence in making inspections.

The Court held that the state could not escape preemption by relying on the general tort doctrine that "one who undertakes, gratuitously or otherwise, to render services to another for the protection of the other's person or things" may be liable for failure to exercise reasonable care. Restatement of Torts (Second) Section 323. This claim, said the Court, could not be described as independent of the collective agreement and was, therefore, also preempted. See Note, *Moving Toward a Clearer Standard of Federal Law Preemption of State Law Claims Under Section 301 of the LMRA,* 37 SAN DIEGO L. REV. 121 (1992); Lorraine Schmall, *Workplace Safety and the Union's Duty After Lueck & Hechler,* 38 KAN. L. REV. 561 (1990).

# CHAPTER IX

## PAYING FOR EMPLOYEE ILLNESS AND INJURY

■ ■ ■

Much of law school study concerns distributing the burdens resulting from illness or injury. The legal systems that determine who pays for employment related illness or injury, and how much each party pays, draw upon several different models, including private insurance, government-sponsored social insurance programs, and common law doctrines for dealing with personal injury. The statistics about workplace injuries underscore both the importance of constructing fair and efficient systems for dealing with these costs, and the extent to which working in America takes a substantial toll on its workers. In 2005, injured workers in this country received more than 55 billion dollars in workers compensation benefits; in August of 2007, 6.9 million disabled workers received Social Security disability payments totaling nearly 7 billion dollars.

## A. THE COMMON LAW RESPONSE TO EMPLOYEE INJURIES

### FARWELL v. BOSTON AND WORCESTER RAIL ROAD CORPORATION

Supreme Judicial Court of Massachusetts, 1842
45 Mass. (4 Metc.) 49

SHAW, C.J.

This is an action of new impression in our courts, and involves a principle of great importance. It presents a case, where two persons are in the service and employment of one company, whose business it is to construct and maintain a rail road, and to employ their trains of cars to carry persons and merchandize for hire. They are appointed and employed by the same company to perform separate duties and services, all tending to the accomplishment of one and the same purpose—that of the safe and rapid transmission of the trains; and they are paid for their respective duties, and the labor and skill required for their proper performance. The question is, whether, for damages sustained by one of the persons so employed, by means of the carelessness and negligence of another, the party injured has a remedy against the common employer. It is an argument against such an action, though certainly not a decisive one, that no such action has before been maintained.

It is laid down by Blackstone, that if a servant, by his negligence, does any damage to a stranger, the master shall be answerable for his neglect. But the damage must be done while he is actually employed in the master's service; otherwise, the servant shall answer for his own misbehavior. 1 Bl.Com. 431. *M'Manus v. Crickett*, 1 East, 106. This rule is obviously founded on the great principle of social duty, that every man, in the management of his own affairs, whether by himself or by his agents or servants, shall so conduct them as not to injure another; and if he does not, and another thereby sustains damage, he shall answer for it. If done by a servant, in the course of his employment, and acting within the scope of his authority, it is considered, in contemplation of law, so far the act of the master, that the latter shall be answerable *civiliter*. But this presupposes that the parties stand to each other in the relation of strangers, between whom there is no privity; and the action, in such case, is an action sounding in tort. The form is trespass on the case, for the consequential damage. The maxim *respondeat superior* is adopted in that case, from general considerations of policy and security.

But this does not apply to the case of a servant bringing his action against his own employer to recover damages for an injury arising in the course of that employment, where all such risks and perils as the employer and the servant respectively intend to assume and bear may be regulated by the express or implied contract between them, and which, in contemplation of law, must be presumed to be thus regulated. * * *

The claim, therefore, is placed, and must be maintained, if maintained at all, on the ground of contract. As there is no express contract between the parties, applicable to this point, it is placed on the footing of an implied contract of indemnity, arising out of the relation of master and servant. It would be an implied promise, arising from the duty of the master to be responsible to each person employed by him, in the conduct of every branch of business, where two or more persons are employed, to pay for all damage occasioned by the negligence of every other person employed in the same service. If such a duty were established by law—like that of a common carrier, to stand to all losses of goods not caused by the act of God or of a public enemy—or that of an innkeeper, to be responsible, in like manner, for the baggage of his guests; it would be a rule of frequent and familiar occurrence, and its existence and application, with all its qualifications and restrictions, would be settled by judicial precedents. But we are of opinion that no such rule has been established, and the authorities, as far as they go, are opposed to the principle. *Priestley v. Fowler*, 3 Mees. & Welsb. 1. *Murray v. South Carolina Rail Road Company*, 1 McMullan, 385.

The general rule, resulting from considerations as well of justice as of policy, is, that he who engages in the employment of another for the performance of specified duties and services, for compensation, takes upon himself the natural and ordinary risks and perils incident to the performance of such services, and in legal presumption, the compensation is adjusted accordingly. And we are not aware of any principle which should except the perils arising from the carelessness and negligence of those who are in the same employment. These are perils which the servant is as likely to know, and against which he can as effectually guard, as the master. They are perils incident to the service, and which can be as distinctly foreseen and provided for in the rate of compensation as any others. To say that the master shall be responsible because the damage is caused by his agents, is assuming the very point which remains to be proved. They are his agents to some extent, and for some purposes; but whether he is responsible, in a particular case, for their negligence, is not decided by the single fact that they are, for some purposes, his agents. * * *

In considering the rights and obligations arising out of particular relations, it is competent for courts of justice to regard considerations of policy and general convenience, and to draw from them such rules as will, in their practical application, best promote the safety and security of all parties concerned. This is, in truth, the basis on which implied promises are raised, being duties legally inferred from a consideration of what is best adapted to promote the benefit of all persons concerned, under given circumstances. To take the well known and familiar cases already cited; a common carrier, without regard to actual fault or neglect in himself or his servants, is made liable for all losses of goods confided to him for carriage, except those caused by the act of God or of a public enemy, because he can best guard them against all minor dangers, and because, in case of actual loss, it would be extremely difficult for the owner to adduce proof of embezzlement, or other actual fault or neglect on the part of the carrier, although it may have been the real cause of the loss. The risk is therefore thrown upon the carrier, and he receives, in the form of payment for the carriage, a premium for the risk which he thus assumes. So of an innkeeper; he can best secure the attendance of honest and faithful servants, and guard his house against thieves. Whereas, if he were responsible only upon proof of actual negligence, he might connive at the presence of dishonest inmates and retainers, and even participate in the embezzlement of the property of the guests, during the hours of their necessary sleep, and yet it would be difficult, and often impossible, to prove these facts. * * *

We are of opinion that these considerations apply strongly to the case in question. Where several persons are employed in the conduct of one common enterprise or undertaking, and the safety of each depends much on the care and skill with which each other shall perform his appropriate duty, each is an observer of the conduct of the others, can give notice of any misconduct, incapacity or neglect of duty, and leave the service, if the common employer will not take such precautions, and employ such agents as the safety of the whole party may require. By these means, the safety of each will be much more effectually secured, than could be done by a resort to the common employer for indemnity in case of loss by the negligence of each other. Regarding it in this light, it is the ordinary case of one sustaining an injury in the course of his own employment, in which he must bear the loss himself, or seek his remedy, if he have any, against the actual wrong-doer.

In applying these principles to the present case, it appears that the plaintiff was employed by the defendants as an engineer, at the rate of wages usually paid in that employment, being a higher rate than the plaintiff had before received as a machinist. It was a voluntary undertaking on his part, with a full knowledge of the risks incident to the employment; and the loss was sustained by means of an ordinary casualty, caused by the negligence of another servant of the company. Under these circumstances, the loss must be deemed to be the result of a pure accident, like those to which all men, in all employments, and at all times, are more or less exposed; and like similar losses from accidental causes, it must rest where it first fell, unless the plaintiff has a remedy against the person actually in default; of which we give no opinion.

It was strongly pressed in the argument, that although this might be so, where two or more servants are employed in the same department of duty, where each can exert some influence over the conduct of the other, and thus to some extent provide for his own security; yet that it could not apply where two or more are employed in different departments of duty, at a distance from each other, and where one can in no degree control or influence the conduct of another. But we think this is founded upon a supposed distinction, on which it would be extremely difficult to establish a practical rule. When the object to be accomplished is one and the same, when the employers are the same, and the several persons employed derive their authority and their compensation from the same source, it would be extremely difficult to distinguish, what constitutes one department and what a distinct department of duty. It would vary with the circumstances of every case. If it were made to depend upon the nearness or distance of the persons from each other, the question would immediately arise, how near or how distant must they be, to be in the same or different departments. In a blacksmith's shop, persons working in the same building, at different fires, may be quite independent of each other, though only a few feet distant. * * *

Besides, it appears to us, that the argument rests upon an assumed principle of responsibility which does not exist. The master, in the case supposed, is not exempt from liability, because the servant has better means of providing for his safety, when he is employed in immediate connection with those from whose negligence he might suffer; but because the implied contract of the master does not extend to indemnify the servant against the negligence of any one but himself; and he is not liable in tort, as for the negligence of his servant, because the person suffering does not stand towards him in the relation of a stranger, but is one whose rights are regulated by contract express or implied. The exemption of the master, therefore, from liability for the negligence of a fellow servant, does not depend exclusively upon the consideration, that the servant has better means to provide for his own safety, but upon other grounds. Hence the separation of the employment into different departments cannot create that liability, when it does not arise from express or implied contract, or from a responsibility created by law to third persons, and strangers, for the negligence of a servant.

In coming to the conclusion that the plaintiff, in the present case, is not entitled to recover, considering it as in some measure a nice question, we would add a caution against any hasty conclusion as to the application of this rule to a case not fully within the same principle. It may be varied and modified by circumstances not appearing in the present case, in which it appears, that no willful wrong or actual negligence was imputed to the corporation, and where suitable means were furnished and suitable persons employed to accomplish the object in view. We are far from intending to say that there are no implied warranties and undertakings arising out of the relation of master and servant. Whether, for instance, the employer would be responsible to an engineer for a loss arising from a defective or ill-constructed steam engine: Whether this would depend upon an implied warranty of its goodness and sufficiency, or upon the fact of willful misconduct, or gross negligence on the part of the employer, if a natural person, or of the superintendent or immediate representative and managing agent, in case of an incorporated company—are questions on which we give no opinion. In the present case, the claim of the plaintiff is not put on the ground that the defendants did not furnish a sufficient engine, a proper rail road track, a well constructed switch, and a person of suitable skill and experience to attend it; the gravamen of the complaint is, that that person was chargeable with negligence in not changing the switch, in the particular instance, by means of which the accident occurred, by which the plaintiff sustained a severe loss. * * * Upon this question, supposing the accident to have occurred, and the loss to have been caused, by the negligence of the person employed to attend to and change the switch, in his not doing so in the particular case, the court are of opinion that it is a loss for which the defendants are not liable, and that the action cannot be maintained.

*Plaintiff nonsuit.*

## NOTES AND QUESTIONS

1. Justice Shaw speaks of the employee taking upon himself the "natural and ordinary risks and perils incident to" the employment and suggests that those risks are reflected in the compensation received. To what extent do these assumptions coincide with your own work world experience? Do workers knowingly assume such risks and obtain commensurate compensation? Even assuming that is true, does the increased compensation give adequate protec-

tion for the worker who suffers a severe injury in the first week, first month, or first year of employment?

2.    If the financial risks of employee injury are shifted to the employer, what impact would you expect that to have upon employer attentiveness to safety? Upon worker attentiveness to safety? Is a shift of the cost to the employer merely transitory; that is, does the employer eventually shift the cost forward to customers or backward to the employees? Justice Pitney, writing for a unanimous Court, once observed: "[J]ust as the employee's assumption of ordinary risks at common law presumably was taken into account in fixing the rate of wages, so the fixed responsibility of the employer, and the modified assumption of risk by the employee under the new [statutory workers compensation] system, presumably will be reflected in the wage scale." *New York Central R.R. v. White*, 243 U.S. 188, 201–02, 37 S.Ct. 247, 252, 61 L.Ed. 667 (1917).

3.    If the employer is liable for a worker's injury or illness under a theory of tort, what measure(s) of damages should be applicable? If the employer is liable for a worker's injury or illness under a theory of implied contract, what measure(s) of damages should be applicable?

4.    Professor Larson, whose treatise is the leading work on the law of workers' compensation, has noted that until 1837 the common law was strangely silent respecting the subject of an employer's liability for employee injuries. ARTHUR. LARSON, THE LAW OF WORKMEN'S COMPENSATION §§ 4.10, 4.20. The issue received high court attention, however, in *Priestley v. Fowler*, 3 M & W 1, 150 Eng.Rep. 1030 (1837), when the British bench rejected the assertion that an employer can be held liable for injuries caused to a worker by the negligence of a fellow employee. There, the British court emphasized the contractual nature of employment and asserted that workers voluntarily assume the risks of their employment. The *Farwell* decision, as we have seen, accepted the rationale of the British court and the Massachusetts decision soon received wide circulation and the influential endorsement of Justice Story's much cited treatise on Agency. JOSEPH STORY, AGENCY § 453d (2d ed.1843). The resulting doctrinal development provided employers with three very effective defenses to suits by employees seeking recovery for work-related injuries even where the worker could overcome the formidable burden of proving his injury was proximately caused by the employer's intentional misconduct or negligence:

- *Contributory negligence.* The employer was relieved of all liability if it showed that the injured worker's own negligence was a proximate cause of the harm.

- *Implied assumption of risk.* The employer was relieved of all liability if it showed the injury resulted from the sort of risk a worker assumed by accepting the particular type of employment.

- *The fellow servant rule.* The employer was relieved of all liability if the injury was caused by a fellow worker of the injured employee.

In addition to overcoming these legal barriers to recovery, the injured worker could anticipate difficulty finding fellow workers or supervisors willing to testify against their employer's interests. Moreover, from a practical perspective few workers had the resources to prosecute a substantial tort claim and small claims weren't worth pursuing. Lying in a hospital bed with no income and medical bills mounting, injured workers were an easy mark to settle tort claims for pennies on the dollar as long as those pennies were received now, when the worker most needed them.

The social impact of the common law policy cannot be fully appreciated without reflecting upon the magnitude of worker injuries during the era of industrialization. In the 1830s, 600 immigrant workers annually died in New Orleans' fever ridden swamps digging the Ponchartrain Canal. They were drawn to the work by high wages. The wages were high because slave owners were unwilling to rent their $900 slaves for such work. Marc Linder, *Fatal Subtractions: Statistical MIAs on the Industrial Battlefield*, 20 J.Legis. 99, 144 (1994). The progress of mechanization did not improve the worker's lot. Thus, the 18th Annual Report of the Interstate Commerce Commission (1904) noted that in 1903, one railroad worker was killed for every 123 employed aboard a train and one trainman was injured for every 10 employed that year. Some of those injuries, no doubt, resulted in permanent, total disability. Given these statistics, what was the prospect of a trainman surviving intact during a forty to fifty year employment life span?

## PEREZ v. McCONKEY

Supreme Court of Tennessee, 1994
872 S.W.2d 897

Anderson, Justice.

In this appeal, we are asked to decide whether and to what extent the common-law doctrine of assumption of risk retains its vitality in view of our recent decision in *McIntyre v. Balentine*, 833 S.W.2d 52 (Tenn.1992). There, we held that contributory negligence no longer serves as a complete bar to a plaintiff's recovery, but is to be considered in apportioning damages according to the principles of modified comparative fault so long as the plaintiff's negligence remains less than the defendant's negligence. * * *

The defendant, Jamie McConkey d/b/a J & V Sales of Englewood, Tennessee, employed the plaintiff, Nancy S. Perez, as an operator of screen printing machinery which was located in the back room of another business. The back room was approximately twenty-five feet wide and thirty feet long. One component of the screen printing equipment Perez used in the discharge of her duties was a dryer which heated up to three hundred and ten (310) degrees Fahrenheit. In addition to the excessive heat generated by the dryer, Perez testified that the printing process itself produced smoke and vapors which caused her to experience flu-like symptoms. Perez contends that on several occasions she complained to the defendant about the oppressive heat and the lack of adequate ventilation, to no avail.

On July 10, 1989, while working on a printing assignment in the back room, Perez testified she fainted and fell due to the heat and vapors. As a result of the fall, she was hospitalized for several days with heat exhaustion and a head injury, and thereafter underwent surgery.

Perez filed a common-law negligence action against the defendant-employer, McConkey,[1] alleging that inadequate ventilation resulted in conditions that rendered the work place unsafe and that, despite her persistent complaints, the defendant negligently failed to remedy the situation.

At the trial, after the plaintiff rested her proof, the defendant moved for a directed verdict, asserting the affirmative defense of implied assumption of risk. The trial court granted the directed verdict motion, finding as a matter of law, that the plaintiff had assumed the risk of the injuries she sustained. The plaintiff appealed. * * *

The Court of Appeals vacated the judgment of the trial court and remanded the matter to the trial court * * *.

### Historical Development

The Latin maxim *volenti non fit injuria*, which means to one who is willing no harm is done, was often described as a synonym for assumption of risk. It was originally applied in Roman–Law as a means of validating the process by which a free citizen sold himself into slavery. Although the date it first appeared in recorded English case law was 1305, the first notable expression of the contemporary common-law doctrine of assumption of risk has been traditionally traced to Lord Abinger's opinion in *Priestly v. Fowler*, 3 M. & W. 1, 150 Eng.Rep. 1030 (Ex.1837). There, the plaintiff, a servant of the defendant, was injured by being thrown to the ground when a "van," overloaded by another of the defendant's servants, broke down.[2] Lord Abinger denied recovery, concluding that "the plaintiff must have known as well as his master, and probably better, whether the van was sufficient, whether it was overloaded, and whether it was likely to carry him safely." Id., 150 Eng.Rep. at 1033. Although Lord Abinger was addressing himself to domestic servants such as chamber maids, coachmen, and footmen, the doctrine of assumption of risk expanded and was extensively applied in master-servant cases during the ensuing industrial revolution where it was interposed to defeat countless claims of injured workers.

Inevitably, the doctrine became a part of American common law as an instrument of public policy to be applied in the American Industrial Revolution. In a refinement of the holding in Priestly, Chief Justice Shaw of the Supreme Judicial Court of Massachusetts in *Farwell v. Boston & Worcester RR Corp.*, 45 Mass. 49 (1842), during our nation's Industrial Revolution, found that a worker's contract of employment impliedly

---

**1.** The plaintiff's claims against the defendant pursuant to the Workers Compensation Act were dismissed because the defendant employed fewer than five persons and, therefore, was not subject to the Act.

**2.** It was also in *Priestly v. Fowler*, supra, that Lord Abinger created the fellow-servant doctrine which this Court recently abandoned in *Glass v. City of Chattanooga*, 858 S.W.2d 312 (1993).

*Modern justification* {

includes the risks of his profession. The court identified three justifications for its holding: (1) the chance of injury is reflected in compensation; (2) the employee is as likely to know of the dangers as the employer; and (3) non-compensation of injuries tends to make workers more careful. Id. The United States Supreme Court thereafter endorsed the doctrine in *Tuttle v. Detroit, Grand Haven & Milwaukee Ry.*, 122 U.S. 189 (1886) as a necessary "rule of public policy, inasmuch as an opposite doctrine would not only subject employers to unreasonable and often ruinous responsibilities, thereby embarrassing all branches of business." Id. 122 U.S. at 196, 7 S.Ct. at 1169.

In Tennessee the doctrine of assumption of risk developed in a similar fashion. * * *

The principal reason for the development of the doctrine was explained by the United States Supreme Court in *Tiller v. Atlantic Coast Line R. Co.*:

> Assumption of risk ... was developed in response to the general impulse of common law courts at the beginning of this period [the industrial revolution] to insulate the employer as much as possible from bearing the "human overhead" which is an inevitable part of the cost—to someone—of the doing of industrialized business. The general purpose behind the development in the common law seems to have been to give maximum freedom to expanding industry.

318 U.S. 54, 58–59, 63 S.Ct. 444, 446–47, 87 L.Ed. 610 (1943). See also Bohlen, Voluntary Assumption of Risk, 20 Harv.L.Rev. 14 (1906). * * *

### Current Status

In contrast to its growth during the first part of this century, the doctrine of implied assumption of risk has lately been on the decline. The proliferation of Workers' Compensation Statutes in all the states and the District of Columbia have abrogated the doctrine in the very context in which it gained acceptance with such unseemly haste. Moreover in other areas of tort law, the doctrine has been a subject of controversy and confusion because * * * the term has been used by courts to refer to at least two different legal concepts, primary and secondary implied assumption of risk, which also overlap both with the basic common-law principles of duty and with aspects of the doctrine of contributory negligence.

In its primary sense, implied assumption of risk focuses not on the plaintiff's conduct in assuming the risk, but on the defendant's general duty of care. The doctrine of primary implied assumption of risk "technically is not a defense, but rather a legal theory which relieves a defendant of the duty which he might otherwise owe to the plaintiff with respect to particular risks." *Armstrong v. Mailand*, 284 N.W.2d 343, 351 (Minn. 1979). * * * Clearly, primary implied assumption of risk is but another way of stating the conclusion that a plaintiff has failed to establish a prima facie case by failing to establish that a duty exists.

On the other hand, secondary implied assumption of risk is an affirmative defense which must be asserted by the defendant after a negligent breach of duty has been established. As Professor Mutter points out in her analysis, this type of implied assumption of risk refers to both unreasonable and reasonable conduct by the plaintiff in assuming a known risk.[3] Secondary implied assumption of risk has been further subdivided by courts and commentators into "unreasonable or qualified" secondary assumption of risk and "reasonable or strict or pure" secondary implied assumption of risk. Qualified or unreasonable secondary assumption of risk is functionally indistinguishable from contributory negligence.

The confusion engendered by the overlap of the doctrine of assumption of risk with the common law concepts of duty and contributory negligence, as well as the harsh results of the defense, has resulted in criticism of the doctrine, and has led legal commentators to call for the doctrine's abrogation. * * *

However, the greatest blow to the doctrine of implied assumption of risk has been the overwhelming acceptance and adoption by most states of comparative fault or comparative negligence principles. Of the forty-five states, other than Tennessee, that apply principles of comparative fault, only five states—Georgia, Nebraska, Mississippi, Rhode Island and South Dakota—retain assumption of risk as a complete bar to recovery. Ten states abolished the doctrine entirely as a separate affirmative defense before, or without any reference to, the adoption of the state's particular comparative-negligence law. Ten other states by statute have abolished or subsumed the defense of assumption of risk into their comparative fault schemes. The remaining nineteen states which have judicially considered the appropriate role of assumption of risk in light of a statutory or judicial adoption of comparative negligence or fault principles have also altered or abolished the common law doctrine.

Whether by statute or by judicial decision, those states which have tailored assumption of risk to mesh with comparative negligence or fault principles appear to follow one of three approaches. Some states have merged secondary implied assumption of risk into the comparative negligence scheme, while retaining the principle of primary implied assumption of risk as a complete bar to recovery. After concluding that the situations to which both primary and secondary implied assumption of risk have been applied are just as amenable to resolution under the common law concepts of duty and comparative fault, other jurisdictions have abolished implied assumption of risk entirely, and dispensed with using assumption of risk terminology. Finally, some jurisdictions have combined the doctrine of primary implied assumption of risk with the common-law concept of duty, while retaining the defense of secondary implied assumption of risk as a factor for comparison in the same manner as any plaintiff's negligence and not as a complete bar to recovery.

---

**3.** C. Mutter, Moving to Comparative Negligence in an Era of Tort Reform: Decisions for Tennessee, 57 Tenn. L. Rev. 190, 286 (1990).

In spite of the diversity of opinion as to the proper role of the various categories of implied assumption of risk in a comparative negligence scheme, commentators and courts almost unanimously agree that even in a system of comparative fault, express assumption of risk should remain an absolute bar to recovery. The uniformity of decision on this issue has been attributed to the fact that "express assumption of risk involves an affirmatively demonstrated, and presumably bargained upon choice by the plaintiff to relieve the defendant of his legal duty. . . ." Prosser and Keeton, § 68, at 496. * * * Tennessee's case law in this area is typical. Specifically, an express release, waiver, or exculpatory words by which one party agrees to assume the risk of harm arising from another party's negligent conduct will be enforced by the courts so long as it does not extend to liability for willful or gross negligence and does not otherwise offend public policy. * * *

After reviewing the wealth of authorities from other jurisdictions, as well as the writings of numerous legal commentators on the subject, we join the vast majority of jurisdictions by concluding that the doctrine of implied assumption of risk no longer operates as a complete bar to recovery in Tennessee. It would be ironic indeed if, after abolishing the all-or-nothing proposition of contributory negligence in *McIntyre*, we were to reinstate it here using the vehicle of assumption of risk. However valid at the time, the policy of insulating business from human overhead, from which assumption of risk developed, now runs directly counter to modern social policy that is typified by the almost universal enactment of workmen's compensation legislation.

* * * The types of issues raised by implied assumption of risk are readily susceptible to analysis in terms of the common-law concept of duty and the principles of comparative negligence law.

* * * Because duty is an element of the plaintiff's prima facie case, the doctrine of primary implied assumption of risk, as an alternate expression of the concept of duty, would serve no productive purpose; indeed it would only confuse and convolute the issues. * * * While we agree that those situations described by commentators as involving the concept of primary implied assumption of risk will preclude recovery under a scheme of comparative fault, the same result will be obtained, without any unnecessary confusion, if Tennessee courts use the common-law concept of duty to analyze the issues.

Moreover, we do not consider it necessary or desirable to retain the doctrine of secondary implied assumption of risk as a separate defense. Rather, the reasonableness of a party's conduct in confronting a risk should be determined under the principles of comparative fault. Attention should be focused on whether a reasonably prudent person in the exercise of due care knew of the risk, or should have known of it, and thereafter confronted the risk; and whether such a person would have behaved in the manner in which the plaintiff acted in light of all the surrounding circumstances, including the confronted risk.

*Conclusion*

Based on the foregoing analysis, we hold that implied assumption of risk is no longer a complete bar to recovery in Tennessee. Instead the doctrine is abolished because the situations to which it applied under the former common law contributory negligence scheme are more clearly and readily amenable to analysis after *McIntyre* in terms of the common-law concept of duty and by reference to principles of comparative fault. Express assumption of risk as it existed under the former common-law contributory negligence regime is unaffected by this holding.

\* \* \* The judgment of the Court of Appeals, as modified, is affirmed. \* \* \*

# GLASS v. CITY OF CHATTANOOGA

Supreme Court of Tennessee, 1993
858 S.W.2d 312

O'BRIEN, JUSTICE.

\* \* \* The circumstances giving rise to this action are \* \* \* undisputed. At the time of the injury the plaintiff, Queen Ann Glass, was employed as a school bus driver by the defendant, City of Chattanooga. On 7 February 1989, Ms. Glass was seated alone in the driver's seat of her parked school bus. Positioned immediately in front of Ms. Glass' bus was another parked school bus operated by Steve May, also an employee of the City of Chattanooga. It is stipulated by the parties that when Mr. May attempted to drive his bus away from the curb, he inadvertently had the transmission in reverse gear and negligently backed into Ms. Glass' parked bus, causing her injury. The plaintiff filed suit against the City alleging she was entitled to damages proximately caused by Steve May's negligence.

*[margin note: Other bus driver reverses + injures Queen]*

Because the City of Chattanooga is not subject to the Tennessee workers' compensation statutes, the issue of the City's liability is governed by common law. T.C.A. 50–6–106(5). \* \* \*

The trial court denied the City's motion to dismiss and the cause proceeded to trial. The trial judge, without the intervention of a jury, found for the plaintiff and awarded damages in the amount of $6,500.00.

*[margin note: Tr Ct: π]*

The City of Chattanooga appealed citing error by the trial court for refusing to apply the fellow servant doctrine. In a split decision, the Court of Appeals ruled that the fellow servant doctrine was indeed applicable and dismissed the case. We granted the plaintiff permission to appeal. \* \* \*

*[margin note: Ct of App's Rev. Fellow servant]*

This common law tort defense was first pronounced by Lord Abinger of the London Court of the Exchequer in the case of *Priestley v. Fowler*, 150 Eng.Rep. 1030 (1837); \* \* \*.

The rule was first adopted in the United States four years after *Priestley* in the case of *Murray v. South Carolina Railroad Co.*, 26 S.C.L.

(1 Mc.Mul.) 385 (1841). The *Murray* case fell into relative obscurity, and the doctrine did not begin to receive wide attention until the next year when the highest court of Massachusetts published *Farwell v. Boston and Worcester Railroad Corp.*, 45 Mass. (4 Met.) 49 (1842); See, Comment, The Creation of a Common Law Rule: The Fellow Servant Rule 1837–1860, 132 U.Pa.L.R. 579 (1984). * * *

By 1858, the doctrine was considered well-settled law in Tennessee, *Goggin v. E.T. Va. R.R. Co.*, 1 Tenn.Cas. (1 Shann.) 85 (1858), and although the doctrine's harsh result was recognized, courts were unwilling to abate the rule altogether. "If this be a hard rule to apply to these unfortunate men who, perhaps, for inadequate wages, perform so much arduous and perilous labor, and so many of whom are injured, it is still a rule too well established to be overthrown by the courts." *Nashville, Chattanooga & St. Louis Railroad Co. v. Wheless*, 78 Tenn. (10 Lea) 741, 748 (1882). Seven years later in 1889, the Court announced that the "state has gone as far as it is deemed prudent or wise to go in recognizing exceptions or modifications to the doctrine of fellow-servants, and we have no desire to extend them one step beyond the point already reached." *Louisville & N.R. Co. v. Martin*, 87 Tenn. 398, 10 S.W. 772 (1889). Despite the holding in *Martin, supra*, courts devised ways to avoid application of the doctrine and its harsh result. * * * See, *Washburn v. The Nashville & Chattanooga Railroad Co.*, 40 Tenn. (3 Head) 638 (1859) (cautioning that care should be taken to apply the doctrine narrowly); *Haynes v. East Tennessee & Georgia Railroad*, 43 Tenn. (3 Cold) 222 (1866) (employer liable for the negligence of fellow employees in different departments); *Knoxville Iron Company v. Dobson*, 75 Tenn. (7 Lea) 367 (1881) (an employer may not escape liability for the negligence of vice-principal); *Virginia Iron, Coal & Coke Co. v. Hamilton*, 107 Tenn. 705, 65 S.W. 401 (1901) (employer liable for negligently failing to provide safe work place); *Memphis Steam Laundry v. Johnson*, 5 Tenn.Civ.App. (5 Higgins) 123 (1915) (an employer is liable for a co-employee's negligent performance of a nondelegable duty); See also, 10 Tenn.Jur. Employer and Employee, §§ 32–38 (1983).

Whatever viability the rule may have offered at the advent of the industrial revolution, by placing the economic costs of work related injury squarely on the shoulders of those employees injured by the negligence of co-workers, has since withered. Legislation in all fifty States has abolished the doctrine as an affirmative defense for claims brought under workers' compensation statutes. Prosser, and Keeton on Torts, Sec. 80 at 573 (5th Ed.1984). Since 1919, the doctrine in Tennessee has been limited in application solely to those employers exempt from workers compensation laws. T.C.A. 50–6–111(2); * * *. In this limited application, the doctrine works as an inherently unjust rule that denies a party, free of fault, the right to recover for injuries sustained through the negligence of another over whose conduct the injured party has no control, merely because of a fortuitous circumstance of employment. *Buckley v. City of New York*, 437 N.E.2d 1088 (N.Y.1982). Clearly, the fellow servant doctrine is in rigorous conflict with contemporary thought on theories of compensation for injuries occurring in the work place.

This Court has not hesitated when it became expedient and appropriate to modify aging common law principles. * * *

In *Buckley, supra*, the New York court elucidated the principle which we now adopt as the standard to be applied for injuries sustained in the course of employer-employee relationships in this State, where no other remedy exists:

> Logically, there appears to be little reason for denying an employee the right which a third party possesses to recover from the employer in *respondeat superior* . . . Moreover, the class of persons most frequently endangered by the negligence of an employee—his fellow workers—should not, without compelling reason, be denied a remedy accorded to the general public. . . .

> The inherent injustice of a rule which denies a person, free of fault, the right to recover for injuries sustained through the negligence of another, over whose conduct he has no control merely because of the fortuitous circumstance that the other is a fellow employee, is manifest. *Poniatowski v. City of New York*, 14 N.Y.2d 76, 77, 198 N.E.2d 237, 238, 248 N.Y.S.2d 849, 850 (1964).

The fellow servant rule was created by judicial fiat and we now declare its demise. It is a rule that has largely been displaced by enactment of the Workers' Compensation statutes and under present conditions serves no useful purpose in the work place. * * * Accordingly, the judgment of the Court of Appeals dismissing plaintiff's claim is reversed. The trial court's judgment is reinstated.

### NOTES AND QUESTIONS

1. As these two cases illustrate, there are still some situations in which tort law is available to employees as a basis for recovering from their employers. This is because the workers compensation laws typically have a number of exemptions from coverage. A dozen states exempt businesses with a small number of employees; most exempt domestic workers in private homes and workers in agriculture. State and local government workers are often exempt, but in many cases there are special benefit programs for those same workers. For example, the federal government provides state and local public safety officers (police officers and fire fighters) or their families with a permanent disability benefit or a death benefit of $100,000 (adjusted for inflation using 1988 as the base year) in the event of injury or death which was "in the line of duty." 42 U.S.C. § 3796.

2. As the opinion in *Glass* indicates, not every American court fully subscribed to the rationale of *Priestley* and *Farwell*. In 1851, the Ohio bench ruled that the fellow servant defense is not available if the negligent fellow employee has managerial responsibilities. *Little Miami R.R. v. Stevens*, 20 Ohio 415 (1851). In time, this qualification, known as the "vice principal"

exception, was adopted by several other states. See, e.g., *Mayor and Board of Aldermen of the City of Vicksburg v. Young*, 616 So.2d 883 (Miss. 1992). Also, a number of states limited the fellow servant defense to situations in which the tortfeasor worked in "habitual association" with the victim's employment activity. *Asbury v. Hecla Mining Co.*, 103 Wash. 542, 175 Pac. 179 (1918). Another inroad upon the employer defenses was a New York decision that held the assumption of the risk defense inapplicable where the injury resulted from the employer's violation of a safety statute. *Fitzwater v. Warren*, 206 N.Y. 355, 99 N.E. 1042 (1912). Similarly, some courts rejected the assumption of the risk defense in those circumstances in which the worker could not abandon apparently dangerous conduct without endangering others. *Olney v. Boston & Me. R.R.*, 71 N.H. 427, 52 Atl. 1097 (1902). Finally, the most extensive inroad upon the doctrine announced in *Farwell* was the concept of nondelegable duties. *Memphis Steam Laundry v. Johnson* [cited in *Glass*].

These changes often carried little practical significance. For one thing, work related injuries were frequently the result of the employee's sole fault. Personal carelessness perhaps brought on by the fatigue of long work hours or by succumbing to distractions from the tedium of mass production, caused a large portion of the injuries suffered by workers. Moreover, even when there was a basis for establishing employer liability, the courts were not readily available to the average worker. Going to court required professional assistance which most workers could not afford except on a contingency fee basis. But if the amount at stake was not substantial, that is, if the injury was not of major proportions, the claim was not likely to be attractive to a lawyer. Also, many in the workforce were newly arrived immigrants who lacked familiarity with the American legal system or sufficient command of English to provide clear, persuasive testimony in favor of their claims. Other workers lacked the legal capacity to bring such suits on their own because they had not attained legal majority. For example, in 1910 about two million children between the ages of 10 and 15 were gainfully employed. Many of these children worked in especially dangerous industries such as mining, textile mills, and canneries. Often, too, their parents and siblings worked for the same employer and, therefore, they were hesitant to sue for redress of any injuries.

3. The changes in tort law in Tennessee are, as the opinions make clear, common in many states. Some jurisdictions, however, continue to apply the fellow servant doctrine, either as a matter of *stare decisis* or because the doctrine has been adopted in a statute. See, e.g., *Mayor and Board of Aldermen of Vicksburg v. Young*, 616 So.2d 883 (Miss. 1992); *Gowin v. Trangsrud*, 571 N.W.2d 824 (N.Dak. 1997) (applying a statute).

## A Note on Economic Theory, Compensating Wages, and Perfecting the Market by Requiring Employer Paid Compensation Insurance

From the perspective of neoclassical economic analysis, the debate over the efficacy of tort law in compensating workers for industrial hazards is of little consequence. Following the logic of the majority in *Farwell*, if an employee bears risk of loss due to injury or illness from a job, either because the employer is not negligent or because the tort system just doesn't work very well, the employee will have to be compensated for that risk in order to get the employee to take the job. These "compensating wages" not only give the employer incentive to make the workplace safer, thereby achieving savings in the wages that must be paid, but also would serve as a source of revenue with which the employee might purchase insurance against losses due to the risk of injury or illness. There is good evidence that compensating wages exist and workers are in fact paid more for jobs that involve risk to personal safety than comparable safer jobs. W. Kip Viscusi, *The Value of Risks to Life and Health*, 31 J. OF ECON. LIT. 1912 (1993). Why do we care whether workers are adequately compensated for injury and illness through the tort system or some other system if they receive *ex ante* compensation for this risk in their paychecks?

The short answer is that, although the mechanism of contract and compensating wages suggested by the neoclassical model does function, it is far from the perfect mechanism suggested by economic theory. Neither employers nor employees have all of the information on potential workplace injury or illness necessary to determine adequate compensating wages. Although some jobs are clearly more risky than others, with the result that some compensating wage is paid, less obvious risks of injury or illness may not be apparent to employees and thus may not enter into the job choice or compensation. Moreover, the neoclassical model assumes that the employee in fact has a choice among comparable jobs, some of which are safer than others and all of which are actively competing for workers. This is of course a very strong assumption to make about all employees in our economy in any place and at any time. Some of the worst cases of under-compensation for risk occur among "exploited workers" who do not have options. See *e.g.* JOSEPH A. PAGE AND MARY-WIN O'BRIEN, BITTER WAGES 59–62 (1973) (during Great Depression workers continued digging tunnel near Gauley Bridge, West Virginia even after hundreds took ill from silicosis and ultimately 476 workers died and 1,500 were disabled); *People v. O'Neil*, 194 Ill.App.3d 79, 141 Ill.Dec. 44, 550 N.E.2d 1090 (1 Dist.,1990) (undocumented immigrant worked over illegal vats of cyanide and died). Finally, there is reason to believe that, in order to deal with extreme risk, people tend to defer it in their minds assuming that other people will suffer the loss, not them. Although this may be an emotionally comforting basis on which to deal with extreme risk day to day, it is a poor basis for the rational negotiation of wages to compensate one for the risk. As a result of these imperfections in information, opportunity and rational decision-making about risk, compensating wages generally do not fully compensate workers for the risks they bear and workers generally do not buy insurance against the risk of injury and illness—even though many should. Susan Rose–Ackerman, *Progressive Law and Economics—And the New Administrative Law*, 98 YALE L.J. 341, 355–57 (1988); but see MICHAEL J. MOORE & W. KIP VISCUSI, COMPENSATION MECHANISMS FOR JOB RISKS 74–75 (1990).

The failure of employers to pay fully compensating wages for job risks has implications for society as well as workers. Because the workers' wages don't fully reflect the costs of job risks imposed on them, the price of the good they produce does not fully reflect the costs of its production. As a result employers don't have adequate incentive to adopt new, safer and more efficient technologies and consumers don't have adequate incentive to consume safely produced goods. Moreover, these costs of work place risks don't just disappear. If the employee can't afford to bear them and maintain his or her household, then the cost of the employee's maintenance and medical care will inevitably be borne by the public at large through bad debt, charity or government programs.

*Less incentive for safety*

However, contractual compensation is a two-way street. Under the neoclassical analysis of compensating wages, would it really hurt employers to promise employees some reasonable level of compensation for workplace injury and illness as part of their contract for employment? If enforceable, such a promise would decrease the employees' risk in taking the job and the employer could forgo paying them compensating wages for that risk. Indeed, one can plausibly argue that if the market worked better and people had access to perfect information and made fully rational decisions about risks, employers would commonly offer employees an employer paid no-frills insurance policy against workplace injury and illness as part of the offer of employment. This is a risk that fully informed employees would rationally insure against and, rather than paying the employees a compensating wage and letting them insure on their own, the employer can more cheaply take care of the problem by purchasing a group policy. The employer is the superior bearer of the risk of workplace injury because the employer has more control over safety in the workplace than individual employees, can more efficiently spread risk through self-insurance and can take advantage of economies of scale in purchasing group insurance. As a result, the employer can insure the risk of workplace injury or illness more cheaply then the individual employees. Prior to workers' compensation employers did not commonly offer such insurance policies because employees could not command adequate compensating wages and thus the employees bore most of the costs of accidents or illnesses, or externalized them on society. One can argue that by requiring employer paid workers' compensation insurance, state regulation is really just perfecting the market.

## B.  SPECIFIC REMEDIES FOR RAILROAD WORKERS AND SEAFARERS

The three cases in the prior section illustrate how the common law process has often worked in the United States. An influential court will decide a case of first impression, its opinion will attract the attention of other courts and of commentators, and if the logic and the policy arguments of the opinion are appealing, that opinion will have a shaping influence on the development of the law. Over time lawyers employed by those who are not well served by the doctrine will persuade courts to limit the scope of operation of those doctrines, and may eventually persuade courts to reject entirely the approach taken by that first opinion, perhaps arguing that circumstances have changed, perhaps that the original policy arguments were flawed. That process of change, however, can take a lot of time. *Farwell* was decided in 1842. New York did not abandon the fellow servant rule until 140 years later; Tennessee followed New York's lead eleven years after that. It is little wonder that advocates for workers turned to the legislature for help. The statutes that ultimately came to dominate in this area are state workers compensation laws. Several groups of workers are not subject to those laws, though. The largest group consists of employees of the federal government, who have their own federal workers compensation statute. Two other substantial groups are the subject of this section: railroad operating employees, and workers who fall within the admiralty jurisdiction of the federal government. Railroads were arguably the first truly "big business" in the U.S., and provided impetus for a number of important developments in the law. JAMES ELY, RAILROADS AND AMERICAN LAW (2001). Much of our administrative law was shaped by cases involving the Interstate Commerce Commission. The ICC played a role also in publicizing the need for greater railroad safety and the plight of injured railroad workers. The 18th Annual Report of the Interstate Commerce Commission (1904) noted that, in 1903, one railroad worker was killed for every 123 employed aboard a train and one train-man was injured for every 10 employed that year. Statistics like that aided advocates of change, and in 1906 the Congress enacted an employers' liability act along the lines of those that had been passed in roughly half the states, limiting the use of the fellow servant defense. The 1906 statute was struck down by the Supreme Court in *Howard v. Illinois Central R.R.*, 207 U.S. 463, 28 S.Ct. 141, 52 L.Ed. 297 (1908) because it covered all railroad employees, not just those involved in operating the trains and therefore exceeded the scope of the federal power to regulate commerce, as the Court then defined that power. A second version of the statute, confined to those employees more directly involved in operating the trains, was found constitutional in *The Second Employers' Liability Cases*, 223 U.S. 1, 32 S.Ct. 169, 56 L.Ed. 327 (1912). The changes the Federal Employers Liability Act (FELA) made in the law are discussed in the case that follows, *Norfolk So. Ry. Co. v. Sorrell*.

The situation of workers subject to the admiralty jurisdiction of the federal government is different in some ways. Like railroad workers, longshore workers and crew members injured in the territorial waters could seek damages under state law in the late 19th and early 20th centuries. Unlike railroad workers, however, seafarers and longshoremen could also seek relief in the federal courts acting as courts of admiralty. In the admiralty they could seek relief under doctrines of "maintenance and cure" and "unseaworthiness" (the latter often described as the "general maritime remedy"). In 1920, the Congress added to the remedies available by enacting two statutes, the Jones Act (extending the FELA to seafarers) and the Death on the High Seas Act (which applies to passengers as well as crew members and is also available to those traveling over the oceans by air). The resulting multiplicity of remedies has resulted in a number of problems for the courts to resolve, as the *Miles* case demonstrates.

Only a small fraction of the workforce can elect these remedies. Why study them, even in so brief a section of this text? In part because they show what the alternatives to the workers compensation system look like—and this may provide clues to why state legislatures made the choice they did, and why some employer groups, at least, found workers compensation a compromise they could live with.

## NORFOLK SOUTHERN RAILWAY CO. v. SORRELL

United States Supreme Court, 2007
549 U.S. 158, 127 S.Ct. 799, 166 L.Ed.2d 638

CHIEF JUSTICE ROBERTS delivered the opinion of the Court.

Timothy Sorrell, respondent in this Court, sustained neck and back injuries while working as a trackman for petitioner Norfolk Southern Railway Company. He filed suit in Missouri state court under the Federal Employers' Liability Act (FELA), 45 U.S.C. §§ 51–60, which makes railroads liable to their employees for injuries "resulting in whole or in part from the negligence" of the railroad, § 51. Contributory negligence is not a bar to recovery under FELA, but damages are reduced "in proportion to the amount of negligence attributable to" the employee, § 53. Sorrell was awarded $1.5 million in damages by a jury; Norfolk objects that the jury instructions reflected a more lenient causation standard for railroad negligence than for employee contributory negligence...

On November 1, 1999, while working for Norfolk in Indiana, Sorrell was driving a dump truck loaded with asphalt to be used to repair railroad crossings. While he was driving between crossings on a gravel road alongside the tracks, another Norfolk truck approached, driven by fellow employee Keith Woodin. * * * According to Sorrell's testimony, Woodin forced Sorrell's truck off the road; according to Woodin, Sorrell drove his truck into a ditch. * * *

Missouri purports to apply different standards of causation to railroad and employee contributory negligence in its approved jury instructions for FELA liability. The instructions direct a jury to find an employee contributorily negligent if the employee was negligent and his negligence "directly contributed to cause" the injury, ... while allowing a finding of railroad negligence if the railroad was negligent and its negligence contributed "in whole or in part" to the injury ...[1]

---

1. Missouri in the past directed a jury to find a railroad liable if the railroad's negligence "directly resulted in whole or in part in injury to plaintiff * * * This language persisted until 1978, when the instruction was modified to its present version ... The commentary explains that the word "direct" was excised because, under FELA, "the traditional doctrine of proximate (direct) cause is not applicable." * * * The contributory negligence instruction, on the other hand, has remained unchanged.

When Sorrell proposed the Missouri approved instruction for employee contributory negligence, Norfolk objected on the ground that it provided a "different" and "much more exacting" standard for causation than that applicable with respect to the railroad's negligence under the Missouri instructions ... The trial court overruled the objection. * * * The Missouri Court of Appeals affirmed. * * *

In briefing and argument before this Court, Norfolk has attempted to expand the question presented to encompass what the standard of causation under FELA should be, not simply whether the standard should be the same for railroad negligence and employee contributory negligence. * * *

Sorrell raises both a substantive and procedural objection in response. Substantively, he argues that this Court departed from a proximate cause standard for railroad negligence under FELA in *Rogers v. Missouri Pacific R. Co.*, 352 U.S. 500 (1957). There we stated: "Under [FELA] the test of a jury case is simply whether the proofs justify with reason the conclusion that employer negligence played any part, even the slightest, in producing the injury or death for which damages are sought ...

"For practical purposes the inquiry in these cases today rarely presents more than the single question whether negligence of the employer played any part, however small, in the injury or death which is the subject of the suit." Id. at 506.508.

Sorrell argues that these passages from Rogers have been interpreted to mean that a plaintiff's burden of proof on the question whether the railroad's negligence caused his injury is less onerous than the proximate cause standard prevailing at common law, citing cases such as *CONRAIL v. Gottshall*, 512 U.S. 532, 542–543 (1994); *Holbrook v. Norfolk Southern R. Co.*, 414 F. 3d 739, 741–742 (CA7 2005); *Hernandez v. Trawler Miss Vertie Mae, Inc.*, 187 F. 3d 432, 436 (CA4 1999); and *Summers v. Missouri Pacific R. System*, 132 F. 3d 599, 606–607 (CA10 1997). * * *

Norfolk counters that Rogers did not alter the established common-law rule of proximate cause, but rather simply rejected a flawed and unduly stringent version of the rule, the so-called "sole proximate cause" test. According to Norfolk, while most courts of appeals may have read Rogers as Sorrell does, several state supreme courts disagree, * * * and "there is a deep conflict of authority on precisely that issue." Reply Brief for Petitioner 20, n. 10.

Sorrell's procedural objection is that we did not grant certiorari to determine the proper standard of causation for railroad negligence under FELA, but rather to decide whether different standards for railroad and employee negligence were permissible under the Act. * * *

We agree with Sorrell that we should stick to the question on which certiorari was sought and granted. * * *

II

In response to mounting concern about the number and severity of railroad employees' injuries, Congress in 1908 enacted FELA to provide a compensation scheme for railroad workplace injuries, pre-empting state tort remedies. * * * Unlike a typical workers' compensation scheme, which provides relief without regard to fault, Section 1 of FELA provides a statutory cause of action sounding in negligence:

> "Every common carrier by railroad . . . shall be liable in damages to any person suffering injury while he is employed by such carrier . . . for such injury or death resulting in whole or in part from the negligence of any of the officers, agents, or employees of such carrier . . ."

45 U.S.C. § 51.

FELA provides for concurrent jurisdiction of the state and federal courts, § 56, although substantively FELA actions are governed by federal law. * * * Absent express language to the contrary, the elements of a FELA claim are determined by reference to the common law. * * * One notable deviation from the common law is the abolition of the railroad's common-law defenses of assumption of the risk, § 54; * * * and, at issue in this case, contributory negligence, § 53. * * *

> "[In all actions under FELA], the fact that the employee may have been guilty of contributory negligence shall not bar a recovery, but the damages shall be diminished by the jury in proportion to the amount of negligence attributable to such employee . . ."

45 U.S.C. § 53.

Both parties agree that at common law the causation standards for negligence and contributory negligence were the same * * *.

Missouri's practice of applying different causation standards in FELA actions is apparently unique. Norfolk claims that Missouri is the only jurisdiction to allow such a disparity, and Sorrell has not identified another.[2] It is of course possible that everyone is out of step except

---

**2.** A review of model and pattern jury instructions in FELA actions reveals a variety of approaches. Some jurisdictions recommend using the "in whole or in part" or "in any part" formulation for both railroad negligence and plaintiff contributory negligence, by using the same language in the respective pattern instructions, including a third instruction that the same causation standard is applied to both parties, or including in commentary an admonition to that effect. See, e.g., 5 L. Sand, J. Siffert, W. Loughlin, S. Reiss, & N. Batterman, Modern Federal Jury Instructions—Civil PP 89.02–89.03, pp. 89–7, 89–44, 89–53 (3d ed. 2006); 4 Fla. Forms of Jury Instruction §§ 161.02, 161.47, 161.60 (2006); Cal. Jury Instr., Civ., Nos. 11.07, 11.14, and Comment (2005); 3 Ill. Forms of Jury Instruction §§ 91.02[1], 91.50[1] (2005); 3 N. M. Rules Ann., Uniform Jury Instr., Civ., Nos. 13–905, 13–909, 13–915 (2004); Model Utah Jury Instr., Civ., Nos. 14.4, 14.7, 14.8 (1993 ed.); Manual of Model Civil Jury Instructions for the District Courts of the Eighth Circuit § 7.03, and n. 7 (2005); Eleventh Circuit Pattern Jury Instructions (Civil Cases) § 7.1 (2005). Other jurisdictions use the statutory formulation ("in whole or in part") for railroad negligence, and do not contain a pattern instruction for contributory negligence. See, e.g., Mich. Non–Standard Jury Instr., Civ., § 12:53 (Supp. 2006). Both Alabama and Virginia use formulations containing language of both proximate cause and in whole or in part. 1 Ala. Pattern Jury Instr., Civ., Nos. 17.01, 17.05 (2d ed. 1993) (railroad negligence "proximately caused, in whole or in part"; plaintiff contributory negligence "proximately contributed to

Missouri, but we find no basis for concluding that Congress in FELA meant to allow disparate causation standards.

We have explained that "although common-law principles are not necessarily dispositive of questions arising under FELA, unless they are expressly rejected in the text of the statute, they are entitled to great weight in our analysis." *Gottshall*, 512 U.S. at 544. In *Gottshall* we "cataloged" the ways in which FELA expressly departed from the common law: it abolished the fellow servant rule, rejected contributory negligence in favor of comparative negligence, prohibited employers from contracting around the Act, and abolished the assumption of risk defense. * * * The fact that the common law applied the same causation standard to defendant and plaintiff negligence, and FELA did not expressly depart from that approach, is strong evidence against Missouri's disparate standards. * * *

Departing from the common-law practice of applying a single standard of causation for negligence and contributory negligence would have been a peculiar approach for Congress to take in FELA. As one court explained, under FELA,

> "as to both attack or defense, there are two common elements, (1) negligence, i.e., the standard of care, and (2) causation, i.e., the relation of the negligence to the injury. So far as negligence is concerned, that standard is the same—ordinary prudence—for both Employee and Railroad alike. Unless a contrary result is imperative, it is, at best, unfortunate if two standards of causation are used."

*Page v. St. Louis S. R. Co.*, 349 F.2d 820 at 823.

As a practical matter, it is difficult to reduce damages "in proportion" to the employee's negligence if the relevance of each party's negligence to the injury is measured by a different standard of causation. Norfolk argues, persuasively we think, that it is far simpler for a jury to conduct the apportionment FELA mandates if the jury compares like with like— apples to apples. * * *

Sorrell argues that FELA does contain an explicit statutory alteration from the common-law rule: Section 1 of FELA—addressing railroad negligence—uses the language "in whole or in part," 45 U.S.C. § 51, while

---

cause"); 1 Va. Jury Instructions §§ 40.01, 40.02 (3d ed. 1998) (railroad negligence "in whole or in part was the proximate cause of or proximately contributed to cause," plaintiff negligence "contributed to cause"). In New York, the pattern instructions provide that railroad causation is measured by whether the injury results "in whole or in part" from the railroad's negligence, and a plaintiff's contributory negligence diminishes recovery if it "contributed to cause" the injury. 1B N. Y. Pattern Jury Instr., Civ., No. 2:180 (3d ed. 2006). Montana provides only a general FELA causation instruction. Mont. Pattern Instr., Civ., No. 6.05 (1997) ("An act or a failure to act is the cause of an injury if it plays a part, no matter how small, in bringing about the injury"). Kansas has codified instructions similar to Missouri's, Kan. Pattern Instr. 3d, Civ., No. 132.01 (2005) (railroad liable when injury "results in whole or in part" from railroad's negligence); id., No. 132.20 (contributory negligence is negligence on the part of the plaintiff that "contributes as a direct cause" of the injury), but the commentary to these instructions cites cases and instructions applying a single standard, id., No. 132.01, and Comment, and in practice the Kansas courts have used the language of in whole or in part for both parties' negligence. See *Merando v. Atchison, T. & S. F. R. Co.*, 232 Kan. 404, 406–409, 656 P.2d 154, 157–158 (1982).

Section 3—covering employee contributory negligence—does not, 45 U.S.C. § 53. This, Sorrell contends, evinces an intent to depart from the common-law causation standard with respect to railroad negligence under Section 1, but not with respect to any employee contributory negligence under Section 3.

The inclusion of this language in one section and not the other does not alone justify a departure from the common-law practice of applying a single standard of causation. It would have made little sense to include the "in whole or in part" language in Section 3, because if the employee's contributory negligence contributed "in whole" to his injury, there would be no recovery against the railroad in the first place. The language made sense in Section 1, however, to make clear that there could be recovery against the railroad even if it were only partially negligent.

Even if the language in Section 1 is understood to address the standard of causation, and not simply to reflect the fact that contributory negligence is no longer a complete bar to recovery, there is no reason to read the statute as a whole to encompass different causation standards. Section 3 simply does not address causation. On the question whether a different standard of causation applies as between the two parties, the statutory text is silent.

Finally, in urging that a higher standard of causation for plaintiff contributory negligence is acceptable, Sorrell invokes FELA's remedial purpose and our history of liberal construction. We are not persuaded. FELA was indeed enacted to benefit railroad employees, as the express abrogation of such common-law defenses as assumption of risk, the contributory negligence bar, and the fellow servant rule make clear. * * * It does not follow, however, that this remedial purpose requires us to interpret every uncertainty in the Act in favor of employees. * * *

We conclude that FELA does not abrogate the common-law approach, and that the same standard of causation applies to railroad negligence under Section 1 as to plaintiff contributory negligence under Section 3. Sorrell does not dispute that Missouri applies different standards ... and accordingly we vacate the judgment below and remand the case for further proceedings. * * *

JUSTICE SOUTER, with whom JUSTICE SCALIA and JUSTICE ALITO join, concurring.

I agree that the same standard of causal connection controls the recognition of both a defendant-employer's negligence and a plaintiff-employee's contributory negligence in Federal Employers' Liability Act (FELA) suits, and I share the Court's caution in remanding for the Missouri Court of Appeals to determine in the first instance just what that common causal relationship must be, if it should turn out that the difference in possible standards would affect judgment on the verdict in this case. * * *

The briefs and arguments here did, however, adequately address the case of ours with which exploration will begin, and I think it is fair to say a word about the holding in *Rogers v. Missouri Pacific R. Co*, 352 U.S. 500 (1957). Despite some courts' views to the contrary, *Rogers* did not address, much less alter, existing law governing the degree of causation necessary for redressing negligence as the cause of negligently inflicted harm; the case merely instructed courts how to proceed when there are multiple cognizable causes of an injury. * * *

FELA changed some rules but, as we have said more than once, when Congress abrogated common law rules in FELA, it did so expressly. * * * FELA said nothing, however, about the familiar proximate cause standard for claims either of a defendant-employer's negligence or a plaintiff-employee's contributory negligence, and throughout the half-century between FELA's enactment and the decision in *Rogers*, we consistently recognized and applied proximate cause as the proper standard in FELA suits. * * *

*Rogers* left this law where it was. We granted certiorari in *Rogers* to establish the test for submitting a case to a jury when the evidence would permit a finding that an injury had multiple causes. * * *

JUSTICE GINSBURG, concurring in the judgment.

The Court today holds simply and only that in cases under the Federal Employers' Liability Act (FELA), railroad negligence and employee contributory negligence are governed by the same causation standard. I concur in that judgment. It should be recalled, however, that the Court has several times stated what a plaintiff must prove to warrant submission of a FELA case to a jury. That question is long settled, we have no cause to reexamine it, and I do not read the Court's decision to cast a shadow of doubt on the matter.

In *CONRAIL v. Gottshall*, 512 U.S. 532, 543 (1994), we acknowledged that "a relaxed causation standard applies under FELA." Decades earlier, in *Crane v. Cedar Rapids & Iowa City R. Co.*, 395 U.S. 164 (1969), we said that a FELA plaintiff need prove "only that his injury resulted in whole or in part from the railroad's violation." Id., at 166 (internal quotation marks omitted). Both decisions referred to the Court's oft-cited opinion in *Rogers v. Missouri Pacific R. Co.*, 352 U.S. 500 (1957), which declared: "Under [FELA] the test of a jury case is simply whether the proofs justify with reason the conclusion that employer negligence played any part, *even the slightest*, in producing the injury or death for which damages are sought." Id., at 506 (emphasis added). *Rogers*, in turn, drew upon *Coray v. Southern Pacific Co.*, 335 U.S. 520, 524 (1949), in which the Court observed: "Congress ... imposed extraordinary safety obligations upon railroads and has commanded that if a breach of these obligations contributes in part to an employee's death, the railroad must pay damages."

* * * Today's opinion leaves in place precedent solidly establishing that the causation standard in FELA actions is more "relaxed" than in tort litigation generally.

A few further points bear emphasis. First, it is sometimes said that *Rogers* eliminated proximate cause in FELA actions. \* \* \* It would be more accurate, as I see it, to recognize that *Rogers* describes the test for proximate causation applicable in FELA suits. That test is whether "employer negligence played any part, even the slightest, in producing the injury or death for which damages are sought." 352 U.S. at 506.

Whether a defendant's negligence is a proximate cause of the plaintiff's injury entails a judgment, at least in part policy based, as to how far down the chain of consequences a defendant should be held responsible for its wrongdoing. \* \* \*

The "slightest" cause sounds far less exacting than "proximate" cause, which may account for the statements in judicial opinions that *Rogers* dispensed with proximate cause for FELA actions. These statements seem to me reflective of pervasive confusion engendered by the term "proximate cause." As Prosser and Keeton explains:

> "The word 'proximate' is a legacy of Lord Chancellor Bacon, who in his time committed other sins. The word means nothing more than near or immediate; and when it was first taken up by the courts it had connotations of proximity in time and space which have long since disappeared. It is an unfortunate word, which places an entirely wrong emphasis upon the factor of physical or mechanical closeness. For this reason 'legal cause' or perhaps even 'responsible cause' would be a more appropriate term."

W. Keeton, D. Dobbs, R. Keeton, & D. Owen, Prosser and Keeton on Law of Torts § 42, p. 273 (5th ed. 1984) (footnotes omitted).

If we take up Prosser and Keeton's suggestion to substitute "legal cause" for "proximate cause," we can state more clearly what *Rogers* held: Whenever a railroad's negligence is the slightest cause of the plaintiff's injury, it is a legal cause, for which the railroad is properly held responsible.

## NOTES AND QUESTIONS

1. What is the scope of disagreement between the two concurring opinions, if any? Why might that have practical importance?

2. How, if at all, is the remedy available to plaintiff Sorrell in the principal case different from that available to plaintiff Glass in her action against the City of Chattanooga?

3. Federal "substantive" law governs in actions brought under the FELA in state court, but the states remain free to apply their own "adjective" or "procedural" law. Defining what is the appropriate characterization of a particular issue is not always easy. In *Gallick v. Baltimore & Ohio R.R.*, 372 U.S. 108, 83 S.Ct. 659, 9 L.Ed.2d 618 (1963), the jury was asked to answer a series of more than twenty questions, under the Ohio special verdict statute. The Ohio Court of Appeals found that the jury's answers to some of the questions were inconsistent, particularly questions dealing with "proximate

cause" and "foreseeability" (perhaps earning them the sympathy of 1L law students struggling with *Palsgraf v. Long Island R.R Co.*, 248 N.Y. 339, 162 N.E. 99 (1928)). The Supreme Court held that the state court had "improperly invaded the function and province of the jury."

4. The extent to which general common law development should govern FELA decisions has divided the Court more than once. In recent years, that has been most noticeable in cases involving emotional distress.

In *Atchison, Topeka & Santa Fe Ry. v. Buell*, 480 U.S. 557, 107 S.Ct. 1410, 94 L.Ed.2d 563 (1987), the Court ruled that grievance and arbitration procedures established under the Railway Labor Act do not preclude a railroad employee from bringing a FELA suit for allegedly suffering severe emotional distress as a result of purported management threats and harassment designed, among other things, to cause the employee to file car inspection reports in an improper manner. The Court expressly declined to reach the question of the extent to which FELA provides a remedy for solely emotional injuries. It reached that question in *Consolidated Rail Corp. v. Gottshall*, 512 U.S. 532, 114 S.Ct. 2396, 129 L.Ed.2d 427 (1994), where it held that negligent infliction of emotional distress is recoverable under the FELA if the plaintiff sustained a "physical impact" or was placed in immediate risk of physical harm by the conduct that caused the emotional distress. The Court explained that it was adopting this "zone of danger" test because "it best reconciles the concerns of the common law with the principles underlying our FELA jurisprudence." 114 S.Ct. at 2410. Justice Ginsburg, in a dissenting opinion joined by Justices Blackmun and Stevens, expressed support for the approach that had been taken by the Court of Appeals for the Third Circuit, which stated that recovery was available if the factual circumstances demonstrated that there had been genuine and serious injury and that the injury resulted from pressures that went beyond the ordinary stress of the job. In *Metro–North Commuter R.R. v. Buckley*, 521 U.S. 424, 117 S.Ct. 2113, 138 L.Ed.2d 560 (1997), the Court held that it would not construe FELA to allow a recovery for emotional damages where the only physical contact involved was breathing asbestos dust. That exposure would not amount to "physical impact," the majority reasoned, since it carried a risk only of possible future harm. The majority opinion emphasizes that most common law courts would deny relief to those who are at the time of trial still free of disease and symptoms. Thus mere fear that exposure to asbestos would eventually cause cancer did not justify a FELA claim for emotional distress nor for the costs of monitoring the worker to determine if and when the disease symptoms become apparent. Justice Ginsburg again dissented in part, arguing that the Court was adopting an approach inconsistent with earlier FELA precedent, and was instead taking a step backward by relying so heavily on what common law courts do. She would have affirmed the decision below allowing recovery of some of the medical monitoring costs the plaintiff would pay because of a reasonable fear of cancer. A defendant in a case of this sort is entitled to an instruction that the plaintiff must show a "genuine and serious" fear of developing cancer. *CSX Transportation, Inc. v. Hensley*, ___ U.S. ___, 129 S.Ct. 2139, 173 L.Ed.2d 1184 (2009).

5. One significant difference between general common law doctrine and principles developed under the FELA concerns the doctrine of negligence per

se. Under that doctrine, proof that an individual violated a statute (or a regulation issued under a statute) serves to establish that that party was negligent; the statute, in essence, sets the standard of conduct in the case, so that the jury need not decided what a "reasonable prudent person" would have done. In general common law, violation of a statute establishes negligence only if the statute was designed to protect the class of persons to which the injured party belongs from the general sort of harm that the party has suffered. In FELA cases, that qualification does not apply. In *Urie v. Thompson*, 337 U.S. 163, 69 S.Ct. 1018, 93 L.Ed. 1282 (1949), for example, the Court found that the plaintiff had established negligence by proving that the railroad had violated a safety regulation requiring "proper sanding apparatus" on locomotives. The purpose of the regulation was to insure that sand could be dropped onto the rails to provide a better braking action, particularly in wet weather. The plaintiffs in the case alleged that they had been injured because the sanding apparatus was poorly adjusted and maintained, so that sand was being dropped onto the rails constantly, with the result that they breathed silica dust and over a long period this led to the development of lung disease. The Court arguably went even further in *Kernan v. American Dredging Co.*, 355 U.S. 426, 78 S.Ct. 394, 2 L.Ed.2d 382 (1958). As the next main case makes clear, the FELA also protects the crews of vessels, because of provisions of the Jones Act. In the *Kernan* case, a crew member was killed by fire when a kerosene lamp on his tugboat ignited fumes from petroleum residues floating on the water of the river the tug was navigating. The kerosene lamp was very close to the surface of the water, instead of being at the eight foot height prescribed by a Coast Guard regulation. That regulation was clearly intended to make the tug visible to other boats, and had nothing to do with the prevention of fire. Nonetheless, the Court held, the survivors of the dead seaman were entitled to recover.

  6. Although pain and suffering are recoverable under FELA, punitive damages are not. See, e.g., *Holmes v. Elgin, Joliet & Eastern Ry.*, 18 F.3d 1393 (7th Cir.1994); *Horsley v. Mobil Oil Corp.*, 15 F.3d 200 (1st Cir.1994). Nor can a surviving spouse recover for loss of companionship in an FELA suit. *Sea–Land Services, Inc. v. Gaudet*, 414 U.S. 573, 94 S.Ct. 806, 39 L.Ed.2d 9 (1974).

  The Supreme Court has held that when calculating the present value of the lost income earning potential of an injured employee, the determination should take into account differences in the tax treatment of earned income as compared with the tax treatment of damages recoveries and applied that federal standard to a FELA recovery in a suit brought in state court. *Norfolk & Western Ry. v. Liepelt*, 444 U.S. 490, 100 S.Ct. 755, 62 L.Ed.2d 689 (1980). In addition, in *Jones & Laughlin Steel Corp. v. Pfeifer*, 462 U.S. 523, 103 S.Ct. 2541, 76 L.Ed.2d 768 (1983), a case involving recovery under the Longshore and Harbor Workers' Compensation Act, the Court permitted trial courts to make a limited adjustment to reflect the anticipated impact of inflation in determining the present value of the lost ability to earn future income. *Culver v. Slater Boat Co.*, 722 F.2d 114 (5th Cir.1983) (en banc), cert. denied 467 U.S. 1252, 104 S.Ct. 3537, 82 L.Ed.2d 842 (1984), discusses the method selected by that court to calculate the pre-tax market rate of interest and the inflation rate to provide a fair current market value of the lost capacity to earn income.

7.   Railroads compete with truck, air and water carriers. Employee injury and disease in the truck and air industries are covered by workers' compensation laws, usually a state legislated and administered program. As seen below, seafarers are protected by FELA for such mishaps but have additional means of recovery as well. Are there sound reasons why competing industries face different types of financial risks from employee injuries and illness?

## GEORGE v. CHESAPEAKE & OHIO RAILWAY CO.

United States District Court, Eastern District of Virginia, 1972
348 F.Supp. 283

WALTER E. HOFFMAN, CHIEF JUDGE

Plaintiff, Luther Earl George, seeks payment from his employer, The Chesapeake and Ohio Railway Company (C & O), for maintenance and cure alleged to be due as a result of an operation which was performed upon the plaintiff at a private hospital. He is also seeking damages by way of attorney's fees for failure to pay maintenance and cure. Recovery is sought solely under the principles of general maritime law.

George has been a marine employee of C & O for 48 years and has achieved the status of a tugboat pilot. Since the tugboats are utilized seven days a week and 24 hours a day, George works a 12–hour shift and is off 24 hours; then 12 hours on and 48 hours off; all of which is the equivalent of a 40–hour workweek. His time off is his own and any recall for extra duty during this time is purely optional on his part. He is paid by the hour with no meals and lodging being provided by the company.

For the past 15 years George has been afflicted with recurrent sores in his mouth and gums. He has treated himself for this condition with warm salt water rinses, such treatments being taken both on board the tugs and at home. In June 1967 while serving as pilot on the Tug A.T. Lowmaster, a sore developed which did not respond to the accustomed treatment. His condition became so aggravated that George went to see Dr. Kupcuoglu, a private ear, nose and throat specialist, who took a biopsy of the lesion.

Upon learning of the ulcer's cancerous nature, George reported to the C & O boatmaster as required by company regulations. The boatmaster sent plaintiff to a local company doctor who, in turn, referred him to the C & O Railway Employee's Hospital Association's hospital at Clifton Forge, Virginia, where he was seen by Dr. Charles. George was given the same diagnosis and advised of alternative remedies—radical surgery or conservative treatment by way of x-ray therapy. Dr. Charles, who represented himself as having been a doctor on a transoceanic passenger liner, told the plaintiff he would perform the surgery, if such course was undertaken.

Due to the very serious nature of the operation which in effect amounted to the removal of one-third of the face, as explained by Dr. Charles to his wife, George elected to undergo the x-ray treatment. While evidence subsequent to the eventual operation revealed that the C & O hospital had a plastic surgeon from Roanoke, Virginia, as a consultant, and indeed Dr. Charles himself might very well have been qualified to perform the operation, none of this information or special qualifications was relayed to the plaintiff at the time of his decision.

The hospital at Clifton Forge was without the proper facilities to administer radiation therapy, so George returned to his home in Newport News, Virginia. The boatmaster did not send George to the Marine Hospital in Norfolk for free treatment but arranged for a series of cobalt treatments at a private hospital, which were paid for without question by the C & O.

Upon his return to Newport News on July 3, 1967, George sought the advice of Dr. Thompson, his family physician. Realizing the gravity of the situation, Dr. Thompson sent the plaintiff to Dr. Charles Horton, a highly qualified plastic surgeon in Norfolk. It was Dr. Horton's considered opinion that such an operation should be performed only by a qualified plastic surgeon due to the extensiveness, the anatomical location, and the pathological grade of the disease; and he was quite emphatic about not having such an operation performed at the Clifton Forge hospital.

Since Dr. Horton believed the x-ray treatments advisable prior to any operation, George pursued that course of action. As a result of such treatments, there was an apparent remission of the disease for six months. Early in February 1968, George noticed a lump in his neck and returned directly to Dr. Horton, without notifying the company boatmaster. The plaintiff was told that, unless he was operated upon immediately, he could not expect to live longer than two months. * * * Norfolk General was designated as the hospital of choice since this was the only location at which the post-operative period of intensive care with constant supervision was available, as required by these critical cases.

The operation was in fact performed at Norfolk General, a private hospital, and George was placed in the intensive care unit for the following five days, being seen at least three times each day by one of several doctors. After a substantial recuperative period George returned and is currently employed by C & O as a tug pilot.

It is important to note that at no time did the C & O boatmaster suggest that George go to the Marine Hospital; nor did the plaintiff request to be sent there. While it is true that George had the authority to issue "hospital tickets" to members of his crew allowing them to enter the Public Health facilities in Norfolk, only the boatmaster could do the same for him as a pilot. * * *

* * * The essential factors of a maintenance and cure case are that he was a seaman and secondly, that his illness occurred, was aggravated, or manifested itself while in the ship's service. No question has been presented as to George's status as a seaman in the general sense. The controversy lies in the interpretation to be placed on the second requirement.

The phrase "in the service of the ship" has become one of art in this field. Since maintenance and cure has been characterized as an implied contractual obligation, *Aguilar v. Standard Oil Co.*, 318 U.S. 724, 730, 63 S.Ct. 930, 87 L.Ed. 1107 (1943), it is obvious that a seaman is thusly engaged while he is performing his assigned tasks on board ship. It is clear, however, that the illness or injury need not arise out of the seaman's employment, nor need it rest on the culpability of the employer. * * * Therefore the Supreme Court, in keeping with the benevolent nature of the remedy, has liberally construed the phrase so as to encompass a seaman who is ashore on authorized leave tending to purely personal business. *Aguilar v. Standard Oil Co.*, *supra*. Additionally, a seaman is deemed to remain "in the service of the ship" as long as he is generally answerable to the call of duty. * * *

Due to the nature of his employment, George no longer remains in the ship's service when he leaves his vessel at the completion of his shift. * * * The philosophy behind extending maintenance and cure to apparently personal adventures stems from the restrictive life led by seamen on lengthy voyages. Such a seaman is in a sense serving the ship while ashore since the time off makes him a more efficient crew member; not to mention the fact that no one would become a sailor if he were denied shore leave. *Aguilar v. Standard Oil Co.*, *supra*. In the present case, the purpose for leaving every night is merely to allow the plaintiff to live a normal home life, and therefore cannot be said to serve the ship to such an extent as to justify his absence on shore leave. * * *

Likewise the plaintiff was not answerable to the call of duty during his off hours. * * *

Since George no longer remains in the ship's service once he leaves the vessel, in order to bring himself within the protection of maintenance and cure his cancer must have either "occurred, become aggravated, or manifested itself" while he was on board his vessel. The application of this test is complicated by the fact that the plaintiff's maladies are merely manifestations of a slow and insidious disease from which he apparently has been suffering for 15 years. This is not the case of some traumatic accident which originates at an identifiable point in time or an illness whose first manifestation is disabling. There is grave doubt as to the exact time the cancer commenced, as well as doubt concerning the location where it first manifested itself, but it may be said with certainty that the disease originated, progressed, and previously manifested itself while George was employed as a seaman for C & O. Obviously this malignancy was present during his daily periods of being in the service of his ship and, therefore, George is entitled to maintenance and cure. * * *

Even though a plaintiff has shown himself to be entitled to maintenance and cure, he may forfeit this right by his own willful misconduct. * * * However, such a defense must be affirmatively alleged and the burden of proof rests upon the defendant. * * * It has been contended that the election of George to be operated upon by a private physician in a private hospital amounted to such willful misconduct as to bar any recovery for maintenance and cure.

As a general rule where an employer has offered hospital services which are voluntarily refused by the seaman, any obligation of maintenance and cure is relieved. * * * While this rule is not applied inflexibly, * * * it is clear that if the proffered medical assistance is rejected on personal grounds without some showing of its inadequacy, all rights have been forfeited. * * * Therefore, George's conduct must be examined in light of all the surrounding circumstances to determine whether it was justified or merely some purely personal choice.

The fact that George went to a private doctor initially for a diagnosis has no effect on his claim for maintenance and cure since a seaman has a right to know whether his condition is such that he should be hospitalized. * * * The important consideration is his compliance with the company regulations upon determining the seriousness of his illness. Likewise, the plaintiff's decision to undergo radiation therapy should not prejudice his rights. * * * It was not unreasonable for George to elect the more conservative treatment based upon the nature of the operation and the apparent qualifications of the staff as related to him at Clifton Forge. * * *

*All this is okay*

This court must look to the reasonableness of George's belief in the inadequacy of the Clifton Forge Hospital as the determinative factor in this case. George had been told by the company's general surgeon in Newport News that he was unable to do the required work. At Clifton Forge he learned of the radical nature of the operation and was told that another general surgeon would operate. Upon talking with his private physician he was advised that the operation should only be performed by a certified plastic surgeon and was strongly advised against having it done at Clifton Forge. When viewed against these facts we must conclude that a reasonably prudent man would have refused treatment at the company hospital and would have sought private help.

*Reasonable*

While it is true that an employer need not be responsible for supplying the best available care for a seaman, the standard of care required is directly proportionate to the seriousness of illness. * * * George was justified in expecting something more than ordinary care for his aggravated condition. He was also justified in relying on the expert recommendation of his doctor. * * * Since there was no representation made to the plaintiff that a plastic surgeon was available at Clifton Forge, he merely sought privately benefits not otherwise obtainable. * * * George made a bona fide attempt to avail himself of the tendered services but, under the circumstances, was forced to obtain appropriate treatment elsewhere, therefore C & O is liable for the reasonable expenses so incurred. * * *

As a final grounds for defense, C & O claims that even if its facilities at Clifton Forge were inadequate, George was still under a duty to avail himself of treatment at the Marine Hospital in Norfolk, Virginia. * * *

There is no rule which says that an employer is obligated to satisfy its duties of care and cure by utilizing the services of the Marine Hospital.

Therefore, when a shipowner elects to satisfy this duty by some other means which turns out to be inadequate, he should not be able to defeat a subsequent claim for maintenance and cure by alleging the seaman's failure to go to the Marine Hospital which was never offered. C & O had, by its conduct, indicated that resort to the Marine Hospital was unnecessary. * * *

The plaintiff has made a claim for damages by way of counsel fees, but this court is not inclined to find this a proper case for such recovery. * * * Clearly there was a substantial question as to George's right to receive reimbursement, which payment was duly considered by C & O Railway and refused. Since they were acting neither callously nor in bad faith, the claim for damages by way of counsel fees must be denied.

## NOTES AND QUESTIONS

1.  One court has held: "[I]t is only the additional maintenance and cure expense which is caused by a seaman's unjustified rejection of public hospital treatment that is not recoverable by the seaman." *Pelotto v. L & N Towing Co.*, 604 F.2d 396, 403 (5th Cir.1979). Beneficiaries of the duty of maintenance and cure include all persons employed aboard a vessel. Thus, hairdressers, musicians, and bartenders are among those awarded such claims. Moreover, injuries are covered whether or not incurred in the line of duty. Accordingly, recreational activities, even when not aboard ship, are covered so long as the ship's voyage has not been completed. However, the Court has indicated that coverage does not extend to contracting venereal disease or injuries resulting from extreme drunkenness or brawling. *Aguilar v. Standard Oil Co. of N.J.*, 318 U.S. 724, 63 S.Ct. 930, 87 L.Ed. 1107 (1943).

2.  The traditional standard for computing maintenance was to provide "food and lodging of the kind and quality he would have received" while on the vessel. *Tate v. American Tugs, Inc.*, 869, 871 (5th Cir. 1981). For many years, that was a "standardized" figure of $8 a day. That approach, however, makes little sense in the case of workers who return home each night to eat in their own homes and sleep in their own beds. It is also of little relevance to those who work on such non-traditional vessels as "floating platform" oil rigs. The courts have thus moved in the direction of making awards based on the actual cost of food and lodging during the period of disability, limited by a standard of reasonableness. See, e.g., *Hall v. Noble Drilling (U.S.), Inc.*, 242 F.3d 582, rehearing denied, 252 F.3d 437 (5th Cir. 2001). In the *Hall* opinion, however, the court indicated that it recognized the clear advantages of using a standardized figure, such as avoiding litigation and making prompt payment of maintenance more likely, and indicated it might be willing to consider arguments in favor of returning to that approach (at a figure well above $8 a day). If so, how much weight should be given a collective bargaining agreement covering an injured worker's job? See *Espinal v. Royal Caribbean Cruises*, 253 F.3d 629 (11th Cir. 2001).

## C. WORKERS' COMPENSATION PROGRAMS

## 1. INTRODUCTION TO THE DEVELOPMENT OF WORKERS' COMPENSATION

By the end of the 19th century, American legislators at both the state and federal levels were generally convinced that the fault-based litigation system was not a good model for dealing with industrial injuries. See generally Donald G. Gifford, *The Death of Causation; Mass Products Torts' Incomplete Incorporation of Social Welfare Principles*, 41 WAKE FOREST L. REV. 943, 952–954 (2006) (hereafter Gifford). Developing sensible alternatives, though, was not an easy task. Americans began looking to Europe for possible guidance, and found appealing models in Britain and Germany.

The 1884 German legislation providing benefits for those injured by industrial accidents was proposed by Prussian Chancellor Otto von Bismarck, a conservative political leader, who thought of it as one means of discouraging the growth of radical socialism in the German Empire. See GERHARD A. RITTER, SOCIAL WELFARE IN GERMANY AND BRITAIN 33–58 (KIM TRAYNOR TRANS. 1983). The program was one part of a broader program of social insurance, including sickness and disability insurance, funded by contributions from both employers and workers. Americans were well aware of the German program through studies, reports, and even a display at the St. Louis World's Fair in 1904. Id. at 7–8; Gifford at 952–955.

It was, however, an English statute, originally enacted in 1897* and influenced by the earlier German law, which provided the immediate drafting model for legislatures in the United States. Conferences were held to discuss a variety of drafting problems; there was even a recommended uniform law. See Ernst Freund, *Unifying Tendencies in American Legislation*, 22 YALE L.J. 96, 105, 112 (1912). Early articles and treatises on workers' compensation statutes in the U.S. often included treatment of the English statute. See Francis Bohlen, *A Problem in the Drafting of Workmen's Compensation Acts*, 25 HARV. L. REV. 328, 401, 517 (1912); *Book Review*, 23 YALE L.J. 702 (1914); Charles Clark, *Book Review*, 26 YALE L.J. 628 (1917).

At the time these statutes were being considered, the Supreme Court took a relatively restrictive view of the power of the Congress to regulate commerce. As mentioned earlier, the Court struck down the first version of the Federal Employers Liability Act because it covered the activities of all employees of railroads, not just those who were themselves engaged in interstate commerce. *Howard v. Illinois Central R. Co.*, 207 U.S. 463, 28 S.Ct. 141, 52 L.Ed. 297 (1908). Most employer-employee matters were thought to be local in nature, a view not abandoned by the Court majority

---

* An Act To Amend the Law with respect to Compensation to Workmen for Accidental Injuries Suffered in the Course of their Employment,1897, 60 & 61 VICT., c. 37.

until 1937. *N.L.R.B. v. Jones & Laughlin Steel Corp.*, 301 U.S. 1, 57 S.Ct. 615, 81 L.Ed. 893 (1937). Enacting workers' compensation laws was therefore largely left to the states. This happened rapidly in most jurisdictions; by 1920, 40 states had passed such laws. There have been suggestions from time to time that a federal law would be better than the varying state statutes; no such proposal has ever advanced very far. Perhaps the closest the Congress has come to considering such a move was the creation of a National Commission on Workers' Compensation Law in 1970. That commission's report recommended a substantial number of changes in typical state laws, but the state by state response was varied, and relatively few major changes occurred. While industrial injury and disease are therefore generally dealt with by state law, there are four federal statutes that provide coverage for significant numbers of workers:

- Federal Employees Compensation Act, 5 U.S.C. §§ 8101–8152. As the name indicates, this is the system used by injured federal workers, who generally are not eligible for state law coverage because of principles of preemption. A very early predecessor of the present statute was enacted in 1908, just as many states were considering taking such a step.

- Longshore and Harbor Workers Compensation Act, 33 U.S.C. §§ 901–950. This statute covers those working on piers, wharves, and adjoining areas, and in the maintenance of vessels. Since coverage extends to areas adjacent to navigable waters, there are times when a given worker may be covered both by the LHWCA and a state law.

- Black Lung Benefits Act, 30 U.S.C. §§ 901–945. This statute applies to coal mine workers totally disabled by pneumoconiosis, and includes provisions to coordinate coverage with state laws.

- Energy Employees Occupational Illness Compensation Program Act, 42 U.S.C. §§ 7384–7385s–15. This statute provides benefits for workers employed by the Department of Energy or by atomic weapons producers who develop illnesses as the result of exposure to radioactive materials or other toxic materials. It overlaps to some extent with a program that covers both employment and non-employment related injuries resulting from radiation exposure, the Radiation Exposure Compensation Act, see 42 U.S.C. § 2210. To date, nearly $5 billion have been paid out under this program.

Since the early state statutes had similar roots, it is hardly surprising that the policy debates in the state legislatures tended to focus on the same themes and that the resulting statutes had many of the same features (although there were variations). One of the themes commonly discussed in the legislative policy debates was what has been referred to as "the historic compromise:" that under workers' compensation employers would give up the common law tort defenses and accept no fault liability in return for lower predictable compensation schedules, while employees would give up the possibility of higher tort damages in return for more modest but sure compensation. A second theme has been referred to as "the compensation principle:" the idea that it is not only fair, but also efficient, that workers be compensated for the costs of industrial accidents and illnesses and that such costs be charged back to the employer and reflected in the price of the good. If employers maintain dangerous work sites they *should* bear higher accident costs giving them incentive to adopt safer work practices, and the price of the employer's good *should* be higher giving consumers incentive to buy other goods with lower costs and prices. Moreover, it was hoped that requiring employers to provide adequate compensation to all injured workers would prevent these workers from becoming wards of the state and passing on the costs of employment injuries to society at large. Finally, it was hoped that workers' compensation would provide a more administratively efficient means of delivering compensation to injured workers than the tort system because workers' compensation was based on a simplified no fault administrative determination rather than costly adjudication through the negligence based tort system. Along these same lines, states sometimes created state insurance funds to eliminate the costs of private insurance companies that are motivated by profits to deny benefits.

The common features of state workers' compensation statutes were generally these:

- *Specific limits on which employees would be covered.* Agricultural workers, domestic service workers, employees of state and local governments were almost always excluded in the early statutes, and remain so in many places. The early statutes usually also excluded small employers; this has become much less common. Employees subject to FELA and FECA are also excluded, doubtless in recognition of doctrines of federal preemption.

- *Taking industrial accident cases out of ordinary court-based litigation.* All but a handful of states created administrative agencies to process claims for benefits, and provided only limited judicial review.

- *Changing the claimant's burden of proof from one of showing fault to showing that the harm the worker has suffered is connected to the employment.* This was generally done by limiting the employer's liability to pay to those injuries that "arise out of and in the course of employment."

- *Eliminating the defenses of contributory negligence, the fellow servant rule, and assumption of risk.* A remnant of the philosophy underlying contributory negligence arguably remains in statutes that disqualify a claimant from benefits whose injury is intentionally self-inflicted.

- *Granting employers a new defense from liability in tort under the "exclusive remedy" clause.* If an employer has complied with the provisions of the workers compensation act by purchasing the required insurance (or meeting self-insured status standards) so that an injured worker is eligible for compensation benefits, that worker cannot sue the employer for damages.

- *Requiring the employer to provide all reasonably necessary medical care for an employment-connected injury.* There are a number of variations on how this is to be done, and the extent of employee freedom to choose a particular treating professional, but the fundamental concept of full employer responsibility has been in these statutes from the beginning.

- *Providing partial replacement of lost wages.* The most common approach originally was to provide the worker with a proportion of wages actually lost during the healing period (two-thirds of the worker's average weekly wage over the prior year was the most common base line figure, and was subject to an upper limit, a "cap"), and if there was permanent damage to the worker's body, to provide some additional benefits, stated as a number of weeks of partial wage replacement, perhaps on the theory that that sort of injury would over time reduce the worker's wage-earning capacity. Most early statutes—and many today—provide this by valuing an arm, say, at 150 weeks, an eye at 200.

- *Providing death benefits to those dependent on a deceased worker for support.* A fair number of statutes established "conclusive presumptions" that certain persons—usually spouses and minor children— are dependent, while others must prove actual dependency. These benefits, too, are often expressed in terms of number of weeks during which the benefits are to be paid.

- *Requiring employers to take out insurance to provide these benefits.* In most states, this was done through private insurers, whose policy forms and claims practices are regulated by the state. Some states set up government insurance funds; of these, a handful are the only entities allowed to issue insurance in that state; in others, the state fund competes with private insurers for business.

The early statutes were often challenged as violating state and federal constitutional principles. The New York Court of Appeals struck down that state's 1910 law, reasoning that its requirement that employers and employees in some industries participate constituted a taking of property without just compensation. *Ives v. South Buffalo Ry.*, 201 N.Y. 271, 94 N.E. 431 (1911). Like other states, New York found a way around that. It made application of the statute "voluntary," but made the choice a fairly easy one; if an employer chose not to be covered, it would lose the benefit of the defenses of assumption of risk, contributory negligence and the fellow servant rule. The United States Supreme Court upheld that statute and two others in 1917 against federal constitutional challenges. *New York Central R.R. v. White*, 243 U.S. 188, 37 S.Ct. 247, 61 L.Ed. 667 (1917); *Hawkins v. Bleakly*, 243 U.S. 210, 37 S.Ct. 255, 61 L.Ed. 678 (1917); *Mountain Timber Co. v. Washington*, 243 U.S. 219, 37 S.Ct. 260, 61 L.Ed.

685 (1917). By 1920, all but eight states had enacted a workers' compensation law.

Whether these statutes were a boon more to worker or to employer has been much debated. A reasonable assessment would probably be that there are winners and losers among both employees and among employers. An employee whose injury is disabling for only a short time, so that bringing a personal injury action against her employer would not be worth the effort, receives free medical treatment and some limited amount of cash compensation—thus a winner. A worker seriously injured by employer negligence cannot seek substantial tort damages from the his or her employer because of the exclusive remedy defense. That worker is thus very possibly a loser. On the other side of the equation, employers in industries with records of many serious employee injuries are very likely winners. Good evidence of this is the effort of railroad employers to move out from the FELA and establish a workers' compensation system in its place by amending the federal legislation. See, e.g., E. BERKOWITZ & M. BERKOWITZ, CHALLENGES TO WORKERS' COMPENSATION: AN HISTORICAL ANALYSIS IN WORKERS' COMPENSATION BENEFITS (WORRALL & APPEL, EDS. 1985) at 158, 159–60.

At all events, the significance of the workers' compensation programs is illustrated by a quick look at a few figures. In 2003, according to the National Academy of Social Insurance, more than 125 million workers were covered by workers' compensation. Just under 55 billion dollars of benefits were paid to injured workers. Forty-five per cent of those benefits were to provide medical care, 55 per cent to provide cash benefits paid to workers and their families. NATIONAL ACADEMY OF SOCIAL INSURANCE, WORKERS' COMPENSATION: BENEFITS, COVERAGE AND COSTS, 2003 (2005).

Over the years, and particularly since the cost of providing medical care began to accelerate so swiftly, the specific provisions in different state statutes have become a bit less similar. The materials that follow, therefore, are simply a sampling of the most common sorts of issues confronted in workers' compensation, not an exhaustive treatment of all the sorts of issues that can arise in any particular jurisdiction.

## 2.  WHAT PARTIES ARE COVERED?

Problems concerning what parties are covered by a workers' compensation statute take several forms. This section introduces a handful of the most common.

- Who fits into the general categories of "employer" and "employee"?

    The definitions of these terms are often circular, using some variant of "employ" as part of the definition. The Vermont statute provides an example: " 'Worker' and 'employee' means an individual who has entered into the employment of, or works under contract of service or apprenticeship with, an employer."

VT. STAT. ANN. TITLE 21, § 601(14). The usual result is for courts to resort to common law decisions about who is an employee, decisions often involving whether a party should be held responsible for the wrongdoing of a person alleged to be that party's employee, under the doctrine of *respondeat superior*.

● Who fits into the categories of specifically included or excluded employees and employers?

The specific inclusion and exclusion provisions are usually more precise than the definitions of employer and employee, but issues arise nonetheless. Is a truck driver who carries freshly harvested produce from the fields to a market an "agricultural worker," or is she in the transportation industry instead?

● Can a single individual have more than one "employer" at the same time?

## (a.) "Employer" and "Employee"

### CLOVERLEAF EXPRESS v. FOUTS

Court of Appeals of Arkansas, Division IV, 2005
91 Ark. App. 4, 207 S.W.3d 576

ROBERT J. GLADWIN, JUDGE.

Appellee Lyle Fouts suffered a cardiac episode on December 15, 2000, while employed by appellant Cloverleaf Express. In an opinion entered on February 20, 2002, the administrative law judge (A.L.J.) found that appellee failed to prove that he was an employee at the time of his injury. The Commission reversed the A.L.J.'s opinion and remanded the matter for resolution of other issues. [On remand, the appellee prevailed.]

Appellants argue that * * *: (1) the facts found by the Commission do not support its determination that appellee was an employee of Cloverleaf; (2) the Commission's finding that appellee was an employee is not supported by substantial evidence; * * *.

Cloverleaf's business involves transporting goods by tractor-trailer truck, and its primary customer is Wal–Mart Stores, Inc. Appellee worked as a truck driver for Cloverleaf and drove one of its two company-owned trucks. On December 15, 2000, appellee was leaving a Wal–Mart facility in Corinth, Mississippi, when a conveyor line fell from the customer's dock as appellee was pulling his truck away from it. Apparently, the conveyor line had not yet been removed from his truck. Wal–Mart personnel requested that appellee help get the conveyor line back in place. Several people were lifting the line, which weighed approximately 800 pounds, when appellee fell onto the ground. He was hospitalized, and Dr. Michael D. Green diagnosed an episode of "sudden cardiac death."

[The court rejects an argument that appellee had voluntarily removed himself from the coverage of the Arkansas statute by signing a "certificate of non-coverage."]

Next, appellants argue that * * * appellee was an independent contractor and not an employee. An independent contractor is one who contracts to do a job according to his own method and without being subject to the control of the other party, except as to the result of the work. * * * The issue of whether one is an employee or an independent contractor is analyzed under two separate tests: (1) the control test; and (2) the relative nature of the work test. On the issue of control, this court has stated:

> The governing distinction is that if control of the work reserved by the employer is control not only of the result, but also of the means and manner of the performance, then the relation of master and servant necessarily follows. But if control of the means be lacking, and the employer does not undertake to direct the manner in which the employee shall work in the discharge of his duties, then the relation of independent contractor exists.

*Massey v. Poteau Trucking Co.*, 221 Ark. 589, 592, 254 S.W.2d 959, 961 (1953). The ultimate question is not whether the employer actually exercises control over the doing of the work, but whether he has the right to control. * * * There is no fixed formula for determining whether a person is an employee or an independent contractor; thus, the determination must be based on the particular facts of each case. * * *

The following factors are to be considered in determining whether one is an employee or independent contractor:

(a) the extent of control which, by the agreement, the master may exercise over the details of the work;

(b) whether or not the one employed is engaged in a distinct occupation or business;

(c) the kind of occupation, with reference to whether in the locality, the work is usually done under the direction of the employer or by a specialist without supervision;

(d) the skill required in the particular occupation;

(e) whether the employer or the workman supplies the instrumentalities, tools, and the place of work for the person doing the work;

(f) the length of time for which the person is employed;

(g) the method of payment, whether by the time or by the job;

(h) whether or not the work is a part of the regular business of the employer;

(i) whether or not the parties believe they are creating the relation of master and servant; and

(j) whether the principal is or is not in business.

* * * The factors pertaining to the nature of the worker's occupation and whether it is a part of the regular business of the employer comprise the "relative nature of the work" test. * * * In *Sandy v. Salter*, 260 Ark.

486, 541 S.W.2d 929 (1976), our supreme court adopted Professor Larson's test for examining the relationship between the worker's occupation and the regular business of the employer. This test requires consideration of two factors: (1) whether and how much the worker's occupation is a separate calling or profession; and (2) what relationship it bears to the regular business of the employer. *Id.* The more the worker's occupation resembles the business of the employer, the more likely the worker is an employee. *Id.*

Appellants maintain that Wal–Mart gave appellee a trailer and a destination and that Cloverleaf's only instruction was "to keep Wal–Mart happy." Appellants argue that it would have incurred contractual liability if it had terminated appellee during one of his hauls because he would be entitled to recover his 27% of the revenue from the haul. Appellants point out that appellee was paid by the job and did not receive an hourly wage. While appellee was free to take passengers with him on hauls, Cloverleaf had no control over those passengers, who may even have chosen to help appellee with his haul. Appellants concede that Cloverleaf furnished the necessary equipment for the job, which weighs in favor of appellee's being considered an employee, but point out that no single factor is determinative. Appellants argue that appellee was engaged in the distinct occupation of truck driver and that transportation of goods by tractor-trailer requires somewhat specialized skills. Appellants argue that appellee's work may be said to be an integral part of Cloverleaf's business but that anytime a business hires someone to perform a task, that task may be said to be in furtherance of the business's enterprise. Appellants argue that appellee's employment was job-to-job with no guarantee of more loads. Appellants also point out that Cloverleaf did not withhold taxes from appellee's pay, which is a circumstance to consider. Finally, appellants argue that appellee understood the certificate of non-coverage and that his signing of the application was evidence that he considered himself an independent contractor.

The Commission found that Cloverleaf exercised control over appellee's work and that appellee's job of driving a truck was an integral part of Cloverleaf's business and not a distinct occupation. Appellee drove one of the two trucks directly owned by Cloverleaf. While Cloverleaf did not pay workers' compensation insurance premiums on appellee, it paid premiums on the person who drove the other company-owned truck. Cloverleaf paid for maintenance, repairs, and fuel for the truck driven by appellee. Cloverleaf instructed appellee as to when he needed to pick up a load from Wal–Mart. Cloverleaf's co-owner Mary Ann Pearson testified that appellee could not hold down any other jobs because the company expected him to be ready to go whenever he was called. Cloverleaf paid appellee 27% of the gross receipts from each haul. The Commission noted that it appeared as though appellee was engaged in at-will employment with Cloverleaf and that either party could terminate the arrangement with no financial consequences. The Commission concluded that the factors indicated that an employee/employer relationship existed and that appellee was not an independent contractor. * * *

We simply cannot say on these facts that there is no substantial evidence to support the Commission's conclusion that appellee was an employee. A reading of the cases involving the issue of employee versus independent contractor indicates that such cases are frequently very close. * * * In many of those cases, a decision either way would have been supported by substantial evidence, and therefore, the appellate court would have been required to affirm, regardless of the result reached by the Commission. Id. When the facts of this case are viewed in the light most favorable to the Commission's findings, it is clear to us that fair-minded persons could have reached the same conclusion as the Commission.

Accordingly, we affirm * * *.

## NOTES AND QUESTIONS

1. The "right to control" test was developed largely in cases involving employer liability under *respondeat superior*. Is that troubling at all?

2. Does the extent of deference given the administrative agency under the "substantial evidence" review standard seem appropriate? Does it contribute to or detract from predictability of decisions? Deference as to fact-finding is very common, but deference on issues of law is more limited. In a few states, deference is given to the findings of the original administrative law judge, rather than to the reviewing board of the agency.

3. Clearly the "employer" here sought to avoid some of the costs associated with an employer-employee relationship. Whether the employer took out insurance (perhaps an umbrella policy of some sort) to protect itself from making an error in this regard the opinion does not state. If not, the employer will be responsible for the entire workers compensation award, and the nature of the injury suggests that will be a substantial figure. If you were counsel to this company, and had advised its management that Mr. Fouts was not an "employee" for purposes of workers' compensation or various other state and federal laws (such as the Internal Revenue Code, Social Security, or unemployment compensation) would you have been guilty of professional negligence?

4. These issues crop up in a large number of contexts beyond workers' compensation and *respondeat superior*. The price tag for error can be high in these as well. A very large corporation with highly respected legal advisers has made the employee-independent contractor call wrongly (at least in the view of one federal circuit) on at least one occasion. See *Vizcaino v. Microsoft Corp.*, 97 F.3d 1187 (9th Cir. 1996), affirmed, 120 F.3d 1006 (9th Cir. en banc 1997), later proceeding, 173 F.3d 713, amended, 184 F.3d 1070 (9th Cir. 1999), cert. denied, 528 U.S. 1105, 120 S.Ct. 844, 145 L.Ed.2d 713 (2000) (stock purchase plan; potential liability in seven figures). Similar litigation involving another multi-million dollar claim by employees in more than two dozen states is making its way through the courts currently. See *In re FedEx Ground Package System, Inc,.* 2007 WL 3027405, 42 Emp. Be. Cases 1020 (N.D. Ind.

2007) (class certification) (ERISA); one aspect of the FedEx litigation involves coverage of worker injury, *Estrada v. FedEx Ground Package System, Inc.*, 154 Cal.App.4th 1, 64 Cal.Rptr.3d 327 (2007) (truck drivers found to be employees; defendant ordered to reimburse them for cost of "work accident" insurance they carried because defendant did not provide workers compensation coverage).

5. The use of a multi-factor test of the sort the court employed in the principal case is common, and is sometimes required by statute. The Maine statute defines "independent contractor" by using a list much like that in *Fouts*, and then states that the administrative agency "may not give any particular factor a greater weight than any other factor." * * * Me. Rev. Stat. Title 39–A, § 102–13. Is that a sound approach, or should one or more factors dominate over others at times?

6. The typical workers compensation insurance contract bases the premium amount on the wages paid by the insured employer to its "employees." Earnings of independent contractors would not count. Insured and insurers sometimes disagree on the classification, resulting in an insurer's suit against its insured for additional premium payments. See *Acuity Mutual Ins. Co. v. Olivas*, 298 Wis.2d 640, 726 N.W.2d 258 (2007).

7. A fourteen year old delivers newspapers each morning to customers on a route assigned by the newspaper. She is charged the wholesale price for delivered papers and keeps the difference between the retail price he collects from customers and any tips. Deliveries must be made by 8 a.m. The carrier's bicycle slips on an icy street one winter morning and she cracks her head and suffers a concussion that permanently impairs her equilibrium. Should she be covered by workers' compensation benefits? See *DaSilva v. Danbury Publishing Co.*, 39 Conn.App. 653, 666 A.2d 440 (Conn.App.Ct.), cert. denied 235 Conn. 936, 668 A.2d 374 (Conn.1995), holding a newspaper carrier to be an independent contractor whose injury is not covered by workers' compensation. Can one too young to have legal capacity to contract enter into an independent contractor relationship? Can the guardian of one too young to have legal capacity to contract agree to a contractual relationship on behalf of the minor even though it exposes the minor to uninsured work hazards? For a condemnation of decisions such as *DaSilva* (and statutory exclusions of news carriers from workers' compensation) see M. Linder, *What's Black and White and Red All Over? The Blood Tax on Newspapers or, How Publishers Exclude Newscarriers from Workers' Compensation*, 3 LOY. POVERTY L.J. 57 (1997).

## (b.) Other Problems in Determining Covered Party Status

### (i.) "Borrowed" Workers

## ALDAY v. PATTERSON TRUCK LINE, INC.

United Sates Court of Appeals, Fifth Circuit, 1985
750 F.2d 375

TATE, CIRCUIT JUDGE:

The plaintiff Alday, a longshoreman, appeals from the dismissal by summary judgment of his maritime personal injury action. Alday's employer was Atchafalaya Industries, Inc. ("Atchafalaya"), which supplies labor to companies that off-load barges and engage in related activities. Alday's first assignment for Atchafalaya was to work unloading barges for the defendant Patterson Truck Lines, Inc. ("Patterson") at the latter's shipyard. While Alday was unloading a barge for Patterson on his first day of work in Atchafalaya's employment, he was injured while on the navigable waters. The district court granted Patterson summary judgment, finding that he was in maritime employment as a "borrowed employee" of Patterson and, therefore, his exclusive remedy against that defendant was for compensation benefits under the Longshoremen's and Harbor Workers' Compensation Act. 33 U.S.C. s 905(a). On Alday's appeal, we reverse, because we find that factual issues precluded summary judgment. * * *

*[Handwritten margin note: Alday unloaded barges for Δ]*

## I.

Our past decisions have enunciated several factors to be evaluated in determining whether an amphibious employee becomes the "borrowed" employee of other than his payroll employer, by virtue of which the employee is entitled upon work-injury to receive longshoremen's compensation from the borrowing employer (while the latter is consequently entitled to claim that such compensation remedy bars the employee's suit in tort against him). * * * *Hall v. Diamond M Company*, 732 F.2d 1246, 1249 (5th Cir.1984); *Gaudet v. Exxon Corporation*, 562 F.2d 351, 355 (5th Cir.1977), cert. denied, 436 U.S. 913, 98 S.Ct. 2253, 56 L.Ed.2d 414 (1978); *Ruiz v. Shell Oil Company*, 413 F.2d 310, 312–13 (5th Cir.1969). As summarized in *Hall, supra*, 732 F.2d at 1249:

Among the considerations for determining whether a servant has been borrowed by another employer are:

(1) Who has control over the employee and the work he is performing, beyond mere suggestion of details or cooperation?

(2) Whose work is being performed?

(3) Was there an agreement, understanding, or meeting of the minds between the original and borrowing employer?

(4) Did the employee acquiesce in the new work situation?

(5) Did the original employer terminate his relationship with the employee?

(6) Who furnished tools and place for performance?

(7) Was the new employment over a considerable length of time?

(8) Who has the right to discharge the employee?

(9) Who had the obligation to pay the employee?

*Ruiz, supra*, the fountainhead of this line of circuit jurisprudence, stated that, although "[t]he factor of control is perhaps the most universally accepted standard for establishing an employer-employee relationship", "no one of these factors [i.e., the criteria above-enumerated], or any combination of them, is decisive, and no fixed test is used to determine the existence of a borrowed-servant relationship." 413 F.2d at 321.

Recognizing this principle, we have nevertheless indicated, in different cases, that certain of these factors may be more important than others, at least in the light of the facts then before the court. * * *

### II.

On the basis of the factual showing, the district court granted summary judgment dismissing Alday's maritime tort suit against Patterson, holding that Alday was Patterson's borrowed employee. * * *

The district court's finding that Alday, although employed and paid by Atchafalaya, was a borrowed employee of Patterson was based: (a) upon Alday's deposition testimony, in which he admitted that during his single day of employment prior to his disabling injury the Patterson foreman instructed and supervised him in the performance of his duties, after he had been dropped off at the Patterson shipyard by Atchafalaya with four or five other non-supervisory Atchafalaya employees; and (b) upon the affidavit of Atchafalaya's president that on the day in question Alday was under the control and supervision of Patterson.

### III.

Nevertheless, despite this factual showing supporting an inference of Patterson's supervisory control of Alday on his single day of work as Atchafalaya's employee on Patterson's work-site, the contract between Atchafalaya and Patterson regulating the relationship between these parties included this provision:

> It is agreed and understood that any work requested by COMPANY [i.e., Patterson]and agreed to be performed by CONTRACTOR [i.e., Atchafalaya] shall be performed under the terms of this Master Service Agreement and that CONTRACTOR shall be and is an independent contractor, COMPANY being interested only in the results obtained, and having the general right of inspection and supervision in order to secure the satisfactory completion of any such work. *Under no circumstance shall an employee of CONTRACTOR be deemed an employee of COMPANY*; neither shall CONTRACTOR act as an agent or employee of COMPANY. (Emphasis added).

This contract contained further provisions attempting to negate any borrowed employee relationship between Patterson and Atchafalaya's employees. It provided, for example, that "any person who is on CONTRACTOR's payroll and receives, has received or is entitled to receive payment from CONTRACTOR in connection with any work performed or to be performed hereunder shall be the employee of CONTRACTOR even though COMPANY reimburses CONTRACTOR for the amount paid such employee." It further provided: "CONTRACTOR shall furnish at its own expense and risk all labor, material, equipment, tools, transportation and other items necessary in the performance of the work or services covered hereby, except such of said items as COMPANY specifically agrees in writing to furnish."

Additionally, in an apparent attempt to prevent subsequent claims of oral modification between the parties, the contract provided: "No waiver of any provision hereof by COMPANY, or Amendment hereto shall be effective unless it is in writing, and expressly refers to this Agreement."

On full development of the evidence, it is true, a trier of fact might find that, in actual working operations, the parties ignored their solemn contract. On the basis at least of the sparse factual showing here, however, we are unable to say that no factual issue is raised by these contractual provisions, which "negate" any intention on the part of the employers to establish a borrowed employee relationship. * * *

These contractual provisions nevertheless raise an issue of fact as to Alday's status as an alleged borrowed employee of Patterson that precludes summary judgment, despite the inferences to the contrary that may be drawn from the unopposed affidavit of Atchafalaya's president and the observations of Alday himself as to his working conditions on his single day at work.

This may perhaps more readily be seen if a converse situation is posed. If a third party was injured by Alday's tort on Patterson's premises and sought to hold Patterson liable under *respondeat superior* as Alday's borrowing employer, such third party plaintiff could not secure a summary judgment holding Patterson liable simply because of a self-serving and conclusory affidavit by Atchafalaya that, contrary to the formal contract between Atchafalaya and Patterson, Atchafalaya had relinquished control of Alday to Patterson, even if Alday's observations (on his single day of work as Atchafalaya's employee on Patterson's premises) seemed to corroborate this testimony. The contractual provision was designed to insulate Patterson from such liability to third persons for Alday's tort. In opposing summary judgment, Patterson would properly urge that, in view of the formal contract between the parties, a trier of fact could conclude— upon further and full development of merit evidence concerning the actual working relationship between the parties under the contract—that indeed Patterson was not liable for the tort of Atchafalaya's employee, since indeed Atchafalaya was an independent contractor conducting general operations under the contract in accordance with the terms agreed upon between the parties.

A third party tort-plaintiff moving for summary judgment could not ignore the contract as creating an issue that required further factual development. In our opinion, neither may Patterson do so, relying only upon a sparse factual showing that merely raises the issue as to whether its responsibility to Atchafalaya's employees was in fact contrary to the formal and apparently binding contractual agreement between it and Atchafalaya.

## IV.

In *Gaudet, supra*, 562 F.2d at 359, it is true, summary judgment was upheld against the employee-plaintiff as "borrowed," despite a somewhat similar provision in the contract between the payroll and borrowing employers. However, unlike the facts so far shown by the present record, in *Gaudet* all factors other than the contract pointed to the acquiescence of both payroll employer and the plaintiff employees to the latter's undisputed transfer to exclusive supervision and control by the borrowing employer over an extended period of time (12 years for one plaintiff, 17 for another), under conditions where the employees fully appreciated and accepted the risks of their borrowed employment. Id., 562 F.2d at 358–59. * * *

To the contrary, in the present case, the factual showing thus far educed does not so unequivocally point to a borrowed employee relationship as to permit a summary judgment. We have already noted as significantly creating a factual issue the Atchafalaya–Patterson contract * * *. In addition, under the showing made, Atchafalaya had the exclusive right to discharge Alday and the exclusive obligation to pay him. Alday had been sent to Patterson only for a single day of work, during which he had been injured, and it can hardly be said as a matter of undisputed fact, without further development, that he acquiesced to the transfer of his employment to Patterson and accepted the risks of Patterson's work. Both under the Atchafalaya–Patterson contract and under Alday's deposition testimony, Atchafalaya (not Patterson) furnished him with a hardhat, gloves, safety shoes, and a work uniform. The record does not reflect that Patterson furnished Alday any equipment to use in unloading the barge. Whether indeed Atchafalaya relinquished control over Alday might also, without further factual development, be regarded as subject to dispute, in view of Alday's deposition testimony and reasonable inferences therefrom that Atchafalaya determined from day to day where Alday would work, transported him to and from the worksites, and furnished him with eating and sleeping facilities when off work, in addition to having the exclusive contractual obligation to pay Alday for the work he did and the sole right to discharge him. * * *

### Conclusion

For the reasons stated, we REVERSE the grant of summary judgment and REMAND for further proceedings consistent with this opinion.

### NOTES AND QUESTIONS

1. The instant case involves two firms doing distinct businesses that complement one another, so that employees of one often work alongside the employees of another for a time, in order to further the hiring employer's business. Sometimes the "borrowing" is more obvious. The importance of temporary staffing agencies and employee leasing firms in the United States has grown substantially since the 1980s. Temporary staffing services (Kelly

Services, Manpower, and the like) typically provide workers for relatively short periods of time to supplement the permanent workforce of a firm. Sometimes, however, the arrangement becomes a long-term one, so that a worker remains in the same establishment for years. In either instance, immediate supervision is provided not by the service furnishing the workers, but rather by the firm where the actual work is performed. Employee leasing services, on the other hand, are a sort of "human resources department" for a small firm. The firm discharges all (or nearly all) its workforce, who immediately become the employees of the leasing service, making the same wages. The leasing firm then becomes responsible for payroll records, tax withholding and remittance, workers compensation coverage, and benefit packages (such as medical insurance) for these workers. Since the workers continue to work in the same place under the same supervision, it clearly makes sense to treat them as "employees" of the old employer—and probably of the employee leasing firm as well.

2. Compare the multi-factor test used in this case to that employed in Cloverleaf to determine employee or independent contractor status. What is similar, what different?

### (ii.) Specific Exclusion and Inclusions

Workers compensation statutes typically include a number of provisions stating that certain parties are or are not "employers" and "employees" for the purposes of that act. Common provisions (as for the most part described in UNITED STATES DEPARTMENT OF LABOR, EMPLOYMENT STANDARDS ADMINISTRATION, STATE WORKERS COMPENSATION LAWS, tables 2–4 (January 2006); available online at workerscompresources.com) include:

- *Exclusion of "casual" workers.* This exclusion is similar to the exclusion of independent contractors in many ways. An employment is said to be "casual" if it is not in the usual course of the alleged employer's business. Many statutes also include a time element. If a business hires an individual to trim trees and shrubs around its premises for a few hours once or twice a year, that tree trimmer is most likely a casual employee, and excluded from coverage, even though he or she is carefully supervised by the manager to make sure the job is done right, and is paid by the hour. If, however, the premises are extensive and the trimmer comes two days a month to work for the same firm, this begins to look less "casual" and coverage would exist unless the trimmer is found to be an independent contractor, running his or her own business.

- *Exclusion of agricultural workers.* This exclusion, once virtually universal, has now become limited in a majority of states to smaller operations, those employing only a few seasonal workers. Only fourteen states, however, cover agricultural workers on exactly the same basis as other workers.

- *Exclusions of small employers.* Once very common, this exclusion is now available in only a dozen or so states. The broadest exclusion (in four states) is of firms that employ fewer than five employees.

- *Exclusions of domestic workers.* Roughly half the states exclude domestic workers in private households entirely. The others provide coverage of domestic workers if they work more than a specified number of hours or make more than a specified amount in a certain time period (week, or month or calendar quarter).

- *Inclusion of "statutory employers," particularly in construction.* The construction of buildings, roads, and the like requires coordination of the work of many firms that are typically independent contractors. The owner for whom the structure is being built will sometimes hire these firms directly, perhaps using the services of a project management firm, or may retain a firm as "general contractor" to select and oversee the work of the contractors. Many of the contractor firms are likely to be small in size, thus posing the problem that they may be too small to be covered by the workers compensation law (roughly a dozen states still have small employer exemptions), or may simply be lax in keeping track of that obligation. Most workers compensation statutes therefore include a "statutory employer" provision, under which a general contractor or owner is liable to pay workers compensation benefits to an injured employee of a sub-contractor that has not paid those benefits. Should this potential workers compensation liability be enough to entitle the general contractor to immunity from a personal injury damages action for negligence, even if the immediate employer has in fact provided workers compensation coverage? The U.S. Supreme Court held "yes" in *Washington Metropolitan Transit Authority v. Johnson*, 467 U.S. 925, 104 S.Ct. 2827 (1984), but the Congress soon overruled that decision. See 33 U.S.C. § 905(a).

- *Inclusion of employers' insurers.* This common provision allows an employer's workers compensation insurer to participate directly in the handling of claims.

- *Exclusion of workers covered by federal statutes.* As mentioned earlier, there are a handful of federal programs covering employment injuries suffered by particular groups, some designed to be exclusive. Deciding where the jurisdiction lies in the case of federal government employees and railroad operating employees has been relatively simple. The lines between state and admiralty jurisdiction, and between longshore worker and crew member, however, have turned out to be elusive, particularly since the 1972 amendments to the Longshore and Harbor Workers Compensation Act. The case that follows is one illustration.

## HARBOR TUG & BARGE CO. v. PAPAI

United States Supreme Court, 1997
520 U.S. 548, 117 S.Ct. 1535, 137 L.Ed.2d 800

JUSTICE KENNEDY delivered the opinion of the Court.

Adjudication to determine whether a maritime employee is a seaman under the Jones Act, 46 U. S. C. App. § 688(a), or a maritime employee covered by the Longshore and Harbor Workers' Compensation Act (LHWCA), 44 Stat. (part 2) 1424, as amended, 33 U.S.C. § 901 et seq., continues to be of concern in our system. The distinction between the two mutually exclusive categories can be difficult to implement, and many cases turn on their specific facts. * * *

On the question of seaman status, there is an issue of significance beyond the facts of this case. Our statement in an earlier case that a worker may establish seaman status based on the substantiality of his connection to "an identifiable group of ... vessels" in navigation, see *Chandris, Inc. v. Latsis*, 515 U. S. 347, 368 (1995), has been subject to differing interpretations, and we seek to provide clarification.

## I

Respondent John Papai was painting the housing structure of the tug Pt. Barrow when a ladder he was on moved, he alleges, causing him to fall and injure his knee. App. 50. Petitioner Harbor Tug & Barge Co., the tug's operator, had hired Papai to do the painting work. Id., at 44. A prime coat of paint had been applied and it was Papai's task to apply the finish coat. Id., at 45. There was no vessel captain on board and Papai reported to the port captain, who had a dockside office. Id., at 36–37. The employment was expected to begin and end the same day, id., at 35, 48, and Papai was not going to sail with the vessel after he finished painting, id., at 51. Papai had been employed by Harbor Tug on 12 previous occasions in the 2 1/2 months before his injury.

Papai received his jobs with Harbor Tug through the Inland Boatman's Union (IBU) hiring hall. He had been getting jobs with various vessels through the hiring hall for about 2¼ years. All the jobs were short term. The longest lasted about 40 days and most were for three days or under. Id., at 29, 34. In a deposition, Papai described the work as coming under three headings: maintenance, longshoring, and deckhand. Id., at 30–32. Papai said maintenance work involved chipping rust and painting aboard docked vessels. Id., at 30, 34–35. Longshoring work required helping to discharge vessels. Id., at 31. Deckhand work involved manning the lines on and offboard vessels while they docked or undocked. Id., at 30. As for the assignments he obtained through the hiring hall over 2 years, most of them, says Papai, involved deckhand work. Id., at 34.

After his alleged injury aboard the Pt. Barrow, Papai sued Harbor Tug in the United States District Court for the Northern District of California, claiming negligence under the Jones Act and unseaworthiness under general maritime law, in addition to other causes of action. His wife joined as a plaintiff, claiming loss of consortium. Harbor Tug sought summary judgment on Papai's Jones Act and unseaworthiness claims, contending he was not a seaman and so could not prevail on either claim. The District Court granted Harbor Tug's motion and later denied Papai's motion for reconsideration. * * *

## II

The LHWCA, a maritime workers' compensation scheme, excludes from its coverage "a master or member of a crew of any vessel," 33 U.S.C. § 902(3)(G). These masters and crewmembers are the seamen entitled to sue for damages under the Jones Act. *Chandris*, 515 U. S., at 355–358. In other words, the LHWCA and the Jones Act are "mutually exclusive." Id. Our recent cases explain the proper inquiry to determine seaman status. We need not restate that doctrinal development, see id., at 355–368; *Wilander*, *supra*, at 341–54, to resolve Papai's claim. It suffices to cite *Chandris*, which held, in pertinent part:

> "The essential requirements for seaman status are twofold. First ... an employee's duties must contribute to the function of the vessel or to the accomplishment of its mission. . . .

> "Second, and most important for our purposes here, a seaman must have a connection to a vessel in navigation (or to an identifiable group of such vessels) that is substantial in terms of both its duration and its nature."

515 U. S., at 368 (citations and internal quotation marks omitted).

The seaman inquiry is a mixed question of law and fact, and it often will be inappropriate to take the question from the jury. Nevertheless, "summary judgment or a directed verdict is mandated where the facts and the law will reasonably support only one conclusion." *Wilander*, *supra*, at 356; see also *Chandris*, 515 U. S., at 368–369. * * *

For the substantial connection requirement to serve its purpose, the inquiry into the nature of the employee's connection to the vessel must concentrate on whether the employee's duties take him to sea. This will give substance to the inquiry both as to the duration and nature of the employee's connection to the vessel and be helpful in distinguishing landbased from seabased employees.

Papai argues, and the Court of Appeals majority held, that Papai meets Chandris' second test based on his employments with the various vessels he worked on through the IBU hiring hall in the 2¼ years before his injury, vessels owned, it appears, by three different employers not linked by any common ownership or control, App. 38. He also did long-shoring work through the hiring hall, id., at 31, and it appears this was for still other employers, id., at 38. As noted above, Papai testified at his deposition that the majority of his work during this period was deckhand work. According to Papai, this satisfies *Chandris* because the group of vessels Papai worked on through the IBU hiring hall constitutes "an identifiable group of ... vessels" to which he has a "substantial connection." 515 U. S., at 368. * * *

[T]he context of our statement in *Chandris* makes clear our meaning, which is that the employee's prior work history with a particular employer may not affect the seaman inquiry if the employee was injured on a new assignment with the same employer, an assignment with different "essential duties" than his previous ones. 515 U. S., at 371. In *Chandris*, the words "particular employer" give emphasis to the point that the inquiry into the nature of the employee's duties for seaman status purposes may concentrate on a narrower, not broader, period than the employee's entire course of employment with his current employer. There was no suggestion of a need to examine the nature of an employee's duties with prior employers. * * * So far as the record shows, each employer was free to hire, assign, and direct workers for whatever tasks and time period they each determined, limited, at most, by the IBU Deckhands Agreement. In deciding whether there is an identifiable group of vessels of relevance for a Jones Act seaman status determination, the question is whether the vessels are subject to common ownership or control. The requisite link is not established by the mere use of the same hiring hall which draws from the same pool of employees.

Considering prior employments with independent employers in making the seaman status inquiry would undermine "the interests of employers and maritime workers alike in being able to predict who will be covered by the Jones Act (and, perhaps more importantly for purposes of the employers' workers' compensation obligations, who will be covered by the LHWCA) before a particular work day begins." *Chandris, supra*, at 363. There would be no principled basis for limiting which prior employments are considered for determining seaman status. * * *

Papai contends his various employers through the hiring hall would have been able to predict his status as a seaman under the Jones Act based on the seagoing nature of some of the duties he could have been hired to perform consistent with his classification as a "qualified deckhand" under the IBU Deckhands Agreement. By the terms of the Agreement, Papai was qualified as a "satisfactory helmsman and lookout," for example, and he could have been hired to serve a vessel while it was underway, in which case his duties would have included "conducting a check of the engine room status a minimum of two (2) times each watch . . . for vessel safety reasons." App. 77. In *South Chicago Coal & Dock Co. v. Bassett*, 309 U.S. 251 (1940), we rejected a claim to seaman status grounded on the employee's job title, which also happened to be "deckhand." "The question," we said, "concerns his actual duties." Id., at 260. . . . The question is what connection the employee had in actual fact to vessel operations, not what a union agreement says. Papai was qualified under the IBU Deckhands Agreement to perform nonseagoing work in addition to the seagoing duties described above. His actual duty on the Pt. Barrow throughout the employment in question did not include any seagoing activity; he was hired for one day to paint the vessel at dockside and he was not going to sail with the vessel after he finished painting it. App. 44, 48, 51. This is not a case where the employee was hired to perform seagoing work during the employment in question, however brief, and we need not consider here the consequences of such an employment. The IBU Deckhands Agreement gives no reason to assume that any particular percentage of Papai's work would be of a seagoing nature, subjecting him to the perils of the sea. In these circumstances, the union agreement does not advance the accuracy of the seaman status inquiry.

Papai argues he qualifies as a seaman if we consider his 12 prior employments with Harbor Tug over the 2½ months before his injury. Papai testified at his deposition that he worked aboard the Pt. Barrow on three or four occasions before the day he was injured, the most recent of which was more than a week earlier. Id., at 35, 44. Each of these engagements involved only maintenance work while the tug was docked. Id., at 34–35. The nature of Papai's connection to the Pt. Barrow was no more substantial for seaman status purposes by virtue of these engagements than the one during which he was injured. * * * In any event, these discrete engagements were separate from the one in question, which was the sort of "transitory or sporadic" connection to a vessel or group of vessels that, as we explained in *Chandris*, does not qualify one for seaman status. 515 U.S., at 368.

Jones Act coverage is confined to seamen, those workers who face regular exposure to the perils of the sea. An important part of the test for determining who is a seaman is whether the injured worker seeking coverage has a substantial connection to a vessel or a fleet of vessels, and the latter concept requires a requisite degree of common ownership or control. The substantial connection test is important in distinguishing between sea- and land-based employment, for land-based employment is inconsistent with Jones Act coverage. This was the holding in *Chandris*, and we adhere to it here ... He failed to meet it. The Court of Appeals erred in holding otherwise. Its judgment is reversed.

It is so ordered.

[The dissent of JUSTICE STEVENS is omitted.]

## NOTES AND QUESTIONS

1. Assume the dockside painting was done by a tugboat worker who normally swabs the deck and ties and unties tow ropes when the vessel is underway. Would his dockside injury while painting the ship's housing structure be covered by the Jones Act or the Longshore and Harbor Workers' Compensation Act? In *Chesapeake & Ohio Ry. v. Schwalb*, 493 U.S. 40, 110 S.Ct. 381, 107 L.Ed.2d 278 (1989), a railroad worker was injured while repairing equipment at a dockside terminal. The Court concluded that because the equipment was essential to loading and unloading vessels, the injury came under the Longshore and Harbor Workers' Compensation Act and was not covered by the Federal Employers Liability Act. Three members of the Court particularly noted that coverage is controlled by the general nature of the work assignment, not the tasks being performed at the time of injury.

2. Because longshoring work occurs not just on piers over navigable waters, but also on adjoining land (under the definition in the 1972 amendments broadening the coverage of the LHWCA), there is a possibility that a state law may apply to the injuries suffered by a longshore worker. In *Sun Ship, Inc. v. Pennsylvania*, 447 U.S. 715, 100 S.Ct. 2432, 65 L.Ed.2d 458

(1980), the Supreme Court held that the LHWCA does not preempt state workers compensation law, so long as the state law is confined to claims that are not exclusively maritime. As Justice Brennan put it: "In 1917, *Southern Pacific Co. v. Jensen*, 244 U.S. 205, 37 S.Ct. 524, 61 L.Ed. 1086 (1917), declared that States were constitutionally barred from applying their compensation systems to maritime injuries ... Subsequent decisions invalidated congressional efforts to delegate compensatory authority to the States within this national maritime sphere. * * * At the same time, the Court began to narrow the *Jensen* doctrine by identifying circumstances in which the subject of litigation might be maritime yet 'local in character,' and thus amenable to relief under state law. * * * Before 1972, then, marine-related injuries fell within one of three jurisdictional spheres ... At the furthest extreme Jensen commanded that nonlocal maritime injuries fall under the LHWCA. 'Maritime but local' injuries 'upon the navigable waters of the United States,' 33 U.S.C. § 903(a), could be compensated under the LHWCA or under state laws. And injuries suffered beyond navigable waters—albeit within the range of federal admiralty jurisdiction—were remediable only under state law. * * * We ... find no sign in the 1972 amendments to the LHWCA that Congress wished to alter the accepted understanding that federal jurisdiction would coexist with state compensation laws in that field in which the latter may constitutionally operate under the Jensen doctrine."

3. The term "vessel" in the LHWCA includes more than ordinary boats. In *Stewart v. Dutra Construction Co.*, 543 U.S. 481, 125 S.Ct. 1118, 160 L.Ed.2d 932 (2005), the Court held that the definition of vessel in the Rules of Construction Act, part of the Revised Statutes of 1873, applies to interpretations of the LHWCA, with the result that a dredge that could move very short distances through the use of its anchors and cables was found to be a vessel. Under that definition the "word 'vessel' includes every description of watercraft or other artificial contrivance used, or capable of being used, as a means of transportation on water." 1 U.S.C. § 3.

## 3. RESOLVING CONTESTED BENEFIT ENTITLEMENT CLAIMS

Processing a workers' compensation claim normally begins when the employee notifies the employer of an injury or claim for benefits. In most jurisdictions a claim is barred unless the employer is notified within a "reasonable time" or within a statutorily specified time after the worker becomes aware of, or should have become aware of, the injury. This requirement, of course, is designed to give the employer an opportunity to: (a) investigate the facts giving rise to the claim while they still are ripe, (b) take preventive measures against additional mishaps, and (c) assure prompt medical attention so as to reduce the possibility of secondary complications. The notification requirement is separate from the statutory limitation of time for filing a claim, though the prompt filing of a claim generally suffices to satisfy the notice requirement.

Most benefits are voluntarily provided to the employee upon presentation of the bills for medical treatment and requests for payment of the indemnity against lost wages. Often, the employer's program of paid sick-leave benefits covers all or part of the indemnity period and provides a benefit rate that is higher than that required by the workers' compensation law (e.g., 100% of normal pay instead of only two-thirds). However, if the employer (or the employer's insurer) refuses to provide benefits, the worker may file a contested claim which, in most jurisdictions, is heard by an administrative hearing officer variously called an administrative law judge, referee, commissioner, or hearing officer, who receives evidence and argument and issues findings and a decision. There are considerable variations in the level of formality and details of procedure. Some states follow judicial rules of evidence; many do not. Typically, hearings are conducted by a hearing officer and that person either issues a decision that may be appealed to the administrative body or makes recommendations that are reviewed by the administrative body. Decisions of that administrative body may be appealed for judicial review. Generally, considerable judicial deference is given to the compensation agency's findings of fact.

In a few states, the trial of questions of fact, as well as law in a contested claim, is heard in the courts and not by administrative tribunals.

### (a.) Time, Place and Manner of Injury: When Does and Injury "Arise Out of and in the Course of Employment"?

All workers' compensation statutes in some form require that, in order to be compensable, an injury or illness must "arise out of and in the course of employment." Courts commonly treat this as two requirements: (1) that the genesis of the injury or illness occurs at a time and place that the employee is engaged "in the course of employment;" and (2) that the risk that gives rise to the injury or illness be one that "arises out of employment." Of course these two issues are intertwined since arguably risks that are encountered in the course of employment logically arise out of employment and in practice a strong case on either issue can make up for a weak argument on the other. Although simple in their objective of ensuring the appropriate nexus between the employee's injury and work, the application of these requirements to the myriad of facts and situations that occur in the workplace is an interesting and important part of understanding the operation of workers' compensation. In this subsection we explore the application of these two requirements and their interaction in various fact situations.

## SANTA ROSA JUNIOR COLLEGE V. WORKERS' COMPENSATION APPEALS BOARD

California Supreme Court, 1985
40 Cal.3d 345, 220 Cal.Rptr. 94, 708 P.2d 673

KAUS, JUSTICE.

The Workers' Compensation Act (Lab. Code, § 3201 et seq.) establishes the liability of an employer "for any injury sustained by his or her employees arising out of and in the course of the employment." Almost 70 years ago, we adopted the "going and coming rule" as an aid in determining whether an injury occurred in the course of the employment. Generally prohibiting compensation for injuries suffered by an employee while commuting to and from work, the going and coming rule has been criticized by courts and commentators alike as being arbitrary and harsh. It has generated a multitude of exceptions which threaten, at times, to defeat the rule entirely. This appeal confronts us with the question of whether one such exception should be dramatically expanded to create, in effect, a "white-collar" nullification of the rule.

Santa Rosa Junior College (college) challenges a decision of the Workers' Compensation Appeals Board (board) awarding death benefits to JoAnne Smyth, widow of a community college instructor who was killed in an automobile accident on his way home from the campus. At issue is the applicability of the going and coming rule to school teachers who regularly take work home. If, in such cases, the home may be fairly regarded as a "second jobsite," the rule does not apply and injuries sustained en route are compensable. If the fact that the employee regularly takes work home does not establish the home as a second jobsite, compensation is barred.

We conclude that—unless the employer requires the employee to labor at home as a condition of the employment—the fact that an employee regularly works there does not transform the home into a second jobsite for purposes of the going and coming rule.

## Facts

Joseph Smyth was a mathematics instructor and head of the mathematics department at the college. At about 6 p.m. on March 16, 1982, he was killed in an accident while driving his personal automobile home from work. His home was located in Ukiah, about 60 miles from the Santa Rosa campus. The family had moved to Ukiah six years earlier for their own convenience: Mrs. Smyth worked in Ukiah, she had a "back problem," and the couple decided that she should be located close to home and to their children's schools.

It is undisputed that at the time of the accident Smyth had with him some student papers he intended to grade that evening. Indeed, Smyth regularly worked at home in the evenings. For several years before the accident, he stayed overnight in Santa Rosa once every two or three weeks and worked at home on some week nights. In 1981–1982, he assumed additional responsibilities as department head. In that school year, he worked late on campus once or twice per week, stayed overnight in Santa Rosa once or twice per week, and brought home one or two hours of work "about every night." At home, he worked in a section of the living room reserved for that purpose, where he kept duplicate copies of necessary books. The work usually consisted of grading papers or exams; occasionally, he would also prepare lesson plans or future class schedules at home. Mrs. Smyth testified that her husband worked at home rather than on campus because on campus, he was subject to interruption by students or other business, and, in addition, he wished to spend time with his family.

Smyth's habit of working at home in the evenings was not unusual for members of the college's faculty; working at home appears to have been the rule, not the exception. * * *

William Wilbur, dean of business services, agreed that there was no rule against taking work home and that working at home is "common to all disciplines." He also stated that neither Smyth nor any other staff member received financial or other consideration to account for the distance and time of their commutes. He knew of no benefit to the employer by reason of the work being done at home rather than on campus.

An office was provided for each instructor at the college. Undisputed evidence shows that Smyth could have eliminated or reduced student interruptions by posting office hours. Moreover, the record shows—not surprisingly—that Smyth was also subject to interruption while working at home.

The workers' compensation judge concluded that Smyth's death did not occur in the course of employment. He found that Smyth had adequate facilities and sufficient time to complete his work on campus and that it was Smyth's choice to work at home.

Acting on a petition for reconsideration, a three-member board panel, by a two-to-one vote, held that the death arose out of and occurred during the course of employment. The board concluded that because of the nature of the work and the frequent interruptions from students and phone calls, Smyth was "essentially required to maintain a second worksite in his home." It reasoned that in this case "[t]he work at home was more a matter of business necessity than of personal convenience." Accordingly, the board awarded death benefits to Mrs. Smyth.

The college seeks review of the board's decision. * * *

We originally adopted the going and coming rule as one means of determining when an accident should be treated as an "accident arising out of and in the course of the employment." * * *

Of course, we recognized that in the broadest sense an injury occurring on the way to one's place of employment is an injury "growing out of and incident to his employment," since "a necessary part of the employment is that the employee shall go to and return from his place of labor." However, the right to an award is founded not "upon the fact that the injury grows out of and is incidental to his employment" but, rather, "upon the fact that the *service* he is rendering at the time of the injury grows out of and is incidental to the employment." (Emphasis original.) Therefore, we reasoned, "an employee going to and from his place of employment is not rendering any service, and begins to render such service only when [arriving at the place of employment]." The rule has also been explained on the theory that "ordinarily the employment relationship is suspended from the time the employee leaves his work to go home until he resumes his work." (*Zenith Nat. Ins. Co. v. Workmen's Comp. App. Bd.* (1967) 66 Cal.2d 944, 947, 59 Cal.Rptr. 622, 428 P.2d 606, quoting *Kobe v. Industrial Acc. Com.* (1950) 35 Cal.2d 33, 35, 215 P.2d 736.)

The going and coming rule resulted from the type of judicial line-drawing frequently required when construing and applying vague or open-ended statutory provisions. [The resulting harshness and arbitrariness of the rule has led to numerous exceptions.] * * *

The trouble is that the facts in this case do not fit convincingly into any of the established limitations or exceptions. Because Smyth's accident occurred miles away from the Santa Rosa campus, exceptions to the "premises line" doctrine[1] cannot reasonably be invoked to render the going and coming rule inapplicable. Smyth received no special or additional compensation for his commute; therefore, the "wage payment or travel expense" exception cannot apply.[2] The college did not require Smyth to furnish his own vehicle on the job. If it had, the "required transportation" exception would have curtailed application of the going and coming rule. (*Smith v. Workmen's Comp. App. Bd.* (1968) 69 Cal.2d 814, 820, 73 Cal.Rptr. 253, 447 P.2d 365; *Hinojosa, supra,* 8 Cal.3d at p. 160, 104 Cal.Rptr. 456, 501 P.2d 1176.)

Smyth's employment at the college in no way created a "special risk." Under that exception, an injury is compensable if, before entry upon the premises, an employee suffers injury from a special risk causally related to employment. (*Gen. Ins. Co. v. Workers' Comp. App. Bd.* (*Chairez*) (1976) 16 Cal.3d 595, 600, 128 Cal.Rptr. 417, 546 P.2d 1361.) "The facts that an accident happens upon a public road and that the danger is one to which the general public is likewise exposed, however, do not preclude the existence of a causal relationship between the accident and the employment if the danger is one to which the employee, by reason of and in connection with his employment, is subjected peculiarly or to an abnormal degree." (*Freire v. Matson Nav. Co.* (1941) 19 Cal.2d 8, 12, 118 P.2d 809.)

---

**1.** For purposes of applying the going and coming rule, the employment relationship begins when the employee enters the employer's premises. We have reaffirmed the "premises line" rule, stating that it "has the advantage of enabling courts to ascertain the point at which employment begins—objectively and fairly." (*Gen. Ins. Co. v. Workers' Comp. App. Bd.* (*Chairez*) 16 Cal.3d 595, 599, 128 Cal.Rptr. 417, 546 P.2d 1361.) However, injuries sustained in close proximity to the employer's premises may, in fact arise out of the employment, especially when the accident occurs in the parking lot used by employees or on public property immediately adjacent to the workplace. Recognizing this, we have defined the course of employment to include a "reasonable margin of time and space necessary to be used in passing to and from the place where the work is to be done." (*Lewis v. Workers' Comp. App. Bd.* (1975) 15 Cal.3d 559, 561, 125 Cal.Rptr. 353, 542 P.2d 225, quoting *Cal. Cas. Ind. Exch. v. Ind. Acc. Com.*, supra, 21 Cal.2d 751, 754, 135 P.2d 158.) Where the employment itself creates a danger to employees entering or leaving the premises, we have posited a "field of risk" or "zone of danger," the extent of which varies from case to case, depending on the degree to which the employer's conduct contributes directly as a proximate cause of the employee's injuries.

**2.** See *Kobe,* supra, 35 Cal.2d at page 35, 215 P.2d 736; *Hinman v. Westinghouse Elec. Co.* (1970) 2 Cal.3d 956, 962, 88 Cal.Rtpr. 188, 471 P.2d 988. The fact that an employer compensates an employee for the commuting time implies an agreement that the employment relationship shall continue during the period of going and coming.

In *Chairez*, we devised a two-prong test to determine applicability of the special risk exception: the exception will apply (1) if "but for" the employment the employee would not have been at the location where the injury occurred and (2) if "the risk is distinctive in nature or quantitatively greater than risks common to the public." While the circumstances of Smyth's accident certainly meet the first requirement (i.e., the accident would not have occurred "but for" the employment), his employment at the college did not subject him to a risk which was distinct or quantitatively greater than that common to the public generally.

We also find no merit in the suggestion that Smyth's accident occurred while he was on "special mission" or "errand" which was reasonably undertaken at the request or invitation of his employer.[3] In relation to his routine duties, there was nothing "extraordinary" about his commute on March 16, 1982. The accident occurred, quite simply, during his regular commute between the college and his home in Ukiah. Smyth's practice of taking work home with him in the evenings cannot convert a routine commute into a "special mission."

Finally, we have recognized a "home as a second jobsite" exception to the going and coming rule. It is this exception—or an extension of it—which the board used in concluding that the rule does not preclude compensation in this case. Generally, "[w]ork done at home may exempt an injury occurring during a regular commute from the going and coming rule if circumstances of the employment—and not mere dictates of convenience to the employee—make the home a second jobsite. If the home becomes a second business situs, the familiar rule applies that injury sustained while traveling between jobsites is compensable." (*Wilson v. Workers' Comp. App. Bd.* (1976) 16 Cal.3d 181, 184, 127 Cal.Rptr. 313, 545 P.2d 225.) We noted that the commute does not constitute a business trip if the employees work at home for their own convenience: "serving the employee's own convenience in selecting an off-premise place to work is a personal and not a business purpose." Ibid. * * *

Applicant in the present case contends that the board properly concluded that it was an implied term or condition of Smyth's employment contract that he take work home in the evenings—that it was "more a matter of business necessity than of personal convenience." On this basis, the board distinguished Wilson, wherein there was no claim that school facilities were not sufficient to allow completion of the required work.

---

**3.** "An injury suffered by an employee during his regular commute is compensable if he was also performing a special mission for his employer." (*Chairez*, supra, 16 Cal.3d at p. 601, 128 Cal.Rptr. 417, 546 P.2d 1361.) The employee's conduct is "special" if it is "extraordinary in relation to routine duties, not outside the scope of employment" (*Schreifer v. Ind. Acc. Com.* (1964) 61 Cal.2d 289, 295, 38 Cal.Rptr. 352, 391 P.2d 832. * * * The closely related "dual purpose" rule also appears inapplicable. In *Lockheed Aircraft Corp. v. Ind. Acc. Com.* (1946) 28 Cal.2d 756, 172 P.2d 1, we held that "where the employee is combining his own business with that of his employer, or attending to both at substantially the same time, no nice inquiry will be made as to which business he was actually engaged in at the time of injury, unless it clearly appears that neither directly or indirectly could he have been serving his employer." The dual purpose situation usually arises when the employees combine their personal business with a "special errand" or "mission."

It is not entirely clear whether the board's determination that Smyth was "implicitly required" to use his home as a second jobsite represents a conclusion of law or a finding of fact. Much of the language used by the board suggests that it was a legal conclusion which the board drew from the uncontradicted evidence in the record: "The picture that emerges from the testimony of the various witnesses is that the decedent was essentially required to maintain a second worksite in his home" (opn. at p. 96 of 220 Cal.Rptr., at p. 675 of 708 P.2d); "... we conclude that the decedent was implicitly authorized to perform part of his duties at home...." (opn. at p. 97 of 220 Cal.Rptr., at p. 676 of 708 P.2d); "Clearly this was an accepted practice. It appears moreover, that this was in effect an implied term or condition of the employment contract" (opn. at p. 97 of 220 Cal.Rptr., at p. 676 of 708 P.2d); "his home was in effect a second worksite due to the fact that he was implicitly required to work at home" (opn. at p. 97 of 220 Cal.Rptr., at p. 676 of 708 P.2d). (Italics added.)

These passages suggest that the board concluded that where an employee works long hours and is subject to interruption at the workplace and where fellow employees commonly take work home with the knowledge and implicit permission of the employer, general principles of workers' compensation law establish that the employee is, as a matter of law, "implicitly required" to use his home as a second jobsite. There is no authority, however, to support such a proposition. * * *

As we observed in Wilson, "[t]he contemporary professional frequently takes work home. There, the draftsman designs on a napkin, the businessman plans at breakfast, the lawyer labors in the evening. But this hearthside activity—while commendable—does not create a white collar exception to the going and coming rule." (16 Cal.3d at p. 185, 127 Cal.Rptr. 313, 545 P.2d 225.) Thus, to the extent that the board's "implicit requirement" determination amounts to a legal conclusion, it cannot be reconciled with Wilson.

Furthermore, we find little to commend the white-collar exception which we refused to establish in Wilson. It would, *a fortiori*, extend workers' compensation benefits to workers injured in the homes themselves, as well as en route to and from their regular work places. Ironically, a white collar exception would probably not diminish the controversy surrounding the going and coming rule; it would merely shift it to a new and equally arbitrary "line" defining the "course of employment." Would the fact that an employee regularly took work-related materials home suffice to create a second jobsite, or would the employee have to show that he actually worked at home? How would we treat employees who work at home on some evenings but not on others, depending on their personal inclinations? And, of course, new problems of the "frolics and detours" variety would plague the new exception.

On the other hand, insofar as the board's determination that the employee was "implicitly required" to maintain his home as a second jobsite was intended as a finding of fact, it is simply not supported by substantial evidence in the record. Although the evidence shows that most faculty members took work home and that the employer was well aware of this practice, there is nothing in the record which indicates that faculty members were required—implicitly or otherwise—to work at home rather than on campus. Rather, the evidence reveals that professors worked at home by choice, not because of the dictates of their employer. On this record, there is no room for a factual finding that working at home was a condition of Smyth's employment.

Therefore, applying established "going and coming rule" principles and precedents, we conclude that the board erred in awarding compensation. We could, of course, abrogate the rule or expand any of its exceptions, for they have evolved simply as "the product of judicial gloss on the statutory conditions of compensability." (*Safeway Stores, supra,* 104 Cal. App.3d at p. 535, 163 Cal.Rptr. 750.) However, they have become an important part of our workers' compensation law. Although the Legislature has enacted significant changes in the Workers' Compensation Act during the last 70 years, it has not disturbed the going and coming rule or its judicially created exceptions. Unless the judiciary can devise rules which are fairer, less arbitrary, less problematic in application, and more clearly consistent with the public policies underlying the act, it should leave to the Legislature the major task of restructuring the rules governing employer liability.

Smyth's accident occurred during a routine commute from college to home. We conclude that the facts of this case are essentially indistinguishable from those of *Wilson v. Workmen's Comp. App. Bd.* and that our holding in *Wilson* should govern here.

The decision of the board is annulled.

[JUSTICE REYNOSO, joined by CHIEF JUSTICE BIRD, dissented emphasizing that "Since Smyth's accident clearly occurred in the course of his employment, it should be compensable."]

## NOTES AND QUESTIONS

1. To what extent might the purpose of workers' compensation be relevant? Should the result in *Santa Rosa* be the same if the purpose of workers' compensation coverage is to spread to the consumers of goods and services the costs of personal risks involved in providing those goods and services? Should the result be the same if the purpose of coverage is to transfer from the worker to the employer the financial burdens of the risks to which the worker would not be exposed but for the work activity? Should the result be the same if the purpose of coverage is to transfer from the worker to the employer the financial burdens of the risks to which he was exposed due to being in the work environment? Should the result be the same if the purpose of coverage is to spread among workers the financial risks of being disabled? Does workers' compensation coverage leave a gap in our social insurance system?

2. Should Joseph Smyth's survivors have recovered workers' compensation benefits if he was accompanied by two students who were joining him for dinner at his home? Should they have recovered if the college provided him with a school-owned vehicle for his transportation uses? Should they have recovered if he was on his way to a cocktail party at the home of a junior member of his department? Or, if he was killed in the parking lot of his neighborhood library where he had been doing research? Is there any principle that can distinguish drawing the line at any one of those places rather than at another? Is it possible to draft a workers' compensation law to ensure the result you think would be appropriate in answer to the above questions?

3. How could Smyth or his family have protected themselves from the risks of a daily 60 mile commute? Would savings be gained by requiring the college to provide a minimum level of medical, disability, and all-risk life and accident insurance for its faculty and staff? What impact would such insurance have upon its liability under the workers' compensation law?

4. How clear cut is the concept of employer "premises" under the California court's approach. Does extending coverage to parking lots make decisions more predictable or fair, or less so? Should it matter whether the employer enjoys some level of control over the parking area? See *Janicki v. Kforce.com, Inc.*, 167 Ohio App.3d 572, 855 N.E.2d 1282 (2006). There, the employee, a nurse, was employed by an agency that supplied health care workers to a variety of facilities, including a hospital, to which the injured worker was assigned for a time. She was injured crossing a street on her way to a parking lot for hospital employees, which she was allowed to use.

5. The "dual purpose" trip concept can result in difficult line drawing as well. Consider the case of an "on call" nurse, required by her job to travel to a variety of patient sites, and required to do paperwork for these visits, which she does at home. Returning from a patient visit she picks up a pizza for the family dinner. She falls while carrying both the necessary paperwork and the pizza. See *Amedisys Home Health, Inc. v. Howard*, 269 Ga.App. 656, 605 S.E.2d 60 (2004).

6. For employees who are required to live on the employer's premises for the convenience of the employer, courts commonly apply what is referred to as the "bunkhouse rule" which establishes that even ordinary risks, such as the risk of burning yourself while cooking, arise out of and in the course of employment when the employee is required to live on the employer's premises and working or even waiting to work. 42 A.L.R.6th 61 (2009). Does this rule meet the purposes of workers' compensation? Is it a good deal or a bad deal for employers if the alternative is tort liability?

## KOLOMIETS v. SYNCOR INTERNATIONAL CORPORATION

Supreme Court of Connecticut, 2000
252 Conn. 261, 746 A.2d 743

NORCOTT, J.

* * * The opinion of the Appellate Court sets forth the following relevant facts. "In January, 1993, the defendant ... hired the plaintiff as

a part-time employee to deliver products from [the defendant's] place of business in Stamford to various hospitals in Connecticut and southern New York. [The defendant] dealt in radioactive products and was subject to regulation by the Nuclear Regulatory Commission. Consequently, [the defendant] maintained manuals at its offices in Stamford outlining the recommended routes its drivers should take when transporting its products. Routes could be changed by the drivers if necessary.

"On February 10, 1993, the plaintiff reported to work and was assigned to deliver products to Lawrence Hospital in Bronxville, New York. The plaintiff used [the defendant's] vehicle to make the deliveries. After making his deliveries, the plaintiff discovered that he had left his wallet and driver's license at home. When the plaintiff returned to Connecticut on Interstate 95, he passed exit 6, which he would have taken to return to [the defendant's] offices, and instead used exit 7 to go to his home to retrieve his wallet and driver's license because he did not know if [the defendant] had any more deliveries for him to make that day. After getting off at exit 7, the plaintiff was involved in a motor vehicle accident as a result of which he suffered injuries.

"Brian Welsh, the plaintiff's supervisor, testified that he would have preferred that the plaintiff call him about the missing license, return to [the defendant's] office and punch out, and then use his own vehicle to go home and retrieve his driver's license and wallet. Welsh also testified that [the defendant] had no additional work for the plaintiff on February 10, 1993, and, therefore, there was no work-related reason for the plaintiff to have his driver's license that afternoon. Subsequently, [the defendant] terminated the plaintiff from its employment because he was involved in a 'preventable accident.'

"On January 5, 1996, the workers' compensation commissioner for the seventh district issued a finding and award for the plaintiff as a result of that accident. The commissioner found that the deviation from the plaintiff's exact job duties was minor and not so unreasonable and unwarranted as to preclude him from receiving workers' compensation benefits. On June 23, 1997, the [workers' compensation review] board reversed the commissioner's finding of compensability. The board found that the plaintiff had finished delivering [the defendant's] products and was engaged in a completely separate side trip when he was injured." Kolomiets v. Syncor International Corp., 51 Conn.App. 523, 524–26, 723 A.2d 1161 (1999).

Pursuant to General Statutes § 31–301b, the plaintiff appealed to the Appellate Court, which reversed the board's decision and directed the board to affirm the commissioner's finding and award. * * *

On appeal to this court, the defendant argues that the Appellate Court improperly concluded that the plaintiff's injuries arose out of and in the course of his employment. * * *

## I

As an initial matter, we set forth the standard of review by which we judge the defendant's appeal. A commissioner's "conclusions . . . from the facts found must stand unless they result from an incorrect application of the law to the subordinate facts or from an inference illegally or unreasonably drawn from them." *Fair v. People's Savings Bank*, 207 Conn. 535, 539, 542 A.2d 1118 (1988). "This rule leads to the conclusion that unless the case lies clearly on the one side or the other the question whether an employee has so departed from his employment that his injury did not arise out of it is one of fact." (Internal quotation marks omitted.) *Spatafore v. Yale University*, 239 Conn. 408, 420, 684 A.2d 1155 (1996).

## II

\* \* \*

### A

We consider first whether the plaintiff's injuries occurred in the course of his employment by the defendant. "It is well settled that we parse [the in the course of] requirement by reference to three factors that we set forth over eighty years ago in *Larke v. John Hancock Mutual Life Ins. Co.*, 90 Conn. 303, 308, 97 A. 320 (1916): In order to establish that [the] injury occurred in the course of employment, the claimant has the burden of proving that the accident giving rise to the injury took place (a) within the period of the employment; (b) at a place [the employee] may reasonably [have been]; and (c) while [the employee was] reasonably fulfilling the duties of the employment or doing something incidental to it \* \* \* *Kish v. Nursing & Home Care, Inc.*, 248 Conn. 379, 383, 727 A.2d 1253 (1999). \* \* \*

In *Kish*, the plaintiff was a registered nurse with twenty-two years of experience who was employed by the defendant on a full-time basis to travel to patients' homes and oversee their care. \* \* \* The plaintiff had reserved a new commode from a supply house for one of her patients because she believed that the commode the patient had been using was unsafe. She was told specifically by her supervisor not to deliver the commode herself, but nonetheless she attempted to make the delivery. On the way to the supply house, the plaintiff stopped her car to get out and hand deliver a personal letter to a mail carrier. While she was stopped, the plaintiff was struck by a car. \* \* \*. Despite these deviations, we affirmed the commissioner's award of compensation benefits. \* \* \*.

Under our holding in *Kish*, the question crucial to our determination of whether an injury occurred in the course of employment is whether the injured employee was performing some task incidental to her employment, or was engaged in a "substantial deviation" from her employment. In answering this question, "no bright line test distinguishes activities that are incidental to employment from those that constitute a substantial deviation therefrom. . . . The question of deviation is typically one of fact for the trier. * * * In deciding whether a substantial deviation has occurred, the trier is entitled to weigh a variety of factors, including the time, place and extent of the deviation; * * *; as well as what duties were required of the employee and the conditions surrounding the performance of his work . . ." * * * Secondary to that inquiry is the issue of employer acquiescence. Contrary to the defendant's assertions, employer acquiescence is a prerequisite to compensability *only* if the deviation previously has been determined to be substantial. * * *.

In *Kish*, we employed these distinctions and reached the conclusion that the plaintiff's arguably unauthorized trip to pick up the new commode, and her subsequent decision to cross the street and mail a letter while she was delivering that commode to one of her patients was a "deviation . . . so minor as to be disregarded as insubstantial." Id. at, 391, 727 A.2d 1253. We are compelled to reach a similar conclusion in the present case. * * *

The commissioner determined that the plaintiff's decision to drive to his house and retrieve his driver's license constituted only a minor deviation. This factual determination was based on evidence that: the plaintiff had followed a recommended, but not required, route; the plaintiff had gone only one exit past the ideal highway terminus to a location within the same city as the company headquarters; and the plaintiff attempted to retrieve a license that would have allowed him legally to fulfill further duties that would have been within the course of employment, and that he reasonably could have expected to be asked to perform.

After a careful review of the record, and bearing in mind the deference we give to a commissioner's factual findings, we conclude that the commissioner's finding that the plaintiff's deviation was minor was not clearly erroneous. * * *

The defendant advances several arguments in an attempt to distinguish this case from *Kish*, and to claim that the plaintiff's injuries did not occur in the course of his employment. None of this is persuasive.

First, the defendant argues that the Appellate Court improperly failed to consider whether the plaintiff's trip to his house fell within the "joint benefit" exception to the coming and going rule. * * *

It is true, as a general matter, that "an injury sustained by an employee on a public highway while traveling to or from his place of employment is not compensable." * * *. The defendant claims that, in order for the plaintiff's injuries to be compensable, his trip would have had to come under the "joint benefit" exception to this rule, which permits compensation for injuries sustained on a public highway "where the employee is injured while using the highway in doing something incidental to his regular employment, for the joint benefit of himself and his employer, with the knowledge and approval of the employer." *Dombach v. Olkon Corp.*, 163 Conn. 216, 222, 302 A.2d 270 (1972). As the plaintiff's trip to his home was unsanctioned, the defendant claims that the coming and going rule bars compensation.

This argument ignores a more general exception to the coming and going rule, namely, "[i]f the work requires the employee to travel on the highways...." Id. In the case of an employee, such as the plaintiff, whose entire job consists of highway travel, this more general exception to the coming and going rule clearly applies * * * In the present case, the plaintiff was hired by the defendant for the express purpose of delivering "products from [the defendant's] place of business in Stamford to various hospitals in Connecticut and southern New York." * * * His job consisted, therefore, almost exclusively of highway travel. The coming and going rule cannot be said, therefore, to bar compensation, regardless of whether the plaintiff drove to his house to retrieve his license without the defendant's knowledge and approval.

Second, the defendant claims that the Appellate Court improperly failed to consider whether the plaintiff's deviation from work was made with the defendant's approval or acquiescence. This argument, too, is unavailing. Our decision in *Kish* draws a clear distinction between minor deviations from work, which do not require employer acquiescence, and substantial deviations from work, which do require such acquiescence. * * *. We already have determined that the commissioner's finding that the deviation in the present case was minor was not clearly erroneous. The defendant's alleged lack of acquiescence, therefore, is not fatal to the plaintiff's claim for compensation.

Finally, the defendant attempts to distinguish the facts of *Kish* from the facts of the present case by drawing our attention to the difference in experience between the plaintiff in *Kish* and the plaintiff in this case. That is a distinction without a difference. Although it may be the case, as the defendant argues, that the plaintiff in this case, as a new employee, had been given virtually no discretion to deviate from his assigned tasks, that fact does not alter the commissioner's factual determination that the actual deviation made by the plaintiff was minor. On that crucial point, *Kish* and the present case are indistinguishable, and the lesson of the former readily may be applied in the latter.

## B

Having concluded that the plaintiff's injuries occurred in the course of his employment, we consider the second part of the compensability test, namely, whether those injuries arose out of his employment. In reversing the board's dismissal of the plaintiff's claim, the Appellate Court impliedly concluded that the plaintiff's injuries had arisen out of his employment. We agree.

Proof that the injury arose out of the employment relates to the "origin and cause of the accident." *Mazzone v. Connecticut Transit Co.*, *supra*, 240 Conn. at 792–93, 694 A.2d 1230. "[T]he essential connecting link of direct causal connection between the personal injury and the employment must be established before the act becomes operative. The personal injury must be the result of the employment and flow from it as the inducing proximate cause. The rational mind must be able to trace resultant personal injury to a proximate cause set in motion by the employment and not by some other agency, or there can be no recovery." * * * *Fair v. People's Savings Bank, supra*, 207 Conn. at 545–46, 542 A.2d 1118.

As with the determination that an injury occurred in the course of employment, the question of whether an injury arose out of employment is one of fact. *Hanson v. Transportation General, Inc., supra*, 245 Conn. at 623, 716 A.2d 857. In the present case, the commissioner found, as a factual matter, that the plaintiff's injuries arose out of his employment by the defendant. Bearing in mind our customary deference to such factual determinations; *Spatafore v. Yale University, supra*, 239 Conn. at 419, 684 A.2d 1155; we conclude that the commissioner's finding on this point was not clearly erroneous. At the time when the plaintiff was injured, he was returning from a delivery made for the defendant, and his objective was to retrieve his driver's license so that he would be able to make more deliveries later that day without violating the law. The notion that the proximate cause of the plaintiff's detour to retrieve his license was his employment hardly causes the rational mind to rebel. Indeed, there exists in the present case a chain of proximate causation that suffices to satisfy a reasonable mind.

The defendant's claim that the causal link between the plaintiff's employment and his injuries is more tenuous a link than this court has in the past required for compensation is unavailing. In support of this proposition, the defendant cites two cases in which injured employees failed to satisfy this requirement. We conclude that both cases are easily distinguished from the facts in the present case.

In *Dennison v. Connecticut Good Humor, Inc.*, 130 Conn. 8, 10, 31 A.2d 332 (1943), an employee was injured while driving a vehicle to which his employer did not allow him access because of the employee's youth and immaturity. The court noted that the employee "understood why the company would not employ him as a driver and he knew he had no authority to operate the truck on the day in question." Id. In *Mason v. Alexandre*, 96 Conn. 343, 344, 113 A. 925 (1921), the plaintiff was struck by a train while walking across the tracks. He was attempting to take an off-road shortcut to reach a doctor's office for medical treatment that would have been paid for by the employer. "In doing so [the employee] subjected himself to an extraordinary peril quite outside of any risk connected with his employment ..." Id., at 345, 113 A. 925.

*Dennison* and *Mason* are readily distinguishable from the present case. * * * In both cases, the events that led to the injuries were unrelated to the employers' assigned tasks. This is in contrast to the present case, in that the essence of the plaintiff's employment involved the possession of a valid driver's license in order to deliver hospital products for the defendant. It was while fulfilling this responsibility that the plaintiff sustained his injuries. Neither case, therefore, affords the defendant's claims any shelter.

In sum, we conclude that the commissioner reasonably found that the injuries suffered by the plaintiff clearly satisfy both prongs of the compensability test of our workers' compensation system. The plaintiff was hurt while performing a minor deviation from his assigned task, a deviation that was necessary to his job as a deliveryman. Therefore, he is entitled to compensation for his injuries.

The judgment of the Appellate Court is *affirmed.*

## Notes and Questions

1. What is a "minor deviation" and what a "frolic of one's own" for an employee hired to travel or sent on an errand depends in part on the nature of the job or errand. For those performing purely local tasks and going home each night, it is the risks of the road that matter. Other workers may travel for weeks or even months at a time on business. For them, the risks associated with transportation are covered, certainly, but also the hazards associated with hotels and other accommodations are certainly "employment risks." Consider an employee whose temporary "home" is a hotel where he stays for business reasons, but where no business itself goes on. His trip to the actual work site is regarded as part of the work, rather than being a commute subject to the "going and coming" doctrine. See the case of the young New Jersey lawyers sent to supervise a class action call center in Minnesota, *Cahalan v. Rohan,* 423 F.3d 815 (8th Cir. 2005). The more difficult line drawing for such workers involves off-duty activities that would be clearly "personal" for a non-traveler. Since a traveling worker must eat (and may even have a meal allowance) routine meals are often thought to be part of the employment risk. Going to a casino is probably not, although even that may count as employment activity in some circumstances. See *Smith v. District II A and B,* 59 S.W.3d 558 (Mo.App. 2001). The line drawing can become quite fine. Consider three sales agents who watch the finals of the NCAA basketball tournament, one in her hotel room, another in her hotel's downstairs bar, a third in a sports bar a half-mile from the hotel. Each is injured when her chair breaks. Would any of these injuries be compensable? Which?

2. Another problem is deciding when a "major" deviation has begun or ended. Consider the employee who goes out from the hotel, where he is clearly authorized to stay, to see an opera. If that is a deviation, does it begin when the employee leaves the room? Leaves the hotel? Gets to the opera house? When does such a deviation end? See *N & L Auto Parts Co. v. Doman,* 111 So.2d 270 (Fla. App. 1959), aff'd. 117 So.2d 410 (Fla. 1960).

## COLEMAN v. ARMOUR SWIFT–ECKRICH

Supreme Court of Kansas, 2006
281 Kan. 381, 130 P.3d 111

The opinion of the court was delivered by Beier, J.:

Workers Compensation claimant Christie R. Coleman appeals from denial of benefits for a back injury she sustained from a coworker's horseplay.

The pertinent facts are simple and undisputed. While waiting for the start of a meeting required by her employer, Armour Swift–Eckrich, Coleman sat on a chair with rollers, with her feet propped up on another chair. A coworker came up behind Coleman, took hold of the back of her chair, and dumped her out of it and onto the floor. The fall injured her back. There was no ill will between Coleman and her coworker, nor had Coleman done anything to provoke or encourage him. There was no evidence that such horseplay was common at Armour Swift–Eckrich or that the company had in some way condoned the coworker's actions.

Relying on long-standing Kansas precedent, the Administrative Law Judge (ALJ) ruled that the horseplay that injured Coleman did not arise out of and in the course of her employment and thus denied Coleman's compensation claim. The Workers Compensation Board affirmed.

The ALJ reluctantly relied on *Stuart v. Kansas City,* 102 Kan. 307, 171 p. 913 (1918). In that case, the injured worker was hurt when a coworker playfully threw mortar into his eye. The trial court instructed the jury to compensate the injured worker if the injury "arose out of and in the course of" employment. This would be true, the court instructed, if the coworker, while engaged in working, either accidently or intentionally struck the plaintiff with mortar, injuring him. The jury so found.

On appeal, this court ruled the instruction misstated the law. *Stuart,* 102 Kan. at 310, 171 p. 913. Recovery should be available, according to this court, only if the injured worker proved that: (1) the coworker injured him in sport; (2) the coworker had a habit of being involved in such dangerous play; and (3) their superiors were aware of the coworker's habits. *Stuart v. Kansas City,* 102 Kan. 563, 171 p. 913 (1918) (opinion on motion for rehearing).

The *Stuart* decision relied primarily on a then-current treatise * * *

This court also observed in *Stuart* that the rule it adopted was consistent with those in other states. * * * Later Kansas cases have maintained the vitality of the *Stuart* rule. * * *

Coleman argues that she should nevertheless be compensated for her injuries because she was an innocent victim of horseplay. She urges us to apply what has become the majority rule in our sister states, as articulated in Larson's Workers' Compensation Law: "[T]he non-participating victim of horseplay may recover compensation." 2 Larson's Workers' Compensation Law, § 23.02, 23–2 (1999). Two members of the Workers Compensation Board (Board) agreed with Coleman, stating in their dissent: "Because of their jobs, workers are placed in close proximity of others ... [I]t is neither unexpected nor surprising that coworkers would occasionally engage in sportive acts. Accordingly, horseplay is a risk of employment" and analogous to other risks, such as broken parts flying from machines. * * *

Armour Swift–Eckrich is correct that our precedent dealing with situations similar to Coleman's is clear and, if adhered to, would deny her relief.

Just a year after *Stuart* was decided, this court issued its opinion in *White,* 104 Kan. 90, 177 p. 522. In that case, a coworker had fastened an electrically charged wire to an iron door as a prank, which "severely shocked" the claimant. 104 Kan. 90, 177 p. 522. The court held that the claimant was entitled to recover because such pranks had become a custom on the employer's premises, and, consequently, qualified as an "incident" of the employment. * * *

The outcome and rationale of another 1919 case were similar. In that case, *Thomas,* 104 Kan. 432, 179 P. 372, a worker was compensated for injuries she sustained during a noon break when, after eating lunch, she and her coworkers took turns pulling each other on a small truck used to transport boxes. The workers had previously asked the employer's permission to ride on the truck, and the employer had approved the activity. *Thomas,* 104 Kan. at 433, 179 P. 372.

The comparatively recent case of *Neal v. Boeing Airplane Co.,* 161 Kan. 322, 167 P.2d 643 (1946), also applied the *Stuart* rule, denying compensation for injuries sustained by an employee as a result of his own horseplay. * * *

Thus Coleman cannot prevail on this appeal unless we are willing to do now what this court was unwilling to do in *Neal* in 1946: Reevaluate the wisdom of the horseplay rule. Sixty years later, we think it is time to do so.

Coleman is correct that the climate has changed since *Stuart* was decided. The Kansas rule, once in the clear majority, is now an anachronism.

As observed in Larson's Workers' Compensation Law treatise: "It is now clearly established that the nonparticipating victim of horseplay may recover compensation. The modern observer may find it hard to believe that such claims were uniformly denied in early compensation law." 2 Larson's Workers' Compensation Law § 23.02, 23–2 (1999); * * *

Larson's treatise also observes that then-Judge Benjamin Cardozo's opinion in *Matter of Leonbruno v. Champlain Silk Mills,* 229 N.Y. 470, 128 N.E. 711 (1920), is considered the starting point of the modern rule permitting recovery to an innocent victim of a coworker's horseplay. In that case, one worker threw an apple at another, which hit the claimant, a bystander, in the eye. Judge Cardozo wrote:

"That [the injury] arose 'in the course of the employment' is unquestioned. That it 'arose out of' employment we now hold. The claimant's presence in a factory in association with other workmen involved exposure to the risk of injury from the careless acts of those about him. He was brought by the conditions of his work 'within the zone of special danger.' [Citation omitted]. Whatever men and boys will do, when gathered together in such surroundings, at all events if it is something reasonably to be expected, was one of the perils of his service.... 'For workmen ... to indulge in a moment's diversion from work to joke with or play a prank upon a fellow workman, is a matter of common knowledge to everyone who employs labor.' ... The risks of such associations and conditions were the risks of employment."

229 N.Y. at 471–72, 128 N.E. 711.

Coleman also directs us to *Kammerer v. United Parcel Service*, 136 Or.App. 200, 901 P.2d 860 (1995), in which a claimant was compensated for injuries when a coworker "flicked" a plastic tag at her that injured her eye, and *Borden Mills, Inc. v. McGaha*, 161 Tenn. 376, 32 S.W.2d 1039 (1930), in which a claimant, sitting on box, was pushed by coworker in jest and the Tennessee court held that the injuries were compensable.

*Tag in eye case*

In addition to these cases from New York, Oregon, and Tennessee a large number of cases from states with workers compensation statutes similar to Kansas' have adopted the interpretation urged by Coleman. * * *

* * * We are clearly convinced here that our old rule should be abandoned. Although appropriate for the time in which it arose, we are persuaded by the overwhelming weight of contrary authority in our sister states and current legal commentary.

Finally, we respond directly to the last argument advanced by counsel for Armour Swift–Eckrich—that it makes no sense to regard an injury to a worker who is a nonparticipant in horseplay as "arising out of" employment when an injury to a worker who is a participant is not so regarded. In fact, however, it makes a great deal of sense. As observed by then-Judge Cardozo, a nonparticipant worker is exposed to the danger created by his or her coworker's horseplay through no choice of his or her own. The mere fact of worker status gives rise to the exposure; any resulting injury arises out of employment. In contrast, a participating worker makes a choice to step away from his or her status and responsibilities as an employee to engage in playful but hazardous conduct. Such a worker's resulting injury is not an artifact of that status or those responsibilities; it does not arise out of employment under the Workers Compensation Act.

Reversed and remanded for further proceedings consistent with this opinion.

## NOTES AND QUESTIONS

1. Toward the end of the opinion, the Kansas court distinguishes between the situations of participants and non-participants in horseplay. Not all jurisdictions do. See *Lubrano v. Malinet*, 65 N.Y.2d 616, 491 N.Y.S.2d 148, 480 N.E.2d 737 (1985), in which a teenager working at a gas station tried to duplicate a trick he had seen performed by a fellow worker, flipping a lighted cigarette into a bucket containing gasoline. Compensation was allowed.

Compensation coverage for an injury caused by horseplay sometimes can be denied based on the typical exclusion for intentional self-inflicted injuries, obviously not applicable to non-participants. The problem of deciding just what sort of "intent" the legislature had in mind is obvious.

If the participant/non-participant distinction is accepted, how would one apply it to the instant case? Suppose, for example, that the claimant had at a prior time pulled a chair out from under another worker, without an injury resulting.

2. The change in understanding of what constitutes a "work risk" rather than a personal risk or a risk common to the entire community has been gradual, obviously, and has not occurred at the same rate of speed in all jurisdictions. The instant case illustrates the fact that state courts of last resort are conscious of what is happening in other jurisdictions and willing to give those opinions attention, and the persuasiveness of that other precedent may be enhanced when endorsed by leading treatises or oft-cited journal articles.

3. Closely related to horseplay is informal recreation activity, often performed on the employment premises. A basketball hoop on the side of a commercial building is, after all, a familiar sight. Sometimes the recreation becomes much more organized. For example, many employers sponsor recreational activities for workers, such as a bowling league or softball league team. Although this can be regarded as a fringe benefit, work performance may be aided by the resulting release of tensions, improved camaraderie, development of leadership skills, and enhanced ability to work as a team. Workers' compensation benefits for resulting injuries are more likely to be provided if there is proof that the activity occurred at facilities provided by the employer which were made available during the course of the work schedule (e.g., during meal breaks) or that the employer urged participation (e.g., weighed participation in evaluating employees) or that the employer gained a significantly enhanced reputation or other benefit beyond the improvement of employee health or morale. See *McNamara v. Town of Hamden*, 176 Conn. 547, 398 A.2d 1161 (1978). In recent years some legislatures have reduced the opportunity for such recoveries by expressly excluding coverage if the employee's participation was voluntary even though the employer paid the costs of the activity. See, for example, *Pickett v. Industrial Commission*, 252 Ill.App.3d 355, 192 Ill.Dec. 109, 625 N.E.2d 69 (1993) and *Laurence W. Bengtson's Case*, 34 Mass.App.Ct. 239, 609 N.E.2d 1229 (1993).

4. The line between what is "personal" and what is "part of the job" is particularly hard to define in the case of workers at isolated sites—members of construction crews in deserted areas who live in employer-provided housing, for instance. The majority and dissenting opinions in an Alaska case are illustrative of the problem. In *Anderson v. Employers Liability Ins. Co.*, 498 P.2d 288 (Alaska 1972), compensation was awarded for injuries sustained  during a pole-climbing contest between two less than totally sober electricians working on Amchitka Island, one of the Aleutians. 305 F.2d 699 (9th Cir. 1962). The majority opinion emphasizes that in this remote location, the workers had little ability to conduct an ordinary social life, and that the employer had recognized the lack of amenities by itself providing a bar, in which the wager that led to the contest was made. Another case, often mentioned because of its distinctive facts is *Self v. Hanson*, 305 F.2d 699 (9th

Cir.1962). Claimant, (Mrs. Self) a clerical worker, was working on the island of Guam for a construction firm. Her injury occurred around 11 p.m., some 10 to 15 miles from her assigned living quarters, when an army weapons carrier backed into a company vehicle in which she and her boss (Mr. Muzzy) were parked. He had arranged to pick her up after classes she taught on a volunteer basis in an adult education program. Claimant and her supervisor asserted they had driven from the school in a direction away from her residence to view a newly arrived ship. The employer urged that the motive was more personal. The court stated:

> There has been some cynicism about the parking. It could be argued that Muzzy and Mrs. Self could not possibly have been looking at the ship because there were intervening high rocks that would have obstructed their view of the ship. But this may not be true. The view would depend on where the truck was parked, and the truck was only approximately located by the witnesses as to its position in the area.

> But whether it was the ship they detoured to see en route to the Builders' Club or the attraction of each other that carried them there, we hold there was coverage.

> Here was a situation where one really had no life but the company's life. Employees were restricted to a most limited portion of the island which itself provided narrow limits of confinement: its area of 206 square miles was covered by very few roads. And the effect of Guam's remoteness from other civilization—particularly Sausalito (or Palo Alto) and the mainland for Mrs. Self—was emphasized by stringent company regulations regarding departure from the island.

> In these circumstances, it is not surprising that MK–PK had to provide inducement for its recruits by providing for their recreation. This they chose to do by sponsoring organized trips and projects and supplying cars for unsupervised recreation. And in these circumstances, it is not surprising to find employees at the end of Crystal Breakwater, where Mrs. Self and Muzzy parked, for this area was patrolled by a military sentry and was one of the very few points on the island's roads where MK–PK employees were authorized to go for recreation.

> No doubt if Muzzy had been injured his case would have been somewhat stronger than Mrs. Self's. But we think in the peculiar circumstances here it was company business for him to go to Harmon and take her home to Edusa. It was company business for her to go back to company quarters from school. Further, although the road traveled was the long way around and it may have been for recreation, still we hold it within the scope of the employment.

305 F.2d at 702–03. See also *State Employees' Retirement System v. Industrial Accident Comm'n*, 97 Cal.App.2d 380, 217 P.2d 992 (1950) (ranger found dead of monoxide poisoning in back of station wagon with scantily clad companion on the reservation, compensable).

# WAIT v. TRAVELERS INDEMNITY CO. OF ILLINOIS

Supreme Court of Tennessee, 2007
240 S.W.3d 220

William M. Barker, C.J.

\* \* \*

## I. FACTUAL BACKGROUND

From October 1998 until September 3, 2004, the plaintiff, Kristina Wait, worked as Senior Director of Health Initiative and Strategic Planning for the American Cancer Society ("ACS"). Because of the lack of office space at its Nashville, Tennessee facilities, the ACS allowed the plaintiff to work from her East Nashville home. The plaintiff converted a spare bedroom of her home into an office, and the ACS furnished the necessary office equipment, including a printer, a facsimile machine, a dedicated business telephone line, and a budget to purchase office supplies. In all respects, the plaintiff's home office functioned as her work place. Not only did the plaintiff perform her daily work for the ACS at her home office, the plaintiff's supervisor and co-workers attended meetings at the office in her house. There is no evidence in the record with respect to any designated hours or conditions of the plaintiff's employment, nature of her work space, or other work rules. Significantly, the plaintiff's work for the ACS did not require her to open her house to the public. In fact, during working hours the plaintiff locked the outside doors of her home and activated an alarm system for her protection. Unfortunately, however, on September 3, 2004, the plaintiff opened her door to a neighbor, Nathaniel Sawyers ("Sawyers"), who brutally assaulted and severely injured the plaintiff.

The plaintiff met Sawyers in May or early June of 2004 at a neighborhood cookout she attended with her husband. [Plaintiff and Sawyers met socially two other times before the incident described here. Once she gave him a ride to a job interview.]

On September 3, 2004, the plaintiff was working alone at her home office. Around noon, the plaintiff was in her kitchen preparing her lunch when Sawyers knocked on her door. The plaintiff answered and invited Sawyers into the house, and he stayed for a short time and then left. However, a moment later, Sawyers returned, telling the plaintiff that he had left his keys in her kitchen. When the plaintiff turned away from the door, Sawyers followed her inside and brutally assaulted the plaintiff without provocation or explanation, beating the plaintiff until she lost consciousness. As a result of this assault, the plaintiff suffered severe injuries, including head trauma, a severed ear, several broken bones, stab wounds, strangulation injuries, and permanent nerve damage to the left side of her body.

On December 12, 2005, the plaintiff filed a complaint seeking workers' compensation benefits from Travelers Indemnity Company of Illinois, the insurer of the ACS. The plaintiff alleged that the she was entitled to workers' compensation benefits for the injuries she sustained in the assault * * *. [Tennessee is one of the few states in which disputed workers' compensation claims are adjudicated by the courts.]

Following discovery, the defendant filed a motion for summary judgment, which the chancery court granted. * * * The plaintiff appealed. * * *

## III.  ANALYSIS

### A.  *The Workers' Compensation Act and Telecommuting*

* * *

This case requires us to apply the [Workers' Compensation] Act to a new and growing trend in the labor and employment market: telecommuting. An employee telecommutes when he or she takes advantage of electronic mail, internet, facsimile machines and other technological advancements to work from home or a place other than the traditional work site. See Brianne M. Sullenger, Comment, Telecommuting: A Reasonable Accommodation Under the Americans With Disabilities Act As Technology Advances, 19 Regent U.L.Rev. 537, 544 (2006–2007) ("Sullenger"). In 2006, approximately thirty-four million American workers telecommuted to some degree. Id.

Telecommuting is a flexible arrangement that affords many benefits not only to the employer and the employee, but also to the community. Employers often use telecommuting as a recruiting tool to attract new employees, and telecommuting has been credited with improving retention, productivity, loyalty, and morale. Id. at 546. Employers often use telecommuting as a way to reduce overhead expenses, such as office space rental. Similarly, employees enjoy many benefits of working at nontraditional work sites, such as reduced travel time and work-related stress, which results in increased time for family and personal activities. Id. at 546–47. Furthermore, society benefits from telecommuting with reductions in traffic congestion and pollution. Id. at 547. * * *

### B.  *Did the plaintiff's injuries occur in the course of her employment?*

It is well settled in Tennessee, and in many other jurisdictions, that for an injury to be compensable under the Act, it must both "arise out of" and occur "in the course of" employment. Tenn.Code Ann. § 50–6–103(a) (2005); *Blankenship v. Am. Ordnance Sys., L.L.S.*, 164 S.W.3d 350, 354 (Tenn.2005); *Clark v. Nashville Mach. Elevator Co.*, 129 S.W.3d 42, 46–47 (Tenn.2004). Although both of these statutory requirements seek to ensure a connection between the employment and the injuries for which benefits are being sought, they are not synonymous. *Blankenship*, 164 S.W.3d at 354 (citing *Sandlin v. Gentry*, 201 Tenn. 509, 300 S.W.2d 897, 901 (1957)). As such, the "arising out of" requirement refers to cause or origin; whereas, "in the course of" denotes the time, place, and circumstances of the injury. *Hill v. Eagle Bend Mfg., Inc.*, 942 S.W.2d 483, 487

(Tenn.1997). Furthermore, we have consistently abstained from adopting any particular judicial test, doctrine, formula, or label that purports to "clearly define the line between accidents and injuries which arise out of and in the course of employment [and] those which do not [.]" *Bell v. Kelso Oil Co.*, 597 S.W.2d 731, 734 (Tenn.1980); accord *Hudson v. Thurston Motor Lines, Inc.*, 583 S.W.2d 597, 600 (Tenn.1979).

In this case, we will consider the second requirement first. An injury occurs in the course of employment "when it takes place within the period of the employment, at a place where the employee reasonably may be, and while the employee is fulfilling work duties or engaged in doing something incidental thereto." *Blankenship*, 164 S.W.3d at 354 (quoting 1 Arthur Larson, Workers' Compensation Law, § 12 (2004)).

Generally, injuries sustained during personal breaks are compensable. *Holder v. Wilson Sporting Goods Co.*, 723 S.W.2d 104, 107 (Tenn.1987). * * * In *Holder*, we affirmed an award of workers' compensation benefits for an employee who slipped and fell in his employer's parking lot while he was putting his lunch box into his vehicle after finishing his meal. Id. at 105. We noted that "[t]he remedial policies of the Worker's Compensation Act would be undermined if too severe a line were drawn controlling the compensability of injuries that occur during the normal course of the work day after employees have arrived for work, have started working, and before they have left for the day." Id. at 107.

Much like the defendant in *Holder*, the defendant here argues that the plaintiff's injuries are not compensable because the plaintiff was not "fulfilling a work duty" in admitting Sawyers into her kitchen. It is true that the plaintiff suffered her injuries while preparing her lunch in the kitchen of her home; however, the plaintiff's work site was located within her home. Under these circumstances, the plaintiff's kitchen was comparable to the kitchens and break rooms that employers routinely provide at traditional work sites. Moreover, the ACS was aware of and implicitly approved of the plaintiff's work site. Her supervisor and co-workers had attended meetings at the plaintiff's home office. It is reasonable to conclude that the ACS realized that the plaintiff would take personal breaks during the course of her working day including "such incidental acts as eating, drinking, smoking, seeking toilet facilities, and seeking fresh air, coolness or warmth." *Carter v. Volunteer Apparel, Inc.*, 833 S.W.2d 492, 495 (Tenn.1992) (citing 1A Arthur Larson, Workmen's Compensation Law, §§ 21.10–21.50 (1990)) (footnote omitted).

Thus, after careful review, we conclude that the injuries the plaintiff sustained while on her lunch break, like the injuries at issue in *Holder*, occurred during the course of the plaintiff's employment. The plaintiff was assaulted at a place where her employer could reasonably expect her to be. The ACS permitted the plaintiff to work from home for approximately four years. The plaintiff's supervisor and co-workers regularly came to her home office for meetings. The record does not suggest that the ACS restricted the plaintiff's activities during working hours or prohibited her from taking personal breaks. The facts do not show that the plaintiff was engaging in any prohibited conduct or was violating any company policy by preparing lunch in her kitchen. It is reasonable to conclude that the ACS would have anticipated that the plaintiff would take a lunch break at her home just as employees do at traditional work sites. See *McCormick v. Aabakus Inc.*, 101 S.W.3d 60, 63 (Tenn.Workers Comp.Panel 2000). Importantly, Sawyer's initial visit was very brief and spontaneous. Unless instructed otherwise by the employer, an employee working from a home office who answers a knock at her door and briefly admits an acquaintance into her home does not necessarily depart so far from her work duties so as to remove her from the course of her employment. This is not to say, however, that situations may never arise where more prolonged or planned social visits might well remove the employee from the course of the employment.

*[handwritten margin note: Admitting Sawyers wasn't serious dev.]*

In arguing that the plaintiff's injury did not occur "in the course of" her employment, the defendant maintains that the plaintiff's decision to admit Sawyers into her home was not a work duty. However, this argument misses the mark on this requirement because the Act does not explicitly state that the employee's actions must benefit the employer; it only requires that the injuries occur in "the course of" the employment. * * * Because the plaintiff was engaged in a permissible personal break incidental to her employment, we reject the defendant's narrow interpretation of the Act. The question is not whether the plaintiff's injuries occurred while she was performing a duty owed to the ACS, but rather whether the time, place, and circumstances demonstrate that the injuries occurred while the plaintiff was engaged in an activity incidental to her employment. Accordingly, we hold that the plaintiff suffered her injuries during the course of her employment and disagree with the chancery court's conclusion on this important point.

### C.   Did the plaintiff's injuries arise out of her employment?

Even though the plaintiff's injuries occurred "in the course of" her employment, we nevertheless hold that they did not "arise out of" her job duties with the ACS. The phrase "arising out of" requires that a causal connection exist between the employment conditions and the resulting injury. *Travelers Ins. Co. v. Googe*, 217 Tenn. 272, 397 S.W.2d 368, 370 (1965). With respect to whether an assault arises out of employment, we have previously delineated assaults into three general classifications:

> (1) assaults with an "inherent connection" to employment such as disputes over performance, pay or termination; (2) assaults stemming from "inherently private" disputes imported into the employment setting from the claimant's domestic or private life and not exacerbated by the employment; and (3) assaults resulting from a "neutral force" such as random assaults on employees by individuals outside the employment relationship.

*[handwritten margin note: 3 kinds of Assaults]*

*Woods v. Harry B. Woods Plumbing Co.*, 967 S.W.2d 768, 771 (Tenn.1998).

When an assault has an "inherent connection" to the employment it is compensable. See *W.S. Dickey Mfg. Co. v. Moore*, 208 Tenn. 576, 347 S.W.2d 493 (1961) (finding injuries stemming from a job performance dispute arose out of the employment). On the other hand, assaults originating from "inherently private" disputes and imported into the work place are not compensable. See *White v. Whiteway Pharm., Inc.*, 210 Tenn. 449, 360 S.W.2d 12 (1962) (denying compensation where a third party murdered an employee on employer's premises over a domestic dispute). However, whether "neutral assaults" are compensable turns on the "facts and circumstances of the employment." *Woods*, 967 S.W.2d at 771; see also *Beck v. State*, 779 S.W.2d 367 (Tenn.1989) (finding a random assault by a third party arose out of employment where the employment exposed the claimant to public risks).

The assault in this case is best described as a "neutral assault." In granting the defendant's motion for summary judgment, the chancery court commented: "[T]here's certainly not any evidence that this person who committed the assault was part of the working employment relationship and was not there on any kind of business related to the [ACS] or really any business with the employee." We agree with the chancery court's conclusions. A "neutral force" assault is one that is "neither personal to the claimant nor distinctly associated with the employment." 1 Arthur Larson, Workers' Compensation Law, § 3.05 (2007); Arthur Larson, The Positional Risk Doctrine in Workers' Compensation, 1973 Duke L.J. 761, 781 (noting that a neutral force is associated with neither the work environment nor the claimant's personal life). The *Woods* categories focus on what catalyst spurred the assault, i.e., was it a dispute arising from a work-related duty, was it a dispute arising from a personal matter, or was it unexplained or irrational? An assault that is spurred by neither a catalyst inherently connected to the employment nor stemming from an inherently private dispute is most aptly labeled as a "neutral force" assault. Here, the undisputed facts clearly show that the assault had neither an inherent connection with the employment, nor did it stem from a personal dispute between Sawyers and the plaintiff. Therefore, we must focus our attention on the facts and circumstances of the plaintiff's employment and its relationship to the injuries sustained by the plaintiff.

Generally, for an injury to "arise out of" employment, it must emanate from a peculiar danger or risk inherent to the nature of the employment. *Blankenship*, 164 S.W.3d at 354. Thus, "an injury purely coincidental, or contemporaneous, or collateral, with the employment ... will not cause the injury ... to be considered as arising out of the employment." *Jackson v. Clark & Fay, Inc.*, 197 Tenn. 135, 270 S.W.2d 389, 390 (1954). However, in limited circumstances, where the employment involves "indiscriminate exposure to the general public," the "street risk" doctrine may supply the required causal connection between the employment and the injury. *Jesse v. Savings Prods.*, 772 S.W.2d 425, 427 (Tenn.1989); see also *Hudson*, 583 S.W.2d at 602 (adopting the "street risk" doctrine).

In *Hudson*, this Court adopted the "street risk" doctrine, which provides that "if the employment exposes the employee to the hazards of the street that it is a risk or danger incident to and inherent in the employment and provides the necessary causal connection between the employment and the injury." *Hudson*, 583 S.W.2d at 602. In that seminal case, unknown assailants assaulted the claimant as he entered the cab of his employer's tractor trailer after purchasing lunch at a fast food restaurant. Id. at 599. The assailants did not steal the claimant's money or anything from the vehicle, and their motives were never discovered. Id. In holding that the "street risk" doctrine supplied the causal connection, we emphasized that the claimant wore a uniform identifying him with his employer, the nature of the claimant's employment exposed him to the general public, and the claimant was charged with safeguarding his employer's property while on duty, even on his lunch break. Id. at 603.

In more recent cases, this Court has applied the "street risk" doctrine in situations that do not actually involve streets and highways. For example, in *Jesse*, 772 S.W.2d at 427, we applied the "street risk" doctrine to supply the causal connection where an employee was raped by a customer on her employer's premises while she was performing her work duties as a convenience store clerk. In that case, we rejected the employer's argument that "an employee so injured must show an employment-related motive on the part of the assailant and that a rape, standing alone, suggests a personal motive." Id. Rather, we held that an assailant's motive is but one factor to consider in deciding whether an assault arises out of the employment. Id. The *Jesse* Court relied on the following rationale of *Hudson*: "the employee's visible identification with his employment and his responsibility as custodian of his employer's valuable property provided a sufficient nexus between the assault and the employment." Id. (citing *Hudson*, 583 S.W.2d at 603). The *Jesse* Court further stated that the street risk doctrine applies where an employee's "indiscriminate exposure to the general public is one of the conditions under which her work [is] required to be performed, and the actions of those persons on the premises are reasonably considered hazards of the employment." *Jesse*, 772 S.W.2d at 427.

Similarly, in *Beck v. State*, 779 S.W.2d 367 (Tenn.1989), we applied the substance of the doctrine to hold that a random assault upon a driver's license examiner, which occurred in her employer's parking lot, arose out of her employment, although we did not use the term "street risk." Id. at 371 (citing *Jesse*, 772 S.W.2d at 427). The assailant in *Beck* came to the claimant's place of employment and inquired: "Where is that mean old [claimant]?" Id. at 368. The assailant waited for the claimant who was administering a driving test. Id. at 368–69. When the claimant returned, she informed her co-workers of an improperly parked car. Id. at 369. The assailant admitted the car was his, but as the claimant turned away, he grabbed her tightly around the waist and whispered, "I want sex, sex, sex." Id. The claimant quickly pulled away from the assailant, but sought workers' compensation benefits based on the incident. Id. at 371.

The *Beck* Court found that the claimant's emotional injuries were compensable and that they arose out of her employment, reasoning that the assailant had access to the claimant because her workplace was open to the public and because her job duties required her to ask the assailant to move his improperly parked vehicle. Id. * * *

Unlike our previous cases in which the facts supported application of the "street risk" doctrine to provide the necessary causal connection, the facts here do not establish that the plaintiff's employment exposed her to a street hazard or that she was singled out for her association with her employer. There is nothing to indicate that she was targeted because of her association with her employer or that she was charged with safeguarding her employer's property. Additionally, the plaintiff was not advancing the interests of the ACS when she allowed Sawyers into her kitchen, and her employment with the ACS did not impose any duty upon the plaintiff to admit Sawyers to her home.

The plaintiff argues that had it not been for her employment arrangement, she would not have been at home to suffer these attacks. However, we have never held that any and every assault which occurs at the work site arises out of employment. Additionally, although Sawyers knew from a previous visit that the plaintiff was home during the day, there is nothing in the record which indicates that there was a causal connection between the plaintiff's employment and the assault. Unlike our prior decisions, the facts do not show that Sawyers attacked the plaintiff because she was identifiable as an ACS employee, or because she was performing a job duty, or because she was safeguarding the ACS's property. The "street risk" doctrine is not a limitless means of allowing recovery for every situation. As such, this case presents us with an opportunity to outline the boundaries of the doctrine. When an employee suffers a "neutral assault" within the confines of her employer's premises—whether the premises be a home office or a corporate office—the "street risk" doctrine will not provide the required causal connection between the injury and the employment unless the proof fairly suggests either that the attacker singled out the employee because of his or her association with the employer or that the employment indiscriminately exposed the employee to dangers from the public. The facts of this case clearly illustrate that the "street risk" doctrine does not apply. There is nothing in the record to fairly suggest or provide any weight to the assertion that the plaintiff's injuries were causally connected with the nature of her employment. Therefore, the chancery court's holding that the plaintiff's injuries did not arise out of her employment is affirmed.

## IV.   CONCLUSION

In sum, the plaintiff's injuries were suffered during the course of her employment; however, they did not arise out of her employment. The plaintiff was engaged in a permissible incidental activity at her sanctioned work site when she was viciously attacked. Under these narrow facts, this injury occurred in the course of the plaintiff's employment. However, the chancery court correctly found that the injuries did not arise out of the plaintiff's employment. We therefore affirm the judgment of the chancery court dismissing the complaint.

### Notes and Questions

1. For a general discussion of employment law application to the telecommuter, see Joan T.A. Gabel and Nancy R. Mansfield, *The Information Revolution and Its Impact on the Employment Relationship: An Analysis of the Cyberspace Workplace*, 40 Am. Bus. L. J. 301 (2003).

2. What if the "assault" is in fact a fight between two employees? The opinion above indicates that if the fight is over how work is to be performed, there is a possibility compensation benefits should be awarded, but not if the fight is over a dispute brought in from outside. What if the fight arises from one worker losing his temper over being referred to in a degrading way over and over again by a fellow worker? See *Hartford Accident & Indemnity Co v. Cardillo*, 72 App. D.C. 52, 112 F.2d 11, cert. denied, 310 U.S. 649, 60 S.Ct. 1100, 84 L.Ed. 1415 (1940); but see *Hill City Trucking v. Christian*, 238 Va. 735; 385 S.E.2d 377 (1989) (applying the actual risk test to deny benefits to a trucker who was robbed and assaulted while on the road because anyone traveling on that road would have been subject to the same risk).

## NIPPERT v. SHINN FARM CONSTRUCTION COMPANY

Nebraska Supreme Court, 1986
223 Neb. 236, 388 N.W.2d 820

Per Curiam.

Dennis W. Nippert appeals the dismissal of a suit filed against his employer, Shinn Farm Construction Company, in the Nebraska Workers' Compensation Court. Nippert seeks compensation for total temporary disability and permanent partial disability suffered as a result of injuries sustained in a tornado on October 18, 1979.

A single judge of the compensation court found, under the "act of nature" doctrine, that the accident which caused Nippert's injury did not "arise out of" his employment as required for recovery under the Workers' Compensation Act, Neb.Rev.Stat. § 48–101 et seq. (Reissue 1984). On rehearing, a three-judge panel affirmed the order of dismissal. We reverse.

Nippert was employed by Shinn Farm Construction Company on October 18, 1979. On this date he and other workers were erecting a hog shed on a farm near Wamego, Kansas. The workers were inside the nearly completed building, preparing to leave the jobsite for the day, when a tornado approached the area at approximately 6 p.m. The weather service had issued tornado warnings, but the construction workers had received no such information. The wind force inside the building was so strong that the workers were unable to move, a phenomenon apparently resulting from the fact that the doors on the southeast and northeast corners of the building had not yet been installed.

*Tornado tosses + hurts him*

At some point the walls of the 40–by–60–foot building collapsed, and the roof fell to the ground intact. Miraculously, no one was injured when the building fell. The wind then subsided for a few moments, but about a minute later the tornado picked Nippert up and hurled him to the ground some 30 feet away. Nippert's leg was fractured, and he later developed back problems.

The storm system that hit the jobsite injured 11 people and caused extensive property damage throughout northeast Kansas. On the farm where the company was erecting the hog shed, Roger Shinn observed extensive damage to two silos, the destruction of a large machine shed and barn, and damaged machinery and equipment, including a truck which was thrown into a feedlot. The storm had also destroyed or damaged buildings on two adjacent farms. The tornado's path was½ to 1½ miles wide, and it traveled approximately 58 miles.

Nippert was treated for his injuries, but he was unable to return to work until November 1980. Shinn Construction Company voluntarily paid Nippert's medical expenses as well as temporary total disability benefits and permanent partial disability benefits based on a 20–percent permanent disability of his left leg. It was not until Nippert filed a petition seeking additional benefits that the company raised a question of liability.

*Shinn paid benefits*

Based upon the increased risk doctrine, the Nebraska Workers' Compensation Court rejected Nippert's claim for benefits. We recently reviewed this doctrine in *McGinn v. Douglas County Social Services Admin.*, 211 Neb. 72, 317 N.W.2d 764 (1982). In a 4–to–3 opinion, the majority held that an employee is entitled to benefits under the provisions of the Nebraska Workers' Compensation Act, § 48–101, only when an accident arises both out of and in the course of employment: "The term 'arising out of' describes the accident and its origin, cause, and character, i.e., whether it resulted from the risks arising from within the scope or sphere of the employee's job." 211 Neb. at 75, 317 N.W.2d at 766–67. An injury caused by the elements arises out of employment only if the employee is exposed to a different hazard than others generally in the area where the injury occurred. *McGinn, supra.*

Nippert's theory on appeal is twofold. First, he asks this court to ① overrule the increased risk test and adopt the positional risk test. Second, ② if the court continues to apply the increased risk test, Nippert asks for reversal on the grounds that the dismissal was against the great weight of evidence that he was exposed to an increased risk of injury in his work environment and, therefore, that his injuries arose out of his employment.

We agree with Nippert's first theory, and to the extent that *McGinn* and earlier cases are inconsistent with it, they are overruled. In *McGinn* we were asked to adopt the positional risk test, the rationale being that an accident arises out of employment when an employee is where he is required to be at the time the act of nature occurs and causes the employee's injury. We rejected the argument and affirmed the increased risk doctrine as the law in this state. The increased risk doctrine requires an employee to demonstrate that his employment duties expose him to a greater risk or hazard than that to which the general public in the area is exposed. * * *

After careful consideration we have concluded that the better rule is the positional risk test espoused by the dissent in *McGinn*. Under this theory an employee's injuries are compensable as long as his employment duties put him in a position that he might not otherwise be in which exposes him to a risk, even though the risk is not greater than that of the general public. In 1 A. Larson, The Law of Workmen's Compensation § 8.12 at 3–23 (1985), the positional risk test is stated as follows:

> "[W]hen one in the course of his employment is reasonably required to be at a particular place at a particular time and there meets with an accident, although one which any other person then and there present would have met with irrespective of his employment, that accident is one 'arising out of' the employment of the person so injured."

The record shows that Nippert's employment required him to be in the area where the tornado struck. The record also reflects that the storm caused Nippert's injuries. The judgment of the Workers' Compensation Court is reversed. * * *

CAPORALE, JUSTICE, dissenting.

I dissent and lament the wound inflicted by the majority upon a venerable but endangered friend: The Rule of Law. *Hahaha*

Reasonable minds schooled in the law are certainly entitled to differ as to whether the "increased risk" or the "positional risk" rule is the better reasoned one. Thus, were this a case of first impression, a majority of this court would have both the right as well as the duty to choose one rule over the other. But this is not a case of first impression. Nor is it a case dealing with a nonstatutory principle of common law.

The Legislature enacted the compensation act 73 years ago. 1913 Neb. Laws, ch. 198, § 1, p. 579. Thirteen years later, this court interpreted the "arising out of and in the course of" language of the act for the first time. *Gale v. Krug Park Amusement Co.*, 114 Neb. 432, 437, 208 N.W. 739, 741 (1926), determined that to be compensable an injury caused by the elements must result from a hazard "greater than that to which the public generally is subjected." During the intervening 60 years, the Legislature has seen fit to let that consistently applied judicial interpretation of its enactment stand. * * *

It seems to me we are not free to ignore the legislative acquiescence rule at our whim.

BOSLAUGH and HASTINGS, JJ. join in this dissent

NOTES AND QUESTIONS

1.  Would the result in *Nippert* have to be different in an "increased risk" jurisdiction? What arguments could you make that the claimant was in a different situation from that of other members of the community?

2.  *A Brief History of the "Arising Out of Employment" Test and the Treatment of "Neutral Risks:"* In determining whether a risk that gives rise to an injury "arises out of employment," there are both easy and hard cases. If an employee imports a "personal risk," for example bringing illegal drugs into the workplace, that gives rise to an injury, it is well established that the injury is not compensable even though it occurs in the course of employment. Similarly, if the employee is exposed to an "occupational risk," for example the grinding gears of the machine he operates on the job, that gives rise to an injury, it is well established that the injury is compensable if it occurs in the course of employment. The courts have had much more trouble in dealing with so-called "neutral risks" that are not clearly personal or inherent to the employees work, for example slipping on ice on a public street, being assaulted by a stranger on a public street, being struck by lightning or being injured by a tornado.

Over the years, the courts have tended to expand the coverage of injuries arising from neutral risks encountered in the course of employment. Initially the courts took a very narrow view requiring that the risk be "proximately caused" or "peculiar" to the job. Under these theories, a door to door salesman who slipped on ice on a public street would not be compensable since all of the public on the street that day were subject to the same risk and it is not proximately caused by or peculiar to the job. *Donahue v. Maryland Casualty Co.*, 226 Mass. 595, 116 N.E. 226 (1917). These doctrines denied compensation for injuries for almost all neutral risks and were particularly harsh in their application to people whose jobs exposed them to many neutral risks, like door to door salesmen. As a result, many courts developed a "street risk" doctrine that said that if a person's job involved exposure to the "perils of the streets," then the he or she was covered for risks inherent to passage in the streets (cars, ice, muggings) but not neutral risks of a "general nature" (lightning, tornadoes). *Katz v. A. Kadans & Co.*, 232 N.Y. 420, 134 N.E. 330 (1922). Today most courts have gone well beyond just a simple street risks exception and apply either an "increased risk" or "positional risk" doctrine in deciding whether injuries from neutral risks are covered. Under the increased risk doctrine, the injury is covered if the person's job increased the level of the person's risk over that of the general public. For example, if the worker's job required climbing a radio tower, he or she would be covered for being struck by lightning, because the job increased his or her risk of being struck. Under the positional risk doctrine, the employee can be compensated for injuries arising from any risk which his or her job brings the employee to the position where they suffer that risk. Under this theory the employee should be compensated because, but for the conditions of employment the employee would not have suffered the risk or the injury. Accordingly the court in *Nippert* decided that the claimant's injuries were compensable, even though the tornado posed a threat to the general public, because Nippert's job took him to the position where he suffered the tornado damage.

3.  Almost all jurisdictions now employ either the increased risk or positional risk doctrines? Which is better? Which is administratively more efficient? Which better fulfills the purposes of workers' compensation? What policy justification, if any, supports a positional risk test? Consider that, prior to the adoption of workers' compensation laws, charities and public welfare programs in localities with large numbers of factory workers often were heavily burdened by the costs of providing treatment and care for severely injured workers and their dependents. Accordingly, it has been suggested that a purpose of workers' compensation was to shift and spread those costs over a broader spectrum of society. Does this purpose justify granting workers' compensation benefits to the worker who, while at work, is injured by a tornado? As an alternative approach, consider that prior to the adoption of workers' compensation programs, a worker could recover from his employer for job-related injuries only by proving the employer's fault and overcoming the common law defenses to such actions. Successful recovery, however, included collateral damages such as pain and suffering. It can be said that a purpose of workers' compensation was to substitute a less generous measure of damages coupled with greater certainty of recovery for the more haphazard common law system of remedies. Does this purpose justify granting workers' compensation benefits to the worker who, while at work, is injured by a tornado? Consider, further, that prior to becoming employed, a person enjoys full freedom of movement and activity and bears for himself the responsibility for his wellbeing. Upon becoming employed, a person surrenders much of his autonomy respecting where he will be and what he will be doing. It can be argued that a purpose of workers' compensation liability is to shift to the employer the risk of the workers' wellbeing in exchange for gaining control over his freedom of movement and activity. Does this purpose justify granting workers' compensation benefits to the worker who, while at work, is injured by a tornado? Consider, also, that prior to becoming employed, a person is entitled to all benefits of his work, but upon becoming employed, a person transfers to his employer the right to reap the rewards of his efforts. Thus, it can be asserted that a purpose of workers' compensation liability is to shift to the employer the risk of injury as part of the remuneration for enjoying the profits generated by the worker risking his wellbeing for the employer's benefit. Does this purpose justify granting workers' compensation benefits to the worker who, while at work, is injured by a tornado?

4.  If a jurisdiction adopts the positional risk test, is it also logically compelled to provide coverage for injuries incurred while commuting to work?

5.  If a jurisdiction covers leisure time injuries in remote sites or traveling employee cases, is it logically compelled to provide coverage in an act of nature case?

## (b.) Nature of Injury

The cases in the prior section show how concerned the courts were about the scope of covered claims when workers' compensation laws were first enacted. As the administering agencies and courts became more accustomed to handling these claims, and to dealing with the hazards posed by working, they became comfortable with a broader view of what constitute employment risks. It is also obvious, however, that even the courts most sympathetic to the claims of workers still recognized fully that the compensation system was limited to employment harms, and was not designed to compensate employees for harms that cannot be traced to the work. The problem of insuring that a harm is truly employment connected becomes more acute when dealing with certain types of harms: mental conditions, heart attacks, generalized deterioration of parts of the body (chronic lower back pain or carpal tunnel syndrome, for instance). The reason is obvious, is it not—there is a very good chance that these sorts of harms may have been caused wholly or partly by non-work stresses and strains. (That is also true of diseases, of course. None of the early statutes provided any substantial benefits for occupational disease as such; that would be added later, usually by legislative amendment. That will be addressed in a later section of this chapter.) The usual catchall term for these sorts of harms is "non-traumatic injury."

The cases in this section illustrate how courts and legislatures have attempted to deal with the appropriateness of compensation for some of these types of injuries. The first opinions are from an influential court that has been relatively demanding in requiring solid proof of employment connection in order to justify award of compensation. They should be read at a single sitting if possible.

## MATTER OF KLIMAS v. TRANS CARIBBEAN AIRWAYS, INC.

Court of Appeals of New York, 1961
10 N.Y.2d 209, 219 N.Y.S.2d 14, 176 N.E.2d 714

FROESSEL, J.

\* \* \*

Decedent was the director of maintenance and engineering of the employer, Trans Caribbean Airways, Inc. On November 8, 1955 one of the two planes which the employer had been operating was grounded by the Civil Aeronautics Authority because of corrosion found on one of the wings. The damaged plane was sent to Brownsville, Texas, for repairs. The employer's president attributed the damage to "sheer negligence", and blamed decedent personally therefor. At a company Christmas party, the president made "quite an issue" of this matter; in the presence of a number of persons he told decedent that "he didn't want any amateurs working for him", and that, if the plane was not out of Brownsville by the end of February, "everybody would be looking for a job." Decedent, understandably, became very much upset.

Thereafter, decedent made several trips to Brownsville in connection with the repair work. In addition, he made an unsuccessful trip to

California in an attempt to procure the required replacement parts, which he ultimately managed to obtain from another airline in Oklahoma.

On March 3, 1956 decedent was directed to go to Brownsville to bring back the plane. The employer's chief pilot arrived in Brownsville on Wednesday, March 7th, expecting to fly the plane back to New York; however, it was not even near readiness. It was on that Wednesday that decedent was "hit with the bill" for the repairs. The chief pilot, who saw him shortly thereafter, testified that decedent's face was "very white", and that he was much disturbed by the amount—$266,000. In a letter written to his wife the following day, decedent stated that he almost "fell over" when he received the bill, and felt "as if its my money I'm spending".

*(margin note: Decedent hit w/ bill)*

During the next three days decedent laboriously checked the bill in detail in an attempt to reduce its amount. Although his normal hours were five days a week from 9:00 A.M. to 5:30 P.M., he worked until late at night on Wednesday and Thursday into Friday morning, as well as all day Friday and Saturday morning. He spent many hours, together with Mr. Taylor, a representative of the repair firm, trying to reduce the amount and clear up what he deemed excessive charges in the bill. No progress was made, however, and on the morning of March 10th they "were just driving their heads against a stone wall". Decedent and Mr. Taylor had been having difficulties, and in a telephone call to his wife decedent said he was very much upset that the plane was still not ready, about the extremely high bill, and that he had a lot of people to argue with in an attempt to reduce it. * * *

*(margin note: Can't reduce bill)*

On Saturday morning, March 10th, decedent was informed that he would have to stay over until at least Monday. He was greatly depressed and aggravated, and, with fear, he communicated with his vice-president in a 40–minute long distance telephone conversation, apparently giving assurances in which he had little hope. Shortly thereafter, he suffered the attack which took his life. In the language of the impartial specialist, "his anxiety was so great throughout that you didn't need much to push it over". The last three-day period was also emphasized by two other doctors as the "climax".

*(margin note: Anxiety + heart attack)*

Although the Appellate Division, in reversing the Workmen's Compensation Board, which awarded death benefits in favor of claimant wife and two minor children, noted that there was "substantial medical testimony in this record connecting decedent's heart attack to the emotional stress of his work", it nevertheless reversed and dismissed the claim, holding that in the absence of a showing of "any physical strain" an industrial accident "cannot be made out". We do not agree.

*(margin note: Comp Board–π App–Δ Here–π)*

Despite the claim to the contrary, there is ample authority in this court and in the Appellate Division sustaining awards of compensation for physical injuries resulting from mental or emotional strain, where the evidence was clear, and our present decision merely follows those precedents. We think it may not be gainsaid that undue anxiety, strain and mental stress from work are frequently more devastating than a mere physical injury, and the courts have taken cognizance of this fact in sustaining awards where no physical impact was present * * *

In [*Matter of Pickerell v. Schumacher*] * * * claimant suffered a cerebral apoplexy as a result of fright when his motor vehicle started to roll backwards and the emergency brake failed to hold. We affirmed an award, holding that compensation may be allowed for physical injuries sustained as the result of an accident where the injuries are fright, mental and nervous shock and consequences thereof, without any physical impact or other physical injury.

In [*Matter of Furtardo v. American Export Airlines*] * * * claimant, 24 years old, was assigned to design and supervise the construction of three shops. The work was considerably harder than his former position and required unusually long hours. During the period August, 1943 to the end of December, 1943, claimant worked 7 days a week, 12 to 14 hours a day, and 3 to 4 hours a night at home in getting the plans ready for the next day. Except for the night work, he continued this schedule until June 10, 1944. He first experienced symptoms of a heart condition in September, 1943, and in October he consulted a company doctor who advised him to take it easy. The pain continued until June, 1944. On June 10th, while at home, he suffered a heart attack which the medical testimony indicated was the result of his overexertion since August, 1943. The board found that the injury was a compensable accident, and the Appellate Division unanimously affirmed. This court denied a motion for leave to appeal.

In [*Matter of Anderson v. New York State Dept. of Labor,*]* * * the board found that claimant, a supervising inspector employed by the State Department of Labor, had sustained accidental injuries in the nature of a coronary occlusion at home as the result of the continued anxiety and excessive exertion at work under trying circumstances. Here, too, claimant worked long hours and was under severe pressure and excessive strain for a period of approximately 18 months before the attack. We again denied leave to appeal from the unanimous affirmance by the Appellate Division of the award of compensation.

*Matter of Church v. County of Westchester* * * * represents a similar recognition that a fatal heart attack brought on by emotional upset and strain is compensable as an industrial accident. There, the decedent was called as a witness in his employer's behalf during the course of a personal injury action. While the decedent was being vigorously cross-examined, he became agitated and nervous and "fenced with the attorney". The board found that the severe cross-examination subjected the decedent to mental stress which caused him to suffer a coronary occlusion from which he died the same day. The award was upheld by a unanimous Appellate Division over objection that there was no proof of accident or causal relation.

In *Matter of Krawczyk v. Jefferson Hotel* * * * decedent, a cook in his employer's hotel, witnessed a fight between two other employees of the hotel. The board found that the quarrel between these two men "caused decedent to suffer from shock and to sustain an emotional upset and strain on the muscles of his heart which resulted in his death on the same day" (278 App. Div. 731). The award was affirmed. * * *

The Appellate Division in the case at bar relied on its former decision in *Matter of Lesnik v. National Carloading Corp.* (285 App. Div. 649, affd. 309 N. Y. 958), a case which, while superficially similar, is readily distinguishable. There the Appellate Division noted that no "stress is shown"; "the record shows no incident of physical stress or *of emotional impact* occurring at the race track"; that "there is certainly no proof of, any physical *or even emotional strain* at the time of its occurrence" (p. 650; emphasis supplied). The medical proof was confusing and uncertain, and was not of the same substantial, virtually conclusive nature as supported the board's determination in the instant case. * * *

As we review the cases, in none of which there was a physical impact, we cannot help but conclude that the board was right in finding that in this unusual case decedent's death "was accidental within the meaning and scope of the Workmen's Compensation Law; that the accident arose out of and in the course of the employment, and that the death was causally related to such accident". This result is not only amply supported by applicable authorities in this State, which we have reviewed above, but also by a host of decisions in other jurisdictions (see 1 Larson, Workmen's Compensation Law, § 42.21, p. 616; 1960 Supp., pp. 217, 221–223). Upon the facts developed in this record, the common-sense viewpoint of the average man would in our opinion be in accord with the board that this was an industrial accident (*Matter of Masse v. Robinson* Co., 301 N. Y. 34, 37).

Accordingly, the order appealed from should be reversed and the award to claimant reinstated, with costs.

CHIEF JUDGE DESMOND, (Dissenting).

This is an unprecedented decision. I have not found anywhere a holding by a New York appellate court that anxiety and worry associated with employment constitute without more an accidental injury justifying an award of workmen's compensation because the injury and anxiety has caused physical deterioration. Not only is there no precedent for sustaining this award, but in the strikingly similar case of *Matter of Lesnik v. National Carloading Corp.* (285 App. Div. 649, affd. 309 N. Y. 958) we held as did the Appellate Division that a heart attack found to have resulted from the mental stresses and worries of a job could not be regarded as an industrial accident.

We have gone far in other heart cases (including the decisions cited in the majority opinion) in sustaining compensation awards where there was proof of definite physical stress and exertion at an ascertainable time, but if we are to go beyond that point and allow compensation to be awarded simply for psychic or nervous strains we will be doing what Judge Finch warned us of in 1938 in *Matter of Goldberg v. 954 Marcy Corp.* (276 N. Y. 313). *We will "make workmen's compensation the equivalent of life and health insurance*" (p. 317). From its earliest days the statute has carefully distinguished between diseases on the one hand and accidental injuries on the other, although a limited number only of specially classified "occupational diseases", not including cardiac ills, were made compensable. Aside from that special list, no idiopathic disease has ever, so far as I know, been held compensable. The heart cases are not authority to the contrary since every decision in this court affirming a compensation award for a heart disability or death is based on a finding that the heart disease was traumatic in the sense of being caused by physical exertion.

There is some justification for the decisions in other States which award compensation for disability resulting from sudden and severe shock during work (see, for instance, *Bailey v. American Gen. Ins. Co.*, 154 Tex. 430; *Bekelski v. Neal Co.*, 141 Neb. 657; *Montgomery v. State Compensation Comr.*, 116 W. Va. 44). An extreme shock or fright directly caused by some work incident may have an effect equivalent to that of a physical blow. But there is nothing like that in this case. The decedent here was worried because inefficient care of his employer's plane was being ascribed to him, and he was fearful that the financial loss resulting therefrom might cause him to lose his position. Such mental or nervous stresses are of a totally different character from the work-related physical injuries covered by workmen's compensation systems. A court, in my opinion, goes far beyond its powers in stretching the Act to cover what is essentially the result of the customary stress and strain of life, not an "accident" or a "physical injury" although in a sense it arises "out of employment". * * *

The order should be *affirmed*.

## MATTER OF WOLFE v. SIBLEY, LINDSAY & CURR CO.

Court of Appeals of New York, 1975
36 N.Y.2d 505, 369 N.Y.S.2d 637, 330 N.E.2d 603

WACHTLER, J.

This appeal involves a claim for workmen's compensation benefits for the period during which the claimant was incapacitated by severe depression caused by the discovery of her immediate supervisor's body after he had committed suicide.

* * * The claimant, Mrs. Diana Wolfe, began her employment with the respondent department store, Sibley, Lindsay & Curr Co. in February 1968. After working for some time as an investigator in the security department of the store she became secretary to Mr. John Gorman, the security director. It appears from the record that as head of security, Mr. Gorman was subjected to intense pressure, especially during the Christmas holidays. Mrs. Wolfe testified that throughout the several years she worked at Sibley's, Mr. Gorman reacted to this holiday pressure by becoming extremely agitated and nervous. She noted, however, that this anxiety usually disappeared when the holiday season was over. Unfortunately, Mr. Gorman's nervous condition failed to abate after the 1970 holidays. * * *

Despite the fact that he followed Mrs. Wolfe's advice to see a doctor, Mr. Gorman's mental condition continued to deteriorate. On one occasion he left work at her suggestion because he appeared to be so nervous. This condition persisted until the morning of June 9, 1971 when according to the claimant, Mr. Gorman looked much better and even smiled and "tousled her hair" when she so remarked.

A short time later Mr. Gorman called her on the intercom and asked her to call the police to room 615. Mrs. Wolfe complied with this request and then tried unsuccessfully to reach Mr. Gorman on the intercom. She entered his office to find him lying in a pool of blood caused by a self-inflicted gunshot wound in the head. Mrs. Wolfe became extremely upset and was unable to continue working that day.

She returned to work for one week only to lock herself in her office to avoid the questions of her fellow workers. Her private physician perceiving that she was beset by feelings of guilt referred her to a psychiatrist and recommended that she leave work, which she did. While at home she ruminated about her guilt in failing to prevent the suicide and remained in bed for long periods of time staring at the ceiling. The result was that she became unresponsive to her husband and suffered a weight loss of 20 pounds. Her psychiatrist, Dr. Grinols diagnosed her condition as an acute depressive reaction.

After attempting to treat her in his office Dr. Grinols realized that the severity of her depression mandated hospitalization. Accordingly, the claimant was admitted to the hospital on July 9, 1971 where she remained for two months during which time she received psychotherapy and medication. After she was discharged, Dr. Grinols concluded that there had been no substantial remission in her depression and ruminative guilt and so had her readmitted for electroshock treatment. These treatments lasted for three weeks and were instrumental in her recovery. She was again discharged and, in mid-January, 1972, resumed her employment with Sibley, Lindsay & Curr.

Mrs. Wolfe's claim for workmen's compensation was granted by the referee and affirmed by the Workmen's Compensation Board. On appeal the Appellate Division reversed citing its opinions in *Matter of Straws v. Fail* (17 AD2d 998, mot for lv to app den 12 NY2d 647); and *Matter of Chernin v. Progress Serv. Co.* (9 AD2d 170, affd 9 NY2d 880), for the proposition that mental injury precipitated solely by psychic trauma is not compensable as a matter of law. We do not agree with this conclusion. * * *

Liability under the act is predicated on accidental injury arising out of and in the course of employment (Workmen's Compensation Law, § 2, subd 7; § 10). Applying these concepts to the case at bar we note that there is no issue raised concerning the causal relationship between the occurrence and the injury. The only testimony on this matter was given by Dr. Grinols who stated unequivocally that the discovery of her superior's body was the competent producing cause of her condition. Nor is there any question as to the absence of physical impact. Accordingly, the focus of our inquiry is whether or not there has been an accidental injury within the meaning of the Workmen's Compensation Law.

Since there is no statutory definition of this term we turn to the relevant decisions. These may be divided into three categories: (1) psychic trauma which produces physical injury, (2) physical impact which produces psychological injury, and (3) psychic trauma which produces psychological injury. (See, generally, 1A Larson, Workmen's Compensation Law, §§ 42.20–42.24; Render, Mental Illness as an Industrial Accident, 31 Tenn L Rev 288.) As to the first class our court has consistently recognized the principle that an injury caused by emotional stress or shock may be accidental within the purview of the compensation law (see, e.g. *Matter of Pickerell v. Schumacher*, 242 NY 577; *Matter of Klimas v. Trans Caribbean Airways*, 10 NY2d 209; * * *) Cases falling into the second category have uniformly sustained awards to those incurring nervous or psychological disorders as a result of physical impact (* * *). As to those cases in the third category the decisions are not as clear.

Of those cases dealing with psychic trauma causing psychological injury, *Matter of Chernin v. Progress Serv. Co.* * * * is the only one to have reached our court. There, a cab driver sought workmen's compensation benefits for a paranoid-schizophrenic condition allegedly arising after his cab struck a pedestrian. The Appellate Division denied recovery on the ground that psychic trauma unaccompanied by physical impact could not be considered an accident compensable under New York law * * * In the Court of Appeals the denial was affirmed despite a vigorous dissent by Judge Dye, on the ground that the claimant's psychic injury was a surfacing of prior internal emotional conflicts which he had previously been able to suppress. Significantly the memorandum left unanswered the question of "whether an occurrence arising out of and in the course of employment which causes psychological trauma may in any case be compensable even though there was no physical injury."

A few months later our court decided *Matter of Klimas v. Trans Caribbean Airways* (*supra*), which reinstated an award for a heart attack caused by work-related anxiety and stress, and *Battalla v. State of New York* (10 NY2d 237), which eliminated the "impact" doctrine in the field of torts. These holdings effectively eroded the underpinnings of the Appellate Division decision in *Chernin* (*supra*), and seemed to presage an affirmative answer to the question reserved by our court in that case.

Subsequently, *Matter of Straws v. Fail* (17 AD2d 998, *supra*;), percolated through the courts. This case involved a claim for compensation by a billiard hall porter who was asked by his employer to accompany a fellow employee to the hospital. En route the coemployee collapsed and died in the claimant's arms. As a result, Straws suffered psychoneurosis and was unable to work for a year. The Appellate Division denied recovery citing its own opinion in *Chernin* (*supra*), and not the Court of Appeals memorandum which had specifically left the question open. Shortly thereafter a motion for leave to appeal was denied thus giving rise to a degree of uncertainty (see 1A Larson, Workmen's Compensation Law, § 42.23).

We hold today that psychological or nervous injury precipitated by psychic trauma is compensable to the same extent as physical injury. This determination is based on two considerations. First, as noted in the psychiatric testimony there is nothing in the nature of a stress or shock situation which ordains physical as opposed to psychological injury. The determinative factor is the particular vulnerability of an individual by virtue of his physical makeup. In a given situation one person may be susceptible to a heart attack while another may suffer a depressive reaction. In either case the result is the same—the individual is incapable of functioning properly because of an accident and should be compensated under the Workmen's Compensation Law.

Secondly, having recognized the reliability of identifying psychic trauma as a causative factor of injury in some cases and the reliability by identifying psychological injury as a resultant factor in other cases, we see no reason for limiting recovery in the latter instance to cases involving physical impact. There is nothing talismanic about physical impact * * *.

We would note in passing that this analysis reflects the view of the majority of jurisdictions in this country and England. * * *

Notwithstanding these considerations the respondents argue that to allow recovery here would be to open the floodgates with no rational way to limit liability. To support this contention they cite *Tobin v. Grossman* (24 NY2d 609), which refused to extend to third parties a cause of action in torts for psychic injury incurred without impact. This assertion however misses the point.

In the instant case, Mrs. Wolfe was not a third party merely witnessing injury to another, she was an active participant. Mr. Gorman's nervous condition had intensely involved her, to the point of her being required to assume his responsibilities and attempting to comfort him. Not only did she consider his suicide a personal failure but she was an integral part of the tragedy by virtue of his last communication and her discovery of his lifeless body. The feeling on her part that she should have been able to foresee and to prevent the tragedy was undoubtedly a competent producing cause of her incapacitation.

Furthermore by seeking to apply the tort concept of foreseeability the respondents disregard the basic policy of workmen's compensation which is that if the injury was accidental and arose in the course of employment then recovery should be allowed (1 Larson, Workmen's Compensation Law, § 2). This is not to say that liability should be extended indefinitely, we must consider the record before us in light of the commonsense viewpoint of the average man (*Matter of Masse v. Robinson Co.*, 301 NY 34). It is enough to say that the claimant was an active participant in the tragedy and as a result suffered disablement, albeit psychological, for which she should be compensated.

Accordingly, the order appealed from should be reversed and the award to the claimant reinstated, with costs.

CHIEF JUDGE BREITEL, Dissenting.

The analytical trichotomy in the majority opinion is intriguing, but does not meet the basis for my disagreement.

True, the courts in this State are now long past difficulty in accepting psychic trauma as compensable even if such trauma be the sole result of a physical event or accident suffered by a claimant or plaintiff * * *. The core problem in the instant case is, however, whether psychic trauma will be accepted as a basis for recovery in tort or compensation where the trauma to the plaintiff or claimant is caused by a physical event or accident which happens to another (e.g., *Tobin v. Grossman*, 24 NY2d 609).

And, of course, the issue should not be addressed as a purely analytical one from the point of view of the logicist. The rules of law and their logic are rooted in the realities of society.

The manifold ramifications of possible psychic trauma to the preconditioned from the impact of events and accidents that occur to other is unlimited, and the lines to be drawn between those proximate or remote to the event or accident are indiscernible on any rational or practical basis (see *Tobin v. Grossman*, 24 NY2d 609, 615–616, *supra*). More important, the vulnerability to psychic trauma, and for this one needs no expert to tell us, is, as the physicians say, idiopathic, that is, causally related to the peculiar makeup of the "bystander", even the concerned bystander, who observed the event or accident. This case is illustrative. The subsequent characterization of claimant as a "pseudoneurotic schizophrenic with paranoid features", of which her "acute depressive reaction" was but one symptomatic manifestation, explains the psychological experience undergone by her after the suicide of her superior. That experience could never have occurred unless she, to begin with, was extraordinarily vulnerable to severe shock at or away from her place of employment or one produced by accident or injury to those close to her in her employment or in her private life.

It is the passive and "unconnected" status of the claimant to the accident or event which evoked her mental symptoms which distinguishes this case from others. Thus, one could agree with the truly vigorous dissent by Judge Dye in *Matter of Chernin v. Progress Serv. Co.* (9 NY2d 880, 882), and yet disagree with the majority in this case. The claimant in the *Chernin* case was the actor in and the "cause" of the unsettling accident. The claimant in this case would be comparable if somehow her conduct "caused" her superior's suicide. * * *

The holding in this case does not open a door, which a reassessment of the rule urged by Judge Dye in the *Chernin* case (*supra*) would do, but tears down a whole side of the structure. One can easily call up a myriad of commonplace occupational pursuits where employees are often exposed to the misfortunes of others which may in the mentally unstable evoke precisely the symptoms which this claimant suffered. Most important, the occasion for extension in the workmen's compensation field is less today, when there exists ordinary disability benefits as there were not in the first half of this century (see Workmen's Compensation Law, art 9).

In an era marked by examples of overburdening of socially desirable programs with resultant curtailment or destruction of such programs, a realistic assessment of impact of doctrine is imperative. An overburdening of the compensation system by injudicious and open-ended expansion of compensation benefits, especially for costly, prolonged, and often only ameliorative psychiatric care, cannot but threaten its soundness or that of the enterprises upon which it depends.

Accordingly, I dissent and vote to affirm the order of the Appellate Division.

JUDGES GABRIELLI, JONES, and FUCHSBERG, concur with JUDGE WACHTLER; CHIEF JUDGE BREITEL dissents and votes to affirm in a separate opinion in which JUDGE JASEN concurs; JUDGE COOKE taking no part.

## MATTER OF DEPAOLI v. GREAT A & P TEA CO.

Court of Appeals of New York, 2000
94 N.Y.2d 377, 725 N.E.2d 1089, 704 N.Y.S.2d 527

CHIEF JUDGE KAYE.

On October 30, 1994, while working as the manager of an A & P supermarket in Goldens Bridge, New York, claimant experienced severe trembling, profuse sweating, palpitations and numbness in his left arm. Fearing a heart attack, claimant went to a nearby hospital, where he was diagnosed with panic disorder. He remained hospitalized for five days, and did not return to work for several months. * * *

Prior to his hospitalization, claimant had been employed by A & P for 25 years and had managed the Goldens Bridge store for approximately two years. According to his testimony before a Workers' Compensation Law Judge, his panic disorder resulted from stress caused by changes in his working conditions during the preceding months. In June and July 1994, A & P replaced two seasoned co-managers with two inexperienced individuals, and shortly thereafter reassigned the store's night crew to the day shift. The night crew had cleaned the store and re-stocked the shelves at a time when there were few customers. After reassignment, their work had to be completed during the day, creating pressure to unload trucks, re-stock shelves and clean the store quickly.

Shortly after these changes were implemented, claimant began to work longer hours in order to maintain the store properly, frequently working seven days and in excess of 70 hours per week. He lost 35 pounds and had difficulty sleeping. Finally, on October 30, 1994, he went to the hospital with the symptoms described above. During claimant's absence from work, both replacement co-managers were fired for incompetence and the night crew was reinstated.

Claimant sought workers' compensation benefits, which A & P opposed. [After an initial adverse ruling, the Workers Compensation Board awarded benefits; the Appellate Division affirmed.] * * *

For purposes of the Workers' Compensation Law, a mental injury is generally compensable to the same extent as a physical injury (see, *Wolfe v. Sibley, Lindsay & Curr Co.*, 36 N.Y.2d 505, 510, 369 N.Y.S.2d 637, 330 N.E.2d 603). In 1990, however, the Legislature made a number of changes to workers' compensation, including amending Workers' Compensation Law § 2(7) to exclude claims for solely mental injuries that are based on work-related stress and "a direct consequence of a lawful personnel decision involving a disciplinary action, work evaluation, job transfer, demotion, or termination taken in good faith by the employer" (L. 1990, ch. 924, § 1). Because there is no dispute that claimant's injury was solely mental and based on work-related stress, the only question for this Court to resolve is whether the injury was a direct consequence of one of the enumerated personnel decisions. We conclude that it was not.

A & P argues that section 2(7) precludes recovery because the replacement of claimant's co-managers and elimination of the night crew were lawful job transfers made in good faith. This argument is unavailing, however, as claimant's injury was not a direct consequence of these personnel decisions. The Legislature's use of the phrase "direct consequence" makes clear that the exclusionary language of section 2(7) applies only when the personnel decision at issue is aimed at the claimant * * *. Here, claimant himself was not the subject of a "personnel decision involving a disciplinary action, work evaluation, job transfer, demotion, or termination" (Workers' Compensation Law § 2[7]). Indeed, he was not the subject of any personnel decision at all. Although the personnel decisions made by A & P regarding the store's co-managers and night crew contributed to claimant's injury, they did so only indirectly, by forcing claimant to work longer hours, take on more responsibility and manage a store that was not performing well.

Finally, although upper management criticized claimant during a number of store visits for not adequately handling the challenges presented by the changed work environment, there is an affirmed finding with support in the record "that claimant's psychiatric condition was caused by ongoing job-related stress and not by a personnel decision which altered or threatened his job status" (257 A.D.2d 912, 684 N.Y.S.2d 47).

Accordingly, the decision appealed from and order of the Appellate Division brought up for review should be *affirmed*, with costs.

## NOTES AND QUESTIONS

1. The two dissenting opinions criticize the court's majority for stretching both beyond the statute itself, and beyond precedent. How much of a shift do you detect?

2.   Chief Judge Breitel forecast a legislative backlash. As the last case in the sequence demonstrates, there was eventually an amendment that narrowed the situations in which benefits would be made available. There was not, however, a drastic change in the workers compensation statute's coverage of either heart attacks or mental conditions. Further narrowing was considered in New York, however. In the 1990s, the legislature asked for a study of the coverage of mental injuries, arguably with a view to making sure that the courts were not expanding coverage to a point such that the costs of non-work related mental conditions were being borne by employers. See NEW YORK STATE WORKERS' COMPENSATION BOARD, WORK-RELATED MENTAL STRESS INJURIES IN THE NYS WORKERS' COMPENSATION SYSTEM (1997). That report listed 21 states requiring evidence of a "physical component" as a prerequisite to recovery of benefits for mental stress harms, 14 states requiring proof that a mental stress injury was the result of "greater than everyday life stress," and seven compensating mental-mental injuries only in cases of "sudden, extreme mental stress."

3.   The requirement that a claimant must be an "active participant" in order to recover benefits for mental injuries resulting from mental stress has not always been easy to apply. In *Matter of Wood v. Laidlaw Transit, Inc.*, 77 N.Y.2d 79, 564 N.Y.S.2d 704, 565 N.E.2d 1255 (1990), the claimant was a school bus driver. While on duty driving a busload of young children to school, she came upon the scene of an automobile accident in which two high school students (whom she knew) were mangled and killed. She saw one of the bodies. She remained on the bus with her passengers, and waited until emergency vehicles arrived. The Appellate Division held she was only a bystander, and was not entitled to workers compensation benefits, but the Court of Appeals reversed.

4.   One major division among the jurisdictions is whether the stress that leads to a heart attack or to a mental condition must be "unusual" or "abnormal." In states that impose such a requirement on claimants, there is then a problem of deciding what is "ordinary" stress for a worker in the claimant's sort of job. The claimant in *Babich v. Workers' Compensation Appeal Board*, 922 A.2d 57 (Pa.Cmwlth. 2007), was a nurse who worked at a maximum security prison, where he was assigned to provide medications to prisoners kept in solitary confinement (the "worst of the worst"). The inmates threatened the claimant, threw urine and feces on him, and would mutilate themselves in front of claimant so that he had to provide care to them on the spot. One inmate slit his jugular vein in claimant's presence. A closely divided court affirmed a finding by the administrative agency that claimant had not been exposed to abnormal working conditions for a prison nurse.

5.   A number of state legislatures have amended their statutes to attempt to deal with employees who have pre-existing heart conditions that make them more likely to suffer a heart attack because of physical or mental stress on the job. See, e.g., Texas Labor Code § 408.008, requiring that "the preponderance of the medical evidence indicates that the employee's work rather than the natural progression of a preexisting heart condition or disease was a substantial contributing factor of the attack" and also denying benefits

to workers whose attacks are the result of "emotional or mental stress factors" unless that stress was a "sudden stimulus."

Courts also have often been willing to consider "life style" factors that may have been more important than work stress in producing a heart attack. See, e.g., *Bearden v. Memphis Dinettes, Inc.*, 690 S.W.2d 862 (Tenn. 1984).

6. Arguably the most extreme cases are claims for benefits for death by suicide, in which the survivors argue that the suicide was the result of job stress. See, e.g., *Martin v. Ketchum, Inc.*, 523 Pa. 509, 568 A.2d 159 (1990).

7. One reason for the different way in which mental injuries are treated may be a suspicion that such injuries are easier to fake than physical injuries. A relatively extreme example of this is a statement made by a physician, Morton Kasdan, M.D., who was at one time chair of the Committee on Ergonomics of the American College of Occupational and Environmental Medicine:

> If you look at people with chronic pain syndrome, some 80 percent of them had some kind of psychological problem while growing up. With many CTD [chronic trauma disorders] patients, if you talk to their employers, you'll find they're not model employees, they're not good workers, and there's usually a precipitating event to that medical claim, such as a reprimand, or are about to lose their job ... If the physician is honest and the employer sends in a patient for evaluation, the doctor will point out that the problem is real, but not work-related. If the problem is not work-related, the employer won't pay the medical bill forcing the physician to collect from the patient. The patient is angry because he wanted to blame it on his employer, and refuses to pay. It's easier for the physician to call the problem work-related and collect his bill. (quoted in P. Feinberg, *Are Workplace Ailments All They're Claimed?*, 39 MODERN OFFICE TECHNOLOGY, 1994, No. 3, p. 27.)

Concern about fraudulent claims has led many legislatures to include specific provisions in their statutes penalizing claimants and others who engage such practices. See, e.g., 33 U.S.C. § 931.

## (c.) Occupational Disease Coverage

Occupational diseases share many of the problems and characteristics of stress related injuries. They can develop years after the initial or even last injurious exposure. For example, asbestosis may not develop in a worker until years after he or she was last exposed on the job. It is sometimes hard to separate whether they are caused by work or other non-job-related factors. For example has a worker developed cancer because of the dangerous chemicals he was exposed to on the job, or because he smoked for fifteen years, or because he has bad genes and cancer runs in his family? Finally, because they often develop over time, it can be hard to allocate responsibility when an employee has had several employers. For example, if a construction worker develops asbestosis, should his last employer have to pay the full compensation bill or should it be allocated among the six construction employers he has had in the last twenty years? Even if it is fair to allocate compensation costs among various employers the employee has had over time, is it administratively efficient to finely hone such determinations?

Early statutes in the United States tended not to provide benefits for disease, but this has gradually changed. Some statutes cover disease through a general provision, such as the definition of "injury" in the Longshoremen and Harbor Workers Compensation Act (LHWCA):

> The term "injury" means accidental injury or death arising out of and in the course of employment, and such occupational disease or infection as arises naturally out of such employment or as naturally or unavoidably results from such accidental injury, and includes an injury caused by the willful act of a third person directed against an employee because of his employment.

Other statutes include more detailed provisions, sometimes listing specific diseases or disease categories, sometimes coupling the disease with a particular type of occupational activity. These listed disease statutes have been expanded regularly over the years. See, e.g., New York Workers Compensation Law § 3.2 (concluding with an "any and all occupational diseases" category) and the North Carolina statute in the case that follows. There are also a handful of federal statutes, mentioned in the introduction to this section, providing benefits only for specific diseases, notably lung diseases of miners.

## JOHNSON v. CITY OF WINSTON–SALEM

Court of Appeals of North Carolina, 2008
188 N.C.App. 383, 656 S.E.2d 608

STEPHENS, JUDGE.

\* \* \*

In an Opinion and Award filed 17 May 2006, Deputy Commissioner Bradley W. Houser held that Plaintiff's employment caused or significantly contributed to the development of his bilateral carpal tunnel syndrome. He further determined that there was insufficient evidence to conclude that Plaintiff's employment caused or significantly contributed to his development of gout or arthritis. Plaintiff was awarded temporary total disability benefits pursuant to N.C. Gen.Stat. § 97–29 and medical expenses related to his bilateral carpal tunnel syndrome. Both parties appealed to the Full Commission.

In an Opinion and Award filed 5 February 2007, a majority of the Full Commission affirmed Deputy Commissioner Houser's Opinion and Award with modifications, finding that Plaintiff was not at maximum medical improvement and ordering further medical treatment for Plaintiff.

From the Opinion and Award of the Full Commission, Defendant appeals.

## I. FACTS

Plaintiff, a 38–year–old high school graduate, worked for Defendant as a recreational center custodian for approximately 15 years. His duties included sweeping, mopping, dusting, polishing, washing windows, washing baseboards, disposing of trash, and removing gum from floors and bleachers. In performing these duties, Plaintiff was required to use a mechanized buffer on the floors and a machine to shampoo the carpet. Additionally, Plaintiff worked some overtime for Defendant on weekends, stripping and waxing gym floors in several recreational centers throughout Winston–Salem. His primary duty during his overtime work was to operate the stripping and buffing machinery, which necessitated the nearly constant gripping and twisting of his hands and wrists. Plaintiff performed all of these duties throughout his 15–year period of employment.

Prior to filing his workers' compensation claim, Plaintiff had been diagnosed with the following: gout, arthritis, hypercholesterolemia, congestive heart failure, underlying idiopathic cardiomyopathy, shortness of breath, chest pain, bilateral knee pain, obesity, atrial fibrillation, tingling and numbness in his hands, hypertension, diabetes, and degenerative joint disease in his knees.

Dr. Anthony DeFranzo, who treated Plaintiff for his carpal tunnel syndrome and was aware of Plaintiff's prior medical conditions, testified to the following: Plaintiff's gout and arthritis were aggravated by his employment but were not caused by his work activities; the combination of Plaintiff's gout, arthritis, and carpal tunnel syndrome resulted in a significant disability in both hands; Plaintiff's employment exposed him to an increased risk of developing carpal tunnel syndrome as opposed to members of the general public not so exposed; and Plaintiff had not yet reached maximum medical improvement.

Dr. James T. Burnette, Ph.D., CPE, an ergonomist, reviewed Plaintiff's work activities and determined that they were repetitive in nature and exposed him to an increased risk of developing bilateral carpal tunnel syndrome as opposed to members of the general public not so exposed.

## II.  DISCUSSION

\* \* \*

### A.  Compensable Injury

\* \* \* For an injury to be compensable under our Workers' Compensation Act, it must be either the result of an "accident arising out of and in the course of employment or an 'occupational disease.'" \* \* \* Although certain "occupational diseases" are specifically listed as compensable conditions under N.C. Gen.Stat. § 97–53, carpal tunnel syndrome is not among them. Thus, this disorder is compensable only if (1) it is "proven to be due to causes and conditions which are characteristic of and peculiar to a particular trade, occupation or employment[,]" and (2) it is not an "ordinary disease of life to which the general public is equally exposed outside of the employment." \* \* \*

"A disease is 'characteristic' of a profession when there is a recogniz-able link between the nature of the job and an increased risk of contract-ing the disease in question." * * *. A disease is "peculiar to the occupa-tion" when the conditions of the employment result in a hazard which distinguishes it in character from employment generally; the disease need not be one that originated exclusively from the employment. Furthermore, the statute does not preclude coverage for all ordinary diseases of life, but only for those " 'to which the general public is equally exposed outside of the employment.' " * * *.

Here, Dr. DeFranzo testified that Plaintiff's job contributed signifi-cantly to the development of Plaintiff's carpal tunnel syndrome. He explained:

> [F]rom what I understand, [Plaintiff] did multiple duties as a custodi-an using his hands to do various tasks all day, but he also used vibrating equipment like floor buffers and things. And when it comes to carpal tunnel syndrome, tools that vibrate are notorious for aggra-vating and causing carpal tunnel syndrome . . .

> [L]ess than one (1) percent-point six (.6) percent of the population develops carpal tunnel syndrome in the general population that do not do repetitive tasks at work. And there is about a six (6) percent incidence of carpal tunnel syndrome in job activities that require repetitive work. So there's about a ten (10) times increase . . . of carpal tunnel syndrome in patients that do lots of work with their hands.

Moreover, when directly asked whether Plaintiff's job duties would "increase his risk of [developing] carpal tunnel syndrome[,]" Dr. DeFran-zo replied, "Yes . . . [P]atients that do repetitive work [with their hands] have an increased incidence of carpal tunnel syndrome." This testimony is sufficient evidence to support the Full Commission's finding that "Plain-tiff's employment with Defendant . . . exposed him to an increased risk of developing bilateral carpal tunnel syndrome as opposed to members of the general public not so exposed."

Accordingly, based on Dr. DeFranzo's testimony * * *, we conclude the evidence was sufficient to support the Full Commission's finding that Plaintiff's carpal tunnel syndrome is a compensable occupational disease.

## NOTES AND QUESTIONS

1. The statute the court is applying in the Johnson case illustrates the changes in approach to occupational disease coverage, some of them favoring claimants, some favoring employers. The 2008 text below has been edited to remove a very detailed provision about hearing loss:

North Carolina General Statutes § 97–53. Occupational diseases enumer-ated; when due to exposure to chemicals

The following diseases and conditions only shall be deemed to be occupa-tional diseases within the meaning of this Article:

(1) Anthrax.

(2) Arsenic poisoning.

(3) Brass poisoning.

(4) Zinc poisoning.

(5) Manganese poisoning.

(6) Lead poisoning. Provided the employee shall have been exposed to the hazard of lead poisoning for at least 30 days in the preceding 12 months' period; and, provided further, only the employer in whose employment such employee was last injuriously exposed shall be liable.

(7) Mercury poisoning.

(8) Phosphorus poisoning.

(9) Poisoning by carbon bisulphide, menthanol, naphtha or volatile halogenated hydrocarbons.

(10) Chrome ulceration.

(11) Compressed-air illness.

(12) Poisoning by benzol, or by nitro and amido derivatives of benzol (dinitrolbenzol, anilin, and others).

(13) Any disease, other than hearing loss covered in another subdivision of this section, which is proven to be due to causes and conditions which are characteristic of and peculiar to a particular trade, occupation or employment, but excluding all ordinary diseases of life to which the general public is equally exposed outside of the employment.

(14) Epitheliomatous cancer or ulceration of the skin or of the corneal surface of the eye due to tar, pitch, bitumen, mineral oil, or paraffin, or any compound, product, or residue of any of these substances.

(15) Radium poisoning or disability or death due to radioactive properties of substances or to roentgen rays, X rays or exposure to any other source of radiation; provided, however, that the disease under this subdivision shall be deemed to have occurred on the date that disability or death shall occur by reason of such disease.

(16) Blisters due to use of tools or appliances in the employment.

(17) Bursitis due to intermittent pressure in the employment.

(18) Miner's nystagmus.

(19) Bone felon due to constant or intermittent pressure in employment.

(20) Synovitis, caused by trauma in employment.

(21) Tenosynovitis, caused by trauma in employment.

(22) Carbon monoxide poisoning.

(23) Poisoning by sulphuric, hydrochloric or hydrofluoric acid.

(24) Asbestosis.

(25) Silicosis.

(26) Psittacosis.

(27) Undulant fever.

(28) Loss of hearing caused by harmful noise in the employment. The following rules shall be applicable in determining eligibility for compensation and the period during which compensation shall be payable: * * *

(29) Infection with smallpox, infection with vaccinia, or any adverse medical reaction when the infection or adverse reaction is due to the employee receiving in employment vaccination against smallpox incident to the Administration of Smallpox Countermeasures by Health Professionals, section 304 of the Homeland Security Act, Pub. L. No. 107–296 (Nov. 25, 2002) (to be codified at 42 U.S.C. § 233(p)), or when the infection or adverse medical reaction is due to the employee being exposed to another employee vaccinated as described in this subdivision.

Occupational diseases caused by chemicals shall be deemed to be due to exposure of an employee to the chemicals herein mentioned only when as a part of the employment such employee is exposed to such chemicals in such form and quantity, and used with such frequency as to cause the occupational disease mentioned in connection with such chemicals.

Since paragraph 13 would seem to provide general coverage, what is the function of the other provisions, some of them added very recently?

2. Medical testimony is often critical in these cases when seeking to determine whether a given disease can fairly be traced to the employment. Provisions like that in the North Carolina statute eliminating the "ordinary diseases of life" underscore that concern. Phrases such as "ordinary diseases" also require courts to distinguish between "disease" and "injury" under many statutes. The Virginia court, for example, has held that post-traumatic stress disorder is not a compensable traumatic injury, but is compensable as an occupational disease. The court held that the proof established as a matter of law that the disorder was not an "ordinary disease of life to which the general public is exposed outside of the employment." *Fairfax County Fire & Rescue Dept. v. Mottram*, 263 Va. 365, 559 S.E.2d 698 (2002). The same court had earlier classed most repetitive trauma conditions, such as carpal tunnel syndrome, as non-compensable ordinary diseases of life, a decision partially overturned by the legislature, as the court notes in *Mottram*.

3. An additional category of compensable diseases comprise those that are the consequential effects of a traumatic injury. If a worker is burned at work so that she must be hospitalized, and contracts pneumonia while in the hospital because of exposure to another patient, that disease is compensable.

4. Occupational diseases are also treated differently from traumatic injuries in other ways in some statutes, particularly in reducing benefits when non-occupational factors play a role in producing disability. See, e.g., Ark. Code Ann. § 11–9–601(c)(1).

5. In 1969, Congress, as part of the Federal Coal Mine Safety Act, adopted a separate system for compensating persons totally disabled by respiratory and pulmonary disorders that typify the poor health of long term underground coal miners. These disorders are commonly known as "black lung disease." The original provisions have been amended several times. Among other things, the amendments have expanded the benefits to surface

miners and altered the operative evidence that must be presented to qualify for benefits.

The method of calculating federal black lung benefits is unique; it uses as a baseline the monthly pay rate for federal employees at the first step of the GS–2 pay level. The minimum benefit is 37½% of that baseline for an individual miner or widow, ($599 in 2008); 50% if there is one surviving dependent, 75% for two qualified dependents and 100% ($1,197 in 2008) for three or more qualified dependents.

Black lung benefits, which include a dependent's annuity as well as disability payments, are available to those who are totally disabled as a result of respiratory or pulmonary disease caused by employment as a coal miner. Total disability is defined by the Act as being prevented "from engaging in gainful employment requiring the skills and abilities comparable to those of any employment in a mine or mines in which he or she previously engaged with some regularity and over a substantial period of time." The Act further states that the fact that a deceased miner was employed in a mine at the time of death shall not be used as conclusive evidence that the miner was not totally disabled. Similarly, a living coal miner's continued work in or around a coal mine is not conclusive evidence of the absence of total disability if there is evidence of reduced performance ability. Accordingly, a worker can be totally disabled for purposes of receiving black lung benefits but still be gainfully employed. However, if the claimant receives earned income, the black lung benefits are reduced in the same manner as is used for reducing social security pension benefits due to current earned income.

To establish the right to benefits, it must also be proved either that: (1) the miner has (or had) complicated pneumoconiosis (the most advanced stage of black lung disease); or (2) that he (a) has (or had) non-complicated pneumoconiosis, (b) that that disease is totally disabling or caused the miner's death, and (c) that the disease arose out of coal mine employment. The latter causation requirement is presumptively satisfied by showing that the employee worked at least ten years as a miner. Proof of pneumoconiosis can be by x-ray findings made by specially qualified physicians, by blood gas analysis, ventilatory analysis, or biopsy.

Proof of complicated pneumoconiosis entitles a claimant to benefits without separate proof of total disability. The Supreme Court, in *Usery v. Turner Elkhorn Mining Co.*, 428 U.S. 1, 96 S.Ct. 2882, 49 L.Ed.2d 752 (1976), rejected a challenge which asserted there was no rational basis for providing disability benefits without proof of income earning incapacity. The Court stated: "[D]estruction of earning capacity is not the sole legitimate basis for compulsory compensation of employees by their employers. . . . We cannot say it would be irrational for Congress to conclude that impairment of health alone warrants compensation." 428 U.S. at 23, 96 S.Ct. at 2896. The Court also observed that the death benefits are intended "not simply as compensation for damages due to the miner's death, but as deferred compensation for injury suffered during the miner's lifetime" and as benefits "for those who were most likely to have already shared the miner's suffering." 428 U.S. at 26, 96 S.Ct. at 2897.

As with other areas of workers' compensation claims, the litigants' bar on both sides of the process has established, to use Justice Douglas' characterization, their respective "stables" of experts. Accordingly, it is not uncommon for the depositions of expert witnesses to read alike, word for word, from one case to the next with only the claimant's name and other identifying data changed.

## 4. CALCULATING BENEFITS AND LIABILITIES

### (a.) Medical Benefits

### AMERICAN MANUFACTURERS MUTUAL INSURANCE CO. v. SULLIVAN

Supreme Court of the United States, 1999
526 U.S. 40, 119 S.Ct. 977, 143 L.Ed.2d 130

CHIEF JUSTICE REHNQUIST delivered the opinion of the Court.

\* \* \*

### I

\* \* \* Pennsylvania's Workers' Compensation Act, Pa. Stat. Ann., Tit. 77, § 1et seq. (Purdon 1992 and Supp.1998) (Act or 77 Pa. Stat. Ann.), first enacted in 1915, creates a system of no-fault liability for work-related injuries and makes employers' liability under this system "exclusive . . . of any and all other liability." § 481(a). All employers subject to the Act must (1) obtain workers' compensation insurance from a private insurer, (2) obtain such insurance through the State Workmen's Insurance Fund (SWIF), or (3) seek permission from the State to self-insure. § 501(a). Once an employer becomes liable for an employee's work-related injury—because liability either is not contested or is no longer at issue—the employer or its insurer must pay for all "reasonable" and "necessary" medical treatment, and must do so within 30 days of receiving a bill. §§ 531(1)(i), (5).

To assure that insurers pay only for medical care that meets these criteria, and in an attempt to control costs, Pennsylvania amended its workers' compensation system in 1993. \* \* \* Most important for our purposes, the 1993 amendments created a "utilization review" procedure under which the reasonableness and necessity of an employee's past, ongoing, or prospective medical treatment could be reviewed before a medical bill must be paid. 77 Pa. Stat. Ann. § 531(6) (Purdon Supp.1998). Under this system, if an insurer "disputes the reasonableness or necessity of the treatment provided," § 531(5), it may request utilization review (within the same 30–day period) by filing a one-page form with the Workers' Compensation Bureau of the Pennsylvania Department of Labor and Industry (Bureau). § 531(6)(i); 34 Pa.Code §§ 127.404(b), 127.452(a) (1998). The form identifies (among other things) the employee, the medical provider, the date of the employee's injury, and the medical treatment to be reviewed. Ibid.; App. 5. The Bureau makes no attempt, as the Court of Appeals stated, to "address the legitimacy or lack thereof of the request," but merely determines whether the form is "properly completed—i.e., that all information required by the form is provided." *Sullivan v. Barnett*, 139 F.3d 158, 163 (C.A.3 1998); see 34 Pa.Code § 127.452(a). Upon the proper filing of a request, an insurer may withhold payment to health care providers for the particular services being challenged. 77 Pa. Stat. Ann. § 531(5) (Purdon Supp.1998); 34 Pa.Code § 208(f).

The Bureau then notifies the parties that utilization review has been requested and forwards the request to a randomly selected "utilization review organization" (URO). § 127.453. URO's are private organizations consisting of health care providers who are "licensed in the same profession and hav[e] the same or similar specialty as that of the provider of the treatment under review," 77 Pa. Stat. Ann. § 531(6)(i) (Purdon Supp. 1998); 34 Pa.Code § 127.466. The purpose of utilization review, and the sole authority conferred upon a URO, is to determine "whether the treatment under review is reasonable or necessary for the medical condition of the employee" in light of "generally accepted treatment protocols." §§ 127.470(a), 127.467. Reviewers must examine the treating provider's medical records, §§ 127.459, 127.460, and must give the provider an opportunity to discuss the treatment under review, § 127.469.[3] Any doubt as to the reasonableness and necessity of a given procedure must be resolved in favor of the employee. § 127.471(b).

URO's are instructed to complete their review and render a determination within 30 days of a completed request. 77 Pa. Stat. Ann. § 531(6)(ii) (Purdon Supp.1998); 34 Pa.Code § 127.465. If the URO finds in favor of the insurer, the employee may appeal the determination to a workers' compensation judge for a de novo review, but the insurer need not pay for the disputed services unless the URO's determination is overturned by the judge, or later by the courts. 77 Pa. Stat. Ann. § 531(6)(iv) (Purdon Supp.1998); 34 Pa.Code § 127.556. If the URO finds in favor of the employee, the insurer must pay the disputed bill immediately, with 10 percent annual interest, as well as the cost of the utilization review. 34 Pa.Code § 127.208(e); 77 Pa. Stat. Ann. § 531(6)(iii) (Purdon Supp.1998).

Respondents are 10 individual employees and 2 organizations representing employees who received medical benefits under the Act. They claimed to have had payment of particular benefits withheld pursuant to the utilization review procedure set forth in the Act. * * * Named as

---

**3.** Although URO's may not request, and the parties may not submit, any "reports of independent medical examinations," 34 Pa.Code § 127.461, employees are allowed to submit a "written personal statement" to the URO regarding their view of the "reasonableness and/or necessity" of the disputed treatment, App. 50. This latter aspect of the process differs from the system in place at the time of the Court of Appeals' decision. Under the law at that time, employees received notice that utilization review had been requested, but were not informed that their medical benefits could be suspended and were not permitted to submit materials to the URO. The Bureau modified its procedures in response to the Court of Appeals' decision, and now provides for more extensive notice and an opportunity for employees to provide at least some input into the URO's decision. Petitioners have not challenged the Court of Appeals' holding with respect to these additional procedures.

defendants were various Pennsylvania officials who administer the Act, the director of the SWIF, the School District of Philadelphia (which self-insures), and a number of private insurance companies who provide workers' compensation coverage in Pennsylvania. Respondents alleged that in withholding workers' compensation benefits without predeprivation notice and an opportunity to be heard, the state and private defendants, acting "under color of state law," deprived them of property in violation of due process. Amended Complaint ¶¶ 265–271, App. 43–44. They sought declaratory and injunctive relief, as well as damages.

The District Court dismissed the private insurers from the lawsuit on the ground that they are not "state actors," *Sullivan v. Barnett*, 913 F.Supp. 895, 905 (E.D.Pa.1996), and later dismissed the state officials who remained as defendants, as well as the school district, on the ground that the Act does not violate due process, App. to Pet. for Cert. 71a.

The Court of Appeals for the Third Circuit disagreed on both issues. 139 F.3d 158 (1998). It held that a private insurer's decision to suspend payment under the Act—what the court called a "supersedeas"—constitutes state action. * * *

We granted certiorari, 524 U.S. 981, 119 S.Ct. 29, 141 L.Ed.2d 789 (1998), to resolve a conflict on the status of private insurers providing workers' compensation coverage under state laws,[7] and to review the Court of Appeals' holding that due process prohibits insurers from withholding payment for disputed medical treatment pending review.

II

To state a claim for relief in an action brought under § 1983, respondents must establish that they were deprived of a right secured by the Constitution or laws of the United States, and that the alleged deprivation was committed under color of state law. Like the state-action requirement of the Fourteenth Amendment, the under-color-of-state-law element of § 1983 excludes from its reach "merely private conduct, no matter how discriminatory or wrongful," *Blum v. Yaretsky*, 457 U.S. 991, 1002, 102 S.Ct. 2777, 73 L.Ed.2d 534 (1982) (quoting *Shelley v. Kraemer*, 334 U.S. 1, 13, 68 S.Ct. 836, 92 L.Ed. 1161 (1948)).

Perhaps hoping to avoid the traditional application of our state-action cases, respondents attempt to characterize their claim as a "facial" or "direct" challenge to the utilization review procedures contained in the Act, in which case, the argument goes, we need not concern ourselves with the "identity of the defendant" or the "act or decision by a private actor or entity who is relying on the challenged law." Brief for Respondents 16. This argument, however, ignores our repeated insistence that state action requires *both* an alleged constitutional deprivation "caused by the exercise of some right or privilege created by the State or by a rule of conduct imposed by the State or by a person for whom the State is responsible," *and* that "the party charged with the deprivation must be a person who

---

7.  Cf. *Barnes v. Lehman*, 861 F.2d 1383 (Ca 5 1988).

may fairly be said to be a state actor." *Lugar v. Edmondson Oil Co.*, 457 U.S. 922, 937, 102 S.Ct. 2744, 73 L.Ed.2d 482 (1982); see *Flagg Bros., Inc. v. Brooks*, 436 U.S. 149, 156, 98 S.Ct. 1729, 56 L.Ed.2d 185 (1978). In this case, while it may fairly be said that private insurers act "with the knowledge of and pursuant to" the state statute, *ibid.* (quoting *Adickes v. S.H. Kress & Co.*, 398 U.S. 144, 162, n. 23, 90 S.Ct. 1598, 26 L.Ed.2d 142 (1970)), thus satisfying the first requirement, respondents still must satisfy the second, whether the allegedly unconstitutional conduct is fairly attributable to the State.

Our approach to this latter question begins by identifying "the specific conduct of which the plaintiff complains." *Blum v. Yaretsky*, 457 U.S., at 1004, 102 S.Ct. 2777; see *id.*, at 1003, 102 S.Ct. 2777 * * *. The complaint alleged that the state and private defendants, acting under color of state law and pursuant to the Act, deprived them of property in violation of due process by withholding payment for medical treatment without prior notice and an opportunity to be heard. All agree that the *public officials* responsible for administering the workers' compensation system and the director of SWIF are state actors. See 139 F.3d, at 167. Thus, the issue we address, in accordance with our cases, is whether a *private insurer's* decision to withhold payment for disputed medical treatment may be fairly attributable to the State so as to subject insurers to the constraints of the Fourteenth Amendment. Our answer to that question is "no."

In cases involving extensive state regulation of private activity, we have consistently held that "[t]he mere fact that a business is subject to state regulation does not by itself convert its action into that of the State for purposes of the Fourteenth Amendment." *Jackson v. Metropolitan Edison Co.*, 419 U.S. 345, 350, 95 S.Ct. 449, 42 L.Ed.2d 477 (1974); see *Blum*, 457 U.S., at 1004, 102 S.Ct. 2777. Faithful application of the state-action requirement in these cases ensures that the prerogative of regulating private business remains with the States and the representative branches, not the courts. Thus, the private insurers in this case will not be held to constitutional standards unless "there is a sufficiently close nexus between the State and the challenged action of the regulated entity so that the action of the latter may be fairly treated as that of the State itself." Ibid. (internal quotation marks omitted). Whether such a "close nexus" exists, our cases state, depends on whether the State "has exercised coercive power or has provided such significant encouragement, either overt or covert, that the choice must in law be deemed to be that of the State." Ibid.;* * * Action taken by private entities with the mere approval or acquiescence of the State is not state action. * * *

Here, respondents do not assert that the decision to invoke utilization review should be attributed to the State because the State compels or is directly involved in that decision. Obviously the State is not so involved. It authorizes, but does not require, insurers to withhold payments for disputed medical treatment. * * *

Respondents do assert, however, that the decision to withhold payment to providers may be fairly attributable to the State because the State has "authorized" and "encouraged" it. Respondents' primary argument in this regard is that, in amending the Act to provide for utilization review and to grant insurers an option they previously did not have, the State purposely "encouraged" insurers to withhold payments for disputed medical treatment. This argument reads too much into the State's reform, and in any event cannot be squared with our cases.

We do not doubt that the State's decision to provide insurers the option of deferring payment for unnecessary and unreasonable treatment pending review can in some sense be seen as encouraging them to do just that. But, as petitioners note, this kind of subtle encouragement is no more significant than that which inheres in the State's creation or modification of any legal remedy. * * *

The State's decision to allow insurers to withhold payments pending review can just as easily be seen as state inaction, or more accurately, a legislative decision not to intervene in a dispute between an insurer and an employee over whether a particular treatment is reasonable and necessary. See *Flagg Bros.*, 436 U.S., at 164–165, 98 S.Ct. 1729. Before the 1993 amendments, Pennsylvania restricted the ability of an insurer (after liability had been established, of course) to defer workers' compensation medical benefits, including payment for unreasonable and unnecessary treatment, beyond 30 days of receipt of the bill. The 1993 amendments, in effect, restored to insurers the narrow option, historically exercised by employers and insurers before the adoption of Pennsylvania's workers' compensation law, to defer payment of a bill until it is substantiated. The most that can be said of the statutory scheme, therefore, is that whereas it previously prohibited insurers from withholding payment for disputed medical services, it no longer does so. Such permission of a private choice cannot support a finding of state action. * * *

Nor does the State's role in creating, supervising, and setting standards for the URO process differ in any meaningful sense from the creation and administration of any forum for resolving disputes. While the decision of a URO, like that of any judicial official, may properly be considered state action, a private party's mere use of the State's dispute resolution machinery, without the "overt, significant assistance of state officials," * * * cannot.

The State, in the course of administering a many-faceted remedial system, has shifted one facet from favoring the employees to favoring the employer. This sort of decision occurs regularly in legislative review of such systems. But it cannot be said that such a change "encourages" or "authorizes" the insurer's actions as those terms are used in our state-action jurisprudence.

We also reject the notion, relied upon by the Court of Appeals, that the challenged decisions are state action because insurers must first obtain "authorization" or "permission" from the Bureau before withholding payment. See 139 F.3d, at 168. As described in our earlier summary of the statute and regulations, the Bureau's participation is limited to requiring insurers to file "a form prescribed by the Bureau," 34 Pa.Code § 127.452, processing the request for technical compliance, and then forwarding the matter to a URO and informing the parties that utilization review has been requested. * * *

Respondents next contend that state action is present because the State has delegated to insurers "powers traditionally exclusively reserved to the State." *Jackson*, 419 U.S., at 352, 95 S.Ct. 449. Their argument here is twofold. Relying on *West v. Atkins*, 487 U.S. 42, 108 S.Ct. 2250, 101 L.Ed.2d 40 (1988), respondents first argue that workers' compensation benefits are state-mandated "public benefits," and that the State has delegated the provision of these "public benefits" to private insurers. They also contend that the State has delegated to insurers the traditionally exclusive government function of determining whether and under what circumstances an injured worker's medical benefits may be suspended. * * *

We think neither argument has merit. West is readily distinguishable: There the State was constitutionally obligated to provide medical treatment to injured inmates, and the delegation of that traditionally exclusive public function to a private physician gave rise to a finding of state action. See 487 U.S., at 54–56, 108 S.Ct. 2250. Here, on the other hand, nothing in Pennsylvania's Constitution or statutory scheme obligates the State to provide either medical treatment or workers' compensation benefits to injured workers. * * *

Nor is there any merit in respondents' argument that the State has delegated to insurers the traditionally exclusive governmental function of deciding whether to suspend payment for disputed medical treatment. Historical practice, as well as the state statutory scheme, does not support respondents' characterization. It is no doubt true that before the 1993 amendments an insurer who sought to withhold payment for disputed medical treatment was required to petition the Bureau, and could withhold payment only upon a favorable ruling by a workers' compensation judge, and then only for prospective treatment.

But before Pennsylvania ever adopted its workers' compensation law, an insurer under contract with an employer to pay for its workers' reasonable and necessary medical expenses could withhold payment, for any reason or no reason, without any authorization or involvement of the State. The insurer, of course, might become liable to the employer (or its workers) if the refusal to pay breached the contract or constituted "bad faith," but the obligation to pay would only arise after the employer had initiated a claim and reduced it to a judgment. That Pennsylvania first recognized an insurer's traditionally private prerogative to withhold payment, then restricted it, and now (in one limited respect) has restored it, cannot constitute the delegation of a traditionally exclusive public function. * * *

Respondents also rely on *Lugar v. Edmondson Oil Co.*, 457 U.S. 922, 102 S.Ct. 2744, 73 L.Ed.2d 482 (1982), which contains general language about "joint participation" as a test for state action. But, as the *Lugar* opinion itself makes clear, its language must not be torn from the context out of which it arose:

> "The Court of Appeals erred in holding that in this context 'joint participation' required something more than invoking the aid of state officials to take advantage of state-created attachment procedures.... Whatever may be true in other contexts, this is sufficient when the State has created a system whereby state officials will attach property on the *ex parte* application of one party to a private dispute."

Id., at 942, 102 S.Ct. 2744.

In the present case, of course, there is no effort by petitioners to seize the property of respondents by an *ex parte* application to a state official.

We conclude that an insurer's decision to withhold payment and seek utilization review of the reasonableness and necessity of particular medical treatment is not fairly attributable to the State. Respondents have therefore failed to satisfy an essential element of their § 1983 claim.

### III

Though our resolution of the state-action issue would be sufficient by itself to reverse the judgment of the Court of Appeals, we believe the court fundamentally misapprehended the nature of respondents' property interest at stake in this case, with ramifications not only for the state officials who are concededly state actors, but also for the private insurers who (under our holding in Part II) are not. If the Court of Appeals' ruling is left undisturbed, SWIF, which insures both public and private employers, will be required to pay for all medical treatment (reasonable and necessary or not) within 30 days, while private insurers will be able to defer payment for disputed treatment pending utilization review.[12] Although we denied the petitions for certiorari filed by the school district, 525 U.S. 824, 119 S.Ct. 69, 142 L.Ed.2d 54 (1998), and the various state officials, 525 U.S. 824, 119 S.Ct. 69, 142 L.Ed.2d 54 (1998), we granted both questions presented in the petition filed by the private insurance companies. The second question therein states:

> "Whether the Due Process Clause requires workers' compensation insurers to pay disputed medical bills prior to a determination that the medical treatment was reasonable and necessary."

Pet. for Cert. (i).

Here, respondents contend that Pennsylvania's workers' compensation law confers upon them a protected property interest in workers' compensation medical benefits. Under state law, respondents assert, once

---

**12.** SWIF, like all insurers and self-insured employers, is entitled to reimbursement from the state *supersedeas* fund for treatment later determined to be unreasonable or unnecessary. See n. 2, supra. Because this fund is maintained through assessments on all insurers, the Court of Appeals' ruling, if left undisturbed, would likely cause distinct injury to private insurers.

an employer's liability is established for a particular work-related injury, the employer is obligated to pay for certain benefits, including partial wage replacement, compensation for permanent injury or disability, and medical care. See 77 Pa. Stat. Ann. §§ 431, 531 (Purdon Supp.1998). It follows from this, the argument goes, that medical benefits are a state-created entitlement, and thus an insurer cannot withhold payment of medical benefits without affording an injured worker due process.

In *Goldberg v. Kelly*, 397 U.S. 254, 90 S.Ct. 1011, 25 L.Ed.2d 287 (1970), we held that an individual receiving federal welfare assistance has a statutorily created property interest in the continued receipt of those benefits. Likewise, in *Mathews, supra*, we recognized that the same was true for an individual receiving Social Security disability benefits. In both cases, an individual's entitlement to benefits had been established, and the question presented was whether predeprivation notice and a hearing were required before the individual's interest in *continued* payment of benefits could be terminated. See *Goldberg, supra*, at 261–263, 90 S.Ct. 1011; *Mathews, supra*, at 332, 96 S.Ct. 893.

Respondents' property interest in this case, however, is fundamentally different. Under Pennsylvania law, an employee is not entitled to payment for *all* medical treatment once the employer's initial liability is established, as respondents' argument assumes. Instead, the law expressly limits an employee's entitlement to "reasonable" and "necessary" medical treatment, and requires that disputes over the reasonableness and necessity of particular treatment must be resolved *before* an employer's obligation to pay—and an employee's entitlement to benefits—arise. See 77 Pa. Stat. Ann. § 531(1)(i) (Purdon Supp.1998) ("The employer shall provide payment ... for *reasonable* surgical and medical services" (emphasis added)); § 531(5) ("All payments to providers for treatment ... shall be made within thirty (30) days of receipt of such bills and records *unless the employer or insurer disputes the reasonableness or necessity of the treatment*" (emphasis added)). Thus, for an employee's property interest in the payment of medical benefits to attach under state law, the employee must clear two hurdles: First, he must prove that an employer is liable for a work-related injury, and second, he must establish that the particular medical treatment at issue is reasonable and necessary. Only then does the employee's interest parallel that of the beneficiary of welfare assistance in *Goldberg* and the recipient of disability benefits in *Mathews*.

Respondents obviously have not cleared both of these hurdles. While they indeed have established their initial *eligibility* for medical treatment, they have yet to make good on their claim that the particular medical treatment they received was reasonable and necessary. Consequently, they do not have a property interest—under the logic of their own argument—in having their providers paid for treatment that has yet to be found reasonable and necessary. To state the argument is to refute it, for what respondents ask in this case is that insurers be required to pay for patently unreasonable, unnecessary, and even fraudulent medical care without any right, under state law, to seek reimbursement from providers. Unsurprisingly, the Due Process Clause does not require such a result.

Having concluded that respondents' due process claim falters for lack of a property interest in the payment of benefits, we need go no further. The judgment of the Court of Appeals is

*Reversed.*

JUSTICE GINSBURG, concurring in part and concurring in the judgment.

I join Part III of the Court's opinion on the understanding that the Court rejects specifically, and only, respondents' demands for constant payment of each medical bill, within 30 days of receipt, pending determination of the necessity or reasonableness of the medical treatment. See *ante*, at 990–991, n. 13. I do not doubt, however, that due process requires fair procedures for the adjudication of respondents' claims for workers' compensation benefits, including medical care. * * *[14]

Part III disposes of the instant controversy with respect to all insurers, the State Workmen's Insurance Fund as well as the private insurers. I therefore do not join the Court's extended endeavor, in Part II, to clean up and rein in our "state action" precedent. * * *

JUSTICE BREYER, with whom JUSTICE SOUTER joins, concurring in part and concurring in the judgment.

I join Parts I and II of the Court's opinion and its judgment. I agree with Part III insofar as it rejects respondents' facial attack on the statute and also points out that respondents "do not contend that they have a property interest in their claims for payment, as distinct from the payments themselves." *Ante*, at 990, n. 13. I would add, however, that there may be individual circumstances in which the receipt of earlier payments leads an injured person reasonably to expect their continuation, in which case that person may well possess a constitutionally protected "property" interest. See, e.g., *Board of Regents of State Colleges v. Roth*, 408 U.S. 564, 577, 92 S.Ct. 2701, 33 L.Ed.2d 548 (1972) ("It is a purpose of the ancient institution of property to protect those claims upon which people rely in their daily lives, reliance that must not be arbitrarily undermined") * * *.

JUSTICE STEVENS, concurring in part and dissenting in part.

Because the individual respondents suffered work-related injuries, they are entitled to have their employers, or the employers' insurers, pay for whatever "reasonable" and "necessary" treatment they may need. Pa. Stat. Ann., Tit. 77, §§ 531(1)(i), (5) (Purdon Supp.1998). That right—whether described as a "claim" for payment or a "cause of action"—is unquestionably a species of property protected by the Due Process Clause of the Fourteenth Amendment. See, e.g., *Tulsa Professional Collection Services, Inc. v. Pope*, 485 U.S. 478, 485, 108 S.Ct. 1340, 99 L.Ed.2d 565 (1988). Disputes over the reasonableness or necessity of particular treat-

---

**14.** I agree with Justice Stevens that, although Pennsylvania's original procedure was deficient, the dispute resolution process now in place meets the constitutional requirement. See post, at 992 (opinion concurring in part and dissenting in part).

ments are resolved by decision makers who are state actors and who must follow procedures established by Pennsylvania law. Because the resolution of such disputes determines the scope of the claimants' property interests, the Constitution requires that the procedure be fair. *Logan v. Zimmerman Brush Co.*, 455 U.S. 422, 102 S.Ct. 1148, 71 L.Ed.2d 265 1982). That is true whether the claim is asserted against a private insurance carrier or against a public entity that self-insures. It is equally clear that the State's duty to establish and administer a fair procedure for resolving the dispute obtains whether the dispute is initiated by the filing of a claim or by an insurer's decision to withhold payment until the reasonableness issue is resolved.

In my judgment, the significant questions raised by this case are: (1) as in any case alleging that state statutory processes violate the Fourteenth Amendment, whether Pennsylvania's procedure was fair when the case was commenced, and (2), if not, whether it was fair after the State modified its rules in response to the Court of Appeals' decision. * * * In my opinion, the Court of Appeals correctly concluded that the original procedure was deficient because it did not give employees either notice that a request for utilization review would automatically suspend their benefits or an opportunity to provide relevant evidence and argument to the state actor vested with initial decisional authority. * * * I do not, however, find any constitutional defect in the procedures that are now in place, and therefore agree that the judgment should be reversed to the extent that it requires any additional modifications. It is not unfair, in and of itself, for a State to allow either a private or a publicly owned party to withhold payment of a state-created entitlement pending resolution of a dispute over its amount. * * *

### NOTES AND QUESTIONS

1. The Pennsylvania statute is typical in requiring that the employer bear the entire cost of medical treatment of injuries covered by workers' compensation. How does this differ from the obligation of a vessel to provide medical treatment under the doctrine of maintenance and cure?

2. Changes in the ways medical care is provided have required amendments to many workers' compensation statutes. The principal case is an illustration: In 1914, the concept of a utilization review procedure would have seemed very strange indeed. Most early statutes were written using private physician fee-for-service as the most common model for providing medical benefits, although most could also accommodate providing health care through a salaried doctor or an employer-owned hospital or clinic. (Those were not unusual in railroading and mining settings.) Managed Care Organizations (MCOs), such as Health Maintenance Organizations (HMOs) and Preferred Provider Organizations (PPOs), were unknown. (The origins of HMOs are disputed, but it is clear there was no widespread use of HMOs until around the time of the enactment of the Health Maintenance Organization Act of 1973, 42 U.S.C. § 300e.) Employers that provide health care through

such institutions are now commonly permitted to use those same institutions to provide workers' compensation medical benefits.

A host of cost control devices appear in workers compensation statutes, many added since 1990. Requirements that medical care providers not charge employers more than their ordinary fees, agency supervision or setting of permitted charges, and utilization reviews of the kind used in Pennsylvania are all being tried as means of cost containment.

3.  Problems arise regularly concerning what constitutes "medical" treatment. Many statutes now specifically deal with such issues as whether homeopathic medicine, treatment by Christian Science practitioners, and other less traditional practices qualify. Insurers have been particularly troubled by counting as "medical" the major renovation of an injured worker's residence to make it more "user friendly" to a disabled person. See, e.g., *Squeo v. Comfort Control Corp.*, 99 N.J. 588, 494 A.2d 313 (1985).

## (b.) Disability Benefits

### JONES v. CRENSHAW

Supreme Court of Tennessee, 1983
645 S.W.2d 238

LLOYD TATUM, SPECIAL JUDGE.

This is a worker's compensation case. It was stipulated that the appellant, Jack Jones, was permanently and totally disabled in a compensable accident that occurred on April 9, 1980 while in the employ of the appellees, Crenshaw and Wortham. The issues presented to us require our determination of whether the trial judge properly computed the appellant's average weekly wage and whether the trial court erred in crediting the appellees with payments made for temporary total disability benefits against the award for permanent total disability benefits. We find that the Circuit Court erred in computing the average weekly wage and that recovery may be had for both temporary total and permanent total disability. * * *

[Discussion of computation errors omitted.]

The appellant next insists that the trial court erred in subtracting 70 weeks' compensation for temporary total disability from 400 weeks' compensation for permanent total disability. We agree with the appellant that temporary total disability benefits are not to be deducted.

The leading case on this question is *Redmond v. McMinn County*, 209 Tenn. 463, 354 S.W.2d 435 (1962). In holding that compensation may be allowed for both temporary total disability and permanent total disability, this court said:

"Our Workmen's Compensation statute (T.C.A. § 50–1007(a), (b), (c), (d)), like the statutes of a number of other states, classifies compensable disabilities into these four distinct classes: '(a) temporary total disability' '(b) temporary partial disability,' '(c) permanent partial disability,' and '(d) permanent total disability.' (citations omitted.)

*[handwritten: 4 types of disability]*

Each of these four kinds of disability is separate and distinct and is separately compensated for by different methods provided by the several sub-sections of § 50–1007; and each of such provisions is independent and unrelated. (citations omitted.)" * * *

"Under statutes like ours, 'temporary total disability' refers to the injured employee's condition while disabled to work by his injury and until he recovers as far as the nature of his injury permits; and it is separate and distinct from any of the other four kinds of disability." * * *

"Under our statute, compensations may be allowed an employee both for '(a) temporary total disability' and '(c) permanent partial disability' as a result of the same injury; *and one is not to be deducted from or credited on the other.* T.C.A. § 50–1007(a), (c). (citations omitted.) (emphasis supplied)

And it seems equally clear that, under the separate provisions of our statute (§ 50–1007(a), (d)), compensations may likewise be allowed for '(a) temporary total disability' and '(d) permanent total disability' as a result of the same injury."

The *Redmond* court held that both types of permanent disability were allowed even though they together exceeded the maximum allowable under subsection (d) of T.C.A. § 50–1007. By a subsequent amendment to T.C.A. § 50–1005, the total liability of the employer for temporary total and permanent total benefits cannot exceed the maximum compensation as specified in T.C.A. § 50–1005(b). * * *

We reaffirm the holding of *Redmond v. McMinn County, supra,* with the modification that the total liability of the employer for temporary total disability and permanent total disability is limited to the maximum specified in T.C.A. § 50–1005(b).

However, we cannot determine the amount of temporary total disability to which the appellant is entitled. The judgment recites that the appellant had been paid compensation for 70 weeks prior to trial but there is no indication in the judgment or elsewhere, as to whether this compensation was for temporary total or permanent total disability. The briefs suggest that both parties might have taken this to be for temporary total disability. There is no evidence in the record concerning the amount of temporary total disability sustained by the appellant, if any. Stipulations in the record indicate that neither party contemplated this to be an issue prior to trial and the dispute apparently first arose when the final judgment was entered. We must, therefore, remand for clarification of that question. * * *

## NOTES AND QUESTIONS

1. A substantial number of jurisdictions, though not all, require payments for temporary disability to be credited to the amount due for permanent disability. The permanency of some injuries is quite apparent, as in the case of an amputation, but the recuperative capacity of individuals and the curative skills of different medical treatment teams can vary greatly. In cases such as *Jones*, what sort of proof should govern to determine when a disability was transformed from temporary to permanent? What impact does a decision such as *Jones* have upon the claimant's receptiveness to proposed methods of treatment or to commencing vocational retraining?

2. The 400 week benefit limit described in *Jones* expires in a little over 7 1/2 years; the temporary total disability benefit in less than a year and a half. How adequate would such a program be in compensating a claimant such as Mr. Squeo, the quadriplegic worker in the New Jersey case cited in note 3 following the prior case (requiring his employer to perform extensive renovation and addition to his home)?

Many statutes do not include "caps" on total liability like the 400 week limit in the Tennessee statute. All, however, have a cap on the maximum weekly benefit. Sometimes that is set as a dollar figure, sometimes as a multiple of average weekly wages (usually in some specified type of employment) in the relevant jurisdiction.

3. Some argue that under-compensation for injuries provides an incentive for workers to be more careful of themselves and co-workers. Others argue that higher compensation for injuries provides an incentive for employers to emphasize accident prevention. Between the early 1970s and the mid–1980s, workers' compensation wage replacement benefits levels as a percentage of the worker's average gross wage increased in thirteen states and remained unchanged in the rest. Although this suggests an overall improvement in such benefits, annually compiled data of occupational injury and illness recordable under OSHA shows that in 1972 there were 3.3 lost work day cases per 100 workers. In 1985 this rate had increased to 4.4 cases, and in 1991 it had increased to 5.5 cases. In addition, the same data reported 47.9 lost work days per 100 workers in 1972, 77.6 lost work days per 100 workers in 1985, and 119.7 lost work days per 100 workers in 1991. It should be noted that during this same period there was a considerable shift of employment away from manufacturing jobs and into service jobs. Improvements in OSHA data reporting and collection may account for part of the recorded change in injury and illness rates. However, it is not the only relevant data suggesting a relationship between workers' compensation benefits and injury rates. Studies of worker compensation systems show that an increase in workers' compensation benefits is accompanied by an increase in the number of claims and longer duration of disability. Are there alternative explanations for these findings? Studies have also shown that higher wage earners experience shorter durations of disability leave than do lower wage earners who suffered the same type of injury. What, if anything, does that finding contribute to your understanding of the relationship between the level of benefits and injury avoidance behavior? Assuming that some workers use disability bene-

fits as a "ticket out of the labor force," does that justify reducing benefits rates or does it call for alternative strategies to improve safety?

## KEENAN v. DIRECTOR FOR THE BENEFITS REVIEW BOARD

United States Court of Appeals, Ninth Circuit, 2004
392 F.3d 1041

GOODWIN, CIRCUIT JUDGE.

This appeal presents the following questions: (1) whether petitioner's shoulder impairment should be compensated as a scheduled disability of the arm under 33 U.S.C. § 908(c)(1); (2) in the alternative, whether he is entitled to unscheduled compensation under 33 U.S.C. § 908(c)(21) on the ground that his shoulder injury prevented him from accepting a more lucrative foreman's position; and (3) whether, if neither form of compensation is granted, petitioner is entitled to a *de minimis* award under 33 U.S.C. § 908(c)(21). * * *

## I. FACTS

Kevin Keenan, then employed as a longshoreman for Eagle Marine Services, suffered a right shoulder injury on January 21, 1988. He underwent two surgeries, experiencing a period of temporary total disability and reaching maximum medical improvement on November 28, 1990. Residual symptoms and partial impairment persist, requiring Keenan to desist from heavy or repetitive overhead work and making it difficult for him to perform strength related activities, especially above chest level. Still, Keenan initially returned to work as a longshoreman, working under medical restrictions, until he was able to secure a mostly clerical position with Eagle, which he continues to hold. Keenan earns significantly more in his new position as a Marine Clerk than he did as a longshoreman, and has no physical trouble performing the job. * * *

## II. ADMINISTRATIVE HISTORY

The dispute arose with respect to Keenan's claim for continuing disability benefits beyond the November 28, 1990 maximum medical improvement point. Keenan argues that he is entitled to receive scheduled benefits from Eagle for permanent partial disability to his arm under 33 U.S.C. § 908(c)(1), or alternatively, that he is entitled to unscheduled benefits for permanent partial disability as defined by his economic losses under 33 U.S.C. § 908(c)(21). In her original decision, the Administrative Law Judge ("ALJ") determined that Keenan's shoulder injury was unscheduled and thus compensable only under 33 U.S.C. § 908(c)(21). She then found that since Keenan suffered no loss in post-injury earning capacity, he was not entitled to unscheduled benefits either. Finally, she awarded Keenan a *de minimis* award of $1/week, as well as medical benefits pursuant to 33 U.S.C. § 907 and attorneys' fees and expenses.

Both parties appealed to the Benefits Review Board ("the Board"). The Board affirmed all of the ALJ's determinations, save the *de minimis* award * * *. During the time the Board's decision was on appeal to the Ninth Circuit, which dismissed the petition for lack of a final appealable order, the Supreme Court had again spoken in *Rambo*, in a decision styled *Metropolitan Stevedore Company v. Rambo*, 521 U.S. 121, 117 S.Ct. 1953, 138 L.Ed.2d 327 (1997) ( "*Rambo II*"). Before the ALJ on remand, Keenan raised a new basis for his § 908(c)(21) claim, namely, that he had been forced to pass up a recent foreman promotion due to his disability. In her second opinion, the ALJ denied this claim as well as the renewed claim for the *de minimis* award. In light of these decisions, the ALJ also declined to reinstate the attorneys' fee award. The Board affirmed on each ground. Keenan timely appeals.

## III.   DISCUSSION

The Longshore and Harbor Workers' Compensation Act, 33 U.S.C. 901 et seq., provides for compensation for permanent partial disabilities resulting from both "scheduled" and "unscheduled" injuries. Disabilities resulting from scheduled injuries are compensated at the rate of 2/3 of average weekly wages at the time of injury for a specified number of weeks, regardless of post-injury earning capacity. Meanwhile, disabilities resulting from unscheduled injuries are compensated at the rate of 2/3 of the *difference* between average weekly wages at the time of injury and post-injury earning capacity, for as long as the disability should last, which is to say in the case of permanent disabilities, indefinitely. The general principle is that the Act should be construed broadly and liberally in light of its purpose of compensating disabled workers, eschewing interpretive nitpicking at the expense of the injured employee. * * *

However, one form of recovery invokes a mechanical formula and the other employs a fact-dependent test; thus, the rule that is the more beneficent in one case may turn out to be less beneficent in another. Indeed, the Supreme Court has acknowledged that the interaction of the schedule and the economic loss formula can produce results that are "incongruous" and even "unfair," and that this in turn poses a dilemma for the courts. *Pepco[ v. Director, OWCP*], 449 U.S. at 282–283, 101 S.Ct. 509 (1980). Because his post-injury earning capacity exceeds his pre-injury wages, Keenan is obviously benefitted by characterizing his injury as scheduled. Yet there are many cases in which present earnings are sufficiently depressed below pre-injury levels to cause the worker to benefit from characterizing his injury as *un*scheduled. The interpretive principle of beneficence is therefore of little help in resolving statutory ambiguities to decide whether a shoulder injury should be treated as scheduled or unscheduled.

We review the Board's decision "for errors of law and adherence to the substantial evidence standard," and should "respect the Board's interpretation of the statute where that interpretation is reasonable and reflects the policy underlying the statute." *Sestich v. Long Beach Container Terminal*, 289 F.3d 1157, 1159 (9th Cir.2002) * * *.

### 1.  Benefits to compensate a scheduled injury under 33 U.S.C. § 908(c)(1)

The question whether Keenan is entitled to scheduled recovery turns on whether his injury qualifies as a partial loss of an arm under § 908(c)(1). The Act provides:

> (c) Permanent partial disability: In case of disability partial in character but permanent in quality the compensation shall be 66 2/3 per centum of the average weekly wages, which shall be in addition to compensation for temporary total disability or temporary partial disability paid in accordance with subdivision (b) or subdivision (e) of this section, respectively, and shall be paid to the employee, as follows:
>
> (1) Arm lost, three hundred and twelve weeks' compensation . . .

33 U.S.C. § 908.

Keenan makes two arguments in support of his claim that his injury should be compensated under § 908(c)(1). First, he argues that the resultant impairment in the use of his arm below the shoulder entitles him to recovery under the meaning of "arm lost." Second, he argues that the shoulder injury itself qualifies as an injury to the arm, insofar as the shoulder is a part of the arm within the meaning of the Act.

As to the first argument, it is relatively well-settled, despite some ambiguity in the statutory language, that an injury to Body Part X resulting in a functional impairment to Body Part Y will be classified according to X and not according to Y under the schedule. Our Circuit was the first to articulate this "situs of the injury" rule, in *Long v. Director, OWCP*, 767 F.2d 1578 (9th Cir.1985), which construed the Act to mandate recovery under § 908(c)(21) rather than under the schedule "for impairments to limbs caused by an accidental injury to a part of the body not specified in the schedule." 767 F.2d at 1582. Since then, the First and Fifth Circuits have both followed *Long*, while no other circuit has taken a contravening approach. * * *

The situs of the injury rule establishes that Keenan cannot recover for his shoulder injury under the schedule on the basis of resultant impairment to his lower arm. However, it does not answer the question whether the shoulder should be considered part of the arm. Keenan asks us to reach this question here.

Keenan's second assertion, that the shoulder is a part of the arm under the meaning of the Act, effectively requires this Court to reject a line of cases holding that a shoulder injury is unscheduled. No Ninth Circuit decision has explicitly held that the shoulder is, or is not, part of the arm for the purposes of § 908(c)(1). Other circuits that have considered how to classify shoulder injuries under the Act have held that they are *per se* unscheduled, without deciding that the shoulder is not a part of the arm. * * * While none of these decisions squarely state that the shoulder is not part of the arm, the proposition is plainly implicit in their conclusions. A survey of relevant medical sources reveals at best an ambiguity in the nomenclature; a mere lexical uncertainty, however, is not sufficiently compelling to reject the clear rule adopted by the Board in *Grimes* and endorsed by our sister circuits. We decline to do so in this case.

### 2. Benefits to compensate an unscheduled injury under 33 U.S.C. § 908(c)(21)

Keenan argues that he should collect § 908(c)(21) benefits according to a hypothetical damages formula, under which the employer must compensate him for the difference between his actual economic position and his hypothetical economic position, which he would have enjoyed but for the injury. However, the statutory formula contemplates wages at time of injury, rather than projected present wages, as the relevant baseline for comparison to actual present earning capacity. 33 U.S.C. § 908(c)(21). Our Circuit recently made explicit this relatively straightforward reading of the statute, ratifying the rule expressed in a number of earlier Board decisions, by holding that under the Act:

> Disability is not defined, as it would be under the tort system, as the inability to earn hypothetical wages that the worker could have earned if he had not been injured. Rather, disability is defined under the Act as the difference between the employee's pre-injury average weekly wages and his post-injury wage-earning capacity.

*Sestich*, 289 F.3d at 1160 (internal quotations omitted). For an unscheduled injury, therefore, the employer is obligated to compensate the worker only up to the level of his wages at time of injury, as the Board and the ALJ correctly held.

* * * It is undisputed that Keenan's actual present wages are significantly higher than his pre-injury wages, and he makes no argument that they do not fairly and reasonably represent his present earning capacity. Therefore, he is not entitled to recovery under § 908(c)(21).

### 3. De minimis award under 33 U.S.C. § 908(c)(21)

The Supreme Court, in *Rambo II*, has clearly endorsed the concept of nominal compensation in cases where the worker suffers a permanent physical disability, but has not yet suffered an economic loss, as the only means of honoring

> the Act's mandate to account for the future effects of disability in fashioning an award, since those effects would not be reflected in the current award and the 1–year statute of limitations for modification after denial of compensation would foreclose responding to such effects on a wait-and-see basis as they might arise.

521 U.S. at 134, 117 S.Ct. 1953. The Court also clarified that "a disability whose substantial [economic] effects are only potential is nonetheless a present disability, albeit a presently nominal one." Id. at 135, 117 S.Ct. 1953. The mechanism of nominal compensation thus neatly reconciles two statutory directives: (1) that awards must account for future economic effects, even potential ones; and (2) that compensable "disabilities" under the Act are economic, not physical, in nature. In the words of the Court, "[i]t is simply reasonable and in the interest of justice (to use the language of § 8(h)) to reflect merely nominal current disability with a correspondingly nominal award." Id. (internal quotations omitted).

The test for nominal compensation is that "there is significant potential that the injury will cause diminished capacity under future conditions" in cases where current earnings exceed pre-injury earnings, thus presently precluding § 908(c)(21) recovery. 521 U.S. at 138, 117 S.Ct. 1953. While the possibility of future decline in wages is "not to be assumed *pro forma* as an administrative convenience in the run of cases," the *Rambo II* test is a liberal one—as befits a conservative award that has no present effect on the parties' interests but simply embodies a "wait-and-see approach to provide for the future effects." Id. at 139, 135, 117 S.Ct. 1953. The existence of a permanent partial disability, moreover, is a crucial factor in the inquiry. The Court held that because Rambo's physical condition had not improved to the point of full recovery, the possibility of future economic loss had been sufficiently raised. * * * Keenan's position is precisely analogous to Rambo's. The Court could not have made it clearer that present employment in which the worker is able to avoid using the impaired body part, far from removing the basis for a *de minimis* award, is exactly the circumstance for which nominal compensation is designed.

* * * If there is a chance of future changed circumstances which, together with the continuing effects of Keenan's injury, create a "significant potential" of future depressed earning capacity, then Keenan is entitled to the possibility of a future modified award under *Rambo II*. That eventuality would come about were Keenan to lose his clerical position due to changed market conditions and find himself on the open market for a longshoreman job, which his physical impairment very possibly would not allow him to perform. This concern, indeed, was acknowledged by the ALJ herself in her original decision, which found that changing market conditions, free trade concerns, and other factors created sufficient doubt to justify a *de minimis* award. While Keenan was not employed as a Marine Clerk at that time, many of the findings—e.g., the likely future market share of the Port, Keenan's work restrictions, and permanent partial disability involving shoulder and arm—apply equally to the present state of affairs. In fact, the ALJ did not withdraw any of her earlier findings; she found only that the additional passage of time outweighed them. However, unless the passage of time has directly removed one of the relevant factors—for example, if some of Keenan's work restrictions were removed, or if market conditions changed for the bet-

ter—the logic of the *Rambo II* test dictates that the mere fact that Keenan is earning above pre-injury levels cannot obviate the basis of the *de minimis* award.

Were Keenan to now lose his clerical position, at least a decade will have passed since he worked as a longshoreman, further increasing the chances of economic loss. Most importantly, it is factually uncontroverted that Keenan's injury is both permanent and substantial. The absence of economic loss thus far does not reflect an underlying absence of loss in physical function. The significance of the injury is a substantial factor in the "significant potential of diminished capacity" test articulated by *Rambo II*. For the foregoing reasons, we elect to follow the conservative "wait and see" approach recommended by *Rambo II* and reverse the Board's denial of the *de minimis* award.

## IV.  CONCLUSION

We affirm the Board's denial of scheduled and unscheduled benefits and reverse the denial of the *de minimis* award, remanding for a determination of the relevant facts under *Rambo II*. In light of this holding, we also reverse the Board's denial of attorneys' fees and remand to the ALJ to resolve the fee question in accordance with her reconsideration of the *de minimis* award.

TALLMAN, CIRCUIT JUDGE, concurring in part and dissenting in part.

I dissent solely from the court's reversal of the Benefits Review Board's ("Board") appropriate denial of a *de minimis* award. In granting a *de minimis* award to Keenan, the court adopts a standard so low that it is difficult to imagine an applicant who will not qualify for compensation if at some point in his prior employment he sustained an injury which might impair his ability to return to that position in the future. * * *

The unrefuted facts before the court are that Keenan earns significantly more money in his post-injury job than he did in his pre-injury job; he has had over ten years of steady post-injury work since reaching his maximum recovery; he is protected by union seniority; he has a college degree; and he has had no injury-related incidents since his injury. Other than the undisputed fact that the injury occurred and that Keenan testified that "it gets worse as time goes by," there is no significant evidence of any potential for future diminished earning capacity. Keenan has therefore failed to meet his preponderance of the evidence burden and we should defer to the Board's decision. * * *

Perhaps in an effort to supplement Keenan's weak showing, the court points out that the loss of physical function is not adequately reflected in the absence of economic loss. * * *. The court may understandably wish to compensate Keenan for the physical injury itself but the Longshore and Harbor Workers' Compensation Act is not a remedy for "physical injury as such, but for economic harm to the injured worker from decreased ability to earn wages." *Rambo II*, 521 U.S. at 126, 117 S.Ct. 1953. The statutory scheme requires him to suffer economic harm or to at least show significant potential of economic harm in order to recover compensation. The "wait and see" approach is only appropriate when a claimant has made a proper showing of potential economic harm; it should not be based simply on sympathy for an uncompensated physical harm. * * *

## NOTES AND QUESTIONS

1. That disability (also referred to as "income replacement") benefits are intended to compensate for loss of earning capacity is widely accepted. But "earning capacity" is obviously an abstraction not capable of precise measurement. Workers' compensation statutes thus use two surrogates for earning capacity: physical impairment and wage loss. Temporary disability benefits are most often based on wage loss, whether total or partial. The use of a "schedule" of permanent physical impairments that governs the number of weeks during which income replacement benefits are to be paid remains common, although not universal. The advantages of such a system include ease of administration and predictability of outcome. It is also obvious that there are disadvantages from not being able to consider more facts about the individual impact of an injury. Loss of a finger, for example, is a very different problem for a pianist than it is for a cab driver. How easy it is to "escape" from the dictates of a schedule varies from jurisdiction to jurisdiction.

2. The fact that most jurisdictions provide a schedule of benefits for common and simple injuries facilitates comparison of workers' compensation benefits between states. In the statutory supplement for this book we have included a table comparing "Maximum and Minimum Workers' Compensation Benefits by Jurisdiction" for 2009 drawn from U.S. CHAMBER OF COMMERCE, 2009 ANALYSIS OF WORKERS' COMPENSATION LAWS. Take a few moments to compare benefit levels in various states and to examine the overall level of benefits in your state. In 2009 the maximum an employee could receive for losing an arm in Alabama was $48,840 while a low-wage worker in Alabama could receive as little as $9,962. Alternatively in 2009 an employee in Illinois would receive from $124,512 to $332,480 for the same arm, depending on the employee's wage. Is this fair? Are compensation levels adequate in Alabama? in Illinois? Similar differences among the jurisdictions exist in the compensation for other body parts and for death and permanent disability. Periodically, policy-makers propose that the federal government set some minimum guidelines for uniformity in workers' compensation programs in the various states, including minimum levels for benefits. Is this a good idea?

3. How a non-schedule injury is to be handled is also the subject of state-to-state variations. The LHWCA, as illustrated by the principal case, moves the determination focus away from physical impairment in the direction of wage loss. Some statutes continue to emphasize physical impairment, sometimes by requiring the evaluator to compare the non-scheduled injury in question to injuries included in the schedule. See, e.g., Wis. Stat. Ann. § 102.55(3). Others assign the "body as a whole" a value stated in terms of number of weeks, and then require the evaluator to determine what proportion of whole body function has been lost because of a particular injury—a lower back strain, for instance. See, e.g., Tenn. Code Ann. § 50–6–207(3)(F). Such comparisons are commonly done using a set of guidelines

prepared by physicians who work in occupational medicine and related specialties. See *American Medical Association Guides to the Evaluation of Permanent Impairment*. Some statutes require the use of a particular edition for this purpose. An updated sixth edition has recently been issued.

## CRELIA v. RHEEM MANUFACTURING CO.

Court of Appeals of Arkansas, 2007
99 Ark.App. 73, 257 S.W.3d 115

JOSEPHINE LINKER HART, JUDGE.

\* \* \*

On August 5, 2002, appellant sustained an admittedly compensable injury to her right hand during her employment with appellee Rheem Manufacturing Company. The injury occurred when four fingers of her right hand were amputated while she was working on a press. Rheem's insurance carrier, Crawford & Company, accepted a sixty-three percent anatomical impairment rating to appellant's right hand. Appellant also received benefits for a compensable injury to her left elbow, epicondylitis.

Appellant argues that the Commission erred when it found that she was not permanently and totally disabled, and she marshals several facts in support of her position.[1] Appellant notes that she was sixty-four years old at the time of the hearing, has a high-school education, and has performed factory work all her life. She further notes that she has had four fingers on her dominant hand amputated, suffers from post-traumatic stress disorder from the accident, has preexisting problems with ulcers on her feet that limit the amount of standing and walking she can do, and has developed epicondylitis in her left arm due to overcompensation with that arm.

"Permanent total disability" is defined as the "inability, because of compensable injury or occupational disease, to earn any meaningful wages in the same or other employment."Ark.Code Ann. § 11–9–519(e)(1) (Repl. 2002). Further, "[t]he burden of proof shall be on the employee to prove inability to earn any meaningful wage in the same or other employment." Ark.Code Ann. § 11–9–519(e)(2). When an appeal is taken from the denial of a claim by the Commission, the substantial-evidence standard of review requires that we affirm the decision if the Commission's opinion displays a substantial basis for the denial of relief. \* \* \*

Here, the ALJ, in an opinion adopted and affirmed by the Commission, considered the facts noted by appellant. The ALJ, however, observed that appellant underwent a functional-capacity examination, which considered the amputation of her fingers and her epicondylitis, and was found to be capable of performing "medium" work. Further, the ALJ noted that

---

**1.** Appellees do not cross-appeal the issue of whether a claimant who has a scheduled injury that does not constitute permanent total disability as set forth in Ark.Code Ann. § 11–9–519(b), may nevertheless be awarded permanent total disability benefits. This issue requires interpretation of Ark.Code Ann. § 11–9–519(c) and (f), and we expressly left this issue open in *McDonald v. Batesville Poultry Equipment*, 90 Ark.App. 435, 206 S.W.3d 908 (2005).

Rheem offered employment in janitorial services that fell within these restrictions and was willing to make accommodations to facilitate appellant's employment, including allowing her to sit as needed and to work only in the administrative offices. Appellant, however, declined this employment. Also, a clinical psychologist, Winston Wilson, recommended that appellant be considered for work that was less demanding than she previously had performed. Further, to alleviate her foot condition, Dr. John Moore directed that she wear compression stockings and limit the amount of time she spent each day in prolonged standing. The burden of proof was on appellant to prove an inability to earn any meaningful wage in the same or other employment, and given the evidence relied on by the Commission, we cannot say that there was not a substantial basis for the denial of relief.

Appellant alternatively argues that the Commission erred in finding that she was not entitled to wage-loss disability over and above her impairment rating to her right hand, noting her previous diagnosis of foot ulcers. * * *

Appellant's injury to her hand was a scheduled injury. We observe that Ark.Code Ann. § 11–9–521(g) (Repl.2002), provides that "[a]ny employee suffering a scheduled injury shall not be entitled to permanent partial disability benefits in excess of the percentage of permanent physical impairment set forth above except as otherwise provided in § 11–9–519(b)." The later provision, Ark.Code Ann. § 11–9–519(b), then describes what constitutes permanent total disability when there is a combination of two scheduled injuries of particular types. Considering these statutes, we hold that a claimant with a scheduled injury is not entitled to [further] permanent partial disability benefits. * * *

*Affirmed.*

## IN THE MATTER OF BARSUK
## v. JOSEPH BARSUK, INC.

Supreme Court of New York, Appellate Division, 2005
24 App.Div.3d 1118, 807 N.Y.S.2d 195

Rose, J.

Appeal from a decision of the Workers' Compensation Board, filed November 17, 2003, which ruled that claimant's work-related injury resulted in a 90% schedule loss of use of the right arm.

In 1997, claimant suffered a near amputation of his right arm when he fell into a scrap metal shearing machine on which he was performing maintenance. As a result of this accident, claimant applied for and received workers' compensation benefits. In 2003, a Workers' Compensation Law Judge rejected claimant's position that he was totally industrially disabled, determined that he had a 90% schedule loss of use of the right arm and made a corresponding award. Upon administrative review, the Workers' Compensation Board affirmed, prompting this appeal by claimant.

A claimant who has a permanent partial disability may nonetheless be classified as totally industrially disabled where the limitations imposed by the work-related disability, coupled with other factors, such as limited educational background and work history, render the claimant incapable of gainful employment * * * Whether a claimant has a total industrial disability is a factual issue to be resolved by the Board and the Board's determination will not be disturbed so long as it is supported by the record * * *. Our review of the record in this case reveals that the medical experts agree that claimant has a 90% loss of use of the right arm and claimant's vocational rehabilitation expert testified that, when this restriction is combined with claimant's age, educational limitations and difficulty focusing, claimant is not a viable candidate for employment in any capacity. As there is no evidence to the contrary, the only conclusion supported by the record is that claimant is totally industrially disabled as a result of his work-related disability. Thus, the Board's decision is without support and cannot be upheld.

ORDERED that the decision is reversed, with costs, and matter remitted to the Workers' Compensation Board for further proceedings not inconsistent with this Court's decision.

## NOTES AND QUESTIONS

1. Obviously the evidence of employability differs in the two preceding cases; is that a sufficient basis for the difference in outcome?

2. Most statutes include "conclusive presumption" provisions that entitle persons to total permanent disability benefits in certain cases, such as the loss of both arms or both legs, or blindness. See the LHWCA provision, for example, 33 U.S.C. § 908(a). Since some individuals—many lawyers, for example—can perform the essential functions of their jobs without the use of their legs, it is possible for them to receive total permanent disability benefits and still be employed. What if one then suffers another injury, such as the loss of a finger? An arm? See *Freeman United Coal Mining Co. v. Industrial Commission*, 99 Ill.2d 487, 77 Ill.Dec. 119, 459 N.E.2d 1368 (1984), awarding temporary total benefits to a maintenance worker who was already receiving permanent total disability benefits under one of the conclusive presumption schedule categories in the Illinois statute.

3. A widely recognized doctrine is often called into play in these cases, the "odd lot" doctrine. If the only work available to a person with the claimant's age, education, experience and disability is an "odd lot" job—one that exists only occasionally, perhaps for only seasonal periods—then the fact that the claimant could perform such work does not bar her from being adjudged totally disabled. See, e.g., *Guyton v. Irving Jensen Co.*, 373 N.W.2d 101 (Iowa 1985). Would a decision such as this perhaps make an employer less likely to hire a worker with limited education, skills, or physical ability? An older worker? Would anti-discrimination laws be of practical help to such persons?

## (c.) Death Benefits

### CAREY'S CASE

Appeals Court of Massachusetts, 2006
66 Mass.App.Ct. 749, 850 N.E.2d 610

BROWN, J.

Adam P. Carey, a minor (employee), died as a result of an injury sustained while operating a golf cart in the course of his part-time (seasonal) employment at the Kernwood Country Club.[1] At the time of his injury, he was sixteen years old, unmarried, and residing with his parents.

The claimants, the employee's parents, filed a claim with the Department of Industrial Accidents for dependency benefits; [following an initial denial of their claim, an] * * * administrative judge awarded the claimants compensation of $39.23 weekly, based on an average weekly wage of $58.90, up until March 2, 2002, the date on which the employee would have reached the age of eighteen, had he lived. The administrative judge denied the claimants' claim for further compensation under G.L. c. 152, §§ 31 and 32, as well as their claim for compensation under G.L. c. 152, § 28. The claimants appealed to the reviewing board pursuant to G.L. c. 152, § 11C.

The reviewing board partially reversed the administrative judge's decision * * *. [Its decision was appealed to a single justice of this court who] issued a memorandum of decision and order essentially affirming the administrative judge's decision in its entirety. * * *

There are three issues before us in this appeal: (1) whether G.L. c. 149, § 62, was violated, thereby allowing the claimants to recover double compensation pursuant to G.L. c. 152, § 28; (2) the correct computation of the employee's average weekly wage for purposes of determining recovery under G.L. c. 152, § 1(1); and (3) whether the claimants should receive the maximum benefits allowed by G.L. c. 152, §§ 31 and 32, based on a determination that they were dependent upon the employee at the time of his injury. * * *

### (1) Section 28.

The claimants contend that the employer committed "serious and willful misconduct" by violating G.L. c. 149, § 62, thereby entitling them to double compensation pursuant to G.L. c. 152, § 28. The reviewing board and the single justice agreed with the administrative judge that, because the golf cart in this case was not used for transportation on a public way, it is not a "motor vehicle[ ] of any description" pursuant to G.L. c. 149, § 62(10). General Laws c. 149, § 62, as in effect when the injury occurred, in 2000, provides, in pertinent part:

---

1. The deceased was earning seven dollars per hour, and had been working for only four weeks.

"No person shall employ a minor under eighteen or permit him to work . . . (10) in operating motor vehicles of any description."

General Laws c. 152, § 28, as amended by St.1934, c. 292, § 2, provides:

"If the employee is injured by reason of the serious and wilful misconduct of an employer . . . the amounts of compensation hereinafter provided shall be doubled. In case the employer is insured, he shall repay to the insurer the extra compensation paid to the employee. . . . The employment of any minor, known to be such, in violation of any provision of sections sixty to seventy-four, inclusive, . . . shall constitute serious and wilful misconduct under this section."

The parties stipulated as follows:

"1. [The Employee's] date of birth was March 2, 1984." . . .

"6. The Employee's job duties included . . . the operation and use of a golf cart on the private property of the [employer]."

"7. On September 16, 2000, the Employee was asked to perform job duties which involved his operation and use of a golf cart on the private property of [the employer]."

"8. The Employee died as a result of his operation and use of a battery powered golf cart during the course of his employment."

"The purpose of G.L. c. 149, § 62, is to prevent minors under eighteen from being exposed to dangers which they might not fully realize on account of their youth, inexperience, lack of foresight and want of restraint." Bagge's Case, 5 Mass.App.Ct. 839, 840, 363 N.E.2d 1321 (1977). It is for this reason that § 62 bars minors' operation of motor vehicles "of any description." The prohibition is not limited to motor vehicles operated on public ways or highways, and the cases cited for this proposition are inapposite. * * *

The purpose of G.L. c. 149, § 62—protecting employees under age eighteen from harm—is quite different from deciding whether a vehicle must be registered or insured. * * * We therefore read narrowly the statute's exceptions to prohibitions against the employment of minors. Cf. Boardman's Case, 365 Mass. 185, 189–190, 310 N.E.2d 593 (1974) (although accident occurred on a working farm, exception to prohibitions of G.L. c. 149, § 62[10], for operating a tractor or trailer on a "farm" did not apply where, under statutes as then in effect, employer was not a "farmer" because he was not engaged "principally in the occupation of farming").

With this view in mind, we turn to the instant matter. The 2002 amendment to § 62, see St.2002, c. 207, explicitly excluded from the prohibition of § 62(10) only the operation of golf carts on a golf course by minors licensed to drive. It is thus apparent that § 62(10), as in effect before the amendment, prohibited minors' operation of golf carts (whether on a golf course or on a way). If this were not so, no amendment would have been required to allow minors' operation of golf carts in the limited circumstances described in St. 2002. Such a reading of the statute satisfies the teaching of *Simmons v. County of Suffolk*, 230 Mass. 236, 237, 119 N.E. 751 (1918), that "[t]he maxim of statutory construction that the expression of one thing is the exclusion of another ... is to be considered with regard to the object sought to be obtained by the entire legislation of which the subject matter to which it relates is but a part." See also G.L. c. 90, § 9, as appearing in St.1977, c. 705, describing golf carts as "motor vehicles":

> We therefore conclude that a golf cart is a "motor vehicle[ ] of any description" within the meaning of G.L. c. 149, § 62(10), and, pursuant to the parties' stipulations, double damages are due under G.L. c. 152, § 28.

### (2) Average weekly wage.

The administrative judge, the reviewing board, and the single justice agreed that the correct calculation of the average weekly wage was $58.90, based on the fact that the employee was a seasonal employee whose wage should be determined by that of comparable employees. See G.L. c. 152, § 1(1). This average weekly wage resulted in a compensation rate of $39.23 per week pursuant to G.L. c. 152, § 31, less than what the insurer had paid to the claimants—the insurer based the compensation rate on an average weekly wage of $69.22. The single justice reasoned:

> "The treatment of the administrative judge and the summary affirmance thereof by the reviewing board were correct. Pursuant to G.L. c. 152, § 1(1), the administrative judge reasonably determined that the employee's work experience of four weeks was too limited to compute the average weekly wage, and he instead applied a rate earned by a similar employee (giving the claimants the benefit of the doubt by selecting the highest rate among the similar employees in question)."

We agree with the single justice's reasoning.

### (3) Dependency benefits.

General Laws c. 152, § 32(e), inserted by St.1926, c. 190, sets out the standard for when a parent is presumed to be dependent upon his or her child:

> "The following persons shall be conclusively presumed to be wholly dependent for support upon a deceased employee: ...

> "(e) A parent upon an unmarried child under the age of eighteen years; provided, that such child was living with the parent at the time of the injury resulting in death."

Before subsection (e) was added to the statute, parents could establish their dependence on their children as matter of fact. See St.1911, c. 751, pt. 2, § 7, now G.L. c. 152, § 32, as amended by St.1950, c. 738, § 4:

"In all other cases questions of dependency, in whole or in part, shall be determined in accordance with the fact as the fact may be at the time of the injury, or at the time of [the employee's] death."

When such dependency was established as matter of fact, the parent-claimants received the maximum benefit set out in the statute, regardless of whether the benefit period extended beyond the deceased child's eighteenth birthday. See, e.g., Murphy's Case, 218 Mass. 278, 279–280, 105 N.E. 635 (1914) (son injured at age fifteen; father received benefits for 300 weeks). * * *

We agree with the single justice and the administrative judge that, in both §§ 31 and 32, presumed eligibility in relation to children—whether they or their parents are the claimants—is generally confined to minors. See, e.g., § 31; § 32(c), (d), (e).

The single justice observed that

"the concept of parental dependency comes about by virtue of the parent's obligation to support the minor child and the concomitant right of the parent to receive any earnings of the child to assist in defraying the support obligation. See *Dembinski's Case*, 231 Mass. 261, 263, 120 N.E. 856 (1918); Nason, Koziol & Wall, Workers' Compensation § 22.2 (3d ed.2003)."

The presumption of parental dependency in c. 152, § 32(e), however, applies only to situations in which an unmarried child, under the age of eighteen and living at home, is working. There is nothing in that statutory provision to suggest the Legislature intended that a child support his parents indefinitely. It was merely to defray the parents' own support obligations. Therefore, any compensation due under subsection (e) ends at eighteen, unless a parent proves that he or she was, in fact, dependent upon the child. We agree with the single justice's reasoning that the purpose of workers' compensation is to replace income that individuals would otherwise receive; its purpose is not to "confer windfalls." "Absent proof of an actual dependency, prolongation of the presumption beyond what would have been the child's eighteenth birthday 'replaces' income that the parents would not have received had there been no injury" and is contrary to the purpose of workers' compensation law.

However, we also agree with the board that by creating a conclusive presumption of dependence for parents of minors living at home, the Legislature did not thereby preclude parents from receiving benefits past the child's eighteenth birthday, as they could before subsection (e) was added to the statute. The administrative judge suggested that, to continue receiving benefits after the deceased child's eighteenth birthday, parent-claimants would have to establish their continuing dependency after that date. His conclusion conflicts with the terms of the statute. See G.L. c. 152, § 32 ("In all other cases questions of dependency ... shall be determined in accordance with the fact as the fact may be *at the time of the injury, or at the time of [the employee's] death*" [emphasis supplied]). Moreover, we think proof of future dependence would often be well-nigh impossible, and most likely would be based upon speculation and conjecture. * * * Instead, we read § 32 to mean that, if parent-claimants are content to receive benefits only up to their deceased child's eighteenth birthday, they may rely exclusively upon the conclusive presumption of subsection (e). If, however, they wish to obtain the maximum benefit, and such benefit would necessarily extend beyond the child's eighteenth birthday, the parent-claimants may, pursuant to the last paragraph of § 32, submit to an administrative judge facts substantiating their dependence upon the child "at the time of the injury, or at the time of [the employee's] death." This practice is well-established, as prior to the insertion of subsection (e), it was the only avenue of recovery for parent-claimants. * * *

### Conclusion.

The judgment is affirmed as to the computation of the employee's average weekly wage. The judgment is reversed as to the violation of G.L. c. 149, § 62, and the claimants' entitlement to double compensation pursuant to G.L. c. 152, § 28. The judgment is vacated as to the claimants' entitlement to the maximum benefits allowed by G.L. c. 152, §§ 31 and 32. The matter is remanded to the reviewing board, where a new decision shall enter remanding to the administrative judge for a determination as to the claimants' entitlement to maximum benefits, and a recalculation of compensation due the claimants in accordance with this opinion. The administrative judge may take new evidence as to the claimants' dependence upon the employee at the time of his injury.

### NOTES AND QUESTIONS

1. The court's decision not to use the deceased worker's own wage to determine the amount of weekly benefits is reasonable, but also unusual. Most statutes require the use of the injured worker's own wages except in the most unusual circumstances. This can create situations of questionable fairness, as in the case of workers already designated for wage increases or decreases. Computation problems can become very technical at times.

2. Adjusting compensation because of employer violation of a safety statute is provided for in a number of jurisdictions. Some also decrease benefits payable to a worker whose injury is the result of deliberate violation of safety rules. See *Van Waters & Rogers v. Workman*, 700 P.2d 1096 (Utah 1985).

3. The use of "conclusive presumptions" of dependency is common, particularly for spouses and minor children. Often (as in the principal case) a claimant must establish both the existence of a relationship and that the deceased worker was "living with" the claimant at the time of injury. "Living with" does not always require actual physical presence in the home, however; a husband absent from the home while working at a distant location or because of ill health is still "living with" the wife. See, e.g., *Shubert v. Steelman*, 214 Tenn. 102, 377 S.W.2d 940 (1964); *Legg's Case*, 358 Mass. 615,

266 N.E.2d 319 (1971); *Lafayette v. General Dynamics Corp.*, 255 Conn. 762, 770 A.2d 1 (2001).

## IN THE MATTER OF LANGAN v. STATE FARM FIRE & CASUALTY

Supreme Court of New York, Appellate Division, 2007
48 A.D.3d 76, 849 N.Y.S.2d 105

KANE, J.

\* \* \*

Claimant and Neal Conrad Spicehandler (hereinafter decedent) were committed domestic partners from 1986 until decedent's death in 2002. In November 2000, claimant and decedent entered into a civil union in Vermont (see Vt. Stat. Ann, tit. 15, § 1201). In February 2002, decedent was struck by a car while he was working for claimant's insurance business, resulting in a serious leg injury. After undergoing surgery on his leg, decedent died. Claimant filed workers' compensation claims for decedent's leg injury, and for death benefits as decedent's surviving spouse pursuant to Workers' Compensation Law § 16(1–a).[1] The workers' compensation carrier accepted the claims as work-related injuries, but questioned whether claimant was decedent's spouse for death benefits purposes. A Workers' Compensation Law Judge found that claimant did not have standing to assert the death benefits claim and the Workers' Compensation Board affirmed.

On claimant's appeal, he makes three arguments: Workers' Compensation Law § 16(1–a) includes a partner to a civil union as a surviving spouse, the doctrine of comity requires New York to recognize claimant as decedent's surviving spouse for death benefits purposes and, if those arguments are not successful, the deprivation of death benefits to same-sex partners of a civil union violates the Equal Protection Clause of the U.S. Constitution. We address each argument in turn.

For purposes of the workers' compensation death benefits provision, which gives first priority to surviving spouses, "the term surviving spouse shall be deemed to mean the legal spouse" of the deceased employee (Workers' Compensation Law § 16[1–a]). Workers' Compensation Law § 16 does not further define the term "legal spouse" (see *Matter of Valentine v. American Airlines*, 17 A.D.3d 38, 40, 791 N.Y.S.2d 217 [2005]). In previously reviewing Workers' Compensation Law § 16(1–a) in the context of a claim for death benefits by a registered domestic partner, we examined the statute's plain language and legislative history and determined that a " 'legal spouse' is a husband or wife of a lawful marriage"(id.). This interpretation is further supported by language in other subdivisions of the same statute, which provide a certain percentage

---

1. Claimant also commenced a wrongful death action against the hospital where decedent's surgery was performed. The Second Department dismissed that action, finding that claimant did not have standing * * *

of the deceased employee's average wages to the surviving spouse during widowhood or widowerhood, with a lump sum payment "upon remarriage" (Workers' Compensation Law §§ 16[1–b], [1–c], [2], [2–a]). Clearly, the term "remarriage" assumes that the surviving spouse was previously a party to a marriage. Claimant acknowledges that a civil union is not a marriage (compare Vt. Stat. Ann, tit. 15, § 1201[2], with § 1201[4]), and he was not married to decedent. If a party to a Vermont civil union was considered a legal spouse for workers' compensation purposes, the statute would have the anomalous result of allowing a surviving civil union partner to continue collecting surviving spouse benefits even after entering into another civil union, because that new civil union is not considered a "remarriage" that would terminate death benefits. As parties to civil unions are not legal spouses under Workers' Compensation Law § 16, claimant was not statutorily entitled to assert the death benefits claim.

The doctrine of comity does not require New York to recognize claimant as decedent's surviving spouse for death benefits purposes. This doctrine is not a mandate to adhere to another state's laws, but an expression of one state's voluntary choice to defer to another state's policy (see *Ehrlich–Bober & Co. v. University of Houston*, 49 N.Y.2d 574, 580, 427 N.Y.S.2d 604, 404 N.E.2d 726 [1980]). Although we may recognize the civil union status of claimant and decedent as a matter of comity, we are not thereby bound to confer upon them all of the legal incidents of that status recognized in the foreign jurisdiction that created the relationship (see *Langan v. St. Vincent's Hosp. of N.Y.*, 25 A.D.3d 90, 102, 802 N.Y.S.2d 476 [Fisher, J., dissenting] [2005], appeal dismissed, 6 N.Y.3d 890, 817 N.Y.S.2d 625, 850 N.E.2d 672 [2006]). Vermont considers parties to a civil union to be "spouses" under that state's law and provides them with all of the benefits, responsibilities and protections of spouses to a marriage, including workers' compensation benefits (see Vt. Stat. Ann, tit. 15, § 1204[a], [b], [e] [9]). But even under Vermont law, such parties are not part of a marriage (see Vt. Stat. Ann, tit. 15, § 1201[2], [4]). While parties to a civil union may be spouses, and even legal spouses, in Vermont, New York is not required to extend to such parties all of the benefits extended to marital spouses. The extension of benefits entails a consideration of social and fiscal policy more appropriately left to the Legislature (see *Langan v. St. Vincent's Hosp. of N.Y.*, 25 A.D.3d at 95, 802 N.Y.S.2d 476). We therefore decline to recognize, as a matter of comity, all of the legal incidents of a civil union that Vermont law provides to such parties in that state.

Having reached the conclusions that Workers' Compensation Law § 16 does not include parties to civil unions as spouses and that we should not extend death benefits to such parties as a matter of comity, we now determine that the deprivation of death benefits to the surviving party of a civil union does not violate the Equal Protection Clause of the U.S. Constitution (see U.S. Const., 14th Amend., § 1). Using the rational basis test to review this allegation of sexual orientation discrimination, the "legislation is presumed to be valid and will be sustained if the classification drawn by the statute is rationally related to a legitimate state interest" * * *. Claimant bears the burden of rebutting this presumption of constitutionality by demonstrating that the denial of death benefits to parties to a civil union serves no legitimate governmental purpose * * *. Prior case law "established that confining marriage and all laws pertaining either directly or indirectly to the marital relationship to different sex couples is not offensive to the Equal Protection Clause" * * *.

Claimant has not set forth any basis for us to depart from precedent. We previously held that Workers' Compensation Law § 16 does not differentiate on the basis of sexual orientation, but on the basis of legal status, and that this classification was rationally related to the state's interest in "swift and orderly processing of death benefits claims" (*Matter of Valentine v. American Airlines*, 17 A.D.3d at 42, 791 N.Y.S.2d 217). While that rationale of administrative efficiency was persuasive in the context of domestic partners, a relationship that could be difficult to define in terms of rights and responsibilities and thus delay the payment of benefits (see id.), existence of a Vermont civil union is easily evidenced by a Vermont Department of Health license and certificate of civil union, similar to proof of a marriage in New York, and the rights of such partners are extensively defined under Vermont law. Even so, there may be other legitimate state interests served by limiting death benefits to marital spouses.

Workers' compensation provides a safety net to a surviving spouse (see *Matter of Landon v. Motorola, Inc.*, 38 A.D.2d 18, 20, 326 N.Y.S.2d 960 [1971], citing *Matter of Post v. Burger & Gohlke*, 216 N.Y. 544, 553, 111 N.E. 351 [1916]). It would not be unreasonable to conclude that the Worker's Compensation Law was enacted, in part, to encourage and protect the traditional family constellation of husband, wife and children. Survivor benefits to the homemaker/child-rearing spouse, who was traditionally not employed or was employed part time, protects that spouse from destitution upon the death of the family breadwinner. It also compensates that spouse for sacrificing his or her own career by remaining at home to raise children. Although some may argue that same-sex couples are as capable of creating a family unit and raising children as opposite-sex couples, the Court of Appeals has already determined that the Legislature's decision to limit marriage to opposite-sex couples is rationally related to this legitimate interest and withstands rational basis scrutiny (see *Hernandez v. Robles*, 7 N.Y.3d at 365, 821 N.Y.S.2d 770, 855 N.E.2d 1). The decision to extend workers' compensation death benefits to a whole new class of beneficiaries, i.e., survivors of same-sex unions, is a decision to be made by the Legislature after appropriate inquiry into the societal obligation to provide such benefits and the financial impact of such a decision. As the statute is rationally related to a legitimate state interest, claimant has not met his burden.

CREW III, J.P., MUGGLIN and LAHTINEN, concur.

ROSE, J. (dissenting).

I respectfully dissent as to the majority's conclusion that the doctrine of comity does not require New York to recognize claimant as decedent's surviving spouse for purposes of the death benefits afforded by Workers' Compensation Law § 16(1–a).

While I certainly agree that the valid Vermont civil union entered into by claimant and decedent does not bind us to confer upon them "all of the incidents which the other jurisdiction attaches to such status" (*Matter of Chase*, 127 A.D.2d 415, 417, 515 N.Y.S.2d 348 [1987]), claimant is not seeking such an incident here. He does not ask us to confer workers' compensation death benefits simply because Vermont would confer them. Rather, claimant asks us only to recognize the legal status of spouse afforded to him by Vermont, as a matter of comity. Once that status is recognized, New York law provides the legal incidents to which claimant would be entitled, including workers' compensation death benefits.

There appears to be no real disagreement that Vermont has defined its civil union as a spousal relationship and conferred upon claimant the legal status of spouse (see Vt. Stat. Ann, tit. 15, § 1204[b]), or that the doctrine of comity requires our recognition of a legal status acquired under the laws of another state (see *Matter of Chase*, 127 A.D.2d at 417, 515 N.Y.S.2d 348). Nor is there any disagreement that Workers' Compensation Law § 16 affords a death benefit to a spouse. Where we diverge appears to be over the question of whether claimant can be a qualifying "legal spouse" in New York in view of our prior holding in *Matter of Valentine v. American Airlines*, 17 A.D.3d 38, 40, 791 N.Y.S.2d 217 [2005], and the use of the term "remarriage" in Workers' Compensation Law § 16(1–b).

In *Matter of Valentine v. American Airlines*, 17 A.D.3d at 40, 791 N.Y.S.2d 217, we dealt only with domestic partnerships, holding that a domestic partner does not fall within the definition of "legal spouse" for purposes of Workers' Compensation Law § 16(1–a). There, unlike here, we were required to determine the legal status of domestic partners because no authority in New York had considered it. Due to the absence of a statutory definition of "legal spouse," we turned to dictionary definitions to find its meaning and concluded that it excluded domestic partners (id. at 40, 791 N.Y.S.2d 217). We did not consider the legal status of Vermont civil union spouses. While Vermont civil unions are not marriages, they are formal spousal relationships between same-sex couples which are sanctioned and recognized by that state (see Vt. Stat. Ann, tit. 15, § 1201), require a court proceeding to dissolve (see Vt. Stat. Ann, tit. 15, § 1206) and obligate each party to provide for the support of the other (see Vt. Stat. Ann, tit. 15, § 1204[c]). Thus, here, we need not construe the term "legal spouse" because a state legislature clearly has conferred that status on claimant, and we need only apply our doctrine of comity to give it effect.

As for the implications of the term "remarriage," it is significant that marriage was the only legally recognized spousal relationship in the

United States when Worker's Compensation Law § 16 was first drafted (see L. 1913, ch. 816) and, thus, the term "remarriage" covered the only conceivable event that could replace the support obligation lost upon a first spouse's death. Since a civil union is now an alternate way to become a legal spouse and replace that obligation, an anomalous result could occur under the majority's strict reading of the statute even if civil union spouses were excluded from workers' compensation death benefits. Under the majority's construction, the term "remarriage" would mean that, upon later entry into a civil union, the surviving spouse of a marriage would not face termination of death benefits because it would not be a remarriage. That result can be avoided by reading the term "remarriage" to mean entry into a subsequent marriage or civil union, thereby treating all spouses the same. The term "remarriage" would then no longer imply that a surviving spouse could only have been previously married rather than having entered a civil union. Such an interpretation of "remarriage," while expansive, would avoid the anomaly, not be unreasonable and, in my view, be preferable "[s]ince the Workers' Compensation Law must be liberally construed in favor of employees in order to achieve its humanitarian purpose" (*Matter of Lashlee v. Pepsi–Cola Newburgh Bottling*, 301 A.D.2d 879, 881, 754 N.Y.S.2d 102 [2003]).

## NOTES AND QUESTIONS

1. The dependency provisions of workers compensation statutes have spawned a significant number of constitutional issues. In *Weber v. Aetna Casualty & Surety Co.*, 406 U.S. 164, 92 S.Ct. 1400, 31 L.Ed.2d 768 (1972), the Court held that a Louisiana statute that denied the same workers compensation benefit entitlement to dependent unacknowledged illegitimate children of a deceased worker that the statute provided to dependent legitimate children of the deceased worker violated the Equal Protection clause.

2. A number of statutes originally provided benefits to "widows" or "wives" but not to "widowers" or "husbands." When challenged, these provisions were found unconstitutional. *Wengler v. Druggists Mut. Ins. Co.*, 446 U.S. 142, 100 S.Ct. 1540, 64 L.Ed.2d 107 (1980). Courts differed about the appropriate remedy. Some decided that the appropriate course of action was to read the language to include both genders. See, e.g., *Russell v. International Paper Co.*, 2 Ark. App. 355, 621 S.W.2d 867 (1981). Others struck down the conclusive presumption for widows and held they must pursue their claims under the "actual dependency" provision of the statute until their legislature decided whether to provide the conclusive dependency presumption to both women and men. See *Insurance Co. of N. America v. Russell*, 246 Ga. 269, 271 S.E.2d 178 (1980).

3. The Alaska Supreme Court recently upheld a statute that provides spousal death benefits to widows or widowers if formally married, but not to a woman who lived with a man for a period of four years without ever marrying him. One argument the claimant made was that denying benefits to unmarried cohabitants violated a state constitutional provision guaranteeing the right to privacy. Her Equal Protection claim was rejected on the ground that

administrative efficiency in the handling of claims was a sufficient governmental interest to justify the requirement of formal marriage. *Ranney v. Whitewater Engineering*, 122 P.3d 214 (Alaska 2005). To what extent do cases such as these and the principal case suggest that the use of the "conclusive presumption" approach may continue to be an appropriate device?

4.   In April 2009, the Vermont legislature enacted a statute providing for same-sex marriage, overriding the governor's veto. Previously, an intermediate appellate court in New York ruled that a county could not deny spousal benefits to a same-sex couple who had legally married in Canada. *Martinez v. County of Monroe*, 50 App.Div.3d 189, 850 N.Y.S.2d 740, leave to appeal dismissed, 10 N.Y.3d 856, 859 N.Y.S.2d 617, 889 N.E.2d 496 (2008). In response to that decision, New York Governor Patterson issued an executive order directing all state agencies to review their regulations to ensure that terms such as "spouse" would be construed "in a manner that encompasses legal same-sex marriages," in the absence of some contravening statute. The governor's action was upheld in *Golden v. Paterson*, 23 Misc.3d 641, 877 N.Y.S.2d 822 (2008).

## (d.) Special Problems: Successive and Concurrent Harms

The tension between the goals of individual fairness and administrative efficiency is particularly obvious in dealing with the problem of successive and concurrent injury and disease. Consider the case of a worker whose knee was injured playing basketball in high school, not badly enough to have to leave the team, but enough so that the worker wears a knee brace when engaging in strenuous activity. A slip and fall at work then aggravates the old injury enough so that standing all day on a hard surface is no longer possible. As you will see in the cases that follow, there is widespread agreement that this worker is entitled to compensation benefits that are not reduced in any way because of the earlier knee injury. As soon as one leaves that simplest case behind, however, varying treatments abound. Should a worker with asbestosis who has been employed by three different companies and was exposed to asbestos fibers at all of them receive benefits from just one of the companies? From all? In what proportions? And there are lurking problems, are there not, even in the simplest case? Would a sensible employer not want to hire only those workers with the very fewest physical limitations, so as to reduce the likelihood of having to pay benefits?

### GEATHERS v. 3V, INC.

Supreme Court of South Carolina, 2007
371 S.C. 570, 641 S.E.2d 29

JUSTICE BURNETT:

\* \* \*

### *FACTUAL/PROCEDURAL BACKGROUND*

In the course of Claimant's employment with 3V, Inc. (Employer), she suffered successive accidental injuries to her back and leg. Her first injury occurred on July 20, 1999. Employer's workers' compensation insurance carrier at the time of this accident was EBI. Claimant returned to work August 24, 1999. She was placed on light duty for two months before she returned to full duty. Claimant testified Dr. Wilkins released her from his care in January 2000, because she reached maximum medical improvement.

Claimant's second injury occurred on May 11, 2000. Employer's workers' compensation insurance carrier at the time of this injury was Liberty. Claimant returned to work on May 23, 2000, and assumed light duty. Employer sent Claimant home two days later because it did not have any more light duty work for her. Claimant has not worked since that time and has not applied for any other jobs.

Claimant filed for workers' compensation benefits for [both injuries, but EBI and Liberty denied liability for benefits.] * * *

At the hearing before the Single Commissioner, EBI argued: (1) Claimant's injuries from the first accident were no longer compensable because she had reached maximum medical improvement; (2) Dr. Wilkins released Claimant from his care in January 2000; and (3) Claimant's injuries from the second accident were not the same as her injuries from the first. Liberty argued Claimant never reached maximum medical improvement and EBI should share liability with Liberty for Claimant's current injuries. * * *

The Single Commissioner found both of Claimant's injuries compensable and found Dr. Wilkins had not released Claimant from his care or given his opinion as to maximum medical improvement based on Dr. Wilkins' records. The Single Commissioner found:

> [The second injury] was intervening, but not totally independent of the [first] accidental injury and that the [second] accidental injury aggravated, exacerbated, and worsened Claimant's condition; and the two injuries from the two accidental injuries are intertwined, indistinguishable, and inseparable beginning May 11, 2000 [the date of the second accident] and remain so as of the date of the hearing.

The Single Commissioner ordered EBI to pay Claimant's benefits for the time period between the first and second accidents, and ordered EBI and Liberty to "share equally in all causally related benefits" from the date of the second accident forward. EBI appealed and the Full Commission affirmed.

EBI appealed to the circuit court which reversed, finding the rule in *Gordon v. E.I. Du Pont Nemours & Co.*, 228 S.C. 67, 76, 88 S.E.2d 844, 848 (1955) (where a non-disabling injury is aggravated with resulting disability, such disability is compensable). The circuit court found no evidence to support the Commission's finding that Dr. Wilkins had not released Claimant as having maximum medical improvement. The circuit court also found the second accident was "clearly distinguishable" from the first accident because Claimant's need for benefits after the second accident was necessitated solely by the second accident. Consequently, Liberty was found to be solely liable for Claimant's entire benefits following the second accident.

The Court of Appeals reversed the decision of the circuit court and reinstated the Commission's decision. * * * We granted Petitioner's petition for writ of certiorari to review the Court of Appeals' decision.

## ISSUES

I.   Does the South Carolina Workers' Compensation Commission have authority to apportion liability between EBI and Liberty for successive injuries to Claimant?

II.   Did the Court of Appeals err in failing to apply the *Gordon v. E.I. Du Pont Nemours & Co.*, 228 S.C. 67, 88 S.E.2d 844 (1955), rule to the facts of this case? * * *.

## LAW/ANALYSIS

### I.   Authority to Apportion

EBI argues the Court of Appeals erred in finding the Commission has the authority to apportion liability for Claimant's second injury and to order EBI to pay benefits related to the second injury when EBI did not provide coverage for Employer on the date of the second injury. We agree.

A "successive-carrier problem" occurs when a worker suffers successive workplace injuries with an intervening change of employers or change of insurance carriers by the same employer. 9 Larson's Workers' Compensation Law § 153.01[1] (2005). There are two possible solutions to the successive-carrier problem.

The apportionment solution has been adopted by many jurisdictions.[1] The leading case establishing apportionment, *Anderson v. Babcock & Wilcox Co.*, 256 N.Y. 146, 175 N.E. 654, 655 (1931), explains the rationale for the approach:

> Unjust it is that the second insurer should bear the entire liability when the second accident was related in large measure to the first. No less unjust it is that the first insurer should bear the entire liability if it appears that without the second accident an earlier recovery might have been had.

The problem with this approach is that it is complicated by statutes of limitations, out-of-state employers, and the difficulty of determining the proportion of liability attributable to each insurer. 9 Larson's Workers' Compensation Law at § 153.01[2]. South Carolina has neither statute nor

---

**1.** See *Employers' Cas. Co. v. U.S. Fid. & Guar. Co.*, 214 Ark. 40, 214 S.W.2d 774 (1948); *Argonaut Ins. Co. v. Indus. Acc. Comm'n*, 231 Cal. App. 2d 111, 41 Cal.Rptr. 628 (1964); *Sauer Indus. Contracting Inc. v. Ditch*, 547 So.2d 276 (Fla.Dist.Ct.App.1989); *Johnson v. Bath Iron Works Corp.*, 551 A.2d 838 (Me.1988); *Arender v. Nat'l Sales, Inc.*, 193 So.2d 579 (Miss.1966); *Calabro v. Campbell Soup Co.*, 244 N.J. Super. 149, 581 A.2d 1318 (App.Div.1990); *Butts v. Ward La France Trucking Corp.*, 85 A.D.2d 814, 445 N.Y.S.2d 628 (1981); *Wilkerson Chevrolet, Inc. v. Mackey*, 367 P.2d 162 (Okla.1961); *Merton Lumber Co. v. Indus. Comm'n*, 260 Wis. 109, 50 N.W.2d 42 (1951)

case law authorizing the apportionment of workers' compensation benefits in successive injury cases.[2]

The second solution to the successive-carrier problem is called the "last injurious exposure rule" and it is the majority rule.[3] Id. at § 153.02[1]. This rule "places full liability upon the carrier covering the risk at the time of the most recent injury that bears a causal relation to the disability." Id. Consistent with the rule that an employer takes its employee as it finds her, the last injurious exposure rule makes the insurer at risk at the time of the second injury liable even if the second injury would have been much less severe in the absence of the prior condition and even if the prior injury significantly contributed to the final condition. Id. at § 153.02[2]. However, if the second injury is merely a recurrence of the first injury, then the insurer on the risk at the time of the original injury remains liable for the second. Id. at § 153.02[4]. The benefit of the last injurious exposure rule is it "provides a reasonably equitable approach to compensation problems in the multi-employer context which is simple, easy to administer, and avoids the difficulties associated with apportionment." 82 Am.Jur.2d Workers' Compensation § 200 (2003).

While South Carolina has not expressly adopted the last injurious exposure rule, both statutory and case law favor adopting the rule rather than the apportionment solution. First, S.C.Code Ann. § 42–9–430 (1985) favors placing sole liability on a single insurer. It states:

> Whenever a dispute arises between two or more parties as to which party is liable for the payment of workers' compensation benefits to an injured employee pursuant to the provisions of this title and there is no genuine issue of material fact as to the employee's employment, his average weekly wage, the occurrence of an injury, the extent of the injury, and the fact that the injury arose out of and in the scope of the employment, the hearing commissioner may, in his discretion, require the disputing parties involved to pay benefits immediately to the employee and to share equally in the payment of those benefits until it is determined which party is solely liable, at which time the liable party must reimburse all other parties for the benefits they have paid to the employee. . . .

---

**2.** Cf. S.C.Code Ann. § 42–13–50 (1985) (authorizing the Commission to apportion liability between employers in cases where an employee suffers ionizing radiation injury, disability, or death attributable in part to exposure received in previous employment); *Hargrove v. Titan Textile Co.*, 360 S.C. 276, 599 S.E.2d 604 (Ct.App.2004) (apportionment allowed when claimant suffered one injury while simultaneously employed by two employers).

**3.** See *McKeever Custom Cabinets v. Smith*, 379 N.W.2d 368 (Iowa 1985); *Carter v. Avondale Shipyards, Inc.*, 415 So.2d 174 (La.1981); *Aseltine v. Leto Constr. Co.*, 43 Mich.App. 559, 204 N.W.2d 262 (Mich.Ct.App.1972); *Jensen v. Kronick's Floor Covering Serv.*, 309 Minn. 541, 245 N.W.2d 230 (1976); *Collett Elec. v. Dubovik*, 112 Nev. 193, 911 P.2d 1192 (1996); *Rose City Van & Storage v. McGuire*, 107 Or.App. 404, 811 P.2d 1387 (1991); *Novak v. C.J. Grossenburg & Son*, 89 S.D. 308, 232 N.W.2d 463 (1975); *Bennett v. Howard Johnsons Motor Lodge*, 714 S.W.2d 273 (Tenn.1986); *Duaine Brown Chevrolet Co. v. Indus. Comm'n*, 29 Utah 2d 478, 511 P.2d 743 (1973).

Second, 25A S.C.Code Ann. Regs. 67–409 (1976) instructs the Commission to presume the policy with the later effective date is in force "when duplicate or dual coverage exists by reason of two different insurance carriers issuing two policies to the same employer securing the same liability." Finally, a number of cases have applied a version of the last injurious exposure rule and declined to follow the apportionment rule when dealing with occupational diseases. * * *

Since South Carolina has adopted neither the apportionment rule nor the last injurious exposure rule, this case presents a novel issue of law. In the absence of authority permitting apportionment and because existing statutory authority expresses a preference for holding a single insurer liable rather than apportioning liability among multiple insurers, we adopt the last injurious exposure rule. Applying this rule, we find the Court of Appeals erred in apportioning liability for Claimant's second injury.

## II.   The *Gordon* Rule

EBI argues the Court of Appeals erred in failing to apply the principle espoused in *Gordon*, that aggravation of a pre-existing condition is compensable. In *Gordon*, this Court held:

> The rule is well established that where a latent or quiescent weakened, but not disabling, condition resulting from disease is by accidental injury in the course and scope of employment aggravated or accelerated or activated, with resulting disability, such disability is compensable. The same principle is equally applicable where the latent, but not disabling, condition has resulted from a prior accidental injury. If the disability is proximately caused by the subsequent accidental injury, compensability is referable to that, and not the earlier one.

Id. at 76, 88 S.E.2d at 848 (internal citations omitted). The Court of Appeals declined to follow *Gordon* because of the "factual-driven nature of the *Gordon* decision." On the contrary, the *Gordon* rule is "well established" and the Court of Appeals erred in limiting *Gordon* to its facts.

The Court of Appeals distinguished Claimant's situation because her injuries were not separate and distinct but "intertwined, indistinguishable, and inseparable." *Gordon*, according to the Court of Appeals, did not apply because it dealt with separate and distinct injuries. The Court of Appeals was correct in determining the Commission's finding of inseparability was supported by substantial evidence. However, such a finding does not preclude the application of *Gordon* because *Gordon* is not limited to its particular facts. *Gordon* applies to the instant case because: (1) Claimant suffered a non-disabling back injury during a workplace accident; (2) Claimant's disability was caused by the second accident; and (3) the second injury "aggravated or accelerated or activated" the pre-existing condition.

Not only does the *Gordon* rule apply to this case, but it also reflects the essence of the last injurious exposure rule which is to hold the insurer on the risk at the time of the second injury solely liable when the second injury aggravates the first injury.

## CONCLUSION

For the foregoing reasons, we reverse the Court of Appeals and reinstate the decision of the circuit court finding Liberty solely liable for Claimant's benefits following her second injury.

REVERSED.

## NOTES AND QUESTIONS

1. As the opinion in the principal case illustrates, a single jurisdiction may deal with different sorts of injuries in different ways. In South Carolina after this decision, most workers who suffer a non-disabling occupational harm followed by another that aggravates the first harm to a point that makes it disabling will receive benefits from only one employer or insurer. Those harmed by exposure to ionizing radiation in successive employment will, however, receive their benefits from multiple sources. There are a number of statutes that include apportionment provisions limited to diseases, sometimes as in South Carolina to very specific diseases. As noted earlier, responsibility for benefits for heart attacks also is often given special treatment. Consider the philosophies underlying workers compensation—certainty of prompt benefits, limiting litigation, and so on—and try to decide which approach better serves those purposes, apportionment or the last injurious exposure doctrine?

2. The decision in *Hargrove v. Titan Textile Co.*, cited by the court, is also relatively unusual. The worker in that case worked for both a textile manufacturer and a chicken processing firm. The work at each involved stressful repetitive use of arms and wrists, although in very different tasks—picking up yarn spools and skinning and eviscerating chickens—and medical testimony indicated that there was a likelihood that each sort of work could contribute to aggravating the claimant's condition. The court majority therefore upheld an award against each employer. A dissenting judge, however, would have exonerated the chicken processing employer, since the claimant had worked there only nine days while she had been at the textile firm off and on for more than eight years.

3. If one is to impose liability on an insurer "on the risk" at a particular time, fixing that time is obviously crucial. In the case of an occupational disease, does it make better sense to fix liability as of the time a worker becomes aware of a potentially disabling disease, or at the time the disease becomes disabling? In a case under the LHWCA, the court put it this way:

> This doubleheader of a case presents not one, but two, interrelated questions. Both questions involve the nexus between occupational disease and the Longshore and Harbor Workers' Compensation Act (LHWCA), 33 U.S.C. §§ 901–950 (1988). First, we must decide whether, as between successive insurance carriers, the primary obligation to provide LHWCA benefits is triggered by a worker's disability or by his awareness of the potential for disability. Second, we must decide whether, as between

successive insurance carriers, the date of disablement is the date on which a worker's long-latency disease is first diagnosed or the date on which he first experiences a decrease in earning capacity. For the reasons that follow, we conclude that congressional intent and administrative convenience are best realized by a system in which, for LHWCA purposes, liability for the effects of an occupational disease falls upon the last responsible insurer on the date of disability, as determined by the date of decreased earning capacity.

*Liberty Mut. Ins. Co. v. Commercial Union Ins. Co.*, 978 F.2d 750 (1st Cir. 1992). Does the court's choice seem the best answer?

## DESCHENES v. TRANSCO, INC.

Supreme Court of Connecticut, 2007
284 Conn. 479, 935 A.2d 625

NORCOTT, J.

The sole issue in this appeal is whether the workers' compensation benefits payable to a claimant with a 25 percent permanent partial disability in each lung, caused in part by work-related asbestos exposure, should be apportioned[1] or reduced by the amount of that disability attributable to a concurrently developing nonoccupational disease, specifically cigarette smoking related emphysema. The defendants, Reed and Greenwood Insulation Company (Reed), and AC & S, Inc. (AC & S), appeal from the decision of the compensation review board (board) affirming the decision of the workers' compensation commissioner for the second district, Stephen Delaney, awarding compensation for a 25 percent permanent partial disability in each lung to the plaintiff, George Deschenes. We conclude that further findings of fact are required because apportionment of benefits is appropriate when a respondent employer is able to prove that: (1) a disability has resulted from the combination of two concurrently developing disease processes, one that is nonoccupational, and the other that is work related; and (2) the conditions of the claimant's occupation have no influence on the development of the nonoccupational disease. Accordingly, we reverse the decision of the board and remand the case for further proceedings.

The record reveals the following facts and procedural history. The plaintiff, who was born in 1945, joined Local 33 of the International Association of Heat and Frost Insulators and Asbestos Workers (union) in 1967. After he joined the union, the plaintiff worked until 1985 as an insulator on numerous commercial construction sites for multiple employ-

---

**1.** Many of the authorities cited herein, and the parties in their briefing of this case, use the term "apportionment" to refer to the reduction of a claimant's benefits based on the degree of disability attributable to an occupational cause. See, e.g., 3 A. Larson, Workers' Compensation Law (2007 Ed.) § 52.06[4][d], pp. 52–79 through 52–81. Under our state law pertaining to workers' compensation, the term "apportionment" has, however, historically been used as a term of art to refer to the proportional division of responsibility among various employers or insurers for a claimant's benefits, rather than to any specific reduction of the benefits owed to the claimant in the first instance. See, e.g., *Pizzuto v. Commissioner of Mental Retardation*, 283 Conn. 257, 277, 927 A.2d 811 (2007); *Hatt v. Burlington Coat Factory*, 263 Conn. 279, 312–13,

ers, including Reed and AC & S. During that time, he was exposed to significant amounts of asbestos, with his last exposure occurring in 1985, while he was employed by Transco. The plaintiff has not been able to work full-time since 1994, when he was diagnosed with asbestos related pleural lung disease.[4]

Asbestos is, however, not the only toxic substance to which the plaintiff's lungs have been exposed. He started smoking cigarettes at the age of seventeen or eighteen, and he smoked one and one-half to two packs per day from the age of twenty-five until 1991, when he had a heart attack requiring coronary artery bypass surgery. At that point, he reduced his smoking, and currently is down to one cigarette after each meal. The plaintiff has, however, developed emphysema as a result of his cigarette smoking.[5]

The plaintiff filed a claim for compensation with the workers' compensation commission in 1994. After a hearing held in 2003, the commissioner for the eighth district, Amado Vargas, found that the plaintiff had suffered a lung injury as a result of his asbestos exposure at work, and "another lung injury" that resulted from his "long history of cigarette smoking. . . ." Vargas, who desired to appoint an independent physician to assess the plaintiff's condition, left open the apportionment and permanent partial disability claims pending that examination. At a subsequent hearing, Delaney adopted Vargas' findings, and concluded that the plaintiff had sustained a 25 percent permanent partial disability to each lung "as a result of [his] asbestos related injury." Delaney noted that the various physicians who testified agreed about the extent of the plaintiff's disability, but disagreed about whether that disability was caused by asbestos exposure or smoking. Delaney found, however, that the "work related asbestos exposure was a substantial contributing factor to this injury and resulting permanency," and ordered the defendants to pay permanent partial disability benefits to the plaintiff equating to 25 percent of each of his lungs, apportioned among the defendants, based on his length of prior service with each.

The defendants petitioned the board for review of Delaney's decision. The board agreed with Delaney that the plaintiff's entire disability was compensable. The board concluded that Delaney's conclusions were adequately supported by the testimony of Mark Cullen, a physician who had testified that the plaintiff's lung impairment was the result of both "his asbestos exposure and . . . his 'former smoking,' rather than . . . any smoking that had occurred after the disease symptoms had begun to

---

**4.** According to expert testimony, which Delaney apparently credited, the plaintiff's asbestos-related impairment is a sign of early asbestosis on the "continuum of asbestos effects," and is characterized by fibrosis, plaques and calcification on the pleura, or surfaces, of both lungs. This condition reduces lung capacity if the plaques thicken sufficiently to entrap the lung " 'like a corset.' "

**5.** Emphysema comes under the umbrella term known as chronic obstructive pulmonary disease, and is characterized by scarring and lesions that obstruct the small airways in the lungs, which leads to reduced diffusion and mixing of gases, including oxygen, in the lungs. Diffusion is the movement of gases through lung tissue into the bloodstream, and vice versa.

develop." The board also noted Cullen's testimony that three quarters of the plaintiff's disability was related to his emphysema, with one quarter of that, or 6.25 percent of the total disability, attributable to the asbestos exposure. The board also stated that Cullen had testified about the "synergistic effects" of the plaintiff's emphysema and asbestos related disease, and specifically "about the interplay between asbestos and smoke exposure that contributes to the [plaintiff's] overall permanency, based on his experience studying 'this population of jointly exposed men.' ... The ongoing effects of the [plaintiff's] asbestos exposure were not described by [Cullen] as being self-limiting. Thus, it was reasonable to conclude that the effects of the asbestos exposure have continued over time to produce an impairment, whether the progression has happened of its own volition, or in conjunction with the [plaintiff's] smoking-induced emphysema."

Relying on its decision in *Strong v. United Technologies Corp.*, No. 4563 CRB–1–02–8 (August 25, 2003), the board further concluded that the plaintiff's "smoking-related emphysema need not be treated separately for the purpose of assigning liability for the lung permanency, even if some doctors calculated the percentage of the impairment that was caused by asbestos exposure. It has long been a fundamental principle of workers' compensation law that an employer takes an employee as it finds him, and that any statutory variation from that principle must be construed to work a minimum encroachment on that rule." The board emphasized that even if the plaintiff's smoking related emphysema is considered a "concurrently developing condition," rather than a preexisting condition, "that argument does not undo the foundational tenet that the employer is responsible for the effects of a compensable injury, even if that injury's toll on a particular claimant is unexpectedly severe because of the way it collaborates with other health problems. Here, the employers and insurers that were on the risk during the [plaintiff's] period of asbestos exposure are responsible for the effects of that occupational exposure on the [plaintiff], with apportionment rights amongst themselves under [General Statutes] § 31–299b. There is no legal remedy that allows those employers to avoid liability for whatever portion of the [plaintiff's] lung impairment might be traceable to non-work-related emphysema, insofar as it was one of two conditions that combined to cause a single impairment." Accordingly, the board affirmed the decision of Delaney. This appeal followed.

On appeal, the defendants claim that the board improperly awarded the plaintiff compensation for the entire 25 percent permanent partial disability in each lung. The defendants first argue that they are responsible for only one quarter of the plaintiff's total disability because the plaintiff has two distinct lung injuries, one occupational, and one not. As a corollary to this argument, the defendants also contend that the 25 percent award is improper because there was no finding that the plaintiff's smoking related emphysema, which was a distinct disease process that had developed concurrently with his asbestos related symptoms and was responsible for 75 percent of his disability, was itself occupational in nature in any way and, therefore, compensable. Emphasizing that there is no evidence that the plaintiff's emphysema was a preexisting condition that was aggravated by the asbestos exposure, they contend that the axiom that an employer takes an employee as it finds him is inapplicable and that, as a policy matter, employers should not have to bear the costs of their employees' smoking habits.

In response, the plaintiff, emphasizing the broad construction and application customarily given to the workers' compensation statutes, contends that, although it "is undisputed that the [plaintiff] has emphysematous changes in his lungs, and it is undisputed that the [plaintiff] has asbestos-related pleural disease . . . it is far from clear that he has two separate and distinct lung injuries." The plaintiff notes the "synergistic and often difficult to separate" effects of asbestos exposure and cigarette smoking, and also claims that there is no practical way to determine whether he would have a lung impairment in the absence of asbestos exposure, or whether the cigarette related impairment would be the same without the asbestos exposure. The plaintiff emphasizes that the defendants all took him as they found him, specifically, as "a man with a history of smoking and a risk for developing smoking-related disease. Each successive employer took a man with a history of asbestos exposure and a risk for developing asbestos-related disease. And each successive employer took a man with both a history of cigarette smoking and asbestos exposure and a risk for developing synergistic lung disease." In light of the evidence adduced before Delaney, we agree with the defendants. * * *

We note at the outset that the legal difficulty in the present case stems from its factual posture, namely, that Delaney did not find that the plaintiff's emphysema was a preexisting condition that was aggravated by his asbestos-related lung condition, a determination that would have entitled the plaintiff to full compensation under General Statutes § 31–275(1)(D). See *Gartrell v. Dept. of Correction, supra,* 259 Conn. at 43, 787 A.2d 541 ("compensating an employee for the exacerbation of a preexisting mental or emotional condition that was caused by a work-related physical injury furthers the beneficent purposes of the Workers' Compensation Act [act]"); see also *Cashman v. McTernan School, Inc.,* 130 Conn. 401, 408–409, 34 A.2d 874 (1943) (statutory limitation on compensation for aggravation of preexisting diseases applicable only to preexisting "occupational diseases"). Similarly, Delaney did not find that the plaintiff's emphysema was a "previous disability" and that the asbestos exposure was a "second injury resulting in a permanent disability caused by both the previous disability and the second injury which is materially and substantially greater than the disability that would have resulted from the second injury alone," which would have entitled him to full compensation under General Statutes § 31–349(a). Instead, the question presented here, namely, whether the act requires the apportionment of benefits when a disability is caused by two separate, but concurrently developing medical conditions, only one of which is occupational in nature, is one of first impression for Connecticut's appellate courts that requires us to fill a gap in our statutes. Accordingly, it presents a question of law subject to plenary review. See, e.g., *Tracy v. Scherwitzky Gutter Co., supra*, 279 Conn. at 272–73, 901 A.2d 1176. * * *.

Our sister states have taken divergent approaches to this issue, and the factual and statutory peculiarities attendant to each state's case law renders it difficult to discern true "majority" or "minority" approaches. The seminal case in this area is *Pullman Kellogg v. Workers' Compensation Appeals Board*, 26 Cal.3d 450, 452–53, 605 P.2d 422, 161 Cal.Rptr. 783 (1980), which involved a pipefitter who had been exposed to numerous toxins, including asbestos, over forty years of work, but who also smoked a pack of cigarettes per day over that period. The pipefitter was diagnosed with chronic obstructive pulmonary disease, specifically chronic bronchitis and emphysema, which a physician's report stated was caused by " 'two factors,' " namely, his occupational exposure and his smoking. Id., at 453,161 Cal.Rptr. 783, 605 P.2d 422. He was rated as having a permanent 40 percent disability, and the workers' compensation commissioner reduced the benefits award by 50 percent to reflect the degree to which the disability had an occupational cause. Id., at 453–54, 161 Cal.Rptr. 783, 605 P.2d 422.

On appeal, the California Supreme Court concluded that the physician's "opinion that 50 percent of [the claimant's] pathology was caused by exposure to harmful substances and the remainder to his smoking habit does *not* provide a basis for apportionment. *It is disability resulting from, rather than a cause of, a disease which is the proper subject of apportionment*; 'pathology' may not be apportioned.... The [physician's] report does not attribute any part of the disability to [the claimant's] smoking of cigarettes; rather, it purports to make an apportionment of 'pathology.' Moreover, it does not state whether [the claimant] would have been disabled as the result of the smoking in the absence of the work-related inhalation of harmful substances. For all that appears in the record, he would not have suffered any disability whatever because of his smoking habit if he had not been exposed to damaging substances in his work. In the absence of such evidence, apportionment was not justified." (Citations omitted; emphasis added.) Id., at 454–55, 161 Cal.Rptr. 783, 605 P.2d 422.

The California Supreme Court further emphasized that "the fact that [the claimant's] disease resulted from both work-related and nonindustrial causes operating concurrently and that the nonindustrial component did not predate the industrial injury does not militate against application of the principles of apportionment. Any part of [the claimant's] lung disease which was due to his smoking preceded his disability, and *the decisive issue ... is whether such disease was accelerated or aggravated by his employment and whether its normal progress would have caused any disability absent the exposure to harmful substances in his work*." (Emphasis added.) Id., at 455, 161 Cal.Rptr. 783, 605 P.2d 422. Finally, the court emphasized that the burden of proving that "none of the disability is due to a preexisting condition" falls to the employer, who is the party that "benefits from a finding of apportionment...." Id., at 455–56, 161 Cal. Rptr. 783, 605 P.2d 422.

We find North Carolina case law even more instructive because that state, like Connecticut, has a statutory gap in this area. In *Morrison v. Burlington Industries*, 304 N.C. 1, 4–5, 282 S.E.2d 458 (1981), the claimant, a textile worker, became totally disabled when she contracted byssinosis, a chronic obstructive lung condition caused by exposure to cotton dust. She also suffered from phlebitis, varicose veins and diabetes. Id., at 6, 282 S.E.2d 458. The compensation commission concluded that the claimant was entitled to only a 55 percent permanent partial disability award, which reflected the portion attributable to the byssinosis. Id., at 7, 282 S.E.2d 458.

On appeal, the North Carolina Supreme Court rejected the claimant's argument that the state workers' compensation act "permits no such apportionment of an award in a case of total incapacity," and that "if an occupational disease acting together with non-job-related infirmities causes total disability the employee is entitled to compensation for total disability." Id., at 11, 282 S.E.2d 458. Noting that the workers' compensation act "is not, and was never intended to be, a general accident and health insurance act," the court stated that "the inquiry here is to determine whether, and to what extent, [the claimant] is incapacitated by that part of her chronic obstructive lung disease caused by her occupation to earn * * * [T]here must be some causal relation between the injury and the employment before the resulting disability or disablement can be said to 'arise out of' the employment." Id., at 11–12, 282 S.E.2d 458. After considering the state's law defining "occupational diseases," the court concluded that the "claimant's disablement resulting from the occupational disease does not exceed 50 to 60 percent and that the remaining 40 to 50 percent of her disability results from bronchitis, phlebitis, varicose veins, diabetes, and that part of her chronic lung disease not caused by her occupation. These ailments were in no way caused, aggravated or accelerated by the occupational disease." Id., at 13, 282 S.E.2d 458. The court stated that the industrial commission, therefore, "had no legal authority to award the claimant compensation for total disability when 40 to 50 percent of her disablement was not occupational in origin and was not aggravated or accelerated by any occupational disease." Id.

The North Carolina Supreme Court concluded by summarizing: "(1) an employer takes the employee as he finds her with all her pre-existing infirmities and weaknesses. (2) When a pre-existing, nondisabling, non-job-related condition is aggravated or accelerated by an accidental injury arising out of and in the course of employment or by an occupational disease so that disability results, then the employer must compensate the employee for the entire resulting disability even though it would not have disabled a normal person to that extent. (3) On the other hand, when a pre-existing, nondisabling, non-job-related disease or infirmity eventually causes an incapacity for work without any aggravation or acceleration of it by a compensable accident or by an occupational disease, the resulting incapacity so caused is not compensable. (4) When a claimant becomes incapacitated for work and part of that incapacity is caused, accelerated or aggravated by an occupational disease and the remainder of that incapacity for work is not caused, accelerated or aggravated by an occupational disease, the Workers' Compensation Act of North Carolina requires compensation only for that portion of the disability caused, accelerated or aggravated by the occupational disease." Id., at 18, 282 S.E.2d 458. * * *

Accordingly, on the basis of these well reasoned decisions, we conclude that apportionment or proportional reduction of benefits is appropriate when a respondent employer is able to prove that: (1) a disability has resulted from the combination of two concurrently developing disease processes, one that is nonoccupational, and the other that is occupational in nature; and (2) the conditions of the claimant's occupation have no influence on the development of the nonoccupational disease. In our view, this conclusion is consistent with the legislature's treatment of the aggravation of preexisting injuries under § 31–275(1)(D), and second injuries under § 31–349(a), in that it accommodates two axiomatic principles of workers' compensation law, namely, that to be compensable, the injury must arise out of and occur in the course of the employment, and also "that an employer takes the employee in the state of health in which it finds the employee." (Internal quotation marks omitted.) *Blakeslee v. Platt Bros. & Co.*, 279 Conn. 239, 245, 902 A.2d 620 (2006). Accordingly, the board, in relying on its decision in Strong v. United Technologies Corp., *supra*, at No. 4563 CRB–1–02–8, applied an incorrect legal standard when it concluded that the plaintiff's "smoking-related emphysema need not be treated separately for the purpose of assigning liability for the lung permanency," and there "is no legal remedy that allows those employers to avoid liability for whatever portion of the claimant's lung impairment might be traceable to non-work related emphysema, insofar as it was one of two conditions that combined to cause a single impairment." Put differently, apportionment or reduction of benefits is appropriate only in those cases wherein different diseases, one of which is occupational in nature, have combined to cause, in effect, two different disabilities, even if they ultimately affect the same bodily part or function.[19]

---

**19.** By way of illustration, we disagree with the analyses in *Jenkins v. Halstead Industries*, 17 Ark.App. 197, 706 S.W.2d 191 (1986), *Anderson v. Brinkhoff*, 859 P.2d 819 (Colo.1993), and *Forte v. Fernando Originals, Ltd.*, 667 A.2d 780 (R.I.1995), wherein the courts apportioned awards in cases involving a disability that resulted from a single disease that was caused by multiple factors, some of which were not occupational. In *Jenkins*, the court upheld an apportionment of the claimant's disability payments, which was attributable only to a single diagnosis of chronic obstructive pulmonary disease, based on 92 percent to his smoking and 8 percent to his occupational exposure to chemical fumes and talc dust. *Jenkins v. Halstead Industries*, supra, at 201, 706 S.W.2d 191. In *Anderson*, the claimant, a carpenter, had a genetic disorder that caused progressive emphysema and cardiac problems, which was aggravated coequally by his cigarette smoking and occupational exposure to sawdust and construction site dust. *Anderson v. Brinkhoff*, supra, 859 P.2d at 820. The administrative law judge had concluded that his smoking and occupational dust exposures were "co-equal aggravating factors" in the acceleration of his emphysema, and ruled that he should receive 50 percent of the benefits to which he otherwise would have been entitled. Id., at 821. On subsequent appeal, the Colorado Supreme Court upheld this order after concluding that "where there is no evidence that occupational exposure [to a hazard] is a necessary precondition to development of the disease," "the claimant [suffers from]

We further conclude that additional fact-finding proceedings are required because the record in the present case does not permit us to uphold the decision of the board under the correct legal standard, and also does not permit us to direct judgment in favor of the defendants because the commissioners have not made any findings with respect to the apportionment or proportional reduction; see footnote 1 of this opinion; of the plaintiff's benefits. Specifically, it has not been claimed that the plaintiff's emphysema is an occupational disease. Similarly, Delaney did not find that the conditions of the plaintiff's occupation influenced the development of his emphysema, or that it was impossible to make that determination. Moreover, although there is evidence in the record, including Cullen's testimony and report, as well as the report of Michael Conway, the physician appointed by a commissioner, to support apportionment of the 25 percent permanent partial disability among the two diseases, Delaney did not make a specific finding of fact corresponding to that evidence.

The decision of the compensation review board is reversed and the case is remanded to the board with direction to reverse the commissioner's decision, and to remand the case to a new commissioner for further proceedings according to law.

### NOTES AND QUESTIONS

1. The court emphasizes that there are two different diseases involved, in footnotes at the beginning of its opinion. How clear is the distinction between the two?

2. Now that you are familiar with both the "last injurious exposure" approach and the "apportionment" approach, which seems more appropriate to you? Is your answer the same for both traumatic injury and occupational disease? For all diseases? What about repeated stress traumatic injury, such as carpal tunnel syndrome?

## E.P. PAUP CO. v. DIRECTOR, OFFICE OF WORKERS COMPENSATION PROGRAMS

United States Court of Appeals, Ninth Circuit, 1993
999 F.2d 1341

SKOPIL, CIRCUIT JUDGE:

This is an appeal from a final decision of the Benefits Review Board ("Board") awarding disability benefits to an injured employee, Arthur

---

an occupational disease only to the extent that the occupational conditions have contributed to the claimant's overall disability." (Internal quotation marks omitted.) Id., at 824–25. Although the court concluded that aggravation of the emphysema was compensable because the "risk associated with the exposure to sawdust and other airborne particulate matter is greater for a carpenter than the risk of exposure outside the workplace," it nevertheless also upheld the 50 percent apportionment because the "occupational dust exposure was a co-equal aggravating factor in the acceleration of [the claimant's] emphysema...." Id., at 825. Similarly, in *Forte*, without a statute providing to the contrary, the court upheld an order that reduced the employer's medical payments obligation by one-half based on testimony that the claimant's "respiratory injury" was caused 50 percent by smoking and 50 percent by his exposure to airborne compounds in the workplace, even though the claimant's "medical treatment was for a single ailment caused by several contributing factors, one of which was the workplace." *Forte v. Fernando Originals, Ltd.*, supra, 667 A.2d at 783–84.

McDougall ("McDougall"), and directing that his employer, E.P. Paup Company ("employer"), reimburse the State of Washington ("state") for benefits previously paid under state workers' compensation law. [The employer's federal workers' compensation carrier is Insurance Company of North America ("INA").]* * *

### Facts and Prior Proceedings

McDougall injured his left hand in a non-work-related car accident in 1978 and did not work for approximately 18 months. In 1979, he injured his lower back while working for employer as a pile buck and he has not worked since that injury. He sought workers' compensation benefits for his back injury under state law and later under the LHWCA. The state paid $53,548.08 in compensation and $16,244.95 in medical expenses before it stopped paying benefits upon learning that LHWCA benefits had been awarded.

*[handwritten margin note: Then hortsback dtaok]*

The parties stipulated at the LHWCA hearing that McDougall was permanently and totally disabled. The Administrative Law Judge ("ALJ") awarded McDougall temporary total disability benefits for two years and permanent total disability benefits thereafter. He determined that Director's special fund would be liable for payments after the expiration of 104 weeks pursuant to 33 U.S.C. § 908(f) because McDougall's permanent total disability was the result of his previous hand injury and his work-related back injury. The ALJ also allowed offsets to INA and Director's special fund pursuant to 33 U.S.C. § 903(e) for compensation McDougall had received from the state. Thus, the ALJ awarded McDougall the difference between state and LHWCA benefits. * * *

On reconsideration of the modification, the ALJ vacated the section 903(e) credit and ordered INA and the special fund to reimburse the state for McDougall's state benefits. The ALJ held that INA was not required to reimburse the state for medical expenses. * * *

The Board affirmed the ALJ's determination that INA was not entitled to an offset under section 903(e). It ordered INA to reimburse the state for benefits it paid to McDougall. It held that the state was entitled to reimbursement for medical expenses if on remand the ALJ determined that McDougall was entitled to medical benefits under the LHWCA. The Board reversed the ALJ's ruling that INA was entitled to special fund relief under section 908(f), holding that the evidence in the record was not sufficient to support the ALJ's determination that McDougall's hand injury contributed to his permanent total disability.

On remand, the parties stipulated that McDougall's medical expenses for his back injury were covered under the LHWCA and represented reasonable charges. The ALJ ordered INA to reimburse the state for those medical expenses. The ALJ rejected INA's offer of proof of additional evidence regarding the section 908(f) issue. The Board affirmed the ALJ's decision on remand and employer, INA and Director timely petition this court for review.

*Discussion*

\* \* \*

I.

INA and Director argue that the Board's order directing INA to reimburse the state for benefits paid to McDougall violates section 903(e) of the LHWCA. That provision gives an employer or its carrier an offset credit when a claimant has received benefits for the same injury under a state workers' compensation law. Section 903(e) provides:

> Notwithstanding any other provision of law, any amounts paid to an employee for the same injury, disability, or death for which benefits are claimed under this chapter pursuant to any other workers' compensation law or section 688 of Title 46 (relating to recovery for injury to or death of seamen) shall be credited against any liability imposed by this chapter. 33 U.S.C. § 903(e).

> The Board held that section 903(e) does not apply here because state law excludes coverage for workers covered under the federal maritime laws. State law provides in part: (1) The provisions of this title shall not apply to a master or member of a crew of any vessel, or to employers and workers for whom a right or obligation exists under the maritime laws for personal injuries or death of such workers. . . . (4) In the event payments are made under this title prior to the final determination under the maritime laws, such benefits shall be repaid by the worker or beneficiary if recovery is subsequently made under the maritime laws. Wash.Rev. Code § 51.12.100 (1990) (amended 1991). INA and Director dispute the Board's holding on several grounds. Director contends that either state law does not apply or its application to these facts is prohibited by federal law. INA argues that the state statute is preempted by the federal legislation.

A.

\* \* \*

B.

INA argues that section 903(e) preempts the state's reimbursement statute. \* \* \*

On first inspection, the plain language of section 903(e) appears to support the argument that state law is preempted. Section 903(e) provides that "[n]otwithstanding any other provision of law" an employer has the right to receive an offset credit for "any amounts paid to an employee . . . pursuant to any other workers' compensation law." 33 U.S.C. § 903(e). . . . A contention could be made that the federal statute covers any and all payments to an employee, even those made erroneously or provisionally.

A closer review, however, satisfies us that Congress did not intend to expressly preempt the state's reimbursement scheme.... Because state law excludes from its coverage workers who are covered under the LHWCA, the benefits here were not paid "pursuant to" the state's workers' compensation law. * * *

The history of the LHWCA demonstrates that since 1972 Congress has intended to allow, but not to require, concurrent state and federal coverage of workers' compensation claims. Congress amended the LHWCA in 1972, in part to raise the amount of compensation and to extend coverage to certain contiguous land areas. *Director, OWCP v. Perini North River Assoc.*, 459 U.S. 297, 313, 103 S.Ct. 634, 645, 74 L.Ed.2d 465 (1983). "In so doing, the Longshoremen's Act became, for the first time, a source of relief for injuries which had always been viewed as the province of state compensation law." *Sun Ship, Inc. v. Pennsylvania*, 447 U.S. 715, 719, 100 S.Ct. 2432, 2436, 65 L.Ed.2d 458 (1980). In Sun Ship the issue was whether extended shoreside coverage under the 1972 amendments had the effect of displacing concurrent state remedies. The Court held that it did not, reasoning that the 1972 extension of federal jurisdiction supplemented rather than supplanted state compensation law. Id. at 720, 100 S.Ct. at 2436.

Congress amended the LHWCA in 1984 to include section 903(e). At that time Congress also considered amending section 905(a) to preclude a worker eligible for LHWCA benefits from receiving an award under state compensation. * * * The amendment passed the Senate but failed in the House.... Congressional rejection of a provision making coverage under the LHWCA exclusive demonstrates that the phrase "notwithstanding any other provision of law" was not intended to preempt state workers' compensation law or to upset the scheme allowing concurrent federal and state coverage.

There is no direct conflict between section 51.12.100 and section 903(e) because nothing in the federal legislation prohibits the state from excluding coverage to workers eligible for LHWCA benefits or from seeking reimbursement of amounts paid to an employee while pursuing a federal remedy. Contra *Bouchard v. General Dynamics Corp.*, 963 F.2d 541, 544 (2d Cir.1992) (Connecticut law determined to conflict with section 903(e)). * * *

Section 903(e) codified the credit doctrine, which permits the deduction of certain types of payments in order to prevent an injured worker from receiving a double recovery. *Todd Shipyards Corp. v. Director, OWCP*, 848 F.2d 125, 126 (9th Cir.1988). Prior to section 903(e), the credit doctrine allowed offset of benefits against LHWCA awards only if prior benefits were awarded under the LHWCA. Id. at 127. Section 903(e) thus broadened the credit doctrine to allow a credit against an LHWCA award of any other workers' compensation benefits or Jones Act benefits. Id.

*[handwritten margin note: No Conflict]*

\* \* \* When it enacted section 903(e) in 1984, Congress intended to overrule *United Brands Co. v. Melson,* 594 F.2d 1068 (5th Cir.1979). See 130 Cong.Rec. 8326 (1984) (explanation of House amendment to § 38); 130 Cong.Rec. 25905 (1984) (remarks of Rep. Erlenborn). In *Melson,* the court held that an employee may recover compensation under both the LHWCA and the state act, and there was no requirement in the LHWCA that the employee's federal award be reduced by the amount of the state settlement. *Melson,* 594 F.2d at 1074–75.

Thus, the legislative history shows that Congress intended to prevent double recovery by broadening an employer's right to receive an offset. Section 51.12.100 does not stand as a direct obstacle to accomplishing that goal. To the contrary, because section 51.12.100(4) requires repayment of state benefits paid to the worker when there is coverage under the LHWCA, the state statute actually furthers the objective of section 903(e) by preventing double recovery. There is no issue here involving double recovery or McDougall's eligibility for benefits under the LHWCA.

Section 903(e) applies only if there is concurrent state and federal coverage. There is nothing in the LHWCA to indicate that a state cannot exclude from its jurisdiction injuries that are covered by federal law. Allowing the state to make such an exclusion does not stand as an obstacle to the Congressional objective of preventing double recovery by broadening an employer's right to recover offsets. \* \* \*

### C.

INA contends that if it is required to pay additional benefits, the Board erred by requiring INA, rather than McDougall, to reimburse the state. INA asserts that the state's statutory scheme does not permit an order of reimbursement from anyone other than a claimant. The ALJ concluded that it was "administratively more efficient" to require direct payment from INA to the state. The Board affirmed that decision without discussion.

We agree that the Board erred when it ordered INA to pay the state directly. That conclusion contravenes Wash.Rev. Code § 51.12.100(4), which provides that benefits shall be "repaid by the worker" if recovery is made under the maritime laws. Furthermore, it contravenes 33 U.S.C. §§ 914(a), 902(12). Section 914(a) provides that compensation shall be paid "directly to the person entitled thereto." \* \* \*

In summary, we conclude that the Board erred when it ordered INA to pay the state directly. Accordingly, we modify the Board's order to require INA to pay McDougall an amount equal to the state payments and require McDougall to pay that amount to the state. \* \* \*

### II.

INA contends that the Board erred by holding that employer was not entitled to special fund relief pursuant to 33 U.S.C. § 908(f). Section 908(f) provides that where an employee is permanently and totally disabled, and the disability is found not to be caused solely by the injury incurred on the job, the employer's liability is limited to a maximum of 104 weeks. See *FMC Corp. v. Director, OWCP*, 886 F.2d 1185, 1186 (9th Cir.1989). After that time period, liability is shifted from the employer to the special fund established by 33 U.S.C. § 944. The purpose of section 908(f) is to encourage hiring of partially disabled people. *Lockheed Shipbuilding v. Director, OWCP*, 951 F.2d 1143, 1144 (9th Cir.1991).

To establish section 908(f) relief, the employer must show: (1) that the employee had an existing permanent partial disability prior to the employment injury; (2) that the disability was manifest to the employer prior to the employment injury; and (3) that the current disability is not due solely to the most recent injury. Id. (quoting Todd Pac. *Shipyards v. Director, OWCP*, 913 F.2d 1426, 1429 (9th Cir.1990)). There is no dispute here that McDougall had a preexisting permanent partial disability that was manifest to employer. INA contends that McDougall's disability was not due solely to his back injury. * * *

INA must demonstrate that the second injury alone did not cause McDougall's permanent total disability. See *FMC*, 886 F.2d at 1186–87. It is not sufficient if the evidence indicates only that his two injuries create a greater disability than would his back injury alone. Id. at 1187. If the later injury was enough to totally disable McDougall, it is not relevant that his preexisting hand injury made his total disability even greater. *See Director, OWCP v. Luccitelli*, 964 F.2d 1303, 1305–06 (2d Cir.1992). * * *

[The court concluded that the ALJ's findings were supported by the record.]

### III.

INA argues that McDougall is not entitled to attorney's fees and costs pursuant to 33 U.S.C. § 928(b) because only the source of his benefits was at issue, not the amount of his compensation. The Board rejected that argument, holding that INA was liable for fees because, "by virtue of the modification proceedings, claimant successfully obtained an inchoate right to additional compensation equivalent to the amount of the Section [90]3(e) credit awarded to employer."

The purpose of section 928 is to authorize attorney's fees against employers when the existence or extent of liability is controverted and the claimant succeeds in establishing liability or obtaining increased compensation. *National Steel & Shipbuilding Co. v. United States Dep't of Labor*, 606 F.2d 875, 882 (9th Cir.1979). The award of fees here serves that purpose. The extent of INA's liability was controverted ever since McDougall sought a modification on the basis of the state's reimbursement order. McDougall succeeded in the administrative proceedings in establishing INA's further liability. Accordingly, we affirm the award of fees and costs imposed by the Board.

*Conclusion*

We agree with the Board that INA is not entitled to a section 903(e) offset credit because the LHWCA does not prohibit a state from excluding from its coverage injuries that are covered under federal workers' compensation law. We modify the reimbursement scheme to require INA to pay McDougall an amount equal to the state payments and require McDougall to pay that amount to the state. We affirm the Board's conclusion that INA is not entitled to special fund relief under section 908(f). Finally, we affirm the award of attorney's fees and costs.

*Affirmed* as Modified.

## NOTES AND QUESTIONS

1. Note that to encourage hiring and retention of disabled workers, Section 908(f) limits an employer's LHWCA liability regardless of whether the prior injury was suffered while in the employ of (a) the current employer, (b) a different employer, or (c) was not work-related. Federal courts have applied the "cautious employer" test in deciding whether a worker is permanently partially disabled within the meaning of that section. That test finds such permanent partial disability if the impairment is so severe as to motivate a cautious employer to discharge the employee because of a greatly increased risk of employment related accident and compensation liability. *Lockheed Shipbuilding v. Director*, 951 F.2d 1143 (9th Cir.1991).

2. The doctrines and procedures discussed in the last three cases began to be developed more than seventy years ago. They must now be viewed against the backdrop of The Americans with Disabilities Act (42 U.S.C. § 12101, et seq.) (ADA), which was enacted in 1990. The ADA, which applies to employers with 15 or more employees, prohibits discrimination against a person who: (a) has, or is regarded as having, a physical or mental impairment that substantially limits one or more major life activities, and (b) can perform the essential functions of a job with or without reasonable accommodation. Financial hardship is a defense to not accommodating the disabled person, but is not a defense to discrimination if reasonable accommodation is not necessary for the individual to perform the essential job tasks. For example, it was a violation of the Rehabilitation Act of 1973, which applies similar standards to employers performing federal contracts, for an employer to justify rejection of a "morbidly obese" job applicant on the ground that it feared a resulting increase in its workers' compensation costs. *Cook v. State of Rhode Island*, 10 F.3d 17 (1st Cir.1993). What should be the ADA's impact upon the "cautious employer" test set out in the previous note?

Section 102(d) of the ADA [42 U.S.C. § 12112(d)] prohibits employers covered by the Act from asking a job applicant about any disabilities, or the severity or nature of a disability. However, a prospective employer may inquire about the applicant's ability to perform job-related functions and an offer of employment can be conditioned upon the results of examinations and inquiries that are related to job function performance and any required accommodations. The EEOC has adopted Enforcement Guidelines explaining what conduct it deems prohibited respecting medical inquiries and examinations. The Guidelines impose a burden on an employer to justify an inquiry or examination based on objective evidence that the targeted medical condition will pose a direct threat to safe or effective performance of essential job functions. Unlike the discrimination prohibitions, a claim based on the ADA's restrictions on medical inquiries and examinations can be brought regardless of whether the claimant is "disabled" within the meaning of the statute.

Clearly a major purpose of the "second injury fund" provisions in the majority of workers' compensation laws was to make employment of workers with a disability more attractive. Does the ADA make that a less important objective? Is a second injury fund more or less important in a jurisdiction that uses an apportionment of liability approach rather than the last injurious exposure approach?

3.  Several courts have ruled that the exclusivity of workers' compensation remedies does not preclude an employee's state or federal damages action asserting that in an effort to reduce future compensation costs, an employer refused to reemploy, provide an accommodating job assignment, or continue the employment of a workers' compensation claimant. See, for example, *Fail v. Community Hospital*, 946 P.2d 573 (Colo.App.1997); *City of Moorpark v. Superior Court of Ventura*, 57 Cal.Rptr.2d 156 (Cal.App., 2d Dist.1996); *Wood v. County of Alameda*, 875 F.Supp. 659 (N.D.Cal.1995).

4.  Most jurisdictions do not impose liability upon second injury funds if the prior injury was not known and was not apparent when the worker was hired. Should such injuries be excluded from second fund coverage?

5.  In addition to second injury funds, various other types of special funds operated in conjunction with workers' compensation systems are designed to spread the costs of providing particular types of benefits in situations in which the immediate employer likely is not in a position to wholly prevent the compensated disability, as in the case of occupational disease, or where the nature of the benefit has a social purpose that goes beyond curative treatment for and financial support of the injured or ill worker—as in the case of vocational rehabilitation.

The other basic category of special fund is the fund that provides financial security to the system in the event the normal source of funds is unavailable. Thus, most jurisdictions that permit coverage by private carriers operate surety funds to cover the liabilities of insolvent carriers, and a considerable number provide similar surety programs for self-insurers. Many jurisdictions also have a special fund to provide benefits to cover the liabilities of uninsured employers; that is, employers who fail to obtain required insurance.

6.  Several months after an employee received treatment for a back injury, he applied for a new job involving some lifting. In his job application he answered "no" to a question asking if he ever experienced a back injury. In the new job he hurt his back once again, aggravating the damage from the prior injury. Should his new employer be liable for workers' compensation benefits? The South Dakota court denied benefits to such a claimant in *Oesterreich v. Canton–Inwood Hospital*, 511 N.W.2d 824 (S.D.1994). The court, relying on what it described as the majority rule, held that a workers' compensation claim is barred if: (1) the employee knowingly and willfully

made a false representation concerning his physical condition, (2) the employer's reliance on that representation was a substantial factor in hiring the worker, and (3) there was a causal connection between the misrepresentation and the injury.

The defense that the claimant materially misrepresented his physical condition when applying for work is codified in some state workers' compensation statutes. See, e.g., *Robinett v. Enserch Alaska Construction*, 804 P.2d 725 (Alaska 1990) (declining, however, to apply the defense to injuries suffered prior to the statutory adoption of the rule). For a decision rejecting the majority rule, see *Blue Bell Printing v. Workmen's Compensation Appeal Board*, 115 Pa.Cmwlth. 203, 539 A.2d 933 (1988).

What impact, if any, do you expect the ADA to have upon the defense of material misrepresentation?

7. The "credit rule" applied under the LHWCA can also be used in situations in which workers' compensation statutes in sister states are both available to an injured worker. That can happen, for instance, in situations in which an employee resides in state A and does most work there (so that her work can be said to be "localized" in state A), but is injured while working in state B. Each of the two states would have a basis for applying its compensation law, and may do so without violating the Full Faith and Credit clause of the federal constitution. *Thomas v. Washington Gas Light Co.*, 448 U.S. 261, 100 S.Ct. 2647, 65 L.Ed.2d 757 (1980). If the injured worker discovers she is entitled to greater benefits in state B but has already received payments in state A, and applies for benefits in B, double recovery is prevented by crediting the payments made in state A against the award in state B. See, e.g., *Lesco Restoration v. Workers' Compensation Appeal Bd.*, 861 A.2d 1002 (Pa. Cmwlth. 2004).

The Defense Bases Act, 42 U.S.C. § 1651, provides that the LHWCA applies to U.S. contractors and their civilian employees working on military installations in foreign countries. In *Lee v. Boeing Co.*, 7 F.Supp.2d 617 (D.Md. 1998), the court held that credit would be allowed to an employer for payments made under the Saudi Social Insurance law, because that law has so many of the characteristics of a typical American workers' compensation statute.

An alternative to using the credit rule is to hold that an injured worker who has sought and received benefits in state A has "elected" that as her remedy, and cannot receive further benefits in state B. See, e.g., Texas Lab. Code Ann. § 406.075 (Vernon 2006). A statute of state A purporting to make its award of benefits exclusive is not necessarily binding, however, on a sister state that rejects the election doctrine. *P.I. & I. Motor Express, Inc. v. Industrial Comm'n*, 368 Ill.App.3d 230, 306 Ill.Dec. 385, 857 N.E.2d 784 (2006).

## 5.  FINANCING BENEFITS

The general scheme of workers' compensation programs is to place benefit costs upon the beneficiary's employer. However, not all costs are allocated in this manner. In large measure this is because it is often difficult to determine who or what caused the ailment or to project, for insurance purposes, what liabilities are likely to be waiting down the road.

When an employer uses a government or private insurance program to meet its responsibilities, premiums are set by methods that are largely, but not totally, dependent upon the claims experience of the employer's workforce. One system used for determining those premiums is known as "manual rates." These set premiums at a specified rate per $100 of payroll based on the claims payment and overhead cost experience of all firms in a given occupational or industry class in the jurisdiction regardless of differences in individual workforce claims experience and regardless of differences in the firms' average levels of remuneration. Generally, unmodified manual rates are used only for the smallest businesses. Other employers' manual rates usually are adjusted ("experience rated") based on their actual loss experiences for the past few years as modified by actuarial considerations that try to take into account the probable future deviations from that past experience. Some states permit employers to be self-insurers. This requires creating special investment accounts used to pay benefits. Generally only large employers find it feasible to self-insure; some of these will also purchase special "umbrella" insurance policies that will provide coverage in the event there is an unusually heavy loss experience in a particular year.

Among the problems in setting a workers' compensation insurance premium is the difficulty of determining how to equitably allocate the administrative costs of benefit programs. Larger enterprises often have greater internal expertise in guiding benefits applicants and preparing claims documentation. This can result in lower per capita administrative costs. Consequently, larger employers normally are given a discount to reflect a smaller allocation of administrative costs per covered employee. On the other hand, in the case of private insurers, such discounts may sometimes be motivated, at least in part, by the desire to capture a larger segment of the business.

To the extent that an employer must pay for the workers' compensation benefits received by its employees, it has a financial motivation to reduce benefits claims. Some alternatives are socially desirable; others are not. One way to do this is by making the workplace and work procedures safer. Other steps can also be taken. The employer can try to hire workers who are healthy and whose personal and family characteristics indicate they are less prone to work related injury or disease, or try to hire workers who are more likely to recuperate quickly from a work related illness or injury, or try to deter ill and injured workers from seeking benefits, or it can try to hide or modify information establishing the work-related nature of an injury or illness or the extensiveness of a worker's disability and medical and rehabilitation needs. The Americans with Disabilities Act, 42 U.S.C. § 12101, places some restraints upon the type of information an employer can request of job applicants and the type of characteristics an employer can use as criteria for personnel decisions. Title II of the Genetic Information Nondiscrimination Act of 2008, 42 U.S.C. §§ 2000ff–2000ff–

11, now forbids the use of genetic data for discriminatory purposes by employers, employment agencies and labor organizations. The Act specifically outlaws employment practices that would have a disparate impact, and also requires that the genetic information an employer may legitimately have must be kept confidential.

Because of the problems in ascertaining cause-effect relationships, as seen in many of the cases in the preceding sections, liability is sometimes pooled among all employers or similarly situated employers with respect to benefits arising out of situations in which injury or illness results from long-term exposure to hazards while employed by multiple employers. In addition, as we have seen, there are situations in which the degree of disability is compounded by pre-existing infirmities, so that some of the benefits costs may be allocated to prior employers. Allocating the burdens can be done in many ways, but there are constitutional due process limits on just how far a state may go in assessing the costs of industrial injury on enterprises other than an immediate employer. See the opinions of a highly divided Court in *Eastern Enterprises v. Apfel*, 524 U.S. 498, 118 S.Ct. 2131, 141 L.Ed.2d 451 (1998). Another deviation from the principle of allocating cost to the beneficiary's employer is the distribution of the burden of paying for the machinery to resolve disputed claims. To a large extent these costs are paid by government from general revenues.

## 6. SCOPE OF THE "EXCLUSIVE REMEDY" DEFENSE

### ALDAY v. PATTERSON TRUCKLINE, INC.

The opinion appears above at p. 689

#### NOTES AND QUESTIONS

1.  Whether a firm (Hypothetically, the XYZ Co.) wishes to be characterized as an "employer" can clearly depend on whether, in the absence of the exclusive remedy defense, it would likely be held liable in tort for substantial damages. Otherwise, the firm is likely to prefer not to be considered an employer, since employer status creates other liabilities—for wages, as defendant in a discrimination case, and so on. The injured worker may be best served if XYZ Co. is characterized as an employer if there is no other source of medical and disability benefits and little likelihood of tort recovery (or if the worker is in acute need of money and damages recovery is likely to take time). If, on the other hand, there is another enterprise paying compensation benefits, there is every reason for the injured worker to want the relationship with XYZ Co. not to be characterized as employment, since that leaves XYZ as a potential tort defendant. The typical worker may well not be aware of all of this in the days following a serious injury. Should an agency administering a workers' compensation law provide advice on this topic, or is that too far outside its proper role?

2. "Statutory employers" (see p. 695) will often include indemnification agreements in their agreements with subcontractors in an attempt to make sure that primary liability for workers' compensation benefits is clearly fixed, and may demand that the subcontractor provide proof of workers' compensation insurance coverage as a condition of entering into the contract. The same is true with firms that supply employees to work for other firms, on either a temporary or long-term basis. While such agreements may be effective between the contracting parties, they do not control the characterization of the relationship by the courts. See *Brown v. Union Oil Co. of California*, 984 F.2d 674 (5th Cir. 1993).

3. Suppose that instead of sending injured workers to independent physicians, a company employs physicians to treat employee on-the-job injuries. An employee of such a company is injured at work and receives medical treatment by a physician hired by her employer. The treatment is incompetent and the victimized worker sues the physician for medical malpractice. Should the suit be allowed? Most jurisdictions that have addressed this question hold that the worker's sole recovery for such malpractice injuries is under the workers' compensation statute; others allow the malpractice suit. What reasoning would support the respective positions? Compare, for example, *McCormick v. Caterpillar Tractor Co.*, 85 Ill.2d 352, 53 Ill.Dec. 207, 423 N.E.2d 876 (1981) (malpractice action dismissed) with *Ducote v. Albert*, 521 So.2d 399 (La.1988) (malpractice action allowed), and *Hendy v. Losse*, 54 Cal.3d 723, 1 Cal.Rptr.2d 543, 819 P.2d 1 (1991) (football player's malpractice suit against a team doctor denied).

# SUAREZ v. DICKMONT PLASTICS CORPORATION

Supreme Court of Connecticut, 1994
229 Conn. 99, 639 A.2d 507

KATZ, ASSOCIATE JUSTICE.

The principal issue on appeal is whether the Appellate Court properly affirmed the trial court's granting of the defendant's motion for summary judgment based on the exclusive remedy provisions of the Workers' Compensation Act (act).[1] * * *

The following facts are undisputed. The plaintiff, Alfonso Suarez, filed a complaint alleging that he had been severely and permanently injured while working for the defendant, Dickmont Plastics Corporation, when,

---

1. General Statutes § 31–284 provides in pertinent part: "BASIC RIGHTS AND LIABILITIES. CIVIL ACTION TO ENJOIN NONCOMPLYING EMPLOYER FROM ENTERING INTO EMPLOYMENT CONTRACTS. NOTICE OF AVAILABILITY OF COMPENSATION. N. (a) An employer shall not be liable to any action for damages on account of personal injury sustained by an employee arising out of and in the course of his employment or on account of death resulting from personal injury so sustained, but an employer shall secure compensation for his employees as provided under this chapter, except that compensation shall not be paid when the personal injury has been caused by the wilful and serious misconduct of the injured employee or by his intoxication. All rights and claims between employer and employees, or any representatives or dependents of such employees, arising out of personal injury or death sustained in the course of employment are abolished other than rights and claims given by this chapter, provided nothing in this section shall prohibit any employee from securing, by agreement with his employer, additional compensation from his employer for the injury or from enforcing any agreement for additional compensation."

while attempting to clear hot molten plastic out of a plastic molding machine, two of his right hand fingers became caught in the machine and were partially amputated. The plaintiff alleged that his injuries, which resulted in a permanent loss of function and use of his master hand and substantial scarring, were caused by the defendant's wilful and serious misconduct. The plaintiff further alleged, inter alia, that the defendant: (1) always required the plaintiff and other employees to clean the plastic molding machine while it was in operation; (2) refused to allow the plaintiff or other employees to use safer cleaning methods; and (3) refused to equip the machine with a protective cover or other device in order to prevent injuries to persons operating or cleaning it.

The defendant moved for summary judgment claiming that, in the absence of proof by the plaintiff that the employer intended to injure the plaintiff, the exclusive remedy provisions of the act barred the plaintiff's claim. By affidavit, the defendant's president denied the plaintiff's allegations and maintained that he had not intended for the plaintiff to be injured. In his opposition to the motion, supported by his own deposition and the affidavit and attached opinion of Michael E. Shanok, a physical engineer, the plaintiff claimed that the defendant's intentional conduct was substantially certain to cause the injuries that occurred. At his deposition, the plaintiff testified that the defendant's foreman, although aware of the dangers involved, had told him that: (1) he could not use a vacuum cleaner to clean the hot material from the machine because it would waste material; (2) the machine could not be turned off during the cleaning because the operator would lose time; and (3) if he used the vacuum cleaner, he would be fired.

In his report, Shanok described the equipment involved as a plunger type horizontal injection molding machine used to melt thermoplastic and thermoset rubber polymers into a mold through the action of a hydraulically operated plunger. Shanok further explained that the material is fed from a small, cylindrical hopper with a conical bottom directly into a feed chute. From the chute, the material falls into an injection chamber. From there, an injection plunger is pushed by a hydraulic ram through a barrel surrounded by electrical heating bands. As the plastic is melted within the barrel, it is further pushed into the mold. * * *

Shanok's report further states that the feed chute should be vacuum cleaned when the material hopper is positioned away from the feed chute, so that raw plastic cannot be fed into the machine during cleaning. Nevertheless, the plaintiff alleges that the foreman had ordered him to clean up during the completion of production, while the machine was still operating, so that the employer could avoid paying personnel overtime. Pursuant to these orders, he was required to reach into the chute with his hand to remove the remaining plastic pellets in the feed chamber to avoid wasting material. On the day of the accident, the plaintiff claims that he had put his hand into the energized machine's feed chute while the machine was operating, thereby causing the plunger to move forward in the injection sleeve and partially amputate two of the plaintiff's right hand fingers.

In addition, Shanok listed in his report several resulting violations of the Occupational Safety and Health Act (OSHA); 29 U.S.C. § 658 et seq.; General Industry Regulations; 29 C.F.R.; and deviations from the recommended requirements of the American National Standard for Safety Requirements for the Construction, Care and Use of Horizontal Injection Molding Machines. American National Standards Institute, B151.1–1976.[2] In particular, Shanok noted that the defendant's alleged conduct violated accepted safety standards by requiring employees to insert their hands into the feed chute of an energized horizontal injection molding surface, adding that the "circumstances which existed at the time of the subject accident caused such action to be even more dangerous, because the hydraulic system was not interlocked to prevent actuation of the plunger and the control panel is so situated that the operator cannot see an individual who is standing at the maintenance platform."

Shanok concluded that the defendant's actions "crossed the boundary between gross negligence and reckless disregard for the safety of its employees," that "there was a total absence of any sign ... that even the slightest consideration for [the plaintiff's] safety had been undertaken," that remedying even one of the numerous unsafe actions could have prevented the injury, and that it was clear from the combination of factors that the plaintiff's injury "would be, sooner or later, a predictable and probable event."

The trial court granted the defendant's motion for summary judgment having determined that the plaintiff's "documentary proof [fell] short of the standard necessary to entitle him to benefit from the exception to the exclusivity provisions of the Connecticut Workers' Compensation Act." * * * The Appellate Court held that the plaintiff's factual allegations could not support a determination either that his employer had intended to harm him, or that his employer had believed the injury that occurred was substantially certain to follow from its acts or conduct. * * * Accordingly, that court affirmed the judgment. Id., at 636, 621 A.2d 1356. We granted the plaintiff's petition for certification limited to the following issues: "(1) Whether an individual may bring a civil action for damages against his employer for injuries sustained at work where such injuries were caused by work conditions intentionally created by the employer which made the injuries substantially certain to occur?" and "(2) Whether there is a genuine issue of material fact as to whether the employer's intentional actions created a situation in which the employee's injuries were substantially certain to occur?" *Suarez v. Dickmont Plastics Corp.*, 225 Conn. 926, 625 A.2d 827 (1993). * * *

---

**2.** Shanok explained in his report that, as opposed to OSHA regulations, which require compliance by law, "[t]he American National Standard is a recommended practice which was developed through the auspices of the Society of the Plastics Industry, Inc., and is in such general use in the plastics industry that it can be considered to be an [authoritative] standard for the custom and practice of maintaining safety in the industry."

We consistently have interpreted the exclusivity provision of the act, General Statutes § 31–284(a), as a total bar to common law actions brought by employees against employers for job related injuries with one narrow exception that exists when the employer has committed an intentional tort or where the employer has engaged in wilful or serious misconduct. *Jett v. Dunlap*, 179 Conn. 215, 217, 425 A.2d 1263 (1979). * * *

* * * In *Jett*, we recognized the distinction between the actor who is "merely a foreman or supervisor," to which attribution of corporate responsibility for his or her conduct is inappropriate, and the actor who "is of such a rank in the corporation that he [or she] may be deemed the alter ego of the corporation under the standards governing disregard of the corporate entity," to which attribution of corporate responsibility is appropriate. Id., at 219, 425 A.2d 1263. This distinction, relying on identification and not agency, was based entirely on status and not on conduct. The pleadings in *Jett*, however, did not allege that the employer had directed or authorized the subject conduct or that the actor could be deemed the "alter ego" of the defendant's organization. Rather, the plaintiff alleged only that the employer had condoned the supervisor's offensive conduct after the fact. Because the injury, if any, resulted not from the employer's subsequent ratification, but rather from the employee's precedent intentional tort, we held that such condoning was not an intentional tort and did not relate back.

In this case, the plaintiff alleged that it was the defendant whose wilful and serious misconduct caused his injuries. Moreover, in his deposition, the plaintiff referred to the foreman's warning that "[i]f they see you, they fire you," in reference to what would have happened had he refused to clean the energized machine manually. The defendant denies requiring the plaintiff to clean the machine while it was in operation, although notably, there is no denial regarding the prohibition against using vacuums, as opposed to hands, to clean the machine. This question of credibility between the parties, however, raises an issue of fact which the trial court cannot resolve on a motion for summary judgment. * * *

Another significant case relied upon by the parties is *Mingachos v. CBS, Inc.*, 196 Conn. 91, 102, 491 A.2d 368 (1985), in which we further delineated the scope of the exception to the act. In that case we declined to "extend judicially the [*Jett v. Dunlap, supra*, 179 Conn. 215, 425 A.2d 1263] exception to § 31–284 to include injuries to employees resulting from 'intentional,' or 'wilful,' or 'reckless' violations by the employer of safety standards established pursuant to federal and state law, such as OSHA." Id., at 100, 491 A.2d 368. * * *

In defining the operative terms, we stated in *Mingachos v. CBS, Inc., supra*, 196 Conn. at 101, 491 A.2d 368, that "intent refers to the consequences of an act ... [and] denote[s] that the actor desires to cause [the] consequences of his act, or that he believes that the consequences are substantially certain to follow from it. 1 Restatement (Second), Torts § 8A

(1965)." (Citation omitted; internal quotation marks omitted.) "A result is intended if the act is done for the purpose of accomplishing such a result or with knowledge that to a substantial certainty such a result will ensue." 1 F. Harper & F. James, Torts (1956) § 3.3, p. 216. An intended or wilful injury "does not necessarily involve the ill will or malevolence shown in express malice," but it is insufficient "to constitute such an [intended] injury that the act ... was the voluntary action of the person involved." *Mingachos v. CBS, Inc.*, *supra*, at 102, 491 A.2d 368. * * *

The substantial certainty test differs from the true intentional tort test but still preserves the statutory scheme and the overall purposes of the act. The problem with the intentional tort test, i.e., whether the employer intended the specific injury, "appears to be that it allows employers to injure and even kill employees and suffer only workers' compensation damages so long as the employer did not specifically intend to hurt the worker." *Beauchamp v. Dow Chemical Co.*, 427 Mich. 1, 25, 398 N.W.2d 882 (1986). Prohibiting a civil action in such a case "would allow a corporation to 'cost-out' an investment decision to kill workers." Blankenship v. Cincinnati Milacron Chemicals, Inc., 69 Ohio St.2d 608, 617, 433 N.E.2d 572 (1982) (Celebrezze, J., concurring). The "substantial certainty" test provides for the "intent to injure" exception to be strictly construed and still allows for a plaintiff to maintain "a cause of action against an employer where the evidence is sufficient to support an inference that the employer deliberately instructed an employee to injure himself." *Gulden v. Crown Zellerbach Corp.*, 890 F.2d 195, 197 (9th Cir.1989).

The issue then is whether the defendant established as a matter of law that the plaintiff's evidence of the defendant's refusal to allow employees to *vacuum* the machinery *after* it has been shut down failed to raise an issue of fact that such conduct was substantially certain to result in injury. * * *

Intent is clearly a question of fact that is ordinarily inferred from one's conduct or acts under the circumstances of the particular case. * * * *Waterbury Petroleum Products, Inc. v. Canaan Oil & Fuel Co.*, 193 Conn. 208, 216–17, 477 A.2d 988 (1984). Thus, whether the actor knows that the consequences of his or her conduct are certain or substantially certain to result from his or her act and still proceeds with the conduct, so that he or she should be treated by the law as though he or she in fact desired to produce the result, is a question of fact for the jury. * * *

Here, a jury could reasonably infer, from all the circumstances viewed in the light most favorable to the plaintiff, that the defendant's conduct constituted more than a mere failure to provide appropriate safety or protective measures, and that the plaintiff's injury was the inevitable and known result of the actions required of him by the defendant. "A specific intent to produce injury is not the only permissible inference to be drawn from [the] defendant's ... [conduct], but is it one that a jury should be permitted to consider. It is for the finder of fact, not the court on summary judgment, to determine what inferences to draw." *Gulden v. Crown Zellerbach Corp., supra,* 890 F.2d at 197. * * *

We are not prepared to say as a matter of law that the refusal to allow employees to vacuum the machinery after it has been shut down did nothing more than merely set the stage for an accidental injury later, or that it was no more than merely a wilful failure to furnish a safe place to work. Under the circumstances of this case, whether the intentional conduct in which the defendant engaged was tantamount to a "deliberate infliction of harm comparable to an intentional left jab to the chin"; 2A A. Larson, Workmen's Compensation (1990) § 68.13, p. 13–71; is a question best left to the jury.

Notably, several other appellate courts also have decided that it is for the jury to evaluate whether the employer's intentional conduct allows the inference that the employer knew that the occurrence of the injury was a substantial certainty. See, e.g., *Gulden v. Crown Zellerbach Corp., supra,* 890 F.2d at 197 (allegations that the defendant was aware that the plaintiffs' contact with PCBs would injure them but nevertheless ordered them to perform their task in a manner requiring them to initiate and maintain such contact were sufficient to allow a jury to decide whether to draw an inference of deliberate intent to injure from those facts); *O'Brien v. Ottawa Silica Co.,* 656 F.Supp. 610, 611–12 (E.D.Mich.1987) (despite knowledge that the plaintiff was contracting respiratory disease, the employer's failure to take precautions to inform the plaintiff of reported health risks might permit an inference that the employer knew injury was substantially certain to occur); *Kachadoorian v. Great Lakes Steel Corp.,* 168 Mich.App. 273, 277, 424 N.W.2d 34 (1988) (the plaintiff's allegations that the plaintiff's decedent had been directed by his foreman to drive his slag-moving machine under a vessel containing molten steel during a blowing process that frequently caused overflow spills of molten steel and that the defendant had disciplined employees for refusing to drive under the vessel during the blowing process, thereby forcing the employee to choose between the substantial certainty of injury and losing his job, were enough to raise an issue of fact as to the defendant's intent); *Kielwein v. Gulf Nuclear Inc.,* 783 S.W.2d 746, 747–48 (Tex.App.1990) (whether the employer's failure to take appropriate measures to protect the plaintiff during the clean up operation of a radiation spill was substantially certain to cause the plaintiff injury and was substantially certain to result in radioactive contamination is "uniquely a fact question for the trier of fact after considering all the relevant evidence").

The defendant also claims, as an alternate ground for affirming the trial court's judgment, that the plaintiff's application for and receipt of workers' compensation benefits bars him from any further recovery against the defendant. According to the defendant, the plaintiff's receipt and retention of benefits under the act constitutes an admission that the incident falls within the scope of the act. * * *

Although courts in some jurisdictions hold that the collection of workers' compensation benefits bars a damage suit, others take a less restrictive approach. In *Millison v. E.I. du Pont de Nemours & Co.*, 101 N.J. 161, 186, 501 A.2d 505 (1985), for example, the New Jersey Supreme Court held that the doctrine of election of remedies did not bar the plaintiffs, who had filed claims under the New Jersey Workers' Compensation Act, from pursuing a civil action for intentional torts even though it was undisputed that the plaintiffs' claims were compensable under that act. The court held that "the best approach is to allow a plaintiff to process his [or her] workers' compensation claim without forfeiting the opportunity to establish that he [or she] was injured as a result of" intentionally wrongful conduct. Id., at 187, 501 A.2d 505. Additionally, to the extent that a damage award would serve as a double recovery, the court held that the employer would be entitled to offset any compensation benefits previously paid against a damage award. Id.[8] * * *

Although the doctrine of election, to the extent that it is designed to prevent double redress for the same injury, has a sound basis, it can also serve to destroy all rights under compensation acts without justification. "Workmen's compensation is above all a security system; a strict election doctrine transforms it into a grandiose sort of double-or-nothing gamble. Such gambles are appealing to those who still think of the judicial process as a glorious game in which formal moves and choices are made at peril, and in which the ultimate result is spectacular victory for one side and utter defeat for the other. The stricken workman is in no mood for this kind of play, and should not be maneuvered into the necessity for gambling with his rights, under the guise of enforcing a supposed penalty against the employer." 2A A. Larson, *supra*, § 67.31, p. 12–133. Because the employer can be reimbursed by way of a setoff, double redress is avoided. * * *

We are not unmindful that our opinion today may trigger concerns among employers regarding their potential exposure to claims on two fronts. We do not believe that our holding, however, will encourage significant additional litigation, for only in those rare instances when an employer's conduct allegedly falls within the very narrow exception to the act will such litigation result. In those very few instances, we believe that it is better to allow employees to accept the well conceived and often vital benefits of the act rather than to gamble all on a potential recovery that is not likely to provide compensation until considerably later. We think the setoff provisions used routinely by our judges in other areas provide

---

**8.** Of those courts that follow the election theory, many, however, will enforce it only where the court is satisfied that the employee had " '[f]irst full knowledge of the nature of the inconsistent rights and the necessity of electing between them [and s]econd, an intention to elect manifested, either expressly or by acts which imply choice and acquiescence.' " *McAlester Corp. v. Wheeler*, 205 Okla. 446, 448, 239 P.2d 409 (1951). Mere acceptance of some compensation benefits by an injured employee will not constitute an election in the absence of some evidence of both his or her conscious intent to elect the remedy under the compensation statutes and to waive his or her other rights. 2A A. Larson, supra, § 67.35, pp. 12–182–12–189 * * *.

adequate protection for employers on those rare occasions where a suit follows recovery under the act.

The judgment of the Appellate Court is reversed and the case is remanded to that court for further proceedings.

BORDEN, ASSOCIATE JUSTICE, dissenting and concurring.

I disagree with the majority that, on this record, the plaintiff has created a question of fact sufficient to bring the defendant's conduct within the intentional tort exception to the exclusivity provision of the Workers' Compensation Act. * * *

I begin, briefly, with the second issue, namely, whether the application for and receipt of workers' compensation benefits bars an employee from later asserting a common law action against his employer based upon the employer's intentionally tortious conduct. For all of the reasons so aptly stated by the majority, I agree, and join that part of the opinion.

I believe, however, that the majority has misapplied the intentional tort exception to the act's exclusivity provision. The gist of the majority opinion is that the plaintiff created a question of fact, sufficient to withstand a motion for summary judgment, on the issue of whether the defendant "believe[d] that the consequences of [its] conduct [were] substantially certain to follow from [that conduct.]" (Internal quotation marks omitted.) *Mingachos v. CBS, Inc.*, 196 Conn. 91, 101, 491 A.2d 368 (1985). Although this case presents a close question, I disagree.

First, there are some "facts" upon which both the plaintiff and the majority rely, that are not properly cognizable on a motion for summary judgment, involving the ordinarily elusive issue of a party's state of mind. These are the assertions in the affidavit of the plaintiff's expert, Michael E. Shanok, that the defendant's conduct exceeded gross negligence and recklessness, and that there was a total absence of indication that the defendant had undertaken "even the slightest consideration for the plaintiff's safety." * * *

I agree with the majority that questions of state of mind, ordinarily provable only by circumstantial evidence, are also ordinarily left to the jury. But that proposition also necessarily implies that such a question, requiring nothing more than the application of common sense and human experience, is not the kind of question that an expert is any more qualified to answer than six lay jurors. Therefore, such a question, calling for an opinion that is not within the expertise of any expert, is properly objectionable. The plaintiff's case, consequently, must be viewed shorn of those assertions by Shanok.

This leaves the plaintiff's case, on the defendant's summary judgment motion, as consisting of the description of the cleaning process that the plaintiff was required to follow, plus Shanok's opinions that: (1) proper cleaning of the feed chute was by vacuum, with the hopper positioned so that it would be unable to continue feeding raw plastic during the cleaning; (2) the cleaning process that the plaintiff was required to follow violated several Occupational Safety and Health Act regulations, industry safety regulations, and certain national safety standards regarding injection molding machines; (3) remedying even one of the unsafe conditions would have prevented the accident; and (4) it was clear from all of these factors that the plaintiff's injury "would be, sooner or later, a predictable and probable event." I conclude that the sum of these facts, even with all of the reasonable inferences to be drawn from them in favor of the plaintiff, was inadequate for a rational inference that the defendant believed that it was substantially certain that the plaintiff's injuries would follow. * * *

This body of case law, therefore, indicates that the language of "substantial certainty," as used in the lexicon of the intentional tort exception to the exclusivity of workers' compensation benefits, is essentially intended to describe a surrogate state of mind for purposefully harmful conduct, but not to describe conduct that, albeit blameworthy, is simply reckless. * * *

In my view, the plaintiff's proper proof adduced in response to the defendant's motion for summary judgment simply cannot be stretched beyond the realm of recklessness. Indeed, this is the import of Shanok's conclusion that the plaintiff's injury "would be, sooner or later, a *predictable* and *probable* event." (Emphasis added.) What is predictable and probable is not certain; if it were, any reckless conduct would also fall within the intentional conduct exception. * * *

### NOTES AND QUESTIONS

1. In a frequently mentioned opinion, *Millison v. E.I. du Pont de Nemours & Co.*, 101 N.J. 161, 501 A.2d 505 (1985), cited in the principal case, the plaintiffs sought tort damages on two grounds: (1) the employer knowingly exposed them to a dangerous work environment, because the ambient air was filled with asbestos fibers, the employer knew this to be dangerous, but did not inform plaintiffs of the danger; (2) doctors working for their employer gave plaintiffs examinations each year the results of which indicated plaintiffs were developing pulmonary diseases, but concealed this information from the plaintiffs for periods up to eight years. Plaintiffs were allowed to proceed on the second count, but not the first. What would account for the different treatment?

2. Stiff lobbying by employers has sometimes resulted in limiting the intentional wrong exclusion to only those cases in which there is evidence that the employer "deliberately intended to harm." Should an employer be able to purchase liability insurance that would cover such cases? (The usual policy issued by most insurers to employers is a combination workers' compensation liability policy, and an "employer's liability" policy that protects the employer in cases in which an employee seeks damages outside the workers' compensation statute.) See the discussion in *Travelers Indemnity Co. v. PCR, Inc.*, 889 So.2d 779 (Fla. 2004). The opinion is also useful for its discussion of various standards for determining what is an intentional wrong. At least one state treats an intentional tort as an "injury" covered by its workers compensation

statute. See *Haddon v. Metropolitan Life Ins. Co.,* 239 Va. 397, 389 S.E.2d 712 (1990). What approach best serves the underlying policies of workers compensation? Of tort law?

## MESSER v. HUNTINGTON ANESTHESIA GROUP, INC.

Supreme Court of Appeals of West Virginia, 2005
218 W.Va. 4, 620 S.E.2d 144, 16 A.D. Cases 1626

BENJAMIN, JUSTICE.

* * * In her complaint, Messer sought recovery under The West Virginia Human Rights Act ("the WVHRA") for both an aggravated or worsened physical injury and non-physical injuries stemming from the alleged refusal of Appellee Huntington Anesthesia Group, Inc., her employer, to accommodate her disability, a herniated disc at L4–L5. The circuit court made two findings in its August 18, 2003, order:

1.   The West Virginia Human Right Act does not create a cause of action for workplace injuries;

2.   Any injuries as alleged and sustained are the exclusive jurisdiction of the Workers' Compensation Act.

Appellant, Messer, asks this Court to reverse the circuit court's August 18, 2003, order [dismissing her complaint]. * * *

### I.   FACTS AND PROCEDURAL BACKGROUND

Since Appellant's complaint was dismissed at the pleading stage, the facts are largely as alleged therein, which, for purposes of a Rule 12(b)(6) motion, are to be taken as true. * * *

The complaint alleges that Messer was employed as a Certified Registered Nurse Anesthetist by Appellees from September 13, 1988, until an unspecified date in September, 2000; and that at all relevant times, she suffered from a herniated disc at L4–L5, which limited her ability to lift, stand, and work. After January, 1998, Messer alleges that her primary treating physician informed Appellees on multiple occasions that Messer was limited to eight-hour work days, lifting restrictions, and that she should refrain from overtime "due to her injury." Messer asserts that Appellees ignored these restrictions and that Appellees failed to accommodate her physical handicap. As a result, Messer claims that her physical condition progressed and worsened to the point in September, 2000, that she was no longer able to perform her duties as a Certified Registered Nurse Anesthetist for Appellees.

The record is not fully developed as to the underlying injury which caused Messer's back problems or Messer's later aggravations. It is apparent to the Court from the thrust of Messer's arguments that her physical claims herein were largely, if not entirely, within the scope of coverage of the Workers' Compensation Act. * * * Appellees argue that Messer "... has received workers' compensation benefits for the injuries she alleges in the instant action." Messer's pleadings are silent as to the nature of her back injury or whether she, in fact, received workers' compensation benefits in whole or in part for the physical injuries alleged herein. Messer merely alleges that she "has at all times relevant hereto suffered from a herniated disc at L4–L5." In reply to Appellees' factual statements, Messer does not expressly deny such representations with respect to Messer filing a workers' compensation claim, reopening the claim, or receiving workers' compensation benefits for the injuries she alleges in the instant action. * * *

## III. DISCUSSION

### A.

#### *The Issue on Appeal and the Nature of Appellant's Claims*

This appeal presents the issue of whether the exclusivity provisions of the West Virginia Workers' Compensation Act shield an employer from the injuries directly caused by its unlawful discriminatory conduct against an employee in the workplace. Stated differently, we consider on this appeal whether an employee may seek to recover under the WVHRA for actual injuries caused not by an injury received in the course of and arising out of his or her employment for which workers' compensation benefits would ordinarily be payable, but rather for actual injuries of a kind for which workers' compensation benefits are not ordinarily payable, which flow directly and uniquely from the employer's unlawful discrimination against the employee. Key to our consideration of the issues presented are the important policies codified within the Workers' Compensation Act and the WVHRA, both systems of legislative creation. This consideration leads us necessarily to distinguish not only the nature of the acts alleged to have caused the claimed injuries, but also the type of injuries for which recovery is claimed and whether or not such injuries depend for their viability upon an injury which was compensable under the Workers' Compensation Act.

The essence of Messer's claims is that she sustained an aggravation or worsening of an underlying physical injury because of Appellees' refusal to abide by her work restrictions and that Appellees violated their obligation of accommodation and interaction under the WVHRA. In addition, she seeks recovery for non-physical injuries, which she describes as "emotional distress, mental distress and anguish," stemming from the same refusal and violation, and for the nonphysical injuries she is seeking, according to her complaint, "damages for mental and emotional distress, lost wages, value of lost benefits, cost and attorney fees, reinstatement, injunctive relief against future violations of the law, and such other and further relief as may upon the premises be appropriate." Messer contends some claimed injuries are not recoverable in a workers' compensation claim, but admits that others are. In its brief as *amicus curiae*, the H[uman] R[ights] C[omission] focuses its attention on Appellees' failure to accommodate, arguing "[a]n action alleging breach of the duty to reasonably accommodate is not an action for workplace injury compensation."

B.

*The Workers' Compensation Act*

(Its Exclusivity)

The essence of the exclusivity of the Workers' Compensation Act for work-related injuries is found at W. Va.Code § 23–2–6 (2003), which provides that an employer "is not liable to respond in damages at common law or by statute for the injury or death of any employee, however occurring." * * *

When considered together, the words "injury" and "however occurring," in W. Va.Code § 23–2–6 (2003) and the expression of legislative intent in W. Va.Code § 23–4–2(d)(1) (2003) provide employers with an expansive immunity from liability outside the workers' compensation system for workplace injuries of employees. This immunity, however, is not absolute. Exceptions to this immunity are set forth specifically and implicitly in the Workers' Compensation Act.

While exceptions to the exclusivity provision of W. Va.Code § 23–2–6 (2003) exist, the Legislature has been extremely restrictive in creating such exceptions. For example, an employer is not immune from lawsuit for workplace injuries if the employer "acted with deliberate intention." W. Va.Code § 23–4–2(d)(2) (2003). Messer does not claim that she comes within this exception.

The Legislature has also specifically set forth private civil remedies outside of the exclusivity provision for certain discriminatory practices by an employer related to employees who have compensable injuries. W. Va.Code § 23–5A–1, et seq.[5] Though Messer apparently does not invoke these anti-discrimination provisions of the Workers' Compensation Act, we do find such provisions revealing with respect to the types of acts and resulting injuries which the Legislature has envisioned to fall within and without of the exclusivity provision of W. Va.Code § 23–2–6 (2003).

These exceptions reveal that the most significant word in the exclusivity provision of W. Va.Code § 23–2–6 (2003) for purposes of the issues before us in the instant matter is the term "injury". In considering any potential exception to the exclusivity provision, i.e., that an employer "is not liable to respond in damages at common law or by statute for the

---

**5.** W. Va.Code § 23–5A–1 (1978), in relevant part, provides: No employer shall discriminate in any manner against any of his present or former employees because of such present or former employee's receipt of or attempt to receive benefits under this chapter. W. Va.Code § 23–5A–2 (1982), in relevant part, provides: Any employer who has provided any type of medical insurance for an employee or his dependents by paying premiums, in whole or in part, on an individual or group policy shall not cancel ... or cause coverage provided to be decreased during the entire period for which that employee ... is claiming or is receiving benefits under this chapter for a temporary disability. ... *This section provides a private remedy for the employee.* ... (Emphasis added.) W. Va.Code § 23–5A–3 (1990), in relevant part, provides: It shall be a discriminatory practice within the meaning of section one [§ 23–5A–1] of this article to terminate an injured employee while the injured employee is off work due to a compensable injury ... unless the injured employee has committed a separate dischargeable offense. ... It shall be a discriminatory practice ... for an employer to fail to reinstate an employee who has sustained a compensable injury. ... Any civil action brought under this section shall be subject to [collective bargaining agreements and related exceptions].

injury or death of any employee, however occurring," we must look to the other provisions of the Workers' Compensation Act to determine the Legislature's intent in defining what is and what is not a compensable "injury" for purposes of the exclusivity provision. Id. W. Va.Code § 23–4–1, et seq., establishes that injuries and defined occupational diseases incurred "in the course of and resulting from [an employee's] covered employment" are compensable injuries. W. Va.Code, § 23–4–1, et seq. Implicit in this statutory definition of "injury" is the limitation that only occupational diseases "as hereinafter defined" are compensable. W. Va. Code § 23–4–1(b) (2003). We must draw from this express limitation that the Legislature intended certain work-related events, here, occupational diseases not "hereinafter defined" to not come within the meaning of "injury" for purposes of the Workers' Compensation Act generally and the exclusivity provision specifically.

The Legislature also expressly exempted other work-related injuries from the definition of what may be a compensable injury for purposes of the Workers' Compensation Act. For instance, W. Va.Code § 23–4–1f (1993) states that "[f]or the purposes of this chapter, no alleged injury or disease shall be recognized as a compensable injury or disease which was solely caused by nonphysical means and which did not result in any physical injury or disease to the person claiming benefits. It is the purpose of this section to clarify that so-called mental-mental claims are not compensable under this chapter."

To this list of work-related injuries exempted from the provisions of the Workers' Compensation Act (and, consequently, from the exclusivity provision of W. Va.Code § 23–2–6 (2003)), are the other express statutory exceptions within the Workers' Compensation Act discussed above; namely, injuries caused by an employer's "deliberate intention," as defined by W. Va.Code § 23–4–2 (2003), and injuries caused by certain discriminatory actions by an employer, as set forth in W. Va.Code § 23–5A–1, et seq. We find these latter two exceptions especially noteworthy for purposes of the matter before us since, in both instances, the Legislature has focused on the acts which underlie the resulting work-related injury as being determinative of whether the exclusivity provision is applicable.

C.

*The West Virginia Human Rights Act*

The purpose of the WVHRA is, among other things, to assure equal employment opportunities to individuals with certain disabilities by making certain discriminatory practices unlawful. W. Va.Code § 5–11–9 (1998). "The term 'discriminate' or 'discrimination' means to exclude from, or fail or refuse to extend to, a person equal opportunities because of ... disability...." W. Va.Code § 5–11–3(h) (1998). Disability means a mental or physical impairment which substantially limits one or more of a person's major life activities. W. Va.Code § 5–11–3(m) (1998).

Effective May 19, 1994, the HRC adopted legislative "Rules Regarding Discrimination Against Individuals With Disabilities," which appear in W. Va.C.S.R. § 77–1–1 et seq. W. Va.C.S.R. § 77–1–4.5 obligates an employer to "make reasonable accommodation to the known physical or mental impairments of qualified individuals with disabilities where necessary to enable a qualified individual with a disability to perform the essential functions of the job."

In *Skaggs v. Elk Run Coal Company, Inc.*, 198 W.Va. 51, 64, 479 S.E.2d 561, 574 (1996), this Court acknowledged that although the WVHRA does not have an explicit provision obligating employers to provide reasonable accommodation for disabled individuals, "the West Virginia [HRC] and this Court have inferred that our [HRA] imposes this duty of reasonable accommodation." * * *

### D.

#### *Employment–Related Injuries: Workers' Compensation and Civil Rights Coverage*

#### Cases From Other Jurisdictions

A review of the status of law regarding the interaction of workers' compensation laws and civil rights laws from other jurisdictions in the United States provides a valuable insight into how other states have considered the issue before us herein. While each state necessarily has its own unique set of workers' compensation and civil rights laws, the underlying public policies for such laws have many similarities to our workers' compensation and civil rights laws. Though not precedential, a look to other states provides us some persuasive direction into our consideration of this appeal.

#### 1.  Arkansas

In *Davis v. Dillmeier Enterprises, Inc.*, 330 Ark. 545, 956 S.W.2d 155 (1997), Davis sustained bilateral carpal syndrome resulting from her employment for which she was compensated under Arkansas' workers' compensation laws. 956 S.W.2d at 156. She was assigned a rating of five percent permanent physical impairment in each upper extremity. Having obtained a release from further treatment, Davis reported to work and was immediately terminated from employment by her employer. She thereupon brought an action against her former employer for discrimination based upon a physical disability, in violation of the Arkansas Civil Rights Act for which she claimed damages in the form of lost wages, mental anguish, and loss of dignity. She also asked for punitive damages. The trial court dismissed the complaint "reasoning that it was the General Assembly's intent that the remedies provided under the Workers' Compensation Act were to be exclusive." Id. at 157.

Distinguishing the injury sustained by Davis by her termination from that caused by her compensable physical injury, the Supreme Court of Arkansas reversed the trial court's dismissal of Davis' complaint and remanded the case to allow Davis to proceed with her termination claim under the Arkansas Civil Rights Act. * * * The Court reasoned as follows:

> * * * the rights and remedies provided by both Acts are considerably different and serve to fulfill different purposes. *Appellant has alleged two separate injuries—one being a work-related physical injury, for which she has received workers' compensation benefits, and one being a subsequent nonphysical injury arising from Appellee's action in terminating her based upon her physical disability. The first injury is exclusively cognizable under the Workers' Compensation Act, while the subsequent injury is of the type envisioned by the Arkansas Civil Rights Act of 1993.*

Id. at 160–61. (Emphasis added.)

### 2.   California

In *City of Moorpark v. Superior Court of Ventura County*, 18 Cal.4th 1143, 77 Cal.Rptr.2d 445, 959 P.2d 752 (1998), plaintiff was an administrative secretary employed by the city who suffered a work-related knee injury. Her supervisor terminated her employment because her injury prevented her from performing essential job functions. Plaintiff filed a lawsuit against the city claiming discrimination based on a physical disability in violation of California's Fair Employment and Housing Act (FEHA). The city defended asserting that plaintiff's action was barred by the exclusivity provisions of the workers' compensation law. The trial court disagreed and the Supreme Court of California affirmed. * * *

We agree with the reasoning of the California court that it would be inconsistent with the purposes of the WVHRA to limit its applicability to physical-injury disabilities unrelated to work. Workers who are discriminated against because of a work-related injury should not be entitled to less protection under the law than workers disabled by non-work-related injuries.

### 3.   Florida

In *Byrd v. Richardson–Greenshields Securities, Inc.*, 552 So.2d 1099 (Fla.1989), the Supreme Court of Florida answered in the negative the following certified question: "Whether the workers' compensation statute [of Florida] provides the exclusive remedy for a claim based on sexual harassment in the workplace." *Byrd*, 552 So.2d at 1100. In its opinion, the court noted that

> workers' compensation is directed essentially at compensating a worker for lost resources and earnings. This is a vastly different concern than is addressed by the sexual harassment laws. While workplace injuries rob a person of resources, sexual harassment robs the person of dignity and self esteem. *Workers' compensation addresses purely economic injury; sexual harassment laws are concerned with a much more intangible injury to personal rights. To the extent these injuries*

*are separable, we believe that they both should be, and can be, enforced separately.*

Id. at 1104 (footnote omitted). (Emphasis added.) * * *

### 4. Louisiana

In *Cox v. Glazer Steel Corporation*, 606 So.2d 518 (La.1992), plaintiff was not rehired because of a compensable injury. After having settled a worker's compensation claim for the physical injury, plaintiff filed a civil claim against his former employer for discrimination against the handicapped under the Louisiana Civil Right Act for Handicapped Persons. The trial court dismissed the claim and the court of appeals affirmed "holding that the discrimination claim was as outgrowth of the industrial accident and thus barred by the exclusive remedy of workers' compensation." *Cox*, 606 So.2d at 520. The Louisiana Supreme Court reversed on the ground that the coverage of the Civil Rights Act is not within the scope of the workers' compensation law and is not barred by that law. Id. In a concurring opinion, two of the justices of the court stated that "plaintiff's cause of action for discrimination is not based on the employer's liability for the injury, but on the employer's liability for subsequent conduct that, although incidentally related to the on-the-job injury, gave rise to entirely separate liability under an entirely separate statute." Id. at 521.

*La = OK*

### 5. Maine

In *King v. Bangor Federal Credit Union*, 568 A.2d 507 (Me.1989), [the court permitted plaintiff to pursue claims under both workers compensation and anti-discrimination statutes. Plaintiff had resigned because her employer declined to accommodate a work-related disability.]

*Me = OK*

### 6. Michigan

In *Boscaglia v. Michigan Bell Telephone Company*, 420 Mich. 308, 362 N.W.2d 642 (1985), Boscaglia filed an action against her former employer alleging violations of Michigan's Fair Employment Practices Act and Civil Rights Act. She claimed she was demoted as a result of sex discrimination. Various employment problems allegedly arose after her demotion, including an accusation by her supervisor of coming to work late. She ultimately sought psychiatric treatment and quit her job. She filed a claim for workers' compensation and was awarded benefits for mental and emotional disability during the pendency of her civil action. A second plaintiff, Pacheco, alleged various acts of [national origin] discrimination against him by his employer * * * He did not file a workers' compensation claim.

*Mich - OK*

In response to what the court described as the "principal question" before it in the two cases, the court held that "the exclusive remedy provision of the workers' compensation act [does not bar] an action seeking recovery for physical, mental, or emotional injury resulting from an employer's violation of the fair employment practices act (FEPA) or the Michigan civil rights act." *Boscaglia*, 362 N.W.2d at 643. The court in its opinion noted that "[t]he evils at which the civil rights acts are aimed are different from those at which the workers' compensation act is directed," Id. at 315, 362 N.W.2d at 645. * * *.

### 7. Minnesota

In *Karst v. F.C. Hayer Co., Inc.*, 447 N.W.2d 180 (Minn.1989), the Supreme Court of Minnesota ruled against an injured employee based upon its perception of the legislature's intent and the election of the plaintiff to recover workers' compensation benefits, which the court said barred his recovery under other theories. The Minnesota Supreme Court said that only one issue was presented to it in the case, namely, "whether the exclusive remedy provision of the Workers' Compensation Act precludes an action by a disabled individual against his former employer for disability discrimination under the Minnesota Human Rights Act where the individual becomes disabled as a result of work-related injuries and the former employer refuses to rehire the individual because of the disability." *Karst*, 447 N.W.2d at 181. The Court resolved the issue in the affirmative principally on the ground that it believed "the legislature intended the decision of whether or not to rehire an injured worker and the consequences flowing from that decision to be within the scope of the Workers' Compensation Act." Id. at 184.The Court concluded its opinion with the statement that "in light of the vital importance of the exclusivity provision to the workers' compensation system and in the absence of a clear legislative intent to impose the liability of the Human Rights Act in addition to that under the Workers' Compensation Act, we decline to interpret the Human Rights Act as applicable here." Id. at 186.

### 8. Ohio

In *Kerans v. Porter Paint Company*, 61 Ohio St.3d 486, 575 N.E.2d 428 (1991), the Ohio Supreme Court held that Ohio's workers' compensation statute is not the exclusive remedy for claims based upon sexual harassment in the workplace. * * *

### 9. Rhode Island

In *Folan v. State/Department of Children, Youth and Families*, 723 A.2d 287 (R.I.1999), plaintiff was sexually harassed in her workplace and was compensated by Rhode Island's workers' compensation system for a resulting occupational stress injury. She subsequently filed a civil complaint under the state's Fair Employment Practices Act and the Civil Rights of People with Disabilities statutes. In holding for plaintiff, the Rhode Island Supreme Court concluded:

> that the Legislature did not intend the exclusivity provision of the Workers' Compensation Act to bar the independent statutory claims created by the FEPA or the CRA ... the exclusivity clause of the Workers' Compensation Act as interpreted by defendants could render the FEPA and the CRA nugatory and ineffective ... under our interpretation, the exclusivity clause does not bar a claim if to do so

would frustrate a broad, fundamental public policy which fulfills paramount purposes, such as a claim under the FEPA or the CRA. Id. at 291–92.

## 10. Washington

* * *

## 11. Wisconsin

* * *

### E.

*Harmonizing the Policies Respecting Workers' Compensation and Human Rights*

The State's Workers' Compensation Law, W. Va.Code Chapter 23, and The West Virginia Human Rights Act, W. Va.Code Chapter 5, Article 11, set forth two significant legislative public policies. We must therefore endeavor to uphold the Legislature's intent by protecting the integrity of both statutory schemes. * * *

Here, Messer's cause of action for discrimination is not based on her employer's liability for a compensable work-related injury within the meaning of the Workers' Compensation Act. Rather, it is based on Appellees' alleged subsequent discriminatory conduct that, although incidentally related to the compensable work-related injury, gives rise to an entirely separate liability under the WVHRA. Any apparent conflict between West Virginia's Workers' Compensation Act and the WVHRA that may arise can be harmonized by recognizing, as many courts have done, that the rights and remedies of the Acts are considerably different and serve to fulfill different purposes. Thus we hold that the first of the two Acts is directed at compensating an employee who has suffered an injury or disease in the course of and resulting from his/her employment and at shielding the employer from liability outside the workers' compensation system for such injury. The second is directed towards actions of an employer in discriminating against an employee because of his or her disability. Since the Acts seek to remedy two separate harms, physical injury and discrimination, no conflict exists between the two Acts and it would be inconsistent with the purposes of the West Virginia Human Rights Act, W. Va.Code § 5–11–1 et seq., to limit its applicability to physical-injury disabilities unrelated to work. The injury that Messer seeks to redress under the WVHRA is the indignity of the alleged discrimination against her because of her disability.

The interpretation which Appellees would attach to the exclusivity clause would render the WVHRA ineffective and useless to a large group of West Virginians who have compensable work-related injuries. Such an interpretation would frustrate a broad, fundamental public policy which fulfills paramount purposes and would effectively relegate one class of employee to an inferior status compared to another class of employee who have injuries or disabilities which are not work-related. Being enacted later in time to the Workers' Compensation Act, the WVHRA makes no distinction between classes of employees to which civil rights protection is extended. Had the Legislature desired to treat employees with work-related disabilities differently, it would have done so within the WVHRA. It did not do so. That the Workers' Compensation Act itself excludes from its immunities injuries caused by certain acts, including deliberate intent acts at W. Va.Code § 23–4–2 and discriminatory acts at W. Va.Code § 23–5A–1, et seq., provides a further measure of assurance that the Legislature intended employees such as Messer to be protected by *both* systems.

Here, Messer has alleged essentially two separate types of injuries. To the extent that a worker's injuries are of the type cognizable under W. Va.Code § 23–4–1 for which workers' compensation benefits may be sought, including aggravations and physical and non-physical conditions which flow directly and uniquely from such injury, we find that the exclusivity provision of the Workers' Compensation Act prohibits recovery outside of the mechanisms set forth in the West Virginia Workers' Compensation Act. To the extent that a worker's injuries are directly and proximately caused by the unlawful discriminatory acts of his or her employer, and are of a type not otherwise recoverable under the Workers' Compensation Act, we hold that the exclusivity provision of the Workers' Compensation Act is inapplicable as the Legislature did not intend such injuries to fall within the types of injuries for which the Workers' Compensation Act was established. Thus, while an aggravation or worsening of an employee's physical injury by the conduct of his/her employer may be compensable under and thus subject to, the exclusive remedy provided by the Workers' Compensation Act, an employee's claim against an employer for violation of The West Virginia Human Rights Act and resulting non-physical injuries, such as mental and emotional distress and anguish, directly and proximately resulting from such violation and not associated with the physical injury or the aggravation or worsening thereof are not barred by the exclusivity provisions of the Workers Compensation Act, W. Va Code § 23–2–6 (2003) and–6a (1949). Such violation and the resulting nonphysical injuries are not within the scope of the Workers' Compensation Act. Rather, they are separate liabilities from the physical injury and were created by The West Virginia Human Rights Act, an entirely different statute from the Workers' Compensation Act with different policy objectives.

## IV.

## CONCLUSION

For the reasons stated above, the circuit court's order of August 18, 2003, in its Civil Action No. 02–C–0635, is affirmed, in part, reversed, in part and remanded to the circuit court * * *

MAYNARD, JUSTICE, dissenting.

Once again, the majority is chipping away at the immunity provided to employers by the Workers' Compensation Act. Ignoring the plain language of the exclusivity provisions of W.Va.Code §§ 23–2–6 and 23–2–6a, the majority has now determined that an employee can pursue both a worker's compensation claim and a human rights claim for the same workplace injury. Because I believe that the statutory provisions of both the Workers' Compensation Act and the West Virginia Human Rights Act clearly establish that the sole recourse for the appellant to recover for her workplace injuries is the workers' compensation system, I dissent to the majority's decision in this case. * * *

Instead of following the clear language of our Workers' Compensation Act and Human Rights Act as set forth above, the majority chose to look to other jurisdictions for guidance. The majority's reliance on what other courts have done in these types of cases was misplaced. Our laws applicable to this issue are unique to this State, and there is simply no basis for comparison with the statutes of other states.

The decision by the majority in this case paves the way for human rights claims to be filed in every instance where an employee suffers an aggravation and/or progression of his or her prior workplace injury. These employees will always allege that their injuries were made worse by their employer's failure to accommodate their disability that resulted from their previous injury. The end result will be more double recoveries for claimants or possibly triple recoveries if a deliberate intention claim is also filed. Whether a claimant could get around the requirements of W.Va.Code § 23–4–2(d)(2)(ii)(C) remains to be seen. * * *

### NOTES AND QUESTIONS

1. Is the statement of the Michigan court different enough from that in the principal case to call for a different outcome? What of the Rhode Island decision?

2. Plaintiff in the principal case chose to pursue her remedy under state law. If she had brought her action under the American with Disabilities Act, she would also have been able to argue that the federal statute preempted the exclusive remedy of the state compensation act. See *Liss v. Nassau County*, 425 F.Supp.2d 335 (E.D.N.Y. 2006)(ADA), applying the general principle that federal civil rights remedies are not preempted by state workers compensation laws developed in *Lopez v. S.B. Thomas, Inc.*, 831 F.2d 1184 (2d Cir. 1987)(42 U.S.C. § 1981).

3. Tort actions for infliction of mental distress have led to disparate results around the nation. Compare *Lasher v. Day & Zimmerman Int'l, Inc.*, 516 F.Supp.2d 565 (D.S.C. 2007) with *Ford v. Revlon, Inc.*, 153 Ariz. 38, 734 P.2d 580 (1987). See also Ruth Vance, *Workers' Compensation and Sexual Harassment in the Workplace*, 11 HOFSTRA LAB. L.J. 141 (1993)

## 7.  MODIFICATION OF AWARDS

### LOWE v. DRIVERS MANAGEMENT, INC.

Supreme Court of Nebraska, 2007
274 Neb. 732, 743 N.W.2d 82

MILLER–LERMAN, J.

\* \* \*

### STATEMENT OF FACTS

In 2001, Lowe sustained an injury arising out of and in the course of his employment with DMI. The injury resulted in neck and radicular arm pain. Lowe filed a petition with the Nebraska Workers' Compensation Court. In an order filed February 11, 2004, he was awarded workers' compensation disability benefits (the initial award). The initial award provided that Lowe receive permanent partial disability benefits based upon a 70–percent loss of earning capacity. The court also approved a vocational rehabilitation plan calling for job placement services. Specifically, the court determined that a vocational rehabilitation plan had "been approved by a vocational rehabilitation specialist, and so [Lowe] should participate in this plan."

It is undisputed that Lowe failed to participate in the plan. The record reflects that the vocational rehabilitation counselor who was to assist Lowe with job placement services "left several [telephone] messages for [Lowe] and sent him a letter dated 3/12/04 asking him to contact [her] but [she] never heard back from him." \* \* \*

In July 2004, as a result of "gradually increasing pain in his neck, left shoulder, and left arm," Lowe began treating with Dr. Gerard H. Dericks. On October 4, 2005, Lowe filed an application to modify the initial award, claiming that he was totally disabled. On April 14, 2006, a modification hearing was held before a trial judge of the workers' compensation court on Lowe's application. A total of 66 exhibits were received into evidence, including Dericks' medical reports and deposition. Lowe appeared and testified during the hearing.

On August 22, 2006, the trial judge entered his "Further Award." The judge found that Lowe had failed to participate in court-ordered vocational rehabilitation services and that he did not have reasonable cause for failing to participate in those services during a period immediately after those services had been awarded. As a result, pursuant to § 48–162.01(7), the judge ordered a partial reduction in the amount of the disability benefits awarded to Lowe prior to the modification proceedings. In his further award, the trial judge also determined that there had been a material and substantial change in Lowe's condition, necessitating a reassessment of Lowe's loss of earning capacity. The judge determined that Lowe was permanently and totally disabled and awarded Lowe disability benefits based upon his permanent and total disability. With respect to Lowe's failure to participate in vocational rehabilitation, the judge did not reduce compensation for Lowe's permanent and total disability going forward, stating "there is reasonable cause not to participate [in vocational rehabilitation] because [Lowe] is totally disabled." * * *

DMI filed for review of the trial judge's further award before the workers' compensation review panel. Lowe also filed for review of that portion of the trial judge's further award that reduced his benefits for failure to participate in the vocational rehabilitation plan. A hearing was held before the review panel on February 6, 2007, and on March 16, the review panel entered its "Order of Affirmance in Part on Review and Reversal in Part on Review." The review panel determined that the trial judge was not clearly wrong when he found that Lowe was permanently and totally disabled, and therefore, it affirmed that portion of the trial judge's further award. However, the review panel determined that the trial judge erred in reducing Lowe's workers' compensation benefits pursuant to § 48–162.01(7), and it reversed that part of the trial judge's further award. DMI appeals. * * *

## ANALYSIS

As its first assignment of error, DMI claims that the review panel erred when it reversed that portion of the trial judge's further award that had reduced the amount of disability benefits owed to Lowe due to his failure to participate in vocational rehabilitation. The statute at issue with respect to this claim is Neb.Rev.Stat. § 48–162.01(7), which currently provides, in pertinent part, as follows:

> If the injured employee without reasonable cause refuses to undertake or fails to cooperate with a physical, medical, or vocational rehabilitation program determined by the compensation court or judge thereof to be suitable for him or her ... the compensation court or judge thereof may suspend, reduce, or limit the compensation otherwise payable under the Nebraska Workers' Compensation Act.

DMI asserts that this statute establishes a two-part test to determine whether benefits should be suspended, reduced, or limited. First, the employee must either refuse to undertake or fail to cooperate with a court-ordered physical, medical, or vocational rehabilitation program. Second, the employee's refusal must be without reasonable cause.

We agree with DMI's assertion that § 48–162.01(7) establishes a two-part test. We further note that it has been held that both parts of this two-part test present factual questions to be determined by the trial judge based upon the evidence. See *Warburton v. M & D Construction Co.*, 1 Neb.App. 498, 498 N.W.2d 611 (1993).

In his decision, the trial judge found that Lowe did not participate in the job placement services he was ordered to participate in under the initial award, a fact that neither party disputes. Further, as we read his order, the trial judge found that during the period from the initial award up to the modification proceedings, Lowe's failure to participate in vocational rehabilitation was without reasonable cause. The record contains evidence supporting this finding of fact. Specifically, the record contains evidence to the effect that immediately following the entry of the February 11, 2004, initial award, Lowe failed to respond to the vocational rehabilitation counselor's efforts to contact him with regard to these services, thereby causing her to submit a case closure report form dated April 20, 2004, to the Nebraska Workers' Compensation Court with the status of "Closed Not Working–Not Interested in VR Services." * * *

* * * Upon appellate review, the findings of fact made by the trial judge of the compensation court have the effect of a jury verdict and will not be disturbed unless clearly wrong. Id. The record contains evidence supporting the trial judge's findings of fact to the effect that Lowe refused to cooperate in vocational rehabilitation without reasonable cause during the time period immediately after the initial award. As a result, the trial judge was not clearly wrong when he ordered a reduction in Lowe's disability benefits for the period of time prior to the modification proceedings and the review panel erred in reversing this portion of the trial judge's further award.

For its second assignment of error, DMI claims that the review panel erred in affirming the trial judge's further award that modified Lowe's initial award and that awarded Lowe permanent total disability benefits. In this regard, DMI argues that the medical evidence does not support an award of permanent total disability benefits and that even if such status is now warranted, because of Lowe's failure to avail himself of vocational rehabilitation services, his situation worsened and Lowe's benefits should be reduced.

The modification of an earlier workers' compensation award is governed by Neb.Rev.Stat. § 48–141 (Reissue 2004), which provides, inter alia, that "at any time after six months from the date of the ... award, an application [for modification] may be made by either party on the ground of increase or decrease of incapacity due solely to the injury." We have previously stated that to obtain a modification of a prior award, "[t]he applicant must prove there exists a material and substantial change for the better or worse in the condition—a change in circumstances that justifies a modification, distinct and different from the condition for which the adjudication had previously been made." *Hagelstein v. Swift–Eckrich*, 261 Neb. 305, 308, 622 N.W.2d 663, 667 (2001).

In support of its assignment of error objecting to the award of permanent total disability benefits, DMI argues that the trial judge erred in relying upon the medical reports and opinions of Dericks because Dericks had not treated Lowe prior to July 2004. Instead, DMI argues that the trial judge should have accepted the opinions of DMI's expert who examined Lowe prior to the initial award and also prior to the modification hearing. * * *

The record from the modification hearing contains evidence that beginning sometime in July 2004, Lowe began treating with Dericks for "gradually increasing pain in his neck, left shoulder, and left arm." Dericks' medical report dated October 19, 2005, indicates that an MRI of Lowe's cervical spine was performed in September 2004, and when he compared it to an MRI conducted in 2001, prior to the initial award, Dericks determined that "it was quite obvious that there was substantially increased posterior herniation of disk material behind the body of C6. That is to say, it appears that the disk has progressed causing further deformation of the spinal canal behind the vertebral body of the C6." Moreover, the record contains a medical questionnaire dated December 23, 2005, in which Dericks answered "Yes" when effectively asked whether Lowe's physical condition noted by Dericks in his October 19 report was "due solely to the injury he sustained as the result of his work accident while employed with" DMI.

In this case, it is apparent that the trial judge found Dericks' opinion to be credible and persuasive. * * * It was within the trial judge's authority to credit Dericks' opinion, and the opinion supports the award. Given our standard of review and the evidence in the record, we cannot say that the review panel erred in affirming the trial judge's further award modifying Lowe's initial award due to a material and substantial change for the worse in Lowe's condition and finding Lowe to be permanently and totally disabled.

Notwithstanding evidence that Lowe was permanently and totally disabled, DMI argues in its brief that under the job placement plan approved by the Workers' Compensation Court in the initial award, there were jobs available to Lowe, and thus "had [Lowe] participated in the plan [he] would have found a job. Had [Lowe] been working at the time of [the modification hearing], it would have been difficult for [Lowe] to argue he was totally disabled." Brief for appellant at 34. At the modification hearing, DMI offered no evidence to support its assertion on appeal that participation in vocational rehabilitation services would have forestalled or prevented Lowe from becoming permanently and totally disabled and that Lowe's failure to participate in vocational rehabilitation was unreasonable as it bore on the issue of permanent and total disability. Rather than referring to evidence in support of its assertion, DMI relies on argument and the provisions of § 48–162.01(7). DMI claims that going forward, the review panel should have reduced Lowe's permanent total disability benefits otherwise payable due to his failure to participate in the court-ordered vocational rehabilitation services during the period between the initial award and the modification proceedings.

We have not previously determined which party bears the burden of proof to establish the two-part test set forth under § 48–162.01(7). However, we have discussed such burden under another provision in the Nebraska Workers' Compensation Act, Neb.Rev.Stat. § 48–120(2)(c) (Supp.2007), which provision contains language similar to § 48–162.01(7). Section 48–120(2)(c) currently provides that if an injured employee "unreasonably refuses or neglects to avail himself or herself of medical or surgical treatment furnished by the employer ... the compensation court or judge thereof may suspend, reduce, or limit the compensation otherwise payable under the Nebraska Workers' Compensation Act." When considering this language, we have stated that "[t]he unreasonableness of the refusal of an injured employee to permit an operation to be performed is a question of fact to be determined by the evidence, and the burden of proof ... is upon the employer." *Simmerman v. Felthauser*, 125 Neb. 795, 798, 251 N.W. 831, 833 (1934).

The language used in § 48–120(2)(c) is comparable to the language used in § 48–162.01(7) now under consideration. Thus, it logically follows that under the provisions of § 48–162.01(7), the employer bears the burden of proof to demonstrate that an injured employee has refused to undertake or failed to cooperate with a physical, medical, or vocational rehabilitation program and that such refusal or failure is without reasonable cause such that the compensation court or judge may properly rely on such evidence to suspend, reduce, or limit the compensation otherwise payable under the Nebraska Workers' Compensation Act.

We have reviewed the record to determine whether DMI has carried its burden of proof. DMI has not directed us to evidence, and we have not located evidence in the record that supports DMI's arguments urging a reduction of benefits for the period after the modification proceedings. The record from the modification hearing contains a "Revised Loss of Earning Power Analysis," dated January 9, 2006, and prepared by a vocational rehabilitation counselor mutually agreed to by Lowe and DMI. In that report, the counselor stated that based upon Dericks' medical reports, "Lowe is not capable of obtaining a job on a full-time or a part-time basis" and that as a result, Lowe had "sustained a loss of earning power of 100% as the result of his February, 2001 work injury." It appears the trial judge relied upon this evidence when, in his consideration of Lowe's claim of permanent and total disability, he stated "there is reasonable cause not to participate [in vocational rehabilitation] because [Lowe] is totally disabled." The record supports this determination.

Earlier in this opinion, we have agreed with DMI and the trial judge that the evidence showed that Lowe lacked reasonable cause for his failure to participate in vocational rehabilitation immediately after the initial award, and we have approved of a reduction of benefits therefore. However, with respect to the period commencing with these modification proceedings, without evidence, this court "will not speculate as to what might" have ensued relative to Lowe's permanent and total disability claim had Lowe participated in the court-approved vocational rehabilitation plan. See *Simmerman v. Felthauser*, 125 Neb. at 800, 251 N.W. at 833. As to the later timeframe, DMI failed to demonstrate that Lowe refused to participate in vocational rehabilitation without reasonable cause and that had he participated in the court-ordered job placement services, he would have been employed at the time of the modification hearing. * * *

*Affirmed In Part, and In Part Reversed and Remanded with Directions.*

## NOTES AND QUESTIONS

1. Compensation statutes vary on how long after an initial award a request for modification may be made. There are also differences about what justifies a modification, with many statutes requiring that the party requesting the change demonstrate that the physical condition of the claimant has altered. Others permit consideration of non-physical factors, such as the case of a claimant who has retrained and now works in a job paying more than the one he formerly held. Which is the better position? See the discussion in *Model Laundry & Dry Cleaning Co. v. Simmons*, 268 Ark. 770, 596 S.W.2d 337 (App. 1980). See also *McDowell v. Citibank*, 734 N.W.2d 1 (S.Dak. 2007), reasoning that a change in physical condition did not justify reopening a settled case where the occupational disability remained the same as at the time of settlement.

2. Responsibility for medical rehabilitation—the restoration of muscle strength, for example, through weight training—is almost always placed on the employer as part of medical benefits. Provisions for vocational rehabilitation vary considerably, in scope of the retraining available, in whether such retraining is a condition of receiving benefits, and in how cost is shared among employer, employee and public agency. Under some statutes an injured worker who is dissatisfied with the quality of rehabilitation services he is receiving may ask to have modification of an initial award in order to obtain more or better rehabilitation. See, e.g., *Liberty Northwest Ins. Corp. v. Jacobson*, 164 Or.App. 37, 988 P.2d 442 (1999).

3. Judging the reasonableness of refusal of medical or rehabilitation services is often difficult. Refusing services because of reasonably perceived substantial risk to one's person is generally acceptable. Compare *Martinez v. Excel Corp.*, 32 Kan.App.2d 139, 79 P.3d 230 (2003) with *Scott v. Alabama Machinery and Supply Co.*, 52 Ala.App. 459, 294 So.2d 160 (1974).

4. Another basis for modification of an award at the request of an employer (in many statutes) is the refusal of a claimant to return to the former job, or to another suitable job offered to the claimant. See *Johnson v. McKee Foods*, 98 Ark.App. 360, 255 S.W.3d 478 (2007).

# D. SOCIAL INSURANCE PROGRAMS

## 1. STATE DISABILITY INSURANCE

Six jurisdictions (California, Hawaii, New Jersey, New York, Puerto Rico, and Rhode Island) require employers to finance a weekly monetary benefit during a worker's total disability due to injury or illness from non-occupational causes. California, for example, requires a weekly benefit of 55% of average wages earned during the statutorily defined base period subject to minimum and maximum limits. For claims filed after January 1, 2008, the minimum weekly benefit in California was $50 and the maximum $917 with a specified maximum number of benefit weeks per claim period. The California disability benefit for nonoccupational causes is administered in conjunction with the unemployment insurance law. (See Calif. Unemployment Ins. Code §§ 2601, 2627, 2629, 2655.) It is financed through a payroll tax. It is possible for employers to substitute a private plan, however, if there is employee consent, if the plan provides equal or better benefits, and if it is approved by the responsible state agency.

New York administers its nonoccupational disability program in conjunction with its workers' compensation law. Benefits are generally financed through private insurance. The benefit is available for a maximum of 26 out of every 52 weeks and is paid at the rate of 50% of the average wage earned during the eight weeks prior to disability subject to a maximum weekly benefit of $170. (See, N.Y. Workers' Comp. Law §§ 201, 204, 205.)

The California statute includes in its definition of disability "illness or injury resulting from pregnancy, childbirth or related medical condition." (Calif. Unemployment Ins. Code § 2626.) Disability benefits are available in a noncomplicated pregnancy for a total of eight weeks under the New York law, and for up to the maximum available benefit period if medical complications cause disability for a longer duration.

In *Shaw v. Delta Air Lines, Inc.*, 463 U.S. 85, 103 S.Ct. 2890, 77 L.Ed.2d 490 (1983), an attempt was made to declare New York's disability law constitutionally invalid under the doctrine of federal preemption based on the 1974 Employee Retirement Income Security Act (ERISA), which subjects employer financed employee pension and welfare benefit plans to a variety of federal regulations designed to assure that such plans are operated in a manner that is fiscally sound and adhere to the purpose of protecting the employees and their dependents. The statutory definition of a welfare benefit plan includes a plan providing benefits in the event of the worker's illness, accident, disability, death, or unemployment. However, ERISA exempts plans from its coverage if "maintained solely for the purpose of complying with applicable workmen's compensation laws or unemployment compensation or disability laws."

Many companies doing business in a variety of jurisdictions maintain a single employee benefits program using "multibenefit" plans that are regulated under ERISA. Multibenefit plans provide a variety of employee welfare benefits—such as paid sick-leave, medical and hospitalization insurance, and disability benefits—administered as a single program. The preemption attack upon the New York disability act was based upon the fact that it let employers meet their obligations either by providing a separately administered disability insurance plan or by providing such benefits as part of a multibenefit plan. The employers challenging the New York law contended that because it allowed compliance through multibenefit plans, the New York law did not come within the explicit ERISA exemption and, therefore, the state law was preempted by this comprehensive federal legislation. They also argued that New York, at the least, was preempted from regulating the program of any employer providing disability benefits through a multibenefit plan.

The Supreme Court ruled that the New York law was preempted insofar as it attempted to regulate any aspect of multibenefit plans. However, the Court refused to strike down the entire state statute. It held that: "while the State may not require an employer to alter its ERISA plan, it may force the employer to choose between providing disability benefits in a separately administered plan and including the state-mandated benefits in its ERISA plan. If the State is not satisfied that the ERISA plan comports with the requirements of its disability insurance law, it may compel the employer to maintain a separate plan that does comply." 463 U.S. at 108, 103 S.Ct. at 2905.

## 2. THE SOCIAL SECURITY DISABILITY INSURANCE PROGRAM

Benefits for long-term, total disability are provided as part of the federal Old–Age and Survivors and Disability Insurance (OASDI) programs. Benefits are financed through a payroll tax on employers, employees and self-employed persons. In 2010 the tax is imposed at a 6.2% rate on the first $106,800 of each worker's wage income. The employer also pays at a 6.2% rate, for total payroll. (No tax for this purpose is imposed on investment income.) Starting in 1954, Congress amended the Social Security Act to provide that a worker who satisfies the Act's eligibility requirements (meets the minimum number of quarters of OASDI tax contributions) and becomes totally disabled, is entitled to retirement benefits at the same age (then 65) as if there had been no work interruption. A program of monthly benefit payments for totally disabled workers under normal retirement age was introduced into the Act in 1956. As of the end of 2009, roughly 7.8 million totally disabled workers received monthly social security disability benefits; additional benefits were paid to a substantial number of spouses and dependent children of those workers. Total payments in December 2009 were 9.1 billion dollars. Questions have been raised about the long-term solvency of the program. The trust fund created by the payroll taxes that finance the program is projected to peak between 2007 and 2014 and then to decline, with possible exhaustion around 2018.

As the following case indicates, "total disability" under the Social Security Act means inability, due to physical or mental impairment that is "demonstrable by medically acceptable clinical and laboratory diagnostic techniques," to engage, considering the worker's age, education and work experience, in any kind of substantial gainful work that exists anywhere in the nation. (It is irrelevant whether the work is available in the area where the claimant lives or whether the claimant would be hired.) The disability must be "long term", which is defined to mean that it has lasted or is expected to last at least 12 months. Finally, there is a five-month waiting period for filing claims. See generally, *Bowen v. Yuckert*, 482 U.S. 137, 107 S.Ct. 2287, 96 L.Ed.2d 119 (1987). Despite this demanding definition, the number of beneficiaries has grown significantly in recent decades.

In *Cleveland v. Policy Management Systems Corp.*, 526 U.S. 795, 119 S.Ct. 1597, 143 L.Ed.2d 966 (1999), the Court was asked whether an individual who applied for Social Security Disability Insurance (SSDI) benefits is barred from asserting a claim under the Americans with Disabilities Act. It concluded that because SSDI eligibility does not weigh the possibility of reasonable accommodation, the two claims are not inherently inconsistent. Such a claimant, however, must proffer a sufficient explanation as to why the ADA claim is not in fact inconsistent with the application for SSDI benefits.

Claims for benefits are evaluated in a multi-stage process. As described in *Heckler v. Day*, 467 U.S. 104, 104 S.Ct. 2249, 81 L.Ed.2d 88 (1984) at 106–07:

> The disability programs administered under Titles II and XVI "are of a size and extent difficult to comprehend." *Richardson v. Perales*, 402 U.S. 389, 399, 91 S.Ct. 1420, 1426, 28 L.Ed.2d 842 (1971). Approximately two million disability claims were filed under these two Titles in fiscal year 1983. Over 320,000 of these claims must be heard by some 800 administrative law judges each year. To facilitate the orderly and sympathetic administration of the disability program of Title II, the Secretary and Congress have established an unusually protective four-step process for the review and adjudication of disputed claims. First, a state agency determines whether the claimant has a disability and the date the disability began or ceased. * * * Second, if the claimant is dissatisfied with that determination, he may request reconsideration of the determination. This involves a de novo reconsideration of the disability claim by the state agency, and in some cases a full evidentiary hearing. * * * Additional evidence may be submitted at this stage, either on the request of the claimant or by order of the agency. Third, if the claimant receives an adverse reconsideration determination, he is entitled by statute to an evidentiary hearing and to a de novo review by an Administrative Law Judge (ALJ). * * * Finally, if the claimant is dissatisfied with the decision of the ALJ, he may take an appeal to the Appeals Council of the Department of Health and Human Services (HHS). * * * These four steps exhaust the claimant's administrative remedies. Thereafter, he may seek judicial review in federal district court.

Once the claim reaches the administrative law judge level, its handling can become complex, as the following opinion demonstrates.

## TACKETT v. APFEL

United States Court of Appeals, Ninth Circuit, 1999
180 F.3d 1094

PREGERSON, CIRCUIT JUDGE:

\* \* \*

### I. *Facts and Prior Proceedings.*

[Claimant Richard] Tackett has had problems with his knees for well over ten years. One of his treating physicians stated that Tackett's left knee was "one of the worst knees" he had ever operated on. It is undisputed that Tackett is currently disabled. To determine whether Tackett was disabled before his fiftieth birthday, a review of the facts is necessary.

In 1988, Tackett had surgery on his right knee under the care of Dr. Michael Lawley. In 1991, he had surgery on his left knee, again under the care of Dr. Lawley. Dr. Lawley thought that Tackett would someday need total replacements of both knees and a hip replacement necessitated by his knee problems.

In September of 1991, Tackett lost his balance and fell while at work. After this accident, Tackett's knee problems got so bad that he had to leave his job as a machinist. In 1994, Tackett took a job at ACE Hardware but could not manage the work because of his knees. He left after a month.

Based on these medical problems, Tackett filed an application for Social Security disability benefits on July 29, 1993, alleging that he has been disabled since September 16, 1991. The Commissioner of the Social Security Administration ("Commissioner") denied both Tackett's application and his request for reconsideration. See 20 C.F.R. §§ 404.901(a)(1)–(2), 404.907. Tackett timely requested and was granted a hearing before the ALJ. See 20 C.F.R. §§ 404.901(a)(3), 404.929–933. On March 21, 1995, the ALJ determined that Tackett became disabled under the Medical–Vocational Guidelines when he turned fifty on February 7, 1995, but that he was not disabled before he turned fifty.

Tackett requested that the Appeals Council review the ALJ's decision insofar as it denied benefits from September 1991 to February 1995. \* \* \* On May 30, 1996, the Appeals Council declined Tackett's request for review. At this point, the ALJ's ruling became the final decision of the Commissioner. \* \* \* Tackett then sought review in federal court. See 42 U.S.C. § 405(g). \* \* \*[T]he district judge referred the matter to a magistrate judge. The magistrate judge recommended that the ALJ's decision be affirmed because it was supported by substantial evidence and was free from errors of law. \* \* \* The district court adopted the magistrate judge's Report and Recommendation on October 30, 1997, and issued an order affirming the ALJ's decision.

Tackett appeals the district court's order affirming the ALJ's decision. He contends that the ALJ's decision to deny benefits from September 1991 to February 1995 was not supported by the evidence and was based on errors of law. * * *

## II. *Standard of Review.*

We review de novo the decision of the district court affirming the decision of the ALJ. * * * This court may set aside the Commissioner's denial of disability insurance benefits when the ALJ's findings are based on legal error or are not supported by substantial evidence in the record as a whole. * * *

Substantial evidence is defined as "more than a mere scintilla but less than a preponderance." * * *

## III. *Establishing Disability Under the Social Security Act.*

To establish a claimant's eligibility for disability benefits under the Social Security Act, it must be shown that: (a) the claimant suffers from a medically determinable physical or mental impairment that can be expected to result in death or that has lasted or can be expected to last for a continuous period of not less than twelve months; and (b) the impairment renders the claimant incapable of performing the work that the claimant previously performed and incapable of performing any other substantial gainful employment that exists in the national economy. See 42 U.S.C. § 423(d)(2)(A). If a claimant meets both requirements, he or she is "disabled."

The Social Security Regulations set out a five-step sequential process for determining whether a claimant is disabled within the meaning of the Social Security Act. See 20 C.F.R. § 404.1520. The burden of proof is on the claimant as to steps one to four.[3] As to step five, the burden shifts to the Commissioner. If a claimant is found to be "disabled" or "not disabled" at any step in the sequence, there is no need to consider subsequent steps. See id.

The five steps are:

Step 1. Is the claimant presently working in a substantially gainful activity?[4] If so, then the claimant is *"not disabled"* within the meaning of the Social Security Act and is not entitled to disability insurance benefits. If the claimant is not working in a substantially gainful activity, then the

---

**3.** As noted by our sister circuit, the application of burdens of proof "is particularly elusive in cases involving social security benefits, in part because the proceedings are not designed to be adversarial." *Donato v. Secretary of Dept. of Health & Human Servs. of the United States,* 721 F.2d 414, 418 (2d Cir.1983) (internal quotations omitted). In addition, the ALJ's affirmative duty to assist a claimant to develop the record further complicates the allocation of burdens. See 20 C.F.R. § 404.1512(d). Notwithstanding the fact that the ALJ shares the burden at each step, we use the term burden of proof for convenience.

**4.** Substantial gainful activity is work activity that is both substantial, i.e., involves significant physical or mental activities, and gainful, i.e., work activity performed for pay or profit. See 20 C.F.R. § 404.1572.

claimant's case cannot be resolved at step one and the evaluation proceeds to step two. * * *

Step 2.   Is the claimant's impairment severe? If not, then the claimant is *"not disabled"* and is not entitled to disability insurance benefits. If the claimant's impairment is severe, then the claimant's case cannot be resolved at step two and the evaluation proceeds to step three. * * *

Step 3.   Does the impairment "meet or equal" one of a list of specific impairments described in the regulations? If so, the claimant is *"disabled"* and therefore entitled to disability insurance benefits. If the claimant's impairment neither meets nor equals one of the impairments listed in the regulations, then the claimant's case cannot be resolved at step three and the evaluation proceeds to step four. * * *

Step 4.   Is the claimant able to do any work that he or she has done in the past? If so, then the claimant is *"not disabled"* and is not entitled to disability insurance benefits. If the claimant cannot do any work he or she did in the past, then the claimant's case cannot be resolved at step four and the evaluation proceeds to the fifth and final step. * * *

Step 5.   Is the claimant able to do any other work? If not, then the claimant is *"disabled"* and therefore entitled to disability insurance benefits. See 20 C.F.R. § 404.1520(f)(1). If the claimant is able to do other work, then the Commissioner must establish that there are a significant number of jobs in the national economy that claimant can do. There are two ways for the Commissioner to meet the burden of showing that there is other work in "significant numbers" in the national economy that claimant can do: (1) by the testimony of a vocational expert, or (2) by reference to the Medical–Vocational Guidelines at 20 C.F.R. pt. 404, subpt. P, app. 2. If the Commissioner meets this burden, the claimant is *"not disabled"* and therefore not entitled to disability insurance benefits. See 20 C.F.R. §§ 404.1520(f), 404.1562. If the Commissioner cannot meet this burden, then the claimant is *"disabled"* and therefore entitled to disability benefits. See id.

### A.   *Steps One and Two are Not in Dispute.*

The ALJ found that Tackett had not engaged in substantial gainful activity since September 16, 1991. The ALJ also found that Tackett had "severe impairments due to degenerative joint disease of both knees." Consequently, Tackett met steps one and two. We proceed to step three.

### B.   *Step Three: The ALJ's Determination that Tackett's Impairments Did Not Meet or Equal a Listed Impairment is Supported by Substantial Evidence.*

At step three, the ALJ determines if a claimant's impairment meets or equals an impairment listed in Appendix 1 to Subpart P of Regulations No. 4. The Listing of Impairments ("the List") describes specific impairments of each of the major body systems "which are considered severe enough to prevent a person from doing any gainful activity." See 20 C.F.R. § 404.1525. * * *

The List describes the characteristics of each impairment. The description includes the "symptoms, signs and laboratory findings" that make up the characteristics of each listed impairment. 20 C.F.R. § 404.1525. To meet a listed impairment, a claimant must establish that he or she meets each characteristic of a listed impairment relevant to his or her claim. To equal a listed impairment, a claimant must establish symptoms, signs and laboratory findings "at least equal in severity and duration" to the characteristics of a relevant listed impairment, or, if a claimant's impairment is not listed, then to the listed impairment "most like" the claimant's impairment. 20 C.F.R. § 404.1526.

If a claimant suffers from multiple impairments and none of them individually meets or equals a listed impairment, the collective symptoms, signs and laboratory findings of all of the claimant's impairments will be evaluated to determine whether they meet or equal the characteristics of any relevant listed impairment. See id. * * *

Tackett claims that he meets or equals Listed Impairment 1.03, which is "[a]rthritis of a major weight-bearing joint." To be found disabled at step three, Tackett had to establish that he met or equaled each of the following characteristics of listed impairment 1.03:

(i)  marked limitation of motion or abnormal motion of the knee;

(ii)  history of persistent joint pain and stiffness;

(iii)  gross anatomical deformity;

(iv)  reconstructive surgery or surgical arthrodesis; and

(v)  a markedly limited ability to walk and stand.

See 20 C.F.R. § 404, Subpt. P, App. 1, 1.03.

The ALJ's medical expert reviewed Tackett's medical records and concluded that Tackett's knee problems met the second through the fifth characteristics listed above. But the expert testified that he could not find clear evidence that Tackett met the first characteristic of "marked limitation of motion or abnormal motion" of the knee, and accordingly the expert would not state that Tackett met all of the above characteristics for listed impairment 1.03. * * *

Consequently, there is substantial evidence to support the ALJ's conclusion that Tackett did not suffer from abnormal motion of either knee and therefore did not meet listed impairment "1.03 Arthritis of a major weight-bearing joint."

Tackett also argues that even if his impairments do not *meet* the five characteristics for a finding of disability under listed impairment 1.03, his impairments are *equal* to listed impairment 1.03. See 20 C.F.R. § 404.1520(d); *Lester v. Chater*, 81 F.3d 821, 828 (9th Cir.1995) ("Claimants are conclusively disabled if their condition either meets or equals a listed impairment."). Tackett asserts that the ALJ's medical expert's testimony that Tackett suffered from "a significant functional problem with respect to his knees" established that Tackett's impairment was equal to listed impairment 1.03. This argument is also without merit. "Medical equivalence must be based on medical findings." 20 C.F.R. § 404.1526. A generalized assertion of functional problems is not enough to establish disability at step three. See id. * * *

C. *Step Four: Tackett is Unable to Return to his Former Work.*

It is undisputed that Tackett's knee problems prevent him from doing the machinist work he did in the past. Therefore, we proceed to the final step, step five.

D. *Step Five: Tackett's Ability to Perform Other Work Was Not Properly Ascertained.*

1. *Vocational Experts and the Medical Vocational Guidelines.*

Once a claimant has established that he or she suffers from a severe impairment that prevents the claimant from doing any work he or she has done in the past, the claimant has made a prima facie showing of disability. At this point—step five—the burden shifts to the Commissioner to show that the claimant can perform some other work that exists in "significant numbers" in the national economy, taking into consideration the claimant's residual functional capacity, age, education, and work experience. 20 CFR § 404.1560(b)(3). There are two ways for the Commissioner to meet the burden of showing that there is other work in "significant numbers" in the national economy that claimant can perform: (a) by the testimony of a vocational expert, or (b) by reference to the Medical–Vocational Guidelines at 20 C.F.R. pt. 404, subpt. P, app. 2. See *Desrosiers v. Secretary of Health and Human Servs.*, 846 F.2d 573, 577–78 (Pregerson, J., concurring) (9th Cir.1988).

(a) *Vocational Expert.*

At step five, the ALJ can call upon a vocational expert to testify as to: (1) what jobs the claimant, given his or her residual functional capacity, would be able to do; and (2) the availability of such jobs in the national economy. At the hearing, the ALJ poses hypothetical questions to the vocational expert that "set out all of the claimant's impairments" for the vocational expert's consideration. *Gamer v. Secretary of Health and Human Servs.*, 815 F.2d 1275, 1279 (9th Cir.1987). The ALJ's depiction of the claimant's disability must be accurate, detailed, and supported by the medical record. See id. at 1279–80. The vocational expert then " 'translates [these] factual scenarios into realistic job market probabilities' by testifying on the record to what kinds of jobs the claimant still can perform and whether there is a sufficient number of those jobs available in the claimant's region or in several other regions of the economy to support a finding of 'not disabled.' " *Desrosiers*, 846 F.2d at 578 (Pregerson, J., concurring) (internal citations omitted.)

### (b) Medical–Vocational Guidelines.

In some cases, it is appropriate for the ALJ to rely on the Medical–Vocational Guidelines to determine whether a claimant can perform some work that exists in "significant numbers" in the national economy. The Medical–Vocational Guidelines are a matrix system for handling claims that involve substantially uniform levels of impairment. See 20 C.F.R. pt. 404, subpt. P, app 2.

The Guidelines present, *in table form*, a short-hand method for determining the availability and numbers of suitable jobs for a claimant. These tables are commonly known as "the grids." The grids categorize jobs by their physical-exertional requirements and consist of three separate tables—one for each category: "[m]aximum sustained work capacity limited to sedentary work," "[m]aximum sustained work capacity limited to light work," and "[m]aximum sustained work capacity limited to medium work." 20 C.F.R. pt. 404, subpt. P, app. 2, rule 200.00. Each grid presents various combinations of factors relevant to a claimant's ability to find work. The factors in the grids are the claimant's age, education, and work experience. For each combination of these factors, e.g., fifty years old, limited education, and unskilled work experience, the grids direct a finding of either "disabled" or "not disabled" based on the number of jobs in the national economy in that category of physical-exertional requirements. See id.

This approach allows the Commissioner to streamline the administrative process and encourages uniform treatment of claims. See *Heckler v. Campbell*, 461 U.S. 458, 460–462, 103 S.Ct. 1952, 76 L.Ed.2d 66 (1983) (discussing the creation and purpose of the Medical–Vocational Guidelines).

The Commissioner's need for efficiency justifies use of the grids at step five where they *completely and accurately* represent a claimant's limitations. See id. at 461. In other words, a claimant must be able to perform the *full range* of jobs in a given category, i.e., sedentary work, light work, or medium work. As explained in *Desrosiers*:

> This court has recognized that significant non-exertional impairments, such as poor vision or inability to tolerate dust or gases, may make reliance on the grids inappropriate. We have also held that pain can be a non-exertional limitation.

> However, the fact that a non-exertional limitation is alleged does not automatically preclude application of the grids. The ALJ should first determine if a claimant's non-exertional limitations significantly limit the range of work permitted by his exertional limitations.

> . . . A non-exertional impairment, if sufficiently severe, may limit the claimant's functional capacity in ways not contemplated by the guidelines. In such a case, the guidelines would be inapplicable.

846 F.2d at 577 (Pregerson, J., concurring) (internal citations omitted). The ALJ may rely on the grids alone to show the availability of jobs for

the claimant "only when the grids accurately and completely describe the claimant's abilities and limitations." *Jones v. Heckler*, 760 F.2d 993, 998 (9th Cir.1985); see also, 20 C.F.R. pt. 404, subpt. P, app. 2, rule 200(e); *Desrosiers*, 846 F.2d at 577. Examples of non-exertional limitations are pain, postural limitations, or environmental limitations. See id.

### 2. *The ALJ Improperly Disregarded Medical Evidence of Tackett's Non–Exertional Limitations and Erred in Failing to Call a Vocational Expert.*

At step five in the instant case, the ALJ concluded that Tackett's limitations were adequately covered by the grids. Consequently, the ALJ did not call a vocational expert to establish the availability of suitable jobs in the national economy. This was error.

#### (a) *The ALJ Erred in Disregarding Medical Evidence That Tackett Suffered From Non–Exertional Limitations.*

Tackett's treating physicians and the ALJ's medical expert expressed the opinion that Tackett was not "totally precluded" from doing some form of sedentary work. But the doctors also expressed the opinion that Tackett's knee problems required him to change positions, shift his body, walk, or stand about *every half hour*. Notwithstanding this medical evidence, the ALJ found that "[Tackett] could sit throughout an eight hour workday with normal breaks *every two hours* to allow for the need to change his position." Consequently, the ALJ determined that Tackett could work the full range of sedentary jobs and that application of the grids was therefore appropriate. In making this determination, the ALJ failed to give proper weight to the opinions of Tackett's treating physicians and the ALJ's own medical expert. * * *

The ALJ's own medical expert expressed the opinion that Tackett could work at a job, sitting "for up to 30 minutes at a time ... so long as he could shift when he needed to." Shifting, the expert explained, meant "[g]etting up and moving around as needed. No prolonged work in a single position, frequent position changes as needed."

There is no medical evidence to support the ALJ's finding that Tackett could work through an eight hour workday with breaks every two hours. Instead of relying on the opinions of the physicians, the ALJ apparently relied on Tackett's testimony of a road trip he took to California. Tackett testified that he moved to California with the hope that "the weather out there would help with the arthritis and things like this." Tackett traveled with his fiancee, driving about 500 miles per day and stopping frequently. * * *

The ALJ acknowledged that, "[the medical expert] felt the evidence showed [Tackett] had the ability to sit throughout an eight hour workday *so long as he could get up briefly or shift positions every 30 minutes or so*." (Emphasis added). But because of Tackett's testimony concerning the California trip, the ALJ found, contrary to the expert's testimony, that

"[Tackett] could sit throughout an eight hour workday with normal breaks *every two hours* to allow for the need to change his position." (Emphasis added).

There is no evidence on how much cross-country driving Tackett did, if any. There is no evidence of the frequency or the duration of the rest stops. There is no evidence whether Tackett rode sitting up, reclining, or lying down in the back seat. Evidence that Tackett took a four-day road trip to California, without more, is insufficient to counter the opinion of Tackett's treating physicians and the ALJ's own medical examiner that Tackett needs to shift positions "every 30 minutes or so."

Consequently, the ALJ's determination that Tackett could sit throughout an eight hour workday for two hours at a time is not supported by substantial evidence in the record as a whole.

*(b) Because Tackett Suffers From Significant Non–Exertional Limitations, i.e., the Need to Shift Positions Every 30 Minutes, the ALJ Erred in Finding Tackett "Not Disabled" at Step Five Without Consulting a Vocational Expert.*

Because the ALJ believed that Tackett could sit through an eight-hour work day with normal breaks every two hours, the ALJ concluded that Tackett's residual functional capabilities allowed him to perform the full range of sedentary work and that use of the grids was appropriate. The ALJ * * * found that as a "younger individual," Tackett was "not disabled" until his fiftieth birthday on February 7, 1995. At that time, Tackett became "an individual approaching advanced age" and the grids directed a finding of "disabled." * * *

"Sedentary work" contemplates work that involves the ability to sit through most or all of an eight hour day:

> Sedentary work involves lifting no more than 10 pounds at a time and occasionally lifting or carrying articles like docket files, ledgers, and small tools. Although *a sedentary job is defined as one which involves sitting,* a certain amount of walking and standing is often necessary in carrying out job duties. Jobs are sedentary if walking and standing are required occasionally and other sedentary criteria are met.

20 C.F.R. § 404.1567(a) (emphasis added). While some sedentary jobs *may* require some walking and/or standing, others may not require any. Thus, to be physically able to work the full range of sedentary jobs, the worker must be able to sit through most or all of an eight hour day.

The grids should be applied only where a claimant's functional limitations fall into a standardized pattern "accurately and completely" described by the grids. *Jones,* 760 F.2d at 998. Tackett's need to shift, stand up, or walk around every 30 minutes is a significant non-exertional limitation not contemplated by the grids. It is easy to imagine the problems this non-exertional limitation would cause in many sedentary jobs which require sitting during most or all of an eight hour day such as some assembly line jobs, or jobs as a phone operator or dispatcher. Eighty-five percent of the unskilled sedentary jobs "are in the machine trades and benchwork occupational categories." 20 C.F.R. pt. 404, subpt. P, app. 2, rule 201.00(a). Because Tackett's non-exertional limitations "significantly limit the range of work" he can perform, mechanical application of the grids was inappropriate. *Desrosiers*, 846 F.2d at 577. Consequently, to determine whether Tackett was disabled before reaching his fiftieth birthday, the ALJ was *required* to take the testimony of a vocational expert. By concluding that Tackett was not disabled without the aid of the testimony of a vocational expert, the ALJ committed reversible error.

## IV. *Conclusion.*

We remand Tackett's case to the Social Security Administration for reconsideration of Tackett's disability status between September of 1991 and February of 1995. * * *

### NOTES AND QUESTIONS

1.  The system for evaluation of claims described above has at times been overwhelmed by the volume of claims. At the beginning of fiscal year 2008, more than 135,000 cases on the dockets of the Office of Disability Adjudication and Review were 900 days old or older. The total number of pending cases awaiting decision by administrative law judges (or other disposition) was 746,744. Social Security Administration, Office of Disability Adjudication and Review, "Plan To Eliminate the Hearing Backlog," (End of Year Fiscal Report 2007) at 3. One possible implication of this is that the solvency problems of the Disability Insurance Trust Fund may become acute more rapidly than earlier forecast. Another source of delay—slowness in initial processing of claims at the first level, by a state agency—was addressed by the Supreme Court in *Heckler v. Day*, 467 U.S. 104, 104 S.Ct. 2249, 81 L.Ed.2d 88 (1984). A federal district court had found the delays in decisions on requests for reconsideration in Vermont were so great that claimants were denied their statutory right to a hearing within a reasonable time. A narrowly divided Court overturned the decision, finding it was an unwarranted intrusion into the executive and congressional supervision of the agency.

2.  May a claimant who has been through all four steps of the administrative process and has now filed her appeal in federal court raise an issue that she did not raise during the administrative stage? The Supreme Court divided sharply on the issue in *Sims v. Apfel*, 530 U.S. 103, 120 S.Ct. 2080, 147 L.Ed.2d 80 (2000). Four justices reasoned that the non-adversarial nature of the administrative process meant that issue exhaustion should not be required; four disagreed. The deciding vote was cast by Justice O'Connor, who decided that issue exhaustion should not be required on the narrow ground that the Social Security Administration had not told claimants that such a rule might be in place.

3.  What if a claimant is found to be able to perform her prior job, but that job is now largely eliminated from the national economy? See *Barnhart v. Thomas*, 540 U.S. 20, 124 S.Ct. 376, 157 L.Ed.2d 333 (2003) (elevator operator).

4.   Use of the Medical–Vocational Guidelines ("the grids") was approved by the Supreme Court in *Heckler v. Campbell*, 461 U.S. 458, 103 S.Ct. 1952, 76 L.Ed.2d 66 (1983) against an argument that the statute contemplates a more individualized determination on that issue. Two separate opinions in the case raise questions about the overall quality of administrative adjudication in disability cases.

5.   In *Richardson v. Belcher*, 404 U.S. 78, 92 S.Ct. 254, 30 L.Ed.2d 231 (1971), the Court upheld an "offset" provision of the statute, under which the amount of a person's disability benefit is reduced by the amount of any workers' compensation benefit attributable to the same time period.

6.   Once an application for benefits has been approved, cash payments begin with the sixth month of disability. The amount of the monthly benefits depends upon (a) the amount of earnings on which the claimant has paid social security taxes, and (b) whether there are eligible dependents.

7.   In addition to cash benefits, recipients of Social Security Disability benefits are eligible for vocational rehabilitation and for participation in Medicare. Evaluation of whether rehabilitation is appropriate is virtually automatic, and an applicant's refusal to participate may result in loss of benefits. See 42 U.S.C. § 422. An applicant becomes eligible for Medicare beginning with the 25th month of disability.

# E.   PRIVATE AND PUBLIC SECTOR INSURANCE PROGRAMS

Sick and injured workers (and their dependents) obtain much of their health care through insurance programs other than workers' compensation and Social Security. While the bulk of this is for conditions not related to work, the increasing integration of workers' compensation health care with that provided as a basic "fringe benefit" means that the lines between them have blurred. In 2005, 161 million Americans, 63% of the population under 65 years of age, had private health insurance (using the term "insurance" broadly, to include not only policies that pay all or part of medical expenses obtained through a traditional "fee for service" transaction, but also Blue Cross style plans, other preferred provider plans and health maintenance organizations) obtained through the workplace, down from 69% two decades earlier. National Center for Health Statistics, Health: United States 2007, Table 137. The reasons for the growth in the uninsured population are complex, but it seems obvious that the main reason is the spiraling inflation in health care costs, a rate that has exceeded the general inflation rate consistently over a long period. *Id.* Table 122 The large number of persons not covered by private insurance has no doubt contributed to an increase in the importance of public funded programs, such as federal Medicaid and a variety of state government programs. The most ambitious of those has probably been in Hawaii, which requires employers to provide health insurance coverage that meets certain minimum standards to the majority of those who work 20 hours a week or more. See Hawaii Prepaid Health Care Act, Hawaii Rev. Stat. ch.

393. Health care was a major topic of debate in the 2008 presidential campaign. After lengthy partisan wrangling, the Congress finally enacted a comprehensive statute in early 2010, the Patient Protection and Affordable Care Act (PPACA), Pub. L. 111–148, with amendments contained in the Health Care and Education Reconciliation Act of 2010 (HCERA), Pub. L. 111–152. This legislation has no direct impact on workers compensation, but some spillover effect may be possible.

Until that happens, the regulation of private insurance will continue to be divided between a variety of state laws and the requirements of the Employee Retirement Income Security Act (ERISA). That statute, despite its title, applies not just to post-retirement benefits, but to "welfare plans"—including health insurance—provided to current workers. One feature of ERISA is a "supersedure" clause, widely referred to as the "preemption clause." That provision displaces state law regulating employee fringe benefits with federal law, except as provided by a "saving clause." The saving clause preserves, inter alia, state laws regulating "insurance." Working out how the preemption clause and saving clause fit together has led to much litigation and a number of proposals for change. That litigation is discussed in Chapter XI of this book. For the purposes of this chapter, it is enough to say that the most common source of legal actions against insurers by insureds under health policies is what is called "coverage" litigation—lawsuits over whether a particular individual, medical condition, or type of treatment is within the scope of the insurer's promise to provide health care in return for the premiums received.

Medicare is a federal program established in the 1960s to provide medical benefits to Social Security recipients. It is financed through a payroll tax and through the collections of premiums from participants. It has two principal components. Part A provides hospital care benefits; coverage is automatic for those receiving old-age benefits. Part B covers physician fees and some laboratory and other medical care costs; coverage is elective, and requires payment of a premium. Both Part A and Part B involve co-pays, deductibles, and the like. Health care providers may choose in some circumstances whether to participate in the care of Medicare patients; those who do must abide by a fee schedule. Recently, a drug coverage was added, Part D, which also has deductibles and co-pays, largely administered through private entities that compete to sell their particular version of the plan. Private insurance policies—often called "medigap" policies—are also available to cover all or part of the co-pays, co-insurance and deductibles involved with Medicare.

Medicaid is a federal-state program to provide health services to persons with limited incomes. In recent years, a number of states have been developing programs to deliver healthcare to groups that include persons other than those who would meet federal indigency guidelines, such as workers in low-wage jobs, using Medicaid funds as one resource to pay for these programs.

Group disability insurance, designed to replace part of the income lost when an individual is unable to work because of illness or injury, is much less common than group health insurance. Just under forty per cent of the private industry work force is covered by policies providing short term benefits, typically three to six months; thirty per cent for longer term benefits. U.S. Department of Labor, Bureau of Labor Statistics, "National Compensation Survey: Employee Benefits in Private Industry in the United States, March 2007," Table 13. The policies vary greatly in coverage and in the amount of benefits paid. The most common benefit is a per cent of lost wages, often 50 per cent, but in some policies as much as two-thirds of the average wage during the prior year. The definition of disability also varies; the most generous policies define it as inability to perform one's usual job, the most restrictive use a definition similar to that of the Social Security program. See generally Couch on Insurance § 147.107 (2007). Many have a clause integrating payment of benefits with what is being paid under workers' compensation; often all or part of the amount of any workers' compensation benefit will be deducted from what is payable under the disability policy.

## BLUE CROSS & BLUE SHIELD OF MISSISSIPPI, INC. v. LARSON

Supreme Court of Mississippi, 1986
485 So.2d 1071

PATTERSON, CHIEF JUSTICE, for the Court:

This appeal concerns the construction of insurance contract provisions. One is a Coordination Of Benefits (C.O.B.) provision in a Blue Cross & Blue Shield group policy of Moss Point Marine covering Kenneth Larson, a participating employee, and his wife, Carolyn, as his dependent. The second is an "Other Insurance" provision contained in the Pascagoula–Moss Point Bank Employee Medical Expense Reimbursement Trust (Trust) covering Carolyn as a bank employee participant.

Carolyn was an employee of the Pascagoula–Moss Point Bank which created the Trust to pay medical expenses of its employees if there was no other medical coverage. Carolyn was also protected by Blue Cross & Blue Shield as a dependent through her husband's policy as an employee of Moss Point Marine. Medical expenses of over $600.00 were incurred by Carolyn for which she unsuccessfully sought reimbursement from Blue Cross. The claim was denied because Blue Cross maintained its obligation was secondary, and that her employer's Trust was primarily liable. Accordingly, it tendered less than $200.00 (excess) to the Larsons as a secondary insurance carrier. * * *

The Blue Cross policy contains a C.O.B. provision to limit benefits for a single medical risk to not more than one hundred percent of the medical expenses. The C.O.B. is intended to avoid duplication of coverage, and thereby avoid twofold payment exceeding the actual medical expenses to a claimant. The C.O.B. provision of the Blue Cross policy follows:

This provision shall apply in determining the benefits as to a person covered under this Contract for any Claim Determination Period if, for the Covered Services incurred as to such person during such period, the sum of the benefits that would be payable under this Contract in the absence of this Provision, and the benefits that would be payable under all other Plans in the absence therein of contractual terms of similar purpose to this Provision would exceed the reasonable cost of such Covered Services.

The Bank's Trust for its employees contained a clause relating to "Other Insurance," viz:

> Reimbursement under this Plan shall be made by the Trust only in the event and to the extent that such reimbursement or payment is not provided for under any other employer sponsored or labor union sponsored insurance policy or policies, regardless of whether the coverage is attributable to the employment of the spouse or a dependent of an enrolled Employee. In the event that there is such a policy or plan in effect, the Employer shall be relieved of any liability hereunder.

Coordination of benefits is a valid method to contain health care cost within reasonable limits by the prevention of duplication of payments in excess of actual medical charges. These provisions provide an orderly procedure for the determination of primary and secondary coverage responsibilities. Complexities have arisen largely because our society supports, and family economics demand, the employment of both spouses outside the family unit. * * *

The procedures for equitably resolving the issues arising from duplicating coverage have been addressed by this Court. In *Travelers Indemnity Co. v. Chappell*, 246 So.2d 498 (Miss.1971), we gave examples of three broad categories of "other insurance" clauses where the phraseology of the policies permitted. The first is a "pro rata" clause in which one company is primary but agrees to pay its pro rata share with other primary insurers. The second category is the "excess" clause, which insures the loss only to the extent it is not paid by other insurance. The third category is the "escape" clause where the insurer disclaims any liability where there is other coverage. We discussed the development of these legal principles stating:

> The courts had little trouble with this rule; that is to say, so long as the escape v. escape clauses, excess v. excess clauses and pro rata v. pro rata clauses were identical, the courts held them to be conflicting and nugatory so as to cancel each other out, and therefore liability under the two policies was prorated between the two insurance policies in the ratio of the limits of liability fixed in each policy which bears to the total limits in all of the policies covering the risk.

246 So.2d at 503.

We observed, however, that if there were conflicting clauses not within similar categories whereby one clause of a policy predominates over a somewhat similar clause of another policy, legal entanglements would likely follow. We observed:

> When there was a conflict between an escape clause and an excess clause, the excess clause ordinarily would be given full effect and would not activate the liability in that policy. Likewise, where an excess clause is in conflict with either an escape clause or a prorata clause in the other policy, the excess clause ordinarily would be given full effect. The courts are thus attempting to give full effect to the intent of the two policies to offer two different levels of coverage.

246 So.2d at 503.

Our interpretation of the C.O.B. provision of Blue Cross encompasses not only its language to achieve the prevention of overpayment of claims; but necessarily entails other considerations in resolving, or attempting to, the procedural steps necessary to the resolution of primary and secondary coverage. One such fact employed in the resolution is the status of the protected employee; i.e., whether a subscribing beneficiary of his employer's protection plan, or whether the claimant is a dependent beneficiary of the subscribing beneficiary, but who is also a primary beneficiary of another program of a different employer. In this circumstance the dependent claimant, by ordinary C.O.B. agreements, would be required to seek primary medical benefit payments from the insurer to whose services he or she subscribes. By this method of determining primary and secondary liability coverage, the claimant's status as a designated beneficiary in coverage provided by a spouse is largely overlooked. By invoking this procedure the liability of Blue Cross in this case is secondary simply because the claimant enjoys or is burdened by the protection plan of her own employer.

Although this expedient procedure undoubtedly has admirable persuasions to support it such as simplicity and the avoidance of litigation with its cost, it overlooks and erodes the privileged right of the several parties to contract, assuming such is not against public policy, by expressing their intentions through the language of their choice. Other well intended devices such as primary and secondary liability being established according to the time in which coverage was attained, in our opinion, detract from the language expressing the intentions of the insurer and the insured.

It is our opinion the issue now before us can best be determined by resolving the protection intended to be afforded by Blue Cross and that intended by the Trust as expressed in their contracts without employment of devices to expedite contractual interpretation. * * *

In *Starks v. Hospital Service Plan of N.J., Inc.*, 182 N.J.Super. 342, 440 A.2d 1353, 25 A.L.R. 4th 1009 (1981), the New Jersey Court held against Blue Cross–Blue Shield because the overall objective of the two policies revealed one policy had primary coverage and the other had only a provision for excess coverage in the event there was primary coverage for the claimant emanating from another policy source. This is to say the claimant's policy never intended to provide primary coverage where another policy existed containing primary coverage for the spouse of the primary beneficiary, but was only secondary or excess coverage if a spouse was protected by the provisions of another policy. In other words, we do not think the C.O.B. provision of Blue Cross and the "Other Insurance" expression in the Trust are compatible to a construction permitting a plan against which the benefits of the two policies could be coordinated.

This appears to be the precise situation now before us. We find *Starks, supra,* to be precisely on point and because this is so, we quote from it somewhat extensively.

> The controversy here arises from the fact that the individual plaintiffs are all direct beneficiaries of the Welfare Fund Plan and each is also the spouse and hence a dependent of a direct subscriber under a Blue Cross/Blue Shield employer group contract. The question then is whether the Welfare Fund Plan is a program against which Blue Cross/Blue Shield is entitled to coordinate benefits, thereby converting its primary responsibility into a secondary or excess one. * * *

> In our judgment the Welfare Fund Plan only intended to be obligated to make payments to its members for reimbursement of medical and hospital expenses to the extent that the cost of those services was not covered by any other source of payment, including employer group contracts such as those issued by Blue Cross/Blue Shield covering its members as dependents of direct subscribers. Its intention thus was to serve as a payment source of absolutely last resort. * * *

> In applying these principles here, it is first evident that in the circumstances before us the Blue Cross/Blue Shield coverage is intended to be primary as to its subscribers and excess as to dependents of subscribers *who are direct beneficiaries of other delimited plans.* Its intention as to these plaintiffs was apparently, therefore, to provide only excess coverage. It is also evident that the Welfare Fund Plan is not intended to be primary in any circumstances.... it is ... the precise nature and purpose of the offered benefits as compared with the precise nature and purpose of those offered by Blue Cross/Blue Shield, which determine whether it constitutes a plan against which Blue Cross/Blue Shield is entitled to coordinate against. We are further persuaded that these considerations preclude such coordination here. * * *

> If the provisions of the two plans here were mutually repugnant, we would unhesitatingly apply the *Cosmopolitan* rule and hold that as to these plaintiffs, Blue Cross/Blue Shield and the Welfare Fund Plan would be obliged to share the payment of benefits pro rata. We do not do so, however, because in our view a comparison of the two operative other-insurance clauses makes it clear that they do not support the predicate of mutual repugnancy. That predicate, as we view it, is the

existence in each of the clauses of language which establishes precisely the same order of payment for each coverage. If there is, however, in either but not both of the clauses a clearly expressed intention of the undertaking of an obligation prior to or subsequent to the other, that intention will ordinarily be enforced by the courts.

Indeed, such expressed intentions constitute the basis of enforcement of the customary excess or secondary payment clause vis-a-vis primary undertaking where the insured is entitled to a single recovery only. (Citations omitted.) Where the two coverages are not, however, primary and secondary but rather secondary and tertiary, there being no primary coverage in the usual sense, the only rational result is to require the secondary coverage to pay first and the tertiary coverage to pay second. *The concept of tertiary coverage, that is, coverage which is intended as excess to ordinary excess coverage is, moreover, not a novel one in insurance usage.... We are persuaded that the Welfare Fund Plan here constitutes just such contingent excess coverage and that this intention could hardly have been more plainly spelled out.* * * *

... [T]he Blue Cross/Blue Shield COB provision is not reasonably construable as having intended that a contingent resource such as that offered by the Welfare Fund Plan would constitute a plan against which its benefits would be coordinated. (Emphasis added.)

440 A.2d at 1356–61.

For the foregoing reasons we are of the opinion the trial court and the circuit court on appeal reached the proper result in the resolution of the issue before them.

We also hold that Blue Cross & Blue Shield is primarily liable to Carolyn Larson for her medical expenses and the Bank Trust is liable only for "Contingent Excess Liability." The judgment of the circuit court on appeal is affirmed.

*Affirmed.*

## NOTES AND QUESTIONS

1. In what circumstances would the Bank Trust have to pay any of an employee's medical expenses? Is such a limited liability so illusory as to be unconscionable, or does it have real value?

2. Under ERISA, employers that set up and administer their own plans are generally not subject to regulation by state insurance authorities under the "deemer" clause. 29 U.S.C. § 1144(b)(2)(B), about which more is said in Chapter XI of this book. ERISA does not, however, provide the Secretary of Labor or other authorities the same sort of policy language approval power enjoyed by some state commissioners. The language of the documents creating the plan is generally held to be totally controlling. See *FMC Corp. v. Holliday,* 498 U.S. 52, 111 S.Ct. 403, 112 L.Ed.2d 356 (1990).

# F. THIRD PARTY RECOVERY

## ALDAY v. PATTERSON TRUCKLINE, INC.

The opinion appears above at 689.

### NOTES AND QUESTIONS

1. Most workers' compensation statutes bar the actions for unintended physical harm against fellow employees, either by explicit language or judicial interpretation. See, e.g., *Rivera v. Safford*, 126 Wis.2d 462, 377 N.W.2d 187 (1985). Granting that immunity has sometimes been held to create issues under state constitutional provisions. See, e.g., *Estabrook v. American Hoist & Derrick, Inc.*, 127 N.H. 162, 498 A.2d 741 (1985) (Souter, J., dissenting).

2. As mentioned earlier, "statutory employer" provisions commonly provide immunity from liability for negligence to an employer "up the chain" from one's own employer if that statutory employer in fact has paid benefits to the injured worker. Some go further to provide that immunity to a general or intermediate contractor that has obtained workers compensation insurance coverage for that worker. Some, such as Oklahoma, at one time went still further, to provide immunity for all employers engaged upon a "common task." See *O'Baugh v. Drilling Well Control, Inc.*, 609 P.2d 355 (Okla. 1980). The Oklahoma state legislature amended its statute soon after, however, to limit the immunity to intermediate and principal contractors, and thereby eliminated the "horizontal immunity" approach. See *Stacy v. Bill Hodges Truck Co., Inc.*, 809 P.2d 1313 (Okla. 1991). There are still occasional provisions that extend the immunity to specific third parties outside a chain of contractorship, such as a Florida law protecting consulting design engineers from liability for damages if the injured party is eligible for workers' compensation benefits. See *Estate of Reyes v. Parsons Brinckerhoff Construction Services, Inc.*, 784 So.2d 514 (Fla. App. 2001).

3. If a general contractor is not entitled to immunity from suit because of the exclusive remedy clause, then questions arise in any tort action against it about the scope of the duties owed by the general contractor in light of the duties owed by the immediate employer as subcontractor. In *Kelley v. Howard S. Wright Construction Co.*, 90 Wash.2d 323, 582 P.2d 500 (1978), the court explored four sources of duty owed by a general contractor: (1) control of the premises where work was being done; (2) inherently dangerous nature of the work being done; (3) statutes such as the Occupational Safety and Health Act; (4) promises made in the general contractor's agreement with the project owner. A concurring opinion in the case argues against using OSHA for negligence *per se* purposes. (The case is also interesting with respect to the contribution issues discussed in notes following the next principal case.)

## ESTATE OF COWART v. NICKLOS DRILLING CO.

United States Supreme Court, 1992
505 U.S. 469, 112 S.Ct. 2589, 120 L.Ed.2d 379

Justice Kennedy delivered the opinion of the Court.

The Longshore and Harbor Workers' Compensation Act (LHWCA or Act)* * * allows injured workers, without forgoing compensation under the Act, to pursue claims against third parties for their injuries. But § 33(g) of the LHWCA, 33 U.S.C. § 933(g), provides that under certain circumstances if a third-party claim is settled without the written approval of the worker's employer, all future benefits including medical benefits are forfeited. The question we must decide today is whether the forfeiture provision applies to a worker whose employer, at the time the worker settles with a third party, is neither paying compensation to the worker nor yet subject to an order to pay under the Act.

### I

The injured worker in this case was Floyd Cowart, and his estate is now the petitioner. Cowart suffered an injury to his hand on July 20, 1983, while working on an oil drilling platform owned by Transco Exploration Company (Transco). The platform was located on the Outer Continental Shelf, an area subject to the Act. 43 U.S.C. § 1333(b). Cowart was an employee of the Nicklos Drilling Company (Nicklos), who along with its insurer Compass Insurance Co. (Compass) are respondents before us. Nicklos and Compass paid Cowart temporary disability payments for 10 months following his injury. At that point Cowart's treating physician released him to return to work, though he found Cowart had a 40% permanent partial disability. App. 75. The Department of Labor notified Compass that Cowart was owed permanent disability payments in the total amount of $35,592.77, plus penalties and interest. This was an informal notice which did not constitute an award. No payments were made.

Cowart, meanwhile, had filed an action against Transco alleging that Transco's negligence caused his injury. On July 1, 1985, Cowart settled the action for $45,000, of which he received $29,350.60 after attorney's fees and expenses. Nicklos funded the entire settlement under an indemnification agreement with Transco, and it had prior notice of the settlement amount. But Cowart made a mistake: He did not secure from Nicklos a formal, prior, written approval of the Transco settlement.

After settling, Cowart filed an administrative claim with the Department of Labor seeking disability payments from Nicklos. Nicklos denied liability on the grounds that under the terms of § 33(g)(2) of the LHWCA, Cowart had forfeited his benefits by failing to secure approval from Nicklos and Compass of his settlement with Transco, in the manner required by § 33(g)(1).

Section 33(g) provides in pertinent part:

(g) Compromise obtained by person entitled to compensation

(1) If the person entitled to compensation (or the person's representative) enters into a settlement with a third person referred to in subsection (a) of this section for an amount less than the compensation to which the person (or the person's representative) would be entitled under this chapter, the employer shall be liable for compensation as determined under subsection (f) of this section only if written approval of the settlement is obtained from the employer and the employer's carrier, before the settlement is executed, and by the person entitled to compensation (or the person's representative). The approval shall be made on a form provided by the Secretary and shall be filed in the office of the deputy commissioner within thirty days after the settlement is entered into.

(2) If no written approval of the settlement is obtained and filed as required by paragraph (1), or if the employee fails to notify the employer of any settlement obtained from or judgment rendered against a third person, all rights to compensation and medical benefits under this chapter shall be terminated, regardless of whether the employer or the employer's insurer has made payments or acknowledged entitlement to benefits under this chapter.

33 U.S.C. § 933(g).

The Administrative Law Judge (ALJ) rejected Nicklos' argument on the basis of prior interpretations of § 33(g) by the Benefits Review Board (Board or BRB). In the first of those decisions, *O'Leary v. Southeast Stevedoring Co.*, 7 BRBS 144 (1977), aff'd mem., 622 F.2d 595 (CA9 1980), the Board held that in an earlier version of § 33(g) the words "person entitled to compensation" referred only to injured employees whose employers were making compensation payments, whether voluntary or pursuant to an award. The *O'Leary* decision held that a person not yet receiving benefits was not a "person entitled to compensation," even though the person had a valid claim for benefits.

The statute was amended to its present form, the form we have quoted, in 1984. In that year Congress redesignated then subsection (g) to what is now (g)(1) and modified its language somewhat, but did not change the phrase "person entitled to compensation." Congress also added the current subsection (g)(2), as well as other provisions. Following the 1984 amendments the Board decided *Dorsey v. Cooper Stevedoring Co.*, 18 BRBS 25 (1986), app. dism'd, 826 F.2d 1011 (CA11 1987). The Board reaffirmed its interpretation in *O'Leary* of the phrase "person entitled to compensation," saying that because the 1984 amendments had not changed the specific language, Congress was presumed to have adopted the Board's previous interpretation. It noted that nothing in the 1984 legislative history disclosed an intent to overrule the Board's interpretations. The Board decided that the forfeiture provisions of subsection (g)(2), including the final phrase providing that forfeiture occurs "regardless of whether the employer ... has made payments or acknowledged entitlement to benefits," was a "separate provisio[n] applicable to separate situations." 18 BRBS, at 29.

The ALJ in this case held that under the reasoning of *O'Leary* and *Dorsey*, Cowart was not a person entitled to compensation because he was not receiving payments at the time of the Transco settlement. Thus, the written-approval provision did not apply and Cowart was entitled to benefits. Cowart's total disability award was for $35,592.77, less Cowart's net recovery from Transco of $29,350.60, for a net award of $6,242.17. In addition, Cowart was awarded interest, attorney's fees, and future medical benefits, the last constituting, we think, a matter of great potential consequence. The Board affirmed in reliance on *Dorsey*. 23 BRBS 42 (1989) (per curiam).

On review, a panel of the Court of Appeals for the Fifth Circuit reversed. 907 F.2d 1552 (1990). * * *

In a *per curiam* opinion, the en banc Court of Appeals confirmed the panel's decision reversing the BRB in its *Cowart* case. 927 F.2d 828 (CA5 1991). The Court of Appeals' majority held that § 33(g) is unambiguous in providing for forfeiture whenever an LHWCA claimant fails to get written approval from his employer of a third-party settlement. The majority acknowledged the well-established principle requiring judicial deference to reasonable interpretations by an agency of the statute it administers, but concluded that the plain language of § 33(g) leaves no room for interpretation. Judge Politz, joined by Judges King and Johnson, dissented on the ground that the OWCP's was a reasonable agency interpretation of the phrase "person entitled to compensation," to which the Court of Appeals should have deferred.

We granted certiorari because of the large number of LHWCA claimants who might be affected by the Court of Appeals' decision. 502 U.S. 1003, 112 S.Ct. 635, 116 L.Ed.2d 653 (1991). We now affirm.

## II

* * *

The controlling principle in this case is the basic and unexceptional rule that courts must give effect to the clear meaning of statutes as written. The principle can at times come into some tension with another fundamental principle of our law, one requiring judicial deference to a reasonable statutory interpretation by an administering agency. *Chevron U.S.A. Inc. v. Natural Resources Defense Council, Inc.*, 467 U.S. 837, 104 S.Ct. 2778, 81 L.Ed.2d 694 (1984); *National Railroad Passenger Corporation v. Boston & Maine Corp.*, 503 U.S. 407, 417, 112 S.Ct. 1394, 1401, 118 L.Ed.2d 52 (1992). Of course, a reviewing court should not defer to an agency position which is contrary to an intent of Congress expressed in unambiguous terms. *K mart Corp. v. Cartier, Inc.*, 486 U.S. 281, 291, 108 S.Ct. 1811, 1817, 100 L.Ed.2d 313 (1988); *Chevron, supra*, 467 U.S., at 842–843, 104 S.Ct., at 2781, 2782. In any event, we need not resolve any tension of that sort here, because the Director of the OWCP and the

Department of Labor have altered their position regarding the best interpretation of § 33(g). The Director appears as a respondent before us, arguing in favor of the Court of Appeals' statutory interpretation, and contrary to his previous position. * * * Because we agree with the federal respondent and the Court of Appeals, and because Cowart concedes that the position of the BRB is not entitled to any special deference, see Brief for Petitioner 25; see also *Potomac Electric Power Co. v. Director, Office of Workers' Compensation Programs*, 449 U.S. 268, 278, n. 18, 101 S.Ct. 509, 514–515, n. 18, 66 L.Ed.2d 446 (1980); *Martin v. Occupational Safety and Health Review Comm'n, supra*, we need not resolve the difficult issues regarding deference which would be lurking in other circumstances.

As a preliminary matter, the natural reading of the statute supports the Court of Appeals' conclusion that a person entitled to compensation need not be receiving compensation or have had an adjudication in his favor. Both in legal and general usage, the normal meaning of entitlement includes a right or benefit for which a person qualifies, and it does not depend upon whether the right has been acknowledged or adjudicated. It means only that the person satisfies the prerequisites attached to the right. * * *

If the language of § 33(g)(1), in isolation, left any doubt, the structure of the statute would remove all ambiguity. First, and perhaps most important, when Congress amended § 33(g) in 1984, it added the explicit forfeiture features of § 33(g)(2), which specify that forfeiture occurs "regardless of whether the employer or the employer's insurer has made payments or acknowledged entitlement to benefits under this chapter." We read that phrase to modify the entirety of subsection (g)(2), including the beginning part discussing the written-approval requirement of paragraph (1). The BRB did not find this amendment controlling because the quoted language is not an explicit modification of subsection (1). This is a strained reading of what Congress intended. Subsection (g)(2) leaves little doubt that the contemplated forfeiture will occur whether or not the employer has made payments or acknowledged liability.

The addition of subsection (g)(2) in 1984 also precludes the primary argument made by the BRB in favor of its decisions in *Dorsey* and this case, and repeated by Cowart to us: That Congress in 1984, by reenacting the phrase "person entitled to compensation," adopted the Board's reading of that language in *O'Leary*. The argument might have had some force if § 33(g) had been reenacted without changes, but that was not the case. In 1984 Congress did more than reenact § 33(g); it added new provisions and new language which on their face appear to have the specific purpose of overruling the prior administrative interpretation. In light of the clear import of § 33(g)(2), the Board erred in relying on the purported lack of legislative history showing an explicit intent to reject the *O'Leary* decision. Even were it relevant, the Board's reading of the legislative history is suspect because as the federal respondent demonstrates, the legislative history of predecessor bills to the eventual 1984 enactment do indicate an intent to overturn *O'Leary*. * * *

*[handwritten margin note: Legis Changes clearly tld to refet O'Leary]*

Our interpretation of § 33(g) is reinforced by the fact that the phrase "person entitled to compensation" appears elsewhere in the statute in contexts in which it cannot bear the meaning placed on it by Cowart. For example, § 14(h) of the LHWCA, 33 U.S.C. § 914(h), requires an official to conduct an investigation upon the request of a person entitled to compensation when, *inter alia*, the claim is controverted and payments are not being made. For that provision, the interpretation championed by Cowart would be nonsensical. Another difficulty would be presented for the provision preceding § 33(g), § 33(f). It mandates that an employer's liability be reduced by the net amount a person entitled to compensation recovers from a third party. Under Cowart's reading, the reduction would not be available to employers who had not yet begun payment at the time of the third-party recovery. That result makes no sense under the LHWCA structure. Indeed, when a litigant before the BRB made this argument, the Board rejected it, acknowledging in so doing that it had adopted differing interpretations of the identical language in §§ 33(f) and 33(g). *Force v. Kaiser Aluminum and Chemical Corp.*, 23 BRBS 1, 4–5 (1989). This result is contrary to the basic canon of statutory construction that identical terms within an Act bear the same meaning. * * *

Yet another reason why we are not convinced by the Board's position is that the Board's interpretation of "person entitled to compensation" has not been altogether consistent; and Cowart's interpretation may not be the same as the Board's in precise respects. At times the Board has said this language refers to an employee whose "employer is actually paying compensation either pursuant to an award or voluntarily when claimant enters into a third party settlement." Dorsey, 18 BRBS, at 28; 23 BRBS, at 44 (case below). At other times, sometimes within the same opinion, the Board has spoken in terms of the employer either making payments *or* acknowledging liability. * * *

We do not believe that Congress' use of the word "employee" in subsection (g)(2), rather than the phrase "person entitled to compensation," undercuts our reading of the statute. The plain meaning of subsection (g)(1) cannot be altered by the use of a somewhat different term in another part of the statute. Subsection (g)(2) does not purport to speak to the question of who is required under subsection (g)(1) to obtain prior written approval.

Cowart's strongest argument to the Court of Appeals was that any ambiguity in the statute favors him because of the deference due the OWCP Director's statutory construction, a deference which Nicklos and Compass concede is appropriate. Brief for Private Respondents 7. As we have said, we are not faced with this difficult issue because the views of the OWCP Director have changed since we granted certiorari. * * *

The history of the Department of Labor regulation goes far toward confirming our view of the significance of the 1984 amendments. The original § 702.281, proposed in 1976 and enacted in final form in 1977, required only that an employee notify his employer and the Department of any third-party claim, settlement, or judgment. 41 Fed.Reg. 34297 (1976); 42 Fed.Reg. 45303 (1977). The sole reference to the forfeiture provisions was a closing parenthetical: "Caution: See 33 U.S.C. § 933(g)." In 1985, in response to the 1984 congressional amendments, the Department proposed to amend § 702.281 by replacing the closing parenthetical with a subsection (b), stating that failure to obtain written approval of settlements for amounts less than the compensation due under the Act would lead to forfeiture of future benefits. 50 Fed.Reg. 400 (1985). In response to comments, the final rulemaking modified § 702.281(b) to clarify that the forfeiture provision applied regardless of whether the employer was paying compensation. 51 Fed.Reg. 4284–4285 (1986). Thus the evolution of § 702.281 suggests that at least some elements within the Department of Labor read the 1984 statutory amendments to adopt a rule different from the Board's previous decisions.

We also reject Cowart's argument that our interpretation of § 33(g) leaves the notification requirements of § 33(g)(2) without meaning. An employee is required to provide notification to his employer, but is not required to obtain written approval, in two instances: (1) Where the employee obtains a judgment, rather than a settlement, against a third party; and (2) Where the employee settles for an amount greater than or equal to the employer's total liability. Under our construction the written-approval requirement of § 33(g)(1) is inapplicable in those instances, but the notification requirement of § 33(g)(2) remains in force. That is why subsection (g)(2) mandates that an employer be notified of "any settlement."

This view comports with the purposes and structure of § 33. Section 33(f) provides that the net amount of damages recovered from any third party for the injuries sustained reduces the compensation owed by the employer. So the employer is a real party in interest with respect to any settlement that might reduce but not extinguish the employer's liability. The written-approval requirement of § 33(g) "protects the employer against his employee's accepting too little for his cause of action against a third party." *Banks v. Chicago Grain Trimmers Assn., Inc.*, 390 U.S. 459, 467, 88 S.Ct. 1140, 1145, 20 L.Ed.2d 30 (1968). In cases where a judgment is entered, however, the employee does not determine the amount of his recovery, and employer approval, even if somehow feasible, would serve no purpose. And in cases where the employee settles for greater than the employer's liability, the employer is protected regardless of the precise amount of the settlement because his liability for compensation is wiped out. Notification provides full protection to the employer in these situations because it ensures against fraudulent double recovery by the employee.

As a final line of defense, Cowart's attorney suggested at oral argument that Nicklos' participation in the Transco settlement brought this case outside the terms of § 33(g)(1). Tr. of Oral Arg. 4–7. Relying on the recent decision of the Court of Appeals for the Fourth Circuit in *I.T.O. Corporation of Baltimore v. Sellman*, 954 F.2d 239, 242–243 (1992), counsel argued that § 33(g)(1) requires written approval only of "settlement[s] with a third person," and that Nicklos' participation in the Transco settlement meant it was not with a *third person*. Without indicating any view on the merits of this contention, we do not address it because it is not fairly included within the question on which certiorari was granted. See this Court's Rule 14.1(a).

We need not today decide the retroactive effect of our decision, nor the relevance of *res judicata* principles for other LHWCA beneficiaries who may be affected by our decision. Cf. *Pittston Coal Group v. Sebben*, 488 U.S. 105, 121–123, 109 S.Ct. 414, 423–425, 102 L.Ed.2d 408 (1988). We do recognize the stark and troubling possibility that significant numbers of injured workers or their families may be stripped of their LHWCA benefits by this statute, and that its forfeiture penalty creates a trap for the unwary. It also provides a powerful tool to employers who resist liability under the Act. Counsel for respondents stated during oral argument that he had used the Transco settlement as a means of avoiding Nicklos' liability under the LHWCA. Tr. of Oral Arg. 23–26. These harsh effects of § 33(g) may be exacerbated by the inconsistent course followed over the years by the federal agencies charged with enforcing the Act. But Congress has spoken with great clarity to the precise question raised by this case. It is the duty of the courts to enforce the judgment of the Legislature, however much we might question its wisdom or fairness. Often we have urged the Congress to speak with greater clarity, and in this statute it has done so. If the effects of the law are to be alleviated, that is within the province of the Legislature. It is Congress that has the authority to change the statute, not the courts.

For the reasons stated, the judgment of the Court of Appeals is

*Affirmed.*

Justice Blackmun with whom Justice Stevens and Justice O'Connor join, dissenting.

For more than 14 years, the Director of the Office of Workers' Compensation Programs interpreted the Longshore and Harbor Workers' Compensation Act (LHWCA or Act), 44 Stat. 1424, as amended, 33 U.S.C. § 901et seq., in the very same way that petitioner Floyd Cowart's estate now urges. Indeed, the Director *advocated* Cowart's position in the Court of Appeals, both before the panel and before that court en banc.

After certiorari was granted, however, and after Cowart's opening brief was filed, the federal respondent informed this Court: "In light of the en banc decision in this case, the Department of Labor reexamined its views on the issue." Brief for Federal Respondent 8, n. 6. The federal respondent now assures us that the interpretation the Director advanced and defended for 14 years is inconsistent with the statute's "plain meaning." The Court today accepts that improbable contention, and in so doing rules that perhaps thousands of employees and their families must be denied death and disability benefits. I cannot agree with the federal respondent's newly discovered interpretation, and still less do I find it to be compelled by the "plain meaning" of the statute. The Court needlessly inflicts additional injury upon these workers and their families. I dissent. * * *

In my view, the language of § 33 in no way compels the Court to deny Cowart's claim. In fact, the Court's reliance on the Act's "plain language," ante, at 2594, is selective: as discussed below, analysis of §§ 33(b) and (f) of the Act shows that, even leaving aside the question whether Cowart is a "person entitled to compensation," a *consistently* literal interpretation of the Act's language would not require Cowart to have obtained Nicklos' written approval of the settlement. Indeed, under a thoroughgoing "plain meaning" approach, Cowart would be entitled to receive *full* LHWCA benefits in addition to his third-party settlement, not just the excess of his statutory benefits over the settlement.

At the same time, a consistently literal interpretation of the Act would commit the Court to positions it might be unwilling to take. The conclusion I draw is not that the Court should adopt a purely literal interpretation of the Act, but instead that the Court should recognize, as it has until today, that the LHWCA must be read in light of the purposes and policies it would serve. Once that point is recognized, then, as suggested by the Court's closing remarks on the "stark and troubling" implications of its interpretation, * * * it follows that recognition of Cowart's claim is fully consistent with the Act.

## A

Were the Court truly to interpret the Act "as written," it would not conclude that Cowart is barred from receiving compensation. Section 33(g)(1) of the LHWCA, on which the Court's "plain meaning" argument relies, provides that if a "person entitled to compensation" settles with a third party for an amount less than his statutory benefits, his employer will be "liable for compensation *as determined under subsection (f)*" only if the "person entitled to compensation" obtains and files the employer's written approval. The "plain language" of subsection (g)(1) does not establish any general written-approval requirement binding either all "persons entitled to compensation," or the subset of those persons who settle for less than their statutory benefits. Instead, it requires written approval only as a condition of receiving compensation "as determined under subsection (f)." Where the "person entitled to compensation" is not eligible for compensation "as determined under subsection (f)," subsection (g)(1) does not require him to obtain written approval.

The "plain language" of subsection (f) in turn suggests that the provision does not apply to Cowart's situation. Subsection (f), by its terms, applies only "[i]f the person entitled to compensation institutes proceedings within the period prescribed in subsection (b)." And the "period prescribed in subsection (b)" begins, by the terms of that subsection, upon the person's "[a]cceptance of compensation under an award in a compensation order filed by the deputy commissioner, an administrative law judge, or the Board." Cowart's third-party suit was clearly *not* instituted within this period: He filed suit *before* any award of LHWCA benefits, and he still has not accepted (or been offered) compensation under any award. Thus, he does not come within the "plain meaning" of subsection (f), and, accordingly, for the reasons given above, he would not be bound by the subsection (g)(1) written-approval requirement. It would also follow that, because Nicklos indisputably received the notice required by subsection (g)(2), that provision would not bar Cowart from receiving LHWCA compensation and medical benefits.

Indeed, if Cowart is not covered by subsection (f), he would appear to have been eligible for a larger award than he sought. Subsection (f) does not authorize compensation otherwise unavailable; instead, it operates as a *limit*, in the specified circumstances, on the employer's LHWCA liability. If read literally, subsection (f) would not bar Cowart from receiving full LHWCA benefits, *in addition to* the amount he received in settlement of the third-party claim.

It is true that § 33(f) has not always been read literally. Subsection (f) has been assumed to be applicable where, for example, the claimant's third-party suit was filed after an employer *voluntarily* began paying LHWCA compensation, not just where compensation was paid pursuant to an award. See, e.g., *I.T.O. Corp. of Baltimore v. Sellman*, 954 F.2d 239, 240, 243–245 (CA4 1992); *Shellman v. United States Lines, Inc.*, 528 F.2d 675, 678–679, n. 2 (CA9 1975) (referring to the availability of an employer's lien, where the employer has paid compensation without an award, as "judicially created" rather than statutory), cert. denied, 425 U.S. 936, 96 S.Ct. 1668, 48 L.Ed.2d 177 (1976). That interpretation is eminently sensible and consistent with the statutory purpose of encouraging employers to make payments "promptly," "directly," and "without an award." See § 14(a). A contrary interpretation would penalize employers who acknowledge liability and commence payments without seeking an award, and it would reward employers who, whether in good faith or bad, contest their liability until faced with a formal award. See *Shellman*, 528 F.2d, at 679, n. 2 ("The purpose of this Act would be frustrated if a different result could be reached merely because the employer pays compensation without entry of a formal award").

It is not obvious, however, that a similar argument from statutory purpose should be available to employers such as Nicklos who refuse to pay benefits and then seek shelter under § 33(f) (and by extension, § 33(g)(1)). And the fact remains that the Court professes to interpret the "clear meaning" of the statute "as written." The Court's interpretation today, however, is no more compelled by the language of the LHWCA than the interpretation Cowart defends: The Court is simply insensible to the fact that it implicitly has relied upon presumed statutory purposes and policy considerations to bring Nicklos and Cowart under the setoff provisions of § 33(f), thus absolving Nicklos of the first $29,000 in LHWCA liability. Only at *that* point does the Court invoke the plain meaning rule and insist on a "literal" interpretation of § 33(g)(1). This selective insistence on "plain meaning" deprives Cowart's estate of the last $6,242.17 Nicklos would otherwise have been bound to pay.

### B

For these reasons, I think it clear that a purely textual approach to the LHWCA cannot justify the Court's holding. In my view, a more sensible approach is to consider § 33(g) as courts always have considered the other parts of § 33—in relation to the history, structure, and policies of the Act.

[The remainder of the opinion is omitted.]

### NOTES AND QUESTIONS

1.  The LHWCA is typical in including detailed provisions with respect to third party recovery. Almost all statutes provide that the employer's payment of compensation benefits entitles the employer to subrogation of some sort with respect to the employee's claim against a third party. Several motivations play a role in this. Two purposes seem particularly important: Avoiding "double recovery," and reducing the cost of workers' compensation coverage. Beyond this, there is the argument that if an injury results from a wrongful act, the wrongdoer should be regarded as "more liable" than the employer, whose liability results from a type of "no-fault" scheme. In this case, however, the indemnification agreement signed by the employer undercuts that argument, does it not? Should such agreements be valid?

Most statutes spell out whether the employee or the employer has the first right to bring an action against the third party, and also provide that if that party does not exercise the right within a certain time, the other party may then bring the action. Most also call for the injured employee to cooperate in an action brought by the employer. Many provide for the division of the ultimate damages award, and of expenses of litigation. Spelling out standards for what is a reasonable refusal to settle is generally left to judicial judgment.

2.  Particularly vexing questions may arise when both an employer and a third party were allegedly negligent in causing the employee's injury. If the worker obtains a judgment against the third party far exceeding the amount of compensation benefits due, the third party is likely to seek contribution or indemnity from the employer. Should that be permitted? If so, should the amount of contribution be limited to the amount of the employer's compensation liability? See *Lambertson v. Cincinnati Corp.*, 312 Minn. 114, 257 N.W.2d 679 (1977). For a case involving a claim for indemnity under the Federal Tort Claims Act, see *Lockheed Aircraft Corp. v. United States*, 460 U.S. 190, 103 S.Ct. 1033, 74 L.Ed.2d 911 (1983). If a jurisdiction allows no recovery by way of contribution or indemnity from the employer, may the third party seek a determination of the employer's level of fault in an action brought by the employee? See *Dresser Industries, Inc. v. Lee*, 880 S.W.2d 750 (1993).

3.  One category of defendant that figures often in third-part actions brought by injured workers is the manufacturer of a product used in the workplace. The reasons for this and for the relatively high rate of success by

plaintiffs in these actions are explored by Professor Weiler in a 1989 article. Paul Weiler, *Workers' Compensation and Product Liability: The Interaction of a Tort and a Non-tort Regime*, 50 OHIO ST. L.J. 825 (1989).

4. *I.B.E.W. v. Hechler*, 481 U.S. 851, 107 S.Ct. 2161, 95 L.Ed.2d 791 (1987), arose after an apprentice electrician was injured when she made contact with energized components at a power substation. She sued the union that represented her in collective bargaining with her employer. Her claim against the union was that it had a duty to ensure she was provided with a safe workplace and not exposed to risks beyond her training and experience. The assertion that the union had such a duty was based upon language in the collective agreement between the union and the injured worker's employer. The Court concluded that because the claim is dependent upon an interpretation of the collectively bargained agreement, the action is controlled by Section 301 of the Labor Management Relations Act (LMRA) and the appropriate federal statute of limitations for suits brought to enforce such agreements. The action was remanded for lower court determination of whether the six-month period of limitations applicable to some suits involving alleged abridgements of collective agreements (the hybrid duty-of-fair-representation action) governs this type of suit.

Survivors of a miner killed in an underground fire were no more successful when they brought a timely action alleging negligence by a union that had a contractual right to make mine safety inspections. In United Steelworkers of *America v. Rawson*, 495 U.S. 362, 110 S.Ct. 1904, 109 L.Ed.2d 362 (1990), it was held, 6–3, that because the union's mine inspection arose out of a right specified in the collective agreement, any resulting liability was controlled by the substantive law developed under LMRA section 301 and not state law. In addition, the Court held that although the union's statutory duty of fair representation was applicable to its conduct as mine inspector, any additional duties had to be found in specific language of the collective agreement. Construing the agreement, the Court ruled that it did not establish a specific contractual obligation toward the employer, the employees or their survivors. Finally, the Court held that because the alleged facts did not go beyond asserting mere negligence by the union, the pleadings failed to assert a breach of the duty of fair representation.

On the other hand, under maritime law a federal appellate court has held that a union may be liable for the death of a seaman killed by a fellow seafarer referred for employment by the union hiring hall where the union did not warn the shipowner of that seafarer's known history of extraordinarily violent conduct. The issue before the court concerned the shipowner's claim that the union had to indemnify it for any liability to the survivors. The indemnity obligation was found to be implied in the job-referral agreement between the union and ship owner. *Miles v. Melrose*, 882 F.2d 976 (5th Cir.1989), cert. denied as to this issue 494 U.S. 1066, 110 S.Ct. 1783, 108 L.Ed.2d 785 (1990). Would it be appropriate to extend this decision to hold the union, as a matter of indemnity, directly liable to the victim of the referred seafarer's violence? In such a situation should the union be liable to the victim's survivors under the theory of breach of its duty of fair representation?

# CHAPTER X

# UNEMPLOYMENT COMPENSATION

■ ■ ■

## A.  BACKGROUND

### 1.  UNEMPLOYMENT

The U.S. Bureau of Labor Statistics conducts a monthly sample household survey to determine the extent of unemployment. The survey classifies as unemployed anyone age 16 or older who in the past week did not have an active job and who in the past four weeks made unsuccessful efforts to find a job. This includes students and others who sought part-time work. Some argue that the resulting unemployment figures under-state the economy's ability to provide work to all who need it because the data includes people, such as students, whose earned income is not relied on for anyone's support. Others argue that the unemployment figures overstate the economy's ability to provide work because the data does not reflect the extent to which people who have been discouraged by past unsuccessful efforts are no longer looking for work nor the extent to which those who are employed have fewer work hours available than they desire.

Since World War II, the unemployment rate in the U.S. has fluctuated between 2.9% (1953) and 9.8% (2010). However, unemployment rates vary dramatically among population subgroups, especially when separated by race, ethnicity, gender, age, education, profession, industry and region. African Americans, Native Americans and Hispanics tend to suffer higher unemployment rates than other racial and ethnic groups. In 2009 the overall unemployment rate was 9.3% and the unemployment rate for African Americans was 14.5%, the rate for Hispanics was 12.1%, the rate for Whites (non-Hispanic) was 8.4% and the rate for Asians was 7.3%. Recently men have suffered higher rates of unemployment than women because they do not enjoy as many educational opportunities as women and because they tend to populate economic sectors (construction and manufacturing) that are more vulnerable to recession. In the recent "mancession," men suffered an unemployment rate (10.3%) over two percentage points higher than women (8.1%) for 2009. Younger workers experience higher levels of unemployment than older workers. During

2009, workers 15–24 years old suffered a 16.7% unemployment rate while the rate for workers 25–44 years old was 8.2% and the rate for workers 45 years old and older was 6.3%. Less educated workers suffer more unemployment than those with more education. In 2009, workers without a high school education had a 17.5% unemployment rate while those with a high school education had a 9.1% unemployment rate and those with a college education had a 4.5% unemployment rate. Bureau of Labor Statistics, *Labor Force Statistics from the Current Population Survey*, tbls.24–34, http://www.bls.gov/cps/tables.htm#charunem (last modified Feb. 24, 2010). Of course these demographic factors can have compounding effects. For example, for the twelve month period ending September 2009, African American men 15–24 years old without a high school education suffered a 48.5% unemployment rate while the relatively privileged White women over 45 years old with a college education enjoyed a 3.7% unemployment rate. Shan Carter, Amanda Cox & Kevin Quealy, *The Jobless Rate for People Like You*, N.Y. TIMES, Nov. 6, 2009, *available at* http://www.ny times.com/interactive/2009/11/06/business/economy/unemployment-lines. html.

There are some marked differences in the unemployment rate by profession, industry and geographic region as well. Although the general unemployment rate in 2009 was 9.3%, manager, professionals and related occupations had only a 4.6% unemployment rate. In 2009 the construction industry suffered the highest unemployment rate (19%) followed by agricultural workers (14. 3%) while government workers had the lowest unemployment rate (3.6%) followed by education and health workers (5.3%). Bureau of Labor Statistics, *Labor Force Statistics from the Current Population Survey*, tbls.24–34 (2010) http://www.bls.gov/cps/tables. htm#charunem (last modified Feb. 24, 2010). For the month of May 2010 when the national rate was 9.7%, the unemployment rate by state ranged from a high of 14% in Nevada and 13.6% in Michigan to a low of 3.6% in North Dakota. Bureau of Labor Statistics, *Local Area Unemployment Statistics—Current Unemployment Rates for States and Historical Highs/ Lows*, http://www.bls.gov/web/laus/lauhsthl.htm (last modified June 18, 2010).

Although the unemployment rate indicates the extent of joblessness throughout the economy, the impact of joblessness on an individual is better measured by the duration of his or her unemployment. As might be expected, the duration of individual unemployment is affected by the unemployment rate. For example, in 2005, when the national unemployment rate was 4.0%, the average duration of joblessness was 12.4 weeks and the median was 5.8 weeks. In 2009, when the national unemployment rate was 9.3%, the average duration of employment was 24.4 weeks and the median duration of unemployment was 15.1 weeks. Of course, just as the unemployment rate can vary based on demographic and geographic factors, so too the duration of employment can vary based on those same factors. In 2009 African Americans suffered an average unemployment duration of 28.9 weeks and Asians had an average unemployment duration of 26.9 while the average duration for Whites (non-Hispanic) was 23.3 weeks and the average duration for Hispanics was 22.6 weeks. On average men tended to stay unemployed longer (24.6 weeks) than women (24.1 weeks) in 2009 and, generally, the older the job seeker, the longer it took to find a job. Duration of employment can also vary by profession and industry. In 2009 managerial and professional workers took on average 25.7 weeks to find a job while production workers endured an average unemployment spell of 24.9 weeks and service employees had an average unemployment duration of 22.8 weeks. Workers in the financial sector had the longest average duration of unemployment in 2009 (28.5 weeks), followed by workers engaged in information industry (28.1 weeks). The shortest average duration of unemployment in 2005 was found in mining (19.9 weeks) followed by the agriculture industry (20.6 weeks). Bureau of Labor Statistics, *Labor Force Statistics from the Current Population Survey*, tbls.24–34, http://www.bls.gov/cps/tables.htm#charunem (last modified Feb. 24, 2010).

Unemployment figures present only part of the joblessness picture. Part-time workers in the U.S. are counted among the employed, however some of them are working part-time because they can't find full-time work. For example, in 2009, about 24.4% of the labor force had part-time employment and about a fourth of those, or 5.8% of the labor force had part-time employment but wanted a full-time job. In periods of higher unemployment the portion of part-timers who want full-time jobs is higher. In addition, especially in times of higher unemployment, many people who want jobs leave the active labor force because they are discouraged by their unsuccessful search for work. In 2009 there were approximately 778,000 people who had left the labor force because they despaired at ever finding a job, a number equal to about 0.5% of the active labor force. Types of workers who experience longer durations of unemployment are more likely to be discouraged workers. Bureau of Labor Statistics, *Labor Force Statistics from the Current Population Survey*, tbls.24–34, http://www.bls.gov/cps/tables.htm#charunem (last modified Feb. 24, 2010).

Comparison of unemployment rates across nations is made difficult by the fact that data collectors for different nations often do not have the same definition of who is in the work force (for example, at what age is one not in school considered part of the work force or how often must one look for a job to be considered in the work force), who is unemployed (for example, should someone be counted as unemployed when receiving a stipend while in a government sponsored skills enhancement program), and use varying degrees of rigor to obtain a count. For example, Sweden has elaborate retraining and public works programs for the unemployed. People engaged in these programs are not included in the unemployment rate. If counted, the Swedish rate would be about double the reported unemployment figure. Similarly, it has been observed that while the U.S. unemployment rate was about 3.5 times the 1992 rate in Japan, if measured by the conventional method used in the U.S. for calculating unemployment, the Japanese rate would be closer to U.S. levels. Sara Elder & Constance Sorrentino, *Japan's Low Unemployment: A BLS Update and Revision*, 116 MONTHLY LAB. REV. 56, 56, Oct. 1, 1993.

Moreover, comparative studies have found that the rate of joblessness is affected by the composition of the workforce with the result that workforce increases in the portion of youths, elderly and women are accompanied by increased unemployment. Todd M. Godbout, *Employment Change and Sectoral Distribution in 10 Countries, 1970–90*, 116 MONTHLY LAB. REV. 3, 3, Oct. 1, 1993. To the extent that these demographics vary across counties, one would expect the unemployment rates in those countries to vary regardless of economic performance. Never-the-less, a standardized measurement procedure adopted by the Organization for Economic Cooperation and Development (OECD) estimated that in January of 2010 the unemployment rate for the U.S. was 9.8%, in Canada it was 8.2%, in the European Community nations overall, it was 9.6%, in France it was 10%, in Germany it was 7.5%, in the U.K. it was 7.7%, and in Japan it was 4.9%. Organization for Economic Co-operation and Development, *Harmonised Unemployment Rates (HURs), OECD Updated: April 2010*, http://www.oecd.org/document/32/0,3343,en_2649_34251_44976934_1_1_1_1,00.html.

## 2. DEVELOPMENT OF UNEMPLOYMENT INSURANCE

Until the last decades of the 19th Century, unemployed industrial workers had to look to their own or their family's resources to tide them over during periods of joblessness or seek the sparse benefits of private charity or public relief that took such forms as soup kitchens. By the 1880s European unions were providing benefits for jobless members and by the 1890s local governments in Belgium, the Netherlands, Germany, Italy and Switzerland were subsidizing such programs. By the early part of the 20th Century, regional or national government subsidies were being provided in most Western European countries in support of union sponsored unemployment benefit plans. Under the political leadership of Winston Churchill, in 1911 Britain adopted the first modern system of unemployment insurance. This program was financed by a combination of compulsory employer, employee and government contributions and was independent of union affiliations. In 1920 the British system was modified to reduce the financial contributions of employers and workers with good records of regular employment. By 1930 most of Western Europe had compulsory unemployment insurance programs. The concept, however, had more difficulty taking hold in the U.S. where, despite average annual joblessness of about 9–10 percent during the first quarter of the century, unemployment insurance proposals met stiff resistance from business and political leaders. Nevertheless, in the 1920s and early 1930s, a few large companies, including General Electric and Eastman Kodak, as well as several dozen smaller companies, voluntarily maintained employer financed or joint employer-employee financed programs to provide benefits for laid off workers.

Also in the 1920s and early 1930s, intensive efforts were mounted in many industrial states seeking adoption of unemployment compensation programs. These made little headway until the dramatic impact of the Great Depression, that quickly followed upon the stock market crash of 1929, and made unemployment a central focus of political attention. (It is estimated that by 1932 one out of four workers was jobless.) As a result, a modest unemployment insurance law was enacted in Wisconsin in 1932 but did not become effective until 1934. In 1935 New York became the second state to adopt an unemployment insurance program. By this time, similar legislative efforts were gaining momentum in California, Massachusetts, Pennsylvania and Ohio. However, the catastrophic, national dimensions of the economic crisis shifted attention to the federal government. Despite concerns respecting its constitutionality, in 1935 Congress adopted, as part of the Social Security Act, a scheme for inducing states to enact compulsory unemployment insurance programs conforming to broad federally established standards. The law's constitutionality was upheld in *Charles C. Steward Machine Co. v. Davis*, 301 U.S. 548, 57 S.Ct. 883, 81 L.Ed. 1279 (1937). *See* DANIEL NELSON, UNEMPLOYMENT INSURANCE: THE AMERICAN EXPERIENCE, 1915–1935 (1969); Kenneth M. Casebeer, *Unemployment Insurance: American Social Wage, Labor Organization and Legal Ideology*, 35 B.C. L. REV. 259, 260–320 (1994).

Canada was similarly slow in adopting a national unemployment insurance scheme but did so in 1935. However, the Canadian Act was declared beyond the scope of federal authority. This was rectified by amendments to the British North America Act and a valid national program was adopted in 1940.

## 3. BASIC CHARACTERISTICS OF UNEMPLOYMENT COMPENSATION INSURANCE

### (a.) Financing Benefits

Today, unemployment insurance programs have been established by the federal government for its workers and by each state, the District of Columbia, Puerto Rico and the Virgin Islands. The Federal Unemployment Tax Act (26 U.S.C. § 3301 *et seq.*) imposes a payroll tax on most employers. In 2010 the rate was 6.2 percent up to the first $7,000 of an employee's pay per year. However, the law provides a credit against Federal tax liability of up to 5.4% to employers who pay state taxes timely under an approved state UI program. This credit is allowed regardless of the amount of the tax paid to the state by the employer. Accordingly, in states meeting the specified requirements, employers pay an effective Federal tax of 0.8%, or a maximum of $56 per covered worker, per year, which is used to pay the federal administrative costs for the program. The 6.2% tax includes a 0.2% tax increase scheduled to terminate June 30,

2011. States can and do have a higher cap for imposing their own unemployment insurance levies. In 2010, Washington had the highest cap ($36,800). Nevertheless, the cap in most states was considerably lower and $15,918 was the national average for the amount of annual pay on which the unemployment insurance tax was levied in 2010. Although the ceiling on the portion of pay that is taxable for unemployment tax purposes resulted in the tax being assessed against about 98% of all wages paid in 1939, because of the growth in average wages in the subsequent decades, that portion has substantially declined. Accordingly, unemployment insurance taxes are now levied on only a small portion of all wages paid in the U.S. United States Department of Labor, *Unemployment Insurance Tax Topic*, http://ows.doleta.gov/unemploy/uitaxtopic.asp (last modified April 20, 2010).

Concern has been expressed regarding the impact tax base ceilings may have upon employer decisions to meet needs for increased work hours since such limits favor adding hours to current work schedules rather than expand the size of the workforce. The current ceilings, therefore, would appear to undercut the goal of reducing the number of people who are unemployed.

Included in the federal guidelines is a requirement that the funds be deposited in trust accounts maintained by the U.S. Treasury. Also included are a number of accounting requirements and regulations respecting the definition of wages on which the payroll tax is to be levied, a requirement that the tax rate reflect the frequency with which unemployment claims are paid to the employer's former workers, and some aspects concerning the measure of and criteria for available benefits payments.

Although the federal payroll tax for unemployment compensation insurance is levied only on employers, Alaska, New Jersey and Pennsylvania impose a levy on employees as well as employers to fund the unemployment compensation system. In large measure the federal tax is used to pay grants to the states to help finance the administrative costs of these programs. In addition, if the funds created by payroll taxes are exhausted during periods of high unemployment, the federal government extends a loan to the state or territorial program's account.

Finally, Congress has provided for federally subsidized benefits extensions for the long term unemployed who are located in areas of high unemployment and have exhausted regular benefits. In addition to standby legislation for extending the duration of unemployment compensation, Congress has adopted temporary extensions during periods of recession. For example, at the height of the 1975 recession, as a result of the federal extended benefits program, it was possible to receive unemployment compensation payments for a combined total of 65 weeks. In more recent years, Congress has been less generous in financing extended benefits, though the expected economic fallout from the terrorist attacks of September 11, 2001, prompted proposals to use extended unemployment insurance as a means of cushioning the dislocations. At the beginning of the

Great Recession, Congress enacted the Emergency Unemployment Compensation Program (EUC), Pub. L. No. 110–252, 105 Stat 1049 (2008) which was signed on June 30, 2008. Because of the depth and duration of the recession, Congress and the President Obama extended the program several times, but in June of 2010 a Republican filibuster in the Senate blocked further extensions until it was overcome in late July. Most often, benefit extensions are for 13–20 weeks and availability is triggered by the state's rate of unemployment compensation claims. However, even when available, the claimant must satisfy separate federal eligibility standards including the requirement that any available work be accepted unless there is evidence of good prospects that the claimant will soon obtain work in his or her customary occupation.

As indicated, above, payroll taxes that finance unemployment compensation are levied at rates that are lower for employers that experience low rates of benefits claims from former or laidoff employees. Experience ratings are based on maintaining separate accounts for each employer's contributions and for benefits paid based on employment with that employer. Experience rating formulas vary; some are geared to shorter term assessment of changes in the employer's work force stability, others to longer term assessments. New employers are subject to a standard tax rate but after a year a state may adjust the rate based on its experience formula. As an illustration of the resulting variations, in 2010, depending on the state, experience ratings could result in a maximum tax rate as high as 10.6% (Tennessee) and a minimum rate as low as 0% in sixteen states. In Indiana the minimum rate was 0.1% and the maximum was 5.6%, in California the minimum was 0.1% and the maximum 6.2%, and in New York the minimum was 0% and the maximum 8.9%. United States Department of Labor, *Comparison of State Unemployment Laws*, ch. 2, http://www.ows.doleta.gov/unemploy/uilawcompar/2009/comparison2009. asp (last modified July 28, 2009).

Of course, the actual cost of unemployment insurance is a combination of the effective federal tax on up to the first $7,000 of compensation, plus the state rate as adjusted by the employer's experience rating and as applied up to the state's tax base ceiling. For the United States as a whole in 2008, the average employer unemployment compensation tax rate was 2.25% of taxable wages. Among the states, the average employer tax rate on taxable wages varied from lows of 0.57% in Utah and 0.73% in Hawaii to a high of 4.72% in Michigan and 4.67% in Pennsylvania. However, because the taxable wage cap varies by state and average wage levels vary by state perhaps a better measure of the impact of unemployment taxes on employer costs is to look at them as a percent of total wages. In 2008 the average employer unemployment compensation tax rate for the United States as a whole was 0.6% of total wages. The average employer tax rate on total wages varied from lows of 0.23% in Virginia and 0.25% in New Hampshire to highs of 1.29% in Alaska and 1.17% in Rhode Island. United States Department of Labor, Employment and Training Financial Data

Handbook 394 Report, Employment and Wage Data Report for 2008, http://ows.doleta.gov/unemploy/finance.asp.

Claims are paid whether or not the responsible employer has a plus balance in its unemployment insurance account and the employer's tax rate is not raised above the maximum. Thus, in effect the state program is the insurer for the benefits claims. As a result, employers with low rates of claims ultimately subsidize the costs of providing benefits for the unemployment claims of those who were employed by entities that maintain prolonged or even permanent negative account balances. This subsidy, however, is less than occurs in the unemployment insurance systems in other countries because the U.S. is relatively unique in using individual employer experience ratings as contrasted with a uniform payroll tax or financing from general revenues. FRANK P. R. BRECHLING & LOUISE LAURENCE, PERMANENT JOB LOSS AND THE U.S. SYSTEM OF FINANCING UNEMPLOYMENT INSURANCE 10 (1995).

As noted, extensions of unemployment insurance are triggered by an individual state's prolonged high rate of claims. The impetus for an extension of benefits goes beyond concerns for worker welfare. Post-Keynesian economists look to unemployment insurance as a valuable mechanism for countering economic cycles. When job opportunities are plentiful the economy is faced with the danger of over-expansion. At such times, the unemployment insurance system takes more money into the U.S. Treasury than it pays out and, to that degree, reduces available investment capital and consumption. (Surplus trust funds are invested in interest bearing bills and notes issued by the Treasury Department.) In contrast, when job opportunities are scarce the economy is faced with the need for greater expansion. At such times the unemployment insurance system is likely to pay out more than it takes in—especially if benefit periods are extended. This helps provide a new source for consumption expenditure and, in turn, encourages capital investment. An alternative to using extended unemployment insurance benefits as a counter-cyclical strategy is to provide new public works jobs for the unemployed in times of economic stress.

Whether the unemployment insurance system in fact serves as a counter-cyclical tool of economic planning depends upon whether government resists: 1) the temptation to lower the tax in response to large reserves during times of high employment (the resulting increase in favorable experience ratings automatically has this impact), and 2) the urge to increase these taxes in response to depleted reserves during periods of prolonged joblessness. A report to the House Committee on Ways and Means prepared by the Library of Congress in 1988 concluded:

> The role of the UC system as an automatic economic stabilizer was diminished during the 1980s. The program's contribution to fiscal stimulus in 1982 was only two-thirds that of 1975 because of UC benefit reductions and tax increases, but a vastly changed fiscal policy during the 1980s lessened the importance of this change in UC. While

deficit reduction and monetary policy now occupy the attention of economic policymakers, changes in UC have reduced its utility as a tool for automatic stimulation or dampening of the economy.*

Benefits paid to the jobless are subject to a maximum weekly amount that generally is based upon an index of average wages received by those with jobs. Because the benchmark for determining the maximum benefit generally exceeds the tax base ceiling, the effect is that the tax imposed on wages earned by higher paid workers represents a smaller ratio of taxes to payable benefits than does the tax imposed on wages earned by lower paid workers.

## (b.) Scope of Coverage and Benefit Levels

Under the minimum federal standard for unemployment insurance coverage, most employers must pay unemployment compensation taxes for all persons on the payroll if at least one person is employed for each of 20 weeks in the current or preceding year or if the employer paid $1,500 or more in wages in the current or preceding calendar quarter. Agricultural employers must pay federal unemployment compensation taxes if their quarterly payroll is at least $20,000 or they employ 10 or more workers for no fewer than twenty weeks a year. An employer of domestic labor must pay unemployment taxes if the employer pays such workers at least $1,000 in a calendar quarter in the current or previous calendar year.

A spouse and a child under 21 who works for his or her parent is exempt from federal unemployment insurance coverage. Similarly exempt are federal and some state employees, and students employed by nonprofit educational institutions. Insurance salespeople who are wholly compensated by commission are exempt, as are a certain news delivery personnel and a few other special categories of workers including seafarers aboard larger vessels. Railroad workers are covered by a separate system of unemployment insurance.

Even though federal unemployment insurance taxes are part of the payroll taxes that must be paid for an employee, the employee is often not qualified for benefits after losing a job. The unemployment compensation insurance system provides benefits only if the employee was employed for a sufficient amount of time during a qualifying period prior to becoming jobless. There are state variations in the system for measuring whether a person had sufficient employment during the qualifying period.

Normally, the qualifying period consists of the first four calendar quarters of the five calendar quarters completed before the worker became jobless. A few states require that to qualify for unemployment benefits, the worker must have had a minimum level of earnings (varying from $1,000 to $2,000) during this base period. To qualify for benefits in some

---

* See also Martin Feldstein, *Unemployment Caused by Unemployment Insurance, in* ECONOMICS OF LABOR IN INDUSTRIAL SOCIETY 57 (Clark Kerr & Paul D. Staudohar, eds., 1986) (arguing that employer's cost of unemployment insurance discourages expansion of job opportunities and worker benefits discourage search for work and their expenditure of the benefits does not provide a fiscal stimulus that would not otherwise be generated through other means).

other states, the minimum amount must have been earned within a specified number of weeks. Many states set the qualifying earnings during the base period at a multiple (for example, 30) of the weekly unemployment benefit to be paid. Whatever the method for measuring the qualifying amount of employment prior to joblessness, many unemployed people are unqualified to receive unemployment compensation benefits because they have not had sufficient recent employment.

In addition, the federally established standards for the unemployment insurance system deny benefits to illegal aliens. Those standards also prohibit making benefit payments to educational employees or to professional athletes during their annually scheduled idle periods so long as the employee has a reasonable expectation of reemployment when seasonal activity resumes. Further, a number of states exclude from coverage work in industries deemed to be seasonal. Others define seasonal employment based on a pattern of periods of operation for less than a specified number of weeks (most often 26 weeks) and exclude such seasonal employment from coverage during the off-season. About a fourth of the jurisdictions also specially provide unemployment benefits for seasonal workers during the industry's normal operating period.

Generally, a worker who qualifies for unemployment insurance benefits receives a weekly payment equal to one half of his or her normal weekly job earnings during that quarter of the qualifying period in which the claimant received the highest earnings. About one out of four states pays a small allowance for each dependent in addition to the payment based on the jobless beneficiary's prior earnings. All states impose minimum and maximum limits for unemployment insurance benefits. Some states set the maximum benefit at a fixed amount which is revised by the state legislature. However, most states index the maximum benefit by establishing it as a set percentage of the periodically determined average weekly wage in the state. In 2008 the national average weekly unemployment insurance benefit was $297. The average weekly benefit ranged from lows of $183 (Mississippi) and $196.23 (Alabama) to highs of $413 (Hawaii) and $391 (Massachusetts). United States Department of Labor, Employment and Training Financial Data Handbook 394 Report, Employment and Wage Data Report for 2008, http://ows.doleta.gov/unemploy/finance.asp.

States can reduce unemployment compensation benefits of an employee who is receiving disability or retirement benefits, but only to the extent that the former employer funded those benefits. About half the states reduce unemployment compensation benefits to the extent of dismissal payments (severance pay) received by the jobless worker.

All states allow some weekly earnings without the employee becoming disqualified from receiving full benefits and provide for partial reduction of benefits for earned income above that allowed income. This encourages unemployed workers to seek part-time employment when full-time employment is unavailable. In many states, however, benefits are not available if the worker is employed a minimum of a stated number of days in a week, e.g., three.

Prior to World War II, across-the-board work schedule reductions—work sharing—was the common response to reduced work opportunities in an establishment. "As the depression wore on, however, labor's view of work sharing soured. Few employers offered any assistance to workers on short time. Workers on short time suffered large pay cuts that often reduced their earnings below subsistence levels. Consequently, work sharing during the Great Depression became widely viewed as a failed experiment." KATHARINE G. ABRAHAM & SUSAN N. HOUSEMAN, JOB SECURITY IN AMERICA: LESSONS FROM GERMANY 134 (1993). By the end of World War II, U.S. employers and workers, especially in unionized establishments, generally accepted the notion that the appropriate response to reduced work opportunities is seniority based layoffs.

Even though employers risk losing trained workers when a layoff is imposed, the impact of financing fixed fringe benefits significantly increases hourly labor costs when there is a cutback in individual work hours. In addition, if the employer is already paying at or near the maximum unemployment insurance tax rate, there is no offsetting cost to selecting a layoff in lieu of work sharing. On the other hand, with a sufficient reduction in work hours, unemployment benefits become a more attractive alternative for many workers, especially those in lower paying jobs (who are not affected by the maximum benefit allowed). Thus, the financial incentive of employers to lay off or dismiss some workers, rather than reduce everyone's hours, is complimented both by the comparable attractiveness of unemployment insurance benefits for lower paid workers and the resistance of more senior and higher paid workers toward work sharing.

A number of states have programs designed to encourage work sharing by providing, under appropriate circumstances, pro-rated unemployment compensation for workers whose hours have been reduced. Studies show that the impact of these programs has not been substantial. A variety of explanations have been offered including, in some states, the impact on an employer's unemployment tax liability if it adopts a work sharing policy, lack of employer awareness respecting the availability of partial unemployment benefits for those on reduced work schedules, and fear of seemingly complex bureaucratic oversight. ABRAHAM & HOUSEMAN, *supra*, at 135–39; California Employment Development Department, *Work Sharing*, http://www.edd.ca.gov/unemployment/work_sharing_claims.htm; Massachusetts Department of Labor and Workforce Development, *Work Sharing*, http://www.mass.gov/?pageID=elwdsubtopic&L=4&L0=Home&L1=Businesses&L2=Businesses+Services+and+Programs&L3=WorkSharing&sid=Elwd.

An alternative approach to work sharing is available in some jurisdictions in which it is possible for an employer to work half its employees one week and the other half the alternating week and qualify all of them to

*Week-*
*scattering*
*as a*
*staff*

receive unemployment insurance benefits for the jobless week. This is because the cumulative number of weeks worked satisfies the state minimum for qualification. If the employer is already paying the top tax rate, it has no disincentive for accommodating its work force in this manner, rather than placing all of them on a reduced work week schedule that would disqualify them from receiving full weekly benefits or permanently laying off a substantial number of them during long periods of reduced activity.

It has been noted that the concept of unemployment benefits is to provide an income safety net for the unemployed at a level of about half of the worker's average compensation. However, as a result of the benefit ceiling, many claimants receive considerably less than that. As mentioned above, in 2008 the national average weekly unemployment insurance benefit was $297. This amounted to only about 34% of the average total weekly wage. Among the states in 2008, they varied from Alaska where the average weekly benefit was $202, which replaced only 23.5% of the state average total wage to Hawaii where the average weekly benefit was $413, which replaced 54.4% of the state average total wage. United States Department of Labor, Employment and Training Financial Data Handbook 394 Report, Employment and Wage Data Report for 2008, http://ows.doleta.gov/unemploy/finance.asp. Also limiting the adequacy of unemployment compensation benefits is the fact that since 1987 these benefits have been fully taxable. However, these average figures can be misleading since they are affected by whether the bulk of the unemployed come from low wage jobs and, therefore, draw low weekly benefits. Moreover, if the duration of unemployment is short, the overall impact of low benefits upon annual income may not be substantial. On the other hand, in assessing the extent to which unemployment insurance provides a meaningful safety net, consideration also should be given to the fact that employment frequently provides additional benefits, such a health insurance and retirement program contributions, in addition to weekly pay. In contrast, unemployment insurance provides only a cash payment.

A comprehensive examination of the policy goals of unemployment insurance and assessment of its actual and potential effectiveness as a method of income redistribution can be found at Gillian Lester, *Unemployment Insurance and Wealth Redistribution*, 49 UCLA L. REV. 335 (2001).

## NOTES AND QUESTIONS

1. Do higher wage earners require a more generous safety net to meet financial obligations during periods of unemployment? Do equitable considerations justify removing or increasing the caps on unemployment benefits? Savings provide an alternative or supplemental means of meeting financial needs during periods of unemployment. Should higher wage earners be required to rely largely or entirely on such resources during periods of unemployment? Alternatively, if unemployment compensation is a system of insurance, should employees be required to pay all or part of the insurance

premium based on their own unemployment experience? Would such direct employee involvement in financing the payment of benefits justify eliminating benefits caps, eliminating waiting periods, and removing the linkage between the duration of benefits and the duration of recent employment?

2. Studies indicate that a wife's employment income increases in response to the husband's unemployment, but that the increase is less for those households receiving higher unemployment insurance benefits than for those receiving lower benefits. Julie Berry Cullen & Jonathon Gruber, *Spousal Labor Supply as Insurance: Does Unemployment Insurance Crowd Out the Added Worker Effect?*, 18 J. OF LAB. ECON. 546 (2000). Research has also demonstrated that although jobless persons often use savings to supplement unemployment insurance benefits, many workers lack such a financial cushion. Indeed, the total savings of almost a third of jobless workers studied was less than 10% of the income they lost due unemployment. Jonathon Gruber, *The Wealth of the Unemployed*, 55 INDUS. & LAB. REL. REV. 79 (2001).

### (c.) Disqualification

The federal standards permit state law to disqualify an otherwise qualified unemployed person from receiving benefits if dismissed from the most recent job for work-related misconduct, for refusing to accept an appropriate job offer, or for making fraudulent claims for unemployment insurance benefits. State laws vary in their treatment of persons who are disqualified from receiving benefits due to prior dismissal for work-related misconduct. Some states disqualify the worker for the full period of unemployment subsequent to that dismissal. Others suspend the worker's right to receive benefits for a period of time but thereafter allow the benefits claim. A few jurisdictions treat good cause dismissal from the most recent job as a basis for reducing the amount of the unemployment insurance benefit.

A basic premise of the unemployment insurance system is that beneficiaries be ready, willing and available to accept full-time work. Therefore, full-time students are not qualified to receive unemployment compensation benefits. However, federal law rejects disqualification where a student, who is otherwise qualified for unemployment benefits, is engaged in a state approved work-training program. Federal law also prohibits a state from disqualifying an employee for refusing a job if the vacancy resulted directly from a labor dispute, if the wages or other conditions of work are "substantially less favorable than those prevailing for similar work in the locality," or if employment is conditioned upon the worker joining a company-dominated union or upon the worker refraining from joining or resigning from a bona fide labor organization. In addition, the federal act prohibits denials of unemployment benefits solely on the basis of pregnancy or the termination of pregnancy.

An informal administrative process is used in making the initial eligibility determination. The employer is informed of the claim and may contest it. Appeals from the eligibility decision are heard by an administrative hearing officer. In most states the hearing officer's decision is appealed to an administrative commission or board. The final administrative decision is appealed to a state court. In most states judicial review initially is by a lower level court but in a few states the appeal is directly to the highest appellate court.

The characteristics of an unemployment insurance "hearing" may not always measure-up to normal perceptions of what takes place at evidentiary presentations. Generally these hearings are quite informal and brief. For example, in refusing to treat an unemployment compensation eligibility determination as having collateral estoppel effect in a lawsuit relating to the employee's dismissal, the Indiana court observed that at the hearing the referee acted as the primary questioner, cross-examination was minimal and ineffective, and neither side was represented by counsel. *McClanahan v. Remington Freight Lines, Inc.*, 517 N.E.2d 390 (Ind.1988). A more extreme example is presented in *Small v. Jacklin Seed Co.*, 109 Idaho 541, 709 P.2d 114 (1985). There the unemployment claimant asserted that she quit because of a supervisor's sexual harassment. The hearing consisted of a recorded telephone conference call in which questions were posed by the Appeals Examiner. The claimant appealed from an adverse decision to the Industrial Commission which affirmed based on its review of the transcript of that phone call. The court reversed and remanded because two exhibits mailed to the agency had not been included in the case record. The court did not question the propriety of this sort of "hearing," though it did observe: "The commissioners may well want to consider a new hearing to obtain an accurate record * * * considering the apparent inadequacies of the telephone conference record presently before the Court." *Id.* at 116. A broad rejection of collateral estoppel based on unemployment hearing findings was announced in *Clapper v. Budget Oil Co.*, 437 N.W.2d 722 (Minn. Ct. App. 1989) (emphasizing the inapplicability of statutory and common law rules of evidence, the potential controlling effect of hearsay, and the high priority given to speedy case resolution). By statute, Minnesota prohibits evidence from unemployment insurance cases being introduced in an arbitration proceeding. MINN. STAT. § 268.19 (2007).

Although labor arbitrators are often presented with attempts to introduce records of unemployment compensation awards, "the conclusions and actions of state unemployment compensation commissions have been given very little weight (often none at all) in arbitration proceedings." FRANK ELKOURI & EDNA ASPER ELKOURI, HOW ARBITRATION WORKS 392 (4th ed. 1985). *See also* MARVIN HILL & ANTHONY V. SINICROPI, EVIDENCE IN ARBITRATION \ 371–75 (2d ed.1987).

Finally, for a variety of reasons, the majority of unemployed workers (55–65% in recent decades) do not apply for unemployment insurance benefits. Of those who decline to apply, most believe themselves ineligible either because they have not worked long enough to qualify for benefits or because they voluntarily left their last job. Another significant portion do not apply because they expect to soon take another job or be recalled by their former employer. Stephen A. Wandner & Andrew Stettner, *Why are*

*Many Jobless Workers Not Applying for Benefits*, 123 MONTHLY LAB. REV. 12, 21 (June 2000).

# B.  DISQUALIFICATION FROM BENEFITS

## 1.  INTERACTION BETWEEN UNEMPLOYMENT AND WORKERS' COMPENSATION INCOME MAINTENANCE

### APPEAL OF PETERSON

Supreme Court of New Hampshire, 1985
126 N.H. 605, 495 A.2d 1266

SOUTER, JUSTICE.

\* \* \*

The appeal tribunal denied the plaintiff's request for unemployment compensation benefits on the ground that the plaintiff had terminated his prior employment voluntarily without good cause attributable to his employer. RSA 282–A:32, I(a) (Supp.1983); N.H.Admin. Rules, Emp. 503.01. We reverse.

The plaintiff was disabled in February, 1982, in the course of employment as an aide at New Hampshire Hospital. The evidence indicates that during the period of disability he was treated as an employee on leave, and although his salary stopped, he received weekly workers' compensation benefits, presumably under RSA 281:25, plus vocational rehabilitation benefits under RSA 281:21–b.

*Got comp + rehab*

Following recovery from surgery for his injury the plaintiff was unable to return to his job. He and a rehabilitation counselor then presented a plan to the New Hampshire Department of Labor under which the plaintiff would receive vocational rehabilitation benefits to defray the expense of attending college, would seek a new job consistent with his college schedule, and would receive other workers' compensation benefits for no more than twelve further weeks.

*Voc rehab for more school*

There was evidence that the department of labor felt that the limitation of further weekly benefits to twelve weeks was not in the plaintiff's interest and that the requested educational benefits were too extensive. The department of labor proposed instead that the plaintiff agree with the State, as his employer, to accept a lump sum benefit under RSA 281:33 (Supp.1983) in lieu of all further workers' compensation benefits, after resigning from his hospital job. The defendant agreed to this and received the lump sum in June, 1983.

*Comp sum*

Before obtaining new employment he sought unemployment compensation benefits under RSA chapter 282–A (Supp.1983). DES denied benefits on the ground that plaintiff had voluntarily left his employment, without good cause within the meaning of RSA 282–A:32, I(a) (Supp. 1983), that is, without good cause attributable to his employer as required

*ok to deny? otherwise? resigned?*

by N.H.Admin. Rules, Emp. 503.01. *See Appeal of the City of Franklin,* 125 N.H. 761, 485 A.2d 295 (1984). The issue before us is whether the appeal tribunal was correct in upholding this denial. *See* RSA 282–A:53 and :67 (Supp.1983). We hold that it was not.

It is elementary law that an employee is not entitled to unemployment compensation benefits after a resignation for personal reasons. *Putnam v. Dep't of Employment Security,* 103 N.H. 495, 497, 175 A.2d 519, 520 (1961). We have held that the combined effect of the statute and administrative regulation applicable here is that an employee who voluntarily leaves employment is not entitled to benefits unless his resignation has "some connection with or relation to the employment * * *." *Nashua Corp. v. Brown,* 99 N.H. 205, 207, 108 A.2d 52, 54 (1954). There is such a connection when the employee quits because an injury received in the course of his employment has left him unable to perform further services for his employer. *Raffety v. Iowa Emp.Sec.Comm.,* 247 Iowa 896, 76 N.W.2d 787 (1956).

In the present case, the plaintiff left his employment at New Hampshire Hospital because an injury suffered in the course of his employment prevented him from discharging his duties and the hospital could offer him no work that he could do. Hence, the plaintiff is entitled to benefits unless it can be said that his agreement to resign and take the lump sum workers' compensation benefit breaks the direct causal connection between the injury and the resignation.

The plaintiff argues that the agreement may not be given any such effect, because to do so would violate the terms of RSA 282–A:157 (Supp.1983), which provides that "[a]ny agreement by an individual to waive, release or commute his rights to benefits or any other rights under this chapter shall be void." In support of this argument the plaintiff has cited cases dealing with the application of such a statute to collective bargaining agreement provisions for mandatory retirement at a given age. *See, e.g., Campbell Soup Co. v. Div. of Employment Security,* 13 N.J. 431, 100 A.2d 287 (1953). Such cases stand for the proposition that employees subject to such an agreement who wish to work after the mandatory retirement age do not voluntarily quit, within the meaning of the unemployment compensation laws. Therefore to construe the retirement provision as disqualifying a claimant from receiving unemployment compensation would offend the prohibition on waiver of unemployment benefits. *Contra Kentucky Unemployment Insurance Commission v. Reynolds Metals Company,* 360 S.W.2d 746 (Ky.1962).

We do not find *Campbell* and like cases on point, however, for they deal with agreements to retire that were not the personal agreements of the employees in question, but were imposed on all employees willy-nilly. Rather, we find a more basic reason for declining to recognize the present agreement as disqualifying the plaintiff.

The effect to be given the plaintiff's agreement must be decided in light of the obvious public policy underlying the law in question, to lighten the burdens of the unemployed. 1981 Laws 408:2. Therefore, unless a resignation agreement between employer and injured employee would provide some valuable benefit to lighten the burden of unemployment, that agreement should not be recognized as breaking the connection between a debilitating work-related injury and the consequent resignation. In determining how valuable an agreed-upon benefit must be in order to recognize the agreement as breaking the connection between injury and resignation, we start with the proposition that the benefit must be one to which the employee would not be entitled without the agreement. For without some incremental benefit under the agreement, the employee would in effect be resigning for nothing; to construe such a naked agreement as disqualifying the employee from unemployment compensation would necessarily turn the agreement into a waiver of benefits. Further, given the remedial nature of the statute, *Appeal of Gallant,* 125 N.H. 832, 835, 485 A.2d 1034, 1037 (1984), the burden should be on the employer to demonstrate that the agreement provided an incremental benefit valuable enough to be considered a reasonable substitute for unemployment compensation.

On the present record, no such benefit could be found. While the agreement provided for a lump sum workers' compensation benefit, there is no indication that the lump sum was intended to be, or was, more valuable than a continuation of other workers' compensation benefits would have been. *Cf. Carter v. Brown,* 102 N.H. 271, 155 A.2d 176 (1959) (lump sum of more than twice maximum remaining periodic benefits). We cannot tell how much of the lump sum was attributable to anticipated vocational rehabilitation benefits under RSA 281:21–b, or how much, if any, was attributable to weekly benefits that would have been deemed to be wages under RSA 282–A:14, III(a) (Supp.1983). Hence, it would be total speculation to suggest that the agreement provided anything more valuable than the benefits that the plaintiff might otherwise have received.

We therefore hold that the agreement before us cannot be regarded as breaking the connection between the work-related injury and the resignation that it caused. The judgment of the appeal tribunal is reversed, and the case is remanded for a calculation of benefits due the plaintiff.

*Reversed.*

All concurred.

## NOTES AND QUESTIONS

1. What are the similarities and differences between the purposes of disability benefits under workers' compensation and the benefits paid by unemployment insurance? Does your answer depend on whether the benefit is for partial or total disability? For example, if a worker is awarded partial disability benefits under workers' compensation, by definition he is able to work. However, he may be laid off from his prior employment. Should that worker continue to draw partial disability benefits while receiving unemploy-

ment compensation payments? Note that while employed he receives both his earned income and the partial disability benefits. Should the workers' compensation benefit be treated as earned income in calculating unemployment benefits and the latter be adjusted based on the claimant's receipt of that earned income?

2. Should the income maintenance aspects of workers' compensation and employer tort liability laws be merged with unemployment compensation insurance? A worker who is prevented from working for nine weeks due to a job related injury receives disability payments regardless of whether he had worked for the previous two years or only for the previous two weeks. A worker who is prevented from working for nine weeks due to the scarcity of raw materials will receive unemployment insurance benefits if he had worked for the previous two years, but not if he had only worked for the previous two weeks. A worker injured in a non-work accident caused by another can receive full lost earnings in a tort action regardless of the duration of prior employment. A worker who is prevented from working for nine weeks due to an injury suffered at home will receive neither workers' compensation disability benefits nor unemployment insurance benefits. Are these differences the by-product of lapses in legislative rationality or do they reflect sound policy judgments?

3. Section 102 of The Americans with Disabilities Act (42 U.S.C. § 12112), protects a qualified person with a disability from discrimination with regard to discharge and terms, conditions and privileges of employment. Had it been in effect when Patterson was asked to resign as a condition of receiving the proposed lump sum settlement of his workers' compensation claim, would the request have violated the Act?

## 2. DISMISSAL—SUBSTANTIVE GROUNDS AND PROOF OF JUST CAUSE

### FONDEL v. UNEMPLOYMENT COMPENSATION BOARD

Commonwealth Court of Pennsylvania, 1987
111 Pa.Cmwlth. 123, 533 A.2d 789

PALLADINO, JUDGE.

Matthew Marion Fondel (Petitioner) appeals from an order of the Unemployment Compensation Board (Board) which affirmed a referee's decision denying benefits to Petitioner for willful misconduct pursuant to section 402(e) of the Unemployment Compensation Law, 43 P.S. § 802(e). We affirm.

Petitioner was employed as an electronics engineer by the Naval Air Development Center (Employer). On May 14, 1986, the Deputy Director for the Center (Petitioner's superior) directed his secretary to arrange a meeting with Petitioner. Petitioner told the Director's secretary that he wanted representation at the meeting. The Director immediately called Petitioner to inform him that the purpose of the meeting was to discuss Petitioner's work product and that he was not entitled to representation.

The Director then asked Petitioner to attend, but Petitioner responded by stating "Are you hard of hearing?" and refused to attend. The Director then issued an order to Petitioner to attend, and Petitioner hung up the telephone.

On May 15, 1986, the Director again contacted Petitioner and ordered him to attend the meeting. Petitioner responded with abusive language and hung up the telephone. Shortly thereafter, Petitioner was discharged for refusal to comply with a reasonable order of his superior.[2] Both the referee and the Board denied benefits on the basis of willful misconduct, and this appeal followed.

Petitioner contends that the Board's findings of fact are not supported by substantial evidence in the record. In addition, he contends that the Board may not deny him benefits for willful misconduct because he is a federal employee and because the Board made no finding that his discharge would promote the efficiency of the federal service.

Our scope of review is limited to whether the Board has committed an error of law or violated any constitutional right, or whether necessary findings of fact are supported by substantial evidence. Section 704 of the Administrative Agency Law, 2 Pa.C.S. § 704.

Petitioner initially contends that the Board's findings of fact are not supported by substantial evidence. We disagree.

\* \* \*

Petitioner denied making any of the alleged abusive statements and accused the director of being a liar. In addition, Petitioner stated that he agreed to attend the meetings but only with representation.

Questions of credibility are within the exclusive province of the Board and are conclusive upon review to this court. _Davis v. Unemployment Compensation Board of Review_, 105 Pa.Commonwealth Ct. 377, 524 A.2d 1033 (1987). In this matter, the Board chose to believe Employer's version of the events surrounding Petitioner's discharge.

Finally, Petitioner argues that the Board is precluded from denying benefits for willful misconduct because 5 U.S.C. § 7513(a) prohibits discharge of federal employees unless such action will promote the efficiency of federal service, and, Petitioner alleges, Employer has made no such showing. This contention is meritless.

5 U.S.C. § 7513 provides cause and procedural requirements for disciplinary action against a federal employee in the form of discharge, suspension, or reduction in pay or rank. Under 5 U.S.C. § 7513(c), an employee against whom such disciplinary action is taken is entitled to appeal such action to the Merit Systems Protection Board. Thus, any allegation Petitioner may raise as to the propriety of his discharge must be

2. On a prior occasion, Petitioner was suspended for conduct similar to the conduct for which he was ultimately discharged. He filed for unemployment compensation benefits for the time he was on suspension. Benefits were denied and an appeal from this denial is pending before this court at No. 2529 C.D. 1986.

appealed pursuant to 5 U.S.C. § 7513(c). With regard to this unemployment compensation appeal, as stated above, findings of fact as to the nature and reason for discharge provided in a military document to the Unemployment Compensation Board of Review are conclusive and unreviewable by this court. * * *

Furthermore, under federal law, the state unemployment compensation authorities are empowered to act as agents of the federal government in providing benefits to eligible federal employees. 5 U.S.C. § 8502; *Lenns v. Unemployment Compensation Board of Review,* 109 Pa.Commonwealth Ct. 48, 530 A.2d 528 (1987). 5 U.S.C. § 8502(b) states, in pertinent part:

> [C]ompensation will be paid by the state to a federal employee in the same amount, on the same terms, and *subject to the same conditions* as the compensation which would be payable to him under the unemployment compensation law of the State * * *. (Emphasis added.)

Under Pennsylvania law, unemployment compensation claimant will be ineligible for benefits if his unemployment is due to his discharge from work for willful misconduct connected with his work. 43 P.S. § 802(e). Under 5 U.S.C. § 8502(b), this condition applies equally to federal employees. We have already concluded that the Board's decision to deny benefits to Petitioner for willful misconduct is supported by substantial evidence. Accordingly, the order of the Board denying benefits to Petitioner is affirmed.

* * *

# LONDON v. UNEMPLOYMENT COMPENSATION BOARD OF REVIEW

Commonwealth Court of Pennsylvania, 1987
111 Pa.Cmwlth. 132, 533 A.2d 792

MacPhail, Judge.

* * *

Claimant was employed by G.T.E. of Pennsylvania (Employer) for approximately seven and one-half years. Her position during the period of her misconduct involved preparation of Employer's telephone directories. Her last day of work was June 11, 1986.

On October 19, 1984, Claimant obtained telephone service by applying for that service under the middle and last names of her husband and son, and using her five-year-old son's Social Security number. At that time, Claimant had five outstanding accounts for telephone service with Employer, under various names, with a total past due amount of $867.47 of which Claimant was aware. Employer discovered Claimant's connection to these accounts upon investigation. On June 11, 1986, Claimant was given the option of resigning or being discharged, and Claimant chose to resign. The Board found that Claimant failed to adequately justify her actions.

The Board, in its brief, contends that the instant case is analogous to the case of *Abbey v. Unemployment Compensation Board of Review,* 50 Pa.Commonwealth Ct. 323, 413 A.2d 3 (1980). We disagree.

The claimant in *Abbey* was employed by the Department of Public Welfare (DPW) as a Mental Retardation Aide I at C. Howard Marcy Hospital. During the course of this employment, Ms. Abbey defrauded DPW by obtaining $6000 from Pennsylvania's public assistance program by lying to her caseworker. This fraud constituted a violation of a state statute which DPW enforces as a state agency. Citing *Nevel v. Unemployment Compensation Board of Review,* 32 Pa.Commonwealth Ct. 6, 377 A.2d 1045 (1977), this Court stated that, "[a] state agency as employer has a right to expect its employees not to violate a statute the agency enforces." *Abbey,* 50 Pa.Commonwealth Ct. at 325, 413 A.2d at 4. Both of these cases specifically relate to employment by state agencies and violation of state statutes enforced by those same agencies. On this basis, *Abbey* is clearly distinguishable from the instant case.

Claimant contends, *inter alia,* that the alleged misconduct was not sufficiently material to her employment to constitute willful misconduct. Our scope of review is limited to a determination of whether any constitutional rights have been violated, an error of law has been committed, or any findings of fact necessary to support the decision of the Board are not supported by substantial evidence. *Estate of McGovern v. State Employees' Retirement Board,* 512 Pa. 377, 517 A.2d 523 (1986). The question of whether Claimant's actions constitute willful misconduct disqualifying her from eligibility for unemployment compensation benefits is a question of law subject to the review of this Court. *Richner v. Unemployment Compensation Board of Review,* 95 Pa.Commonwealth Ct. 572, 505 A.2d 1375 (1986).

Section 402(e) of the Law provides that, "An employe shall be ineligible for compensation for any week * * * In which his unemployment is due to his discharge or temporary suspension from work for willful misconduct *connected with his work* * * *." (Emphasis added.) Our careful review of the record leads us to conclude that the Claimant's misconduct was not connected with her work and is therefore not covered under Section 402(e) of the Law. In *Barnett v. Unemployment Compensation Board of Review,* 47 Pa.Commonwealth Ct. 360, 408 A.2d 195 (1979), we held that in order for concealed or falsified information to be disqualifying for unemployment compensation benefits, such information had to be material to the qualifications of claimant's employment. Claimant's misconduct here was only connected with Employer as a consumer. While Claimant's misconduct may well be proper grounds for terminating Claimant or forcing her resignation, it is not sufficiently connected to her job involving preparation of Employer's telephone directories. Consequently, Claimant cannot be denied unemployment compensation benefits based on these circumstances, and the decision of the Board must be reversed.

## NOTES AND QUESTIONS

1. If, as suggested by the court, there was justification for terminating the employment of Ms. London, why would the legislature want her to receive unemployment insurance benefits?

2. In *Fondel,* the Pennsylvania court says that questions of credibility are within the exclusive province of the Board and are conclusive upon the court. What is the justification for this rule? Is your answer dependent upon whether the Board itself hears the witness or merely reviews a record in a hearing presided over by a referee? Is it dependent upon the degree of formality of the hearing and the type of representation typically received by the claimant, if any?

3. In *London,* the Pennsylvania court says the scope of judicial review includes determining whether material findings of fact are not supported by substantial evidence. Under that authority, is it possible for the court occasionally to set aside the Board's credibility findings?

4. Assume that Fondel appealed his discharge to the Merit System Review Board pursuant to the federal statute, and London appealed her discharge to an arbitrator pursuant to a collectively bargained agreement. Should the unemployment insurance decision have a *res judicata* or collateral estoppel impact on the Merit System Review Board or labor arbitration proceedings? Should it have such an impact in a suit for wrongful discharge? *Compare Ryan v. New York Tel. Co.*, 62 N.Y.2d 494, 478 N.Y.S.2d 823, 467 N.E.2d 487 (1984) (claims against the employer for false arrest, defamation and wrongful discharge collaterally estopped absent proof that the employee lacked a full and fair opportunity to litigate in the unemployment insurance proceeding) *with McClanahan v. Remington Freight Lines, Inc.*, 517 N.E.2d 390 (Ind. 1988) (described in the Subsection A(3)(c) note above). In *Rue v. K–Mart Corp.*, 552 Pa. 13, 713 A.2d 82 (1998), it was held that an unemployment compensation finding respecting an employee's alleged theft could not be used as evidence in a defamation action because the rules of evidence for an unemployment hearing are too relaxed, there is no pre-hearing discovery, unemployment compensation hearings are designed for expeditious resolutions, and the goal is to aid the unemployed claimant.

5. Given the cap on unemployment insurance payments, the limited duration of benefits, and the termination of benefits upon finding new employment, does it pay for a worker or employer to litigate an adverse unemployment claim decision? The party whose position is supported by the administrative agency's determination can simply rely on the agency to represent that interest in court. But what about the party that is displeased with the agency's determination? Although the costs of going to court often exceed the employer's liability for the claim, the prospect of future claims of a similar nature may give an employer a sufficient financial stake to justify the costs of overturning the precedent of an award favoring a particular claimant.

But what motivates a disappointed claimant to litigate? A survey of the first twenty cases in the chapter that involve claimant appeals indicates that some litigants minimize the expense by taking their appeal without the benefit of legal representation. In many jurisdictions, if the employee is poor enough, a legal aid, legal services, or law school clinic program will provide free representation in pursuing an appeal. (These two categories combined represented forty percent of the surveyed cases.) Other employees receive similar free representation from their union. Often, though, the claimant is represented by private counsel. In many such cases, there is collateral or potential collateral litigation for which the lawyer may have been retained and the unemployment proceedings could have some value in developing facts, establishing a basis for collateral estoppel, or influencing settlements by demonstrating the strength or weakness of relative positions taken in the collateral proceedings. Included are situations in which criminal charges could be pending (e.g., drug testing cases) or damages actions might be brought based on assertions such as breach of confidentiality, abuse of fiduciary duties, unfair trade practices, or violation of privacy rights. Finally, there are those situations in which an employee may be investing in an expected vindication that will demonstrate to prospective employers that the job termination was not attributable to the employee's misbehavior or inadequacies.

## MERLINO v. UNEMPLOYMENT COMPENSATION BOARD OF REVIEW

Commonwealth Court of Pennsylvania, 1988
113 Pa.Cmwlth. 209, 536 A.2d 863

MacPhail, Judge.

\* \* \*

Claimant was employed by Nordic Fisheries, Inc. (Employer) in both its wholesale operation and retail fish business. On July 16, 1986, Claimant and her husband, who was the manager of Employer's fresh fish department, informed Employer that they were going to open their own retail fish store three miles from Employer's store, in the Squirrel Hill section of Pittsburgh. As found by the Board, Employer draws a substantial portion of its business from Squirrel Hill. Board's Finding of Fact No. 8. Upon discovering that Claimant and her husband intended to remain in Employer's employ, Employer advised them that their new store would be a conflict of interest and that the Merlinos could not continue as employees while in competition with Employer. Employer subsequently discharged both Claimant and her husband when they refused to resign.

Claimant was denied benefits by both the Office of Employment Security and the referee, based on willful misconduct. The Board, after making findings of fact consistent with those of the referee, concluded that Claimant's actions in operating a competing fish store with her husband constituted a conflict of interest sufficient to support a finding of willful misconduct. Claimant's appeal of this order is now before our Court.

\* \* \*

Claimant argues here that the Board's findings are not supported by substantial evidence and that the Board erred as a matter of law in concluding that Claimant committed willful misconduct.

"Willful misconduct," which renders a claimant ineligible for benefits under Section 402(e), has been defined by this Court to include the wanton and willful disregard of the employer's interest, the deliberate violation of rules, the disregard of standards of behavior an employer can rightfully expect, or negligence manifesting culpability, wrongful intent, evil design, or intentional and substantial disregard of the employer's interests or the employee's duties and obligations. *Kentucky Fried Chicken of Altoona, Inc. v. Unemployment Compensation Board of Review,* 10 Pa. Commonwealth Ct. 90, 309 A.2d 165 (1973). Such conduct must be *willful* and not merely that which *appears* to be contrary to the employer's interests. *Penflex, Inc. v. Bryson,* 506 Pa. 274, 485 A.2d 359 (1984).

In this case, the Board concluded that because the testimony established that Claimant was involved in the operation of her husband's competing fish store, Employer had met its burden of proving Claimant's willful misconduct based on a conflict of interest. We agree with Claimant, however, that there is nothing in the record to support a finding of willful misconduct.

The Board's findings of fact, on which its conclusion of conflict of interest is based, include the following:

> 9. Claimant made no statement at the meeting on July 16, 1986, to indicate that she would not be involved in her husband's business and it was the employer's clear understanding, of which claimant was aware, that both claimant and her husband would be operating the retail store.

> \* \* \*

> 16. The ownership of the new retail fish store was placed only in the claimant's husband's name and the lease was only signed by claimant's husband even though the employer had been advised by the husband, with no dissent from claimant, that the ownership and the lease were in both names and that both were involved in the ownership and operation of the new store.

The Board found, additionally, that notices of the new store's opening were distributed in both the Squirrel Hill area, where the new store was located, and near Employer's store, and that an advertisement had been placed in a local ethnic newspaper. *See* Board's Finding of Fact No. 13.

We conclude that the Board's findings do not support the conclusion that Claimant's husband's fish store presented a conflict of interest with *Claimant's* employment with Employer. At the time of Claimant's discharge, the only action she, individually, had taken on behalf of her husband's business was to use a personal day off from Employer to assist in the store's opening day and to sign a health department inspection report. *See* Board's Findings of Fact Nos. 12 and 14. This conduct does not manifest a willful disregard of Employer's interests or any degree of misconduct sufficient to sustain Employer's burden of proving Claimant's willful misconduct.

We, accordingly, reverse the Board's order denying benefits to Claimant for willful misconduct.[2]

\* \* \*

### NOTES AND QUESTIONS

1. What alternative reasons may have motivated Nordic to fire the claimant? Which of those fits the phrase "willful misconduct"?

2. Does this decision require Nordic to help finance its competitor's start-up in business? In *Jordan v. Unemployment Compensation Board of Review*, 119 Pa.Cmwlth. 375, 547 A.2d 811 (1988), a claim was denied where the claimant was dismissed for engaging on his own time in the same business as his employer. There was no evidence that the claimant carried on his own activities on his employer's time, solicited his employer's customers, or competed with his employer for particular jobs.

3. In *Heins v. Unemployment Compensation Board of Review*, 111 Pa. Cmwlth. 604, 534 A.2d 592 (1987), the employer discontinued giving assignments to the claimant, who was employed an average of two days a week for about two years as an on-call driver and dock worker, when he refused to complete a written examination, called a Reid test, that purports to determine the extent of an employee's honesty. The test was required of all employees. In support of his refusal to complete the test, the claimant asserted that it posed unduly intrusive questions and was unreliable. The court, in upholding the denial of unemployment insurance benefits, did not assess the test's degree of intrusiveness nor its reliability. Rather, it noted the claimant's failure to provide objective proof of the test's inadequacy and added: "In any event, the fact that the test may not have been of the highest reliability does not necessarily render Employer's request or decision to use it unreasonable." *Id.* at 595. The court made special note that such tests are not analogous to polygraphic examinations which are illegal as a matter of state law in Pennsylvania.

In contrast, applying state constitutional and statutory protections of privacy, religious and political liberty and life style choice, a California court granted injunctive relief and upheld a damages cause of action against an employer that required certain employees to take a psychological test that inquired into sexual preferences and religious beliefs. *Soroka v. Dayton*

*[handwritten margin note: Emp'ee wouldn't take "honesty" test]*

---

**2.** In so holding, we are mindful of the cases in which this Court has affirmed a finding of willful misconduct under circumstances more clearly exhibiting "conflict of interest." *See, e.g., Burke v. Unemployment Compensation Board of Review,* 99 Pa. Commonwealth Ct. 500, 512 A.2d 1367 (1986) (claimant deliberately referred away employer's business); *Lee v. Unemployment Compensation Board of Review,* 73 Pa. Commonwealth Ct. 264, 458 A.2d 629 (1983) (claimant revealed confidential information to a business competitor); *Cahill v. Unemployment Compensation Board of Review,* 42 Pa. Commonwealth Ct. 566, 401 A.2d 405 (1979) (contrary to a supervisor's directive, claimant helped a competitor's employee install a dishwasher manufactured by the competitor and not claimant's employer).

*Hudson Corp.*, 1 Cal.Rptr.2d 77 (Cal. Ct. App. 1991), *appeal dismissed by parties' stipulation*, 24 Cal.Rptr.2d 587, 862 P.2d 148 (1993).

4. A fire fighter informed his supervisor he had learned he contracted AIDS. Being advised by two physicians that if the firefighter engaged in rescue missions, it would pose a danger of HIV transmission, the department assigned him to light duty tasks such as maintaining fire hydrants, doing errands and checking the town dump. In time the firefighter found this work demeaning and eventually was dismissed when he refused to perform some of these duties on the ground that he feared it was bad for his health. The fire fighter's discrimination claim, brought under the Rehabilitation Act of 1973, was rejected 2–1 on the ground that the facts did not establish that the dismissal was solely on the basis of handicap. *Severino v. North Fort Myers Fire Control Dist.*, 935 F.2d 1179 (11th Cir. 1991). Should the dismissed firefighter receive unemployment insurance benefits? Is your answer dependent upon whether the physician's advice was medically sound? Is your answer dependent upon whether the fire district normally dismissed personnel based on a single incident of insubordination? Suppose the firefighter was dismissed for withholding from the employer the information that he had been diagnosed with AIDS and that department regulations required disclosure of "any illness, condition or injury that could possibly affect a firefighter's fitness for duty." Would the dismissed firefighter be entitled to unemployment compensation?

## STEPP v. EMPLOYMENT SECURITY DIVISION REVIEW BOARD

Indiana Court of Appeals, Fourth District, 1988
521 N.E.2d 350

CONOVER, JUDGE.

Plaintiff–Appellant Dorothe Stepp (Stepp) appeals the decision of the Review Board of the Indiana Employment Security Division (Review Board) finding she was dismissed for just cause by the Medical Laboratory of Indianapolis, Indiana (Laboratory) when she refused to perform her assigned tasks on vials of bodily fluids with Acquired Immune Deficiency Syndrome (AIDS) warnings attached.

We affirm.

Stepp presents two issues for review,

1. whether the Review Board erred in finding Stepp had been dismissed for just cause, and

2. whether the Laboratory waived its right to compel Stepp to perform any tasks on fluids with an AIDS warning label attached.

\* \* \*

The Laboratory performs chemical examinations on bodily fluids submitted by physicians. Some of the fluids come from individuals who may have AIDS. These fluids are in vials with warning labels attached. Stepp was employed by the Laboratory as a staff technician from April 1,

1977, until her discharge on February 27, 1987. Her duties included performing tests on fluids submitted to the Laboratory.

Stepp's supervisor, Christy Zurface (Zurface), had discussions with Stepp concerning AIDS specimens being tested at the Laboratory and the proper safety procedures to be used with these specimens. Subsequent to this discussion, Stepp refused to perform tests on specimens with AIDS warning labels attached. On February 10, 1987, Stepp was asked by Zurface to perform a test on a specimen with the AIDS precautionary label. She refused. On February 13, Stepp was informed a refusal to perform a test on any specimen would be considered insubordination and subject her to termination. Again, Stepp refused to test samples with AIDS precautionary labels. For this refusal, Stepp was suspended for three days in accordance with the Laboratory's disciplinary policy for insubordination.

*Suspended for refusal*

On February 16, Stepp, Zurface and the Laboratory's business manager, Patricia Wynne (Wynne), met to discuss Stepp's suspension. Stepp contended she had refused to perform the tests for more than a year and was therefore exempt. Zurface and Wynne discussed with Stepp the safety precautions for handling specimens with AIDS precautionary labels. Stepp said she was not concerned with safety and refused to perform the tests because "AIDS is God's plague on man and performing the tests would go against God's will."

*Uh... crazy.*

The Laboratory had a safety manual informing employees of precautions they should take when performing tests on potentially infectious specimens. The Laboratory provided masks, aprons, gloves and disinfectants for protecting workers from infectious specimens. Although the Laboratory had no specific safety policy for the handling of AIDS specimens, the topic was discussed at inservice education seminars and meetings.

*Precautions*

After returning from her suspension, Stepp was again asked to perform tests on specimens with AIDS precautionary labels. Stepp refused and was discharged. After Stepp was discharged she sought unemployment compensation. * * *

*Fired*

Stepp contends the Laboratory failed to provide a safe work place and she was justified in refusing to perform a dangerous task.

Under Section 11(c)(1) of the Occupational Safety and Health Act of 1970 (OSHA) an employer is prohibited from discharging any employee who exercises any right afforded by OSHA. One of the protected rights is "the right of an employee to choose not to perform his assigned task because of a reasonable apprehension of death or serious injury coupled with a reasonable belief that no less drastic alternative is available." *Whirlpool Corp. v. Marshall* (1980), 445 U.S. 1, 100 S.Ct. 883, 885, 63 L.Ed.2d 154.

*OSHA*

The *Whirlpool* court laid out a two part test. First, an employee must reasonably believe the working conditions pose an imminent risk of

*(1)*

serious bodily injury, and second, the employee must have a reasonable belief there is not sufficient time or opportunity either to seek effective redress from his employer or to apprise OSHA of the danger.

The facts of this case reveal Stepp has failed both parts of this test.

In a discharge case, the burden of establishing just cause initially rests with the employer. When the employer establishes a prima facie case the burden shifts to the employee to introduce competent evidence to rebut the employer's case. On appeal the burden is upon the employee to establish reversible error exists. *Sloan v. Review Board* (1983), Ind.App., 444 N.E.2d 862, 865.

Whether a safe working condition exists is a question of fact. On appeal, we will neither reweigh the evidence nor assess the credibility of witnesses. We review to determine whether there is substantial evidence having probative value supporting the Board's determination. We will consider only the evidence most favorable to the award, including any and all reasonable inferences deducible from the proven facts.

\* \* \*

The facts of *Whirlpool* are distinguishable from the present case. In *Whirlpool*, the trial court found the employees were justified in refusing to obey the orders. Here, no such finding was made.

The Laboratory presented evidence it had taken proper precautions to protect employees and had followed the guidelines set out by The Center for Disease Control in Atlanta. No evidence was presented these precautions were not effective.

Stepp failed to prove the precautions taken by the Laboratory were not effective in preventing the spread of the disease. Stepp testified she had "heard" of workers contacting AIDS from contaminated fluids. She did not present evidence of how these workers contracted AIDS. Instead, she presented only her own hearsay evidence.

Furthermore, Stepp had sufficient time to contact OSHA about the alleged unsafe working conditions, yet she failed to take these measures. Stepp was first warned she would be required to perform tests on the specimens, then suspended for not performing the tests and finally discharged. (Stepp does not contest the suspension in this action).

The Review Board could have reasonably found safety was not the reason for Stepp's refusal to perform the tests; rather, it was Stepp's religious beliefs which formed the basis of Stepp's refusal to perform her assigned tasks.

The Review Board did not abuse its discretion by finding Stepp was not faced with a threat of serious bodily injury or death to which no less drastic alternative existed.

Stepp also claims she was exempted from performing tests on AIDS contaminated fluids and therefore the Laboratory had waived its right to enforce the employment contract.

\* \* \*

Here, the Laboratory claimed it never waived its right to require Stepp to perform any tests. Wynne testified all employees were required to perform tests on AIDS related materials and no employee was exempted from this rule. Furthermore, Stepp was warned, suspended, then discharged for insubordination. She was clearly required to perform a task which she refused to do. The evidence most favorable to the Laboratory reveals no waiver occurred.

The Review Board is in all things affirmed.

MILLER, P.J., and STATON, J., concur.

### NOTES AND QUESTIONS

1. If Stepp performed the tests but the precautionary measures proved inadequate or Stepp inadvertently failed to follow a precaution and became infected with AIDS, what remedy would be available to her?

2. If a jobless laboratory technician who is receiving unemployment insurance benefits is offered a job testing AIDS suspected specimens, should benefits eligibility be lost if the technician rejects the job on the ground that it involves an unacceptable risk?

3. Title VII of the Civil Rights Act of 1964 imposes a burden on employers to accommodate employee religious beliefs if such an accommodation can be achieved without undue hardship to the employer. Should the medical laboratory be held to a similar standard if it seeks to avoid unemployment compensation liability upon discharging an employee who sincerely fears for her health if she handles AIDS infected materials? That is, should she be entitled to benefits if dismissed even though the lab could have assigned her to entirely non-AIDS work?

See the U.S. Supreme Court's *Hobbie* decision, presented below in subchapter B(4), for an examination of the effect of the 14th Amendment's due process and equal protection clauses upon available justifications for withholding unemployment compensation.

4. Would the result have been different in *Stepp* if the case was decided under the Pennsylvania statute's "willful misconduct" standard?

5. Courts have divided over the question of whether unemployment benefits are available to an employee who was dismissed because a mandatory urinalysis test indicated off-the-job exposure to marijuana. For example, it has been held that "In the absence of evidence that an employee's drug usage had actual on-the-job impact, an employee's dismissal for failing a urine drug test based on off-the-job drug usage does not disqualify the employee from receiving unemployment compensation benefits." *National Gypsum Co. v. State Employment Sec. Bd. of Review*, 244 Kan. 678, 772 P.2d 786, 793 (1989). In accord with this result, the Arizona appellate court observed that a failed drug screen did not establish work performance impairment due to marijuana consumption nor the extent or nature of the exposure that produced the positive test result. Pointing to the lack of evidence of on-the-job marijuana use, the court stated: "The company rule must reasonably address a real threat to the employer's legitimate business interests without excessive prying

into the bodies and private lives of its employees. * * * An employer's moral support for a general public policy against drug abuse is not connected with the employee's work. This is the rule in every case of employee misconduct—even when a worker is discharged from employment for an alleged violation of public law." *Weller v. Arizona Dep't of Econ. Sec.*, 176 Ariz. 220, 860 P.2d 487, 495 (App. 1993). In contrast, *Johnson v. Department of Employment Security*, 782 P.2d 965 (Utah Ct. App. 1989) held that a rocket manufacturer was entitled to have a drug free work force and, therefore, off-the-job use of illegal drugs is "culpable conduct" justifying the denial of unemployment benefits.

The appellate court in Oregon allowed the payment of unemployment benefits to an employee who was dismissed due to the results of a random urine screen for drugs that indicated marijuana exposure, but denied benefits to a fellow employee who was dismissed for refusing to submit to such a test even though there was no evidence suggesting a need to test the latter employee. *Glide Lumber Prods. Co. v. Employment Div.*, 86 Or.App. 669, 741 P.2d 907 (1987); *Glide Lumber Prods. Co. v. Employment Div.*, 87 Or.App. 152, 741 P.2d 904 (1987).

In a few jurisdictions, the unemployment insurance statute expressly withholds unemployment benefits from those who lose their jobs because they refused to take or failed a drug test.

6. <u>Courts respond with varying degrees of sympathy when workers are dismissed for violating an employee appearance code</u>. *See, e.g.*, Claim of Apodaca, 108 N.M. 175, 769 P.2d 88 (1989) (absent evidence of customer complaint, benefit granted to waitress discharged for dying hair purple); *Whitacre v. Employment Division*, 102 Or.App. 229, 793 P.2d 1390 (1990) (benefit granted to Vietnam veteran who, on psychologist's advice, did not shave even though no-beard rule was imposed to facilitate wearing a respirator); *Ellis v. Unemployment Comp. Bd. of Review*, 68 Pa.Cmwlth. 617, 449 A.2d 881 (1982) (benefit withheld from waitress who refused to wear a badge); *Kentucky Unemployment Ins. Comm'n v. Murphy*, 539 S.W.2d 293 (Ky. 1976) (no benefit for waitress who insisted on wearing pants suit).

7. <u>If a jurisdiction wants to adopt a scheme of protection against unfair dismissal, would the existing administrative machinery for determining unemployment insurance eligibility</u> provide an appropriate or desirable structure for enforcing that substantive job security protection? Professor Janice Bellace has proposed such an approach, urging that it would avoid the expenses and delays of litigation without requiring the creation of an additional bureaucracy. She notes that if such a system is adopted, the unemployment compensation hearing officer will have to rule separately on the question of unemployment insurance eligibility as distinguished from unfair dismissal because there may be cases in which it is appropriate to grant unemployment benefits even though a remedy should not be provided based upon unfair dismissal. As an example, she poses the situation in which a mother frequently is absent from work to care for sick children because alternative child care arrangements are unavailable. "An employer is certainly entitled to discharge a person who is repeatedly absent from work because the needs of the business demand that the job be performed. It is equally clear, however, that the woman has not acted willfully [the ineligibility standard used in Pennsylva-

nia, the jurisdiction Prof. Bellace uses for her example—ed.] to destroy the employment relationship. Accordingly, the state referee would determine that the woman is entitled to unemployment benefits for there is no reason to deny her the safety net of unemployment compensation. Nevertheless, the employer did have just cause to discharge the woman." Janice R. Bellace, *A Right of Fair Dismissal: Enforcing a Statutory Guarantee*, 16 U. MICH. J.L. REFORM 207, 239 (1983).

## 3. CONCERTED WITHHOLDING OF WORK

Most states disqualify claimants from unemployment compensation benefits if their joblessness is the result of a labor dispute and their employer has not hired replacements for them. In *New York Telephone Co. v. New York State Department of Labor*, 440 U.S. 519, 99 S.Ct. 1328, 59 L.Ed.2d 553 (1979), the Court held that the National Labor Relations Act's policy promoting collective bargaining free from government interference does not prevent a state from granting unemployment compensation benefits for striking workers even though the funds providing those benefits are paid by employers at rates reflecting the extent to which benefits are received by their employees. Based on its examination of the legislative history, the Court concluded that Congress intended the states to be free to permit or prohibit unemployment compensation payments to strikers. It also noted that although an employer's premiums are adjusted to reflect its workforce's unemployment experience, due to maximum contribution rates there is less than a 100% correlation between that experience and the employer's contribution to financing the unemployment insurance system.

On the other hand, the Supreme Court allows states to disqualify jobless workers from unemployment insurance benefits if their unemployment is related to a labor dispute, despite the fact that the claimants themselves are not on strike. Accordingly, the Court held in *Ohio Bureau of Employment Services v. Hodory*, 431 U.S. 471, 97 S.Ct. 1898, 52 L.Ed.2d 513 (1977), that the federal guidelines for unemployment insurance programs do not prevent a state from disqualifying a worker where the worker's joblessness results from a work stoppage engaged in by some other group in the employer's workforce. In 1967, the United Auto Workers conducted a work stoppage while negotiating a new collective agreement with Ford Motor Company. During the strike, the union substantially increased its dues, on a temporary basis, to augment its strike fund. Before strike benefits could be paid to striking Ford employees, an agreement was reached and the union next turned its attention to General Motors. Although a national agreement was reached with GM without a work stoppage, in early 1968 the union went on selective local strikes in support of bargaining demands at three GM foundries. By that time, the special dues assessment had been rescinded because substantial strike funds had been accumulated. The funds, raised from that special assessment, were used to pay benefits of $4 to $6 a day to the striking GM foundry workers. GM responded to the local strikes by shutting down operations at 24 other plants whose activities were integrated with the striking foundries. The laid off employees' unemployment compensation claims were rejected by the state court on the ground that the claimants were disqualified under the state law as a result of having helped finance the labor dispute that gave rise to their unemployment. The U.S. Supreme Court affirmed that ruling and rejected the union's assertion that the National Labor Relations Act's protection of the right of workers to give mutual support to other employees preempts a state from penalizing workers for contributing to a strike fund. *Baker v. General Motors Corp.*, 478 U.S. 621, 106 S.Ct. 3129, 92 L.Ed.2d 504 (1986). The Court reasoned that these claimants had done more than give mutual support to fellow workers; they facilitated a work stoppage whose impact would predictably result in their own unemployment. It concluded that under such circumstances, federal statutory policy under the Social Security and Labor Relations Acts permits a state to choose to withhold unemployment insurance benefits. Justice Brennan, joined by Justices Blackmun and Marshall, dissented on the thesis that the legislative history of the Social Security Act supports only a state's option to disqualify actual strikers. Although accepting the proposition that this justifies disqualifying those who help finance a strike knowing that it will result in their own layoff, the dissenters argued that there was insufficient reason to assume that the GM workers anticipated their own layoff when they contributed to a special strike fund initiated during the work stoppage at Ford.

*Hodory* upheld a worker's ineligibility for benefits despite the fact that the worker had no interest in the underlying labor dispute, no influence on the stoppage and no participation in any aspect of the dispute or stoppage. Although it made no direct suggestion of any deficiency in the *Hodory* decision, in *Baker* the Court emphasized that the distinction between voluntary and involuntary unemployment is at the core of determining the right to benefits under the federal standard.

Work stoppages can be initiated by employers as well as by workers. In some jurisdictions, workers locked out by an employer during a labor dispute are qualified for unemployment compensation benefits. This often raises factual issues such as who initiated the stoppage and whether the stoppage occurred only after one of the parties did not live up to basic responsibilities of the employment relationship or made unilateral changes in the terms or conditions of employment and, therefore, was responsible for the event that initiated the work stoppage.

In Britain, unemployment benefits are denied to claimants who are "directly interested" in the outcome of the labor dispute that caused their unemployment. Where production workers represented by one union were laid-off as a result of a strike by maintenance engineers who were represented by a different union, the "directly interested" principle was used to deny benefits to the production workers because the employer normally extended to them any benefits granted the other group of workers. See discussion of *Presho v. Department of Health and Security*, 1 All E.R. 97 (H.L.1984) in Susan H. Ephron, *Redefining Neutrality: Alter-*

*native Interpretations of the Labor Dispute Disqualification in Unemployment Compensation*, 8 COMP. LAB. L.J. 89, 99–100 (1986).

What is the appropriate role of unemployment compensation in work stoppages? Does the governmental decision to grant or withhold benefits inevitably intrude into the parties' comparative bargaining strength? Is your answer influenced by whether the benefits program is financed exclusively by taxes paid by the employer or by payroll taxes paid by workers as well? Does the imposition of a payroll tax solely on the employer inevitably have an impact on the workers' remuneration and, if so, should that affect your answer? Is the purpose of unemployment compensation benefits to provide a financial cushion during times of involuntary joblessness? Is joblessness involuntary if an employer has locked out the workers in support of its bargaining demands? Is it involuntary if a strike is provoked by an employer's refusal to offer concessions in the face of reasonable bargaining demands? Is it sound policy to permit an administrative or judicial tribunal to determine whether such demands are reasonable?

## 4. QUITTING WORK AND ELIGIBILITY FOR BENEFITS

### *PROBLEM*

Peg Crane, a maintenance electrician, injured her back when her foot slipped on a ladder while she was carrying a burnt-out 45 pound motor that she had just removed from an overhead conveyor belt. She was off from work for two weeks. During that time she spent 6 days in traction and received daily physical and drug therapy. At the end of her treatment period, she reported experiencing moderate to severe pain from prolonged standing and from bending more than 15 degrees from a complete vertical or horizontal position. Her orthopedist's report states that she has a compressed disk which can be treated surgically with a 60% prospect of providing substantial relief. It also states that continued physical therapy and no further traumas will probably eliminate most of the pain after six months to a year but that without surgery there is little prospect of her ever again being able to lift more than 10 to 15 pounds without experiencing considerable pain and risking further spinal damage.

Enderby Manufacturing, Crane's employer, removed her from the maintenance electrician job on the ground that it requires frequent lifting of objects weighing 20–50 pounds and often necessitates prolonged periods of standing and bending. Enderby transferred Crane to the job of electrical parts assembly inspector. This job can be performed sitting down, involves no lifting above 5 pounds, and rarely requires bending. It pays $8.85 an hour while the maintenance electrician job paid $14.44 an hour.

Peg rejects the assembly inspector job and is laid-off. Her application for unemployment insurance benefits is denied. She appeals, and at her administrative hearing explains she is a certified electrician, having served a three year apprenticeship learning her line of work. While most electrician jobs involve substantial lifting, bending and standing, she knows that there are some in the community that do not—though she is unaware of any such openings at the moment. She is very depressed and upset at the idea of doing repetitive work on an assembly line, being under constant supervision, having little or no discretion, and earning barely more than half of an electrician's pay. She says she would prefer to survive on unemployment compensation until she can find an appropriate job rather than have the humiliation of doing underpaid, unskilled factory work. What should be the result and why?

## HOLBROOK v. MINNESOTA MUSEUM OF ART

Minnesota Court of Appeals, 1987
405 N.W.2d 537

LANSING, JUDGE.

Relator Mary Holbrook challenges a determination by the Department of Jobs and Training that she voluntarily quit, without good cause, her job with respondent Minnesota Museum of Art. We reverse.

### Facts

The Minnesota Museum of Art hired Mary Holbrook in October 1981 to work 15 hours per week as a curatorial assistant. At the time she was hired, Holbrook held a Bachelor of Arts degree from the University of Minnesota and had finished the necessary class work for a Masters degree in the classics area. She had a background in research and library work.

During Holbrook's first few years at the museum, she performed primarily clerical work, although when she was hired she was assured that research would be an important part of her job. In November 1983 she wrote a letter to her supervisor complaining about her duties and requesting additional responsibilities involving research, collection, cataloging and teaching.

Holbrook was subsequently promoted to the position of assistant curator and her hours were eventually increased from 15 to 27.5 hours per week. Her responsibilities also increased and, by 1985, the bulk of her time was spent on research and documentation. Holbrook spent approximately one-third of her time performing secretarial or clerical work; however, the curatorial department had no support staff and all employees in that department—even the head curator—performed some clerical duties.

In the summer of 1985 Holbrook learned that, due to funding limitations, her position as assistant curator would be eliminated and she would be reassigned to two half-time positions in other departments. The positions were primarily clerical in nature, but Holbrook was informed that if she accepted them, a review would be held in three months, at which time the positions might be upgraded. Holbrook refused to accept the reassignment and left the museum when her assistant curator position ended. Her claim for unemployment compensation benefits was denied on the basis that she did not have good cause to decline the clerical positions.

## Issue

Did Holbrook have good cause to refuse the two clerical positions when her position as assistant curator was eliminated?

## Analysis

Minn.Stat. § 268.09, subd. 1(1) (1986), states that an individual is disqualified from receiving unemployment compensation benefits for quitting a job "voluntarily and without good cause attributable to the employer." The Commissioner's representative determined that Holbrook did not have good cause to turn down the two half-time clerical positions and was therefore disqualified from receiving unemployment compensation benefits.

When, as here, the relevant facts are undisputed, the question of whether an employee had good cause to quit is one of law, to be independently determined by this court. *Forsberg v. Depth of Field/Fabrics,* 347 N.W.2d 284, 286 (Minn.Ct.App.1984). "Good cause" does not require a finding that the employer was at fault or acted wrongfully. *Helmin v. Griswold Ribbon and Typewriter,* 345 N.W.2d 257, 262 (Minn. Ct.App.1984), *pet. for rev. denied,* (Minn. June 12, 1984) (citing *Hanson v. IDS Properties Management Company,* 308 Minn. 422, 425 n. 1, 242 N.W.2d 833, 835 n. 1 (1976)). Rather, this court has stated:

> The proper test for "good cause attributable to the employer" is whether the employee's reason for quitting was compelling, real and not imaginary, substantial and not trifling, reasonable and not whimsical and capricious.

*Kratochwill v. Los Primos,* 353 N.W.2d 205, 207 (Minn.Ct.App.1984) (citing *Ferguson v. Department of Employment Services,* 311 Minn. 34, 44, 247 N.W.2d 895, 900 (1976)).

The Commissioner's representative cited several reasons for believing that Holbrook did not have good cause to reject the two clerical positions. First, he noted that Holbrook would have continued to receive the same hourly wage she had been receiving as assistant curator. In fact, the increase from her 27 1/2 hour–per–week position as assistant curator to 40 hours per week from both half-time clerical positions would have actually resulted in an increase in Holbrook's weekly pay. In addition, she would have received more benefits by working 40 hours per week.

The fact that Holbrook would not have received a reduction in pay by accepting the clerical positions is not determinative. In *Marty v. Digital Equipment Corporation,* 345 N.W.2d 773 (Minn.1984), a personnel assistant with a maximum potential salary of $10.18 was offered a sales position with a maximum potential salary of $9.30 per hour. Although her salary would have initially been the same, she refused the transfer, believing it would reduce her opportunities for advancement and future pay. The supreme court agreed, concluding that the employee had good cause to refuse the new position:

> We have recognized that a claimant has a right to reject, without loss of benefits, a job which requires substantially less skill than she possesses. *Id.* at 775.

*Less advancement is ok person*

Holbrook had advanced to a position requiring only limited clerical work. The half-time clerical positions would have involved less responsibility and there was evidence that the pay scales for those positions were lower than the pay scale for her assistant curator position.

The Commissioner's representative relied on *Simonson v. Thin Film Technology Corporation,* 392 N.W.2d 363 (Minn.Ct.App.1986), *Heisler v. B. Dalton Bookseller,* 368 N.W.2d 314 (Minn.Ct.App.1985), and *Forsberg* as authority for his conclusion that Holbrook did not have good cause to refuse the transfer. These cases are distinguishable. In *Simonson* the employee was reassigned to a lower-grade position with a reduction in pay after she returned from a two-month leave of absence. In addition, the employer had a policy of rotating its employees to different positions. In *Heisler* the employee was demoted after she failed to improve her job performance. In *Forsberg* the employee's increased responsibilities were intended to be temporary, lasting only three months. Holbrook had not taken a leave of absence or received poor performance reviews, nor did the museum have an established policy of rotating its employees to different positions. There has been no claim that Holbrook's assistant curator responsibilities were intended to be temporary. In addition, there is no indication in the *Forsberg* opinion that the employee was overqualified for the offered position. Holbrook was clearly overqualified for the primarily clerical positions.

The Commissioner's representative also concluded that Holbrook did not have good cause to quit because the two half-time positions were not totally clerical:

> Some of the duties were: maintaining the art work in the "kid space," assisting in the supervising of "kid space" interns; and serving as "an information resource person for the community, answering inquiries on all activities of the Museum, particularly those sponsored by the Museum school"; performing other duties as may be assigned.

The Commissioner also found that everyone in the curatorial department did some clerical work, and job descriptions were not totally accurate. Nevertheless, the representative specifically found that the two half-time positions were "primarily" clerical in nature. In view of this finding, the proposed reassignment constituted good cause for Holbrook to quit.

The Commissioner's representative relied heavily on the "possibility" that the two clerical positions might have been upgraded in three months and concluded that Holbrook's separation was premature. While we have held that an employer should be given an opportunity to correct unfavorable working conditions, *see, e.g., McLane v. Casa de Esperanza,* 385

N.W.2d 416, 417–18 (Minn.Ct.App.1986), none of those cases involved a demotion. To hold that Holbrook should have performed primarily clerical duties for three months to see if she might ever be promoted would be a departure from our previous holdings.

Finally, the Commissioner's representative determined that Holbrook did not have good cause to turn down the clerical positions because the museum's offer was not unreasonable or unfair. This consideration is not relevant to eligibility for unemployment compensation. *Helmin,* 345 N.W.2d at 262 (citing *Hanson v. IDS Properties Management Company,* 308 Minn. 422, 425 n. 1, 242 N.W.2d 833, 835 n. 1 (1976)).

### Decision

The Commissioner's representative erroneously concluded that Holbrook did not have good cause to quit.

Reversed.

*Rvd.*

*Good cause*

## MURPHY v. EMPLOYMENT SECURITY DEPARTMENT

Court of Appeals of Washington, 1987
47 Wash.App. 252, 734 P.2d 924

MUNSON, JUDGE.

Leo E. Murphy appeals the Superior Court affirmance of the Employment Security Department (Department) denying his unemployment benefits. Mr. Murphy challenges the commissioner's conclusion that he did not demonstrate "good cause" for leaving his employment. We reverse.

Mr. Murphy, age 50, worked for Kaiser Aluminum & Chemical Corporation for 17 years as a brick mason. On January 25, 1985, Kaiser informed him that due to a cutback in employees, his services as a brick mason were not needed. Kaiser offered him a position in the pot room with a 5 percent reduction in salary. He voluntarily quit his job refusing to accept the position in the pot room.

*Pot room job for 5% less*

As a brick mason, Mr. Murphy spent much of his time maintaining the furnaces and occasionally running a jack hammer. The work was strenuous at times, but did not involve much lifting; the temperature in the working area was sometimes 100° F. Although he would have been transferred to the pot room as a laborer, it is likely he would have spent more than half his day working as a carbon setter, standing on a narrow catwalk 6 to 12 inches above vats of molten steel at 1100° F. to 1300° F., breaking the crust on the metal with a heavy crowbar. A carbon setter typically wears a cape, chaps, mask, and long underwear to protect himself from the heat and gases escaping from the molten metal.

*New job= Carbon setter*

Mr. Murphy said he would not work in the pot room because of the extreme heat and gases. Because the work was so strenuous, he described it as a "young man's" job. The job is generally a stepping point; when a carbon setter gets some seniority, he transfers to a job that is less

*Pot room is stepping pt.*

physically demanding. Kaiser claimed Mr. Murphy had no physical restrictions on his medical chart and felt he could adapt to the strenuous work.

The Job Service Center granted Mr. Murphy unemployment compensation; Kaiser appealed; the Office of Administrative Hearings (OAH), after taking testimony and reviewing exhibits, made the following determination:

> 4.  * * * The five percent reduction in salary, although important, would not constitute by itself a substantial deterioration of the work factor. . . . Although claimant's job as a mason was certainly not easy, the job was much less intense in terms of strenuous work and extreme heat. We note that very few of the workers in the pot room are fifty years of age or older. The work in the pot room is extremely demanding and performed under adverse conditions. Although claimant might have been able to perform the work, we find that the reduction in salary coupled with the change to a more strenuous, harder, and less desirable position to be a substantial involuntary deterioration of the work factor. Claimant has established good cause for quitting his job pursuant to RCW 50.20.050(1). . . .

Kaiser appealed to the commissioner of the Department. The commissioner, after reviewing the record, set aside the decision of the OAH, adopting the findings of fact and conclusions of law, except for conclusion 4 (above), stating:

> Pursuant to the statute and regulations cited at Conclusion 1, a claimant, to show good cause for quitting work, must establish that he or she quit work due to a compelling work factor after having made a reasonable effort to preserve his or her employment. It has not been demonstrated in the present case that work in the pot room would adversely affect claimant's health or safety within the contemplation of RCW 50.20.050(3). Absent such a showing, it cannot be concluded that he had a compelling reason for quitting that work.

The Superior Court affirmed the commissioner's decision. Mr. Murphy repaid the $2,220 received as unemployment compensation; he has found mason work since leaving Kaiser. Mr. Murphy appeals.

The sole issue is whether the commissioner of the Department erred in concluding Mr. Murphy voluntarily left his employment without good cause. The scope of this court's review is governed by RCW 34.04.130(6) which provides:

> The court may affirm the decision of the agency or remand the case for further proceedings; or it may reverse the decision if the substantial rights of the petitioners may have been prejudiced because the administrative findings, inferences, conclusions, or decisions are:

* * *

> (d) affected by other error of law; or

(e) clearly erroneous in view of the entire record as submitted and the public policy contained in the act of the legislature authorizing the decision or order; or

(f) arbitrary or capricious.

Which standard to apply depends on whether the issue is one of fact, law, or a mixed question of law and fact. *Rasmussen v. Department of Empl. Sec.,* 98 Wash.2d 846, 849–50, 658 P.2d 1240 (1983); *Franklin Cy. Sheriff's Office v. Sellers,* 97 Wash.2d 317, 324–30, 646 P.2d 113 (1982), *cert. denied,* 459 U.S. 1106, 103 S.Ct. 730, 74 L.Ed.2d 954 (1983). A factual issue is reviewable under the "clearly erroneous" standard. *Franklin Cy. Sheriff's Office,* at 324–25, 646 P.2d 113. The error of law standard is applied whenever a question of law or a mixed question of law and fact is presented. *Renton Educ. Ass'n v. Public Employment Relations Comm'n,* 101 Wash.2d 435, 440–41, 680 P.2d 40 (1984).

When the dispute involves inferences drawn from raw facts and an interpretation of the term "good cause," the error of law standard applies. *Grier v. Department of Empl. Sec.,* 43 Wash.App. 92, 95, 715 P.2d 534, *review denied,* 106 Wash.2d 1003 (1986). Although Washington courts accord substantial weight to an administrative agency's construction of statutory language, they also recognize the countervailing principle that it is ultimately for the court to determine the purpose and meaning of statutes even when contrary to that of the agency. * * *

Here, the commissioner found Mr. Murphy had not established good cause because he had not demonstrated that work in the pot room would adversely affect his health or safety within the contemplation of RCW 50.20.050(3), the pertinent portion of which provides:

> In determining under this section whether an individual has left work voluntarily without good cause, the commissioner shall only consider work-connected factors such as the degree of risk involved to the individual's health, safety, and morals, the individual's physical fitness for the work, the individual's ability to perform the work, and such other work connected factors as the commissioner may deem pertinent, including state and national emergencies.

Apparently the commissioner reads the statute to require a claimant to demonstrate that the work must adversely affect his or her health or safety. We disagree. The statute merely limits the commissioner's consideration to work-connected factors *such as* the risk to the claimant's health and safety. Having determined the commissioner erred in applying RCW 50.20.050 to these facts, this court may make a de novo review of the record to determine if Mr. Murphy has established "good cause" for leaving his employment. * * *

The purpose of the Employment Security Act is to combat involuntary unemployment by providing benefits for "persons unemployed through no fault of their own." RCW 50.01.010. To establish good cause for becoming voluntarily unemployed, a claimant must demonstrate (1) he or she left work primarily because of a work-connected factor of such a compelling nature that a reasonably prudent person would have left his or her employment, and (2) he or she first exhausted all reasonable alternatives prior to termination. * * *

RCW 50.20.050(3) further provides:

> Good cause shall not be established for voluntarily leaving work because ... of any other significant work factor which was generally known and present at the time he or she accepted employment, unless the related circumstances have so changed as to amount to a substantial involuntary deterioration of the work factor or unless the commissioner determines that other related circumstances would work an unreasonable hardship on the individual were he or she required to continue in the employment.

The Department contends a reasonably prudent person in Mr. Murphy's circumstances would not quit simply because the work was strenuous and normally performed by younger workers. The Department argues Mr. Murphy should have at least tried the carbon setter job.

Whether a work-connected factor of such a compelling nature would cause a reasonably prudent person to leave his or her employment exists is determined by the particular facts in each case.

> It is undoubtedly true that an employee might be justified in voluntarily terminating his employment, if called upon to work for substantially reduced wages or under less favorable conditions; but each phase would be a matter of degree, and the circumstances surrounding each case should certainly be considered by any authority called upon to determine whether or not the employee had good cause to leave his employment.

> An employee might well be justified in terminating his employment, if transferred from available work to work of a substantially different nature, or even of the same nature but paying a lower wage or requiring work under less favorable conditions.

> On the other hand, a different situation would be presented if the employer no longer had occasion to use the employee in the work he had formerly performed, either permanently or temporarily, but could continue the employment in some lesser but related capacity.

*In re Anderson,* 39 Wash.2d 356, 361–62, 235 P.2d 303 (1951) (a 20 percent per hour reduction in pay and a loss of opportunity to be placed on another shift at a $.10 per hour increase is not sufficient to establish good cause for voluntary unemployment). *See also Sweitzer v. Department of Empl. Sec.,* 43 Wash.App. 511, 718 P.2d 3 (1986) (sexual harassment is good cause for leaving employment); *Grier v. Department of Empl. Sec., supra* (a 33 percent reduction in pay is a compelling reason for terminating one's employment); *Johns v. Department of Empl. Sec., supra* (philosophical differences with supervisors, lack of communication, and dissatisfaction with responsibilities and salary are not sufficient to compel a reasonably prudent person to leave his or her employment); . . . *Cowles Pub'g Co. v. Department of Empl. Sec.*, 15 Wash.App. 590, 550 P.2d 712 (1976) (personal dissatisfaction with low wages and lack of promotional opportunity is not good cause for leaving employment), *review denied*, 88 Wash.2d 1001 (1977).

The act does not require a claimant, whose particular services are no longer required by the employer, to accept whatever position the employer offers. Several cases in other jurisdictions have held that a bricklayer may refuse a position as a laborer and remain eligible for unemployment compensation. In *United States Steel Corp. v. Unemployment Compensation Bd. of Review*, 10 Pa.Commw. 295, 310 A.2d 94 (1973), a bricklayer, who had been laid off due to lack of work, declined the employer's offer for work as a laborer. The court affirmed the board's finding the position as a laborer was not "suitable work" because (1) although the claimant first worked as a laborer for approximately 2 years, he completed a bricklayer apprenticeship program which required a minimum of 4 years to complete; (2) as a laborer he would use none of these skills; and (3) he had only one week to seek work as a bricklayer. In *Green v. Republic Steel Corp.*, 44 A.D.2d 345, 355 N.Y.S.2d 192 (1974), a bricklayer, who had been laid off due to lack of work, was offered a position by his employer as a laborer. The court affirmed the agency's finding of good cause for the claimant's refusal to accept the position as a laborer because (1) the claimant had always worked as a bricklayer and never as a laborer, (2) a laborer's duties entail substantially less skill and discretion than those of a bricklayer, and (3) the claimant would suffer a 15 percent reduction in pay.

Here, Mr. Murphy had several reasons for declining to accept the position as a carbon setter: (1) he had worked 17 years at Kaiser as a brick mason and was asked to accept a position as an unskilled laborer; (2) the new job was to be performed in extreme heat: a carbon setter stands on a catwalk between 6 and 12 inches above vats of molten steel at 1100° F. to 1300° F., wearing a cape, chaps, mask, and long underwear to protect himself from the heat and escaping gases; (3) the new job was extremely strenuous—a great deal of the work is done with a heavy crowbar; (4) very few of the carbon setters are 50 years old; (5) Mr. Murphy would suffer a 5 percent reduction in pay; and (6) Mr. Murphy was required to accept the new position immediately.

Although we consider the above factors as a whole, we find the nature of the alternative position offered to Mr. Murphy particularly significant. The change to a more strenuous and less desirable position as an unskilled laborer is a work-connected factor of such a compelling nature as to cause a reasonably prudent 50–year–old person to leave his or her employment. This constitutes a substantial involuntary deterioration of the work factor.

The Department contends Mr. Murphy should be denied benefits because he refused to try the job as carbon setter; thus, he failed to exhaust all reasonable alternatives prior to leaving his employment. He is not required to try just any position offered by his employer. He was given a choice—carbon setter or nothing. Because of the nature of the newly offered position, Mr. Murphy did not act unreasonably and, therefore, did not fail to exhaust all reasonable alternatives.

The judgment of the Superior Court is reversed. Mr. Murphy is entitled to attorney fees in the amount of $1,326 and costs in the amount of $201.29. * * *

## NOTES AND QUESTIONS

1.  In most instances the unemployment insurance benefit is significantly less than full time earnings. Why would a worker seek such benefits in lieu of suitable employment? Does your answer to that question provide an appropriate guide for determining what burden of proof and burden of persuasion rules and what presumptions should apply in claims and litigation processing? What other considerations should guide those rules and presumptions?

2.  When new owners took over management of a rest home, an employee who for eleven years had been in charge of preparing breakfast and lunch for patients, working from 6 a.m. to 2 p.m., was given reduced work hours from 11 a.m. to 6 p.m. and was assigned cleaning duties in addition to helping a cook to prepare lunch and dinner. The court ruled that the employee had the burden of proving eligibility for unemployment benefits and that the inconvenience of the change in hours that resulted from not being able to prepare her husband's dinner did not justify her leaving the job. However, the court observed that she was nevertheless entitled to unemployment compensation if the new tasks were clearly antithetical to that for which she was initially employed, and remanded for further findings on that issue. *Uvello v. Director of Div. of Employment Sec.*, 396 Mass. 812, 489 N.E.2d 199 (1986). Suppose the new owner had dismissed the employee because there were complaints about the quality of her cooking. Would that be reason to disqualify her from receiving unemployment benefits? Suppose she was dismissed for allegedly neglecting her cleaning duties and resisting the directions of the new cook. Who would have the burden of proving whether she was entitled to unemployment compensation benefits?

Courts are divided over the extent to which family responsibilities, especially child care, justify rejecting a work schedule change. See cases collected in George L. Blum, Annotation, *Unemployment Compensation: Eligibility as Affected by Claimant's Refusal to Work at Particular Times or on Particular Shifts for Domestic or Family Reasons*, 2 A.L.R. 5th 475 (1992).

3.  Compare the roles of the administrators and the courts in reviewing the determination of whether there was good cause to quit. Are these merely formal distinctions or do they have a substantive impact? Which entity would you expect to be more sympathetic to the claimant: the administrative agency or the court?

4.  Assume that prior to working at her most recent job, an employment benefits claimant worked cleaning motel and hospital rooms. At her most recent job she was given a chance to demonstrate her cooking skills and succeeded in obtaining a promotion to a higher paid position as a short-order

cook. The employer went out of business and the jobless claimant, who is seeking work as a short-order cook, turned down a work opportunity cleaning motel rooms. Should she be denied unemployment compensation benefits? If she accepted the motel cleaning job but quit after two weeks because she decided that such work is no longer suitable, should she be entitled to resume receiving unemployment payments? If an overqualified person is forced to take a less desirable job, what impact does that have on that worker, on the employer, on less qualified job seekers, on society?

5.   Federal law protects a worker's eligibility for unemployment insurance benefits where the worker refuses to accept new work "if the wages, hours, or other conditions of the work offered are substantially less favorable to the individual than those prevailing for similar work in the locality." Does that federal standard for unemployment insurance programs offer guidance for dealing with the situation of the employee whose job has become less attractive?

6.   Courts have displayed widely divergent attitudes toward the extent to which a reduction in compensation must be suffered before an employee is justified in quitting a job. For example, in *Nason v. Louisiana Department of Employment Security*, 475 So.2d 85 (La. Ct. App. 2 Cir. 1985), *writ denied*, 478 So.2d 149 (La. 1985), the court held that a claimant was entitled to unemployment benefits when he quit his firefighter job after seven years because mandatory wage deductions for employee benefits programs had reduced his take-home pay almost 10%. In contrast, a laid off claimant who had been working five days a week for $8.90/hour was denied benefits when he declined recall to his job for four days a week at $8.20/hour. Claim of D'Allesandro, 186 A.D.2d 954, 589 N.Y.S.2d 113 (N.Y. A.D. 3 Dept., 1992).

A Pennsylvania court allowed unemployment compensation benefits for a worker who quit when her employer discontinued providing full medical insurance coverage after the insurance premiums had risen over the six years of her employment from $101.55/month to $235.16/month. The court noted that because the employee was a diabetic, this coverage was an important part of her original employment contract and that the employer's offer to contribute $64.48 toward her cost of continuing the coverage constituted more than a 14% reduction in her compensation. *Steinberg Vision Assoc. v. Unemployment Comp. Bd. of Review*, 154 Pa.Cmwlth. 486, 624 A.2d 237 (1993). Was the reduction in the employer's support of medical insurance a compelling reason to leave the job? What medical benefits will the employee receive after leaving? Is there a difference in the nature of the justification for leaving due to reduction of benefits or change of job tasks or responsibilities, and the justification for leaving due to family responsibilities?

An employer that seeks to avoid unemployment compensation costs charged against its account (and experience rating) in lieu of laying off or terminating a worker may be tempted to make a job so intolerable that the employee quits. To what extent should deterrence of that improper motive for changing job assignments or conditions be weighed in determining whether a quit was justified?

7.   An employee who is eligible for unemployment compensation benefits based on past full-time employment loses the full-time job. The employee also

has a part time job that she quits. Should benefits be paid minus the lost part-time earnings? Should she continue to get the full benefits from the lost full-time job? Courts have endorsed both results. *Compare Campeanu v. Unemployment Appeals Comm'n*, 629 So.2d 1015 (Fla. App. 4 Dist., 1993) *with Rodgers v. Department of Employment Sec.*, 186 Ill.App.3d 194, 134 Ill.Dec. 168, 542 N.E.2d 168 (2 Dist., 1989).

8.   In reading what follows, consider whether there are other reasons for allowing workers, without losing unemployment insurance benefits, to quit in response to significant changes in the terms or conditions of their jobs.

An argument posed for resisting efforts to increase unemployment insurance benefits is that such payments create a work disincentive. Efforts to study this proposition are complicated by a number of factors. For example, there is evidence that higher unemployment insurance benefits induce workers to file claims more promptly. If that occurs, the increased benefit amount will be accompanied by benefits payments for a longer duration even if the actual period of unemployment remains the same or is slightly reduced. Nevertheless, studies show that increased benefits do tend to extend, to a small degree, the period of a beneficiary's unemployment, particularly where that person's earnings are not the sole source of household income. On the other hand, the prolonged duration of individual unemployment sometimes carries offsetting benefits. Thus, there is evidence that the resulting prolonged job search increases the probability that the worker will get higher future earnings than would have been received if the employee returned to the former employment. Presumably, that means that the added time spent unemployed aids the worker in finding a more suitable match for his or her abilities. In addition, there is some evidence indicating that more generous benefits induce some benefit recipients who would otherwise abandon the search for a job to continue those efforts in order to qualify for the benefits.[*]

Although there are obvious short-term program costs when unemployment claimants receive benefits for a longer duration, one study suggests that an offsetting benefit is improved job opportunities for unemployed persons who are ineligible for unemployment insurance benefits. Phillip B. Levine, *Spillover Effects Between the Insured and Uninsured Unemployed*, 47 Indus. & Lab. Rel. Rev. 73 (1993).

A study of Canadian experience indicates that duration of unemployment is affected not only by the benefit level, but also by the claimant's prior unemployment history. It was found that claimants tend to collect benefits for longer durations with each successive claim. Does this pattern suggest that unemployment is "addictive," that the stigma fades with repeated experience resulting in less vigorous efforts to find new work? Or is the explanation to be found in the proposition that repeated joblessness has a "scarring" effect that discourages the claimant's search for new work? Or is the better hypothesis that potential employers are weary of hiring a job applicant whose work

[*] *See generally* Daniel S. Hamermesh, Jobless Pay and the Economy (Policy Studies in Employment and Welfare) (1977); Raymond Munts & Irwin Garfinkel, The Work Disincentive Effects of Unemployment Insurance (1974). *See also* John J. Antel, *The Wage Effects of Voluntary Labor Mobility With and Without Intervening Unemployment*, 44 Indus. & Lab. Rel. Rev. 299 (1991) (finding that those who are unemployed when they seek a new job get better paying work than those who find a new job while still employed elsewhere).

history shows frequent episodes of joblessness? Miles Corak, *Is Unemployment Insurance Addictive? Evidence from the Benefit Durations of Repeat Users*, 47 INDUS. & LAB. REL. REV. 62 (1993).

9. Largely because of the combined effects of the various benefit qualifications and the limited duration of benefits, at any given time in the past couple of decades, 25–65% of unemployed workers have either exhausted their unemployment benefits, have not been qualified for such benefits, or have not applied even though qualified. It has been estimated that as many as ten percent of those not receiving benefits fall within the latter group. One hypothesis is that lower paid and part-time workers have less information about unemployment insurance benefits and are less likely to apply for them.

As a result of the earnings requirements during the qualifying period preceding unemployment, new entrants to the job market and reentrants who have been out of the work force for an extended period cannot qualify for unemployment insurance benefits. Because of the long period of high unemployment rates in the first part of the 1980s, some states exhausted program funds. In response, they reduced the duration of their benefit programs and made eligibility more difficult. Similar tightening of eligibility standards were also imposed by the federal government respecting the conditions for providing extensions of the benefit coverage period in states with especially high rates of unemployment. Thus, benefits were exhausted more quickly and it took longer for reemployed workers to requalify in the event of subsequent resumption of unemployment.

Generally, that tightening of eligibility requirements has remained unchanged and the problem of benefits exhaustion has increased. Thus, by November 1992, nearly 40% of those receiving unemployment insurance benefits were exhausting their regular state benefits without finding new employment. The comparable exhaustion rate for the prerecessionary period had been running between 25 and 30%. The problem of increased exhaustion of unemployment benefits may be at least partially related to a structural change in the causes of joblessness. In earlier decades, close to half of unemployed persons were on layoff from jobs to which they would return after several weeks or months. In contrast, in the recession of the early 1990s, it was estimated that only 14% of unemployed persons had a reasonable expectation of returning to their former jobs. Rita L. DiSimone, *Unemployment Insurance: New Emergency Benefits Extension*, 56 Soc. SECURITY BULL. 87, 87 (Jan. 1993).

Workforce distribution changes and related changes in the geographical impact of recessions present another structural explanation for at least part of the increase in exhaustion of unemployment benefits. A study of the marked decline of jobless persons receiving unemployment insurance benefits in the early 1980s found that half of that decline resulted from the shift of joblessness from the northeastern to the southern and western states where eligibility requirements long had been more stringent. Rebecca M. Blank & David E. Card, *Recent Trends in Insured and Uninsured Employment: Is There an Explanation*, 106 Q. J. ECON. 1157 (1991).

Professor Mary O'Connell has argued that the general pattern of qualification requirements for unemployment compensation benefits, as well as for other employee benefit programs, provides special rewards for the person deemed "the good worker," the worker who has a long-term relationship with a single employer or industry and whose encounters with unemployment are relatively brief. Professor O'Connell contends that the system disenfranchises certain occupational groups that characteristically have significant numbers of women, black, and Hispanic workers, and that it is based on the false premise that those who make an honest effort will be included in the good worker group. In contrast, she observes:

> The last decade has seen a dramatic expansion in the number of part-time, temporary, and contract workers. Economists and labor analysts explain this shift as one that enhances efficiency. Contemporary business has apparently concluded that it is strategically wise to expand and contract the work force to match demand. Layoffs, however, harm worker morale and may increase unemployment insurance premiums. The ideal situation would allow the employer to trim the work force without layoffs. The use of temporary or contract workers produces this result. These employees are hired on an as-needed basis with no expectation of long-term affiliation with the employer. When they are no longer needed, they simply disappear, and the employer incurs labor costs only as required to produce his output.

> From the employer's perspective, the use of contingent workers provides a flexible and cheap source of labor. But the ability to make these workers disappear on cue is, of course, a fantasy. The employer's vaunted savings are in reality a mere shift in costs from employer to employee. * * *

>> What happens to these workers? Some, of course, are the dependents of good workers and obtain derivatively what they are denied directly. But the myth that the part-time and temporary work force is made up exclusively of married women who elect their work patterns ("mothers' hours") is not borne out by the empirical data. The number of "involuntary" part-time workers—those who want, but are unable to find, full-time work—is growing at twice the rate of the voluntary part-time or temporary work force.

Mary E. O'Connell, *On the Fringe: Rethinking the Link Between Wages and Benefits*, 67 TUL. L. REV. 1421, 1476–77 (1993).

10. One commentator has observed:

Unemployment insurance primarily benefits the employer by reducing some of the costs of employing workers from the primary labor market. That is, unemployment insurance provides a reserve labor pool which enables an employer to lay off and later recall the insured worker without having to train a new employee. * * *

The operation of the unemployment insurance system as a mechanism for the individual worker to ensure a rational, personal skill progression which has been earned by his or her past contributions to society has been rendered unthinkable. Kenneth M. Casebeer, *Unemployment Insurance: American Social Wage, Labor Organization and Legal Ideology*, 35 B.C. L. REV. 259, 325, 342–43 (1994).

Does the above assessment accurately describe the effect of our system of unemployment compensation insurance? What other social and economic purposes are served or should be served by unemployment insurance?

## WIMBERLY v. LABOR AND INDUSTRIAL RELATIONS COMMISSION

United States Supreme Court, 1987
479 U.S. 511, 107 S.Ct. 821, 93 L.Ed.2d 909

JUSTICE O'CONNOR delivered the opinion of the Court.

\* \* \*

### I

In August 1980, after having been employed by the J.C. Penney Company for approximately three years, petitioner requested a leave of absence on account of her pregnancy. Pursuant to its established policy, the J.C. Penney Company granted petitioner a "leave without guarantee of reinstatement," meaning that petitioner would be rehired only if a position was available when petitioner was ready to return to work. Petitioner's child was born on November 5, 1980. On December 1, 1980, when petitioner notified J.C. Penney that she wished to return to work, she was told that there were no positions open.

*[handwritten margin note: Leave, but no guar. of coming back + can't]*

Petitioner then filed a claim for unemployment benefits. The claim was denied by the Division of Employment Security (Division) pursuant to Mo.Rev.Stat. § 288.050.1(1) (Supp.1984), which disqualifies a claimant who "has left his work voluntarily without good cause attributable to his work or to his employer." A deputy for the Division determined that petitioner had "quit because of pregnancy," App. to Pet. for Cert. A53, and therefore had left work "voluntarily and without good cause attributable to [her] work or to [her] employer." *Id.,* at A52. Petitioner appealed the decision to the Division's appeals tribunal, which, after a full evidentiary hearing, entered findings of fact and conclusions of law affirming the deputy's decision. The Labor and Industrial Relations Commission denied petitioner's petition for review.

*[handwritten margin note: Quit b/c of preg. Voluntary]*

\* \* \*

### II

The Federal Unemployment Tax Act (Act), 26 U.S.C. § 3301 *et seq.,* enacted originally as Title IX of the Social Security Act in 1935, 49 Stat. 639, envisions a cooperative federal-state program of benefits to unemployed workers. See *St. Martin Evangelical Lutheran Church v. South Dakota,* 451 U.S. 772, 775, 101 S.Ct. 2142, 2144, 68 L.Ed.2d 612 (1981). The Act establishes certain minimum federal standards that a State must satisfy in order for a State to participate in the program. See 26 U.S.C. § 3304(a). The standard at issue in this case, § 3304(a)(12), mandates that "no person shall be denied compensation under such State law solely on the basis of pregnancy or termination of pregnancy."

Apart from the minimum standards reflected in § 3304(a), the Act leaves to state discretion the rules governing the administration of unemployment compensation programs. See *Steward Machine Co. v. Davis*, 301 U.S. 548, 57 S.Ct. 883, 81 L.Ed. 1279 (1937). State programs, therefore, vary in their treatment of the distribution of unemployment benefits, although all require a claimant to satisfy some version of a three-part test. First, all States require claimants to earn a specified amount of wages or to work a specified number of weeks in covered employment during a one-year base period in order to be entitled to receive benefits. Second, all States require claimants to be "eligible" for benefits, that is, they must be able to work and available for work. Third, claimants who satisfy these requirements may be "disqualified" for reasons set forth in state law. The most common reasons for disqualification under state unemployment compensation laws are voluntarily leaving the job without good cause, being discharged for misconduct, and refusing suitable work.

\* \* \*

The treatment of pregnancy-related terminations is a matter of considerable disparity among the States. Most States regard leave on account of pregnancy as a voluntary termination for good cause. Some of these States have specific statutory provisions enumerating pregnancy-motivated termination as good cause for leaving a job, while others, by judicial or administrative decision, treat pregnancy as encompassed within larger categories of good cause such as illness or compelling personal reasons.[1] A few States, however, like Missouri, have chosen to define "leaving for good cause" narrowly.[2] In these States, all persons who leave their jobs are disqualified from receiving benefits unless they leave for reasons directly attributable to the work or to the employer.

Petitioner does not dispute that the Missouri scheme treats pregnant women the same as all other persons who leave for reasons not causally connected to their work or their employer, including those suffering from other types of temporary disabilities. \* \* \* She contends, however, that § 3304(a)(12) is not simply an antidiscrimination statute, but rather that it mandates preferential treatment for women who leave work because of pregnancy. According to petitioner, § 3304(a)(12) affirmatively requires States to provide unemployment benefits to women who leave work because of pregnancy when they are next available and able to work,

---

**1.** States with statutory provisions that specifically treat pregnancy as good cause for leaving work include Arkansas, South Dakota, and Tennessee. See Ark.Stat.Ann. § 81–1106(a) (1976 and Supp.1985); S.D. Codified Laws § 61–6–3 (1978); Tenn. Code Ann. § 50–7–303(a)(1) (Supp.1986). For an example of a State that has reached the same result by administrative determination, see Cal.Admin. Code, Tit. 22, § 1256–15(b), reprinted in 2 CCH Unempl.Ins.Rep. ¶ 5219 O (Apr. 8, 1982).

**2.** See, *e.g.*, Okla.Stat., Tit. 40, §§ 2–404, 2–405 (1981); Vt.Stat.Ann., Tit. 21, § 1344(a)(3) (1978 and Supp.1986).

regardless of the State's treatment of other similarly situated claimants. * * *

Contrary to petitioner's assertions, the plain import of the language of § 3304(a)(12) is that Congress intended only to prohibit States from singling out pregnancy for unfavorable treatment. The text of the statute provides that compensation shall not be denied under state law "solely on the basis of pregnancy." The focus of this language is on the basis for the State's decision, not the claimant's reason for leaving her job. Thus, a State could not decide to deny benefits to pregnant women while at the same time allowing benefits to persons who are in other respects similarly situated: the "sole basis" for such a decision would be on account of pregnancy. On the other hand, if a State adopts a neutral rule that incidentally disqualifies pregnant or formerly pregnant claimants as part of a larger group, the neutral application of that rule cannot readily be characterized as a decision made "solely on the basis of pregnancy." For example, under Missouri law, *all* persons who leave work for reasons not causally connected to the work or the employer are disqualified from receiving benefits. To apply this law, it is not necessary to know that petitioner left because of pregnancy: all that is relevant is that she stopped work for a reason bearing no causal connection to her work or her employer. Because the State's decision could have been made without ever knowing that petitioner had been pregnant, pregnancy was not the "sole basis" for the decision under a natural reading of § 3304(a)(12)'s language.

We have, on other occasions, construed language similar to that in § 3304(a)(12) as prohibiting disadvantageous treatment, rather than as mandating preferential treatment. In *Monroe v. Standard Oil Co.*, 452 U.S. 549, 101 S.Ct. 2510, 69 L.Ed.2d 226 (1981), for example, the Court considered 38 U.S.C. § 2021(b)(3), a provision of the Vietnam Era Veterans' Readjustment Assistance Act of 1974, which provides that a person "shall not be denied retention in employment * * * because of any obligation" as a member of the Nation's Reserve Forces. The *Monroe* Court concluded that the intent of the provision was to afford reservists "the same treatment afforded their co-workers without military obligations," 452 U.S., at 560, 101 S.Ct., at 2517; it did not create an "employer responsibility to provide preferential treatment." *Id.*, at 562, 101 S.Ct., at 2518. Similarly, in *Southeastern Community College v. Davis*, 442 U.S. 397, 99 S.Ct. 2361, 60 L.Ed.2d 980 (1979), we considered § 504 of the Rehabilitation Act of 1973, 29 U.S.C. § 794, which provides that an "otherwise qualified handicapped individual" shall not be excluded from a federally funded program "solely by reason of his handicap." We concluded that the statutory language was only intended to "eliminate discrimination against otherwise qualified individuals," and generally did not mandate "affirmative efforts to overcome the disabilities caused by handicaps." 442 U.S., at 410, 99 S.Ct., at 2369.

Even petitioner concedes that § 3304(a)(12) does not prohibit States from denying benefits to pregnant or formerly pregnant women who fail to satisfy neutral eligibility requirements such as ability to work and availability for work.... Nevertheless, she contends that the statute prohibits the application to pregnant women of neutral *disqualification* provisions.... But the statute's plain language will not support the distinction petitioner attempts to draw. The statute does not extend only to disqualification rules. It applies, by its own terms, to any decision to deny compensation. In both instances, the scope of the statutory mandate is the same: the State cannot single out pregnancy for disadvantageous treatment, but it is not compelled to afford preferential treatment.

The legislative history cited by petitioner does not support her view that § 3304(a)(12) mandates preferential treatment for women on account of pregnancy.... As petitioner notes, the House Report on the bill containing the language now found in § 3304(a)(12) refers to "nineteen states" that had "special disqualification provisions pertaining to pregnancy." H.R.Rep. No. 94–755, at 7. The Report goes on to observe that "[s]everal of these provisions hold pregnant women unable to work and unavailable for work; the remainder disqualify a claimant because she left work on account of her condition or because her unemployment is a result of pregnancy." *Ibid.* Although the Report does not specify which 19 States had "special disqualification provisions pertaining to pregnancy," the parties agree that Congress most probably was referring to the 19 States listed in a program letter issued by the Department of Labor a week before the Committee Report was filed. See Unemployment Insurance Program Letter No. 33–75 (Dec. 8, 1975). In that letter, the agency called for the repeal of state laws which "still include special disqualifications for pregnancy or automatically consider unavailable for work any pregnant claimant." *Id.*, at 2. In an attached summary, the letter discussed the statutory provisions of 19 States relating to pregnancy.

Neither Missouri nor any State with a rule like Missouri's is included in the list of 19 States having special disqualification provisions pertaining to pregnancy. The summary includes only state provisions that disqualify women from receiving unemployment compensation for a defined period around the date of childbirth (the kind of provision at issue in *Turner v. Department of Employment Security of Utah,* 423 U.S. 44, 96 S.Ct. 249, 46 L.Ed.2d 181 (1975)); provisions that specifically disqualify women who leave work because of pregnancy; and miscellaneous provisions that otherwise single out pregnancy for disadvantageous treatment. * * *

The focus of the House Report clearly was on "*discriminatory* disqualifications because of pregnancy," H.R.Rep. No. 94–755, at 50 (emphasis added); there is no hint in the House Report of any disagreement with state provisions that neutrally disqualify workers who leave their jobs for reasons unrelated to their employment.

The Senate Report also focuses exclusively on state rules that single out pregnant women for disadvantageous treatment. In *Turner v. Department of Employment Security, supra,* this Court struck down on due process grounds a Utah statute providing that a woman was disqualified for 12 weeks before the expected date of childbirth and for 6 weeks after childbirth, even if she left work for reasons unrelated to pregnancy. The Senate Report used the provision at issue in *Turner* as representative of the kind of rule that § 3304(a)(12) was intended to prohibit:

"In a number of States, an individual whose unemployment is related to pregnancy is barred from receiving any unemployment benefits. In 1975 the Supreme Court found a *provision of this type* in the Utah unemployment compensation statute to be unconstitutional. * * * A number of other States have similar provisions although most appear to involve somewhat shorter periods of disqualification." S.Rep. No. 94–1265, at 19, 21, U.S. Code Cong. & Admin. News 1976, pp. 6013, 6015 (emphasis added).

In short, petitioner can point to nothing in the Committee Reports, or elsewhere in the statute's legislative history, that evidences congressional intent to mandate preferential treatment for women on account of pregnancy. * * *

Because § 3304(a)(12) does not require States to afford preferential treatment to women on account of pregnancy, the judgment of the Missouri Supreme Court is affirmed.

*It is so ordered.*

JUSTICE BLACKMUN took no part in the decision of this case.

### NOTES AND QUESTIONS

1.  One commentator has stated:

Although Congress has traditionally recognized society's interest in preserving the unique and important rights of procreation and family life, the *Wimberly* Court refused to recognize that Congress intended to mandate a discriminatory program as it relates to pregnancy. At the core of the issue is the underlying perception that, while the economic impact on pregnant and formerly pregnant claimants for unemployment compensation insurance is adverse, it is not a consequence which the marketplace ought to be obligated to insure against. In essence, the pregnant employee is regarded as subordinating the interests of the labor force to the individual interests of the family.

Patricia Kurp Masten, Note, *Unemployment Compensation—Pregnancy—Federal Employment Tax Act 26 U.S.C. 3304(a)(12) Recent Decision*, 26 DUQ. L. REV. 485, 507 (1987).

Is the decision to pay or not pay unemployment benefits to employees who leave work due to pregnancy likely to have an impact on family planning? If so, what result, if any, should be dictated by national, regional or local population growth policies? Assuming that a legislative judgment is made to provide a financial cushion for those who leave work due to pregnancy, should it also apply to those who leave work due to adoption? To both spouses? Should the benefit be financed by charging the unemployment benefit against the former employer's individual account? Against a pooled account? By some other scheme?

For a critical analysis of the Court's reasoning in *Wimberly,* see Mary F. Radford, *Wimberly and Beyond: Analyzing the Refusal to Award Unemployment Compensation to Women Who Terminate Prior Unemployment Due to Pregnancy,* 63 N.Y.U. L. REV. 532 (1988).

2. Although the Family and Medical Leave Act (FLMA) preserves the worker's job during a mandated pregnancy leave, it does not render the *Wimberly* decision moot. The FLMA does not apply to employers with fewer than 50 employees, to workers with fewer than 12 months' prior employment with the current employer, or to pregnancy leaves that, by themselves or in combination with other leaves, continue for more than 12 weeks during the previous twelve months. Moreover, if the job disappears during the leave, the returning worker must seek unemployment benefits.

3. Other nations have adopted a variety of ways to protect the job and income status of workers affected by childbirth and child rearing responsibilities. In Hong Kong, for example, an employee who has worked for an employer for at least 26 weeks is entitled to a leave of absence while disabled due to pregnancy. (Excluded are non-manual workers earning more than HK $10,500 a month—as of mid–1994, about $1,350/month.) Normally, this is the four week period before expected childbirth and six weeks after completion of the pregnancy. In addition, if the woman worked for the employer for at least 40 weeks and has less than two surviving children, she is entitled to receive two-thirds of her normal pay during the four week pre-delivery leave period.

European Council Directive 92/85, adopted October 19, 1992, requires all member nations to retain existing pregnancy benefits to the extent that they exceed the European Communities' minimum standards. At the same time, the Council Directive adopted a minimum standard requiring that a woman who has worked for at least 12 months prior to her expected date of delivery receive a total of 14 successive weeks of pregnancy leave compensated at a minimum level equivalent to the pay the worker would receive if on disability leave. Pregnant workers are also entitled to take unpaid time off from work for pre-natal medical examinations.

Previously established Italian law ensures the employee five months of maternity leave during which compensation is received from the social security system at 80% of her regular pay and mandates that the maternity leave time be counted as though worked for purposes of determining vacation and seniority benefits. The Italian law also gives the mother a right to take an additional six months of leave. During that extended leave the social security system pays 30% of her regular pay. Finally, a mother, or the father if he has custody, has a right to take time off from work to attend an ill child until the child is age 3.

French law provides social security compensation during maternity leave at 90% of the base wage. Because the benefit is tax exempt, it is reported to be substantially equal to normal wage earnings.

Japanese law entitles a pregnant worker to take six weeks leave prior to the expected date of birth. This right is expanded to ten weeks in the event of an expected multiple birth. In addition, the woman is prohibited from working for six weeks after giving birth, having a stillbirth, a late-term abortion (after four months), or a miscarriage. For an additional two weeks the woman can request to work only with her physician's consent. During these leave periods the woman is entitled to receive from the health insurance fund a stipend equal to 60% of her standardized daily wage. In addition, the leave period must be counted as though worked when calculating her vacation benefit entitlement.

For further details, see INTERNATIONAL ENCYCLOPEDIA FOR LABOUR LAW AND INDUSTRIAL RELATIONS: EUROPEAN WORKS COUNCIL, France ¶ 189, Hong Kong ¶ 187–91, Italy ¶ 173 (Roger Blanpain ed., 1998); KAZUO SUGENO, JAPANESE LABOR LAW 311 (Leo Kanowitz trans., 1992).

4.  Health care is often provided within the family unit. If that care requires constant attention, a family member may be forced temporarily to leave the work market. When the medical crisis has been resolved, should the care provider be treated as a new labor market entrant and, therefore, ineligible for unemployment insurance benefits? *Compare Moore v. Unemployment Comp. Bd. of Review*, 103 Pa.Cmwlth. 154, 520 A.2d 80 (1987) (where an employee who quit to care for her brother's recently orphaned children was denied her claim on the ground that she did not demonstrate that there was no reasonable alternative to quitting to provide care for the children) *with Morse v. Daniels*, 271 Ark. 402, 609 S.W.2d 80 (App. 1980) (where the court, on the grounds of the compelling nature of the emergency and the worker's efforts to preserve her job, upheld the claim of a worker whose employer rejected a leave of absence request to care for parents who were unable to care for themselves).

5.  The growth of dual career families poses the question of whether unemployment benefits are payable when one spouse leaves a job to accompany the other who has moved to a new location for the purpose of preserving his or her existing employment or obtaining new or improved employment. Some states reject such claims on the ground that the benefits are payable under the state law only if the employer caused the worker to quit and that quitting in such circumstances is for personal reasons. *See, e.g., Department of the Air Force v. Unemployment Appeals Comm'n*, 486 So.2d 632 (Fla. Dist. Ct. App. 1986) (held no benefit payable to civilian Air Force employee who left job to accompany husband, an Air Force military employee, who was transferred to a distant base); *Schroeder v. Department of Employment Serv.*, 479 A.2d 1281 (D.C. 1984) (held that employee who quits to follow spouse to a new job location is not entitled to benefits because the quit did not result from a work-connected cause). In one case, unemployment compensation benefits were granted to an unmarried employee when she quit her job to go to the new work location of the man with whom she had been living for thirteen years. *Reep v. Commissioner of the Dep't of Employment and Training*, 412 Mass. 845, 593 N.E.2d 1297 (1992). Some states' statutes explicitly preserve the benefit claim of the accompanying spouse. In California, such claims are paid out of a pooled fund rather than out of the prior employer's individual account. *Altaville Drug Store, Inc. v. Employment Dev. Dep't*, 44 Cal.3d 231, 242 Cal.Rptr. 732, 746 P.2d 871 (1988).

Virginia's rejection of unemployment compensation benefits to a spouse who left her job to follow her husband to a new locality, because she was required to do so by her religious beliefs, withstood constitutional challenge as an infringement upon both constitutional protections of the marital status and free exercise of religion. *Austin v. Berryman*, 878 F.2d 786 (4th Cir.) (en banc), *cert. denied*, 493 U.S. 941, 110 S.Ct. 343, 107 L.Ed.2d 331 (1989). The court said the proximate cause of unemployment was the distance between the claimant's job and residence, not her religious beliefs.

What is the societal impact of denying unemployment benefits to a spouse who moves to maintain the family unit at another location? If you think benefits should not be denied to someone who quits under that type of compulsion, whom do you think should bear the costs of providing the benefit? *See* Martin H. Malin, *Unemployment Compensation in a Time of Increasing Work–Family Conflicts*, 29 U. M**ICH**. J.L. R**EFORM** 131 (1996).

## TRU–STONE CORPORATION v. GUTZKOW

Minnesota Court of Appeals, 1987
400 N.W.2d 836

F**OLEY**, J**UDGE**.

\* \* \*

Gutzkow applied for unemployment compensation. A claims deputy denied him benefits, determining that he did not have good cause to quit. Gutzkow appealed to a Department referee, who affirmed the claims deputy's decision, reasoning that Gutzkow "simply did not give the employer a reasonable amount of time to remedy the situation." Gutzkow appealed again, this time to a Commissioner's representative, who reversed the referee's decision, finding:

> The evidence demonstrates that the employer knew for several weeks that the claimant was being harassed substantially, but took no decisive steps to end these acts. Indeed, the claimant's immediate superior joined in on the threats, intimidation and humiliation of the claimant. The claimant had no reason to expect that the president of the employer would in fact exert sufficient control to give him real relief.

*No good ave. Rvd.*

### Issue

Does the record support the Commissioner's determination that Gutzkow had good cause to quit his job with Tru–Stone?

### Analysis

An individual who voluntarily quits his job is disqualified from receiving unemployment compensation benefits unless he can prove that his resignation was for "good cause attributable to the employer." Minn.Stat. § 268.09, subd. 1(1) (1984); *Zepp v. Arthur Treacher Fish & Chips*, 272 N.W.2d 262, 263 (Minn.1978). "Good cause" may be established if the employee has been subjected to harassment on the job and can demonstrate that he gave his employer notice of the harassment and an opportunity to correct the problem. *See Larson v. Department of Economic Security,* 281 N.W.2d 667 (Minn.1979); *Burtman v. Dealers Discount Supply,* 347 N.W.2d 292, 294 (Minn.Ct.App.1984). Then, if the employee is "provided with the expectation of assistance from his employer" in eliminating the harassment, the employee must continue to apprise the employer of additional harassment. *Larson,* 281 N.W.2d at 669.

Here, the Commissioner's representative found that Gutzkow had received no real expectation of assistance from Tru–Stone. The Commissioner's findings must be upheld if there is any evidence in the record which reasonably tends to sustain them. *Chellson v. State Div. of Employment and Security,* 214 Minn. 332, 336, 8 N.W.2d 42, 45 (1943).

There is evidence in the record that Gutzkow's superiors did not provide him with a reasonable expectation of assistance. Gutzkow himself testified:

> [T]hen [the plant manager] got both me and Dan [the co-worker] together and he told us * * * that he couldn't put up with this child-like stuff, he's not a babysitter, and then he said that he's going to have the two of us working together every day for the next six months till we can learn to get along.

*Evi* [handwritten margin note]

Tru–Stone's president testified that he assured Gutzkow he would look into the problem and then delegated everything to the plant manager. The plant manager testified:

*Prez's retort* [handwritten margin note]

> I tried to get [Gutzkow] and [the co-worker] to work along, you know. You've got to work together in a shop.

This was the plant manager's sole testimony regarding his response to the harassment. We concur with the Commissioner's finding that, in view of the plant manager's failure to respond, Gutzkow was not actually provided with a "reasonable expectation of assistance."

The record also indicates that Gutzkow's section leader participated in the harassment. Gutzkow testified without contradiction that the section leader was similar to a foreman, i.e., a direct supervisor. According to Gutzkow, some time after he had complained to the president, the section leader called him names such as "slime," "scum" and "son-of-a-bitch," called his wife a slut, and told him that he was "never going to be off the shit list around here", that nobody liked him, and that he would make Gutzkow quit or get him fired.

*§ leader bullied* [handwritten margin note]

The supreme court has stated that a manager's knowledge should be imputed to an employer where the manager "performs basically a 'first level supervisory and managerial function.'" *McNabb v. Cub Foods,* 352 N.W.2d 378, 383 (Minn.1984). In *Dura Supreme v. Kienholz,* 381 N.W.2d 92 (Minn.Ct.App.1986), this court declined to hold that the employer had offered reasonable assurances of assistance where the employee's supervisor told the employee to take the harassment as a joke. Similarly, in *Porrazzo v. Nabisco Inc.,* 360 N.W.2d 662 (Minn.Ct.App.1985), we held that an employer was deemed to have had knowledge of continuing harassment where the supervisor was the source of many of the employee's problems.

Thus, here, the harassment by Gutzkow's section leader must be imputed to Tru–Stone. This harassment, in combination with the plant manager's failure to respond to the situation, negated the president's assurances of assistance. Since Gutzkow therefore received no real expectation of assistance, he had no duty to keep Tru–Stone apprised of the continuing harassment. Continued notification is necessary only after the employee has received an expectation of assistance. *See Larson,* 281 N.W.2d at 669; *Porrazzo,* 360 N.W.2d at 664.

Tru–Stone argues that because Gutzkow somehow "incited" the harassment, he did not have good cause to quit. We do not consider this issue, since there was no evidence that it was ever presented to the Commissioner's representative for review. *See Ruzynski v. Cub Foods, Inc.,* 378 N.W.2d 660, 663 (Minn.Ct.App.1985). However, we do note that neither the Commissioner's representative nor the referee found that Gutzkow incited the harassment. To the contrary, the Commissioner's representative found that Gutzkow's fighting was in response to the harassment.

### Decision

The record supports the Commissioner's determination that Gutzkow had good cause to quit his job due to harassment.

Affirmed.

### NOTES AND QUESTIONS

1. "Shop talk" (coarse or harsh language used without an intent to threaten, intimidate or cause emotional distress) and "horseplay" (physical interactions not intended to cause serious pain or harm) are a common means of relieving the tedium and tensions of work. The line between such conduct and abusive interactions is quite often thin and a matter of personal perception. Frequently, the fact patterns are not as clear as they appear to be in the *Tru–Stone* case. One way management can deal with the problem of knowing when that thin line has been crossed is to prohibit and penalize all observed or reported instances of shop talk and horseplay. Is that sound management policy? Is it sound public policy to encourage management to adopt that approach?

2. State and federal civil rights laws protect employees from sexual harassment. However, enforcement of such laws is time consuming and less than 100% effective. As an interim or an alternative measure, an employee may decide to take the self-help avenue of leaving the employment. Courts have held that sexual harassment need not reach the point of being unbearable before it justifies quitting. If the employee has called the harassment problem to management's attention and management has not provided relief, the employee may quit without losing eligibility for unemployment insurance

benefits. *See, e.g., McNabb v. Cub Foods*, 352 N.W.2d 378 (Minn. 1984). In *Chapman v. Indus. Comm'n*, 700 P.2d 1099 (Utah 1985), the claimant tolerated harassment for five years without complaining to management, and then quit. The court held that she did not have just cause to quit inasmuch as she had not given her employer an opportunity to resolve the problem, and there was no showing that a request for management's intervention would have been futile. Nevertheless, the court concluded that principles of equity and the act's protective purpose entitled the claimant to receive unemployment benefits.

3. In addition to unemployment benefits, if harassment or an abusive work environment is based on sex, race, religion or national origin, the victim has a claim for relief under Title VII of the Civil Rights Act of 1964, 42 U.S.C. § 2000e–2(a)(1). *Harris v. Forklift Sys., Inc.*, 510 U.S. 17, 114 S.Ct. 367, 126 L.Ed.2d 295 (1993).

4. In *NLRB v. Gullett Gin Co.*, 340 U.S. 361, 71 S.Ct. 337, 95 L.Ed. 337 (1951), the Court held that backpay remedies under the National Labor Relations Act need not be reduced by the amount of unemployment compensation the claimant received. The Court did not reach the issue of whether the NLRB would violate the Act if it allowed such deductions. A majority of federal appeals courts have held that unemployment compensation may not be deducted from backpay in remedying prohibited employment discrimination. The rationale supporting this conclusion is that such deductions reduce the remedy's deterrent impact and that the public interest served by such protective legislation requires a remedy that deters as well as makes whole. A few circuits permit the trial court to make such deductions in the exercise of its discretion to shape an appropriate remedy. *Gaworski v. ITT Commercial Finance Corp.*, 17 F.3d 1104, 1113 (8th Cir.1994).

## HOBBIE v. UNEMPLOYMENT APPEALS COMMISSION

United States Supreme Court, 1987
480 U.S. 136, 107 S.Ct. 1046, 94 L.Ed.2d 190

JUSTICE BRENNAN delivered the opinion of the Court.

Appellant's employer discharged her when she refused to work certain scheduled hours because of sincerely-held religious convictions adopted after beginning employment. The question to be decided is whether Florida's denial of unemployment compensation benefits to appellant violates the Free Exercise Clause of the First Amendment of the Constitution, as applied to the States through the Fourteenth Amendment.[1]

### I

Lawton and Company (Lawton), a Florida jeweler, hired appellant Paula Hobbie in October 1981. She was employed by Lawton for 2 1/2 years, first as trainee and then as assistant manager of a retail jewelry store. In April 1984, Hobbie informed her immediate supervisor that she

---

1. An employer's duty to accommodate the religious beliefs of employees is governed by Title VII of the Civil Rights Act of 1964, 42 U.S.C. § 2000e *et seq.* Hobbie has not sought relief pursuant to Title VII in this action.

was to be baptized into the Seventh–Day Adventist Church and that, for religious reasons, she would no longer be able to work on her Sabbath, from sundown on Friday to sundown on Saturday. The supervisor devised an arrangement with Hobbie: she agreed to work evenings and Sundays, and he agreed to substitute for her whenever she was scheduled to work on a Friday evening or a Saturday.

This arrangement continued until the general manager of Lawton learned of it in June 1984. At that time, after a meeting with Hobbie and her minister, the general manager informed appellant that she could either work her scheduled shifts or submit her resignation to the company. When Hobbie refused to do either, Lawton discharged her.

On June 4, 1984, appellant filed a claim for unemployment compensation with the Florida Department of Labor and Employment Security. Under Florida law, unemployment compensation benefits are available to persons who become "unemployed through no fault of their own." Fla. Stat. § 443.021 (1985). Lawton contested the payment of benefits on the ground that Hobbie was "disqualified for benefits" because she had been discharged for "misconduct connected with [her] work." § 443.101(1)(a).

* * *

## II

Under our precedents, the Appeals Commission's disqualification of appellant from receipt of benefits violates the Free Exercise Clause of the First Amendment, applicable to the States through the Fourteenth Amendment. *Sherbert v. Verner,* 374 U.S. 398, 83 S.Ct. 1790, 10 L.Ed.2d 965 (1963); *Thomas v. Review Board of the Indiana Employment Security Div.,* 450 U.S. 707, 101 S.Ct. 1425, 67 L.Ed.2d 624 (1981). In *Sherbert* we considered South Carolina's denial of unemployment compensation benefits to a Sabbatarian who, like Hobbie, refused to work on Saturdays. The Court held that the State's disqualification of Sherbert

> "force[d] her to choose between following the precepts of her religion and forfeiting benefits, on the one hand, and abandoning one of the precepts of her religion in order to accept work, on the other hand. Governmental imposition of such a choice puts the same kind of burden upon the free exercise of religion as would a fine imposed against [her] for her Saturday worship." 374 U.S., at 404, 83 S.Ct., at 1794.

We concluded that the State had imposed a burden upon Sherbert's free exercise rights that had not been justified by a compelling state interest.

In *Thomas,* too, the Court held that a State's denial of unemployment benefits unlawfully burdened an employee's right to free exercise of religion. Thomas, a Jehovah's Witness, held religious beliefs that forbade his participation in the production of armaments. He was forced to leave his job when the employer closed his department and transferred him to a division that fabricated turrets for tanks. Indiana then denied Thomas unemployment compensation benefits. The Court found that the employee had been "put to a choice between fidelity to religious belief or cessation of work" and that the coercive impact of the forfeiture of benefits in this situation was undeniable:

> " 'Not only is it apparent that appellant's declared ineligibility for benefits derives solely from the practice of * * * religion, but the pressure upon [the employee] to forego that practice is unmistakable.' " *Thomas,* 450 U.S., at 717, 101 S.Ct., at 1431 (quoting *Sherbert, supra,* 374 U.S., at 404, 83 S.Ct., at 1794).

We see no meaningful distinction among the situations of Sherbert, Thomas, and Hobbie. We again affirm, as stated in *Thomas:*

> "Where the state conditions receipt of an important benefit upon conduct proscribed by a religious faith, *or where it denies such a benefit because of conduct mandated by religious belief, thereby putting substantial pressure on an adherent to modify his behavior and to violate his beliefs,* a burden upon religion exists. While the compulsion may be indirect, the infringement upon free exercise is nonetheless substantial." *Id.,* 450 U.S. at 717–718, 101 S.Ct., at 1431–1432 (emphasis added).

Both *Sherbert* and *Thomas* held that such infringements must be subjected to strict scrutiny and could be justified only by proof by the State of a compelling interest. The Appeals Commission does not seriously contend that its denial of benefits can withstand strict scrutiny; rather it urges that we hold that its justification should be determined under the less rigorous standard articulated in Chief Justice Burger's opinion in *Bowen v. Roy,* 476 U.S. 693, 707–708, 106 S.Ct. 2147, 2156, 90 L.Ed.2d 735 (1986): "the Government meets its burden when it demonstrates that a challenged requirement for governmental benefits, neutral and uniform in its application, is a reasonable means of promoting a legitimate public interest." Five Justices expressly rejected this argument in *Roy.* . . . We reject the argument again today. * * *

The Appeals Commission also suggests two grounds upon which we might distinguish *Sherbert* and *Thomas* from the present case. First, the Appeals Commission points out that in *Sherbert* the employee was deemed completely ineligible for benefits under South Carolina's unemployment insurance scheme because she would not accept work that conflicted with her Sabbath. The Appeals Commission contends that, under Florida law, Hobbie faces only a limited disqualification from receipt of benefits, and that once this fixed term has been served, she will again "be on an equal footing with all other workers, provided she avoids employment that conflicts with her religious beliefs." * * *

This distinction is without substance. The immediate effects of ineligibility and disqualification are identical, and the disqualification penalty is substantial. Moreover, *Sherbert* was given controlling weight in *Thomas,* which involved a disqualification provision similar in all relevant respects to the statutory section implicated here. See *Thomas,* 450 U.S., at 709–710, n. 1, 101 S.Ct., at 1427–1428, n. 1.

The Appeals Commission also attempts to distinguish this case by arguing that, unlike the employees in *Sherbert* and *Thomas,* Hobbie was the "agent of change" and is therefore responsible for the consequences of the conflict between her job and her religious beliefs. In *Sherbert* and *Thomas,* the employees held their respective religious beliefs at the time of hire; subsequent changes in the conditions of employment made *by the employer* caused the conflict between work and belief. In this case, Hobbie's beliefs changed during the course of her employment, creating a conflict between job and faith that had not previously existed. The Appeals Commission contends that "it is * * * unfair for an employee to adopt religious beliefs that conflict with existing employment and expect to continue the employment without compromising those beliefs" and that this "intentional disregard of the employer's interests * * * constitutes misconduct." Brief for Appellee Appeals Comm'n 20–21.

In effect, the Appeals Commission asks us to single out the religious convert for different, less favorable treatment than that given an individual whose adherence to his or her faith precedes employment. We decline to do so. The First Amendment protects the free exercise rights of employees who adopt religious beliefs or convert from one faith to another after they are hired. The timing of Hobbie's conversion is immaterial to our determination that her free exercise rights have been burdened; the salient inquiry under the Free Exercise Clause is the burden involved. In *Sherbert, Thomas,* and the present case, the employee was forced to choose between fidelity to religious belief and continued employment; the forfeiture of unemployment benefits for choosing the former over the latter brings unlawful coercion to bear on the employee's choice.

Finally, we reject the Appeals Commission's argument that the awarding of benefits to Hobbie would violate the Establishment Clause. This Court has long recognized that the government may (and sometimes must) accommodate religious practices and that it may do so without violating the Establishment Clause. See *e.g., Wisconsin v. Yoder,* 406 U.S. 205, 92 S.Ct. 1526, 32 L.Ed.2d 15 (1972) (judicial exemption of Amish children from compulsory attendance at high school); *Walz v. Tax Comm'n,* 397 U.S. 664, 90 S.Ct. 1409, 25 L.Ed.2d 697 (1970) (tax exemption for churches). As in *Sherbert,* the accommodation at issue here does not entangle the State in an unlawful fostering of religion:

> "In holding as we do, plainly we are not fostering the 'establishment' of the Seventh-day Adventist religion in South Carolina, for the extension of unemployment benefits to Sabbatarians in common with Sunday worshippers reflects nothing more than the governmental obligation of neutrality in the face of religious differences, and does not represent the involvement of religious with secular institutions

which it is the object of the Establishment Clause to forestall." 374 U.S., at 409, 83 S.Ct., at 1796.[11]

### III

We conclude that Florida's refusal to award unemployment compensation benefits to appellant violated the Free Exercise Clause of the First Amendment. Here, as in *Sherbert* and *Thomas,* the State may not force an employee "to choose between following the precepts of her religion and forfeiting benefits, * * * and abandoning one of the precepts of her religion in order to accept work." *Sherbert, supra,* at 404, 83 S.Ct., at 1794. The judgment of the Florida Fifth District Court of Appeal is therefore

*Reversed.*

[In a concurring opinion Justice Powell noted that the *Roy* case reference to a standard less rigorous than the compelling interest test explicitly did not refer to a religiously oriented exemption mechanism created by the government. Justice Stevens also concurred separately in an opinion that asserted that denying the unemployment benefit is a religiously based denial of equal treatment. Chief Justice Rehnquist dissented on the ground that he adhered to his dissent in *Thomas.*]

### NOTES AND QUESTIONS

1.   Recall the *Stepp* case, above at subchapter B(2). At one point Stepp asserted that her unwillingness to work with body fluids from suspected AIDS patients was based on her religious belief that "AIDS is God's plague on man and performing the tests would go against God's will." Does the 14th Amendment protect her right to unemployment insurance benefits if she quits rather than violates that religious belief?

2.   Alfred Smith and Galen Black were discharged from employment by a private drug rehabilitation organization in Oregon because they ingested peyote as part of the sacrament at a ceremony of the Native American Church. Peyote is a bitter tasting plant whose ingestion induces hallucinations. Although its possession, transfer and use are generally prohibited as a controlled substance, federal regulations and the laws of almost half the states

---

**11.** The Appeals Commission contends that this Court's recent decision in *Estate of Thornton v. Caldor,* 472 U.S. 703, 105 S.Ct. 2914, 86 L.Ed.2d 557 (1985), reveals that the accommodation sought by Hobbie would constitute an unlawful establishment of religion. In *Thornton,* we held that a Connecticut statute that provided employees with an absolute right not to work on their Sabbath violated the Establishment Clause. The Court determined that the State's "unyielding weighting in favor of Sabbath observers over all other interests * * * ha[d] a primary effect that impermissibly advance[d] a particular religious practice," *id.,* at 710, 105 S.Ct., at 2918, and placed an unacceptable burden on employers and co-workers because it provided no exceptions for special circumstances regardless of the hardship resulting from the mandatory accommodation.

In contrast, Florida's provision of unemployment benefits to religious observers does not single out a particular class of such persons for favorable treatment and thereby have the effect of implicitly endorsing a particular religious belief. Rather, the provision of unemployment benefits generally available within the State to religious observers who must leave their employment due to an irreconcilable conflict between the demands of work and conscience neutrally accommodates religious beliefs and practices, without endorsement.

permit its use in religious ceremonies. Oregon, however, does not provide for such an exclusion. Nevertheless, no effort was made to prosecute Smith or Black and there was only one reported case in Oregon of a prosecution for religious use of peyote. Smith and Black were denied unemployment insurance benefits on the theory that they had been dismissed for good cause, and by a six-to-three vote, that decision was upheld by the U.S. Supreme Court. The majority reasoned that because the controlled substance law is not aimed at religious activity, its constitutionality is not subject to strict scrutiny standards. Therefore, it found the prohibition against peyote use a valid prohibition against socially harmful conduct and concluded it was constitutionally permissible to treat the dismissal as a legally justified disqualification from receiving unemployment benefits. *Employment Div. v. Smith*, 494 U.S. 872, 110 S.Ct. 1595, 108 L.Ed.2d 876 (1990). Putting aside the First Amendment issue that divided the Court, would it have been appropriate to treat such off-the-job activity as "misconduct" had the employer not been a drug rehabilitation organization?

In November of 1993, the Religious Freedom Restoration Act, Pub. L. No. 103–141, 107 Stat. 1488 (codified at 42 U.S.C. § 2000b), was signed into law. The Act's statement of findings asserts: "[I]n *Employment Division v. Smith*, 494 U.S. 872, 110 S.Ct. 1595, 108 L.Ed.2d 876 (1990) the Supreme Court virtually eliminated the requirement that the government justify burdens on religious exercise imposed by laws neutral toward religion * * *." Pub. L. No. 103–141, § 2(a)(4). Section 3 of Pub. L. No. 103–141 declares that "government shall not substantially burden a person's exercise of religion even if the burden results from a rule of general applicability" unless it "demonstrates that application of the burden to the person—(1) is in furtherance of a compelling governmental interest; and (2) is the least restrictive means of furthering that compelling governmental interest." Does Pub. L. No. 103–141 overrule the Court's holding in *Smith?* The Court resolved that question in *City of Boerne v. Flores*, 521 U.S. 507, 117 S.Ct. 2157, 138 L.Ed.2d 624 (1997), when it declared the Act unconstitutional.

## C. GROUP HEALTH PLAN CONTINUATION

The Consolidated Omnibus Budget Reconciliation Act of 1986 (CO-BRA) was a massive piece of legislation that, among other things, added to the Employee Retirement Income Security Act (ERISA) provisions that imposed certain requirements for group health benefits plans sponsored by employers of 20 or more workers. These requirements enable workers and their dependents to continue their participation in the medical benefits, at their own expense, after the worker's employment is terminated or after the relationship qualifying the dependent as a plan beneficiary has ended. This right similarly applies when an employee's work hours are reduced below the plan's threshold for participation. [See the Employee Retirement Income Security Act in the Appendix at 29 U.S.C. §§ 1161–67.] The right to continued participation in a group health plan is valuable because individual health insurance is generally much more costly.

The right to continuation of benefits is not available to an employee who was dismissed for "gross misconduct." The duration for which the employee or dependents must be allowed to continue to participate is 18 months if the covered worker was dismissed from employment; in other situations the available duration of continued participation is 36 months. For example, when an employee's children cease to be qualified dependents under the plan, due to reaching majority or leaving school, they can elect to continue the insurance coverage, at their own expense, for three more years. Similarly, a deceased worker's spouse or a divorced spouse is entitled to make the same election. The Act permits an employer to add up to 2% to the premium cost for such continued participation. There is a 60–day period during which the claimant can elect to exercise the right to continue in the group health plan.

The COBRA amendments do not require an employer to continue the group health plan itself. Thus, if the plan is terminated, all participants— current workers, former workers and their dependents—lose their medical insurance protection. *See, e.g., Local 217, Hotel & Restaurant Employees Union v. MHM, Inc.*, 976 F.2d 805 (2d Cir. 1992).

The issue of health insurance benefits continuation arises in other contexts addressed by ERISA, which was amended in 1996 to add prohibitions against employer sponsored group health insurance plans establishing eligibility rules based on prior or current health, genetic or claims history. Similarly, the amendments prohibit charging different premiums based on such variable characteristics in a covered individual's background. Another 1996 change, the Mental Health Parity Act, prohibits imposing more stringent coverage limits on mental health treatment benefits than are imposed for other types of health care benefits.

## D.  FEDERAL PLANT CLOSING ACT

Between 1969 and 1976, 25 million jobs were created by new plant openings, or an average of 3.6 million jobs a year. In the same period, 22 million jobs were lost by plant closings, an average loss of 3.2 million jobs a year. In other words, for every 110 jobs created, about 100 were lost. This trend continued into the 1980s. Thus, between 1981–86, approximately 2.2 million jobs were dislocated annually. Moreover, in recent years, newly created jobs have been very different—in educational level, skill, wages, and employment conditions—from those lost. BARRY BLUE-STONE & BENNETT HARRISON, THE DEINDUSTRIALIZATION OF AMERICA: PLANT CLOSINGS, COMMUNITY ABANDONMENT AND THE DISMANTLING OF BASIC INDUSTRY 29–31 (1982); Francis W. Horvath, *The Pulse of Economic Change: Displaced Workers of 1981–1985*, 110 MONTHLY LAB. REV. 3 (Jun. 1987).

The enormous economic and emotional impact on the individuals directly affected by massive job dislocation, and on the communities in which they live, has become a topic of serious discussion. Although many employers have made efforts to reduce these burdens, others have not. As reported to Congress:

> According to a recent GAO survey of employers with more than 100 employees, a full 20% of such employers provide no "general notice"

to those affected that the plant will be closed or that a permanent layoff will take place (general notice is information that the closing or layoff will take place specifying neither the particular workers affected nor the date of the closure). A quarter provide between one day and two weeks general notice. Only 18% provide general notice of three months or more. Similarly, such employers have not been forthcoming with "specific notice" of a closing or mass layoff, i.e., information that specific workers will lose their jobs on a particular day. Distressingly, almost a quarter—23%—provide *no specific notice at all*. More than half—54%—provide two weeks or less. Only 9% provide specific notice of 3 months or more for a plant closing or mass layoff.

When these figures are disaggregated and the notice given blue collar workers is studied, the results are even less impressive. Thirty percent of the employers studied provide their blue collar workers with no specific notice at all that jobs will be lost. Sixty-five percent give less than two weeks specific notice. The average non-union blue collar worker receives two days of specific notice.

S. Rep. No. 100–62, 100th Cong., 1st Sess., at 12–13 (1987) (emphasis in original).

Those supporting legislation protecting employees in plant closing or mass layoff situations argued that effective programs for assisting dislocated workers depend upon adequate notice of impending displacement. A study published shortly after Congress heeded such arguments examined the events surrounding and subsequent to the job displacement of over 2,500 workers whose plant was closed or relocated. The study found that, to a statistically significant degree, workers receiving at least 60 days' advance notice of their impending job loss were unemployed for shorter periods and suffered less lost earnings than those who did not receive such notice. The study also found that shorter periods of advance layoff notice had no significant impact on unemployment or lost earnings. Stephen Nord & Yuan Ting, *The Impact of Advance Notice of Plant Closings on Earnings and the Probability of Unemployment*, 44 INDUS. & LAB. REL. REV. 681, 688 (1991). Additionally, it has been noted that every industrialized Western nation, as well as Japan, has more elaborate worker protections than an advance notice requirement.

The position of those opposed to such requirements were encapsulated in the separate statement of Professor Krueger in a report published by the National Academy of Sciences:

Advance notification of layoffs is undoubtedly beneficial to those workers who will lose their jobs. If there were no negative side effects associated with advance notification, it would clearly be beneficial to all.

There will be several side effects, however, if notification is mandatory. First, the necessary enforcement apparatus would increase the cost of doing business. Second, for all firms, especially for risky ones, knowledge that layoffs could not be made on short notice would increase incentives to use capital and hire fewer workers. To the extent that fewer jobs would be created, the proposed requirement would hurt the employment prospects of those the proposal is designed to assist. That mandatory periods prior to layoffs can result in smaller levels of employment has been well documented in a number of developing countries. Third, requirements of advance notification reduce the flexibility of firms already in difficulty. The requirement is, in effect, the same as a tax for these firms.

NAT'L ACAD. OF SCI. ET AL., REPORT, TECHNOLOGY AND EMPLOYMENT: INNOVATION AND GROWTH IN THE U.S. ECONOMY 216 (Richard M. Cyert & David C. Mowery eds., 1987).

The Worker Adjustment and Retraining Notification Act (WARN), which emerged from this debate, imposes on all but smaller employers, a duty to give employees or their collective bargaining representative, and the local government unit, sixty days advance notice of: a) shut downs of a single employment facility resulting, for at least 50 full-time employees, in termination or long term layoff or reduction of work hours by more than half, and b) long term layoffs affecting the lesser of at least a third of the work force or 500 employees. Generally, employers with fewer than 100 full time employees are excluded from the Act.

An employer that fails to give the required advance notice is liable to the employees for backpay equal to the normal weekly compensation, including benefits and contributions to benefit funds, they would have received during the notice period. In effect, the Act provides the employee with mandatory severance pay in lieu of the advance notice. This statutory claim is in addition to any other contractual or statutory rights or remedies the employees may have. Furthermore, unless it promptly pays that equivalent to mandatory severance pay, the employer can be held liable for a civil penalty of up to $500 for each day it failed to give advance notice to the local government. In the event of transfer of a business, the buyer becomes the employer responsible for satisfying the notice provisions as of the day after the effective date of the sale.

The Act's provisions do not apply to situations in which the employees knew when they were hired that the employment would be for a limited duration. Neither does it apply if the layoff or termination is caused by a natural disaster. Nor does it apply to work stoppages initiated in the course of collective bargaining, nor to the replacement of economic strikers. The notice requirement is also excused when the layoff or termination results from a relocation or consolidation of the enterprise and, within six months, the workers will have the opportunity to transfer to a new worksite within commuting distance from the former one. Similarly, the notice requirement is excused if, within six months of termination at the old site the worker accepts a transfer to new employment, no matter how distant, and the worker was given at least 30 days to weigh the transfer offer. In addition, the required notice period is reduced to the extent that the employer was actively seeking capital or business that would be sufficient to postpone the shutdown and had a good faith belief that giving the notice would preclude the employer from obtaining that business or capital. The notice period is also reduced to the extent that it resulted from unforeseeable business circumstances.

No provision is made in the federal plant closing law for an indemnity fund to ensure that workers will in fact be able to collect compensation due in the event they are unable to collect from the employer. Nor is there any provision establishing the bankruptcy priority of the employee's claim if the employer fails to provide the pay in lieu of giving the required 60 days notice. Although severance pay is expressly included in the limited third priority claim available under the Bankruptcy Code for pre-bankruptcy petition earnings, it is unclear whether the mandatory payment due in lieu of notice should be treated as severance pay for purposes of the Code. If all or part of the notice period occurs after the bankruptcy petition, the issue is further clouded by the fact that it is unclear whether severance pay claims arising after the petition, let alone this statutory payment in lieu of notice, are entitled to any priority under the Bankruptcy Code.

The Act is silent, too, regarding employee rights to seek alternative employment during the notice period. Many other countries that give workers a right to pretermination notice include entitlement to use a specific amount of paid work time during the notice period (e.g., a half day a week) to search for other employment.

One commentator has observed that because WARN excludes a large portion of part time workers, it is less protective of women than of men. Catherine Connolly, *The Failure of WARN to Warn: Hidden Gender Discrimination in the Worker Adjustment and Retraining Notification Act*, 29 LAND & WATER L. REV. 557 (1994).

Courts have divided over the impact of WARN payments on unemployment compensation claims. For example, in *Capitol Castings, Inc. v. Arizona Department of Economic Security*, 171 Ariz. 57, 828 P.2d 781 (App. 1992), the court concluded that WARN payments for failure to provide the statutory notice are not wages since they are payable regardless of whether the worker has found new employment. Accordingly, it reasoned that such payments do not defeat or reduce the worker's unemployment compensation claim. In contrast, in *Labor & Industrial Relations Commission v. Division of Employment Security*, 856 S.W.2d 376 (Mo. Ct. App. 1993), the court reasoned that unemployment compensation is available only when the worker cannot rely on receiving wages and that since there is no insecurity respecting WARN payments, those payments "are fully deductible from Missouri unemployment benefits." The Missouri decision does not explain whether that deduction means that the period for which unemployment benefits begin is delayed until the period of the WARN payments has been exhausted or whether the WARN payments supplant unemployment benefits and the period is part of the total duration for which unemployment benefits may be received.

Federal appellate courts are split over the question of whether the notice remedy is sixty days of wages less the number of days for which notice was given or whether it is only for the number of work days for which the employee would have been scheduled to work during the period for which notice was not given. The former approach was adopted in *United Steelworkers of America v. North Star Steel Company, Inc.*, 5 F.3d 39 (3d Cir. 1993), *cert. denied*, 510 U.S. 1114, 114 S.Ct. 1060, 127 L.Ed.2d 380 (1994). The court explained that the required notice is counted in calendar days, not work days, that the Act makes no mention of work days, and therefore, the payment in lieu of notice is for each calendar day of violation. The court also pointed out that the remedy is not merely for lost earnings, as evidenced by the fact that no deduction is made for subsequent earnings if the worker is dismissed without any notice. However, a different approach was adopted in *Carpenters District Council of New Orleans & Vicinity v. Dillard Department Stores, Inc.*, 15 F.3d 1275 (5th Cir. 1994), *cert. denied*, 513 U.S. 1126, 115 S.Ct. 933, 130 L.Ed.2d 879 (1995). The latter court reasoned that the remedy is to replace what the employee would have been able to earn had sixty days of notice been given and, therefore, the proper damages measurement should look to what the worker normally earned during a sixty-day period. As in the latter decision, most courts hold that the notice period is 60 calendar days starting with the day after termination or layoff, and damages are calculated on the basis of what the employees would have earned had the employer allowed them to work during the entire notice period, less what they in fact were compensated during the period of notice. *See, e.g., Breedlove v. Earthgrains Baking Co., Inc.*, 140 F.3d 797 (8th Cir. 1998), *cert. denied*, 525 U.S. 921, 119 S.Ct. 276, 142 L.Ed.2d 228 (1998).

In early 1993, a Congressionally sponsored eleven state study of the impact of the federal plant closing law reported that over half of the employers that closed plants or laid off workers were not obligated by federal law to provide the sixty-day notice because the work disruption did not affect a large enough segment of the work force. The study also found that about half of the employers involved in circumstances requiring that the statutory notice be given failed to provide it and almost 30% of the remaining employers gave less than the full sixty days of notice. Despite the widespread violations, the study revealed that local officials are reluctant to seek civil penalties under the Act for fear that the community will gain a reputation of being anti-business. Additionally, it was reported that lawyers are reluctant to take plant closing cases because of the expense and difficulty of learning whether the circumstances came within the Act's parameters and whether the exemption conditions were applicable. Finally, about 29% of the employers that gave notice claimed they detected some reduction in productivity after notice was given.

A study comparing employer practices in giving pre-layoff notice before and after the adoption of WARN concluded: "The evidence suggests that *at most* there was only a slight increase in the length in the notice specifically provided under the Act." John T. Addison & McKinley L.

Blackburn, *The Worker Adjustment and Retraining Notification Act: Effects on Notice Provision*, 47 INDUS. & LAB. REL. REV. 650, 660 (1994) (emphasis in original).

## NOTES AND QUESTIONS

1.  Why mandate pretermination notice in situations involving substantial long-term layoffs and mass terminations but not in situations involving short-term layoffs or long-term layoffs or terminations involving small segments of the workforce?

2.  A foundation was established to receive endowments for the support of a hospital. The foundation trustees were appointed by the hospital's board of directors from among the members of the hospital's board. For several years the hospital's operating deficits were covered by income distributions from the foundation. Due to increased hospital deficits, distributions were increased to the point that invasions were made on the corpus of the foundation's funds. After several years of invading the corpus, the foundation was advised by legal counsel that such activity might jeopardize the foundation's tax exempt status and subject the trustees to liability. It was further advised to discontinue distributions to the hospital until the corpus was restored or a favorable ruling was received from the I.R.S. The hospital board weighed this advice on February 26, at which time the hospital administrator estimated that current cash receipts would allow it to remain open only another two weeks. The board then announced to its employees that the hospital would be closed as of March 14. It did not pay the employees for the additional notice period. According to the employees who sought a WARN recovery, the foundation's legal advice was erroneous because its charter, approved by the I.R.S., expressly permitted invasions of principal. The employees' suit was rejected in *Jurcev v. Central Community Hospital*, 7 F.3d 618 (7th Cir. 1993), *cert. denied*, 511 U.S. 1081, 114 S.Ct. 1830, 128 L.Ed.2d 459 (1994). The court found that the hospital did not control the foundation and could not force it to distribute funds to the hospital because the board members who held both posts had separate fiduciary responsibilities in their capacity as foundation trustees. The court concluded that the termination of fund distributions left the hospital in a financial situation that caused it to close and therefore, excused it from the additional notice period. Perhaps most significantly, the court ruled that the hospital was not required to prove that it had inadequate assets to enable it to stay open for the full sixty days.

3.  Are not the benefits granted by the Worker Adjustment and Retraining Notification Act largely illusory? To the extent that the benefits are not illusory, does this type of legislation injure workers by impeding management's flexibility in adjusting to technological, market and financial changes?

A study has shown that when combined with an active program of assisting employees with placement counseling and related services, "all industrial plants studied noted improvements in quality and productivity in the final phase of the facility's operation." RONALD E. BERENBEIM, COMPANY PROGRAMS TO EASE THE IMPACT OF SHUTDOWNS 14 (1986). Management officials surveyed attributed this, among other things, to the release of anxiety once the uncertainty of the plant's future had been resolved and good will generated by an active placement program. Additionally, it has been observed that employees actively seeking new employment may be particularly diligent in their current job performance to obtain good references for prospective new employment. Contrast these observations with the survey of management that reported 29% stating there was a notable loss of productivity after the WARN notice was given.

4. The loss of highly qualified employees who find other jobs soon after they learn the "ship is sinking" need not be viewed as an adverse consequence of mandatory advance notice. From the perspective of social costs, does the community not benefit from them putting their talents to work for better managed organizations? *See* John T. Addison & Petro Portugal, *The Effect of Advance Notification of Plant Closings on Unemployment*, 41 INDUS. & LAB. REL. REV. 3, 13 (1987).

5. Professor Bob Hepple of Cambridge University notes that throughout the world, employment law "generally draws a distinction between (1) the power of the employer to terminate the employment relationship when the job itself will continue to exist; and (2) the power of the employer to make workforce reductions for economic, technical or organizational reasons." Bob Hepple, *Flexibility and Security of Employment, in* COMPARATIVE LABOUR LAW AND INDUSTRIAL RELATIONS IN INDUSTRIALIZED MARKETS, 277, 280 (Robert Blanpain ed., 6th ed. 1998). Hepple observes that because work force reductions have the potential of creating serious social and economic problems for the community, often the decision to make such reductions is subject to special rules. In some countries, such as Norway and Sweden, employees have a right to be transferred to any suitable work within the enterprise before they can be dismissed for a lack of work in their normal job positions. Similarly, employers often are required to share reduced work hours among the workforce by eliminating overtime and placing workers on shortened work schedules. Many European nations provide workers on such reduced schedules with pay subsidies funded either from the unemployment insurance program or special government funds. Similar programs are available in Canada and Japan.

Notice requirements and mandatory severance pay are imposed by statute or collective agreement in many countries to give employers a financial disincentive to resort to workforce reductions. Such payments also provide a further cushion for the employee so long as such payments are not eventually absorbed by being treated as deductible from unemployment insurance benefits. An alternative is to require the employer to supplement the worker's unemployment insurance benefit so as to pay a larger percentage of the worker's most recent wage.

Another form of restriction on workforce reductions that has been adopted in other countries is the establishment of legally enforceable criteria to guide the selection of those who are to be severed. Typically, these criteria look to factors such as job or enterprise seniority, age, and even the number of dependents.

6. In *First National Maintenance Corp. v. NLRB*, 452 U.S. 666, 101 S.Ct. 2573, 69 L.Ed.2d 318 (1981), the Supreme Court held that, at the least,

an employer whose workforce has a collective bargaining representative must negotiate with that representative at a meaningful time respecting the impact of a decision that will result in substantial work force dislocation. What is the effect of the federal plant closing law on that obligation?

7. Would it be more rational to integrate the financial responsibility of the employer under the federal plant closing law into unemployment compensation legislation? How does the financial responsibility established by the plant closing law differ from that created by unemployment insurance? How does the benefit differ? If Congress moves to provide some type of insurance funding to guaranty payment of the plant closing law benefit for failure to provide the statutory notice, should the premiums for that insurance be shared by employers and employees?

# E. RETURN TO WORK PROGRAMS

The most effective way to provide income security to jobless persons is to find them or help them find new employment. Worker efforts to find new jobs can be hampered not only by the scarcity of work, but also by inefficiencies in available methods of matching job seekers with job vacancies, mismatches between job needs and worker skills and experience, and inadequate motivation to obtain reemployment. A number of government programs are designed to overcome these employment barriers.

Lack of work experience, either in general or in the specific type of work, appears to be one factor that causes difficulty in efforts to find employment. Recent economic trends have increased the impact of this hurdle in searching for employment. For example, a study of 5.6 million workers age 20 or older with at least three years work experience who were jobless at some point in the five year period from 1987 to 1992 found that 52.1% lost their employment because the establishment where they worked closed or moved to a distant location and another 16.3% became unemployed because their job or shift had been abolished. As a result, "just over half of all displaced workers who had lost private nonagricultural wage and salary jobs, and who were reemployed in January 1992, had found jobs in different major industries." Jennifer M. Gardner, *Recession Swells Count of Displaced Workers*, 116 MONTHLY LAB. REV. 14, 14, 15, 17 (Jun. 1993). In the mid–1980s the portion finding jobs in new industries was even higher—60%. Older workers generally have greater difficulty finding new work under such circumstances. As a result, while the median duration of unemployment during the period of the above study was 8.3 weeks, it was 9.3 weeks for workers age 45–54 and 10.4 weeks for those 55 and older. J. Gardner, above at p. 17. Moreover, even when they find new employment, nearly half accept an earnings reduction. In the January 1992 study, 32% percent suffered earnings reductions of 20% or more. On the other hand, about 25% reported finding new employment paying 20% or more above their prior level of earnings.

For several decades, Congress has used two approaches to improve employment opportunities for certain workers who have special difficulties obtaining and retaining jobs. One approach is a tax credit that subsidizes the initial cost of employing such workers, the other finances or subsidizes the costs of job training and placement.

The Targeted Job Tax Credit (26 U.S.C. § 51) targets eight categories of unemployed persons based either on their family's low income or the worker's personal history and job search difficulties. Among the targeted groups are military veterans, ex-felons, youths from impoverished families, recipients of welfare benefits, and persons referred by vocational rehabilitation programs. Employers that hire workers who qualify under the target criteria can take a tax credit of 40% of the first $6,000 in wages paid during the worker's first year on the job. An employer that hires targeted youths for summer employment can take the credit for up to the first $3,000 in wages paid. Additional requirements are designed to prevent an employer from churning such workers through its workforce solely to obtain the tax credit.

For several decades Congress had piecemeal adopted various programs to encourage job training and placement for the chronically unemployed. These were administered through a variety of agencies including the Department of Defense, Department of Veterans Affairs, and Department of Education as well as the Department of Labor. In 1994, the Department of Labor issued a study that urged consolidation and restructuring of the numerous programs. In 1998, Congress consolidated and modified existing programs under the title Workforce Investment Act. Below are excerpts from the Department of Labor's 1994 report.

The evidence of growth in long-term unemployment, and the inability of our current approaches to respond effectively, is compelling:

—In 1992, 75 percent of laid-off workers were on permanent lay-off—the highest annual proportion since tracking began in 1967. The same proportion holds for 1993.

—The length of unemployment spells has increased over the last two decades. During the 1970s, an average of 11 percent of the unemployed were out of work for six months or longer. In the 1980s, long-term unemployment averaged 15 percent of total unemployment, and thus far in the 1990s it averages 16 percent. Last year 21 percent of the unemployed hadn't worked in six months—the second highest annual level since the end of World War II. Regular unemployment benefits, meanwhile, are only available for six months in most States.

—Between 1984 and 1989, an average of 1.8 million full-time workers were displaced annually due to plant closures, production cutbacks, or lay-offs. In 1990, the total reached 2.2 million. 1993's total is expected to be similar.

—A year after they lose their jobs, more than half of all displaced workers are still unemployed, or are employed in jobs paying less than 80 percent of their former wages.

—Workers who had held their jobs for six or more years experience particularly substantial losses in earnings. In Pennsylvania, five years after such workers were displaced, their average earnings were still 25 percent below their previous levels. The emotional and financial costs of job uncertainty and dislocation to workers, their families, and communities are substantial. The societal costs of a system that does not help its workers make smooth transitions in the labor market are mounting:

—Economic output and tax revenues decline when workers are idle or underemployed.

—The cost of regular unemployment insurance benefits, which are financed by taxes on employers, has averaged $24 billion a year (adjusting for inflation) over the past 5 years.

—The temporary emergency unemployment compensation program— targeted to reach the long-term unemployed who have exhausted their regular benefits—was enacted in November 1991, and had distributed $27 billion in benefits through December 1993.

—Despite the magnitude of these regular and temporary emergency UI costs, virtually none of these expenditures were systematically linked to reemployment services to ensure that the long-term unemployed received the help they need to obtain employment.

—As a result, some jobless workers also turn to other benefit programs for support, such as welfare and food stamps, thereby increasing budget outlays for other Federal and State programs. Some of these costs are expected to decline as the American economy continues to recover from recession, but cyclical recovery will only mitigate, not erase, the challenge of structural change.

\* \* \*

# CHAPTER XI

## RETIREMENT AND WELFARE BENEFIT PROGRAMS

■ ■ ■

## A. INTRODUCTION

Employer-provided pensions, health care, and insurance were virtually unknown at the dawn of the 20th century in the United States. The American Express Co. had a pension plan as early as 1875, but it applied to only a handful of the firm's employees, those with 20 years or more of service who were 60 years of age or older. At the time, many workers obtained benefits like these by joining one or more mutual aid societies, such as the Ancient Order of United Workman or the Ladies of the Maccabees. Some railroads began to establish pension programs at the end of the nineteenth century, and they were fairly common for railroads by the time of the First World War. These early pensions often included "no-binding-effect" clauses, but even if they didn't, courts commonly treated pensions and other deferred benefits as mere "gratuities" offered by the employer, that could be changed or revoked by the employer at any time before they were actually granted. See, e.g *Dolge v. Dolge*, 70 A.D. 517, 75 N.Y.S. 386 (1902). As the twentieth century went on, benefits provided by the employer increased in importance, while the role of the societies declined. Any number of factors contributed to the increased importance of employer provided benefits: the increased mobility of the population, the decision by many unions to make improved benefits a major bargaining objective, favorable tax treatment for employer provided pensions and benefits, and many others. Later in the century, the broadest implications of the 'gratuity theory' of pensions and other deferred benefits were largely discredited, and the theory was replaced with alternative theories for enforcing deferred benefit agreements including: promissory estoppel, unilateral contract, and deferred wages. See B. AARON, LEGAL STATUS OF EMPLOYEE BENEFIT RIGHTS UNDER PRIVATE PENSION PLANS 4–14 (1961). But even these improved theories left a need for legislation to protect employee interests.

By the end of the twentieth century, well over a quarter of compensation costs consisted of the cost of benefits. Thus far, the trend has continued into the twenty-first century. In a News Release on March 12, 2008, the Bureau of Labor Statistics offered this summary of compensation costs for employers in December 2007:

> Employer costs for employee compensation for civilian workers averaged $28.11 per hour worked in December 2007 * * *. Wages and salaries, which averaged $19.62, accounted for 69.8 percent of these costs, while benefits, which averaged $8.49, accounted for the remaining 30.2 percent. * * * Employers averaged $2.23 or 7.9 percent of total compensation for legally required benefits for every hour worked in December 2007. Legally required benefits—which include Social Security, Medicare, federal and state unemployment insurance, and workers' compensation—is only one of several benefit categories * * *.
>
> Employer costs for insurance benefits—life, health, and disability—averaged $2.34 per hour (8.3 percent of total compensation). Paid leave benefits (vacations, holidays, sick leave, and other leave) averaged $1.96 (7.0 percent); retirement and savings averaged $1.24 (4.4 percent); and supplemental pay averaged 72 cents (2.6 percent) per hour worked.

Obviously, benefits costs are now a very important component of compensation.

The first significant federal regulation of employee benefits was a 1909 tax code provision listing what benefit costs could be deducted by corporations as part of the reasonable cost of doing business. Tax provisions continue to provide powerful incentives in determining the structure of employer benefit packages because plans that meet statutory requirements are eligible for current employer tax deductions while the benefits from the plan are received by the employees on either a tax free or tax deferred basis. Federal labor relations law came into play in deciding what sorts of benefits constituted mandatory and permissive subjects of bargaining. See *Ford Motor Co. v. N.L.R.B.*, 441 U.S. 488, 99 S.Ct. 1842, 60 L.Ed.2d 420 (1979); *Inland Steel Co. v. N.L.R.B.*, 170 F.2d 247 (7th Cir. 1948), cert. denied, 336 U.S. 960, 69 S.Ct. 887, 93 L.Ed. 1112 (1949). When the courts decided that employee benefits were a mandatory subject of bargaining under the National Labor Relations Act, this allowed unions to bargain for such benefits to the point of impasse and strike. In many industries, it became common practice for a benefit program to be operated under the auspices of a union, making it possible for a construction worker or truck driver to maintain the same benefit package as he moved from one employer to another. A provision of the Taft–Hartley Act set some basic standards for how the funds involved in these programs were to be handled. See 29 U.S.C. § 186(c)(5). While the majority of these programs were well run, a few, including some sizable ones, were poorly managed or, in some instances, infiltrated by organized crime figures. Some went bankrupt. As a result, the Congress enacted the Pension and Welfare Plan Disclosure Act in 1958. Its objective was to make the plans "transparent," by requiring plan administrators to disclose their financial data periodically to beneficiaries. The statute was soon amended to require further reporting to the United States Department of Labor. Relatively few beneficiaries were able to follow all the intricacies of benefits accounting.

State law also provided some protection to beneficiaries. Many benefits were provided through insurance companies, for example, and regulation of those benefits had been turned back over to the states by the McCarran Ferguson Act, ch. 20, 59 Stat. 33 (1945) (codified as amended at 15 U.S.C. §§ 1011–1015 (2006)). Pension fund administrators could be treated as fiduciaries in some states under some state trust laws. (A few states were in the process of enacting more rigorous protections at the time ERISA was moving through the Congress.)

In the 1960s, pressure began to develop for more extensive regulation of benefit plans. This was fueled in part by the widely reported failure of the pension plan at a Studebaker automobile plant in Indiana. In that plant closure, over 4,000 workers, ranging in ages from forty to sixty, lost about eighty-five percent of the value of their vested retirement benefits.  James A. Wooten, *"The Most Glorious Story of Failure in the Business": The Studebaker–Packard Corporation and the Origins of ERISA*, 49 BUFF. L. REV. 683 (2001). Public concerns included not only the appropriate funding and termination of pensions, but also individual rights to pension credits in the face of employer discretion. A cabinet level committee, the President's Committee on Corporate Pension Funds, appointed by President Kennedy in 1962, issued its final report in 1964. The report recommended: (1) minimum vesting standards, (2) minimum funding standards, (3) further study of portable pension credits for employees changing jobs, (4) plan termination insurance, (5) a dollar limitation on contributions or benefits, (6) a limitation on the amount of employer securities used to fund a plan, and (7) disclosure provisions. *See generally* President's Committee On Corporate Pension Funds and Other Private Retirement and Welfare Programs, Public Policy and Private Pension Programs, A Report to the President on Private Employee Retirement Plans (Jan. 1965). It would be a decade later, however, before the final legislative product, the Employee Retirement Income Securities Act of 1974 (ERISA), would reach the desk of President Gerald Ford and be signed into law. 29 U.S.C. §§ 1001–1461.

As the statute's name indicates, the bulk of debate and discussion centered on standards for the funding and operation of retirement plans. The scope of the statute is broader than that, however. The Congress took the opportunity to amend the employee benefit provisions of the tax code and the disclosure requirements of the Pension and Welfare Plan Disclosure Act and included these in ERISA. As a result, ERISA covers not only pensions, but medical benefits and many other important deferred employee benefits.

The central focus on pensions, however, can be readily understood. Life expectancy has been on the increase in the United States, so that a worker who turns 61 will, on average, live to age 80 or beyond. Since the proportion of people who work full time starts to drop off fairly sharply at 62, this means that retirees need to plan for at least 20 to 30 years of income after they cease working. Moreover, some living expenses—particularly health care—may well increase during this period. It is a complex transaction to credit employees for years of service, finance deferred benefits based on that service and pay those benefits over a period of years. It is thus not surprising that it takes a very complex system of regulation, ERISA, to ensure that these benefits are properly funded, insured and paid despite employer incentives to not fund and to deny benefits.

In March 2010, Congress enacted the Patient Protection and Affordable Care Act (PPACA), Pub. L. 111–148, with amendments contained in the Health Care and Education Reconciliation Act of 2010 (HCERA), Pub. L. 111–152, following extended, and at times rancorous, debate. Some of its provisions will affect ERISA, such as a provision extending to all group health insurance the ERISA requirement that health plans provide an appeals mechanism (often arbitration) to challenge denials of coverage. The new statute's provisions are to be phased in over time, with most fully effective in 2014. The statute provides additional incentives for employers to provide health care plans for employees and their families; large employers who do not will pay a penalty. PPACA § 1511 et seq, as amended by HCERA § 1003. Small businesses that initiate health coverage will receive tax credits. PPACA § 1421 More than ninety per cent of the population will be required to obtain health insurance, either at work or through some other means, such as health benefit exchanges created under the new law. PPACA § 1501, as amended by HCERA § 1002; (for heath benefit exchanges see PPACA § 1521). Those who fail to do so will pay a penalty. Persons with very low income will be exempted from the penalty; a further set of exemptions deal with religious beliefs and members of Indian tribes.

## B. GENERAL STRUCTURE OF ERISA

ERISA was organized into four titles, three of them codified into Title 29, the "labor" title of United States Code. Title I is the most relevant to those practicing employment law. It sets standards about:

- what information must be maintained and disclosed to employees and to the Secretary of Labor (29 U.S.C. §§ 1021–1031);
- what rules a plan may have about who is entitled to participate, and about when an employee's rights to benefits vest (Id. §§ 1051–1061);
- funding of plans, particularly pension plans (Id. §§ 1081–1085);
- responsibilities of "fiduciaries" (Id. §§ 1101–1114);

- circumstances in which a former employee must be allowed to continue to participate in an employer's group health plan, usually at the employee's expense, after being fired or laid off (Id. §§ 1161–1169) (often referred to as "COBRA coverage"); and

- coverage and portability provisions of group health plans (Id. §§ 1181–1185c).

Title I also includes provisions for how these standards are to be administered and enforced. 29 U.S.C.A. §§ 1131–1148.

Title II contains tax law provisions as amendments to the Internal Revenue Code. 26 U.S.C.A. §§ 401–418E. ERISA does not require that an employer offer any benefit whatever to its workers. The tax rules on employee benefits do, however, offer a "carrot" to employers to encourage them to establish certain types of plans. For example, if a pension plan set up by an employer meets the standards of Title II, so that it constitutes a "qualified" plan, that employer is allowed to take a deduction for any money it pays into the pension trust fund in the year in which that contribution is made. The benefited employees, however, do not report that sum as income in the year when the employer contributes, nor do they report any share of the trust fund's earnings as income until they actually receive pension payments from that fund. This deferral of taxes is a substantial benefit, and it means that the ultimate payment of pension benefits can be achieved with far fewer dollars of employer contribution than would otherwise be the case. The cost to the U.S. government in tax forbearance or deferral for qualified employee benefit plans was over $292 billion in 2009.*

A similar situation exists with respect to health insurance. An individual can deduct medical expenses from taxable income only after those expenses exceed 7.5% of adjusted gross income. An employer, however, can deduct the full cost of an employee group health care plan that meets tax code standards, while none of the payments made to health care providers on behalf of the employee will be treated as taxable income. The converse of this favorable treatment of "qualified" plans is, as one would expect, a variety of tax liabilities if standards are not met. Sometimes the adverse consequence is primarily visited on the employer, through denial of a deduction; at other times an employee may also feel the pinch, by being required to pay tax on "imputed" income, including income that the employee has not yet received in cash. These tax benefits—granting deductions to employers and not treating benefits as income, or postponing taxes until a future time—offer powerful incentives for conforming with the standards set in the tax code provisions that were so extensively amended by ERISA's Title II. These health care tax code provisions are affected in significant ways by the PPACA, Pub. L. 111–148, as amended

---

* The approximate "tax expenditure" of the U.S. government received by employers and employees in forgone or deferred taxes on employee benefits in 2009 was as follows: medical benefits, $180 billion; employer pension plans, $48 billion; 401(k) plans, $46 billion; Keogh plans, $13 billion; parking benefits, $3 billion; life insurance, $2 billion. U.S DEPARTMENT OF COMMERCE, STATISTICAL ABSTRACT OF THE UNITED STATES: 2008, 127TH ED, 311 (2009).

by the HCERA, Pub. L. 111–152, particularly PPACA Title I, subtitles D, F and Title IX.

Many of the standards that must be met in order to "qualify" for favorable tax treatment have to do with Congressional judgments concerning what provisions in a plan are fair and equitable to the beneficiaries. Some of these "fairness" provisions mirror standards that appear in Title I of ERISA. Both 29 U.S.C.A. § 1056(d)(1) and Internal Revenue Code § 401(a)(13) require that a pension plan include a provision that "benefits under the plan may not be assigned or alienated," for example, thus protecting those benefits from most creditors. Other "fairness" provisions in the tax code are aimed at limiting the extent to which a benefit plan may be structured to favor more highly paid employees over those earning lower wages. These "anti discrimination" requirements often require detailed calculations and can be treacherous in application. There are, however, some relatively easy-to-understand "safe harbor" provisions available to employers that are willing to contribute at least 3% of employee salaries to a 401(k) plan. Other tax code provisions are aimed not so much at notions of fairness as at limiting the amount of loss of current tax revenues. These include limits on the amounts that can be contributed to various deferred compensation plans on behalf of an individual employee, and requiring that employees begin to receive minimum pension payouts by a certain age, so that taxes can start to be assessed against the investment income that has accumulated. Other standards have to do with maintaining the integrity of trust funds used to pay benefits, by imposing fiduciary standards and limiting conflicts of interests. As in the case of many "fairness" standards, these often have parallels in the labor law title.

Title III is devoted to additional provisions related to the jurisdiction, administration, and enforcement of ERISA. Subtitle A calls for coordination between the Secretaries of Labor and the Treasury, and articulates which department will have primary responsibility for certain areas. 29 U.S.C.A. §§ 1201–1204. Subtitle B created a number of study groups, all of them required to submit reports back to the Congress. 29 U.S.C. §§ 1221–1232. Subtitle C created the Joint Board for the Enrollment of Actuaries. 29 U.S.C. §§ 1241–1242.

Finally, Title IV created the Pension Benefit Guaranty Corporation and established a system of employee plan termination insurance, including special provisions for multiemployer plans. Id. §§ 1301–1461.

## C.  COVERAGE

The basic coverage provision, 29 U.S.C. § 1003 states that ERISA covers "any employee benefit plan if it is established or maintained (1) by any employer engaged in commerce or in any industry or activity affecting commerce; or (2) by any employee organization or organizations representing employees engaged in commerce or in any industry or activity affecting commerce; or (3) by both." There are five principal exceptions: (1) a "governmental plan" (primarily plans sponsored by the federal government or state and local governments); (2) a "church plan" (one sponsored by a church or association of churches); (3) a plan "maintained solely for the purpose of complying with applicable workmen's compensation laws or unemployment compensation or disability insurance laws"; (4) a plan maintained outside of the United States primarily for the benefit of persons substantially all of whom are nonresident aliens; or (5) an "excess benefit plan" (generally one providing more generous benefits to certain higher paid executives, without any advance funding).

The sweep of the statute is thus very broad, since virtually any employer's business, no matter how small, can be said to "affect commerce." See *Katzenbach v. McClung*, 379 U.S. 294, 85 S.Ct. 377, 13 L.Ed.2d 290 (1964). Not every employee benefit, however, is subject to ERISA, as the following opinion makes clear.

## FORT HALIFAX PACKING CO., INC. v. COYNE

Supreme Court of the United States, 1987
482 U.S. 1, 107 S.Ct. 2211, 96 L.Ed.2d 1

JUSTICE BRENNAN delivered the opinion of the Court.

In this case we must decide whether a Maine statute requiring employers to provide a one-time severance payment to employees in the event of a plant closing, * * * is pre-empted by either the Employee Retirement Income Security Act of 1974, 88 Stat. 832, as amended, 29 U.S.C. §§ 1001–1381 (ERISA), or the National Labor Relations Act, 49 Stat. 452, as amended, 29 U.S.C. §§ 157–158 (NLRA). * * *

### I

In 1972, Fort Halifax Packing Company (Fort Halifax or Company) purchased a poultry packaging and processing plant that had operated in Winslow, Maine, for almost two decades. The Company continued to operate the plant for almost another decade, until, on May 23, 1981, it discontinued operations at the plant and laid off all its employees except several maintenance and clerical workers. At the time of closing, over 100 employees were on the payroll. Forty-five had worked in the plant for over 10 years, 19 for over 20 years, and 2 for 29 years. * * *

On October 30, 1981, 11 employees filed suit in Superior Court seeking severance pay pursuant to Me. Rev. Stat. Ann., Tit. 26, § 625–B (Supp.1986–1987). This statute * * * provides that any employer that terminates operations at a plant with 100 or more employees, or relocates those operations more than 100 miles away, must provide one week's pay for each year of employment to all employees who have worked in the plant at least three years. The employer has no such liability if the employee accepts employment at the new location, or if the employee is covered by a contract that deals with the issue of severance pay. § 625–B(2), (3). Under authority granted by the statute, the Maine Director of the Bureau of Labor Standards also commenced an action to enforce the provisions of the state law, which action superseded the suit filed by the employees.

* * * [The Maine courts] found that eligible employees were entitled to severance pay due to the closure of the plant at Winslow.

## II

Appellant's basic argument is that any state law pertaining to a type of employee benefit listed in ERISA necessarily regulates an employee benefit plan, and therefore must be pre-empted. Because severance benefits are included in ERISA, see 29 U.S.C. § 1002(1)(B), appellant argues that ERISA pre-empts the Maine statute. In effect, appellant argues that ERISA forecloses virtually all state legislation regarding employee benefits. This contention fails, however, in light of the plain language of ERISA's pre-emption provision, the underlying purpose of that provision, and the overall objectives of ERISA itself.

## A

The first answer to appellant's argument is found in the express language of the statute. ERISA's pre-emption provision does not refer to state laws relating to "employee benefits," but to state laws relating to "employee benefit plans":

> "[T]he provisions of this subchapter ... shall supersede any and all State laws insofar as they may now or hereafter *relate to any employee benefit plan* described in § 1003(a) of this title and not exempt under § 1003(b) of this title." 29 U.S.C. § 1144(a) (emphasis added).

We have held that the words "relate to" should be construed expansively: "[a] law 'relates to' an employee benefit plan, in the normal sense of the phrase, if it has a connection with or reference to such a plan." *Shaw v. Delta Airlines, Inc.*, 463 U.S. 85, 96–97, 103 S. Ct. 2890, 2900, 77 L. Ed. 2d 490 (1983). Nothing in our case law, however, supports appellant's position that the word "plan" should in effect be read out of the statute. Indeed, Shaw itself speaks of a state law's connection with or reference to a plan. Ibid. The words "benefit" and "plan" are used separately throughout ERISA, and nowhere in the statute are they treated as the equivalent of one another. Given the basic difference between a "benefit" and a "plan," Congress' choice of language is significant in its pre-emption of only the latter.

Thus, as a first matter, the language of the ERISA presents a formidable obstacle to appellant's argument. The reason for Congress' decision to legislate with respect to plans rather than to benefits becomes plain upon examination of the purpose of both the pre-emption section and the regulatory scheme as a whole.

B

The second answer to appellant's argument is that pre-emption of the Maine statute would not further the purpose of ERISA pre-emption. In analyzing whether ERISA's pre-emption section is applicable to the Maine law, "as in any pre-emption analysis, 'the purpose of Congress is the ultimate touchstone.'" *Metropolitan Life Ins. Co. v. Massachusetts*, 471 U.S. 724, 747, 105 S. Ct. 2380, 2393, 85 L. Ed. 2d 728 (1985) (quoting *Malone v. White Motor Corp.*, 435 U.S. 497, 504, 98 S. Ct. 1185, 1190, 55 L. Ed. 2d 443 (1978)). Attention to purpose is particularly necessary in this case because the terms "employee benefit plan" and "plan" are defined only tautologically in the statute, each being described as "an employee welfare benefit plan or employee pension benefit plan or a plan which is both an employee welfare benefit plan and an employee pension benefit plan." 29 U.S.C. § 1002(3).

Statements by ERISA's sponsors in the House and Senate clearly disclose the problem that the pre-emption provision was intended to address. In the House, Representative Dent stated that "with the preemption of the field [of employee benefit plans], we round out the protection afforded participants by eliminating the threat of conflicting and inconsistent State and local regulation." 120 Cong. Rec. 29197 (1974). Similarly, Senator Williams declared: "It should be stressed that with the narrow exceptions specified in the bill, the substantive and enforcement provisions of the conference substitute are intended to preempt the field for Federal regulations, thus eliminating the threat of conflicting or inconsistent State and local regulation of employee benefit plans." Id., at 29933.

These statements reflect recognition of the administrative realities of employee benefit plans. An employer that makes a commitment systematically to pay certain benefits undertakes a host of obligations, such as determining the eligibility of claimants, calculating benefit levels, making disbursements, monitoring the availability of funds for benefit payments, and keeping appropriate records in order to comply with applicable reporting requirements. The most efficient way to meet these responsibilities is to establish a uniform administrative scheme, which provides a set of standard procedures to guide processing of claims and disbursement of benefits. Such a system is difficult to achieve, however, if a benefit plan is subject to differing regulatory requirements in differing States. A plan would be required to keep certain records in some States but not in others; to make certain benefits available in some States but not in others; to process claims in a certain way in some States but not in others; and to comply with certain fiduciary standards in some States but not in others. * * *

It is thus clear that ERISA's pre-emption provision was prompted by recognition that employers establishing and maintaining employee benefit plans are faced with the task of coordinating complex administrative activities. A patchwork scheme of regulation would introduce considerable inefficiencies in benefit program operation, which might lead those employers with existing plans to reduce benefits, and those without such plans to refrain from adopting them. Pre-emption ensures that the administrative practices of a benefit plan will be governed by only a single set of regulations. See, e.g., H.R. Rep. No. 93–533, p. 12 (1973), U.S. Code Cong. & Admin. News 1974, pp. 4639, 4650 ("[A] fiduciary standard embodied in Federal legislation is considered desirable because it will bring a measure of uniformity in an area where decisions under the same set of facts may differ from state to state").

The purposes of ERISA's pre-emption provision make clear that the Maine statute in no way raises the types of concerns that prompted pre-emption. * * *

The Maine statute neither establishes, nor requires an employer to maintain, an employee benefit plan. The requirement of a one-time, lump-sum payment triggered by a single event requires no administrative scheme whatsoever to meet the employer's obligation. The employer assumes no responsibility to pay benefits on a regular basis, and thus faces no periodic demands on its assets that create a need for financial coordination and control. Rather, the employer's obligation is predicated on the occurrence of a single contingency that may never materialize. The employer may well never have to pay the severance benefits. To the extent that the obligation to do so arises, satisfaction of that duty involves only making a single set of payments to employees at the time the plant closes. To do little more than write a check hardly constitutes the operation of a benefit plan. Once this single event is over, the employer has no further responsibility. The theoretical possibility of a one-time obligation in the future simply creates no need for an ongoing administrative program for processing claims and paying benefits.

This point is underscored by comparing the consequences of the Maine statute with those produced by a state statute requiring the establishment of a benefit plan. In *Standard Oil Co. of California v. Agsalud*, 633 F.2d 760 (CA9 1980), summarily aff'd, 454 U.S. 801, 102 S. Ct. 79, 70 L. Ed. 2d 75 (1981), for instance, Hawaii had required that employers provide employees with a comprehensive health care plan. The Hawaii law was struck down, for it posed two types of problems. First, the employer in that case already had in place a health care plan governed by ERISA, which did not comply in all respects with the Hawaii Act. If the employer sought to achieve administrative efficiencies by integrating the Hawaii plan into its existing plan, different components of its single plan would be subject to different requirements. If it established a separate plan to administer the program directed by Hawaii, it would lose the benefits of maintaining a single administrative scheme. Second, if Hawaii could demand the operation of a particular benefit plan, so could other States, which would require that the employer coordinate perhaps dozens of programs. Agsalud thus illustrates that whether a State requires an existing plan to pay certain benefits, or whether it requires the establishment of a separate plan where none existed before, the problem is the same. Faced with the difficulty or impossibility of structuring administrative practices according to a set of uniform guidelines, an employer may decide to reduce benefits or simply not to pay them at all.

By contrast, the Maine law does not put the employer to the choice of either: (1) integrating a state-mandated ongoing benefit plan with an existing plan or (2) establishing a separate plan to process and pay benefits under the plan required by the State. * * *

## C

The third answer to appellant's argument is that the Maine statute not only fails to implicate the concerns of ERISA's pre-emption provision, it fails to implicate the regulatory concerns of ERISA itself. The congressional declaration of policy, codified at 29 U.S.C. § 1001, states that ERISA was enacted because Congress found it desirable that "disclosure be made and safeguards be provided with respect to the establishment, operation, and administration of [employee benefit] plans." § 1001(a). Representative Dent, the House sponsor of the legislation, represented that ERISA's fiduciary standards "will prevent abuses of the special responsibilities borne by those dealing with plans." 120 Cong. Rec. 29197 (1974). Senator Williams, the Senate sponsor, stated that these standards would safeguard employees from "such abuses as self-dealing, imprudent investing, and misappropriation of plan funds." Id. at 29932. * * *

The foregoing makes clear both why ERISA is concerned with regulating benefit "plans" and why the Maine statute does not establish one. Only "plans" involve administrative activity potentially subject to employer abuse. The obligation imposed by Maine generates no such activity. There is no occasion to determine whether a "plan" is "operated" in the interest of its beneficiaries, because nothing is "operated." No financial transactions take place that would be listed in an annual report, and no further information regarding the terms of the severance pay obligation is needed because the statute itself makes these terms clear. It would make no sense for pre-emption to clear the way for exclusive federal regulation, for there would be nothing to regulate. Under such circumstances, pre-emption would in no way serve the overall purpose of ERISA.

## III

[Discussion of the principles of preemption under the National Labor Relations Act is omitted.]

## IV

We hold that the Maine severance pay statute is not pre-empted by ERISA, since it does not "relate to any employee benefit plan" under that statute. 29 U.S.C. § 1144(a). We hold further that the law is not pre-empted by the NLRA, since its establishment of a minimum labor standard does not impermissibly intrude upon the collective-bargaining process. The judgment of the Maine Supreme Judicial Court is therefore

AFFIRMED.

JUSTICE WHITE, with whom THE CHIEF JUSTICE, JUSTICE O'CONNOR, and JUSTICE SCALIA join, dissenting.

The Court rejects appellant's pre-emption challenge to Maine's severance pay statute by reasoning that the statute does not create a "plan" under ERISA because it does not require an "administrative scheme" to administer the payment of severance benefits. By making pre-emption turn on the existence of an "administrative scheme," the Court creates a loophole in ERISA's pre-emption statute, 29 U.S.C. § 1144, which will undermine Congress' decision to make employee-benefit plans a matter of exclusive federal regulation. The Court's rule requiring an established "administrative scheme" as a prerequisite for ERISA pre-emption will allow States to effectively dictate a wide array of employee benefits that must be provided by employers by simply characterizing them as non-"administrative." The Court has also chosen to ignore completely what precedent exists as to what constitutes a "plan" under ERISA. I dissent because it is incredible to believe that Congress intended that the broad pre-emption provision contained in ERISA would depend upon the extent to which an employer exercised administrative foresight in preparing for the eventual payment of employee benefits. * * *

## NOTES AND QUESTIONS

1. How much "administrative scheme" should be necessary in order to have a "plan" for ERISA purposes? What if an employer had a consistent policy of paying discharged employees their unused vacation time at the time of discharge, would this be an administrative scheme under ERISA? The amount involved would be calculated from records kept by the employer as part of its regular accounting practices, and would be paid from general assets, not from a separate fund. *Massachusetts v. Morash*, 490 U.S. 107, 109 S.Ct. 1668, 104 L.Ed.2d 98 (1989) (not a "plan"; unanimous opinion).

2. Since the statute itself does not have a comprehensive definition of "plan," the Secretary of Labor has issued regulations that seek to fill the gap. See 29 C.F.R. § 2510.3–1. Those regulations indicate that a number of benefits will not be treated as "plans" if paid for out of general assets. These include holiday bonuses and continued payment of wages during temporary periods of disability or during military duty (often referred to as "payroll practices"). Other exempted benefit programs include providing meal facilities, selling goods or services to employees at a discount, and providing on-site medical care. The regulation also exempts certain group insurance schemes, so long as the employer does not contribute to the payment of premiums, endorse the program or provide any administrative services, but simply permits an insurer to publicize the program to employees. For a discussion of the regulation and the deference due it, see *Stern v. International Business Machines Corp.*, 326 F.3d 1367 (11th Cir. 2003).

3. The statute applies to "employers" and "employees" (among other entities) but without defining the terms with any precision. In *Yates v. Hendon*, 541 U.S. 1, 124 S.Ct. 1330, 158 L.Ed.2d 40 (2004), the Court held that a "working owner" may be treated as an employee protected by ERISA if

he or she is a participant in a plan that also enrolls at least one "common law employee."

# D.  TRANSPARENCY: REPORTING AND DISCLOSURE

A major portion of ERISA consisted of new and tightened requirements of reporting and disclosure, building on the earlier 1958 legislation. More have been added since, particularly by the Pension Protection Act of 2006. The principal requirements are these:

- Annual reports. Sections 103 and 104, 29 U.S.C. §§ 1023, 1024, require that reports be filed with the Secretary of Labor each year, providing a variety of information, largely financial. The specific requirements depend on the nature of the plan, with "pay-as-you-go" welfare plans treated differently from advance funded pension plans, for example. After many years of revision, the various annual report forms have been consolidated into a single form ("Form 5500"). Most reporting is now done electronically. Beneficiaries and participants are entitled to this information, but must request it. Plans with fewer than 100 participants may be exempt from many of these requirements.

- Benefit statements furnished to participants and beneficiaries. The requirements imposed by section 105, 29 U.S.C. § 1025, much amended in 2006, vary with the sort of pension plan involved. As discussed *infra* p. 981–983, ERISA regulates two types of pension plans: "defined benefit plans" in which the employer promises to pay a defined benefit upon retirement, generally based on average income and years of service, and "defined contribution plans" in which the employer promises to make a defined contribution to an account for the employee's retirement for each period of service, perhaps along with an employee contribution for the same purpose.

  - For defined benefit plans the requirement is relatively lighter: The plan administrator must provide a statement not less than every three years to each individual who (a) has a non-forfeitable accrued benefit, and (b) is currently employed by the employer maintaining the plan. The statement must tell the participant the amount of benefit accrued, the amount that is non-forfeitable, and the date on which accrued benefits will become non-forfeitable.

  - For defined contribution plans, a statement must be furnished at least once a year to each participant or beneficiary with an account in the plan. If the participant has the right under the plan to direct how the account is to be invested, then a statement must be furnished each calendar quarter.

- Defined benefit plan annual funding notice. This requirement once applied only to multiemployer plans, but now extends to single employer plans as well, although the details differ somewhat between the two. The information that is to be included is largely financial, such as the plan's assets and liabilities, funding policies, and numbers of participants. It is to be provided to the Pension Benefit Guarantee Corporation, to plan participants and beneficiaries, and to labor organizations representing those participants and beneficiaries. See 29 U.S.C. § 1021(f).

- Notice of eligibility to divest employer securities. This relatively new requirement is in response to the dire situation of many employees whose defined contribution plan accounts are almost entirely invested in the stock of their employers; a state of affairs that was demonstrated to be very undesirable when the Enron Corporation and WorldCom entered bankruptcy in 2001 and 2002. A plan administrator must inform a participant at least 30 days in advance of the participant's right to divest these securities. The drafters of the requirement clearly hoped that this notice would lead many individuals to reduce their reliance on a single investment in favor of a more diversified portfolio. See 29 U.S.C. § 2021(m).

- Summary Plan Description (SPD). This must ordinarily be furnished to a participant within 90 days of becoming one. It must provide basic information about the nature of the plan and the benefits to be provided and "shall be written in a manner calculated to be understood by the average plan participant." The SPD has become an important source of employee protection as the cases that follow indicate. 29 U.S.C. §§ 1021(a), 1022, 1024(b), 1191b.

- Summary of Material Modifications (SMM). Plan administrators must provide a summary of any "material modification" in the terms of a plan within 210 days after the close of the plan year during which the modification was made. What constitutes a material modification is not defined in the statute. 29 U.S.C. § 1021(b).

## HICKS v. FLEMING COMPANIES, INC.

United States Court of Appeals, Fifth Circuit, 1992
961 F.2d 537

WIENER, CIRCUIT JUDGE:

We are here presented with this court's first opportunity to consider the appropriate test for determining when a document constitutes a summary plan description (SPD) for purposes of the Employment Retirement Income Security Act (ERISA). * * *

### I. FACTS AND PROCEDURAL HISTORY

The facts in this case are largely uncontested. Hicks worked for White Swan, Inc. (White Swan), a subsidiary of Fleming Companies, Inc. (Fleming), first as a truck loader and later as a truck driver. As fringe benefits for its employees, White Swan sponsors a number of ERISA benefit plans, one of which is a long-term disability benefits plan (the plan) available to clerical employees under the age of seventy and to employees, also under the age of seventy, whose employment is considered exempt under the provisions of the Fair Labor Standards Act of 1938. As a truck driver and hourly employee, Hicks did not fall within either category, and thus was ineligible for long-term disability benefits under the terms of the plan. White Swan did not represent to Hicks at the time he was hired that he would be eligible to participate in this plan.

In January 1988, Hicks received a six-page booklet from Fleming, entitled "Your 1988 Total Compensation Report," which purported to summarize the main elements of Fleming's various employee benefit plans, including health care, survivor, retirement, and long-term disability benefits. The booklet was "individualized" for Hicks, that is, it contained personal information about Hicks, including his date of birth, social security number, date of hire, and his elections under various plans. Apparently through some computer glitch, the section of Hicks' booklet concerning the long-term disability benefits plan did not reflect his ineligibility but stated:

> After 180 days of disability, you can receive $1,615 a month, including social security. Payments can continue during total disability: Up to age 65 or longer if disability begins after age 62. The maximum family amount from all sources combined is 80% of your pay when disabled.

In its introduction, the booklet represented that it was a "simple but comprehensive summary" containing "personalized information" on Fleming benefits. The booklet also contained several disclaimers, warning that the information contained in the booklet was merely a summary, that benefit amounts were not final, and that its terms were subject to those in the various benefit plans themselves. The booklet did not say that it was an SPD, and Fleming apparently did not intend that it be one. Fleming furnished participants and beneficiaries with copies of an SPD for the long-term disability benefits plan as required by ERISA, but Hicks, like other non-participants, was not furnished one.

In May 1988, Hicks was injured on the job and became disabled. When he inquired into his long-term disability benefits, White Swan informed him, after some initial confusion, that he was ineligible for that plan. Hicks then brought this ERISA suit against White Swan and Fleming, alleging that he was wrongfully denied his long-term disability benefits. Invoking the venerable "walks like a duck, quacks like a duck" argument, Hicks contended that the booklet is an SPD because it looks like an SPD, contains information required in an SPD, and purports to serve the same purposes as an SPD. As such, Hicks argued, the booklet's terms govern his entitlement to long-term disability benefits. Fleming, on the other hand, asserted that the booklet is not an SPD and thus any variance between the booklet's terms and those of the plan is irrelevant under ERISA. (Subsequently, in *Hansen v. Continental Ins. Co.*, decided after this suit was filed, this court held "that if there is a conflict between the summary plan description and the terms of the policy, the summary plan description shall govern.")

After completion of discovery, Fleming filed a motion for summary judgment, contending that the booklet was not an SPD because it did not meet the minimum content and information requirements of ERISA as set forth in § 1022(b). The district court agreed with Fleming and granted summary judgment, holding as a matter of law that the booklet was not an SPD. * * *

Hicks appealed to this court.

## II.   ANALYSIS

### A.   STATUTORY AND REGULATORY REQUIREMENTS FOR SPD

ERISA requires that welfare benefit plans be governed by formal written plan documents that are prepared and filed in compliance with ERISA's reporting and disclosure rules. One such document, the SPD, is the statutory plain-language mechanism for informing plan participants of the terms of the plan and its benefits. ERISA provides that the plan administrator must furnish the SPD to each participant and beneficiary. ERISA does not define the term "Summary Plan Description"—hence the dispute in this case. Instead, it sets out with great specificity how the SPD must be written and what information it must contain. These requirements are found in §§ 1022(a) and (b):

> (a)(1). * * * The summary plan description shall include the information described in subsection (b) of this section, shall be written in a manner calculated to be understood by the average plan participant, and shall be sufficiently accurate and comprehensive to reasonably apprise such participants and beneficiaries of their rights and obligations under the plan....

> (b).   The plan description and summary plan description shall contain the following information: The name and type of administration of the plan; the name and address of the person designated as agent for the service of legal process, if such person is not the administrator; the name and address of the administrator; names, titles, and addresses of any trustee or trustees (if they are persons different from the administrator); a description of the relevant provisions of any applicable collective bargaining agreement; the plan's requirements respecting eligibility for participation and benefits; a description of the provisions providing for nonforfeitable pension benefits; circumstances which may result in disqualification, ineligibility, or denial or loss of benefits; the source of financing of the plan and the identity of any organization through which benefits are provided; the date of the end of the plan year and whether the records of the plan are kept on a calendar, policy, or fiscal year basis; the procedures to be followed in presenting claims for benefits under the plan and the remedies

available under the plan for the redress of claims which are denied in whole or in part (including procedures required under section 1133 of this title).

ERISA also requires that the plan administrator file the SPD with the Secretary of Labor. Assuming the Secretary finds it adequate under the law, the SPD is available for public inspection.

DOL regulations significantly extend and amplify ERISA's statutory requirements on the types of information that must be contained in the SPD. * * *

## B.  THE APPROPRIATE TEST

There are three widely-cited cases that consider whether a document constitutes an SPD: *Kochendorfer v. Rockdale Sash & Trim Co. Inc., Alday v. Container Corp. of America and Gridley v. Cleveland Pneumatic Co.* In *Kochendorfer*, the first case to consider this issue, an Illinois district court found that a "record-keeping booklet" was an SPD, "albeit an abridged one." The court stated:

> We do not believe that Congress intended to exclude from the term "summary plan description" every document which lacks some of the information required in section 1022(b). Rather, any document a plan distributes to its participants which contains all or substantially all of the information the average participant would deem crucial to a knowledgeable understanding of his benefits under the plan shall be deemed a summary plan description. The crucial information which any document must contain before it could be deemed a summary plan description includes an explanation of the benefits and the circumstances which may disqualify a participant from securing benefits.

*Kochendorfer* went on to rule that the booklet in question was an SPD because it described, in a manner calculated to be understood by the average plan participant, such things as the plan's purpose, the source and amounts of money contributed, the method by which shares are determined, when and how payment is received, and how funds are invested.

In *Alday*, the Eleventh Circuit ruled that an individualized booklet, which was entitled "Summary of Personal Benefits" and which said nothing more about the company's health insurance plan than "health insurance is available to you and your dependents at a modest cost," was not an SPD under ERISA. The court reasoned that the booklet did not satisfy the requirements in § 1022; specifically, the booklet neither described the plan's terms, specified the plan's benefits or coverage, defined the plan's eligibility requirements, nor otherwise gave participants the information necessary to participate in the plan's health insurance program.

In the most complete treatment of this issue to date, the Third Circuit, in Gridley, adopted a fact-intensive approach in determining that a brochure, entitled "Employee Benefits Summary," was not an SPD for a life insurance plan, even though the booklet purported to provide an overview of the company's plan. Gridley based its decision on four factors: (1) the brochure instructed employees to refer to their SPDs, hence no reasonable reader could have thought the brochure an SPD; (2) the brochure lacked ten of twelve categories of information required under § 1022(b); (3) the brochure was a perfunctory description of subjects treated in other documents that were SPDs; and (4) the brochure was an updated version of an earlier brochure that was not an SPD.

In this case, Hicks asserts that *Kochendorfer* supplies the appropriate test for deciding whether a document is an SPD under ERISA. Hicks characterizes *Kochendorfer* as looking to the employee's subjective understanding of the document. Hence, he argues, the booklet is an SPD, and its terms are binding on Fleming under ERISA, because he understood the booklet to mean that he was eligible for long-term disability benefits. As the foregoing quotation shows, however, Hicks misunderstands *Kochendorfer* because that case quite obviously adopts an objective, "reasonable participant" test.

Fleming, on the other hand, contends that the booklet cannot be an SPD as it does not contain all twelve categories of information required by § 1022(b). Fleming asserts that the operative word in the first sentence of § 1022(b) is "shall," indicating that ERISA itself requires this rule of strict compliance. Hicks counters that Fleming's approach is not strictly mandated by ERISA-§ 1022(b) states that an SPD must contain twelve categories of information, not that a document that does not include all twelve categories is not an SPD.

We believe that Fleming urges the better rule, although we acknowledge Hicks's point that this rule is not strictly required by ERISA. We reject *Kochendorfer's* premise that Congress did not intend to exclude as an SPD every document that lacks § 1022(b) information because such a premise would set a trap for the unwary employer who circulates benefit information in writing and at the same time would have a chilling effect on the cautious employer who might otherwise write freely to his or her employees about their benefit plans. We believe that speculation as to congressional intent on this point would be more accurate if phrased in the converse: We do not believe Congress intended the term SPD to include every document that contains some of the information required in § 1022(b).

We hold, therefore, that the appropriate test for determining if a document constitutes an SPD under ERISA is to see whether it contains all or substantially all categories of information required under 29 U.S.C. § 1022(b) and the DOL's regulations at 29 C.F.R. § 2520.102–3 for the type of benefit in question. We emphasize that DOL's regulations * * * are especially critical to this determination because they expand on the requirements in § 1022(b) and clarify the information required for each of type of benefit plan.

In large part, we adopt this bright-line approach because we are unwilling to declare that a document could constitute an SPD under ERISA even though it does not satisfy the information requirements in § 1022(b) and § 2520.102–3, and, thus, would not be accepted by the Secretary of Labor for filing and publication. If a document is to be afforded the legal effects of an SPD, such as conferring benefits when it is at variance with the plan itself, that document should be sufficient to constitute an SPD for filing and qualification purposes. Quite simply, there should be no accidental or inadvertent SPDs. In addition, "reasonable participant" or case-by-case tests—with their inevitable hair-splitting factual distinctions and litigation-encouraging ambiguities—would introduce considerable uncertainty into this area of law, to the ultimate detriment, no doubt, of all parties.

## C.   APPLICATION OF TEST TO THE BOOKLET

When we compare the information required in § 1022(b) and § 2520.102–3 to the booklet at issue here, it is clear that the booklet is not an SPD. Frankly, the question is not even close. Although the booklet includes some cursory information on monthly payments under the long-term disability benefits plan, it contains none of the information required under § 1022(b) and § 2520.102–3 on the plan's management and rules, such as the name and type of administration of the plan; the name and address of the person designated as agent for the service of legal process; the source of financing of the plan and the identity of any organization through which benefits are provided; the date of the end of the plan year and whether the records of the plan are kept on a calendar, policy, or fiscal year basis; the procedures to be followed in presenting claims for benefits under the plan and the remedies available under the plan for the redress of claims that are denied in whole or in part. Neither does the booklet contain the information required by DOL regulations alone, such as the employer identification number assigned by the IRS to the plan sponsor; the plan number assigned to the plan sponsor; and the so-called statement of ERISA rights.

## III.   CONCLUSION

We hold that a document is a summary plan description under ERISA if it contains all or substantially all categories of information required under 29 U.S.C. § 1022(b) and Department of Labor regulations at 29 C.F.R. § 2520.102–3. Finding that the booklet in this case does not meet this test, we AFFIRM the judgment of the district court.

## BERGT v. RETIREMENT PLAN FOR PILOTS EMPLOYED BY MARKAIR, INC.

United States Court of Appeals, Ninth Circuit, 2002
293 F.3d 1139

BREWSTER, SENIOR DISTRICT JUDGE.

* * *

## I.  Facts and Procedural History

[Neil G.] Bergt, previously a pilot with MarkAir, Inc. ("the Company"), served as its President and Chairman of the Board of Directors from 1975 to 1995. Beginning in 1976, Bergt participated in the company-sponsored profit-sharing plan and from 1984, he participated in the Employee Stock Ownership Plan ("ESOP"). In 1980, the Company created an ERISA retirement plan that allowed employees who were pilots, or former pilots, to participate. Section 3.03 of the retirement plan, however, excluded otherwise eligible employees who were "participants in any other pension, profit sharing, or retirement plan which is 'qualified' by the Internal Revenue Service and to which the Company is contractually obligated to contribute. . . ." The Company also issued a summary of the retirement plan, called a Summary Plan Document ("SPD"), that specified "if you are a member of another Company-sponsored retirement or profit sharing plan, you cannot be a member of this plan."

On March 22, 1996, Bergt filed a claim for benefits under the ERISA retirement plan. On April 28, 1998, the committee to oversee the administration of the retirement plan ("Committee") denied his request, claiming that he was ineligible based on Section 3.03 because he was a participant in the Company's profit-sharing plan. On June 30, 1998, Bergt petitioned the Committee for reconsideration. In denying his request, the Committee found that Section 3.03 of the retirement plan was ambiguous. Examining the SPD and extrinsic evidence, the Committee held the profit-sharing plan was " 'qualified' by the Internal Revenue Service" and constituted a plan "to which the Company was contractually obligated to contribute." In the alternative, the Committee ruled that the phrase, "which is 'qualified' by the Internal Revenue Service and to which the Company is contractually obligated to contribute," only modified "retirement plan," and did not modify "pension" or "profit sharing." Therefore, according to the Committee, an employee who participated in any profit-sharing plan was excluded from participating in the retirement plan. Thus, the Committee found Berg ineligible to participate on both grounds.

Bergt appealed the Committee's decision to the United States District Court for the District of Alaska. * * * The district court denied Bergt's motion for summary judgment and granted summary judgment affirming the Committee, but for a different reason. First, the court found the profit sharing plan was not a binding obligation on the Company. The lower court then ruled that although the language in the plan master document was unambiguous, when viewed in light of the conflicting SPD, an ambiguity was created as to whether Bergt was eligible to participate in the retirement plan. Since the court found an ambiguity, it considered extrinsic evidence, concluding that Bergt was not eligible to participate in the retirement plan because the understanding of the parties was that an employee could not be a participant in both the retirement plan and a company-sponsored profit-sharing plan. Although the court reviewed the Committee's decision for an abuse of discretion, it noted that it would have granted summary judgment even if it had applied a de novo review.

## II.  Discussion

### A.  Standard of Review

We review a district court's grant or denial of a motion for summary judgment de novo. * * *. We also determine which standard of review to apply to a committee's decision de novo. * * *. In *Firestone Tire & Rubber Co. v. Bruch*, 489 U.S. 101, 115, 109 S. Ct. 948, 103 L. Ed. 2d 80 (1989), the Supreme Court said that when an ERISA plan grants discretionary authority to the plan administrator to determine plan eligibility, the court will ordinarily review a committee's decision to deny benefits for an abuse of discretion. [The court rejects arguments for a more stringent review standard in this case.] * * *

### B.  Summary Judgment

#### *SPD part of ERISA Plan*

The lower court committed legal error when it determined that the Committee did not abuse its discretion when it refused Bergt benefits under the retirement plan. As a preliminary matter, we conclude the SPD is a plan document and should be considered when interpreting an ERISA plan. The ERISA statute requires the plan fiduciaries to act solely "in accordance with the *documents and instruments* governing the plan. . . ." 29 U.S.C. § 1104(a)(1)(D) (emphasis added). Employers are required to provide participants with a copy of an SPD (not the plan master document) that describes the "circumstances which may result in disqualification, ineligibility, or denial or loss of benefits" and shall "be written in a manner calculated to be understood by the average plan participant, and shall be sufficiently accurate and comprehensive to reasonably apprise such participants and beneficiaries of their rights and obligations under the plan." 29 U.S.C. § 1022(a)–(b). Furthermore, the SPD is the "statutorily established means of informing participants of the terms of the plan and its benefits" and the employee's primary source of information regarding employment benefits * * *. For these reasons, we follow the other courts that have held that the SPD is part of the ERISA plan. * * *

*Need to provide copies of SPD*

#### *Plan Master Document*

In this case, the ERISA plan contains two conflicting plan documents: the plan master document and the SPD. The provisions in the plan master document show Bergt was eligible to participate in the retirement plan, which says that an employee who is a pilot, or a former pilot, is a member unless he "participates in another profit, pension, or retirement plan which is IRS qualified and to which the company was contractually obligated to contribute."

The initial issue is whether the provisions of the plan master document are ambiguous, which would justify the Committee's use of extrinsic evidence to determine whether Bergt was eligible to participate in the retirement plan. * * *

The lower court found the provisions of the plan master document unambiguous. We agree. * * *. The phrase, "to which the company was contractually obligated to contribute," simply means the Company is legally obligated, pursuant to a contract, to contribute. This phrase is not reasonably susceptible to a different interpretation. And as the lower court noted, the terms "pension" and "profit sharing," are not followed by the word "plan." As a result, the term "plan" relates to the words "pension," "profit sharing," and "retirement" making the qualifying phrase "plan which is . . ." applicable to all three.

The next issue is whether, based on the unambiguous provisions of the plan master document, Bergt is eligible to participate in the retirement plan. The Committee conceded that Bergt was an employee and a former pilot, but decided that he was ineligible to participate in the retirement plan because he was a(1) member of a profit-sharing plan, (2) which was qualified by the IRS, and (3) to which the Company was contractually obligated to contribute.

Although the lower court did not determine whether Bergt was a member of a profit-sharing plan that was qualified by the IRS, it held the Company was not contractually obligated to contribute to it. Again, we agree with the lower court. The profit-sharing plan states, in relevant part:

> Employer Contributions: For each Year, the Employer shall contribute such amount as its Board of Directors shall deem be made on account of such Year. . . .

Although the profit-sharing plan uses the word "shall," it does not require the Company to contribute anything. For the Company to have been contractually obligated, it must have had a legal duty to contribute and someone must be entitled to a remedy if it does not. * * *. In this case, the Company did not promise to a pay an objectively determinable amount each profitable year, which may have constituted a contractual obligation * * *.

According to the plan master document, Bergt was clearly eligible to participate in the retirement plan because he was an employee, was a former pilot, and did not participate in another pension or profit-sharing plan to which the company was contractually obligated to contribute.

### Summary Plan Document

Although Bergt qualifies to participate in the retirement plan by the terms of the plan master document, the SPD unambiguously prevents him from participating. The SPD states, "if you are member of another Company-sponsored retirement or profit-sharing plan, you cannot be a member of this plan." Therefore, a conflict exists between the plan master document and the SPD.

### The Plan Master Document Controls

The critical issue in this case is how to interpret an ERISA plan when the plan master document unambiguously qualifies an employee as a member of the retirement plan, but the SPD unambiguously excludes him. The lower court held that this created an ambiguity, and then looked to extrinsic evidence to resolve it. See, e.g., *Richardson*, 112 F.3d at 985 (9th Cir.1997) ("Typically, however, when a plan is ambiguous, a court will examine extrinsic evidence to determine the intent of the parties."); *Vizcaino v. Microsoft Corp.*, 97 F.3d 1187, 1194 (9th Cir.1996). The court, after considering the evidence, concluded the long-standing understanding of the parties was that an employee who participated in the profit-sharing plan could not be a member of the retirement plan.

The lower court correctly noted the contradiction between the plan master document and the SPD created an ambiguity as to whether Bergt was eligible to participate in the retirement plan. * * * The district court's consideration of extrinsic evidence to resolve the conflict, however, was erroneous. In this case, we are not dealing with an ambiguous word or phrase, or conflicting provisions in the same document, as we were in Vizcaino and Richardson, but with a substantially more egregious ambiguity arising from an inconsistency between the plan master document and plan summary.

The other courts that have encountered ERISA plans where the plan master document conflicted with the SPD did not consider extrinsic evidence of the parties' intent to resolve the inconsistency. * * * In these cases, the SPD conflicted with, and was more favorable to the employee, than the plan master document. Instead of relying on extrinsic evidence, however, these courts held that it would be unfair to have the employees bear the burden of a conflicting SPD and plan master document and, thus, decided that the provision more favorable to the employee controlled. *Chiles*, 95 F.3d at 1518; *Hansen*, 940 F.2d at 982; *Heidgerd*, 906 F.2d at 907–08; *Edwards*.

We follow this same reasoning to conclude that when the plan master document is more favorable to the employee than the SPD, and unambiguously allows for eligibility of an employee, it controls, despite contrary unambiguous provisions in the SPD. The plan master document is the main document that specifies the terms of the plan, and employees should be entitled to rely on its unambiguous provisions. The SPD, on the other hand, should simply summarize the relevant portions of the plan master document. Specifically, we adopt the reasoning of the Fifth Circuit, which stated:

> Any burden of uncertainty created by careless or inaccurate drafting of the summary must be placed on those who do the drafting, and who are most able to bear that burden, and not on the individual employee, who is powerless to affect the drafting of the summary or the policy and ill equipped to bear the financial hardship that might result from a misleading or confusing document. Accuracy is not a lot to ask.

### III. Conclusion

In this case, the unambiguous provisions of the plan master document control. As a result, the Committee abused its discretion by refusing to provide Bergt benefits under the retirement plan. * * * We reverse the ruling of the lower court and instruct it to enter judgment in favor of the appellant.

### NOTES AND QUESTIONS

1. If an employer fails to provide a summary plan description or any of the several types of reports required by ERISA, affected participants and beneficiaries may bring a civil action under § 502 to recover a civil penalty of up to $100 per day. 29 U.S.C. § 1132(a)(1), (c). The Secretary of Labor is authorized to assess civil penalties ranging from $100 to $1,100 a day for failure to file the required annual report, and for other reporting deficiencies. See 29 U.S.C. § 1132(c)(2), (4) through (8).

2. The changes made by ERISA in requiring disclosure once a plan is in place represented a substantial step forward from the common law protection available in many jurisdictions. Prior to ERISA, if an employer kept its welfare plan secret, potential beneficiaries who had no knowledge of the plan might well lack either a contractual or estoppel basis for claiming benefits. See *Alfaro v. Stauffer Chemical Co.*, 173 Ind.App. 89, 362 N.E.2d 500 (1977), finding no right of action for severance pay by employees who were severed prior to the adoption of ERISA even though their prior employer had a written severance pay policy to which only management had access.

Under ERISA, once an employee benefit plan is established, it is subject to the Act's disclosure, information, and reporting requirements. Thus, in *Donovan v. Dillingham*, 688 F.2d 1367 (11th Cir. 1982), it was held that if an employer establishes and maintains a plan it must comply with ERISA even though the plan is informal and unwritten. The court observed that purchase of employee benefits insurance may serve as evidence of the establishment of such a plan. In an unusual and perhaps debatable case, an employer that maintained a written but unpublished severance benefits plan, but failed both to provide employees with a summary statement of the plan's provisions and also to include a claims procedure in the plan was found to have violated ERISA. In addition, in that situation the court ruled that claimants could enforce the plan based upon its written provisions, even though they did not learn the contents of those provisions prior to bringing suit and even though in practice the employer administered the plan in a manner that modified some of those provisions. *Blau v. Del Monte Corp.*, 748 F.2d 1348 (9th Cir. 1984), cert. denied 474 U.S. 865, 106 S.Ct. 183, 88 L.Ed.2d 152 (1985). In order for such a duty to exist, the benefit program must, of course, constitute a "plan" within the meaning of cases such as *Fort Halifax Packing Co. v. Coyne.* See *Sandstrom v. Cultor Food Science, Inc.*, 214 F.3d 795 (7th Cir. 2000).

3. Is an employer, administering a pension plan, required to disclose its deliberations about the possible adoption of new or more advantageous retirement benefits to prospective retirees in advance of actual adoption of the

changes? *Berlin v. Michigan Bell Tel. Co.*, 858 F.2d 1154 (6th Cir. 1988), held that adversely affected persons have an ERISA right to relief if they are misled by the employer's false statements regarding such impending changes, and *Lembo v. Texaco, Inc.*, 194 Cal.App.3d 531, 239 Cal.Rptr. 596 (Cal. App. 2 Dist. 1987), upheld such an action under ERISA based on the employer's concealment of impending changes upon being questioned by a senior employee respecting the available retirement options. In the latter case, the court treated the suit as an ERISA action even though the federal statute was not cited in the complaint and the pleadings were cast in terms of state law theories of relief. See also *Bins v. Exxon Co.*, 220 F.3d 1042 (9th Cir. 2000) (en banc), holding that when a plan participant inquires about potential plan changes, the employer has a duty to respond truthfully and completely about changes that are under serious consideration. However, in the absence of an inquiry, the employer does not have an affirmative duty to volunteer information prior to final adoption of a change unless the employer agreed to do so. Accord, *Fischer v. Philadelphia Electric Co.*, 994 F.2d 130 (3d Cir.), cert. denied, 510 U.S. 1020, 114 S.Ct. 622, 126 L.Ed.2d 586 (1993). One court has criticized the holdings in *Bins* and *Fischer II* because imposing such a duty might hamper the normal decision making process of an employer with respect to changes, and make it unduly difficult for the employer to conduct its regular business. *Martinez v. Schlumberger, Ltd.*, 338 F.3d 407 (5th Cir. 2003).

# E.  MINIMUM PLAN CONTENT STANDARDS

ERISA does not require an employer to provide any benefit plan at all. If an employer chooses to do so—as many do, as a means of attracting and retaining a work force—the statute requires that many of the plans meet certain basic standards in order to be tax deductible. Because ERISA governs so many different types of benefit plans, many of the standards are made specific to the type of plan involved. Health plans have one set of provisions, ESOPs another, pension plans yet others, and so on. Given the variety and complexity of these standards, this text will provide an introduction only to a sampling of the minimum standards dealing with health care plans and the most common sorts of pension plans.

## 1.  HEALTH CARE PLANS

*HIPPA*—Several basic standards were added to the statute by the Health Insurance Portability and Accountability Act of 1996 (HIPPA), 110 Stat. 1936 (1996) (codified beginning at 29 U.S.C. § 1181). Probably the most important provisions have to do with what persons cannot be excluded from participating in a plan, and what a plan may do to exclude coverage of preexisting conditions. The Patient Protection and Affordable Care Act, Pub. L. 111–148, will gradually eliminate the bulk of such exclusions.

*Eligibility of individuals for coverage.* "Group health plans" and "health insurance issuers" cannot:

- exclude an otherwise eligible person from coverage because of medical history, disability, or genetic information;

- exclude from coverage an otherwise eligible dependent child, if the participant enrolled the child in "creditable coverage" coverage within 30 days of birth or adoption and there has not been a significant gap (more than 63 days) in the coverage of that child.

*Exclusion of conditions.* "Group health plans" and "health insurance issuers" cannot:

- exclude from coverage a "preexisting health condition" for more than 12 months (18 months in the case of a person who does not enroll in a plan promptly when eligible) (This exclusion period may be shortened if the participant has been covered under another health plan—including Medicare and Medicaid—without a break in coverage of more than 63 days.);

- treat as a preexisting condition a condition for which the individual has not had medical consultation or treatment within the prior six months;

- exclude pregnancy as a preexisting condition under any circumstances.

A plan may, however, exclude a condition by name, or include annual and lifetime limits on the total amount of benefits to be paid, so long as these limitations are uniformly applied to all participants. These provisions will be of little importance as the 2010 health care reform legislation takes effect. That legislation, for instance, allows adults with pre-existing conditions to become insured by joining a high-risk pool beginning in June 2010; this pool will be replaced by a "health care exchange" in 2014. Lifetime dollar limits and "unreasonable" annual limits on spending for an individual's care are also to be eliminated. Patient Protection and Affordable Care Act § 1001, amending the Public Health Service Act.

*COBRA*—The Consolidated Omnibus Budget Reconciliation Act of 1985 (COBRA), 100 Stat. 227 (1985) (codified beginning at 29 U.S.C. § 1161) requires health plans to allow participants and beneficiaries who would otherwise lose their coverage because of a "qualified event" to purchase ongoing coverage for a period, usually of up to 18 months. "Qualified event" includes death of a covered employee, reduction in hours for the employee, termination from the job (except for "gross misconduct," a term not defined in the statute), or becoming entitled to Medicare benefits.

*MHPA*—The Mental Health Parity Act (MHPA), 110 Stat. 2847 (1996), 29 U.S.C. § 1185a, does not require a health plan to provide mental health coverage. It does, however, require that if a plan provides that coverage, the annual and lifetime dollar limits must not be lower than those for medical and surgical benefits. This requirement does not extend to treatment for substance abuse or chemical dependency. As mentioned earlier, many caps on spending for a particular individual's care will be phased out under 2010 legislation.

*NMHPA*—The Newborns' and Mothers' Health Protection Act (NMHPA), 110 Stat. 2935 (1996), 29 U.S.C. § 1185(a)(1), forbids a plan to limit a hospital stay for childbirth to less than 48 hours for a "normal" childbirth, 96 hours for a caesarean section.

*Mastectomy Coverage*—The Women's Health and Cancer Rights Act, 112 Stat. 2681—436 (1998), see 29 U.S.C. § 1185b, requires a plan that covers a mastectomy to include coverage of prosthetic devices and reconstructive surgery.

## 2. PENSION PLANS

### CENTRAL LABORERS' PENSION FUND v. HEINZ

Supreme Court of the United States, 2004
541 U.S. 739, 124 S.Ct. 2230, 159 L.Ed.2d 46

JUSTICE SOUTER delivered the opinion of the Court.

With few exceptions, the "anti-cutback" rule of the Employee Retirement Income Security Act of 1974 (ERISA) prohibits any amendment of a pension plan that would reduce a participant's "accrued benefit." 88 Stat. 858, 29 U.S.C. § 1054(g). The question is whether the rule prohibits an amendment expanding the categories of postretirement employment that trigger suspension of payment of early retirement benefits already accrued. We hold such an amendment prohibited.

I

Respondents Thomas Heinz and Richard Schmitt (collectively, Heinz) are retired participants in a multiemployer pension plan (hereinafter Plan) administered by petitioner Central Laborers' Pension Fund. Like most other participants in the Plan, Heinz worked in the construction industry in central Illinois before retiring, and by 1996, he had accrued enough pension credits to qualify for early retirement payments under a defined benefit "service only" pension. This scheme pays him the same monthly retirement benefit he would have received if he had retired at the usual age, and is thus a form of subsidized benefit, since monthly payments are not discounted even though they start earlier and are likely to continue longer than the average period.

Heinz's entitlement is subject to a condition on which this case focuses: the Plan prohibits beneficiaries of service only pensions from certain "disqualifying employment" after they retire. The Plan provides that if beneficiaries accept such employment their monthly payments will be suspended until they stop the forbidden work. When Heinz retired in 1996, the Plan defined "disqualifying employment" as any job as "a union or non-union construction worker." Brief for Respondents 6. This condition did not cover employment in a supervisory capacity, however, and when Heinz took a job in central Illinois as a construction supervisor after retiring, the Plan continued to pay out his monthly benefit.

In 1998, the Plan's definition of disqualifying employment was expanded by amendment to include any job " 'in any capacity in the construction industry (either as a union or non-union construction worker).' " Ibid. The Plan took the amended definition to cover supervisory work and warned Heinz that if he continued on as a supervisor, his monthly pension payments would be suspended. Heinz kept working, and the Plan stopped paying.

Heinz sued to recover the suspended benefits on the ground that applying the amended definition of disqualifying employment so as to suspend payment of his accrued benefits violated ERISA's anti-cutback rule. * * *.

II

A

There is no doubt about the centrality of ERISA's object of protecting employees' justified expectations of receiving the benefits their employers promise them. * * *

ERISA's anti-cutback rule is crucial to this object, and (with two exceptions of no concern here) provides that "[t]he accrued benefit of a participant under a plan may not be decreased by an amendment of the plan...." 29 U.S.C. § 1054(g)(1). After some initial question about whether the provision addressed early retirement benefits, * * * a 1984 amendment made it clear that it does. Retirement Equity Act of 1984, § 301(a)(2), 98 Stat. 1451. Now § 204(g) provides that "a plan amendment which has the effect of ... eliminating or reducing an early retirement benefit ... with respect to benefits attributable to service before the amendment shall be treated as reducing accrued benefits." 29 U.S.C. § 1054(g)(2).

Hence the question here: did the 1998 amendment to the Plan have the effect of "eliminating or reducing an early retirement benefit" that was earned by service before the amendment was passed? The statute, admittedly, is not as helpful as it might be in answering this question; it does not explicitly define "early retirement benefit," and it rather circularly defines "accrued benefit" as "the individual's accrued benefit determined under the plan...." § 1002(23)(A). Still, it certainly looks as though a benefit has suffered under the amendment here, for we agree with the Seventh Circuit that, as a matter of common sense, "[a] participant's benefits cannot be understood without reference to the conditions imposed on receiving those benefits, and an amendment placing materially greater restrictions on the receipt of the benefit 'reduces' the benefit just as surely as a decrease in the size of the monthly benefit payment." 303 F.3d, at 805. Heinz worked and accrued retirement benefits under a plan with terms allowing him to supplement retirement income by certain employment, and he was being reasonable if he relied on those terms in planning his retirement. The 1998 amendment undercut any such reliance, paying retirement income only if he accepted a substantial curtailment of his opportunity to do the kind of work he knew. We simply do not see how, in any practical sense, this change of terms could not be viewed as shrinking the value of Heinz's pension rights and reducing his promised benefits.

### B

The Plan's responses are technical ones, beginning with the suggestion that the "benefit" that may not be devalued is actually nothing more than a "defined periodic benefit the plan is legally obliged to pay," Brief for Petitioner 28, so that § 204(g) applies only to amendments directly altering the nominal dollar amount of a retiree's monthly pension payment. A retiree's benefit of $100 a month, say, is not reduced by a postaccrual plan amendment that suspends payments, so long as nothing affects the figure of $100 defining what he would be paid, if paid at all. Under the Plan's reading, § 204(g) would have nothing to say about an amendment that resulted even in a permanent suspension of payments. But for us to give the anti-cutback rule a reading that constricted would take textual force majeure, and certainly something closer to irresistible than the provision quoted in the Plan's observation that accrued benefits are ordinarily "expressed in the form of an annual benefit commencing at normal retirement age,"29 U.S.C. § 1002(23)(A).

The Plan also contends that, because § 204(g) only prohibits amendments that "eliminat[e] or reduc[e] an early retirement benefit," the anti-cutback rule must not apply to mere suspensions of an early retirement benefit. This argument seems to rest on a distinction between "eliminat[e] or reduc[e]" on the one hand, and "suspend" on the other, but it just misses the point. No one denies that some conditions enforceable by suspending benefit payments are permissible under ERISA: conditions set before a benefit accrues can survive the anti-cutback rule, even though their sanction is a suspension of benefits. Because such conditions are elements of the benefit itself and are considered in valuing it at the moment it accrues, a later suspension of benefit payments according to the Plan's terms does not eliminate the benefit or reduce its value. The real question is whether a new condition may be imposed after a benefit has accrued; may the right to receive certain money on a certain date be limited by a new condition narrowing that right? In a given case, the new condition may or may not be invoked to justify an actual suspension of benefits, but at the moment the new condition is imposed, the accrued benefit becomes less valuable, irrespective of any actual suspension.

### C

Our conclusion is confirmed by a regulation of the Internal Revenue Service (IRS) that adopts just this reading of § 204(g). When Title I of ERISA was enacted to impose substantive legal requirements on employee pension plans (including the anti-cutback rule), Title II of ERISA amended the Internal Revenue Code to condition the eligibility of pension plans for preferential tax treatment on compliance with many of the Title I requirements. Employee Benefits Law 47, 171–173 (S. Sacher et al. eds., 2d ed.2000). The result was a "curious duplicate structure" with nearly verbatim replication in the Internal Revenue Code of whole sections of text from Title I of ERISA. Langbein & Wolk 91, ¶ 6. The anti-cutback rule of ERISA § 204(g) is one such section, showing up in substantially identical form as 26 U.S.C. § 411(d)(6). This duplication explains the provision of the Reorganization Plan No. 4 of 1978, § 101, 43 Fed. Reg. 47713 (1978), 92 Stat. 3790, giving the Secretary of the Treasury the ultimate authority to interpret these overlapping anti-cutback provisions. * * * Although the pertinent regulations refer only to the Internal Revenue Code version of the anti-cutback rule, they apply with equal force to ERISA § 204(g). See 53 Fed. Reg. 26050, 26053 (1988) ("The regulations under section 411 are also applicable to provisions of [ERISA] Title I").

The IRS has formally taken the position that the anti-cutback rule does not keep employers from specifying in advance of accrual that "[t]he availability of a section 411(d)(6) protected benefit [is] limited to employees who satisfy certain objective conditions...." 26 CFR § 1.411(d)–4, A–6(a)(1) (2003). Without running afoul of the rule, for example, plans may say from the outset that a single sum distribution of benefits is conditioned on the execution of a covenant not to compete. § 1.411(d)–4, A–6(a)(2). And employers are perfectly free to modify the deal they are offering their employees, as long as the change goes to the terms of compensation for continued, future employment: a plan "may be amended to eliminate or reduce section 411(d)(6) protected benefits with respect to benefits not yet accrued...." § 1.411(d)–4, A–2(a)(1). The IRS regulations treat such conditions very differently, however, when they turn up as part of an amendment adding new conditions to the receipt of benefits already accrued. The rule in that case is categorical: "[t]he addition of ... objective conditions with respect to a section 411(d)(6) protected benefit that has already accrued violates section 411(d)(6). Also, the addition of conditions (whether or not objective) or any change to existing conditions with respect to section 411(d)(6) protected benefits that results in any further restriction violates section 411(d)(6)." § 1.411(d)–4, A–7. So far as the IRS regulations are concerned, then, the anti-cutback provision flatly prohibits plans from attaching new conditions to benefits that an employee has already earned.

The IRS has, however, told two stories. The Plan points to a provision of the Internal Revenue Manual that supports its position: "[a]n amendment that reduces IRC 411(d)(6) protected benefits on account of [a plan's disqualifying employment provision] does not violate IRC 411(d)(6)." Internal Revenue Manual 4.72.14.3.5.3(7) (May 4, 2001), available at http:// www. irs. gov/ irm/ part 4/ ch 50 s 19. html. And the United States as amicus curiae says that the IRS has routinely approved amendments to plan definitions of disqualifying employment, even when they apply retroactively to accrued benefits. But neither an unreasoned statement in the manual nor allegedly longstanding agency practice can trump a formal regulation with the procedural history necessary to take on the force of law. See generally Note, Omnibus Taxpayers' Bill of Rights Act: Taxpayers' Remedy or Political Placebo? 86 Mich. L. Rev. 1787, 1799–1801 (1988) (discussing legal status of the Internal Revenue Manual). Speaking in its most authoritative voice, the IRS has long since approved the interpretation of § 204(g) that we adopt today.

### III

In criticizing the Seventh Circuit's reading of § 204(g), the Plan and the United States rely heavily on an entirely separate section of ERISA § 203(a)(3)(B), 29 U.S.C. § 1053(a)(3)(B). Here they claim to find specific authorization to amend suspension provisions retroactively, in terms specific enough to trump any general prohibition imposed by § 204(g). Section 203(a)(3)(B) provides that

> [a] right to an accrued benefit derived from employer contributions shall not be treated as forfeitable solely because the plan provides that the payment of benefits is suspended for such period as [beneficiaries like respondents are] employed . . . in the same industry, in the same trade or craft, and the same geographic area covered by the plan, as when such benefits commenced.

29 U.S.C. § 1053(a)(3)(B).

The Plan's arguments notwithstanding, § 203(a)(3)(B) is irrelevant to the question before us, for at least two reasons.

First, as a technical matter, § 203(a) addresses the entirely different question of benefit forfeitures. This is a distinct concept: § 204(g) belongs to the section of ERISA that sets forth requirements for benefit accrual (the rate at which an employee earns benefits to put in his pension account), see 29 U.S.C. § 1054, whereas § 203(a)(3)(B) is in the section that regulates vesting (the process by which an employee's already-accrued pension account becomes irrevocably his property), see 29 U.S.C. § 1053. See generally *Nachman Corp.*, 446 U.S., at 366, n. 10, 100 S. Ct. 1723 ("Section 203(a) is a central provision in ERISA. It requires generally that a plan treat an employee's benefits, to the extent that they have vested by virtue of his having fulfilled age and length of service requirements no greater than those specified in § 203(a)(2), as not subject to forfeiture"). To be sure, the concepts overlap in practical effect, and a single act by a plan might raise both vesting and accrual concerns. But it would be a non sequitur to conclude that, because an amendment does not constitute a prohibited forfeiture under § 203, it must not be a prohibited reduction under § 204. Just because § 203(a)(3)(B) failed to forbid it would not mean that § 204(g) allowed it.

Second, read most simply and in context, § 203(a)(3)(B) is a statement about the terms that can be offered to plan participants up front and enforced without amounting to forfeiture, not as an authorization to adopt retroactive amendments. Section 203(a), 29 U.S.C. § 1053(a), reads that "[e]ach pension plan shall provide that an employee's right to his normal retirement benefit is nonforfeitable upon the attainment of normal retirement age." This is a global directive that regulates the substantive content of pension plans; it adds a mandatory term to all retirement packages that a company might offer. Section 203(a)(3)(B), in turn, is nothing more than an explanation of this substantive requirement. Congress wanted to allow employers to condition future benefits on a plan participant's agreement not to accept certain kinds of postretirement employment, see n. 1, *supra*, and it recognized that a plan provision to this effect might be seen as rendering vested benefits improperly forfeitable. Accordingly, adding § 203(a)(3)(B) made it clear that such suspension provisions were permissible in narrow circumstances. But critically for present purposes, § 203(a)(3)(B) speaks only to the permissible substantive scope of existing ERISA plans, not to the procedural permissibility of plan amendments. The fact that ERISA allows plans to include a suspension provision going to benefits not yet accrued has no logical bearing on the analysis of how ERISA treats the imposition of such a condition on (implicitly) bargained-for benefits that have accrued already. Section 203(a)(3)(B) is no help to the Plan.

The judgment of the Seventh Circuit is AFFIRMED.

It is so ordered.

JUSTICE BREYER, with whom THE CHIEF JUSTICE, JUSTICE O'CONNOR, and JUSTICE GINSBURG join, concurring.

I join the opinion of the Court on the assumption that it does not foreclose a reading of the Employee Retirement Income Security Act of 1974 that allows the Secretary of Labor, or the Secretary of the Treasury, to issue regulations explicitly allowing plan amendments to enlarge the scope of disqualifying employment with respect to benefits attributable to already-performed services. Cf. *Christensen v. Harris County*, 529 U.S. 576, 589, 120 S. Ct. 1655, 146 L. Ed. 2d 621 (2000) (SOUTER, J., concurring).

## NOTES AND QUESTIONS

1. There can be little question about Justice Souter's statement of ERISA's central purpose with respect to pensions: "ERISA's object of protecting employees' justified expectations of receiving the benefits their employers promise them." The provision that is the focus of the principal case is aimed at "partial forfeiture" problems—loss of a part of what the employee reasonably expects. This reflects a view that retirement benefits are simply a form of postponed earnings, compensation fully earned already, but not yet in the paycheck.

The "anti-cutback" provision applies to pension plans, but not welfare plans. In some cases, it may be challenging to determine where the line should be drawn between the two categories. See *Kerber v. Qwest Pension Plan*, 572 F.3d 1135 (10th Cir. 2009).

Other provisions mentioned in the opinion, but not central to this case, have the same central purpose but deal with different reasons why employer promises may prove illusory. These are standards for "accrual," "eligibility to participate" and "vesting."

2. "Accrual" standards target the rate at which pension benefits are earned, a concern with many defined benefit plans. Prior to ERISA, some plans were very heavily "backloaded," so that an employee would earn pension entitlement very slowly in early years, but rapidly after twenty or thirty years of service. For example, a pension plan might provide a benefit at the plan's normal retirement age (assume 65) consisting of a certain percentage of the worker's annual average wage for each of the last five years of employment. The percentage would be based on years of employment: 1% for all years up to the last three worked, and 5% for each of those three. An employer that spends considerable time and money in training a work force would find such a plan desirable, as an inducement for those trained workers to remain with the firm. From an employee perspective the plan is less attractive. The "lock in" effect is obvious; so also is the likelihood that a worker who needed to retire early for a reason such as poor health would experience serious financial difficulty.

Section 204 of ERISA, 29 U.S.C. § 1054, limits backloading, by requiring employers to use one of three methods for computing accruals under a defined benefit plan:

- The participating employee must earn at least 3% of that worker's "anticipated normal retirement benefit" in each year of participation, up to a maximum of 33 1/3 years.

- The worker must earn a fraction of the anticipated benefit each year, the fraction denominator being the number of years between the time the employee begins working for the sponsoring employer and the "normal retirement age" specified under the plan. Suppose a worker begins working for the employer at age 30, and works until age 60. The employer's plan specifies 65 as the normal retirement age. That worker would be credited with having earned 30/35 of his or her maximum credit toward a pension.

- Under the so-called "133 1/3" rule, a later rate of accrual for one year of plan participation must not exceed 133 1/3 per cent of the rate of accrual for any other year. The opposite of backloading, which disadvantages younger workers, would be provisions discriminating against older workers, such as decreasing rates of contribution for workers over 55. That is forbidden both by the Age Discrimination in Employment Act, 29 U.S.C. §§ 621–634, and by ERISA itself. 29 U.S.C. § 1054(b)(1)(H), (b)(2)(A).

3. "Eligibility to participate" standards reflect some of the same concerns that prompted the accrual standards. Reserving eligibility to participate for those with many years of service would disadvantage both younger workers and those who want to seek better jobs with a different employer at various points in their working life. Section 202 of ERISA, 29 U.S.C. § 1052, generally requires a plan to be open to any worker with one "year of service" (a 12–month period during which the employee has worked 1,000 hours or

more) who is 21 years old or above. The major exception is for plans with 100% "vesting" (see the next note) after a maximum of two years of service; such plans may postpone eligibility to participate for two years rather than one. Once a worker is eligible to participate, that worker's application to enroll must be honored within six months (or on the first day of the plan year, if that is earlier).

4.   "Vesting" standards, like the anti-cutback rule, are designed to limit how much of an accrued benefit a worker may lose if a certain contingency occurs—usually leaving the job voluntarily or being fired. If a pension benefit has vested, that benefit cannot be taken away. Under many plans, an employee with a vested benefit may have options available upon leaving the job before retirement age. One option is to remain a plan participant and receive benefits at the normal retirement age; another common option is to receive the present value of the vested future benefit as a lump sum. If the employee does the latter, it is important that he or she "roll over" that distribution into another qualified plan (often a "rollover IRA") in order to avoid paying taxes and tax penalties on the distribution. Employers tend to prefer for employees to take lump sum settlements, since that simplifies record keeping and does away with the problem of staying in touch with plan participants who are no longer employees.

Two of the ERISA vesting rules are so commonsensical they are easy to remember:

- Any contribution made by the employee vests immediately. (This does not mean the value may not change, of course. Suppose in the case of a defined contribution plan, for example, the employee directs the plan to invest all contributions in the stock of XYZ, Inc. The plan buys the stock at $50 a share, at a point when the employee's account has $2,000 in it. The stock then goes to $100 a share; the employee's account is now worth $4,000. Then XYZ has a bad earnings year or two and the stock goes to $10 a share. The employee's account is now worth $400.)

- All accrued benefits vest at the plan's "normal retirement age." (All defined benefit plans must have such an age; if a plan does not specify a normal retirement age, then it is the later of the time the participant turns 65 or the fifth anniversary of the time when the employee became a plan participant.) See 26 U.S.C. § 411(a)(8).

The remainder of the vesting rules are a bit more complicated, although the basic principles are simple enough. ERISA permits employer contributions to vest in either of two ways: "Cliff vesting" and "graded vesting." As the term implies, cliff vesting is a system in which all employer contributions vest at once on a certain date, so that an employee who leaves the job the day before that date has no claim to employer-contribution based benefits at all. ERISA sets five "years of service" as the maximum for cliff vesting for defined benefit plans, three years for defined contribution plans. If the sponsors of a plan choose to use "graded" vesting, then the percentage of employer contributions that must be vested must meet a minimum schedule. For defined benefit plans the present schedule requirement is that at least 20% must vest after three "years of service," 40% after four years, 60% after five years, 80% after six years, and 100% at seven years. For defined contribution plans, the requirement accelerates one year, so that at least 20% must vest at the end of two years of service, 40% after three years, 60% after four years, 80% after five years, and 100% at the end of six years. (There are special rules for some collectively bargained plans and for employees whose employment is interrupted by breaks in service.) See generally ERISA section 203(b), 29 U.S.C. § 1053(b).

5. As the principal opinion states, an employer is generally free to modify or terminate a plan unless it was established through collective bargaining. All vested benefits rights must be provided to plan participants, however.

6. If a plan was established through collective bargaining, then modifications must be bargained for, unless the union has waived its right to insist on that bargaining. See generally, *Southern Nuclear Operating Co. v. N.L.R.B.*, 524 F.3d 1350 (D.C. Cir. 2008) (some bargaining rights waived, others not).

## KENNEDY v. PLAN ADMINISTRATOR FOR DUPONT SAVINGS AND INVESTMENT PLAN

Supreme Court of the United States, 2009
___ U.S. ___, 129 S.Ct. 865, 172 L.Ed.2d 662, 77 USLW 4082

JUSTICE SOUTER delivered the opinion of the Court.

The Employee Retirement Income Security Act of 1974 (ERISA), 88 Stat. 829, 29 U.S.C. § 1001 et seq., generally obligates administrators to manage ERISA plans "in accordance with the documents and instruments governing" them.§ 1104(a)(1)(D). At a more specific level, the Act requires covered pension benefit plans to "provide that benefits ... under the plan may not be assigned or alienated,"§ 1056(d)(1), but this bar does not apply to qualified domestic relations orders (QDROs), § 1056(d)(3). The question here is whether the terms of the limitation on assignment or alienation invalidated the act of a divorced spouse, the designated beneficiary under her ex-husband's ERISA pension plan, who purported to waive her entitlement by a federal common law waiver embodied in a divorce decree that was not a QDRO. We hold that such a waiver is not rendered invalid by the text of the antialienation provision, but that the plan administrator properly disregarded the waiver owing to its conflict with the designation made by the former husband in accordance with plan documents.

I

The decedent, William Kennedy, worked for E.I. DuPont de Nemours & Company and was a participant in its savings and investment plan (SIP), with power both to "designate any beneficiary or beneficiaries ... to receive all or part" of the funds upon his death, and to "replace or revoke such designation." App. 48. The plan requires "[a]ll authorizations, designations and requests concerning the Plan [to] be made by employees in the manner prescribed by the [plan administrator]," id., at

52, and provides forms for designating or changing a beneficiary, id., at 34, 56–57. If at the time the participant dies "no surviving spouse exists and no beneficiary designation is in effect, distribution shall be made to, or in accordance with the directions of, the executor or administrator of the decedent's estate." Id., at 48.

The SIP is an ERISA" 'employee pension benefit plan,' * * * and the parties do not dispute that the plan satisfies ERISA's antialienation provision, § 1056(d)(1), which requires it to "provide that benefits provided under the plan may not be assigned or alienated." The plan does, however, permit a beneficiary to submit a "qualified disclaimer" of benefits as defined under the Tax Code, see 26 U.S.C. § 2518, which has the effect of switching the beneficiary to an "alternate ... determined according to a valid beneficiary designation made by the deceased." Supp. Record 86–87 (Exh. 15).

In 1971, William married Liv Kennedy, and, in 1974, he signed a form designating her to take benefits under the SIP, but naming no contingent beneficiary to take if she disclaimed her interest. 497 F.3d, at 427. William and Liv divorced in 1994, subject to a decree that Liv "is ... divested of all right, title, interest, and claim in and to ... [a]ny and all sums ... the proceeds [from], and any other rights related to any ... retirement plan, pension plan, or like benefit program existing by reason of [William's] past or present or future employment." App. to Pet. for Cert. 64–65. William did not, however, execute any documents removing Liv as the SIP beneficiary, 497 F.3d, at 428, even though he did execute a new beneficiary-designation form naming his daughter, Kari Kennedy, as the beneficiary under DuPont's Pension and Retirement Plan, also governed by ERISA.

On William's death in 2001, petitioner Kari Kennedy was named executrix and asked DuPont to distribute the SIP funds to William's Estate. DuPont, instead, relied on William's designation form and paid the balance of some $400,000 to Liv. The Estate then sued respondents DuPont and the SIP plan administrator (together, DuPont), claiming that the divorce decree amounted to a waiver of the SIP benefits on Liv's part, and that DuPont had violated ERISA by paying the benefits to William's designee.

* * * The Court of Appeals held that Liv's waiver constituted an assignment or alienation of her interest in the SIP benefits to the Estate, and so could not be honored. Id., at 430. The court relied heavily on the ERISA provision for bypassing the antialienation provision when a marriage breaks up: under 29 U.S.C. § 1056(d)(3), a court order that satisfies certain statutory requirements is known as a qualified domestic relations order, which is exempt from the bar on assignment or alienation. Because the Kennedys' divorce decree was not a QDRO, the Fifth Circuit reasoned that it could not give effect to Liv's waiver incorporated in it, given that "ERISA provides a specific mechanism—the QDRO—for addressing the elimination of a spouse's interest in plan benefits, but that mechanism is not invoked." 497 F.3d, at 431.

We granted certiorari to resolve a split among the Courts of Appeals and State Supreme Courts over a divorced spouse's ability to waive pension plan benefits through a divorce decree not amounting to a QDRO. We subsequently realized that this case implicates the further split over whether a beneficiary's federal common law waiver of plan benefits is effective where that waiver is inconsistent with plan documents * * *.

## II

### A

By its terms, the antialienation provision, § 1056(d)(1), requires a plan to provide expressly that benefits be neither "assigned" nor "alienated," the operative verbs having histories of legal meaning: to "assign" is "[t]o transfer; as to assign property, or some interest therein," Black's Law Dictionary 152 (4th rev. ed.1968), and to "alienate" is "[t]o convey; to transfer the title to property," id., at 96. We think it fair to say that Liv did not assign or alienate anything to William or to the Estate later standing in his shoes.

The Fifth Circuit saw the waiver as an assignment or alienation to the Estate, thinking that Liv's waiver transferred the SIP benefits to whoever would be next in line; without a designated contingent beneficiary, the Estate would take them. The court found support in the applicable Treasury Department regulation that defines "assignment" and "alienation" to include

> [a]ny direct or indirect arrangement (whether revocable or irrevocable) whereby a party acquires from a participant or beneficiary a right or interest enforceable against the plan in, or to, all or any part of a plan benefit payment which is, or may become, payable to the participant or beneficiary.

26 CFR § 1.401(a)–13(c)(1)(ii) (2008).

* * * Casting the alienation net this far, though, raises questions that leave one in doubt. * * *

Our doubts, and the exceptions that call the Fifth Circuit's reading into question, point us toward authority we have drawn on before, the law of trusts that "serves as ERISA's backdrop." *Beck v. PACE Int'l Union*, 551 U.S. 96, 101, 127 S. Ct. 2310, 168 L. Ed. 2d 1 (2007). We explained before that § 1056(d)(1) is much like a spendthrift trust provision barring assignment or alienation of a benefit, see *Boggs, supra*, at 852, and the cognate trust law is highly suggestive here. Although the beneficiary of a spendthrift trust traditionally lacked the means to transfer his beneficial interest to anyone else, he did have the power to disclaim prior to accepting it, so long as the disclaimer made no attempt to direct the interest to a beneficiary in his stead. See 2 Restatement (Third) of Trusts § 58(1), Comment c, p. 359 (2001) ("A designated beneficiary of a spendthrift trust is not required to accept or retain an interest prescribed by the terms of the trust.... On the other hand, a purported disclaimer by which the beneficiary attempts to direct who is to receive the interest is a precluded transfer"); * * *

We do not mean that the whole law of spendthrift trusts and disclaimers turns up in § 1056(d)(1), but the general principle that a designated spendthrift can disclaim his trust interest magnifies the improbability that a statute written with an eye on the old law would effectively force a beneficiary to take an interest willy-nilly. Common sense and common law both say that "[t]he law certainly is not so absurd as to force a man to take an estate against his will." *Townson v. Tickell*, 3 Barn. & Ald. 31, 36, 106 Eng. Rep. 575, 576–577 (K.B.1819).

The Treasury is certainly comfortable with the state of the old law, for the way it reads its own regulation "no party 'acquires from' a beneficiary a 'right or interest enforceable against the plan' pursuant to a beneficiary's waiver of rights where the beneficiary does not attempt to direct her interest in pension benefits to another person." Brief for United States as Amicus Curiae 18. * * *

In sum, Liv did not attempt to direct her interest in the SIP benefits to the Estate or any other potential beneficiary, and accordingly we think that the better view is that her waiver did not constitute an assignment or alienation rendered void under the terms of § 1056(d)(1). * * *

### III

The waiver's escape from inevitable nullity under the express terms of the antialienation clause does not, however, control the decision of this case, and the question remains whether the plan administrator was required to honor Liv's waiver with the consequence of distributing the SIP balance to the Estate. We hold that it was not, and that the plan administrator did its statutory ERISA duty by paying the benefits to Liv in conformity with the plan documents.

ERISA requires "[e]very employee benefit plan [to] be established and maintained pursuant to a written instrument," 29 U.S.C. § 1102(a)(1), "specify[ing] the basis on which payments are made to and from the plan," § 1102(b)(4). The plan administrator is obliged to act "in accordance with the documents and instruments governing the plan insofar as such documents and instruments are consistent with the provisions of [Title I] and [Title IV] of [ERISA]," § 1104(a)(1)(D), and the Act provides no exemption from this duty when it comes time to pay benefits. On the contrary, § 1132(a)(1)(B) (which the Estate happens to invoke against DuPont here) reinforces the directive, with its provision that a participant or beneficiary may bring a cause of action "to recover benefits due to him under the terms of his plan, to enforce his rights under the terms of the plan, or to clarify his rights to future benefits under the terms of the plan."

The Estate's claim therefore stands or falls by "the terms of the plan," * * *

We express no view regarding the ability of a participant or beneficiary to bring a cause of action under 29 U.S.C. § 1132(a)(1)(B) where the terms of the plan fail to conform to the requirements of ERISA and the party seeks to recover under the terms of the statute.

And the cost of less certain rules would be too plain. Plan administrators would be forced "to examine a multitude of external documents that might purport to affect the dispensation of benefits," *Altobelli v. IBM Corp.*, 77 F.3d 78, 82–83 (C.A.4 1996) (Wilkinson, C. J., dissenting), and be drawn into litigation like this over the meaning and enforceability of purported waivers. * * *

The Estate of course is right that this guarantee of simplicity is not absolute. The very enforceability of QDROs means that sometimes a plan administrator must look for the beneficiaries outside plan documents notwithstanding § 1104(a)(1)(D); § 1056(d)(3)(J) provides that a "person who is an alternate payee under a [QDRO] shall be considered for purposes of any provision of [ERISA] a beneficiary under the plan." * * *

These are good and sufficient reasons for holding the line, just as we have done in cases of state laws that might blur the bright-line requirement to follow plan documents in distributing benefits. Two recent preemption cases are instructive here. *Boggs v. Boggs*, 520 U.S. 833, 117 S. Ct. 1754, 138 L. Ed. 2d 45, held that ERISA preempted a state law permitting the testamentary transfer of a nonparticipant spouse's community property interest in undistributed pension plan benefits. We rejected the entreaty to create "through case law ... a new class of persons for whom plan assets are to be held and administered," explaining that "[t]he statute is not amenable to this sweeping extratextual extension." Id., at 850. And in Egelhoff we held that ERISA preempted a state law providing that the designation of a spouse as the beneficiary of a nonprobate asset is revoked automatically upon divorce. 532 U.S., at 143. We said the law was at fault for standing in the way of making payments "simply by identifying the beneficiary specified by the plan documents," id., at 148, and thus for purporting to "undermine the congressional goal of 'minimiz[ing] the administrative and financial burden[s]' on plan administrators," id., at 149–150 * * *.

What goes for inconsistent state law goes for a federal common law of waiver that might obscure a plan administrator's duty to act "in accordance with the documents and instruments." See *Mertens v. Hewitt Associates*, 508 U.S. 248, 259, 113 S. Ct. 2063, 124 L. Ed. 2d 161 (1993) ("The authority of courts to develop a 'federal common law' under ERISA ... is not the authority to revise the text of the statute"). And this case does as well as any other in pointing out the wisdom of protecting the plan documents rule. Under the terms of the SIP Liv was William's designated beneficiary. The plan provided an easy way for William to change the designation, but for whatever reason he did not. The plan provided a way to disclaim an interest in the SIP account, but Liv did not purport to follow it. The plan administrator therefore did exactly what

§ 1104(a)(1)(D) required: "the documents control, and those name [the ex-wife]." *McMillan v. Parrott*, 913 F.2d 310, 312 (C.A.6 1990).

\* \* \* It is uncontested that the SIP and the summary plan description are "documents and instruments governing the plan." See Curtiss–Wright Corp., 514 U.S., at 84 (explaining that 29 U.S.C. §§ 1024(b)(2) and (b)(4) require a plan administrator to make available the "governing plan documents"). Those documents provide that the plan administrator will pay benefits to a participant's designated beneficiary, with designations and changes to be made in a particular way. William's designation of Liv as his beneficiary was made in the way required; Liv's waiver was not.

## IV

Although Liv's waiver was not rendered a nullity by the terms of § 1056, the plan administrator properly distributed the SIP benefits to Liv in accordance with the plan documents. The judgment of the Court of Appeals is affirmed on the latter ground.

It is so ordered.

### NOTES AND QUESTIONS

1. The "qualified domestic relations order" (QDRO) exception to the anti-alienation provision is designed to protect primarily the interests of spouses and children of workers. In order for one of these state court orders to "qualify" it must protect the interest of an individual who is an "alternate payee" under the relevant plan, and must in general conform to the terms of that plan. The order cannot, for example, require the payment of a benefit any greater than what the plan provides. Failure to comply with the detailed procedural and substantive requirements of 29 U.S.C. § 1056(d)(3) will result in an order that is ineffective under the anti-alienation provision.

2. The federal Bankruptcy Code provides that "a restriction on the transfer of a beneficial interest of the debtor in a trust that is enforceable under applicable nonbankruptcy law, is enforceable in a [bankruptcy case.]" 11 U.S.C. § 541(c)(2) Therefore a beneficiary's interest in an ERISA-governed pension plan is not to be included in that beneficiary's bankruptcy estate.

In *In re Nelson*, 322 F.3d 541 (8th Cir. 2003), Ronald Nelson had acquired an interest in his ex-wife Denise's ERISA-governed pension plan by virtue of a QDRO that was entered by the court that granted Nelson and his former wife their divorce. The bankruptcy court at first ruled that Ronald's interest in Denise's plan was includable in the bankruptcy estate. The court reasoned that Ronald was not to be treated as a beneficiary of the retirement plan (and thus entitled to the benefit of the anti-alienation provision), since he had acquired his interest by way of a QDRO. The Bankruptcy Appeal Panel and the Eighth Circuit Court of Appeals, however, reached the opposite conclusion. They noted that Ronald, as a spouse, was an alternate payee under the retirement plan, and that ERISA provides beneficiary status to alternate payees under a QDRO.

As the Nelson opinion indicates, however, once a benefit has been paid out to an individual, it becomes part of that individual's estate, and is subject to garnishment and attachment just as any other of the individual's property would be. Thus, Ronald's interest in the corpus of funds in Denise's plan would be protected by the anti-alienation provision, but any payout he received—a monthly annuity payment, for example—would not be protected.

3. ERISA also protects the interests of spouses by requiring that a pension plan include a provision that "(1) in the case of a vested participant who does not die before the annuity starting date, the accrued benefit payable to such participant shall be in the form of a qualified joint and survivor annuity; and (2) in the case of a vested participant who dies before the annuity starting date and who has a surviving spouse, a qualified preretirement survivor annuity shall be provided to the surviving spouse of such participant." 29 U.S.C. § 1055(a). A spouse can under some circumstances waive some of this protection. 29 U.S.C. § 1055 (c), (g), (k).

4. Another exception to the anti-alienation provision is one that permits a participant to borrow from the plan, and use her accrued vested benefit in the plan as security, so long as the plan permits that, and the loan does not constitute a "prohibited transaction." In *Yates v. Hendon*, 541 U.S. 1, 124 S.Ct. 1330, 158 L.Ed.2d 40 (2004), a "working owner"—the sole shareholder and president of a professional corporation—established a profit sharing plan in which he and others employed by the corporation participated. He then borrowed from the plan, and failed to make timely repayments as the loan document required, until he repaid the entire loan three weeks before declaring bankruptcy. The lower courts decided that this was a transaction that should be set aside as a voidable preferential transfer under the Bankruptcy Code, and that the repaid money should be treated as part of the bankruptcy estate available to pay off creditors. They reasoned that an owner should not be treated as a "participant" in the plan for purposes of the anti-alienation provision. The Supreme Court reversed, and held that so long as one other person who would have the status of a common law employee participated in a plan, the working owner should be treated as a participant protected by ERISA as well. The Court did not, however, address any other questions about whether the Bankruptcy Code's voidable preference provisions should be given greater weight than the ERISA-required anti-alienation clause. That issue was sent back to the lower courts.

5. In 1997, the Congress added subsection 29 U.S.C. § 1056(d)(4), and resolved an issue on which the circuit courts were sharply divided: Should a person who is both plan fiduciary and plan participant, and who violates his fiduciary responsibilities in a way that reduces the assets of the plan, be able to use the anti-alienation provision to prevent the plan from offsetting the monetary damage he has done to the plan against any benefits the individual might otherwise be due from the plan? The statute now specifically allows such an offset, but in limited circumstances. The wrongdoing participant must (a) have been convicted of a crime, (b) be the subject of a civil judgment based on violation of the fiduciary duties imposed by ERISA, or (c) have entered into a settlement with the Secretary of Labor or the Pension Benefit Guaranty Corporation involving an alleged violation of a fiduciary rule. In the latter two

cases, the offset must be included in the judgment or agreement. For a discussion of the prior split, see *Coar v. Kazimir*, 990 F.2d 1413 (3d Cir. 1993).

6. It is generally agreed that the anti-alienation provision does not extend to welfare benefit plans, but that those plans are free to adopt such a provision. Orders entered in divorce proceedings sometimes require that a participant in a health plan maintain coverage for a child. ERISA requires group health plans to honor such orders, provided they meet standards similar to those that apply to pension plans. See 29 U.S.C. § 1169(a).

# F. FIDUCIARY STATUS AND CONDUCT

## LARUE v. DEWOLFF, BOBERG & ASSOCIATES, INC.

Supreme Court of the United States, 2008
552 U.S. 248, 128 S.Ct. 1020, 169 L.Ed.2d 847

JUSTICE STEVENS delivered the opinion of the Court.

In *Massachusetts Mut. Life Ins. Co. v. Russell*, 473 U.S. 134, 105 S. Ct. 3085, 87 L. Ed. 2d 96 (1985), we held that a participant in a disability plan that paid a fixed level of benefits could not bring suit under § 502(a)(2) of the Employee Retirement Income Security Act of 1974 (ERISA), 88 Stat. 891, 29 U.S.C. § 1132(a)(2), to recover consequential damages arising from delay in the processing of her claim. In this case we consider whether that statutory provision authorizes a participant in a defined contribution pension plan to sue a fiduciary whose alleged misconduct impaired the value of plan assets in the participant's individual account. * * *

I

Petitioner filed this action in 2004 against his former employer, DeWolff, Boberg & Associates (DeWolff), and the ERISA-regulated 401(k) retirement savings plan administered by DeWolff (Plan). The Plan permits participants to direct the investment of their contributions in accordance with specified procedures and requirements. Petitioner alleged that in 2001 and 2002 he directed DeWolff to make certain changes to the investments in his individual account, but DeWolff never carried out these directions. Petitioner claimed that this omission "depleted" his interest in the Plan by approximately $150,000, and amounted to a breach of fiduciary duty under ERISA. The complaint sought " 'make-whole' or other equitable relief as allowed by [§ 502(a)(3)]," as well as "such other and further relief as the court deems just and proper." * * *

Respondents filed a motion for judgment on the pleadings, arguing that the complaint was essentially a claim for monetary relief that is not recoverable under § 502(a)(3). Petitioner countered that he "d[id] not wish for the court to award him any money, but ... simply want[ed] the plan to properly reflect that which would be his interest in the plan, but for the breach of fiduciary duty." * * * The District Court concluded, however, that since respondents did not possess any disputed funds that rightly belonged to petitioner, he was seeking damages rather than equitable relief available under § 502(a)(3). Assuming, *arguendo*, that respondents had breached a fiduciary duty, the District Court nonetheless granted their motion. [The Court of Appeals affirmed.] * * *

Section 502(a)(2) provides for suits to enforce the liability-creating provisions of § 409, concerning breaches of fiduciary duties that harm plans. The Court of Appeals cited language from our opinion in *Russell* suggesting that that these provisions "protect the entire plan, rather than the rights of an individual beneficiary." 473 U.S., at 142, 105 S. Ct. 3085. It then characterized the remedy sought by petitioner as "personal" because he "desires recovery to be paid into his plan account, an instrument that exists specifically for his benefit," and concluded:

> We are therefore skeptical that plaintiff's individual remedial interest can serve as a legitimate proxy for the plan in its entirety, as [§ 502(a)(2)] requires. To be sure, the recovery plaintiff seeks could be seen as accruing to the plan in the narrow sense that it would be paid into plaintiff's plan account, which is part of the plan. But such a view finds no license in the statutory text, and threatens to undermine the careful limitations Congress has placed on the scope of ERISA relief.

450 F.3d, at 574.

The Court of Appeals also rejected petitioner's argument that the make-whole relief he sought was "equitable" within the meaning of § 502(a)(3). Although our grant of certiorari, 551 U.S. 1130, 127 S. Ct. 2971, 168 L. Ed. 2d 702 (2007), encompassed the § 502(a)(3) issue, we do not address it because we conclude that the Court of Appeals misread § 502(a)(2).

## II

As the case comes to us we must assume that respondents breached fiduciary obligations defined in § 409(a), and that those breaches had an adverse impact on the value of the plan assets in petitioner's individual account. Whether petitioner can prove those allegations and whether respondents may have valid defenses to the claim are matters not before us. * * * Although the record does not reveal the relative size of petitioner's account, the legal issue under § 502(a)(2) is the same whether his account includes 1% or 99% of the total assets in the plan.

As we explained in *Russell*, and in more detail in our later opinion in *Varity Corp. v. Howe*, 516 U.S. 489, 508–512, 116 S. Ct. 1065, 134 L. Ed. 2d 130 (1996), § 502(a) of ERISA identifies six types of civil actions that may be brought by various parties. The second, which is at issue in this case, authorizes the Secretary of Labor as well as plan participants, beneficiaries, and fiduciaries, to bring actions on behalf of a plan to recover for violations of the obligations defined in § 409(a). The principal statutory duties imposed on fiduciaries by that section "relate to the proper management, administration, and investment of fund assets," with an eye toward ensuring that "the benefits authorized by the plan" are ultimately paid to participants and beneficiaries. * * * The misconduct alleged by the petitioner in this case falls squarely within that category.

The misconduct alleged in Russell, by contrast, fell outside this category. The plaintiff in Russell received all of the benefits to which she was contractually entitled, but sought consequential damages arising from a delay in the processing of her claim. 473 U.S., at 136–137, 105 S. Ct. 3085. In holding that § 502(a)(2) does not provide a remedy for this type of injury, we stressed that the text of § 409(a) characterizes the relevant fiduciary relationship as one "with respect to a plan," and repeatedly identifies the "plan" as the victim of any fiduciary breach and the recipient of any relief. See id., at 140, 105 S. Ct. 3085. The legislative history likewise revealed that "the crucible of congressional concern was misuse and mismanagement of plan assets by plan administrators." Id., at 141, n. 8, 105 S. Ct. 3085. Finally, our review of ERISA as a whole confirmed that §§ 502(a)(2) and 409 protect "the financial integrity of the plan," id., at 142, n. 9, 105 S. Ct. 3085, whereas other provisions specifically address claims for benefits. See id., at 143–144, 105 S. Ct. 3085 (discussing §§ 502(a)(1)(B) and 503). We therefore concluded:

> "A fair contextual reading of the statute makes it abundantly clear that its draftsmen were primarily concerned with the possible misuse of plan assets, and with remedies that would protect the entire plan, rather than with the rights of an individual beneficiary."

Id., at 142, 105 S. Ct. 3085.

Russell's emphasis on protecting the "entire plan" from fiduciary misconduct reflects the former landscape of employee benefit plans. That landscape has changed.

Defined contribution plans dominate the retirement plan scene today. In contrast, when ERISA was enacted, and when Russell was decided, "the [defined benefit] plan was the norm of American pension practice." J. Langbein, S. Stabile, & B. Wolk, Pension and Employee Benefit Law 58 (4th ed.2006); * * *. Unlike the defined contribution plan in this case, the disability plan at issue in Russell did not have individual accounts; it paid a fixed benefit based on a percentage of the employee's salary. See *Russell v. Massachusetts Mut. Life Ins. Co.*, 722 F.2d 482, 486 (C.A.9 1983).

The "entire plan" language in Russell speaks to the impact of § 409 on plans that pay defined benefits. Misconduct by the administrators of a defined benefit plan will not affect an individual's entitlement to a defined benefit unless it creates or enhances the risk of default by the entire plan. It was that default risk that prompted Congress to require defined benefit plans (but not defined contribution plans) to satisfy complex minimum funding requirements, and to make premium payments to the Pension Benefit Guaranty Corporation for plan termination insurance. * * *

For defined contribution plans, however, fiduciary misconduct need not threaten the solvency of the entire plan to reduce benefits below the amount that participants would otherwise receive. Whether a fiduciary breach diminishes plan assets payable to all participants and beneficiaries, or only to persons tied to particular individual accounts, it creates the kind of harms that concerned the draftsmen of § 409. Consequently, our references to the "entire plan" in Russell, which accurately reflect the operation of § 409 in the defined benefit context, are beside the point in the defined contribution context.

Other sections of ERISA confirm that the "entire plan" language from Russell, which appears nowhere in § 409 or § 502(a)(2), does not apply to defined contribution plans. Most significant is § 404(c), which exempts fiduciaries from liability for losses caused by participants' exercise of control over assets in their individual accounts. See also 29 CFR § 2550.404c–1 (2007). This provision would serve no real purpose if, as respondents argue, fiduciaries never had any liability for losses in an individual account.

We therefore hold that although § 502(a)(2) does not provide a remedy for individual injuries distinct from plan injuries, that provision does authorize recovery for fiduciary breaches that impair the value of plan assets in a participant's individual account. Accordingly, the judgment of the Court of Appeals is vacated, and the case is remanded for further proceedings consistent with this opinion.

It is so ordered.

[Concurring opinions of CHIEF JUSTICE ROBERTS (joined by JUSTICE KENNEDY) and JUSTICE THOMAS (joined by JUSTICE SCALIA) are omitted.]

## A Note on Defined Benefit Plans and Defined Contribution Plans

As discussed in the case, ERISA regulates two types of pension plans: defined benefit plans and defined contribution plans. Under a defined benefit plan, the employer promises to pay a specified monthly benefit at retirement. The promised benefit might be a specific dollar amount, such as $1000 per month, or based on a plan formula—for example, one percent of the average salary for the last five years of employment for every year of service the employee has with the employer. The employer is responsible for setting aside enough money and investing it wisely so that there are enough proceeds in the pension fund to pay benefits when they become due. Under a defined contribution plan, the employer promises to make specified regular contributions to a retirement account for the employee, perhaps in conjunction with contributions by the employee, and this account yields unspecified retirement income for the employee. The employer contributions are typically a percent of the income earned by the employee working for the employer and the retirement income depends on the amount of contributions made, the return the employee earns on the retirement account and how fast the employee decides to withdraw money from the account. The account could also be used to buy a life annuity based on the size of the account and the life expectancy of the employee at the time of retirement. Examples of defined contribution plans include 401(k) plans, 403(b) plans, employee stock ownership plans, and profit-sharing plans.

There are various advantages and disadvantages to defined benefit plans and defined contribution plans for employers and employees. Employees tend to prefer defined benefit plans because the risk that plan investments will go sour (or grow) is on the employer and there is some protection for inflation because plan benefits are generally based on the employee's income during the last five years of service—which will rise with inflation. Very mobile employees may prefer a defined contribution plan since individual retirement accounts are more portable than defined benefit credits. Employers tend to favor defined contribution plans because pension contributions are limited and predictable, the risk that fund investments will go sour (or grow) is on the employee, and these plans are simpler to administer. In practice when employers change from a defined benefit plan to a defined contribution plan, employer pension contributions are reduced. Also in practice, employee managed individual retirement accounts under defined contribution plans have fared more poorly in their returns than professionally managed group plans under defined benefit plans. Alicia H. Munnell, Mauricio Soto, Jerilyn Libby, and John Prinzivalli, Investment Returns: Defined Benefit vs. 401(k) Plans, Issue in Brief No. 52, Center for Retirement Research at Boston College (Sept. 2006). As a result, employee retirement benefits are generally higher and much more predictable under a defined benefit plan than under a defined contribution plan. *Legislator's Guide to Nebraska Retirement Systems,* December 1998. A 1998 study of the State of Nebraska retirement system found that, ten years after retirement, retirees under a defined benefit plan enjoyed pension benefits approximately 50% higher than employees with comparable employment records under a defined contribution plan. Jeff Opdyke, The Wall Street Journal, *"State Worker's Pension Plans Spark Debate,"* May 5, 2000.

In recent years the private employer retirement system in the United States has undergone a dramatic transformation as the percent of employers offering defined benefit plans has decreased and the percent of employers offering defined contribution plans has increased. In 1975, 68% of all workers with pensions had defined benefit plans and these plans accounted for two-thirds of all pension plan assets. Defined benefit plans at this time were minimal. However by 2004, only 20% of workers with pensions were enrolled in defined benefit plans while 63% of workers with pension coverage were enrolled in defined contribution plans. Samuel Estreicher and Laurence Gold, *The Shift From Defined Benefit Plans to Defined Contribution Plans*, 11 LEWIS & CLARK L. REV. 331, 331–32 (2007). This transformation has come about for a number of reasons. First, the manufacturing sector in which employees traditionally enjoyed defined benefit plans has declined since the 1970's. Second, employees have become more mobile in the modern economy and defined contribution plans fit mobile employees better. Finally, with the decline of unions in the United States and the rise of the global economy, American employers now enjoy more bargaining power relative to their employees and prefer defined contribution pensions.

## QUESTION

From a national perspective, what are the implications of the shift from defined benefit plans to defined contribution plans for Americans' preparation for retirement? How will this affect the planned retirement ages of employees?

## METROPOLITAN LIFE INSURANCE CO. v. GLENN

Supreme Court of the United States, 2008
554 U.S. 105, 128 S.Ct. 2343, 171 L.Ed.2d 299

JUSTICE BREYER delivered the opinion of the Court.

The Employee Retirement Income Security Act of 1974 (ERISA) permits a person denied benefits under an employee benefit plan to challenge that denial in federal court. 88 Stat. 829, as amended, 29 U.S.C. § 1001 et seq.; see § 1132(a)(1)(B). Often the entity that administers the plan, such as an employer or an insurance company, both determines whether an employee is eligible for benefits and pays benefits out of its own pocket. We here decide that this dual role creates a conflict of interest; that a reviewing court should consider that conflict as a factor in determining whether the plan administrator has abused its discretion in denying benefits; and that the significance of the factor will depend upon the circumstances of the particular case. See *Firestone Tire & Rubber Co. v. Bruch*, 489 U.S. 101, 115, 109 S. Ct. 948, 103 L. Ed. 2d 80 (1989).

I

Petitioner Metropolitan Life Insurance Company (MetLife) serves as both an administrator and the insurer of Sears, Roebuck & Company's long-term disability insurance plan, an ERISA-governed employee benefit plan. * * * The plan grants MetLife (as administrator) discretionary authority to determine whether an employee's claim for benefits is valid; it simultaneously provides that MetLife (as insurer) will itself pay valid benefit claims. * * *

Respondent Wanda Glenn, a Sears employee, was diagnosed with severe dilated cardiomyopathy, a heart condition whose symptoms include fatigue and shortness of breath. She applied for plan disability benefits in June 2000, and MetLife concluded that she met the plan's standard for an initial 24 months of benefits, namely, that she could not "perform the material duties of [her] own job." * * * MetLife also directed Glenn to a law firm that would assist her in applying for federal Social Security disability benefits (some of which MetLife itself would be entitled to receive as an offset to the more generous plan benefits). In April 2002, an Administrative Law Judge found that Glenn's illness prevented her not

*Soc Sect benes* [handwritten margin note]

only from performing her own job but also "from performing any jobs [for which she could qualify] existing in significant numbers in the national economy." * * * The Social Security Administration consequently granted Glenn permanent disability payments retroactive to April 2000. Glenn herself kept none of the backdated benefits: three-quarters went to MetLife, and the rest (plus some additional money) went to the lawyers.

To continue receiving Sears plan disability benefits after 24 months, Glenn had to meet a stricter, Social–Security-type standard, namely, that her medical condition rendered her incapable of performing not only her own job but of performing "the material duties of any gainful occupation for which" she was "reasonably qualified." * * * MetLife denied Glenn this extended benefit because it found that she was "capable of performing full time sedentary work." * * *

After exhausting her administrative remedies, Glenn brought this federal lawsuit, seeking judicial review of MetLife's denial of benefits. See 29 U.S.C. § 1132(a)(1)(B); 461 F.3d 660, 665 (C.A.6 2006). The District Court denied relief. Glenn appealed to the Court of Appeals for the Sixth Circuit. Because the plan granted MetLife "discretionary authority to . . . determine benefits," the Court of Appeals reviewed the administrative record under a deferential standard. Id., at 666. In doing so, it treated "as a relevant factor" a "conflict of interest" arising out of the fact that MetLife was "authorized both to decide whether an employee is eligible for benefits and to pay those benefits." Ibid.

The Court of Appeals ultimately set aside MetLife's denial of benefits in light of a combination of several circumstances: (1) the conflict of interest; (2) MetLife's failure to reconcile its own conclusion that Glenn could work in other jobs with the Social Security Administration's conclusion that she could not; (3) MetLife's focus upon one treating physician report suggesting that Glenn could work in other jobs at the expense of other, more detailed treating physician reports indicating that she could not; (4) MetLife's failure to provide all of the treating physician reports to its own hired experts; and (5) MetLife's failure to take account of evidence indicating that stress aggravated Glenn's condition. See id., at 674.

MetLife sought certiorari, asking us to determine whether a plan administrator that both evaluates and pays claims operates under a conflict of interest in making discretionary benefit determinations. The Solicitor General suggested that we also consider " 'how' " any such conflict should " 'be taken into account on judicial review of a discretionary benefit determination.' " * * *

II

In *Firestone Tire & Rubber Co. v. Bruch*, 489 U.S. 101, 109 S. Ct. 948, 103 L. Ed. 2d 80, this Court addressed "the appropriate standard of judicial review of benefit determinations by fiduciaries or plan administrators under"§ 1132(a)(1)(B), the ERISA provision at issue here. * * * *Firestone* set forth four principles of review relevant here.

(1) In "determining the appropriate standard of review," a court should be "guided by principles of trust law"; in doing so, it should analogize a plan administrator to the trustee of a common-law trust; and it should consider a benefit determination to be a fiduciary act (i.e., an act in which the administrator owes a special duty of loyalty to the plan beneficiaries). Id., at 111–113, 109 S. Ct. 948. * * *

(2) Principles of trust law require courts to review a denial of plan benefits "under a de novo standard" unless the plan provides to the contrary. Firestone, 489 U.S., at 115, 109 S. Ct. 948; see also id., at 112, 109 S. Ct. 948 (citing, inter alia, 3 A. Scott & W. Fratcher, Law of Trusts § 201, p. 221 (4th ed.1988); G. Bogert & G. Bogert, Law of Trusts and Trustees § 559, pp. 162–168 (2d rev. ed.1980) (hereinafter Bogert); 1 Restatement (Second) of Trusts § 201, Comment b (1957) (hereinafter Restatement)).

(3) Where the plan provides to the contrary by granting "the administrator or fiduciary *discretionary authority* to determine eligibility for benefits," Firestone, 489 U.S., at 115, 109 S. Ct. 948 (emphasis added), "[t]rust principles make a *deferential standard* of review appropriate," id., at 111, 109 S. Ct. 948 (citing Restatement § 187 (abuse-of-discretion standard); Bogert § 560, at 193–208; emphasis added).

(4) If "a benefit plan gives discretion to an administrator or fiduciary who *is operating under a conflict of interest*, that conflict must be *weighed as a 'factor* in determining whether there is an abuse of discretion.'" *Firestone, supra*, at 115, 109 S. Ct. 948 (quoting Restatement § 187, Comment d; emphasis added; alteration omitted).

The questions before us, while implicating the first three principles, directly focus upon the application and the meaning of the fourth.

### III

The first question asks whether the fact that a plan administrator both evaluates claims for benefits and pays benefits claims creates the kind of "conflict of interest" to which Firestone's fourth principle refers. In our view, it does.

That answer is clear where it is the employer that both funds the plan and evaluates the claims. In such a circumstance, "every dollar provided in benefits is a dollar spent by ... the employer; and every dollar saved ... is a dollar in [the employer's] pocket." *Bruch v. Firestone Tire & Rubber Co.*, 828 F.2d 134, 144 (C.A.3 1987). The employer's fiduciary interest may counsel in favor of granting a borderline claim while its immediate financial interest counsels to the contrary. Thus, the employer has an "interest ... conflicting with that of the beneficiaries," the type of conflict that judges must take into account when they review the discretionary acts of a trustee of a common-law trust. Restatement § 187, Comment d; * * *.

Indeed, Firestone itself involved an employer who administered an ERISA benefit plan and who both evaluated claims and paid for benefits. See 489 U.S., at 105, 109 S. Ct. 948. And thus that circumstance quite possibly was what the Court had in mind when it mentioned conflicted administrators. See id., at 115, 109 S. Ct. 948. The Firestone parties, while disagreeing about other matters, agreed that the dual role created a conflict of interest of some kind in the employer. See Brief for Petitioners 6–7, 27–29, Brief for Respondents 9, 26, and Brief for United States as Amicus Curiae 22, in *Firestone Tire & Rubber Co. v. Bruch*, O.T.1988, No. 87–1054.

MetLife points out that an employer who creates a plan that it will both fund and administer foresees, and implicitly approves, the resulting conflict. But that fact cannot change our conclusion. At trust law, the fact that a settlor (the person establishing the trust) approves a trustee's conflict does not change the legal need for a judge later to take account of that conflict in reviewing the trustee's discretionary decisionmaking. See Restatement § 107, Comment f (discretionary acts of trustee with settlor-approved conflict subject to "careful scrutiny")* * *

MetLife also points out that we need not follow trust law principles where trust law is "inconsistent with the language of the statute, its structure, or its purposes." *Hughes Aircraft Co. v. Jacobson*, 525 U.S. 432, 447, 119 S. Ct. 755, 142 L. Ed. 2d 881 (1999) (internal quotation marks omitted). MetLife adds that to find a conflict here is inconsistent (1) with ERISA's efforts to avoid complex review proceedings, see *Varity Corp. v. Howe*, 516 U.S. 489, 497, 116 S. Ct. 1065, 134 L. Ed. 2d 130 (1996); (2) with Congress' efforts not to deter employers from setting up benefit plans, see ibid., and (3) with an ERISA provision specifically allowing employers to administer their own plans, see 29 U.S.C. § 1108(c)(3).

But we cannot find in these considerations any significant inconsistency. As to the first, we note that trust law functions well with a similar standard. As to the second, we have no reason, empirical or otherwise, to believe that our decision will seriously discourage the creation of benefit plans. As to the third, we have just explained why approval of a conflicted trustee differs from review of that trustee's conflicted decisionmaking. As to all three taken together, we believe them outweighed by "Congress' desire to offer employees enhanced protection for their benefits." *Varity*, *supra*, at 497, 116 S. Ct. 1065 (discussing "competing congressional purposes" in enacting ERISA).

The answer to the conflict question is less clear where (as here) the plan administrator is not the employer itself but rather a professional insurance company. Such a company, MetLife would argue, likely has a much greater incentive than a self-insuring employer to provide accurate claims processing. That is because the insurance company typically charges a fee that attempts to account for the cost of claims payouts, with the result that paying an individual claim does not come to the same extent from the company's own pocket. It is also because the marketplace (and regulators) may well punish an insurance company when its products, or ingredients of its products, fall below par. And claims processing, an ingredient of the insurance company's product, falls below par when it seeks a biased result, rather than an accurate one. * * *

Conceding these differences, we nonetheless continue to believe that for ERISA purposes a conflict exists. For one thing, the employer's own conflict may extend to its selection of an insurance company to administer its plan. An employer choosing an administrator in effect buys insurance for others and consequently (when compared to the marketplace customer who buys for himself) may be more interested in an insurance company with low rates than in one with accurate claims processing. Cf. Langbein, Trust Law as Regulatory Law, 101 Nw. U. L. Rev. 1315, 1323–1324 (2007) (observing that employees are rarely involved in plan negotiations).

For another, ERISA imposes higher-than-marketplace quality standards on insurers. It sets forth a special standard of care upon a plan administrator, namely, that the administrator "discharge [its] duties" in respect to discretionary claims processing "solely in the interests of the participants and beneficiaries" of the plan, § 1104(a)(1); it simultaneously underscores the particular importance of accurate claims processing by insisting that administrators "provide a 'full and fair review' of claim denials," Firestone, 489 U.S., at 113, 109 S. Ct. 948 (quoting § 1133(2)); and it supplements marketplace and regulatory controls with judicial review of individual claim denials, see § 1132(a)(1)(B). * * *

## IV

We turn to the question of "how" the conflict we have just identified should "be taken into account on judicial review of a discretionary benefit determination." 552 U.S. 1161, 128 S. Ct. 1117 (2008). In doing so, we elucidate what this Court set forth in Firestone, namely, that a conflict should "be weighed as a 'factor in determining whether there is an abuse of discretion.'" 489 U.S., at 115, 109 S. Ct. 948 (quoting Restatement § 187, Comment d; alteration omitted).

We do not believe that Firestone's statement implies a change in the standard of review, say, from deferential to de novo review. Trust law continues to apply a deferential standard of review to the discretionary decisionmaking of a conflicted trustee, while at the same time requiring the reviewing judge to take account of the conflict when determining whether the trustee, substantively or procedurally, has abused his discretion. * * *

Nor would we overturn Firestone by adopting a rule that in practice could bring about near universal review by judges de novo—i.e., without deference—of the lion's share of ERISA plan claims denials. * * * Had Congress intended such a system of review, we believe it would not have left to the courts the development of review standards but would have said more on the subject. See Firestone, supra, at 109, 109 S. Ct. 948 ("ERISA does not set out the appropriate standard of review for actions under § 1132(a)(1)(B)''); * * *

We believe that Firestone means what the word "factor" implies, namely, that when judges review the lawfulness of benefit denials, they will often take account of several different considerations of which a conflict of interest is one. This kind of review is no stranger to the judicial system. Not only trust law, but also administrative law, can ask judges to determine lawfulness by taking account of several different, often case-specific, factors, reaching a result by weighing all together. * * *

In such instances, any one factor will act as a tiebreaker when the other factors are closely balanced, the degree of closeness necessary depending upon the tiebreaking factor's inherent or case-specific importance. The conflict of interest at issue here, for example, should prove more important (perhaps of great importance) where circumstances suggest a higher likelihood that it affected the benefits decision, including, but not limited to, cases where an insurance company administrator has a history of biased claims administration. See Langbein, *supra*, at 1317– 1321 (detailing such a history for one large insurer). It should prove less important (perhaps to the vanishing point) where the administrator has taken active steps to reduce potential bias and to promote accuracy, for example, by walling off claims administrators from those interested in firm finances, or by imposing management checks that penalize inaccurate decisionmaking irrespective of whom the inaccuracy benefits. See Herzel & Colling, The Chinese Wall and Conflict of Interest in Banks, 34 Bus. Law 73, 114 (1978) (recommending interdepartmental information walls to reduce bank conflicts); Brief for Blue Cross and Blue Shield Association as Amicus Curiae 15 (suggesting that insurers have incentives to reward claims processors for their accuracy); cf. generally J. Mashaw, Bureaucratic Justice (1983) (discussing internal controls as a sound method of producing administrative accuracy).

The Court of Appeals' opinion in the present case illustrates the combination-of-factors method of review. The record says little about MetLife's efforts to assure accurate claims assessment. The Court of Appeals gave the conflict weight to some degree; its opinion suggests that, in context, the court would not have found the conflict alone determinative. See 461 F.3d, at 666, 674. The court instead focused more heavily on other factors. In particular, the court found questionable the fact that MetLife had encouraged Glenn to argue to the Social Security Administration that she could do no work, received the bulk of the benefits of her success in doing so (the remainder going to the lawyers it recommended), and then ignored the agency's finding in concluding that Glenn could in fact do sedentary work. See id., at 666–669. This course of events was not only an important factor in its own right (because it suggested procedural unreasonableness), but also would have justified the court in giving more weight to the conflict (because MetLife's seemingly inconsistent positions were both financially advantageous). And the court furthermore observed that MetLife had emphasized a certain medical report that favored a denial of benefits, had deemphasized certain other reports that suggested a contrary conclusion, and had failed to provide its independent vocational and medical experts with all of the relevant evidence. See id., at 669–674. All these serious concerns, taken together with some degree of conflicting interests on MetLife's part, led the court to set aside MetLife's discretionary decision. See id., at 674–675. We can find nothing improper in the way in which the court conducted its review.

We AFFIRM the decision of the Court of Appeals.

It is so ordered.

CHIEF JUSTICE ROBERTS, concurring in part and concurring in the judgment.

I join all but Part IV of the Court's opinion. I agree that a third-party insurer's dual role as a claims administrator and plan funder gives rise to a conflict of interest that is pertinent in reviewing claims decisions. I part ways with the majority, however, when it comes to how such a conflict should matter. The majority would accord weight, of varying and indeterminate amount, to the existence of such a conflict in every case where it is present. * * *

I would instead consider the conflict of interest on review only where there is evidence that the benefits denial was motivated or affected by the administrator's conflict. No such evidence was presented in this case. I would nonetheless affirm the judgment of the Sixth Circuit, because that court was justified in finding an abuse of discretion on the facts of this case-conflict or not. * * *

I would therefore affirm the judgment below.

JUSTICE KENNEDY, concurring in part and dissenting in part. (omitted)

JUSTICE SCALIA, with whom JUSTICE THOMAS joins, dissenting.

I agree with the Court that petitioner Metropolitan Life Insurance Company (hereinafter petitioner) has a conflict of interest. A third-party insurance company that administers an ERISA-governed disability plan and that pays for benefits out of its own coffers profits with each benefits claim it rejects. * * *

The more important question is how the existence of a conflict should bear upon judicial review of the administrator's decision, and on that score I am in fundamental disagreement with the Court. [H]owever, this is not a question to be solved by this Court's policy views; our cases make clear that it is to be governed by the law of trusts. Under that law, a fiduciary with a conflict does not abuse its discretion unless the conflict actually and improperly motivates the decision. There is no evidence of that here. * * *

"Abuse of discretion," as the Restatement uses the term, refers specifically to four distinct failures: the trustee acted dishonestly; he acted with some other improper motive; he failed to use judgment; or he acted beyond the bounds of a reasonable judgment. See Restatement (Second) of Trusts § 187, Comment e. * * *

*Naïve?*

Respondent essentially asks us to presume that all fiduciaries with a conflict act in their selfish interest, so that their decisions are automatically reviewed with less than total deference (how much less is unspecified). But if one is to draw any inference about a fiduciary from the fact that he made an informed, reasonable, though apparently self-serving discretionary decision, it should be that he suppressed his selfish interest (as the settlor anticipated) in compliance with his duties of good faith and loyalty. * * * Only such a presumption can vindicate the trust principles and ERISA provisions that permit settlors to appoint fiduciaries with a conflict in the first place. * * *

### II

Applying the Restatement's guidelines to this case, I conclude that the only possible basis for finding an abuse of discretion in this case would be unreasonableness of petitioner's determination of no disability. The principal factor suggesting that is the finding of disability by the Social Security Administration (SSA). But ERISA fiduciaries need not always reconcile their determinations with the SSA's, nor is the SSA's conclusion entitled to any special weight. Cf. *Black & Decker Disability Plan v. Nord*, 538 U.S. 822, 834, 123 S. Ct. 1965, 155 L. Ed. 2d 1034 (2003). The SSA's determination may have been wrong, and it was contradicted by other medical opinion.

We did not take this case to make the reasonableness determination, but rather to clarify when a conflict exists, and how it should be taken into account. I would remand to the Court of Appeals for its determination of the reasonableness of petitioner's denial, without regard to the existence of a conflict of interest.

### NOTES AND QUESTIONS

1. Why is a benefit determination to be treated as a "fiduciary act" under ERISA? Deciding that a particular act is a fiduciary act can be critical. For example:

- In *Mertens v. Hewitt Associates*, 508 U.S. 248, 113 S.Ct. 2063, 124 L.Ed.2d 161 (1993), the plaintiffs claimed that defendant actuary acted improperly by failing to disclose that actuarial assumptions made by its client, the sponsor of a retirement plan, were faulty because they failed to take into account the impact of a large number of early retirements. The Court held (5–4) that, assuming the actuary was an advisor to a fiduciary, not a fiduciary itself, it could not be required to make the pension fund whole for the losses resulting from failure to disclose the use of those faulty actuarial assumptions. A fiduciary, however, can be held liable for such "make whole" relief. See 29 U.S.C. § 1109(a).

- An employer acting as a "settlor" of a plan (establishing it, terminating it, modifying its terms) is not acting in a fiduciary capacity and therefore need not consider beneficiary interests in making such a decision. See *Lockheed Corp. v. Spinks*, 517 U.S. 882, 116 S.Ct. 1783, 135 L.Ed.2d 153 (1996) (pension plan amendment); *Curtiss–Wright Corp. v. Schoonejongen*, 514 U.S. 73, 115 S.Ct. 1223, 131 L.Ed.2d 94 (1995) (welfare plan amendment). There are, obviously, a number of ERISA provisions that govern these sorts of actions, without regard to fiduciary status.

2.   As the next opinion states, it is not necessary to be named as a fiduciary in order to be treated as one for ERISA purposes. In *Varity Corp. v. Howe*, 516 U.S. 489, 116 S.Ct. 1065, 134 L.Ed.2d 130 (1996), a corporation decided to spin off several divisions that were losing money into a separate new corporation. In order to induce employees to transfer their services to this new entity the employer sponsored meetings during which employees were assured by corporate representatives that their benefit plans would be the same under the new corporation as under the former one. They were also told a number of things about the new corporation's prospects for success, some of them misleading because they were based upon unrealistic evaluations of assets and clearly over-optimistic projections of business growth. The benefit plans in question were administered by each employer directly. When the new corporation failed after less than two years, employees who had become employees of the new entity sought relief under ERISA on the basis of the misleading statements made to them in order to induce them to transfer. The Varity Court (6–3) concluded that the District Court was justified in holding that the non-pension benefit plan participants reasonably understood their employer's representative to be speaking to them both as employer and also as administrator of the plans—and thus a fiduciary. This is based on several factors, the chief being the heavy emphasis placed on benefits in the oral and written communications to employees at the time of the spin-off. The Court also found that making such misleading statements constitutes a violation of fiduciary duty, rejecting an argument that only decisions to grant or deny benefits, to make disclosures on request, or to make certain investments fall in this category. The majority also held that the district court had the power to require the reinstatement of the misled employees to the non-pension benefit plans that their former employer had continued in place as "appropriate equitable relief."

3.   ERISA recognizes a broader category of persons and firms that may have responsibilities in the control or operation of a plan, "parties in interest," defined in 29 U.S.C. § 1102(14). Section 406(a) of the statute forbids a fiduciary to engage in certain categories of transactions with a party in interest. 29 U.S.C. § 1106(a). In *Harris Trust and Savings Bank v. Salomon Smith Barney, Inc.*, 530 U.S. 238, 120 S.Ct. 2180, 147 L.Ed.2d 187 (2000), a plan sponsor/administrator and that plan's trustee (both fiduciaries) sued National Investment Services of America (NISA), an investment manager hired by the sponsor/administrator to exercise investment control over part of the plan's assets (its control of those assets makes NISA a fiduciary), and Salomon Smith Barney, a firm that provided broker-dealer services to the plan (thus being a "party in interest"—but not a "fiduciary" since it had no discretion in regard to how assets would be invested). NISA decided to invest some of the plan assets in interests in motel properties; these interests were

sold to the plan by Salomon. When the real estate "bust" of the late 1980s hit, these interests became virtually worthless. Salomon argued that section 406(a) imposes a duty only on a fiduciary, not on a party in interest, and that it therefore could not be sued under section 502(a)(3), 29 U.S.C. § 1132(a)(3). The Court, in an opinion by Justice Scalia, agreed that section 406(a) imposes a duty only on a fiduciary. Despite that, the Court concluded, an action for restitution is available under section 502(a)(3) against a non-fiduciary that is a "knowing participant" in a breach of a fiduciary's duty. The Court decided this must be true because section 502(*l*), 29 U.S.C. § 1132 (*l*) authorizes the recovery of a civil penalty for "knowing participation" in such a breach by "any other person" and the amount of the penalty is determined by looking to the amount "ordered by a court to be paid by such . . . other person" under section 502(a)(2) or (5). The wording of section 502(a)(5) is virtually identical to that of section 502(a)(3), except that the former authorizes an action by the Secretary of Labor, while the latter authorizes an action "by a participant, beneficiary or fiduciary." The case was remanded to the lower courts for determination of whether there was enough knowledge on the part of the non-fiduciary that the transaction was forbidden.

4. The issuers of publicly traded securities do not become ERISA fiduciaries simply because a covered pension plan buys and holds those securities, whether shares of stock in a corporation, or shares of a mutual fund. Some investment trusts, however, do not sell interests in the open market and are not traded in the conventional way. Hedge funds are one example. Determining when the managers of such a fund become fiduciaries is not an easy matter, but may have been made simpler by a provision added by the Pension Protection Act. See generally I. Lee Falk and Daniel R. Kleinman, *What To Do if Your Fund Becomes Subject to ERISA*, 14 THE INVESTMENT LAWYER 1 (2007).

The bankruptcy of the Enron Corporation was one of the most significant business failures of the past several decades. Founded in 1985 by Ken Lay through the merger of Houston Natural Gas and InterNorth pipeline, Enron aspired to be "The World's Leading Company" (as a banner in its corporate offices proclaimed) and by 2001 it ranked as the seventh largest company in the United States. Under Jeff Skilling, Enron began dealing in energy futures and long-run contracts for guaranteed supplies of gas at a fixed price. When times were good, Enron was known for high management salaries and lavish corporate expenditures and parties. However, in gambling on gas prices Enron eventually guessed wrong and when a number of its operations started losing money, it disguised these losses through accounting methods, approved by Arthur Andersen, LLP, that used a maze of financial partnerships to conceal mounting debts. In the end game, Enron executives made fraudulent misrepresentations about the company's health so they could cash out stock options while stockholders and employees were left holding the bag. Enron's Chief Financial Officer, Andrew Fastow, agreed to a 10 year jail term and forfeiture of $23.8 million in ill-gotten profits for his part in the fraud and turned state's evidence against other Enron executives. A federal jury found Ken Lay and Jeff Skilling guilty on multiple counts, and they were each given sentences in excess of 20 years. Ken Lay died before he surrendered to be jailed but Skilling is currently serving time. Enron's bankruptcy resulted in extensive litigation, with opinions running into thousands of pages. The following opinion from one class action has been reduced roughly 90 per cent, but may still provide an impression of some of the complexities that arise for employees when their employer fails.

## IN RE ENRON CORPORATION SECURITIES, DERIVATIVE & "ERISA" LITIGATION

United States District Court, S.D. Texas, Houston Division, 2003
284 F. Supp. 2d 511

HARMON, DISTRICT JUDGE

### RE TITLE DEFENDANTS' MOTIONS TO DISMISS

[This] * * * action is brought on behalf of Enron Corporation ("Enron") employees who were participants in three employee pension benefit plans governed by the Employment Retirement Income Security Act of 1974 ("ERISA"), § 3(2), 29 U.S.C. § 1002(2), specifically the Enron Corporation Savings Plan ("Savings Plan"), the Enron Corporation Employee Stock Ownership Plan ("ESOP"), and the Enron Corporation Cash Balance Plan ("Cash Balance Plan"), * * *

### I. OVERVIEW OF CAUSES OF ACTION AND PENDING MOTIONS

Defendants fall into five groups: (1) Enron and individual officers and directors of the company; (2) committees, trustees, and individuals that administered the three pension plans [the "Enron ERISA defendants]; (3) Enron's accountant Arthur Andersen LLP and some of its individual partners and employees * * *; (4) Enron's outside law firm Vinson & Elkins L.L.P. and some of its individual partners * * *; and (5) five investment banks (J.P. Morgan Chase & Co., Merrill Lynch & Co., Inc., Credit Suisse First Boston, Citigroup, Inc., and Salomon Smith Barney, Inc).

The complaint asserts its causes of action in nine counts: five under ERISA, two under RICO, one under Texas common-law negligence, and the last under Texas common-law civil conspiracy.

Count I originally asserted a claim on behalf of the Savings Plan and the ESOP against Defendants Enron, [a group of Enron officers and directors known as the Enron Defendants], former CEOs Lay and Skilling * * * and Arthur Andersen, at a time when Enron, the Enron ERISA Defendants, Lay, and Skilling knew or should have known that Enron stock was an imprudent investment choice, for breaches of their fiduciary and co-fiduciary duties of prudence, care and loyalty under 29 U.S.C. §§ 1104(a)(1)(A)–(D) and 1105, for (1) allowing Savings Plan participants the ability to direct the Plan's fiduciaries to purchase Enron stock for their individual accounts from monies the participants contributed as deductions from their salaries; (2) inducing the participants to direct the fiduciaries to purchase Enron stock for their individual accounts in exchange for funds they contributed to the Plan; (3) causing and allowing the Savings Plan to purchase or accept Enron's matching contributions in the form of Enron stock; (4) imposing and maintaining age restrictions and other restrictions on the participants' ability to direct the Savings Plan fiduciaries to transfer both Savings Plan and ESOP assets out of Enron stock; and (5) inducing the Savings Plan and ESOP participants to direct or allow the fiduciaries of both Plans to maintain investments in Enron stock. Arthur Andersen is charged with breaching its fiduciary duty under § 502(a)(3) of ERISA, 29 U.S.C. § 1132(a)(3), by * * * actively concealing from the Plan fiduciaries and Plan participants the actual financial condition of Enron and the imprudence of investing in Enron stock.

Count II is brought on behalf of the Savings Plan and the ESOP against Defendants Enron, the Enron ERISA Defendants, Lay, * * * and the Northern Trust Company ("Northern Trust"), for breach of their fiduciary duties under 29 U.S.C. §§ 1104(a)(1)(A)–(D) and 1105, based on the lockdown (freeze, blackout) of the two Plans, without adequate notice to participants, effectually from October 17, 2001 until November 14, 2001, while the Plans were switched to a new record keeper and trustee, during which time the price of Enron stock fell from $33.84 to $10.00 per share.

In Count III, Plaintiffs, on behalf of the Savings Plan, assert a breach of fiduciary duty in violation of 29 U.S.C. § 1104(a)(1)(D) against Enron, the Enron ERISA Defendants (excluding the ESOP Administrative Committee and the Cash Balance Administrative Committee), Lay, Skilling, * * * and the Northern Trust Company for their failure to diversify the Savings Plan assets, i.e., to liquidate the Enron stock, in accordance with the terms of the plan, because Defendants knew or should have known that investment in Enron stock was imprudent.

In Count IV Plaintiffs on behalf of Certain Retirement Plan Participants and Beneficiaries assert * * * another claim of breach of fiduciary duty, this time with respect to offsets (reductions) of accrued pension benefits that were based on the artificially inflated price of Enron stock from 1998–2000. The Enron Corp. Cash Balance Plan and its predecessor, the Enron Corp. Retirement Plan, constituted a "defined benefit plan" under 29 U.S.C. § 1002(35) and was fully funded by Enron. In essence Plaintiffs allege that until January 1, 1996, the retirement benefits provided to a plan participant of five years or more service were determined by adding different percentages of final average pay multiplied by levels of years of accrued service, and then offset by the annuity value of a portion of that participant's account in the ESOP ("Offset Account") as of certain determination dates * * *. Effective January 1, 1996, the Retirement Plan was amended, renamed the Enron Corp. Cash Balance Plan, and the benefit formula was changed from an average pay formula to a cash balance formula, while the offset arrangement between the Plan and the ESOP was to be phased out over the coming five-year period. Under the new plan, a plan participant's accrued benefit under the Cash Balance Plan was based on his employment from 1987–1994 and was offset over the five-year phase-out period by the value of his ESOP stock based on a formula set out in §§ 5.1–5.5 of the Plan. Each January 1st from 1996–2000, the value of one-fifth of the shares of Enron stock credited to each participant's Offset Account was to be calculated based on the stock's market price on that date as reported at closing time on the New York Stock Exchange and was thereafter permanently fixed at that amount. Plaintiffs allege that Defendants knew or should have known that the market price of Enron stock from 1998 to 2000 was artificially inflated and not representative of its true value, and that Defendants breached their fiduciary duty by not computing the component of the offset at its true, much lower value. As a result, participants and beneficiaries who accrued benefits under the Retirement Plan between January 1, 1987 and December 31, 1994 have suffered losses because their retirement benefits would be offset by the inflated market price of one-fifth of the shares of Enron stock in their ESOP Offset Account in 1998, 1999, and 2000.

Count V, brought on behalf of the Savings Plan, the ESOP, and the Cash Balance Plan against Enron and the Compensation Committee Defendants, alleges another breach of fiduciary and co-fiduciary duties under 29 U.S.C. § 1104(a)(1)(A)–(D) and § 1105 relating to their failure to appoint and monitor other plan fiduciaries and their failure to disclose to the investing fiduciaries material information about Enron's true financial condition. * * *

[The opinion then lists the non-ERISA counts and the various motions to dismiss before the court.]

## II.  APPLICABLE LAW

### A.  ERISA

#### 1.  Fiduciary Liability

The issue of fiduciary status is a mixed question of law and fact. *Reich v. Lancaster*, 55 F.3d 1034, 1044 (5th Cir.1995).

#### a.  Expansive Definition of Fiduciary

Under ERISA, a person or entity may be deemed a fiduciary either by assumption of the fiduciary obligations (the functional or de facto method) or by express designation by the ERISA plan documents. * * *

Section 409(a) of ERISA, 29 U.S.C. § 1109(a), provides, "Any person who is a fiduciary with respect to a plan who breaches any of the responsibilities, obligations, or duties imposed upon fiduciaries by this subchapter shall be personally liable." It makes no distinction between the functional definition of a trustee and the formal designation of a fiduciary named by the plan documents or by following the procedure in those documents for designating a fiduciary and thus applies to both.

#### b.  Fiduciary Duties

* * * The most fundamental duty of ERISA plan fiduciaries is a duty of complete loyalty, under 29 U.S.C. § 1104(a)(1)(B), to insure that they discharge their duty "solely in the interests of the participants and

beneficiaries," and to "exclude all selfish interest and all consideration of the interests of third persons." Id. Fiduciaries must discharge their duties with respect to the plan "solely in the interest of the participants and the beneficiaries," i.e., "for the exclusive purpose of (i) providing benefits to participants and their beneficiaries; and (ii) defraying reasonable expenses of administering the plan." 29 U.S.C. § 1104(a)(1)(A). Thus among the responsibilities and duties imposed on fiduciaries by ERISA is avoidance of conflicts of interest. * * *

Second, the fiduciary must meet a "prudent man" standard under 29 U.S.C. § 1104(a)(1)(B), to act "with the care, skill, prudence and diligence under the circumstances then prevailing that a prudent man acting in a like capacity and familiar with such matters would use" and "with single-minded devotion" to these plan participants and beneficiaries. * * *

Regarding this overlapping duty of "care, skill, prudence, and diligence under the circumstances then prevailing that a prudent man acting in a like capacity and familiar with such matters would use," the Fifth Circuit has stated,

> In determining compliance with ERISA's prudent man standard, courts objectively assess whether the fiduciary, at the time of the transaction, utilized proper methods to investigate, evaluate and structure the investment; acted in a manner as would others familiar with such matters; and exercised independent judgment when making investment decisions. " '[ERISA's] test of prudence . . . is one of conduct, and not a test of the result of performance of the investment. The focus of the inquiry is how the fiduciary acted in his selection of the investment, and not whether his investments succeeded or failed.' " * * *

Furthermore, the standard of the prudent man is an objective standard, and good faith is not a defense to a claim of imprudence. * * * *Donovan v. Cunningham*, 716 F.2d at 1467 ("this is not a search for subjective good faith—a pure heart and an empty head are not enough").

Third, the ERISA fiduciary must diversify the plan's investments to minimize risk of loss unless, under the circumstances, it is clearly prudent not to diversify. 29 U.S.C. § 1104(a)(1)(C). The legislative history offers some guidance about diversifying the assets of an ERISA plan:

> The degree of investment concentration that would violate this requirement to diversify cannot be stated as a fixed percentage, because a fiduciary must consider the facts and circumstances of each case. The factors to be considered include (1) the purposes of the plan; (2) the amount of the plan assets; (3) financial and industrial conditions; (4) the type of investment, whether mortgages, bonds or shares of stock or otherwise; (5) distribution as to geographical location; (6) distribution as to industries; (7) dates of maturity.

*Metzler v. Graham*, 112 F.3d 207, 208–09 (5th Cir.1997), citing H.R. Rep. No. 1280, 93d Cong., 2d Sess. (1974), reprinted in 1974 U.S.C.C.A.N. 5038, 5084–85 (Conf. Rpt. at 304). * * *

To prevail on a claim that a fiduciary violated its duty to diversify, a plaintiff must show that the portfolio, on its face, is not diversified. The burden then shifts to the defendant to demonstrate that it was "clearly prudent" not to diversify, the express statutory exception to the duty to diversify. * * *

Fourth, the plan fiduciary must follow the documents and instruments governing the plan to the extent that they are consistent with ERISA. 29 U.S.C. § 1104(a)(1)(D). "In case of a conflict, the provisions of the ERISA policies as set forth in the statute and regulations prevail over those of the Fund guidelines." *Laborers Nat. Pension Fund v. Northern Trust Quantitative Advisors, Inc.,* 173 F.3d at 322. * * *

### c. "Two–Hat" Doctrine

Unlike the trustee at common law, who must wear only his fiduciary hat when he acts in a manner to affect the beneficiary of the trust, an ERISA trustee may wear many hats, although only one at a time, and may have financial interests that are adverse to the interests of the beneficiaries but in the best interest of the company. * * * For example a fiduciary may wear the hat of an employer and fire a beneficiary for reasons not related to the ERISA plan, or the hat of a plan sponsor and modify the terms of a plan to be less generous to the beneficiary. Pegram, 530 U.S. at 225, 120 S. Ct. 2143. When making fiduciary decisions, however, a fiduciary may wear only his fiduciary hat. Id. * * *

### d. Power to Appoint/Remove Plan Fiduciaries

A person or entity that has the power to appoint, retain and/or remove a plan fiduciary from his position has discretionary authority or control over the management or administration of a plan and is a fiduciary to the extent that he or it exercises that power. * * *

### e. Duty to Disclose

* * * The fiduciary's duty to disclose is an area of developing and controversial law. * * *

In Varity Corp., 516 U.S. at 506, 116 S. Ct. 1065, the Supreme Court chose not to "reach the question whether ERISA fiduciaries have any fiduciary duty to disclose truthful information on their own initiative, or in response to employee inquiries." * * *

Courts have generally agreed that where an ERISA fiduciary makes statements about future benefits that misrepresent present facts, these misrepresentations are material if they would induce a reasonable person to rely on them. * * *

A number of the Circuit Courts of Appeals have held that after an ERISA participant/beneficiary requests information from his plan's fiduciary, who is informed of that participant/beneficiary's circumstances, the fiduciary has a duty to provide full and accurate information material to the participant/beneficiary's situation, including information about which the participant/beneficiary did not specifically ask. * * *

Thus some Circuits have concluded that there is an additional affirmative duty, beyond a full and accurate response triggered by a participant/beneficiary's specific question, to disclose material information to plan participants and beneficiaries. The Third Circuit, one of the most aggressive courts in this area, has held, "[I]t is a breach of fiduciary duty for an employer to knowingly make material misleading statements about the stability of a benefits plan." * * *

In comparison, in the very few cases in which the Fifth Circuit has addressed a fiduciary duty to disclose, and then only in narrow circumstances, the Fifth Circuit appears to impose such a duty cautiously. * * * Like many courts, it views the plan administrator as having a fiduciary duty to plan participants as a whole, but not to individual participants with particular problems who do not make a specific request for information. * * *

* * * Certain Committee and Outside Directors ("Compensation Committee") Defendants have argued that if these Defendants met their duty of loyalty by selectively disclosing only to the plan participants nonpublic information about material accounting irregularities and financial improprieties, so that the participants could make an informed decision not to purchase additional shares or to sell their currently held shares of Enron stock before the market and the public found out and the price plunged, Defendants would be violating insider trading laws under the federal securities laws. * * *

Defendants' argument that despite the duty of loyalty, a fiduciary should make no disclosure to the plan participants, because under the securities laws he cannot selectively disclose nonpublic information, translates in essence into an argument that the fiduciary should both breach his duty under ERISA and, in violation of the securities laws, become part of the alleged fraudulent scheme to conceal Enron's financial condition to the continuing detriment of current and prospective Enron shareholders, which include his plan's participants. This Court does not believe that Congress, ERISA or the federal securities statutes sanction such conduct or such a solution, i.e., violating all the statutes and conning the public. * * *

At the same time, a fiduciary's duty of loyalty should also not be construed to require him to enable and encourage plan participants to violate the law, i.e., to sell their stock at artificially high prices to make a profit or avoid loss before disclosure of Enron's financial condition was made public. * * *

The Court finds that the Secretary [of Labor]'s brief appropriately addresses the issue and suggests practical ways to resolve the alleged tension between ERISA and the federal securities statutes so that both can be followed:

Defendants' duty to "disclose or abstain" under the securities laws does not immunize them from a claim that they failed in their conduct as ERISA fiduciaries. To the contrary, while their Securities Act and ERISA duties may conflict in some respects, they are congruent in others, and there are certain steps that could have been taken that would have satisfied both duties to the benefit of the plans. First and foremost, nothing in the securities laws would have prohibited them from disclosing the information to other shareholders and the public at large, or from forcing Enron to do so. * * * The duty to disclose the relevant information to the plan participants and beneficiaries, which the Plaintiffs assert these Defendants owed as ERISA fiduciaries, is entirely consistent with the premise of the insider trading rules: that corporate insiders owe a fiduciary duty to disclose material nonpublic information to the shareholders and trading public. * * *

Second it would have been consistent with the securities law for the Committee to have eliminated Enron stock as a participant option and as the employer match under the Savings Plan. * * *

### f.  Personal Liability of Corporate Employees

Courts are divided about if and under what circumstances the officers or employees of a corporation that is the named fiduciary in plan instruments may be personally liable for a breach of their fiduciary duty. In light of the traditional rule that the employees of a corporation acting within the course and scope of their employment cannot be personally liable for their actions, some courts have held that the individual corporate employee must have an individual discretionary role in the plan administration to be liable as a fiduciary under ERISA. * * *

In view of the broad language, the functional and flexible definition of "fiduciary," and the expansive liability policy of the statute, as well as the holding in Musmeci, this Court agrees with those courts which reject a per se rule of nonliability for corporate officers acting on behalf of the corporation and instead make a functional, fact-specific inquiry to assess "the extent of responsibility and control exercised by the individual with respect to the Plan" to determine if a corporate employee, and thus also the corporation, has exercised sufficient discretionary authority and control to be deemed an ERISA fiduciary and thus personally liable for a fiduciary breach. *Bell v. Executive Committee of United Food and Commercial Workers Pension Plan for Employees*, 191 F. Supp.2d 10, 15 (D.D.C. 2002) * * *.

### g.  Professional Liability

Even where a person exercises some control over the plan's operations or assets, if he is providing only traditional professional services to the plan, he is not a "fiduciary" for such services and is not subject to an ERISA suit for breach of fiduciary duties. "[A]n attorney rendering legal and consulting advice to a plan" will not be considered to be a fiduciary unless he exercises authority over the plan "in a manner other than by usual professional functions" and thus cannot be sued for breach of fiduciary duty under ERISA for pursuing a lawyer's traditional services. * * * The same is true for providers of other professional services, including accountants and banks. * * * The Department of Labor's guidelines for interpreting ERISA's definition of "fiduciary" in 29 U.S.C. 1002(21)(A) note that "attorneys, accountants, actuaries, and consultants will ordinarily not be considered fiduciaries." Interpretive Bulletin 75–5, 29 C.F.R. § 2509.75–5 (1987).

ERISA does not permit a civil action for legal damages against a non-fiduciary charged with knowing participation in a fiduciary breach. *Reich v. Rowe*, 20 F.3d 25, 26, 28 (1st Cir.1994), citing *Mertens v. Hewitt Associates*, 508 U.S. 248, 113 S. Ct. 2063, 124 L. Ed. 2d 161 (1993). As an alternative to fiduciary liability, a nonfiduciary may be liable as a "party in interest," but only for "appropriate equitable relief," including injunctions and equitable restitution, in civil actions brought by plan participants under 29 U.S.C. § 1132(a)(3). * * * A party in interest of an employee benefit plan is defined in 29 U.S.C. § 1002(14) and includes inter alia any fiduciary (administrator, officer, trustee, custodian, etc.), a person that provides services to the plan (such as an accountant, attorney), an employer of any employees covered by the plan and an employee organization including any members covered by the plan. Such non-fiduciaries may be held liable for such "appropriate equitable relief" if they are "parties in interest" and, with actual or constructive knowledge, they participate in a fiduciary's breach of its duties in transactions between the plan and a party in interest that are expressly prohibited under § 406(a) of ERISA, 29 U.S.C. § 1106(a). * * *

Even though generally a lawyer or accountant providing services to a plan is a party in interest and not a fiduciary, it has been recognized that at times a professional consultant or advisor may go beyond his normal, traditional advisory function and, because of his special expertise and influence, in effect exercise the discretionary authority or control over the management or administration of an ERISA plan to the point that he has assumed the fiduciary obligations and has transmuted into a fiduciary as defined under ERISA, 29 U.S.C. § 1102(21)(A). * * * To meet the "authority or control" element under 29 U.S.C. § 1002(21)(A)(i), a plaintiff must show that the consultant or advisor did not merely influence the plan fiduciary, but "caused [the] trustee . . . to relinquish his independent discretion in investing the plan's funds and follow the course prescribed" by the consultant. * * *

There is no per se rule regarding the rendering of professional advice and the point at which a professional may become subject to fiduciary liability. * * *

h.  Section 404(c) Plans

Section 404(c) of ERISA, 29 U.S.C. § 1104(c) * * * provides that a plan fiduciary is not liable if (1) the plan is an "individual account plan", (2) the plan participants can exercise control over the assets allocated to their accounts, and (3) the plan participants actually do exercise control over their accounts in a manner proscribed under the regulations. Under § 404(c), the plan participants that exercise such control over their accounts will not be treated as fiduciaries, and neither the plan participants nor the other plan fiduciaries will be liable for any loss or breach that results from the plan participants' exercise of control over the plan administration; in other words, no one is liable for the participants' loss that results from the participants' own informed investment choices. * * *

Many 401(k) plans are established to qualify as § 404(c) plans. Plaintiffs argue that the Savings Plan does not qualify as a § 404(c) plan because under article XV.3, it imposes a duty to diversify on all Plan fiduciaries unless it would be prudent under the circumstances not to do so. Moreover the regulations require that the fiduciaries provide participants with "complete and accurate information" about investment alternatives, a range of investments, procedures to permit transfers and to deal with conflicts of interest, as well as notice that the plan qualifies under § 404(c), none of which were met according to Plaintiffs. Furthermore, as Plaintiffs point out, the employer's matching contributions went directly into Enron stock, where it remained until the employee reached fifty years of age; the employee never had the requisite independent control over this portion of his plan assets. Under 29 C.F.R. § 2550.404(c)–1(c)(2), a plan participant also lacks independent control where he "is subjected to improper influence by a plan fiduciary or plan sponsor with respect to the transaction or where a plan fiduciary has concealed material non-public facts regarding the investment from the participant or beneficiary. . . ." Plaintiffs have alleged such concealment occurred at Enron. * * *

Because § 404(c) in essence exempts a fiduciary from liability that he normally would have under 29 U.S.C. § 1109(a), the fiduciary seeking protection under § 404(c), and not the plaintiff, has the burden of demonstrating that it applies. * * *

Even if the Savings Plan were to qualify as a § 404(c) plan, relating to the Savings Plan and the ESOP in the Department of Labor's Final Regulation Regarding Participant Directed Individual Account Plans, Preamble, 57 Fed. Reg. 46,906, 924 n. 27 (1992), the agency emphasized,

> [T]he act of designating investment alternatives . . . is a fiduciary function . . . [and] [a]ll of the fiduciary provisions of ERISA *remain applicable to both the initial designation of investment alternatives and investment managers and the ongoing determination that such alternatives and managers remain suitable and prudent investment alternatives for the plan* [emphasis added].

* * *

### i. Causation

Defendants contend that Plaintiffs have failed to plead facts showing that the alleged breaches of fiduciary duty caused the loss to the plans.

There is division of opinion about who bears the burden of proving the fiduciary caused the alleged losses to a plan.

The Sixth and Second Circuits have placed the burden of demonstrating causation on the plaintiff. * * *

The Fifth and Eighth Circuits have held that the plaintiff initially must prove a breach of fiduciary duty and a prima facie case of loss by the plan under § 1109(a), and then the burden shifts to the defendant fiduciary to prove that the loss was not caused by the breach of the fiduciary duty. * * * Thus Plaintiffs need not plead causation. * * * Moreover, because at this point Plaintiffs have pleaded under Counts II and III both fiduciary breach and injury, i.e., that Defendants' participation in the lockdowns and failure to diversify caused the plans, and indirectly the plaintiffs, to lose hundreds of millions of dollars, Plaintiffs have stated a claim and demonstrated standing to sue, even though they have not alleged that "but for the lockdown" or "but for the failure of the fiduciaries to diversify investments of the Plan," they, themselves, would have timely diversified their investments or sold the Enron stock in their individual accounts.

### 2. Co–Fiduciary Liability

* * * The elements of a claim brought under § 405(a)(1), 29 U.S.C. § 1105(a)(1), are "(1) that a co-fiduciary breached a duty to the plan, (2) that the fiduciary knowingly participated in the breach or undertook to conceal it, and (3) damages resulting from the breach." * * *

Under § 405(a)(2), 29 U.S.C. § 1105(a)(2), providing the broadest type of co-fiduciary liability without any requirement of knowledge about what the co-fiduciary is doing, to impose liability a plaintiff must prove that the fiduciary "failed to comply with its duties under ERISA, and thereby enabled a co-fiduciary to commit a breach." * * *.

For a cause of action under § 405(a)(3), 29 U.S.C. § 1105(a)(3), the elements are that the fiduciary had knowledge of the co-fiduciary's breach and that the losses "resulted from" the co-fiduciary defendant's failure to take reasonable steps to remedy the breach. Id. at 1337. Under Department of Labor Interpretive Bulletin, 29 C.F.R. § 2509.75–5FR–10, a fiduciary must take all legal and reasonable steps to prevent or remedy a breach by a co-fiduciary, including taking legal action against the co-fiduciary or informing the Department or the plan sponsor.

### 3. Directed Trustee Liability

There is a factual dispute in Tittle as to whether Northern Trust was a "directed" or discretionary trustee. Plaintiffs argue that it was the latter. * * *

Northern Trust contends that it was a "directed" trustee, as opposed to a "discretionary" trustee, under provisions in the plan documents and trust agreement that subjected it to direction by the Administrative Committee [the "named fiduciary"], that the Administrative Committee exercised total authority and discretion over the plan assets and management, and that Northern Trust thus had no responsibility or liability for the lockdown. * * *

While case law addressing the duties of a directed trustee is minimal, it is also in conflict with respect to the extent, if any, of the duty and potential liability of a directed trustee. * * *

After extensive research, this Court concludes for the reasons discussed [in a review of legislative history, regulations and case law omitted here] that even where the named fiduciary appears to have been granted full control, authority and/or discretion over that portion of activity of plan management and/or plan assets at issue in a suit and the plan trustee is directed to perform certain actions within that area, the directed trustee still retains a degree of discretion, authority, and responsibility that may expose him to liability, as reflected in the structure and language of provisions of ERISA. At least some fiduciary status and duties of a directed trustee are preserved, even though the scope of its "exclusive authority and discretion to manage and control the assets of the plan" has been substantially constricted by the directing named fiduciary's correspondingly broadened role, and breach of those duties may result in liability.

In any ERISA retirement plan, where the plaintiffs, as in [this case], allege with factual support that the directed trustee knew or should have known from a number of significant waving red flags and/or regular reviews of the company's financial statements that the employer company was in financial danger and its stock greatly diminished in value, yet the named fiduciary, to which the plan allocated all control over investments by the plan, directed the trustee to continue purchasing the employer's stock, there is factual question whether the evidence is sufficient to give rise to a fiduciary duty by the directed trustee to investigate the advisability of purchasing the company stock to insure that the actions in compliance with ERISA as well as the plan.

Finally, even if the Court construed § 403(a) to require only that the trustee find that the directions he received from the named fiduciary are "proper" and facially in compliance with the terms of the plan and of ERISA, it finds that the Tittle Plaintiffs still state a claim: "Plaintiffs submit that any order to proceed with lockdowns on its face violated the duties of prudence and loyalty mandated by ERISA" because the alleged exigent circumstances, laid out in the complaint, made its timing highly suspect and clearly injurious to plan participants and beneficiaries. * * *

[The opinion's extended discussions of standing, remedies and preemption issues are omitted.]

### III.  APPLICATION OF THE LAW TO COMPLAINT'S ALLEGATIONS

* * *

## C.  ERISA BREACH OF FIDUCIARY AND CO–FIDUCIARY DUTY

* * *

### 1.  Count I * * * and Count V

With respect to Counts I–V generally, the provisions of the Enron Corporation Savings Plan (Ex. A to #322) set out the fiduciary obligations of the various players and echo the law established under ERISA, discussed previously. * * *

As a threshold matter, the Court finds that Plaintiffs' pleadings have raised material issues as to whether the Savings Plan qualifies as a § 404(c) plan, entitling Defendants to immunity from liability for investment decisions controlled by plan participants, by allegations that the plan did not provide the requisite broad range of diversified investment options, liberal opportunities to transfer assets among allocations, and sufficient information to make sound investment decisions, nor notice to plan participants that it intended to qualify as such a plan. * * *

With respect to the claims in Count I, the Court finds that Plaintiffs have stated a claim, which is intertwined with Plaintiffs' contention that the fiduciaries failed to meet the requirements for a § 404(c) plan, against those Defendants who were authorized by the Plans to invest the Plan assets and who allegedly induced their uninformed Savings Plan participants to direct the fiduciaries to buy more or maintain Enron stock for their individual accounts, in breach of their duties of loyalty and prudence.

Second, some of the allegations under Court I relate to plan design, a settlor function, and do not trigger fiduciary duties: * * *

Nevertheless, outside of challenging the establishment of these terms by the employer in its settlor, not fiduciary, capacity, * * * Plaintiffs have stated a claim for breach of their fiduciary duties of loyalty and prudence based on Defendants' alleged inducement of the plan participants to direct the trustee to invest in Enron stock for their individual Savings Plan accounts and inducing Savings Plan and ESOP participants to direct or allow the fiduciaries of both Plans to maintain such investments, under the circumstances from 1998–2000 set forth in the complaint. They also state a claim for breach of fiduciary duty in causing and allowing the Savings Plan to purchase or accept Enron's matching contributions in the form of Enron stock once the fiduciaries allegedly knew or should have known of the inherent risk of such stock * * *.

A claim has also been stated in Count I against Enron and the Compensation Committee for breach of their fiduciary duty of providing information necessary for Plan Administration because they allegedly withheld from the Administrative Committee (which in turn purportedly failed in its fiduciary duty to investigate) material information regarding the actual financial condition of Enron. * * *

Members of both the Administrative and the Compensation Committees, Enron, and Olson, when they spoke about plan investments, had a fiduciary obligation not to materially mislead plan participants and beneficiaries about Defendants' concealment of Enron's precarious financial condition by means of erroneous accounting and about the risk involved in investing their assets in and retaining its stock. * * *

Count V addresses breach of the fiduciary duty to appoint, monitor and remove. As indicated earlier, as a matter of law, because Enron (i.e., a corporation acting through employees who perform functions on behalf of the corporation) has authority and control over appointments of fiduciaries to administer the plan and control its investments, it also has a fiduciary duty to monitor its appointees.

*[handwritten margin note: Fid duty for Counts]*

The ESOP * * * designates Enron as the Plan administrator, which is authorized under § 14.1 to appoint a Committee for Administration of the Plan. * * *

[O]utside Directors argue that the Savings Plan did not invest them with any power of appointment. As indicated in the summary of the relevant terms of the Savings Plan, Enron had and exercised the power of appointment, which, as a corporation, it necessarily did through its Board of Directors. Under the holding of Curtiss–Wright Corp., 514 U.S. at 80–81, 115 S. Ct. 1223, an ERISA plan need not specify individuals or bodies within the "Company" to show who has the authority to perform the action on behalf of the corporation.

The Court finds that Plaintiffs on behalf of the Savings Plan and the ESOP have stated claims in Count V for breach of fiduciary duties of loyalty and prudence under ERISA against Enron, Enron ERISA Defendants, including Members of the Compensation and Management Development Committee ("Compensation Committee") * * * because they were given the power to appoint, retain and remove plan fiduciaries (Enron to appoint members of the Administrative Committee of both plans, and all three Defendants to select, appoint and remove fiduciaries of the Savings Plan and the ESOP) and because they allegedly exercised that discretionary authority of appointment over the management or administration of a plan under § 3(21)(A) of ERISA, 29 U.S.C. § 1002(21)(A).

The complaint has also stated a claim in Counts I and V against these Defendants for co-fiduciary liability under § 502(a)(3), 29 U.S.C. § 1132(a)(3), for knowingly participating in or concealing their knowledge of and/or failing to make reasonable efforts to remedy their co-fiduciaries' breach of fiduciary duties in violation of § 404(a), 29 U.S.C. § 1104(a). * * *

### 2.   Count II: Lockdowns

* * * Plaintiffs have stated a claim for breach of fiduciary and co-fiduciary duties to the ESOP and Savings Plan participants and beneficiaries against Enron, the Enron ERISA Defendants * * * and the named fiduciary and trustee Northern Trust, whether deemed a directed trustee or not, for proceeding with a previously scheduled lockdown of the Savings Plan and the ESOP on October 26, 2001 and October 20, 2001, respectively, in spite of the extraordinary circumstances, enumerated below, that

obviously made the lockdowns an extreme threat to the participants' interests in their employee benefit plans. Plaintiffs have stated a claim that these exigent circumstances should have triggered the trustee's fiduciary duties to its plan participants and beneficiaries to postpone or at least to limit the duration of the scheduled lockdowns, as Defendants had the ability to do.

First, the complaint asserts that Enron shocked Wall Street with the announcement on October 16, 2001 that it had lost $618 million in the quarter and was writing down $1.2 billion of its net worth. The media were filled with stories raising questions about the corporation's financial stability. Concerned employees urged Northern Trust and Enron to postpone the lockdowns. Their questions may have triggered the fiduciaries' duties to respond with truthful and complete information that would apply to the plans as a whole. Even without questions from the plan participants and beneficiaries, the fiduciaries had a duty to disclose to the participants and beneficiaries material facts affecting their interests in the plans' assets of which they were unaware and which threatened their retirement funds. * * *

Second, on October 22, 2001, Enron announced that the SEC was informally investigating the company.

Third, two days later Fastow was forced to leave his position of Chief Financial Officer, which was taken over by McMahon, who had earlier voiced many of the same concerns about Enron's purportedly massive accounting improprieties as Watkins.

Furthermore, the complaint asserts that in the face of a swell of complaints and demands from panicked Plan participants, Enron actually did inquire about possible postponement of the lockdown and was told by Northern Trust and Hewitt Associates that a postponement was physically possible. Nevertheless, according to the complaint, although they knew or should have known the likely harm that would result for plan participants and although they had the discretion and power to delay the lockdowns, Enron decided that a postponement would be "inconvenient"; * * *.

Plaintiffs have further complained that these Defendants had a duty to provide timely and informative notice of the lockdown to Savings Plan participants so they had an opportunity to safeguard their rights and direct Northern Trust to sell the Enron stock allocated to their individual accounts; instead Enron sent notice to participants by e-mail on October 25, 2001 at 11:44 p.m., the day before the lockdown, and employees did not receive it until they came to work on the day of the lockdown. The complaint asserts they had no reasonable time to "review [their] overall strategy and carefully weigh the potential earnings of each investment choice against its risk before making investment decisions that are aligned with [their] long-term financial plans and [their] risk tolerance," as directed by the e-mail. * * * Given the timing of the e-mail and the lack of opportunity for this kind of detailed portfolio review, the fiduciaries knew or should have known that the notice was clearly inadequate, maintain Plaintiffs. * * *

Finally, Plaintiffs have stated a claim for co-fiduciary liability against the Enron ERISA Defendants, Northern Trust, Olson, and the Administrative Committee relating to their action or inaction in knowingly participating in the lockdowns and failing to make reasonable efforts to remedy the breaches of their co-fiduciaries.

### 3.   Count III: Failure to diversify Savings Plan assets

Plaintiffs have also stated a claim against the Enron ERISA Defendants, including the Administrative Committee, and against Northern Trust for failure to diversify Savings Plan assets in accordance with the plan's provisions and ERISA. * * *

[W]hile § 1.1 of the Savings Plan Trust agreement (Ex. B to #322) states that the Administrative Committee "has the responsibility . . . for monitoring the diversification of the investments of the Funds," § 6.2 mandates that, subject to its duty of loyalty and the prudent man standard, "the Trustee shall diversify the investments of that portion of the Fund of which it has investment responsibility so as to minimize the risk of large losses. . . ." Furthermore § 6.3 recites that subject to its duty of loyalty and the prudent man standard, "the Trustee shall, with respect to that portion of the Fund of which it has investment responsibility, follow the investment guidelines established by the Administrative Committee and shall act in accordance with the direction of the Administrative Committee. . . ." Thus the Savings Plan mandates that the Administrative Committee and the Trustee share a fiduciary responsibility to diversify plan assets where prudent. The trustee furthermore has a duty to plan participants not to follow the Administrative Committee's directions where they are contrary to ERISA, i.e., where they would lead to an imprudent result harmful to the plan participants and beneficiaries. * * *

Under 29 U.S.C. § 1104(a)(1)(C), a plan fiduciary has a duty to "diversif [y] the investments of the Plan so as to minimize the risk of large losses, unless under the circumstances it is clearly prudent not to do so." * * *

Plaintiffs concede in their complaint * * * that ERISA explicitly exempts defined contribution plans (a/k/a "individual account plans") from the diversification requirement to the extent that the employee benefit plan invests in the employer's own stock. * * * Nevertheless, since an employer may establish the conditions and terms of its plan as long as these conditions and terms do not violate ERISA, and because neither the statute nor the plan mandates non-diversification in the individual account plan, Plaintiffs argue that § XV.3 of the Savings Plan, charging the Administrative Committee and Northern Trust with the duty of "diversifying the investments of the Plan so as to minimize the risk of large losses," controls over § 404(a)(2), 29 U.S.C. § 1104(a)(2).

Urging that Plaintiffs cannot state a claim for failure of the fiduciaries to diversify the Savings Plan, Defendants highlight a different provision in the Plan, which they claim is contrary to § XV.3, i.e., § XIX.5, which provides, "The Plan is specifically authorized to acquire and hold up to 100% of its assets in 'qualifying employer securities' as such term is defined in Section 407(d) of [ERISA]." Moreover, Section V.16 of the Savings Plan * * * provides that Enron's 50% match of employees' contributions would be made "primarily" in Enron stock and remain in such stock until participants reach the age of 50. * * *

After examining the text of the Savings Plan, the Court concludes the provisions are not in conflict and that Plaintiffs can state a claim under the key "clearly prudent under the circumstances" standard established in § XV.3(c): "[e]ach fiduciary ... *shall discharge his duties and responsibilities* with respect to the Plan *by inter alia diversifying the investments of the Plan* so as to minimize the risk of large losses, *unless under the circumstances it is clearly not prudent* to do so [emphasis added]." While the plan authorizes the trustee to hold "up to 100% of its assets" in Enron stock, it does not mandate that the trustee hold 100%, or even 30% or 20%, of its assets in Enron stock, and, in fact, seemingly allows complete discretion in how much may be invested in Enron stock where the circumstances make such investment imprudent. There also is substantial discretion permitted in § V.16's requirement that employer matching contributions be "primarily," but not wholly, in Enron stock. The language and grammatical structure of the Savings Plan's § XV.3 indicate that diversification is the general rule, not the exception, and where diversification is not effected, there is a burden to justify that the absence of diversification was clearly prudent under the circumstances. As most investment advisors inform their clients, putting all of one's eggs in a single basket is clearly a risky investment strategy; it is the rare case where diversification "is clearly not prudent." According to the parallel provision to § XV.3(c) in ERISA (§ 404(a)(1)(C)) and, as noted earlier, to case law construing it, if the fiduciary trustee decides not to diversify and is subsequently sued for breach of fiduciary duty, once a plaintiff meets the minimal burden of showing that the portfolio is not diversified on its face, the trustee then bears the much heavier burden to show that the choice was clearly prudent under the circumstances. *Metzler*, 112 F.3d at 209.

The complaint meets its light burden by alleging as facts that immediately before the lockdown, and in light of the red lights and rapidly deteriorating circumstances described in the pleadings, the Plan assets were dangerously overweighted in Enron stock, which constituted 60% of its investments, as Olson conceded during her testimony before Congress. It charges that Defendants breached their responsibility to protect the investments and to diversify. * * *

4.  Count IV: (Plaintiffs on behalf of certain retirement plan participants and beneficiaries sue Enron and the Enron ERISA Defendants for breach of fiduciary duties to the Cash Balance Plan participants and beneficiaries from 1998–2000 relating to offsets based on the inflated value of Enron stock)

* * * With respect to the amendment of the Cash Balance Plan effective in 1996, and its computation of the offset to a plan participant's

average pay for retirement benefits under § 5.2(g) of the amended Cash Balance Plan, Plaintiffs have asserted that Enron and the ERISA Defendants, because they knew or should have known that the market price of Enron stock did not reflect its actual value, breached their fiduciary duty by (1) failing to use the true value of Enron stock, which Defendants knew or should have known, rather than the artificially inflated market price, to compute the offset; (2) failing to fix permanently the market value component of the offset because it did not reflect the stock's real value at the close of the market on the first day of each year from 1996 to 2000; and/or (3) failing to disclose to participants and beneficiaries that the value of the stock used for the offset was artificially inflated or not the actual value of the stock on the relevant dates. * * *

According to the complaint, beginning in 1998, the company diversified, acquired more and new businesses, and the price of Enron stock increased substantially through 2000; at some point, not clearly pinpointed, the price became fraudulently inflated. While the amount of the offset under the Cash Balance Plan also increased, thereby reducing the participants' and beneficiaries' accrued pension benefits, had that rise in value of Enron reflected Enron's actual worth, the larger offset amount would not have injured Plaintiffs because their ESOP account holdings would also have increased substantially. Thus in essence the target of Plaintiffs' claim is not the new pension benefit plan formula established by the amendment. The cause of the injury is not the structure of the plan itself, but the purported fraud that allegedly began to occur a couple of years after the 1995 amendment became effective and which caused the market value of the stock to rise when the actual financial condition of the company was deteriorating, thereby making the application of the plan's formula injurious to plan participants and beneficiaries.

Plaintiffs have characterized their claim as a breach of fiduciary duty on the grounds that once Defendants knew or should have known that Enron's precarious financial condition and fraudulent accounting made evident that Enron stock was overpriced (identified by the complaint * * * as "the three-year period 1998–2000"), the plan fiduciaries should have disregarded the terms of the plan for those three years, determined what the true value of the stock should have been, and computed each component of the offset with that true value, or refused to fix the component permanently at the artificially inflated closing price as the plan mandated, or disclosed to plan participants and beneficiaries that the values of the stock were artificially inflated. Instead Defendants proceeded according to the plan amendment's formula even though they knew that the new formula would unfairly reduce the plan participants' pension benefits. Moreover, in the context of the larger scheme to defraud, Plaintiffs have also charged Defendants with a conflict of interest because at least some of the savings to Enron in paying Plaintiffs with, and reducing the amount of their benefits by use of, artificially inflated stock in their ESOP accounts allegedly went into higher bonuses and salaries for Defendants' personal gain, another breach of fiduciary duty because

Defendants had the authority to amend the pension benefits and the discretion to exercise it.

* * * The Court agrees that Plaintiffs have stated a claim for breach of fiduciary duty; it is two of their particular remedies with which this Court takes issue because they offend policies behind ERISA. It addresses the Plaintiffs' proposed remedies first.

Plaintiffs plead that the plan administrators should have not only "disregarded" terms of the amended plan established by the employer in his settlor capacity, even though they facially complied with the statute, but also that the administrators should affirmatively have determined for themselves the real value of Enron stock for each of the last three years and used that amount and/or not fixed the price of the artificially inflated stock as a permanent component of the offset. Plaintiffs cannot mandate to the plan administrators what they should have done; and a court can only determine after the fact whether the path the administrators took was prudent in light of the circumstances and available options. A fiduciary must independently investigate and examine the prudence of possible options and determine which to follow, with an eye to the policies underlying ERISA. There is a substantial difference between "disregarding" a plan term and mandating a specific new one that offends the employer/settlor's authority.

The two proposed remedies appear not merely to restrict the administrators' options, but are contrary to ERISA's policies. These proposed remedial actions in essence would constitute a plan amendment without reference to plan procedures. The Court finds no authority for and is not willing to impose as a fiduciary duty on the trustee or plan administrators, as a matter of law, writing such specific terms into the plan; plan amendment is a settlor function, and in the case sub judicia, is reserved by the Cash Balance Plan's express terms solely to the Company. * * * The settlor function protection was created to encourage employers to establish plans. There are other options open to the trustee to "disregard" the plan's terms under the circumstances.

Second, the proposed task (of determining the true worth of Enron stock) would have been complex, costly, and unlikely to yield certain or verifiable figures in light of the alleged fraud. ERISA was enacted not only to provide plan participants and beneficiaries with a vested right to receive benefits when they reach normal retirement age, but also, as a balance, to hold down the impact of cost increases and burdens on employers, again to induce them to create such plans.

Alternatively Plaintiffs assert that Defendants had a fiduciary duty to disclose the artificially inflated price of the stock to protect the plan participants and beneficiaries. Here Plaintiffs have stated a more appropriate option under the circumstances: affirmative disclosure of the artificially high price of the stock, which, as noted previously, would, because of the securities laws' insider trading provisions, also necessitate a duty to find a means to disclose to all investors and the public at large the fraudulent acts and concealment that inflated the value of Enron stock. * * *

Plaintiffs insist they do not assert a § 502(a)(1) claim for denied plan benefits, which would require the Court to determine (1) whether the plan administrator made the correct legal interpretation of the plan and (2) whether the administrator interpreted the plan uniformly. * * * Plaintiffs emphasize that their claim does not fall under § 502(a)(1) because they agree that the plan is clear and unambiguous, they are not contending that Defendants did not interpret it properly, and they are not seeking to recover benefits under the terms of the plan. The Court agrees. They seek not to recover benefits, enforce rights, or clarify rights to future benefits under the plan; they seek to nullify the provision in dispute as it applies to certain plan participants from 1998–2000. * * * Here Plaintiffs have dismissed the Cash Balance Plan. Because Plaintiffs have consciously framed their claim under § 502(a)(3) as a breach of fiduciary duty, they therefore must meet the burdens of proving a claim for which relief is provided under that statute.

In their complaint, Plaintiffs are vague about the equitable remedy prayer with respect to the Cash Balance Plan. According to the complaint they seek to enjoin Defendants from computing the value of each component of the ESOP offset according to the market value of the Enron shares on each January 1st of the three-year period 1998–2000 and order those defendants to redress all damages flowing from prior Cash Balance payments made pursuant to the offset arrangement. * * * In their memorandum * * * they assert that they seek "injunctive and declaratory relief from those now in charge of the plan" and from each Committee Member "monetary make-whole relief that was 'typically available in equity.'" They cite as authority Great–West, 122 S. Ct. at 712, which ironically may be their undoing. * * *

The remedy of an injunction to maintain the status quo * * * would be to enjoin a three-year practice of offsetting pension benefits with the inflated value of Enron stock; that practice ended in 2000 and thus injunctive relief "to preserve the status quo" is a moot issue. Moreover it would not be an injunction under the language of § 502(a)(3) "to enjoin any act or practice which violates the terms of the plan" since implementation of that offset was in compliance with the terms of the plan. * * *

Under § 503(a) a prayer for equitable relief such as disgorgement or restitution to redress violations such as breaches of fiduciary duty must refer to "those categories of relief that were typically available in equity" under Great–West. Remedies of equitable restitution and disgorgement would have to meet the standard set out in Great–West, i.e., remedies that were typically available in a court of equity and that are not compensatory damages punishing Defendants for Plaintiffs' loss, but restoration of property subject to imposition of a constructive trust or equitable lien in which money belonging in good conscience to Plaintiffs can clearly be traced to particular funds in the Defendants' possession.

Plaintiffs' complaint alleges that they are seeking "monetary make-whole relief" from Committee Members' personal assets, in essence a claim for the difference in value between what their pensions would have been if calculated by a formula using the true worth of Enron stock and what they were allocated under the inflated value calculation from 1998–2000. As discussed earlier, under Great–West such monetary relief is actually compensatory relief for their loss, the imposition of personal liability on these Defendants' individual resources, unless Plaintiffs can trace some or all of the sum of money to which they claim entitlement, but which was never received by them or by the plan, through Enron's enormous business into the bonuses and increased salaries that went into these particular Defendants' personal pockets and which remains within their possession and control. Plaintiffs have set themselves a daunting task. At this stage of the litigation the Court cannot state that there is no possibility that Plaintiffs can satisfy their burden of proof, but their relief is limited to that defined as typical equitable restitution in Great–West.

[The court's discussions of non-ERISA claims and a recital of rulings on each motion to dismiss are omitted.]

## NOTES AND QUESTIONS

1. The "lockdown" problem was addressed in the Pension Protection Act of 2006 by an amendment to section 404(c), 29 U.S.C. § 1004(c), that states that a beneficiary is not to be treated as in control of an individual account during a period when there is a lockdown preventing that beneficiary from actually exercising control.

2. The Pension Protection Act also made changes in the treatment of "company stock" (stock authorized by the company's board of directors to be issued, but held in the company's treasury instead of having been sold to the public) issued to individual retirement accounts. Section 901 of that act requires that an employee be able to divest her individual account of publicly traded employer securities sooner than in the past. (Roughly speaking, after three years.) Another new provision, section 101(m), 29 U.S.C. § 1021(m) requires that notice be given to the owner of an individual account 30 days in advance that he will have the right to divest the account of an employer security as of a certain date and "describe[s] the importance" of diversification.

The use of company stock as a means of funding retirement plans has distinct advantages to an employer. It avoids the need to use up cash resources, for example, and the administrative costs are low. Moreover, a contribution can be made quickly, taking advantage of good market conditions. Some argue that an employee with an investment stake in her company is likely to work more effectively. The risks to employees are made painfully obvious in this case. Not only does an employee of a bankrupt firm find himself out of a job, he has also lost much of the value of his retirement account.

Defined benefit plans are in general forbidden to hold more than 10% of their assets in company stock. 29 U.S.C. § 1107. Even so, problems can arise for fiduciaries in deciding when that stock is a good buy (or a good investment to hold on to). In *Donovan v. Bierwirth*, 680 F.2d 263 (2d Cir.), cert. denied, 459 U.S. 1069, 103 S.Ct. 488, 74 L.Ed.2d 631 (1982), the defendants were executives of the Grumman Corporation and also trustees of one of its pension plans. A hostile takeover bid for Grumman was made by a conglomerate. The defendants decided both to hold onto Grumman stock in the pension fund, and to buy more, which make the takeover attempt harder. The court recognized that these executives were in a conflict of interest situation: in the event of a takeover they might well lose their jobs. Given that conflict, the court reasoned, these trustees should have recused themselves from making decisions about whether to buy, hold or tender the company stock. Not having done so, they were liable to the plan. As it happened, the defendants had made a decision that turned out well. The takeover attempt failed, the company did well, and the price of the company's stock went up, beyond any price paid by the pension plan they served as trustees. Thus, their individual liability was very limited (to costs of litigation and the like). Had the market gone into a slide, however, they could have been liable for very substantial sums.

3.  The bankruptcy of any substantial firm is likely to generate claims for benefits promised to employees but not provided, such as contributions that should have been made to pension plans. Assembling a group of plaintiffs to pursue employee claims can sometimes be a challenge, if only because of the up-front costs involved. This is particularly true if the employer in question is not unionized, as was the case with Enron. If a defined benefit plan is involved, the Pension Benefit Guaranty Corporation (PBGC) is very likely to become a party, and to try to see to it that assets of the bankrupt firm are used to make up any underfunding. That was true, for example, with the defined benefit plan at Portland General Electric, an Enron subsidiary. When PGE was ultimately sold, proceeds of the sale were put into a separate interest-bearing account for a time until the extent of the pension fund losses could be determined and paid for out of those proceeds. The Department of Labor also played a role in the Enron situation, bringing suit in 2004 alleging violations of ERISA and seeking appointment of different fiduciaries for the pension plans. That action was handled together with the class actions insofar as possible.

4.  Many bankrupt firms, like Enron, file under Chapter 11 of the Bankruptcy Code, seeking to remain in business, at least for a time, rather than to liquidate immediately. This presents additional challenges for workers who may need to balance their need for a better funded retirement plan against the need for a current job with whatever firm emerges from the bankruptcy proceedings. In the case of Enron, a reorganization plan was in fact approved in 2004. Once the plan was approved, the surviving corporation (eventually renamed Enron Creditors Recovery Corporation) devoted itself to selling off the assets of the firm. The last substantial sale (of Prisma Energy International, Inc., a subsidiary) occurred in the fall of 2007. The Enron stock in retirement accounts proved to be virtually worthless. It is not possible to determine accurately how many jobs were lost, since some of the buyers of Enron subsidiaries kept portions of their workforces on. The class actions, Labor Department actions and securities litigation eventually resulted in

settlement and judgments against Enron itself that became claims in the administration of the bankruptcy estate (for over $350 million). The claims in the litigation that produced the opinion above also resulted in settlement of claims against the accounting firm ($1.25 million) and Northern Trust Co. ($37.5 million). Pursuit of claims against former Enron chairman Kenneth Lay became complicated because of his death soon after being convicted of criminal fraud. That death prior to the time for an appeal resulted in abatement of the conviction, which plaintiffs had sought to use in the civil litigation. A settlement was ultimately reached that provided pension funds a $12 million claim against his estate. The claims against former Enron president Jeffrey Skilling were dealt with in a settlement package ($85 million) that involved many other former executives and directors. While situations differed at the various Enron subsidiaries, a rough estimate is that the typical Enron employee lost more than 80% of the value of her pension plan assets.

5. Bankruptcy proceedings often involve proposals by the bankrupt and non-employee creditors to discontinue benefit plans, and in many instances, the bankruptcy court grants such requests, applying a four-part test. 29 U.S.C. § 1341(c)(2)(B)(ii). See, e.g., *In re Falcon Prods., Inc.*, 497 F.3d 838 (8th Cir. 2007). When the plan is part of a collective bargaining agreement, the Bankruptcy Code requires that specific findings be made by the bankruptcy court before the agreement can be set aside. 11 U.S.C. § 1113. See, e.g., *In re Northwest Airlines*, 346 B.R. 307 (Bankr. S.D.N.Y. 2006) (revisions of medical benefits; closing of defined benefit pension plan; establishment of defined contribution plan).Whether court-approved disavowal of a collective agreement should be treated as a breach of contract, generating additional claims against the debtor, has been a troubling issue. See *Northwest Airlines Corp. v. Association of Flight Attendants*, 483 F.3d 160 (2d Cir. 2007) (court-approved disavowal not a breach but an "abrogation"). In some cases, the PBGC plays a role, and may have interests that are not identical to those of the workers involved. See, e.g., *Air Line Pilots Ass'n Int'l v. P.B.G.C.*, 193 F. Supp. 2d 209 (D.D.C. 2002). In that case, the PBGC urged rapid termination of a pension plan because of underfunding; PBGC did not want the obligations for future pensions to continue to pile up. The pilots' union argued against the termination.

When the assets of a firm are enough so that paying off the claims of "secured" creditors do not exhaust them, the priority given to the unsecured claims becomes important. Some employee claims are given priority status. See the discussion in *Howard Delivery Service, Inc. v. Zurich American Ins. Co.*, 547 U.S. 651, 126 S.Ct. 2105, 165 L.Ed.2d 110 (2006), refusing to treat unpaid workers compensation insurance premiums as entitled to the priority given to contributions to employee benefit plans.

A number of critics have argued that the existing law does not provide adequate protection to the interests of workers, and have proposed changes. See Carol Pettit, Rejection of Collective Bargaining Agreements in Chapter 11 Bankruptcies: Legal Analysis of Changes to 11 U.S.C. Section 1113 Proposed in H.R. 3652 (Congressional Research Service Report RL 34486) (2008).

6. Why is the designation of investment alternatives treated as a fiduciary rather than a settlor function? Does this mean that the defense provided by

section 404(c) of ERISA is not available when the participant's claim is an improper choice of alternatives? Compare *Langbecker v. Electronic Data Systems Corp.*, 476 F.3d 299 (5th Cir. 2007) with *In re Tyco Int'l, Ltd. Multidistrict Litigation*, 606 F. Supp. 2d 166 (D.N.H. 2009).

# G.  PLAN TERMINATION AND FUNDING

## BECK v. PACE INTERNATIONAL UNION

Supreme Court of the United States, 2007
551 U.S. 96, 127 S.Ct. 2310, 168 L.Ed.2d 1

JUSTICE SCALIA delivered the opinion of the Court.

We decide in this case whether an employer that sponsors and administers a single-employer defined-benefit pension plan has a fiduciary obligation under the Employee Retirement Income Security Act of 1974 (ERISA), 88 Stat. 829, as amended, 29 U.S.C. § 1001 et seq., to consider a merger with a multiemployer plan as a method of terminating the plan.

I

Crown Paper and its parent entity, Crown Vantage (the two hereinafter referred to in the singular as Crown), employed 2,600 persons in seven paper mills. PACE International Union, a respondent here, represented employees covered by 17 of Crown's defined-benefit pension plans. * * * In such a plan, the employer generally shoulders the investment risk. It is the employer who must make up for any deficits, but also the employer who enjoys the fruits (whether in the form of lower plan contributions or sometimes a reversion of assets) if plan investments perform beyond expectations. See *Hughes Aircraft Co. v. Jacobson*, 525 U.S. 432, 439–440, 119 S. Ct. 755, 142 L. Ed. 2d 881 (1999). In this case, Crown served as both plan sponsor and plan administrator.

In March 2000, Crown filed for bankruptcy and proceeded to liquidate its assets. ERISA allows employers to terminate their pension plans voluntarily * * *and in the summer of 2001, Crown began to consider a "standard termination," a condition of which is that the terminated plans have sufficient assets to cover benefit liabilities. § 1341(b)(1)(D). * * * Crown focused in particular on the possibility of a standard termination through purchase of annuities, one statutorily specified method of plan termination. See § 1341(b)(3)(A)(i). PACE, however, * * * proposed that, rather than buy annuities, Crown instead merge the plans covering PACE union members with the PACE Industrial Union Management Pension Fund (PIUMPF), a multiemployer or "Taft–Hartley" plan. See § 1002(37). Under the terms of the PACE-proposed agreement, Crown would be required to convey all plan assets to PIUMPF; PIUMPF would assume all plan liabilities.

Crown took PACE's merger offer under advisement. As it reviewed annuitization bids, however, it discovered that it had overfunded certain of its pension plans, so that purchasing annuities would allow it to retain a projected $5 million reversion for its creditors after satisfying its obligations to plan participants and beneficiaries. See § 1344(d)(1) (providing for reversion upon plan termination where certain conditions are met). Under PACE's merger proposal, by contrast, the $5 million would go to PIUMPF. What is more, the Pension Benefit Guaranty Corporation (PBGC), which administers an insurance program to protect plan benefits, agreed to withdraw the proofs of claim it had filed against Crown in the bankruptcy proceedings if Crown went ahead with an annuity purchase. Crown had evidently heard enough. It consolidated 12 of its pension plans into a single plan, and terminated that plan through the purchase of an $84 million annuity. That annuity fully satisfied Crown's obligations to plan participants and beneficiaries and allowed Crown to reap the $5 million reversion in surplus funds.

PACE and two plan participants, also respondents here (we will refer to all respondents collectively as PACE), thereafter filed an adversary action against Crown in the Bankruptcy Court, alleging that Crown's directors had breached their fiduciary duties under ERISA by neglecting to give diligent consideration to PACE's merger proposal. The Bankruptcy Court * * * found that the decision whether to purchase annuities or merge with PIUMPF was a fiduciary decision, and that Crown had breached its fiduciary obligations by giving insufficient study to the PIUMPF proposal. Rather than ordering Crown to cancel its annuity (which would have resulted in a substantial penalty payable to Crown's annuity provider), the Bankruptcy Court instead issued a preliminary injunction preventing Crown from obtaining the $5 million reversion. It subsequently approved a distribution of that reversion for the benefit of plan participants and beneficiaries, which distribution was stayed pending appeal.

Petitioner, the trustee of the Crown bankruptcy estates, appealed the Bankruptcy–Court decision to the District Court, which affirmed in relevant part, as did the Court of Appeals for the Ninth Circuit. * * *

## II

Crown's operation of its defined-benefit pension plans placed it in dual roles as plan sponsor and plan administrator; an employer's fiduciary duties under ERISA are implicated only when it acts in the latter capacity. * * *.

It is well established in this Court's cases that an employer's decision whether to terminate an ERISA plan is a settlor function immune from ERISA's fiduciary obligations. * * * But PACE says that its proposed merger was different, because the PIUMPF merger represented a method of terminating the Crown plans. And just as ERISA imposed on Crown a fiduciary obligation in its selection of an appropriate annuity provider when terminating through annuities, see 29 CFR §§ 2509.95–1, 4041.28(c)(3) (2006), so too, PACE argues, did it require Crown to consider merger.

The idea that the decision whether to merge could switch from a settlor to a fiduciary function depending upon the context in which the merger proposal is raised is an odd one. But once it is realized that a merger is simply a transfer of assets and liabilities, PACE's argument becomes somewhat more plausible: The purchase of an annuity is akin to a transfer of assets and liabilities (to an insurance company), and if Crown was subject to fiduciary duties in selecting an annuity provider, why could it automatically disregard PIUMPF simply because PIUMPF happened to be a multiemployer plan rather than an insurer? There is, however, an antecedent question. In order to affirm the judgment below, we would have to conclude (as the Ninth Circuit did) that merger is, in the first place, a permissible form of plan termination under ERISA. That requires us to delve into the statute's provisions for plan termination.

ERISA sets forth the exclusive procedures for the standard termination of single-employer pension plans. § 1341(a)(1); * * * Those procedures are exhaustive, setting detailed rules for, inter alia, notice by the plan to affected parties, § 1341(a)(2), review by the PBGC, § 1341(b)(2)(A), (C), and final distribution of plan funds, § 1341(b)(2)(D), § 1344. * * * At issue in this case is § 1341(b)(3)(A), the provision of ERISA setting forth the permissible methods of terminating a single-employer plan and distributing plan assets to participants and beneficiaries. Section 1341(b)(3)(A) provides as follows:

> In connection with any final distribution of assets pursuant to the standard termination of the plan under this subsection, the plan administrator shall distribute the assets in accordance with section 1344 of this title. In distributing such assets, the plan administrator shall—
>
> (i) purchase irrevocable commitments from an insurer to provide all benefit liabilities under the plan, or
>
> (ii) in accordance with the provisions of the plan and any applicable regulations, otherwise fully provide all benefit liabilities under the plan. . . .

The PBGC's regulations impose in substance the same requirements. * * *

The parties to this case all agree that § 1341(b)(3)(A)(i) refers to the purchase of annuities, see 29 CFR § 4001.2 (defining "irrevocable commitment"), and that

§ 1341(b)(3)(A)(ii) allows for lump-sum distributions at present discounted value (including rollovers into individual retirement accounts). As PACE concedes, purchase of annuity contracts and lump-sum payments are "by far the most common distribution methods." * * * To affirm the Ninth Circuit, we would have to decide that merger is a permissible method as well. And we would have to do that over the objection of the PBGC, which (joined by the Department of Labor) disagrees with the Ninth Circuit, taking the position that § 1341(b)(3)(A) does not permit merger as a method of termination because (in its view) merger is an alternative to (rather than an example of) plan termination. * * * We have traditionally deferred to the PBGC when interpreting ERISA, for "to attempt to answer these questions without the views of the agencies responsible for enforcing ERISA, would be to embar[k] upon a voyage without a compass." *Mead Corp. v. Tilley*, 490 U.S. 714, 722, 725–726, 109 S. Ct. 2156, 104 L. Ed. 2d 796 (1989) * * * In reviewing the judgment below, we thus must examine "whether the PBGC's policy is based upon a permissible construction of the statute." Id., at 648, 110 S. Ct. 2668.

We believe it is. PACE has "failed to persuade us that the PBGC's views are unreasonable," *Mead Corp.*, *supra*, at 725. At the outset, it must be acknowledged that the statute, with its general residual clause in § 1341(b)(3)(A)(ii), is potentially more embracing of alternative methods of plan termination (whatever they may be) than longstanding ERISA practice, which appears to have employed almost exclusively annuities and lump-sum payments. But we think that the statutory text need not be read to include mergers, and indeed that the PBGC offers the better reading in excluding them. Most obviously, Congress nowhere expressly provided for merger as a permissible means of termination. * * * PACE nevertheless maintains that merger is clearly covered under § 1341(b)(3)(A)(ii)'s residual clause, which refers to a distribution of assets that "otherwise fully provide[s] all benefit liabilities under the plan." By PACE's reasoning, annuities are covered under § 1341(b)(3)(A)(i); annuities are—by virtue of the word "otherwise"—an example of a means by which a plan may "fully provide all benefit liabilities under the plan,"§ 1341(b)(3)(A)(ii); and therefore, "at the least," any method of termination that is the "legal equivalent" of annuitization is permitted, * * * Merger, PACE argues, is such a legal equivalent.

We do not find the statute so clear. Even assuming that PACE is right about "otherwise"—that the word indicates that annuities are one example of satisfying the residual clause in § 1341(b)(3)(A)(ii)—we still do not find mergers covered with the clarity necessary to disregard the PBGC's considered views. Surely the phrase "otherwise fully provide all benefit liabilities under the plan" is not without some teeth. And we think it would be reasonable for the PBGC to determine both that merger is not like the purchase of annuities in its ability to "fully provide all benefit liabilities under the plan," and that the statute's distinct treatment of merger and termination provides clear evidence that one is not an example of the other. Three points strike us as especially persuasive in these regards.

First, terminating a plan through purchase of annuities (like terminating through distribution of lump-sum payments) formally severs the applicability of ERISA to plan assets and employer obligations. Upon purchasing annuities, the employer is no longer subject to ERISA's multitudinous requirements, such as (to name just one) payment of insurance premiums to the PBGC, § 1307(a). And the PBGC is likewise no longer liable for the deficiency in the event that the plan becomes insolvent; there are no more benefits for it to guarantee. The assets of the plan are wholly removed from the ERISA system, and plan participants and beneficiaries must rely primarily (if not exclusively) on state-contract remedies if they do not receive proper payments or are otherwise denied access to their funds. Further, from the standpoint of the participants and beneficiaries, the risk associated with an annuity relates solely to the solvency of an insurance company, and not the performance of the merged plan's investments.

Merger is fundamentally different: it represents a continuation rather than a cessation of the ERISA regime. If Crown were to have merged its pension plans into PIUMPF, the plan assets would have been combined with the assets of the multiemployer plan, where they could then be used to satisfy the benefit liabilities of participants and beneficiaries other than those from the original Crown plans. Those assets would remain within ERISA's purview, the PBGC would maintain responsibility for them, and if Crown continued to employ the plan participants it too would remain subject to ERISA. Finally, plan participants and beneficiaries would have their recourse not through state-contract law, but through the ERISA system, just as they had prior to merger.

Second, in a standard termination ERISA allows the employer to (under certain circumstances) recoup surplus funds, § 1344(d)(1), (3), as Crown sought to do here. But ERISA forbids employers to obtain a reversion in the absence of a termination:

> Third, the structure of ERISA amply (if not conclusively) supports the conclusion that § 1341(b)(3)(A)(ii) does not cover merger. * * * Section 1058, the general merger provision, in fact quite clearly contemplates that merger and termination are not one and the same, forbidding merger "unless each participant in the plan would *(if the plan then terminated)* receive a benefit immediately after the merger ... which is equal to or greater than the benefit he would have been entitled to receive immediately before the merger ... *(if the plan had then terminated).*

(Emphasis added).

As for the different rules and procedures governing termination and merger: Most critically, plans seeking to terminate must provide advance notice to the PBGC, as well as extensive actuarial information. § 1341(b)(2)(A). The PBGC has the authority to halt the termination if it determines that plan assets are insufficient to cover plan liabilities. § 1341(b)(2)(C). Merger, by contrast, involves considerably less PBGC oversight, and the PBGC has no similar ability to cancel, * * * And while mergers between multiemployer plans do require 120–days advance notice, § 1411(b)(1), this still differs from the general notice provision for termination of single-employer plans, which requires notice to the PBGC "[a]s soon as practicable" after notice is given to affected parties, § 1341(b)(2)(A). * * *

PACE believes that these procedural differences can be ironed over rather easily. It insists:

> Many plan mergers take place without intent to terminate a plan; in those cases, the requirements for plan merger can be followed without consulting the requirements for plan termination. Conversely, many plan terminations take place without an associated merger; in those cases there is no need to consult the requirements for mergers. But if a plan sponsor intends to use merger as a method of implementing a plan termination, it simply must follow the rules for both merger and termination.

Brief for Respondents 36.

PACE similarly explains that while the PBGC does not approve "ordinary merger [s]," PBGC approval would be necessary when a merger is designed to terminate a plan. Id., at 37. The confusion invited by PACE's proposed framework is alone enough to condemn it. How could a plan be sure that it was in one box rather than the other? To avoid the risk of liability, should it simply follow both sets of rules all of the time? PACE's proposal is flawed for another reason as well: It has no apparent basis in the statute. The separate provisions governing termination and merger quite clearly treat the two as wholly different transactions, with no exception for the case where merger is used for termination.

For all of the foregoing reasons, we believe that the PBGC's construction of the statute is a permissible one, and indeed the more plausible. Crown did not breach its fiduciary obligations in failing to consider PACE's merger proposal because merger is not a permissible form of termination. Even from a policy standpoint, the PBGC's choice is an eminently reasonable one, since termination by merger could have detrimental consequences for plan beneficiaries and plan sponsors alike. When a single-employer plan is merged into a multiemployer plan, the original participants and beneficiaries become dependent upon the financial well-being of the multiemployer plan and its contributing members. Assets of the single-employer plan (which in this case were capable of fully funding plan liabilities) may be used to satisfy commitments owed to other participants and beneficiaries of the (possibly underfunded) multiemployer plan. The PBGC believes that this arrangement creates added risk for participants and beneficiaries of the original plan, particularly in view of the lesser guarantees that the PBGC provides to multiemployer plans, compare § 1322 with § 1322a. * * *

We hold that merger is not a permissible method of terminating a single-employer defined-benefit pension plan. The judgment of the Court of Appeals is reversed, and the case is remanded * * *.

## NOTES AND QUESTIONS

1. When an employer withdraws from a multiemployer plan, it incurs a withdrawal liability, under amendments to ERISA in the Multiemployer

Pension Plan Amendments Act of 1980, Pub L. 96–364, 94 Stat. 1208. Under those provisions, the employer is typically required to make periodic payments to the plan from which it has withdrawn, based on the plan sponsor's computation of that employer's share of the plan's "unfunded vested benefits." For a review of the background of these provisions, see *Pension Benefit Guaranty Corp. v. R.A. Gray & Co.*, 467 U.S. 717, 104 S.Ct. 2709, 81 L.Ed.2d 601 (1984). Disputes over the amount of liability are typically dealt with by arbitration, in which the plan sponsor's calculations are entitled to the benefit of presumptions of correctness. See *Concrete Pipe & Prods. of California, Inc. v. Construction Laborers Pension Trust for S. California*, 508 U.S. 602, 113 S.Ct. 2264, 124 L.Ed.2d 539 (1993) (approving the constitutionality of the use of presumptions although finding them inartfully phrased).

2. The original provisions of ERISA governing the funding of single employer defined benefit plans were designed in part to cope with the problem that fund assets, particularly publicly traded stocks, fluctuate in value. The "smoothing" mechanisms in the statute involved allowing plan sponsors to "average" fund values over periods of years. One result was that some sponsors were not required to make contributions to plans even in years when those plans were underfunded. A widely publicized example involved Bethlehem Steel, a firm that had lawfully not made contributions for a substantial time, with the result that when the company failed, the PBGC was saddled with between three and four billion dollars of unfunded liability. These provisions were amended substantially by the Pension Protection Act of 2006 (PPA), with the bulk of the changes to take effect in 2008. The language is highly technical in nature, and there are special provisions for particular industries (notably airlines). Overall, however, the objective of the PPA is to make the calculation of the current value of future liabilities more accurate, and to require any funding shortfalls to be made up more quickly than in the past. There are also requirements that plans notify participants when funding is below the 80% level. Whether the assumptions that underlie the statute are sound enough so that the risk of future defined benefit plan failure has been reduced is debatable, but probably the new statute on balance represents progress. See the critical treatment in Eric D. Chason, *Outlawing Pension Funding Shortfalls*, 26 VA. TAX REV. 519 (2007). Questions have been raised about whether there should be any limit on the compensation paid to a firm's executives at times when that firm's pension plans are underfunded. See GAO Report 10–77 (October 2009), Private Pensions: Sponsors of 10 Underfunded Plans Paid Executives Approximately $350 Million in Compensation Shortly Before Termination.

3. Overfunded plans also present hazards. In *Mead Corp. v. Tilley*, 490 U.S. 714, 109 S.Ct. 2156, 104 L.Ed.2d 796 (1989), Mead Corporation sold a wholly-owned subsidiary which had a fully funded defined-benefit plan. Under the plan, full retirement benefits were payable at age 65 and the amount was calculated based on the participant's earnings and years of service. At age 55, participants were eligible for early retirement benefits, calculated in the same manner as normal retirement benefits, but reduced by 5% for each year by which a participant's retirement preceded the normal retirement age. A subsidized or unreduced early retirement benefit, equal to that payable at age 65, was available to participants who had 30 or more years of service and

elected to retire after age 62. The plan did not specify how benefits were to be paid upon plan termination.

When the Mead subsidiary was sold, its defined-benefit plan was terminated, and payments equal to the present dollar value of vested claims were paid to the employees. Only those who met both the age (minimum of 62) and years of service (minimum of 30) requirements for full pension benefits were paid the equivalent of their full early retirement benefits. The distribution was reduced for any worker who at the time of the plan's termination had not reached age 62. Four already had 30 years of credited service and a fifth had 28 and would have 30 years had he remained employed by the subsidiary until age 62. Had they been paid the present value of the unreduced early retirement benefits, each of these employees would have received on average nine thousand dollars more. After Mead finished distributing plan assets to plan participants, nearly $11 million remained in the Plan's fund. Mead recouped this money pursuant to the Plan. The employees who received the reduced payments sued asserting that § 4044(a) of the Employee Retirement Income Security Act requires a plan administrator to pay plan participants unreduced early retirement benefits provided under the plan before residual assets may revert to an employer. They argued that they are entitled to such benefits because contingent early retirement benefits, even if unaccrued, are "benefits under the plan" under category 6, § 4044(a)(6), and therefore must be distributed before the employer can recoup any residual plan assets.

The Supreme Court held that § 4044(a)(6) does not create benefit entitlements but simply provides for the orderly distribution of plan assets. However, it remanded for the lower court to consider whether unreduced early retirement benefits may qualify either as "accrued benefits" under ERISA or as "liabilities" within the meaning of § 4044(d)(1)(A). On remand, the Court of Appeals, in a 2–1 decision, noted that the plan stated that Mead was entitled to the reversion of "any surplus remaining in the Retirement Fund, due to actuarial error, after the satisfaction of all benefit rights or contingent benefit rights accrued under the Plan." The court concluded that "unreduced early retirement benefits were 'contingent rights' because the Plan was obligated to pay them on a contingency, i.e., the plaintiff's satisfaction of the age and service requirements." *Tilley v. Mead Corp.*, 927 F.2d 756, 762 (4th Cir. 1991). Accordingly, the court ruled that Tilley had a contractual right to recover the unreduced early retirement benefit.

4. During the 1980s, a large number of plans were liquidated by employers in order to obtain surpluses in those plans' funds. A number of studies concluded that the effect of premature termination on workers was very harsh, and that this was particularly true with the oldest workers. In an attempt to discourage such "raiding" of overfunded plans, Congress imposed an excise tax on fund reversions. The general rate is 20% of the amount of assets recaptured by the employer. See 26 U.S.C. § 4980. A higher rate can be imposed if the employer fails to provide either a replacement plan or some level of benefit increase at the time of termination. Some critics have argued that one effect is to discourage employers from establishing defined benefit plans, or from funding them adequately. See Richard Ippolito, *The Reversion Tax's Perverse Result*, REGULATION (Spring 2002) at 46 (publication of the CATO Institute).

5.  For some older workers, conversion of a traditional defined benefit pension plan, under which the benefit amount is set as a percentage of the worker's average wage in the last few years of work (generally years of higher income for most workers), to a "cash balance" plan may also have harsh effects. Challenges to the propriety of such conversions resulted in mixed outcomes in the courts. The Pension Protection Act of 2006 specifically allows such conversions so long as they meet certain standards. Whether the new solution is an adequate one is a matter of debate. See generally, Stephen Befort, *The Perfect Storm of Retirement Insecurity: Fixing the Three-legged Stoll of Social Security, Pensions and Private Savings*, 91 MINN. L. REV. 938 at 952, 973–976 (2007).

# H.  INTERFERENCE WITH BENEFIT ACCRUAL

## INTER–MODAL RAIL EMPLOYEES ASSOC. v. ATCHISON, TOPEKA & SANTA FE RAILWAY CO.

Supreme Court of the United States, 1997
520 U.S. 510, 117 S.Ct. 1513, 137 L.Ed.2d 763

O'CONNOR, J., delivered the opinion for a unanimous Court.

Section 510 of the Employee Retirement Income Security Act of 1974 (ERISA), 88 Stat. 895, makes it unlawful to "discharge, fine, suspend, expel, discipline, or discriminate against a participant or beneficiary [of an employee benefit plan] . . . for the purpose of interfering with the attainment of any right to which such participant may become entitled under the plan." 29 U.S.C. § 1140. The Court of Appeals for the Ninth Circuit held that § 510 only prohibits interference with the attainment of rights that are capable of "vesting," as that term is defined in ERISA. We disagree.

I

The individual petitioners are former employees of respondent Santa Fe Terminal Services, Inc. (SFTS), a wholly owned subsidiary of respondent The Atchison, Topeka and Santa Fe Railway Co. (ATSF), which was responsible for transferring cargo between railcars and trucks at ATSF's Hobart Yard in Los Angeles, California. While petitioners were employed by SFTS, they were entitled to retirement benefits under the Railroad Retirement Act of 1974, 88 Stat. 1312, as amended, 45 U.S.C. § 231 et seq., and to pension, health, and welfare benefits under collective bargaining agreements involving SFTS and the Teamsters Union. SFTS provided its workers with pension, health, and welfare benefits through employee benefit plans subject to ERISA's comprehensive regulations.

In January 1990, ATSF entered into a formal "Service Agreement" with SFTS to have SFTS do the same "inter-modal" work it had done at the Hobart Yard for the previous 15 years without a contract. Seven weeks later, ATSF exercised its right to terminate the newly formed Agreement and opened up the Hobart Yard work for competitive bidding. Respondent

In–Terminal Services (ITS) was the successful bidder, and SFTS employees who declined to continue employment with ITS were terminated. ITS, unlike SFTS, was not obligated to make contributions to the Railroad Retirement Account under the Railroad Retirement Act. ITS also provided fewer pension and welfare benefits under its collective bargaining agreement with the Teamsters Union than had SFTS. Workers who continued their employment with ITS "lost their Railroad Retirement Act benefits" and "suffered a substantial reduction in Teamsters benefits." 80 F.3d 348, 350 (C.A.9 1996) (per curiam).

Petitioners sued respondents SFTS, ATSF, and ITS in the United States District Court for the Central District of California, alleging that respondents had violated § 510 of ERISA by "discharging" petitioners "for the purpose of interfering with the attainment of . . . rights to which" they would have "become entitled" under the ERISA pension and welfare plans adopted pursuant to the SFTS–Teamsters collective bargaining agreement. . . . Had SFTS remained their employer, petitioners contended, they would have been entitled to assert claims for benefits under the SFTS–Teamsters benefits plans, at least until the collective bargaining agreement that gave rise to those plans expired. The substitution of ITS for SFTS, however, precluded them from asserting those claims and relegated them to asserting claims under the less generous ITS–Teamsters benefits plans. According to petitioners, the substitution "interfered with the attainment" of their "right" to assert those claims and violated § 510. Respondents moved to dismiss these § 510 claims, and the District Court granted the motion. [The appellate court found that the retirement benefits had vested and, therefore, allowed the suit with respect to the retirement benefits claims. However, it found no vesting of the health and welfare benefits and, therefore, agreed with the dismissal of that portion of the suit. * * *

## II

The Court of Appeals' holding that § 510 bars interference only with vested rights is contradicted by the plain language of § 510. As noted above, that section makes it unlawful to "discharge . . . a [plan] participant or beneficiary . . . for the purpose of interfering with the *attainment of any right* to which such participant may become entitled under *the plan.*" 29 U.S.C. § 1140 (emphasis added). ERISA defines a "plan" to include both "an employee welfare benefit plan [and] an employee pension benefit plan," § 1002(3), and specifically exempts "employee welfare benefit plans" from its stringent vesting requirements, see § 1051(1). Because a "plan" includes an "employee welfare benefit plan," and because welfare plans offer benefits that do not "vest" (at least insofar as ERISA is concerned), Congress' use of the word "plan" in § 510 all but forecloses the argument that § 510's interference clause applies only to "vested" rights. Had Congress intended to confine § 510's protection to "vested" rights, it could have easily substituted the term "pension plan," see 29 U.S.C. § 1002(2), for "plan," or the term "nonforfeitable" right, see

§ 1002(19), for "any right." But § 510 draws no distinction between those rights that "vest" under ERISA and those that do not.

The right that an employer or plan sponsor may enjoy in some circumstances to unilaterally amend or eliminate its welfare benefit plan does not, as the Court of Appeals apparently thought, justify a departure from § 510's plain language. It is true that ERISA itself "does not regulate the substantive content of welfare-benefit plans." *Metropolitan Life Ins. Co. v. Massachusetts*, 471 U.S. 724, 732 (1985). Thus, unless an employer contractually cedes its freedom, see, e.g., *Adcox v. Teledyne, Inc.*, 21 F.3d 1381, 1389 (CA6), cert. denied, 513 U.S. 871 (1994), it is "generally free under ERISA, for any reason at any time, to adopt, modify, or terminate [its] welfare plan." *Curtiss–Wright Corp. v. Schoonejongen*, 514 U.S. 73, 78 (1995).

The flexibility an employer enjoys to amend or eliminate its welfare plan is not an accident; Congress recognized that "requiring the vesting of these ancillary benefits would seriously complicate the administration and increase the cost of plans." S. Rep. No. 93–383, p. 51 (1973). Giving employers this flexibility also encourages them to offer more generous benefits at the outset, since they are free to reduce benefits should economic conditions sour. If employers were locked into the plans they initially offered, "they would err initially on the side of omission." *Heath v. Varity Corp.*, 71 F.3d 256, 258 (C.A.7, 1995). Section 510 counterbalances this flexibility by ensuring that employers do not "circumvent the provision of promised benefits." *Ingersoll–Rand Co.*, 498 U.S. at 143 (citing S. Rep. No. 93–127, pp. 35–36 (1973); H. R. Rep. No. 93–533, p. 17 (1973)). In short, "§ 510 helps to make promises credible." *Heath, supra*, at 258. An employer may, of course, retain the unfettered right to alter its promises, but to do so it must follow the formal procedures set forth in the plan. See 29 U.S.C. § 1102(b)(3) (requiring plan to "provide a procedure for amending such plan"); *Schoonejongen, supra*, at 78 (observing that the "cognizable claim [under ERISA] is that the company did not [amend its welfare benefit plan] in a permissible manner"). Adherence to these formal procedures "increases the likelihood that proposed plan amendments, which are fairly serious events, are recognized as such and given the special consideration they deserve." *Schoonejongen, supra*, at 82. The formal amendment process would be undermined if § 510 did not apply because employers could "informally" amend their plans one participant at a time. Thus, the power to amend or abolish a welfare benefit plan does not include the power to "discharge, fine, suspend, expel, discipline, or discriminate against" the plan's participants and beneficiaries "for the purpose of interfering with [their] attainment of ... rights ... under the plan." To be sure, when an employer acts without this purpose, as could be the case when making fundamental business decisions, such actions are not barred by § 510. But in the case where an employer acts with a purpose that triggers the protection of § 510, any tension that might exist between an employer's power to amend the plan and a participant's rights under § 510 is the product of a careful balance of competing interests, and is most surely not the type of "absurd or glaringly unjust" result, *Ingalls Shipbuilding Inc. v. Director, Office of Workers' Compensation Programs,* 519 U.S. 248, 261 (1997), that would warrant departure from the plain language of § 510.

Respondents argue that the Court of Appeals' decision must nevertheless be affirmed because § 510, when applied to benefits that do not "vest," only protects an employee's right to cross the "threshold of eligibility" for welfare benefits.... In other words, argue respondents, an employee who is eligible to receive benefits under an ERISA welfare benefits plan has already "attained" her "rights" under the plan, so that any subsequent actions taken by an employer cannot, by definition, "interfere" with the "attainment of ... rights" under the plan. According to respondents, petitioners were eligible to receive welfare benefits under the SFTS–Teamsters plan at the time they were discharged, so they cannot state a claim under § 510. The Court of Appeals' approach precluded it from evaluating this argument, and others presented to us, and we see no reason not to allow it the first opportunity to consider these matters on remand.

We therefore vacate the judgment of the Court of Appeals and remand for proceedings consistent with this opinion.

### NOTES AND QUESTIONS

1. The Court observes that ERISA allows an employer to unilaterally amend or terminate a health or welfare benefit plan so long as it follows the amendment procedure which, under § 1102(b)(3) of ERISA, must be included in the plan. Compliance with ERISA procedures also would include satisfying the summary plan notification and reporting requirements of § 1021. In the Inter–Modal situation the railroad did not have unilateral authority to amend or terminate the health and welfare benefits plan because the workers had a collective bargaining agent. Therefore, under the Railway Labor Act the employer was required to bargain collectively to impasse before changing the benefits.

2. On remand, the ERISA claim eventually was dismissed as barred by the one-year state statute of limitations, which the court found applicable to ERISA wrongful termination actions. *Inter–Modal Rail Employees Ass'n v. Burlington,* 210 F.3d 383 (9th Cir.), cert. denied 530 U.S. 1262, 120 S.Ct. 2718, 147 L.Ed.2d 983 (2000).

3. In *Hazen Paper Co. v. Biggins,* 507 U.S. 604, 113 S.Ct. 1701, 123 L.Ed.2d 338 (1993), it was held that although ERISA § 510 (29 U.S.C. § 1140) is violated if an employer dismisses a 62–year–old employee to prevent him from gaining sufficient duration of service for his retirement plan rights to vest, the dismissal does not violate the Age Discrimination in Employment Act. On the other hand, the Court noted that it was not reaching the question of whether there may be liability under both statutes if vesting of pension benefits is based on age and the dismissal is to prevent that vesting. Note that the potential recovery may be greater under the Age

Discrimination in Employment Act than under ERISA because the latter statute does not provide for punitive damages in such actions. See 29 U.S.C. § 1132 and *Dependahl v. Falstaff Brewing Corp.* 653 F.2d 1208 (8th Cir. 1981), cert. denied 454 U.S. 968, 102 S.Ct. 512, 70 L.Ed.2d 384 and 454 U.S. 1084, 102 S.Ct. 641, 70 L.Ed.2d 619 (1981).

4. *Gavalik v. Continental Can Co.*, 812 F.2d 834 (3d Cir.), cert. denied 484 U.S. 979, 108 S.Ct. 495, 98 L.Ed.2d 492 (1987), involved a class action asserting that in order to avoid triggering future vesting of employee pension claims, the employer had shifted work among its plants and established plant production loads based on an analysis of vested and unvested liability for pension claims by the workforces at its various plants. The court ruled that regardless of whether the employer succeeded in its strategy, the combination of an intention to discriminate in order to avoid the vesting of the interests of those whose pension rights had not yet vested, plus conduct in furtherance of that goal, constituted a violation of § 510 of ERISA. Accordingly, any employees who were laid off as a result of the plan were entitled to relief for the loss of work resulting from the implementation of the pension benefits avoidance plan.

5. In *Ingersoll–Rand Co. v. McClendon*, 498 U.S. 133, 111 S.Ct. 478, 112 L.Ed.2d 474 (1990), the Court held that ERISA preempted a state law claim for wrongful discharge in order to prevent plaintiff from becoming eligible for benefits.

# I. PREEMPTION

The so-called "preemption clause" of ERISA, section 514(a), 29 U.S.C. § 1144(a) does not in fact use that term, but speaks of "supersedure." This broadly written provision states:

> Except as provided in subsection (b) ... the provisions of this [statute] ... shall supersede any and all State laws insofar as they may now or hereafter relate to any employee benefit plan ... not exempt under section 1003(b)....

Subsection (b)(2)(A) is the "saving" clause:

> Except as provided in [the "deemer" clause] ... nothing in this [statute] ... shall be construed to exempt or relieve any person from any law of any State which regulates insurance, banking, or securities.

Subsection (b)(2)(B) is the "deemer" clause:

> Neither an employee benefit plan ..., nor any trust established under such a plan, shall be deemed to be an insurance company or to be engaged in the business of insurance or banking for the purposes of any law of any State purporting to regulate insurance companies, insurance contracts, banks, trust companies, or investment companies.

Section 1003(b), referred to in the "supersedure" clause, exempts from ERISA coverage several categories of plans, including those "maintained solely for the purpose of complying with applicable workers compensation laws or unemployment compensation or disability insurance laws."

In its early ERISA cases, the Court treated section 514 as an instance of "explicit" preemption. Over time, however, it has become increasingly clear to many of the Justices that the language is so non-specific that it is more appropriate to apply approaches traditionally used in "conflict" and "field" preemption. The following table sets out results in cases involving statutory regulation.

## Pre–2000 ERISA Preemption Cases Involving Statutory Regulation

| Case style | Nature of "regulation" | "Relate to" a "plan"? | "Savings clause" applicable? | Plan excluded under section 1003(b)? |
|---|---|---|---|---|
| Alessi v. Raybestos–Manhattan, Inc., 451 U.S. 504 (1981) | Statute forbids integration of workers compensation benefits and pension benefits | Yes | No | No, since regulated plan not maintained "solely" for workers compensation purposes |
| Shaw v. Delta Air Lines, Inc., 463 U.S. 85 (1983) | State disability benefits law requires payment of sick leave benefits to pregnant employees | Perhaps, if there is "reference to" or "connection with" a plan | No | Depends on whether sick leave benefits are provided under general plan subject to ERISA or under plan adopted solely to provide mandated disability benefits |
| Metro. Life Ins. Co. v. Massachusetts, 471 U.S. 724 (1985) | Insurance code mandates including mental health benefits in coverage of health insurance policies | Yes | Yes | |
| Fort Halifax Packing Co. v. Coyne, 482 U.S. 1 (1987) | Statute requires one-time severance payment to longer-term employees not covered by severance plan provision in contract | No, no "plan" involved | No | |
| Mackey v. Lanier Collection Agency & Serv., Inc., 486 U.S. 825 (1988) | Garnishment law excludes ERISA plans from garnishment | Yes, makes "reference to" ERISA plans | No | |
| Massachusetts v. Morash, 490 U.S. 107 (1989) | Statute requires payment of all "wages" due at time of discharge, includ- | Depends on whether a vacation "plan" includes certain vested accumu- | No | |

| Case style | Nature of "regulation" | "Relate to" a "plan"? | "Savings clause" applicable? | Plan excluded under section 1003(b)? |
|---|---|---|---|---|
| | ing vacation benefits | lation provisions | | |
| FMC Corp. v. Holliday, 498 U.S. 52 (1990) | Financial responsibility law bans provisions in health plans that would permit reimbursement of plan from ultimate tort recovery | Yes | Yes, but "deemer clause" prevents applying it to health plan operated as self-funded entity | |
| District of Columbia v. Greater Washington Board of Trade, 506 U.S. 125 (1992) | Workers compensation ordinance requires benefit-liable employer to maintain health insurance for worker during disability | Yes | No | |
| New York State Conference of Blue Cross & Blue Shield Plans v. Travelers Ins. Co., 514 U.S. 645 (1995) | Statute imposing surcharge on health care bills paid by commercial insurers, but not on those paid by Blues | No "reference to" plans; no "connection with" since effect indirect in area of traditional state regulation | Not reached, but arguable | |
| California Division of Labor Standards Enforcement v. Dillingham Construction, N.A., Inc., 519 U.S. 316 (1997). | Contractors on public works projects may pay below "prevailing wage" rates to participants in approved apprenticeship plans | No "reference to" since some apprenticeship plans may not be ERISA governed; no "connection with" since law does not require plan to do anything | Not reached (would be no) | |
| De Buono v. NYSA–ILA Med. and Clinical Servs. Fund, 520 U.S. 806 (1997) | Tax imposed on gross receipts for patient treatment at hospitals, treatment centers, and other medical facilities, including those directly operated by a Plan | No "reference to" plan, only to possible providers; no "connection with" even though there is direct impact on a particular plan, in area of traditional state regulation | Not reached (would probably be no, although such a tax on HMOs and other PPOs might be considered a type of insurance regulation depending on how it was structured) | |

# KENTUCKY ASSOCIATION OF HEALTH PLANS, INC. v. MILLER

Supreme Court of the United States, 2003
538 U.S. 329, 123 S.Ct. 1471, 155 L.Ed.2d 468

JUSTICE SCALIA delivered the opinion of the Court.

Kentucky law provides that "[a] health insurer shall not discriminate against any provider who is located within the geographic coverage area of the health benefit plan and who is willing to meet the terms and conditions for participation established by the health insurer, including the Kentucky state Medicaid program and Medicaid partnerships." Ky. Rev. Stat. Ann. § 304.17A–270 (West 2001). Moreover, any "health benefit plan that includes chiropractic benefits shall . . . [p]ermit any licensed chiropractor who agrees to abide by the terms, conditions, reimbursement rates, and standards of quality of the health benefit plan to serve as a participating primary chiropractic provider to any person covered by the plan."§ 304.17A171(2). We granted certiorari to decide whether the Employee Retirement Income Security Act of 1974 (ERISA) pre-empts either, or both, of these "Any Willing Provider" (AWP) statutes.

## I

Petitioners include several health maintenance organizations (HMOs) and a Kentucky-based association of HMOs. In order to control the quality and cost of health-care delivery, these HMOs have contracted with selected doctors, hospitals, and other health-care providers to create exclusive "provider networks." Providers in such networks agree to render health-care services to the HMOs' subscribers at discounted rates and to comply with other contractual requirements. In return, they receive the benefit of patient volume higher than that achieved by non-network providers who lack access to petitioners' subscribers.

Kentucky's AWP statutes impair petitioners' ability to limit the number of providers with access to their networks, and thus their ability to use the assurance of high patient volume as the quid pro quo for the discounted rates that network membership entails. Petitioners believe that AWP laws will frustrate their efforts at cost and quality control, and will ultimately deny consumers the benefit of their cost-reducing arrangements with providers.

In April 1997, petitioners filed suit against respondent, the Commissioner of Kentucky's Department of Insurance, in the United States District Court for the Eastern District of Kentucky, asserting that ERISA, 88 Stat. 832, as amended, pre-empts Kentucky's AWP laws. ERISA pre-empts all state laws "insofar as they may now or hereafter relate to any employee benefit plan,"29 U.S.C. § 1144(a), but state "law[s] . . . which regulat[e] insurance, banking, or securities" are saved from pre-emption, § 1144(b)(2)(A). The District Court concluded that although both AWP statutes "relate to" employee benefit plans under § 1144(a), each law "regulates insurance" and is therefore saved from pre-emption by § 1144(b)(2)(A). App. to Pet. for Cert. 64a84a. In affirming the District Court, the Sixth Circuit also concluded that the AWP laws "regulat[e] insurance" and fall within ERISA's saving clause. *Kentucky Assn. of Health Plans, Inc. v. Nichols*, 227 F.3d 352, 363–372 (2000). * * * Finding that the laws passed both the "common sense" test and the McCarran–Ferguson "checking points," the Sixth Circuit upheld Kentucky's AWP statutes. * * *

II

To determine whether Kentucky's AWP statutes are saved from pre-emption, we must ascertain whether they are "law[s] … which regulat[e] insurance" under § 1144(b)(2)(A).

[1] It is well established in our case law that a state law must be "specifically directed toward" the insurance industry in order to fall under ERISA's saving clause; laws of general application that have some bearing on insurers do not qualify. *Pilot Life Ins. Co. v. Dedeaux*, 481 U.S. 41, 50, 107 S. Ct. 1549, 95 L. Ed. 2d 39 (1987); see also *Rush Prudential HMO, Inc. v. Moran*, 536 U.S. 355, 366, 122 S. Ct. 2151, 153 L. Ed. 2d 375 (2002); *FMC Corp. v. Holliday*, 498 U.S. 52, 61, 111 S. Ct. 403, 112 L. Ed. 2d 356 (1990). At the same time, not all state laws "specifically directed toward" the insurance industry will be covered by § 1144(b)(2)(A), which saves laws that regulate insurance, not insurers. As we explained in Rush Prudential, insurers must be regulated "with respect to their insurance practices,"536 U.S., at 366, 122 S. Ct. 2151. Petitioners contend that Kentucky's AWP laws fall outside the scope of § 1144(b)(2)(A) for two reasons. First, because Kentucky has failed to "specifically direc[t]" its AWP laws toward the insurance industry; and second, because the AWP laws do not regulate an insurance practice. We find neither contention persuasive.

A

Petitioners claim that Kentucky's statutes are not "specifically direct-ed toward" insurers because they regulate not only the insurance industry but also doctors who seek to form and maintain limited provider networks with HMOs. That is to say, the AWP laws equally prevent providers from entering into limited network contracts with insurers, just as they prevent insurers from creating exclusive networks in the first place. We do not think it follows that Kentucky has failed to specifically direct its AWP laws at the insurance industry.

Neither of Kentucky's AWP statutes, by its terms, imposes any prohibitions or requirements on health-care providers. See Ky. Rev. Stat. Ann. § 304.17A–270 (West 2001) (imposing obligations only on "health insurer[s]" not to discriminate against any willing provider); § 304.17A171 (imposing obligations only on "health benefit plan[s] that includ[e] chiropractic benefits"). And Kentucky health-care providers are still capable of entering exclusive networks with insurers who conduct business outside the Commonwealth of Kentucky or who are otherwise not covered by §§ 304.17A–270 or 304.17A–171. Kentucky's statutes are transgressed only when a "health insurer," or a "health benefit plan that includes chiropractic benefits," excludes from its network a provider who is willing and able to meet its terms.

It is of course true that as a consequence of Kentucky's AWP laws, entities outside the insurance industry (such as health-care providers) will be unable to enter into certain agreements with Kentucky insurers. But the same could be said about the state laws we held saved from pre-emption in FMC Corp. and Rush Prudential. Pennsylvania's law prohibiting insurers from exercising subrogation rights against an insured's tort recovery, see *FMC Corp.*, *supra*, at 55, n. 1, 111 S. Ct. 403, also prevented insureds from entering into enforceable contracts with insurers allowing subrogation. Illinois' requirement that HMOs provide independent review of whether services are "medically necessary," *Rush Prudential*, *supra*, at 372, 122 S. Ct. 2151, likewise excluded insureds from joining an HMO that would have withheld the right to independent review in exchange for a lower premium. Yet neither case found the effects of these laws on noninsurers, significant though they may have been, inconsistent with the requirement that laws saved from pre-emption by § 1144(b)(2)(A) be "specifically directed toward" the insurance industry. Regulations "directed toward" certain entities will almost always disable other entities from doing, with the regulated entities, what the regulations forbid; this does not suffice to place such regulation outside the scope of ERISA's saving clause.

Petitioners claim that the AWP laws do not regulate insurers with respect to an insurance practice because, unlike the state laws we held saved from pre-emption in *Metropolitan Life Ins. Co. v. Massachusetts*, 471 U.S. 724, 105 S. Ct. 2380, 85 L. Ed. 2d 728 (1985), UNUM, and Rush Prudential, they do not control the actual terms of insurance policies. Rather, they focus upon the relationship between an insurer and third-party providers—which in petitioners' view does not constitute an "insurance practice."

In support of their contention, petitioners rely on *Group Life & Health Ins. Co. v. Royal Drug Co.*, 440 U.S. 205, 210, 99 S. Ct. 1067, 59 L. Ed. 2d 261 (1979), which held that third-party provider arrangements between insurers and pharmacies were not "the 'business of insurance'" under § 2(b) of the McCarran–Ferguson Act. ERISA's saving clause, however, is not concerned (as is the McCarran–Ferguson Act provision) with how to characterize conduct undertaken by private actors, but with how to characterize state laws in regard to what they "regulate." It does not follow from Royal Drug that a law mandating certain insurer-provider relationships fails to "regulate insurance." Suppose a state law required all licensed attorneys to participate in 10 hours of continuing legal education (CLE) each year. This statute "regulates" the practice of law—even though sitting through 10 hours of CLE classes does not constitute the practice of law—because the State has conditioned the right to practice law on certain requirements, which substantially affect the product delivered by lawyers to their clients. Kentucky's AWP laws operate in a similar manner with respect to the insurance industry: Those who wish to provide health insurance in Kentucky (any "health insurer") may not discriminate against any willing provider. This "regulates" insurance by imposing conditions on the right to engage in the business of insurance; whether or not an HMO's contracts with providers constitute "the business of insurance" under Royal Drug is beside the point.

We emphasize that conditions on the right to engage in the business of insurance must also substantially affect the risk pooling arrangement between the insurer and the insured to be covered by ERISA's saving clause. Otherwise, any state law aimed at insurance companies could be deemed a law that "regulates insurance," contrary to our interpretation of § 1144(b)(2)(A) in Rush Prudential, 536 U.S., at 364, 122 S. Ct. 2151. A state law requiring all insurance companies to pay their janitors twice the minimum wage would not "regulate insurance," even though it would be a prerequisite to engaging in the business of insurance, because it does not substantially affect the risk pooling arrangement undertaken by insurer and insured. Petitioners contend that Kentucky's AWP statutes fail this test as well, since they do not alter or affect the terms of insurance policies, but concern only the relationship between insureds and third-party providers, Brief for Petitioners 29. We disagree. We have never held that state laws must alter or control the actual terms of insurance policies to be deemed "laws ... which regulat[e] insurance" under § 1144(b)(2)(A); it suffices that they substantially affect the risk pooling arrangement between insurer and insured. By expanding the number of providers from whom an insured may receive health services, AWP laws alter the scope of permissible bargains between insurers and insureds in a manner similar to the mandated-benefit laws we upheld in Metropolitan Life, the notice-prejudice rule we sustained in UNUM, and the independent-review provisions we approved in Rush Prudential. No longer may Kentucky insureds seek insurance from a closed network of health-care providers in exchange for a lower premium. The AWP prohibition substantially affects the type of risk pooling arrangements that insurers may offer.

## III

Our prior decisions construing § 1144(b)(2)(A) have relied, to varying degrees, on our cases interpreting §§ 2(a) and 2(b) of the McCarran–Ferguson Act. In determining whether certain practices constitute "the *business of* insurance" under the McCarran–Ferguson Act (emphasis added), our cases have looked to three factors: "first, whether the practice has the effect of transferring or spreading a policyholder's risk; second, whether the practice is an integral part of the policy relationship between the insurer and the insured; and third, whether the practice is limited to entities within the insurance industry." *Pireno*, 458 U.S., at 129, 102 S. Ct. 3002.

We believe that our use of the McCarran–Ferguson case law in the ERISA context has misdirected attention, failed to provide clear guidance to lower federal courts, and, as this case demonstrates, added little to the relevant analysis. That is unsurprising, since the statutory language of § 1144(b)(2)(A) differs substantially from that of the McCarran–Ferguson Act. Rather than concerning itself with whether certain practices constitute "[t]he business of insurance," 15 U.S.C. § 1012(a), or whether a state law was "enacted ... *for the purpose of* regulating the business of insurance,"§ 1012(b) (emphasis added), 29 U.S.C. § 1144(b)(2)(A) asks merely whether a state law is a "law ... which regulates insurance, banking, or securities." What is more, the McCarran–Ferguson factors were developed in cases that characterized conduct by private actors, not state laws. See *Pireno, supra*, at 126, 102 S. Ct. 3002 ("The only issue before us is *whether petitioners' peer review practices* are exempt from antitrust scrutiny as part of the 'business of insurance'" (emphasis added)); Royal Drug, 440 U.S., at 210, 99 S. Ct. 1067 ("The only issue before us is whether the Court of Appeals was correct in concluding that these *Pharmacy Agreements* are not the 'business of insurance' within the meaning of § 2(b) of the McCarran–Ferguson Act" (emphasis added)).

Our holdings in UNUM and Rush Prudential—that a state law may fail the first McCarran–Ferguson factor yet still be saved from pre-emption under § 1144(b)(2)(A)—raise more questions than they answer and provide wide opportunities for divergent outcomes. May a state law satisfy *any* two of the three McCarran–Ferguson factors and still fall under the saving clause? Just one? What happens if two of three factors are satisfied, but not "securely satisfied" or "clearly satisfied," as they were in UNUM and Rush Prudential? 526 U.S., at 374, 119 S. Ct. 1380,536 U.S., at 373, 122 S. Ct. 2151. Further confusion arises from the question whether the *state law itself* or the *conduct regulated by that law* is the proper subject to which one applies the McCarran–Ferguson factors. In Pilot Life, we inquired whether Mississippi's *law of bad faith* has the effect of transferring or spreading risk, 481 U.S., at 50, 107 S. Ct. 1549, whether *that law* is integral to the insurer-insured relationship, id., at 51, 107 S. Ct. 1549, and whether *that law* is limited to the insurance industry, ibid. Rush Prudential, by contrast, focused the McCarran–Ferguson inquiry on the *conduct regulated* by the state law, rather than the state law itself. 536 U.S., at 373, 122 S. Ct. 2151 ("It is obvious enough that the independent review requirement *regulates* 'an integral part of the policy relationship between the insurer and insured'" (emphasis added)); id., at 374, 122 S. Ct. 2151 ("The final factor, that the law be aimed at a *'practice* ... limited to entities within the insurance industry' is satisfied ..." (emphasis added; citation omitted)).

We have never held that the McCarran–Ferguson factors are an essential component of the § 1144(b)(2)(A) inquiry. Metropolitan Life initially used these factors only to buttress its previously reached conclusion that Massachusetts' mandated-benefit statute was a "law ... which regulates insurance" under § 1144(b)(2)(A). 471 U.S., at 742–743, 105 S. Ct. 2380. Pilot Life referred to them as mere "considerations [to be] weighed" in determining whether a state law falls under the saving clause. 481 U.S., at 49, 107 S. Ct. 1549. UNUM emphasized that the McCarran–Ferguson factors were not "'require[d]'" in the saving clause analysis, and were only "checking points" to be used after determining whether the state law regulates insurance from a "common-sense" understanding. 526 U.S., at 374, 119 S. Ct. 1380. And Rush Prudential called the factors "guideposts," using them only to "confirm our conclusion" that Illinois' statute regulated insurance under § 1144(b)(2)(A). 536 U.S., at 373, 122 S. Ct. 2151.

Today we make a clean break from the McCarran–Ferguson factors and hold that for a state law to be deemed a "law ... which regulates insurance" under § 1144(b)(2)(A), it must satisfy two requirements. First, the state law must be specifically directed toward entities engaged in insurance. See *Pilot Life*, *supra*, at 50, 107 S. Ct. 1549, *UNUM*, *supra*, at 368, 119 S. Ct. 1380; *Rush Prudential*, *supra*, at 366, 122 S. Ct. 2151. Second, as explained above, the state law must substantially affect the risk pooling arrangement between the insurer and the insured. Kentucky's law satisfies each of these requirements. * * *

For these reasons, we affirm the judgment of the Sixth Circuit.

## NOTE

The following table outlines the pre–2000 Supreme Court decisions dealing with claims for damages for injury resulting from sponsor or fiduciary activity.

### Pre–2000 ERISA Preemption Cases Involving Individual Non–Regulatory Claims

| Case style | State law claim | "Relate to" a Plan? | "Savings clause" applicable? | Plan excluded under 1003(b)? |
|---|---|---|---|---|
| Pilot Life Ins. Co. v. Dedeaux, 481 U.S. 41 (1987) | Action for bad faith refusal to pay insurance benefits under group disability | Yes | No, largely because Congress intended ERISA's own remedies to be exclusive | No |
| Metro. Life Ins. Co. v. Taylor, 481 U.S. 58 (1987) | Action for breach of promise to pay benefits; defendant seeks removal to federal court | Yes | No, citing *Dedeaux* and its reasoning; case therefore removable | No |
| Ingersoll–Rand Co. v. McClendon, 498 U.S. 133 (1990) | Common law cause of action for wrongful discharge in order to evade pension obligations | Yes | No, since ERISA provides a remedy under section 510 | No |
| Unum Life Ins. Co. of Am. v. Ward, 526 U.S. 358 (1999) | 1. "Notice-prejudice" rule (lack of timely notice to insurer does not bar claim unless insurer prejudiced by lateness):<br><br>2. Notice to employer is notice to insurer under group policy | 1. Stipulated by parties<br><br><br>2. Yes | 1. Yes<br><br><br>2. No, since there is a potential conflict with ERISA structuring of responsibilities for administering a Plan | No |

## AETNA HEALTH INC. v. DAVILA

Supreme Court of the United States, 2004
542 U.S. 200, 124 S.Ct. 2488, 159 L.Ed.2d 312

JUSTICE THOMAS delivered the opinion of the Court.

In these consolidated cases, two individuals sued their respective health maintenance organizations (HMOs) for alleged failures to exercise ordinary care in the handling of coverage decisions, in violation of a duty imposed by the Texas Health Care Liability Act (THCLA), Tex. Civ. Prac. & Rem. Code Ann. §§ 88.001–88.003 (2004 Supp. Pamphlet). We granted certiorari to decide whether the individuals' causes of action are completely pre-empted by the "interlocking, interrelated, and interdependent remedial scheme," *Massachusetts Mut. Life Ins. Co. v. Russell*, 473 U.S. 134, 146 (1985), found at § 502(a) of the Employee Retirement Income Security Act of 1974 (ERISA), 88 Stat. 891, as amended, 29 U.S.C. § 1132(a) et seq. 540 U.S. 981, (2003). We hold that the causes of action are completely pre-empted and hence removable from state to federal court. * * *

### I

### A

Respondent Juan Davila is a participant, and respondent Ruby Calad is a beneficiary, in ERISA-regulated employee benefit plans. Their respective plan sponsors had entered into agreements with petitioners, Aetna Health Inc. and CIGNA Healthcare of Texas, Inc., to administer the plans. * * *

Respondents both suffered injuries allegedly arising from Aetna's and CIGNA's decisions not to provide coverage for certain treatment and services recommended by respondents' treating physicians. Davila's treating physician prescribed Vioxx to remedy Davila's arthritis pain, but Aetna refused to pay for it. Davila did not appeal or contest this decision, nor did he purchase Vioxx with his own resources and seek reimbursement. Instead, Davila began taking Naprosyn, from which he allegedly suffered a severe reaction that required extensive treatment and hospitalization. Calad underwent surgery, and although her treating physician recommended an extended hospital stay, a CIGNA discharge nurse determined that Calad did not meet the plan's criteria for a continued hospital stay. CIGNA consequently denied coverage for the extended hospital stay. Calad experienced postsurgery complications forcing her to return to the hospital. She alleges that these complications would not have occurred had CIGNA approved coverage for a longer hospital stay.

Respondents brought separate suits in Texas state court against petitioners. Invoking THCLA § 88.002(a), respondents argued that petitioners' refusal to cover the requested services violated their "duty to exercise ordinary care when making health care treatment decisions," and that these refusals "proximately caused" their injuries. Ibid. Petitioners removed the cases to Federal District Courts, arguing that respondents' causes of action fit within the scope of, and were therefore completely pre-empted by, ERISA § 502(a). The respective District Courts agreed, and declined to remand the cases to state court. Because respondents refused to amend their complaints to bring explicit ERISA claims, the District Courts dismissed the complaints with prejudice.

## B

Both Davila and Calad appealed the refusals to remand to state court. * * * The Court of Appeals recognized that state causes of action that "duplicate or fall within the scope of an ERISA § 502(a) remedy" are completely pre-empted and hence removable to federal court. * * * After examining the causes of action available under § 502(a), the Court of Appeals determined that respondents' claims could possibly fall under only two: § 502(a)(1)(B), which provides a cause of action for the recovery of wrongfully denied benefits, and § 502(a)(2), which allows suit against a plan fiduciary for breaches of fiduciary duty to the plan.

Analyzing § 502(a)(2) first, the Court of Appeals concluded that, under *Pegram v. Herdrich*, 530 U.S. 211 (2000), the decisions for which petitioners were being sued were "mixed eligibility and treatment decisions" and hence were not fiduciary in nature. 307 F.3d at 307–308. The Court of Appeals next determined that respondents' claims did not fall within § 502(a)(1)(B)'s scope. It found significant that respondents "assert tort claims," while § 502(a)(1)(B) "creates a cause of action for breach of contract," id., at 309, and also that respondents "are not seeking reimbursement for benefits denied them," but rather request "tort damages" arising from "an external, statutorily imposed duty of 'ordinary care.'" Ibid. From *Rush Prudential HMO, Inc. v. Moran*, 536 U.S. 355, (2002), the Court of Appeals derived the principle that complete pre-emption is limited to situations in which "States . . . duplicate the causes of action listed in ERISA § 502(a)," and concluded that "because the THCLA does not provide an action for collecting benefits," it fell outside the scope of § 502(a)(1)(B). 307 F.3d at 310–311.

## II

## A

Under the removal statute, "any civil action brought in a State court of which the district courts of the United States have original jurisdiction, may be removed by the defendant" to federal court. 28 U.S.C. § 1441(a). One category of cases of which district courts have original jurisdiction are "federal question" cases: cases "arising under the Constitution, laws, or treaties of the United States." § 1331. We face in these cases the issue whether respondents' causes of action arise under federal law.

Ordinarily, determining whether a particular case arises under federal law turns on the " 'well-pleaded complaint' " rule. * * * The Court has explained that "whether a case is one arising under the Constitution or a law or treaty of the United States, in the sense of the jurisdictional statute[,] ... must be determined from what necessarily appears in the plaintiff's statement of his own claim in the bill or declaration, unaided by anything alleged in anticipation of avoidance of defenses which it is thought the defendant may interpose." *Taylor v. Anderson*, 234 U.S. 74, 75–76 (1914).

In particular, the existence of a federal defense normally does not create statutory "arising under" jurisdiction. * * *

### B

ERISA's * * * integrated enforcement mechanism, ERISA § 502(a), 29 U.S.C. § 1132(a), is a distinctive feature of ERISA, and essential to accomplish Congress' purpose of creating a comprehensive statute for the regulation of employee benefit plans. As the Court said in *Pilot Life Ins. Co. v. Dedeaux*, 481 U.S. 41(1987):

> The detailed provisions of § 502(a) set forth a comprehensive civil enforcement scheme that represents a careful balancing of the need for prompt and fair claims settlement procedures against the public interest in encouraging the formation of employee benefit plans. The policy choices reflected in the inclusion of certain remedies and the exclusion of others under the federal scheme would be completely undermined if ERISA-plan participants and beneficiaries were free to obtain remedies under state law that Congress rejected in ERISA. 'The six carefully integrated civil enforcement provisions found in § 502(a) of the statute as finally enacted ... provide strong evidence that Congress did not intend to authorize other remedies that it simply forgot to incorporate expressly.'

Id. at 54 (quoting *Russell, supra*, at 146).

Therefore, any state-law cause of action that duplicates, supplements, or supplants the ERISA civil enforcement remedy conflicts with the clear congressional intent to make the ERISA remedy exclusive and is therefore pre-empted. See 481 U.S., at 54–56; see also *Ingersoll–Rand Co. v. McClendon*, 498 U.S. 133, 143–145(1990). * * *

### III

### A

ERISA § 502(a)(1)(B) provides:

"A civil action may be brought—(1) by a participant or beneficiary—... (B) to recover benefits due to him under the terms of his plan, to enforce his rights under the terms of the plan, or to clarify his rights to future benefits under the terms of the plan." 29 U.S.C. § 1132(a)(1)(B).

This provision is relatively straightforward. If a participant or beneficiary believes that benefits promised to him under the terms of the plan are not provided, he can bring suit seeking provision of those benefits. \* \* \*

It follows that if an individual brings suit complaining of a denial of coverage for medical care, where the individual is entitled to such coverage only because of the terms of an ERISA-regulated employee benefit plan, and where no legal duty (state or federal) independent of ERISA or the plan terms is violated, then the suit falls "within the scope of" ERISA § 502(a)(1)(B). *Metropolitan Life, supra,* 481 U.S., at 66. In other words, if an individual, at some point in time, could have brought his claim under ERISA § 502(a)(1)(B), and where there is no other independent legal duty that is implicated by a defendant's actions, then the individual's cause of action is completely pre-empted by ERISA § 502(a)(1)(B).

To determine whether respondents' causes of action fall "within the scope" of ERISA § 502(a)(1)(B), we must examine respondents' complaints, the statute on which their claims are based (the THCLA), and the various plan documents. Davila alleges that Aetna provides health coverage under his employer's health benefits plan. \* \* \* Davila also alleges that after his primary care physician prescribed Vioxx, Aetna refused to pay for it. \* \* \* The only action complained of was Aetna's refusal to approve payment for Davila's Vioxx prescription. Further, the only relationship Aetna had with Davila was its partial administration of Davila's employer's benefit plan. \* \* \*

Similarly, Calad alleges that she receives, as her husband's beneficiary under an ERISA-regulated benefit plan, health coverage from CIGNA. \* \* \* She \* \* \* alleges that CIGNA, acting through a discharge nurse, refused to authorize more than a single day despite the advice and recommendation of her treating physician. \* \* \* Calad contests only CIGNA's decision to refuse coverage for her hospital stay. \* \* \* And, as in Davila's case, the only connection between Calad and CIGNA is CIGNA's administration of portions of Calad's ERISA-regulated benefit plan. \* \* \*

It is clear, then, that respondents complain only about denials of coverage promised under the terms of ERISA-regulated employee benefit plans. Upon the denial of benefits, respondents could have paid for the treatment themselves and then sought reimbursement through a § 502(a)(1)(B) action, or sought a preliminary injunction \* \* \*.

Respondents contend, however, that the complained-of actions violate legal duties that arise independently of ERISA or the terms of the employee benefit plans at issue in these cases. Both respondents brought suit specifically under the THCLA, alleging that petitioners "controlled, influenced, participated in and made decisions which affected the quality of the diagnosis, care, and treatment provided" in a manner that violated "the duty of ordinary care set forth in §§ 88.001 and 88.002." \* \* \* Respondents contend that this duty of ordinary care is an independent legal duty. \* \* \*

The duties imposed by the THCLA in the context of these cases, however, do not arise independently of ERISA or the plan terms. The THCLA does impose a duty on managed care entities to "exercise ordinary care when making health care treatment decisions," and makes them liable for damages proximately caused by failures to abide by that duty. § 88.002(a). However, if a managed care entity correctly concluded that, under the terms of the relevant plan, a particular treatment was not covered, the managed care entity's denial of coverage would not be a proximate cause of any injuries arising from the denial. Rather, the failure of the plan itself to cover the requested treatment would be the proximate cause. More significantly, the THCLA clearly states that "the standards in Subsections (a) and (b) create no obligation on the part of the health insurance carrier, health maintenance organization, or other managed care entity to provide to an insured or enrollee treatment which is not covered by the health care plan of the entity." § 88.002(d). Hence, a managed care entity could not be subject to liability under the THCLA if it denied coverage for any treatment not covered by the health care plan that it was administering.

Thus, interpretation of the terms of respondents' benefit plans forms an essential part of their THCLA claim, and THCLA liability would exist here only because of petitioners' administration of ERISA-regulated benefit plans. Petitioners' potential liability under the THCLA in these cases, then, derives entirely from the particular rights and obligations established by the benefit plans.

Hence, respondents bring suit only to rectify a wrongful denial of benefits promised under ERISA-regulated plans, and do not attempt to remedy any violation of a legal duty independent of ERISA. We hold that respondents' state causes of action fall "within the scope of" ERISA § 502(a)(1)(B), Metropolitan Life, 481 U.S., at 66, 95 L. Ed. 2d 55, 107 S. Ct. 1542, and are therefore completely pre-empted by ERISA § 502 and removable to federal district court.

### B

The Court of Appeals came to a contrary conclusion for several reasons, all of them erroneous. First, the Court of Appeals found significant that respondents "assert a tort claim for tort damages" rather than "a contract claim for contract damages," and that respondents "are not seeking reimbursement for benefits denied them." 307 F.3d at 309. But, distinguishing between pre-empted and non-pre-empted claims based on the particular label affixed to them would "elevate form over substance and allow parties to evade" the pre-emptive scope of ERISA simply "by relabeling their contract claims as claims for tortious breach of contract." *Allis–Chalmers, supra,* 471 U.S., at 211. Nor can the mere fact that the state cause of action attempts to authorize remedies beyond those authorized by ERISA § 502(a) put the cause of action outside the scope of the ERISA civil enforcement mechanism. In Pilot Life, Metropolitan Life, and Ingersoll–Rand, the plaintiffs all brought state claims that were labeled either tort or tort-like. * * * And, the plaintiffs in these three cases all sought remedies beyond those authorized under ERISA. See *Pilot Life*, *supra*, 481 U.S., at 43 (compensatory and punitive damages); *Metropolitan Life, supra*, 481 U.S., at 61 (mental anguish); *Ingersoll–Rand, supra*, 498 U.S., at 136(punitive damages, mental anguish). And, in all these cases, the plaintiffs' claims were pre-empted. The limited remedies available under ERISA are an inherent part of the "careful balancing" between ensuring fair and prompt enforcement of rights under a plan and the encouragement of the creation of such plans. * * *

Second, the Court of Appeals believed that "the wording of [respondents'] plans is immaterial" to their claims, as "they invoke an external, statutorily imposed duty of 'ordinary care.' " 307 F.3d at 309. But as we have already discussed, the wording of the plans is certainly material to their state causes of action, and the duty of "ordinary care" that the THCLA creates is not external to their rights under their respective plans. * * *

## C

Respondents also argue—for the first time in their brief to this Court—that the THCLA is a law that regulates insurance, and hence that ERISA § 514(b)(2)(A) saves their causes of action from pre-emption (and thereby from complete pre-emption). This argument is unavailing. The existence of a comprehensive remedial scheme can demonstrate an "overpowering federal policy" that determines the interpretation of a statutory provision designed to save state law from being pre-empted. Rush Prudential, 536 U.S. at 375. ERISA's civil enforcement provision is one such example. See ibid.

As this Court stated in Pilot Life, "our understanding of [§ 514(b)(2)(A)] must be informed by the legislative intent concerning the civil enforcement provisions provided by ERISA § 502(a), 29 U.S.C. § 1132(a)." 481 U.S. at 52. The Court concluded that "the policy choices reflected in the inclusion of certain remedies and the exclusion of others under the federal scheme would be completely undermined if ERISA-plan participants and beneficiaries were free to obtain remedies under state law that Congress rejected in ERISA." Id., 481 U.S., at 54. * * *

Pilot Life's reasoning applies here with full force. Allowing respondents to proceed with their state-law suits would "pose an obstacle to the purposes and objectives of Congress." Id., 481 U.S., at 52. As this Court has recognized in both Rush Prudential and Pilot Life, ERISA § 514(b)(2)(A)must be interpreted in light of the congressional intent to create an exclusive federal remedy in ERISA § 502(a). Under ordinary principles of conflict pre-emption, then, even a state law that can arguably be characterized as "regulating insurance" will be pre-empted if it provides a separate vehicle to assert a claim for benefits outside of, or in addition to, ERISA's remedial scheme.

IV

Respondents, their *amici*, and some Courts of Appeals have relied heavily upon *Pegram v. Herdrich*, 530 U.S. 211 (2000), in arguing that ERISA does not pre-empt or completely pre-empt state suits such as respondents'. * * *

*Pegram* cannot be read so broadly. In *Pegram*, the plaintiff sued her physician-owned-and-operated HMO (which provided medical coverage through plaintiff's employer pursuant to an ERISA-regulated benefit plan) and her treating physician, both for medical malpractice and for a breach of an ERISA fiduciary duty. See 530 U.S., at 215–216. The plaintiff's treating physician was also the person charged with administering plaintiff's benefits; it was she who decided whether certain treatments were covered. See id., 530 U.S., at 228. We reasoned that the physician's "eligibility decision and the treatment decision were inextricably mixed." Id., 530 U.S., at 229. We concluded that "Congress did not intend [the defendant HMO] or any other HMO to be treated as a fiduciary to the extent that it makes mixed eligibility decisions acting through its physicians." Id., 530 U.S., at 231.

A benefit determination under ERISA, though, is generally a fiduciary act. * * *

Pegram, in highlighting its conclusion that "mixed eligibility decisions" were not fiduciary in nature, contrasted the operation of "traditional trustees administering a medical trust" and "physicians through whom HMOs act." 530 U.S., at 231–232. A traditional medical trust is administered by "paying out money to buy medical care, whereas physicians making mixed eligibility decisions consume the money as well." Ibid. And, significantly, the Court stated that "private trustees do not make treatment judgments." Id., 530 U.S., at 232. But a trustee managing a medical trust undoubtedly must make administrative decisions that require the exercise of medical judgment. Petitioners are not the employers of respondents' treating physicians and are therefore in a somewhat analogous position to that of a trustee for a traditional medical trust. ERISA itself and its implementing regulations confirm this interpretation.

ERISA defines a fiduciary as any person "to the extent . . . he has any discretionary authority or discretionary responsibility in the administration of [an employee benefit] plan," § 3(21)(A)(iii), 29 U.S.C. § 1002(21)(A)(iii). When administering employee benefit plans, HMOs must make discretionary decisions regarding eligibility for plan benefits, and, in this regard, must be treated as plan fiduciaries. * * * Also, ERISA § 503, which specifies minimum requirements for a plan's claim procedure, requires plans to "afford a reasonable opportunity to any participant whose claim for benefits has been denied for a full and fair review by the appropriate named fiduciary of the decision denying the claim." 29 U.S.C. § 1133(2). This strongly suggests that the ultimate decisionmaker in a plan regarding an award of benefits must be a fiduciary and must be acting as a fiduciary when determining a participant's or beneficiary's claim. * * *

Since administrators making benefits determinations, even determinations based extensively on medical judgments, are ordinarily acting as plan fiduciaries, it was essential to Pegram's conclusion that the decisions challenged there were truly "mixed eligibility and treatment decisions," 530 U.S., at 229, i.e., medical necessity decisions made by the plaintiff's treating physician qua treating physician and qua benefits administrator. Put another way, the reasoning of Pegram "only makes sense where the underlying negligence also plausibly constitutes medical maltreatment by a party who can be deemed to be a treating physician or such a physician's employer." *Cicio*, 321 F.3d at 109 (Calabresi, J., dissenting in part). Here, however, petitioners are neither respondents' treating physicians nor the employers of respondents' treating physicians. Petitioners' coverage decisions, then, are pure eligibility decisions, and *Pegram* is not implicated.

### V

We hold that respondents' causes of action, brought to remedy only the denial of benefits under ERISA-regulated benefit plans, fall within the scope of, and are completely pre-empted by, ERISA § 502(a)(1)(B), and thus removable to federal district court. The judgment of the Court of Appeals is reversed, and the cases are remanded for further proceedings consistent with this opinion.

It is so ordered.

JUSTICE GINSBURG, with whom JUSTICE BREYER joins, concurring.

The Court today holds that the claims respondents asserted under Texas law are totally preempted by § 502(a) of the Employee Retirement Income Security Act of 1974 (ERISA or Act), 29 U.S.C. § 1132(a). That decision is consistent with our governing case law on ERISA's preemptive scope. I therefore join the Court's opinion. But, with greater enthusiasm, as indicated by my dissenting opinion in *Great–West Life & Annuity Ins. Co. v. Knudson*, 534 U.S. 204 (2002), I also join "the rising judicial chorus urging that Congress and [this] Court revisit what is an unjust and increasingly tangled ERISA regime." *DiFelice v. AETNA U.S. Healthcare*, 346 F.3d 442, 453 (CA3 2003) (Becker, J., concurring).

Because the Court has coupled an encompassing interpretation of ERISA's preemptive force with a cramped construction of the "equitable relief" allowable under § 502(a)(3), a "regulatory vacuum" exists: "Virtually all state law remedies are preempted but very few federal substitutes are provided." Id., at 456 (internal quotation marks omitted).

A series of the Court's decisions has yielded a host of situations in which persons adversely affected by ERISA-proscribed wrongdoing cannot gain make-whole relief. First, in *Massachusetts Mut. Life Ins. Co. v. Russell*, 473 U.S. 134 (1985), the Court stated, in dicta: "There is a stark absence—in [ERISA] itself and in its legislative history—of any reference to an intention to authorize the recovery of extracontractual damages" for consequential injuries. Id., 473 U.S. 134, at 148. Then, in *Mertens v. Hewitt Associates*, 508 U.S. 248 (1993), the Court held that § 502(a)(3)'s term " 'equitable relief'. . . refers to those categories of relief that were *typically* available in equity (such as injunction, mandamus, and restitution, but not compensatory damages)." Id., 508 U.S., at 256 (emphasis in original). Most recently, in Great–West, the Court ruled that, as "§ 502(a)(3), by its terms, only allows for *equitable* relief," the provision excludes "the imposition of personal liability . . . for a contractual obligation to pay money." 534 U.S. at 221 (emphasis in original).

As the array of lower court cases and opinions documents, see, e.g., *DiFelice; Cicio v. Does*, 321 F.3d 83 (CA2 2003), cert. pending sub nom. *Vytra Healthcare v. Cicio*, No. 03–69, fresh consideration of the availability of consequential damages under § 502(a)(3) is plainly in order. See 321 F.3d at 106, 107 (Calabresi, J., dissenting in part) ("gaping wound" caused by the breadth of preemption and limited remedies under ERISA, as interpreted by this Court, will not be healed until the Court "starts over" or Congress "wipes the slate clean"); *DiFelice*, 346 F.3d at 467 ("The vital thing . . . is that either Congress or the Court act quickly, because the current situation is plainly untenable."); Langbein, What ERISA Means by "Equitable": The Supreme Court's Trail of Error in Russell, Mertens, and Great–West, 103 Colum. L. Rev. 1317, 1365 (2003) (hereinafter Langbein) ("The Supreme Court needs to . . . realign ERISA remedy law with the trust remedial tradition that Congress intended [when it provided in § 502(a)(3) for] 'appropriate equitable relief.' ").

The Government notes a potential amelioration. Recognizing that "this Court has construed Section 502(a)(3) not to authorize an award of money damages against a non-fiduciary," the Government suggests that the Act, as currently written and interpreted, may "allow at least some forms of 'make-whole' relief against a breaching fiduciary in light of the general availability of such relief in equity at the time of the divided bench." Brief for United States as Amicus Curiae 27–28, n. 13 (emphases added); cf. ante, at 19 ("entity with discretionary authority over benefits determinations" is a "plan fiduciary"); Tr. of Oral Arg. 13 ("Aetna is [a fiduciary]—and CIGNA is for purposes of claims processing."). As the Court points out, respondents here declined the opportunity to amend their complaints to state claims for relief under § 502(a); the District Court, therefore, properly dismissed their suits with prejudice. See ante, at 20, n. 7. But the Government's suggestion may indicate an effective remedy others similarly circumstanced might fruitfully pursue.

"Congress . . . intended ERISA to replicate the core principles of trust remedy law, including the make-whole standard of relief." Langbein 1319. I anticipate that Congress, or this Court, will one day so confirm.

### NOTES AND QUESTIONS

1. The literature discussing (often criticizing) the Court's ERISA preemption doctrine is immense. See, e.g., Elizabeth Barnidge, *What Lies Ahead*

For ERISA's Preemption Doctrine After a Judicial Call To Action Is Issued in Aetna Health Care Inc. v. Davila, *43 Hous. L. Rev. 125 (2006) (reviewing much of the prior literature); Donald Bogan,* Protecting Patient Rights Despite ERISA: Will the Supreme Court Allow the States to Regulate Managed Care?, *74 Tul. L. Rev. 951 (2000).*

2.   As the discussion of *Pegram* demonstrates, deciding what is a medical decision by a treating provider rather than a fiduciary denial of benefit can in some instances be challenging. If the act is not subject to ERISA, then tort law can be applied. Some have argued that the extensive preemption of claims like those in Davila may lead to increased litigation against medical practitioners.

3.   The lack of any damages remedy for wrongful denial of medical treatment has troubled many commentators and courts, as the two articles cited in Note 1, and the article by Professor Langbein cited by Justice Ginsburg indicate. Those defending these outcomes argue that to have a wide-ranging damages remedy would discourage employers from offering health care plans, due to added costs.

# J.  MANDATED BENEFIT PROGRAMS

## 1.  WORKERS COMPENSATION, STATE DISABILITY INSURANCE, AND SOCIAL SECURITY DISABILITY INSURANCE

Please see Chapter IX pages 680–846.

## 2.  UNEMPLOYMENT COMPENSATION

Please see Chapter X pages 865–926.

## 3.  FAMILY AND MEDICAL LEAVE ACT

### RAGSDALE v. WOLVERINE WORLD WIDE, INC.

Supreme Court of the United States, 2002
535 U.S. 81, 122 S.Ct. 1155, 152 L.Ed.2d 167

JUSTICE KENNEDY delivered the opinion of the Court.

Qualifying employees are guaranteed 12 weeks of unpaid leave each year by the Family and Medical Leave Act of 1993 (FMLA or Act), 107 Stat. 6, as amended, 29 U.S.C. § 2601 et seq. (1994 ed. and Supp. V). The Act encourages businesses to adopt more generous policies, and many employers have done so. Respondent Wolverine World Wide, Inc., for example, granted petitioner Tracy Ragsdale 30 weeks of leave when cancer kept her out of work in 1996. Ragsdale nevertheless brought suit under the FMLA. She alleged that because Wolverine was in technical violation of certain Labor Department regulations, she was entitled to more leave.
\* \* \*

## I

Ragsdale began working at a Wolverine factory in 1995, but in the following year she was diagnosed with Hodgkin's disease. Her prescribed treatment involved surgery and months of radiation therapy. Though unable to work during this time, she was eligible for seven months of unpaid sick leave under Wolverine's leave plan. Ragsdale requested and received a 1–month leave of absence on February 21, 1996, and asked for a 30–day extension at the end of each of the seven months that followed. Wolverine granted the first six requests, and Ragsdale missed 30 consecutive weeks of work. Her position with the company was held open throughout, and Wolverine maintained her health benefits and paid her premiums during the first six months of her absence. Wolverine did not notify her, however, that 12 weeks of the absence would count as her FMLA leave.

In September, Ragsdale sought a seventh 30–day extension, but Wolverine advised her that she had exhausted her seven months under the company plan. Her condition persisted, so she requested more leave or permission to work on a part-time basis. Wolverine refused and terminated her when she did not come back to work.

Ragsdale filed suit in the United States District Court for the Eastern District of Arkansas. Her claim relied on the Secretary's regulation, which provides that if an employee takes medical leave "and the employer does not designate the leave as FMLA leave, the leave taken does not count against an employee's FMLA entitlement." 29 CFR § 825.700(a) (2001). The required designation had not been made, so Ragsdale argued that her 30 weeks of leave did "not count against [her] FMLA entitlement." Ibid. It followed that when she was denied additional leave and terminated after 30 weeks, the statute guaranteed her 12 more weeks. She sought reinstatement, backpay, and other relief.

When the parties filed cross-motions for summary judgment, Wolverine conceded it had not given Ragsdale specific notice that part of her absence would count as FMLA leave. It maintained, however, that it had complied with the statute by granting her 30 weeks of leave—more than twice what the Act required. The District Court granted summary judgment to Wolverine. In the court's view the regulation was in conflict with the statute and invalid because, in effect, it required Wolverine to grant Ragsdale more than 12 weeks of FMLA-compliant leave in one year. The Court of Appeals for the Eighth Circuit agreed. 218 F.3d 933 (2000).

We granted certiorari, * * * and now affirm.

## II

Wolverine's challenge concentrates on the validity of a single sentence in § 825.700(a). This provision is but a small part of the administrative structure the Secretary devised pursuant to Congress' directive to issue regulations "necessary to carry out" the Act. 29 U.S.C. § 2654 (1994 ed.). The Secretary's judgment that a particular regulation fits within this statutory constraint must be given considerable weight. \* \* \* Our deference to the Secretary, however, has important limits: A regulation cannot stand if it is "arbitrary, capricious, or manifestly contrary to the statute." \* \* \* To determine whether § 825.700(a) is a valid exercise of the Secretary's authority, we must consult the Act, viewing it as a "symmetrical and coherent regulatory scheme." *Gustafson v. Alloyd Co.*, 513 U.S. 561, 569, 115 S. Ct. 1061, 131 L. Ed. 2d 1 (1995).

The FMLA's central provision guarantees eligible employees 12 weeks of leave in a 1–year period following certain events: a disabling health problem; a family member's serious illness; or the arrival of a new son or daughter. 29 U.S.C. § 2612(a)(1). During the mandatory 12 weeks, the employer must maintain the employee's group health coverage. § 2614(c)(1). Leave must be granted, when "medically necessary," on an intermittent or part-time basis.§ 2612(b)(1). Upon the employee's timely return, the employer must reinstate the employee to his or her former position or an equivalent. § 2614(a)(1). The Act makes it unlawful for an employer to "interfere with, restrain, or deny the exercise of" these rights, § 2615(a)(1), and violators are subject to consequential damages and appropriate equitable relief, § 2617(a)(1).

A number of employers have adopted policies with terms far more generous than the statute requires. Congress encouraged as much, mandating in the Act's penultimate provision that "[n]othing in this Act … shall be construed to discourage employers from adopting or retaining leave policies more generous than any policies that comply with the requirements under this Act." § 2653. Some employers, like Wolverine, allow more than the 12–week annual minimum; others offer paid leave. U.S. Dept. of Labor, D. Cantor et al., Balancing the Needs of Families and Employers: Family and Medical Leave Surveys 5–10, 5–12 (2001) (22.9% of FMLA-covered establishments allow more than 12 weeks of leave per year; 62.7% provide paid disability leave). As long as these policies meet the Act's minimum requirements, leave taken may be counted toward the 12 weeks guaranteed by the FMLA. See 60 Fed. Reg. 2230 (1995) ("[E]mployers may designate paid leave as FMLA leave and offset the maximum entitlements under the employer's more generous policies").

With this statutory structure in place, the Secretary issued regulations requiring employers to inform their workers about the relationship between the FMLA and leave granted under company plans. The regulations make it the employer's responsibility to tell the employee that an absence will be considered FMLA leave. 29 CFR § 825.208(a) (2001). Employers must give written notice of the designation, along with detailed information concerning the employee's rights and responsibilities under the Act, "within a reasonable time after notice of the need for leave is given by the employee—within one or two business days if feasible." § 825.301(c).

The regulations are in addition to a notice provision explicitly set out in the statute. Section 2619(a) requires employers to "keep posted, in conspicuous places ..., a notice ... setting forth excerpts from, or summaries of, the pertinent provisions of this subchapter and information pertaining to the filing of a charge." According to the Secretary, the more comprehensive and individualized notice required by the regulations is necessary to ensure that employees are aware of their rights when they take leave. See 60 Fed. Reg. 2220 (1995). We need not decide today whether this conclusion accords with the text and structure of the FMLA, or whether Congress has instead "spoken to the precise question" of notice, * * * and so foreclosed the notice regulations. Even assuming the additional notice requirement is valid, the categorical penalty the Secretary imposes for its breach is contrary to the Act's remedial design.

The penalty is set out in a separate regulation, § 825.700, which is entitled "What if an employer provides more generous benefits than required by the FMLA?" This is the sentence on which Ragsdale relies:

> "If an employee takes paid or unpaid leave and the employer does not designate the leave as FMLA leave, the leave taken does not count against an employee's FMLA entitlement."

29 CFR § 825.700(a) (2001).

This provision punishes an employer's failure to provide timely notice of the FMLA designation by denying it any credit for leave granted before the notice. The penalty is unconnected to any prejudice the employee might have suffered from the employer's lapse. If the employee takes an undesignated absence of 12 weeks or more, the regulation always gives him or her the right to 12 more weeks of leave that year. The fact that the employee would have acted in the same manner if notice had been given is, in the Secretary's view, irrelevant. Indeed, as we understand the Secretary's position, the employer would be required to grant the added 12 weeks even if the employee had full knowledge of the FMLA and expected the absence to count against the 12–week entitlement. An employer who denies the employee this additional leave will be deemed to have violated the employee's rights under § 2615 and so will be liable for damages and equitable relief under § 2617.

The categorical penalty is incompatible with the FMLA's comprehensive remedial mechanism. To prevail under the cause of action set out in § 2617, an employee must prove, as a threshold matter, that the employer violated § 2615 by interfering with, restraining, or denying his or her exercise of FMLA rights. Even then, § 2617 provides no relief unless the employee has been prejudiced by the violation: The employer is liable only for compensation and benefits lost "by reason of the violation," § 2617(a)(1)(A)(i)(I), for other monetary losses sustained "as a direct result of the violation," § 2617(a)(1)(A)(i)(II), and for "appropriate" equitable relief, including employment, reinstatement, and promotion, § 2617(a)(1)(B). The remedy is tailored to the harm suffered. * * *

Section 825.700(a), Ragsdale contends, reflects the Secretary's understanding that an employer's failure to comply with the designation requirement might sometimes burden an employee's exercise of basic FMLA rights in violation of § 2615. Consider, for instance, the right under § 2612(b)(1) to take intermittent leave when medically necessary. An employee who undergoes cancer treatments every other week over the course of 12 weeks might want to work during the off weeks, earning a paycheck and saving six weeks for later. If she is not informed that her absence qualifies as FMLA leave—and if she does not know of her right under the statute to take intermittent leave—she might take all 12 of her FMLA-guaranteed weeks consecutively and have no leave remaining for some future emergency. In circumstances like these, Ragsdale argues, the employer's failure to give the notice required by the regulation could be said to "deny," "restrain," or "interfere with" the employee's exercise of her right to take intermittent leave.

This position may be reasonable, but the more extreme one embodied in § 825.700(a) is not. The penalty provision does not say that in certain situations an employer's failure to make the designation will violate § 2615 and entitle the employee to additional leave. Rather, the regulation establishes an irrebuttable presumption that the employee's exercise of FMLA rights was impaired—and that the employee deserves 12 more weeks. There is no empirical or logical basis for this presumption, as the facts of this case well demonstrate. Ragsdale has not shown that she would have taken less leave or intermittent leave if she had received the required notice. * * * In fact her physician did not clear her to work until December, long after her 30–week leave period had ended. Even if Wolverine had complied with the notice regulations, Ragsdale still would have taken the entire 30–week absence. Blind to this reality, the Secretary's provision required the company to grant Ragsdale 12 more weeks of leave—and rendered it liable under § 2617 when it denied her request and terminated her.

The challenged regulation is invalid because it alters the FMLA's cause of action in a fundamental way: It relieves employees of the burden of proving any real impairment of their rights and resulting prejudice. In the case at hand, the regulation permitted Ragsdale to bring suit under § 2617, despite her inability to show that Wolverine's actions restrained her exercise of FMLA rights. Section 825.700(a) transformed the company's failure to give notice—along with its refusal to grant her more than 30 weeks of leave—into an actionable violation of § 2615. This regulatory sleight of hand also entitled Ragsdale to reinstatement and backpay, even though reinstatement could not be said to be "appropriate" in these circumstances and Ragsdale lost no compensation "by reason of" Wolverine's failure to designate her absence as FMLA leave. By mandating these results absent a showing of consequential harm, the regulation worked an end run around important limitations of the statute's remedial scheme.

In defense of the regulation, the Government notes that a categorical penalty requiring the employer to grant more leave is easier to administer than one involving a fact-specific inquiry into what steps the employee would have taken had the employer given the required notice. "Regardless of how serious the problem an administrative agency seeks to address, however, it may not exercise its authority 'in a manner that is inconsistent with the administrative structure that Congress enacted into law.' " * * *. By its nature, the remedy created by Congress requires the retrospective, case-by-case examination the Secretary now seeks to eliminate. The purpose of the cause of action is to permit a court to inquire into matters such as whether the employee would have exercised his or her FMLA rights in the absence of the employer's actions. To determine whether damages and equitable relief are appropriate under the FMLA, the judge or jury must ask what steps the employee would have taken had circumstances been different-considering, for example, when the employee would have returned to work after taking leave. Though the Secretary could not enact rules purporting to make these kinds of determinations for the courts, § 825.700(a) has this precise effect. * * *

Furthermore, even if the Secretary were authorized to reconfigure the FMLA's cause of action for her administrative convenience, this particular rule would be an unreasonable choice. As we have noted in other contexts, categorical rules—such as the rule of per se antitrust illegality—reflect broad generalizations holding true in so many cases that inquiry into whether they apply to the case at hand would be needless and wasteful. * * * That said, the generalization made by the Secretary's categorical penalty—that the proper redress for an employer's violation of the notice regulations is a full 12 more weeks of leave—holds true in but few cases. The employee who would have taken the absence anyway, of course, would need no more leave; but the regulation provides 12 additional weeks. Even the employee who would have chosen to work on an intermittent basis— say, every other week, * * * could claim an entitlement not to 12 weeks of leave but instead to the 6 weeks he or she would not have taken. To be sure, 12 more weeks might be an appropriate make-whole remedy for an employee who would not have taken any leave at all if the notice had been given. It is not a "fair assumption," *United States v. O'Hagan*, 521 U.S. at 676, 117 S. Ct. 2199, however, that this fact pattern will occur in any but the most exceptional of cases.

To the extent the Secretary's penalty will have no substantial relation to the harm suffered by the employee in the run of cases, it also amends the FMLA's most fundamental substantive guarantee—the employee's entitlement to "a total of 12 workweeks of leave during any 12–month period." § 2612(a)(1). Like any key term in an important piece of legislation, the 12–week figure was the result of compromise between groups with marked but divergent interests in the contested provision. Employers wanted fewer weeks; employees wanted more. See H.R. Rep. No. 102–135, pt. 1, p. 37 (1991). Congress resolved the conflict by choosing a middle ground, a period considered long enough to serve "the needs of families" but not so long that it would upset "the legitimate interests of employers." § 2601(b).

Courts and agencies must respect and give effect to these sorts of compromises. * * * The Secretary's chosen penalty subverts the careful balance, for it gives certain employees a right to more than 12 weeks of FMLA-compliant leave in a given 1–year period. * * *

That the Secretary's penalty is disproportionate and inconsistent with Congress' intent is evident as well from the sole notice provision in the Act itself. As noted above, § 2619 directs employers to post a general notice informing employees of their FMLA rights. See *supra*, at 1160. This provision sets out its own penalty for noncompliance: "Any employer that willfully violates this section may be assessed a civil monetary penalty not to exceed $100 for each separate offense." § 2619(b). Congress believed that a $100 fine, enforced by the Secretary, was the appropriate penalty for willful violations of the only notice requirement specified in the statute. The regulation, in contrast, establishes a much heavier sanction, enforced not by the Secretary but by employees, for both willful and inadvertent violations of a supplemental notice requirement.

Section 825.700(a) is also in considerable tension with the statute's admonition that "[n]othing in this Act ... shall be construed to discourage employers from adopting or retaining leave policies more generous than any policies that comply with the requirements under this Act." § 2653. The FMLA was intended to pull certain employers up to the minimum standard, but Congress was well aware of the danger that it might push more generous employers down to the minimum at the same time. * * *

Although § 825.700(a) itself is directed toward employers "provid[ing] more generous benefits than required by the FMLA," its severe and across-the-board penalty could cause employers to discontinue these voluntary programs. Compliance with the designation requirement is easy enough for companies meeting only the minimum federal requirements: All leave is given the FMLA designation. Matters are quite different for companies like Wolverine, which offer more diverse and expansive options to their employees. In addition to allowing more than 12 weeks of leave per year, these employers might also provide leave for non-FMLA reasons, or to employees who are not yet FMLA eligible-leave the Secretary may not permit to be designated as FMLA leave. * * *

These considerations persuade us that § 825.700(a) effects an impermissible alteration of the statutory framework and cannot be within the Secretary's power to issue regulations "necessary to carry out" the Act under § 2654. In so holding we do not decide whether the notice and designation requirements are themselves valid or whether other means of enforcing them might be consistent with the statute. Whatever the bounds of the Secretary's discretion on this matter, they were exceeded here. The FMLA guaranteed Ragsdale 12—not 42—weeks of leave in 1996.

The judgment of the Court of Appeals is affirmed.

JUSTICE O'CONNOR, with whom JUSTICE SOUTER, JUSTICE GINSBURG, and JUSTICE BREYER join, dissenting.

The Court today holds that the Family and Medical Leave Act of 1993 (FMLA or Act), 29 U.S.C. § 2601 et seq. (1994 ed. and Supp. V), clearly precludes the Secretary of Labor from adopting a rule requiring an employer to give an employee notice that leave is FMLA qualifying before the leave may be counted against the employer's 12–week obligation. Because I believe the Secretary is justified in requiring such individualized notice and because I think that nothing in the Act constrains the Secretary's ability to secure compliance with that requirement by refusing to count the leave against the employer's statutory obligation, I respectfully dissent. * * *

## NOTES AND QUESTIONS

1. The Family and Medical Leave Act, 29 U.S.C. §§ 2601–2654, was enacted in 1993 as the first major legislative program of the Clinton administration. As the opinion in the principal case indicates, it was the subject of intense lobbying. It was preceded by a handful of state laws providing parental leave (particularly for pregnant women). In general, however, the patterns of state legislation and official practice were found by the Congress in the prefatory sections of FMLA to reflect widely held stereotypes about gender differences. In *Nevada Dept. of Human Resources v. Hibbs*, 538 U.S. 721, 123 S.Ct. 1972, 155 L.Ed.2d 953 (2003), a majority of the Court found that this situation justified the Congressional decision to make state governments liable for damages for violations of FMLA. In his opinion for the Court, Chief Justice Rehnquist stated: "the States' record of unconstitutional participation in, and fostering of, gender-based discrimination in the administration of leave benefits is weighty enough to justify the enactment of prophylactic [XIVth Amendment] § 5 legislation." 538 U.S. at 735.

2. The coverage provisions of FMLA are different from those in most employment laws, particularly the coverage of employers. An employer is covered only if it has a minimum of fifty employees within a 75–mile radius. An employee is an "eligible employee" if she has worked for the employer a minimum of 12 months and has worked 1250 hours within that 12–month period. The combined effect of these requirements is that something between thirty and forty per cent of workers are probably not covered by the statute at any given time. Counting hours can sometimes be challenging. See *Pirant v. United States Postal Service*, 542 F.3d 202 (7th Cir. 2008) (employee 1.2 hours short of qualifying for FMLA protection).

What if an eligible employee leaves the employer, but after a hiatus returns to the same place of employment? Is that worker covered immediately because of the prior eligibility? See *Rucker v. Lee Holding Co.*, 471 F.3d 6 (1st Cir. 2006); Benjamin Davis, *Case Comment*, 41 SUFFOLK U.L. REV. 425 (2008); *O'Connor v. Busch's, Inc.*, 492 F. Supp. 2d 736 (E.D. Mich. 2007). The Department of Labor announced in April 2008 that it intended to develop regulations dealing with the issue.

3. The 12–week unpaid leave provided by the FMLA is a considerably lesser benefit than that available in most industrialized nations, particularly

in Europe. See the broad review of parental leave benefits in Saul Levmore, *Parental Leave and American Exceptionalism*, 58 CASE W.L. REV. 203 (2007).

The 12 weeks of leave are to be provided in four situations:

● Birth of a child to the employee (and "in order to care for" that newborn);

● Placement of a child with the employee for adoption or foster care;

● Care of a spouse, son, daughter or parent of the employee, if that person has a "serious health condition";

● The employee is unable to perform work because of a "serious health condition." 29 U.S.C. § 2612.

A "serious health condition" is defined as "an illness, injury, impairment, or physical or mental condition that involves (a) inpatient care in a hospital, hospice, or residential medical care facility; or (b) continuing treatment by a health care provider." 29 U.S.C. § 2611(11). Thus, care of chronic conditions that require intermittent leave (migraine headaches, for example) is covered only if the condition is one being treated by a health practitioner on an ongoing basis.

4. The "Family" in FMLA is in some respects at least a traditional one; "spouse" is defined as "husband or wife," for example. One result is that FMLA-required leave is not generally available for the care of partners in non-traditional relationships. Care of newborns by the biological parent or an adopting parent would be covered, but the situation of a non-traditional partner of such a parent would be problematic. Many private and public employers have adopted leave policies that extend leave programs to such non-traditional partners. One commentator has suggested that it would be wise to extend this benefit to friends who serve as surrogate parents or children. See Laura A. Rosenbury, "Friends with Benefits?," 106 Mich. L. Rev. 189 (2007).

# 4. SOCIAL SECURITY

The modern concept of government-sponsored retirement insurance has its origins in a German Old Age Insurance statute adopted in 1889. In the early phases of the industrial revolution in the United States, elderly in need either sought refuge with family members, received aid from mutual aid societies to which they belonged, turned to local charities, or engaged in some combination of these. The inadequacies of this "system" were evident and by the mid–1920s serious attention was being devoted by American scholars and social reformers to examining the merits of government-sponsored old age insurance programs which by then had become firmly established in European industrial countries such as Germany, Britain, and Belgium. The issue was forced to center stage when the economic collapse of the early 1930s magnified the problem of meeting the needs of retired workers whose private pensions had vanished (where they ever existed). Because too few families were left with the resources to meet basic needs and welfare resources were overwhelmed, voters looked to government for help. Resulting populist proposals, such as the Townsend Movement, which called for a grant of $200 for every person over age 60, offered quick but often impractical answers. However, they added to the political urgency to find a manageable solution to a problem with which most electors by then could personally identify.

Congressional studies of retirement welfare programs in other nations suggested a variety of approaches to financing and measuring benefits. When the Social Security Act was adopted in 1935, some basic policy choices were made that to a substantial degree continue to characterize the U.S. approach. They include the requirements that participation is compulsory, financing is shared by employer and employee contributions, benefits are paid largely from the program's current income ("pay as you go," but with a small reserve) which is levied in the form of a tax on personal earnings, eligibility is based upon prior participation in financing benefits, and benefits are paid on the basis of prior contributions and family responsibilities rather than financial need.

Another basic characteristic of the Social Security retirement income program is the effort to adjust benefits to reflect current living costs. Until 1975 this was accomplished by ad hoc Congressional modifications in the benefits schedule. Since then such increases have been automatically tied to changes in the Consumer Price Index (CPI). Because the system's income is tied to employee earnings, inflationary pressures that push-up benefits expenditures generally are accompanied by payroll expansions that increase the program's income.

Initially, the Social Security retirement system covered about 60% of the working population. A few groups, such as railroad workers and government employees, were excluded because they were covered by existing government-imposed retirement income programs. Others were excluded because it was feared that the extra payroll expense or administrative burdens of tax payment would reduce the level of employment. Still others were excluded due to political neglect. For many years the self-employed were excluded, later were given the right to optional participation, and eventually were brought within mandatory coverage. By mid–2000, it was estimated that 93% of men and 83% of women over age 20 had earned a sufficient number of contribution quarters to qualify for Social Security retirement benefits. The largest groups of uncovered workers are state and local government employees in jurisdictions that have not elected to participate, and federal employees hired prior to 1984. However, many workers in both of the latter categories have Social Security retirement protection either because of prior employment in covered jobs or as a spouse of a covered worker.

The Social Security retirement system operated for many years on the assumption that 65 is the normal retirement age. A person who retires earlier can start drawing benefits from the system starting at age 62 but the benefit level of those retiring prior to reaching 65 is reduced so as to result, in the average case, in total payouts equivalent to what would have been received had benefits not begun until age 65. Beginning in the year 2000, the normal retirement age increases 2 months each year until it reaches age 67 in the year 2022. The reduction in benefits resulting from early retirement will be adjusted to reflect that change.

A beneficiary can increase the monthly payment amount by delaying when he or she begins drawing benefits. Up to age 70, the amount of the monthly retirement benefit increases by a small percentage for each month of delay. In 2007, the average benefit for an individual was $1,055 for an individual and $1,722 for a couple (both receiving benefits).

Beneficiaries drawing Social Security retirement who are at full retirement age can continue to earn income without any reduction of those benefits. (Deductions are not taken for unearned income; that is, income from investments or other unearned sources.) The benefits of all non-disabled beneficiaries under full retirement age are reduced to reflect wage earnings. These benefits are not subject to federal income tax for those individuals whose income is less than $25,000; for couples filing jointly, the figure is $32,000. For those individuals earning more than $34,000, or couples earning more than $44,000, up to 85% of the social security benefit may be taxable.

In addition to monthly retirement income, Social Security Medicare provides beneficiaries with certain health care insurance. Also, Social Security survival benefits extend to some dependents other than a retiree's surviving spouse.

Entitlement to Social Security benefits depends, then, on two things: age, and whether one has paid social security taxes in enough different time periods on enough earnings. There is no needs test. There are occasional contests of Social Security Administration determinations both of age and earnings records. Contests with respect to age are relatively rare compared to early years of the system, because birth records are generally more adequate than in the early 20th century. There are still some challenges every year, however, many involving immigrants to the United States claiming that records from home countries or on entry-into-the-US documents were flawed. See, e.g., *Panetis v. Barnhart*, 95 Fed. Appx. 454 (3d Cir. 2004) (challenge denied); *Yang v. Shalala*, 22 F.3d 213 (9th Cir. 1994) (challenge allowed; claimant allowed recovery of costs under Equal Access to Justice Act).

Some urge that government-administered support should be provided solely on the basis of need. Providing Social Security retirement benefits only to low income elderly people would make it possible either to reduce the tax rate or increase the benefits level. Merton and Joan Bernstein explain the Act's preference for a status test over a needs test:

> Social Security avoids needs or means testing for several very good reasons. Administering such needs-test procedures increases program costs prodigiously. While the Social Security cash programs (for retirees, survivors, the disabled, and their families) incur slightly more than 1 percent of payments for administrative expenses, Supple-

mental Security Income (SSI), which pays benefits to a comparable population but on a needs-tested basis, costs 7.05 percent to operate. Additionally, designers and defenders of the Social Security program argue that the program does not require needs testing because most recipients do in fact need a substitute for lost earnings in order to maintain living standards.

The system can dispense with a needs test because, among other reasons, Social Security pays its own way from funds provided primarily by contributions by employers, employees, and the self-employed; not everyone knows that Social Security is self-sustaining. Having paid contributions throughout their working life, recipients regard benefits as earned. Benefits derive from deferred pay earned quite as much as our cash pay. In a sense, all of us who work maintain and build the economy from which benefits are ultimately derived. Further, the absence of a needs test encourages savings to supplement program benefits. Were a needs test used, many would not save and some would even "spend down" in order to qualify.

The absence of a means test and the view by most people that they earn their benefits are factors that undoubtedly account for the enormous popularity of the system.

M. BERNSTEIN & J. BERNSTEIN, SOCIAL SECURITY: THE SYSTEM THAT WORKS AT 13–14 (1988).

On the other hand, Social Security retirement benefits are not wholly based upon what the recipient provided as a contributor to funding the program. For example, a cap is placed upon the monthly benefit that does not permit the average participant who has made maximum payments for a full work life to receive a total payback in constant (uninflated) dollars. That payback is partially reduced, as well, for the beneficiary who continues to earn a substantial income beyond the "normal" retirement age. In the same way, the provision of minimum benefits provides many low income recipients with a payback that may well exceed their contributions. (The extent of those differences, however, is modified by the generally longer life expectancy of higher income and the shorter life expectancy of lower income earners.) What policy choices do you think might justify deviations from a pure earned-benefit approach? Is it administratively feasible to achieve a pure earned-benefits program of retirement insurance?

## PARKER v. SULLIVAN

United States Court of Appeals, Seventh Circuit, 1990
898 F.2d 578

POSNER, CIRCUIT JUDGE.

For fifteen years, Rithie Parker has been trying to establish her entitlement to widow's benefits under the Social Security Act. She had married George Parker in 1970, but two years before his death in 1975 he had obtained a decree of divorce in a state court in Indiana, where the couple lived. He obtained the decree by fraud. In support of the petition for divorce he had submitted an affidavit in which he swore that his wife had left the state and that her whereabouts were unknown; in fact, as he well knew, she was living in the marital residence in Indiana. He did not, of course, serve her with a copy of the complaint, or any other pleading in the suit. The only service was by publication in that widely read weekly Info Inc. Mrs. Parker did not learn about the suit from that or any other source (illustrating once again that the operative meaning of constructive notice is no notice), and Mr. Parker was therefore granted the divorce by default. When Mrs. Parker learned of the decree, she brought suit in an Indiana state court to have it set aside as fraudulent; but fifteen months later, when her husband died, the suit was dismissed as moot.

The Social Security Administration held that Mrs. Parker was not George Parker's widow, because the divorce decree was not void, but merely voidable. She sought review in federal district court, and in 1983 the court, doubting its power or that of the Social Security Administration to determine the validity of a divorce under state law, remanded the matter to the agency for further consideration. The court suggested in its order of remand that Mrs. Parker reopen the proceeding in state court to set aside the divorce decree and point out to that court that the validity of the decree was germane to her application for social security benefits and therefore had not been rendered moot by George Parker's death after all. *Beavers v. Bess*, 58 Ind. App. 287, 300, 108 N.E. 266, 270 (1915). She did not follow this advice and on remand the Social Security Administration reaffirmed its earlier denial of benefits. She again appealed to the district court, which again affirmed, agreeing with the agency that since the decree was voidable rather than void, it was valid until set aside. 713 F. Supp. 277 (N.D. Ind. 1989). At argument the Administration repeated the district court's earlier suggestion that Mrs. Parker try to reopen the seventeen-year-old divorce proceeding.

The parties have devoted most of their forensic efforts to debating the question whether the divorce decree was void or voidable. We think this misses the point. The Social Security Act provides that for purposes of the Act an applicant is a widow if the courts of the state (Indiana) in which her alleged husband was domiciled at the time of his death "would find that such applicant and such insured individual [i.e., the putative husband] were validly married at [such] time." 42 U.S.C. § 416(h)(1)(A). The statute does not say, if they are validly married, but instead, if the state courts would find that they are validly married. Moreover, section 416(h)(1)(B) describes subsection (A), the subsection applicable here, as including both the case in which the applicant "is" married, in the sense that all relevant papers are in apple-pie order, and the case in which she is "deemed to be" married because the irregularity, such as a divorce decree procured by fraud, is one that the state courts would cure in a suitable proceeding. The Social Security Administration is required, therefore, to predict whether the Indiana courts would have held that the Parkers were validly married if Mrs. Parker had been or would be allowed to press to completion her suit to set aside the decree as fraudulently procured. *Chlystek v. Califano*, 599 F.2d 1270 (3d Cir.1979); *Cain v. Secretary*, 377 F.2d 55 (4th Cir.1967); cf. *White v. Harris*, 504 F. Supp. 153, 155 (C.D.Ill.1980). And—this is the novel issue in the case—the Administration cannot shift the burden of ascertaining state law to the applicant by the heartless expedient of forcing her to conduct a lawsuit in state court for the sole purpose of determining her entitlement to federal benefits; the fact that Mrs. Parker is on public assistance makes the suggestion a joke, but an especially unfunny one when we recall that she has been on the receiving end of a bureaucratic runaround for fifteen years now. Of course the Administration cannot grant or rescind a divorce, but that is not the point; it can determine marital status for purposes of entitlement to social security benefits, as *Chlystek* and *Cain* and many other cases ... hold. What it particularly cannot do, so far as regards this case, is to conscript a state court to serve as a special master for determining entitlements to federal benefits.

If Mrs. Parker had pressed her suit to completion, the divorce decree would have been set aside; of that there is no doubt, for the administrative law judge found that George Parker had procured his divorce by fraud, and we are given no reason to suppose that a state court would have found differently or that having found fraud it would nonetheless have refused to set aside the decree, if only she had satisfied the court that her suit was not moot. The only doubt is whether, unless and until formally set aside, the decree retains any legal force. Let us assume with the Social Security Administration that it does, that in other words it is not void. Then for some purposes the divorce decree is valid. But it is valid only because it has not been set aside, and that is not the sense of validity that matters to entitlement to social security benefits unless the widow is required to bring a state lawsuit in order to establish her entitlement. She is not. Obviously a decree may be immune to certain forms of collateral attack and hence not void, without being "valid" in the substantive sense that it would withstand a collateral attack if one could be brought; otherwise "void" and "voidable" would mean the same thing. Unless the Social Security Act makes entitlements depend on substantive validity, rather than on nonvoidness, persons in Mrs. Parker's position will be required to bring state-court suits for the sole purpose of qualifying for federal benefits. That would be an affront to federalism as well as an unneeded and unwanted expense to persons often of limited monetary means and legal sophistication. It is not, we think, what Congress had in mind in making state law determinative of entitlement to widow's benefits, or what it said in requiring the Social Security Administration to determine whether a state court would find that the applicant had been married or in other words would deem the applicant married despite an irregularity in the marriage's chain of title.

Therefore, the validity of a marriage for purposes of the Social Security Act depends not on the contents of an ex parte order by a state trial court, but on what the highest court of the state would do with that order if it were challenged by the method provided by the state for such challenges. *Cain v. Secretary, supra; Orr v. Bowen,* 648 F. Supp. 1510 (D.Nev.1986); *McGuire v. Califano,* 440 F. Supp. 1031, 1034–35 (D.Neb. 1977). The required finding is hypothetical. The applicant is not required to institute state court proceedings, and by the same token should not be penalized if as here the proceedings are instituted, but abandoned before completion.

The judgment is reversed and the Social Security Administration is instructed to grant the application for widow's benefits.

## NOTES AND QUESTIONS

1. A spouse of a worker or retired worker who is qualified to receive Social Security retirement benefits normally is entitled to his or her own spousal benefit (derivative benefit) in an amount equal to one half of the benefit payable to the qualified worker or retired worker if the marriage has continued for at least one year. Under some circumstances this derivative spousal benefit is available even though the marriage has been of shorter duration. Thus, the household of a retired worker who has a spouse of retirement age gets more in benefits than does that of a retired worker who is unmarried or whose spouse has not yet reached retirement age. However, since the spouse may also be entitled to benefits based upon his or her own employment earnings, a maximum Social Security benefit limit is imposed on the household.

If either spouse requests, separate checks are issued by the Social Security Administration dividing the benefit among the household beneficiaries.

A surviving spouse normally is entitled to the same benefit as would have been payable to the deceased worker, or retired worker, up to the "family maximum." The derivative benefit paid to a surviving spouse is suspended during any period of remarriage. Under some circumstances the survivor's benefit is not available to a spouse who was married to the deceased for fewer than nine months.

2. Under current law, a divorced legal spouse of retirement age who was married for at least ten years is entitled to a benefit equal to half of the prior spouse's primary Social Security retirement insurance amount. This benefit is not altered by the fact that the former spouse remarries or that there has been a succession of marriages for ten or more years. Nor does it reduce the benefit payable to the former spouse. Accordingly, because the marriage was not of sufficient duration to qualify her for a divorced spouse's benefit, the claimant in the Parker case was entitled to a survivor's benefit only if she still was married to George Parker when he died.

The Social Security Act treats a claimant as though married to a worker who qualifies for Social Security retirement benefits if in good faith and not knowing of an impediment to getting married, the claimant entered into a marriage ceremony with the covered worker and was living in the same household as that worker at the time of the covered worker's retirement or death. (Prior to an amendment that became effective in 1991, several federal courts had permitted recovery by such claimants only if no other divorced or legal spouse was entitled to benefits.)

3.   What is the basis for a spouse's or ex-spouse's claim to retirement benefits either during the wage earner's life or upon the wage earner's death? Professor Grace Ganz Blumberg reports that "for marital property purposes, pensions are generally treated as a form of deferred compensation.... [T]hus, to the extent that the right to the benefit is earned during marriage, it usually will be treated as an asset subject to distribution at divorce." Grace Ganz Blumberg, *Marital Property Treatment of Pensions, Disability Pay, Workers' Compensation, and Other Wage Substitutes: An Insurance, or Replacement, Analysis*, 33 UCLA L. REV. 1250, 1257 (1986). As such, most jurisdictions, in dividing marital assets, use one formula or another to try to project the future retirement benefits that will be received based upon work performed during the marriage. The rationale underlying treating future pension benefits as a marital asset is that, however funded, providing retirement benefits is a substitute for higher current earnings that otherwise would have been enjoyed by the couple or would have resulted in greater savings by them. (Professor Blumberg's analysis, accordingly, emphasizes the character of retirement benefits as a form of savings.) Although in dividing marital assets a court cannot alter the distribution of Social Security benefits, there is nothing to prevent it from taking account of the rules regarding their distribution in making its division of the marital res.

4.   The amount of the Social Security benefit available to a qualified former spouse is determined not only by the contributions made during the marriage but also by the former spouse's post-divorce earnings. Moreover, the derivative benefit is the same for a former spouse whose marriage lasted 10 years, a second former spouse whose marriage lasted 15 years, and a current spouse who has been married three years. Is there a sound rationale to support this benefit structure?

A proposed alternative is to credit Social Security accounts of married couples on the basis of "earnings sharing". As explained by Bernstein and Bernstein:

> Under earnings sharing, the earnings of both spouses during each year of marriage would be added together and half of the total then credited to the account of each. Such an arrangement would produce equal treatment for all couples with equal total earnings regardless of whether or how much either spouse worked for pay. The arrangement would for the first time give credits (half the couple's total) to nonworking spouses. In the event of divorce, a non-working spouse would have earned credits for the years of marriage in which the other partner worked. Similarly, a spouse working part time would obtain credit for some of the pay received by the higher-earning spouse.
>
> Earnings sharing accomplishes four things: it equalizes the benefits of all couples with equal earnings; it credits current earnings to both partners so that in the event of divorce the spouse with the lower cash earnings or none will get equal treatment with the spouse for the period

of the marriage; it takes account of all the couple's earnings in providing a retirement benefit; and, very importantly, earnings sharing facilitates qualifying as "disability insured" for women who work in the home or sporadically outside of it. The disability feature accounts for the greatest portion of earnings-sharing costs.

In one respect, earnings sharing saves money for the trust funds by no longer paying a spouse's benefit based on a life-time record for a marriage that lasts less time. It also avoids paying a full spouse's benefits to each former mate of a multiply-divorced insured. Under current law, the higher-earning spouse, generally the husband, suffers no financial ill effects from divorce, no matter how often divorced and no matter how many former spouses qualify for spouse's benefits on that record. Indeed, the family maximum does not apply to multiple spouses' benefits for divorced people. Spouses with fewer than ten years of marriage, however, get nothing from their spouse's records for those years under Social Security.

Earnings sharing results in higher benefits for the lower-earning spouse and lower benefits for the higher-earning spouse when each comes to draw on his or her own record. In the event of divorce, such an outcome seems appropriate—divorcing couples divvy up their common property, either by agreement or court-imposed apportionment. Community property states treat property acquired during marriage as owned equally by husband and wife. In the typical divorce situation, earnings sharing usually will result in lower Social Security benefits for the former husband. * * *

M. Bernstein & J. Bernstein, Social Security: The System That Works 218–19 (1988). For a more complete analysis of the impact of earnings sharing and alternative approaches to reforming Social Security spousal benefits, see Bernstein & Bernstein at pp. 216–23.

5.  Compare ERISA's model for protecting spousal interests in retirement benefits with the Social Security model and with the Bernsteins' proposed revision of the latter. Are there sound reasons for applying different rules for dealing with this issue under ERISA as compared with Social Security? Which model best serves society's interest in strengthening the family unit? In promoting equitable distribution of wealth? In rewarding initiative and effort? In reducing destitution?

6.  The complexities of calculating Social Security benefits inevitably lead both to excessive and deficient payments. Both types of errors respecting the same claimant can accumulate for years before being discovered. The Act authorizes the Social Security Administration to rectify payment errors but specifies that in the event of overpayment, "there shall be no adjustment of payments to, or recovery by the United States from, any person who is without fault if such adjustment would defeat the purpose of this subchapter or would be against equity and good conscience." 42 U.S.C. § 404(b). In *Sullivan v. Everhart*, 494 U.S. 83, 110 S.Ct. 960, 108 L.Ed.2d 72 (1990) the Court held, 5–4, that the Act is not violated when payment excesses and deficiencies are netted for the full period covered by any calculation errors and results in recoupment of overpayments by substantially reducing monthly

payments for long periods. The dissenters argued that the Act requires separate procedures to correct underpayments and overpayments. Thus, an underpayment would be corrected by paying the deficiency to the claimant; an overpayment would be corrected by first conducting a hearing to decide whether the above-quoted waiver is appropriate and if not appropriate then seeking cash recoupment or recoupment through reduced future benefits. The Court expressly did not reach the question of whether procedural due process is violated because under the regulations a finding of deficiency results in the reduction of monthly payments prior to holding an administrative hearing respecting the § 404(b) request for waiver.

## SOCIAL SECURITY AND OLDER WORKERS

Michael V. Leonesio
56 Social Security Bulletin, Summer 1993, p. 47

Viewed in total, the evidence indicates that the OASI program has contributed to the decline in the labor-force participation of older men but that the direct financial effects appear to be modest. The Social Security system has contributed to the popularity of retirement at ages 62 and 65, . . . but appears to be a minor force in the long post-World War II trend to retire at earlier ages. * * *

[E]conomic research indicates that the Social Security retirement test plays a relatively small role in determining the aggregate labor supply of older workers. There appear to be several explanations for these findings. First, research suggests that retirement decisions are influenced by the availability and generosity of Social Security and private pensions, health status, job characteristics, wage offers, family circumstances, and personal preferences for work versus leisure time. These other contributing factors that encourage or enable retirement appear to be dominant. Second, other Social Security provisions, particularly the actuarial adjustment for early retirement, the delayed retirement credit, and the automatic benefit recomputation feature, significantly offset the apparent penalty of the test. Third, the retirement test has been substantially liberalized over the years, permitting beneficiaries to earn more money without loss of benefits. Although earlier, more stringent forms of the test may have posed significant work disincentives, the current rules are far less restrictive. Fourth, some beneficiaries are undoubtedly sensitive to the retirement test and respond by making important adjustments in their lifetime labor supply plans. Nonetheless, the relatively small size of this group limits any impact that their response can have when the aggregate behavior of many millions of people is measured. Finally, many workers have limited control over the number of hours they work and therefore may exhibit little reaction to changes in the retirement test in the short run.

Social Security probably causes a reduction in the labor-force activity of older Americans. This conclusion is consistent with two widely cited rationales for the existence of Social Security, both of which imply that the system promotes earlier retirement. As pointed out by Hagens [Ref. deleted—Ed.], according to the forced saving rationale, individuals are often myopic and must be induced to save for their old age. If the program accomplishes this, individuals will enter their later years with greater personal wealth and will be able to afford more of all commodities, including their own leisure, so they will retire earlier. According to the insurance rationale, OASI provides insurance against the loss of earnings. The retirement date is uncertain when workers are young, and Social Security provides insurance for this risk. If retirement occurs late, workers might have more savings than they need to finance continuation of their normal lifestyles; however, early retirement can result in inadequate savings levels. The Social Security system can transfer resources from the former group to the latter if adjustments made to benefit payments in response to changes in the retirement date are less than actuarially fair. If late retirees effectively subsidize early retirees, the system encourages early retirement. Retirement neutrality has never been a primary goal of the OASI program, and it is inherently at odds with both the forced savings and insurance rationales.

Of course, it is possible that the conclusions about the influence of the OASI program on labor supply are in error and that somehow the economic studies have produced evidence that is a poor guide to what might be anticipated in the future. There are several reasons for hesitating to embrace these conclusions fully, particularly in predicting behavior in the 1990's and beyond.

1. Perusal of the historical evidence offers circumstantial evidence that the development of the Social Security system had an important impact on American retirement patterns. Ransom and Sutch found that retirement rates among nonagricultural workers declined over the 1870–1930 period. In contrast, retirement rates for older men increased from 1940 until the mid–1980's. Although there are numerous possible causes for this turnaround apart from the advent of Social Security, the results from the microeconometric studies are—at least on the surface—somewhat at odds with this pattern.

2. Although the economic and statistical modeling displays impressive skills and industry on the part of the researchers, even the best retirement models ignore what would appear to be significant facets of the individual decision-making process and are consequently misspecified. The most sophisticated models bypass some or all factors such as uncertainty, liquidity constraints, replanning, the physical demands imposed by jobs, employer-imposed constraints on work choices, and unmeasured individual differences among workers. No single study attempts to address more than one or two of these phenomena. Only modest attention has been given to the way financial incentives might interact with other factors such as health status, the physical demands of jobs, and other nonmonetary influences. Most of the research reviewed in this chapter was conducted at a time when the labor-force participation rates of older men had been falling for decades. This long-term decline apparently stopped in the mid–1980's, and men's rates have risen slightly during the ensuing six years. Whether this represents a temporary halt in a trend that will

shortly resume or a historic turnaround is not yet evident. At this point, however, the Department of Labor is forecasting a 1.1 percentage point increase in the participation rate for men aged 55–64 during 1988–2000 (following a decline of 8 percentage points from 1976 to 1988). * * *

The evidence argues against the view that there are politically acceptable changes in Social Security policy that are likely to result in a substantial increase in the labor-force participation of older workers. Nonetheless, in their focus on monetary incentives, economic models might be missing a key element of Social Security's influence. That is, because it is the single largest source of retirement income, it may establish an important social norm. One aspect of policies such as an increase in the normal retirement age or elimination of the retirement test involves changes in financial incentives. Such changes also send strong messages about society's expectations concerning work and retirement. There can be little doubt that over the years Social Security and other institutions have consistently signaled that early retirement is desirable and well deserved. Policies that clearly indicate that longer work lives are expected and will be rewarded may well generate larger work responses than changes in monetary incentives alone might suggest. At this time, there appears to be no solid evidence that this would be the case. * * *

### NOTES AND QUESTIONS

The development of computer data banks that store an array of information about individuals has been accompanied by the transformation of the Social Security Number (SSN) into a standardized personal identification number (PIN). The SSN thereby has become a central tool for compiling and accessing personal dossiers for each person in our society. Congress' reaction to this development has been inconsistent. It has taken some steps designed to reduce the potential intrusion on privacy, but it has taken other steps that facilitate use of the SSN as a universal PIN.

Public Law 93–579 (1974) made it unlawful for state or federal entities to withhold a right, benefit or privilege from an individual for refusing to disclose his or her Social Security Number (SSN) unless such disclosure was required by law or regulation prior to 1975 or was specifically authorized by law. However, as a result of the then existing government use of the SSN as an identifying code and subsequent legislation expressly authorizing particular uses, PL 93–579 has had minimal impact upon the expanded use of the SSN as the primary means of identifying information stored by government agencies. Government officials and others, such as employers, who are required by law to obtain private information are subject to penalties for unauthorized disclosure of such information, including the SSN (see, e.g., 5 U.S.C. § 552a, 26 U.S.C. § 6109, 42 U.S.C. § 405) and section 313 of the Social Security Independence and Program Improvements Act of 1994, amending 42 U.S.C. § 408, increased the severity of those penalties.

A person's SSN is generally available through sources other than government agencies or persons, such as employers, required by law to obtain an

SSN. For example, some states use the SSN as the driver's license identification number. Since the driver's license has become a standard means of personal identification for all sorts of transactions, there is no protection against what, as a practical matter, amounts to compelled SSN disclosure by persons residing in such states. In addition, private parties are not prohibited by federal law from insisting upon disclosure of the SSN as a condition for transacting business and then using the SSN as the identification code for storing, transferring, sharing, and even selling any information gathered from that person. For many types of business transactions and most types of financial transactions, the federal tax code requires such disclosure in order to be able to receive full payment of accounts or in order to be able to engage in the transaction. Moreover, the Social Security Act, at 42 U.S.C. § 408(a)(7), makes it a felony to obtain anything of value from another with the intent to deceive by falsely representing a number to be the SSN assigned by the government. Thus, if someone who seeks to minimize the extent to which investigators may obtain information about him, uses a false SSN in filling out a bank loan form, he has committed a federal felony even though he has the financial ability to pay back the loan, intends to pay back the loan, and has provided accurate financial data and adequate identifying information to the bank.

# INDEX

## References are to Pages

References are to Pages

References are to Pages

†